P9-BBQ-110

International Marketing

International Marketing

Seventeenth edition

Philip R. Cateora
FELLOW, ACADEMY OF INTERNATIONAL
BUSINESS, UNIVERSITY OF COLORADO

Mary C. Gilly
UNIVERSITY OF CALIFORNIA, IRVINE

John L. Graham
UNIVERSITY OF CALIFORNIA, IRVINE

R. Bruce Money
BRIGHAM YOUNG UNIVERSITY

McGraw Hill Education

INTERNATIONAL MARKETING, SEVENTEENTH EDITION

Published by McGraw-Hill Education, 2 Penn Plaza, New York, NY 10121. Copyright © 2016 by McGraw-Hill
Education. All rights reserved. Printed in the United States of America. Previous editions © 2013, 2011, and
2009. No part of this publication may be reproduced or distributed in any form or by any means, or stored in a
database or retrieval system, without the prior written consent of McGraw-Hill Education, including, but not
limited to, in any network or other electronic storage or transmission, or broadcast for distance learning.

Some ancillaries, including electronic and print components, may not be available to customers outside the
United States.

This book is printed on acid-free paper.

2 3 4 5 6 7 8 9 DOW 21 20 19 18 17 16

ISBN 978-0-07-784216-1
MHID 0-07-784216-2

Senior Vice President, Products & Markets: *Kurt L. Strand*
Vice President, General Manager, Products & Markets: *Michael Ryan*
Vice President, Content Design & Delivery: *Kimberly Meriwether David*
Managing Director: *Susan Gouijnstook*
Brand Manager: *Kim Leistner*
Director, Product Development: *Meghan Campbell*
Product Developer: *Heather Darr*
Marketing Manager: *Elizabeth Schonagen*
Digital Product Analyst: *Kerry Shanahan*
Director, Content Design & Delivery: *Terri Schiesl*
Program Manager: *Faye M. Herrig*
Content Project Managers: *Jessica Portz, Keri Johnson, Karen Jozefowicz*
Buyer: *Laura M. Fuller*
Design: *Tara McDermott*
Content Licensing Specialist: *DeAnna Dausener*
Cover Image: *© Stocktrek Images/Getty Images/RF*
Compositor: *MPS Limited*
Printer: *R. R. Donnelley*

All credits appearing on page or at the end of the book are considered to be an extension of the copyright page.

Library of Congress Cataloging-in-Publication Data
Cateora, Philip R., author.
   International marketing / Philip R. Cateora, Mary C. Gilly, John L. Graham, R. Bruce Money.
   Seventeenth edition. | New York, NY : McGraw-Hill Education, [2016]
   LCCN 2015036297 | ISBN 9780077842161 (alk. paper)
   LCSH: Export marketing. | International business enterprises.
   LCC HF1416 .C375 2016 | DDC 658.8/4—dc23 LC record available at http://lccn.loc.gov/2015036297

The Internet addresses listed in the text were accurate at the time of publication. The inclusion of a website does
not indicate an endorsement by the authors or McGraw-Hill Education, and McGraw-Hill Education does not
guarantee the accuracy of the information presented at these sites.

mheducation.com/highered

To Steve Jobs, the best international
marketer and inventive negotiator
of his generation

WALKTHROUGH

A quick look at the new edition

International Marketing by Cateora, Gilly, and Graham has always been a pioneer in the field of international marketing. The authors continue to set the standard in this edition with new and expanded topics that reflect the swift changes of an expanding competitive global market, as well as increased coverage of technology's impact on the international market arena. We are happy that Bruce Money has now joined our team.

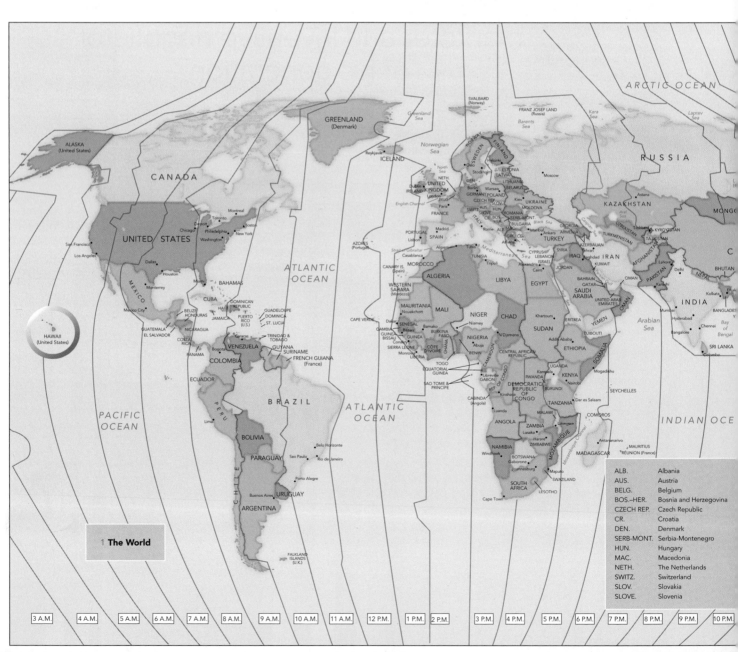

1 **The World**

ALB.	Albania
AUS.	Austria
BELG.	Belgium
BOS.–HER.	Bosnia and Herzegovina
CZECH REP.	Czech Republic
CR.	Croatia
DEN.	Denmark
SERB-MONT.	Serbia-Montenegro
HUN.	Hungary
MAC.	Macedonia
NETH.	The Netherlands
SWITZ.	Switzerland
SLOV.	Slovakia
SLOVE.	Slovenia

3 A.M. | 4 A.M. | 5 A.M. | 6 A.M. | 7 A.M. | 8 A.M. | 9 A.M. | 10 A.M. | 11 A.M. | 12 P.M. | 1 P.M. | 2 P.M. | 3 P.M. | 4 P.M. | 5 P.M. | 6 P.M. | 7 P.M. | 8 P.M. | 9 P.M. | 10 P.M.

4-Color Design

New color maps and exhibits allow for improved pedagogy and a clearer presentation of international symbols and cultural meanings in marketing and advertising. In addition, photos that depend on full color for maximum impact easily bring many global examples to life. This visually stimulating combination works together to make the text material reader-friendly and accessible for both instructors and students.

Chapter Openers

A Chapter Outline provides students an at-a-glance overview of chapter topics, while Chapter Learning Objectives summarize the chapter's goals and focus. Each chapter is introduced with a Global Perspective, a real-life example of company experiences that illustrates significant issues discussed in the chapter. Companies featured in the Global Perspective vignettes range from exporters to global enterprises.

PART ONE

Chapter 1

The Scope and Challenge of International Marketing

CHAPTER OUTLINE

Global Perspective: Global Commerce Causes Peace

The Internationalization of U.S. Business

International Marketing Defined

The International Marketing Task

- Marketing Decision Factors
- Aspects of the Domestic Environment
- Aspects of the Foreign Environment

Environmental Adaptation Needed

The Self-Reference Criterion and Ethnocentrism: Major Obstacles

Developing a Global Awareness

Stages of International Marketing Involvement

- No Direct Foreign Marketing
- Infrequent Foreign Marketing
- Regular Foreign Marketing
- International Marketing
- Global Marketing

The Orientation of *International Marketing*

CHAPTER LEARNING OBJECTIVES

What you should learn from Chapter 1:

- **LO1** The benefits of international markets
- **LO2** The changing face of U.S. business
- **LO3** The scope of the international marketing task
- **LO4** The importance of the self-reference criterion (SRC) in international marketing
- **LO5** The increasing importance of global awareness
- **LO6** The progression of becoming a global marketer

Global Perspective

GLOBAL COMMERCE CAUSES PEACE

Global commerce thrives during peacetime. The economic boom in North America during the late 1990s was in large part due to the end of the Cold War and the opening of the formerly communist countries to the world trading system. However, we should also understand the important role that trade and international marketing play in producing peace.

Boeing Company, one of America's largest exporters, is perhaps the most prominent example. Although many would argue that Boeing's military sales (aircraft and missiles) do not exactly promote peace, over most of the company's history, that business has constituted only about 20–25 percent of the company's commercial activity. The company still counts customers in more than 150 countries, and its 169,000 employees work in 65 countries.[1] The new 787 Dreamliner uses parts from around the world, including Australia, France, India, Italy, Japan, Russia, and Sweden. Its more than 12,000 commercial jets in service worldwide carry about 1 billion travelers per year. Its NASA Services division is the lead contractor in the construction and operation of the 16-country International Space Station, first manned by an American and two Russians in the fall of 2000. The Space and Intelligence Systems Division also produces and launches communications satellites affecting people in every country.

All the activity associated with the development, production, and marketing of commercial aircraft and space vehicles requires millions of people from around the world to work together. Moreover, no company does more[2] to enable people from all countries to meet face-to-face for both recreation and commerce. All this interaction yields not just the mutual gain associated with business relationships but also personal relationships and mutual understanding. The latter are the foundation of global peace and prosperity.

Another group of companies that promotes global dialogue and therefore peace is the mobile phone industry. By 2015, the number of mobile phone subscribers exceeded 7.0 billion. Samsung (South Korea), Nokia (Finland), and Apple (United States) are the market leaders.

Individuals and small companies also make a difference—perhaps a subtler one than large multinational companies, but one just as important in the aggregate. Our favorite example is Daniel Lubetzky's company, PeaceWorks. Mr. Lubetzky used a fellowship at Stanford Law School to study how to foster joint ventures between Arabs and Israelis. Then, following his own advice, he created a company that combined basil pesto from Israel with other raw materials and glass jars supplied by an Arab partner to produce the first product in a line he called Moshe & Ali's Gourmet Foods. The company now sells four different product lines in 15,000 stores in the United States and has its headquarters on Park Avenue in New York, as well as business operations in Israel, Egypt, Indonesia, Turkey, and Sri Lanka. Again, beyond the measurable commercial benefits of cooperation between the involved Arabs, Israelis, and others is the longer-lasting and more fundamental appreciation for one another's circumstances and character.

International marketing is hard work. Making sales calls is no vacation, even in Paris, especially when you've been there 10 times before. But international marketing is important work. It can enrich you, your family, your company, and your country. And ultimately, when international marketing is done well, by large companies or small, the needs and wants of customers in other lands are well understood, and prosperity and peace are promoted along the way.[3]

Sources: For more details, see http://boeing.com; http://airbus.com; http://peaceworks.com; Heidi Vogt, "Making Change: Mobile Pay in Africa," *The Wall Street Journal*, January 2, 2015, p. B6. Cell phone sales data are available at http://www.mobithinking.com.

[1] Boeing's 2014 Annual Report (http://www.boeing.com).

[2] The European commercial aircraft manufacturer Airbus is beginning to catch up, employing 63,000 people around the world (see Airbus's 2014 Annual Report, http://www.airbus.com).

[3] In response to criticisms of globalization catalyzed by the riots in Seattle in 1999, a growing literature argues for trade as a fundamental cause of peace. For a variety of such arguments, see Jagdish Bhabwati, *In Defense of Globalization* (Oxford: Oxford University Press, 2004); Thomas L. Friedman, *The World Is Flat* (New York: Farrar, Straus, and Giroux, 2005); Clifford J. Schultz III, Timothy J. Burkink, Bruno Grbac, and Natasa Renko, "When Policies and Marketing Systems Explode: An Assessment of Food Marketing in the War-Ravaged Balkans and Implications for Recovery, Sustainable Peace, and Prosperity," *Journal of Public Policy & Marketing* 24, no. 1 (2005), pp. 24–37; William Hernandez Requejo and John L. Graham, *Global Negotiation: The New Rules* (New York: Palgrave Macmillan, 2008), Chapter 13; Steven Pinker, *The Better Angels of Our Nature: Why Violence Has Declined* (New York: Viking, 2011; Hernando de Soto, "The Capitalist Cure for Terrorism," *Wall Street Journal*, October 10, 2014, online.)

PART TWO

Chapter 6

The Political Environment:

A CRITICAL CONCERN

CHAPTER OUTLINE

Global Perspective: World Trade Goes Bananas

The Sovereignty of Nations

Stability of Government Policies

- Forms of Government
- Political Parties
- Nationalism
- Targeted Fear and/or Animosity
- Trade Disputes

Political Risks of Global Business

- Confiscation, Expropriation, and Domestication
- Economic Risks
- Political Sanctions
- Political and Social Activists and Nongovernmental Organizations
- Violence, Terrorism, and War
- Cyberterrorism and Cybercrime

Assessing Political Vulnerability

- Politically Sensitive Products and Issues
- Forecasting Political Risk

Lessening Political Vulnerability

- Joint Ventures
- Expanding the Investment Base
- Licensing/Franchising
- Planned Domestication
- Political Bargaining
- Political Payoffs

Government Encouragement

CHAPTER LEARNING OBJECTIVES

What you should learn from Chapter 6:

- **LO1** What the sover`eignty of nations means and how it can affect the stability of government policies
- **LO2** How different governmental types, political parties, nationalism, targeted fear/animosity, and trade disputes can affect the environment for marketing in foreign countries
- **LO3** The political risks of global business and the factors that affect stability
- **LO4** The importance of the political system to international marketing and its effect on foreign investments
- **LO5** The impact of political and social activists, violence, and terrorism on international business
- **LO6** How to assess and reduce the effect of political vulnerability
- **LO7** How and why governments encourage foreign investment

Global Perspective

WORLD TRADE GOES BANANAS

Rather than bruising Chiquita Bananas, the wrath of politics instead hammered Prosciutto di Parma ham from Italy, handbags from France, and bath oils and soaps from Germany. These and a host of other imported products from Europe were all slapped with a 100 percent import tariff as retaliation by the U.S. government against EU banana-import rules that favored Caribbean bananas over Latin American bananas. Keep in mind that no bananas are exported from the United States, yet the United States has been engaged in a trade war over the past 7 years that has cost numerous small businesses on both sides of the Atlantic millions of dollars. But how can this be, you ask? Politics, that's how!

One small business, Reha Enterprises, for example, sells bath oil, soaps, and other supplies imported from Germany. The tariff on its most popular product, an herbal foam bath, was raised from 5 percent to 100 percent. The customs bill for 6 months spiraled to $37,783 from just $1,851—a 1,941 percent tax increase. For a small business whose gross sales are less than $1 million annually, it was crippling. When the owner of Reha heard of the impending "banana war," he called everyone—his congressperson, his senator, the United States Trade Representative (USTR). When he described his plight to the USTR, an official there expressed amazement. "They were surprised I was still importing," because they thought the tariff would cut off the industry entirely. That was their intention, which of course would have meant killing Reha Enterprises as well.

In effect, he was told it was his fault that he got caught up in the trade war. He should have attended the hearings in Washington, just like Gillette and Mattel, and maybe his products would have been dropped from the targeted list, just as theirs were. Scores of European products, from clothing to stoves to glass Christmas ornaments, dolls, and ballpoint pens, that were originally targeted for the retaliatory tariffs escaped the tariff. Aggressive lobbying by large corporations, trade groups, and members of Congress got most of the threatened imported products off the list. The USTR had published a list of the targeted imports in the Federal Register, inviting affected companies to testify. Unfortunately, the Federal Register was not on Reha's owner's reading list.

In that case, he was told, he should have hired a lobbyist in Washington to keep him briefed. Good advice—but it doesn't make much sense to a company that grosses less than $1 million a year. Other advice received from an official of the USTR included the off-the-record suggestion that he might want to change the customs number on the invoice so it would appear that he was importing goods not subject to the tariff, a decision that could, if he were caught, result in a hefty fine or jail. Smaller businesses in Europe faced similar problems as their export business dried up because of the tariffs.

How did this banana war start? The European Union imposed a quota and tariffs that favored imports from former colonies in the Caribbean and Africa, distributed by European firms, over Latin American bananas distributed by U.S. firms. Chiquita Brands International and Dole Food Company, contending that the EU's "illegal trade barriers" were costing $520 million annually in lost sales to Europe, asked the U.S. government for help. The government agreed that unfair trade barriers were damaging their business, and 100 percent tariffs on selected European imports were levied. Coincidentally, Chiquita Brands' annual political campaign contributions increased from barely over $40,000 in 1991 to $1.3 million in 1998.

A settlement was finally reached that involved high tariffs on Latin America bananas and quotas (with no tariffs) on bananas from Europe's former colonies. But the bruising over bananas continued, and not in a straightforward way! In 2007 the issue shifted to banana bending. That is, bananas from Latin America tend to be long and straight, while those from the non-tariff countries are short and bent. Because the latter are not preferred by the shippers or retailers (the bendier ones don't stack as neatly and economically), the bananas from the former colonies were still not preferred. And new regulations were adopted by the European Commission that mandated that bananas must be free from "abnormal curvature of the fingers." So the bendy banana producers threatened to renege on the whole agreement. Circa 2007 everyone involved found this prospect very unappealing.

The tale does have a happy ending though. In 2009, after marathon meetings among all parties in Geneva, the 16-year banana split was finally healed: The European Union cut import tariffs on bananas grown in Latin America by U.S. firms. Most recently, there's also an epilogue. Chiquita has now become a Brazilian brand. The U.S. corporation was purchased recently by two South American investors for $742 million.

Sources: "U.S. Sets Import Tariffs in Latest Salvo in Ongoing Battle over Banana Trade," *Minneapolis Star Tribune*, March 4, 1999; Timothy Dove, "Hit by a $200,000 Bill from the Blue," *Time*, February 7, 2000, p. 54; Geneva Agreement on Trade in Bananas, signed May 31, 2010, http://www.ec.europa.eu.; "Chiquita's Top Banana? Two Brazilians Win Bid," *Associated Press*, October 27, 2014, online.

Crossing Borders Boxes

These invaluable boxes offer anecdotal company examples. These entertaining examples are designed to encourage critical thinking and guide students through topics ranging from ethical to cultural to global issues facing marketers today.

CROSSING BORDERS 13.2 — Seeds of Fashion: Eastern vs. Western Counter-Culture Movements and a Look at the Gothic Lolitas of Harajuku, Japan

Where do new ideas come from? Since its origin, the Gothic Lolita subculture of Harajuku has continued to fascinate people around the world. This group is just one example of the counterculture fashion movements that have emerged from the Harajuku district of Japan, each group identified by a specific look that conveys a visual message. Gothic Lolita fashion infuses Victorian-era clothing with elements of Goth and Japanese *anime* to create a unique form of dress. Adherents take notes from the *Gothic & Lolita Bible* (a quarterly magazine with an estimated circulation of 100,000) and rely on their distinctive appearance to proclaim their subcultural identity. As in other counterculture movements, youths' fantasies of liberation, rebellion, and revolution have become embedded in the cultural mode of a changing nation.

By examining the fashion of the Harajuku, we can gain a more in-depth understanding of group affiliation and construction of self in counterculture movements. Definitive of a counterculture, the Gothic Lolita's in-group behavior and fashion evokes opposition and displays a symbolic rebellion against mainstream Japanese culture. These attitudes are reflected in norm-breaking and attention-grabbing styles.

In the past, youth subcultures generally have emerged from Western society and diffused globally. But the Harajuku subculture began in the East and is moving West, marking a shift in the cultural current. The Harajuku subculture is also an example of the difference between Eastern and Western counterculture movements. Whereas maturity in Western cultures is associated with authority and individuality, in Confucian Japan, maturity is the ability to cooperate with a group, accept compromises, and fulfill obligations to society. Therefore, rebellion in Japanese youth culture means rebellion against adulthood as well. Rather than engaging in sexually provocative or aggressive behaviors to emphasize their maturity and independence, as occurs among Western rebels, Japanese Gothic Lolitas display themselves in a childlike and vulnerable manner to emphasize their immaturity and inability to meet the social responsibilities and obligations of adulthood.

Likely because of this refusal to cooperate with social expectations, mainstream Japan views the subculture as selfish, especially considering its indulgent consumption behaviors. Unlike contemporary Western youth cultures, such as punk and grunge, the Gothic Lolita subculture does not condemn materialism or other aspects of modern consumer culture. Instead, one outfit (as seen in the accompanying photo) can cost as much as $300–$1,000! Because personal consumption is regarded as both antisocial and immoral in Japanese society, the subculture opposes normative social values by indulging in the conspicuous consumption.

Most participants (aged 13–30 years) are students or have jobs that require them to wear a uniform every day. On Sundays, they feel they have reached the time they can truly be themselves. Their lifestyle is frowned upon, making it very common to see teenagers carrying bags with their "harajuku outfit" on the train and changing at the park so their parents never see their outfits. Others wear the clothing as their normal daily dress, but the vast majority save it for Sundays, when they congregate at Jingu Bridge and Yoyogi Park to show off their fashions, hang out, and meet others like them. Some go just to have their pictures taken by the subculture's magazine photographers, who search for shots of new trends, or by tourists.

Japanese women in an ad for Angelic Pretty fashions appearing in the Gothic & Lolita Bible.

Source: Kristen Schiele, "How Subcultures Regain Control through Reclamation: A Case of Commodification in Japan," working paper, Merage School of Business, University of California, Irvine, 2015.

When analyzing a product for a second market, the extent of adaptation required depends on cultural differences in product use and perception between the market the product was originally developed for and the new market. The greater these cultural differences between the two markets, the greater the extent of adaptation that may be necessary.[26] Research has also shown that firms with strong organizational identities can

[26] An excellent new book on this topic is John A. Quelch and Katherine E. Jocz's *All Business is Local* (New York: Portfolio/Penguin, 2012).

NEW Cases

New cases accompany the seventeenth edition, enlivening the material in the book and class discussions while broadening a student's critical thinking skills. These cases bring forth many of the topics discussed in the chapters and demonstrate how these concepts are dealt with in the real world. These cases can be found in Connect and SmartBook.

PART SIX

Cases 3 ASSESSING GLOBAL MARKET OPPORTUNITIES

OUTLINE OF CASES

CASE 3-5 A Sea Launch Recovery?

CIRCA 2008

Sea Launch engineers say the three-week round-trip journey across the Pacific Ocean is the most rewarding part of their jobs. The cruise is the culmination of nearly two months of work preparing the rocket, payload, and launch teams for the mission. Prior to operations at Home Port, about 18 months goes into the planning, flight design, and logistics. "It's really nice to know most of the reviews are over and we're finally ready to launch," said Bill Ragcvan, mission director for the company's next flight.

More than 300 people take the trip to the company's equatorial launch site about 1,400 miles south of Hawaii. The crew includes workers from several nations, including: Ukraine, Russia, Norway, the Philippines, and the United States. Ukraine-based Yuzhnoye and Yuzhmash build the Zenit 3SL rocket's first and second stages, while Energia of Russia manufactures the Block DM-SL upper stage for the rocket. Norwegian ship officers manage marine operations, and Filipino deckhands work on both the *Sea Launch Commander* and the *Odyssey* launch platform. U.S. employees from the Boeing Co. fill management roles and provide the flight design, payload fairing, and satellite adapter. Astrotech, a contractor, oversees processing of customer payloads inside a clean room at the company's Payload Processing Facility at Home Port in Long Beach, California.

After 27 missions in nine years of business, Sea Launch is thriving in the do-or-die commercial launch industry. The company's Zenit 3SL rocket has suffered three setbacks in that time. Two were total failures. The rocket's success rate places it among the top tier of heavy-lift launchers on the commercial market, and the company's launch backlog seems to confirm that. Sea Launch

is already booking payloads for launch in the future. Next year is sold out, according to company officials.

Sea Launch Home Port is a decommissioned U.S. Navy facility on the tip of a manmade peninsula at the Port of Long Beach. The Sea Launch buildings are all left over from the Navy except for the Payload Processing Facility, which the company built in the late 1990s. The company's pier is home to two one-of-a-kind vessels—the *Sea Launch Commander* and the *Odyssey* launch platform. The *Sea Launch Commander* carries about 240 people, ranging from rocket technicians and corporate leaders to chefs and helicopter pilots. The *Commander* houses a state-of-the-art launch control center divided between two sections designed for Ukrainian and Russian engineers and American engineers and managers. The cavernous rocket assembly and checkout hall is located on the command ship's lower deck and stretches nearly the entire length of the vessel. The facility is capable of supporting two simultaneous launch campaigns using staging and integration compartments and a fueling cell. Giant cranes inside the high bays lift rocket stages, which sits on Russian-gauge rails on the floor integration room floor. The rocket's ground support equipment inside the *Sea Launch Commander* is virtually identical to hardware used for Zenit launches at the Baikonur Cosmodrome in Kazakhstan, according to Sea Launch officials.

The *Sea Launch Commander* was specially constructed for Sea Launch at a Scotland shipyard by the maritime unit of Kvaerner, then a leading Norwegian industrial company. Measuring 656 feet long and 105 feet wide, the command ship was outfitted with more than 600 tons of rocket support equipment in Russia before sailing to Long Beach in 1998. The massive ship's crew quarters are home to Sea Launch's international employees during their stay in the United States.

The Sea Launch Commander and the Odyssey platform are seen here docked at Home Port.

Credit: Chris Miller/Spaceflight Now

A Wealth of Supplements

Global Perspectives

At the beginning of each chapter, Global Perspectives give examples of current company experiences in global marketing. Illustrating chapter concepts, these profiles help students to combine the theory they read about with real-life application.

Global Perspective
GLOBAL COMMERCE CAUSES PEACE

Global commerce thrives during peacetime. The economic boom in North America during the late 1990s was in large part due to the end of the Cold War and the opening of the formerly communist countries to the world trading system. However, we should also understand the important role that trade and international marketing play in producing peace.

Boeing Company, one of America's largest exporters, is perhaps the most prominent example. Although many would argue that Boeing's military sales (aircraft and missiles) do not exactly promote peace, over most of the company's history, that business has constituted only about 20–25 percent of the company's commercial activity. The company still counts customers in more than 150 countries, and its 169,000 employees work in 65 countries.[1] The new 787 Dreamliner uses parts from around the world, including Australia, France, India, Italy, Japan, Russia, and Sweden. Its more than 12,000 commercial jets in service worldwide carry about 1 billion travelers per year. Its NASA Services division is the lead contractor in the construction and operation of the 16-country International Space Station, first manned by an American and two Russians in the fall of 2000. The Space and Intelligence Systems Division also produces and launches communications satellites affecting people in every country.

All the activity associated with the development, production, and marketing of commercial aircraft and space vehicles requires millions of people from around the world to work together. Moreover, no company does more[2] to enable people from all countries to meet face-to-face for both recreation and commerce. All this interaction yields not just the mutual gain associated with business relationships but also personal relationships and mutual understanding. The latter are the foundation of global peace and prosperity.

Another group of companies that promotes global dialogue and therefore peace is the mobile phone industry. By 2015, the number of mobile phone subscribers exceeded 7.0 billion. Samsung (South Korea), Nokia (Finland), and Apple (United States) are the market leaders.

Individuals and small companies also make a difference—perhaps a subtler one than large multinational companies, but one just as important in the aggregate. Our favorite example is Daniel Lubetzky's company, PeaceWorks. Mr. Lubetzky used a fellowship at Stanford Law School to study how to foster joint ventures between Arabs and Israelis. Then, following his own advice, he created a company that combined basil pesto from Israel with other raw materials and glass jars supplied by an Arab partner to produce the first product in a line he called Moshe & Ali's Gourmet Foods. The company now sells four different product lines in 15,000 stores in the United States and has its headquarters on Park Avenue in New York, as well as business operations in Israel, Egypt, Indonesia, Turkey, and Sri Lanka. Again, beyond the measurable commercial benefits of cooperation between the involved Arabs, Israelis, and others is the longer-lasting and more fundamental appreciation for one another's circumstances and character.

International marketing is hard work. Making sales calls is no vacation, even in Paris, especially when you've been there 10 times before. But international marketing is important work. It can enrich you, your family, your company, and your country. And ultimately, when international marketing is done well, by large companies or small, the needs and wants of customers in other lands are well understood, and prosperity and peace are promoted along the way.[3]

Sources: For more details, see http://boeing.com, http://airbus.com, http://peaceworks.com; Heidi Vogt, "Making Change: Mobile Pay in Africa," *The Wall Street Journal*, January 2, 2015, p. B6. Cell phone sales data are available at http://www.mobithinking.com.

[1]Boeing's 2014 Annual Report (http://www.boeing.com).

[2]The European commercial aircraft manufacturer Airbus is beginning to catch up, employing 63,000 people around the world (see Airbus's 2014 Annual Report, http://www.airbus.com).

[3]In response to criticisms of globalization catalyzed by the riots in Seattle in 1999, a growing literature argues for trade as a fundamental cause of peace. For a variety of such arguments, see Jagdish Bhabwati, *In Defense of Globalization* (Oxford: Oxford University Press, 2004); Thomas L. Friedman, *The World Is Flat* (New York: Farrar, Straus, and Giroux, 2005); Clifford J. Schultz III, Timothy J. Burkink, Bruno Grbac, and Natasa Renko, "When Policies and Marketing Systems Explode: An Assessment of Food Marketing in the War-Ravaged Balkans and Implications for Recovery, Sustainable Peace, and Prosperity," *Journal of Public Policy & Marketing* 24, no. 1 (2005), pp. 24–37; William Hernandez Requejo and John L. Graham, *Global Negotiation: The New Rules* (New York: Palgrave Macmillan, 2008), Chapter 13; Steven Pinker, *The Better Angels of Our Nature: Why Violence Has Declined* (New York: Viking, 2011), Hernando de Soto, "The Capitalist Cure for Terrorism," *Wall Street Journal*, October 10, 2014, online.)

Required=Results

McGraw-Hill Connect®
Learn Without Limits

Connect is a teaching and learning platform that is proven to deliver better results for students and instructors.

Connect empowers students by continually adapting to deliver precisely what they need, when they need it, and how they need it, so your class time is more engaging and effective.

Course outcomes improve with Connect.

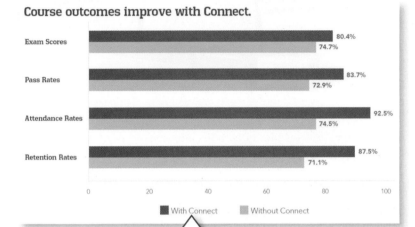

	With Connect	Without Connect
Exam Scores	80.4%	74.7%
Pass Rates	83.7%	72.9%
Attendance Rates	92.5%	74.5%
Retention Rates	87.5%	71.1%

88% of instructors who use **Connect** require it; instructor satisfaction **increases** by 38% when **Connect** is required.

Using **Connect** improves passing rates by **10.8%** and retention by **16.4%**.

Analytics

Connect Insight®

Connect Insight is Connect's new one-of-a-kind visual analytics dashboard—now available for both instructors and students—that provides at-a-glance information regarding student performance, which is immediately actionable. By presenting assignment, assessment, and topical performance results together with a time metric that is easily visible for aggregate or individual results, Connect Insight gives the user the ability to take a just-in-time approach to teaching and learning, which was never before available. Connect Insight presents data that empowers students and helps instructors improve class performance in a way that is efficient and effective.

Connect helps students achieve better grades

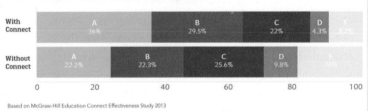

	A	B	C	D	F
With Connect	36%	29.5%	22%	4.3%	
Without Connect	22.2%	22.3%	25.6%	9.8%	

Based on McGraw-Hill Education Connect Effectiveness Study 2013

Students can view their results for any **Connect** course.

Mobile

Connect's new, intuitive mobile interface gives students and instructors flexible and convenient, anytime–anywhere access to all components of the Connect platform.

Adaptive

THE FIRST AND ONLY **ADAPTIVE READING EXPERIENCE** DESIGNED TO TRANSFORM THE WAY STUDENTS READ

> More students earn **A's** and **B's** when they use McGraw-Hill Education **Adaptive** products.

SmartBook®

Proven to help students improve grades and study more efficiently, SmartBook contains the same content within the print book, but actively tailors that content to the needs of the individual. SmartBook's adaptive technology provides precise, personalized instruction on what the student should do next, guiding the student to master and remember key concepts, targeting gaps in knowledge and offering customized feedback, and driving the student toward comprehension and retention of the subject matter. Available on smartphones and tablets, SmartBook puts learning at the student's fingertips—anywhere, anytime.

> Over **4 billion questions** have been answered, making McGraw-Hill Education products more intelligent, reliable, and precise.

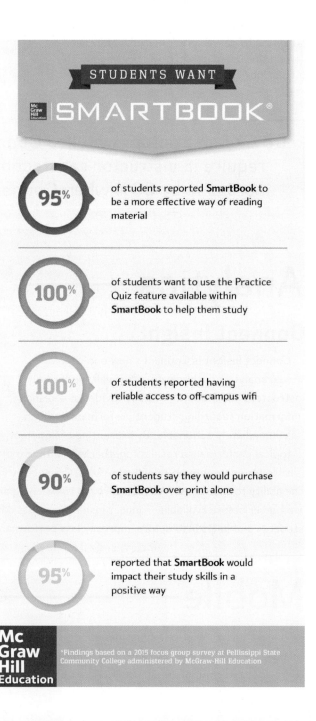

STUDENTS WANT

SMARTBOOK®

95% of students reported **SmartBook** to be a more effective way of reading material

100% of students want to use the Practice Quiz feature available within **SmartBook** to help them study

100% of students reported having reliable access to off-campus wifi

90% of students say they would purchase **SmartBook** over print alone

95% reported that **SmartBook** would impact their study skills in a positive way

*Findings based on a 2015 focus group survey at Pellissippi State Community College administered by McGraw-Hill Education

Mc Graw Hill Education

CONNECT INSTRUCTOR LIBRARY

Instructor's Manual: The custom-designed Instructor's Manual includes chapter summaries, learning objectives, an extended chapter outline, key terms, description of text boxes, discussion questions, summary of end-of-chapter cases, and additional activities.

Test Bank: The Test Bank has been revised and updated to reflect the content of the Seventeenth edition of the book. Each chapter includes multiple-choice, true/false, and essay questions.

PowerPoint: The slides include lecture material, additional content to expand concepts in the text, and the PowerPoint slides also include detailed teaching notes.

Videos: International *Marketing,* seventeenth edition, offers links to videos accompanied by instructional notes and discussion questions.

Cases: New cases accompany the seventeenth edition. These cases bring forth many of the topics discussed in the chapters and demonstrate how these concepts are dealt with in the real world. These cases are available in Connect.

Country Notebook: This writing guide will help students develop a marketing plan that contains information a marketer should be aware of when making decisions involving a specific country market.

Binder-Ready Loose-Leaf Text (ISBN 1259305708)

This full-featured text is provided as an option to the price-sensitive student. It is a four-color text that's three-hole punched and made available at a discount to students. It is also available in a package with Connect.

Tegrity Campus: Lectures 24/7

Tegrity Campus is a service that makes class time available 24/7 by automatically capturing every lecture in a searchable format for students to review when they study and complete assignments. With a simple one-click start-and-stop process, you capture all computer screens and corresponding audio. Students can replay any part of any class with easy-to-use browser-based viewing on a PC or Mac.

Educators know that the more students can see, hear, and experience class resources, the better they learn. In fact, studies prove it. With Tegrity Campus, students quickly recall key moments by using Tegrity Campus's unique search feature. This search helps students efficiently find what they need, when they need it, across an entire semester of class recordings. Help turn all your students' study time into learning moments immediately supported by your lecture.

To learn more about Tegrity, watch a two-minute Flash demo at http://tegritycampus.mhhe.com.

Assurance of Learning Ready

Many educational institutions today are focused on the notion of *assurance of learning,* an important element of some accreditation standards. *International Marketing* is designed specifically to support your assurance of learning initiatives with a simple, yet powerful solution. Each test bank question for *International Marketing* maps to a specific chapter learning outcome/objective listed in the text. You can use *Connect Marketing* to easily query for learning outcomes/objectives that directly relate to the learning objectives for your course.

McGraw-Hill Higher Education and Blackboard

McGraw-Hill Higher Education and Blackboard have teamed up. What does this mean for you?

1. **Your life, simplified.** Now you and your students can access McGraw-Hill's Connect™ and Create™ right from within your Blackboard course—all with one single sign-on. Say good-bye to the days of logging in to multiple applications.

2. **Deep integration of content and tools.** Not only do you get single sign-on with Connect™ and Create™, you also get deep integration of McGraw-Hill content

and content engines right in Blackboard. Whether you're choosing a book for your course or building Connect™ assignments, all the tools you need are right where you want them—inside of Blackboard.

3. **Seamless Gradebooks.** Are you tired of keeping multiple gradebooks and manually synchronizing grades into Blackboard? We thought so. When a student completes an integrated Connect™ assignment, the grade for that assignment automatically (and instantly) feeds your Blackboard grade center.

4. **A solution for everyone.** Whether your institution is already using Blackboard or you just want to try Blackboard on your own, we have a solution for you. McGraw-Hill and Blackboard can now offer you easy access to industry leading technology and content, whether your campus hosts it, or we do. Be sure to ask your local McGraw-Hill representative for details.

AACSB Statement

The McGraw-Hill Companies is a proud corporate member of AACSB International. Understanding the importance and value of AACSB accreditation, *International Marketing,* Seventeenth Edition, recognizes the curricula guidelines detailed in the AACSB standards for business accreditation by connecting selected questions in the test bank to the six general knowledge and skill guidelines in the AACSB standards.

The statements contained in *International Marketing,* Seventeenth Edition, are provided only as a guide for the users of this textbook. The AACSB leaves content coverage and assessment within the purview of individual schools, the mission of the school, and the faculty. While *International Marketing,* Seventeenth Edition, and the teaching package make no claim of any specific AACSB qualification or evaluation, we have within International Marketing, Seventeenth Edition, labeled selected questions according to the six general knowledge and skills areas.

McGraw-Hill Campus

McGraw-Hill Campus is a new one-stop teaching and learning experience available to users of any learning management system. This institutional service allows faculty and students to enjoy single sign-on (SSO) access to all McGraw-Hill Higher Education materials, including the award-winning McGraw-Hill Connect platform, from directly within the institution's website. With McGraw-Hill Campus, faculty receive instant access to teaching materials (e.g., eBooks, test banks, PowerPoint slides, animations, learning objects, etc.), allowing them to browse, search, and use any instructor ancillary content in our vast library at no additional cost to instructor or students.

McGraw-Hill Education Customer Care Contact Information

At McGraw-Hill, we understand that getting the most from new technology can be challenging. That's why our services don't stop after you purchase our products. You can e-mail our Product Specialists 24 hours a day to get product-training online. Or you can search our knowledge bank of Frequently Asked Questions on our support website. For Customer Support, call **800-331-5094,** e-mail hmsupport@mcgraw-hill.com, or visit www.mhhe.com/support. One of our Technical Support Analysts will be able to assist you in a timely fashion.

ABOUT THE AUTHORS

Philip R. Cateora Professor Emeritus, The University of Colorado at Boulder. Received his Ph.D. from the University of Texas at Austin where he was elected to Beta Gamma Sigma. In his academic career at the University of Colorado he has served as Division Head of Marketing, Coordinator of International Business Programs, Associate Dean, and Interim Dean. His teaching has spanned a range of courses in marketing and international business, from fundamentals through the doctoral level. He received the University of Colorado Teaching Excellence Award and the Western Marketing Educator's Association's Educator of the Year Award.

Professor Cateora has conducted faculty workshops on internationalizing principles of marketing courses for the AACSB and participated in designing and offering similar faculty workshops under a grant by the Department of Education. In conjunction with these efforts, he co-authored *Marketing: An International Perspective,* a supplement to accompany principles of marketing texts. Professor Cateora has served as consultant to small export companies as well as multinational companies, served on the Rocky Mountain Export Council, and taught in management development programs. He is a Fellow of the Academy of International Business.

Mary C. Gilly Professor of Marketing at the Paul Merage School of Business, University of California, Irvine. She received her B.A. from Trinity University in San Antonio, Texas; her M.B.A. from Southern Methodist University in Dallas, Texas; and her Ph.D. from the University of Houston. At UCI, Dr. Gilly has served as Vice Dean, Associate Dean, Director of the Ph.D. Program, Faculty Chair in the School of Business, Associate Dean of Graduate Studies, and Chair of the Academic Senate for the campus. She was elected Chair of the UC Academic Council and served at the UC Office of the President from 2013 through 2015. She has been on the faculties of Texas A&M University and Southern Methodist University and has been a visiting professor at the Madrid Business School and Georgetown University. Professor Gilly has been a member of the American Marketing Association since 1975 and has served that organization in a number of capacities, including Marketing Education Council, President, Co-Chair of the 1991 AMA Summer Educators' Conference, and member and chair of the AMA–Irwin Distinguished Marketing Educator Award Committee. She currently serves as Academic Director for the Association for Consumer Research. Professor Gilly has published her research on international, cross-cultural, and consumer behavior topics in *Journal of Marketing*, *Journal of Consumer Research*, *Journal of Retailing*, *California Management Review*, and other venues. In 2011, she received the Williams-Qualls-Spraten Multicultural Mentoring Award of Excellence.

John L. Graham Professor Emeritus of International Business and Marketing at the Paul Merage School of Business, University of California, Irvine. At UCI he is the Director of the Center for Global Leadership and has served as Associate Dean, Director of the John & Marilyn Long US-China Institute for Business & Law, and Director of the Center for Citizen Peacebuilding; Visiting Scholar, Georgetown University School of Business; Visiting Professor at Madrid Business School in Spain; and Associate Professor, University of Southern California. Before beginning his doctoral studies at UC Berkeley, he worked for a division of Caterpillar Tractor Co. and served as an officer in the U.S. Navy Underwater Demolition/SEAL Teams. Professor Graham is the author of (with Lynda Lawrence and William Hernandez Requejo), Inventive Negotiation: *Getting Beyond Yes*, Palgrave-Macmillan, 2014; (with William Hernandez Requejo) of *Global Negotiation: The New Rules*, Palgrave-Macmillan, 2008; (with N. Mark Lam) of *China Now, Doing Business in the World's Most Dynamic Market,* McGraw-Hill, 2007; (with Yoshihiro Sano and James Hodgson, former U.S. Ambassador to Japan) of *Doing Business with the New Japan,* Rowman & Littlefield, 4th edition, 2008; and editor (with Taylor Meloan) of *Global and International Marketing,* Irwin, 2nd edition, 1997. He has published articles in publications such as *Harvard Business Review, Journal of Marketing, Journal of International Business Studies, Strategic Management Review, Journal of Consumer Research, Journal of International Marketing,* and *Marketing Science.* Excerpts of his work have been read into the *Congressional Record,* and his research on business negotiation styles in 20 cultures was the subject of an article in the January 1988 issue of *Smithsonian.* His 1994 paper in *Management Science* received a citation of excellence from the Lauder Institute at the Wharton School of Business. He was selected for the 2009 International Trade Educator of the Year Award, given by the North American Small Business International Trade Educators' Association.

R. Bruce Money

Fred Meyer Professor of International Business and Marketing; Director of the Whitmore Global Management Center, Marriott School, Brigham Young University. Professor Money has been teaching and researching international marketing for more than 20 years. He holds a B.A. from BYU, an M.B.A. from the Harvard Business School, and a Ph.D. in marketing from the University of California, Irvine. Prior to joining BYU, he served nine years on the faculty of the University of South Carolina, perennially ranked as one of the top international business programs in the country. His international marketing research has been published in leading academic outlets such as *Journal of Marketing, Journal of International Business Studies* and *Harvard Business Review* (in abstract). He has won seven teaching awards at the undergraduate, MBA, and executive MBA program levels. Prior to his academic career, Dr. Money gained 10 years of professional and nonprofit experience, mostly in the international marketing of financial services. Proficient in Japanese, his most recent business position was vice president in the Los Angeles office of The Sakura Bank, Ltd. (now Sumitomo Mitsui), one of the world's largest banks. There, he directed the bank's marketing strategy for *Fortune* 100 prospects for the western United States (11 states). Dr. Money also served as partner in a consultancy to William E. Simon, former U.S. Secretary of the Treasury, for whom he initiated a Japanese joint venture program. He also directed $1 billion in Japanese debt and equity relationships for the Koll Company (now CB Richard Ellis), the West Coast's largest real estate developer at that time. Dr. Money has taught in dozens of executive education programs for clients such as Nissan's Tokyo headquarters, Bosch Corporation, Bayer, CSX, and Norsk Hydro. He has also been a visiting professor of international marketing at business schools in Austria and Greece.

PREFACE

At the start of the last millennium, the Chinese were the preeminent international traders. Although a truly global trading system would not evolve until some 500 years later, Chinese silk had been available in Europe since Roman times.

At the start of the last century, the British military, merchants, and manufacturers dominated the seas and international commerce. Literally, the sun did not set on the British Empire.

At the start of this century, the United States had surged past a faltering Japan to retake the lead in global commerce. The American domination of information technology has since been followed by the political upheaval of 9/11 and the economic shocks of 2001 and 2008. China started the 21st century as the largest military threat to the United States, and within a decade it had become a leading, often difficult trading partner.

What surprises do the new decade, century, and millennium hold in store for all of us? In this century, natural disasters and wars hampered commerce and human progress. Just in the last decade, we have witnessed the human tragedy and economic disaster of a 1000-year earthquake and tsunami and a nuclear meltdown in Japan; protests and revolutions—the so-called Arab Spring—across the Middle East and North Africa (MENA); widespread economic protests across the developed countries; and the ongoing potential for a financial meltdown in the European Union. The battle to balance economic growth and stewardship of the environment continues. The globalization of markets has certainly accelerated through almost universal acceptance of the democratic free enterprise model and new communication technologies, including cell phones and the Internet. Which will prove the better, Chinese gradualism or the Russian big-bang approach to economic and political reform? Will the information technology boom of the previous decade be followed by a demographics bust as American baby boomers continue to retire in greater numbers. Or will NAFTA and the young folks in Mexico provide a much needed demographic balance? Ten years out the debate about global warming should be settled—more data and better science will yield the answers. Will the economic tsunami of 2008–2009 evolve into something even worse? So far the recovery in the United States in Europe, and Japan has been both tepid and uneven. China's growth is slowing; will the landing be a hard or soft one? What unforeseen advances or disasters will the biological sciences bring us? Will we conquer AIDS/HIV in Africa? Will weapons and warfare become obsolete?

International marketing will play a key role in providing positive answers to all these questions. We know that trade causes peace and prosperity by promoting creativity, mutual understanding, and interdependence. Markets recently burgeoning in emerging economies in eastern Europe, the Commonwealth of Independent States, China, Indonesia, Korea, India, Mexico, Chile, Brazil, Argentina, and across sub-Sahara Africa have begun sputtering. These emerging economies still hold the promise of huge markets in the future. In the more mature markets of the industrialized world, opportunity and challenge also abound as consumers' tastes become more sophisticated and complex and as the hoped for rebound in purchasing power provides consumers with new means of satisfying new demands.

With the recent downturn in the industrialized countries and the stalled growth in emerging markets has come a new competitive landscape, one vastly different from that earlier period when U.S. multinationals dominated world markets. From the late 1940s through the 1960s, multinational corporations (MNCs) from the United States had little competition; today, companies from almost all the world's nations vie for global markets.

The economic, political, and social changes that have occurred over the last decade have dramatically altered the landscape of global business. Consider the present and future impact of the following:

- The ever-present threat of global terrorism as represented by the September 11, 2001, attacks

- Major armed conflicts in sub-Saharan Africa and the Middle East

- The potential global recession emanating from the United States

- The emerging markets in eastern Europe, Asia, and Latin America, where more than 75 percent of the growth in world trade over the next 20 years is expected to occur
- The reunification of Hong Kong, Macau, and China, which finally puts all of Asia under the control of Asians for the first time in over a century
- The European Monetary Union and the successful switch from local-country currencies to one monetary unit for Europe, the euro, and its apparent fragility
- The rapid move away from traditional distribution structures in Japan, Europe, and many emerging markets
- The shrinking of middle-income households the world over
- The continued struggles of regional market groups such as the European Union (EU), the North American Free Trade Area (NAFTA), the Central American Free Trade Area (CAFTA), ASEAN Free Trade Area (AFTA), the Southern Cone Free Trade Area (Mercosur), and the Asia-Pacific Economic Cooperation (APEC)
- The so far unsuccessful completion of the Uruguay Round of the General Agreement on Tariffs and Trade (GATT) and the creation of the World Trade Organization (WTO), the latter now including China and Taiwan
- The restructuring, reorganizing, and refocusing of companies in telecommunications, entertainment, and biotechnology, as well as in traditional smokestack industries around the world
- The continuing integration of the Internet and cell phones into all aspects of companies' operations and consumers' lives

These are not simply news reports. These changes affect the practice of business worldwide, and they mean that companies will have to constantly examine the way they do business and remain flexible enough to react rapidly to changing global trends to be competitive.

As global economic growth occurs, understanding marketing in all cultures is increasingly important. *International Marketing* addresses global issues and describes concepts relevant to all international marketers, regardless of the extent of their international involvement. Not all firms engaged in overseas marketing have a global perspective, nor do they need to. Some companies' foreign marketing is limited to one country; others market in a number of countries, treating each as a separate market; and still others, the global enterprises, look for market segments with common needs and wants across political and economic boundaries. All, however, are affected by competitive activity in the global marketplace. It is with this future that the seventeenth edition of *International Marketing* is concerned.

Emphasis is on the strategic implications of competition in different country markets. An environmental/cultural approach to international marketing permits a truly global orientation. The reader's horizons are not limited to any specific nation or to the particular ways of doing business in a single nation. Instead, the book provides an approach and framework for identifying and analyzing the important cultural and environmental uniqueness of any nation or global region. Thus, when surveying the tasks of marketing in a foreign milieu, the reader will not overlook the impact of crucial cultural issues.

The text is designed to stimulate curiosity about management practices of companies, large and small, seeking market opportunities outside the home country and to raise the reader's consciousness about the importance of viewing international marketing management strategies from a global perspective.

Although this revised edition is infused throughout with a global orientation, export marketing and the operations of smaller companies are also included. Issues specific to exporting are discussed where strategies applicable to exporting arise, and examples of marketing practices of smaller companies are examined.

New and Expanded Topics in This Edition

University students around the country (and the world) are particularly interested in the threats of global climate change, thousands even protesting on the topic. The major improvement in the 17th edition is the strengthened emphasis on how international marketing can help. The new material starts with the cover which demonstrates the use of electricity (that is, energy) around the world. We focus on Europe because that continent has done the best job of reducing their carbon footprint. The image also reflects the high population density in India, the continuing reductions in the polar icecaps, and the brightness of our immense consumption of energy in North America. Seven different chapters include new information on fossil and renewable energy and sustainability.

Other new and expanded topics in this seventeenth edition reflect issues in competition, changing marketing structures, ethics and social responsibility, negotiations, and the development of the manager for the 21st century. Competition is raising the global standards for quality, increasing the demand for advanced technology and innovation, and increasing the value of customer satisfaction. The global market is swiftly changing from a seller's market to a buyer's market. This is a period of profound social, economic, and political change. To remain competitive globally, companies must be aware of all aspects of the emerging global economic order.

Additionally, the evolution of global communications and its known and unknown impacts on how international business is conducted cannot be minimized. In the third millennium, people in the "global village" will grow closer than ever before and will hear and see each other as a matter of course. An executive in Germany can routinely connect via VoIP (Voice over Internet Protocol) to hear and see his or her counterpart in an Australian company or anywhere else in the world. In many respects (time zone differences is a prominent exception), geographic distance is becoming irrelevant.

Telecommunications, the Internet, and satellites are helping companies optimize their planning, production, and procurement processes. Information—and, in its wake, the flow of goods—is moving around the globe at lightning speed. Increasingly powerful networks spanning the globe enable the delivery of services that reach far beyond national and continental boundaries, fueling and fostering international trade. The connections of global communications bring people all around the world together in new and better forms of dialogue and understanding.

This dynamic nature of the international marketplace is reflected in the number of substantially improved and expanded topics in this sixteenth edition, including the following:

- All data, text, pictures, and exhibits have been updated throughout the text. Out-of-date materials have been deleted. More than 100 new academic articles and their findings have been also integrated and cited throughout.

- **Chapter 1** New material on the role of entrepreneurship in international marketing and environmental issues has been added to Chapter 1.

- **Chapter 2** The bumpy road of international marketing is exemplified by new trade talks between America and its Pacific and Atlantic neighbors. Meanwhile the United States and China agree to collaborate on reducing carbon emissions in the midst of a trade dispute over solar panels.

- **Chapter 3** Population growth and emerging economies both put new pressures on the international marketing system with respect to environmental impact. Both challenges and opportunities are created.

- **Chapter 4** This chapter includes a discussion of how culture and language are evolving in the environment of new communication technologies, from thumb typing to emoji.

- **Chapter 5** A new Crossing Borders box about how women's roles are changing in Japan has been added.
- **Chapter 6** Data, text, pictures, and exhibits have been updated. New material on how governments support environmental projects is provided.
- **Chapter 7** We continue the narrative of how technological changes push government policies (taxes, censorship, and cyberterrorism) around the world.
- **Chapter 8** Another scary new story about privacy and data collection is added in a new Crossing Borders box.
- **Chapter 9** The data included on Cuba suggest the international marketing potential now that the half-century embargo by the United States is being lifted.
- **Chapter 10** New emphasis is placed on the political/economic problems of Russia's annexation of Crimea and its ongoing dispute with the Ukraine and the associated trade sanctions imposed by both the EU and the United States.
- **Chapter 11** New Crossing Borders include a discussion of spam (both the meat and Internet sort) and how Asian culture affects the United States (think Gangnam Style). Also, American marketing errors in China are discussed in some detail.
- **Chapter 12** Market entry strategies are discussed for American media producers such as Netflix selling content and services in Europe.
- **Chapter 13** A section further describing how diversity yields innovation is added, and a new section extends the definition of product quality to include public health and safety concerns.
- **Chapter 14** Toyota's revolutionary introduction of hydrogen fuel cell vehicles is discussed along with innovations in the use of wood pellets as carbon neutral fuels in the European Union.
- **Chapter 15** Crossing Borders boxes are added on American-style food trucks in Paris and the importance of shipping container technology. The section on Marriott Internet technology approaches is updated, and a rare error made by Alibaba in China is noted.
- **Chapter 16** The continuing decline of print, the coming decline of TV, and the growing dominance of the Internet are charted. A new Crossing Borders further demonstrates the challenges associated with translation of advertising messages. The distinction between public relations and advertising is illustrated through a marketing mistake made by Samsung in Italy.
- **Chapter 17** New emphasis on the importance of learning foreign languages is presented.
- **Chapter 18** A new Global Perspective provides details about chocolate and sugar price volatility and controls, both affecting the price of Oreos around the world. Also, new data on oil price volatility is presented.
- **Chapter 19** New materials on the topic of inventive international negotiation are included.
- **Three new cases:** (1) Club Med and the Global Consumption of Leisure, (2) Pricing Gillette's New Razor for the Developing World, and (3) Child Labor in IKEA's Global Supply Chain. All the cases will be available within Connect and SmartBook.

Structure of the Text

The text is divided into six parts. The first two chapters, Part 1, introduce the reader to the environmental/cultural approach to international marketing and to three international marketing management concepts: domestic market expansion, multidomestic marketing, and global marketing. As companies restructure for the global economic and competitive rigors of the 21st century, so too must tomorrow's managers. The successful manager must be globally aware and have a frame of reference that goes beyond a country, or even a region, and encompasses the world. What global awareness means and how it is acquired is discussed early in the text; it is at the foundation of global marketing.

Chapter 2 focuses on the dynamic environment of international trade and the competitive challenges and opportunities confronting today's international marketer. The importance of the creation of the World Trade Organization, the successor to GATT, is fully explored. The growing importance of cell phones and the Internet in conducting international business is considered, creating a foundation on which specific applications in subsequent chapters are presented.

The five chapters in Part 2 deal with the cultural environment of global marketing. A global orientation requires the recognition of cultural differences and the critical decision of whether it is necessary to accommodate them.

Geography and history (Chapter 3) are included as important dimensions in understanding cultural and market differences among countries. New emphasis is placed on the concern for the deterioration of the global ecological environment and the multinational company's critical responsibility to protect it.

Chapter 4 presents a broad review of culture and its impact on human behavior as it relates to international marketing. Specific attention is paid to Geert Hofstede's study of cultural values and behavior. The elements of culture reviewed in Chapter 4 set the stage for the indepth analyses in Chapters 5, 6, and 7 of business customs and the political and legal environments. Ethics and social responsibility are presented in the context of the dilemma that often confronts the international manager, that is, balancing corporate profits against the social and ethical consequences of his or her decisions.

We have organized Part 3 of the book into four chapters on assessing global market opportunities. As markets expand, segments grow within markets; as market segments across country markets evolve, marketers are forced to understand market behavior within and across different cultural contexts. Multicultural research, qualitative and quantitative research, and the Internet as a tool in the research task are explored in Chapter 8.

Separate chapters on economic development and the Americas (Chapter 9); Europe, Africa, and the Middle East (Chapter 10); and the Asia Pacific Region (Chapter 11) reflect the evolving marketing organizations of many multinational companies in response to the costs of travel and communications across time zones, as well as the steady creation and growth of regional market groups in all three regions. The discussions in all three chapters include details about both established and emerging markets present in each region.

The strategic implications of the dissolution of the Soviet Union and the emergence of new independent republics, the shift from socialist-based to market-based economies in Eastern Europe, and the return of South Africa, Cuba, and Vietnam to international commerce are examined. Attention is also given to the efforts of the governments of China and India and many Latin American countries to reduce or eliminate barriers to trade, open their countries to foreign investment, and privatize state-owned enterprises.

These political, social, and economic changes that are sweeping the world are creating new markets and opportunities, making some markets more accessible while creating the potential for greater protectionism in others.

In Part 4, Developing Global Marketing Strategies, planning and organizing for global marketing is the subject of Chapter 12. The discussion of collaborative relationships, including strategic alliances, recognizes the importance of relational collaborations among firms, suppliers, and customers in the success of the global marketer. Many multinational companies realize that to fully capitalize on opportunities offered by global markets, they must have strengths that often exceed their capabilities. Collaborative relationships can provide technology, innovations, productivity, capital, and market access that strengthen a company's competitive position.

Chapters 13 and 14 focus on product and services management, reflecting the differences in strategies between consumer and industrial offerings and the growing importance in world markets for both consumer and business services. Additionally, the discussion on the development of global offerings stresses the importance of approaching the adaptation issue from the viewpoint of building a standardized product/service platform that can be adapted to reflect cultural differences. The competitive importance in today's global market of quality, innovation, and technology as the keys to marketing success is explored.

Chapter 15 takes the reader through the distribution process, from home country to the consumer in the target country market. The structural impediments to market entry imposed by a country's distribution system are examined in the framework of a detailed presentation of the Japanese distribution system. Additionally, the rapid changes in channel structure that are occurring in Japan, as well as in other countries, and the emergence of the World Wide Web as a distribution channel are presented.

Chapter 16 covers advertising and addresses the promotional element of the international marketing mix. Included in the discussion of global market segmentation are recognition of the rapid growth of market segments across country markets and the importance of market segmentation as a strategic competitive tool in creating an effective promotional message. Chapter 17 discusses personal selling and sales management and the critical nature of training, evaluating, and controlling sales representatives.

Price escalation and ways it can be lessened, countertrade practices, and price strategies to employ when the dollar is strong or weak relative to foreign currencies are concepts presented in Chapter 18.

In Part 5, Chapter 19 is a thorough presentation of negotiating with customers, partners, and regulators. The discussion stresses the varying negotiation styles found among cultures and the importance of recognizing these differences at the negotiation table.

Pedagogical Features of the Text

The text portion of the book provides thorough coverage of its subject, with a subject emphasis on the planning and strategic problems confronting companies that market across cultural boundaries.

The use of the Internet as a tool of international marketing is stressed throughout the text. On all occasions in which data used in the text originated from an Internet source, the web address is given. Problems that require the student to access the Internet are included with end-of-chapter questions. Internet-related problems are designed to familiarize the student with the power of the Internet in his or her research, to illustrate data available on the Internet, and to challenge the reader to solve problems using the Internet. Many of the examples, illustrations, and exhibits found in the text can be explored in more detail by accessing the web addresses that are included.

Current, pithy, sometimes humorous, and always relevant examples are used to stimulate interest and increase understanding of the ideas, concepts, and strategies presented in emphasizing the importance of understanding cultural uniqueness and relevant business practices and strategies.

Each chapter is introduced with a Global Perspective, a real-life example of company experiences that illustrates salient issues discussed in the chapter. Companies featured in the Global Perspectives range from exporters to global enterprises.

The boxed Crossing Borders, an innovation of the first edition of *International Marketing*, have always been popular with students. They reflect contemporary issues in international marketing and can be used to illustrate real-life situations and as the basis for class discussion. They are selected to be unique, humorous, and of general interest to the reader.

The book is presented in full color, allowing maps to depict geographical, cultural, and political boundaries and features more easily. Color also allows us to better communicate the intricacies of international symbols and meanings in marketing communications. New photographs of current and relevant international marketing events are found throughout the text—all in color.

The Country Notebook—A Guide for Developing a Marketing Plan, found in Part 6, Supplementary Material, is a detailed outline that provides both a format for a complete cultural and economic analysis of a country and guidelines for developing a marketing plan.

In addition to The Country Notebook, the seventeenth edition comprises a selection of short and long cases located in Connect. The short cases focus on a single problem, serving as the basis for discussion of a specific concept or issue. The longer, more integrated cases are broader in scope and focus on more than one marketing management problem; new cases focus on services marketing, pricing, and ethics. The cases can be analyzed using the information provided. They also lend themselves to more in-depth analysis, requiring the student to engage in additional research and data collection.

Acknowledgments

The success of a text depends on the contributions of many people, especially those who take the time to share their thoughtful criticisms and suggestions to improve the text.

We would especially like to thank the following reviewers who gave us valuable insights into this revision:

Anthony Di Benedetto
Temple University

Richard Nasby
Regis University

Stefanie Mayfield-Garcia
University of Central Florida

Ruth Taylor
Texas State University

We appreciate the help of all the many students and professors who have shared their opinions of past editions, and we welcome their comments and suggestions on this and future editions of *International Marketing*.

A very special thanks to Susan Gouijnstook, Kim Leister, Heather Darr, Elizabeth Schonagen, Jessica Portz, and Kerry Shanahan, whose enthusiasm, creativity, constructive criticisms, and commitment to excellence have made this edition possible.

Philip R. Cateora
Mary C. Gilly
John L. Graham
R. Bruce Money

BRIEF CONTENTS

PART ONE

AN OVERVIEW

PART TWO

THE CULTURAL ENVIRONMENT OF GLOBAL MARKETS

PART THREE

ASSESSING GLOBAL MARKET OPPORTUNITIES

PART FOUR

DEVELOPING GLOBAL MARKETING STRATEGIES

PART FIVE

IMPLEMENTING GLOBAL MARKETING STRATEGIES

PART SIX

SUPPLEMENTARY MATERIAL

LIST OF "CROSSING BORDERS" BOXES

International Marketing

Chapter 1

The Scope and Challenge of International Marketing

Global Perspective

GLOBAL COMMERCE CAUSES PEACE

Global commerce thrives during peacetime. The economic boom in North America during the late 1990s was in large part due to the end of the Cold War and the opening of the formerly communist countries to the world trading system. However, we should also understand the important role that trade and international marketing play in producing peace.

Boeing Company, one of America's largest exporters, is perhaps the most prominent example. Although many would argue that Boeing's military sales (aircraft and missiles) do not exactly promote peace, over most of the company's history, that business has constituted only about 20–25 percent of the company's commercial activity. The company still counts customers in more than 150 countries, and its 169,000 employees work in 65 countries.[1] The new 787 Dreamliner uses parts from around the world, including Australia, France, India, Italy, Japan, Russia, and Sweden. Its more than 12,000 commercial jets in service worldwide carry about 1 billion travelers per year. Its NASA Services division is the lead contractor in the construction and operation of the 16-country International Space Station, first manned by an American and two Russians in the fall of 2000. The Space and Intelligence Systems Division also produces and launches communications satellites affecting people in every country.

All the activity associated with the development, production, and marketing of commercial aircraft and space vehicles requires millions of people from around the world to work together. Moreover, no company does more[2] to enable people from all countries to meet face-to-face for both recreation and commerce. All this interaction yields not just the mutual gain associated with business relationships but also personal relationships and mutual understanding. The latter are the foundation of global peace and prosperity.

Another group of companies that promotes global dialogue and therefore peace is the mobile phone industry. By 2015, the number of mobile phone subscribers exceeded 7.0 billion. Samsung (South Korea), Apple (United States), and Lenovo (China) are the market leaders.

Individuals and small companies also make a difference—perhaps a subtler one than large multinational companies, but one just as important in the aggregate. Our favorite example is Daniel Lubetzky's company, PeaceWorks. Mr. Lubetzky used a fellowship at Stanford Law School to study how to foster joint ventures between Arabs and Israelis. Then, following his own advice, he created a company that combined basil pesto from Israel with other raw materials and glass jars supplied by an Arab partner to produce the first product in a line he called Moshe & Ali's Gourmet Foods. The company now sells four different product lines in 15,000 stores in the United States and has its headquarters on Park Avenue in New York, as well as business operations in Israel, Egypt, Indonesia, Turkey, and Sri Lanka. Again, beyond the measurable commercial benefits of cooperation between the involved Arabs, Israelis, and others is the longer-lasting and more fundamental appreciation for one another's circumstances and character.

International marketing is hard work. Making sales calls is no vacation, even in Paris, especially when you've been there 10 times before. But international marketing is important work. It can enrich you, your family, your company, and your country. And ultimately, when international marketing is done well, by large companies or small, the needs and wants of customers in other lands are well understood, and prosperity and peace are promoted along the way.[3]

Sources: For more details, see http://boeing.com; http://airbus.com; http://peaceworks.com; Heidi Vogt, "Making Change: Mobile Pay in Africa," *The Wall Street Journal*, January 2, 2015, p. B6. Cell phone sales data are available at http://www.mobithinking.com.

---

[1]Boeing's 2014 Annual Report (http://www.boeing.com).

[2]The European commercial aircraft manufacturer Airbus is beginning to catch up, employing 63,000 people around the world (see Airbus's 2014 Annual Report, http://www.airbus.com).

[3]In response to criticisms of globalization catalyzed by the riots in Seattle in 1999, a growing literature argues for trade as a fundamental cause of peace. For a variety of such arguments, see Jagdish Bhabwati, *In Defense of Globalization* (Oxford: Oxford University Press, 2004); Thomas L. Friedman, *The World Is Flat* (New York: Farrar, Straus, and Giroux, 2005); Clifford J. Schultz III, Timothy J. Burkink, Bruno Grbac, and Natasa Renko, "When Policies and Marketing Systems Explode: An Assessment of Food Marketing in the War-Ravaged Balkans and Implications for Recovery, Sustainable Peace, and Prosperity," *Journal of Public Policy & Marketing* 24, no. 1 (2005), pp. 24–37; William Hernandez Requejo and John L. Graham, *Global Negotiation: The New Rules* (New York: Palgrave Macmillan, 2008), Chapter 13; Steven Pinker, *The Better Angels of Our Nature: Why Violence Has Declined* (New York: Viking, 2011; Hernando de Soto, "The Capitalist Cure for Terrorism," *Wall Street Journal*, October 10, 2014, online.)

The relationships between mobile phones and riots is well demonstrated by these two pictures. Mobile devices enable demonstrators to communicate and organize to great effect, even supporting successful revolutions such as those in Egypt in 2009. Particularly valuable are the photographic capabilities now available, which deliver the world as a witness to violence. Pictured on the left is Silicon Valley entrepreneur Micha Benoliel during the 2014 democracy protests in Hong Kong. His start-up, Open Garden, has produced an app branded as FireChat that allows smartphones to talk directly to one another via their embedded Bluetooth and Wi-Fi radios. He happened to be in Hong Kong on a layover between visits to potential customers in India and China. The tech-savvy demonstrators (Hong Kong has the highest concentration of cell phones of any city at 2.39 per person) appreciate the app—it allows them to organize even if the government shuts down cell phone services.[4] Meanwhile, nobody in the world works harder to keep order than the Chinese authorities in Beijing. The 2012 riot over unavailability of the latest Apple iPhone is, of course, nothing like those in Cairo or Hong Kong, and even might seem a little bit humorous, except that people were injured there as well.

LO1

The benefits of international markets

Never before in American history have U.S. businesses, large and small, been so deeply involved in and affected by international business. A global economic boom, unprecedented in modern economic history, has been under way as the drive for efficiency, productivity, and open, unregulated markets sweeps the world. Powerful economic, technological, industrial, political, and demographic forces are converging to build the foundation of a new global economic order on which the structure of a one-world economic and market system will be built.

When we wrote those words 15 years ago to open the eleventh edition of this book, the world was a very different place. The nation was still mesmerized by the information technology boom of the late 1990s. Most did not visualize the high-tech bust of 2001 or the Enron and WorldCom scandals. No one could have imagined the September 11, 2001 disasters, not even the perpetrators. The wars in Afghanistan and Iraq were not on the horizon. The major international conflict grabbing headlines then was the series of diplomatic dustups among China, Taiwan, and the United States. Who could have predicted the disruptions associated with the 2003 SARS outbreak in Asia? The great Indian Ocean tsunami of 2004 was perhaps impossible to anticipate. Oil priced at more than $100 per barrel was also unthinkable then—the price seemed to have peaked at about $40 per barrel in late 2000. Then in 2015, the world price of oil collapsed again to below $50 per barrel from more than $100 per barrel a few months earlier. We wrote about the promise of the space program and the international space station, whose future is now clouded by the demise of the space shuttle program and NASA budget cuts.

Through all these major events, American consumers had continued to spend, keeping the world economy afloat. Layoffs at industrial icons such as United Airlines and Boeing and a generally tough job market did not slow the booming American housing market until the fall of 2007. Lower government interest rates had yielded a refinancing stampede, distributing the cash that fueled the consumer spending, which finally began flagging in early 2008. Then in September and October of that year, the housing bubble burst, and the world financial system teetered on collapse. The ever faithful American consumer stopped buying, and world trade

---

[4] Noam Cohen, "Hong Kong Protests Propel FireChat Phone-to-Phone App," *New York Times*, October 5, 2014, online; and "It's Not Over," *The Economist*, January 2, 2015, pp. 16–17.

experienced its deepest decline in more than 50 years, a drop of 12.0 percent. It had dropped only twice during the previous half century: in 1975 by −3.1 percent after the OPEC oil crisis and in 1992 by −0.3 percent. Then in 2011, the earthquake and tsunami that hit Japan and floods in Thailand caused major trade disruptions. And seeing into the future is harder now than ever. Most experts expect global terrorism to increase, and the carnage in Bali, Madrid, London, and Mumbai seem to prove the point. Finally, as the global economy tries to recover, international trade tensions take on new importance. Competition from new Chinese companies continues to raise concerns in the United States. Brazilian and Indian multinationals are stepping up competitive pressures as well, particularly as their and other emerging economies fared better during the most recent global downturn.[5] Perhaps the best news in these rather glum times is that we have not experienced a dramatic nationalistic rise of trade protectionism, as in the 1930s. Additionally, the steady growth of the U.S. trade and balance of payments deficits dramatically abated during 2009, along with American consumer spending.

More recently, the turn of the decade brought astonishing surprises in the form of global protests and violence in response to the inequities that marked the financial losses suffered by citizens, both within and across countries. The so-called Arab Spring was ignited by a Tunisian street vendor's self-immolating protest of economic conditions and police harassment. Large-scale protests ensued in 15 countries in North Africa and the Middle East, resulting in the overthrow of autocratic governments in Tunisia, Egypt, and Libya. Along the Mediterranean coast, Greece, Italy, and Spain are feeling the pain of the global recession, creating the potential for a new north-south schism in the European Union. The protests in Greece were particularly violent. Both China and India experienced widespread protests against the heavy hands of governments there. In the United States, the Occupy Wall Street protests were imitated in several other cities around the nation and the world.

The continuing violence in the Middle East has again drawn the United States and an array of allies into the conflicts in Iraq and Syria. No one sees an end to this ongoing tragedy, and many believe outside interventions will make little difference, or just make things worse. The West African ebola debacle transformed from a scare into a real threat for the rest of the world.[6] The oil and gas boom caused by new discoveries and technologies has

Trade also is easing tensions between Taiwan and China[7] and among North Korea, its close neighbors, and the United States. Here a rail link between North and South Korea has opened for the first time in nearly 60 years to provide transportation of raw materials and managers from the South, bound for a special economic development zone at Kaesong in the North.[8]

[5]"Counting Their Blessings," *The Economist*, January 2, 2010, pp. 25–28.

[6]Manny Fernandez and Jack Healy, "CDC Says It Should Have Responded Quicker to Dallas Ebola Case," *New York Times*, October 15, 2014, p. A19.

[7]Andrew Jacobs, "Ma Ying-jeou Is Re-Elected Taiwan President, a Result that Is Likely to Please China," *The New York Times,* January 14, 2012.

[8]Bruce Wallace, "2 Trains Cross Korean Border," *Los Angeles Times*, May 17, 2007, p. A4.

Close neighbors are going in different directions. The European Parliament votes to start discussions with Turkey about joining the European Union. Trade is beginning to bridge the religious divide between Christian Europe and Muslim Asia Minor. Despite this positive vote, European equivocation is pushing Turkey toward building stronger trade links with its Arab neighbors. Ultimately, this may be a positive turn of events if Turkey is finally invited to join the European Union. Meanwhile, as Turkey grows economically, Greek citizens protest austerity measures forced on them by other EU nations. Ultimately Greece's continued membership in the EU is being threatened by its continuing economic malaise.[9]

been a pleasant surprise in the United States. However, environmentalists decry the consequent increases in use of fossil fuels and the dangers of fracking. While the U.S. and U.K. economies are weakly recovering from the 2009 economic earthquake, the rest of the world continues to struggle.

International marketing is affected by and affects all these things. In particular, the costs of risks in the politically and financially unstable North Africa/Middle East region have burgeoned. The potential economic disruptions in the European Union affect the forecasts and prospects for all multinational firms around the world. Even before the 2009 financial crisis, and for the first time in its history, McDonald's had closed its operations in a few Middle Eastern and Latin American countries. Damaged economies, increasing competition, and anti-Americanism have affected sales revenues everywhere. Indeed, the salient lesson for those involved in international commerce is to expect the unexpected. Any executive experienced in international business will verify that things never go as planned in global commerce. You still have to plan and forecast, but markets, particularly international ones, are ultimately unpredictable. The natural fluctuations in markets are best managed through building strong interpersonal and commercial relationships and broad portfolios of businesses. Flexibility means survival.

Perhaps now, more than ever, whether or not a U.S. company wants to participate directly in international business, it cannot escape the effects of the ever-increasing number of North American firms exporting, importing, and manufacturing abroad. Nor can it ignore the number of foreign-based firms operating in U.S. markets, the growth of regional trade areas, the rapid growth of world markets, and the increasing number of competitors for global markets.

---

[9] "The Euro's Next Crisis, Greece's Election," *The Economist*, January 3, 2015, p. 10.

Of all the events and trends affecting global business today, four stand out as the most dynamic, the ones that will influence the shape of international business beyond today's "bumpy roads" and far into the future: (1) the rapid growth of the World Trade Organization and new free trade agreements around the world; (2) the trend toward the acceptance of the free market system among developing countries in Latin America, Asia, and eastern Europe; (3) the burgeoning impact of the Internet, mobile phones, and other global media on the dissolution of national borders; and (4) the mandate to manage the resources and global environment properly for the generations to come.

Today most business activities are global in scope. Technology, research, capital investment, and production, as well as marketing, distribution, and communications networks, all have global dimensions. Every business must be prepared to compete in an increasingly interdependent global economic and physical environment, and all businesspeople must be aware of the effects of these trends when managing either a domestic company that exports or a multinational conglomerate. As one international expert noted, every American company is international, at least to the extent that its business performance is conditioned in part by events that occur abroad. Even companies that do not operate in the international arena are affected to some degree by the success of the European Union, the export-led growth in South Korea, the revitalized Mexican economy, the economic changes taking place in China, military conflicts in the Middle East, and climate change.

The challenge of international marketing is to develop strategic plans that are competitive in these intensifying global markets. For a growing number of companies, being international is no longer a luxury but a necessity for economic survival. These and other issues affecting the world economy, trade, markets, and competition are discussed throughout this text.

The Internationalization of U.S. Business

LO2

The changing face of U.S. business

Current interest in international marketing can be explained by changing competitive structures, coupled with shifts in demand characteristics in markets throughout the world. With the increasing globalization of markets, companies find they are unavoidably enmeshed with foreign customers, competitors, and suppliers, even within their own borders. They face competition on all fronts—from domestic firms and from foreign firms. A huge portion of all consumer products—from automobiles to dinnerware—sold in the United States is foreign made. Sony, Norelco, Samsung, Toyota, and Nescafé are familiar brands in the United States, and for U.S. industry, they are formidable opponents in a competitive struggle for U.S. and world markets.

Many familiar U.S. companies are now foreign controlled or headed in that direction. When you drop in at a 7-Eleven convenience store or buy Firestone tires, you are buying directly from Japanese companies. Some well-known brands no longer owned by U.S. companies are Carnation (Swiss), *The Wall Street Journal* (Australian), and the all-American Smith & Wesson handgun that won the U.S. West, which is owned by a British firm. The last U.S.-owned company to manufacture TV sets was Zenith, but even it was acquired by South Korea's LG Electronics Inc., which manufactures Goldstar TVs and other products. Pearle Vision, Universal Studios, and many more are currently owned or controlled by foreign multinational businesses (see Exhibit 1.1). Foreign direct investment in the United States is more than $3 trillion.[10] Companies from the United Kingdom lead the group of investors, with companies from the Japan, the Netherlands, Canada, and France following, in that order.

Other foreign companies that entered the U.S. market through exporting their products into the United States realized sufficient market share to justify building and buying manufacturing plants in the United States. Honda, BMW, and Mercedes are all manufacturing in the United States. Investments go the other way as well. Ford bought and sold Volvo; PacifiCorp acquired Energy Group, the United Kingdom's largest electricity supplier and second-largest gas distributor; and Wisconsin Central Transportation, a medium-sized U.S. railroad, controls all U.K. rail freight business and runs the Queen's private train via its English, Welsh & Scottish Railway unit. It has also acquired the company that runs rail

---

[10]http://www.bea.gov.

Exhibit 1.1
Foreign Acquisitions of
U.S. Companies

Sources: Compiled from annual reports
of listed firms, 2015.

U.S. Companies/Brands	Foreign Owner
7-Eleven	Japan
Ben & Jerry's (ice cream)	U.K.
Budweiser	Belgium
Chrysler	Italy
Chrysler Building (NYC)	Abu Dhabi
Church's Chicken	Bahrain
CITGO	Venezuela
Columbia Pictures (movies)	Japan
French's Mustard (not France!)	U.K.
Firestone (tires)	Japan
Frigidaire	Sweden
Genentech	Switzerland
Gerber	Switzerland
Holiday Inn	U.K.
Huffy Corp. (bicycles)	China
Oroweat (breads)	Mexico
Random House (publishing)	Germany
RCA (televisions)	France/China
Smith & Wesson (guns)	U.K.
Swift & Company (meatpacking)	Brazil
The Wall Street Journal	Australia
T-Mobile	Germany
Waldorf Astoria Hotel (NYC)	China

shuttles through the Channel Tunnel. Investments by U.S. multinationals abroad are nothing new. Multinationals have been roaming the world en masse since the end of World War II, buying companies and investing in manufacturing plants. What is relatively new for U.S. companies is having their global competitors competing with them in "their" market, the United States. One of the more interesting new entrants is Chivas USA, a Mexican-owned soccer team that plays its matches in Southern California.

Once the private domain of domestic businesses, the vast U.S. market that provided an opportunity for continued growth must now be shared with a variety of foreign companies and products. Companies with only domestic markets have found increasing difficulty in sustaining their customary rates of growth, and many are seeking foreign markets in which

Along with NAFTA have come two of Mexico's most prominent brand names. Gigante, one of Mexico's largest supermarket chains, now has several stores in Southern California, including this one in Anaheim. On store shelves are a variety of Bimbo bakery products. Grupo Bimbo, a growing Mexican multinational, has recently purchased American brand-named firms such as Oroweat, Webers, Sara Lee, and Mrs. Baird's Bread.

CROSSING BORDERS 1.1   *Blanca Nieves, La Cenicienta, y Bimbo* (Snow White, Cinderella, and Bimbo)

Bimbo is a wonderful brand name. It so well demonstrates the difficulties of marketing across borders. In *Webster's Dictionary* "bimbo" is defined as ". . . a term of disparagement, an attractive, but empty-headed person, a tramp."

Meanwhile, in Spain, Mexico, and other Spanish-speaking countries, the word "bimbo" has no pejorative meaning. Indeed, it is often simply associated with the little white bear logo of Bimbo brand bread. Bimbo is the most popular brand of bread in Mexico and, with the North American Free Trade Agreement (NAFTA), is stretching its corporate arms north and south. For example, the Mexican firm most recently acquired the U.S. brands Sara Lee and Bestfoods; Mrs. Baird's Bread, the most popular local brand in Dallas, Texas; and Fargo, the most popular bread brand in Argentina. And you can now see 18-wheelers pulling truckloads of Bimbo products north on Interstate 5 toward Latino neighborhoods in Southern California and beyond.

Perhaps Bimbo is the reason the city leaders in Anaheim so feared Gigante's entrance into their city. Gigante, the Mexican-owned supermarket chain, features Bimbo buns, tomatillos, cactus pears, and other Latino favorites. Gigante already had three stores in Los Angeles County. But it was denied the city's permission to open a new market near the "Happiest Place on Earth." One has to wonder if Disneyland, Anaheim's biggest employer, may have been fretting over the juxtaposition of the Bimbo brand and its key characters, blonde, little, all-American Alice and her cinema sisters. Actually, a better case can be made that the Gigante–Anaheim imbroglio was more a matter of a mix of nationalism, xenophobia, and even racism. The city council eventually was forced to allow Gigante to open.

American firms have often run into similar problems as they have expanded around the world. Consider French nationalism. French farmers are famous for their protests—throwing lamb chops at their trade ministers and such. Or better yet, Culture Minister Jack Lang's comments about the U.S. Cartoon Network: "We must fight back against this American aggression. It is intolerable that certain North American audiovisual groups shamelessly colonize our countries."

Consider our own fear and loathing of "Japanese colonization" in both the 1920s and the 1980s. This apparent xenophobia turned to racism when Americans stoned Toyotas and Hondas but not Volkswagens and BMWs or when we decried Japanese takeovers of American firms and ignored Germany's gorging on the likes of Bankers Trust, Random House, and Chrysler.

PEMEX's current ban on American investments in the oil and gas industry in Mexico is a good example of nationalism. However, when British Petroleum buying ARCO is no problem, but Mexican cement giant CEMEX buying Houston's Southdown is, that's racism at work.

A cruel irony regarding Gigante's problems in Anaheim is well revealed by a quick drive around Tijuana. During the last few decades, the change in Tijuana's retail facade has been remarkable. In this border town, after NAFTA, McDonald's, Costco, Smart & Final, and other American brands now dominate the signage.

Sources: John L. Graham, "Blanca Nieves, La Cenicienta, y Bimbo," *La Opinion*, February 22, 2002, p. C1 (translated from the Spanish); Culture Minister Jack Lang quoted in Scott Kraft, "Culture Clash: New Turner Network Is Galling the French", *Los Angeles Times*, September 25, 1993; Clifford Kraus, "New Accents in the U.S. Economy," *The New York Times*, May 2, 2007, pp. C1, C14; "Sara Lee Completes Sale to Bimbo," *Chicago Sun-Times*, November 7, 2011; http://www.GrupoBimbo.com, accessed 2015.

to expand. Companies with foreign operations find that foreign earnings are making an important overall contribution to total corporate profits. A four-year Conference Board study of 1,250 U.S. manufacturing companies found that multinationals of all sizes and in all industries outperformed their strictly domestic U.S. counterparts. They grew twice as fast in sales and earned significantly higher returns on equity and assets. Furthermore, U.S. multinationals reduced their manufacturing employment, both at home and abroad, more than domestic companies. Another study indicates that despite the various difficulties associated with internationalization, on average, firm value is increased by global diversification.[11] Indeed, at least periodically, profit levels from international ventures exceed those from domestic operations for many multinational firms.

Exhibit 1.2 illustrates how important revenues generated on investments abroad are to U.S. companies. In many cases, foreign sales were greater than U.S. sales, demonstrating the global reach of these American brands. Apple's performance has been most impressive, with total revenues exploding from just $6 billion in 2003 to $24 billion in 2007, $108 billion

---

[11]John A. Doukas and Ozgur B. Kan, "Does Global Diversification Destroy Firm Value?" *Journal of International Business Studies* 37 (2006), pp. 352–71.

Part 1 An Overview

Exhibit 1.2
Selected U.S. Companies
and Their International
Sales

Source: S&P 500, 2013: Global Sales
Year in Review (September 2014).

Company	Global Revenues (billions)	Percent Revenues from Outside the U.S.
Apple	$170.9	61.3%
Avon	10.0	85.4
Boeing	86.6	56.6
Chevron	211.6	75.9
Direct TV	31.8	21.0
Ford	146.9	41.8
IBM	99.8	65.1
Intel	52.7	82.8
Johnson & Johnson	71.3	55.3
Mondelez (Oreos, etc.)	35.3	80.2
Walmart	474.3	29.0

in 2011 and $171 billion in 2013. Now the company's foreign sales are more than 60 percent the total revenues.

Companies that never ventured abroad until recently are now seeking foreign markets. Companies with existing foreign operations realize they must be more competitive to succeed against foreign multinationals. They have found it necessary to spend more money and time improving their market positions abroad because competition for these growing markets is intensifying. For firms venturing into international marketing for the first time and for those already experienced, the requirement is generally the same: a thorough and complete commitment to foreign markets and, for many, new ways of operating.

International Marketing Defined

International marketing is the performance of business activities designed to plan, price, promote, and direct the flow of a company's goods and services to consumers or users in more than one nation for a profit. The only difference between the definitions of domestic marketing and international marketing is that in the latter case, marketing activities take place in more than one country. This apparently minor difference, "in more than one country," accounts for the complexity and diversity found in international marketing operations. Marketing concepts, processes, and principles are universally applicable, and the marketer's task is the same, whether doing business in Dimebox, Texas, or Dar es Salaam, Tanzania. Business's goal is to make a profit by promoting, pricing, and distributing products for which there is a market. If this is the case, what is the difference between domestic and international marketing?

The answer lies not with different concepts of marketing but with the environment within which marketing plans must be implemented. The uniqueness of foreign marketing comes from the range of unfamiliar problems and the variety of strategies necessary to cope with different levels of uncertainty encountered in foreign markets.

Competition, legal restraints, government controls, weather, fickle consumers, natural disasters, and any number of other uncontrollable elements can, and frequently do, affect the profitable outcome of good, sound marketing plans. Generally speaking, the marketer cannot control or influence these uncontrollable elements but instead must adjust or adapt to them in a manner consistent with a successful outcome. What makes marketing interesting is the challenge of molding the controllable elements of marketing decisions (product, price, promotion, distribution, and research) within the framework of the uncontrollable elements of the marketplace (competition, politics, laws, consumer behavior, level of technology, and so forth) in such a way that marketing objectives are achieved. Even though marketing principles and concepts are universally applicable, the environment within which the marketer must implement marketing plans can change dramatically from country to country or region to region. The difficulties created by different environments are the international marketer's primary concern.

The International Marketing Task

LO3

The scope of the international marketing task

The international marketer's task is more complicated than that of the domestic marketer because the international marketer must deal with at least two levels of uncontrollable uncertainty instead of one. Uncertainty is created by the uncontrollable elements of all business environments, but each foreign country in which a company operates adds its own unique set of uncontrollable factors.

Exhibit 1.3 illustrates the total environment of an international marketer. The inner circle depicts the controllable elements that constitute a marketer's decision area, the second circle encompasses those environmental elements at home that have some effect on foreign-operation decisions, and the outer circles represent the elements of the foreign environment for each foreign market within which the marketer operates. As the outer circles illustrate, each foreign market in which the company does business can (and usually does) present separate problems involving some or all of the uncontrollable elements. Thus, the more foreign markets in which a company operates, the greater is the possible variety of foreign environmental factors with which to contend. Frequently, a solution to a problem in country market A is not applicable to a problem in country market B.

Marketing Decision Factors

The successful manager constructs a marketing program designed for optimal adjustment to the uncertainty of the business climate. The inner circle in Exhibit 1.3 represents the area under the control of the marketing manager. Assuming the necessary overall corporate resources, structures, and competencies that can limit or promote strategic choice, the marketing manager blends price, product, promotion, channels-of-distribution, and research activities to capitalize on anticipated demand. The controllable elements can be altered in the long run and, usually, in the short run to adjust to changing market conditions, consumer tastes, or corporate objectives.

Exhibit 1.3
The International Marketing Task

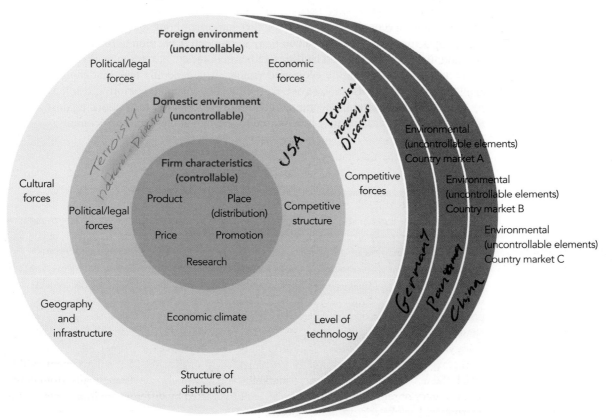

The outer circles surrounding the marketing decision factors represent the levels of uncertainty created by the domestic and foreign environments. Although the marketer can blend a marketing mix from the controllable elements, the uncontrollable elements are precisely that; the marketer must actively evaluate and, if needed, adapt. That effort—the adaptation of the marketing mix to these environmental factors—determines the outcome of the marketing enterprise.

Aspects of the Domestic Environment

The second circle in Exhibit 1.3 represents the aspects of the domestic environment uncontrollables. These include home-country elements that can have a direct effect on the success of a foreign venture: political and legal forces, economic climate, and competition.

A political decision involving foreign policy can have a direct effect on a firm's international marketing success. For example, the U.S. government placed a total ban on trade with Libya to condemn Libyan support for terrorist attacks, imposed restrictions on trade with South Africa to protest apartheid, and placed a total ban on trade with Iraq, whose actions were believed to constitute a threat to the national security of the United States and its allies. More recently, trade sanctions have been leveled against both Russia and Iran. In each case, the international marketing programs of U.S. companies, whether IBM, Exxon, or Hawg Heaven Bait Company, were restricted by these political decisions. The U.S. government has the constitutional right to restrict foreign trade when such trade adversely affects the security or economy of the country or when such trade is in conflict with U.S. foreign policy.

Conversely, positive effects occur when changes in foreign policy offer countries favored treatment. Such were the cases when South Africa abolished apartheid and the embargo was lifted and when the U.S. government decided to uncouple human rights issues from foreign trade policy and grant permanently normalized trade relations (PNTR) status to China, paving the way for its entry into the World Trade Organization (WTO). In both cases, opportunities were created for U.S. companies. Finally, note that on occasion, companies can exercise a controversially high degree of influence over such legislation in the United States. Recall that it is Congress's responsibility to regulate business, not vice versa. Indeed, in the case of PNTR for China, companies with substantial interests there, such as Boeing and Motorola, lobbied hard for the easing of trade restrictions.

The domestic economic climate is another important home-based uncontrollable variable with far-reaching effects on a company's competitive position in foreign markets. The capacity to invest in plants and facilities, either in domestic or foreign markets, is to a large extent a function of domestic economic vitality. It is generally true that capital tends to flow toward optimum uses; however, capital must be generated before it can have mobility. Furthermore, if internal economic conditions deteriorate, restrictions against foreign investment and purchasing may be imposed to strengthen the domestic economy.

A Citibank branch in the heart of Brazil on a rainy day. The address on the Avenida Paulista is 1776—how American! One of the world's great multinational corporations barely survived the financial debacle of October 2008. Perhaps its red, white, and blue umbrella logo protected it from "adverse weather" on Wall Street? Indeed, during the past few years, its international operations have performed much better than its domestic ones. In particular, emerging markets such as China, India, and Brazil proved relatively resilient for the first few years after the global financial crisis that began in 2008.

Competition within the home country can also have a profound effect on the international marketer's task. For more than a century, Eastman Kodak dominated the U.S. film market and could depend on achieving profit goals that provided capital to invest in foreign markets. Without having to worry about the company's lucrative base, management had the time and resources to devise aggressive international marketing programs. However, the competitive structure changed when Fuji Photo Film became a formidable competitor by lowering film prices in the United States, opening a $300 million plant, and soon gaining 12 percent of the U.S. market. Since then, the acceptance of digital photography, with Canon, from Japan, leading the market, has further disrupted Kodak's domestic business. Even though Kodak redirected its energy and resources back into the United States, it was not able to avoid filing for Chapter 11 bankruptcy protection in 2012. Fujifilm has managed to survive the digital onslaught by broadening its strategic portfolio, away from film and toward pharmaceuticals and liquid-crystal displays.[12] Competition within its home country affects a company's domestic as well as international plans.

Aspects of the Foreign Environment

In addition to uncontrollable domestic elements, a significant source of uncertainty is foreign environment uncontrollables (depicted in Exhibit 1.3 by the outer circles). A business operating in its home country undoubtedly feels comfortable forecasting the business climate and adjusting business decisions to these elements. The process of evaluating the uncontrollable elements in an international marketing program, however, often involves substantial doses of cultural, political, and economic shock.

A business operating in a number of foreign countries might find polar extremes in political stability, class structure, and economic climate—critical elements in business decisions. The dynamic upheavals in some countries further illustrate the problems of dramatic change in cultural, political, and economic climates over relatively short periods of time. A case in point is China, which has moved from a communist legal system in which all business was done with the state to a transitional period while a commercial legal system develops. In this transitional phase, new laws are passed but left to be interpreted by local authorities, and confusion often prevails about which rules are still in force and which rules are no longer applicable.

For example, commercial contracts can be entered into with a Chinese company or individual only if that company or person is considered a "legal person." To be a legal person in China, the company or person must have registered as such with the Chinese government. To complicate matters further, binding negotiations may take place only with "legal representatives" of the "legal person." So if your company enters into negotiations with a Chinese company or person, you must ask for signed legal documents establishing the right to do business. The formalities of the signature must also be considered. Will a signature on a contract be binding, or is it necessary to place a traditional Chinese seal on the document? Even when all is done properly, the government still might change its mind. Coca-Cola had won approval for its plan to build a new facility to increase production for its increasing Chinese market share. But before construction began, the Chinese parliament objected that Coca-Cola appeared to be too successful in China, so negotiations continued delaying the project. Such are the uncertainties of the uncontrollable political and legal factors of international business.

The more significant elements in the uncontrollable international environment, shown in the outer circles of Exhibit 1.3, include political/legal forces, economic forces, competitive forces, level of technology, structure of distribution, geography and infrastructure, and cultural forces. These forces constitute the principal elements of uncertainty an international marketer must cope with in designing a marketing program. Although each will be discussed in depth in subsequent chapters, consider the level of technology and political/legal forces as illustrations of the uncontrollable nature of the foreign environment.

The level of technology is an uncontrollable element that can often be misread because of the vast differences that may exist between developed and developing countries.

---

[12]Kana Inagaki and Juro Osawa, "Fujifilm Thrived by Changing Focus," *The Wall Street Journal*, January 20, 2012, p. B5.

CROSSING BORDERS 1.2

Mobile Phones, Economic Development, and Shrinking the Digital Divide

Wedged between stalls of dried fish and mounds of plastic goods, a red shipping container is loaded with Coca-Cola bottles. The local distributor for Soweto market, located in a tatty corner of Zambia's capital city, Lusaka, sells all its stock every few days. A full load costs 10m kwacha (about $2,000). In cash, this amount can be hard to get hold of, takes ages to count, and—being 10 times the average annual wage—is tempting to thieves. So Coca-Cola now tells its 300 Zambian distributors to pay for deliveries not in cash but by sending text messages from their mobile phones. The process takes about 30 seconds, and the driver issues a receipt. Far away computers record the movement of money and stock. Coca-Cola is not alone. Around the corner from the market, a small dry-cleaning firm lets customers pay for laundry using their phones. So do Zambian petrol stations and dozens of bigger shops and restaurants.

This is just one example of the many innovative ways in which mobile phones are being used in the poorest parts of the world. Anecdotal evidence of mobile phones' ability to boost economic activity is abundant: They enable fishermen or farmers to check prices at different markets before selling produce and make it easier for people to look for jobs and prevent wasted journeys. Mobile phones reduce transaction costs, broaden trade networks, and substitute for costly physical transport. They are of particular value when other means of communication (such as roads, post, or fixed-line phones) are poor or nonexistent.

This importance can be hard for people in affluent countries to understand, because the ways in which mobile phones are used in low-income countries are so different. In particular, phones are widely shared. One person in a village buys a mobile phone, perhaps using a microcredit loan. Others then rent it out by the minute; the small profit margin enables its owner to pay back the loan and make a living. When the phone rings, its owner carries it to the home of the person being called, who then takes the call. Other entrepreneurs set up as "text message interpreters," sending and receiving text messages (which are generally cheaper than voice calls) on behalf of their customers, who may be illiterate. So though the number of phones per 100 people is low by affluent-world standards, they still make a big difference.

Yet mobile phone technologies also can be controversial. Chinese authorities imposed a blackout on communications (Internet access, international phone service, and text messaging) in the northwest region of Xinjiang province in the wake of ethnic violence in the area in July 2009. The government there said it severed communications to ease tensions that it claims were inflamed by social networking sites and text messages.

Sources: *The Economist*, "Economics Focus, Calling across the Divide," March 12, 2005, p. 74; Bruce Meyerson, "Skype Takes Its Show on the Road," *BusinessWeek*, October 29, 2007, p. 38; Andrew Jacobs, "China Restores Text Messaging in Xinjiang," *The New York Times*, January 18, 2010, p. A9.

A marketer cannot assume that an understanding of the concept of preventive maintenance for machinery is the same in other countries as in the United States. Technical expertise may not be available at a level necessary for product support, and the general population may not have an adequate level of technical knowledge to maintain equipment properly. In such situations, a marketer will have to take extra steps to make sure that the importance of routine maintenance is understood and carried out. Furthermore, if technical support is not readily available, local people will have to be specially trained, or the company will have to provide support.

Political and legal issues face a business, whether it operates at home or in a foreign country. However, the issues abroad are often amplified by the "alien status" of the company, which increases the difficulty of properly assessing and forecasting the dynamic international business climate. The alien status of a foreign business has two dimensions: It is alien in that foreigners control the business and in that the culture of the host country is alien to management. The alien status of a business means that, when viewed as an outsider, it can be seen as an exploiter and receive prejudiced or unfair treatment at the hands of politicians, legal authorities, or both. Political activists can rally support by advocating the expulsion of the "foreign exploiters," often with the open or tacit approval of authorities. The Indian government, for example, gave Coca-Cola the choice of either revealing its secret formula or leaving the country. The company chose to leave. When it was welcomed back several years later, it faced harassment and constant interference in its operations from political activists, often inspired by competing soft drink companies.

Masai tribesmen in Tanzania with their cell phones. Competition is fierce among carriers in burgeoning markets like Tanzania. There were some 6 billion cell phone subscribers in the world in 2012. Both Celtel and Vodacom provide paint for local stores and houses. Here you see the bright Celtel yellow and red, which goes nicely with the colorful garb of local customers. Vodacom blue is at a disadvantage there. But at the time of this picture, Celtel was a subsidiary of Zain Group, a Kuwaiti company that is now owned by Bharti Airtel of India. So goes the fast pace of global telecommunications. Finally, we imagine the ear lobe "carrying case" makes it easy to hear the ring but hard to dial!

Furthermore, in a domestic situation, political details and the ramifications of political and legal events are often more transparent than they are in some foreign countries. For instance, whereas in the United States, each party in a dispute has access to established legal procedures and due process, legal systems in many other countries are still evolving. In many foreign countries, corruption may prevail, foreigners may receive unfair treatment, or the laws may be so different from those in the home country that they are misinterpreted. The point is that a foreign company is foreign and thus always subject to the political whims of the local government to a greater degree than a domestic firm. Google's conflicts with the Chinese government regarding censorship and confidentiality are pertinent here.[13]

Political/legal forces and the level of technology are only two of the uncontrollable aspects of the foreign environment that are discussed in subsequent chapters. The uncertainty of different foreign business environments creates the need for a close study of the uncontrollable elements within each new country. Thus, a strategy successful in one country can be rendered ineffective in another by differences in political climate, stages of economic development, level of technology, or other cultural variations.

Environmental Adaptation Needed

To adjust and adapt a marketing program to foreign markets, marketers must be able to interpret effectively the influence and impact of each of the uncontrollable environmental elements on the marketing plan for each foreign market in which they hope to do business. In a broad sense, the uncontrollable elements constitute the culture; the difficulty facing the marketer in adjusting to the culture lies in recognizing its impact. In a domestic market, the reaction to much of the environment's (cultural) impact on the marketer's activities is automatic; the various cultural influences that fill our lives are simply a part of our socialization, and we react in a manner acceptable to our society without consciously thinking about it.

The task of cultural adjustment, however, is the most challenging and important one confronting international marketers; they must adjust their marketing efforts to cultures to which they are not attuned. In dealing with unfamiliar markets, marketers must be aware of the frames of reference they are using in making their decisions or evaluating the potential

---

[13]Jay Yarow, "Google Is Diving back into China with Search that Can't Be Censored," *Business Insider*, January 12, 2012; Julie Makinen, "China Broadens Crackdown on Google Services," *Los Angeles Times*, June 13, 2014, online.

of a market, because judgments are derived from experience that is the result of acculturation in the home country. Once a frame of reference is established, it becomes an important factor in determining or modifying a marketer's reaction to situations—social and even nonsocial.

For example, time-conscious Americans are not culturally prepared to understand the culturally nuanced meaning of time to Latin Americans. Such a difference must be learned to avoid misunderstandings that can lead to marketing failures. Such a failure occurs every time sales are lost when a "long waiting period" in the outer office of a Latin American customer is misinterpreted by an American sales executive. Cross-cultural misunderstandings can also occur when a simple hand gesture has a number of different meanings in different parts of the world. When wanting to signify something is fine, many people in the United States raise a hand and make a circle with the thumb and forefinger. However, this same hand gesture means "zero" or "worthless" to the French, "money" to the Japanese, and a general sexual insult in Sardinia and Greece. A U.S. president sent an unintentional message to some Australian protesters when he held up his first two fingers with the back of his hand to the protesters. Meaning to give the "victory" sign, he was unaware that in Australia, the same hand gesture is equivalent to holding up the middle finger in the United States.

Cultural conditioning is like an iceberg—we are not aware of nine-tenths of it. In any study of the market systems of different peoples, their political and economic structures, religions, and other elements of culture, foreign marketers must constantly guard against measuring and assessing the markets against the fixed values and assumptions of their own cultures. They must take specific steps to make themselves aware of the home cultural reference in their analyses and decision making.[14]

The Self-Reference Criterion and Ethnocentrism: Major Obstacles

LO4

The importance of the self-reference criterion (SRC) in international marketing

The key to successful international marketing is adaptation to environmental differences from one market to another. Adaptation is a conscious effort on the part of the international marketer to anticipate the influences of both the foreign and domestic uncontrollable factors on a marketing mix and then to adjust the marketing mix to minimize the effects.

The primary obstacles to success in international marketing are a person's **self-reference criterion (SRC)** and an associated ethnocentrism. The SRC is an unconscious reference to one's own cultural values, experiences, and knowledge as a basis for decisions. Closely connected is ethnocentrism, that is, the notion that people in one's own company, culture, or country know best how to do things. Ethnocentrism was particularly a problem for American managers at the beginning of the 21st century because of America's dominance in the world economy during the late 1990s. Ethnocentrism is generally a problem when managers from affluent countries work with managers and markets in less affluent countries. Both the SRC and ethnocentrism impede the ability to assess a foreign market in its true light.

When confronted with a set of facts, we react spontaneously on the basis of knowledge assimilated over a lifetime—knowledge that is a product of the history of our culture. We seldom stop to think about a reaction; we simply react. Thus, when faced with a problem in another culture, our tendency is to react instinctively and refer to our SRC for a solution. Our reaction, however, is based on meanings, values, symbols, and behavior relevant to our own culture and usually different from those of the foreign culture. Such decisions are often not good ones.

To illustrate the impact of the SRC, consider misunderstandings that can occur about personal space between people of different cultures. In the United States, unrelated individuals keep a certain physical distance between themselves and others when talking or in groups. We do not consciously think about that distance; we just know what feels right without thinking. When someone is too close or too far away, we feel uncomfortable and either move farther away or get closer to correct the distance. In doing so, we are relying on our SRC.

---

[14] Emily Maltby, "Expanding Abroad? Avoid Cultural Gaffes," *The Wall Street Journal*, January 19, 2010, p. B5.

In some cultures, the acceptable distance between individuals is substantially less than that which is comfortable for Americans. When someone from another culture approaches an American too closely, the American, unaware of that culture's acceptable distance, unconsciously reacts by backing away to restore the proper distance (i.e., proper by American standards), and confusion results for both parties. Americans assume foreigners are pushy, while foreigners assume Americans are unfriendly and literally "standoffish." Both react according to the values of their own SRCs, making both victims of a cultural misunderstanding.

Your self-reference criterion can prevent you from being aware of cultural differences or from recognizing the importance of those differences. Thus, you might fail to recognize the need to take action, you might discount the cultural differences that exist among countries, or you might react to a situation in a way offensive to your hosts. A common mistake made by Americans is to refuse food or drink when offered. In the United States, a polite refusal is certainly acceptable, but in Asia or the Middle East, a host is offended if you refuse hospitality. Although you do not have to eat or drink much, you do have to accept the offering of hospitality. Understanding and dealing with the SRC are two of the more important facets of international marketing.

Ethnocentrism and the SRC can influence an evaluation of the appropriateness of a domestically designed marketing mix for a foreign market. If U.S. marketers are not aware, they might evaluate a marketing mix based on U.S. experiences (i.e., their SRC) without fully appreciating the cultural differences that require adaptation. Certainly, having a great cup of coffee handy at a major tourist attraction seems like a great idea. So Starbucks opened a store in the Forbidden City in Beijing. While American tourists were happy to buy, Chinese took great umbrage with the tactic. It took Starbucks six years to correct the error. Women's clothing maker Zara headquartered in Spain fixed things much faster. They had offered online a striped blouse with a yellow six-pointed star emblazoned across the heart. For Jews, it was reminiscent of World War II concentration camp uniforms. Consumers complained, and Zara took the product off the market immediately. Damage was still done.[15] Both of these examples were real mistakes made by major companies stemming from their reliance on their SRC in making a decision.

When marketers take the time to look beyond their own self-reference criteria, the results are more positive. A British manufacturer of chocolate biscuits (cookies, in American English), ignoring its SRC, knew that it must package its biscuits differently to accommodate the Japanese market. Thus, in Japan, McVitie's chocolate biscuits are wrapped individually, packed in presentation cardboard boxes, and priced about three times higher than in the United Kingdom—the cookies are used as gifts in Japan and thus must look and be perceived as special. Unilever, appreciating the uniqueness of its markets, repackaged and reformulated its detergent for Brazil. One reason was that the lack of washing machines among poorer Brazilians made a simpler soap formula necessary. Also, because many people wash their clothes in rivers, the powder was packaged in plastic rather than paper so it would not get soggy. Finally, because the Brazilian poor are price conscious and buy in small quantities, the soap was packaged in small, low-priced packages. Even McDonald's modifies its traditional Big Mac in India, where it is known as the Maharaja Mac. This burger features two mutton patties, because most Indians consider cows sacred and don't eat beef. In each of these examples, had the marketers' own self-reference criteria been the basis for decisions, none of the necessary changes would have been readily apparent based on their home-market experience.

The most effective way to control the influence of ethnocentrism and the SRC is to recognize their effects on our behavior. Although learning every culture in depth and being aware of every important difference is obviously humanly impossible, an awareness of the need to be sensitive to differences and to ask questions when doing business in another culture can help you avoid many of the mistakes possible in international marketing. Asking the appropriate question helped the Vicks Company avoid making

[15]Danny Hakim, "Sara Withdraws T-Shirts over Anti-Semitisim Claims," *The New York Times*, August 28, 2014, p. B4.

a mistake in Germany. It discovered that in German, "Vicks" sounds like the crudest slang equivalent of "intercourse," so it changed the name to "Wicks" before introducing the product.

Be aware, also, that not every activity within a marketing program is different from one country to another; indeed, there probably are more similarities than differences. For example, the McVitie's chocolate biscuits mentioned earlier are sold in the United States in the same package as in the United Kingdom. Such similarities, however, may lull the marketer into a false sense of apparent sameness. This apparent sameness, coupled with the self-reference criterion, is often the cause of international marketing problems. Undetected similarities do not cause problems; however, the one difference that goes undetected can create a marketing failure.

To avoid errors in business decisions, the knowledgeable marketer will conduct a cross-cultural analysis that isolates the SRC influences and maintain vigilance regarding ethno-centrism. The following steps are suggested as a framework for such an analysis.

1. Define the business problem or goal in home-country cultural traits, habits, or norms.
2. Define the business problem or goal in foreign-country cultural traits, habits, or norms through consultation with natives of the target country. Make no value judgments.

CROSSING BORDERS 1.3   Spy vs. Spy and the Waldorf Astoria

Cultural icons—nobody likes it when foreigners invade them. At the apex of Japanese financial strength in 1990, investors from that golf-loving culture bought the Pebble Beach Golf Course. It took almost a decade before a consortium of investors, including Arnold Palmer, Richard Ferris, Peter Ueberroth, and Clint Eastwood, returned the links to American ownership. A bench overlooking the 18th hole commemorates its return.

The Forbidden City in Beijing was home to 24 Chinese emperors. In 2000, Starbucks Coffee was granted space for at 200-square-foot store on the premises. It took seven years before the company bowed to pressure from Chinese citizens and closed the location.

Now a Chinese insurance company has bought the Waldorf Astoria Hotel across from Central Park in New York City. The Waldorf salad was born there in 1897. Presidents Hoover and Eisenhower and General Douglas MacArthur all retired there. Both Nikola Tesla and Marilyn Monroe also called it home for short stints. Among the 20 or so movies shot at the hotel have been *Scent of a Woman, Serendipity,* and *Coming to America.* Beijing-based Anbang Insurance Group paid American-based Hilton International $1.95 billion for the property.

Before New Yorkers even had a chance to complain, the U.S. government began an investigation into the purchase. Not only is the Waldorf a matter of American culture, it is also apparently a matter of American national security.

The hotel serves as the home to the U.S. Ambassador to the United Nations and hosts the American president and hundreds of U.S. diplomats during the annual U.N. General Assembly. Specifically American security experts are concerned about the potential for espionage associated with a planned refurbishment of the hotel.

At the time the, *Associated Press* reported that the U.S. government warns diplomats and business executives to be concerned about security in foreign countries in general, regarding physical and electronic surveillance and, in particular, laptop computers in hotel rooms. Trade secrets, negotiating positions, and other sensitive commercial information are of special concern. Of course, the U.S. government issues no such warnings about the National Security Administration ubiquitous surveillance here at home.

Part of the irony of this political, security, cultural dustup is that Hilton will not only manage the Waldorf in New York, but also the Waldorf Astoria Shanghai on the Bund. Moreover, Chinese leader Deng Xiaoping stayed in the hotel and met with Henry Kissinger in 1974. Now his grandson-in-law just happens to run Anbang Insurance. Nice.

Sources: Matthew Lee, "Government to Investigate Chinese Firm's $2 Billion Purchase of Waldorf Astoria," *Associated Press,* October 13, 2014, online, used with permission; David Barboza, "Chinese Return to the Waldorf, With $2 Billion," *The New York Times,* October 8, 2014, online.

3. Isolate the SRC influence in the problem and examine it carefully to see how it complicates the problem.

4. Redefine the problem without the SRC influence and solve for the optimum business goal situation.

An American sales manager newly posted to Japan decided that his Japanese sales representatives did not need to come into the office every day for an early morning meeting before beginning calls to clients in Tokyo. After all, that was how things were done in the United States. However, the new policy, based on both the American's SRC and a modicum of ethnocentrism, produced a precipitous decline in sales performance. In his subsequent discussions with his Japanese staff, he determined that Japanese sales representatives are motivated mostly by peer pressure. Fortunately, he was able to recognize that his SRC and his American "business acumen" did not apply in this case in Tokyo. A return to the proven system of daily meetings brought sales performance back to previous levels.

The cross-cultural analysis approach requires an understanding of the culture of the foreign market as well as one's own culture. Surprisingly, understanding one's own culture may require additional study, because much of the cultural influence on market behavior remains at a subconscious level and is not clearly defined.

Developing a Global Awareness

LO5

The increasing importance of global awareness

Opportunities in global business abound for those who are prepared to confront myriad obstacles with optimism and a willingness to continue learning new ways. The successful businessperson in the 21st century will have global awareness and a frame of reference that goes beyond a region or even a country and encompasses the world.[16] To be globally aware is to have (1) tolerance of and a willingness to learn about cultural differences and (2) knowledge of cultures, history, world market potential, and global economic, social, and political trends. Close akin to global awareness is what others have called "cultural intelligence" or CQ. Aspects of the latter have been shown to enhance international marketing efforts.[17]

Tolerance for cultural differences is crucial in international marketing. Tolerance is understanding cultural differences and accepting and working with others whose behaviors may be different from yours. You do not have to accept as your own the cultural ways of another, but you must allow others to be different and equal. For example, the fact that punctuality is less important in some cultures does not make them less productive, only different. The tolerant person understands the differences that may exist between cultures and uses that knowledge to relate effectively.

A globally aware person is knowledgeable about cultures and history. Knowledge of cultures is important in understanding behavior in the marketplace or in the boardroom. Knowledge of history is important because the way people think and act is influenced by their history. Some Latin Americans' reluctance toward foreign investment or Chinese reluctance to open completely to outsiders can be understood better if you have a historical perspective.

Global awareness also involves knowledge of world market potentials and global economic, social, and political trends. Over the next few decades, enormous changes will take place in the market potentials in almost every region of the world, all of which a globally aware person must continuously monitor. Finally, a globally aware person will keep abreast of global economic, social, and political trends, because a country's prospects can change as these trends shift direction or accelerate. The former republics of the Soviet Union, along with Russia, eastern Europe, China, India, Africa, and Latin America, are undergoing economic, social, and political changes that have already altered the course of trade and

---

[16]Gary A. Knight and Daekwan Kim, "International Business Competence and the Contemporary Firm," *Journal of International Business Studies* 40, no. 2 (2009), pp. 255–73.

[17]Peter Magnusson, Stanford A. Westjohn, Alexey V. Semenov, Arilova A. Randrianasolo, and Srdan Zdravkovic, "The Role of Cultural Intelligence in Marketing Adaptation and Export Performance," *Journal of International Marketing* 21, no. 4 (2013), pp. 44–61.

defined new economic powers. The knowledgeable marketer will identify opportunities long before they become evident to others. It is the authors' goal in this text to guide the reader toward acquiring global awareness.

Global awareness can and should be built into organizations using several approaches. The obvious strategy is to select individual managers specifically for their demonstrated global awareness. Global awareness can also be obtained through personal relationships in other countries. Indeed, market entry is very often facilitated through previously established social ties. Certainly, successful long-term business relationships with foreign customers often result in an organizational global awareness based on the series of interactions required by commerce. Foreign agents and partners can help directly in this regard. But perhaps the most effective approach is to have a culturally diverse senior executive staff or board of directors. Unfortunately, American managers seem to see relatively less value in this last approach than managers in most other countries.

Stages of International Marketing Involvement

LO6

The progression of becoming a global marketer

Once a company has decided to go international, it has to decide the degree of marketing involvement and commitment it is prepared to make. These decisions should reflect considerable study and analysis of market potential and company capabilities—a process not always followed.[18] Research has revealed a number of factors favoring faster internationalization: (1) Companies with either high-technology and/or marketing-based resources appear to be better equipped to internationalize than more traditional manufacturing kinds of companies;[19] (2) smaller home markets and larger production capacities appear to favor internationalization; and (3) firms with key managers well networked internationally are able to accelerate the internationalization process. Many companies begin tentatively in international marketing, growing as they gain experience and gradually changing strategy and tactics as they become more committed. Others enter international marketing after much research and with fully developed long-range plans, prepared to make investments to acquire a market position and often evincing bursts of international activities. Studies suggest that striking a balance between the two approaches may actually work best,[20] with a variety of conditions and firm characteristics to be evaluated.

Regardless of the means employed to gain entry into a foreign market, a company may make little or no actual market investment—that is, its marketing involvement may be limited to selling a product with little or no thought given to the development of market control. Alternatively, a company may become totally involved and invest large sums of money and effort to capture and maintain a permanent, specific position in the market. In general, one of five (sometimes overlapping) stages can describe the international marketing involvement of a company. Although the stages of international marketing involvement are presented here in a linear order, the reader should not infer that a firm progresses from one stage to another; quite to the contrary, a firm may begin its international involvement at any one stage or be in more than one stage simultaneously. For example, because of a short product life cycle and a thin but widespread market for many technology products, many high-tech companies, large and small, see the entire world, including their home market, as a single market and strive to reach all possible customers as rapidly as possible.

---

[18]Protiti Dastidar, "International Corporate Diversification and Performance: Does Firm Self-Selection Matter?" *Journal of International Business Studies* 40, no. 1 (2009), pp. 71–85.

[19]Chiung-Hui Tseng, Patriya Tansuhaj, William Hallagan, and James McCullough, "Effects of Firm Resources on Growth in Multinationality," *Journal of International Business Studies* 38 (2007), pp. 961–74; Niron Hashai, "Sequencing the Expansion of Geographic Scope and Foreign Operations by 'Born Global' Firms," *Journal of International Business Studies* 42 (2011), pp. 995–1015.

[20]Harry G. Barkema and Rian Drogendijk, "Internationalizing in Small, Incremental or Larger Steps?" *Journal of International Business Studies* 38 (2007), pp. 1132–48; Peter Lamb, Jorgen Sandberg, and Peter W. Liesch, "Small Firm Internationalization Unveiled through Phenomenography," *Journal of International Business Studies* 42 (2010), pp. 672–93.

No Direct Foreign Marketing

A company in this stage does not actively cultivate customers outside national boundaries; however, this company's products may reach foreign markets. Sales may be made to trading companies as well as foreign customers who directly contact the firm. Or products may reach foreign markets via domestic wholesalers or distributors who sell abroad without the explicit encouragement or even knowledge of the producer. As companies develop websites, many receive orders from international Internet users. Often an unsolicited order from a foreign buyer is what piques the interest of a company to seek additional international sales.

Infrequent Foreign Marketing

Temporary surpluses caused by variations in production levels or demand may result in infrequent marketing overseas. The surpluses are characterized by their temporary nature; therefore, sales to foreign markets are made as goods become available, with little or no intention of maintaining continuous market representation. As domestic demand increases and absorbs surpluses, foreign sales activity is reduced or even withdrawn. In this stage, little or no change is seen in the company organization or product lines. However, few companies fit this model today because customers around the world increasingly seek long-term commercial relationships. Furthermore, evidence suggests that financial returns from such short-term international expansions are limited.

The first two stages of international marketing involvement are more reactive in nature and often do not represent careful strategic thinking about international expansion. Indeed, putting strategic thinking on the back burner has resulted in marketing failures for even the largest companies.

The consensus of researchers and authors[21] in this area suggests three relatively distinct approaches to strategic decisions in firms involved in international markets:

1. Regular foreign marketing
2. Multidomestic or international marketing
3. Global marketing

Next we discuss each of the three stages (and their associated strategic orientations) in turn.

Regular Foreign Marketing

At this level, the firm has permanent productive capacity devoted to the production of goods and services to be marketed in foreign markets. A firm may employ foreign or domestic overseas intermediaries, or it may have its own sales force or sales subsidiaries in important foreign markets. The primary focus of operations and production is to service domestic market needs. However, as overseas demand grows, production is allocated for foreign markets, and products may be adapted to meet the needs of individual foreign markets. Profit expectations from foreign markets move from being seen as a bonus in addition to regular domestic profits to a position in which the company becomes dependent on foreign sales and profits to meet its goals.

Meter-Man, a small company (25 employees) in southern Minnesota that manufactures agricultural measuring devices, is a good example of a company in this stage.[22] In 1989, the 35-year-old company began exploring the idea of exporting; by 1992 the company was shipping product to Europe. Today, one-third of Meter-Man's sales are in 35 countries, and soon the company expects international sales to account for about half of its business. "When you start exporting, you say to yourself, this will be icing on the cake," says the director of sales and marketing. "But now I say going international has become critical to our existence." Recently Meter-Man was purchased by Komelon, Inc., a larger, more diversified international company with operations in Washington state, South Korea, China, and Europe.

---

[21]A seminal paper in this genre is by Yorum Wind, Susan P. Douglas, and Howard V. Perlmutter, "Guidelines for Developing International Marketing Strategy," *Journal of Marketing*, April 1973, pp. 14–23.

[22]See http://www.komelon.com for its Meter-Man product line and other details.

James Neff quoted in "So You Think The World Is Your Oyster", June 08, 1997, *Bloomberg Business*.

International Marketing

Companies in this stage are fully committed to and involved in international marketing activities. Such companies seek markets all over the world and sell products that are a result of planned production for markets in various countries. This planning generally entails not only the marketing but also the production of goods outside the home market. At this point, a company becomes an international or multinational marketing firm.

The experience of Fedders, a manufacturer of room air conditioners, typifies that of a company that begins its international business at this stage.[23] Even though it is the largest manufacturer of air conditioners in the United States, the firm faced constraints in its domestic market. Its sales were growing steadily, but sales of air conditioners (the company's only product) are seasonal, and thus, domestic sales at times do not even cover fixed costs. Furthermore, the U.S. market is mature, with most customers buying only replacement units. Any growth would have to come from a rival's market share, and the rivals, Whirlpool and Matsushita, are formidable. Fedders decided that the only way to grow was to venture abroad.

Fedders decided that Asia, with its often steamy climate and expanding middle class, offered the best opportunity. China, India, and Indonesia were seen as the best prospects. China was selected because sales of room air conditioners had grown from 500,000 units to more than 4 million in five years, which still accounted for only 12 percent of the homes in cities like Beijing, Shanghai, and Guangzhou. The company saw China as a market with terrific growth potential. After careful study, Fedders entered a joint venture with a small Chinese air conditioner company that was looking for a partner; a new company, Fedders Xinle, formed. The company immediately found that it needed to redesign its product for this market. In China, air conditioners are a major purchase, seen as a status symbol, not as a box to keep a room cool, as in the United States. The Chinese also prefer a split-type air conditioner, with the unit containing the fan inside the room and the heat exchanger mounted on a wall outside. Because Fedders did not manufacture split models, it designed a new product that is lightweight, energy efficient, and packed with features, such as a remote control and an automatic air-sweeping mechanism.

The joint venture appears to be successful, and the company is exploring the possibility of marketing to other Asian markets and maybe even back to the United States with the new product that it developed for the Chinese market. As Fedders expands into other markets and makes other commitments internationally, it continues to evolve as an international or multinational company. Finally, Fedders's successes internationally made it an attractive acquisition candidate, and in 2008 it was purchased by a French firm, Airwell, that has distributors in more than 80 countries around the world.

Global Marketing

At the global marketing level, the most profound change is the orientation of the company toward markets and associated planning activities. At this stage, companies treat the world, including their home market, as one market. Market segmentation decisions are no longer focused on national borders. Instead, market segments are defined by income levels, usage patterns, or other factors that frequently span countries and regions. Often this transition from international marketing to global marketing is catalyzed by a company's crossing the threshold at which more than half its sales revenues come from abroad. The best people in the company begin to seek international assignments, and the entire operation—organizational structure, sources of finance, production, marketing, and so forth—begins to take on a global perspective.

The example of Coca-Cola's transition from international to global is instructive. Coca-Cola had actually been a global company for years; the mid-1990s' organizational redesign was the last step in recognizing the changes that had already occurred. Initially, all international divisions reported to an executive vice president in charge of international operations, who, along with the vice president of U.S. operations, reported to the president. The new organization consists of six international divisions. The U.S.

---

[23]See http://www.airwell-fedders.com for details about the company.

business unit accounts for about 20 percent of profits and has been downgraded to just part of one of the six international business units in the company's global geographic regions. The new structure does not reduce the importance of the company's North American business; it just puts other areas on an equal footing. It represents the recognition, however, that future growth is going to come from emerging markets outside the United States.

International operations of businesses in global marketing reflect the heightened competitiveness brought about by the globalization of markets, interdependence of the world's

CROSSING BORDERS 1.4   Risks and Payoffs in International Marketing

After the 2009 financial crash, the U.S. government approved the Advanced Technology Vehicle Manufacturing (ATVM) Loan Program. Half-billion-dollar loans were made to two new motor vehicle companies, Tesla Motors (Palo Alto, California) and Fisker Automotive (Anaheim, California).

Karmas were sold in both Europe and North America. Perhaps the most prominent sale was an all-chrome model purchased by Justin Bieber. After producing about 2,400 Karmas, four-door sports cars, Fisker declared bankruptcy in 2013.

Alternatively, Tesla reported its first quarterly profits in 2014. Tesla has been a success in both the U.S. and foreign markets and has sold some 35,000 vehicles globally. It has opened sales locations in both Europe and China and has launched right-hand drive vehicles in the UK, Hong Kong, Japan, and Australia.

As can be seen below, both products were nicely designed, at least on the outside. Tesla is all electric, and Karma was a plug-in hybrid. The Tesla Model S is also a four-door luxury sedan, and both the S and Karma sold for more than $70,000 in the United States. Tesla also markets a two-seat roadster and will begin offering a Model X SUV in 2015.

At this writing, Tesla has about 125 stores and service locations around the world. With such a small volume, so far they are selling through company-owned stores, and the cars are serviced in wholly owned subsidiaries. Both

Texas and Maryland require new automobiles to be sold in dealerships, and Tesla can sell cars to customers in those states only online.

Expansion of Tesla's production is limited by both the availability of batteries and charging stations. The firm recently chose Nevada as the location for its new battery production plant. It is investing in Supercharging stations around the country and world.

Tesla also sells its technology to both Toyota and Daimler Benz. You can now buy a small Mercedes SUV or a Toyota RAV-4 with a Tesla all-electric drive train. Both companies also have major investments in Tesla. Speaking of investors, in the past few years, the firm issued successful initial public offerings (IPOs). And much to the delight of the U.S. government, Tesla settled its outstanding balance from the ATVM program *in advance.*

The opportunities are great for Tesla as the importance of clean energy continues to grow. The major threat is another general economic downturn in which luxury cars would suffer disproportionately. Tesla CEO Elon Musk is planning a fully autonomous operating system (the car drives itself) in about five years. We assume the machines will be very good at finding charging stations!

Sources: Various company news releases from Tesla.com; stock analysts reports such as *Zacks Investment Research*, October 8, 2014, online; Mike Ramsey, "Tesla CEO Musk Sees Fully Autonomous Car Ready in Five or Six Years," *The Wall Street Journal*, September 17, 2014, online.

Fisker Karma

Tesla S

economies, and the growing number of competing firms from developed and developing countries vying for the world's markets. *Global companies* and *global marketing* are terms frequently used to describe the scope of operations and marketing management orientation of companies in this stage.

As the competitive environment facing U.S. businesses becomes more internationalized the most effective orientation for many firms engaged in marketing in another country will be a global orientation. This orientation means operating as if all the country markets in a company's scope of operations (including the domestic market) were approachable as a single global market and standardizing the marketing mix where culturally feasible and cost effective. It does not, however, mean a slavish adherence to one strategic orientation.[24] Depending on the product and market, other orientations may make more marketing sense. For example, Procter & Gamble may pursue a global strategy for disposable diapers but a multidomestic strategy in Asian markets for detergents.

The Orientation of *International Marketing*

Most problems encountered by the foreign marketer result from the strangeness of the environment within which marketing programs must be implemented. Success hinges, in part, on the ability to assess and adjust properly to the impact of an unfamiliar circumstance. The successful international marketer possesses the best qualities of the anthropologist, sociologist, psychologist, diplomat, lawyer, prophet, and businessperson.

In light of all the variables involved, with what should a textbook in foreign marketing be concerned? It is the opinion of the authors that a study of foreign marketing environments, people, and cultures[25] and their influences on the total marketing process is of primary concern and is the most effective approach to a meaningful presentation. Our views are supported by the most recent ranking of countries on their extent of globalization—see Exhibit 1.4.

The United States may be the largest economy in the world, yet both China and Germany exported more goods and services last year.[26] Moreover, the United States ranked only 32nd on the most recent KOF Globalization Index.[27] The 23 variables used to calculate the KOF Globalization Index include many per capita measures, so most of the countries ranked in the top ten are small. As the three summary categories show, the United States does well with respect to political globalization (#18) but poorly on economic globalization (#87). When we take an even closer look at the data we find that U.S. strength in social globalization (#28) is mostly related to technological connectivity, ranking #11 in Internet users and #12 in television ownership among all countries. Yet the United States ranks only 53rd in international tourism. That is, compared with folks in other countries, Americans generally do not experience foreign environments and have had little contact with people in other cultures. This lack is the very gap on which this book focuses.

Consequently, the orientation of this text can best be described as an environmental/cultural approach to international strategic marketing. By no means is it intended to present principles of marketing; rather, it is intended to demonstrate the unique problems of

---

[24]Susan P. Douglas and C. Samuel Craig, "Convergence and Divergence: Developing a Semiglobal Marketing Strategy," *Journal of International Marketing* 19, no. 1 (2011), pp. 82–101; Garzia D. Santangelo and Klaus E. Meyer, "Extending the Internationalization Process Model: Increases and Decreases of MNE Commitment in Emerging Economies," *Journal of International Business Studies* 42 (2011), pp. 894–909.

[25]Tricia Bisoux, "Trade Secrets: An Interview with Caterpillar CEO, Jim Owens," *BizEd*, September/October 2009, pp. 20–27; Udo Zander and Lena Zander, "Opening the Grey Box: Social Communities, Knowledge and Culture in Acquisitions," *Journal of International Business Studies* 41, no. 1 (2010), pp. 27–37.

[26]See http://www.WTO.org.

[27]See http://www.kof.ethz.ch.

Exhibit 1.4

The KOF Globalization Index (top ten plus selected other countries)

The countries that top the charts in economic, social, political links to the rest of the world

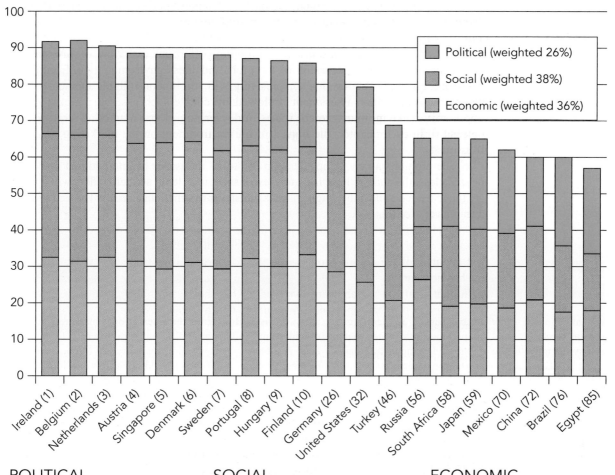

POLITICAL
GLOBALIZATION
MEASURES

Trade flows

Foreign direct investment flows

Income payments to foreigners

Mean tariff rates

Taxes on international trade

SOCIAL
GLOBALIZATION
MEASURES

Telephone traffic

International tourism

Foreign population

Internet users

Televisions

ECONOMIC
GLOBALIZATION
MEASURES

Embassies in country

Membership in
    international organizations

International treaties

Participation in UN
    missions

Source: http://www.kof.ethz.ch.

international marketing. It attempts to relate the foreign environment to the marketing process and to illustrate the many ways in which culture can influence the marketing task. Although marketing principles are universally applicable, the cultural environment within which the marketer must implement marketing plans can change dramatically from country to country. It is with the difficulties created by different environments that this text is primarily concerned.

The text addresses issues relevant to any company marketing in or into any other country or groups of countries, however slight the involvement or the method of involvement.

Hence this discussion of international marketing ranges from the marketing and business practices of small exporters, such as a Colorado-based company that generates more than 50 percent of its $40,000 annual sales of fish-egg sorters in Canada, Germany, and Australia, to the practices of global companies such as Microsoft, Mary Kay, and Johnson & Johnson, all of which generate more than 50 percent of their annual profits from the sales of multiple products to multiple country-market segments all over the world.

The first section of *International Marketing* offers an overview of international marketing, including a discussion of the global business environment confronting the marketer. The next section deals exclusively with the uncontrollable elements of the environment and their assessment, followed by chapters on assessing global market opportunities. Then, management issues in developing global marketing strategies are discussed. In each chapter, the impact of the environment on the marketing process is illustrated.

Space prohibits an encyclopedic approach to all the issues of international marketing; nevertheless, the authors have tried to present sufficient detail so that readers will appreciate the real need to do a thorough analysis whenever the challenge arises. The text provides a framework for this task.

Summary

The internationalization of American business is accelerating. The globalization of markets and competition necessitates that all managers pay attention to the global environment. International marketing is defined as the performance of business activities, including pricing, promotion, product, and distribution decisions, across national borders. The international marketing task is made more daunting because environmental factors such as laws, customs, and cultures vary from country to country. These environmental differences must be taken into account if firms are to market products and services at a profit in other countries.

Key obstacles facing international marketers are not limited to environmental issues. Just as important are difficulties associated with the marketer's own self-reference criteria and ethnocentrism. Both limit the international marketer's abilities to understand and adapt to differences prevalent in foreign markets. A global awareness and sensitivity are the best solutions to these problems, and they should be nurtured in international marketing organizations.

Three different strategic orientations are found among managers of international marketing operations. Some see international marketing as ancillary to the domestic operations. A second kind of company sees international marketing as a crucial aspect of sales revenue generation but treats each market as a separate entity. Finally, a global orientation views the globe as the marketplace, and market segments are no longer based solely on national borders—common consumer characteristics and behaviors come into play as key segmentation variables applied across countries.

Key Terms

International marketing
Controllable elements
Uncontrollable elements

Domestic environment
    uncontrollables

Foreign environment
    uncontrollables

Self-reference criterion (SRC)
Global awareness

Questions

1. Define the key terms listed above.
2. "The marketer's task is the same whether applied in Dimebox, Texas, or Dar es Salaam, Tanzania." Discuss.
3. How can the increased interest in international marketing on the part of U.S. firms be explained?
4. Discuss the five phases of international marketing involvement.
5. Discuss the conditions that have led to the development of global markets.
6. Differentiate between a global company and a multinational company.

7. Differentiate among the three international marketing concepts.

8. Prepare your lifelong plan to be globally aware.

9. Discuss the three factors necessary to achieve global awareness.

10. Define and discuss the idea of global orientation.

11. Visit the Bureau of Economic Analysis homepage (http://www.bea.doc.gov). Select the section "International articles" and find the most recent information on foreign direct investments in the United States. Which country has the highest dollar amount of investment in the United States? Second highest?

Chapter 2

The Dynamic Environment of International Trade

Global Perspective

TRADE BARRIERS—AN INTERNATIONAL MARKETER'S MINEFIELD

We all know the story about U.S. trade disputes with Japan. Japan has had so many trade barriers and high tariffs that U.S. manufacturers are unable to sell in Japan as much as Japanese companies sell in the United States. The Japanese claimed that "unique" Japanese snow requires skis made in Japan, and U.S. baseballs are not good enough for Japanese baseball. Even when Japan opened its rice market, popular California rice had to be mixed and sold with inferior grades of Japanese rice.

However, the Japanese are not alone; every country seems to take advantage of the open U.S. market while putting barriers in the way of U.S. exports. The French protect their film and broadcast industry from foreign competition by limiting the number of American shows that can appear on television, the percentage of American songs broadcast on radio, and the proportion of U.S. movies that can be shown in French theaters. Not only do these barriers and high tariffs limit how much U.S. companies can sell, they also raise prices for imported products much higher than they sell for in the United States.

Another trade protection tactic even involved Britain's Supreme Court of Judicature, which has finally answered a question that has long puzzled late-night dorm-room snackers: What, exactly, is a Pringle? With citations ranging from Baroness Hale of Richmond to Oliver Wendell Holmes, Lord Justice Robin Jacob concluded that legally it is a potato chip. The decision was bad news for Procter & Gamble U.K., which then owed $160 million in value-added taxes to the state. It is thus good news for Her Majesty's Revenue and Customs—and for fans of no-nonsense legal opinions. In Britain, most foods are exempt from the value-added tax (VAT), but potato chips (known there as crisps) and "similar products made from the potato, or from potato flour" are taxable. Procter & Gamble argued that Pringles are about 40 percent potato flour and also contain corn, rice, and wheat and therefore should not be considered potato chips or "similar products." Rather, they are "savory snacks."

The VAT and Duties Tribunal disagreed, ruling that Pringles, marketed in the United States as "potato chips," are taxable. "There are other ingredients," the Tribunal agreed, but a Pringle is "made from potato flour in the sense that one cannot say that it is not made from potato flour, and the proportion of potato flour is significant being over 40 percent."

In 2010, the Chinese government began restricting sales of rare earth metals to the United States, Japan, and the European Union. China produces 90 percent of the world's rare earths used in the manufacture of hybrid car batteries, wind turbines, and energy-efficient lighting. Prices exploded. The three governments complained to the World Trade Organization (WTO) that the Chinese quotes gave Chinese firms an unfair advantage on world markets for these high-tech products. The WTO ruled the Chinese restrictions were unjustified and should be eliminated.

Barriers to trade, whatever form they take, both tariff and nontariff, are one of the major issues confronting international marketers. Nations continue to use trade barriers for a variety of reasons: some rational, some not so rational. Fortunately, tariffs generally have been reduced to record lows, and substantial progress has been made on eliminating nontariff barriers. And work continues around the world to further reduce these pesky hurdles to peace and prosperity.

Sources: Adapted from Todd G. Buchholz, "Free Trade Keeps Prices Down," *Consumers' Research Magazine*, October 1995, p. 22; Tomas Kellner, "What Gaul!" *Forbes*, April 28, 2003, p. 52; Jonathan Lynn, "WTO Negotiators to Tackle Obstacles to Farm Deal," *Reuters News*, January 3, 2008; Adam Cohen, "The Lord Justice Hath Ruled: Pringles Are Potato Chips," *The New York Times*, June 1, 2009; Tom Barkley, "China Loses WTO Appeal on Raw-Materials," *The Wall Street Journal*, January 30, 2012; "China Loses Appeal of WTO Ruling on Rare Earth Exports," *Reuters*, August 7, 2014, online.

Yesterday's competitive market battles were fought in western Europe, Japan, and the United States; now competitive battles have extended to Latin America, eastern Europe, Russia, China, India, Asia, and Africa as these emerging markets continue to open to trade. More of the world's people, from the richest to the poorest, will participate in the world's growing prosperity through global trade. The emerging global economy brings us into worldwide competition, with significant advantages for both marketers and consumers. Marketers benefit from new markets opening and smaller markets growing large enough to become viable business opportunities. Consumers benefit by being able to select from the widest range of goods produced anywhere in the world at the lowest prices.

Bound together by burgeoning international communications media and global companies, consumers in every corner of the world are demanding an ever-expanding variety of goods and services. As Exhibit 2.1 illustrates, world trade is an important economic activity. Because of this importance, the inclination is for countries to attempt to control international trade to their own advantage. As competition intensifies, the tendency toward protectionism gains momentum. If the benefits of the social, political, and economic changes now taking place are to be fully realized, free trade must prevail throughout the global marketplace. The creation of the World Trade Organization (WTO) is one of the biggest victories for free trade in history.

Exhibit 2.1

Top Ten 2014 U.S. Trading Partners ($ billions, merchandise trade)

Source: http://www.census.gov/foreign-trade/statistics/highlights/top/index.html, 2015.

Rank	Country	Total Trade	Exports	Imports	Balance
—	Total	3969.1	1623.3	2345.8	−722.5
1	Canada	658.1	312.0	346.1	−34.1
2	China	590.7	124.0	466.7	−342.7
3	Mexico	534.5	240.3	133.9	−106.4
4	Japan	200.9	67.0	133.9	−66.9
5	Germany	172.6	49.4	123.2	−73.8
6	South Korea	114.1	44.5	69.6	−25.1
7	United Kingdom	107.9	53.9	54.0	−0.1
8	France	78.2	31.2	47.0	−15.8
9	Brazil	72.8	42.4	30.3	12.1
10	Taiwan	67.4	26.8	40.6	−13.8

Trade statistics such as those listed in Exhibit 2.1 have often served to focus the attention of government officials around the world.[1] But readers of this text and analysts alike need to look a bit deeper than these macro statistics. For example, it is quite clear that China is the United States's biggest trade problem; the imbalance of trade is more than four times greater than that with Mexico. However, often U.S. imports from China include a majority of parts actually made in other countries. A prominent example is Apple's products, assembled in and imported from China. The iPhone includes parts made in several other countries (see Exhibit 2.2). Thus, trade balance statistics are greatly distorted, particularly

Exhibit 2.2

Sources of Distortion in Prominent Trade Statistics

Sources: Andrew Batson, "Not Really 'Made in China'," *The Wall Street Journal*, December 16, 2010, pp. B1–2; "iPadded," *The Economist*, January 12, 2012, p. 84.

Value of iPhone Shipped from China to U.S. (components and labor)	Value of Apple iPad Shipped from China Globally (costs and profits)
Japan 34%	Chinese labor 2%
Germany 17%	Non-Chinese labor 5%
South Korea 13%	Cost of materials 31%
United States 6%	Distribution & retail 15%
China 3.6%	Apple profits 30%
Others 27%	Other U.S. profits 2%
	S. Korean profits 7%
	Taiwanese profits 2%
	Others' profits 6%

---

[1]Christi Parsons and Kathleen Hennessey, "Obama Pushes His Manufacturing Plan," *Los Angeles Times*, January 26, 2012, p. A8; Jeanna Smialek, "Trade Gap Shrank in 2013 as U.S. Fuel Exports Climbed," *Bloomberg News*, February 6, 2014, online.

with respect to China, because consumer electronics constitute a large portion of American imports from the Middle Kingdom. In 2015, Apple iPads shipped to the United States from China alone amounted to approximately $8 billion of America's reported trade deficit.

This chapter briefly surveys the United States's past and present role in global trade and some concepts important for understanding the relationship between international trade and national economic policy. A discussion of the logic and illogic of protectionism, the major impediment to trade, is followed by a review of the General Agreement on Tariffs and Trade (GATT) and its successor, the World Trade Organization (WTO), two multinational agreements designed to advance free trade.

The Twentieth to the Twenty-First Century

At no time in modern economic history have countries been more economically interdependent, have greater opportunities for international trade existed, or has the potential for increased demand existed than now, at the beginning of the 21st century. This statement remains true even with due regard to the global financial crisis that began in 2008. In contrast, in the preceding 100 years, world economic development was erratic.

The first half of the 20th century was marred by a major worldwide economic depression that occurred between two world wars that all but destroyed most of the industrialized world. The last half of the century, while free of a world war, was marred by struggles between countries espousing the socialist Marxist approach and those following a democratic capitalist approach to economic development. As a result of this ideological split, traditional trade patterns were disrupted.

LO1

The basis for the reestablishment of world trade following World War II

After World War II, as a means to dampen the spread of communism, the United States set out to infuse the ideal of capitalism throughout as much of the world as possible. The Marshall Plan to assist in rebuilding Europe, financial and industrial development assistance to rebuild Japan, and funds channeled through the Agency for International Development and other groups designed to foster economic growth in the underdeveloped world were used to help create a strong world economy. The dissolution of colonial powers created scores of new countries in Asia and Africa. With the striving of these countries to gain economic independence and the financial assistance offered by the United States, most of the noncommunist world's economies grew, and new markets were created.

Even though the John Deere tractors lined up for shipment from its Waterloo, Iowa, plant appear impressive, the Hyundai cars stacked up by the water in Ulsan, South Korea, headed for the United States dwarf their numbers. The juxtaposition of the two pictures aptly reflects the persistence of America's broader merchandise trade deficit.

The benefits of the foreign economic assistance given by the United States flowed both ways. For every dollar the United States invested in the economic development and rebuilding of other countries after World War II, hundreds of dollars more returned in the form of purchases of U.S. agricultural products, manufactured goods, and services. This overseas demand created by the Marshall Plan and other programs[2] was important to the U.S. economy because the vast manufacturing base built to supply World War II and the swelling labor supply of returning military created a production capacity well beyond domestic needs. The major economic boom and increased standard of living the United States experienced after World War II were fueled by fulfilling pent-up demand in the United States and the demand created by the rebuilding of war-torn countries of Europe and Asia. In short, the United States helped make the world's economies stronger, which enabled them to buy more from us.

In addition to U.S. economic assistance, a move toward international cooperation among trading nations was manifest in the 1986–1994 negotiation of the General Agreement on Tariffs and Trade (GATT). International trade had ground to a halt following World War I when nations followed the example set by the U.S. passage of the Smoot-Hawley Act (1930), which raised average U.S. tariffs on more than 20,000 imported goods to levels in excess of 60 percent. In retaliation, 60 countries erected high tariff walls, and international trade stalled, along with most economies. A major worldwide recession catapulted the world's economies into the Great Depression when trade all but dried up.[3]

Determined not to repeat the economic disaster that followed World War I, world leaders created **GATT**, a forum for member countries to negotiate a reduction of tariffs and other barriers to trade. The forum proved successful in reaching those objectives. With the ratification of the Uruguay Round agreements, the GATT became part of the World Trade Organization (WTO) in 1995, and its 117 original members moved into a new era of free trade.

World Trade and U.S. Multinationals

The rapid growth of war-torn economies and previously underdeveloped countries, coupled with large-scale economic cooperation and assistance, led to new global marketing opportunities. Rising standards of living and broad-based consumer and industrial markets abroad created opportunities for American companies to expand exports and investment worldwide. During the 1950s, many U.S. companies that had never before marketed outside the United States began to export, and others made significant investments in marketing and production facilities overseas.

At the close of the 1960s, U.S. multinational corporations (MNCs) were facing major challenges on two fronts: resistance to direct investment and increasing competition in export markets. Large investments by U.S. businesses in Europe and Latin America heightened the concern of these countries about the growing domination of U.S. multinationals. The reaction in Latin American countries was to expropriate direct U.S. investments or to force companies to sell controlling interests to nationals. In Europe, apprehension manifested itself in strong public demand to limit foreign investment. Concerns, even in Britain, that they might become a satellite with manufacturing but no determination of policy led to specific guidelines for joint ventures between British and U.S. companies. In the European Community, U.S. multinationals were rebuffed in ways ranging from tight control over proposed joint ventures and regulations covering U.S. acquisitions of European firms to strong protectionism laws.

The threat felt by Europeans was best expressed in the popular book *The American Challenge*, published in 1968, in which the French author J. J. Servan-Schreiber wrote:

> Fifteen years from now it is quite possible that the world's third greatest industrial power, just after the United States and Russia, will not be Europe but American Industry in Europe. Already, in the ninth year of the Common Market, this European market is basically American in organization.[4]

Servan-Schreiber's prediction did not come true for many reasons, but one of the more important was that American MNCs confronted a resurgence of competition from all over

---

[2]The Organization for Economic Cooperation and Development (OECD) was a direct result of the Marshall Plan.

[3]David M. Kennedy and Lizabeth Cohen, *The American Pageant*, 15th ed. (Boston: Houghton Mifflin, 2012).

[4]J. J. Servan-Schreiber, *The American Challenge* (New York: Atheneum Publishers, 1968), p. 3.

Exhibit 2.3

The Nationality of the World's 100 Largest Industrial Corporations (size measured by annual revenues)

Source: "2014 Global 500," *Fortune*, http://www.fortune.com.

	1963	1979	1984	1996	2000	2005	2011	2014
United States	67	47	47	24	36	33	29	34
Germany	13	13	8	13	12	15	11	8
Britain	7	7	5	2	5	10	8	
United Kingdom								5
France	4	11	5	13	11	10	10	8
Japan	3	7	12	29	22	12	11	7
Italy	2	3	3	4	3	3	4	4
Netherlands–United Kingdom	2	2	2	2	2	1		
Netherlands	1	3	1	2	5	2	2	2
Switzerland	1	1	2	5	3	4	2	2
Luxembourg							1	
Belgium		1	1		1		1	
Norway						1	1	1
Finland								
Brazil		1					1	1
Canada		2	3					
India				1			1	1
Kuwait				1				
Mexico		1	1	1		1	1	1
Venezuela		1	1	1			1	1
South Korea			4	4		1	3	3
Sweden			1					
Spain						1	3	1
Russia							2	3
China					2	1	6	15
Malaysia							1	1
Taiwan							1	1
Thailand								1

the world. The worldwide economic growth and rebuilding after World War II was beginning to surface in competition that challenged the supremacy of American industry. Competition arose on all fronts; Japan, Germany, most of the industrialized world, and many developing countries were competing for demand in their own countries and looking for world markets as well. Countries once classified as less developed were reclassified as newly industrialized countries (NICs). Various NICs such as Brazil, Mexico, South Korea, Taiwan, Singapore, and Hong Kong experienced rapid industrialization in select industries and became aggressive world competitors in steel, shipbuilding, consumer electronics, automobiles, light aircraft, shoes, textiles, apparel, and so forth. In addition to the NICs, developing countries such as Venezuela, Chile, and Bangladesh established state-owned enterprises (SOEs) that operated in other countries. One state-owned Venezuelan company has a subsidiary in Puerto Rico that produces canvas, cosmetics, chairs, and zippers; there are also Chilean and Colombian companies in Puerto Rico; in the U.S. state of Georgia, a Venezuelan company engages in agribusiness; and Bangladesh, the sixth largest exporter of garments to the United States, also owns a mattress company in Georgia.

In short, economic power and potential has become more evenly distributed among countries than was the case when Servan-Schreiber warned Europe about U.S. multinational domination. Instead, the U.S. position in world trade is now shared with other countries. For example, in 1950, the United States represented 39 percent of world gross national product (GNP), but by 2014, it represented less than 23 percent. In the meantime, however, the global GNP grew much larger, as did the world's manufacturing output—all countries shared in a much larger economic pie. This change was reflected in the fluctuations in the growth of MNCs from other countries as well. Exhibit 2.3 reflects the dramatic changes between 1963 and 2014. In 1963, the United States had 67 of the world's largest industrial corporations. By 1996, that number had dropped to a low of 24, while Japan moved from having 3 of the largest to 29 and South Korea from 0 to 4. And following the great economic boom in the late 1990s in the United States, 36 of the largest companies were American, only 22 Japanese, and none were Korean. Most recently, GAZPROM, the Russian natural gas giant, was the first eastern European entrant into the top 100 global firms, ranking number 17 in the most recent *Fortune* list. The decline in Japanese and dramatic increase in Chinese companies' rankings are prominent as well.

Another dimension of world economic power, the balance of merchandise trade, also reflected the changing role of the United States in world trade. Between 1888 and 1971, the United States sold more to other countries than it bought from them; that is, the United States had a favorable balance of trade. By 1971, however, the United States had a trade deficit of $2 billion that grew steadily until it peaked at $160 billion in 1987. After that, the deficit in merchandise trade declined to $74 billion in 1991 but began increasing again and by 2007 had surpassed $700 billion. With the continued weakness in the U.S. dollar, the trade deficit began to abate some in the fall of 2007.[5] The positive consequence of the global financial crisis that began in 2008 in the United States was the halving of the U.S. trade deficit during 2009 from its high in 2007. But in 2011, the deficit was again more than $700 billion.

The heightened competition for U.S. businesses during the 1980s and early 1990s raised questions similar to those heard in Europe two decades earlier: how to maintain the competitive strength of American business, to avoid the domination of U.S. markets by foreign MNCs, and to forestall the "buying of America." In the 1980s, the United States saw its competitive position in capital goods such as computers and machinery erode sharply. From 1983 to 1987, almost 70 percent of the growth of the merchandise trade deficit was in capital goods and automobiles. At the time, those were America's high-wage, high-skill industries. But U.S. industry got a wake-up call and responded by restructuring its industries, in essence, "getting lean and mean." By the late 1990s, the United States was once again holding its own in capital goods, particularly with trade surpluses in the high-tech category.

Among the more important questions raised in the 1980s were those concerning the ability of U.S. firms to compete in foreign markets and the fairness of international trade policies of some countries. Trade friction revolved around Japan's sales of autos and electronics in the United States and Japan's restrictive trade practices. The United States, a strong advocate of free trade, was confronted with the dilemma of how to encourage trading partners to reciprocate with open access to their markets without provoking increased protectionism. In addition to successfully pressuring Japan to open its markets for some types of trade and investment, the United States was a driving force behind the establishment of the WTO.

By the last decade of the 20th century, profound changes in the way the world would trade were already under way. The continuing integration of the countries of the European Union, the creation of NAFTA[6] and the American Free Trade Area (AFTA), and the rapid evolution of the Asia-Pacific Economic Cooperation Conference (APEC) are the beginnings of global trading blocks that many experts expect to dominate trade patterns in the future. With the return of Hong Kong in 1997 and Macao in 2000 to China, all of Asia is now controlled and managed by Asians for the first time in 400 years. During the decades since World War II, the West set the patterns for trade, but increasingly, Asia will be a major force, if not the leading force.

Beyond the First Decade of the Twenty-First Century

The unprecedented and precipitous growth of the U.S. economy in the late 1990s slowed dramatically in the last few years, and of course dramatically so in 2009. Growth in most of the rest of the world followed suit, with the exception of China. The Organization for Economic Cooperation and Development (OECD) estimates that the economies of member countries will expand an average of 3 percent annually for the next 25 years, the same rate as in the past 25 years. Conversely, the economies of the developing world will grow at faster rates—from an annual rate of 4 percent in the past quarter century to a rate of

---

[5]Alex Kowalski, "U.S. Trade Deficit Widens More Than Economists Forecast as Exports Decline," Bloomberg.com, January 13, 2012.

[6]Jenalia Moreno, "Trade Tariffs End, Making NAFTA a Milestone," *Houston Chronicle*, January 2, 2008.

6 percent for the next 25 years. Their share of world output will rise from about one-sixth to nearly one-third over the same period. The World Bank estimates that five countries—Brazil, China, India, Indonesia, and Russia—whose share of world trade is barely one-third that of the European Union will, by 2020, have a 50 percent higher share than that of the European Union. As a consequence, economic power and influence will move away from industrialized countries—Japan, the United States, and the European Union—to countries in Latin America, eastern Europe, Asia, and Africa.

This shift does not mean that markets in Europe, Japan, and the United States will cease to be important; those economies will continue to produce large, lucrative markets, and the companies established in those markets will benefit. It does mean that if a company is to be a major player in the 21st century, now is the time to begin laying the groundwork. How will these changes that are taking place in the global marketplace impact international business? For one thing, the level and intensity of competition will change as companies focus on gaining entry into or maintaining their position in emerging markets, regional trade areas, and the established markets in Europe, Japan, and the United States.

Companies are looking for ways to become more efficient, improve productivity, and expand their global reach while maintaining an ability to respond quickly and deliver products that the markets demand. For example, large Chinese state-owned companies are investing heavily in developing economies. Nestlé is consolidating its dominance in global consumer markets by acquiring and vigorously marketing local-country major brands. Samsung of South Korea has invested $500 million in Mexico to secure access to markets in the North American Free Trade Area. Whirlpool, the U.S. appliance manufacturer, which secured first place in the global appliance business by acquiring the European division of the appliance maker Royal Dutch Philips, immediately began restructuring itself into its version of a global company. These are a few examples of changes that are sweeping multinational companies as they gear up for the rest of the 21st century.

Global companies are not the only ones aggressively seeking new market opportunities. Smaller companies are using novel approaches to marketing and seeking ways to apply their technological expertise to exporting goods and services not previously sold abroad. A small Midwestern company that manufactures and freezes bagel dough for supermarkets to bake and sell as their own saw opportunities abroad and began to export to Japan. International sales, though small initially, showed such potential that the company sold its U.S. business to concentrate on international operations. Other examples of smaller companies include Nochar Inc., which makes a fire retardant it developed a decade ago for the Indianapolis 500. The company now gets 32 percent of its sales overseas, in 29 countries. The owner of Buztronics Inc., a maker of promotional lapel buttons, heard from a friend that his buttons, with their red blinking lights, would "do great" in Japan. He made his first entry in exporting to Japan, and after only a year, 10 percent of Buztronics sales came from overseas. While 50 of the largest exporters account for 30 percent of U.S. merchandise exports, the rest come from middle- and small-sized firms like those just mentioned. The business world is weathering a flurry of activity as companies large and small adjust to the internationalization of the marketplace at home and abroad.

Balance of Payments

When countries trade, financial transactions among businesses or consumers of different nations occur. Products and services are exported and imported, monetary gifts are exchanged, investments are made, cash payments are made and cash receipts received, and vacation and foreign travel occur. In short, over a period of time, there is a constant flow of money into and out of a country. The system of accounts that records a nation's international financial transactions is called its **balance of payments**.

LO2

The importance of balance-of-payment figures to a country's economy

A nation's balance-of-payments statement records all financial transactions between its residents and those of the rest of the world during a given period of time—usually one year. Because the balance-of-payments record is maintained on a double-entry bookkeeping

Exhibit 2.4
U.S. Current Account by
Major Components, 2014
($ billions)

Exports	
Goods	$ 1635
Services	709
Income receipts	813
Imports	
Goods	−2371
Services	−478
Income payments	−586
Unilateral current transfers, net	164
Current account balance	−114

system, it must always be in balance. As on an individual company's financial statement, the assets and liabilities or the credits and debits must offset each other. And like a company's statement, the fact that they balance does not mean a nation is in particularly good or poor financial condition. A balance of payments is a record of condition, not a determinant of condition. Each of the nation's financial transactions with other countries is reflected in its balance of payments.

A nation's balance-of-payments statement presents an overall view of its international economic position and is an important economic measure used by treasuries, central banks, and other government agencies whose responsibility is to maintain external and internal economic stability. A balance of payments represents the difference between receipts from foreign countries on one side and payments to them on the other. On the plus side of the U.S. balance of payments are merchandise export sales; money spent by foreign tourists; payments to the United States for insurance, transportation, and similar services; payments of dividends and interest on investments abroad; return on capital invested abroad; new foreign investments in the United States; and foreign government payments to the United States.

On the minus side are the costs of goods imported, spending by American tourists overseas, new overseas investments, and the cost of foreign military and economic aid. A deficit results when international payments are greater than receipts. It can be reduced or eliminated by increasing a country's international receipts (i.e., gain more exports to other countries or more tourists from other countries) and/or reducing expenditures in other countries. A balance-of-payments statement includes three accounts: the current account, a record of all merchandise exports, imports, and services plus unilateral transfers of funds; the *capital account*, a record of direct investment, portfolio investment, and short-term capital movements to and from countries; and the official *reserves account*, a record of exports and imports of gold, increases or decreases in foreign exchange, and increases or decreases in liabilities to foreign central banks. Of the three, the current account is of primary interest to international business.

The *current account* is important because it includes all international merchandise trade and service accounts, that is, accounts for the value of all merchandise and services imported and exported and all receipts and payments from investments and overseas employment. Exhibit 2.4 gives the current account calculations for the United States in 2014.

Since 1971, the United States has had a favorable current account balance (as a percentage of GDP) in only a few years—see Exhibit 2.5. The imbalances resulted primarily from U.S. demand for oil, petroleum products, cars, consumer durables, and other merchandise. Because of the huge increases in domestic oil production in 2013 and 2014, the merchandise trade deficit has fallen back below the $700 billion mark. Still, such imbalances have drastic effects on the balance of payments and therefore the value of U.S. currency in the world marketplace. Factors such as these eventually require an adjustment through a change in exchange rates, prices, and/or incomes. In short, once the wealth of a

Exhibit 2.5
U.S. Current Account Balance (% of GDP)

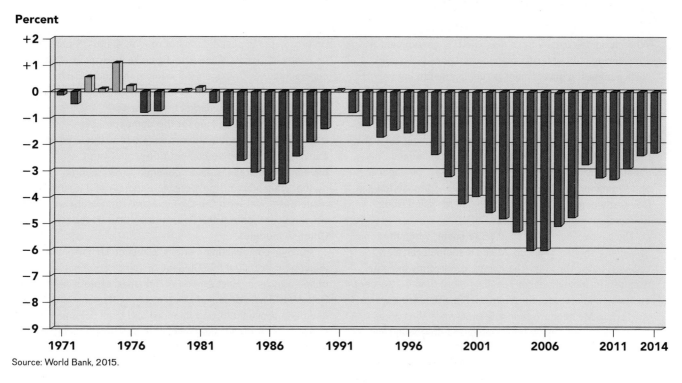

Percent

Source: World Bank, 2015.

country whose expenditures exceed its income has been exhausted, that country, like an individual, must reduce its standard of living. If its residents do not do so voluntarily, the rates of exchange of its money for foreign monies decline, and through the medium of the foreign exchange market, the purchasing power of foreign goods is transferred from that country to another.

As the U.S. trade deficit has grown, pressures have begun to push the value of the dollar to lower levels. And when foreign currencies can be traded for more dollars, U.S. products (and companies) are less expensive for the foreign customer and exports increase, and foreign products are more expensive for the U.S. customer and the demand for imported goods is dampened. Likewise, investments in dollar-denominated equities and such invest-ment goods become less attractive. Indeed, the dollar itself becomes less useful as a global currency.

Protectionism

LO3

The effects of protectionism on world trade

International business executives understand the reality that this is a world of tariffs, quo-tas, and nontariff barriers designed to protect a country's markets from intrusion by foreign companies. Although the World Trade Organization has been effective in reducing tariffs, countries still resort to measures of **protectionism**. Nations utilize legal barriers, exchange barriers, and psychological barriers to restrain the entry of unwanted goods. Businesses work together to establish private market barriers, while the market structure itself may provide formidable barriers to imported goods. Most recently, the United States and other countries have accused China of keeping the value of its currency artificially low to boost exports and limit exports. The complex distribution system in Japan, as will be detailed in Chapter 15, is a good example of a market structure creating a barrier to trade. However, as effective as it is in keeping some products out of the market, in a legal sense, it cannot be viewed as a trade barrier.

CROSSING BORDERS 2.1

Running in Different Directions, with Scissors

When it comes to running shoes, the U.S. government is considering cutting tariffs on imported shoes. But, with solar panels, the government is running fast to cut imports of solar panels from China in the opposite direction.

Among the many new trade agreements on the table for the Obama administration is the so-called Trans-Pacific Partnership (TPP), a free-trade agreement among 11 Pacific Rim nations (Australia, Brunei Darussalam, Canada, Chile, Japan, Malaysia, Mexico, New Zealand, Peru, Singapore, and Vietnam). The TPP is a smaller-scale approach toward free trade begun in response to the so-far-failed Doha Round of global free-trade talks.

The rubber meets the road, so to speak, when the topic of running shoes comes up. Maine manufacturer, New Balance, hates the idea. The company currently benefits from tariffs, in some cases reaching more than 60 percent on shoes manufactured in Vietnam. New Balance pays its workers in Maine more than $10/hour, while Vietnamese shoe makers are paying their employees 46¢/hour. Nike would like to import more shoes of its U.S.-designed shoes from Vietnam, so consumers could pay lower prices. On the jobs issue, Nike argues that TPP will create high-paying jobs in the United States for positions from designers to product engineers. Nike and other supporters of TPP argue tariff barriers that save jobs in one industry often make little sense in the context of overall risks and benefits to Americans.

Meanwhile, the U.S. government has succeeded in cutting by half imports of solar panels from China. American solar panel manufacturers are cheering. In 2012, the United States imposed duties of roughly 24 to 36 percent on imported panels made from Chinese solar cells after concluding that Chinese solar companies had received unfair subsidies from their government and dumped products on the American market below costs.

But the tariffs have upset the domestic solar industry. Many manufacturers have been squeezed to bankruptcy by intense competition from China, while developers, installers, and consumers have been helped by the availability of inexpensive panels. Amid a similar trade case overseas, the Chinese and the European Union agreed on a price floor and volume quota for Chinese modules.

Further complicating matters, a Justice Department indictment accusing five Chinese military personnel of online attacks against American industrial targets cited SolarWorld as a prominent victim, saying its computers had been broken into, and financial and legal documents stolen, after it filed trade complaints against Chinese manufacturers. And, of course, the Chinese government has complained loudly about the tariffs. You will notice that China is not included in the ongoing TPP talks.

Finally, as solar energy becomes more expensive, the world becomes more polluted.

Sources: Eric Marting, "New Balance Wants Its Tariffs, Nike Doesn't," *Bloomberg BusinessWeek*, May 13, 2012, pp. 14–15; Peter Coy, "Mapping the Way to a Global Free-Trade Deal," *Bloomberg BusinessWeek*, June 20, 2012, pp. 24–26; Diane Carwell and Keith Bradher, "Solar Industry ins Rebalanced by U.S. Pressure on China," *The New York Times*, July 26, 2014, pp. B1–2; "China Condemns US in Solar Trade Battle," *Reuters*, July 29, 2014, online.

Protection Logic and Illogic

Countless reasons to maintain government restrictions on trade are espoused by protectionists, but essentially all arguments can be classified as follows: (1) protection of an infant industry, (2) protection of the home market, (3) need to keep money at home, (4) encouragement of capital accumulation, (5) maintenance of the standard of living and real wages,[7] (6) conservation of natural resources, (7) industrialization of a low-wage nation, (8) maintenance of employment and reduction of unemployment,[8] (9) national defense, (10) enhancement of business size, and (11) retaliation and bargaining. Economists in general recognize as valid only the arguments regarding infant industry, national defense, and industrialization of underdeveloped countries. The resource conservation argument becomes increasingly valid in an era of environmental consciousness and worldwide shortages of raw materials and agricultural commodities. A case might be made for temporary protection of markets with excess productive capacity or excess labor when such protection could facilitate an orderly transition. Unfortunately such protection often becomes long term and contributes to industrial inefficiency while detracting from a nation's realistic adjustment to its world situation.

---

[7] Jeff Madrick, "Our Misplaced Faith in Free Trade," *The New York Times*, October 5, 2014, p. SR5.
[8] Ibid.

Exhibit 2.7
Growth of Consumer Purchasing Power 1990–2013 (GDP per capital, PPP, constant 2011 $s)

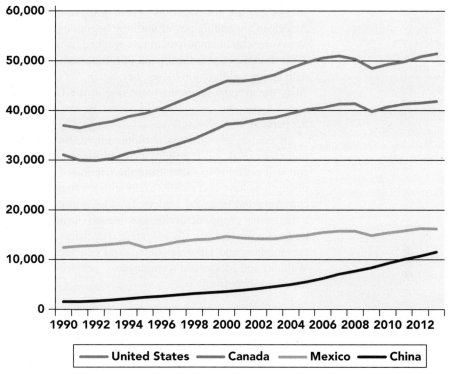

Source: World Bank, World Development Indicators, 2015.

To give you some idea of the cost to the consumer, consider the results of a recent study of 21 protected industries. The research showed that U.S. consumers pay about $70 billion per year in higher prices because of tariffs and other protective restrictions. On average, the cost to consumers for saving one job in these protected industries was $170,000, much higher than the wages and benefits of the average America manufacturing worker. Unfortunately, protectionism is politically popular, particularly during times of declining wages[9] and/or high unemployment, but it rarely leads to renewed growth in a declining industry. And the jobs that are saved are saved at a very high cost, which constitutes a tax that consumers unknowingly pay.

The larger view of how free trade has affected participating nations during the last three decades is presented in Exhibit 2.7. There, we look at the growth in purchasing power of the average consumer since 1990 in the United States, Canada, Mexico, and China. During the time period 1990–2013, consumers in all four countries have enjoyed a growth in their income: United States 39 percent, Canada 35 percent, Mexico 31 percent, and China an astonishing 640 percent.

The two big breakthroughs in free trade in those years for the United States were (1) the North American Free Trade Agreement (NAFTA) in 1994 and (2) the granting of Permanent Normalized Trade Relationship (PNTR) in 2000. China's entry into the World Trade Organization (WTO) in 2001 followed the next year. We discuss both in some detail in sections of the book to come.

Incomes of average Canadians and Americans continued to climb smartly after the agreement with Mexico. The average Mexican consumer lost about $1,000 in purchasing power in 1995 but regained it by 1997. Since then, NAFTA has yielded growth in all

---

[9]"Seeking Protection," *The Economist*, January 14, 2012, pp. 35–36.

three economies. Moreover, when we do a similar analysis of unemployment in the United States, we can find no evidence of NAFTA causing a loss of jobs for Americans.

After the declaration of PNTR for China, the average American's purchasing power took a one-year drop of $21 in 2001. Note this was also the year of the September 11 terrorist attacks and the dot-com bust. Then, 2002 began a six-year period of steady increases in American's spending power until the beginnings of the so-called Great Recession in 2008. The American unemployment rate reached its nadir for the period at an even 4.0 percent in 2000. It climbed to a local peak of 6.0 percent in 2002. One might blame the agreements with China for these job losses, but, again, 9/11 and the dot-com bust confuse the analysis. Also, the average unemployment rate in the United States during the 1990–2013 period was 5.8 percent; excluding the Great Recession years of 2009–2013, the average was 5.2 percent.

Of course, our analysis is quite simple. But we think it is hard to conclude that free trade hurt incomes or employment during the past three decades. Many Americans have and will continue to suffer from the friction of a vacillating economy. Indeed, the biggest disruptions have had mostly to do with shortsightedness and omissions of American policymakers and financial leaders. In at least three of the countries included in our analysis, a dangerous economic divide has opened during the past three decades. Many blame free trade. But the real culprits are internal decisions made about distribution of wealth, income tax policies, and labor relations. You can see the beginnings of corrections when both Walmart and McDonald's employees—services workers—begin to protest low wages and expensive benefits.

Trade Barriers

LO4

The several types of trade barriers

To encourage development of domestic industry and protect existing industry, governments may establish such barriers to trade as U.S. tariffs and a variety of nontariff barriers including quotas, boycotts, monetary barriers, and market barriers (see Exhibit 2.8 for a complete listing). Barriers are imposed against imports and against foreign businesses. While the inspiration for such barriers may be economic or political, they are encouraged by local industry. Whether or not the barriers are economically logical, the fact is that they exist.

Tariffs.   A tariff, simply defined, is a tax imposed by a government on goods entering at its borders. Tariffs may be used as revenue-generating taxes or to discourage the importation of goods, or for both reasons. Tariff rates are based on value or quantity or a

Exhibit 2.8
Trade Barrier Categories

- **Import policies** (*e.g.*, tariffs and other import charges, quantitative restrictions (quotas), import licensing, customs barriers, boycotts, embargoes, and other market access barriers);
- **Sanitary and phytosanitary measures** and technical barriers to trade;
- **Government procurement** (*e.g.*, "buy national" policies and closed bidding);
- **Export subsidies** (*e.g.*, export financing on preferential terms and agricultural export subsidies that displace U.S. exports in third country markets);
- **Lack of intellectual property protection** (*e.g.*, inadequate patent, copyright, and trademark regimes and enforcement of intellectual property rights);
- **Services barriers** (*e.g.*, limits on the range of financial services offered by foreign financial institutions, regulation of international data flows, restrictions on the use of foreign data processing, and barriers to the provision of services by foreign professionals);

- **Monetary barriers** (*e.g.*, limitations on foreign equity participation and on access to foreign government-funded research and development programs, local content requirements, technology transfer requirements and export performance requirements, and restrictions on repatriation of earnings, capital, fees and royalties);
- **Government-tolerated anticompetitive conduct** of state-owned or private firms that restricts the sale or purchase of U.S. goods or services in the foreign country's markets;
- **Trade restrictions affecting electronic commerce** (*e.g.*, tariff and nontariff measures, burdensome and discriminatory regulations and standards, and discriminatory taxation); and

Source: Adapted from 2015 National Trade Estimate Report on FOREIGN TRADE BARRIERS Office of the United States Trade Representative, pages 1–2.

CROSSING BORDERS 2.2 — Crossing Borders with Monkeys in His Pants

Robert Cusack smuggled a pair of endangered pygmy monkeys into the United States—in his pants! On June 13, 2002, a U.S. Fish and Wildlife Service special agent was called to Los Angeles International Airport after Cusack was detained by U.S. Customs on arrival from Thailand. Officials soon also discovered that Cusack had four endangered tropical birds and 50 protected orchids with him. "When one of the inspectors opened up his luggage, one of the birds flew out," tells one official. "He had to go catch the bird." After finding the other purloined birds and exotic flowers, the inspectors asked, "Do you have anything else you should tell us about?" Cusack answered, "Yes, I have monkeys in my pants." The monkeys ended up in the Los Angeles Zoo, and the smuggler ended up in jail for 57 days. He also paid a five-figure fine.

Similarly, Wang Hong, a Chinese exporter, pleaded guilty to smuggling sea turtles into the United States. He didn't have them in his pants; instead, the sea turtle "parts" came in the form of shells and violin bows, among other things.

However, Kai Xu, a Canadian turtle smuggler, was caught with 51 turtles in his pants in the Detroit-Windsor tunnel, according to a U.S. Attorney Sara Woodward. A Detroit judge ordered him to be held without bond. If convicted, a ten-year jail term is in Xu's future.

Smuggling isn't just a game played by sneaky individuals. Multinational companies can also get into the act. In recent years, convictions have come down for smuggling cell phones into Vietnam, cigarettes into Iraq and Canada, and platinum into China. In perhaps the biggest ever corporate case, after a nine-year lawsuit, Amway Corporation agreed to pay the Canadian government $38.1 million to settle charges it had avoided customs duties by undervaluing merchandise it exported from the United States to Canadian distributors over a six-year period. As long as there have been trade barriers, smuggling has been a common response. Indeed, Rudyard Kipling wrote some 100 years ago:

Five and twenty ponies trotting through the dark—
Brandy for the Parson, 'baccy for the clerk;
Laces for a lady, letters for a spy;
And watch the wall, my darling, while the Gentlemen go by!

Sources: "Amway Pays $38 Million to Canada," *Los Angeles Times*, September 22, 1989, p. 3; Patricia Ward Biederman, "Smuggler to Pay for Pocketing Monkeys," *Los Angeles Times*, December 19, 2002, p. B1; "Chinese National Pleads Guilty of Smuggling Protected Sea Turtles," *Associated Press*, January 3, 2008; Raymond Fisman, "Measuring Tariff Evasion and Smuggling," *NBER Reporter*, No. 3, 2009, pp. 8–10; Robert Snell, "Feds Lift Veil on International Turtle Smuggling Ring" *Detroit News*, September 26, 2014, online.

Rudyard Kipling, "'A Smuggler's Song"

combination of both. In the United States, for example, the types of customs duties used are classified as follows: (1) ad valorem duties, which are based on a percentage of the determined value of the imported goods; (2) specific duties, a stipulated amount per unit weight or some other measure of quantity; and (3) a compound duty, which combines both specific and ad valorem taxes on a particular item, that is, a tax per pound plus a percentage of value. Because tariffs frequently change, published tariff schedules for every country are available to the exporter on a current basis.[10] In general, tariffs:

Increase	Inflationary pressures.
	Special interests' privileges.
	Government control and political considerations in economic matters.
	The number of tariffs (they beget other tariffs via reciprocity).
Weaken	Balance-of-payments positions.
	Supply-and-demand patterns.
	International relations (they can start trade wars).
Restrict	Manufacturers' supply sources.
	Choices available to consumers.
	Competition.

In addition, tariffs are arbitrary, are discriminatory, and require constant administration and supervision. They often are used as reprisals against protectionist moves of trading

---

[10]The entire Harmonized Tariff Schedule of the United States can be downloaded or accessed via an interactive tariff database at http://www.usitc.gov; select the Harmonized Tariff Schedule.

partners. In a dispute with the European Union over pasta export subsidies, the United States ordered a 40 percent increase in tariffs on European spaghetti and fancy pasta. The European Union retaliated against U.S. walnuts and lemons. The pasta war raged on as Europe increased tariffs on U.S. fertilizer, paper products, and beef tallow, and the United States responded in kind. The war ended when the Europeans finally dropped pasta export subsidies. Less developed countries are increasingly voicing complaints about American and European tariffs on agricultural products.

Quotas and Import Licenses.   A quota is a specific unit or dollar limit applied to a particular type of good. Great Britain limits imported television sets; Germany has established quotas on Japanese ball bearings; Italy restricts Japanese motorcycles; and the United States has quotas on sugar, textiles, and, of all things, peanuts. Quotas put an absolute restriction on the quantity of a specific item that can be imported. When the Japanese first let foreign rice into their country, it was on a quota basis, but since 2000 the quotas have been replaced by tariffs.[11] Even more complicated, the banana war between the United States and the European Union resulted in a mixed system wherein a quota of bananas is allowed into the European Union with a tariff, then a second quota comes in tariff-free. In early 2010, as *Avatar* dominated cinema around the world, China ordered its movie houses to limit showings to the 3D version only. Like tariffs, quotas tend to increase prices. The U.S. quotas on textiles are estimated to add 50 percent to the wholesale price of clothing.

As a means of regulating the flow of exchange and the quantity of a particular imported commodity, countries often require import licenses. The fundamental difference between quotas and import licenses as a means of controlling imports is the greater flexibility of import licenses over quotas. Quotas permit importing until the quota is filled; licensing limits quantities on a case-by-case basis.

Voluntary Export Restraints.   Similar to quotas are the voluntary export restraints (VERs) or *orderly market agreements* (OMAs). Common in textiles, clothing, steel, agriculture, and automobiles, the VER is an agreement between the importing country and the exporting country for a restriction on the volume of exports. For many years Japan had a VER on automobiles to the United States; that is, Japan agreed to export a fixed number of automobiles annually. When televisions were still manufactured in the United States, Japan signed an OMA limiting Japanese color television exports to the United States to 1.56 million units per year. However, Japanese companies began to adjust their strategies by investing in television manufacturing in the United States and Mexico, and as a result, they regained the entire market share that had been lost through the OMA, eventually dominating the entire market. A VER is called voluntary because the exporting country sets the limits; however, it is generally imposed under the threat of stiffer quotas and tariffs being set by the importing country if a VER is not established.

Boycotts and Embargoes.   A government boycott is an absolute restriction against the purchase and importation of certain goods and/or services from other countries. This restriction can even include travel bans, like the one once in place for Chinese tourists; the Beijing government refused to designate Canada as an approved tourism destination. Officials in Beijing were not forthcoming with explanations, even after three years of complaints by and negotiations with their Canadian counterparts, but most believe it had to do with Canada's unrelenting criticism of Chinese human rights policies. An embargo is a

NYK Line (Nippon Yusen Kaisha) brings automobiles from Japan to Aqaba, Jordan, on the Red Sea for delivery to other countries in the area, but not for neighboring Israel. Because of the Arab boycott of Israel, separate shipments of cars are made to the adjacent port of Eilat. Ironically, automobiles now are imported into neighboring Jordan through a second route: through the Israeli port of Haifa.

---

[11]See the USA Rice Federation's website for details, http://www.usarice.com; also see Hodgson et al., *Doing Business in the New Japan.* See James Day Hodgson, Yoshihiro Sano, and John L. Graham, *Doing Business in the New Japan, Succeeding in America's Richest Foreign Market* (Boulder, CO: Rowman & Littlefield, 2008) for the complete story.

refusal to sell to a specific country. A public boycott can be either formal or informal and may be government sponsored or sponsored by an industry. The United States uses boycotts and embargoes against countries with which it has a dispute. For example, both Iran and North Korea have long-standing sanctions imposed by the United States. In 2014, the United States imposed new trade sanctions on Russia, and President Obama has moved to lift the decades-long trade embargo against Cuba.[12] It is not unusual for the citizens of a country to boycott goods of other countries at the urging of their government or civic groups. Nestlé products were boycotted by a citizens' group that considered the way Nestlé promoted baby formula in less developed countries misleading to mothers and harmful to their babies.

Monetary Barriers. A government can effectively regulate its international trade position by various forms of exchange-control restrictions. A government may enact such restrictions to preserve its balance-of-payments position or specifically for the advantage or encouragement of particular industries. Two such barriers are blocked currency and government approval requirements for securing foreign exchange.

Blocked currency is used as a political weapon or as a response to difficult balance-of-payments situations. In effect, blockage cuts off all importing or all importing above a certain level. Blockage is accomplished by refusing to allow an importer to exchange its national currency for the sellers' currency.

Government approval to secure foreign exchange is often used by countries experiencing severe shortages of foreign exchange. At one time or another, most Latin American and East European countries have required all foreign exchange transactions to be approved by a central minister. Thus, importers who want to buy a foreign good must apply for an exchange permit, that is, permission to exchange an amount of local currency for foreign currency.

The exchange permit may also stipulate the rate of exchange, which can be an unfavorable rate depending on the desires of the government. In addition, the exchange permit may stipulate that the amount to be exchanged must be deposited in a local bank for a set period prior to the transfer of goods. For example, Brazil has at times required funds to be deposited 360 days prior to the import date. This requirement is extremely restrictive because funds are out of circulation and subject to the ravages of inflation. Such policies cause major cash flow problems for the importer and greatly increase the price of imports. Clearly, these currency-exchange barriers constitute a major deterrent to trade.

Standards. Nontariff barriers of this category include standards to protect health, safety, and product quality. The standards are sometimes used in an unduly stringent or discriminating way to restrict trade, but the sheer volume of regulations in this category is a problem in itself. A fruit content regulation for jam varies so much from country to country that one agricultural specialist says, "A jam exporter needs a computer to avoid one or another country's regulations." Different standards are one of the major disagreements between the United States and Japan. The size of knotholes in plywood shipped to Japan can determine whether or not the shipment is accepted; if a knothole is too large, the shipment is rejected because quality standards are not met. Other examples include the following: In the Netherlands, all imported hen and duck eggs must be marked in indelible ink with the country of origin; in Spain, imported condensed milk must be labeled to show fat content if it is less than 8 percent fat; and in the European Union, strict import controls have been placed on beef and beef products imported from the United Kingdom because of mad cow disease. Add to this list all genetically modified foods, which are meeting stiff opposition from the European Union as well as activists around the world.

The United States and other countries require some products (automobiles in particular) to contain a percentage of "local content" to gain admission to their markets. The North American Free Trade Agreement (NAFTA) stipulates that all automobiles coming from member countries must have at least 62.5 percent North American content to deter foreign car makers from using one member nation as the back door to another.

---

[12]"American and Cuba, the New Normal," *The Economist*, January 3, 2015, pp. 11–12.

Cracker Jack invented the toy-with-candy promotion back in 1912. However, the Italian chocolatier Ferrero took things much further. Its milk chocolate Kinder eggs contain "sopresas" that kids enjoy in 37 countries around the world. The product is unavailable in the United States because of concerns about choking hazards. The product pictured is produced in Argentina for sale in Mexico, and it includes a warning label regarding kids under three years of age. Cracker Jack has had to eliminate many of the cool little toys it put in the packages for the same reason. Nestlé introduced a product similar to Kinder eggs in the U.S. market in the late 1990s but had to withdraw it for safety reasons. Wonderball is the latest version, but it has edible chocolate figures inside. See http://www.ferrero.com.ar and http://www.crackerjack.com for more details. Toys must be larger than the dimensions of the plastic tube (25.4 mm by 57.1 mm) pictured on the right to meet the U.S. safety standard.

Antidumping Penalties.   Historically, tariffs and nontariff trade barriers have impeded free trade, but over the years, they have been eliminated or lowered through the efforts of the GATT and WTO. Now there is a newer nontariff barrier: antidumping laws that have emerged as a way of keeping foreign goods out of a market. Antidumping laws were designed to prevent foreign producers from "predatory pricing," a practice whereby a foreign producer intentionally sells its products in the United States for less than the cost of production to undermine the competition and take control of the market. This barrier was intended as a kind of antitrust law for international trade. Violators are assessed "antidumping" duties for selling below cost and/or "countervailing duties" to prevent the use of foreign government subsidies to undermine American industry. Many countries have similar laws, and they are allowed under WTO rules.

Recent years have seen a staggering increase in antidumping cases in the United States. In one year, 12 U.S. steel manufacturers launched antidumping cases against 82 foreign steelmakers in 30 countries. In 2014, the United States imposed antidumping duties of up to 78 percent on China and Taiwan[13], despite President Barack Obama's agreement with other G20 leaders "to avoid protectionist measures at a time of great economic peril" in April of that year.[14] In 2014 more than 700 antidumping notices were posted in the U.S. Federal Register. Many economists felt that these antidumping charges were unnecessary because of the number of companies and countries involved; supply and demand could have been left to sort out the best producers and prices. And of course, targeted countries have complained as well. Nevertheless, antidumping cases are becoming de facto trade barriers. The investigations are very costly, they take a long time to resolve, and until they are resolved, they effectively limit trade. Furthermore, the threat of being hit by an antidumping charge is enough to keep some companies out of the market.

Domestic Subsidies and Economic Stimuli.   Agricultural subsidies in the United States and Europe have long been the subject of trade complaints in developing countries. However, the economic doldrums beginning in 2008 triggered new, huge,

---

[13]Diane Cardwell, "U.S. Imposes Steep Tariffs on Chinese Solar Panels," *The New York Times*, December 17, 2014, p. B2.

[14]Rapozza, "Obama's Half Truths," op. cit. Kenneth Rapozza, "Obama's Half-Truth on China Tire Tariffs," forbes.com, January 25, 2012.

domestic bailout packages in the larger economies for banks and automakers, to name just a couple. Developing countries complained that such subsidies of domestic industries gave companies in those countries unfair advantages in the global marketplace. Smaller countries defended themselves with a variety of tactics; for example, Malaysia limited the number of ports that could accept inbound goods, Ecuador increased tariffs on 600 types of goods, and Argentina and 15 other countries asked the WTO to examine whether stimuli and bailouts were "industrial subsidies," in which case, under WTO rules, trading partners have the right to retaliate. Similarly, the U.S. government complained about Chinese policies, including continuing currency controls, tax breaks on exports, and requirements that force government entities to buy Chinese products.

Easing Trade Restrictions

Lowering the trade deficit has been a priority of the U.S. government for a number of years. Of the many proposals brought forward, most deal with fairness of trade with some of our trading partners instead of reducing imports or adjusting other trade policies. Many believe that too many countries are allowed to trade freely in the United States without granting equal access to U.S. products in their countries. Japan was for two decades the trading partner with which we had the largest deficit and which elicited the most concern about fairness. The Omnibus Trade and Competitiveness Act of 1988 addressed the trade fairness issue and focused on ways to improve U.S. competitiveness. At the turn of the century, China took over from Japan as America's number one "trade problem," as can be seen in Exhibit 2.1.

The Omnibus Trade and Competitiveness Act

The *Omnibus Trade and Competitiveness Act of 1988* is many faceted, focusing on assisting businesses to be more competitive in world markets as well as on correcting perceived injustice in trade practices. The trade act was designed to deal with trade deficits, protectionism, and the overall fairness of our trading partners. Congressional concern centered on the issue that U.S. markets were open to most of the world but markets in Japan, western Europe, and many Asian countries were relatively closed. The act reflected the realization that we must deal with our trading partners based on how they actually operate, not on how we want them to behave. Some see the act as a protectionist measure, but the government sees it as a means of providing stronger tools to open foreign markets and to help U.S. exporters be more competitive. The bill covers three areas considered critical in improving U.S. trade: market access, export expansion, and import relief.

LO5

The provisions of the Omnibus Trade and Competitiveness Act

The issue of the openness of markets for U.S. goods is addressed as *market access*. Many barriers restrict or prohibit goods from entering a foreign market. Unnecessarily restrictive technical standards, compulsory distribution systems, customs barriers, tariffs, quotas, and restrictive licensing requirements are just a few. The act gives the U.S. president authority to restrict sales of a country's products in the U.S. market if that country imposes unfair restrictions on U.S. products. Furthermore, if a foreign government's procurement rules discriminate against U.S. firms, the U.S. president has the authority to impose a similar ban on U.S. government procurement of goods and services from the offending nation.

Besides emphasizing market access, the act recognizes that some problems with U.S. export competitiveness stem from impediments on trade imposed by U.S. regulations and export disincentives. Export controls, the Foreign Corrupt Practices Act (FCPA), and export promotion were specifically addressed in the *export expansion* section of the act. Export licenses could be obtained more easily and more quickly for products on the export control list. In addition, the act reaffirmed the government's role in being more responsive to the needs of the exporter. Two major contributions facilitating export trade were computer-based procedures to file for and track export license requests and the creation of the National Trade Data Bank (NTDB) to improve access to trade data.

Export trade is a two-way street: We must be prepared to compete with imports in the home market if we force foreign markets to open to U.S. trade. Recognizing that foreign penetration of U.S. markets can cause serious competitive pressure, loss of market

The billboard overlooking a busy shopping district in Beijing proclaims the importance of China's space technology to all passersby. Meanwhile, Boeing and Hughes had to pay $32 million in a settlement with the U.S. government for allegedly giving the Chinese sensitive space technology in the middle 1990s. The restrictions on technology sales to this day have rendered American high-tech firms less competitive in international markets even beyond China, such as Canada.

share, and, occasionally, severe financial harm, the *import relief* section of the Omnibus Trade and Competitiveness Act provides a menu of remedies for U.S. businesses adversely affected by imports. Companies seriously injured by fairly traded imports can petition the government for temporary relief while they adjust to import competition and regain their competitive edge.

The act has resulted in a much more flexible process for obtaining export licenses, in fewer products on the export control list, and in greater access to information and has established a basis for negotiations with India, Japan, and other countries to remove or lower barriers to trade. However, since a 1999 congressional report (accusing China of espionage regarding defense technology), restrictions on exports of many high-tech products have again been tightened for national security reasons.

As the global marketplace evolves, trading countries have focused attention on ways to eliminate tariffs, quotas, and other barriers to trade. Four ongoing activities to support the growth of international trade are GATT, the associated WTO, the International Monetary Fund (IMF), and the World Bank Group.

General Agreement on Tariffs and Trade

LO6

The importance of GATT and the World Trade Organization

Historically, trade treaties were negotiated on a bilateral (between two nations) basis, with little attention given to relationships with other countries. Furthermore, they tended to raise barriers rather than extend markets and restore world trade. The United States and 22 other countries signed the *General Agreement on Tariffs and Trade (GATT)* shortly after World War II. Although not all countries participated, this agreement paved the way for the first effective worldwide tariff agreement. The original agreement provided a process to reduce tariffs and created an agency to serve as watchdog over world trade. The GATT's agency director and staff offer nations a forum for negotiating trade and related issues. Member nations seek to resolve their trade disputes bilaterally; if that fails, special GATT panels are set up to recommend action. The panels are only advisory and have no enforcement powers.

The GATT treaty and subsequent meetings have produced agreements significantly reducing tariffs on a wide range of goods. Periodically, member nations meet to reevaluate trade barriers and establish international codes designed to foster trade among members. In general, the agreement covers these basic elements: (1) trade shall be conducted on a nondiscriminatory basis; (2) protection shall be afforded domestic industries through customs tariffs, not through such commercial measures as import quotas; and (3) consultation shall be the primary method used to solve global trade problems.

Since GATT's inception, eight "rounds" of intergovernmental tariff negotiations have been held. The most recently completed was the Uruguay Round (1994), which built on the successes of the Tokyo Round (1974)—the most comprehensive and far-reaching undertaken by GATT up to that time. The Tokyo Round resulted in tariff cuts and set out new international rules for subsidies and countervailing measures, antidumping, government procurement, technical barriers to trade (standards), customs valuation, and import licensing. While the Tokyo Round addressed nontariff barriers, some areas that were not covered continued to impede free trade.

In addition to market access, there were issues of trade in services, agriculture, and textiles; intellectual property rights; and investment and capital flows. The United States was especially interested in addressing services trade and intellectual property rights, since neither had been well protected. On the basis of these concerns, the eighth set of negotiations (Uruguay Round) was begun in 1986 at a GATT Trade Minister's meeting in Punta del Este, Uruguay, and finally concluded in 1994. By 1995, 80 GATT members, including the United States, the European Union (and its member states), Japan, and Canada, had accepted the agreement.

The market access segment (tariff and nontariff measures) was initially considered to be of secondary importance in the negotiations, but the final outcome went well beyond the initial

Uruguay Round goal of a one-third reduction in tariffs. Instead, virtually all tariffs in 10 vital industrial sectors with key trading partners were eliminated. This agreement resulted in deep cuts (ranging from 50 to 100 percent) in tariffs on electronic items and scientific equipment and the harmonization of tariffs in the chemical sector at very low rates (5.5 to 0 percent).

An important objective of the United States in the Uruguay Round was to reduce or eliminate barriers to international trade in services. The *General Agreement on Trade in Services (GATS)* was the first multilateral, legally enforceable agreement covering trade and investment in the services sector. It provides a legal basis for future negotiations aimed at eliminating barriers that discriminate against foreign services and deny them market access. For the first time, comprehensive multilateral disciplines and procedures covering trade and investment in services were established. Specific market-opening concessions from a wide range of individual countries were achieved, and provision was made for continued negotiations to liberalize telecommunications and financial services further.

Equally significant were the results of negotiations in the investment sector. *Trade-Related Investment Measures (TRIMs)* established the basic principle that investment restrictions can be major trade barriers and therefore are included, for the first time, under GATT procedures. As a result of TRIMs, restrictions in Indonesia that prohibit foreign firms from opening their own wholesale or retail distribution channels can be challenged. And so can investment restrictions in Brazil that require foreign-owned manufacturers to buy most of their components from high-cost local suppliers and that require affiliates of foreign multinationals to maintain a trade surplus in Brazil's favor by exporting more than they sell within.

Another objective of the United States for the Uruguay Round was achieved by an agreement on *Trade-Related Aspects of Intellectual Property Rights (TRIPs)*. The TRIPs agreement establishes substantially higher standards of protection for a full range of intellectual property rights (patents, copyrights, trademarks, trade secrets, industrial designs, and semiconductor chip mask works) than are embodied in current international agreements, and it provides for the effective enforcement of those standards both internally and at the border.

The Uruguay Round also includes another set of improvements in rules covering antidumping, standards, safeguards, customs valuation, rules of origin, and import licensing. In each case, rules and procedures were made more open, equitable, and predictable, thus leading to a more level playing field for trade. Perhaps the most notable achievement of the Uruguay Round was the creation of a new institution as a successor to the GATT—the World Trade Organization.

According to the U.S. government, you can't call it a "catfish" unless it's grown in America. Vietnamese are producing filets in flooded rice paddies at about $1.80 a pound at wholesale. American fish farmers are charging about $2.80. Neither consumers nor ichthyologists can tell the difference between the Asian and American fish, but Uncle Sam has stepped in anyway. The congressional claim on the "catfish" name has forced the United States to stifle its own protests about Europeans claiming exclusive rights to the name "herring." Most recently, the catfish issue is getting even sticker. The 10 Pacific Rim nations involved in the TPP negotiations have joined Vietnam's complaints about the U.S. catfish program.[15]

World Trade Organization[16]

At the signing of the Uruguay Round trade agreement in Marrakech, Morocco, in April 1994, U.S. representatives pushed for an enormous expansion of the definition of trade issues. The result was the creation of the World Trade Organization (WTO), which encompasses the current GATT structure and extends it to new areas not adequately covered in the past. The WTO is an institution, not an agreement as was GATT. It sets many rules governing trade among its 160 members, provides a panel of experts to hear and rule on trade disputes among members, and, unlike GATT, issues binding decisions. It requires, for the first time, the full participation of all members in all aspects of the current GATT and the Uruguay Round agreements, and, through its enhanced stature and scope, provide a permanent, comprehensive forum to address the trade issues of the 21st century global market.

---

[15]Ron Nixon, "U.S. Catfish Program Could Stymie Pacific Trade Pact, 10 Nationals Say," *The New York Times*, June 29, 2014, p. A15.

[16]See http://wto.org.

All member countries have equal representation in the WTO's ministerial conference, which meets at least every two years to vote for a director general, who appoints other officials. Trade disputes, such as those swirling around genetically modified foods, export taxes, and quotas for raw materials, as well as subsidies for aircraft companies and country-of-origin labeling, are heard by a panel of experts selected by the WTO from a list of trade experts provided by member countries. The panel hears both sides and issues a decision; the winning side is authorized to retaliate with trade sanctions if the losing country does not change its practices. Although the WTO has no means of enforcement, international pressure to comply with WTO decisions from other member countries is expected to force compliance. The WTO ensures that member countries agree to the obligations of all the agreements, not just those they like. For the first time, member countries, including developing countries (the fastest growing markets of the world), undertake obligations to open their markets and to be bound by the rules of the multilateral trading system.

The World Trade Organization provision of the Uruguay Round encountered some resistance before it was finally ratified by the three superpowers: Japan, the European Union (EU), and the United States. A legal wrangle among European Union countries centered on whether the EU's founding treaty gives the European Commission the sole right to negotiate for its members in all areas covered by the WTO.

In the United States, ratification was challenged because of concern for the possible loss of sovereignty over its trade laws to WTO, the lack of veto power (the U.S. could have a decision imposed on it by a majority of the WTO's members), and the role the United States would assume when a conflict arises over an individual state's laws that might be challenged by a WTO member. The GATT agreement was ratified by the U.S. Congress, and soon after, the European Union, Japan, and more than 60 other countries followed. All 117 members of the former GATT supported the Uruguay agreement. Since almost immediately after its inception on January 1, 1995, the WTO's agenda has been full with issues ranging from threats of boycotts and sanctions and the membership of Iran and Russia.[17] Indeed, a major event in international trade was China's 2001 entry into the WTO. Instead of waiting for various "rounds" to iron out problems, the WTO offers a framework for a continuous discussion and resolution of issues that retard trade. Russia was finally admitted in 2012 and has jumped into the game quite quickly. The European Union has filed complaints over Russian import duties.[18] Meanwhile, the Russians have claimed that EU and U.S. economic sanctions over the dustup with Ukraine are violations of WTO rules.[19]

The WTO has its detractors, but from most indications it is gaining acceptance by the trading community. The number of countries that have joined and those that want to become members is a good measure of its importance. Another one is its accomplishments since its inception: It has been the forum for successful negotiations to opening markets in telecommunications and in information technology equipment, something the United States had sought for the last two rounds of GATT. It also has been active in settling trade disputes, and it continues to oversee the implementation of the agreements reached in the Uruguay Round. But with its successes come other problems: namely, how to counter those countries that want all the benefits of belonging to WTO and also want to protect their markets. Indeed, the latest multilateral initiative, dubbed the "Doha Round" for the city of Qatar where the talks began in 2001, has been stalled with little progress.[20]

Skirting the Spirit of GATT and WTO

Unfortunately, as is probably true of every law or agreement, since its inception there have been those who look for loopholes and ways to get around the provisions of the WTO. For example, China was asked to become a member of the WTO, but to be accepted it had to

---

[17]Laura M. Brank, "Embracing Russia's WTO Entry," cnbc.com, January 23, 2012.

[18]Matthew Dalton, "EU Files Complaint over Russian Import Duties," *The Wall Street Journal*, May 21, 2014, online.

[19]Alexander Kolyandr, "Russia's Putin Slam Sanctions as Breach of WTO Rules," *The Wall Street Journal*, September 18, 2014, online.

[20]Daniel Pruzin, "WTO Ministrerial Ends with Whimper as Discussions over Doha Round Stall," globalwatch.com, January 5, 2010.

show good faith in reducing tariffs and other restrictions on trade. To fulfill the requirements to join the WTO, China reduced tariffs on 5,000 product lines and eliminated a range of traditional nontariff barriers to trade, including quotas, licenses, and foreign exchange controls. At the same time, U.S. companies began to notice an increase in the number and scope of technical standards and inspection requirements. As a case in point, China applied safety and quality inspection requirements on such seemingly benign imported goods as jigsaw puzzles. It also has been insisting that a long list of electrical and mechanical imports undergo an expensive certification process that requires foreign companies but not domestic companies to pay for on-site visits by Chinese inspection officials. Under WTO rules, China now must justify the decision to impose certain standards and provide a rationale for the inspection criteria. In 2009, the WTO ruled Chinese restrictions on imports of movies, music, and books to be illegal.

The previously mentioned antidumping duties are becoming a favorite way for nations to impose new duties. Indeed, following the example of the United States, the region's most prolific user of antidumping cases, Mexico and other Latin American countries have increased their use as well. China also has accused the United States of dumping cars into its markets,[21] even as the United States accused South Korea of dumping appliances.[22] The WTO continues to fight these new, creative barriers to trade.

Finally, frustrated with the slow progress of the most recent round of WTO trade negotiations, several countries are negotiating bilateral trade agreements.[23] For example, the United States has signed free trade with twenty countries including Peru, Colombia, Panama, and South Korea.[24] The European Union is engaged in similar activities with South American countries. Perhaps most notable, China and Taiwan have begun free trade talks. South Korea and India have also signed a free trade pact as have five East African countries. To the extent that the bilateral talks ultimately lead to multilateral concessions, such activities are not inconsistent with WTO goals and aspirations.

In this same vein, the United States in the last few years has begun talks on multilateral free-trade pacts with both Pacific Rim countries and the European Union. The Obama administration has been nursing along the Trans-Pacific Partnership among 11 neighboring countries (Australia, Brunei Darussalam, Canada, Chile, Japan, Malaysia, Mexico, New Zealand, Peru, Singapore, and Vietnam) and the Trans Atlantic Trade and Investment Partnership with the EU.[25] Political and economic uncertainties in the United States and abroad threaten both initiatives circa 2015.[26]

The International Monetary Fund and World Bank Group

LO7

The emergence of the International Monetary Fund and the World Bank Group

The **International Monetary Fund (IMF)**[27] and the World Bank Group[28] are two global institutions created to assist nations in becoming and remaining economically viable. Each plays an important role in the environment of international trade by helping maintain stability in the financial markets and by assisting countries that are seeking economic development and restructuring.

[21]Stefanie Qi, "China to Levy Duties on Vehicles from U.S.," *The Wall Street Journal*, December 14, 2011.

[22]James Hagerty and Bob Tita, "Whirlpool Accuses Samsung, LG of Dumping Washers," *The Wall Street Journal*, December 31, 2011.

[23]Jayant Menon, "Dealing with the Proliferation of Bilateral Free Trade Agreements," *World Economy* 32 (October 2009), pp. 1381–407; Elizabeth Williamson and Tom Barkley, "Congress Approves Trade Pacts," *The Wall Street Journal,* October 23, 2011.

[24]http://www.ustr.gov, 2012.

[25]Brian Wingfield, "The Biggest Trade Deal Ever," *Bloomberg BusinessWeek*, July 8–14, 2013, pp. 24–25; Jack Ewing, "Carmakers Are Central Voice in U.S.-Europe Trade Talks," *The New York Times*, July 15, 2014, pp. B1, 4.

[26]Jackie Calmes, "A Proposal to Speed Up Action on Trade Accords," *The New York Times*, January 10, 2014, p. B2.

[27]http://www.imf.org.

[28]http://www.worldbank.org.

Inadequate monetary reserves and unstable currencies are particularly vexing problems in global trade. So long as these conditions exist, world markets cannot develop and function as effectively as they should. To overcome these particular market barriers that plagued international trading before World War II, the *International Monetary Fund (IMF)* was formed. Originally 29 countries signed the agreement; now 188 countries are members. Among the objectives of the IMF are the stabilization of foreign exchange rates and the establishment of freely convertible currencies to facilitate the expansion and balanced growth of international trade. Member countries have voluntarily joined to consult with one another to maintain a stable system of buying and selling their currencies so that payments in foreign money can take place between countries smoothly and without delay. The IMF also lends money to members having trouble meeting financial obligations to other members. Argentina, Turkey, and Greece have recently received such help from the IMF, but the results have been mixed.

To cope with universally floating exchange rates, the IMF developed *special drawing rights (SDRs)*, one of its more useful inventions. Because both gold and the U.S. dollar have lost their utility as the basic medium of financial exchange, most monetary statistics relate to SDRs rather than dollars. The SDR is in effect "paper gold" and represents an average base of value derived from the value of a group of major currencies. Rather than being denominated in the currency of any given country, trade contracts are frequently written in SDRs because they are much less susceptible to exchange-rate fluctuations. Even floating rates do not necessarily accurately reflect exchange relationships. Some countries permit their currencies to float cleanly without manipulation (clean float), whereas other nations systematically manipulate the value of their currency (dirty float), thus modifying the accuracy of the monetary marketplace. Although much has changed in the world's monetary system since the IMF was established, it still plays an important role in providing short-term financing to governments struggling to pay current account debts.

Although the International Monetary Fund has some severe critics,[29] most agree that it has performed a valuable service and at least partially achieved many of its objectives. To be sure, the IMF proved its value in the financial crisis among some Asian countries in 1997. The impact of the crisis was lessened substantially as a result of actions taken by the IMF. During the financial crisis, the IMF provided loans to several countries including Thailand, Indonesia, and South Korea. Had these countries not received aid ($60 billion to Korea alone), the economic reverberations might have led to a global recession. As it was, all the major equity markets reflected substantial reductions in market prices, and the rate of economic growth in some countries was slowed.

Sometimes confused with the IMF, the *World Bank Group* is a separate institution that has as its goal the reduction of poverty and the improvement of living standards by promoting sustainable growth and investment in people. The bank provides loans, technical assistance, and policy guidance to developing country members to achieve its objectives. The World Bank Group has five institutions, each of which performs the following services: (1) lending money to the governments of developing countries to finance development projects in education, health, and infrastructure; (2) providing assistance to governments for developmental projects to the poorest developing countries (per capita incomes of $925 or less); (3) lending directly to help strengthen the private sector in developing countries with long-term loans, equity investments, and other financial assistance; (4) providing investors with investment guarantees against "noncommercial risk," such as expropriation and war, to create an environment in developing countries that will attract foreign investment; and (5) promoting increased flows of international investment by providing facilities for the conciliation and arbitration of disputes between governments and foreign investors. It also provides advice, carries out research, and produces publications in the area of foreign investment law.

---

[29]Naomi Klein, *The Shock Doctrine* (New York: Picador, 2007); Krishna Guha, "Watchdog Calls on IMF to Curb Loan Conditions," *Financial Times*, January 4, 2008, p. 4.

Since their inception, these institutions have played a pivotal role in the economic development of countries throughout the world and thus contributed to the expansion of international trade since World War II.

Protests against Global Institutions

Beginning in 1999, what some are calling "anticapitalist protesters" began to influence the workings of the major global institutions described previously. The basic complaint against the WTO, IMF, and others is the amalgam of unintended consequences of globalization: environmental concerns, worker exploitation and domestic job losses, cultural extinction, higher oil prices, and diminished sovereignty of nations. The antiglobalization protests first caught the attention of the world press during a WTO meeting in Seattle in November 1999. Then came the World Bank and IMF meetings in April in Washington, DC, the World Economic Forum in Melbourne, Australia, in September, and IMF/World Bank meetings in Prague, also in September 2000. Some 10,000 protesters faced some 11,000 police in Prague. The protesters have established websites associated with each event, labeled according to the respective dates. The websites, the Internet, and mobile phones have proved to be important media aiding organizational efforts. And the protests and violence have continued at other meetings of world leaders regarding economic issues, such as WTO meetings in Geneva, Switzerland, and in individual countries affected by the IMF. Tragically, the terrorism in London was most likely timed to coincide with the G8 meetings in Scotland in 2005.[30] Many observers also suggest a direct influence of the WTO/IMF protests on recent "Occupy" activism around the world.[31]

Three kinds of antiglobalization protests: the photo on this page and the two photos on the next. Gifford Myers showed this sculpture *Object (Globalization)–2001* in Faenza, Italy, as a peaceful protest.

[30]Mark Rice-Osley, "Overshadowed by Terrorism, G-8 Summit Still Secures Debt Relief," *Christian Science Monitor*, July 11, 2005, p. 7.

[31]Naomi Klein, "Learning from Globalization Protests," *The New York Times*, October 6, 2011.

Starbucks may be replacing McDonald's as the American brand foreigners most love to hate. Here local police fail to stop anti–World Trade Organization rioters in Seattle from breaking windows close to home.

And, finally, protest of the deadly sort. Terrorists maim and kill those aboard the classic red London double-deck bus (you can see the pieces in the street).

The protest groups, some of them with responsible intent, have affected policy. For example, "antisweatshop" campaigns, mostly in America and mostly student-led, have had effects beyond college campuses. A coalition of nongovernmental organizations, student groups, and UNITE (the textile workers' union) recently sued clothing importers, including Calvin Klein and The Gap, over working conditions in the American commonwealth of Saipan in the Pacific. Faced with litigation and extended public campaigns against their brands, 17 companies settled, promising better working conditions.

Given the apparent previous successes associated with the generally peaceful grassroots efforts to influence policy at these global institutions, we can expect more of the same in the future. But predicting the consequences of the terrorism and associated violence apparently being added to the mix of protestation is impossible.

Summary

Regardless of the theoretical approach used in defense of international trade, the benefits from an absolute or comparative advantage clearly can accrue to any nation. Heightened competition around the world has created increased pressure for protectionism from every region of the globe at a time when open markets are needed if world resources are to be developed and utilized in the most beneficial manner. And though market protection may be needed in light of certain circumstances and may be beneficial to national defense or the encouragement of infant industries in developing nations, the consumer seldom benefits from such protection.

Free international markets help underdeveloped countries become self-sufficient, and because open markets provide new customers, most industrialized nations have, since World War II, cooperated in working toward freer trade. Such trade will always be partially threatened by various governmental and market barriers that exist or are created for the protection of local businesses. However, the trend has been toward freer trade. The changing economic and political realities are producing unique business structures that continue to protect certain major industries. The future of open global markets lies with the controlled and equitable reduction of trade barriers.

Key Terms

GATT	Nontariff barriers	World Trade Organization	International Monetary Fund
Balance of payments	Tariff	(WTO)	(IMF)
Current account	Voluntary export restraints		
Protectionism	(VERs)		

Questions

1. Define the key terms listed above.

2. Discuss the globalization of the U.S. economy.

3. Differentiate among the current account, balance of trade, and balance of payments.

4. Explain the role of price as a free market regulator.

5. "Theoretically, the market is an automatic, competitive, self-regulating mechanism which provides for the maximum consumer welfare and which best regulates the use of the factors of production." Explain.

6. Interview several local businesspeople to determine their attitudes toward world trade. Furthermore, learn if they buy or sell goods produced in foreign countries. Correlate the attitudes with their commercial experience and report on your findings.

7. What is the role of profit in international trade? Does profit replace or complement the regulatory function of pricing? Discuss.

8. Why does the balance of payments always balance, even though the balance of trade does not?

9. Enumerate the ways in which a nation can overcome an unfavorable balance of trade.

10. Support or refute each of the various arguments commonly used in support of tariffs.

11. France exports about 18 percent of its gross domestic product, while neighboring Belgium exports 46 percent. What areas of economic policy are likely to be affected by such variations in exports?

12. Does widespread unemployment change the economic logic of protectionism?

13. Review the economic effects of major trade imbalances such as those caused by petroleum imports.

14. Discuss the main provisions of the Omnibus Trade and Competitiveness Act of 1988.

15. The Tokyo Round of GATT emphasized the reduction of nontariff barriers. How does the Uruguay Round differ?

16. Discuss the impact of GATS, TRIMs, and TRIPs on global trade.

17. Discuss the evolution of world trade that led to the formation of the WTO.

18. Visit www.usitc.gov/taffairs.htm (U.S. Customs tariff schedule) and look up the import duties on leather footwear. You will find a difference in the duties on shoes of different value, material composition, and quantity. Using what you have learned in this chapter, explain the reasoning behind these differences. Do the same for frozen and/or concentrated orange juice.

19. The GATT has had a long and eventful history. Visit www.wto.org/wto/about/about.htm and write a short report on the various rounds of GATT. What were the key issues addressed in each round?

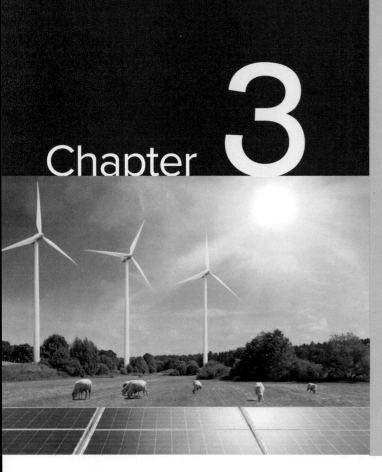

Chapter 3

History and Geography:

THE FOUNDATIONS OF CULTURE

CHAPTER LEARNING OBJECTIVES

What you should learn from Chapter 3:

LO1   The importance of history and geography in understanding international markets

LO2   The effects of history on a country's culture

LO3   How culture interprets events through its own eyes

LO4   How long-past U.S. international policies still affect customer attitudes abroad

LO5   The effect of geographic diversity on economic profiles of a country

LO6   Why marketers need to be responsive to the geography of a country

LO7   The economic effects of controlling population growth and aging populations

LO8   Communication infrastructures are an integral part of international commerce

Global Perspective

DO YOU REMEMBER...

the date of this speech by President Obama? Every Cuban does.

There's a complicated history between the United States and Cuba. I was born in 1961—just over two years after Fidel Castro took power in Cuba, and just a few months after the Bay of Pigs invasion, which tried to overthrow his regime. Over the next several decades, the relationship between our countries played out against the backdrop of the Cold War, and America's steadfast opposition to communism. We are separated by just over 90 miles. But year after year, an ideological and economic barrier hardened between our two countries.

Neither the American, nor Cuban people are well served by a rigid policy that is rooted in events that took place before most of us were born. Consider that for more than 35 years, we've had relations with China—a far larger country also governed by a Communist Party. Nearly two decades ago, we reestablished relations with Vietnam, where we fought a war that claimed more Americans than any Cold War confrontation.

That's why—when I came into office—I promised to re-examine our Cuba policy. As a start, we lifted restrictions for Cuban Americans to travel and send remittances to their families in Cuba... While I have been prepared to take additional steps for some time, a major obstacle stood in our way—the wrongful imprisonment, in Cuba, of a U.S. citizen and USAID sub-contractor Alan Gross for five years. Over many months, my administration has held discussions with the Cuban government about Alan's case, and other aspects of our relationship. His Holiness Pope Francis issued a personal appeal to me, and to Cuba's President Raul Castro, urging us to resolve Alan's case, and to address Cuba's interest in the release of three Cuban agents who have been jailed in the United States for over 15 years.

Today, Alan returned home—reunited with his family at long last. Alan was released by the Cuban government on humanitarian grounds. Separately, in exchange for the three Cuban agents, Cuba today released one of the most important intelligence agents that the United States has ever had in Cuba, and who has been imprisoned for nearly two decades.

First, I've instructed Secretary Kerry to immediately begin discussions with Cuba to reestablish diplomatic relations that have been severed since January of 1961. Going forward, the United States will reestablish an embassy in Havana, and high-ranking officials will visit Cuba.

Where we can advance shared interests, we will—on issues like health, migration, counterterrorism, drug trafficking and disaster response. Indeed, we've seen the benefits of cooperation between our countries before. It was a Cuban,

Carlos Finlay, who discovered that mosquitoes carry yellow fever; his work helped Walter Reed fight it. Cuba has sent hundreds of health care workers to Africa to fight Ebola, and I believe American and Cuban health care workers should work side by side to stop the spread of this deadly disease.

Second, I've instructed Secretary Kerry to review Cuba's designation as a State Sponsor of Terrorism. This review will be guided by the facts and the law. Terrorism has changed in the last several decades. At a time when we are focused on threats from al Qaeda to ISIL, a nation that meets our conditions and renounces the use of terrorism should not face this sanction.

Third, we are taking steps to increase travel, commerce, and the flow of information to and from Cuba. This is fundamentally about freedom and openness, and also expresses my belief in the power of people-to-people engagement. With the changes I'm announcing today, it will be easier for Americans to travel to Cuba, and Americans will be able to use American credit and debit cards on the island.

I believe that American businesses should not be put at a disadvantage, and that increased commerce is good for Americans and for Cubans. So we will facilitate authorized transactions between the United States and Cuba. U.S. financial institutions will be allowed to open accounts at Cuban financial institutions. And it will be easier for U.S. exporters to sell goods in Cuba.

I believe in the free flow of information. Unfortunately, our sanctions on Cuba have denied Cubans access to technology that has empowered individuals around the globe. So I've authorized increased telecommunications connections between the United States and Cuba. Businesses will be able to sell goods that enable Cubans to communicate with the United States and other countries.

These are the steps that I can take as President to change this policy. The embargo that's been imposed for decades is now codified in legislation. As these changes unfold, I look forward to engaging Congress in an honest and serious debate about lifting the embargo.

Change is hard—in our own lives, and in the lives of nations. And change is even harder when we carry the heavy weight of history on our shoulders. But today we are making these changes because it is the right thing to do. Today, America chooses to cut loose the shackles of the past so as to reach for a better future—for the Cuban people, for the American people, for our entire hemisphere, and for the world.

Source: Excerpts from President Barak Obama, The White House, December 17, 2014.

LO1

The importance of
history and geography
in understanding
international markets

Here we begin the discussion of the Cultural Environment of Global Markets. *Culture* can be defined as a society's accepted basis for responding to external and internal events. To understand fully a society's actions and its points of view, you must have an appreciation for the influence of historical events and the geographical uniqueness to which a culture has had to adapt. To interpret behavior and attitudes in a particular culture or country, a marketer must have some idea of a country's history and geography.

The goal of this chapter is to introduce the reader to the impact of history and geography on the marketing process. The influence of history on behavior and attitudes and the influence of geography on markets, trade, and environmental issues are examined in particular.

Historical Perspective in Global Business

History helps define a nation's "mission," how it perceives its neighbors, how it sees its place in the world, and how it sees itself. Insights into the history of a country are important for understanding attitudes about the role of government and business, the relations between managers and the managed, the sources of management authority, and attitudes toward foreign corporations.

To understand, explain, and appreciate a people's image of itself and the attitudes and unconscious fears that are reflected in its view of foreign cultures, it is necessary to study the culture as it is now as well as to understand the culture as it was—that is, a country's history. Finally, we must learn that history also influences business decisions such as foreign direct investments,[1] market entry, and even personnel choices.

History and Contemporary Behavior

LO2

The effects of history on a
country's culture

Most Americans know the most about European history, even though our major trading partners are now to our west and south. Circa 2008, China became a hot topic in the United States. It was back in 1776 as well. In a sense, American history really begins with China. Recall the Boston Tea Party: Our complaint then was the British tax and, more important, the British prohibition against Yankee traders dealing directly with merchants in Canton. So it is worthwhile to dwell for a few moments on a couple of prominent points in the history of the fast burgeoning market that is modern-day China. James Day Hodgson, former U.S. Labor Secretary and Ambassador to Japan, suggested that anyone doing business in another country should understand at least the encyclopedic version of the people's past as a matter of politeness, if not persuasion.[2] As important examples we offer a few perhaps surprising glimpses of the past that continues to influence U.S.–Asia trade relations even today.

First Opium War and the Treaty of Nanjing (1839–1842). During the early 1800s, the British taste for tea was creating a huge trade deficit with China. Silver bullion was flowing fast in an easterly direction. Of course, other goods were being traded, too. Exports from China also included sugar, silk, mother-of-pearl, paper, camphor, cassia, copper and alum, lacquer ware, rhubarb, various oils, bamboo, and porcelain. The British "barbarians" returned cotton and woolen textiles, iron, tin, lead, carnelian, diamonds, pepper,

---

[1]Shige Makino and Eric W.K. Tsang, "Historical Ties and Foreign Direct Investment," *Journal of International Business Studies* 42 (2011), pp. 545–57.

[2]James Day Hodgson, Yoshihiro Sano, and John L. Graham, *Doing Business in the New Japan, Succeeding in America's Richest Foreign Market* (Latham, MD: Rowman & Littlefield, 2008).

1000 First millennium ends; Y1K problem overblown—widespread fear of the end of the world proved unfounded
1000 Vikings settle Newfoundland
1004 Chinese unity crumbles with treaty between the Song and the Liao, giving the Liao full autonomy; China will remain fractured until the Mongol invasion in the 13th century (see 1206)

1025 Navy of Cholas in southern India crushes the empire of Srivijaya in modern Myanmar to protect its trade with China
1054 Italy and Egypt formalize commercial relations
1066 William the Conqueror is victorious over Harold II in the Battle of Hastings, establishing Norman rule in England and forever linking the country with the continent

1081 Venice and Byzantium conclude a commercial treaty (renewed in 1126)
1095 First of the crusades begins; Pope Urban II calls on Europe's noblemen to help the Byzantines repel the Turks; the crusaders' travel, stories, and goods acquired along the way help increase trade across Europe and with the Mediterranean and Asia; eighth major crusade

ends—Syria expels the Christians
1100 Japan begins to isolate itself from the rest of the world, not really opening up again until the mid-19th century (see 1858)
1100 China invents the mariner's compass and becomes a force in trade; widespread use of paper money also helps increase trade and prosperity

betel nuts, pearls, watches and clocks, coral and amber beads, birds' nests and shark fins, and foodstuffs such as fish and rice. But the tea-for-silver swap dominated the equation.

Then came the English East India Company's epiphany: opium. Easy to ship, high value to volume and weight ratios, and addicting to customers—what a great product! At the time, the best opium came from British India, and once the full flow began, the tea-caused trade deficit disappeared fast. The Emperor complained and issued edicts, but the opium trade burgeoned. One of the taller skyscrapers in Hong Kong today is the Jardine Matheson Trading House.[3] Its circular windows are reminiscent of the portholes of its clipper-ship beginnings in the opium trade.

In 1836 some high-ranking Chinese officials advocated legalizing opium. The foreign suppliers boosted production and shipments in anticipation of exploding sales. Then the Emperor went the opposite direction and ordered the destruction of the inventories in Canton (now known as Guangzhou). By 1839 the trade was dead. The British responded by sinking junks in the Pearl River and blockading all Chinese ports.

The "magically accurate" British cannon pointed at Nanjing yielded negotiations there in 1842. The Chinese ceded Hong Kong and $21 million pounds to the British. Ports at Xiamen, Fuzhou, Ningbo, and Shanghai were opened to trade and settlement by foreigners. Hong Kong thus became the gateway to a xenophobic China, particularly in the last half of the 20th century. Perhaps most important, China recognized for the first time its loss of great power status.

Ultimately the Opium War became about foreign access to Chinese trade, and the treaty of Nanjing really didn't settle the issue. A second Opium War was fought between 1857 and 1860. In that imbroglio, British and French forces combined to destroy the summer palace in Beijing. Such new humiliations yielded more freedoms for foreign traders; notably, the treaty specifically included provisions allowing Christian evangelism throughout the realm.

Taiping Rebellion (1851–1864).

One consequence of the humiliation at the hands of foreigners was a loss of confidence in the Chinese government. The resulting disorder came to a head in Guangxi, the southernmost province of the Empire. The leader of the uprising was a peasant who grew up near Guangzhou. Hong Xiuquan aspired to be a civil servant but failed the required Confucian teachings–based exam. When in Guangzhou for his second try at the exam, he came in contact with Protestant Western missionaries and later began to have visions of God.

After flunking the exam for a fourth time in 1843, he began to evangelize, presenting himself as Christ's brother. In the next seven years, he attracted 10,000 followers. In 1851, he was crowned by his followers as the "Heavenly King" of the "Heavenly Kingdom of Peace." Despite their adopted label, they revolted, cut off their pigtails in defiance of the ruling Manchus, and began to march north. With the fervor of the religious zealots they were, they fought their way through the capital at Nanjing and almost to Tianjing by 1855.

But then things started to unravel. Chinese opposition forces organized. Because foreigners appreciated neither Hong's interpretation of the scriptures, nor his 88 concubines,

---

[3]In a very interesting paper, the authors argue that choices made by Jardine's and Swire's (trading houses) in Asia today, for example, are an outgrowth of strategic choices first in evidence more than a century ago! *See* Geoffrey Jones and Tarun Khanna, "Bringing History (Back) into International Business," *Journal of International Business Studies* 37 (2006), pp. 453–68.

---

nor his attacks on Shanghai, they formed another army against him. Hong took his own life just before the final defeat and the recapture of Nanjing.

Estimates of the death toll from the Taiping Rebellion stand between 20 and 40 million people. We repeat: 20–40 million Chinese lives were lost. By contrast, "only" 2 million were killed in the 1949 Communist Revolution. The Taiping Rebellion is the single most horrific civil war in the history of the world. (although one estimate of the lost lives from famine during Chairman Mao's Great Leap Forward in 1958–1962 is 36 million).[4] Surely Hong Xiuquan was insane. Other rebellions also occurred in China during this time; the Muslim one in the northwest is most notable (1862–78). However, based on these events in the mid-1800s, it is easy to see why the Chinese leadership has remained wary of foreign influences in general, and religious movements in particular, even today.[5]

History and Japan.   Trade with Japan was a hot topic in the United States in both the 1850s and the 1980s. Likewise, unless you have a historical sense of the many changes that have buffeted Japan—seven centuries under the shogun feudal system, the isolation before the arrival of Commodore Perry in 1853, the threat of domination by colonial powers, the rise of new social classes, Western influences, the humiliation of World War II, and involvement in the international community—you will have difficulty fully understanding its contemporary behavior. Why do the Japanese have such strong loyalty toward their companies? Why is the loyalty found among participants in the Japanese distribution systems so difficult for an outsider to develop? Why are decisions made by consensus? Answers to such questions can be explained in part by Japanese history (and geography).

Loyalty to family, to country, to company, and to social groups and the strong drive to cooperate, to work together for a common cause, permeate many facets of Japanese behavior and have historical roots that date back thousands of years. Historically, loyalty and service, a sense of responsibility, and respect for discipline, training, and artistry were stressed to maintain stability and order. Confucian philosophy, taught throughout Japan's history, emphasizes the basic virtue of loyalty "of friend to friend, of wife to husband, of child to parent, of brother to brother, but, above all, of subject to lord," that is, to country. A fundamental premise of Japanese ideology reflects the importance of cooperation for the collective good. Japanese achieve consensus by agreeing that all will unite against outside pressures that threaten the collective good. A historical perspective gives the foreigner in Japan a basis on which to begin developing cultural sensitivity and a better understanding of contemporary Japanese behavior.

History Is Subjective

LO3

How culture interprets events through its own eyes

History is important in understanding why a country behaves as it does, but history from whose viewpoint? Historical events always are viewed from one's own biases and self-reference criteria (SRC), and thus, what is recorded by one historian may not be what another records, especially if the historians are from different cultures. Historians traditionally try to be objective, but few can help filtering events through their own cultural biases.

Our perspective not only influences our view of history but also subtly influences our view of many other matters. For example, maps of the world sold in the United States generally show the United States at the center, whereas maps in Britain show Britain at the center, and so on for other nations.

[4]"Millennial Madness," *The Economist*, October 27, 2012, pp. 83–84.

[5]N. Mark Lam and John L. Graham, *Doing Business in China Now, the World's Most Dynamic Marketplace* (New York: McGraw-Hill, 2007).

Mongol Empire extending from China to eastern Europe
1300 The early stirrings of the Renaissance begin in Europe as people are exposed to other cultures, primarily through merchants and trade; trade fairs are held in numerous European cities
1315 A great famine hits Europe, lasting two years, more widespread and longer than any before

1348 The Plague (the Black Death) kills one-fourth to one-third of the population in Europe (25 million people) in just three years, disrupting trade as cities try to prevent the spread of the disease by restricting visitors; it likely started in Asia in the 1320s; massive inflation took hold, because goods could only be obtained locally; serfs were in high demand and began moving to higher

wage payers, forever altering Europe's labor landscape
1358 German Hanseatic League officially forms by the Hansa companies of merchants for trade and mutual protection, eventually encompassing more than 70 cities and lasting nearly 300 years
1375 Timur Lang the Turk conquers lands from Moscow to Delhi

1381 English rioters kill foreign Flemish traders as part of the 100,000-strong peasant rebellion against Richard II, which was led by Wat Tyler in a failed attempt to throw off the yoke of feudalism
1392 England prohibits foreigners from retailing goods in the country
1400 Koreans develop movable-type printing (see 1450)

A crucial element in understanding any nation's business and political culture is the subjective perception of its history. Why do Mexicans have a love–hate relationship with the United States? Why were Mexicans required to have majority ownership in most foreign investments until recently? Why did dictator General Porfírio Díaz lament, "Poor Mexico, so far from God, so near the United States"? Why? Because Mexicans see the United States as a threat to their political, economic, and cultural sovereignty.

Most citizens of the United States are mystified by such feelings. After all, the United States has always been Mexico's good neighbor. Most would agree with President John F. Kennedy's proclamation during a visit to Mexico that "Geography has made us neighbors, tradition has made us friends." North Americans may be surprised to learn that most Mexicans "felt it more accurate to say 'Geography has made us closer, tradition has made us far apart.' "[6]

Citizens of the United States feel they have been good neighbors. They see the Monroe Doctrine as protection for Latin America from European colonization and the intervention of Europe in the governments of the Western Hemisphere. Latin Americans, in contrast, tend to see the Monroe Doctrine as an offensive expression of U.S. influence in Latin America. To put it another way, "Europe keep your hands off —Latin America is only for the United States," an attitude perhaps typified by former U.S. President Ulysses S. Grant, who, in a speech in Mexico in 1880, described Mexico as a "magnificent mine" that lay waiting south of the border for North American interests.

United States Marines sing with pride of their exploits "from the halls of Montezuma to the shores of Tripoli." To the Mexican, the exploit to which the "halls of Montezuma" refers is remembered as U.S. troops marching all the way to the center of Mexico City and extracting as tribute 890,000 square miles that became Arizona, California, New Mexico, and Texas (see Exhibit 3.1). A prominent monument at the entrance of Chapultepec Park recognizes *Los Niños Heroes* (the boy heroes), who resisted U.S. troops, wrapped themselves in Mexican flags, and jumped to their deaths rather than surrender. Mexicans recount the heroism of *Los Niños Heroes*[7] and the loss of Mexican territory to the United States every September 13, when the president of Mexico, the cabinet, and the diplomatic corps assemble at the Mexico City fortress to recall the defeat that led to the "*despojo territorial* " (territorial plunder).

The Mexican Revolution, which overthrew the dictator Díaz and launched the modern Mexican state, is particularly remembered for the expulsion of foreigners—most notably North American businessmen who were the most visible of the wealthy and influential entrepreneurs in Mexico.

---

[6]For an insightful review of some of the issues that have affected relations between the United States and Mexico, see John Skirius, "Railroad, Oil and Other Foreign Interest in the Mexican Revolution, 1911–1914," *Journal of Latin American Studies*, February 2003, p. 25.

[7]When the United Nations recommended that all countries set aside a single day each year to honor children, Mexico designated April 30 as "Dia de Los Niños." Interestingly, this holiday often coincides with Saint Patrick's Day celebrations, which include recognition of the San Patricios, the Irish-American battalion that fought with the Mexicans in the Mexican–American War.

Porfirio Diaz, Translator Ralph Keyes, *The Quote Verifier: Who Said What, Where, and When*, St. Martin's Griffin; 1st edition (May 30, 2006)

John F. Kennedy: "Address by the President at a Luncheon Given in His Honor by President Lopez Matcos.," June 29, 1962.

W.E. Christian, *Rhymes of the Rookies*, 1917, Dodd, Mead and Company

---

1404   Chinese prohibit private trading in foreign countries, but foreign ships may trade in China with official permission
1415   Chinese begin significant trading with Africa through government expeditions—some believe they sailed to North America as well in 1421
1425   Hanseatic city of Brugge becomes the first Atlantic seaport to be a major trading center

1427   Aztec Empire is created by Itzcotl; it will encompass about 6 million people before its destruction in 1519
1430   Portuguese Prince Henry the Navigator explores wêst African coast to promote trade
1441   Mayan Empire collapses as the city of Mayapán is destroyed in a revolt
1450   Renaissance takes hold in Florence, its traditional birthplace

1450   Gutenberg Bible is first book printed with movable type; the ability to mass produce books creates an information revolution
1453   Byzantine Empire is destroyed as Muhammad II sacks Constantinople (renaming it Istanbul)
1464   French royal mail service established by Louis XI
1470   Early trademark piracy committed by Persians

who copy mass-produced Chinese porcelain to capitalize on its popularity in foreign countries
1479   Under the Treaty of Constantinople, in exchange for trading rights in the Black Sea, Venice agrees to pay tribute to the Ottoman Empire
1482   English organize a postal system that features fresh relays of horses every 20 miles

The Monumento de Los Niños Heroes honors six young cadets who, during the Mexican–American War of 1847, chose death over surrender. The Mexican–American War is important in Mexican history and helps explain, in part, Mexico's love–hate relationship with the United States. *(© Dave G. Houser/ Corbis)*

Manifest Destiny and the Monroe Doctrine

Manifest Destiny and the Monroe Doctrine were accepted as the basis for U.S. foreign policy during much of the 19th and 20th centuries.[8] Manifest Destiny, in its broadest interpretation, meant that Americans were a chosen people ordained by God to create a model society. More specifically, it referred to the territorial expansion of the United States from the Atlantic to the Pacific. The idea of Manifest Destiny was used to justify the U.S. annexation of Texas, Oregon, New Mexico, and California and, later, U.S. involvement in Cuba, Alaska, Hawaii, and the Philippines. Exhibit 3.1 illustrates when and by what means the present United States was acquired.

The Monroe Doctrine, a cornerstone of early U.S. foreign policy, was enunciated by President James Monroe in a public statement proclaiming three basic dicta: no further European colonization in the New World, abstention of the United States from European political affairs, and nonintervention by European governments in the governments of the Western Hemisphere.

After 1870, interpretation of the Monroe Doctrine became increasingly broad. In 1881, its principles were evoked in discussing the development of a canal across the Isthmus of Panama. Theodore Roosevelt applied the Monroe Doctrine with an extension that became known as the Roosevelt Corollary. The corollary stated that not only would the United States prohibit non-American intervention in Latin American affairs, but it would also police the area and guarantee that Latin American nations met their international obligations. The corollary

---

[8]Some say even into the 21st century. See "Manifest Destiny Warmed Up?" *The Economist*, August 14, 2003. Of course, others disagree. See Joseph Contreras, "Roll Over Monroe: The Influence the United States Once Claimed as a Divine Right in Latin America is Slipping away Fast," *Newsweek International*, December 10, 2007; Daniel Larison, "Gingrich the Historian and the Monroe Doctrine," *The Conservative American*, January 26, 2012.

1488 Bartolomeu Dias sails around the coast of Africa; this, along with the voyages of Christopher Columbus, ushers in the era of sea travel
1492 Christopher Columbus "discovers" the New World
1494 Portugal and Spain divide the unexplored world between them with the Treaty of Tordesillas
1500 Rise of mercantilism, the accumulation of wealth by the

state to increase power, in western Europe; states without gold or silver mines try to control trade to maintain a surplus and accumulate gold and silver; Englishman Thomas Mun was one of the great proponents in 1600, who realized that the overall balance of trade was the important factor, not whether each individual trade resulted in a surplus

1500 Slave trade becomes a major component of commerce
1504 Regular postal service established among Vienna, Brussels, and Madrid
1520 First chocolate brought from Mexico to Spain
1521 Mexico is conquered by Hernán Cortés after Aztec ruler Montezuma is accidentally killed
1522 Magellan's expedition completes its three-year sail

around the world; it is the first successful circumnavigation
1531 Antwerp stock exchange is the first exchange to move into its own building, signifying its importance in financing commercial enterprises throughout Europe and the rising importance of private trade and commerce; Antwerp emerges as a trading capital
1532 Brazil is colonized by the Portuguese

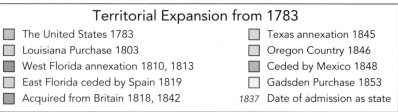

Exhibit 3.1

Territorial Expansion of United States from 1783

The United States expanded westward to the Pacific through a series of financial deals, negotiated settlements, and forcible annexations. The acquisition of territory from Mexico began with the Battle of San Jacinto in 1836, when Texas staged a successful revolt against the rule of Mexico and became The Republic of Texas—later to join the Union in 1845. The Mexican War (1846–1848) resulted in Mexico ceding California and a large part of the West to the United States.

Source: Cartography © Philip's. Reprinted with permission of Octopus Publishing Group.

Territorial Expansion from 1783

■ The United States 1783	■ Texas annexation 1845
■ Louisiana Purchase 1803	■ Oregon Country 1846
■ West Florida annexation 1810, 1813	■ Ceded by Mexico 1848
■ East Florida ceded by Spain 1819	■ Gadsden Purchase 1853
■ Acquired from Britain 1818, 1842	*1837* Date of admission as state

sanctioning American intervention was applied in 1905 when Roosevelt forced the Dominican Republic to accept the appointment of an American economic adviser, who quickly became the financial director of the small state. It was also used in the acquisition of the Panama Canal Zone from Colombia in 1903 and the formation of a provisional government in Cuba in 1906.

The manner in which the United States acquired the land for the Panama Canal Zone typifies the Roosevelt Corollary—whatever is good for the United States is justifiable.

According to U.S. history, these Latin American adventures were a justifiable part of our foreign policy; to Latin Americans, they were unwelcome intrusions in Latin American affairs. This perspective has been constantly reinforced by U.S. intervention in Latin America since 1945 (see Exhibit 3.2). The way historical events are recorded and interpreted in one culture can differ substantially from the way those same events are recorded and interpreted in another. From the U.S. view, each of the interventions illustrated in Exhibit 3.2 was justified. A comparison of histories goes a long way in explaining the differences in outlooks and behavior of people on both sides of the border. Many Mexicans believe that their "good neighbor" to the north is not reluctant to throw its weight around when it wants something. Suspicions that self-interest is the primary motivation for good relations with Mexico abound.

History viewed from a Latin American perspective explains how a national leader, under adverse economic conditions, can point a finger at the United States or a U.S. multinational

LO4

How long-past U.S. international policies still affect customer attitudes abroad

---

1534 English break from the Catholic Church, ending its dominance of politics and trade throughout Europe, as Henry VIII creates the Church of England
1553 South American Incan Empire ends with conquest by Spanish; the Incas had created an extensive area of trade, complete with an infrastructure of roads and canals

1555 Tobacco trade begins after its introduction to Europe by Spanish and Portuguese traders
1557 Spanish crown suffers first of numerous bankruptcies, discouraging cross-border lending
1561 Via Dutch traders, tulips come to Europe from Near East for first time
1564 William Shakespeare is born; many of his plays are stories of merchant traders

1567 Typhoid fever, imported from Europe, kills two million Indians in South America
1588 Spanish Armada defeated by British, heralding Britain's emergence as the world's greatest naval power; this power will enable Britain to colonize many regions of the globe and lead to its becoming the world's commercially dominant power for the next 300 years

1596 First flush toilet is developed for Britain's Queen Elizabeth I
1597 Holy Roman Empire expels English merchants in retaliation for English treatment of Hanseatic League
1600 Potatoes are brought from South America to Europe, where they quickly spread to the rest of world and become a staple of agricultural production

Exhibit 3.2
U.S. Intervention in Latin America Since 1945

1 USA attempts to thwart election of Perón (1946)

2 Popular Revolution neutralized by US economic pressure (1952)

3 CIA-organized invasion overthrows Arbenz (1954) following expropriation of United Fruit Company lands

4 Nationalist revolution (1959) and alliance with USSR (1960). USA declares economic embargo, and CIA organizes failed Bay of Pigs invasion (1961). Cuban Missile Crisis (1962).

5 Covert intervention by USA against elected Marxist government of Popular Unity (1970–73)

6 Military intervention to suppress possible communist influence (1965)

7 Revolution (1979): USA funds counter-revolutionary movement (1980s)

8 Covert intervention by USA to defeat left-wing guerrillas (1980–88)

9 US invasion to restore stable government (1983)

10 US invasion to arrest President Noriega on charges of drug trafficking (1989)

11 "Negotiated" US invasion to restore democracy (1994)

12 North American Free Trade Agreement (1994)

US Intervention in Latin America since 1945

● Direct military action by USA   ■ Economic and political intervention by USA   ◆ Direct military action by USSR

Source: Cartography © Philip's. Reprinted with permission of Octopus Publishing Group.

corporation and evoke a special emotional, popular reaction to divert attention away from the government in power. As a case in point, after the U.S. House of Representatives voted to censure Mexico for drug corruption, President Ernesto Zedillo came under pressure to take a hard stand with Washington. He used the anniversary of Mexico's 1938 expropriation of the oil industry from foreign companies to launch a strong nationalist attack. He praised the state oil monopoly Pemex as a "symbol of our historical struggles for sovereignty." Union members cheered him on, waving a huge banner that read: "In 1938 Mexico was 'decertified' because it expropriated its oil and it won—today we were decertified for defending our dignity and sovereignty." Apparently Venezuelan President Hugo Chavez was listening, based on his more recent nationalization of foreign oil company assets in the Orinoco River Basin[9] and his recent renaming of the country the Bolivarian Republic of Venezuela.

---

[9]"Venezuela: Spirit of the Monroe Doctrine," *Washington Times*, June 10, 2007, p. B5; Girish Gupta, "ExxonMobile's Loss in Venezuela Sobers Investors," *globalpost.com*, January 18, 2012.

1600   Japan begins trading silver for foreign goods
1600   Britain's Queen Elizabeth I grants charter to the East India Company, which will dominate trade with the East until its demise in 1857
1601   France makes postal agreements with neighboring states
1602   Dutch charter their own East India Company, which will

dominate the South Asian coffee and spice trade
1607   British colony of James-town built
1609   Dutch begin fur trade through Manhattan
1611   Japan gives Dutch limited permission to trade
1612   British East India Company builds its first factory in India
1620   *Mayflower* sails for the New World

1620   Father of the Scientific Revolution, Francis Bacon, publishes *Novum Organum*, promoting inductive reasoning through experimentation and observation
1625   Dutch jurist Hugo Grotius, sometimes called the father of international law, publishes *On the Laws of War and Peace*
1636   Harvard University founded

1637   Dutch "tulip mania" results in history's first boom–bust market crash
1651   English pass first of so-called Navigation Acts to restrict Dutch trade by forcing colonies to trade only with English ships
1654   Spain and Germany develop hereditary land rights, a concept that will help lead to the creation of great wealth in single families and thus to

CROSSING BORDERS 3.1 Microsoft Adapts Encarta to "Local History"

Adapting to the local culture is an important aspect of strategy for many products. Understanding a country's history helps achieve that goal. Microsoft has nine different editions reflecting local "history" to be sure that its Encarta multimedia encyclopedia on CD-ROM does not contain cultural blunders. As a consequence, it often reflects different and sometimes contradictory understandings of the same historical events. For example, who invented the telephone? In the U.S., U.K., and German editions, it is Alexander Graham Bell, but ask the question in the Italian edition, and your answer is Antonio Meucci, an Italian-American candle maker whom Italians believe beat Bell by five years. For electric light bulbs, it is Thomas Alva Edison in the United States, but in the United Kingdom, it is the British inventor Joseph Swan. Other historical events reflect local perceptions. The nationalization of the Suez Canal, for example, in the U.S. edition is a decisive intervention by superpowers. In the French and U.K. editions, it is summed up as a "humiliating reversal" for Britain and France—a phrase that does not appear in the U.S. edition.

Although Microsoft is on the mark by adapting these events to their local historical context, it has, on occasion, missed the boat on geography. South Korean ire was raised when the South Korean island of Ullung-do was placed within Japan's borders and when the Chon-Ji Lake, where the first Korean is said to have descended from

heaven, was located in China. And finally, an embarrassed Microsoft apologized to the people of Thailand for referring to Bangkok as a commercial sex center, assuring the women's activists group that protested that the revised version would "include all the great content that best reflects its rich culture and history."

Microsoft also bows to political pressure. The government of Turkey stopped distribution of an Encarta edition with the name Kurdistan used to denote a region of southeastern Turkey on a map. Hence Microsoft removed the name Kurdistan from the map. Governments frequently lobby the company to show their preferred boundaries on maps. When the border between Chile and Argentina in the southern Andes was in dispute, both countries lobbied for their preferred boundary, and the solution both countries agreed to was—no line.

But our fun stories about changes to Encarta must come to an end, because the online encyclopedia has itself become a topic of history. Microsoft folded the entire Encarta operation without explanation in 2009; most analysts agree Wikipedia simply did it in.

Sources: Kevin J. Delaney, "Microsoft's Encarta Has Different Facts for Different Folks," *The Wall Street Journal*, June 25, 1999, p. A1; "Why You Won't Find Kurdistan on a Microsoft Map of Turkey," *Geographical*, November 1, 2004; Nick Winfield, "Microsoft to Shut Encarta as Free Sites Alter Market," *The Wall Street Journal*, March 31, 2009, p. B3.

These leaders might be cheered for expropriation or confiscation of foreign investments, even though the investments were making important contributions to their economies. To understand a country's attitudes, prejudices, and fears, it is necessary to look beyond the surface of current events to the inner subtleties of the country's entire past for clues. Three comments by Mexicans best summarize this section:

> History is taught one way in Mexico and another way in the United States—the United States robbed us but we are portrayed in U.S. textbooks as bandits who invaded Texas.

> We may not like gringos for historical reasons, but today the world is dividing into commercial blocks, and we are handcuffed to each other for better or worse.

> We always have been and we continue to be a colony of the United States.

the development of private commercial empires
1687 Apple falling on Newton's head leads to his publication of the law of gravity
1694 The Bank of England is established; it offers loans to private individuals at 8 percent interest
1698 First steam engine is invented
1719 French consolidate their trade in Asia into one

company, the French East India Company; rival British East India Company maintains its grip on the region's trade, however, and the French revert to individual company trading 60 years later
1725 Rise of Physiocrats, followers of the economic philosopher François Quesnay, who believed that production, not trade, created wealth and

that natural law should rule, which meant producers should be able to exchange goods freely; movement influenced Adam Smith's ideas promoting free trade
1740 Maria Theresa becomes empress of the Holy Roman Empire (until 1780); she ends serfdom and strengthens the power of the state
1748 First modern, scientifically drawn map, the Carte Géomé

trique de la France, comprising 182 sheets, was authorized and subsequently drawn by the French Academy; Louis XV proclaimed that the new map, with more accurate data, lost more territory than his wars of conquest had gained
1750 Benjamin Franklin shows that lightning is a form of electricity by conducting it through the wet string of a kite

Most recently, the issue of illicit drugs again has put Mexico and the United States at odds. Vicente Fox, Mexico's first opposition party president, was elected in 2000 to a six-year term of office to change things (Cambio). He grew steadily dissatisfied with trying to manage the drug problem with force, sending in the federal troops to quell the cartel violence.

He proposed legalizing everything for users—cocaine, heroin, LSD, marijuana, PCP, opium, synthetic opioids, mescaline, peyote, psilocybin mushrooms, amphetamines, and meth. The law allowed for substantial quantities for personal use. Fox's list was revolutionary. The Mexican Congress passed the measure, and Fox, of course, promised a signature. Then he had conversations with the Bush administration and changed his mind. A few months, later he left office, and the violence in Mexico really began to accelerate as the Colombian cartels lost control.

Then in 2009, after Bush had left office, the next Mexican president, Felipe Calderon, signed off on an almost identical bill. Use was decriminalized, and Mexican government forces could focus on the cartels and the flow of illicit drugs through the country to the United States. The Obama administration has taken a wait-and-see attitude.

Geography and Global Markets

Geography, the study of Earth's surface, climate, continents, countries, peoples, industries, and resources, is an element of the uncontrollable environment that confronts every marketer but that receives scant attention. The tendency is to study the aspects of geography as isolated entities rather than as important causal agents of the marketing environment. Geography is much more than memorizing countries, capitals, and rivers. It also includes an understanding of how a society's culture and economy are affected as a nation struggles to supply its people's needs within the limits imposed by its physical makeup. Thus, the study of geography is important in the evaluation of markets and their environment.[10]

LO5

The effect of geographic diversity on economic profiles of a country

This section discusses the important geographic characteristics a marketer needs to consider when assessing the environmental aspects of marketing. Examining the world as a whole provides the reader with a broad view of world markets and an awareness of the effects of geographic diversity on the economic profiles of various nations. Climate and topography are examined as facets of the broader and more important elements of geography. A brief look at Earth's resources and population—the building blocks of world markets—completes the presentation on geography and global markets.

Climate and Topography

Altitude, humidity, and temperature extremes are climatic features that affect the uses and functions of products and equipment.[11] Products that perform well in temperate zones may deteriorate rapidly or require special cooling or lubrication to function adequately in tropical zones. Manufacturers have found that construction equipment used in the United States requires extensive modifications to cope with the intense heat and dust of the Sahara Desert. A Taiwanese company sent a shipment of drinking glasses to a buyer in the Middle East.

---

[10]See Philip Parker's extensive research on the relationship among geography, consumer behavior, and marketing. For example, Philip Parker, *Physioeconomics* (Cambridge, MA: MIT Press, 2000).

[11]Elizabeth Holmes, "Hot H&M Targets Cool Climes," *The Wall Street Journal*, May 10, 2010, p. B7.

1750 Industrial Revolution begins and takes off with the manufacture, in 1780, of the steam engine to drive machines—increased productivity and consumption follow (as do poor working conditions and increased hardships for workers)
1760 Chinese begin strict regulation of foreign trade to last nearly a century when they permit

Europeans to do business only in a small area outside Canton and only with appointed Chinese traders
1764 British victories in India begin Britain's dominance of India, Eastern trade, and trade routes
1764 British begin numbering houses, making mail delivery more efficient and providing the means for the development of

direct mail merchants centuries later
1773 Boston Tea Party symbolizes start of American Revolution; impetus comes from American merchants trying to take control of distribution of goods that were being controlled exclusively by Britain
1776 American Declaration of Independence proclaims the colonies' rights to determine their

own destiny, particularly their own economic destiny
1776 Theory of modern capitalism and free trade expressed by Adam Smith in *The Wealth of Nations*; he theorized that countries would only produce and export goods that they were able to produce more cheaply than could trading partners; he demonstrates that mercantilists were wrong: It is not gold or silver that

LO6

Why marketers need to be responsive to the geography of a country

The glasses were packed in wooden crates with hay used as dunnage to prevent breakage. The glasses arrived in shards. Why? When the crates moved to the warmer, less humid climate of the Middle East, the moisture content of the hay dropped significantly and shriveled to a point that it offered no protection.

Within even a single national market, climate can be sufficiently diverse to require major adjustments. In Ghana, a product adaptable to the entire market must operate effectively in extreme desert heat and low humidity and in tropical rainforests with consistently high humidity. Bosch-Siemens washing machines designed for European countries require spin cycles to range from a minimum spin cycle of 500 rpm to a maximum of 1,600 rpm. Because the sun does not shine regularly in Germany or in Scandinavia, washing machines must have a 1,600 rpm spin cycle because users do not have the luxury of hanging them out to dry. In Italy and Spain, however, clothes can be damp, because the abundant sunshine is sufficient to justify a spin cycle speed of 500 rpm.

Different seasons between the northern and southern hemispheres also affect global strategies. JCPenney had planned to open five stores in Chile as part of its expansion into countries below the equator. It wanted to capitalize on its vast bulk buying might for its North American, Mexican, and Brazilian stores to provide low prices for its expansion into South America. After opening its first store in Chile, the company realized that the plan was not going to work—when it was buying winter merchandise in North America, it needed summer merchandise in South America. The company quickly sold its one store in Chile; its expansion into South America was limited to much larger Brazil.

Mountains, oceans, seas, jungles, and other geographical features can pose serious impediments to economic growth and trade. For example, mountain ranges cover South America's west coast for 4,500 miles, with an average height of 13,000 feet and a width of 300 to 400 miles. This natural, formidable barrier has precluded the establishment of commercial routes between the Pacific and Atlantic coasts. South America's natural barriers inhibit both national and regional growth, trade,[12] and communication. Geographic hurdles have a direct effect on a country's economy, markets, and the related activities of communication and distribution in China, Russia, India, and Canada as well. As countries seek economic opportunities and the challenges of the global marketplace, they invest in infrastructure to overcome such barriers. Once seen as natural protection from potentially hostile neighbors, physical barriers that exist within Europe are now seen as impediments to efficient trade in an integrated economic union.

For decades the British resisted a tunnel under the English Channel—they did not trust the French or any other European country and saw the channel as protection. But when they became members of the European Union, economic reality meant the channel tunnel had to be built to facilitate trade with other EU members. Now you can take a bullet train through the Chunnel, but even a decade after it opened, its finances were still a bit shaky, and recently, undocumented workers have tried to walk the underwater route to reach England.

From the days of Hannibal, the Alps have served as an important physical barrier and provided European countries protection from one another. But with the EU expansion, the Alps became a major impediment to trade. Truck traffic between southern Germany and northern Italy, which choked highways through some of Switzerland's most treacherous

[12]Jared M. *Diamond, Guns, Germs, and Steel* (New York: Norton, 1999).

will enhance the state, but the *material* that can be purchased with it
1783   Treaty of Paris officially ends the American Revolution following British surrender to American troops at Yorktown in 1781
1787   U.S. Constitution approved; it becomes a model document for constitutions for at least the next two centuries; written constitutions will help stabilize many

countries and encourage foreign investment and trade with them
1789   French Revolution begins; it will alter the power structure in Europe and help lead to the introduction of laws protecting the individual and to limited democracy in the region
1792   Gas lighting introduced; within three decades, most major European and U.S. cities will use gas lights

1804   Steam locomotive introduced; it will become the dominant form of transport of goods and people until the 20th century, when trucks and airplanes become commercially viable
1804   Napoleon crowns himself emperor, overthrowing the French revolutionary government, and tries to conquer Europe (after already occupying Egypt as a means of cutting off British trade

with the East), the failure of which results in the redrawing of national boundaries in Europe and Latin America
1807   Robert Fulton's steamboat is the first to usher in a new age of transport when his *Clermont* sails from New York to Albany
1807   French Napoleonic Code issued and eventually becomes a model of civil law adopted by many nations around the world

CROSSING BORDERS 3.2

Innovation and the Water Shortage, from Fog to Kid Power

Fog Catchers

When you live in Chungungo, Chile, one of the country's most arid regions with no nearby source of water, you drink fog. Of course! Thanks to a legend and resourceful Canadian and Chilean scientists, Chungungo now has its own supply of drinkable water after a 20-year drought. Before this new source of water, Chungungo depended on water trucks that came twice a week.

Chungungo has always been an arid area, and legend has it that the region's original inhabitants used to worship trees. They considered them sacred because a permanent flow of water sprang from the treetops, producing a constant interior rain. The legend was right— the trees produced rain! Thick fog forms along the coast. As it moves inland and is forced to rise against the hills, it changes into tiny raindrops, which are in turn retained by the tree leaves, producing the constant source of rain. Scientists set out to take advantage of this natural phenomenon.

The nearby ancient eucalyptus forest of El Tofo Hill provided the clue that scientists needed to create an ingenious water-supply system. To duplicate the water-bearing effect of the trees, they installed 86 "fog catchers" on the top of the hill—huge nets supported by 12-foot eucalyptus pillars, with water containers at their base. About 1,900 gallons of water are collected each day and then piped into town. This small-scale system is cheap (about one-fifth as expensive as having water trucked in), clean, and provides the local people with a steady supply of drinking water.

PlayPump: Part I

[This material is as we have had it in the 14th and 15th editions of this book. Make sure you read the update in Part II to come!]

In sub-Saharan Africa, inventive folks have come up with a new way to bring water up from wells. A life-changing and life-saving invention—the PlayPump water system—provides easy access to clean drinking water, brings joy to children, and leads to improvements in health, education, gender equality, and economic development in more than 1,000 rural villages in South Africa, Swaziland, Mozambique, and Zambia. The PlayPump systems are innovative, sustainable, patented water pumps powered by children at play. Installed near schools, the PlayPump system doubles as a water pump and a merry-go-round. The PlayPump system also provides one of the only ways to reach rural and peri-urban communities with potentially life-saving public health messages. Please see the accompanying pictures of a new solution to one of humankind's oldest problems.

PlayPump: Part II

[Oops! In the 14th and 15th editions of *International Marketing*, we made the same mistake many others have made with respect to PlayPumps. We are contrite, but we also see the great value in reporting the complete Play-Pump story as it has unfolded. We thanks Laura Freschi for her excellent reporting.]

At the primary schools in South Africa, where the first of these merry-go-rounds were installed, kids got a place to play, their communities got free drinking water, and girls and women—who bear much of the burden of collecting water for their families—got time to attend school or pursue other activities. Billboards lining the raised water tank brought in advertising revenue to fund the pumps' maintenance, as well as spread public health messages about hygiene or safe sex.

In 2000, the PlayPumps idea won the World Bank's Development Marketplace award. In 2006, Laura Bush announced $16 million in funding from USAID/PEPFAR and private foundations, with the goal of raising $45 million more to install 4,000 pumps in Africa by 2010. Jay-Z pitched in with concerts and an MTV documentary. Play-Pumps announced plans to expand, first to Mozambique, Swaziland, and Zambia, and then into Lesotho, Malawi, Ethiopia, Kenya, Tanzania, and Uganda. The nonprofit launched a sophisticated social networking campaign and successfully raised money for "100 Pumps in 100 Days" on World Water Days in 2007 and 2008.

Sadly, somewhere along the way, PlayPumps stopped being a smart homegrown idea and became a donor-pleasing, top-down solution that simply did not fit many of the target communities.

In response, the charity WaterAid wrote a position paper on why it did not adopt the PlayPumps technology. For one, it said, PlayPumps are too expensive. At $14,000 each, they cost four times as much as traditional pump systems. The mechanism requires specialized skills to repair and so cannot be fixed with local labor. Spare parts are hard to find and expensive to replace. WaterAid also decried the system's "reliance on child labour." A recent critical commentary in the *Guardian* (UK) calculated that children would have to "play" for 27 hours every day to meet PlayPumps' stated targets of providing 2,500 people per pump with their daily water needs.

An aid worker and engineer in Malawi documented some of these problems in a brilliant series of blog posts. His anecdotes and pictures give limited but compelling evidence that PlayPumps in his area are not being used as the inventors intended: "Each time I've visited a PlayPump, I've always found the same scene: a group of women and children struggling to spin it by hand so they can draw water."

He also suggests one reason PlayPumps might be slow to get that crucial feedback: "[A]s soon as the foreigner with a camera comes out (aka me), kids get excited. And when they get excited, they start playing. Within 5 minutes, the thing looks like a crazy success. . . . I've always figured that as soon as I leave the excitement wears off and the pump reverts back to its normal state: being spun manually by women and kids."

Does the story of PlayPumps carry a broader lesson about the aid world? Suppose the organization had charged ahead with a Twitter campaign to raise millions for *the* solution to water problems in Africa, even as reality kept diverging farther from the rosy picture. Then PlayPumps would represent the triumph of bad but photogenic solutions in a broken aid marketplace.

But last fall, the CEO announced instead that its inventory would be turned over to the organization Water for People, where PlayPumps would be just one option out of "a portfolio of technologies from which communities can choose." This seems like the right outcome. We can ask why it took so long to see the flaws in the PlayPumps model. But in contrast to the official aid world, where old, failed solutions keep getting recycled across 60 years, this relatively quick response represents real progress!

We forecast (and hope) that the €8 smokeless stoves described on page 160 will perform betterin the emerging market marketplace than the $14,000 PlayPumps. Stay tuned.

Sources: "Drinking Fog," *World Press Review*; "Silver Lining," *The Economist*, February 5, 2000, p. 75; "UNESCO Water Portal Weekly Update No. 89: Fog," April 15, 2005, http://www.unesco.org/water/news/newsletter/89. shtml; http://www.playpumps.org, 2008; Aliah D. Wright, "Dive into Clean Water," *HRMagazine* 54, no. 6 (2009), p. 4.; Laura Freschi, "Some NGOs CAN Adjust to Failure: The PlayPumps Story," *aidwatchers.com*, February 19, 2010. Used with permission; Andrew Chambers, "Africa's Not-so-Roundabout," *guaradian. co.uk*, November 24, 2009.

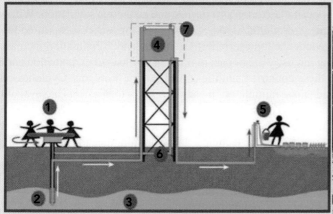

While children have fun spinning on the PlayPump merry-go-round, (1) clean water is pumped (2) from underground (3) into a 2,500-liter tank, (4) standing seven meters above the ground. A simple tap (5) makes it easy for adults and children to draw water. Excess water is diverted from the storage tank back down into the base hole (6). The water storage tank (7) provides rare opportunities to advertise to outlying communities. All four sides of the tank are leased as billboards, with two sides for consumer advertising and the other two sides for health and educational messages. The revenue generated from this unique model pays for pump maintenance. Capable of producing up to 1,400 liters of water per hour at 16 rpm from a depth of 40 meters, it is effective up to a depth of 100 meters. See http://www.playpumps.org. *(right: © Frimmel Smith/PlayPump)*

mountain roads and pristine nature areas, was not only burdensome for all travelers but also becoming economically unacceptable. The solution, the 21-mile Loetschberg Tunnelo which opened in 2007, burrows under the Alps and trims the time trains need to cross between Germany and Italy from a three-and-a-half-hour trip to less than two hours. By 2016, the 36-mile Gotthard Tunnel will provide additional rail coverage for the area and be the world's longest rail tunnel.

Geography, Nature, and Economic Growth

Always on the slim margin between subsistence and disaster, less-privileged countries suffer disproportionately from natural and human-assisted catastrophes.[13] The slow recovery from the Haitian earthquake disaster of 2010 is perhaps the prominent example, particularly when

---

[13]"Honda Sees Sharp Drop in Profit on Thai Floods," *Associated Press,* January 31, 2012; Thomas Fuller, "Floodwaters Are Gone, but Supply Chain Issues Linger," *The New York Times*, January 20, 2012.

This advertisement provides the only time we have seen a human vomiting to market a product. The product advertised treats altitude sickness. The billboard appears in the Lima, Peru, airport, targeting tourists traveling from sea level to Cuzco and Machu Picchu (pictured in the scenic background). Cuzco, the old Inca capital, is at more than 11,000 feet in altitude, and many foreign tourists visiting there suffer this particular sort of *tourista*.

juxtaposed with the progress of Japan's recovery from its 2011 earthquake/tsunami/nuclear power plant disaster.[14] Climate and topography coupled with civil wars, poor environmental policies, and natural disasters push these countries further into economic stagnation. Without irrigation and water management, droughts, floods, and soil erosion afflict them, often leading to creeping deserts that reduce the long-term fertility of the land.[15] Population increases, deforestation, and overgrazing intensify the impact of drought and lead to malnutrition and ill health, further undermining these countries' abilities to solve their problems. Cyclones cannot be prevented, nor can inadequate rainfall, but means to control their effects are available. Unfortunately, each disaster seems to push developing countries further away from effective solutions. Countries that suffer the most from major calamities are among the poorest in the world. Many have neither the capital nor the technical ability to minimize the effects of natural phenomena; they are at the mercy of nature.

As countries prosper, natural barriers are overcome. Tunnels and canals are dug, air conditioning systems are constructed,[16] and bridges and dams are built in an effort to control or to adapt to climate, topography, and the recurring extremes of nature. Humankind has been reasonably successful in overcoming or minimizing the effects of geographical barriers and natural disasters, but as they do so, they must contend with problems of their own

---

[14]Japan is experiencing longer term problems as well though. See Julie Makinen, "Disasters Add New Theme to Tokyo Disney: Hardship," *Los Angeles Times*, April 5, 2011, pp. B1, B3.

[15]See Map 2, "Global Climate," in the World Maps section for a view of the diversity of the world's climate. The climatic phenomenon of El Niño wreaks havoc with weather patterns and is linked to crop failures, famine, forest fires, dust and sand storms, and other disasters associated with either an overabundance or a lack of rain.

[16]"No Sweat," *The Economist*, January 5, 2013, pp. 45–46.

1807 U.S. President Thomas Jefferson bans trade with Europe in an effort to convince warring British and French ships to leave neutral U.S. trading ships alone
1810 Frenchman Nicolas Appert successfully cans food and prevents spoilage
1810 Following Napoleon's invasion of Spain and Portugal, Simón Bolivar begins wars of independence for Spanish colonies

in Latin America, leading to new governments in Bolivia, Columbia, Ecuador, Peru, and Venezuela
1814 First practical steam locomotive is built by George Stephenson in England, leading to the birth of railroad transportation in 1825 with the first train carrying 450 passengers at 15 miles per hour
1815 Napoleon defeated at Battle of Waterloo and gives up throne days later

1815 British build roads of crushed stone, greatly improving the quality and speed of road travel
1817 David Ricardo publishes *Principles of Political Economy and Taxation*, in which he proposes modern trade theory: Comparative advantage drives trade; countries will produce and export goods for which they have a *comparative* advantage as opposed to

Adam Smith's *absolute* advantage (see 1776)
1821 Britain is first to adopt gold standard to back the value of its currency
1823 U.S. President James Monroe promulgates the doctrine bearing his name that declares the Americas closed to colonization in an attempt to assert U.S. influence over the region

making. The construction of dams is a good example of how an attempt to harness nature for good has a bad side. Developing countries consider dams a cost-effective solution to a host of problems. Dams create electricity, help control floods, provide water for irrigation during dry periods, and can be a rich source of fish. However, there are side effects; dams displace people (the Three Gorges Dam in China has displaced 1.3 million people), and silt that ultimately clogs the reservoir is no longer carried downstream to replenish the soil and add nutrients. Similarly, the Narmada Valley Dam Project in India will provide electricity, flood control, and irrigation, but it has already displaced tens of thousands of people, and as the benefits are measured against social and environmental costs, questions of its efficacy are being raised. In short, the need for gigantic projects such as these must be measured against their social and environmental costs.

As the global rush toward industrialization and economic growth accelerates, environmental issues become more apparent.[17] Disruption of ecosystems, relocation of people, inadequate hazardous waste management, and industrial pollution are problems that must be addressed by the industrialized world and those seeking economic development. The problems are mostly by-products of processes that have contributed significantly to economic development and improved lifestyles. During the last part of the 20th century, governments and industry expended considerable effort to develop better ways to control nature and to allow industry to grow while protecting the environment.[18]

Social Responsibility and Environmental Management

Nations, companies, and people reached a consensus during the close of the last decade: Environmental protection is not an optional extra; it is an essential part of the complex process of doing business. Many view the problem as a global issue rather than a national issue and as one that poses common threats to humankind and thus cannot be addressed by nations in isolation. Of special concern to governments and businesses are ways to stem the tide of pollution and to clean up decades of neglect.

Companies looking to build manufacturing plants in countries with more liberal pollution regulations than they have at home are finding that regulations everywhere have gotten stricter. Many governments are drafting new regulations and enforcing existing ones. Electronic products contain numerous toxic substances that create a major disposal problem in landfills where inadequate disposal allows toxins to seep into groundwater. The European Union, as well as other countries, has laws stipulating the amount and types of potentially toxic substances it will require a company to take back to recycle. A strong motivator is the realization that pollution is on the verge of getting completely out of control.

China is now the world's top polluter in almost all respects.[19] By 2020 its greenhouse-gas emissions will be more than double the closest rival, the United States. An examination of rivers, lakes, and reservoirs in China revealed that toxic substances polluted 21 percent and that 16 percent of the rivers were seriously polluted with excrement. China has 16 of

---

[17]Ram Mudambi, "Approaches to Climate Change: Technology and Institutions," *Journal of International Business Studies* 42 (2011), p. 974.

[18]Visit http://www.gemi.org for information on the Global Environmental Management Initiative, an organization of U.S. multinational companies dedicated to environmental protection.

[19]"Chinese Air Pollution, Clearing the Air?" *The Economist*, January 14, 2012, pp. 41–42.

1837 Reign of Britain's Queen Victoria begins; she oversees the growth of the British Empire and Britain's emergence as an industrial power (she dies in 1901)
1837 Electronic telegraph begins wide commercial use, transmitting information, including production orders, swiftly
1839 Process for recording negative images on paper is introduced in England, the

precursor to modern film technology
1841 Briton David Livingstone begins 30 years of exploring in Africa
1842 Hong Kong ceded to Britain with the Treaty of Nanjing following the Opium War; the city will become a financial and trading center for Asia
1844 Chinese open five ports to U.S. ships

1847 First government-backed postage stamps issued by United States, leading to more certain and efficient communication by post
1848 John Stuart Mill publishes *Principles of Political Economy*, completing the modern theory of trade by stating that gains from trade are reflected in the strength of the *reciprocal* demand for imports and exports and that gains would come from better terms of trade (see 1817)

1848 *The Communist Manifesto,* by Germans Karl Marx and Friedrich Engels, is issued; it will become the basis for the communist movements of the 20th century
1851 First international world's fair held in London, showcasing new technology
1856 Declaration of Paris recognizes the principle of free movement for trade, even in wartime—blockades could only extend

Two kinds of pollution in Cambodia. The monkey with the Coke can may seem kind of funny, until you think about it as an eyesore on the steps of the pristine Angkor Wat temple grounds. We'd also guess that caffeine, sugar, sharp-edged aluminum cans, and monkeys don't mix too well. The land mines still in the ground from a decades past war are not funny. Here, Germany is helping clean up the deadly mess.

the world's 20 most polluted cities.[20] The very process of controlling industrial wastes leads to another and perhaps equally critical issue: the disposal of hazardous waste, a by-product of pollution controls. Estimates of hazardous wastes collected annually exceed 300 million tons; the critical issue is disposal that does not simply move the problem elsewhere. Countries encountering increasing difficulty in the disposal of wastes at home are seeking countries willing to assume the burden of disposal. Waste disposal is legal in some developing countries as governments seek the revenues that are generated by offering sites for waste disposal. In other cases, illegal dumping is done clandestinely. A treaty among members of the Basel Convention that required prior approval before dumping could occur was later revised to a total ban on the export of hazardous wastes by developed nations. The influence and leadership provided by this treaty are reflected in a broad awareness of pollution problems by businesses and people in general.[21]

Governments, organizations, and businesses[22] are becoming increasingly concerned with the social responsibility and ethical issues surrounding the problem of maintaining economic growth while protecting the environment for future generations.[23] However, the commitment made by governments and companies varies dramatically around the world. For example, with one of the highest pollution rates on a per capita basis, the United States

---

[20]Barbara Demick, "U.S. Tweets Stir Beijing's Air," *Los Angeles Times*, October 30, 2011, pp. A1, A8.

[21]For a comprehensive view of OECD programs, including environmental issues, visit http://www.oecd.org.

[22]Leonadis C. Leonidou, Constantine S. Katsikeas, Thomas A. Fotiadis, and Paul Christodoulides, "Antecedents and Consequences of a Eco-Friendly Export Marketing Strategy: The Moderating Role of Foreign Public Concern and Competitive Intensity," *Journal of International Marketing* 21, no. 3 (2013), pp. 22–46.

[23]Jonatan Pinkse and Ans Kolk, "Multinational Enterprises and Climate Change: Exploring Institutional Failures and Embeddedness," *Journal of International of Business Studies* 43 (2012), pp. 332–41.

---

along the enemy's coast; it also establishes the practice of allowing the accession to treaties of nations other than the original signatories

1857 Russia and France sign trade treaty

1858 Ansei Commercial Treaties with Japan open the formerly closed country to trade with the West (treaties follow "opening" of Japan to the West by American Matthew Perry in 1854)

1860 The Cobden Treaty aims to create free trade by reducing or eliminating tariffs between Britain and France; also leads to most-favored-nation status in bilateral agreements and eventually to multilateral agreements

1860 Passports are introduced in the United States to regulate foreign travel

1866 The principle of the electric dynamo is found by German Werner

Siemens, who will produce the first electric power transmission system

1866 The trans-Atlantic cable is completed, allowing nearly instant (telegraphic) communication between the United States and Europe

1869 Suez Canal completed after 11 years of construction; the canal significantly cuts the time for travel between Europe and Asia, shortening, for example, the

tripbetween Britain and India by 4,000 miles

1869 First U.S. transcontinental rail route is completed, heralding a boon for commerce; first commercially viable typewriter patented; until computer word processing becomes common more than a century later, the typewriter enables anyone to produce documents quickly and legibly

Exhibit 3.3

A Comparison of Greenhouse-Gas Emission Rates and Pledges for Reductions

Source: EuroMonitor International, 2014; Intergovernmental Panel on Climate Change.

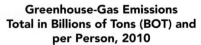

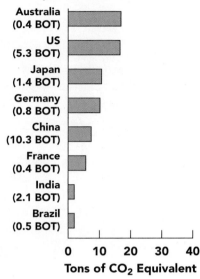

Greenhouse-Gas Emissions
Total in Billions of Tons (BOT) and per Person, 2010

Australia (0.4 BOT)
US (5.3 BOT)
Japan (1.4 BOT)
Germany (0.8 BOT)
China (10.3 BOT)
France (0.4 BOT)
India (2.1 BOT)
Brazil (0.5 BOT)

0 10 20 30 40
Tons of CO$_2$ Equivalent

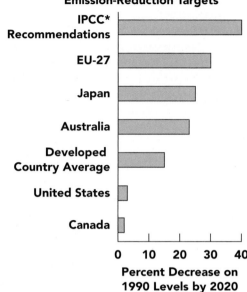

Pledged Greenhouse-Gas Emission-Reduction Targets

IPCC* Recommendations
EU-27
Japan
Australia
Developed Country Average
United States
Canada

0 10 20 30 40
Percent Decrease on 1990 Levels by 2020

*Intergovernmental Panel on Climate Change

lags behind almost all major competitors in agreeing to greenhouse emission standards (see Exhibit 3.3). The Organization for Economic Cooperation and Development, the United Nations,[24] the European Union, and international activist groups are undertaking programs to strengthen environmental policies. In many ways China, because it has the most urgent and greatest pollution problems, is leading the charge in new green technology. Many large multinational companies such as Petrobras,[25] Walmart, and Nike are not only cleaning up their own operations around the world but also pushing their suppliers to do the same.

The issue that concerns everyone is whether economic development and protection for the environment can coexist. Sustainable development is a joint approach among those (e.g., governments, businesses, environmentalists, and others) who seek economic growth with "wise resource management, equitable distribution of benefits and reduction of negative effects on people and the environment from the process of economic growth." Sustainable development is not about the environment or the economy or society. It is about striking a lasting balance between all of these. More and more companies are embracing the idea of sustainable development as a "win–win" opportunity.[26] Responsibility for protecting the environment does not rest solely with governments, businesses, or activist

---

[24]"Three Essential Facts about the U.N. Climate Summit," *Time*, October 6, 2014, p. 18.

[25]Jose Sergio Gabrielli de Azevedo, "The Greening of Petrobras," *Harvard Business Review*, March 2009, pp. 43–47.

[26]Visit http://www.oecd.org, the OECD website, for a directory and complete coverage of sustainable development.

1873 United States adopts the gold standard to fix the international value of the dollar
1875 Universal Postal Union created in Switzerland to provide for an international mail service
1876 Alexander Graham Bell is granted a patent for the telephone, which will revolutionize communications
1880 Thomas Edison creates first electric power station, after

inventing the electric light in 1878, which lights New York City and starts a revolution in culture and business—making a truly 24-hour day and paving the way for electronic machines
1881 Zoopraxiscope, which shows pictures in motion, is developed
1884 The basis for establishing standard time and measuring the longitude of any spot in the world is created with the designation of

Greenwich, England,as the prime meridian (0° longitude)
1886 American Federation of Labor founded, becoming a model for workers around the world to unite against management and gain higher pay and better working conditions
1901 Italian Guglielmo Marconi sends the first radio message; the radio could be said to spark thestart of globalization because

of the speed with which information is able to be transmitted
1903 First successful flight of an airplane, piloted by Orville Wright, takes place at Kitty Hawk, North Carolina
1904 First vacuum tube is developed by John Fleming, allowing alternating current to become direct current and helping create widespread use of the radio

Here in São Paulo, Shell sells two kinds of fuel: alcohol made primarily from sugarcane and gasoline made from dirtier fossil fuels. Flexible-fuel engines in Brazilian cars can burn either kind of fuel or any mixture of the two. Although the price per liter is quite different, so is the mileage per liter. Brazilians make their choice of fuel based on the kind of driving they anticipate, city versus highway.

groups; however, each citizen has a social and moral responsibility to include environmental protection among his or her highest goals.[27] This idea is particularly a problem in the United States, where consumers are often more interested in style than in sustainability, public opinion polls favor growth over the environment, and high school students receive relatively little environmental education.[28] A recent study has also shown that governments with pluralistic constituencies may have relatively more trouble persuading important minority groups to agree to their environmental efforts.[29]

Resources   The availability of minerals and the ability to generate energy are the foundations of modern technology. The locations of Earth's resources, as well as the available sources of energy, are geographic accidents. The world's nations are not equally endowed, and no nation's demand for a particular mineral or energy source necessarily coincides with domestic supply.

In much of the underdeveloped world, human labor provides the preponderance of energy. The principal supplements to human energy are animals, wood, fossil fuel, nuclear power, and, to a lesser and more experimental extent, the ocean's tides, geothermal power, and the

---

[27]Visit http://www.webdirectory.com for the *Amazing Environmental Organization Web Directory*, a search engine with links to an extensive list of environmental subjects.

[28]"Are U.S. Teenagers 'Green' Enough?" *Chronicle of Higher Education*, November 20, 2009, p. A4.

[29]Amir Grinstein and Udi Nisan, "Demarketing, Minorities, and National Attachment," *Journal of Marketing* 73, no. 2 (2009), pp. 105–22.

1913   Assembly line introduced by Henry Ford; it will revolutionize manufacturing

1914   The first war to involve much of the world begins with the assassination of Archduke Francis Ferdinand and lasts four years; construction of Panama Canal is completed, making trade faster and easier

1917   Lenin and Trotsky lead Russian revolution, creating a living economic model that will

affect trade (adversely) for the rest of the century

1919   First nonstop trans Atlantic flight completed, paving the way for cargo to be transported quickly around the globe

1920   League of Nations created, establishing a model for international cooperation (though it failed to keep the peace)

1923   Vladimir Zworykin creates first electronic television, which will eventually help integrate cultures and consumers across the world

1929   Great Depression starts with crash of U.S. stock market

1930   Hawley-Smoot Tariff passed by U.S. Senate, plunging the world deeper into the Great Depression

1935   Radar developed in Britain; it will allow travel on ships and planes even when there is no visibility, enabling the goods to keep to a transport schedule (eventually allowing the development of just-in-time and other cost-saving processes)

1938   American Chester Carlson develops dry copying process for documents (xerography), which, among other things, will enable governments to require that multiple forms be filled out to move goods

1939   World War II begins with German invasion of Poland; over 50 million people will die

1943   The first programmable computer, Colossus I, is created in England at Bletchley Park; it helps to crack German codes

The best: There are at least four sources of renewable energy pictured here. What are they? The answers are to this little guessing game are listed at the bottom of page 84.

The worst: Coal being loaded on a titanic ship, aptly named for the Prometheus, the Titan of Greek mythology. The irony is heavy here. Prometheus was sentenced to eternal misery for defying the gods and giving humanity fire. Here, the titan loads an Olympus-sized mountain of Canadian coal near Vancouver. She will then head to Dangjin, South Korea, to fuel the newest and most efficient power plants in the world just completed by Siemens and turned over to the customer, a Korean utility.

sun. Of all the energy sources, oil and gas contribute over 60 percent of world energy consumption.[30] Because of petroleum's versatility and the ease with which it is stored and transported, petroleum-related products continue to dominate energy usage.[31] (See Exhibit 3.4.)

Many countries that were self-sufficient during much of their early economic growth have become net importers of petroleum during the past several decades and continue to become increasingly dependent on foreign sources. A spectacular example is the United States, which was almost completely self-sufficient until 1942, became a major importer by 1950, and between 1973 and 2011 increased its dependency from 36 percent to over 66 percent of its annual requirements. From the perspective of 2015, with the oil production burgeoning from new discoveries and new technologies, and assuming increases in renewable sources, U.S. dependence on foreign oil imports is expected to decline to between 50 and 60 percent by the middle of the century. This is still a problem, but a smaller one than that predicted just a few short years ago. Exhibit 3.4 compares North American domestic energy consumption with other world regions. Total world energy consumption for 2013 was 12.7 billion tonnes. The increases in renewable energy sources (wood, peat, dung, wind, solar, and geothermal) have increased tenfold during the last three years. Remarkable! Europe consumes more energy than

---

[30]Visit http://www.eia.doe.gov and search for "International Energy Outlook (most current year)" for details of production, use, and so forth.

[31]See Map 3, "Oil and Gas Production and Consumption," for a global view of the flow and uses of petroleum.

1944 Bretton Woods Conference creates basis for economic coop eration among 44 nations and the founding of the International Monetary Fund to help stabilize exchange rates

1945 Atomic weapons introduced; World War II ends; United Nations founded

1947 General Agreement on Tariffs and Trade signed by 23 countries to try to reduce barriers to trade around the world

1948 Transistor is invented; it replaces the vacuum tube, starting a technology revolution

1949 People's Republic of China founded by Mao Zedong, which will restrict access to the largest single consumer market on the globe

1957 European Economic Community (EEC) established by Belgium, France, West Germany, Italy, Luxembourg, and the Netherlands, the precursor to today's European Union

1961 Berlin Wall is erected, creating Eastern and Western

Europe with a physical and spiritual barrier

1964 Global satellite communications network established with INTELSAT (International Telecommunications Satellite Organization)

1965 *Unsafe at Any Speed* published by Ralph Nader, sparking a revolution in consumer information and rights

1967 European Community (EC) established by uniting the EEC, the European Coal and Steel

Community, and the European Atomic Energy Community

1971 First microprocessor produced by Intel, which leads to the personal computer; communist China joins the United Nations, making it a truly global representative body

1971 United States abandons gold standard, allowing the international monetary system to base exchange rates on perceived values instead of ones fixed in relation to gold

Exhibit 3.4
World Energy Consumption

Sources: BP Statistics Review of World Energy 2014 and International Energy Outlook 2014, U.S. Department of Energy, both accessed 2015.

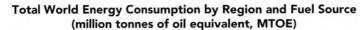
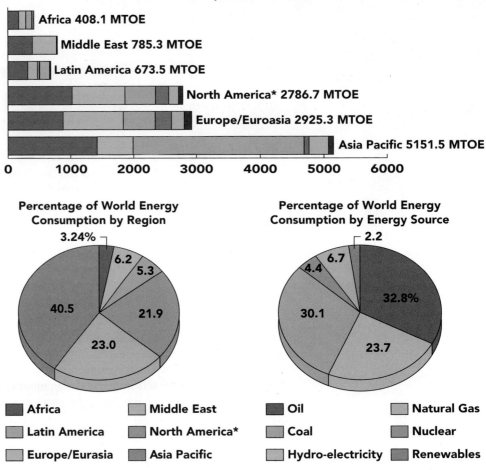

Total World Energy Consumption by Region and Fuel Source (million tonnes of oil equivalent, MTOE)

Africa 408.1 MTOE
Middle East 785.3 MTOE
Latin America 673.5 MTOE
North America* 2786.7 MTOE
Europe/Euroasia 2925.3 MTOE
Asia Pacific 5151.5 MTOE

Percentage of World Energy Consumption by Region
3.24% · 6.2 · 5.3 · 40.5 · 21.9 · 23.0

Percentage of World Energy Consumption by Energy Source
2.2 · 6.7 · 4.4 · 32.8% · 30.1 · 23.7

Africa · Middle East · Latin America · North America* · Europe/Eurasia · Asia Pacific

Oil · Natural Gas · Coal · Nuclear · Hydro-electricity · Renewables

* Includes Mexico

North America (as shown in Exhibit 3.4). Also notice that oil is emphasized in North America, coal in Asia, and natural gas in Europe. Although the United States continues to consume the second greatest quantities of energy of any country (about 17% of the world total), China is first (at more than 23%). Finally, there is some good news on this topic. China is beginning to curtail its use of coal in favor of renewables, with demand there predicted to peak before 2020.[32] Also, the United States and China recently agreed on targets to cut carbon emissions, spurring the global efforts for cutting greenhouse gases.[33]

[32]James Richards, "China Is Losing Some of Its Appetite for Coal," *Bloomberg Business Week*, January 11, 2015, pp. 16–17.
[33]Mark Landler, "U.S. and China Reach Agreement on Climate in Step to Cut Carbon Emissions," *The New York Times*, December 12, 2014, pp. A1, 11.

1972 One billion radios on the planet
1973 Arab oil embargo jolts industrial world into understanding the totally global nature of supply and demand
1980 CNN founded, providing instant and common information the world over, taking another significant step in the process of globalization started by the radio in 1901

1987 ISO issues ISO 9000 to create a global quality standard
1988 One billion televisions on the planet
1989 Berlin Wall falls, symbolizing the opening of the East to the West for ideas and commerce
1991 Soviet Union formally abandons communism, as most formerly communist states move toward capitalism and the trade it fosters; Commonwealth of Independent

States (CIS) established among Russia, Ukraine, and Belarus
1993 NAFTA ratified by U.S. Congress; European Union created from the European Community, along with a framework for joint security and foreign policy action, by the 1991 Maastricht Treaty on European Union; the EEC is renamed the EC
1994 The Chunnel (Channel Tunnel) is opened between France

and Britain, providing a ground link for commerce between the continent and Britain
1995 World Trade Organization (WTO) set up as successor of GATT; by 2000 more than 130 members will account for over 90 percent of world trade.
1997 Hong Kong, a world trading and financial capital and bastion of capitalism, is returned to communist Chinese control; *Pathfinder*

Cattle dung, which is used both as farmyard manure and, dried into cakes, as household fuel, is being carried to a local market in India. India's cattle produce enormous quantities of dung, which some studies suggest provide the equivalent of 10,000 megawatts of energy annually. The Chulla stove described in Chapters 5 and 13 is designed to safely burn the cattle dung pictured on this fellow's head.

This Masai woman of Tanzania put to good use both cow dung and urine in building her hut pictured here in her family village (or boma). The semi-nomadic Masai graze their cattle during the day but enclose them within the acacia bush boma at night to protect them from predators.

Since World War II, arguments about the limitless availability of seemingly inexhaustible supplies of petroleum have been prominent.[34] The dramatic increase in economic growth in the industrialized world and the push for industrialization in the remaining world have put tremendous pressure on Earth's energy resources. Unfortunately, as countries industrialize, energy sources are not always efficiently utilized. China, for example, spends three times the world average on energy (all sources) to produce one dollar of gross national product (GNP). In comparison with Japan, possibly the world's most efficient user of energy, where less than 5 ounces of oil is needed to generate $1 in GNP, in China, approximately 80 ounces of oil is needed. The reasons for China's inefficient oil use are numerous, but the worst culprit is outdated technology.

The location, quality, and availability of resources will affect the pattern of world economic development and trade well into the 21st century. In addition to the raw materials of industrialization, an economically feasible energy supply must be available to transform resources into usable products. As the global demand for resources intensifies and prices rise, resources will continue to increase in importance among the uncontrollable elements of the international marketer's decisions.

---

[34]Stanley Reed, "Endless Oil," *BusinessWeek*, January 18, 2010, pp. 47–49.

lands on Mars, and *Rover* goes for a drive but finds no one with whom to trade
1999   Euro introduced in 11 European Union nations, pavingthe way for the creation of a true trade union and trade bloc
1999   Seattle Round of WTO negotiations attracts the first great protest against globalization

1999   Control of the Panama Canal, a major trade lane, is returned to Panama
2000   Second millennium arrives, predicted computer problems are a non-event
2001   September 11 terrorist attack on the World Trade Center in New York City and the Pentagon in Washington, DC; one billion mobile phones on the planet

2002   United States attacks Taliban in Afghanistan
2003   United States attacks regime of Saddam Hussein in Iraq
2004   Great Indian Ocean tsunami kills 500,000 people
2006   One billion personal computers on the planet
2008   Beijing hosts the Olympics
2009   Great Recession causes largest decline in world trade since World War II; even so,

almost 4 billion mobile phone subscribers around the globe
2010   Earthquake in Haiti kills more than 200,000 people
2011   Japan earthquake and tsunami; Arab Spring protest and revolutions begin;
2016   Toyota sells first mass-produced hydrogen fuel cell automobile
2055   The United Nations' earliest estimate for the world population to begin shrinking due to the global decline of fertility

Exhibit 3.5
World Population by Region, 2014–2050 (millions)

Source: *World Population Prospects, The 2014 Revision*, United Nations Economic and Social Affairs, http://www.unpopulation.org, 2012. Reprinted with permission.

Regions	Population (in millions)	
	2014	2050
World	7,243	9,550
More developed regions*	1,255	1,350
Less developed regions†	5,986	8,247
Least developed regions‡	918	1,810
Africa	1,137	2,047
Asia	4,342	5,156
Europe	742	708
Latin America	662	781
Northern America	357	446
Oceania	49	57

*More developed regions comprise all regions of Europe and Northern America, Australia, New Zealand, and Japan.

†Less developed regions comprise all regions of Africa, Asia (excluding Japan), and Latin America and the regions of Melanesia, Micronesia, and Polynesia.

‡Least developed regions, as defined by the United Nations General Assembly, include 48 countries, of which 33 are in Africa, 9 in Asia, 1 in Latin America, and 5 in Oceania. They are also included in the less developed regions.

Dynamics of Global Population Trends

Current population, rural/urban population shifts, rates of growth, age levels, and population control help determine today's demand for various categories of goods.[35] Although not the only determinant, the existence of sheer numbers of people is significant in appraising potential consumer markets. Changes in the composition and distribution of population among the world's countries will profoundly affect future demand. Moreover, it now appears that demand for goods worldwide can affect migration patterns, in a reversal of the traditional causal relationship. Specifically, the global financial crisis that began in 2008 appears to have caused a (perhaps temporary) reversal of migrations from urban to rural areas within countries and from developed back to developing countries internationally as employment opportunities dry up in response to the decline in demand for goods and services worldwide.

Recent estimates place world population at more than 7 billion people, a number expected to grow to about 9.5 billion by 2050. However, seemingly small differences in assumptions about fertility rates can make big differences in growth forecasts. One possible scenario put forth by United Nations experts suggests the planet's population may peak at about 8 billion and then begin to decline after 2040. All scenarios agree though that almost all of the projected growth up to 2050 will occur in less developed regions. Exhibit 3.5 shows that 85 percent of the population will be concentrated in less developed regions by 2050. The International Labor Organization estimates that 1.2 billion jobs must be created worldwide to accommodate these new entrants through 2025. Furthermore, most of the new jobs will need to be created in urban areas where most of the population will reside.

Controlling Population Growth

LO7

The economic effects of controlling population growth and aging populations

Faced with the ominous consequences of the population explosion, it would seem logical for countries to take steps to reduce growth to manageable rates, but procreation is one of the most culturally sensitive, uncontrollable factors. Economics, self-esteem, religion, politics, and education all play critical roles in attitudes about family size. All these considerations make the impact of China's long-term enforcement of its one-child policies most

---

[35]A book written in 1998 predicted the Great Recession of 2008–2009 ten years in advance, based on demographic projections of consumer demand. For a very interesting read, see Harry S. Dent, *The Roaring 2000s* (Touchstone: New York, 1998); also see John L. Graham, "2020 Is 23 Years from Now," *UCInsight*, Spring 1997, pp. 3, 13 for a similar, demographics-based prediction.

remarkable. And most recently it appears that China is now having problems implementing their new relaxed policy on family size. For many one child is enough.[36]

The prerequisites to population control are adequate incomes, higher literacy levels, education for women, universal access to healthcare, family planning, improved nutrition, and, perhaps most important, a change in basic cultural beliefs regarding the importance of large families. Unfortunately, minimum progress in providing improved living conditions and changing beliefs has occurred. India serves as a good example of what is happening in much of the world. India's population was once stable, but with improved health conditions leading to greater longevity and lower infant mortality, its population will exceed that of China by 2050, when the two will account for about 50 percent of the world's inhabitants. The government's attempts to institute change are hampered by a variety of factors, including political ineptitude and slow changes in cultural norms. Nevertheless, the government continues to pass laws with the intended purpose of limiting the number of births. A novel example was a law that bars those with more than two children from election to the national Parliament and state assemblies. This rule would mean that many now in office could not seek reelection because of their family size.

Perhaps the most important deterrent to population control is cultural attitudes about the importance of large families. In many cultures, the prestige of a man, whether alive or dead, depends on the number of his progeny, and a family's only wealth is its children. Such feelings are strong. Prime Minister Indira Gandhi found out how strong when she attempted mass sterilization of men, which reportedly was the main cause of her defeat in a subsequent election. Additionally, many religions discourage or ban family planning and thus serve as a deterrent to control. Nigeria has a strong Muslim tradition in the north and a strong Roman Catholic tradition in the east, and both faiths favor large families. Most traditional religions in Africa encourage large families; in fact, the principal deity for many is the goddess of land and fertility.

Family planning and all that it entails is by far the most universal means governments use to control birthrates, but some economists believe that a decline in the fertility rate is a function of economic prosperity and will come only with economic development. Ample anecdotal evidence suggests that fertility rates decline as economies prosper. For example, before Spain's economy began its rapid growth in the 1980s, families had six or more children; now, Spain has one of the lowest fertility rates in Europe, an average of 1.4 children per woman.[37] Similar patterns have followed in other European countries as economies have prospered.

Rural/Urban Migration

Migration from rural to urban areas, which can consist of domestic or international moves,[38] is largely a result of a desire for greater access to sources of education, healthcare, and improved job opportunities. In the early 1800s, less than 3.5 percent of the world's people were living in cities of 20,000 or more and less than 2 percent in cities of 100,000 or more; today, more than 54 percent[39] of the world's people are urbanites, and the trend is accelerating. Once in the city, perhaps three out of four migrants achieve some economic gains. The family income of a manual worker in urban Brazil, for example, is almost five times that of a farm laborer in a rural area.

By 2030, estimates indicate that more than 61 percent of the world's population will live in urban areas[40] (up from 49 percent in 2005, with similar changes across all regions), and at least 27 cities will have populations of 10 million or more, 23 of which will be in the less

---

[36]Laurie Burkitt, "China Struggles to Implement Relaxed Policy on Family Size," *The Wall Street Journal*, March 6, 2014, online.

[37]Please note the difference between the statistics: **fertility rate** is the average number of children born per woman in her lifetime, and **birthrate** is the number of children born per 1,000 women per year.

[38]"The Magic of Diasporas," *The Economist*, November 19, 2011, p. 13.

[39]World Urbanization Prospects, *The 2014 Revision* (New York: United Nations), 2014.

[40]Dexter Roberts, "Premier Li Wants More Chinese in the Cities," *Bloomberg BusinessWeek*, June 6, 2013, online.

developed regions. Tokyo has already overtaken Mexico City as the largest city on Earth, with a population of 38 million, a jump of almost 8 million since 1990.

Although migrants experience some relative improvement in their living standards, intense urban growth without investment in services eventually leads to serious problems. Slums populated with unskilled workers living hand to mouth put excessive pressure on sanitation systems, water supplies, and social services. At some point, the disadvantages of unregulated urban growth begin to outweigh the advantages for all concerned.

Consider the conditions that exist in Mexico City today. Besides smog, garbage, and pollution brought about by its increased population, Mexico City faces a severe water shortage. Local water supplies are nearly exhausted and in some cases are unhealthy. Water consumption from all sources is about 16,000 gallons per second, but the underground aquifers are producing only 2,640 gallons per second. Water comes from hundreds of miles away and has to be pumped up to an elevation of 7,444 feet to reach Mexico City. Such problems are not unique to Mexico; throughout the developing world, poor sanitation and inadequate water supplies are consequences of runaway population growth. An estimated 768 million people are currently without access to clean drinking water, and almost 3 billion lack access to sanitation services. Estimates are that 40 percent of the world's population, 2.5 billion people, will be without clean water if more is not invested in water resources. Prospects for improvement are not encouraging, because most of the world's urban growth will take place in the already economically strained developing countries.

Population Decline and Aging

While the developing world faces a rapidly growing population, the industrialized world's population is in decline and rapidly aging. Birthrates in western Europe and Japan have been decreasing since the early or mid-1960s; more women are choosing careers instead of children, and many working couples are electing to remain childless. As a result of these and other contemporary factors, population growth in many countries has dropped below the rate necessary to maintain present levels.[41] Just to keep the population from falling, a nation needs a fertility rate of about 2.1 children per woman. Not one major industrialized country has sufficient internal population growth to maintain itself, and this trend is expected to continue for the next 50 years.

At the same time that population growth is declining in the industrialized world, there are more aging people today than ever before. Global life expectancy has grown more in the past 50 years than over the previous 5,000 years. Until the Industrial Revolution, no more than 2 or 3 percent of the total population was over the age of 65 years. Today in the developed world, the over-age-65 group amounts to 14 percent, and by 2030, this group will reach 25 percent in some 30 different countries. Furthermore, the number of "old old" will grow much faster than the "young old." The United Nations projects that by 2050, the number of people aged 65 to 84 years worldwide will grow from 400 million to 1.3 billion (a threefold increase), while the number of people aged 85 years and over will grow from 26 million to 175 million (a sixfold increase)—and the number aged 100 years and over will increase from 135,000 to 2.2 million (a sixteenfold increase). Exhibit 3.6 illustrates the disparity in aging between more developed countries (that is, North America, Europe, Japan, and Australia) and less developed countries. Countries like Kenya, with a high proportion of young people, face high education and healthcare costs, whereas countries like the United Kingdom, with top-heavy population pyramids, face high pension and healthcare costs for the elderly with fewer wage earners to bear the burden.

Europe, Japan, and the United States epitomize[42] the problems caused by an increasing percentage of elderly people who must be supported by a declining number of skilled

---

[41]"Child Bribe," *The Economist*, June 1, 2013, p. 40; "Make More Babies," *The Economist*, June 7, 2014, p. 53.

[42]Philip Longman, "Think Again, Global Aging," *Foreign Policy*, November 2010; "The Incredible Shrinking Country," *The Economist*, May 31, 2014, p. 35.

Exhibit 3.6
Age Density for World and Japan

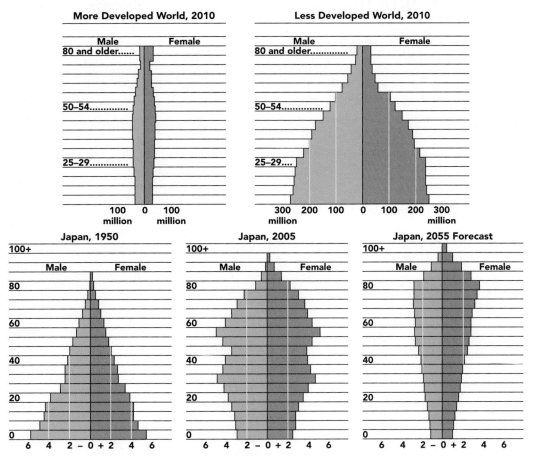

Source: Adapted from "There Will Soon Be Seven Billion People on the Planet," *National Geographic Magazine*, January 2011. p. 51; "A Special Report on Japan," *The Economist*, November 10, 2010, p. 4.

workers. Compare the data for Japan in Exhibit 3.6, then contemplate the consequences of its extremely stringent immigration policies. In 1998, Japan crossed a threshold anticipated with fear by the rest of the developed world: The point at which retirees withdrawing funds from the pension system exceeded the workers contributing to it. The elderly require higher government outlays for healthcare and hospitals, special housing and nursing homes, and pension and welfare assistance, but the workforce that supports these costs is dwindling. The part of the world with the largest portion of people over 65 years is also the part of the world with the fewest number of people under age 15 years. This disparity means that there will be fewer workers to support future retirees, resulting in an intolerable tax burden on future workers, more of the over-65 group remaining in the labor force, or pressure to change existing laws to allow mass migration to stabilize the worker-to-retiree ratio. No one solution is without its problems.

Worker Shortage and Immigration

For most countries, mass immigration is not well received by the resident population. However, a recent report from the United Nations makes the strongest argument for change in immigration laws as a viable solution. The free flow of immigration will help ameliorate the dual problems of explosive population expansion in less developed countries and worker shortage in industrialized regions. Europe is the region of the world most affected by aging and thus by a steadily decreasing worker-to-retiree ratio. The proportion of older persons will increase from 20 percent in 1998 to 35 percent in 2050. The country with the largest share of old people will be Spain, closely followed by Italy.

CROSSING BORDERS 3.3   Where Have All the Women Gone?

Three converging issues in China have the potential of causing a serious gender imbalance:

- China, the world's most populous country, had a strict one-child policy to curb population growth.

- Traditional values dictate male superiority and a definite parental preference for boys.

- Prenatal scanning allows women to discover the sex of their fetuses and thereby abort unwanted female fetuses.

The first wave of children born under the one-child policy is reaching marriageable age, and there are far too few brides to go around. The ratio of males to females is unnaturally high, hovering around 118 boys for every 100 girls in 2005. Thus, men in their 20s have to deal with the harsh reality of six bachelors for every five potential brides. So what is a desperate bachelor to do?

The shortage has prompted some parents to acquire babies as future brides for their sons. Infants are considered more appealing because they are less likely to run away, will look on their buyers as their own parents, and are cheaper than buying a teenage bride. Buying a baby girl can cost as little as $100 and won't result in the fines imposed on couples who violate birth control limits. Such fines can equal as much as six years' income.

Another alternative is to marry a relative. At age 20 years, with his friends already paired off, Liu found himself the odd man out. His parents, farmers in a small back water village, could not raise the $2,000 required to attract a bride for their son. Desperate, Liu's mother asked her sister for a favor: Could she ask Hai, her daughter, to be Liu's bride? Young women like Hai are not likely to defy their parents. And so Liu and Hai were wed.

Chinese officials are starting to worry about the imbalance and have announced a raft of new programs to reverse the trend. These offers include cash payments for couples who have a daughter and let her live, along with privileges in housing, employment, and job training. Some families with girls will also be exempt from paying school fees. Even though the government staunchly defends its one-child policy, it is experimenting with allowing couples whose firstborn is a girl to have a second child. In the meantime and until the new policy results in more girls, today's 20-year-old men will just have to compete if they want a wife.

Sources: Nicholas Zamiska, "China's One-Child Policy Gets Wider Enforcement," *The Wall Street Journal Asia*, January 8, 2008, p. 10; Mark R. Rosenzweig and Junse Zhang, "Do Population Control Policies Induce More Human Capital Investment?" *Review of Economic Studies* 76, no. 3 (2009), pp. 1149–74; Andrea de Boer and Valerie M. Hudson, "The Security Risks of China's Abnormal Demographics," *Washington Post*, April 30, 2014, online.

Recognizing the problem, Spain has changed immigration laws to open its borders to all South Americans of Spanish descent. To keep the worker-to-retiree ratio from falling, Europe will need 1.4 billion immigrants over the next 50 years, while Japan and the United States will need 600 million immigrants between now and 2050. Immigration will not help ameliorate the problem though if political and cultural opposition to immigration cannot be overcome.

The trends of increasing population in the developing world, with substantial shifts from rural to urban areas, declining birthrates in the industrialized world, and global population aging, will have profound effects on the state of world business and world economic conditions. Without successful adjustments to these trends, many countries will experience slower economic growth, serious financial problems for senior retirement programs, and further deterioration of public and social services, leading to possible social unrest.

World Trade Routes

Trade routes bind the world together, minimizing distance, natural barriers, lack of resources, and the fundamental differences between peoples and economies. As long as one group of people in the world wants something that another group somewhere else has and there is a means of travel between the two, there is trade. Early trade routes were over land; later came sea routes, air routes, and, finally, some might say, the Internet to connect countries.

| CROSSING BORDERS 3.4 | History, Geography, and Population Collide in America: Returning to Multigenerational Family Living |

As pension systems, healthcare systems, and retirement plans continue to crumble under the weight of Baby Boom numbers, we all will need to rely more on the strength of family ties and remember the fundamental human characteristic of interdependence. The problem is that such remembrance is particularly hard for Americans, as opposed to all other peoples on the planet.

America started with The Declaration of Independence. On July 4, 1776, the founding fathers broke from the tyranny of England to form a new country. That document and the idea of independence represent the essence of being American, and the concept is literally the most celebrated notion of the nation. Indeed, the goal of mainstream American parenting is to inculcate this idea into the thinking of children: We ensure they make their own beds, make their own lunches, wash their own clothes, do their own homework, drive their own cars, and so forth. How else can they become independent adults?

There are at least three problems with this American obsession with independence. First, it stigmatizes the burgeoning numbers of both boomerang kids and grandparents living with their grandchildren as families across America smartly reunite. According to the most recent U.S. Census figures, there are 22 million adult children living with their parents and 6 million grandparents living in three-generation households, and both numbers are growing fast. Second, teaching independence actually hasn't worked anyway. And third, there is really no such thing as independence anyway. There is only interdependence.

This American overemphasis on independence is now being recognized by the most independent-minded of all Americans, CEOs. In Bill George's wonderful book, *Authentic Leadership*, he argues that the job of chief executive depends on six constituencies. Without surprise, the former CEO of Medtronic lists shareholders, employees, customers, vendors, and the larger community. But what is unique, and perhaps even revolutionary, in his list is his own family. He recognizes that his own success as a CEO in part depended of the quality of his family life. Thus, he organized his executive team and responsibilities such that he had time to attend kids's soccer matches and such. Remarkable!

Source: Sharon G. Niederhaus and John L. Graham, *All in the Family: A Practical Guide to Successful Multigenerational Living* (Boulder, CO: Taylor Trade), 2013.

Trade routes among Europe, Asia, and the Americas were well established by the 1500s. The Spanish empire founded the city of Manila in the Philippines to receive its silver-laden galleons bound for China. On the return trip, the ship's cargo of silk and other Chinese goods would be offloaded in Mexico, carried overland to the Atlantic, and put on Spanish ships to Spain. What we sometimes fail to recognize is that these same trades routes remain important today and that many Latin American countries have strong relationships with Europe, Asia, and the rest of the world that date back to the 1500s. The commodities traded have changed between the 1500s and today, but trade and the trade routes continue to be important. Today, instead of offloading goods in Mexico and carrying them on mule carts overland to the Atlantic, ships travel from the Pacific to the Atlantic via the Panama Canal. And ships too large for the canal offload their containers onto a railroad that crosses the Isthmus of Panama to be met by another container ship. The Panama Canal is now being widened and deepened to handle even larger cargo ships. It will be interesting to see how fast the Arctic ice melts before that 2016 completion date.[43]

Trade routes represent the attempts of countries to overcome economic and social imbalances created in part by the influence of geography. The majority of world trade is among the most industrialized and industrializing countries of Europe, North America, and Asia. It is no surprise that the trade flow, as depicted in Map 8 at the end of this chapter, links these major trading areas. We must also note though that the fastest growing trade routes are not the traditional ones—now trade among developing nations is burgeoning as never before.[44]

---

[43]"California's Ports, The Fickle Asian Container," *The Economist*, January 28, 2012, pp. 30–31; "Dead Locks," *The Economist*, February 8, 2014, page 64.

[44]Simon Kennedy, Matthew Bristow, and Shamim Adam, "There's a New Silk Road, and It Doesn't Lead to the U.S." *Bloomberg Businessweek*, August 9, 2010, pp. 13–14.

Climate change opens up a new trade route that may compete with the Panama Canal, cutting costly days off the travel time between Western Europe and Asia. Here a German commercial vessel follows a Russian icebreaker through the proverbial Northwest Passage.[45]

Communication Links

LO8

Communication infrastructures are an integral part of international commerce

An underpinning of all commerce is effective communications—knowledge of where goods and services exist and where they are needed and the ability to communicate instantaneously across vast distances. Continuous improvements in electronic communications have facilitated the expansion of trade. First came the telegraph, then the telephone, television, satellites, mobile phones, the computer, the Internet, and combinations of them all. Map 5 in the following pages illustrates the importance of fiber optic cable and satellites in providing global communications. Each revolution in technology has had a profound effect on human conditions, economic growth, and the manner in which commerce functions. Each new communications technology has spawned new business models; some existing businesses have reinvented their practices to adapt to the new technology, while other businesses have failed to respond and thus ceased to exist. The Internet and mobile phone revolutions will be no different; they too affect human conditions, economic growth, and the manner in which commerce operates. As we discuss in subsequent chapters, the combination of the Internet and the dramatic increase in mobile phone subscribers worldwide has already begun to shape how international business is managed. However, as the combinations of new technologies permeate the fabric of the world's cultures, the biggest changes are yet to come![46]

---

[45]"Climate Change in the Artic, Beating a Retreat," *The Economist*, September 24, 2011, pp. 99–100. "Frozen Conflict," *The Economist*, January 2, 2015, p. 89; "The Roar of Ice Cracking," *The Economist*, February 2, p. 89.

[46]Ben Charny, "Steve Jobs Reveals New iPad Device," *The Wall Street Journal*, January 27, 2010.

During ancient times the Port of Corinth was a crucial trading center and port serving Greece and its neighbors. The isthmus on which the city is built linked central Greece with the Peloponnesian Peninsula by land before the 6 kilometer canal pictured was completed in 1893. In ancient times ships were unloaded in Corinth and literally dragged across the 6 kilometer isthmus and reloaded, all to save the weeks-long voyage by sail between the Agean and Ionian Seas.

Summary

One British authority admonishes foreign marketers to study the world until "the mere mention of a town, country, or river enables it to be picked out immediately on the map." Although it may not be necessary for the student of foreign marketing to memorize the world map to that extent, a prospective international marketer should be reasonably familiar with the world, its climate, and topographic differences. Otherwise, the important marketing characteristics of geography could be completely overlooked when marketing in another country. The need for geographical and historical knowledge goes deeper than being able to locate continents and their countries. Geographic hurdles must be recognized as having a direct effect on marketing and the related activities of communications and distribution. For someone who has never been in a tropical rainforest with an annual rainfall of at least 60 inches (and sometimes more than 200 inches), anticipating the need for protection against high humidity is difficult. Likewise, someone who has never encountered the difficult problems caused by dehydration in constant 100-degrees-plus heat in the Sahara region will find them hard to comprehend. Indirect effects from the geographical ramifications of a society and culture ultimately may be reflected in marketing activities. Many of the peculiarities of a country (i.e., peculiar to the foreigner) would be better understood and anticipated if its history and geography were studied more closely. Without a historical understanding of a culture, the attitudes within the marketplace may not be fully understood.

Aside from the simpler and more obvious ramifications of climate and topography, history and geography exert complex influences on the development of the general economy and society of a country. In this case, the study of history and geography is needed to provide the marketer with an understanding of why a country has developed as it has rather than as a guide for adapting marketing plans. History and geography are two of the environments of foreign marketing that should be thoroughly understood and that must be included in foreign marketing plans to a degree commensurate with their influence on marketing effort.

Key Terms

Opium Wars	Manifest Destiny	Expropriation	Sustainable development
Taiping Rebellion	Monroe Doctrine	Greenhouse-gas	
Confucian philosophy	Roosevelt Corollary	emissions	

Questions

1. Define the key terms listed above.

2. Why study geography in international marketing?

3. Why study a country's history?

4. How does an understanding of history help an international marketer?

5. Why is there a love–hate relationship between Mexico and the United States?

6. Some say the global environment is a global issue rather than a national one. What does this mean?

7. Pick a country and show how employment and topography affect marketing within the country.

8. Pick a country, other than Mexico, China, or Japan, and show how significant historical events have affected the country's culture.

9. Discuss the bases of world trade. Give examples illustrating the different bases.

10. The marketer "should also examine the more complex effect of geography on general market characteristics, distribution systems, and the state of the economy." Comment.

11. The world population pattern is shifting from rural to urban areas. Discuss the marketing ramifications.

12. Select a country with a stable population and one with a rapidly growing population. Contrast the marketing implications of these two situations.

13. "World trade routes bind the world together." Discuss.

14. Discuss how your interpretations of Manifest Destiny and the Monroe Doctrine might differ from those of a native of Latin America.

15. The telegraph, the telephone, television, satellites, the computer, mobile phones, and the Internet have all had an effect on how international business operates. Discuss how each of these communications innovations affects international business management.

Answers to quiz on page 73

The following four items are all products of the sun's rays: solar, wind, wood (see Chapter 14 for details), and cow manure. The last is used extensively in less-developed countries (see page 75), as it was in the United States in the 1800s. Wood and dung, although burned, are current carbon, already on the surface of the earth. The coal is, of course, fossil fuel and, before mining, is not part of the atmosphere. By the way, Zeus is the Greek god of weather—wind, sun, and lightning (electricity)—and Artemis is the goddess of the forest. When it comes to beliefs/religion and cows, you have to go with the Hindu sacred cow in India.

key world views

Key World Views

GREENLAND
(Denmark)

Greenland Sea

ALASKA
(United States)

Reykjavik ICELAND

Norwegian Sea

North Sea

NETH.

CANADA

Dublin UNITED
IRELAND KINGDOM
London BELG.
English Channel Paris
FRANCE

Montreal
Toronto
Detroit Boston
Chicago Philadelphia New York
UNITED STATES Washington

Madrid
PORTUGAL SPAIN
Lisbon

San Francisco

Los Angeles

AZORES
(Portugal)
Algiers
Strait of Gibraltar
Casablanca
CANARY IS. MOROCCO
(Spain)

Dallas

ATLANTIC
OCEAN

Houston

Miami BAHAMAS

WESTERN
SAHARA
(Morocco)

ALGERIA

MEXICO

Monterrey

CUBA
DOMINICAN
REPUBLIC
HAITI
JAMAICA PUERTO
RICO
(U.S.)

MAURITANIA
Nouakchott

MALI

Mexico City

GUADELOUPE
DOMINICA
ST. LUCIA

CAPE VERDE

Dakar
GAMBIA SENEGAL
GUINEA- Bissau Bamako BURKINA
BISSAU GUINEA FASO
Conakry
SIERRA LEONE CÔTE GHANA
D'IVOIRE
Monrovia
LIBERIA

BELIZE
HONDURAS

GUATEMALA
EL SALVADOR NICARAGUA

HAWAII
(United States)

COSTA
RICA Caracas TRINIDAD &
TOBAGO
Bogota VENEZUELA GUYANA
SURINAME
PANAMA
COLOMBIA FRENCH GUIANA
(France)

TOGO
EQUATORIAL
GUINEA

SAO TOME &
PRINCIPE

ECUADOR

P
E
R
U

Lima

BRAZIL

ATLANTIC
OCEAN

PACIFIC
OCEAN

BOLIVIA

Belo Horizonte

PARAGUAY Sao Paulo
Rio de Janeiro

Porto Alegre

C
H
I
L
E

Buenos Aires URUGUAY

ARGENTINA

1 **The World**

FALKLAND
ISLANDS
(U.K.)

Key World Views

ARCTIC OCEAN

FRANZ JOSEF LAND (Russia)

Barents Sea
Kara Sea
Laptev Sea
East Siberian Sea

RUSSIA

ESTONIA
ATVIA
THUANIA
BELARUS
Moscow

Kiev
UKRAINE
MOLDOVA
ROMANIA
SERB.-MONT.
BULGARIA
MAC.
GREECE
Athens
Istanbul
Ankara
TURKEY
CYPRUS
LEBANON
ISRAEL
Alexandria
Cairo
Mediterranean Sea

Black Sea
GEORGIA
ARMENIA
AZERBAIJAN
Tehran
SYRIA
IRAQ
Baghdad
IRAN
KUWAIT
JORDAN
BAHRAIN
QATAR
UNITED ARAB EMIRATES
SAUDI ARABIA
Persian Gulf
Red Sea

Caspian Sea
Aral Sea
KAZAKHSTAN
Astana
UZBEKISTAN
Tashkent
TURKMENISTAN
TAJIKISTAN
KYRGYZSTAN
AFGHANISTAN
PAKISTAN
Lahore
Karachi

MONGOLIA

Lake Baikal

Shenyang
Beijing
Tianjin
NORTH KOREA
Seoul
SOUTH KOREA
Sea of Japan (East Sea)
JAPAN
Tokyo
Osaka

CHINA

Chongqing
Shanghai

Delhi
NEPAL
BHUTAN
Sea Of Okhotsk

Bering Sea

Guangzhou
Taipei
TAIWAN
East China Sea

BYA
EGYPT
LYBA
CHAD
Khartoum
SUDAN
'Djamena
CENTRAL AFRICAN REPUBLIC
ERITREA
ETHIOPIA
Addis Ababa
DJIBOUTI
SOMALIA
YEMEN

OMAN

Arabian Sea

Mumbai
Hyderabad
Bangalore
INDIA
Kolkata
Dhaka
BANGLADESH
Chennai
Bay of Bengal
MYANMAR
Yangon
LAOS
Hanoi
VIETNAM
THAILAND
Bangkok
CAMBODIA
Hong Kong
Macau
South China Sea
Manila
PHILIPPINES
Philippine Sea

PACIFIC OCEAN

PALAU

FEDERATED STATES OF MICRONESIA

SRI LANKA
Colombo

Ho Chi Minh City
BRUNEI
Kuala Lumpur
MALAYSIA
SINGAPORE

CONGO
UGANDA
Kampala
RWANDA
BURUNDI
DEMOCRATIC REPUBLIC OF CONGO
Kinshasa
KENYA
Nairobi
Mogadishu

SEYCHELLES

INDONESIA

PAPUA NEW GUINEA
Port Moresby
SOLO. IS.

nda
TANZANIA
Dar es Salaam
MALAWI
COMOROS

Mozambique Channel

Jakarta
Surabaya
TIMOR-LESTE

Coral Sea
VANUA

NGOLA
ZAMBIA
Lusaka
Lilongwe
Harare
ZIMBABWE
MOZAMBIQUE
Antananarivo
MADAGASCAR
MAURITIUS
RÉUNION (France)

INDIAN OCEAN

MIBIA
BOTSWANA
Gaborone
Joannesburg
SOUTH AFRICA
SWAZILAND
LESOTHO
Maputo

AUSTRALIA

Sydney
Melbourne
Tasman Sea
NEW ZEALAND
Wellington

ALB.	Albania
AUS.	Austria
BELG.	Belgium
BOS.–HER.	Bosnia and Herzegovina
CZECH REP.	Czech Republic
CR.	Croatia
DEN.	Denmark
SERB-MONT.	Serbia and Montenegro
HUN.	Hungary
MAC.	Macedonia
NETH.	The Netherlands
SWITZ.	Switzerland
SLOV.	Slovakia
SLOVE.	Slovenia

| 4 P.M. | 5 P.M. | 6 P.M. | 7 P.M. | 8 P.M. | 9 P.M. | 10 P.M. | 11 P.M. | 12 A.M. | 1 A.M. | 2 A.M. | 3 A.M. |

POLAR EASTERLIES

POLAR EASTERLIES

Labrador Current

Alaska Current

North Pacific Current

North Equatorial Current

California Current

WESTERLIES

WESTERLIES

WESTERLIES

Gulf Stream

NORTH AMERICA

E

NORTHEAST TRADE WINDS

Canary Current

NORTHEAST TRADE WINDS

North Equatorial Current

A

Equatorial Counter Current

South Equatorial Current

South Equatorial Current

SOUTHEAST TRADE WINDS

Peru (Humboldt) Current

El Niño

SOUTH AMERICA

Brazil Current

SOUTHEAST TRADE WINDS

Benguela Current

Falkland Current

El Niño

Up to 30 times in a century, the El Niño effect occurs, when east-to-west trade winds sweeping over the Pacific Ocean become unusually weak, allowing warm water, normally held back by the winds, to flow eastward along the equator. The current creates a warm band of water and an area of low atmospheric pressure with violent storms right across the eastern Pacific. The global weather machine is thrown into chaos; random and unusual weather events, such as hurricanes, heatwaves, freak floods, and droughts, occur around the globe, bringing devastation in their wake.

WESTERLIES

West Wind Drift

West Wind Drift

WESTERLIES

POLAR EASTERLIES   WESTERLIES

POLAR EASTERLIES   WESTERLIES

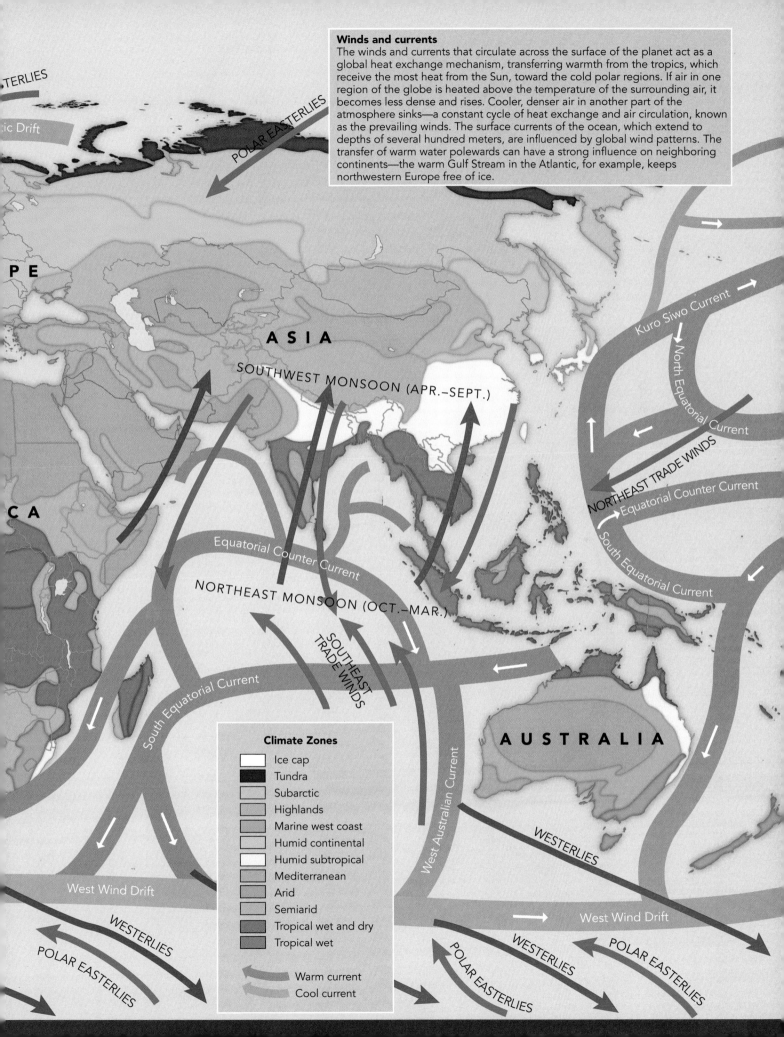

Winds and currents
The winds and currents that circulate across the surface of the planet act as a global heat exchange mechanism, transferring warmth from the tropics, which receive the most heat from the Sun, toward the cold polar regions. If air in one region of the globe is heated above the temperature of the surrounding air, it becomes less dense and rises. Cooler, denser air in another part of the atmosphere sinks—a constant cycle of heat exchange and air circulation, known as the prevailing winds. The surface currents of the ocean, which extend to depths of several hundred meters, are influenced by global wind patterns. The transfer of warm water polewards can have a strong influence on neighboring continents—the warm Gulf Stream in the Atlantic, for example, keeps northwestern Europe free of ice.

TERLIES

tic Drift

POLAR EASTERLIES

PE

CA

ASIA

SOUTHWEST MONSOON (APR.–SEPT.)

Equatorial Counter Current

NORTHEAST MONSOON (OCT.–MAR.)

South Equatorial Current

SOUTHEAST TRADE WINDS

Kuro Siwo Current

North Equatorial Current

NORTHEAST TRADE WINDS

Equatorial Counter Current

South Equatorial Current

West Australian Current

AUSTRALIA

West Wind Drift

WESTERLIES

WESTERLIES

WESTERLIES

POLAR EASTERLIES

West Wind Drift

POLAR EASTERLIES

WESTERLIES

POLAR EASTERLIES

Climate Zones

- Ice cap
- Tundra
- Subarctic
- Highlands
- Marine west coast
- Humid continental
- Humid subtropical
- Mediterranean
- Arid
- Semiarid
- Tropical wet and dry
- Tropical wet

Warm current
Cool current

3 Oil and Gas Production and Consumption

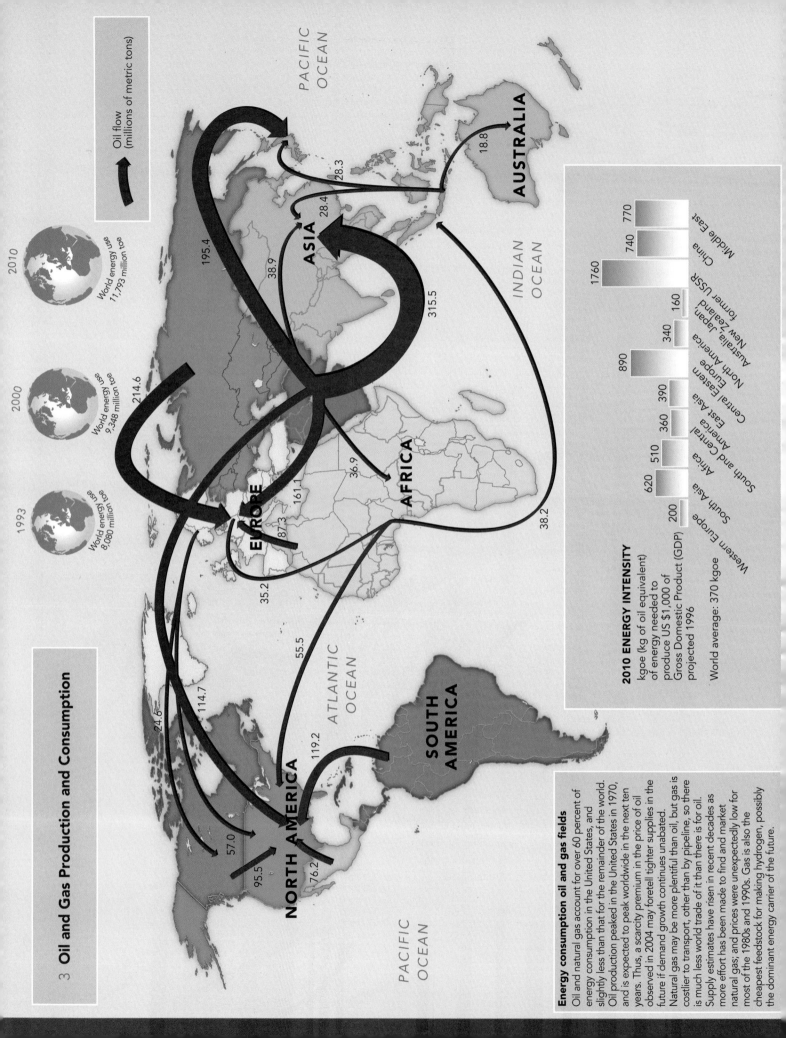

Oil flow
(millions of metric tons)

1993

World energy use
8,080 million toe

2000

World energy use
9,348 million toe

2010

World energy use
11,793 million toe

PACIFIC OCEAN

AUSTRALIA

18.8

28.3

28.4

ASIA

38.9

195.4

214.6

315.5

INDIAN OCEAN

EUROPE

87.3

161.1

36.9

AFRICA

38.2

35.2

55.5

ATLANTIC OCEAN

SOUTH AMERICA

119.2

76.2

NORTH AMERICA

95.5

57.0

24.6

114.7

PACIFIC OCEAN

2010 ENERGY INTENSITY

kgoe (kg of oil equivalent)
of energy needed to
produce US $1,000 of
Gross Domestic Product (GDP)
projected 1996

World average: 370 kgoe

1760	former USSR
770	Middle East
740	China
890	Central/Eastern Europe
340	Australia, Japan, New Zealand
160	North America
390	East Asia
360	Central and South America
510	Africa
620	South Asia
200	Western Europe

Energy consumption oil and gas fields

Oil and natural gas account for over 60 percent of energy consumption in the United States, and slightly less than that for the remainder of the world. Oil production peaked in the United States in 1970, and is expected to peak worldwide in the next ten years. Thus, a scarcity premium in the price of oil observed in 2004 may foretell tighter supplies in the future if demand growth continues unabated. Natural gas may be more plentiful than oil, but gas is costlier to transport, other than by pipeline, so there is much less world trade of it than there is for oil. Supply estimates have risen in recent decades as more effort has been made to find and market natural gas; and prices were unexpectedly low for most of the 1980s and 1990s. Gas is also the cheapest feedstock for making hydrogen, possibly the dominant energy carrier of the future.

4 **Water**

THE WORLD'S WATER
1993 percentages

salt water
97.5%

fresh water
2.5%

69% glaciers
and permanent
snow cover

30% fresh
groundwater

0.3%
freshwater lakes
and river flows

0.9%
other, including
soil moisture,
ground ice, and
swamp water

WATER SHORTAGES
proportion of world's population
facing water shortages
1995 and 2050

2050
scarcity 18%
stress 24%
relative sufficiency 58%
world population 9.4 billion

1995
stress 5%
scarcity 3%
relative sufficiency 92%
world population 5.7 billion

2050
FRESH WATER
Availability per person per year
cubic meters
projected 1997
borders 1998

water scarcity:
under 1,000 cubic meters
per person
chronic water shortages
impede economic
development and cause
environmental degradation

water stress:
1,000–1,700 cubic meters
per person
chronic and widespread
water supply problems

relative water sufficiency:
over 1,700 cubic meters
per person
intermittent or localized
shortages

relative sufficiency in 1995
although shortage predicted
for 2050

Note: Based on
UN population data 1996

CANADA

U.S.A.

MEXICO

CUBA

JAMAICA
BELIZE
HAITI
GUATEMALA
EL SALVADOR
HONDURAS
NICARAGUA
COSTA RICA
PANAMA

DOM REP
BARBADOS

COLOMBIA
VENEZUELA
GUYANA
SURINAME
FRENCH GUIANA (Fr.)
ECUADOR

PERU

BRAZIL

BOLIVIA
PARAGUAY

CHILE
ARGENTINA
URUGUAY

FALKLAND
ISLANDS
(U.K.)

ICELAND

IRELAND
U.K.
NORWAY
SWEDEN
FINLAND
DENMARK
NETH.
BEL.
LUX.
GERMANY
FRANCE
SWITZ.
SPAIN
PORTUGAL
POLAND
CZECH
SLO.
AUS.
HUNG.
ITALY
CRO.
B.-H.S.-M.
SLOV.
ALB.
MACE.
GREECE
BULG.
ROMANIA
MOL.
UKRAINE
BELARUS
EST.
LAT.
LITH.

RUSSIA

MOROCCO
WESTERN
SAHARA
(Morocco)
ALGERIA
LIBYA
TUNISIA
MALTA
EGYPT

MAURITANIA
MALI
NIGER
CHAD
SUDAN

CAPE VERDE
SENEGAL
GAMBIA
GUINEA-BISSAU
GUINEA
SIERRA LEONE
LIBERIA
COTE D'
IVOIRE
BURKINA
FASO
GHANA
TOGO
BENIN
NIGERIA
CAMEROON
EQ. GUINEA
GABON
CONGO
CENT.
AFR. REP.
DEM. REP.
OF THE
CONGO
ANGOLA
NAMIBIA
BOTSWANA
SOUTH
AFRICA
LESOTHO
SWAZILAND
ZIMB.
MOZAMBIQUE
ZAMBIA
MALAWI
TANZANIA
KENYA
UGA.
RWA.
BUR.
ETHIOPIA
ERITREA
DJIBOUTI
SOMALIA
COMOROS
MADAGASCAR
MAURITIUS

TURKEY
CYPRUS
LEB.
ISRAEL
JOR.
SYRIA
IRAQ
IRAN
KUWAIT
BAHRAIN
QATAR
U.A.E.
SAUDI
ARABIA
YEMEN
OMAN
GEORGIA
ARM.
AZER.
TURKMENISTAN
UZBEKISTAN
KAZAKHSTAN
KYRGYSTAN
TAJ.
AFGHANISTAN
PAKISTAN
NEPAL
INDIA
SRI LANKA
MONGOLIA
CHINA

5 Global Communications

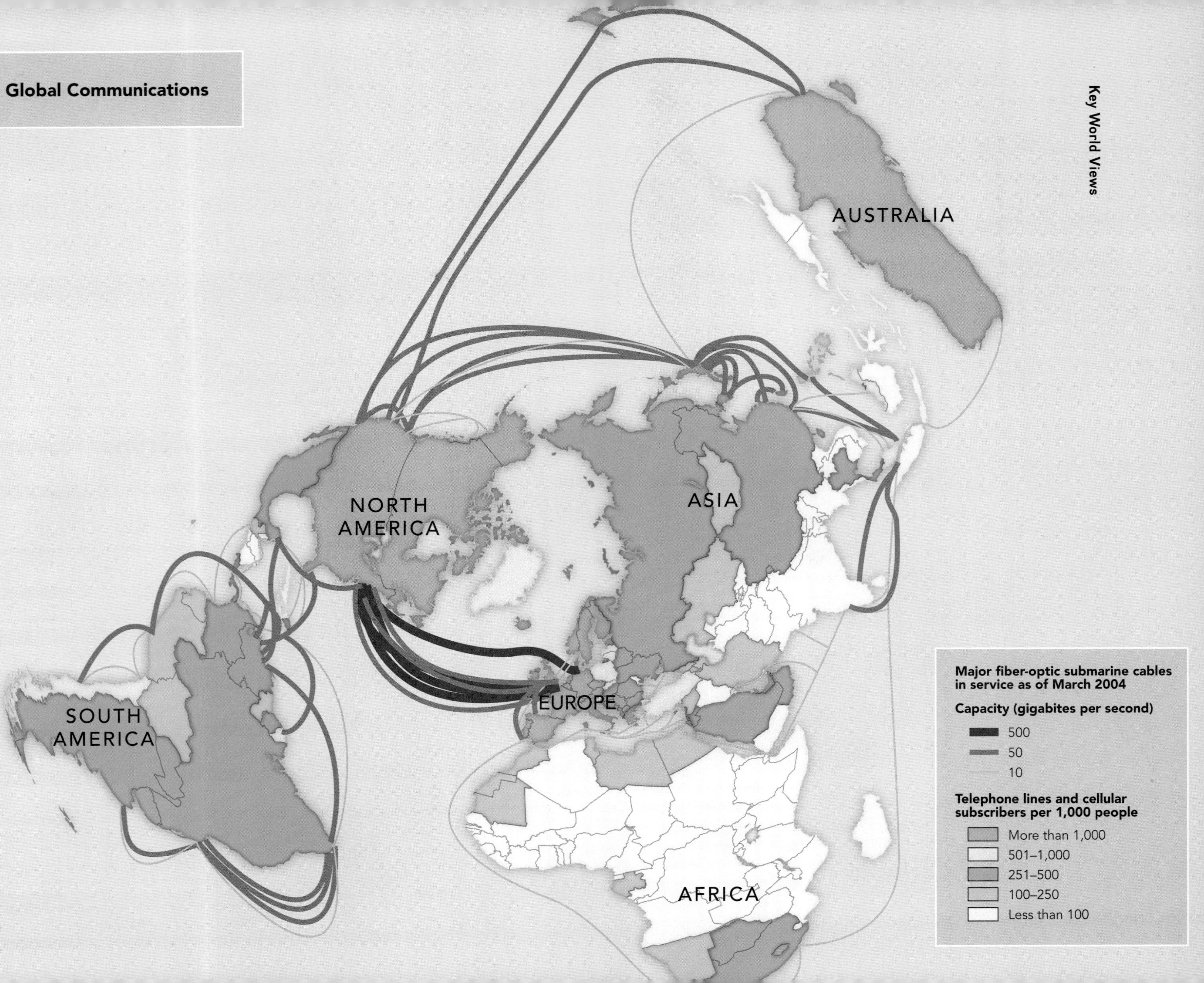

AUSTRALIA

ASIA

AFRICA

EUROPE

NORTH
AMERICA

SOUTH
AMERICA

**Major fiber-optic submarine cables
in service as of March 2004**

Capacity (gigabites per second)

500

50

10

**Telephone lines and cellular
subscribers per 1,000 people**

More than 1,000

501–1,000

251–500

100–250

Less than 100

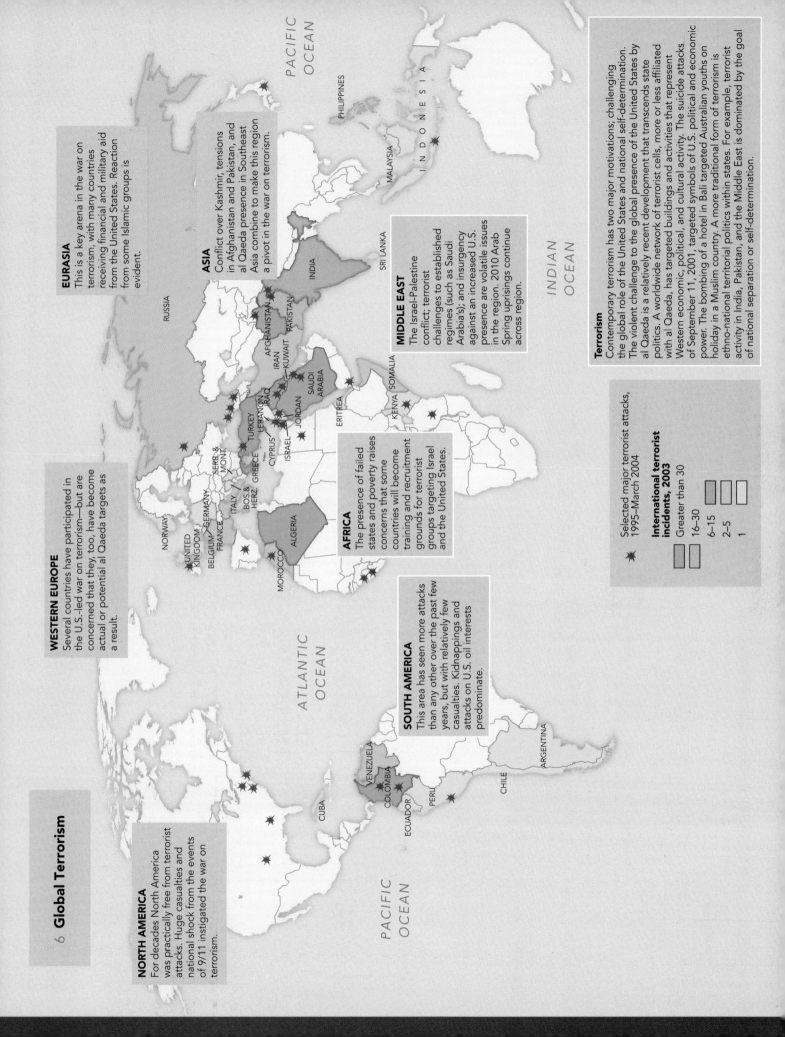

6 Global Terrorism

NORTH AMERICA
For decades North America was practically free from terrorist attacks. Huge casualties and national shock from the events of 9/11 instigated the war on terrorism.

WESTERN EUROPE
Several countries have participated in the U.S.-led war on terrorism—but are concerned that they, too, have become actual or potential al Qaeda targets as a result.

EURASIA
This is a key arena in the war on terrorism, with many countries receiving financial and military aid from the United States. Reaction from some Islamic groups is evident.

ASIA
Conflict over Kashmir, tensions in Afghanistan and Pakistan, and al Qaeda presence in Southeast Asia combine to make this region a pivot in the war on terrorism.

MIDDLE EAST
The Israel-Palestine conflict; terrorist challenges to established regimes (such as Saudi Arabia's); and insurgency against an increased U.S. presence are volatile issues in the region. 2010 Arab Spring uprisings continue across region.

AFRICA
The presence of failed states and poverty raises concerns that some countries will become training and recruitment grounds for terrorist groups targeting Israel and the United States.

SOUTH AMERICA
This area has seen more attacks than any other over the past few years, but with relatively few casualties. Kidnappings and attacks on U.S. oil interests predominate.

Terrorism
Contemporary terrorism has two major motivations; challenging the global role of the United States and national self-determination. The violent challenge to the global presence of the United States by al Qaeda is a relatively recent development that transcends state politics. A worldwide network of terrorist cells, more or less affiliated with al Qaeda, has targeted buildings and activities that represent Western economic, political, and cultural activity. The suicide attacks of September 11, 2001, targeted symbols of U.S. political and economic power. The bombing of a hotel in Bali targeted Australian youths on holiday in a Muslim country. A more traditional form of terrorism is ethno-national territorial politics within states. For example, terrorist activity in India, Pakistan, and the Middle East is dominated by the goal of national separation or self-determination.

* Selected major terrorist attacks, 1995–March 2004

International terrorist incidents, 2003

Greater than 30
16–30
6–15
2–5
1

PACIFIC OCEAN

ATLANTIC OCEAN

PACIFIC OCEAN

INDIAN OCEAN

PHILIPPINES
MALAYSIA
INDONESIA
RUSSIA
INDIA
SRI LANKA
AFGHANISTAN
PAKISTAN
IRAN
KUWAIT
IRAQ
SAUDI ARABIA
JORDAN
LEBANON
TURKEY
CYPRUS
ISRAEL
GREECE
SERB. & MONT.
BOS. & HERZ.
ITALY
FRANCE
BELGIUM
GERMANY
UNITED KINGDOM
NORWAY
ALGERIA
MOROCCO
ERITREA
SOMALIA
KENYA
VENEZUELA
COLOMBIA
ECUADOR
PERU
CHILE
ARGENTINA
CUBA

7 **Religions**

RELIGIONS

- Atheism (and Communism)
- Buddhism
- Hindu
- Muslim
- Traditional/Tribal
- Others
- Christian (Orthodox)
- Christian (no major sect)
- Christian (Protestant)
- Christian (Roman Catholic)

- Christian (no major sect), Muslim, Hindu
- Christian (no major sect), Traditional, Buddhism
- Christian (no major sect), Traditional, Hindu, Muslim
- Christian (no major sect), Christian (Roman Catholic), Hindu, Muslim, Others
- Christian (Roman Catholic), Buddhism, Others

- Christian (Roman Catholic), Muslim, Traditional
- Christian (no major sect), Muslim, Traditional
- Christian (Orthodox), Muslim, Atheism
- Christian (Roman Catholic), Muslim, Others

PACIFIC OCEAN

ASIA

AUSTRALIA

INDIAN OCEAN

AFRICA

EUROPE

ATLANTIC OCEAN

SOUTH AMERICA

NORTH AMERICA

PACIFIC OCEAN

8 Global Economy and World Trade

Trade flow

The circling paths of trade between continents show just how interconnected the world's economies truly are. The richest countries, such as those in North America, western Europe, and the Far East, trade mostly with each other, exchanging different varieties of similar goods such as automobiles. However, trade also flows between higher- and lower-income regions. In those cases, the high-income countries typically provide more complex goods, such as electronic equipment, while low-income countries provide primary goods such as minerals. Smaller, poorer countries are more likely to be dependent on exporting a single commodity, such as coffee or petroleum. In general, poor, labor-abundant countries tend to export labor-intensive goods, such as textiles and shoes, and the countries rich in arable land will export foods such as grains.

AUSTRALIA

ASIA

EUROPE

NORTH AMERICA

AFRICA

SOUTH AMERICA

World economies

High income
Upper-middle income
Lower-middle income
Low income
No income data

World merchandise trade
(in billions of U.S. dollars)

Greater than 200
101–200
31–100
5–30
Less than 5

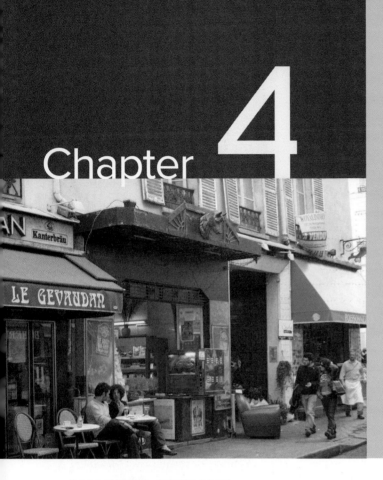

Chapter 4

Cultural Dynamics in Assessing Global Markets

CHAPTER OUTLINE

Global Perspective: Equities and eBay—Culture Gets in the Way

Culture's Pervasive Impact

Definitions and Origins of Culture

    Geography
    History
    The Political Economy
    Technology
    Social Institutions

Elements of Culture

    Cultural Values
    Rituals
    Symbols
    Beliefs
    Thought Processes
    Cultural Sensitivity and Tolerance

Cultural Change

    Cultural Borrowing
    Similarities: An Illusion
    Resistance to Change
    Planned and Unplanned Cultural Change

CHAPTER LEARNING OBJECTIVES

What you should learn from Chapter 4:

LO1   The importance of culture to an international marketer

LO2   The origins of culture

LO3   The elements of culture

LO4   The impact of cultural borrowing

LO5   The strategy of planned change and its consequences

Global Perspective

EQUITIES AND eBAY—CULTURE GETS IN THE WAY

Two trillion dollars! That's about 200 trillion yen. Either way you count it, it's a lot of money. American brokerage houses such as Fidelity Investments, Goldman Sachs, and Merrill Lynch rushed new investment products and services to market in Japan to try to capture the huge capital outflow expected from 10-year time deposits, then held in the Japanese postal system. Liberalization of Japan's capital markets in recent years gave Japanese consumers more freedom of choice in their investments. Post office time deposits still yield about a 2 percent return in Japan, and bank savings yields have been around 0. But Compared to traditional American returns on e-trading investments, that meant an electronic flood of money moving out of the post offices and into the stock markets. Right?

However, Japan is not America. There is no American-style risk-taking culture among Japanese investors. The volume of stock trading in Japan is about one-tenth that of the United States. In Japan, only 10 percent of household financial assets are directly invested in stocks and a mere 7 percent in mutual funds. In contrast, about half of U.S. households own stock. Says one analyst, "Most of the population [in Japan] doesn't know what a mutual fund is." So will the flood be just a trickle? And what about online stock trading? Internet use in Japan has burgeoned—there are now some 110 million users in Japan. That's a little greater percentage than in the United States. But the expected deluge into equities has been a dribble. Merrill Lynch and others cut back staff as fast as they built it just a couple of years before.

Making matters worse, for the Japanese, the transition into a more modern and trustworthy securities market has not been a smooth one. At the time, an astounding transaction took place on the Tokyo Stock Exchange (TSE); instead of placing a small order of 1 share for 610,000 yen of J-Com, a trader with Mizuho Securities Co. mistakenly placed a sell order for 610,000 shares for 1 yen. Mizuho ended up losing 40 billion yen ($344 million) due to a simple computer glitch that ultimately led to the resignation of TSE president Takuo Tsurushima. Ouch!

A French firm is trying to break through a similar aversion to both e-trading and equities in France. That is, about 55 million people use the Internet in France, and one-third of that number own stocks. The French have long shied away from stock market investments, seeing them as schemes to enrich insiders while fleecing novices. After the Enron (2001) and Lehman Bros. (2008) debacles in the United States, you could almost hear the chortling in the sidewalk cafés there. But even in France, investment preferences are beginning to change, especially since the real estate market has turned so volatile. At the same time, the liberalization of Europe's financial services sector is bringing down transaction costs for institutional and retail investors alike.

eBay, the personal online auction site so successful in the United States, is running into comparable difficulties in both Japan and France. For the Japanese, it is embarrassing to sell castoffs to anyone, much less buy them from strangers. Garage sales are unheard of. In France, eBay founder Pierre Omidyar's country of birth, the firm runs up against French laws that restrict operations to a few government-certified auctioneers.

Based on our knowledge of the differences in these cultural values between the United States and both Japan and France, we should expect a slower diffusion of these high-tech Internet services in the latter two countries. E-trading and e-auctions have both exploded on the American scene. However, compared with those in many other countries, U.S. investors are averse to neither the risk and uncertainties of equity investments nor the impersonal interactions of online transactions.

Sources: Sang Lee, "Japan and the Future of Electronic Trading," *Securities Industry News*, November 5, 2007; "Japan Equity Mutual Funds See Large Inflows on New Tax-Break Scheme," *Reuters*, February 14, 2014, online; *World Development Indicators*, World Bank, 2015.

LO1

The importance of
culture to an international
marketer

Culture deals with a group's design for living. It is pertinent to the study of marketing, especially international marketing. If you consider the scope of the marketing concept—the satisfaction of consumer needs and wants at a profit—the successful marketer clearly must be a student of culture. For example, when a promotional message is written, symbols recognizable and meaningful to the market (the culture) must be used. When designing a product, the style, uses, and other related marketing activities must be made culturally acceptable (i.e., acceptable to the present society) if they are to be operative and meaningful. In fact, culture is pervasive in all marketing activities—in pricing, research, promotion, channels of distribution, product, packaging, and styling—and the marketer's efforts actually become a part of the fabric of culture. How such efforts interact with a culture determines the degree of success or failure of the marketing effort.

The manner in and amount which people consume, the priority of needs and wants they attempt to satisfy, and the manner in which they satisfy them are functions of their culture that temper, mold, and dictate their style of living. Culture is the human-made part of human environment—the sum total of knowledge, beliefs, art, morals, laws, customs, and any other capabilities and habits acquired by humans as members of society.[1]

Markets constantly change; they are not static but evolve, expand, and contract in response to marketing effort, economic conditions, and other cultural influences. Markets and market behavior are part of a country's culture. One cannot truly understand how markets evolve or how they react to a marketer's effort without appreciating that markets are a result of culture. Markets are the result of the three-way interaction of a marketer's efforts, economic conditions, and all other elements of the culture. Marketers are constantly adjusting their efforts to cultural demands of the market, but they also are acting as *agents of change* whenever the product or idea being marketed is innovative. Whatever the degree of acceptance, the use of something new is the beginning of cultural change, and the marketer becomes a change agent.

This is the first of four chapters that focus on culture and international marketing. A discussion of the broad concept of culture as the foundation for international marketing is presented in this chapter. The next chapter, "Culture, Management Style, and Business Systems," discusses culture and how it influences business practices and the behaviors and thinking of managers. Chapters 6 and 7 examine elements of culture essential to the study of international marketing: the political environment and the legal environment.

This chapter's purpose is to heighten the reader's sensitivity to the dynamics of culture. It is neither a treatise on cultural information about a particular country nor a thorough marketing science or epidemiological study of the various topics. Rather, it is designed to emphasize the importance of cultural differences to marketers and the need to study each country's culture(s) and all its origins and elements, as well as point out some relevant aspects on which to focus.

Culture's Pervasive Impact

Culture affects every part of our lives, every day, from birth to death, and everything in between.[2] It affects how we spend money and how we consume in general. It even affects how we sleep. For example, we are told that Spaniards sleep less than other Europeans, and Japanese children often sleep with their parents. You can clearly see culture operating in the birthrate tables in Exhibit 4.1. When you look across the data from the three countries, the gradual declines beginning in the 1960s are evident. As countries move from agricultural to industrial to services economies, birthrates decline. Immediate causes may be government policies and birth control technologies, but a global change in values is also occurring. Almost everywhere, smaller families are becoming favored. This cultural change now leads experts to predict that the planet's population may actually

---

[1] An interesting website that has information on various cultural traits, gestures, holidays, language, religions, and so forth is http://www.culturegrams.com.

[2] A most important summary of research in the area of culture's impact on consumption behavior is Eric J. Arnould and Craig J. Thompson, "Consumer Culture Theory (CCT): Twenty Years of Research," *Journal of Consumer Research* 3, no. 2 (March 2005), pp. 868–82.

Exhibit 4.1

Birthrates (per 1,000 women)

Source: World Bank, *World Development Indicators* by International Bank for Reconstruction and Development, 2012. Copyright © 2012 by World Bank. Reproduced with permission of World Bank via Copyright Clearance Center.

■ United States Birthrate

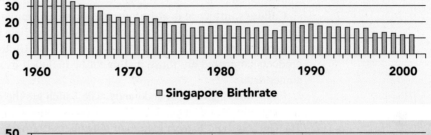

▣ Singapore Birthrate

▣ Japan Birthrate

begin to decline after the middle of the century unless major breakthroughs in longevity intervene, as some predict.

But a closer look at the tables reveals even more interesting consequences of culture. Please notice the little peaks in 1976 and 1988 in the Singapore data. The same pattern can be seen in birthrate data from Taiwan. Those "extra" births are not a matter of random fluctuation. In Chinese cultures, being born in the Year of the Dragon[3] (12 animals—dogs, rats, rabbits, pigs, etc.—correspond to specific years in the calendar) is considered good luck. Such birthrate spikes have implications for sellers of diapers, toys, schools, colleges, and so forth in successive years in Singapore. However, culture-based superstitions[4] have an even stronger influence on the birthrates in Japan, as shown in Exhibit 4.1. A one-year 20 percent drop in Japanese fertility rates in 1966 was caused by a belief that women born in the Year of the Fire Horse, which occurs every 60 years, will lead unhappy lives and perhaps murder their husbands. This sudden and substantial decline in fertility, which has occurred historically every 60 years since Japan started keeping birth records, reflects abstinence, abortions, and birth certificate fudging. This superstition has resulted in the stigmatization of women born in 1966 and had a large impact on market potential for a wide variety of consumer goods and services in Japan. It will be interesting to see how technological innovations and culture will interact in Japan in 2026, the next Year of the Fire Horse.[5]

---

[3]Vinicy Chan, "A Dragon May Give China's Economy a Lift," *Bloomberg BusinessWeek*, December 12, 2011, pp. 33, 36.

[4]We know that superstitions can influence other kinds of consumers judgments as well. See Thomas Kramer and Lauren Block, "Conscious and Nonconscious Components of Superstitious Beliefs in Judgment and Decision Making," *Journal of Consumer Research* 34, no. 2 (2008), pp. 783–93.

[5]Robert W. Hodge and Naohiro Ogawa, *Fertility Change in Contemporary Japan* (Chicago: University of Chicago Press, 1991).

Exhibit 4.2

Patterns of Consumption
(annual, per capita)

Source: CBI Marketing Information Data Base, "CBI Tradewatch for Cut Flowers and Foliage," http://www.cbi.eu, 2012 and 2015. EuroMonitor International, 2015.

Country	Cut Flowers (€)	Chocolate (kg)	Fish and Seafood (kg)	Dried Pasta (kg)	Wine (liters)	Tobacco (sticks)
France	42	4.3	5.2	9.2	37.9	682
Germany	48	8.1	8.6	9.0	24.6	980
Italy	45	2.5	8.3	24.7	35.1	1147
Netherlands	49	4.9	4.8	3.7	25.7	659
Spain	23	2.1	28.2	5.2	19.5	911
United Kingdom	38	8.0	11.3	4.7	21.2	568
Japan	46	1.1	32.1	8.0	7.2	1490
United States	32	4.4	5.0	2.2	9.9	874

Culture's influence is also illustrated in the consumption data presented in Exhibit 4.2. The focus there is on the six European Union countries, but data from the two other major markets of affluence in the world—Japan and the United States—are also included. The products compared are those that might be included in a traditional (American) romantic dinner date.

First come the flowers and candy. The Dutch are the champion consumers of cut flowers, and this particular preference for petals will be explored further in the pages to come. The Germans and British love their chocolates. Perhaps the cooler temperatures have historically allowed for easier storage and better quality in the northern countries. At least among our six EU countries, per capita chocolate consumption appears to decline with latitude.

In Europe, the Spaniards are the most likely to feast on fish. But they are still well behind the Japanese preference for seafood. From the data in the table, one might conclude that being surrounded by water in Japan explains the preference for seafood. However, what about the British? The flat geography in England and Scotland allows for the efficient production of beef, and a bit later in this section, we consider the consequences of their strong preference for red meat. The Italians eat more pasta—not a surprise. History is important. The product was actually invented in China, but in 1270, Marco Polo is reputed to have brought the innovation back to Italy, where it has flourished. Proximity to China also explains the high rate of Japanese noodle (but not dried pasta) consumption.

How about alcohol and tobacco? Grapes grow best in France and Italy, so a combination of climate and soil conditions explains at least part of the pattern of wine consumption seen in Exhibit 4.2. Culture also influences the laws, age limits, and such related to alcohol. The legal environment also has implications for the consumption of cigarettes. Although expenditures on tobacco generally are rising in these countries because of increasing taxes, the amount consumed is declining universally. We've been monitoring these data for more than two decades now, and the single most astonishing change has been the halving of cigarette consumption in Spain during the last six years. The average decline for all eight countries for the same time period was about 20 percent. The steep decline had already begun there in 2009, but the 2011 anti-smoking law that prohibited smoking in all bars and restaurants appears to have accelerated the decline in consumption. Overall, these dramatic declines represent a huge cultural shift that the world seldom sees.

Any discussion of tobacco consumption leads immediately to consideration of the consequences of consumption. One might expect that a high consumption of the romance products—flowers, candy, and wine—might lead to a high birthrate. Reference to Exhibit 4.3 doesn't yield any clear conclusions. The Germans have some of the highest consumption levels of the romantic three but the lowest birthrate among the six European countries. During the last six years, the German birthrate has increased slightly, while the Japanese birthrate continues its steady decline.

Perhaps the Japanese diet's emphasis on fish yields them the longest life expectancy. But length of life among the eight affluent countries represented in the table shows little variation. How people die, however, does vary substantially across the countries. The influence of fish versus red meat consumption on the incidence of heart problems is easy to see.

Finding horse or donkey as your entrée would not be romantic or even appetizing in most places around the world. Even though horse consumption is generally declining in France, here in Paris you can still buy a steed steak at the local *bouchers chevaleries*. Escargot *oui*, Eeyore *oui*! And we note a recent article in *The Wall Street Journal* advocating the consumption of dog in the United States, including a recipe. Yikes! Meanwhile, it should be pointed out that horse meat is appreciated by some in other countries such as Italy and China[7].

As the evidence that sugar is toxic continues to accumulate,[6] the connection between chocolate (sugar) consumption and heart disease is apparent in our data. Among the countries listed, the diabetes mellitus death rates have declined in five of the countries, with America showing the largest improvement over 2009–2014. Over the same time period, the numbers are worse in both Italy and Germany, with the increases of 4 and 13 percent, respectively.

The most interesting datum in the table is the extremely high incidence of stomach cancer in Japan. The latest studies suggest two culprits: (1) salty foods such as soy sauce and (2) the bacterium *Helicobacter pylori*. The latter is associated with the unsanitary conditions prevalent in Japan immediately after World War II, and it is still hurting health in Japan today. Finally, because stomach cancer in Japan is so prevalent, the Japanese have developed the most advanced treatment of the disease, that is, both procedures and instruments. Even though the death rate is highest, the treatment success rate is likewise the highest in Japan. Whether you are in Tacoma, Toronto, or Tehran, the best medicine for stomach cancer may be a ticket to Tokyo. Indeed, this last example well demonstrates that culture not only affects consumption; it also affects production (of medical services in this case)!

The point is that culture matters.[8] It is imperative for foreign marketers to learn to appreciate the intricacies of cultures different from their own if they are to be effective in foreign markets.

[6]Robert H. Lustig, *Fat Chance: Sugar, Processed Food, Obesity, and Disease* (New York: Plume, 2012).
[7]Jonathan Safran Foer, "Let Them Eat Dog," *The Wall Street Journal*, October 31, 2009, p. W10.
[8]"After the Horse Has Been Bolted," *The Economist*, February 16, 2013, pp. 64–65.

Exhibit 4.3
Consequences of Consumption

| Country | Birthrates (per 1,000) | Life Expectancy | Death Rate per 100,000 | | | |
			Ischemic Heart Disease	Diabetes Mellitus	Lung Cancer	Stomach Cancer
France	13.1	82.2	58.6	18.3	52.2	7.8
Germany	8.6	81.2	161.3	30.8	56.7	12.6
Italy	8.9	82.6	120.2	35.2	60.6	16.8
Netherlands	10.7	81.3	57.8	16.4	64.8	8.5
Spain	9.5	82.6	77.6	22.4	48.0	12.5
United Kingdom	12.8	81.2	121.0	9.7	56.4	7.7
Japan	7.9	83.3	62.1	11.7	56.5	39.4
United States	12.7	78.9	120.1	22.3	51.6	3.7

Source: EuroMonitor 2015.

The Floriad, the biggest exhibition of flowers on earth, happens once every decade. You can go to the next one in 2022.

Outside the Aalsmeer Flower Auction—notice the jet landing at nearby Schiphol Airport, which serves both Amsterdam and Aalsmeer.

The Pope in St. Peter's Square for the holiest Christian ritual, the celebration of Easter Sunday. The pageantry includes the colorful Swiss guards and flowers sent by the Dutch.

The Amsterdam flower market—a busy place for local consumers and tourists.

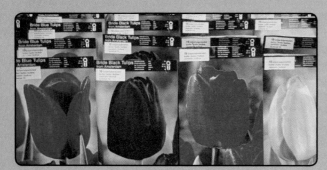
Four hundred years later, the one-dollar black tulip is available in the Amsterdam flower market.

We all love flowers. But for the Dutch, flowers are more important than that. For them, it's more like a national fascination, fixation, or even a fetish for flowers. Why?

The answer is an instructive story about culture and international markets, the broader subjects of this chapter. The story starts with geography, goes through the origins and elements of culture, and ends with the Dutch being the masters of the exhibition, consumption, and production of flowers.

Geography.
The rivers and the bays make the Netherlands a great trading country. But the miserable weather, rain, and snow more than 200 days per year make it a colorless place, gray nearly year-round. The Flying Dutchmen not only went to the Spice Islands for spice for the palate; they also went to the eastern Mediterranean for spice for the eyes. The vibrant colors of the tulip first came to Europe from the Ottoman Empire on a Dutch ship in 1561.

History.
The Dutch enthusiasm for the new "visual drug" was great. Its most potent form was, ironically, the black tulip. Prices exploded, and speculators bought and sold promissory notes guaranteeing the future delivery of black tulip bulbs. This derivatives market yielded prices in today's dollars of $1 million or more for a single bulb, enough to buy a 5-story house in central Amsterdam today. Not only did the tulip mania create futures markets, it also caused the first great market bust in recorded history. Prices plummeted when the government took control in 1637. Now at the Amsterdam flower market, you can buy a black tulip bulb for about a dollar!

A view of a Dutch harbor with trading ships circa 1600.

Inside Aalsmeer, 150 football fields of cut flowers, 20 million per day, are readied for auction.

The bidders in four huge auction rooms pay attention to the "clock" as high starting prices tick down. The wholesale buyer that stops the clock pays the associated price in this the archetypical "Dutch auction."

Technology and Economics.

The technology in the story comes in the name of Carolus Clusius, a botanist who developed methods for manipulating the colors of the tulips in the early 1600s. This manipulation added to their appeal and value, and the tulip trade became international for the Dutch.

Social Institutions.

Every Easter Sunday, the Pope addresses the world at St. Peter's Square in Rome reciting, "Bedankt voor bloemen." Thus, he thanks the Dutch nation for providing the flowers for this key Catholic ritual. The Dutch government, once every tenth year, sponsors the largest floriculture exhibition in the world, the Floriad. You can go next in 2022. Finally, at the Aalsmeer Flower Auction near Amsterdam, the prices are set for all flowers in all markets around the world. The Dutch remain the largest exporters of flowers (60 percent global market share), shipping them across Europe by trucks and worldwide by air freight.

Outside again at Aalsmeer, trucks are loaded for shipment by land across Europe and airfreight worldwide.

Cultural Values.

The high value the Dutch place on flowers is reflected in many ways, not the least of which is their high consumption rate, as seen in Exhibit 4.2.

Aesthetics as Symbols.

Rembrandt Van Rijn's paintings, including his most famous *Night Watch* (1642, Rijksmuseum, Amsterdam), reflect a dark palette. Artists generally paint in the colors of their surroundings. A quarter century later, his compatriot Vincent Van Gogh used a similar bleak palette when he worked in Holland. Later, when Van Gogh went to the sunny and colorful south of France, the colors begin to explode on his canvases. And, of course, there he painted flowers!

Rembrandt's *Night Watch*.

Van Gogh's *Vase with Fifteen Sunflowers*, painted in the south of France in 1889, and sold to a Japanese insurance executive for some $40 million in 1987, at the time the highest price ever paid for a single work of art. The Japanese are also big flower consumers—see Exhibit 4.2.

Van Gogh's *Potato Eaters*, painted in The Netherlands in 1885.

CROSSING BORDERS 4.1   Human Universals: The Myth of Diversity?

Yes, culture's influence is pervasive. But as anthropologist Donald E. Brown correctly points out, we are all human. And since we are all of the same species, we actually share a great deal. Here's a few of the hundreds of traits we share:

Use metaphors

Have a system of status and roles

Are ethnocentric

Create art

Conceive of success and failure

Create groups antagonistic to outsiders

Imitate outside influences

Resist outside influences

Consider aspects of sexuality private

Express emotions with face

Reciprocate

Use mood-altering drugs

Overestimate objectivity of thought

Have a fear of snakes

Recognize economic obligations in exchanges of goods and services

Trade and transport goods

Indeed, the last two suggest that we might be characterized as the "exchanging animal."

Source: Donald E. Brown, *Human Universals* (New York: McGraw-Hill, 1991). Reprinted with permission of The McGraw-Hill Companies.

Definitions and Origins of Culture

LO2

The origins of culture

There are many ways to think about culture. Dutch management professor Geert Hofstede refers to culture as the "software of the mind" and argues that it provides a guide for humans on how to think and behave; it is a problem-solving tool.[9] Anthropologist and business consultant Edward Hall provides a definition even more relevant to international marketing managers: "The people we were advising kept bumping their heads against an invisible barrier. . . . We knew that what they were up against was a completely different way of organizing life, of thinking, and of conceiving the underlying assumptions about the family and the state, the economic system, and even Man himself."[10] The salient points in Hall's comments are that cultural differences are often invisible and that marketers who ignore them often hurt both their companies and careers. Finally, James Day Hodgson, former U.S. ambassador to Japan, describes culture as a "thicket."[11] This last metaphor holds hope for struggling international marketers. According to the ambassador, thickets are tough to get through, but effort and patience often lead to successes.

Most traditional definitions of culture center around the notion that culture is the sum of the *values, rituals, symbols, beliefs,* and *thought processes* that are *learned* and *shared* by a group of people,[12] then *transmitted* from generation to generation.[13] So culture resides in the individual's mind. But the expression "a culture" recognizes that large collectives of people can, to a great degree, be like-minded.

---

[9]Geert Hofstede, Gert Jan Hofstede, and Michael Minkov, *Cultures and Organizations*, 3rd ed. (New York: McGraw-Hill, 2011). Susan P. Douglas, "Exploring New Worlds: The Challenge of Global Marketing," *Journal of Marketing*, January 2001, pp. 103–9.

[10]Edward T. Hall, *The Silent Language* (New York: Doubleday, 1959), p. 26.

[11]James D. Hodgson, Yoshihiro Sano, and John L. Graham, *Doing Business in the New Japan, Succeeding in America's Richest Foreign Market* (Latham, MD: Rowman & Littlefield, 2008).

[12]Please note that the group may be smaller than that defined by nation. See Rosalie Tung, "The Cross-Cultural Research Imperative: The Need to Balance Cross-Cultural and Intra-National Diversity," *Journal of International Business Studies* 39 (2008), pp. 41–46; Jean-Francois Ouellet, "Consumer Racism and Its Effects on Domestic Cross-Ethnic Product Purchase: An Empirical Test in the United States, Canada, and France," *Journal of Marketing* 71 (2007), pp. 113–28.

[13]Melvin Herskovitz, *Man and His Works* (New York: Alfred A. Knopf, 1952), p. 634. See also Chapter 10, "Culture," in Raymond Scupin and Christopher R. Decorse, *Anthropology: A Global Perspective*, 6th ed. (Englewood Cliffs, NJ: Prentice Hall, 2005).

Exhibit 4.4
Origins, Elements, and Consequences of Culture

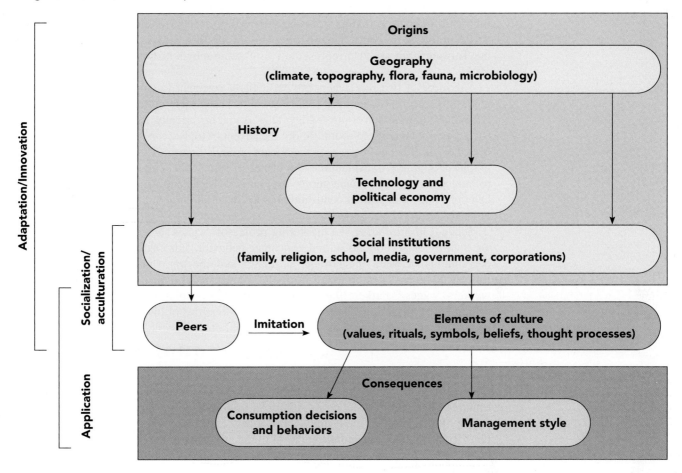

The best international marketers will not only appreciate the cultural differences pertinent to their businesses, but they will also understand the origins of these differences. Possession of the latter, deeper knowledge will help marketers notice cultural differences in new markets and foresee changes in current markets of operation. Exhibit 4.4 depicts the several causal factors and social processes that determine and form cultures and cultural differences. Simply stated, humans make *adaptations* to changing environments through *innovation*. Individuals learn culture from social institutions through *socialization* (growing up) and *acculturation* (adjusting to a new culture). Individuals also absorb culture through role modeling, or imitation of their peers. Finally, people make decisions about consumption and production through *application* of their cultural-based knowledge. More details are provided below.

Geography   In the previous chapter, we described the immediate effects of geography on consumer choice. But geography exercises a more profound influence than just affecting the sort of jacket you buy. Indeed, geography (broadly defined here to include climate, topography, flora, fauna, and microbiology) has influenced history, technology, economics, what is farmed and eaten,[14] our social institutions, perhaps even the boy-to-girl birth ratio,[15]

---

[14]"You Are What You Eat," *The Economist*, May 10, 2014, p. 78.

[15]Nicholoas Bakalar, "Why Does Latitude Affect Boy-Girl Ratios?" *International Herald Tribune*, April 23, 2009, p. 10.

and, yes, our ways of thinking.[16] Geographical influences manifest themselves in our deepest cultural values developed through the millennia, and as geography changes, humans can adapt almost immediately. One sees the latter happening in the new interaction rituals evolving from the HIV/AIDS disaster or more recently the 2003 SARS outbreak in China. The ongoing cultural divides across the English Channel or the Taiwan Strait are also representative of geography's historical salience in human affairs.

The ideas of two researchers are particularly pertinent to any discussion of geography's influence on everything from history to present-day cultural values. First, Jared Diamond,[17] a professor of physiology, tells us that historically, innovations spread faster east to west than north to south. Before the advent of transoceanic shipping, ideas flowed over the Silk Road but not across the Sahara or the Isthmus of Panama. He uses this geographical approach to explain the dominance of Euro-Asian cultures, with their superior technology and more virulent germs, over native African and American cultures. Indeed, Diamond's most important contribution is his material on the influence of microbiology on world history.

Second, Philip Parker,[18] a marketing professor, argues for geography's deep influence on history, economics, and consumer behavior. For example, he reports strong correlations between the latitude (climate) and the per capita GDP of countries. Empirical support can be found in others' reports of climate's apparent influence on workers' wages.[19] Parker, like Diamond before him, explains social phenomena using principles of physiology. The management implications of his treatise have to do with using ambient temperature as a market segmentation variable. We return to this issue in Chapter 8.

History

The impact of specific events in history can be seen reflected in technology, social institutions, cultural values, and even consumer behavior. Diamond's book is filled with examples. For instance, much of American trade policy has depended on the happenstance of tobacco (i.e., the technology of a new cash crop) being the original source of the Virginia colony's economic survival in the 1600s. In a like manner, the Declaration of Independence, and thereby Americans' values and institutions, was fundamentally influenced by the coincident 1776 publication of Adam Smith's *The Wealth of Nations*. Notice too that the military conflicts in the Middle East in 2003 bred new cola brands as alternatives to Coca-Cola—Mecca Cola, Muslim Up, Arab Cola, and ColaTurka.[20] Perhaps most important are the ripple effects of World War II. For example, Germany's long-standing mistrust of propaganda has yielded a variety of unusual limitations on marketing practices.[21] The post-War baby boom still affects consumption patterns around the world.[22]

[16]Richard E. Nisbett, *The Geography of Thought: How Asians and Westerners Think Differently . . . and Why* (New York: The Free Press, 2003).

[17]Jared Diamond's *Guns, Germs and Steel: The Fates of the Human Societies* (New York: Norton, 1999) is a Pulitzer Prize winner, recipient of the Phi Beta Kappa Award in Science, and a wonderful read for anyone interested in history and/or innovation. PBS also has produced a video version of *Guns, Germs and Steel.* Also see Diamond's more recent book, *Collapse* (New York: Viking, 2005).

[18]Philip Parker's *Physioeconomics* (Cambridge, MA: MIT Press, 2000) is a data-rich discussion of global economics well worth reading.

[19]Evert Van de Vliert, "Thermoclimate, Culture, and Poverty as Country-Level Roots of Workers' Wages," *Journal of International Business Studies* 34, no. 1 (2003), pp. 40–52.

[20]See http://www.colaturka.com.tr.

[21]Pamela E. Sweet, S. Jonathan Wiesen, and Jonathan R. Zatlin, eds., *Selling Modernity: Advertising in Twentieth-Century Germany* (Durham, NC: Duke University Press, 2007).

[22]John L. Graham, "Solution to US Debt Woes Isn't Economic, Its Social," *Christian Science Monitor,* July 27, 2011; Sharon G. Niederhaus, and John L. Graham, *All in the Family: A Practical Guide to Successful Multigenerational Living* (Boulder, CO: Taylor Trade, 2013).

The Political Economy

For most of the 20th century, four approaches to governance competed for world dominance: colonialism, fascism, communism, and democracy/free enterprise. Fascism fell in 1945. Colonialism was also a casualty of World War II, though its death throes lasted well into the second half of the century. Communism crumbled in the 1990s.[23] One pundit even declared the "end of history."[24] Unfortunately, we have September 11 and the conflicts in the Middle East to keep the list of bad things growing. Much more detail is included in Chapters 6 and 7 on the influences of politics and the legal environment on the culture of commerce and consumption, so we will leave this important topic until then. The main point here is for you to appreciate the influence of the political economy on social institutions and cultural values and ways of thinking.

Technology

Sit back for a moment and consider what technological innovation has had the greatest impact on institutions and cultural values in the past 100 years in the United States. Seriously, stop reading, look out your window, and for a moment consider the question.

There are many good answers, but only one best one. Certainly jet aircraft, air conditioning, televisions,[25] computers, mobile phones, and the Internet all make the list. But the best answer is most likely the pill.[26] That is, the birth control pill, or more broadly birth control techniques, have had a huge effect on everyday life for most Americans and people around the world. Mainly, it has freed women to have careers and freed men to spend more time with kids. Before the advent of the pill, men's and women's roles were proscribed by reproductive responsibilities and roles. Now half the marketing majors in the United States are women, and 10 percent of the crews on U.S. Navy ships are women. Before the pill, these numbers were unimaginable.

Obviously, not everyone is happy with these new "freedoms." For example, in 1968, the Roman Catholic Church forbade use of the birth control pill. But the technology of birth control undeniably has deeply affected social institutions and cultural values. Families are smaller, and government and schools are forced to address issues such as abstinence and condom distribution.

Finally, the reader will notice that technology does not solve all problems. For example, few would argue with the idea that the United States leads the world in healthcare technology, yet this technological leadership doesn't deliver the best healthcare system. Other aspects of culture make a difference. Thus, citizens in many countries around the world have greater longevity (the most objective measure of the quality of healthcare delivery in a country), as mentioned earlier in this chapter. Consumer lifestyle choices and the financial structure affect the U.S. healthcare system dramatically as well. Please see Exhibit 4.5 for a quick comparison of systems across countries.

Social Institutions

Social institutions including *family, religion, school, the media, government,* and *corporations* all affect the ways in which people relate to one another, organize their activities to live in harmony with one another, teach acceptable behavior to succeeding generations, and govern themselves. The positions of men and women in society, the family, social classes,[27] group behavior, age groups, and how societies define decency

---

[23]Some might argue that communism has survived in North Korea, Cuba, or the Peoples' Republic of China, but at least in the last two cases, free enterprise is on the ascendancy. The three look more like dictatorships to most.

[24]Francis Fukuyama, *The End of History and the Last Man* (New York: The Free Press, 1992).

[25]Sandra K. Smith Speck and Abhijit Roy, "The Interrelationships between Television Viewing, Values, and Perceived Well-Being: A Global Perspective," *Journal of International Business Studies* 39, no. 7 (2008), pp. 1197–219.

[26]Bernard Asbell, *The Pill: A Biography of the Drug that Changed the World* (New York: Random House, 1995).

[27]Tuba Ustuner and Douglas B. Holt, "Toward a Theory of Consumption in Less Industrialized Countries," *Journal of Consumer Research* 37, no. 1 (2010), pp. 37–56.

Exhibit 4.5
Comparison of Healthcare Systems

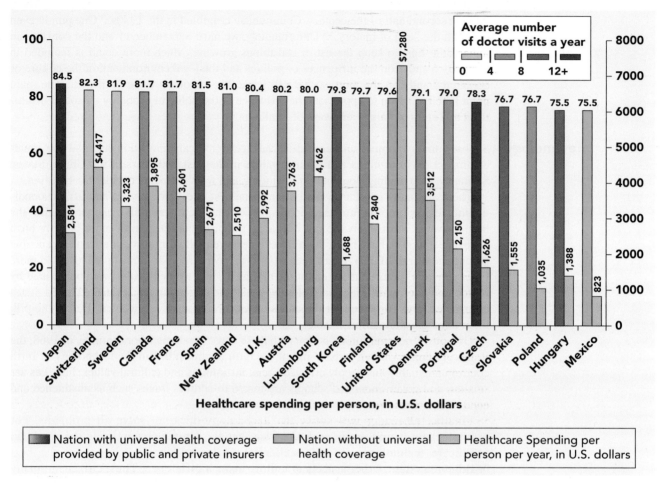

Healthcare spending per person, in U.S. dollars

Average number of doctor visits a year
0   4   8   12+

- ■ Nation with universal health coverage provided by public and private insurers
- ■ Nation without universal health coverage
- ■ Healthcare Spending per person per year, in U.S. dollars

Source: Michelle Andrews, "Health, The Cost of Care," *National Geographic Magazine*, December 2009. Oliver Uberti/National Geographic Stock. Reprinted with permission.

and civility are interpreted differently within every culture. In cultures in which the social organizations result in close-knit family units, for example, a promotion campaign aimed at the family unit is usually more effective than one aimed at individual family members. Travel advertising in culturally divided Canada has pictured a wife alone for the English-speaking market segment but a man and wife together for the French-speaking segments of the population, because the latter are traditionally more closely bound by family ties.

The roles and status positions found within a society are influenced by the dictates of social institutions. The caste system in India is one such institution. The 1997 election of K.R. Narayanan, a low-caste person—once called an "untouchable"—as president made international news because it was such a departure from traditional Indian culture. Decades ago, brushing against an untouchable or even glancing at one was considered enough to defile a Hindu of high status. Even though the caste system has been outlawed, it remains a part of the culture.

Family.   The technology of birth control has tremendously affected families and reduced family sizes around the world, as described earlier. Women are not only putting off child bearing, but in some countries, they are putting off marriage as well. In

America, single women are chosing to have children without marriage.[28] This trend is particularly notable in Asia, where the percentages of women aged 35–39 years who have never married has burgeoned to more than 15 percent, up from about 5 percent in 1970.[29] In Japan where this circumstance has led to a fast shrinking population, government is taking action. The federal government now provides monthly allowances of $150 per child. One provincial government has established an online dating service called the Fukui Marriage Hunting Cafe.[30] Despite all this, apparently some younger Japanese are simply preferring celibacy and avoiding dating.[31] Other governments are in the dating game too, as evidenced by Singapore's LoveByte website. Of course, in India the tradition is for arranged marriages, now supported by online services.[32]

Yet family forms and functions also vary substantially around the world, even around the country.[33] For example, whereas nepotism is seen as a problem in American organizations, it is more often seen as an organizing principle in Chinese and Mexican[34] firms. Or consider the Dutch executive who lives with his mother, wife, and kids in a home in Maastricht that his family has owned for the last 300 years. Then there's the common practice of the high-income folks in Cairo buying an apartment house and filling it up with the extended family—grandparents, married siblings, cousins, and kids. Or how about the Japanese mother caring for her two children pretty much by herself, often sleeping with them at night, while her husband catches up on sleep during his four hours a day commuting via train. And there's the American family in California—both parents work to support their cars, closets, and kids in college, all the while worrying about aging grandparents halfway across the country. In the States technology is also getting into the game in other ways. It is now easy to track your kids, although privacy issues are controversial.[35]

Even the ratio of male to female children is affected by culture (as well as latitude). In most European countries the ratio is about fifty-fifty. However, the gender percentage of boys aged one to six years is 52 in India and of those aged one to four years is 55 in China. Obviously these ratios have long-term implications for families and societies. Moreover, the favoritism for boys is deep-seated in such cultures. For example, you can find the gender discrimination in poetry in China circa 800 BC.

All these differences lead directly to differences in how children think and behave. For example, individualism is being taught the first night the American infant is tucked into her own separate bassinette. Values for egalitarianism are learned the first time Dad washes the dishes in front of the kids or Mom heads off to work or the toddler learns that both Grandpa and little brother are properly called "you." And there is some good news about gender

[28]"The Fraying Knot," *The Economist*, January 12, 2013, pp. 27–28.

[29]"The Flight from Marriage," *The Economist,* August 20, 2011, pp. 21–24.

[30]Aki Ito with Monami Yui, "Bureaucrats Play Matchmaker in Japan," *Bloomberg BusinessWeek,* September 5, 2010, p. 12.

[31] Abigail Hayworth, "(No) Sex in the City," *Marie Claire*, August 2013, pp. 109–115.

[32] Diane Brady, "In India, Arranged Marriages Hit the Web," *Bloomberg BusinessWeek*, April 8, 2013, pp. 18–19.

[33]Michael Finkel's description of a hunter-gather tribe's everyday life, as observed in Tanzania, is important as a representation of family life and structure in people's primordial state. See "The Hadza," *National Geographic*, December 2009, pp. 94–118; also see John L. Graham, "Solution to US Debt Woes Isn't Economic, Its Social," *Christian Science Monitor,* July 27, 2011; *All in the Family,* Niederhaus and Graham, 2013.

[34]Anabella Davila and Marta M. Elvira, "Culture and Human Resource Management in Latin America." In *Managing Human Resources in Latin America*, ed. Marta M. Elvira and Anabella Davila. (London: Routledge, 2005), pp. 3–24.

[35] "Chips Off the Old Block," *The Economist,* January 12, 2013, pp. 53–54.

In the United States, kids attend school 180 days per year; in China, they attend over 220 days—that's six days a week. There's a great thirst for the written word in China—here children read books rented from a street vendor.

equality to share: The education gap between men and women is narrowing in many places around the world—for example, the majority of university students in the United States are now women.

Religion.   In most cultures, the first social institution infants are exposed to outside the home takes the form of a church, mosque, shrine, or synagogue. The impact of religion on the value systems of a society and the effect of value systems on marketing must not be underestimated.[36] For example, Protestants believe that one's relationship with God is a personal one, and confessions are made directly through prayer. Alternatively, Roman Catholics confess to priests, setting up a hierarchy within the Church. Thus some scholars reason that Protestantism engenders egalitarian thinking. But no matter the details, religion clearly affects people's habits, their outlook on life, the products they buy, the way they buy them, and even the newspapers they read.

The influence of religion is often quite strong, so marketers with little or no understanding of a religion may readily offend deeply. For example, the South African government banned an Axe deodorant advertisement from television, when it portrayed angels tossing their halos— an image that offended Christians there.[37] One's own religion is often not a reliable guide to another's beliefs. Most people do not understand religions other than their own, and/or what is "known" about other religions is often incorrect. The Islamic religion is a good example of the need for a basic understanding of all major religions. More than one billion people in the world embrace Islam, yet major multinational companies often offend Muslims. The French fashion house of Chanel unwittingly desecrated the Koran by embroidering verses from the sacred book of Islam on several dresses shown in its summer collections. The designer said he had taken the design, which was aesthetically pleasing to him, from a book on India's Taj Mahal and that he was unaware of its meaning. To placate a Muslim group that felt the use of the verses desecrated the Koran, Chanel had to destroy the dresses with the offending designs, along with negatives of the photos taken of the garments. Chanel certainly had no intention of offending Muslims, since some of its most important customers embrace Islam. This example shows how easy it is to offend if the marketer, in this case the designer, has not familiarized him- or herself with other religions.

School.   Education, one of the most important social institutions, affects all aspects of the culture, from economic development to consumer behavior. The literacy rate of a country is a potent force in economic development. Numerous studies indicate a direct link between the literacy rate of a country and its capability for rapid economic growth. According to the World Bank, no country has been successful economically with less than 50 percent literacy, but when countries have invested in education, the economic rewards

[36]Praveen K. Kopalle, Donald R. Lehmann, and John U. Farley, "Consumer Expectations and Culture: The Effect of Belief in Karma in India," *Journal of Consumer Research* 37 (2010), pp. 251–68.

[37]Lindsey Goltwert, "Axe 'Angels' Deodorant Ad Yanked for Offending Christians," *New York Daily News,* October 29, 2011.

Exhibit 4.6

OECD Program for International Student Assessment (PISA) Selected Scores and (Rankings) for 15-Year-Olds, 2013

Source: OECD, PISA, http://www.economist.com/node/21529014, 2015.

Top Ten and Selected Others

Country	Reading	Math	Science
Shanghai, China	570 (1)	613 (1)	580 (1)
Hong Kong, China	545 (2)	561 (3)	555 (2)
Singapore	542 (3)	573 (2)	551 (3)
Japan	538 (4)	536 (7)	547 (4)
South Korea	536 (5)	554 (5)	538 (7)
Finland	524 (6)	519 (12)	545 (5)
Taiwan	523 (7)	560 (4)	523 (13)
Canada	523 (7)	518 (13)	525 (10)
Ireland	523 (7)	501 (20)	522 (14)
Poland	518 (10)	518 (13)	526 (9)
Vietnam	508 (19)	511 (17)	528 (8)
Germany	508 (19)	514 (16)	524 (12)
France	505 (21)	495 (20)	499 (26)
United States	498 (24)	481 (36)	497 (28)
Spain	488 (30)	484 (33)	496 (29)
Russia	475 (41)	482 (34)	486 (37)
Turkey	475 (41)	448 (44)	463 (43)
Mexico	424 (52)	413 (53)	415 (55)
Brazil	410 (55)	391 (58)	405 (59)
Indonesia	396 (60)	375 (64)	382 (64)

have been substantial. Literacy has a profound effect on marketing. Communicating with a literate market is much easier than communicating with one in which the marketer must depend on symbols and pictures. Increasingly, schools are seen as leading to positive cultural changes and progress across the planet.

The Media.   The four social institutions that most strongly influence values and culture are schools, churches, families, and, most recently, the media. In the United States during the past 30 years, women have joined the workforce in growing numbers, substantially reducing the influence of family on American culture. Media time (TV and increasingly the Internet and mobile phones) has replaced family time—much to the detriment of American culture, some argue. At this time, it is hard to gauge the long-term effects of the hours spent with Bart Simpson or an EverQuest cleric-class character. Indeed, the British Prime Minister's cameo on *The Simpsons* reflects its prominence around the world.

American kids spend only 180 days per year in school. Contrast that with around 220 days per year in China, Japan, and Germany.[38] Indeed, Chinese officials are recognizing the national disadvantages of too much school—narrow minds. Likewise, Americans more and more complain about the detrimental effects of too much media. Many decry the declining American educational system as it produces a lower percentage of college graduates than 12 other countries, including Russia, Japan, and France. Many see the relative performance of educational systems, as represented in Exhibit 4.6, as a leading indicator of economic competitiveness.

Government.   Compared with the early (during childhood) and direct influences of family, religion, school, and the media, governments hold relatively little sway. Cultural values and thought patterns are pretty much set before and during adolescence. Most

[38]"Time in School: How Does the U.S. Compare," http://www.centerforpubliceducation.org, posted 2011; "School Days around the World," *norberthaupt.com*, accessed 2015.

often governments try to influence the thinking and behaviors of adult citizens for the citizens' "own good." For example, the French government has been urging citizens to procreate since the time of Napoleon. Now the government is offering a new "birth bonus" of $800, given to women in their seventh month of pregnancy—despite France having one of the highest fertility rates in the European Union (see Exhibit 4.3). Likewise the Japanese government is spending $225 million to expand day-care facilities toward increasing the falling birthrate and better employing women in the workforce. Or notice the most recent French and British government-allowed bans of *hijabs* (head scarves worn by Muslim schoolgirls) or the Dutch government initiative to ban *burkas* in that country (full-body coverings warn by Muslim women)[39] or the Swiss government's ban of the construction of minarets. Also, major changes in governments, such as the dissolution of the Soviet Union, can have noticeable impacts on personal beliefs and other aspects of culture.

Of course, in some countries, the government owns the media and regularly uses propaganda to form "favorable" public opinions. Other countries prefer no separation of church and state—Iran is currently ruled by religious clerics, for example. Governments also affect ways of thinking indirectly, through their support of religious organizations and schools. For example, both the Japanese and Chinese governments are currently trying to promote more creative thinking among students through mandated changes in classroom activities and hours. Finally, governments influence thinking and behavior through the passage, promulgation, promotion, and enforcement of a variety of laws affecting consumption and marketing behaviors. The Irish government is newly concerned about its citizens' consumption of Guinness and other alcoholic products. Their studies suggest excessive drinking costs the country 2 percent of GDP, so to discourage underage drinking, the laws are being tightened (see the end of Chapter 16 for more details).

Corporations.   Of course, corporations get a grip on us early through the media. But more important, most innovations are introduced to societies by companies, many times multinational companies. Indeed, merchants and traders have throughout history been the primary conduit for the diffusion of innovations, whether it be over the Silk Road or via today's air freight and/or the Internet. Multinational firms have access to ideas from around the world. Through the efficient distribution of new products and services based on these new ideas, cultures are changed, and new ways of thinking are stimulated. The crucial role of companies as change agents is discussed in detail in the last section of this chapter.

Elements of Culture

LO3

The elements of culture

Previously culture was defined by listing its five elements: values, rituals, symbols, beliefs, and thought processes. International marketers must design products, distribution systems, and promotional programs with due consideration of each of the five.

Cultural Values

Underlying the cultural diversity that exists among countries are fundamental differences in cultural values, that is, the importance of things and ideas. The most useful information on how cultural values influence various types of business and market behavior comes from seminal work of Geert Hofstede.[40] Studying more than 90,000 people in 66 countries, he found that the cultures of the nations studied differed along four primary dimensions. Subsequently, he and hundreds of other researchers have determined that a wide

---

[39]"The War of French Dressing," *The Economist,* January 16, 2010, pp. 49–50.
[40]Hofstede, and Minkov, *Cultures and Organizations.*

Exhibit 4.7

Hofstede's Indices, Language, and Linguistic Distance

Source: Geert Hofstede, Gert Jan Hofstede, and Michael Minkov, Culture and Organizations: *Software of the Mind*, 3rd ed. (New York: McGraw-Hill, 2011); Joel West and John L. Graham, "A Linguistics-Based Measure of Cultural Distance and Its Relationship to Managerial Values," *Management International Review* 44, no.3 (2004), pp. 239–60.

Country	IDV Score	PDI Score	UAI Score	Primary Language	Distance from English
Arab countries	38	80	68	Arabic	5
Australia	90	36	51	English	0
Brazil	38	69	76	Portuguese	3
Canada	80	39	48	English, French	0, 3
Colombia	13	67	80	Spanish	3
Finland	63	33	59	Finnish	4
France	71	68	86	French	3
Germany	67	35	65	German	1
Great Britain	89	35	35	English	0
Greece	35	60	112	Greek	3
Guatemala	6	95	101	Spanish	3
India	48	77	40	Dravidian	3
Indonesia	14	78	48	Bahasa	7
Iran	41	58	59	Farsi	3
Japan	46	54	92	Japanese	4
Mexico	30	81	82	Spanish	3
Netherlands	80	38	53	Dutch	1
New Zealand	79	22	49	English	0
Pakistan	14	55	70	Urdu	3
South Korea	18	60	85	Korean	4
Taiwan	17	58	69	Taiwanese	6
Turkey	37	66	85	Turkish	4
United States	91	40	46	English	0
Uruguay	36	61	100	Spanish	3
Venezuela	12	81	76	Spanish	3

variety of business and consumer behavior patterns are associated with three of those four dimensions.[41] The four[42] dimensions are as follows: the Individualism/Collective Index (IDV), which focuses on self-orientation; the Power Distance Index (PDI), which focuses on authority orientation; the Uncertainty Avoidance Index (UAI), which focuses on risk orientation; and the Masculinity/Femininity Index (MAS), which focuses on assertiveness and achievement. The Individualism/Collectivism dimension has proven the most useful of the four dimensions, justifying entire books on the subject.[43] Because the MAS has proven least useful, we will not consider it further here. Please see Exhibit 4.7 for details.

During the 1990s, Robert House[44] and his colleagues developed a comparable set of data, more focused on values related to leadership and organizations. Their data are by themselves quite valuable, and aspects of their study nicely coincide with Hofstede's data,

[41]Debanjan Mitra and Peter N. Golder, "Whose Culture Matters? Near-Market Knowledge and Its Impact on Foreign Market Entry Timing," *Journal of Marketing Research* 39, no. 3 (August 2002), pp. 350–65; Boonghee Yoo and Naveen Donthu, "Culture's Consequences, a Book Review," *Journal of Marketing Research* 39, no. 3 (August 2002), pp. 388–89.

[42]In a subsequent study, a fifth dimension, Long-Term Orientation (LTO), was identified as focusing on cultures' temporal orientations. See Geert Hofstede and Michael Harris Bond, "The Confucius Connection," *Organizational Dynamics* 16, no. 4 (Spring 1988), pp. 4–21; Hofstede, and Minkov, *Cultures and Organizations*.

[43]Harry C. Triandis, *Individualism and Collectivism* (Boulder, CO: Westview Press, 1995).

[44]Robert J. House, Paul J. Hanges, Mansour Javidan, Peter W. Dorfman, and Vipin Gupta (eds.), *Culture, Leadership, and Organizations: The Globe Study of 62 Societies* (Thousand Oaks, CA: Sage, 2004).

collected some 25 years earlier. The importance of this work has yielded important criticisms and discussion.[45]

Individualism/Collectivism Index.

The Individualism/Collective Index refers to the preference for behavior that promotes one's self-interest. Cultures that score high in IDV reflect an "I" mentality and tend to reward and accept individual initiative, whereas those low in individualism reflect a "we" mentality and generally subjugate the individual to the group. This distinction does not mean that individuals fail to identify with groups when a culture scores high on IDV but rather that personal initiative and independence are accepted and endorsed. Individualism pertains to societies in which the ties between individuals are loose; everyone is expected to look after him- or herself and his or her immediate family. Collectivism, as its opposite, pertains to societies in which people from birth onward are integrated into strong, cohesive groups, which throughout people's lifetimes continue to protect them in exchange for unquestioning loyalty. Such differences seem to be reflected in stories that parents tell their children—Western, individualistic cultures favor autobiographical personal stories.[46]

Power Distance Index.

The Power Distance Index measures the tolerance of social inequality, that is, power inequality between superiors and subordinates within a social system. Cultures with high PDI scores tend to be hierarchical, with members citing social roles, manipulation, and inheritance as sources of power and social status. Those with low scores, in contrast, tend to value equality and cite knowledge and achievement as sources of power. Thus, people from cultures with high PDI scores are more likely to have a general distrust of others (not those in their groups) because power is seen to rest with individuals and is coercive rather than legitimate. High PDI scores tend to indicate a perception of differences between superior and subordinate and a belief that those who hold power are entitled to privileges. A low PDI score reflects more egalitarian views.

---

[45]Bradley L. Kirkman, Kevin B. Lowe, and Cristina Gibson, "A Quarter Century of Cultures' Consequences: A Review of Empirical Research Incorporating Hofstede's Cultural Values Framework," *Journal of International Business Studies* 37 (2006), pp. 285–320; Kwock Leung, "Editor's Introduction to the Exchange between Hofstede and GLOBE," *Journal of International Business Studies* 37 (2006), p. 881; Geert Hofstede, "What Did GLOBE Really Measure? Researchers' Minds versus Respondents' Minds," *Journal of International Business Studies* 37 (2006), pp. 882–96; Mansour Javidan, Robert J. House, Peter W. Dorfman, Paul J. Hanges, and Mary Sully de Luque, "Conceptualizing and Measuring Cultures and Their Consequences: A Comparative Review of GLOBE's and Hofstede's Approaches," *Journal of International Business Studies* 37 (2006), pp. 897–914; Peter B. Smith, "When Elephants Fight, the Grass Gets Trampled: The GLOBE and Hofstede Projects," *Journal of International Business Studies* 37 (2006), pp. 915–21; P. Christopher Earley, "Leading Cultural Research in the Future: A Matter of Paradigms and Taste," *Journal of International Business Studies* 37 (2006), pp. 922–31; Rosalie L. Tung and Alain Verbeke, "Beyond Hofstede and GLOBE: Improving the Quality of Cross-Cultural Research," *Journal of International Business Studies* 41, no. 8 (2010), pp. 1259–74; George R.Franke and R. Glenn Richey Jr., "Improving Generalizations from Multi-Country Comparisons in International Business Research," *Journal of International Business Studies* 41, no. 8 (2010), pp. 1275–93; Sunil Vernaik and Paul Brewer, "Avoiding Uncertainty in Hofstede and GLOBE," *Journal of International Business Studies* 41, no. 8 (2010) pp. 1294–1324; Robbert Maseland and Andre van Hoom, "Values and Marginal Preferences in International Business," *Journal of International Business Studies* 41, no. 8 (2010), pp. 1325–30; Vas Taras, Piers Steel, and Bradley L. Kirkman, "Negative Practice-Value Correlations in the GLOBE Data: Unexpected Findings, Questionnaire Limitations, and Research Directions," *Journal of International Business Studies* 41, no. 8 (2010), pp. 1330–38; Geert Hofstede, "The GLOBE Debate: Back to Relevance," *Journal of International Business Studies* 41, no. 8, pp. 1339–1346; Paul Brewer and Sunil Venaik, "Individualism-Collectivism in Hofstede and GLOBE," *Journal of International Business Studies* 42, no. 3 (2011), pp. 436–445.

[46]Qi Wang, *The Autobiographical Self in Time and Culture* (Oxford, UK: Oxford University Press, 2013).

Uncertainty Avoidance Index.   The Uncertainty Avoidance Index measures the tolerance of uncertainty and ambiguity among members of a society. Cultures with high UAI scores are highly intolerant of ambiguity and as a result tend to be distrustful of new ideas or behaviors. They tend to have a high level of anxiety and stress and a concern with security and rule following. Accordingly, they dogmatically stick to historically tested patterns of behavior, which in the extreme become inviolable rules. Those with very high UAI scores thus accord a high level of authority to rules as a means of avoiding risk. Cultures scoring low in uncertainty avoidance are associated with a low level of anxiety and stress, a tolerance of deviance and dissent, and a willingness to take risks. Thus, those cultures low in UAI take a more empirical approach to understanding and knowledge, whereas those high in UAI seek absolute truth.

Cultural Values and Consumer Behavior.   A variety of studies have shown cultural values can predict such consumer behaviors as word-of-mouth communications,[47] impulsive buying,[48] responses of both surprise[49] and disgust,[50] the propensity to complain,[51] responses to service failures,[52] movie preferences,[53] and the influence of perceptions of product creativity.[54] Returning to the e-trading example that opened this chapter, we can see how Hofstede's notions of cultural values might help us predict the speed of diffusion of such new consumer services as equity investments and electronic auctions in Japan and France. As shown in Exhibit 4.7, the United States scores the highest of all countries on individualism, at 91, with Japan at 46 and France at 71. Indeed, in America, where individualism reigns supreme, we might predict that the "virtually social" activity of sitting alone at one's computer might be most acceptable. In both Japan and France, where values favor group activities, face-to-face conversations with stockbrokers and neighbors might be preferred to impersonal electronic communications.

Similarly, both Japan (92) and France (86) score quite high on Hofstede's Uncertainty Avoidance Index, and America scores low (46). Based on these scores, both Japanese and French investors might be expected to be less willing to take the risks of stock market investments—and indeed, the security of post office deposits or bank savings accounts is preferred. So in both instances, Hofstede's data on cultural values suggest that the diffusion of these innovations will be slower in Japan and France than in the United States. Such predictions are consistent with research findings that cultures scoring higher on individualism and lower on uncertainty avoidance tend to be more innovative.[55]

[47]Desmond Lam, Alvin Lee, and Richard Mizerski, "The Effects of Cultural Values in Word-of-Mouth Communication," *Journal of International Marketing* 17, no. 3 (2009), pp. 55–70.

[48]Yinlong Zhang, Karen Page Winterich, and Vikas Mittal, "Power-Distance Belief and Impulsive Buying," *Journal of Marketing Research* 47 (2010), pp. 945–54.

[49]Ana Valenzuela, Barbar Mellers, and Judi Strebel, "Pleasurable Surprises: A Cross-Cultural Study of Consumer Responses to Unexpected Incentives," *Journal of Consumer Research* 36 (2010).

[50]Daisann McLane, "Tackling the Yuck Factor," *National Geographic Traveler*, January 2010, pp. 26–28.

[51]Piotr Chelminski and Robin A. Coulter, "The Effects of Cultural Individualism and Self-Confidence on Propensity to Voice: From Theory to Measurement to Practice," *Journal of International Marketing* 15 (2007), pp. 94–118.

[52]Haksin Chan, Lisa C. Wan, and Leo Y. M. Sin, "The Contrasting Effects of Culture on Consumer Tolerance: Interpersonal Face and Impersonal Fate," *Journal of Consumer Research* 36, no. 2 (2009), pp. 292–304; Haskin Chan and Lisa C. Wan, "Consumer Responses to Service Failures: A Resource Preference Model of Cultural Influences," *Journal of International Marketing* 16, no. 1 (2008), pp. 72–97.

[53]J. Samuel Craig, William H. Greene, and Susan P. Douglas, "Culture Matters: Consumer Acceptance of U.S. Films in Foreign Markets," *Journal of International Marketing* 13 (2006), pp. 80–103.

[54]Gaia Rubera, Andrea Ordanini, and David A. Griffith, "Incorporating Cultural Values for Understanding the Influence of Perceived Product Creativity on Intention to Buy: An Examination of Italy and the US," *Journal of International Business Studies* 42, no, 4 (2011), pp. 459–76.

[55]Jan-Benedict E. M. Steenkamp, Frenkel ter Hofstede, and Michel Wedel, "A Cross-National Investigation into the Individual and National Cultural Antecedents of Consumer Innovativeness," *Journal of Marketing* 63 (April 1999), pp. 55–69.

CROSSING BORDERS 4.2   Culture, Genes, and Take-out Slides

East Asians' collectivism may be encoded in their genes. Joan Chiao, a cultural neuroscientist at Northwestern University, noticed a 2003 study showing that carriers of a short allele in the serotonin transporter gene are more prone to depression than their long-alleled peers. But the finding raised a conundrum: Whereas Caucasians are equally likely to carry the short or long allele, about 80 percent of East Asians carry the short one, without any apparent ill effects. Why would they have genetically selected for the "bad" allele?

The 2003 study looked only at white New Zealanders, so Chiao broadened the pool to 29 countries and noticed that nations where the short allele flourished (e.g., Japan, and China) were twice as likely to be collectivistic than individualistic. Chiao had a hunch that the short allele might confer protection from contagious pathogens; she mapped out her data and saw that in countries where infectious diseases historically ran rampant, collectivism— and the short allele—prevail.

"It's natural selection," Chiao suggests. She believes the short allele boosted fitness in regions teeming with diseases—carriers were less likely to stray from the pack and catch something. In contrast, in low-pathogen regions of the West, successful people tend to be leaders and standouts, so the short allele is not selected for (and may even be associated with negative outcomes, as the 2003 study suggests). It's becoming clear that culture isn't a product of nurture alone; traits are coded into our genes, evolving in response to the environment.

[Please note that Professor Chiao's interpretations are consistent with our views that aspects of geography, such as crowding and diseases affect both genes and cultural values, and the latter two apparently interact in interesting ways.]

When Nick Swisher slid hard into second base and broke Minnesota Twins rookie Tsuyoshi Nishioka's leg, the pundits in baseball circles generally wrote it off as a gritty play. But considering the historical precedent of Japanese middle infielders suffering major injuries in similar fashion, Nishioka's situation suggests an alarming trend.

There have been four Japanese middle infielders to play in the major leagues. Three of them—Nishioka, Kazuo Matsui and Akinori Iwamura—spent significant time on the disabled list as a result of an opponent's aggressive slide. The fourth, Tadahito Iguchi, was upended by vicious take-out slides in 2006 and 2007 but escaped serious injury.

Bobby Valentine, the big-league skipper who spent seven seasons managing in Japan's Pacific League, said Japanese infielders come to the United States somewhat unprepared for the often dangerous slides common around the bag. American players—and Latin players exposed to American-style baseball at a younger age— are schooled in what Valentine calls an "anything goes" approach to breaking up double plays. In Japan, baserunners are taught to slide low, making contact with the infielder's instep or ankle, not wanting to injure their fellow competitors. Nishioka had barely been exposed to the type of slide that cost him at least a month of play.

Sources: Sujata Gupta, "Societal Pressure, Culture May Actually Shape Genes," *Psychology Today*, September 6, 2011; Jared Diamond, "The Cultural Divide of 'Takeout Slides'" *The Wall Street Journal*, April 13, 2011, p. D6.

Perhaps the most interesting application of cultural values and consumer behavior regards a pair of experiments done with American and Chinese students.[56] Both groups were shown print ads using other-focused emotional appeals (that is, a couple pictured having fun on the beach) versus self-focused emotional appeals (an individual having fun on the beach). The researchers predicted that the individualistic Americans would respond more favorably to the self-focused appeals and the collectivistic Chinese to the other-focused appeals. They found the opposite. Their second experiment helped explain these unexpected results. That is, in both cases, what the participants liked about the ads was their *novelty* vis-à-vis their own cultures. So, even in this circumstance, cultural values provide useful information for marketers. However, the complexity of human behavior, values, and culture is manifest.

Rituals   Life is filled with rituals, that is, patterns of behavior and interaction that are learned and repeated. The most obvious ones are associated with major events in life. Marriage ceremonies and funerals are good examples. Perhaps the one most important to most readers of this book is the hopefully proximate graduation ritual—*Pomp and Circumstance*, funny

---

[56]Jennifer L. Aaker and Patti Williams, "Empathy vs. Pride: The Influence of Emotional Appeals across Cultures," *Journal of Consumer Research* 25 (December 1998), pp. 241–61.

Every Muslim is enjoined to make the hajj, or pilgrimage, to Mecca, once in his or her lifetime if physically able. Here, some 2 million faithful come from all over the world annually to participate in what is one of the largest ritual meetings on Earth.

hats, long speeches, and all. Very often these rituals differ across cultures. Indeed, there is an entire *genre* of foreign films about weddings.[57] Perhaps the best is *Monsoon Wedding*. Grooms on white horses and edible flowers are apparently part of the ceremony for high-income folks in New Delhi.

Life is also filled with little rituals, such as dinner at a restaurant or a visit to a department store or even grooming before heading off to work or class in the morning. In a nice restaurant in Madrid, dessert may precede the entrée, but dinner often starts at about

---

[57]Other excellent films in this genre include *Cousin, Cousine* (French), *Four Weddings and a Funeral* (U.K.), *Bend It Like Beckham* (U.K., Asian immigrants), *Wedding in Galilee* (Palestine/Israel), and *The Wedding Banquet* (Taiwan).

[58]Joanna Sugden, "The 80 Million-Pilgrm March," *The Wall Street Journal*, February 2–3, 2013, p. C3.

Dressed in the ritual color of saffron (orange), thousands of pilgrims of the Lord Shiva descend one of the over 100 *Ghats* in Varanasi, India, to perform *puja* (ritual cleansing of the soul). Varanasi (also known as Benares or Banaris) is one of the oldest and holiest cities in India. It is believed to be the home of Lord Shiva (Hindu god) and the location of the first sermon by Buddha, so followers of numerous religions flock to Varanasi on a daily basis. Each day at sunrise and sunset, pilgrims crowd the *Ghats* (steps to the holy river/Mother Ganga/the River Ganges) to immerse themselves in the water and perform *puja*. The 55-day festival attracts some 60–80 million pilgrims.[58] On the busiest day of the ritual, estimate are that tens of millions participate (according to Professor Rika Houston). Meanwhile, televised rituals such as the Academy Awards and World Cup soccer draw billions in the form of virtual crowds.

midnight, and the entire process can be a three-hour affair. Walking into a department store in the United States often yields a search for an employee to answer questions. Not so in Japan, where the help bows at the door as you walk in. Visit a doctor in the States and a 15-minute wait in a cold exam room with nothing on but a paper gown is typical. In Spain the exams are often done in the doctor's office. There's no waiting, because you find the doctor sitting at her desk.

Rituals are important. They coordinate everyday interactions and special occasions. They let people know what to expect. In the final chapter of the text, we discuss the ritual of business negotiations, and that ritual varies across cultures as well.

Symbols

Anthropologist Edward T. Hall tells us that culture is communication. In his seminal article about cultural differences in business settings, he talks about the "languages" of time, space, things,[59] friendships, and agreements.[60] Indeed, learning to interpret correctly the symbols that surround us is a key part of socialization. And this learning begins immediately after birth, as we begin to hear the language spoken and see the facial expressions and feel the touch and taste the milk of our mothers.[61] We begin our discussion of symbolic systems with language, the most obvious part and the part that most often involves conscious communication.

Language.

We should mention that for some around the world, language is itself thought of as a social institution, often with political importance. Certainly the French go to extreme lengths and expense to preserve the purity of their *français*. In Canada, language has been the focus of political disputes including secession, though things seem to have calmed down there most recently. Unfortunately, as the number of spoken languages continues to decline worldwide, so does the interesting cultural diversity of the planet.

The importance of understanding the language of a country cannot be overestimated, particularly if you're selling your products in France! The successful international marketer must achieve expert communication, which requires a thorough understanding of the language as well as the ability to speak it. Advertising copywriters should be concerned less with obvious differences between languages and more with the idiomatic and symbolic[62] meanings expressed. It is not sufficient to say you want to translate into Spanish, for instance, because across Spanish-speaking Latin America, the language vocabulary varies widely. *Tambo*, for example, means a roadside inn in Bolivia, Colombia, Ecuador, and Peru; a dairy farm in Argentina and Uruguay; and a brothel in Chile. If that gives you a problem, consider communicating with the people of Papua New Guinea. Some 750 languages, each distinct and mutually unintelligible, are spoken there. This crucial issue of accurate translations in marketing communications is discussed further in Chapters 8 and 16.

The relationship between language and international marketing is important in another way. Recent studies indicate that a new concept, linguistic distance, is proving useful to marketing researchers in market segmentation and strategic entry decisions. Linguistic distance has been shown to be an important factor in determining differences in values across countries and the amount of trade between countries.[63] The idea is that crossing "wider" language differences increases transaction costs.

---

[59]Tuba Ustuner and Douglas B. Holt, "Toward a Theory of Status Consumption in Less Industrialized Countries," *Journal of Consumer Research* 37 (2010), pp. 37–52.

[60]Edward T. Hall, "The Silent Language in Overseas Business," *Harvard Business Review*, May–June 1960, pp. 87–96. A discussion of the salience of Hall's work appears in John L. Graham, "Culture and Human Resources Management." In *The Oxford Handbook of International Business*, 2nd ed., Alan M. Rugman and Thomas L. Brewer (Oxford: Oxford University Press, 2009), pp. 503–36.

[61]The spices a nursing mother consumes actually affect the flavor of the milk she produces.

[62]Eric Yorkston and Gustavo E. De Mello, "Linguistic Gender Marking and Categorization," *Journal of Consumer Research* 32 (2005), pp. 224–34.

[63]Jennifer D. Chandler and John L. Graham, "Relationship-Oriented Cultures, Corruption, and International Marketing Success," *Journal of Business Ethics* 92(2) (2010), pp. 251–67.

CROSSING BORDERS 4.3 | How Social Media Changes Language

Aurelie Filippetti, the French minister for culture, had to retract a tweet this week after making a glaring spelling mistake. As she is the official guardian of the French language, this was more than a bit embarrassing. Twitter's spontaneity invites carelessness; and the minister duly blamed a sloppy aide. But for linguistic purists, the incident touched on a far broader issue concerning social media's mangling of French and the accelerating invasion of franglais.

The French have long used rules to defend their language from the creeping advance of English, particularly in advertising. By law, any brand's English slogan—such as Nespresso's "What else?"—must be translated with a subtitle (*Quoi d'autre?*). This produces comical results. Quick, a fast-food chain popular across France, introduced le *French burger* to its menu, helpfully translating it as le *burger à la française*. Advertisers merrily twist the rules, using a tiny font for the translation or inventing logos in indigestible franglais. *Very irrésistible* is a perfume by Givenchy, a French luxury brand. Fashion magazines liberally sprinkle their texts with references to le *must*, le *look*, or le *street style*.

The spread of social media is battering French anew. As French is more prolix than English, Twitter's limit of 140 characters per tweet creates an extra squeeze. French tweets, like mobile text messages, are filled with abbreviations: *koi* for *quoi* (what) or *C* for *c'est* (it is).

Neologisms abound. Somebody who tweets can be *followé* by others. A French mobile-telephone operator has launched a service called "Sosh," short for "social media." *Twitter* has itself been transmuted from an English noun into a French verb. One official tweeted recently that "*nous live-twitterons*" regarding a minister's speech.

An official French body tries to fend off anglicisms with French alternatives. For cloud computing, it recommends *informatique en nuage*. A hashtag, used on Twitter with the symbol #, should be *mot-dièse*. In reality, such gimmicks rarely catch on.

What is catching on around the world is emoji. How would you say that in French? Named by combining the Japanese words for picture (*e-*) and character (*moji*), emoji are the alphanumeric-sized graphics that tweeters, texters, and e-mailers around the world are now using millions of times every day. They are the ♥ meant to show affection or the ☺ for humor at the end of a text.

The panda faces and winking ghosts may be easy fodder for Grandpa's next screed about how kids are ruining the English language, but many scholars have come to see emoji as an important tool, helping restore the text that has been lost as in-person communication has given way to inboxes.

Sources: Excerpted from "Nous Twitterons," *The Economist*, August 10, 2014, p. 48; Katy Steinmetz, "Not Just a Smiley Face. The Emoji Boom Is Changing the Way We Communicate," *Time*, July 28, 2014, pp. 52–53.

IBM uses the same copy in print ads targeting industrial customers in both the French and the English-speaking countries Notice the footnotes on the English slogans that protect the French language by leading the reader to the French government required subtitled translations. This is a good example of the language problem described in Crossing Borders 4.3 just above.

Over the years, linguistics researchers have determined that languages around the world conform to family trees[64] based on the similarity of their forms and development. For example, Spanish, Italian, French, and Portuguese are all classified as Romance languages because of their common roots in Latin. Distances can be measured on these linguistic trees. If we assume English[65] to be the starting point, German is one branch away, Danish two, Spanish three, Japanese four, Hebrew five, Chinese six, and Thai seven. These "distance from English" scores are listed for a sampling of cultures in Exhibit 4.7.

Other work in the area is demonstrating a direct influence of language on cultural values, expectations, and even conceptions of time. For example, as linguistic distance from English increases, individualism decreases.[66] These studies are among the first in this genre, and much more work needs to be done. However, the notion of linguistic distance appears to hold promise for better understanding and predicting cultural differences in both consumer and management values, expectations, and behaviors.

Another area of new research interest is the relationship between bilingualism/biculturalism and consumer behaviors and values. For example, bilingual consumers process advertisements differently if heard in their native versus second language,[67] and bicultural consumers, different from bilingual only consumers, can switch identities and perception frames.[68]

Moreover, the relationship between language spoken and cultural values holds deeper implications. That is, as English spreads around the world via school systems and the Internet, cultural values of individualism and egalitarianism will spread with it. For example, both Chinese Mandarin speakers and Spanish speakers must learn two words for "you" (*ni* and *nin* and *tu* and *usted*, respectively). The proper use of the two depends completely on knowledge of the social context of the conversation. Respect for status is communicated by the use of *nin* and *usted*. In English there is only one form for "you."[69] Speakers can ignore social context and status and still speak correctly. It's easier, and social status becomes less important. *Français* beware!

Aesthetics as Symbols.   Art communicates. Indeed, Confucius is reputed to have opined, "A picture is worth a thousand words." But, of course, so can a dance or a song. As we acquire our culture, we learn the meaning of this wonderful symbolic system represented in its aesthetics, that is, its arts, folklore, music, drama, dance, dress, and cosmetics. Customers everywhere respond to images, myths, and metaphors that help them define their personal and national identities and relationships within a context of culture and product benefits. The uniqueness of a culture can be spotted quickly in symbols having distinct meanings. Think about the subtle earth tones of the typical Japanese restaurant compared with the bright reds and yellows in the decor of ethnic Chinese restaurants. Similarly, a long-standing rivalry between the Scottish Clan Lindsay and Clan Donald caused McDonald's Corporation some consternation when it chose the Lindsay tartan design for new uniforms for its workers. Godfrey Lord Macdonald, Chief of Clan Donald, was outraged and complained that McDonald's had

---

[64]For the most comprehensive representation of global linguistic trees, see Jiangtian Chen, Robert R. Sokal, and Merrit Ruhlen, "Worldwide Analysis of Genetic and Linguistic Relationships of Human Populations," *Human Biology* 67, no. 4 (August 1995), pp. 595–612.

[65]We appreciate the ethnocentricity in using English as the starting point. However, linguistic trees can be used to measure distance from any language. For example, analyses using French or Japanese as the starting point have proven useful as well.

[66]Joel West and John L. Graham, "A Linguistics-Based Measure of Cultural Distance and Its Relationship to Managerial Values," *Management International Review* 44, no. 3 (2004), pp. 239–60; "The Evolution of Language: Babel or Babble?" *The Economist,* April 16, 2011, pp. 85, 86.

[67]Stefano Puntoni, Bart de Langhe, and Stijn M.J. van Osselaer, "Bilingualism and the Emotional Intensity of Advertising Language," *Journal of Consumer Research* 35 (2009), pp. 1012–25.

[68]David Luna, Torsten Ringberg, and Laura A. Peracchio, "One Individual, Two Identities: Frame Switching Biculturals," *Journal of Consumer Research* 35, no. 2 (2008), pp. 279–93.

[69]In English, there was historically a second second-person form. That is, "thee" was the informal form up until the last century. Even in some Spanish-speaking countries, such as Costa Rica, the "tu" is being dropped in a similar manner.

Exhibit 4.8
Metaphorical Journeys
through 23 Nations

Source: From Martin J. Gannon, and
Rajnandini K. Pillai *Understanding
Global Cultures, Metaphorical Journeys
through 31 Nations*, 5th ed. (Thousand
Oaks, CA: Sage, 2012).

The Thai Kingdom	The Traditional British House
The Japanese Garden	The Malaysian *Balik Kampung*
India: The Dance of Shiva	The Nigerian Marketplace
Bedouin Jewelry and Saudi Arabia	The Israeli Kibbutzim and Moshavim
The Turkish Coffeehouse	The Italian Opera
The Brazilian Samba	Belgian Lace
The Polish Village Church	The Mexican Fiesta
Kimchi and Korea	The Russian Ballet
The German Symphony	The Spanish Bullfight
The Swedish *Stuga*	The Portuguese Bullfight
Irish Conversations	The Chinese Family Altar
American Football	

a "complete lack of understanding of the name." Of course, the plaid in the uniforms is now the least of the firm's worries as British consumers have become more concerned about health-related matters.

Without culturally consistent interpretations and presentations[70] of countries' aesthetic values, a host of marketing problems can arise. Product styling must be aesthetically pleasing to be successful, as must advertisements and package designs. Insensitivity to aesthetic values can offend, create a negative impression, and, in general, render marketing efforts ineffective or even damaging. Strong symbolic meanings may be overlooked if one is not familiar with a culture's aesthetic values. The Japanese, for example, revere the crane as being very lucky because it is said to live a thousand years. However, the use of the number four should be avoided completely because the word for four, *shi*, is also the Japanese word for death. Thus teacups are sold in sets of five, not four, in Japan. And speaking of inappropriate cups, recently Swiss retail giant Migros put images of Hitler and Mussolini on the labels of their coffee creamers. Hitler was not a hit with Swiss consumers. They complained to the local press via a mobile phone shot and Migros executives apologized for, in their completely accurate words, "the unforgivable incident." Then they immediately withdrew 2000 containers from 100 coffee shops.[71]

Finally, one author has suggested that understanding different cultures' metaphors is a key doorway to success. In Exhibit 4.8, we list the metaphors Martin Gannon[72] identified to represent cultures around the world. In the fascinating text, he compares "American Football" (with its individualism, competitive specialization, huddling, and ceremonial celebration of perfection) to the "Spanish Bullfight" (with its pompous entrance parade, audience participation, and the ritual of the fight) to the "Indian Dance of the Shiva" (with its cycles of life, family, and social interaction). Empirical evidence is beginning to accumulate supporting the notion that metaphors matter.[73] Any good international marketer would see fine fodder for advertising campaigns in the insightful descriptions depicted.

Beliefs   Of course, much of what we learn to believe comes from religious training. But to consider matters of true faith and spirituality adequately here is certainly impossible. Moreover, the relationship between superstition and religion is not at all clear. For example, one explanation of the origin about the Western aversion to the number 13 has to do with Jesus sitting with his 12 disciples at the Last Supper.

---

[70]Michael W. Allen, Richa Gupta, and Arnaud Monnier, "The Interactive Effect of Cultural Symbols and Cultural Values on Taste Evaluations," *Journal of Consumer Research* 35, no. 2 (2008), pp. 294–308.

[71]Dan Bilesfsky, "For Swiss, A Distasteful Jolt with Coffee: Hitler Creamer," *The New York Times*, October 23, 2014, p. A5.

[72]Martin J. Gannon, and Rajnandini K. Pillai *Understanding Global Cultures, Metaphorical Journeys through 31 Nations*, 5th ed. (Thousand Oaks, CA: Sage, 2012).

[73]Cristina B. Gibson and Mary E. Zeller-Bruhn, "Metaphors and Meaning: An Intercultural Analysis of the Concept of Work," *Administrative Science Quarterly* 46, no. 2 (2001), pp. 274–303.

Russian Orthodox priests prepare to bless an assembly line at a Niva sport-utility plant near Moscow, part of a joint venture between General Motors and AvtoVaz. The Niva is the best-selling SUV in Russia, making a profit for GM. Comrade Lenin would have had a tough time with this one!

However, many of our beliefs are secular in nature. What Westerners often call superstition may play quite a large role in a society's belief system in another part of the world. For example, in parts of Asia, ghosts, fortune telling, palmistry, blood types, head-bump reading, phases of the moon, faith healers, demons, and soothsayers can all be integral elements of society. Surveys of advertisements in Greater China show a preference for an "8" as the last digit in prices listed—the number connotes "prosperity" in Chinese culture. The Beijing Olympics started on 8–8–08 at 8:08 p.m. for a reason! And recall the Japanese concern about Year of the Fire Horse discussed earlier.

Called art, science, philosophy, or superstition—depending on who is talking—the Chinese practice of *feng shui* is an important ancient belief held by Chinese, among others. Feng shui is the process that links humans and the universe to *ch'i*, the energy that sustains life and flows through our bodies and surroundings, in and around our homes and workplaces. The idea is to harness this ch'i to enhance good luck, prosperity, good health, and honor for the owner of a premises and to minimize the negative force, *sha ch'i*, and its effects. Feng shui requires engaging the services of a feng shui master to determine the positive orientation of a building in relation to the owner's horoscope, the date of establishment of the business, or the shape of the land and building. It is not a look or a style, and it is more than aesthetics: Feng shui is a strong belief in establishing a harmonious environment through the design and placement of furnishings and the avoidance of buildings facing northwest, the "devil's entrance," and southwest, the "devil's backdoor." Indeed, Disney even "feng-shuied" all its new rides in Hong Kong Disneyland.

Too often, one person's beliefs are another person's funny story. To discount the importance of myths, beliefs, superstitions, or other cultural beliefs, however strange they may appear, is a mistake because they are an important part of the cultural fabric of a society and influence all manner of behavior. For the marketer to make light of superstitions in other cultures when doing business there can be an expensive mistake. Making a fuss about being born in the right year under the right phase of the moon or relying heavily on handwriting and palm-reading experts, as in Japan, can be difficult to comprehend for a Westerner who refuses to walk under a ladder, worries about the next seven years after breaking a mirror, buys a one-dollar lottery ticket, and seldom sees a 13th floor in a building.

Thought Processes

We are now learning in much more detail the degree to which ways of thinking vary across cultures. For example, research has demonstrated cultural differences in consumer impatience[74] and in how consumers make decisions about products—culture seems to matter more in snap judgments than in longer deliberations.[75] Still other studies are demonstrating a deeper impact of culture on sensory perceptions themselves, particularly aromas.[76]

Richard Nisbett, in his wonderful book *The Geography of Thought*,[77] broadly discusses differences in "Asian and Western" thinking. He starts with Confucius and Aristotle and develops his arguments through consideration of historical and philosophical writings and findings from more recent behavioral science research, including his own social-psychological experiments. Although he acknowledges the dangers surrounding generalizations about Japanese, Chinese, and Korean cultures, on the one hand, and European and American cultures, on the other, many of his conclusions are consistent with our own work related to international negotiations, cultural values, and linguistic distance.

A good metaphor for his views involves going back to Confucius's worthy picture. Asians tend to see the whole picture and can report details about the background and foreground. Westerners alternatively focus on the foreground and can provide great detail about central figures but see relatively little in the background. This difference in perception—focus versus big picture—is associated with a wide variety of differences in values, preferences, and expectations about future events. Nisbett's book is essential reading for anyone marketing products and services internationally. His insights are pertinent to Japanese selling in Jacksonville or Belgians selling in Beijing.

Each of the five cultural elements must be evaluated in light of how they might affect a proposed marketing program. Newer products and services and more extensive programs involving the entire cycle, from product development through promotion to final selling, require greater consideration of cultural factors. Moreover, the separate origins and elements of culture we have presented interact, often in synergistic ways. Therefore, the marketer must also take a step back and consider larger cultural consequences of marketing actions.

Cultural Sensitivity and Tolerance

Successful foreign marketing begins with cultural sensitivity—being attuned to the nuances of culture so that a new culture can be viewed objectively, evaluated, and appreciated. Cultural sensitivity, or cultural empathy, must be carefully cultivated. That is, for every amusing, annoying, peculiar, or repulsive cultural trait we find in a country, others see a similarly amusing, annoying, or repulsive trait in our culture. For example, we bathe, perfume, and deodorize our bodies in a daily ritual that is seen in many cultures as compulsive, while we often become annoyed with those cultures less concerned with natural body odor. Just because a culture is different does not make it wrong. Marketers must understand how their own cultures influence their assumptions about another culture. The more exotic the situation, the more sensitive, tolerant, and flexible one needs to be. Being culturally sensitive will reduce conflict and improve communications and thereby increase success in collaborative relationships.

Besides knowledge of the origins and elements of cultures, the international marketer also should have an appreciation of how cultures change and accept or reject new ideas. Because the marketer usually is trying to introduce something completely new (such as e-trading) or to improve what is already in use, how cultures change and the manner in which resistance to change occurs should be thoroughly understood.

[74]Haipen (Allan) Chen, Sharon Ng, and Akshay R. Rao, "Cultural Differences in Consumer Impatience," *Journal of Marketing Research* 42 (2007), pp. 291–301.

[75]Donnel A. Briley and Jennifer L. Aaker, "When Does Culture Matter? Effects of Personal Knowledge on the Correction of Culture-Based Judgments," *Journal of Marketing Research* 43 (2008), pp. 395–408.

[76]T.M Lurmann, "Can't Place that Smell? You Must Be American," *The New York Times*, September 7, 2014, p. SR6.

[77]Nisbett, *The Geography of Thought*.

Cultural Change

Culture is dynamic in nature; it is a living process.[78] But the fact that cultural change is constant seems paradoxical, because another important attribute of culture is that it is conservative and resists change. The dynamic character of culture is significant in assessing new markets even though changes face resistance. Societies change in a variety of ways. Some have change thrust upon them by war (for example, the changes in Japan after World War II) or by natural disaster. More frequently, change is a result of a society seeking ways to solve the problems created by changes in its environment. One view is that culture is the accumulation of a series of the best solutions to problems faced in common by members of a given society. In other words, culture is the means used in adjusting to the environmental and historical components of human existence.

Accidents have provided solutions to some problems; invention has solved many others. Usually, however, societies have found answers by looking to other cultures from which they can borrow ideas. Cultural borrowing is common to all cultures. Although each society has a few unique situations facing it (such as stomach cancer in Japan), most problems confronting societies are similar in nature.

Cultural Borrowing

LO4

The impact of cultural borrowing

Cultural borrowing is a responsible effort to learn from others' cultural ways in the quest for better solutions to a society's particular problems. Thus cultures unique in their own right are the result, in part, of imitating a diversity of others. Some cultures grow closer together and some further apart with contact.[79] Consider, for example, American (U.S.) culture and a typical U.S. citizen, who begins breakfast with an orange from the eastern Mediterranean, a cantaloupe from Persia, or perhaps a piece of African watermelon. After her fruit and first coffee, she goes on to waffles, cakes made by a Scandinavian technique from wheat domesticated in Asia Minor. Over these she pours maple syrup, invented by the Native Americans of the eastern U.S. woodlands. As a side dish, she may have the eggs of a species of bird domesticated in Indochina or thin strips of the flesh of an animal domesticated in eastern Asia that have been salted and smoked by a process developed in northern Europe. While eating, she reads the news of the day, imprinted in characters invented by the ancient Semites upon a material invented in China by a process also invented in China. As she absorbs the accounts of foreign troubles, she will, if she is a good conservative citizen, thank a Hebrew deity in an Indo-European language that she is 100 percent American.[80]

Actually, this citizen is correct to assume that she is 100 percent American, because each of the borrowed cultural facets has been adapted to fit her needs, molded into uniquely American habits, foods, and customs. Americans behave as they do because of the dictates of their culture. Regardless of how or where solutions are found, once a particular pattern of action is judged acceptable by society, it becomes the approved way and is passed on and taught as part of the group's cultural heritage. Cultural heritage is one of the fundamental differences between humans and other animals. Culture is learned; societies pass on to succeeding generations solutions to problems, constantly building on and expanding the culture so that a wide range of behavior is possible. The point is, of course, that though many behaviors are borrowed from other cultures, they are combined in a unique manner that becomes typical for a particular society. Indeed, there is no better place to observe this cultural change process than

---

[78]Indeed, aspects of Hofstede's values scores have been shown to vary over time. See Steve Jenner, Bren MacNab, Donnel Briley, Richard Brislin, and Reg Worthley, "Culture Change and Marketing," *Journal of International Marketing* 21, no. 2 (2008), pp. 161–72.

[79]Kwok Leung, Rabi S. Bhagat, Nancy B. Buchan, Miriam Erez, and Cristina Gibson, "Culture and International Business: Recent Advances and Their Implications for Future Research," *Journal of International Business Studies* 36 (2006), pp. 357–78.

[80]Ralph Linton, *The Study of Man* (New York: Appleton-Century-Crofts, 1936), p. 327.

in the growing number of mixed-culture marriages around the world.[81] To the foreign marketer, this similar-but-different feature of cultures has important meaning in gaining cultural empathy.

Similarities: An Illusion

For the inexperienced marketer, the similar-but-different aspect of culture creates illusions of similarity that usually do not exist. Several nationalities can speak the same language or have similar race and heritage, but it does not follow that similarities exist in other respects—that a product acceptable to one culture will be readily acceptable to the other, or that a promotional message that succeeds in one country will succeed in the other. Even though people start with a common idea or approach, as is the case among English-speaking Americans and the British, cultural borrowing and assimilation to meet individual needs translate over time into quite distinct cultures. A common language does not guarantee a similar interpretation of words or phrases. Both British and Americans speak English, but their cultures are sufficiently different that a single phrase has different meanings to each and can even be completely misunderstood. In England, one asks for a lift instead of an elevator, and an American, when speaking of a bathroom, generally refers to a toilet, whereas in England a bathroom is a place to take a tub bath. Also, the English "hoover" a carpet, whereas Americans vacuum. The movie title *The Spy Who Shagged Me* means nothing to most Americans but much to British consumers. Indeed, anthropologist Edward Hall warns that Americans and British have a harder time understanding each other because of their *apparent* and *assumed* cultural similarities.

The growing economic unification of Europe has fostered a tendency to speak of the "European consumer." Many of the obstacles to doing business in Europe have been or will be eliminated as the European Union takes shape, but marketers, eager to enter the market, must not jump to the conclusion that an economically unified Europe means a common set of consumer wants and needs. Cultural differences among the members of the European Union are the product of centuries of history that will take centuries to ameliorate.[82] The United States itself has many subcultures that even today, with mass communications and rapid travel, defy complete homogenization. To suggest that the South is in all respects culturally the same as the northeastern or midwestern parts of the United States would be folly, just as it would be folly to assume that the unification of Germany has erased cultural differences that arose from over 40 years of political and social separation.

Marketers must assess each country thoroughly in terms of the proposed products or services and never rely on an often-used axiom that if it sells in one country, it will surely sell in another. As worldwide mass communications and increased economic and social interdependence of countries grow, similarities among countries will increase, and common market behaviors, wants, and needs will continue to develop. As this process occurs, the tendency will be to rely more on apparent similarities when they may not exist. A marketer is wise to remember that a culture borrows and then adapts and customizes to its own needs and idiosyncrasies; thus, what may appear to be the same on the surface may be different in its cultural meaning.

Resistance to Change

A characteristic of human culture is that change occurs. That people's habits, tastes, styles, behavior, and values are not constant but are continually changing can be verified by

---

[81]Samantha N. N. Cross and Mary C. Gilly, "Cultural Competence and Cultural Compensatory Mechanisms in Binational Households," *Journal of Marketing* 78, no.3 (May 2014), pp. 121–39.

[82]Tuba Ustuner and Douglas B. Holt, "Dominated Consumer Acculturation: The Social Construction of Poor Migrant Women's Consumer Identity Projects in a Turkish Squatter," *Journal of Consumer Research* 34 (2007), pp. 41–56.

MTV meets Mom in Mumbai (formerly Bombay), India. Culture does change—dress and even names of major cities! Even so, a local resident tells us everyone still calls it Bombay despite the official alteration.

reading 20-year-old magazines. However, this gradual cultural growth does not occur without some resistance; new methods, ideas, and products are held to be suspect before they are accepted, if ever. Some even describe cultural borrowing in a negative light. Reminiscent of French fears about the purity of their language, President Hu Jintao has urged his people to resist Western attempts to dominate Chinese culture by strengthening "Chinese cultural production."[83] Interestingly, research shows that consumers in different cultures display differing resistance.[84]

The degree of resistance to new patterns varies. In some situations, new elements are accepted completely and rapidly; in others, resistance is so strong that acceptance is never forthcoming. Studies show that the most important factors in determining what kind and how much of an innovation will be accepted is the degree of interest in the particular subject, as well as how drastically the new will change the old—that is, how disruptive the innovation will be to presently acceptable values and behavior patterns. Observations indicate that those innovations most readily accepted are those holding the greatest interest within the society and those least disruptive. For example, rapid industrialization in parts of Europe has changed many long-honored attitudes involving time and working women. Today, there is an interest in ways to save time and make life more productive; the leisurely continental life is rapidly disappearing. With this time consciousness has come the very rapid acceptance of many innovations that might have been resisted by most just a few years ago. Instant foods, labor-saving devices, and fast-food establishments, all supportive of a changing attitude toward work and time, are rapidly gaining acceptance.

An understanding of the process of acceptance of innovations is of crucial importance to the marketer. The marketer cannot wait centuries or even decades for acceptance but must gain acceptance within the limits of financial resources and projected profitability periods. Possible methods and insights are offered by social scientists who are concerned with the

---

[83]Edward Wong, "China's President Pushes Back against Western Culture," *The New York Times,* January 3, 2012.

[84]Mark Cleveland, Michel Laroche, and Nicolas Papadopoulos, "Cosmopolitanism, Consumer Ethnocentrism, and Materialism: An Eight-Country Study of Antecedents and Outcomes," *Journal of International Marketing* 17, no. 1 (2009), pp. 116–46; Gerald J. Tellis, Eden Yen, and Simon Bell, "Global Consumer Innovativeness: Cross-Country Differences and Commonalities," *Journal of International Marketing* 17, no. 2 (2009), pp. 1–22.

concepts of planned social change. Historically, most cultural borrowing and the resulting change has occurred without a deliberate plan, but increasingly, changes are occurring in societies as a result of purposeful attempts by some acceptable institution to bring about change, that is, planned change.

Planned and Unplanned Cultural Change

LO5

The strategy of planned change and its consequences

The first step in bringing about planned change in a society is to determine which cultural factors conflict with an innovation, thus creating resistance to its acceptance. The next step is an effort to change those factors from obstacles to acceptance into stimulants for change. The same deliberate approaches used by the social planner to gain acceptance for hybrid grains, better sanitation methods, improved farming techniques, or protein-rich diets among the peoples of underdeveloped societies can be adopted by marketers to achieve marketing goals.[85]

Marketers have two options when introducing an innovation to a culture: They can wait for changes to occur, or they can spur change. The former requires hopeful waiting for eventual cultural changes that prove their innovations of value to the culture; the latter involves introducing an idea or product and deliberately setting about to overcome resistance and to cause change that accelerates the rate of acceptance. The folks at Fidelity Investments in Japan, for example, pitched a tent in front of Tokyo's Shinjuku train station and showered commuters with investment brochures and demonstrations of Japanese-language WebXpress online stock trading services to encourage faster changes in Japanese investor behavior. However, as mentioned previously, the changes have not happened fast enough for most foreign firms targeting this business and similar financial services.

Obviously not all marketing efforts require change to be accepted. In fact, much successful and highly competitive marketing is accomplished by a strategy of cultural congruence. Essentially this strategy involves marketing products similar to ones already on the market in a manner as congruent as possible with existing cultural norms, thereby minimizing resistance. However, when marketing programs depend on cultural change to be successful, a company may decide to leave acceptance to a strategy of unplanned change—that is, introduce a product and hope for the best. Or a company may employ a strategy of planned change—that is, deliberately set out to change those aspects of the culture offering resistance to predetermined marketing goals.

As an example of unplanned cultural change, consider how the Japanese diet has changed since the introduction of milk and bread soon after World War II. Most Japanese, who were predominantly fish eaters, have increased their intake of animal fat and protein to the point that fat and protein now exceed vegetable intake. As many McDonald's hamburgers are likely to be eaten in Japan as the traditional rice ball wrapped in edible seaweed, and American hamburgers are replacing many traditional Japanese foods. Burger King purchased Japan's homegrown Morinaga Love restaurant chain, home of the salmon burger—a patty of salmon meat, a slice of cheese, and a layer of dried seaweed, spread with mayonnaise and stuck between two cakes of sticky Japanese rice pressed into the shape of a bun—an eggplant burger, and other treats. The chain was converted and now sells Whoppers instead of the salmon-rice burger.

The Westernized diet has caused many Japanese to become overweight. To counter this trend, the Japanese are buying low-calorie, low-fat foods to help shed excess weight and are flocking to health clubs. All this began when U.S. occupation forces introduced bread, milk, and steak to Japanese culture. The effect on the Japanese was unintentional, but nevertheless, change occurred. Had the intent been to introduce a new diet—that is, a strategy of planned change—specific steps could have been taken to identify resistance

---

[85]Two very important books on this topic are Everett M. Rogers, *Diffusion of Innovations*, 4th ed. (New York: The Free Press, 1995), and Gerald Zaltman and Robert Duncan, *Strategies for Planned Change* (New York: John Wiley & Sons, 1979).

to dietary change and then to overcome these resistances, thus accelerating the process of change.

Marketing strategy is judged culturally in terms of acceptance, resistance, or rejection. How marketing efforts interact with a culture determines the degree of success or failure. All too often marketers are not aware of the scope of their impact on a host culture. If a strategy of planned change is implemented, the marketer has some responsibility to determine the consequences of such action.

Summary

A complete and thorough appreciation of the origins (geography, history, political economy, technology, and social institutions) and elements (cultural values, rituals, symbols, beliefs, and ways of thinking) of culture may well be the single most important advantage for a foreign marketer in the preparation of marketing plans and strategies. Marketers can control the product offered to a market—its promotion, price, and eventual distribution methods—but they have only limited control over the cultural environment within which these plans must be implemented. Because they cannot control all the influences on their marketing plans, they must attempt to anticipate the eventual effect of the uncontrollable elements and plan in such a way that these elements do not preclude the achievement of marketing objectives. They can also set about to affect changes that lead to quicker acceptance of their products or marketing programs.

Planning marketing strategy in terms of the uncontrollable elements of a market is necessary in a domestic market as well, but when a company is operating internationally, each new environment that is influenced by elements unfamiliar and sometimes unrecognizable to the marketer complicates the task. For these reasons, special effort and study are needed to absorb enough understanding of the foreign culture to cope with the uncontrollable features. Perhaps it is safe to generalize that of all the tools the foreign marketer must have, those that help generate empathy for another culture are the most valuable. Each of the cultural elements is explored in depth in subsequent chapters. Specific attention is given to business customs, political culture, and legal culture in the following chapters.

Key Terms

Culture	Rituals	Cultural sensitivity	Cultural congruence
Social institutions	Linguistic distance	Cultural borrowing	Planned change
Cultural values	Aesthetics		

Questions

1. Define the key terms listed above.
2. What role does the marketer play as a change agent?
3. Discuss the three cultural change strategies a foreign marketer can pursue.
4. "Culture is pervasive in all marketing activities." Discuss.
5. What is the importance of cultural empathy to foreign marketers? How do they acquire cultural empathy?
6. Why should a foreign marketer be concerned with the study of culture?
7. What is the popular definition of culture? Where does culture come from?
8. "Members of a society borrow from other cultures to solve problems that they face in common." What does this mean? What is the significance to marketing?
9. "For the inexperienced marketer, the 'similar-but-different' aspect of culture creates an illusion of similarity that usually does not exist." Discuss and give examples.
10. Outline the elements of culture as seen by an anthropologist. How can a marketer use this cultural scheme?
11. Social institutions affect culture and marketing in a variety of ways. Discuss, giving examples.
12. "Markets are the result of the three-way interaction of a marketer's efforts, economic conditions, and all other elements of the culture." Comment.

13. What are some particularly troublesome problems caused by language in foreign marketing? Discuss.

14. Suppose you were asked to prepare a cultural analysis for a potential market. What would you do? Outline the steps and comment briefly on each.

15. Cultures are dynamic. How do they change? Are there cases in which changes are not resisted but actually preferred? Explain. What is the relevance to marketing?

16. How can resistance to cultural change influence product introduction? Are there any similarities in domestic marketing? Explain, giving examples.

17. Innovations are described as either functional or dysfunctional. Explain and give examples of each.

18. Defend the proposition that a multinational corporation has no responsibility for the consequences of an innovation beyond the direct effects of the innovation, such as the product's safety, performance, and so forth.

19. Find a product whose introduction into a foreign culture may cause dysfunctional consequences and describe how the consequences might be eliminated and the product still profitably introduced.

Chapter 5

Culture, Management Style, and Business Systems

CHAPTER LEARNING OBJECTIVES

What you should learn from Chapter 5:

LO1 The necessity for adapting to cultural differences

LO2 How and why management styles vary around
the world

LO3 The extent and implications of gender bias in
other countries

LO4 The importance of cultural differences in business
ethics

LO5 The differences between relationship-oriented and
information-oriented cultures

Global Perspective

DO BLONDES HAVE MORE FUN IN JAPAN?

Recounts one American executive, "My first trip to Japan was pretty much a disaster for several reasons. The meetings didn't run smoothly because every day at least 20, if not more, people came walking in and out of the room just to look at me. It is one thing to see a woman at the negotiation table, but to see a woman who happens to be blonde, young, and very tall by Japanese standards (5'8" with no shoes) leading the discussions was more than most of the Japanese men could handle."

"Even though I was the lead negotiator for the Ford team, the Japanese would go out of their way to avoid speaking directly to me. At the negotiation table I purposely sat in the center of my team, in the spokesperson's strategic position. Their key person would not sit across from me, but rather two places down. Also, no one would address questions and/or remarks to me—to everyone (all male) on our team—but none to me. They would never say my name or acknowledge my presence. And most disconcerting of all, they appeared to be laughing at me. We would be talking about a serious topic such as product liability, I would make a point or ask a question, and after a barrage of Japanese they would all start laughing."

Another example regards toys and consumer behavior. For years, Barbie dolls sold in Japan looked different from their U.S. counterparts. They had Asian facial features, black hair, and Japanese-inspired fashions.

Then about a decade ago, Mattel Inc. conducted consumer research around the world and learned something surprising: The original Barbie, with her yellow hair and blue eyes, played as well in Hong Kong as it did in Hollywood. Girls didn't care if Barbie didn't look like them, at least if you believed their marketing research.

"It's all about fantasies and hair," said Peter Broegger, general manager of Mattel's Asian operations. "Blonde Barbie sells just as well in Asia as in the United States."

So Mattel began rethinking one of the basic tenets of its $55 billion global industry—that children in different countries want different playthings. The implications were significant for kids, parents, and particularly the company. In the past, giants such as Mattel, Hasbro Inc., and Lego Co. produced toys and gear in a variety of styles. But Mattel went the other direction, designing and marketing one version worldwide. Sales plummeted, forcing a Barbie makeover that most recently includes Hello Kitty clothes and a new video game, iDesign. Then, even at age 50, Barbie began making money again.

Sources: James D. Hodgson, Yoshihiro Sano, and John L. Graham, *Doing Business with the New Japan, Succeeding in America's Richest International Market* (Latham, MD: Rowman & Littlefield, 2008); Lisa Banon and Carlta Vitzthum, "One-Toy-Fits-All: How Industry Learned to Love the Global Kid," *The Wall Street Journal*, April 29, 2003, p. A1; John Kell and Melodie Warner, "Mattel Posts Strong Results, Raises Dividend," *The Wall Street Journal*, January 12, 2012.

Perhaps nothing causes more problems for Americans negotiating in other countries than their impatience. Everyone around the world knows that delaying tactics work well against time-conscious U.S. bargainers.

Culture, including all its elements, profoundly affects management style and overall business systems. This is not a new idea. German sociologist Max Weber made the first strong case back in 1930.[1] Culture not only establishes the criteria for day-to-day business behavior but also forms general patterns of values and motivations. Executives are largely captives of their heritages and cannot totally escape the elements of culture they learned growing up.

In the United States, for example, the historical perspective of individualism and "winning the West" seems to be manifest in individual wealth or corporate profit being dominant measures of success. Japan's lack of frontiers and natural resources and its dependence on trade have focused individual and corporate success criteria on uniformity, subordination to the group, and society's ability to maintain high levels of employment. The feudal background of southern Europe tends to emphasize maintenance of both individual and corporate power and authority while blending those feudal traits with paternalistic concern for minimal welfare for workers and other members of society. Various studies identify North Americans as individualists, Japanese as consensus oriented and committed to the group, and central and southern Europeans as elitists and rank conscious. Although these descriptions are stereotypical, they illustrate cultural differences that are often manifest in business behavior and practices. Such differences also coincide quite well with Hofstede's scores listed in Exhibit 4.7 in the last chapter.[2]

A lack of empathy for and knowledge of foreign business practices can create insurmountable barriers to successful business relations.[3] Some businesses plot their strategies with the idea that their counterparts from other business cultures are similar to themselves and are moved by similar interests, motivations, and goals—that they are "just like us." Even though that may be true in some respects, enough differences exist to cause frustration, miscommunication, and, ultimately, failed business opportunities if these differences are not understood and responded to properly.

Knowledge of the *management style*—that is, the business culture, management values, and business methods and behaviors—existing in a country and a willingness to accommodate the differences are important to success in an international market. Unless marketers remain flexible by accepting differences in basic patterns of thinking, local business tempo, religious practices, political structure, and family loyalty, they are hampered, if not prevented, from reaching satisfactory conclusions to business transactions. In such situations, obstacles take many forms, but it is not unusual to have one negotiator's business proposition accepted over another's simply because "that one understands us."

This chapter focuses on matters specifically related to management style. Besides an analysis of the need for adaptation, it reviews differences in management styles and ethics and concludes with a discussion of culture's influence on strategic thinking.

Required Adaptation

LO1

The necessity for adapting to cultural differences

Adaptation is a key concept in international marketing, and willingness to adapt is a crucial attitude. Adaptation, or at least accommodation, is required on small matters as well as large ones. In fact, small, seemingly insignificant situations are often the most crucial. More than tolerance of an alien culture is required. Affirmative acceptance, that is, open tolerance, may be needed as well. Through such affirmative acceptance, adaptation becomes easier because empathy for another's point of view naturally leads to ideas for meeting cultural differences.

As a guide to adaptation, all who wish to deal with individuals, firms, or authorities in foreign countries should be able to meet 10 basic criteria: (1) open tolerance, (2) flexibility, (3) humility, (4) justice/fairness, (5) ability to adjust to varying tempos, (6) curiosity/interest, (7) knowledge

[1]Max Weber, *The Protestant Ethic and Spirit of Capitalism* (London: George Allen & Unwin, 1930, 1976).

[2]Geert Hofstede, *Culture's Consequences*, 2nd ed. (Thousand Oaks, CA: Sage, 2001).

[3]An important book on this topic is by Soon Ang and Linn Van Dyne, eds., *Handbook of Cultural Intelligence* (Armonk, NY: M.E. Sharpe, 2008).

of the country, (8) liking for others, (9) ability to command respect, and (10) ability to integrate oneself into the environment. In short, add the quality of adaptability to the qualities of a good executive for a composite of the successful international marketer. It is difficult to argue with these 10 items. As one critic commented, "They border on the 12 points of the Boy Scout Law." However, as you read this chapter, you will see that it is the obvious that we sometimes overlook.

Degree of Adaptation

Adaptation does not require business executives to forsake their ways and change to local customs; rather, executives must be aware of local customs and be willing to accommodate those differences that can cause misunderstandings. Essential to effective adaptation is awareness of one's own culture and the recognition that differences in others can cause anxiety, frustration, and misunderstanding of the host's intentions. The self-reference criterion (SRC) is especially operative in business customs. If we do not understand our foreign counterpart's customs, we are more likely to evaluate that person's behavior in terms of what is familiar to us. For example, from an American perspective, a Brazilian executive interrupting frequently during a business meeting may seem quite rude, even though such behavior simply reflects a cultural difference in conversational coordination.

The key to adaptation is to remain American but to develop an understanding of and willingness to accommodate the differences that exist. Studies show that remaining open to new ideas, although more difficult in the face of operating in a country other than one's own, is extremely beneficial for managing in multinational situations.[4] A successful marketer knows that in China it is important to make points without winning arguments; criticism, even if asked for, can cause a host to lose face. In Germany, it is considered discourteous to use first names unless specifically invited to do so. Instead, address a person as Herr, Frau, or Fraulein with the last name. In Brazil, do not be offended by the Brazilian inclination to touch during conversation. Such a custom is not a violation of your personal space but rather the Brazilian way of greeting, emphasizing a point, or making a gesture of goodwill and friendship. A Chinese, German, or Brazilian does not expect you to act like one of them. After all, you are American, not Chinese, German, or Brazilian. Further it would be foolish for an American to give up the ways that have contributed so notably to American success. It would be equally foolish for others to give up their ways. When different cultures meet, open tolerance and a willingness to accommodate each other's differences are necessary. Once a marketer is aware of cultural differences and the probable consequences of failure to adapt or accommodate, the seemingly endless variety of customs must be assessed. Where does one begin? Which customs should be absolutely adhered to? Which others can be ignored? Fortunately, among the many obvious differences that exist between cultures, only a few are troubling.

Imperatives, Electives, and Exclusives

Business customs can be grouped into *imperatives*, customs that must be recognized and accommodated; *electives*, customs to which adaptation is helpful but not necessary; and *exclusives*, customs in which an outsider must not participate. An international marketer must appreciate the nuances of cultural imperatives, cultural electives, and cultural exclusives.

Cultural Imperatives.

Cultural imperatives are the business customs and expectations that must be met and conformed to or avoided if relationships are to be successful. Successful businesspeople know the Chinese word *guanxi*,[5] the Japanese *ningen kankei*, or the Latin American *compadre*. All refer to friendship, human relations, or attaining a level of trust.[6] They also know there is no substitute for establishing friendship in some cultures before effective business negotiations can begin.

[4]Christian Troster and Daan van Knippenberg, "Leader Openness, National Dissimilarity, and Voice in Multinational Teams," *Journal of International Business Studies* 43 (2012), pp. 591–613.

[5]Alaka N. Rao, Jone L. Pearce, and Katherine Xin, "Governments, Reciprocal Exchange, and Trust Among Business Associates," *Journal of International Business Studies* 36 (2005), pp. 104–18; Kam-hon Lee, Gong-ming Qian, Julie H. Yu, and Ying Ho, "Trading Favors for Marketing Advantage: Evidence from Hong Kong, China, and the United States," *Journal of International Marketing* 13 (2005), pp. 1–35.

[6]Srilata Zaheer and Akbar Zaheer, "Trust across Borders," *Journal of International Business Studies* 37 (2006), pp. 21–29.

Informal discussions, entertaining, mutual friends, contacts, and just spending time with others are ways *guanxi*, *ningen kankei*, *compadre*, and other trusting relationships are developed. In those cultures in which friendships are a key to success, the businessperson should not slight the time required for their development. Friendship motivates local agents to make more sales, and friendship helps establish the right relationship with end users, which leads to more sales over a longer period. Naturally, after-sales service, price, and the product must be competitive, but the marketer who has established *guanxi*, *ningen kankei*, or *compadre* has the edge. Establishing friendship is an imperative in many cultures. If friendship is not established, the marketer risks not earning trust and acceptance, the basic cultural prerequisites for developing and retaining effective business relationships.

The significance of establishing friendship cannot be overemphasized, especially in those countries where family relationships are close. In China, for example, the outsider is, at best, in fifth place in order of importance when deciding with whom to conduct business. The family is first, then the extended family, then neighbors from one's hometown, then former classmates, and only then, reluctantly, strangers—and the last only after a trusting relationship has been established.

In some cultures, a person's demeanor is more critical than in other cultures. For example, it is probably never acceptable to lose your patience, raise your voice, or correct someone in public, no matter how frustrating the situation. In some cultures such behavior would only cast you as boorish, but in others, it could end a business deal. In Asian cultures it is imperative to avoid causing your counterpart to lose face. In China, to raise your voice, to shout at a Chinese person in public, or to correct one in front of his or her peers will cause that person to lose face. However, to apologize for one's own oversights or mistakes in cultures like China and Japan, where errors harm the collective good, is mandatory. Moreover, if a corporation is involved, the apology should be widely publicized.[7]

A complicating factor in cultural awareness is that what may be an imperative to avoid in one culture is an imperative to do in another. For example, in Japan, prolonged eye contact is considered offensive, and it is imperative that it be avoided. However, with Arab and Latin American executives, it is important to make strong eye contact, or you run the risk of being seen as evasive and untrustworthy.

Cultural Electives. Cultural electives relate to areas of behavior or to customs that cultural aliens may wish to conform to or participate in but that are not required. In other words, following the custom in question is not particularly important but is permissible. The majority of customs fit into this category. One need not greet another man with a kiss (a custom in some countries), eat foods that disagree with the digestive system (so long as the refusal is gracious), or drink alcoholic beverages (if for health, personal, or religious reasons). However, a symbolic attempt to participate in such options is not only acceptable but also may help establish rapport. It demonstrates that the marketer has studied the culture. Japanese do not expect a Westerner to bow and to understand the ritual of bowing among Japanese, yet a symbolic bow indicates interest and some sensitivity to Japanese culture that is acknowledged as a gesture of goodwill. It may help pave the way to a strong, trusting relationship.

A cultural elective in one county may be an imperative in another. For example, in some cultures, one can accept or tactfully and politely reject an offer of a beverage, whereas in other cases, the offer of a beverage is a special ritual and to refuse it is an

BEIJING, CHINA: German Chancellor Angela Merkel and Chinese Prime Minister Wen Jiabao toast after the EU–China Business Summit at the Great Hall of the People in Beijing. The summit was boosted by the settlement of a trade row that had left 80 million Chinese-made garments piled up in European seaports, unable to be delivered to shops under a quota pact agreed to at the time. Drinking half a bottle is a cultural elective, but taking a sip is more of an imperative in this case.

[7]Christopher Bodeen, "Apple CEO Apologizes to China for Repair Policies," *Associated Press*, April 2, 2013; Takashi Mochizuki and Eric Pfanner, "Sony Warns of Deeper Woes," *The Wall Street Journal*, September 18, 2014, pp. B1, B6.

insult. In the Czech Republic, an aperitif or other liqueur offered at the beginning of a business meeting, even in the morning, is a way to establish goodwill and trust. It is a sign that you are being welcomed as a friend. It is imperative that you accept unless you make it clear to your Czech counterpart that the refusal is because of health or religion. Chinese business negotiations often include banquets at which large quantities of alcohol are consumed in an endless series of toasts. It is imperative that you participate in the toasts with a raised glass of the offered beverage, but to drink is optional. Your Arab business associates will offer coffee as part of the important ritual of establishing a level of friendship and trust; you should accept, even if you only take a ceremonial sip. Cultural electives are the most visibly different customs and thus, more obvious. Often, it is compliance with the less obvious imperatives and exclusives that is more critical.

Cultural Exclusives.   Cultural exclusives are those customs or behavior patterns reserved exclusively for the locals and from which the foreigner is barred. For example, a Christian attempting to act like a Muslim would be repugnant to a follower of Mohammed. Equally offensive is a foreigner criticizing or joking about a country's politics, mores, and peculiarities (that is, peculiar to the foreigner), even though locals may, among themselves, criticize such issues. There is truth in the old adage, "I'll curse my brother, but if you curse him, you'll have a fight." Few cultural traits are reserved exclusively for locals, but a foreigner must carefully refrain from participating in those that are.

You should always stay away from politics (handwritten note)

Foreign managers need to be perceptive enough to know when they are dealing with an imperative, an elective, or an exclusive and have the adaptability to respond to each. There are not many imperatives or exclusives, but most offensive behaviors result from not recognizing them. It is not necessary to obsess over committing a faux pas. Most sensible businesspeople will make allowances for the occasional misstep. But the fewer you make, the smoother the relationship will be. By the way, you can ask for help. That is, if you have a good relationship with your foreign counterparts, you can always ask them to tell you when and how you have "misbehaved."

The Impact of American Culture on Management Style   There are at least three reasons to focus briefly on American culture and management style. First, for American readers, it is important to be aware of the elements of culture influencing decisions and behaviors. Such a self-awareness will help American readers adapt to working with associates in other cultures. Second, for readers new to American culture, it is useful to better understand your business associates from the States. The U.S. market is the biggest export market in the world, and we hope this knowledge will help everyone be more patient while conducting business across borders. Third, since the late 1990s, American business culture has been exported around the world, just as in the 1980s Japanese management practices were imitated almost everywhere. Management practices developed in the U.S. environment will not be appropriate and useful everywhere. That is clear. So understanding their bases will help everyone make decisions about applying, adapting, or rejecting American practices. Indeed, most often Peter Drucker's advice will apply: "Different people have to be managed differently."[8]

There are many divergent views regarding the most important ideas on which normative U.S. cultural concepts are based. Those that occur most frequently in discussions of cross-cultural evaluations are represented by the following:

- "Master of destiny" viewpoint.
- Independent enterprise as the instrument of social action.
- Personnel selection and reward based on merit.
- Decisions based on objective analysis.
- Wide sharing in decision making.

---

[8]Peter F. Drucker, *Management Challenges for the 21st Century* (New York: HarperBusiness, 1999), p. 17.

- Never-ending quest for improvement.
- Competition produces efficiency.

The "master of destiny" philosophy is fundamental to U.S. management thought. Simply stated, people can substantially influence the future; they are in control of their own destinies. This viewpoint also reflects the attitude that though luck may influence an individual's future, on balance, persistence, hard work, a commitment to fulfill expectations, and effective use of time give people control of their destinies. In contrast, many cultures have a more fatalistic approach to life. They believe individual destiny is determined by a higher order and that what happens cannot be controlled.

In the United States, approaches to planning, control, supervision, commitment, motivation, scheduling, and deadlines are all influenced by the concept that individuals can control their futures. Recall from Chapter 4 that the United States scored highest on Hofstede's individualism scale.[9] In cultures with more collectivistic and fatalistic beliefs, these good business practices may be followed, but concern for the final outcome is different. After all, if one believes the future is determined by an uncontrollable higher order, then what difference does individual effort really make? In individualistic cultures, where one's effort determines more of one's destiny, issues of fairness in opportunity loom large. For example, heavy workloads distributed unequally between employees in collectivist countries are seen less onerous and unfair than similar workloads in individualist cultures, where such conditions lead to lower morale and higher turnover.[10]

The acceptance of the idea that *independent enterprise* is an instrument for social action is the fundamental concept of U.S. corporations. A corporation is recognized as an entity that has rules and continuity of existence and is a separate and vital social institution. This recognition can result in strong feelings of obligation to serve the company. Indeed, the company may take precedence over family, friends, or activities that might detract from what is best for the company. This idea is in sharp contrast to the attitudes held by Mexicans, who feel strongly that personal relationships are more important in daily life than work and the company, and Chinese, who consider a broader set of stakeholders as crucial.

Consistent with the view that individuals control their own destinies is the belief that personnel selection and reward must be made on *merit*. The selection, promotion, motivation, or dismissal of personnel by U.S. managers emphasizes the need to select the best-qualified persons for jobs, retaining them as long as their performance meets standards of expectations and continuing the opportunity for upward mobility as long as those standards are met. In other cultures where friendship or family ties may be more important than the vitality of the organization, the criteria for selection, organization, and motivation are substantially different from those in U.S. companies. In some cultures, organizations expand to accommodate the maximum number of friends and relatives. If one knows that promotions are made on the basis of personal ties and friendships rather than on merit, a fundamental motivating lever is lost. However, in many other cultures, social pressure from one's group often motivates strongly. Superstitions can even come into play in personnel selection; in Japan, a person's blood type can influence hiring decisions![11]

The very strong belief in the United States that business decisions are based on *objective analysis* and that managers strive to be scientific has a profound effect on the U.S. manager's attitudes toward objectivity in decision making and accuracy of data. Although judgment and intuition are important tools for making decisions, most U.S. managers believe decisions must be supported and based on accurate and relevant information. Thus, in U.S. business, great emphasis is placed on the collection and free flow of information to all levels within the organization and on frankness of expression in the evaluation of business opinions or decisions. In other cultures, such factual and rational support for decisions is not as important; the accuracy

[9]Hofstede, *Culture's Consequences.*

[10]Liu-Qin Yang and 28 others, "Individualism-Collectivism as a Moderator of the Work Demands-Strains Relationship: A Cross-Level and Cross-National Examination," *Journal of International Business Studies* 43 (2012), pp. 424–43.

[11]"The Importance of Blood Type in Japanese Culture," *Japan Today*, January 20, 2012.

of data and even the proper reporting of data are not prime prerequisites. Furthermore, existing data frequently are for the eyes of a select few. The frankness of expression and openness in dealing with data, characteristic of U.S. businesses, do not fit easily into some cultures.

Compatible with the views that one controls one's own destiny and that advancement is based on merit is the prevailing idea of *wide sharing in decision making*. Although decision making is not a democratic process in U.S. businesses, there is a strong belief that individuals in an organization require and, indeed, need the responsibility of making decisions for their continued development. Thus, decisions are frequently decentralized, and the ability as well as the responsibility for making decisions is pushed down to lower ranks of management. In many cultures, decisions are highly centralized, in part because of the belief that only a few in the company have the right or the ability to make decisions. In the Middle East, for example, only top executives make decisions.

A key value underlying the American business system is reflected in the notion of a *never-ending quest for improvement*. The United States has always been a relatively activist society; in many walks of life, the prevailing question is "Can it be done better?" Thus, management concepts reflect the belief that change is not only normal but also necessary, that nothing is sacred or above improvement. Results are what count; if practices must change to achieve results, then change is in order. In other cultures, the strength and power of those in command frequently rest not on change but on the premise that the status quo demands stable structure. To suggest improvement implies that those in power have failed; for someone in a lower position to suggest change would be viewed as a threat to another's private domain rather than the suggestion of an alert and dynamic individual.

Perhaps most fundamental to Western management practices is the notion that *competition is crucial for efficiency*, improvement, and regeneration. Gordon Gekko put it most banally in the movie *Wall Street:* "Greed is good." Adam Smith in his *The Wealth of Nations* wrote one of the most important sentences in the English language: "By pursuing his own interests he frequently promotes that of the society more effectually than when he really intended to promote it."[12] This "invisible hand" notion justifies competitive behavior because it improves society and its organizations. Competition among salespeople (for example, sales contests) is a good thing because it promotes better individual

---

[12]Adam Smith, *The Wealth of Nations*, Book IV (1776; reprint, New York: Modern Library, 1994), p. 485.

What's different about Adam Smith's, "By pursuing his own interests he frequently promotes that of society more effectually than when he really intended to promote it," and Gordon Gekko's, "Greed is good" statements? It's the adverb. Smith didn't say "always," "most of the time," or even "often." He said "frequently." Today many on Wall Street ignore this crucial difference.

performance and, consequently, better corporate performance. In fact, recent research has shown how Adam Smith's ideas actually complement and improve modern international business theory and practice, centuries later.[13] However, managers and policymakers in other cultures often do not share this "greed is good" view. Cooperation is more salient, and efficiencies are attained through reduced transaction costs. These latter views are more prevalent in collectivistic cultures such as China and Japan.

Management Styles around the World[14]

Because of the diverse structures, management values, and behaviors encountered in international business, there is considerable variation in the ways business is conducted.[15] No matter how thoroughly prepared a marketer may be when approaching a foreign markct, a certain amount of cultural shock occurs when differences in the contact level, communications emphasis, tempo, and formality of foreign businesses are encountered. Ethical standards differ substantially across cultures, as do rituals such as sales interactions and negotiations. In most countries, the foreign trader is also likely to encounter a fairly high degree of government involvement. Among the four dimensions of Hofstede's cultural values discussed in Chapter 4, the Individualism/Collectivism Index (IDV) and Power Distance Index (PDI) are especially relevant in examining methods of doing business cross-culturally.

LO2

How and why management styles vary around the world

Authority and Decision Making

Business size, ownership, public accountability, and cultural values that determine the prominence of status and position (PDI) combine to influence the authority structure of business. In high-PDI countries such as Mexico and Malaysia, understanding the rank and status of clients and business partners is much more important than in more egalitarian (low-PDI) societies such as Denmark and Israel. In high-PDI countries, subordinates are not likely to contradict bosses, but in low-PDI countries, they often do. Although the international businessperson is confronted with a variety of authority patterns that can complicate decision making in the global environment, most are a variation of three typical patterns: top-level management decisions, decentralized decisions, and committee or group decisions.

Top-level management decision making is generally found in situations in which family or close ownership[16] gives absolute control to owners and businesses are small enough to allow such centralized decision making. In many European businesses, such as those in France, decision-making authority is guarded jealously by a few at the top who exercise tight control. In other countries, such as Mexico and Venezuela, where a semifeudal, land-equals-power heritage exists, management styles are characterized as autocratic and paternalistic. Decision-making participation by middle management tends to be deemphasized; dominant family members make decisions that tend to please the family members more than to increase productivity. This description is also true for government-owned companies in which professional managers have to follow decisions made by politicians, who generally lack any working knowledge about management. In Middle Eastern countries, the top executive makes all decisions and prefers to deal only with other executives with decision-making powers. There, one always does business with an individual per se rather than an office or title.

---

[13]Peter J. Buckley, "Adam Smith's Theory of Knowledge and International Business Theory and Practice." *Journal of International Business Studies* 45 (2014), pp. 102–9.

[14]A website that provides information about management styles around the world is http://www.globalnegotiationresources.com.

[15]Sam Han, Tony Kang, Stephen Salter, and Yong Keun Yoo, "A Cross-Country Study on the Effects of National Culture on Earnings Management," *Journal of International Business Studies* 41 (2010), pp. 123–41.

[16]Several researchers have empirically demonstrated the influence and downside of such authority structures. See Kathy Fogel, "Oligarchic Family Control, Social Economic Outcomes, and the Quality of Government," *Journal of International Business Studies* 37 (2006), pp. 603–22; Naresh Kharti, Eric W. K. Tsang, and Thomas M. Begley, "Cronyism: A Cross-Cultural Analysis," *Journal of International Business Studies* 37 (2006), pp. 61–75; Ekin K. Pellegrini and Terri A. Scandura, "Leader-Member Exchange (LMX), Paternalism, and Delegation in the Turkish Business Culture: An Empirical Investigation," *Journal of International Business Studies* 37 (2006), pp. 264–79; Narjess Boubakri, Omrane Guedhami, and Dev Mishra, "Family Control and the Implied Cost of Equity: Evidence before and after the Asian Financial Crisis," *Journal of International Business Studies* 41, no. 3 (2010), pp. 451–74.

CROSSING BORDERS 5.1   Don't Beat Your Mother-in-Law!

The crowding and collectivism of Chinese culture provide fertile ground for hierarchy. Add in a little Confucian advice, and status relationships become central for understanding Chinese business systems. Confucius's teachings were the foundation for Chinese education for 2,000 years, until 1911. He defined five cardinal relationships: between ruler and ruled, husband and wife, parents and children, older and younger brothers, and friends. Except for the last, all relationships were hierarchical. The ruled, wives, children, and younger brothers, were all counseled to trade obedience and loyalty for the benevolence of their rulers, husbands, parents, and older brothers, respectively. Strict adherence to these vertical relations yielded social harmony, the antidote for the violence and civil war of his time.

Obedience and deference to one's superiors remain strong values in Chinese culture. The story of the Cheng family illustrates the historical salience of social hierarchy and high power distance:

In October 1865, Cheng Han-cheng's wife had the insolence to beat her mother-in-law. This was regarded as such a heinous crime that the following punishment was meted out: Cheng and his wife were both skinned alive, in front of the mother, their skin displayed at city gates in various towns and their bones burned to ashes. Cheng's granduncle, the eldest of his close relatives, was beheaded; his uncle and two brothers, and

the head of the Cheng clan, were hanged. The wife's mother, her face tattooed with the words "neglected the daughter's education," was paraded through seven provinces. Her father was beaten 80 strokes and banished to a distance of 3,000 *li*. The heads of the family in the houses to the right and left of Cheng's were beaten 80 strokes and banished to Heilung-kiang. The educational officer in town was beaten 60 strokes and banished to a distance of 1,000 *li*. Cheng's nine-month-old boy was given a new name and put in the county magistrate's care. Cheng's land was to be left in waste "forever." All this was recorded on a stone stele, and rubbings of the inscriptions were distributed throughout the empire.

We recommend you have your children read this story! But seriously, notice the authorities held responsible the entire social network for the woman's breach of hierarchy. Status is no joke among Chinese. Age and rank of executives and other status markers must be taken into account during business negotiations with Chinese. American informality and egalitarianism will not play well on the western side of the Pacific.

Sources: Dau-lin Hsu, "The Myth of the 'Five Human Relations' of Confucius," *Monumenta Sinica* 1970, pp. 29, 31, quoted in Gary G. Hamilton, "Patriarchalism in Imperial China and Western Europe: A Revision of Weber's Sociology of Domination," *Theory and Society* 13, pp. 393–425; N. Mark Lam and John L. Graham, *China Now, Doing Business in the World's Most Dynamic Market* (New York: McGraw-Hill, 2007).

As businesses grow and professional management develops, there is a shift toward decentralized management decision making. Decentralized decision making allows executives at different levels of management to exercise authority over their own functions. As mentioned previously, this approach is typical of large-scale businesses with highly developed management systems, such as those found in the United States. A trader in the United States is likely to be dealing with middle management, and title or position generally takes precedence over the individual holding the job. In other countries, the influence of a Chief Marketing Officer (CMO), for example, has been shown to be culturally dependent. That is, in cultures high in collectivism and uncertainty avoidance, CMOs have been shown to be given higher levels of trust.[17]

Committee decision making is by group or consensus. Committees may operate on a centralized or decentralized basis, but the concept of committee management implies something quite different from the individualized functioning of the top management and decentralized decision-making arrangements just discussed. Because Asian cultures and religions tend to emphasize harmony and collectivism, it is not surprising that group decision making predominates there. Despite the emphasis on rank and hierarchy in Japanese social structure, business emphasizes group participation, group harmony, and group decision making—but at the top management level.

The demands of these three types of authority systems on a marketer's ingenuity and adaptability are evident. In the case of the authoritative and delegated societies, the chief problem is to identify the individual with authority. In the committee decision setup, every committee member must be convinced of the merits of the proposition or product in question. The marketing approach to each of these situations differs.

---

[17]Andreas Englelen, Fritz Lackhoff, and Susanne Schmidt, "How Can Chief Marketing Officers Strengthen Their Influence? A Social Capital Study Across Six Country Groups," *Journal of International Marketing* 21 (2013), pp. 88–109.

Management Objectives and Aspirations

The internationalization of top executives throughout the world is a topic of increasing study and importance.[18] The training and background (i.e., cultural environment) of managers significantly affect their personal and business outlooks.[19] Society as a whole establishes the social rank or status of management, and cultural background dictates patterns of aspirations and objectives among businesspeople. One study reports that higher CEO compensation is found in Scandinavian firms exposed to Anglo-American financial influence and in part reflects a pay premium for increased risk of dismissal.[20] These cultural influences affect the attitude of managers toward innovation, new products, and conducting business with foreigners. To fully understand another's management style, one must appreciate an individual's values, which are usually reflected in the goals of the business organization and in the practices that prevail within the company. In dealing with foreign business, a marketer must be particularly aware of the varying objectives and aspirations of management.

Security and Mobility.   Personal security and job mobility relate directly to basic human motivation and therefore have widespread economic and social implications. The word *security* is somewhat ambiguous, and this very ambiguity provides some clues to managerial variation. To some, security means a big paycheck and the training and ability required for moving from company to company within the business hierarchy; for others, it means the security of lifetime positions with their companies; to still others, it means adequate retirement plans and other welfare benefits. European companies, particularly in the more hierarchical (PDI) countries, such as France and Italy, have a strong paternalistic orientation, and it is assumed that individuals will work for one company for the majority of their lives. For example, in Britain, managers place great importance on individual achievement and autonomy, whereas French managers place great importance on competent supervision, sound company policies, fringe benefits, security, and comfortable working conditions. French managers have much less mobility than British. Finally, research has shown such differences to be general—commitment of workers to their companies tended to be higher in countries lower in individualism (IDV) and higher in power distance (PDI).[21] Such cultural influences on personnel patterns regarding security are are reflected in companies' investment behavior–cultures higher in individualism (IDV) make risker R&D investments, having less fear of harming the collective good of the firm.[22]

Personal Life.   For many individuals, a good personal and/or family life takes priority over profit, security, or any other goal. In his worldwide study of individual aspirations, David McClelland[23] discovered that the culture of some countries stressed the virtue of a good personal life as far more important than profit or achievement. The hedonistic outlook of ancient Greece explicitly included work as an undesirable factor that got in the way of the search for pleasure or a good personal life. Alternatively, according to Max Weber,[24] at least part of the standard of living that we enjoy in the United States today can be attributed to the hard-working Protestant ethic from which we derive much of our business heritage.

To the Japanese, personal life is company life. Many Japanese workers regard their work as the most important part of their overall lives. The Japanese work ethic—maintenance of

[18]Lars Oxelheim, Aleskandra Gregoric, Trond Randoy, and Steen Thomsen, "On the Internationalization of Corporate Boards: The Case of Nordic Firms," *Journal of International Business Studies* 44 (2013), pp. 73–194.

[19]Ted Baker, Eric Gedajlovic, and Michael Lubatkin, "A Framework for Comparing Entrepreneurship Processes across Nations," *Journal of International Business Studies* 36 (2005), pp. 492–504.

[20]Lars Oxelheim and Trond Randoy, "The Anglo-American Financial Influence on CEO Compensation in non–Anglo-American Firms," *Journal of International Business Studies* 36 (2005), pp. 470–83.

[21]Ronald Fischer and Angela Mansell, "Commitment across Cultures: A Meta-Analytic Approach," *Journal of International Business Studies* 40 (2009), pp. 1339–58.

[22]Liang Shao, Cuck C. Y. Kwok, and Ran Zhang, "National Culture and Corporate Investment," *Journal of International Business Studies* 44 (2013), pp. 745–63.

[23]David C. McClelland, *The Achieving Society* (New York: The Free Press, 1985).

[24]Weber, *The Protestant Ethic*.

Exhibit 5.1
Annual Hours Worked

Source: OECD, Labor Market
Indicators, 2012.

	2000	**2010**
United Kingdom	1700	1647
Canada	1775	1702
Germany	1473	1419
Netherlands	1435	1377
Japan	1821	1733
Norway	1455	1414
United States	1814	1778
S. Korea	2512	2193
Mexico	1888	1866
Italy	1861	1778

a sense of purpose—derives from company loyalty and frequently results in the Japanese employee maintaining identity with the corporation. Although this notion continues to be true for the majority, strong evidence indicates that the faltering Japanese economy has affected career advancement patterns[25] and has moved the position of the Japanese "salary man" from that of one of Japan's business elite to one of some derision. Japan's business culture is gradually shifting away from the lifelong employment that led to intense company loyalty. Now even Japanese formality at the office is bowing to higher oil prices; ties and buttoned collars are being shed to leave air-conditioning thermostats set at 82 degrees.

We can get some measure of the work–personal life trade-off made in different cultures with reference to Exhibit 5.1. As a point of reference, 40 hours per week times 50 weeks equals 2,000 hours. The Americans appear to be in the middle of hours worked, far above the northern Europeans[26] and way below the South Koreans. Most Americans are getting about two weeks of paid vacation, while in Europe they are taking between four and six weeks! In South Korea and other Asian nations, Saturday is a workday. Although we do not list the numbers for China, the new pressures of free enterprise are adding hours and stress there as well. However, the scariest datum isn't in the table. Even though hours worked in the United States have decreased in the past five years, Americans still work 20 hours more per year than they did in 1990, with 40 percent of Americans leaving vacation days unused.[27] Trends show that those with more education actually enjoy less leisure time than the educated.[28] Thank you Max Weber! We wonder: How will things be in 2020?

Affiliation and Social Acceptance.   In some countries, acceptance by neighbors and fellow workers appears to be a predominant goal within business. The Asian outlook is reflected in the group decision making so important in Japan, and the Japanese place high importance on fitting in with their group. Group identification is so strong in Japan that when a worker is asked what he does for a living, he generally answers by telling you he works for Sumitomo or Mitsubishi or Matsushita, rather than that he is a chauffeur, an engineer, or a chemist. Indeed, Mitsubishi has a corporate mausoleum, where employees' ashes may rest with those of colleagues, extending company loyalty from cradle to grave—and beyond!

Power and Achievement.   Although there is some power seeking by business managers throughout the world, power seems to be a more important motivating force in South American countries. In these countries, many business leaders are not only profit oriented but also use their business positions to become social and political leaders. Related, but different, are the motivations for achievement also identified by management researchers in the United States. One way to measure achievement is by money in the bank; another is high rank—both aspirations particularly relevant to the United States.

[25]George Graen, Ravi Dharwadkar, Rajdeep Grewal, and Mitsuru Wakabayashi, "Japanese Career Progress: An Empirical Examination," *Journal of International Business Studies* 37 (2006), pp. 148–61.

[26]The long-standing practice in France, however, of taking Wednesdays off, is increasingly under attack. See "Weird About Wednesday," *The Economist*, September 21, 2013.

[27]"What Makes Americans Skip Vacations?" *The New York Times*, September 7, 2014, p. 9.

[28]"Nice Work if You Can Get Out," *The Economist*, April 19, 2014, p. 67.

CROSSING BORDERS 5.2   The American Tourist and the Mexican Fisherman

An American tourist was at the pier of a small coastal Mexican village when a small boat with just one fisherman docked. Inside the small boat were several large yellowfin tuna. The tourist complimented the Mexican on the quality of the fish and asked how long it took to catch them.

The Mexican replied, "Only a little while."

The tourist then asked, "Why didn't you stay out longer and catch more fish?"

The Mexican replied, "With this I have enough to support my family's needs."

The tourist then asked, "But what do you do with the rest of your time?"

The Mexican fisherman said, "I sleep late, fish a little, play with my children, take a siesta with my wife, Maria, stroll into the village each evening where I sip wine and play guitar with my amigos. I have a full and busy life."

The tourist scoffed, "I can help you. You should spend more time fishing and with the proceeds, buy a bigger boat. With the proceeds from the bigger boat you could buy several boats. Eventually you would have a fleet of fishing boats. Instead of selling your catch to a middleman you could sell directly to the processor, eventually opening your own cannery. You would control the product, processing, and distribution. You could leave this small village and move to Mexico City, then Los Angeles, and eventually to New York City where you could run your ever-expanding enterprise."

The Mexican fisherman asked, "But, how long will this take?"

The tourist replied, "15 to 20 years."

"But what then?" asked the Mexican.

The tourist laughed and said, "That's the best part. When the time is right you would sell your company stock to the public and become very rich, you would make millions."

"Millions?... Then what?"

The American said, "Then you would retire. Move to a small coastal fishing village where you would sleep late, fish a little, play with your grandkids, take a siesta with your wife, stroll to the village in the evenings where you could sip wine and play your guitar with your amigos."

Source: Author unknown.

Communication Styles

Edward T. Hall, professor of anthropology and for decades a consultant to business and government on intercultural relations, tells us that communication involves much more than just words. His article "The Silent Language of Overseas Business," which appeared in the *Harvard Business Review* in 1960,[29] remains a most worthwhile read. In it he describes the symbolic meanings (silent languages) of *time*, *space*, *things*, *friendships*, and *agreements* and how they vary across cultures. Office space, for example, is managed differently in America—often as a personal perk—than in other countries[30] In 1960 Hall could not have anticipated the innovations brought on by the Internet. However, all of his ideas about

---

[29]*Harvard Business Review*, May–June 1960, pp. 87–96.

[30]"Don't Get Too Cozy," *Bloomberg BusinessWeek*, September 22, 2014, pp. 51–52; Rachel Reintzeig, "Bosses Take a Stand on Where Workers Sit," *The Wall Street Journal*, October 9, 2013, p. B8.

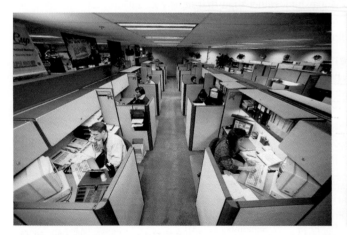

Speaking of office space: Notice the individualism reflected in the American cubicles and the collectivism demonstrated by the Japanese office organization.

cross-cultural communication apply to that medium as well. We begin here with a discussion of communication in the face-to-face setting and then move to the electronic media.

Face-to-Face Communication. No language readily translates into another because the meanings of words differ widely among languages. For example, the word "marriage," even when accurately translated, can connote very different things in different languages—in one it may mean love, in another restrictions. Although language is the basic communication tool of marketers trading in foreign lands, managers, particularly from the United States, often fail to develop even a basic understanding of just one other language, much less master the linguistic nuances that reveal unspoken attitudes and information. Indeed, in the corporate setting, how languages are integrated in multinational companies where several different tongues are spoken is a daunting and difficult task, to be undertaken with care.[31] The formation of trust, for example, in multinational teams is affected by the diversity of language,[32] which may contribute to an "us vs. them" attitude.[33]

On the basis of decades of anthropological fieldwork, Hall[34] places 11 cultures along a high-context/low-context continuum (see Exhibit 5.2). Communication in a high-context

Exhibit 5.2
Context, Communication, and Cultures: Edward Hall's Scale

Note: Patterned after E. T. Hall.

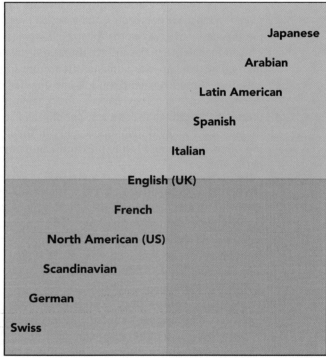

High Context
(Implicit, Emphasis on Conte<u>x</u>t of Communication)

Japanese

Arabian

Latin American

Spanish

Italian

English (UK)

French

North American (US)

Scandinavian

German

Swiss

Low Context
(Explicit, Emphasis on Conte<u>nt</u> of Communication)

[31]Vesa Peltokorpi and Eero Vaara, "Language Policies and Practices in Wholly-owned Foreign Subsidiaries: A Recontextualization Perspective," *Journal of International Business Studies* 43 (2012), pp. 808–33.

[32]Helene Tanzer, Markus Pudelko, and Anne-Wil Harzing, "The Impact of Language Barriers on Trust Formation in Multinational Teams," *Journal of International Business Studies* 45 (2014), pp. 508–35.

[33]Pamela J. Hinds, Tsedal B. Neeley, and Catherine Durnell Cramton, "Language as a Lightning Rod: Power Contests, Emotion Regulation, and Subgroup Dynamics in Global Teams," *Journal of International Business Studies* 45 (2014), pp. 536–61.

[34]Edward T. Hall, "Learning the Arabs' Silent Language," *Psychology Today*, August 1979, pp. 45–53. Hall has several books that should be read by everyone involved in international business, including *The Silent Language* (New York: Doubleday, 1959), *The Hidden Dimension* (New York: Doubleday, 1966), and *Beyond Culture* (New York: Anchor Press-Doubleday, 1976).

culture depends heavily on the contextual (*who* says it, *when* it is said, *how* it is said) or nonverbal aspects of communication, whereas the low-context culture depends more on explicit, verbally expressed communications.[35]

A brief exemplar of the high-/low-context dimension of communication style regards an international marketing executive's description of a Los Angeles business entertainment event: "I picked him [a German client] up at his hotel near LAX and asked what kind of food he wanted for dinner. He said, 'Something local.' Now in LA local food is Mexican food. I'd never met anyone that hadn't had a taco before! We went to a great Mexican place in Santa Monica and had it all, guacamole, salsa, enchiladas, burritos, a real Alka-Seltzer kind of night. When we were done I asked how he liked the food. He responded rather blandly, 'It wasn't very good.'"

The American might have been taken aback by his client's honest, and perhaps too direct, answer. However, the American knew well about German frankness[36] and just rolled with the "blow." Germans, being very low-context oriented, just deliver the information without any social padding. Most Americans would soften the blow some with an answer more like, "It was pretty good, but maybe a bit too spicy." And a high-context oriented Japanese would really pad the response with something like, "It was very good. Thanks." But then the Japanese would never order Mexican food again.

An American or German might view the Japanese response as less than truthful, but from the Japanese perspective, he was just preserving a harmonious relationship. Indeed, the Japanese have two words for truth, *honne* (true mind) and *tatemae* (official stance).[37] The former delivers the information, and the latter preserves the relationship. And in high-context Japan, the latter is often more important. Even eye contact varies among cultures—Americans tend to look one another in the eye during conversations, whereas Asians do so when they have a direct response to your comment or question.[38] Furthermore, in bilingual contexts, people tend to express strong opinions in their native tongue and less emotional statements in their second language.[39] Lack of understanding of such differences in expression can hamper understanding and even a company's performance.[40]

Internet Communications.   The message on a business-to-business website is an extension of the company and should be as sensitive to business customs as any other company representative would be. Once a message is posted, it can be read anywhere, at any time. As a consequence, the opportunity to convey an unintended message is infinite. Nothing about the Web will change the extent to which people identify with their own languages and cultures; thus, language should be at the top of the list when examining the viability of a company's website.

Estimates are that 78 percent of today's website content is written in English, but an English e-mail message cannot be understood by 35 percent of all Internet users. A study of businesses on the European continent highlights the need for companies to respond in the languages of their websites. One-third of the European senior managers surveyed said they would not tolerate English online. They do not believe that middle managers can use English well enough to transact business on the Internet.

---

[35]*Bloomberg Businessweek*, "Office Cultures: A Global Guide," June 13, 2013, p. 15.

[36]Interestingly, the etymology of the term "frankness" has to do with the Franks, an ancient Germanic tribe that settled along the Rhine. This is not mere coincidence; it's history again influencing symbols (that is, language)!

[37]James D. Hodgson, Yoshihiro Sano, and John L. Graham, *Doing Business with the New Japan* (Boulder, CO: Rowman & Littlefield, 2008).

[38]Erin Meyer, "Looking Another Culture in the Eye," *The New York Times*, September 14, 2014, p. 8.

[39]Catherine L. Caldwell-Harris, "Kill One to Save Five? In Another Language, Your Own Thoughts May Be Foreign to You," *Scientific American Mind*, September–October 2014, pp. 71–73.

[40]Adrei Kuzenetsov and Olga Kuznetsova, "Building Professional Discourse in Emerging Markets: Language, Context, and the Challenge of Sensemaking," *Journal of International Business Studies* 45 (2014), pp. 583–99.

At the extreme are the French, who even ban the use of English terms. The French Ministry of Finance issued a directive that all official French civil service correspondence must avoid common English-language business words such as *start-up* and *e-mail;* instead, *jeune pousse* (literally, "a young plant") and *courrier électronique* are recommended.

The solution to the problem is to have country-specific websites, like those of IBM and Marriott. Dell Computer, for example, makes its Premier Pages websites built for its business clients, available in 12 languages. A host of companies specialize in website translations; in addition, software programs are available to translate the company message into another language. However, cultural and linguistic correctness remains a problem with machine translation. If not properly done, English phrases are likely to be translated in a way that will embarrass or even damage a company. One way to avoid this issue is to prepare the original source material in easy-to-translate English, devoid of complicated phrases, idioms, or slang. Unfortunately, no machine translation is available that can manage all the nuances of language or syntax.

It would be ideal if every representative of your company spoke fluently the language of and understood the culture of your foreign customers or business associates; but that is an impossible goal for most companies. However, there is no reason why every person who accesses a company's website should not be able to communicate in his or her own language if a company wants to be truly global.

Finally, e-mail use and usage rates by managers are also affected by culture. That is, businesspeople in high-context cultures do not use the medium to the same extent as those in low-context cultures. Indeed, the structure of the Japanese language has at least hindered the diffusion of Internet technologies in that country.[41] Moreover, businesspeople in Hong Kong behave less cooperatively in negotiations using e-mail than in face-to-face encounters.[42] Much of the contextual information so important in high-context cultures simply cannot be signaled via the computer.

Formality and Tempo

The breezy informality and haste that seem to characterize American business relationships appear to be American exclusives that businesspeople from other countries not only fail to share but also fail to appreciate. A German executive commented that he was taken aback when employees of his Indiana client called him by his first name. He noted, "In Germany you don't do that until you know someone for 10 years—and never if you are at a lower rank." This apparent informality, however, does not indicate a lack of commitment to the job. Comparing British and American business managers, an English executive commented about the American manager's compelling involvement in business: "At a cocktail party or a dinner, the American is still on duty."

Even though Northern Europeans seem to have picked up some American attitudes in recent years, do not count on them being "Americanized." As one writer says, "While using first names in business encounters is regarded as an American vice in many countries, nowhere is it found more offensive than in France," where formality still reigns. Those who work side by side for years still address one another with formal pronouns. France is higher on Hofstede's Power Distance Index (PDI) than the United States, and such differences can lead to cultural misunderstandings. For example, the formalities of French business practices as opposed to Americans' casual manners are symbols of the French need to show rank and Americans' tendency to downplay it. Thus, the French are dubbed snobbish by Americans, while the French consider Americans crude and unsophisticated.

---

[41]Hodgson, Sano, and Graham, *Doing Business with the New Japan.*

[42]Guang Yang and John L. Graham, "The Impact of Computer-Mediated Communications on the Process and Outcomes of Buyer–Seller Negotiations," working paper, University of California, Irvine, 2012.

Carol Hymowitz, "As U.S. Companies Go Global, Managers Must Bridge Gaps", *The Wall Street Journal,* Aug. 15, 2000

Business Week, Bloomberg L.P., 1977

Haste and impatience are probably the most common mistakes of North Americans attempting to trade in the Middle East. Most Arabs do not like to embark on serious business discussions until after two or three opportunities to meet the individual they are dealing with; negotiations are likely to be prolonged. Arabs may make rapid decisions once they are prepared to do so, but they do not like to be rushed, and they do not like deadlines. The managing partner of the Kuwait office of KPMG Peat Marwick says of the "fly-in visit" approach of many American businesspeople, "What in the West might be regarded as dynamic activity—the 'I've only got a day here' approach—may well be regarded here as merely rude."

Marketers who expect maximum success have to deal with foreign executives in ways that are acceptable to the foreigner. Latin Americans depend greatly on friendships but establish these friendships only in the South American way: slowly, over a considerable period of time. A typical Latin American is highly formal until a genuine relationship of respect and friendship is established. Even then, the Latin American is slow to get down to business and will not be pushed. In keeping with the culture, *mañana* (tomorrow) is good enough. How people perceive time helps explain some of the differences between U.S. managers and those from other cultures.

P-Time versus M-Time

Research has demonstrated that managers in Anglo cultures such as the United States tend to be more concerned with time management than managers from either Latin or Asian cultures.[43] Our stereotype of Latin cultures, for example, is "they are always late," and their view of us is "you are always prompt." Neither statement is completely true, though both contain some truth. What is true, however, is that the United States is a very time-oriented society—time is money to us—whereas in many other cultures, time is to be savored, not spent.

Edward T. Hall defines two time systems in the world: monochronic and polychronic time. *M-time*, or *monochronic time*, typifies most North Americans, Swiss, Germans, and Scandinavians. These Western cultures tend to concentrate on one thing at a time. They divide time into small units and are concerned with promptness. M-time is used in a linear way, and it is experienced as almost tangible, in that one saves time, wastes time, bides time, spends time, and loses time. Most low-context cultures operate on M-time. *P-time*, or *polychronic time*, is more dominant in high-context cultures, where the completion of a human transaction is emphasized more than holding to schedules. P-time is characterized by the simultaneous occurrence of many things and by "a great involvement with people." P-time allows for relationships to build and context to be absorbed as parts of high-context cultures.

One study comparing perceptions of punctuality in the United States and Brazil found that Brazilian timepieces were less reliable and public clocks less available than in the United States. Researchers also found that Brazilians more often described themselves as late arrivers, allowed greater flexibility in defining *early* and *late*, were less concerned about being late, and were more likely to blame external factors for their lateness than were Americans.[44] Please see comparisons of 31 countries in Exhibit 5.3. We note that one study has found the index useful as it well predicts the number of days necessary for obtaining a business license in the 31 countries.[45]

The American desire to get straight to the point and get down to business is a manifestation of an M-time culture, as are other indications of directness. The P-time system gives rise to looser time schedules, deeper involvement with individuals, and a wait-and-see-what-develops attitude. For example, two Latin colleagues conversing would likely opt to

[43]Glen H. Brodowsky, Beverlee B. Anderson, Camille P. Schuster, Ofer Meilich, and M. Ven Venkatesan, "If Time Is Money Is It a Common Currency? Time in Anglo, Asian, and Latin Cultures," *Journal of Global Marketing* 21, no. 4 (2008), pp. 245–58.

[44]Robert Levine, *The Geography of Time* (New York: Basic Books, 1998).

[45]Runtian Jing and John L. Graham, "Regulation vs. Values: How Culture Plays Its Role," *Journal of Business Ethics* 80, no. 4 (2008), pp. 791–806.

Exhibit 5.3
Speed Is Relative

Rank of 31 countries for overall pace of life [combination of three measures: (1) minutes downtown pedestrians take to walk 60 feet, (2) minutes it takes a postal clerk to complete a stamp-purchase transaction, and (3) accuracy in minutes of public clocks].

Source: Robert Levine, "The Pace of Life in 31 Countries," *American Demographics*, November 1997. Reprinted with permission of Robert Levine.

Overall Pace	Country	Walking 60 Feet	Postal Service	Public Clocks
1	Switzerland	3	2	1
2	Ireland	1	3	11
3	Germany	5	1	8
4	Japan	7	4	6
5	Italy	10	12	2
6	England	4	9	13
7	Sweden	13	5	7
8	Austria	23	8	9
9	Netherlands	2	14	25
10	Hong Kong	14	6	14
11	France	8	18	10
12	Poland	12	15	8
13	Costa Rica	16	10	15
14	Taiwan	18	7	21
15	Singapore	25	11	4
16	United States	6	23	20
17	Canada	11	21	22
18	South Korea	20	20	16
19	Hungary	19	19	18
20	Czech Republic	21	17	23
21	Greece	14	13	29
22	Kenya	9	30	24
23	China	24	25	12
24	Bulgaria	27	22	17
25	Romania	30	29	5
26	Jordan	28	27	19
27	Syria	29	28	27
28	El Salvador	22	16	31
29	Brazil	31	24	28
30	Indonesia	26	26	30
31	Mexico	17	31	26

be late for their next appointments rather than abruptly terminate the conversation before it came to a natural conclusion. P-time is characterized by a much looser notion of being on time or late. Interruptions are routine, delays to be expected. It is not so much putting things off until *mañana* as it is the concept that human activity is not expected to proceed like clockwork.

Most cultures offer a mix of P-time and M-time behavior but have a tendency to adopt either more P-time or M-time with regard to the role time plays. Some are similar to Japan, where appointments are adhered to with the greatest M-time precision but P-time is followed once a meeting begins. The Japanese see U.S. businesspeople as too time bound and driven by schedules and deadlines that thwart the easy development of friendships.

When businesspeople from M-time and P-time meet, adjustments need to be made for a harmonious relationship. Often clarity can be gained by specifying tactfully, for example, whether a meeting is to be on "Mexican time" or "American time." An American who has been working successfully with the Saudis for many years says he has learned to take plenty of things to do when he travels. Others schedule appointments in their offices so they can work until their P-time friend arrives. The important thing for the U.S. manager to learn is adjustment to P-time in order to avoid the anxiety and frustration that comes from being out of synchronization with local time. As global markets expand, however, more businesspeople from P-time cultures are adapting to M-time. For example, the president of Peru instigated a national campaign entitled "La Hora Sin Demora," or "Time Without Delay," to encourage his country to become more punctual. Spain is considering similar measures to adapt to a siesta-less world.[46]

Negotiations Emphasis

Business negotiations are perhaps the most fundamental commercial rituals. All the just-discussed differences in business customs and culture come into play more frequently and more obviously in the negotiating process than in any other aspect of business. The basic elements of business negotiations are the same in any country: They relate to the product, its price and terms, services associated with the product, and, finally, friendship between vendors and customers. But it is important to remember that the negotiating process is complicated, and the risk of misunderstanding increases when negotiating with someone from another culture.

Attitudes brought to the negotiating table by each individual are affected by many cultural factors and customs often unknown to the other participants and perhaps unrecognized by the individuals themselves. His or her cultural background conditions each negotiator's understanding and interpretation of what transpires in negotiating sessions. The possibility of offending one another or misinterpreting others' motives is especially high when one's self-reference criteria (SRC) is the basis for assessing a situation. One standard rule in negotiating is "know thyself" first and "know your counterpart" second. The SRC of both parties can come into play here if care is not taken. How business customs and culture influence negotiations is the focus of Chapter 19.

Marketing Orientation

The extent of a company's *marketing orientation* has been shown to relate positively to profits. Although American companies are increasingly embracing this notion (and marketing in general),[47] firms in other countries have not been so fast to change from the more traditional *production* (consumers prefer products that are widely available), *product* (consumers favor products that offer the best quality, performance, or innovative features), and *selling* (consumers and businesses alike will not buy enough without prodding) orientations. For example, in many countries, engineers dominate corporate boards, and the focus is more toward a product orientation. However, more profitable American firms have adopted strong marketing orientations wherein everyone in the organization (from shop floor to finance) is encouraged to, and even receive rewards if, they generate, disseminate, and respond to marketing intelligence (that is, consumers' preferences, competitions' actions, and regulators' decisions). Recently researchers have empirically verified that for various complex reasons, including cultural explanations, a marketing orientation is less prevalent in a number of other countries;[48] and it can be difficult to encourage such an orientation across diverse business units in global companies.[49]

Gender Bias in International Business

LO3

The extent and implications of gender bias in other countries

The gender bias against female managers that exists in some countries, coupled with myths harbored by male managers, creates hesitancy among U.S. multinational companies to offer women international assignments. Although women now constitute Nearly 60 percent of the professional and technical U.S. workforce,[50] they represent relatively small percentages of the employees who are chosen for international assignments—less than 20 percent. Why? Some argue that deep-seated negative attitudes

[46]Jim Yardley, "Spain, Land of 10 P.M. Dinner, Asks if it's Time to Reset the Clock," *The New York Times*, February 18, 2014, pp. A1, A12.

[47]John F. Gaski and Michael J. Etzel, "National Aggregate Consumer Sentiment toward Marketing: A Thirty-Year Retrospective and Analysis," *Journal of Consumer Research* 31 (2005), pp. 859–67.

[48]Sin et al., "Marketing Orientation"; John Kuada and Seth N. Buatsi, "Market Orientation and Management Practices in Ghanaian Firms: Revisiting the Jaworski and Kohli Framework," *Journal of International Marketing* 13 (2005), pp. 58–88; Reto Felix and Wolfgang Hinck, "Market Orientation of Mexican Companies," *Journal of International Marketing* 13 (2005), pp. 111–27.

[49]Paul D. Ellis, "Distance, Dependence and Diversity of Markets: Effects on Market Orientation," *Journal of International Business Studies* 38 (2007), pp. 374–86.

[50]U.S. Department of Labor, Women's Bureau, http://www.dol.gov/wb; Department for Professional Employees, AFL-CIO, http://www.dpeaflcio.org.

toward women have roots in ancient agriculture.[51] The most frequently cited reason is the inability for women to succeed abroad. As one executive was quoted as saying, "Overall, female American executives tend not to be as successful in extended foreign work assignments as are male American executives." Unfortunately, such attitudes are shared by many and probably stem from the belief that the traditional roles of women in male-dominated societies preclude women from establishing successful relationships with host-country associates. An often-asked question is whether it is appropriate to send women to conduct business with foreign customers in cultures where women are typically not in managerial positions. To some, it appears logical that if women are not accepted in managerial roles within their own cultures, a foreign woman will not be any more acceptable.

In many cultures—Asian, Middle Eastern, and Latin American—women are not typically found in upper levels of management (see Exhibit 5.4), and men and women are treated very differently. Moreover, the preferred leadership prototypes of male and female leaders varies across countries as well.[52] Indeed, the scariest newspaper headline ever written may have been "Asia, Vanishing Point for as Many as 100 Million Women." The article, appearing in the *International Herald Tribune* in 1991,[53] points out that the birthrate in most countries around the world is about 105 boys for every 100 girls. However, in countries like the United States or Japan, where generally women outlive men, there are about 96 men per 100 women in the population. The current numbers of men per 100 women in other Asian countries are as follows: Korea 105, China 106, India 108, and Pakistan 106.[54] The article described systematic discrimination against females from birth. Now illegal everywhere, ultrasound units are still being used for making gender-specific abortion decisions, and all this prejudice against females is creating disruptive shortages of women. The latest birth statistics are even more chilling: Today in India, there are 112 boys born for every 100 girls, and in China, the ratio is 117 boys to 100 girls, with some villages reaching 150/100.

---

[51]"The Plough and the Now," *The Economist,* July 23, 2011, p. 74.

[52]Lori D. Paris, Jon P. Howell, Peter W. Dorfman, and Paul J. Hanges, "Preferred Leadership Prototypes of Male and Female Leaders in 27 Countries," *Journal of International Business Studies* 40 (2009), pp. 1396–405.

[53]See January 7, 1991, p. 1. Two decades later, with the widespread availability of portable sonograms, the problem appears to be getting worse. See Jonathan V. Last, "The War against Girls," *The Wall Street Journal*, June 18, 2011.

[54]Central Intelligence Agency, "Sex Ratio," *The World Factbook*, http://www.cia.gov.

Two ways to prevent the harassment of women. Mika Kondo Kunieda, a consultant at the World Bank in Tokyo explains, "I ride in a special women-only metro car that runs between 7:20 and 9:20 am. The cars were created in 2005 due to frequent complaints that women were being groped and sexually harassed. I was a victim a few times when I was younger, and it was—and still is—a humiliating experience. I had to learn how to position myself against moves even in the most overcrowded train. Now, I've seen a few men get visibly anxious when they realize they've accidentally boarded a car during women-only time!" One interpretation of the Koran specifies the cover-up pictured here in Riyadh, Saudi Arabia.

Despite the substantial prejudices toward women in foreign countries, evidence suggests that prejudice toward foreign women executives may be exaggerated and that the treatment local women receive in their own cultures is not necessarily an indicator of how a foreign businesswoman is treated. It would be inaccurate to suggest that there is no difference in how male and female managers are perceived in different cultures. However, this difference does not mean that women cannot be successful in foreign postings.

A key to success for both men and women in international business often hinges on the strength of a firm's backing. When a female manager receives training and the strong backing of her firm, she usually receives the respect commensurate with the position she holds and the firm she represents. For success, a woman needs a title that gives immediate credibility in the culture in which she is working and a support structure and reporting relationship that will help her get the job done.[55] In short, with the power of the corporate organization behind her, resistance to her as a woman either does not materialize or is less troublesome than anticipated. Once business negotiations begin, the willingness of a business host to engage in business transactions and the respect shown to a foreign businessperson grow or diminish depending on the business skills he or she demonstrates, regardless of gender. As one executive stated, "The most difficult aspect of an international assignment is getting sent, not succeeding once sent."

The number of women in managerial positions (all levels) in most European countries, with the exception of Germany, is comparable to the United States. The International Labor Organization notes that in the United States, 43 percent of managerial positions are held by women, in Britain 33 percent, and in Switzerland 28 percent. In Germany, however, the picture is different. According to one economic source, German female executives hold just 9.2 percent of management jobs and meet stiff resistance from their male counterparts when they vie for upper-level positions. But the good news is an indication that some German businesses are attempting to remedy the situation. One step taken to help boost women up the executive ladder is a so-called cross-mentoring system organized by Lufthansa and seven other major corporations. High-ranking managers in one company offer advice to female managers in another firm in an effort to help them develop the kind of old-boy network that allows male managers to climb the corporate ladder successfully.[56] Increasingly, governments are mandating gender equality in the boardroom based in large part to Norway's leadership on the matter, as reflected in Exhibit 5.4. From 2010 to 2013, the average increase in women's membership on corporate boards across all EU countries was 5.9 percent. The largest increase was in France, at 17.4 percent.[57] In Brazil, 27 percent of senior managers are women, compared with a global average of 21 percent.[58]

Exhibit 5.4

Few and Far Between

Source: "All Aboard: The World in 2012," *The Economist.* Copyright © The Economist Newspaper Limited, London, November 17, 2011.

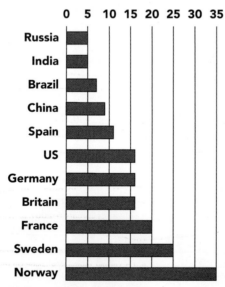

Female directors on corporate boards as a percentage of total.

---

[55]Nancy J. Adler, *International Dimensions of Organizational Behavior* (Mason, OH: Southwestern College Publishing, 2007).

[56]For broader information about global women's equality (including scores for economic participation and opportunity), go to http://www.weforum.org for the *World Economic Forum's Gender Gap Index,* 2014. On the economic opportunity scale, Norway ranks fifth, the United States sixth, Germany thirty-second, Japan one hundredth, and Saudi Arabia one hundred thirty-first, close to last on the list of 135 countries; also see "Closing the Gap," *The Economist,* November 26, 2011, insert, pp. 1–19.

[57]"Gender Balance on Corporate Boards—Europe Is Cracking the Glass Ceiling," European Commission report, March 2014, accessed at http://www.ec.europa.eu. Also see Lisa Abend, *"Boys Won't be Boys,"* *Time,* December 16, 2013, pp. 39–44.

[58]*The Economist,* "Redeemers of a Macho Society," June 15, 2013, p. 70.

CROSSING BORDERS 5.3

Hofstede's Dimensions and the Gender Divide—Who Is mas MAS? Japan and its "Devil Wives"

In Hofstede's dimensions of national culture, Masculinty (MAS) has more to do with how gender roles are defined and separated than with machismo. That is, cultures high in Masculinty are characterized by men doing one thing in society, and women quite another, and the roles do not blend. Scandinavian countries, who typically score low on Masculinity (high in Femininity) view men and women's roles more interchangebly than many other countries, as evidenced by Exhibit 5.4: Norway and Sweden top the list of the number of women on corporate boards. In Scandinavia, men and women are granted equal amounts of time off when a baby is born to the household. The "daddy track" (taking a lesser job to take a larger role at home) is no shame; neither is the "mommy track."

It's quite a different story in Japan, ranked number one in world in the Masculinity scores in Hofstede's data. Although "women only" buses and trolley cars exist in many countries (such as Mexico and Malaysia), Japan takes the role separation of MAS to new heights. The Japanese corporate world is a male's world, where legions of "salarymen" toil long into each night for the greater good of "Japan Inc." Women stay home, retaining complete control of the household budgets, children's activities, and vacation plans. At the opposite end of the spectrum from Scandinavia, only 2 percent of Japanese corporate boards are comprised of women.

This is more than an economic division of labor. It's deeply rooted MAS culture. Terue Suzuki had a baby, but also "had [a] satisfying job and really wanted to go back to it," she says. A woman choosing to do so, instead of staying home to look after the needs of children and husband (as 70 percent do), is called an *oniyome*, or "devil wife." A newspaper article about Suzuki's rare case popularized the term, which gained widespread awareness when national television aired an 11-episode drama called *Oniyome Nikki*, or *Diary of a Devil Wife.*

Public policy officials, from the prime minister on down, are trying to change all that, for more reasons than a discriminatory national culture. With a near world-low fertility rate of 1.41 children per woman—well below population replacement rates—social benefit programs for the burgeoning retired population cannot be supported by an ever-dwindling workforce. Relatedly, the current Japanese economy, now in its third decade of listless performance, can largely be revived by larger numbers of women in the workforce, according to Prime Minister Abe: "Enhancing opportunities for women to work and be active in society is no longer a matter of choice for Japan. It is instead a matter of the greatest urgency," he said. "Abenomics will not work without Womenomics."

One company is trying. Lawson Inc. (which operates 11,000 24-hour convenience stores in Japan, comparable to 7-Eleven) has 20 percent of its workforce of 6,500 comprised of women, partly because of a former Japanese regulation that prohibited women from working after 10 p.m. In recent years, however, half of its new hires have been women. Currently, only one of the company's 28 executives is female, but the company has set a goal to increase the number of women senior vice presidents to 30 percent within five years.

With 7 out of 10 of Japan's employers in a recent survey saying that starting a family makes a woman less employable, such efforts face an uphill battle—and don't count on the currents of culture shifting any time soon. The latest popular hot spots (with an 80-minute stay limit) for singles these days are called "butler cafés"—exclusively for women. Men dressed impeccably in long-tail tuxedos and white gloves cater to the female (mostly working young women) patrons' every wish, greeting them with "Good evening, princess." You've heard of geisha girls? Meet the geisha guys!

Sources: "Reviving Japan with 'Devil Wives,'" *Bloomberg Business Week*, November 12, 2012, p. 13; "Holding Back Half the Nation," *The Economist*, March 29, 2014, pp. 23–24; "Where Japanese Women Rule," Time, February 5, 2007, p. 47; "Untapped Talent," *The Economist*, July 7, 2014, p. 62; Don Lee, "Japan is Pulling for Its Female Workforce," *Los Angeles Times*, August 21, 2013, pp. B1, B6; Kirk Spitzer, "Japan Looks for a Few Good Women to Revive Economy," *USA Today*, January 17, 2014, p. 7A; Hiroko Tabuchi, "Shaking Up the Boardroom in Japan," *The New York Times*, June 25, 2014, pp. B1, B4.

As world markets become more global and international competition intensifies, U.S. companies need to be represented by the most capable personnel available, from entry level to CEO. Research shows that global companies are requiring international experience for top executive positions. Executives who have had international experience are more likely to get promoted, have higher rewards, and have greater occupational tenure. The lack of international experience should not be a structural barrier to breaking through the glass ceiling in corporate America; to limit the talent pool simply because of gender seems shortsighted. The good news is that things are improving worldwide for women in management, and the topic of gender in multinational companies is receiving increasing research attention as well.[59] One study showed that companies with at least one woman director are 40 percent less likely to need to restate quarterly and annual earnings.[60]

So what about our female Ford executive mentioned at the start of the chapter? She was having no fun in Japan when we left her story. However, by all accounts (from peers, supervisors, and even Japanese counterparts) that first encounter was not representative of her continuing successes with the Japanese. She attributes her subsequent effectiveness to the strong support of her male Ford team members and her own recognition of the importance of building personal relationships with the Japanese. She explains:

> My husband, also a Ford manager working with Japanese clients, and I decided to have a few of our Mazda associates over for an "All-American" dinner during their next trip to Detroit. So, we started out inviting three people to our home. We thought this would be a nice intimate way to get to know one another and provide the Japanese with an honest-to-goodness homemade American meal. By the eve of the dinner word had gotten out and we had thirteen for dinner. They sort of invited themselves, they changed their meetings around, and some even flew in from the Chicago Auto Show. We had a wonderful time and for the first time they saw me as a person. A mom and a wife as well as a business associate. We talked about families, some business, not particulars, but world economics and the auto industry in general. The dinner party was a key turning point in my relationships with Mazda.[61]

Business Ethics

LO4

The importance of cultural differences in business ethics

The moral question of what is right or appropriate poses many dilemmas for domestic marketers. Even within a country, ethical standards are frequently not defined or always clear. The problem of business ethics is infinitely more complex in the international marketplace because value judgments differ widely among culturally diverse groups.[62] That which is commonly accepted as right in one country may be completely unacceptable in another, though at least one study has shown relative consistency across 41 countries in the ethics of persuading superiors.[63] Giving business gifts of high value, for example, is generally condemned in the United States, but in many countries of the world, gifts are not only accepted but also expected.[64]

Corruption Defined

Indeed, consistent with the discussions about language, the meaning of the word corruption varies considerably around the world. In formerly communist countries where Marxism was an important part of the educational system for many, *profits* can be seen as a kind of corruption. What American managers view as essential, others view as a sign of exploitation. The *individualism* so important to Americans can also be seen as a kind of corruption. The Japanese have an expression: "The nail that sticks up gets hammered down." In India many attribute the decline in the society there to the *rampant consumerism*, such as that promoted on MTV. Of course, such rampant consumerism is what kept the American economy afloat right after the turn of the century. In some countries, there is no greater Satan

---

[59]For example, see Estefania Santacreu-Vasut, Oded Shankar, and Amir Shoham, "Linguistic Gender Marking and its International Business Ramifications," *Journal of International Business Studies* 45 (2014), pp. 1170–78; K. Praveen Parboteeah, Martin Hoegl, and John B. Cullen, "Managers' Gender Role Attitudes: A Country Institutional Profile Approach," *Journal of International Business Studies* 39, no. 5 (2008), pp. 795–813; William Newburry, Liuba Y. Belkin, and Paradis Ansari, "Perceived Career Opportunities from Globalization Capabilities and Attitudes towards Women in Iran and the U.S.," *Journal of International Business Studies* 39, no. 5 (2008), pp. 814–32.

[60] Melissa Korn, "Maybe Math Isn't So Hard," *The Wall Street Journal*, November 28, 2012, p. B.6.

[61]Hodgson, Sano, and Graham, *Doing Business with the New Japan*.

[62]Pallab Paul, Abhijit Roy, and Kausiki Mukjhopadhyay, "The Impact of Cultural Values on Marketing Ethical Norms: A Study in India and the United States," *Journal of International Marketing* 14 (2006), pp. 28–56; Jatinder J. Singh, Scott J. Vitell, Jamal Al-Khatif, and Irvine Clark III, "The Role of Moral Intensity and Personal Moral Philosophies in the Ethical Decision Making of Marketers: A Cross-Cultural Comparison of China and the United States," *Journal of International Marketing* 15 (2007), pp. 86–112; Srivatsa Seshadri and Greg M. Broekemier, "Ethical Decision Making: Panama-United States Differences in Consumer and Marketing Contexts," *Journal of Global Marketing* 22 (2009), pp. 299–311.

[63]David A. Ralston, Carolyn P. Egri, Maria Teresa de la Garza Carranza, and Prem Ramburuth, and 44 colleagues, "Ethical Preferences for Influencing Superiors: A 41 Society Study," *Journal of International Business Studies* 40 (2009), pp. 1022–45.

[64]See http://www.ethics.org and http://www.business-ethics.org for more pertinent information.

Pope Benedict XVI wrote that the Harry Potter books and movies can "deeply distort Christianity in the soul, before it can grow properly." Meanwhile, Antonio Banderas perhaps helped improve European acceptability for *Shrek 2* when he showed up for the Madrid premiere. In any case, products and services directed at kids get special attention from parents and regulators around the world.

than *R-rated American movies* with their sex and violence. In China, *missionaries* and religious movements are viewed by the government as potentially dangerous and disruptive. Many in sub-Saharan Africa view Western *intellectual property laws* as a kind of exploitation that prevents treatment of AIDS for millions. During the 1997–1998 financial crisis, many government leaders in Southeast Asia decried *currency speculation* as the worst kind of corruption. To this point, studies show that countries high in collectivism, such as Asian countries, perceive higher levels of corruption in bank lending practices than individualistic cultures, regardless of government policies and other possible explanations.[65]

Finally, please recall the 2003 homogenization of Barbie described at the beginning of the chapter. Here's what we predicted in a previous edition of this text: "And then there is *Barbie* having great fun in Japan these days. We hope the love affair lasts, but we are not confident it will. The article does describe the extensive marketing research Mattel did with kids. But there is no mention made about marketing research with their parents.[66] We guarantee that selling a big-busted, blonde doll to their daughters will be viewed as a kind of corruption by some Asian parents, and perhaps governmental officials as well. Particularly, if America is perceived as pursuing military and economic hegemony, a strong reaction against symbols of America will follow. Watch out Barbie, GI Joe, and your other toy store friends."

Our criticism of Mattel then was on the mark in three ways. First, sales of Barbie declined worldwide after the global standardization. Second, parents and governments did react. Most recently the Iranian authorities began enforcing a ban against sales of Barbie, literally removing products from toy store shelves in Tehran. The government's reasoning involved the "destructive cultural and social consequences" of the marketing of the American product.[67] Third, Mattel's strategy boosted the sales of its competitors, MGA Entertainment, Inc.'s, multiethnic Bratz, Razanne, and, in the Arabian Gulf states, Fulla. Razanne and Fulla were both designed with Muslim girls and Muslim parents in mind. Fulla has waist-length black hair with red streaks, a round face with big brown eyes, a tan, a flatter chest than Barbie, and clothes that conceal her elbows and knees. We will again touch on this topic as it pertains to marketing research in Chapter 8. But for now, we switch from Barbie to bribery, another kind of corruption.

[65]Xiaolan Zheng, Sadok El Ghoul, Omrane Guedhami, and Chuck C. Y. Kwok, "Collectivism and Corruption in Bank Lending," *Journal of International Business Studies* 44 (2013), pp. 363–90.

[66]Lisa Bannon and Carlta Vitzthum, "One-Toy-Fits-All," *The Wall Street Journal*, April 29, 2003, p. A1.

[67]Alexandra Sifferlin, "'Morality Police' Officers Give Barbie Dolls the Boot in Iran," *Time,* newsfeed .time.com, January 18, 2012.

HOME-GROWN BUSINESS? As the global economy slowed and China's exports slumped, Beijing cut sales taxes on car and real-estate purchases in certain situations, in hopes of revving up its own consumer engine. At right, a man and woman took a break outside a shop selling Barbie dolls in October. Apparently blonde Barbie doesn't appear to corrupt kids in China!

The Western Focus on Bribery

Before the Enron, WorldCom, and Madoff scandals, to most Americans, the word corruption meant bribery. Now in the domestic context, fraud has moved to the more prominent spot in the headlines.[68] But high-profile foreign cases of bribery, such as those involving the German giant Siemens (which, in connection with its case, paid for 1.5 million billable attorney hours!) and the execution of China's top food and drug official for accepting bribes, underscore the ethical and legal complexities of international business. During the 1970s, for U.S. companies engaged in international markets, bribery became a national issue with public disclosure of political payoffs to foreign recipients by U.S. firms. At the time, the United States had no laws against paying bribes in foreign countries. But for publicly held corporations, the Securities and Exchange Commission's (SEC) rules required accurate public reporting of all expenditures. Because the payoffs were not properly disclosed, many executives were faced with charges of violating SEC regulations.

The issue took on proportions greater than that of nondisclosure because it focused national attention on the basic question of ethics. The business community's defense was that payoffs were a way of life throughout the world: If you didn't pay bribes, you didn't do business. The decision to pay a bribe creates a major conflict between what is ethical and proper and what appears to be profitable and sometimes necessary for business. Many global competitors perceive payoffs as a necessary means to accomplish business goals. A major complaint of U.S. businesses was that other countries did not have legislation as restrictive as does the United States. The U.S. advocacy of global antibribery laws has led to a series of accords by the member nations of the Organization for Economic Cooperation and Development (OECD), the Organization of American States (OAS), and the United Nations Convention against Corruption (UNCAC). Long considered almost a way of business life, bribery and other forms of corruption are now being increasingly criminalized and the enforcement gap between the United States and the rest of the world gratefully seems to be shrinking.[69] The United Kingdom, Brazil, and Canada have all enacted their own antibribery laws in recent years. China is cutting executive pay and perks at state-owned firms in an effort to reduce corruption.[70]

Leaders around the world realize that democracy depends on the confidence the people have in the integrity of their government and that corruption undermines economic liberalization. The actions of the OAS, OECD, and UNCAC will obligate a majority of the world's trading nations to maintain a higher standard of ethical behavior than has existed before.

[68]Robert J. Rhee, "The Madoff Scandal, Market Regulatory Failure and the Business Education of Lawyers," *Journal of Corporation Law* 35, no. 2 (2010), pp. 363–92; perhaps the best book on this topic is Naomi Klein's *Shock Doctrine* (New York: Picador, 2007); also see "Bill Moyers: 6 Movies You Have to See About the Financial Crisis," AlterNet.org, February 2, 2012.

[69] Ben DiPietro, "Global Bribe Focus Hardens," *The Wall Street Journal*, August 14, B5, 2014.

[70] Lingling Wei and Bob Davis, "China to Cut Top Pay at State Firms," *The Wall Street Journal*, October 27, 2014, pp. B1, B2.

Exhibit 5.5
Transparency International Corruption Perceptions Index 2013

Higher numbers correspond to a perceived lower level of public sector corruption. The top 25 (4 tied for #22), the BRIC countries, and the bottom 20 are shown; see http://www.transparency.org for the most complete and up-to-date listings. http://cpi.transparency.org/cpi3013/ for the complete 2013 listings.

Rank	Country	CPI Score	Rank	Country	CPI Score
1	Denmark	91	**BRIC Countries**		
2	New Zealand	91	72	Brazil	91
3	Finland	89	80	China	40
4	Sweden	89	94	India	36
5	Norway	86	127	Russia	28
5	Singapore	86	**Bottom 20**		
7	Switzerland	85	153	Angola	23
8	Netherlands	83	154	Republic of Congo	22
9	Australia	81	154	Democratic Republic of Congo	22
9	Canada	81	154	Tajikistan	22
11	Luxemborg	80	157	Burndi	21
12	Germany	78	157	Myanmar	21
12	Iceland	78	157	Zimbabwe	21
14	United Kingdom	76	160	Cambodia	20
15	Barbados	75	160	Eitrea	20
15	Belgium	75	160	Venezuela	20
15	Hong Kong	75	163	Chad	19
18	Japan	74	163	Equatorial Guinea	19
19	United States	73	163	Haiti	19
19	Uruguay	73	167	Yemen	18
21	Ireland	72	168	Syria	17
22	Bahamas	71	168	Turkmenistan	17
22	Chile	71	168	Uzbekistan	17
22	France	71	171	Iraq	16
22	Santa Lucia	71	172	Libya	15
			173	South Sudan	14
			174	Sudan	11
			175	Afghanistan	8
			175	North Korea	8
			175	Somalia	8

Source: Corruption Perceptions Index 2013, www.transparency.org. Reprinted from Corruption Perceptions Index. Copyright © 2013, Transparency International: the global coalition against corruption. Used with permission. For more information, visit http://www.transparency.org

An international organization called Transparency International (TI)[71] is dedicated to "curbing corruption through international and national coalitions encouraging governments to establish and implement effective laws, policies and anti-corruption programs." The brand name "Transparency International" has proven most insightful, as more scholars are finding a clear relationship between the availability of information and lower levels of corruption.[72] Among its various activities, TI conducts an international survey[73] of businesspeople, political analysts, and the general public to determine their perceptions of corruption in 182 countries. In the 2013 Corruption Perception Index (CPI), shown in part in Exhibit 5.5, Denmark and New Zealand, both with scores of 91 out of a maximum of 100, were perceived to be the least corrupt, and Afghanistan, North Korea, and Somalia, with scores of 8, as the most corrupt. TI also ranks 28 bribe-paying countries, and the ranking

---

[71]http://www.transparency.org.

[72]Cassandra E. DiRienzo, Jayoti Das, Kathryn T. Cort, and John Burbridge Jr., "Corruption and the Role of Information," *Journal of International Business Studies* 38 (2007), pp. 320–32.

[73]For an analysis of the potential biases in surveys on corruption, see Nathan M. Jensen, Quan Li, and Aminur Rahman, "Understanding Corruption and Firm Responses in Cross-National Firm-Level Surveys," *Journal of International Business Studies* 41, no. 9 (2010), pp. 1481–504.

Exhibit 5.6

Transparency International
Bribe Payers Index 2011*

The Index ranks the likelihood
of companies from 28 leading
economies to win business
abroad by paying bribes—higher
scores correspond to perceived
lower levels of bribe paying
internationally.

Source: Bribe Payers Index 2011,
www.transparency.org. Reprinted from
Bribe Payers Index. Copyright © 2011,
Transparency International: the global
coalition against corruption. Used with
permission. For more information, visit
http://www.transparency.org.

Rank	Country	Score
1	Netherlands	8.8
1	Switzerland	8.8
3	Belgium	8.7
4	Germany	8.6
4	Japan	8.6
6	Australia	8.5
6	Canada	8.5
8	Singapore	8.3
8	United Kingdom	8.3
10	United States	8.1
11	France	8.0
11	Spain	8.0
13	South Korea	7.9
14	Brazil	7.7
15	Hong Kong	7.6
15	Italy	7.6
15	Malaysia	7.6
15	South Africa	7.6
19	Taiwan	7.5
19	India	7.5
19	Turkey	7.5
22	Saudi Arabia	7.4
23	Argentina	7.3
23	United Arab Emirates	7.3
25	Indonesia	7.1
26	Mexico	7.0
27	China	6.5
28	Russia	6.1

*Based on responses to questions such as: In the business sectors with which you are most familiar, please indicate how likely companies from the following countries are to pay or offer bribes to win or retain business in this country (respondent's country of residence).

is reported in Exhibit 5.6 in its entirety. TI is very emphatic that its intent is not to expose villains and cast blame but to raise public awareness that will lead to constructive action. As one would expect, those countries receiving low scores are not pleased; however, the effect has been to raise public ire and debates in parliaments around the world—exactly the goal of TI.

The most notable data in the in TI's CPI rankings are those allowing the comparison of the positions of the United States and Japan over the years. In the 1998 CPI rankings, the United States was #17 and Japan #25. In Exhibit 5.5, you will observe that now the United States is #19 and Japan is #18. In the 2011 index, the United States was #24! The analysts at TI warn that because the countries considered and the survey data used vary from year to year, making longitudinal comparisons are problematic. However, it is our opinion that Japan should be lauded for improving its record on corruption during the last decade. We cannot say the same for the United States, which took a large dip in the last few years and still has not returned completely to its 1998 level.

Indeed, Japan's successes in reducing corruption in its business system are all the more remarkable because of its relationship-oriented culture, which would be predicted by many to favor bribery. Finally, the critics are strangely mute regarding the influence of outside pressure, in the form of the aforementioned OECD antibribery convention, which Japan joined in 1999 (the United States also joined the OECD convention in 1999). Long-time observers argue that major changes within Japan often result from such outside influences. Thus, the years 1999–2001 appear to represent the key turning point in Japan's fight against corruption.

Transparency International's CPI is also proving useful in academic studies of the causes and consequences of bribery. Completely consistent with our discussion of the origins and elements of culture in Chapter 4 (see Exhibit 4.4), higher levels of bribery have been perceived in low-income nations and nations with a communist past, both aspects of the political economy. Additionally, higher levels of bribery have been found in collectivistic (IDV) and high power distance (PDI) countries. Moreover, higher levels of bribery and legal constraints such as the Foreign Corrupt Practices Act (FCPA) have deterred firms' participation in such countries.[74] Firms seem generally to eschew investments in corrupt countries as well.[75] Finally, when executives of multinational firms behave ethically in such countries, they also tend to promote more ethical business behaviors among their host country counterparts.[76]

Bribery: Variations on a Theme

Although bribery is a legal issue, it is also important to see bribery in a cultural context to understand different attitudes toward it. Culturally, attitudes about bribery are significantly different among different peoples. Some cultures seem to be more open about taking bribes, whereas others, like the United States, are publicly contemptuous of such practices. But U.S. firms are far from virtuous—we believe the TI "grade" of a C (7.3) to be about right. Regardless of where the line of acceptable conduct is drawn, there is no country where the people consider it proper for those in position of political power to enrich themselves through illicit agreements at the expense of the best interests of the nation. A first step in understanding the culture of bribery is to appreciate the limitless variations that are often grouped under the word *bribery*. The activities under this umbrella term range from extortion through subornation to lubrication.

Bribery and Extortion. The distinction between bribery and extortion depends on whether the activity resulted from an offer or from a demand for payment. Voluntarily offered payment by someone seeking unlawful advantage is bribery. For example, it is bribery if an executive of a company offers a government official payment in exchange for the official incorrectly classifying imported goods so the shipment will be taxed at a lower rate than the correct classification would require. However, it is *extortion* if payments are extracted under duress by someone in authority from a person seeking only what he or she is lawfully entitled to. An example of extortion would be a finance minister of a country demanding heavy payments under the threat that a contract for millions of dollars would be voided.

On the surface, extortion may seem to be less morally wrong because the excuse can be made that "if we don't pay, we don't get the contract" or "the official (devil) made me do it." But even if it is not legally wrong, it is morally wrong—and in the United States it is legally wrong.

Lubrication and Subornation. Another variation of bribery is the difference between lubrication and subornation. Lubrication involves a relatively small sum of cash, a gift, or a service given to a low-ranking official in a country where such offerings are not prohibited by law. The purpose of such a gift is to facilitate or expedite the normal, lawful performance of a duty by that official. This practice is common in many countries of the world. A small payment made to dock workers to speed up their pace so that unloading a truck takes a few hours rather than all day is an example of lubrication.

Subornation, in contrast, generally involves giving large sums of money—frequently not properly accounted for—designed to entice an official to commit an illegal act on behalf of the one offering the bribe. Lubrication payments accompany requests for a person to do a job more rapidly or more efficiently; subornation is a request for officials to turn their heads, to not do their jobs, or to break the law.

Agent's Fees. A third type of payment that can appear to be a bribe but may not be is an agent's fee. When a businessperson is uncertain of a country's rules and regulations, an agent may be hired to represent the company in that country. For example, an attorney

[74]H. Rika Houston and John L. Graham, "Culture and Corruption in International Markets: Implications for Policy Makers and Managers," *Consumption, Markets, and Culture* 4, no. 3 (2000), pp. 315–40; Jennifer D. Chandler and John L. Graham, "Relationship-Oriented Cultures, Corruption, and International Marketing Success," *Journal of Business Ethics* 92, no. 2 (2010), pp. 251–67.

[75]Utz Weitzel and Sjors Berns, "Cross-Border Takeovers, Corruption, and Related Aspects of Governance," *Journal of International Business Studies* 37 (2006), pp. 786–806; Alvaro Cuervo-Cazurra, "Who Cares about Corruption," *Journal of International Business Studies* 37 (2006), pp. 807–22.

[76]Yadong Luo, "Political Behavior, Social Responsibility, and Perceived Corruption: A Structural Perspective," *Journal of International Business Studies* 37 (2006), pp. 747–66; Chuck C. Y. Kwok and Solomon Tadesse, "The MNC as an Agent of Change for Host-Country Institutions: FDI and Corruption," *Journal of International Business Studies* 37 (2006), pp. 767–85.

may be hired to file an appeal for a variance in a building code on the basis that the attorney will do a more efficient and thorough job than someone unfamiliar with such procedures. While this practice is often a legal and useful procedure, if a part of that agent's fee is used to pay bribes, the intermediary's fees are being used unlawfully. Under U.S. law, an official who knows of an agent's intention to bribe may risk prosecution and jail time. The FCPA prohibits U.S. businesses from paying bribes openly or using intermediaries as conduits for a bribe when the U.S. manager knows that part of the intermediary's payment will be used as a bribe. Attorneys, agents, distributors, and so forth may function simply as conduits for illegal payments. The process is further complicated by legal codes that vary from country to country; what is illegal in one country may be winked at in another and be legal in a third.

The answer to the question of bribery is not an unqualified one. It is easy to generalize about the ethics of political payoffs and other types of payments; it is much more difficult to make the decision to withhold payment of money when the consequences of not making the payment may affect the company's ability to do business profitably or at all. With the variety of ethical standards and levels of morality that exist in different cultures, the dilemma of ethics and pragmatism that faces international business cannot be resolved until the anticorruption accords among the OECD, UN, and OAS members are fully implemented and multinational businesses refuse to pay extortion or offer bribes.

The Foreign Corrupt Practices Act, which prohibits American executives and firms from bribing officials of foreign governments, has had a positive effect. According to the latest Department of Commerce figures, since 1994, American businesses have bowed out of 294 major overseas commercial contracts valued at $145 billion rather than paying bribes. This information corroborates the academic evidences cited previously. Even though there are numerous reports indicating a definite reduction in U.S. firms paying bribes, the lure of contracts is too strong for some companies. Lockheed Corporation made $22 million in questionable foreign payments during the 1970s. More recently the company pled guilty to paying $1.8 million in bribes to a member of the Egyptian national parliament in exchange for lobbying for three air cargo planes worth $79 million to be sold to the military. Lockheed was caught and fined $25 million, and cargo plane exports by the company were banned for three years. Lockheed's actions during the 1970s were a major influence on the passing of the FCPA. The company now maintains one of the most comprehensive ethics and legal training programs of any major corporation in the United States.

It would be naive to assume that laws and the resulting penalties alone will put an end to corruption. Change will come only from more ethically and socially responsible decisions by both buyers and sellers and by governments willing to take a stand.

Ethical and Socially Responsible Decisions

Behaving in an ethically and socially responsible way should be the hallmark of every businessperson's behavior, domestic or international. Most of us know innately the socially responsible or ethically correct response to questions about knowingly breaking the law, harming the environment, denying someone his or her rights, taking unfair advantage, or behaving in a manner that would bring bodily harm or damage. Meanwhile, the complex relationships among politics, corruption, and corporate social responsibility are only now beginning to receive attention on the part of scholars and practitioners.[77] Unfortunately, the difficult issues are not the obvious and simple right-or-wrong ones, and differences in cultural values influence the judgment of managers.[78] In many countries, the international marketer faces the

---

[77]Peter Rodriguez, Donald S. Siegel, Amy Hillman, and Lorraine Eden, "Three Lenses on the Multinational Enterprise: Politics, Corruption, and Corporate Social Responsibility," *Journal of International Business Studies* 37 (2006), pp. 733–46.

[78]David A. Waldman, Mary Sully de Luque, Nathan Washburn, Robert J. House, Bolanle Adetoun, Angel Barrasa, Mariya Bobina, Muzaffer Bodur, Yi-jung Chen, Sukhendu Debbarma, Peter Dorfman, Rosemary R. Dzuvichu, Idil Evcimen, Pingping Fu, Mikhail Grachev, Roberto Gonzalez Duarte, Vipin Gupta, Deanne N. Den Hartog, Annebel H.B. de Hoogh, Jon Howell, Kuen-yung Jone, Hayat Kabasakal, Edvard Konrad, P. L. Koopman, Rainhart Lang, Cheng-chen Lin, Jun Liu, Boris Martinez, Almarie E. Munley, Nancy Papalexandris, T. K. Peng, Leonel Prieto, Narda Quigley, James Rajasekar, Francisco Gil Rodriguez, Johannes Steyrer, Betania Tanure, Henk Theirry, V. M. Thomas, Peter T. van den Berg, and Celeste P. M. Wilderom, "Cultural Leadership Predictors of Corporate Social Responsibility Values of Top Management: A GLOBE Study of 15 Countries," *Journal of International Business Studies* 37 (2006), pp. 823–37.

dilemma of responding to sundry situations where local law does not exist, where local practices appear to condone a certain behavior, or where a company willing to "do what is necessary" is favored over a company that refuses to engage in certain practices. In short, being socially responsible and ethically correct are not simple tasks for the international marketer.[79]

Ethical Decisions. In normal business operations, difficulties arise in making decisions, establishing policies, and engaging in business operations in five broad areas: (1) employment practices and policies, (2) consumer protection, (3) environmental protection, (4) political payments and involvement in political affairs of the country, and (5) basic human rights and fundamental freedoms. In many countries, laws may help define the borders of minimum ethical or social responsibility, but the law is only the floor above which one's social and personal morality is tested. The statement that "there is no controlling legal authority" may mean that the behavior is not illegal, but it does not mean that the behavior is morally correct or ethical. Ethical business conduct should normally exist at a level well above the minimum required by law or the "controlling legal authority." In fact, laws are the markers of past behavior that society has deemed unethical or socially irresponsible.

Perhaps the best guides to good business ethics are the examples set by ethical business leaders. However, three ethical principles also provide a framework to help the marketer distinguish between right and wrong, determine what ought to be done, and properly justify his or her actions. Simply stated, they are as follows:

- **Utilitarian ethics.** Does the action optimize the "common good" or benefits of all constituencies? And who are the pertinent constituencies?

- **Rights of the parties.** Does the action respect the rights of the individuals involved?

- **Justice or fairness.** Does the action respect the canons of justice or fairness to all parties involved?

Answers to these questions can help the marketer ascertain the degree to which decisions are beneficial or harmful and right or wrong and whether the consequences of actions are ethical or socially responsible. Perhaps the best framework to work within is defined by asking: Is it legal? Is it right? Can it withstand disclosure to stockholders, to company officials, to the public?

Although the United States has clearly led the campaign against international bribery, European firms and institutions are apparently putting more effort and money into the promotion of what they are calling "corporate social responsibility." For example, the watchdog group CSR (Corporate Social Responsibility) Europe, in cooperation with INSEAD (the European Institute of Administrative Affairs) business school outside Paris, is studying the relationship between investment attractiveness and positive corporate behaviors on several dimensions. Their studies find a strong link between firms' social responsibility and European institutional investors' choices for equity investments.[80] All this is not to say that European firms do not still have their own corporate misbehaviors. However, we expect more efforts in the future to focus on measuring and monitoring corporate social responsibility around the world.

Initiatives. Social responsibility is climbing ever higher on many corporate agendas these days. But whereas in the past, companies may have given cash donations to nongovernmental organizations (NGOs), a new trend is now emerging. Known generally as strategic philanthropy, it usually involves companies applying their expertise or products to sponsorship projects, targeted at local communities or specific segments of the population. The return on this participation is not measured in terms of profit but by other indicators like an increase in brand equity[81] and

---

[79]Shurti Gupta, Julie Pirsch, and Tulay Girard, "An Empirical Examination of a Multinational Ethical Dilemma: The Issue of Child Labor," *Journal of Global Marketing* 23, no. 4 (2010), pp. 288–305.

[80]See http://www.csreurope.org.

[81]Karen L. Becker-Olsen, Charles R. Taylor, Ronald Paul Hill, and Goksel Yalcinkaya, "A Cross-Cultural Examination of Corporate Social Responsibility Marketing Communications in Mexico and the United States: Strategies for Global Brands," *Journal of International Marketing* 19, no. 2 (2011), pp. 30–44.

new learning to generate innovative sustainable solutions, although product quality and, internationally, distance from headquarters, affect the positive impact of such initiatives.[82] Here we provide two very different social responsibility examples: Philips[83] and Mary Kay.[84]

At Philips Design (a division of Royal Philips Electronics, located in the Netherlands, with 2014 revenues of $28 billion), this approach is known as Philanthropy by Design, a term coined by Stefano Marzano, CEO and Chief Creative Director. In short, it means leveraging design creativity to provide meaningful solutions to empower some of the more fragile categories of society. An excellent example of this approach is the development of the Chulha cook stove described in Chapter 3's Global Perspective. "Not only does it help many people living at very low income, it is also very beneficial for us," says Simona Rocchi, Director of Sustainable Design at Philips Design in Eindhoven. "It develops brand equity and trust, it is good for employees' motivation and can act as a source of inspiration. It also shows new ways of co-creating value through cooperation with 'unconventional' partners such as NGOs, local entrepreneurs and self-help groups for women."

But this project is about much more than just designing a healthier, safer, and more efficient way of cooking. The whole business model surrounding the Chulha is aimed at helping it gain widespread acceptance, even if that means using what many would consider unconventional means. Take intellectual property (IP) as an example. "We allow local stakeholders to use the IP and design for free as our philanthropic contribution to sustainable development," says Rocchi. "In this way we make it much easier to achieve widespread distribution of the stoves and help keep costs down. This will not only create better living conditions for the users, but also stimulate local entrepreneurial activities with a low environmental impact." Local players have been identified who will take care of manufacturing and distribution. "We have found a number of companies with suitable facilities for making the stoves," says Unmesh Kulkarni, a senior manager at Philips Design Pune, India. "We are helping them to work with more robust moulds from glass-fiber reinforced plastic because they last longer than steel moulds and enable more complex shapes to be created. These moulds are then used by the NGOs to actually make the stoves." A complete support package is being created that includes not just the details of the stove's physical design but also marketing information for entrepreneurs, communication materials, a training program for NGOs, and installation instructions.

"It is all about appropriate technology," adds Kulkarni. "We tackled a huge problem using a minimum amount of resources. In many ways this is more challenging than designing a very advanced, high-tech solution. It certainly gives a great deal of satisfaction." And, as Rocchi points out, it also makes business sense. "This project saw us supporting social innovation on one hand while contributing to business innovation on the other. Everyone benefits. That's why it is our intention to carry out at least one Philanthropy by Design project each year."

The Mary Kay Company, headquartered in Dallas, is one of the largest direct sellers of skin care and cosmetics in the world, with operations in more than 35 countries. 2.4 million people sold more than $3.5 billion of products during 2012. The company is "committed to changing the lives of women and children around the world" through both its direct selling operations and its corporate social responsibility activities centered on the Mary Kay Foundation. Since 1996 the Foundation has awarded over $28 million to shelters and domestic violence programs and $16 million to cancer researchers and related causes in the United States and Canada. Beyond North America, Mary Kay supports a variety of charitable organizations in more than 23 countries. We briefly outline a few prominent examples.

---

[82]Thomas J. Madden, Martin S. Roth, and William R. Dillon, "Global Product Quality and Corporate Social Responsibility Perceptions: A Cross-National Study of Halo Effects," *Journal of International Marketing* 20 (2012), pp. 42–57; Joanna Tochman Campbell, Lorraine Eden, and Stewart R. Miller, "Multinationals and Corporate Social Responsibility in Host Countries: Does Distance Matter?" *Journal of International Business Studies* 43 (2012), pp. 84–106.

[83]Kerry Capell and Nandini Lakshman, "Philips: Philanthropy by Design," *BusinessWeek,* September 11, 2008; http://www.design.philips.com.

[84]*Pink Changing Lives* (Dallas, TX: Mary Kay Corporate Social Responsibility, 2012); see also http://www.MaryKay.com.

In the Mary Kay Latin America region, the company dedicates its time and resources to helping end domestic violence. Funds have been donated to provide refuge for children. Free psychological, medical, and legal support is given to help women and children suffering from domestic violence. Mary Kay Mexico also cosponsors an international education seminar for shelters and a campaign to create awareness about violence against women. The company provided funding for a related hotline.

In the Europe region, the CSR focus also remains steadfast on women and children. Efforts include Mary Kay Ukraine's commitment to breast cancer awareness and care and Mary Kay Armenia's provision of food, academic assistance, and medical and psychological assistance to children and the elderly. In Germany, the company supports children with disabilities; in Kazakhstan contributions are directed toward surgeries for children with limited auditory abilities; and in Russia, free operations for children with facial injuries and cancer are provided.

Throughout the Asia Pacific region, the company supports a variety of women's issues. Examples include donations to support building libraries in South Korea. Mary Kay also partners with the United Nations Development Program and the China Women's Development Foundation to promote female entrepreneurship in China.

Finally, we mention three notable examples of corruption fighting, ranging across the levels of government, corporate, and individual initiatives. First, the government of Norway is investing its vast oil profits in only ethical companies; it recently withdrew funds from companies such as Walmart, Boeing, and Lockheed Martin, in line with its ethical criteria. Second, Alan Boekmann, CEO of the global construction company Fluor Corp., is fed up with the corruption in his own business. He, along with colleagues at competitor firms, has called for a program of outside auditors to determine the effectiveness of firms' antibribery programs. Third, in 2001, Alexandra Wrage founded Trace International, an Annapolis, Maryland, nonprofit that provides corruption reports about potential foreign clients and training for executives involved in business in difficult areas.[85] We laud all such efforts.

Culture's Influence on Strategic Thinking

Perhaps Lester Thurow provided the most articulate description of how culture influences managers' thinking about business strategy.[86] Others are now examining his ideas in even deeper detail.[87] Thurow distinguished between the British–American "individualistic" kind of capitalism and the "communitarian" form of capitalism in Japan and Germany. The business systems in the latter two countries are typified by cooperation among government, management, and labor, particularly in Japan. Contrarily, adversarial relationships among labor, management, and government are more the norm in the United Kingdom, and particularly in the United States. We see these cultural differences reflected in Hofstede's results—on the IDV scale, the United States is 91, the United Kingdom is 89, Germany is 67, and Japan is 46. In cross-national relationships between retailers and suppliers, Uncertainty Avoidance (UAI) and Long-Term Orientation (LTO) have been found to increase the importance of fairness, while Power Distance (PDI) slightly decreases it.[88]

We also find evidence of these differences in a comparison of the performance of American, German, and Japanese firms.[89] In the less individualistic cultures, labor and

[85] See http://www.traceinternational.org.

[86] Lester Thurow, *Head to Head* (New York: William Morrow, 1992).

[87] Gordon Redding, "The Thick Description and Comparison of Societal Systems of Capitalism," *Journal of International Business Studies* 36, no. 2 (2005), pp. 123–55; Michael A. Witt and Gordon Redding, "Culture, Meaning, and Institutions: Executive Rationale in Germany and Japan," *Journal of International Business Studies* 40 (2009), pp. 859–85; Gerald Albaum, Julie Yu, Nila Wiese, Joel Herche, Felicitas Evangelista, and Brian Murphy, "Culture-Based Values and Management Style of Marketing Decision Makers in Six Western Pacific Rim Countries," *Journal of Global Marketing* 23, no. 2 (2010), pp. 139–51; Carlos M.P. Sousa, Emilio Ruzo, and Fernando Losada, "The Key Role of Managers' Values in Exporting: Influence on Customer Responsiveness and Export Performance," *Journal of International Marketing* 18, no. 2 (2010), pp. 1–19.

[88] Donald L. Lund, Lisa K. Scheer, and Irina V. Kozlenkova, "Culture's Impact on the Importance of Fairness in Interorganizational Relationships," *Journal of International Marketing* 21 (2013), pp. 21–43.

[89] Cathy Anterasian, John L. Graham, and R. Bruce Money, "Are U.S. Managers Superstitious about Market Share?" *Sloan Management Review* 37, no. 4 (1996), pp. 67–77.

WORK WANTED: Chinese migrant workers advertise their skills while waiting for employers in the Sichuan city of Chengdu. The government expects the total number of migrants looking for jobs this year to reach at least 25 million. Maintaining steady growth is the country's foremost priority and also its most challenging task.

management cooperate—in Germany labor is represented on corporate boards, and in Japan, management takes responsibility for the welfare of the labor force. Because the welfare of the workforce matters more to Japanese and German firms, their sales revenues are more stable over time. American-style layoffs are eschewed. The individualistic American approach to labor–management relations is adversarial—each side takes care of itself. So we see damaging strikes and huge layoffs that result in more volatile performance for American firms. Studies have uncovered stability as one of global investors' key criteria.[90]

Circa 2000, the American emphasis on competition looked like the best approach, and business practices around the world appeared to be converging on the American model. But it is important to recall that key word in Adam Smith's justification for competition—"frequently." It's worth repeating here: "By pursuing his own interest he frequently promotes that of society. . . ." Smith wrote *frequently*, not *always*. A competitive, individualistic approach works well in the context of an economic boom. During the late 1990s, American firms dominated Japanese and European ones. The latter seemed stodgy, conservative,

---

[90]Vincentiu Covrig, Sie Tin Lau, and Lilian Ng, "Do Domestic and Foreign Fund Managers Have Similar Preferences for Stock Characteristics? A Cross-Country Analysis," *Journal of International Business Studies* 37 (2006), pp. 407–29.

After more than two decades of stagnation in Japan, the social contract of lifetime employment is softening. This change is reflected in more frequent corporate layoffs, frustrating job searches, and "tent villages" in public places such as Ueno Park in Tokyo. But even at their worst point in history, Japanese jobless are just a trickle compared with the torrent of pink slips and homeless folks when the American economy heads south.

and slow in the then-current hot global information economy. However, downturns in a competitive culture can be ugly things.[91] For example, the instability and layoffs at Boeing during the commercial aircraft busts of the late 1990s and early 2000s were damaging not only to employees and their local communities, but also to shareholders. And during the dramatic economic downturn in 2008–2009, Asian firms tended to eschew layoffs, compared with their American counterparts,[92] and even rejected the U.S. as the benchmark for best management practices.[93] It should also be mentioned that Thurow and others writing in this area omitted a fourth kind of capitalism—that common in Chinese cultures.[94] Its distinguishing characteristics are a more entrepreneurial approach and an emphasis on *guanxi* (one's network of personal connections)[95] as the coordinating principle among firms. This fourth kind of capitalism is also predicted by culture. Chinese cultures are high on PDI and low on IDV, and the strong reciprocity implied by the notion of *guanxi* fits the data well. Additionally, entrepreneurial tendencies are stronger in countries with lower UAI (e.g China), as people in those cultures tend to prefer venturing out on their own rather than the known of working for an established company.[96]

Synthesis: Relationship-Oriented vs. Information-Oriented Cultures

LO5

The differences between relationship-oriented and information-oriented cultures

Cultural distance as a multidimensional concept continues to be quite useful in the area of international marketing research.[97] However, with increasing frequency, studies note a strong relationship between Hall's high-/low-context and Hofstede's Individualism/Collective and Power Distance indices. For example, low-context American culture scores relatively low on power distance and high on individualism, whereas high-context Arab cultures score high on power distance and low on individualism. This result is not at all surprising, given that Hofstede[98] leans heavily on Hall's ideas in developing and labeling the dimensions of culture revealed via his huge database. Indeed, the three dimensions—high/low context, IDV, and PDI—are correlated above the $r = 0.6$ level, suggesting all three dimensions are largely measuring the same thing.[99] Likewise, when we compare linguistic distance (to English) and Transparency International's Corruption Perception Index to the other three, we see similar levels of correlations among all five dimensions. And while metrics for other dimensions of business culture do not yet exist, a pattern appears to be evident (see Exhibit 5.7).

---

[91]For a deep description of "how ugly," see Klien's *Shock Doctrine*.

[92]Evan Ramsatd, "Koreans Take Pay Cuts to Stop Layoffs," *The Wall Street Journal*, March 3, 2009.

[93]"China Rethinks the American Way," *BusinessWeek*, June 15, 2009, p. 32.

[94]Don Y. Lee and Philip L. Dawes, "Guanxi, Trust, and Long-Term Orientation in Chinese Business Markets," *Journal of International Marketing* 13, no. 2 (2005), pp. 28–56; Flora Gu, Kineta Hung, and David K. Tse, "When Does Guanxi Matter? Issues of Capitalization and Its Darkside," *Journal of Marketing* 72, no. 4 (2008), pp. 12–28; Roy Y. J. Chua, Michael W. Morris, and Paul Ingram, "Guanxi vs. Networking: Distinctive Configurations of Affect- and Cognition-Based Trust in the Networks of Chinese vs. American Managers," *Journal of International Business Studies* 40, no. 3 (2009), pp. 490–508.

[95]Mark Lam and John L. Graham, *Doing Business in the New China, The World's Most Dynamic Market* (New York: McGraw-Hill, 2007).

[96] Erkko Autio, Saurav Pathak, and Karl Wennberg, "Consequenses of Cultural Practices for Entrepreneurial Behaviors," *Journal of International Business Studies* 44 (2013), pp. 334–62.

[97]Heather Berry, Mauro F. Guillen, and Nan Zhou, "An Institutional Approach to Cross-National Distance," *Journal of International Business Studies* 41, no. 9 (2010), pp. 1460–80; Joanna Tochman Campbell, Lorraine Eden, and Stewart R. Miller, "Multinationals and Corporate Social Responsibility in Host Countries: Does Distance Matter?" *Journal of International Business Studies* 43, no. 1 (2012), pp. 84–106; Oded Shenkar, "Cultural Distance Revisited: Toward a More Rigorous Conceptualization and Measurement of Cultural Differences," *Journal of International Business Studies* 43, no. 1 (2012), pp. 1–11; Oded Shenkar, "Beyond Cultural Distance: Switching to a Friction Lens in the Study of Cultural Differences," *Journal of International Business Studies* 43, no.1 (2012), pp. 12–17; Srilata Zaheer, Margaret Spring Shomaker, and Lilach Nachum, "Distance without Direction: Restoring Credibility to a Much-Loved Construct," *Journal of International Business Studies* 43, no. 1 (2012), pp. 18–27.

[98]Hofstede, *Culture's Consequences*.

[99]This continuum has also been labeled "social context salience" by H. Rika Houston and John L. Graham, "Culture and Corruption in International Markets: Implications for Policy Makers and Managers," *Consumption, Markets, and Culture* 4, no. 3 (2000), pp. 315–40.

Exhibit 5.7
Dimensions of Culture:
A Synthesis

Information-Oriented (IO)	Relationship-Oriented (RO)
Low context	High context
Individualism	Collectivism
Low power distance	High power distance (including gender)
Bribery less common	Bribery more common*
Low distance from English	High distance from English
Linguistic directness	Linguistic indirectness
Monochronic time	Polychronic time
Internet	Face-to-face
Focus on the foreground	Background
Competition	Reduce transaction costs

*We note that Singapore, Hong Kong, Japan, and Chile do not fit all the rules here. Most would agree that all four are relationship-oriented cultures.

The pattern displayed is not definitive, only suggestive. Not every culture fits every dimension of culture in a precise way. However, the synthesis is useful in many ways. Primarily, it gives us a simple yet logical way to think about many of the cultural differences described in Chapters 4 and 5. For example, American culture is low context, individualistic (IDV), low power distance (PDI), obviously close to English, monochronic time–oriented, linguistically direct, and foreground focused,[100] and it achieves efficiency through competition; therefore, it is categorized hereafter in this book as an *information-oriented culture*. Alternatively, Japanese culture is high context, collectivistic, high power distance, far from English, polychronic (in part), linguistically indirect, and background focused, and it achieves efficiency through reduction of transaction costs; therefore, it is properly categorized as a *relationship-oriented culture*. All these differences exist even though the United States and Japan are both high-income democracies. Both cultures do achieve efficiency but through different emphases. The American business system uses competition, whereas the Japanese depend more on reducing transaction costs. What has been come to be known as "relationship marketing" is 55 percent more effective, interestingly, outside the United States in the BRIC countries (Brazil, Russia, India, and China).[101]

The most managerially useful aspect of this synthesis of cultural differences is that it allows us to make predictions about unfamiliar cultures. Managers who can do so—and manage uncertainty well—have been shown to be much more effective in cross-cultural situations.[102] Reference to the three metrics available gives us some clues about how consumers and/or business partners will behave and think. Hofstede has provided scores for 78 countries and regions, and we have included them in the appendix to this chapter. Find a country on his lists, and you have some information about that market and/or person. One might expect Trinidad to be an information-oriented culture and Russia a relationship-oriented culture, and so on. Moreover, measures of linguistic distance (any language can be used as the focal one, not just English) are available for every country and, indeed, every person. Thus, we would expect that someone who speaks Javanese as a first language to be relationship oriented.

In closing, we are quite encouraged by the publication of the important book *Culture Matters*.[103] We obviously agree with the sentiment of the title and hope that the book will help rekindle the interest in culture's pervasive influences that Max Weber and others initiated so long ago.

---

[100]Richard E. Nisbett, *The Geography of Thought* (New York: The Free Press, 2003).

[101]Stephen A. Samaha, Joshua T. Beck, and Robert W. Palmatier, "The Role of Culture in International Relationship Marketing," *Journal of Marketing* 78 (2014), pp. 78–98.

[102]C. Lakshman, "Bicultural and Attributional Complexity: Cross-cultural Leadership Effectiveness," *Journal of International Business Studies* 44 (2013), pp. 922–40.

[103]Lawrence I. Harrison and Samuel P. Huntington (eds.), *Culture Matters* (New York: Basic Books, 2000).

Summary

Management styles differ around the world. Some cultures appear to emphasize the importance of information and competition, while others focus more on relationships and transaction cost reductions. However, there are no simple answers, and the only safe generalization is that businesspersons working in another country must be sensitive to the business environment and must be willing to adapt when necessary. Unfortunately, to know when such adaptation is necessary is not always easy; in some instances adaptation is optional, whereas in others, it is actually undesirable. Understanding the culture you are entering is the only sound basis for planning.

Business behavior is derived in large part from the basic cultural environment in which the business operates and, as such, is subject to the extreme diversity encountered among various cultures and subcultures. Environmental considerations significantly affect the attitudes, behavior, and outlook of foreign businesspeople. Motivational patterns of such businesspeople depend in part on their personal backgrounds, their business positions, their sources of authority, and their own personalities.

Varying motivational patterns inevitably affect methods of doing business in different countries. Marketers in some countries thrive on competition; in others, they do everything possible to eliminate it. The authoritarian, centralized decision-making orientation in some nations contrasts sharply with democratic decentralization in others. International variation characterizes contact level, ethical orientation, negotiation outlook, and nearly every part of doing business. The foreign marketer can take no aspect of business behavior for granted.

The new breed of international businessperson that has emerged in recent years appears to have a heightened sensitivity to cultural variations. Sensitivity, however, is not enough; the international trader must be constantly alert and prepared to adapt when necessary. One must always realize that, no matter how long in a country, the outsider is not a local; in many countries, that person may always be treated as an outsider. Finally, one must avoid the critical mistake of assuming that knowledge of one culture will provide information about, let alone, acceptability in another.

Key Terms

Cultural imperative	Silent languages	Polychronic time (P-time)	Lubrication
Cultural elective	Monochronic time (M-time)	Bribery	Subornation
Cultural exclusive			

Questions

1. Define the key terms listed above.
2. "More than tolerance of an alien culture is required; there is a need for affirmative acceptance of the concept 'different but equal.'" Elaborate.
3. "We should also bear in mind that in today's business-oriented world economy, the cultures themselves are being significantly affected by business activities and business practices." Comment.
4. "In dealing with foreign businesses, the marketer must be particularly aware of the varying objectives and aspirations of management." Explain.
5. Suggest ways in which persons might prepare themselves to handle unique business customs that may be encountered in a trip abroad.
6. Business customs and national customs are closely interrelated. In which ways would one expect the two areas to coincide, and in which ways would they show differences? How could such areas of similarity and difference be identified?
7. Identify both local and foreign examples of cultural imperatives, electives, and exclusives. Be prepared to explain why each example fits into the category you have selected.
8. Contrast the authority roles of top management in different societies. How do the different views of authority affect marketing activities?
9. Do the same for aspirational patterns.
10. What effects on business customs might be anticipated from the recent rapid increases in the level of international business activity?
11. Interview some foreign students to determine the types of cultural shock they encountered when they first came to your country.
12. Differentiate between:

    Private ownership and family ownership

    Decentralized and committee decision making
13. In which ways does the size of a customer's business affect business behavior?
14. Compare three decision-making authority patterns in international business.
15. Explore the various ways in which business customs can affect the structure of competition.
16. Why is it important that the business executive be alert to the significance of differing management styles?
17. Suggest some cautions that an individual from a relationship-oriented culture should bear in mind when dealing with someone from an information-oriented culture.
18. Political payoffs are a problem. How would you react if you faced the prospect of paying a bribe? What if you knew that by

not paying, you would not be able to complete a $10 million contract?

19. Differentiate among the following:

    bribery

    extortion

    lubrication

    subornation

20. Distinguish between P-time and M-time.

21. Discuss how a P-time person reacts differently from an M-time person in keeping an appointment.

22. What is meant by "laws are the markers of past behavior that society has deemed unethical or socially irresponsible"?

23. What are the three ethical principles that provide a framework to help distinguish between right and wrong? Explain.

24. Visit Transparency International's website and check to see how the CPI Index for countries listed in Exhibits 5.4 and 5.5 have changed. After searching TI's databank, explain why the changes have occurred. The site is found at http://www.transparency.org.

25. Discuss the pros and cons of "there is no controlling legal authority" as a basis for ethical behavior.

26. "The *company.com* page is a company's front door and that doorway should be global in scope." Discuss. Visit several web pages of major multinational companies and evaluate their "front door" to the global world.

27. Visit the websites of Shell and Nike and compare their statements on corporate values. What are the major issues each addresses? Do you think their statements are useful as guides to ethical and socially responsible decision making?

28. Go to your favorite Web reference source and access some recent news articles on Nike and alleged human rights violations. Access the Nike statement on corporate values and write a brief statement on the alleged violations and Nike's statement of corporate values.

Appendix: Index Scores for Countries and Regions

Country	Power Distance	Uncertainty Avoidance	Individualism/ Collectivism	Masculinity/ Femininity	Long-Term/ Short-Term Orientation	Primary Language	Distance from English
Argentina	49	86	46	56		Spanish	3
Australia total	36	51	90	61	31	English	0
Aborigines	80	128	89	22	10	Australian	7
Austria	11	70	55	79	31	German	1
Bangladesh	80	60	20	55	40	Bengali	3
Belgium total	65	94	75	54	38	Dutch	1
Dutch speakers	61	97	78	43		Dutch	1
French speakers	67	93	72	60		French	3
Brazil	69	76	38	49	65	Portuguese	3
Bulgaria	70	85	30	40		Bulgarian	3
Canada total	39	48	80	52	23	English	0
French speakers	54	60	73	45	30	French	3
Chile	63	86	23	28		Spanish	3
China	80	30	20	66	118	Mandarin	6
Colombia	67	80	13	64		Spanish	3
Costa Rica	35	86	15	21		Spanish	3
Czech Republic	57	74	58	57	13	Czech	3
Denmark	18	23	74	16	46	Danish	1
Ecuador	78	67	8	63		Spanish	3
Estonia	40	60	60	30		Estonian	4
Finland	33	59	63	26	41	Finnish	4
France	68	86	71	43	39	French	3
Germany	35	65	67	66	31	German	1
Great Britain	35	35	89	66	25	English	0
Greece	60	112	35	57		Greek	3
Guatemala	95	101	6	37		Spanish	3
Hong Kong	68	29	25	57	96	Cantonese	6
Hungary	46	82	80	88	50	Hungarian	4
India	77	40	48	56	61	Dravidian	3
Indonesia	78	48	14	46		Bahasa	7
Iran	58	59	41	43		Farsi	3
Ireland	28	35	70	68	43	English	0
Israel	13	81	54	47		Hebrew	5
Italy	50	75	76	70	34	Italian	3
Jamaica	45	13	39	68		English	0
Japan	54	92	46	95	80	Japanese	4
Korea (South)	60	85	18	39	75	Korean	4
Luxembourg	40	70	60	50		Luxembourgish	1
Malaysia	104	36	26	50		Malay	7
Malta	56	96	59	47		Maltese	5
Mexico	81	82	30	69		Spanish	3

						Language	
Morocco	70	68	46	53	44	Arabic	5
Netherlands	38	53	80	14	30	Dutch	1
New Zealand	22	49	79	58	44	English	0
Norway	31	50	69	8	0	Norwegian	1
Pakistan	55	70	14	50		Urdu	3
Panama	95	86	11	44		Spanish	3
Peru	64	87	16	42		Spanish	3
Philippines	94	44	32	64	19	Tagalog	7
Poland	68	93	60	64	32	Polish	3
Portugal	63	104	27	31	30	Portuguese	3
Romania	90	90	30	42		Romanian	3
Russia	93	95	39	36		Russian	3
Salvador	66	94	19	40		Spanish	3
Singapore	74	8	20	48	48	Mandarin	6
Slovakia	104	51	52	110	38	Slovak	3
South Africa	49	49	65	63		Afrikaans	1
Spain	57	86	51	42	19	Spanish	3
Surinam	85	92	47	37		Dutch	1
Sweden	31	29	71	5	33	Swedish	1
Switzerland total	34	58	68	70	40	German	1
German speakers	26	56	69	72		German	1
French speakers	70	70	64	58		French	3
Taiwan	58	69	17	45	87	Taiwanese	6
Thailand	64	64	20	34	56	Thai	7
Trinidad	47	55	16	58		English	0
Turkey	66	85	37	45		Turkish	4
United States	40	46	91	62	29	English	0
Uruguay	61	100	36	38		Spanish	3
Venezuela	81	76	12	73		Spanish	3
Vietnam	70	30	20	40	80	Vietnamese	7
Yugoslavia total	76	88	27	21		Serbo-Croatian	3
Croatia (Zagreb)	73	80	33	40		Serbo-Croatian	3
Serbia (Beograd)	86	92	25	43		Serbo-Croatian	3
Slovenia (Ljubljana)	71	88	27	19		Slovene	3
Regions							
Arab countries	80	68	38	53	25	Arabic	5
East Africa	64	52	27	41			8
West Africa	77	54	20	46	16		8

Source: Geert Hofstede, *Culture's Consequences: Comparing Values, Behaviors, Institutions and Organizations Across Nations*, 2nd ed. (Thousand Oaks, CA: Sage, 2001). Reprinted with permission of Geert Hofstede.

Chapter 6

The Political Environment:

A CRITICAL CONCERN

CHAPTER LEARNING OBJECTIVES

What you should learn from Chapter 6:

LO1 What the sovereignty of nations means and how it can affect the stability of government policies

LO2 How different governmental types, political parties, nationalism, targeted fear/animosity, and trade disputes can affect the environment for marketing in foreign countries

LO3 The political risks of global business and the factors that affect stability

LO4 The importance of the political system to international marketing and its effect on foreign investments

LO5 The impact of political and social activists, violence, and terrorism on international business

LO6 How to assess and reduce the effect of political vulnerability

LO7 How and why governments encourage foreign investment

Global Perspective

WORLD TRADE GOES BANANAS

Rather than bruising Chiquita Bananas, the wrath of politics instead hammered Prosciutto di Parma ham from Italy, handbags from France, and bath oils and soaps from Germany. These and a host of other imported products from Europe were all slapped with a 100 percent import tariff as retaliation by the U.S. government against EU banana-import rules that favored Caribbean bananas over Latin American bananas. Keep in mind that no bananas are exported from the United States, yet the United States has been engaged in a trade war over the past 7 years that has cost numerous small businesses on both sides of the Atlantic millions of dollars. But how can this be, you ask? Politics, that's how!

One small business, Reha Enterprises, for example, sells bath oil, soaps, and other supplies imported from Germany. The tariff on its most popular product, an herbal foam bath, was raised from 5 percent to 100 percent. The customs bill for 6 months spiraled to $37,783 from just $1,851—a 1,941 percent tax increase. For a small business whose gross sales are less than $1 million annually, it was crippling. When the owner of Reha heard of the impending "banana war," he called everyone—his congressperson, his senator, the United States Trade Representative (USTR). When he described his plight to the USTR, an official there expressed amazement. "They were surprised I was still importing," because they thought the tariff would cut off the industry entirely. That was their intention, which of course would have meant killing Reha Enterprises as well.

In effect, he was told it was his fault that he got caught up in the trade war. He should have attended the hearings in Washington, just like Gillette and Mattel, and maybe his products would have been dropped from the targeted list, just as theirs were. Scores of European products, from clothing to stoves to glass Christmas ornaments, dolls, and ballpoint pens, that were originally targeted for the retaliatory tariffs escaped the tariff. Aggressive lobbying by large corporations, trade groups, and members of Congress got most of the threatened imported products off the list. The USTR had published a list of the targeted imports in the Federal Register, inviting affected companies to testify. Unfortunately, the Federal Register was not on Reha's owner's reading list.

In that case, he was told, he should have hired a lobbyist in Washington to keep him briefed. Good advice—but it doesn't make much sense to a company that grosses less than $1 million a year. Other advice received from an official of the USTR included the off-the-record suggestion that he might want to change the customs number on the invoice so it would appear that he was importing goods not subject to the tariff, a decision that could, if he were caught, result in a hefty fine or jail. Smaller businesses in Europe faced similar problems as their export business dried up because of the tariffs.

How did this banana war start? The European Union imposed a quota and tariffs that favored imports from former colonies in the Caribbean and Africa, distributed by European firms, over Latin American bananas distributed by U.S. firms. Chiquita Brands International and Dole Food Company, contending that the EU's "illegal trade barriers" were costing $520 million annually in lost sales to Europe, asked the U.S. government for help. The government agreed that unfair trade barriers were damaging their business, and 100 percent tariffs on selected European imports were levied. Coincidentally, Chiquita Brands' annual political campaign contributions increased from barely over $40,000 in 1991 to $1.3 million in 1998.

A settlement was finally reached that involved high tariffs on Latin America bananas and quotas (with no tariffs) on bananas from Europe's former colonies. But the bruising over bananas continued, and not in a straightforward way! In 2007 the issue shifted to banana bending. That is, bananas from Latin America tend to be long and straight, while those from the non-tariff countries are short and bent. Because the latter are not preferred by the shippers or retailers (the bendier ones don't stack as neatly and economically), the bananas from the former colonies were still not preferred. And new regulations were adopted by the European Commission that mandated that bananas must be free from "abnormal curvature of the fingers." So the bendy banana producers threatened to renege on the whole agreement. Circa 2007 everyone involved found this prospect very unappealing.

The tale does have a happy ending though. In 2009, after marathon meetings among all parties in Geneva, the 16-year banana split was finally healed: The European Union cut import tariffs on bananas grown in Latin America by U.S. firms. Most recently, there's also an epilogue. Chiquita has now become a Brazilian brand. The U.S. corporation was purchased recently by two South American investors for $742 million.

Sources: "U.S. Sets Import Tariffs in Latest Salvo in Ongoing Battle over Banana Trade," *Minneapolis Star Tribune,* March 4, 1999; Timothy Dove, "Hit by a $200,000 Bill from the Blue," *Time,* February 7, 2000, p. 54; Geneva Agreement on Trade in Bananas, signed May 31, 2010, http://www.ec.europa.eu.; "Chiquita's Top Banana? Two Brazilians Win Bid," *Associated Press,* October 27, 2014, online.

No company, domestic or international, large or small, can conduct business without considering the influence of the political environment within which it will operate. One of the most undeniable and crucial realities of international business is that both host and home governments are integral partners. A government reacts to its environment by initiating and pursuing policies deemed necessary to solve the problems created by its particular circumstances. Reflected in its policies and attitudes toward business are a government's ideas of how best to promote the national interest, considering its own resources and political philosophy. A government controls and restricts a company's activities by encouraging and offering support or by discouraging and banning or restricting its activities—depending on the pleasure of the government.

International law recognizes the sovereign right of a nation to grant or withhold permission to do business within its political boundaries and to control where its citizens conduct business. Thus, the political environment of countries is a critical concern for the international marketer. This chapter examines some of the more salient political considerations in assessing global markets.

The Sovereignty of Nations

LO1

What the sovereignty of nations means and how it can affect the stability of government policies

In the context of international law, a *sovereign state* is independent and free from all external control; enjoys full legal equality with other states; governs its own territory; selects its own political, economic, and social systems; and has the power to enter into agreements with other nations. Sovereignty refers to both the powers exercised by a state in relation to other countries and the supreme powers exercised over its own members.[1] A state sets requirements for citizenship, defines geographical boundaries, and controls trade and the movement of people and goods across its borders. Additionally, a citizen is subject to the state's laws even when beyond national borders. It is with the extension of national laws beyond a country's borders that much of the conflict in international business arises. This reasoning is especially true when another country considers its own sovereignty to be compromised.

Nations can and do abridge specific aspects of their sovereign rights to coexist with other nations. The European Union, North American Free Trade Agreement (NAFTA), North Atlantic Treaty Organization (NATO), and World Trade Organization (WTO) represent examples of nations voluntarily agreeing to give up some of their sovereign rights to participate with member nations for a common, mutually beneficial goal. The leaders of the G20 nations ceded some sovereignty in their hugely important April 2009 agreement to "reject protectionism" at the nadir of the 2009 crash, when world trade had declined more

---

[1]For those interested in learning more about the concept of sovereignty, see Stephen D. Krasner (ed.), *Problematic Sovereignty* (New York: Columbia University Press, 2001).

A great moment for free trade! U.S. President Barack Obama, Italian Prime Minister Silvio Berlusconi, and Russian President Dmitry Medvedev mugged for the camera during a group photo after a G-20 summit in London aimed at fixing the crises-wracked global economy. All leaders of the G20 nations signed a joint communiqué promising to "resist protectionism." Their April 2009 agreement nadir of the world trade bust (a decline of more than 12 percent) that marked the year. The celebration symbolizes their successful dodging of the Smoot-Hawley tariff bullet that dramatically exacerbated the Great Depression of the 1930s.

Targeted Fear and/or Animosity

It is important for marketers not to confuse nationalism, whose animosity is directed generally toward *all* foreign countries, with a widespread fear or animosity directed at a particular country. This confusion was a mistake made by Toyota in the United States in the late 1980s and early 1990s. Sales of Japanese cars were declining in the States, and an advertising campaign was designed and delivered that assumed the problem was American nationalism. However, nationalism was clearly not the problem, because sales of German cars were not experiencing the same kinds of declines. The properly defined problem was "Americans' *fear* of Japan." Indeed, at the time, Americans considered the economic threat from Japan greater than the military threat from the Soviet Union. So when Toyota spent millions on an advertising campaign showing Camrys being made by Americans in a Toyota plant in Kentucky, it may well have exacerbated the fear that the Japanese were "colonizing" the United States. The long-term animosity of Chinese consumers for Japanese branded product based on the latter's military aggression in the 1930s and 1940s is another example of how history affects international marketing.[15]

Best-selling titles in France, including *The World Is Not Merchandise, Who Is Killing France? The American Strategy*, and *No Thanks Uncle Sam*, epitomize its animosity toward the United States. Although such attitudes may seem odd in a country that devours U.S. movies, eats U.S. fast foods, views U.S. soap operas, and shops at U.S. Walmart stores, national animosity—whatever the cause—is a critical part of the political environment. The United States is not immune to the same kinds of directed negativism either. The rift between France and the United States over the Iraq–U.S. war led to hard feelings on both sides and an American backlash against French wine, French cheese, and even products Americans thought were French. French's mustard felt compelled to issue a press release stating that it is an "American company founded by an American named 'French.'" Thus, it is quite clear that no nation-state, however secure, will tolerate penetration by a foreign company into its market and economy if it perceives a social, cultural, economic, or political threat to its well-being.

Trade Disputes

Finally, narrow trade disputes themselves can roil broader international markets. At the beginning of the chapter we discussed our favorite example—bananas. Among several hot issues circa 2015 were solar panels, Internet trade, steel, trade sanctions against Russia, farm subsidies in developed countries, and the long-simmering AIRBUS–Boeing battle over subsidies. Any of these disputes might boil over and affect other aspects of international trade, but at least at this writing, cooler heads seem to be prevailing—along with the WTO dispute resolution processes.

Political Risks of Global Business[16]

LO3

The political risks of global business and the factors that affect stability

Issues of sovereignty, differing political philosophies, and nationalism are manifest in a host of governmental actions that enhance the risks of global business. Risks can range from confiscation, the harshest, to many lesser but still significant government rules and regulations, such as exchange controls, import restrictions, and price controls that directly affect the performance of business activities. Although not always officially blessed initially, social or political activist groups can provoke governments into actions that prove harmful to business. Of all the political risks, the most costly are those actions that result in a transfer of equity from the company to the government, with or without adequate compensation.

---

[15]Malcolm Smith and Qianpin Li, "The Role of Occupation in an Integrated Boycott Model: A Cross-Regional Study in China," *Journal of Global Marketing* 23, no. 2 (2010), pp. 109–26.

[16]An excellent discussion of a variety of issues regarding political risk can be found in the *Journal of International Business Studies* 41, no. 5 (2010), pp. 759–860. See in particular the following articles: Witold J. Henisz, Edward D. Manisfield, and Mary Ann Von Glinow, "Conflict, Security, and Political Risk: International Business in Challenging Times"; Quan Li and Tatiana Vashchilko, "Dyadic Military Conflict, Security Alliances, and Bilateral FDI Flows"; Reid W. Click and Robert J. Weiner, "Resource Nationalism Meets the Market: Political Risk and the Value of Petroleum Reserves"; Oana Branzei and Samer Abdelnour, "Another Day, Another Dollar: Enterprise Resilience under Terrorism in Developing Countries"; Michael R. Czinkota, Gary Knight, Peter W. Liesch, and John Steen, "Terrorism and International Business: A Research Agenda"; and Walid Hejazi and Eric Santor, "Foreign Asset Risk Exposure, DOI, and Performance: An Analysis of Canadian Banks."

Confiscation, Expropriation, and Domestication

LO4

The importance of the political system to international marketing and its effect on foreign investments

The most severe political risk is confiscation, that is, the seizing of a company's assets without payment. Two notable confiscations of U.S. property occurred when Fidel Castro became the leader in Cuba and later when the Shah of Iran was overthrown. Confiscation was most prevalent in the 1950s and 1960s when many underdeveloped countries saw confiscation, albeit ineffective, as a means of economic growth.

Less drastic, but still severe, is expropriation, where the government seizes an investment but makes some reimbursement for the assets. For example, in 2008 the Chavez regime in Venezuela expropriated Mexico's CEMEX operations, paying a negotiated price. Often the expropriated investment is nationalized; that is, it becomes a government-run entity. A third type of risk is domestication, which occurs when host countries gradually cause the transfer of foreign investments to national control and ownership through a series of government decrees that mandate local ownership and greater national involvement in a company's management. The ultimate goal of domestication is to force foreign investors to share more of the ownership, management, and profits with nationals than was the case before domestication.

Rather than a quick answer to economic development, expropriation and nationalization have often led to nationalized businesses that were inefficient, technologically weak, and noncompetitive in world markets. Risks of confiscation and expropriation appear to have lessened over the last two decades (with exceptions in Latin America, particularly Venezuela), because experience has shown that few of the desired benefits materialize after government takeover. Today, countries often require prospective investors to agree to share ownership, use local content, enter into labor and management agreements, and share participation in export sales as a condition of entry; in effect, the company has to become domesticated as a condition for investment.

Countries now view foreign investment as a means of economic growth. As the world has become more economically interdependent, it has become obvious that much of the economic success of countries such as South Korea, Singapore, and Taiwan is tied to foreign investments. Nations throughout the world that only a few years ago restricted or forbade foreign investments are now courting foreign investors as a much needed source of capital and technology. Additionally, they have begun to privatize telecommunications, broadcasting, airlines, banks, railroads, and other nationally owned companies as a means of enhancing competition and attracting foreign capital.

The benefits of privatizing are many. In Mexico, for example, privatization of the national telephone company resulted in almost immediate benefits when the government received hundreds of millions of dollars of much needed capital from the sale and immediate investment in new telecommunications systems. A similar scenario has played out in Brazil, Argentina, India, and many eastern European countries. Ironically, many of the businesses that were expropriated and nationalized in earlier periods are now being privatized.

Economic Risks

Even though expropriation and confiscation are waning as risks of doing business abroad, international companies are still confronted with a variety of economic risks that can occur with little warning. Restraints on business activity may be imposed under the banner of national security to protect an infant industry, to conserve scarce foreign exchange, to raise revenue, or to retaliate against unfair trade practices, among a score of other real or imagined reasons. These economic risks are an important and recurring part of the political environment that few international companies can avoid.

Exchange Controls.   Exchange controls stem from shortages of foreign exchange held by a country. When a nation faces shortages of foreign exchange and/or a substantial amount of capital is leaving the country, controls may be levied over all movements of capital or selectively against the most politically vulnerable companies to conserve the supply of foreign exchange for the most essential uses. A recurrent problem for the foreign investor is getting profits in and out of the host country without loss of value, which can occur when a currency is devalued. Many countries maintain regulations for control of currency, and should an economy suffer a setback or foreign exchange reserves decline severely, the controls on convertibility are imposed quickly.

Local-Content Laws.   In addition to restricting imports of essential supplies to force local purchase, countries often require a portion of any product sold within the country to have local content, that is, to contain locally made parts. Thailand, for example, requires that all milk products contain at least 50 percent milk from local dairy farmers. Contrary to popular belief, local-content requirements are not restricted to Third World countries. The European Union has had a local-content requirement as high as 45 percent for "screwdriver operations," a name often given to foreign-owned assemblers, and NAFTA requires 62 percent local content for all cars coming from member countries.

Import Restrictions.   Selective restrictions on the import of consumer products, raw materials, machines, and spare parts are fairly common strategies to force foreign industry to purchase more supplies within the host country and thereby create markets for local industry. Although this restriction is an attempt to support the development of domestic industry, the result is often to hamstring and sometimes interrupt the operations of established industries. The problem then becomes critical when there are no adequately developed sources of supply within the country. Perhaps our favorite example in this area is France's restriction on the use of ketchup in its public school cafeterias.[17]

Tax Controls.   Taxes must be classified as a political risk when used as a means of controlling foreign investments. In such cases, they are raised without warning and in violation of formal agreements. India seems to be particularly tough in this regard[18]—for example, the government there taxes PepsiCo and the Coca-Cola Company 40 percent on all soda bottled in India. And, using a different angle of attack, India is attempting to collect $40 million in taxes on travel tickets sold online from Sabre's (an airlines reservations service) data center in Tulsa, Oklahoma. The Indian government contends that Sabre has a permanent establishment in India in the form of data flows between Sabre's Tulsa processing center and the desktop computers of travel agents in India. To underdeveloped countries with economies constantly threatened with a shortage of funds, unreasonable taxation of successful foreign investments appeals to some government officials as the handiest and quickest means of finding operating funds. As the Internet grows in importance, countries will surely seize on Internet transactions as a lucrative source of revenue.[19]

Price Controls.   Essential products that command considerable public interest, such as pharmaceuticals, food, gasoline, and cars, are often subjected to price controls. Such controls applied during inflationary periods can be used to control the cost of living. They also may be used to force foreign companies to sell equity to local interests. A side effect on the local economy can be to slow or even stop capital investment.

Labor Problems.   In many countries, labor unions have strong government support that they use effectively in obtaining special concessions from business. Layoffs may be forbidden, profits may have to be shared, and an extraordinary number of services may have to be provided. In fact, in many countries, foreign firms are considered fair game for the demands of the domestic labor supply. In France, the belief in full employment is almost religious in fervor; layoffs of any size, especially by foreign-owned companies, are regarded as national crises. We should also note that some multinational companies are more powerful than local labor unions. Walmart closed a store in Quebec rather than let it be unionized.

Political Sanctions   In addition to economic risks, one or a group of nations may boycott another nation, thereby stopping all trade between the countries, or may issue sanctions against the trade of specific products. The United States has long-term boycotts of trade with Cuba and Iran and has come under some criticism for its demand for continued sanctions against Cuba[20]

---

[17]Kim Wissher, "In France, a Ban on Ketchup," *Los Angeles Times,* October 6, 2011, p. A3.

[18]Dhanya Ann Thoppil, "Vodafone Challenges India Tax Body's Claims on Transfer Pricing," *The Wall Street Journal,* February 24, 2012.

[19]Devorah Lauter, "France Considers Taxing Google and Other Internet Portals," *Los Angeles Times*, January 8, 2010.

[20] Ernesto Londono, "Still Pondering U.S.-Cuba Relations, Fidel Castro Responds," *The New York Times*, October 14, 2014, online.

and its threats of future sanctions against countries that violate human rights issues. Trade sanctions against Russia for its continued aggressions toward Ukraine are controversial, even within the United States. Russian has retaliated against McDonald's closing stores in Moscow[21] and banning imports of European food imports[22].

Russia

The consequences of the U.S. embargo of Cuba: A relatively new Chinese Chery Q (red provisional plate), and one of the newest American cars you can find on the island, a 1957 Chevy (yellow citizen's plate), certainly with a refurbished engine. A variety of other European and Asian brands ply the streets of Havana, almost all recent models. No new American models are in sight.

History indicates that sanctions are almost always unsuccessful in reaching desired goals, particularly when other major nations' traders ignore them. For example, the Chinese recently signed an agreement with Iran that will bring $70 billion of natural gas to China, and China's imports of Iranian crude oil have risen steadily during the boycott by the United States and European countries.[23] Please see Crossing Borders 6.2 for more on this issue. This lack of success is the case with Cuba, North Korea, and Iran, where the undesirable behavior that the sanctions were imposed to change continues, and the only ones who seem to be hurt are the people[24] and companies that get caught in the middle. China imports of Iranian crude oil have risen steadily during the boycott by the United States and European countries.[25]

Political and Social Activists and Nongovernmental Organizations

Although not usually officially sanctioned by the government, the impact of political and social activists (PSAs) can also interrupt the normal flow of trade. PSAs can range from those who seek to bring about peaceful change to those who resort to violence and terrorism to effect change. When well organized, the actions of PSAs can succeed.

The protestors pictured on pages 184–185 use creativity to make a point. We do not recommend the destructive and/or violent sort of protest often seen in other venues.

One of the most effective and best-known PSA actions was against Nestlé due to the sale of baby formula in Third World markets. The worldwide boycott of Nestlé products resulted in substantial changes in the company's marketing. More recently, activists of the Free Burma Campaign (FBC) have applied enough pressure to cause several U.S. garment companies to stop importing textiles from Myanmar. Furthermore, activists on several U.S.

LO5

The impact of political and social activists, violence, and terrorism on international business

---

[21]James Marson and Julie Jargon, "Moscow Advances on McDonald's," *The Wall Street Journal*, August 21, 2014, p. B1, 2.

[22]Gabi Thesing and Whitney McFerron, "How Putin Lowered the Price of Europe's Apples," *Bloomberg BusinessWeek*, September 11, 2014, online.

[23]Wayne Ma, "China's Oil Imports from Iran Jump," *The Wall Street Journal*, January 21, 2012.

[24]Barbara Demick, "North Koreans' Misery Amplified a Hundredfold," *Los Angeles Times*, February 3, 2010, pp. A1, A7.

[25]Patrick Barta, "EU to Ease Some Myanmar Sanctions," *The Wall Street Journal*, January 23, 2012.

CROSSING BORDERS 6.2

Trade Does Not Work as a Stick, Only as a Carrot

It was 1807 when Thomas Jefferson proposed trade sanctions as an innovation in diplomacy. The donkeys he endeavored to persuade were quite big and quite stubborn—England and France. The goal was to get these warring nations to leave American ships alone on the high seas. Lacking a competitive navy, our third president dreamed up the trade embargo; rather than using trade as a carrot, he planned to withhold trade and use it as a stick. However, instead of changing French or English policies and behaviors, Jefferson's policy actually endangered New England traders. They complained:

> Our ships all in motion, once whiten'd the ocean;
> They sail'd and return'd with a Cargo;
> Now doom'd to decay, they are fallen a prey,
> To Jefferson, worms, and EMBARGO.

Jefferson's embargo fell apart in just 15 months. Only the War of 1812 settled the problems with English aggression at sea.

Consider the track record of trade sanctions in the last century. In 1940 the United States told the Japanese to get out of China, and the ensuing embargo of gasoline and scrap metal led directly to the Pearl Harbor attack. Since 1948 Arab countries have boycotted Israel. Given that countries trade most with their close neighbors, you have to wonder how much this lack of trade has promoted the continuing conflicts in the area. Israel is still there. In 1959 Fidel Castro took over Cuba, and for the next 50+ years, the United States has boycotted sugar and cigars, but Castro remained in charge. OPEC's 1973 oil flow slowdown was intended to get America to stop supporting Israel. However, the dollars still flow fast to Israel and now Egypt as well.

In 1979 the United States told the Soviets to get out of Afghanistan. They refused. America boycotted the Moscow Olympics and stopped selling the Soviets grain and technology. The Soviet response: They continued to kill Afghans (and, by the way, Soviet soldiers) for another 10 years. Moreover, in 1984 they and their allies' athletes stayed away from the Olympics in Los Angeles. And the high-tech embargo didn't work anyway. A San Diego division of Caterpillar lost millions of dollars in service contracts for Soviet natural gas pipelines in the mid-1970s. These revenues were lost permanently, because the Soviets taught themselves how to do the maintenance and overhauls. In 1989 a Moscow weapons research facility had every brand of computer then available in the West: IBMs, Apples, and the best from Taiwan and Japan as well.

Perhaps the 1980s' multilateral trade sanctions imposed on South Africa hastened apartheid's demise. But look how well the world's 10-year embargo of Iraq changed policy there. Using trade as a weapon killed kids while Saddam Hussein celebrated at $12 million birthday parties. Indeed, the best prescription for Middle East peace (and American taxpayers' wallets, by the way) is all sides dropping all embargoes.

The end of the last century witnessed great strides in the elimination of ill-conceived trade sanctions. Perhaps most important was the U.S. Senate's and President's approvals of permanently normalized trade relations (PNTR) with China. However, other important steps were the relaxation of some of the trade restrictions on Vietnam, North Korea, Iran, and Cuba. Indeed, as a result of President Clinton's diplomacy, North and South Koreans marched together at the Sydney Olympics; Americans can now buy pistachio nuts and carpets from Tehran, and U.S. firms can sell medical supplies and services in Havana. Remarkable!

These same kinds of carrots need to be thrown in the direction of the other countries on America's blacklist—Myanmar, Angola, Libya, Sudan, and Syria. Be certain that the chorus of criticism regarding human rights, freedom of the press, and democracy should continue, loud and clear. But instead of dropping bombs (or threatening to), we should be selling them computers and Internet connections. The cost of a cruise missile is about the same as 2,000 Apple computers! And at the most fundamental level, coercion does not work. Exchange does.

Source: John L. Graham, "Trade Brings Peace," http://www .orangetreepartners.net/pdfs/Jerusalem-Olympics.pdf, accessed 2015.

college campuses boycotted Pepsi Cola drinks and PepsiCo-owned Pizza Hut and Taco Bell stores, saying that the company's commercial activities contributed to the abysmal human rights in Myanmar. The results of the boycott were serious enough that PepsiCo sold its stake in its joint venture in Myanmar and withdrew from that market. The concern was that potential losses in the United States outweighed potential profits in Myanmar. Holland's Heineken and Denmark's Carlsberg beer companies withdrew from Myanmar for similar reasons.

The rather broad issue of globalization is the also the focus of many PSA groups. The demonstrations in Seattle during a 1999 WTO meeting and in Washington, DC, against the World Bank and the International Monetary Fund (IMF), along with similar demonstrations in other countries, reflect a growing concern about a global economy. Whether (or not)

The most entertaining protest technique was pioneered by French farmers. Perhaps they were inspired by that American export, *Animal House*. In any case, French farmers like to throw their food. Here they tossed tomatoes and such at McDonald's; they've also lobbed lamb chops at their own trade ministers and herded their sheep into the Louvre Museum.[26]

THE NEW POWER OF PEACEFUL PROTESTS

I like to believe that people in the long run are going to do more to promote peace than our governments. Indeed, I think that people want peace so much that one of these days governments had better get out of the way and let them have it.

—Dwight D. Eisenhower

Dwight D. Eisenhower, TV talk with Prime Minister Macmillan (31 August 1959) - Presidency

Apparently they pay attention in Taiwan. Most recently, fishermen pitched perch in Taipei to protest the Japanese fishing fleet's presence in their waters.

We believe that peace happens because people want it to, not because politicians ordain it so. Our ideas are not new. Karl Popper's *Open Society*[27] and Jonathan Schell's *Unconquerable World*[28] make the same kinds of arguments. We just think in today's world of punitive trade sanctions and military muscle, it is important to remind folks that there are more viable alternatives for international relations and global persuasion.[29]

The organizers (PSAs) of these various demonstrations understand that two things are important in protests:
(1) getting large numbers of people to show up and
(2) producing memorable pictures. On these pages are

PROTESTING MILK PRICES: A farmer sprayed milk on police forces during a protest against falling milk prices outside the European Commission headquarters in Brussels. European dairy farmers are seeking more aid to cope with a sharp drop in milk prices. An udderly fantastic shot!

Some have called this Silicon Valley versus Hollywood. The issue is the propose U.S. Stop Online Piracy Act (SOPA). Music and film industry executives believe the law will prevent abuse of their intellectual property. The main problem they see is with explosion of online pirated material posted by foreign companies. Folks like Google, Wikipeida, and other start-up internet companies complain that the law will stifle innovation and enable censorship in the U.S. Chinese internet users applauded the protest and the freedom of expression it reflects in the U.S.[30] Finally, the protest seems to have worked. At this writing SOPA is on hold.

BARING THEIR DISMAY: Members of the Pirate Party parade through Berlin's Tegel Airport in their underwear to protest government plans to test full-body scans as an invasion of citizens' privacy.

some of our favorite pictures. Please note that to the extent that the Sea Shepherd Conservation Society activists used force to board the Japanese ship (below), we cannot condone their methods. Property damage and violence are never justified; and their use demonstrates a pathetic lack of creative thinking about integrated marketing communications (see Chapter 16).

Activists of the Bharatiya Janata Party wearing "evil" masks shout antigovernment slogans near the Union Carbide plant in the central Indian city of Bhopal on the eve of World Environment Day. The activists protested to draw the attention of the government to chemical waste and demanded the cleanup of hazardous waste in the area. The leak from the Union Carbide pesticide plant in 1984 was one of the world's worst industrial accidents, killing 3,000 people and leaving thousands of others with lifetime illnesses.

They were "pirates" to some, "hostages" to others. But two anti-whaling activists (an Australian and a Briton from the Sea Shepherd Conservation Society) who drew global attention by forcibly boarding a Japanese harpoon ship in Antarctic waters have demonstrated how the emotional clash over Japan's annual whale hunt can disrupt even the best international friendships.

[26]"Sheep Herded into Louvre by Protesting Farmers," *SkyNews*, March 31, 2014, online.

[27]Karl R. Popper, *The Open Society and Its Enemies*, 5th ed. (Princeton, NJ: Princeton University Press, 1966).

[28]Jonathan Schell, *The Unconquerable World: Power, Nonviolence, and the Will of the People* (New York: Metropolitan Books, 2003).

[29]Taken from John L. Graham, *Trade Brings Peace*, 2011.

[30]David Pierson, "Chinese Laud U.S. Website Blackout," *Los Angeles Times*, January 20, 2012, pp. B1, B4.

misguided, uninformed, or just "wackos," as they have been described, PSAs can be a potent force in rallying public opinion and are an important political force that should not be dismissed, as companies such as Nike, McDonald's, and Nestlé know.

The Internet and cell phones have together become effective tools of PSAs to spread the word about whatever cause they sponsor. During protest rallies against the U.S.–Iraq war, organizers were able to coordinate protest demonstrations in 600 cities worldwide and to disseminate information easily. A Google search for "peace protest" during that time (2003) resulted in 788,000 entries (about 660,000 in 2008), including news briefs, website for peace organizations, online petitions for peace, where to show up with your placard, where to send your dollars, and how to write your member of Congress.

Often associated with political activism, nongovernmental organizations (NGOs) are increasingly affecting policy decisions made by governments.[31] Many are involved in peaceful protests, lobbying, and even collaborations with governmental organizations. Many also are involved in mitigating much of the human misery plaguing parts of the planet. Some NGOs have received global recognition—the Red Cross and Red Crescent, Amnesty International, Oxfam, UNICEF, Care, and Habitat for Humanity are examples—for their good works, political influence, and even their brand power.[32]

Violence, Terrorism, and War

Although not usually government initiated, violence is another related risk for multinational companies to consider in assessing the political vulnerability of their activities. Oftentimes, peaceful protests turn violent as we have seen in recent years in many nations, including

---

[31]Hildy Teegen, Jonathan P. Doh, and Sushil Vachani, "The Importance of Non-Governmental Organizations (NGOs) in Global Governance and Value Creation: An International Business Research Agenda," *Journal of International Business Studies* 35, no. 6 (2004), pp. 463–83.

[32]See the excellent book by John A. Quelch and Nathalie Laidler-Kylander, *The New Global Brands: Managing Non-Governmental Organizations in the 21st Century* (Mason, OH: South-Western, 2006).

[33]Eric Pfanner, "Davos Attendees Confront a New Wave of Anger," *The New York Times*, January 24, 2012.

POLITICAL DISASTER STRIKES KENYA: In the Nairobi slum of Kibera, supporters of opposition leader Raila Odinga tear up a key railway that ran from the coast to Uganda. As many as 12 people were killed in the associated clashes. Of course, this destruction will do great damage to commerce and progress to all the countries in Eastern Africa, including the World Economic Forum in Davos, Switzerland.[33] Let's hope the highway and international airport south of Nairobi stay intact, as they supply all of Europe with flowers from the burgeoning greenhouses in the area, and flower exports are a key source of revenue for the formerly thriving Kenyan economy.

Exhibit 6.2

U.S. State Department Travel Warnings (in order of date of posting, most recent first)

Source: http://travel.state.gov/travel/, 2015.

Somalia	Iraq	Venezuela
Mexico	Saudi Arabia	Iran
Mauritania	Pakistan	North Korea
Lesotho	Nigeria	Philippines
Yemen	Liberia	Central African Republic
Eritrea	Cameroon	Sudan
Israel, West Bank, Gaza	Libya	Burundi
Afghanistan	Chad	Niger
Ukraine	Honduras	Mali
Lebanon	Kenya	Haiti
Sierra Leone	South Sudan	
Algeria	Djibouti	

the United States, Russia, Egypt, and most recently Hong Kong. Both sides usually blame the other for the initiation of violence, and, as in any dispute, culpability is often unclear.[34]

The world continues to be victimized by thousands of terrorist attacks each year. Terrorism has many different goals. Multinationals are targeted to embarrass a government and its relationship with firms, to generate funds by kidnapping executives to finance terrorist goals, to use as pawns in political or social disputes not specifically directed at them, and to inflict terror within a country, as did the events of September 11, 2001.

September 11 has raised the cost of doing business domestically and internationally. The dominance of the United States in world affairs exposes U.S. businesses to a multitude of uncertainties, from the growing danger of political violence to investment risks in emerging markets. In the past 30 years, 80 percent of terrorist attacks against the United States have been aimed at American businesses. Since September 11, McDonald's, KFC, and Pizza Hut combined have been bombed in more than 10 countries, including Turkey, Saudi Arabia, Russia, Lebanon, and China; most attacks have been linked with militant Islamic groups. There are reasons to expect that businesses will become increasingly attractive to terrorists, both because they are less well defended than government targets and because of what they symbolize. Based on the threats of terrorism and other violence, the U.S. State Department posts travel warnings on its website (see Exhibit 6.2 for a recent listing). However, many international travelers appear to regularly ignore those warnings. Based on recent studies of firms' responses

---

[34]Michael Forsythe and Alan Wong, "Protestors in Hong Kong on Edge as Police Track Their Online Footprints," *The New York Times*, October 29, 2014, p. A8.

The communist government of Cuba disallows private advertising. Here at the corner of 23rd and L, the "Times Square" of Havana, the only signage you can see are the names of the movies and a political ad about the Cuban 5. Pictured are five Cuban nationals that were held until 2015 in American prisons, convicted of espionage against the United States. The Cuban government considers the five to be heroes that were infiltrating terrorist groups in south Florida, intent on attacking Cuba.

Exhibit 6
"The Waning of War: World-wide Battle Deaths per 100,000 People"

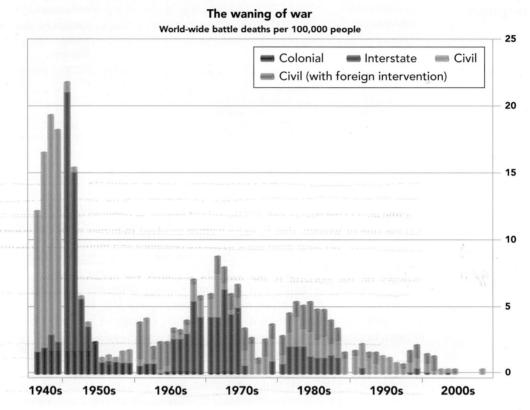

The waning of war
World-wide battle deaths per 100,000 people

Colonial   Interstate   Civil
Civil (with foreign intervention)

1940s   1950s   1960s   1970s   1980s   1990s   2000s

Source: Human Security Report, Project the Uppsala Conflict Data Project, and the Peace Research Institute of Oslo

to political conflict and violence, two decision criteria are important: the proximity of the violence[35] and the advice and influence of both local and foreign stake holders.[36]

Finally, we note strong reasons to believe that international warfare is fast becoming obsolete. The number of wars has declined steadily since the end of the Cold War. Even though politicians in almost all countries use xenophobia to consolidate their own political power, the threat of one country attacking another is declining fast. Some predict a coming war in space, with satellites used as weapons, but the multinational collaboration on the International Space Station makes such a possibility seem remote. In 1996, political scientist Samuel Huntington[37] notoriously predicted a clash of civilizations. In his vision, the world was already divided up into nine civilizations (or cultural groupings): Western, Latin America, African, Islamic, Sinic, Hindu, Orthodox, Buddhist, and Japanese. This prediction reminds us of several others in the early 1990s who suggested the world would soon devolve into three spheres of influence based on trade, dominated by Japan, the European Union, and the United States. There may be some sense to the latter classification; time zones exercise an important influence on trade patterns that favor north–south exchanges. However, both theories oversimplify power and trade relations as they are unfolding. Both theories also ignore the successes of the World Trade Organization and the fast multiplying bilateral trade agreements, such as that between the United States and South Korea. And certainly the facts included in Exhibit 6.3 suggest that these warnings about a new clash

[35]Li Dai, Lorraine Eden, and Paul Beamish, "Place, Space, and Geographical Exposure: Foreign Subsidiary Survival in Conflict Zones," *Journal of International Business Studies* 44 (2013), pp. 554–78.

[36]Jennifer Oetzel and Kathleen Getz, "Why and How Might Firms Respond Strategically to Violent Conflicts?" *Journal of International Business Studies* 43 (2012), pp. 166–86.

[37]Samuel P. Huntington, *The Clash of Civilizations and the Remaking of the World Order* (New York: Simon and Schuster, 1996); Fouad Ajami, "The Clash," *The New York Times*, January 6, 2008.

of civilizations are off the mark. Rather than state-to-state or civilization-to-civilization military action, the greater threats to peace and commerce for the 21st century remain civil strife and terrorism. Finally, we note with some hope that civil conflicts can be settled through negotiation: Consider as examples the recent histories of the relatively peaceful dissolution of the Soviet Union, the divorce of the Czech and Slovak Republics, the marriage of East and West Germany, the Hong Kong handover to China by the United Kingdom, the current trade overtures between China and Taiwan,[38] and even the almost bloodless annexation of Crimea by Russia.[39] In the same vein, voters in both Quebec and Scotland agreed not to secede while Catalonians still consider leaving Spain.[40]

Finally, we celebrate Steven Pinker's important book, *The Better Angels of Our Nature*, as it makes the most detailed argument about the current state of peace on the planet. He provides strong evidence for the steady decline of violence among humankind over the millennia, suggesting that humans have never had less to fear about crime and warfare. Moreover, research demonstrates that humans are not violent by nature.[41] Or, consider that more than 99.9 percent humans have not killed another. This peaceful state is so despite the frequent news coverage of warfare and violence. He reasons that the four causes of this wonderful decline are (1) the rule of law; (2) the rule of reason, as opposed to superstition and the like; (3) the rule of women, that is, more women involved in higher places in government; and (4) commerce, because trade leads to interdependence and mutual understanding.[42]

Cyberterrorism and Cybercrime

Always on the horizon is the growing potential for cyberterrorism and cybercrime. Although still in its infancy, the Internet provides a vehicle for terrorist and criminal attacks by foreign and domestic antagonists wishing to inflict damage on a company with little chance of being caught. One problem in tracing cyberterrorists and criminals is that it is hard to determine if a cyberattack has been launched by a rogue state, a terrorist, or a hacker as a prank. The "I Love You" worm, which caused an estimated $25 billion in damage, was probably just an out-of-control prank. However, the Melissa virus and the denial of service (DoS) attacks that overloaded the websites of CNN, ZDNet, Yahoo!, and Amazon.com with a flood of electronic messages, crippling them for hours, were considered purposeful attacks on specific targets. The government of China has been criticized for blocking text messaging in strife-torn regions and disrupting the local operations of Google.[43] Many of America's largest commercial organizations—the most prominent example is Chase Bank—have been hacked into for reasons yet to be determined. On the list are espionage, robbery, political punishment, and potential national security attacks. A variety of data have been stolen. The FBI continues its investigations,[44] but the latest security analyses are more often pointing to Russian government supported hackers as the most serious threat.[45]

Each wave of viruses gets more damaging and spreads so rapidly that considerable harm is done before it can be stopped. The "Slammer," for example, brought Internet service to a crawl. It doubled its numbers every 8.5 seconds during the first minute of its attack and infected more than 75,000 hosts within 10 minutes.[46] After infecting hundreds of thousands

---

[38]"Reunification by Trade?" *The Economist*, August 8, 2009, pp. 37–38; Ralph Jennings and Barbara Demick, "Taiwan President Ma Ying-jeou Reelected, Vows Closer China Ties," *Los Angeles Times*, January 15, 2012.

[39]Neil MacFarquhar, "After Annexing Crimea, Euphoric Russia Turns Thoughts to Ukraine," *The New York Times*, June 14, 2014, online.

[40]Raphael Minder, "Meeting Fails to Forestall Catalonia Secession Vote," *The New York Times*, July 31, 2014, p. A10.

[41]Luke Glowacki, "Are We Violent by Nature," *Los Angeles Times*, January 19, 2014, p. A24.

[42]Steven Pinker, *The Better Angels of Our Nature* (New York: Viking, 2011).

[43]Johanna Neuman, "Google's China Move Wakes Washington," *Los Angeles Times*, January 15, 2010.

[44]Ellen Nakashima and Andrea Peterson, "FBI Probes Hack into Computers of JPMorgan Chase, Other U.S. Banks," *Washington Post*, August 27, 2014, online.

[45]Nicole Perlroth, "Online Security Experts Link more Breaches to Russian Government," *The New York Times*, October 29, 2014, p. B3.

[46]For more information, see http://www.silicondefense.com.

of computers in Europe and North America, the "Goner worm" traveled to Australia overnight and brought down government agencies, financial and manufacturing sites, and at least 25 MNCs. Whether perpetrated by pranksters or hackers out to do harm, these incidents show that tools for cyberterrorism can be developed to do considerable damage to a company, an entire industry, or a country's infrastructure.

Because of mounting concern over the rash of attacks, business leaders and government officials addressed a Group of 8[47] conference convened to discuss cybercrime, expressing the urgent need for cooperation among governments, industry, and users to combat the growing menace of cybercrime. As the Internet grows, "it's only a matter of time before every terrorist, anarchist, thief, and prankster with a PC and a phone line will be waging a virtual war and inflicting real harm."[48] Perhaps the most disturbing news in this area is evidence of the U.S. National Security Agency listening in on German Chancellor Angela Merkel's mobile phone calls. Our European allies are understandably outraged.[49]

Assessing Political Vulnerability

LO6

How to assess and reduce the effect of political vulnerability

There are at least as many reasons for a company's political vulnerability as there are political philosophies, economic variations, and cultural differences. Some companies appear to be more politically vulnerable than others, in that they receive special government attention. Depending on the desirability of a company, this special attention may result in positive actions toward the company or in negative attention.

Unfortunately, a marketer has no absolute guidelines to follow to determine whether a company and its products will be subject to political attention. Countries seeking investments in high-priority industries may well excuse companies from taxes, customs duties, quotas, exchange controls, and other impediments to investment. In a bid to attract foreign investment and increase exports, India announced a new trade policy that eases restraints and offers tax breaks for companies developing and maintaining infrastructure. Conversely, firms either marketing products not considered high priority or that fall from favor for some other reason often face unpredictable government restrictions.

As a case in point, Continental Can Company's joint venture to manufacture cans for the Chinese market faced a barrage of restrictions when the Chinese economy weakened. China decreed that canned beverages were wasteful and must be banned from all state functions and banquets. Tariffs on aluminum and other materials imported for producing cans were doubled, and a new tax was imposed on canned-drink consumption. For Continental Can, an investment that had the potential for profit after a few years was rendered profitless by a change in the attitude of the Chinese government.

Politically Sensitive Products and Issues

Although there are no specific formulas to determine a product's vulnerability at any point, there are some generalizations that help identify the tendency for products to be politically sensitive. Products that have or are perceived to have an effect on the environment, exchange rates, national and economic security, and the welfare of people (and particularly children—recall the story of Barbie in Saudi Arabia from the previous chapter) or that are publicly visible, subject to public debate, or associated with their country of origin are more likely to be politically sensitive.

---

[47]The Group of 8 (G8) nations consists of government representatives from Britain, Canada, France, Germany, Italy, Japan, Russia, and the United States who convene periodically to examine issues that affect the group. Most recently the group has been expanded to the G20.

[48]Mark Mazzetti, "Senators Warned of Terror Attack by July," *The New York Times*, February 3, 2010, p. A6; "Hacking Corporate Networks, Losing the Plot," *The Economist*, January 3, 2015, p. 12; Kelly Buzby and Caroline Winter, "No Nation Is an Island," *Bloomberg BusinessWeek*, January 11, 2015, pp. 52–57; "America and Cuba, The New Normal," *The Economist*, January 3, 2015, pp. 11–12.

[49]Henry Chu, "Europe Miffed over Spy Talk," *Los Angeles Times*, July 2, 2013, p. A3.

Fast-food restaurants, which are intended to be visible, have often been lightning rods for groups opposed to foreign companies. Authorities closed a KFC restaurant for health reasons (two flies were seen in the kitchen) after months of protesters arguing that foreign investment should be limited to high technology. "India does not need foreign investment in junk-food," said the leader of a protesting farmers' group. The store was later reopened by court order.

Health is often the subject of public debate, and products that affect or are affected by health issues can be sensitive to political concerns. The European Union has banned hormone-treated beef for more than a decade. There is a question about whether the ban is a valid health issue or just protection for the European beef industry. The World Trade Organization concluded in 1989 that the ban had no scientific basis; nevertheless, Europe has yet to lift the ban. Reluctance to respond to the WTO directive may have been the result of the outcry against genetically modified (GM) foods that has, for all practical purposes, caused GM foods to be banned in Europe. Public opinion against Frankenfood has been so strong that Unilever announced that it would stop using GM ingredients in all its products in Britain. Additionally, 11 leading restaurant chains, including McDonald's, Pizza Hut, Wimpy, and Burger King, have gone GM-free. The issue in the United States has not risen to the same level of concern as in Europe; to forestall such adverse public opinion, many U.S. companies are slowing the introduction of GM foods. Fearing a strong public reaction as in Europe, McDonald's has decided to stop using genetically modified potatoes for its french fries in its U.S. stores.

Forecasting Political Risk

In addition to qualitative measures of political vulnerability, a number of firms are employing systematic methods of measuring political risk.[50] Political risk assessment is an attempt to forecast political instability to help management identify and evaluate political events and their potential influence on current and future international business decisions. Perhaps the greatest risk to international marketers is the threat of the government actually failing, causing chaos in the streets and markets. *Foreign Policy* magazine uses 12 criteria to rank countries on its "Failed States Index."[51] The list of criteria includes demographic pressures, human flight, uneven development, and the like. (See Exhibit 6.4.)

Risk assessment is used to estimate the level of risk a company is assuming when making an investment and to help determine the amount of risk it is prepared to accept. In the former Soviet Union and in China, the risk may be too high for some companies, but stronger and better financed companies can make longer-term investments in those countries that will be profitable in the future. Additionally, one study found that compared with American and Japanese managers, French managers' market entry decisions appear to be more influenced by concerns about political risk in foreign markets.[52] Early risk is accepted in exchange for being in the country when the economy begins to grow and risk subsides.

---

[50]See http://www.prsgroup.com for a wealth of information on political risk assessments.

[51]"The Fragile States Index," *Foreign Policy,* August 2014.

[52]Jennifer D. Chandler and John L. Graham, "Relationship-Oriented Cultures, Corruption, and International Marketing Success," *Journal of Business Ethics* 92, no. 2 (2010), pp. 251–67.

Nanjunda Swamy, leader of the farmers group that has led the Bangalore protests, from John F. Burns, "India Nationalists Oppose Presence of a U.S. Chain," *The New York Times,* September 14, 1995.

Exhibit 6.4
20 Most Fragile States (ranked in order of closest to failure)

Source: From *Foreign Policy,* "Fragile States Index," August 2014, pp. 72–77.

South Sudan	Yemen	Syria
Somalia	Haiti	Guinea Bissau
Central African Republic	Pakistan	Nigeria
Democratic Republic of Congo	Zimbabwe	Kenya
Sudan	Guinea	Ethiopia
Chad	Ivory Coast	Niger
Afghanistan		

During the chaos that arose after the political and economic changes in the Soviet Union, the newly formed republics were eager to make deals with foreign investors, yet the problems and uncertainty made many investors take a wait-and-see attitude. However, as one executive commented, "If U.S. companies wait until all the problems are solved, somebody else will get the business." Certainly the many companies that are investing in the former Soviet Union or China do not expect big returns immediately; they are betting on the future. For a marketer doing business in a foreign country, a necessary part of any market analysis is an assessment of the probable political consequences of a marketing plan, since some marketing activities are more susceptible to political considerations than others.

Lessening Political Vulnerability

Although a company cannot directly control or alter the political environment of the country within which it operates, a specific business venture can take measures to lessen its degree of susceptibility to politically induced risks. Indeed, one study has shown some multinational firms actually may see opportunities in financial and political crises.[53]

Foreign investors frequently are accused of exploiting a country's wealth at the expense of the national population and for the sole benefit of the foreign investor. This attitude is best summed up in a statement made by a recent president of Peru: "We have had massive foreign investment for decades but Peru has not achieved development. Foreign capital will now have to meet government and social goals." Such charges are not wholly unsupported by past experiences.

As long as these impressions persist, the political climate for foreign investors will continue to be hostile. Companies must manage external affairs in foreign markets to ensure that the host government and the public are aware of their contributions to the economic, social, and human development of the country. Relations between governments and MNCs are generally positive if the investment (1) improves the balance of payments by increasing exports or reducing imports through import substitution; (2) uses locally produced resources; (3) transfers capital, technology, and/or skills; (4) creates jobs; and/or (5) makes tax contributions.

In addition to the economic contributions a company makes, corporate philanthropy also helps create positive images among the general population. Many MNCs strive to benefit countries through their social programs, which polish their image as well. For example, Microsoft, recognizing that developing countries need sophisticated technical assistance, pledged more than $100 million in technology and training as part of a deal to put government services online in Mexico. Cisco Systems, the leading maker of Internet hardware, relies on nonprofit organizations to run its 10,000 networking academies, which train college and high school students to create computer networks in 150 countries. In China, Procter & Gamble is helping local schools and universities train and educate leaders. And in Malaysia, Motorola and Intel have instituted training programs to enhance the skills of local workers.

Merck, the pharmaceutical company, developed a pill to fight river blindness in Africa and Latin America. River blindness is a parasitic disease transmitted to humans through the bite of the black fly commonly found along the riverbanks in some African countries. The parasite infiltrates, multiplies, and spreads throughout the body for as long as 15 years, causing acute skin rashes, terrible itching, and sometimes disfigurement or blindness. The pill is taken just once a year and has been proven to prevent the disease. Merck contributed millions of doses to fight the disease in developing countries with great success.[54]

---

[53]Christopher Williams and Candace A. Martinez, "Government Effectiveness, the Global Financial Crisis, and Multinational Enterprise Internationalization," *Journal of International Marketing* 20, no. 3 (2012), pp. 65–78.

[54]David Shook, "Merck Is Treating the Third World," *BusinessWeek Online*, October 10, 2002.

Donald Kendall, former CEO of PepsiCo

Quoted in Sree Rama Rao, 'Lessening Political Vulnerability', FEBRUARY 7, 2010, CiteManagement Article Repository Of Cite.Co

Although companies strive to become good corporate citizens in their host countries, political parties seeking publicity or scapegoats for their failures often serve their own interests by focusing public opinion on the negative aspects of MNCs, whether true or false. Companies that establish deep local roots and show by example, rather than meaningless talk, that their strategies are aligned with the long-term goals of the host country stand the best chance of overcoming a less than positive image. "In times like these," says one executive, "global citizenship is perhaps more important than ever."An effective defense for the multinational company is to actively participate in improving the lives of local citizens.

In addition to corporate activities focused on the social and economic goals of the host country and good corporate citizenship, MNCs can use other strategies to minimize political vulnerability and risk.

Joint Ventures

Typically less susceptible to political harassment, joint ventures can be with locals or other third-country multinational companies; in both cases, a company's financial exposure is limited. A joint venture with locals helps minimize anti-MNC feelings, and a joint venture with another MNC adds the additional bargaining power of a third country.

Expanding the Investment Base

Including several investors and banks in financing an investment in the host country is another strategy. This approach has the advantage of engaging the power of the banks whenever any kind of government takeover or harassment is threatened. This strategy becomes especially powerful if the banks have made loans to the host country; if the government threatens expropriation or other types of takeover, the financing bank has substantial power with the government.

Licensing /Franchising

A strategy that some firms find eliminates almost all risks is to license technology for a fee. Licensing can be effective in situations in which the technology is unique and the risk is high. Of course, there is some risk assumed, because the licensee can refuse to pay the required fees while continuing to use the technology. A similar approach is franchising—Starbucks and MacDonald's are prominent examples.

Planned Domestication

In those cases in which a host country is demanding local participation, the most effective long-range solution is planned phasing out, that is, planned domestication. This method is not the preferred business practice, but the alternative of government-initiated domestication can be as disastrous as confiscation. As a reasonable response to the potential of domestication, planned domestication can be profitable and operationally expedient for the foreign investor. Planned domestication is, in essence, a gradual process of participating with nationals in all phases of company operations.

Political Bargaining

Multinational companies clearly engage in lobbying and other sorts of political bargaining to avoid potential political risks.[55] At least one study has shown that such political ties can have a positive influence on international marketing efforts.[56] Mattel issued an extraordinary apology to China over the recall of Chinese-made toys, saying the items were defective

---

[55]Amy J. Hillman and William P. Wan, "The Determinants of MNE Subsidiaries' Political Strategies: Evidence of Institutional Duality," *Journal of International Business Studies* 36, no. 3 (2005), pp. 322–40; Shibin Sheng, Kevin Zheng Zhou, and Julie Juan Li, "The Effects of Business and Political Ties on Firm Performance: Evidence from China," *Journal of Marketing* 75, no. 1 (2011), pp. 1–15; Pei Sun, Kamel Mellahi, and Eric Thun, "The Dynamic Value of MNE Political Embeddedness: The Case of the Chinese Automobile Industry," *Journal of International Business Studies* 41, no. 7 (2010), pp. 1161–82; Charles J.P. Chen, Yuan Ding, and Chansong (Francis) Kim, "High-Level Politically Connected Firms, Corruption, and Analyst Forecast Accuracy around the World," *Journal of International Business Studies* 41, no. 9 (2010), pp. 1505–24.

[56]Maggie Chuoyan Dong, Caroline Bingxin Li and David K. Tse, "Do Business and Political Ties Differ in Cultivating Marketing Channels for Foreign and Local Firms in China?" *Journal of International Marketing* 21, no. 1 (2013), pp. 39–56.

Debra L. Dunn, the senior Hewlett-Packard executive quoted in SUSAN E. REED, 'Business; Technology Companies Take Hope in Charity', *The New York Times*, March 23, 2003.

POLITICAL AND ECONOMIC AID IN ACTION, WHERE EVERYBODY WINS: The Japanese government has paid for the construction of a new highway that connects key safari tourism areas in Tanzania. Foreign tourism becomes more efficient, comfortable, and profitable for the Tanzanian company (and others) pictured—Kibo is one of the best in the country. The Japanese designers, consultants, and contractors involved make money on the work. And the road ultimately pays for itself in the form of lower warranty expenses on the armada of Toyota Land Cruisers that regularly ply the path between the Makuyuni and Ngorongoro animal preserves.

because of Mattel's design flaws rather than faulty manufacturing. In doing so, Mattel was (1) protecting the huge and all-important head of its value chain; (2) recognizing that it would be easier to fix its design and inspection routines than quickly affect manufacturing practices in China; and (3) uniquely for an American firm, publicly admitting its own very real culpability. On the other side of the Pacific, Toyota once considered raising prices of its cars in the American market to "help" its ailing American competitors. The Japanese government has set quotas on auto exports in the past as American car companies have struggled. And in the face of growing American and European criticism, China has agreed to put quotas on its exports of textiles and to float its currency. Now the question remains, when? Finally, a cynical way to look at the motivation behind corporate social responsibility in general is its use as a bargaining chip with foreign publics and governments.

Political Payoffs

One approach to dealing with political vulnerability is the political payoff—an attempt to lessen political risks by paying those in power to intervene on behalf of the multinational company. This choice is not an approach we recommend in any way. However, your competitors may use such a tactic, so beware. Political payoffs, or bribery, have been used to lessen the negative effects of a variety of problems. Paying heads of state to avoid confiscatory taxes or expulsion, paying fees to agents to ensure the acceptance of sales contracts, and providing monetary encouragement to an assortment of people whose actions can affect the effectiveness of a company's programs are decisions that frequently confront multinational managers and raise ethical questions.

Bribery poses problems for the marketer at home and abroad, because it is illegal for U.S. citizens to pay a bribe even if it is a common practice in the host country. Political payoffs may offer short-term benefits, but in the long run, the risks are high, and bribery is an untenable option. This issue is discussed in more detail in Chapters 5 and 7.

Government Encouragement

LO7

How and why governments encourage foreign investment

Governments, both foreign and U.S.,[57] encourage foreign investment as well as discourage it. In fact, within the same country, some foreign businesses may fall prey to politically induced harassment, while others may be placed under a government

---

[57]Jasmine Wang, Kyunghee Park, and Natasha Khan, "Secretary of Commerce," *Bloomberg BusinessWeek*, January 14–20, 2013, pp. 20–21.

umbrella of protection and preferential treatment. The difference lies in the evaluation of a company's contribution to the nation's interest.

The most important reason to encourage foreign investment is to accelerate the development of an economy. An increasing number of countries are encouraging foreign investment with specific guidelines aimed toward economic goals. Multinational corporations may be expected to create local employment, transfer technology, generate export sales, stimulate growth and development of local industry, conserve foreign exchange, or meet a combination of these expectations as a requirement for market concessions. Recent investments in China, India, and the former republics of the Soviet Union include provisions stipulating specific contributions to economic goals of the country that must be made by foreign investors.

During the recent economic downturn, the U.S. government has been particularly creative in helping promote American exports. For example, visa rules are being changed to spur tourism[58] and home sales,[59] and diplomats help push sales of jetliners on the global market.[60] The U.S. government (similar to governments in most other countries)[61] is motivated for economic as well as political reasons to encourage American firms to seek business opportunities in countries worldwide, including those that are politically risky. It seeks to create a favorable climate for overseas business by providing the assistance that helps minimize some of the more troublesome politically motivated financial risks of doing business abroad. The Department of Commerce (DOC) at http://www.doc.gov is the principal agency that supports U.S. business abroad. The International Trade Administration (ITA) at http://www.ita.gov, a bureau of the DOC, is dedicated to helping U.S. business compete in the global marketplace.[62] Other agencies that provide assistance to U.S. companies include:

- Export-Import Bank (Ex-Im Bank) underwrites trade and investments for U.S. firms.[63] http://www.exim.gov

- Foreign Credit Insurance Association (FCIA), an agency of the Ex-Im Bank, provides credit insurance that minimizes nonpayment risk caused by financial, economic, or political uncertainties. It includes insurance against confiscation, civil disturbances, and the cancellation or restriction of export or import licenses. http://www.fcia.com

- The Agency for International Development (AID) provides aid to underdeveloped countries and has limited protection in support of "essential" projects in approved countries and for approved products. http://www.usaid.gov

- The Overseas Private Investment Corporation (OPIC) provides risk insurance for companies investing in less-developed countries. http://www.opic.gov

We close this section with brief mention of the incentives governments around the world are providing for clean energy commercial initiatives. See Exhibit 6.5. Many of these incentives are available only to local firms. However, a good many are also available to firms from other countries and international joint ventures. You will also notice that local circumstances influence each government's choices about incentives—Brazil favors biofuels, and Mexico favors hydrocarbon remediation projects. Feed-in tariffs are long-term

[58]Scott Powers and Sara K. Clarke, "Visa Rules Aim to Spur Tourism," *Los Angeles Times, January* 20, 2012, p. A9.

[59]Jim Puzzanghera and Lauren Beale, "Buy a Pricey Home, Get a U.S. Visa?" *Los Angeles Times*, October 21, 2011, pp. B1–2.

[60]Eric Lipton, Nicola Clark, and Andrew W. Lehren, "Diplomats Help Push Sales of Jetliners on the Global Market," *New York Times, January* 2, 2012.

[61]Leonidas C. Leonidou, Dayananda Palihawandana, and Marios Thodosiou, "National Export-Promotion Programs as Drivers of Organizational Resources and Capabilities: Effects on Strategy, Competitive Advantage, and Performance," *Journal of International Marketing* 19, no. 2 (2011), pp. 1–29.

[62]"Obama to Ask Congress for Power to Merge Agencies," *Associated Press,* January 13, 2012.

[63]Nicola Clark, "Boeing Optimistic Congress Will Renew Financing for Export-Import Bank," *The New York Times*, July 14 2014, p. B4.

Exhibit 6.5

Examples of Government
Incentives for Renewable
Energy Projects

Source: KPMG International Cooperative,
www.kpmg.com, accessed 2015.

Australia – investment funds for R&D and production projects, subsidies, tax incentives, and feed-in tariffs

Brazil – tax incentives (particularly related to biofuels), operating subsidies, and feed-in tariffs for wind, biomass, and hydro technology projects

Japan – feed-in tariffs for all renewable energy projects, green investment tax incentives

Mexico – tax incentives for renewable energy projects, government investments in renewable energy projects, also funding for new technologies related to hydrocarbon pollution reduction and remediation

South Africa – tax incentives for emission reductions, capital and R&D allowances, grants and subsidies

United Kingdom – feed-in tariffs, renewable resource mandates, tax exemptions, carbon tax floor, EU emissions trading exemptions

price contracts often tied to costs of production. These provide a stable platform of income derived in an otherwise volatile energy price environment. Indeed, in Chapter 18 we will take a close look at how price volatility in oil can affect international markets and marketing. Moreover, government incentives for renewable energies are also affected by oil and gas price volatility. If oil prices stay below $85/barrel, countries will make adjustments to their clean energy policies.

Summary

Vital to every marketer's assessment of a foreign market is an appreciation for the political environment of the country within which he or she plans to operate. Government involvement in business activities abroad, especially foreign-controlled business, is generally much greater than business is accustomed to in the United States. The foreign firm must strive to make its activities politically acceptable, or it may be subjected to a variety of politically condoned harassment. In addition to the harassment that can be imposed by a government, the foreign marketer frequently faces the problem of uncertainty of continuity in government policy.

As governments change political philosophies, a marketing firm accepted under one administration might find its activities undesirable under another. An unfamiliar or hostile political environment does not necessarily preclude success for a foreign marketer if the company becomes a local economic asset and responds creatively to the issues raised by political and social activists. The U.S. government may aid an American business in its foreign operations, and if a company is considered vital to achieving national economic goals, the host country often provides an umbrella of protection not extended to others.

Key Terms

Sovereignty	Expropriation	Political and social activists	Nongovernmental
Nationalism	Domestication	(PSAs)	organizations (NGOs)
Confiscation			

Questions

1. Define the key terms listed above.
2. Why would a country rather domesticate than expropriate?
3. "A crucial fact when doing business in a foreign country is that permission to conduct business is controlled by the government of the host country." Comment.
4. What are the main factors to consider in assessing the dominant political climate within a country?
5. Why is a working knowledge of political party philosophy so important in a political assessment of a market? Discuss.

6. How can a change in the political party in power affect an investor? Discuss and give examples.

7. What are the most common causes of instability in governments? Discuss.

8. Discuss how governmental instability can affect marketing.

9. What are the most frequently encountered political risks in foreign business? Discuss.

10. Expropriation is considered a major risk of foreign business. Discuss ways in which this particular type of risk can be minimized somewhat as a result of company activities. Explain how these risks have been minimized by the activities of the U.S. government.

11. How do exchange controls impede foreign business? Discuss.

12. How do foreign governments encourage foreign investment? Discuss.

13. How does the U.S. government encourage foreign investment?

14. What are the motives behind U.S. government encouragement for foreign investment? Explain.

15. Discuss measures a company might take to lessen its political vulnerability.

16. Select a country and analyze it politically from a marketing viewpoint.

17. The text suggests that violence is a politically motivated risk of international business. Comment.

18. There is evidence that expropriation and confiscation are less frequently encountered today than just a few years ago. Why? What other types of political risks have replaced expropriation and confiscation in importance?

19. You are an executive in a large domestic company with only minor interests in international markets; however, corporate plans call for major global expansion. Visit the home page of Control Risks Group (CRG) at http://www.crg.com. After thoroughly familiarizing yourself with the services offered by CRG, write a brief report to management describing how its services could possibly help with your global expansion.

20. Visit the website http://www.politicalresources.net/ and select the Political Site of the Week. Write a brief political analysis highlighting potential problem areas for a company interested in investing in that country.

21. Search the Web for information about the activities of PSAs outside the United States and write a briefing paper for international management on potential problems.

22. Discuss ways the companies discussed in the Global Perspective could have minimized their losses in the banana wars.

23. Discuss any ethical and socially responsible issues that may be implied in the Global Perspective.

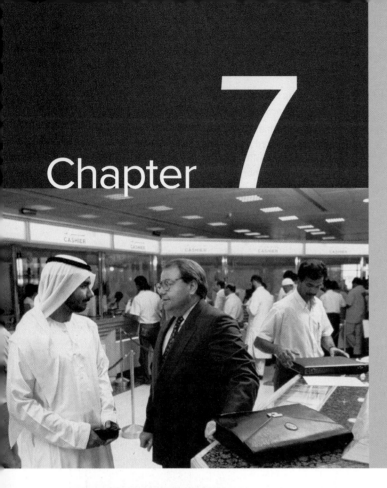

Chapter 7

The International Legal Environment:

PLAYING BY THE RULES

CHAPTER LEARNING OBJECTIVES

What you should learn from Chapter 7:

LO1   The four heritages of today's legal systems

LO2   The important factors in the jurisdiction of legal
disputes

LO3   The various methods of dispute resolution

LO4   The unique problems of protecting intellectual
property rights internationally

LO5   How to protect against piracy and counterfeiting

LO6   The many issues of evolving cyberlaw

LO7   The legal differences between countries and how
those differences can affect international marketing
plans

LO8   The different ways U.S. laws can be applied to U.S.
companies operating outside the United States

LO9   The steps necessary to move goods across country
borders

Global Perspective

THE PAJAMA CAPER

Six headlines illustrate the entanglements possible when U.S. law, host-country law, and a multinational company collide:

- "Wal-Mart's Cuban-Made Pajamas Defy Embargo"
- "Wal-Mart Ignites Row by Pulling Cuban Pajamas off Shelves in Canada"
- "Canada, U.S. Wager Diplomatic Capital in a High-Stakes Pajama Game"
- "Cuban Quandary: Wal-Mart in Hot Water for Yanking Pajamas"
- "Canada Probes Wal-Mart Move against Cuban Pajamas"
- "Wal-Mart Puts Cuban Goods Back on Sale"

The controversy arose over a U.S. embargo forbidding U.S. businesses to trade with Cuba and concern whether or not the embargo could be enforced in Canada. Walmart was selling Cuban-made pajamas in Canada. When Walmart officials in the United States became aware of the origin of manufacture, they issued an order to remove all the offending pajamas because it is against U.S. law (the Helms-Burton Act) for a U.S. company or any of its foreign subsidiaries to trade with Cuba. Canada was incensed at the intrusion of U.S. law on Canadian citizens. The Canadians felt they should have the choice of buying Cuban-made pajamas.

Walmart was thus caught in the middle of conflicting laws in Canada and the United States and a Canada–U.S. foreign policy feud over the extraterritoriality of U.S. law. Walmart Canada would be breaking U.S. law if it continued to sell the pajamas, and it would be subject to a million-dollar fine and possible imprisonment of its managers. However, if the company pulled the pajamas out of Canadian stores as the home office ordered, it would be subject to a $1.2 million fine under Canadian law. After discussion with Canadian authorities, Walmart resumed selling the pajamas. Canada was upset with the United States for attempting to impose its laws on Canadian companies (Walmart Canada is a subsidiary of Walmart U.S.), while the United States says that Walmart was violating its laws in not abiding by the boycott against Cuba. The situation illustrates the reality of the legal environment and international marketing—companies are subject to both home-country laws and host-country laws when doing business in another country. The federal government finally settled with Walmart, and the pajama caper was finally closed. However, as indicated in the previous chapter, the governments of Cuba and the United States have yet to settle.

Sources: *Boston Globe,* March 3, 1997; *St. Louis Post-Dispatch,* March 9, 1997; *Washington Post,* March 14, 1997, p. A6; *The Wall Street Journal,* March 14, 1997, p. B4; John W. Boscariol, "An Anatomy of a Cuban Pyjama Crisis," *Law and Policy in International Business,* Spring 1999, p. 439; Victoria Burnett, "Cuba Unleashes the Pent-Up Energy of Real Estate Dreams," *The New York Times,* February 15, 2012.

How would you like to play a game in which the stakes were high, there was no standard set of rules to play by, the rules changed whenever a new player entered the game, and, when a dispute arose, the referee used the other players' rules to interpret who was right? This game fairly well describes the international legal environment. Because no single, uniform international commercial law governing foreign business transactions exists, the international marketer must pay particular attention to the laws of each country within which it operates. An American company doing business with a French customer has to contend with two jurisdictions (United States and France), two tax systems, two legal systems, and other supranational sets of European Union laws and WTO regulations that may override commercial laws of the countries. The situation is similar when doing business in Japan, Germany, or any other country. Laws governing business activities within and between countries are an integral part of the legal environment of international business.

The legal systems of different countries are so disparate and complex that it is beyond the scope of this text to explore the laws of each country individually. There are, however, issues common to most international marketing transactions that need special attention when operating abroad. Jurisdiction, dispute resolution, intellectual property, the extraterritoriality of U.S. laws, cyberlaw, and associated problems are discussed in this chapter to provide a broad view of the international legal environment. Although space and focus limit an in-depth presentation, the material presented should be sufficient for the reader to conclude that securing expert legal advice is a wise decision when doing business in another country. The foundation of a legal system profoundly affects how the law is written, interpreted, and adjudicated. The place to begin is with a discussion of the different legal systems.

Bases for Legal Systems

LO1

The four heritages of today's legal systems

Four heritages form the bases for the majority of the legal systems of the world: (1) common law, derived from English law and found in England, the United States, Canada,[1] and other countries once under English influence; (2) civil or code law, derived from Roman law and found in Germany, Japan, France, and non-Islamic and non-Marxist countries; (3) Islamic law, derived from the interpretation of the Koran and found in Pakistan, Iran, Saudi Arabia, and other Islamic states; and (4) a commercial legal system in the Marxist–socialist economies of Russia and the republics of the former Soviet Union, Eastern Europe, China, and other Marxist–socialist states whose legal system centered on the economic, political, and social policies of the state. As each country moves toward its own version of a free market system and enters the global market, a commercial legal system is also evolving from Marxist–socialist tenets. China has announced that it will adopt a constitution-based socialist legal system with Chinese characteristics.

The differences among these four systems are of more than theoretical importance because due process of law may vary considerably among and within these legal systems. Even though a country's laws may be based on the doctrine of one of the four legal systems, its individual interpretation may vary significantly—from a fundamentalist interpretation of Islamic law as found in Pakistan to a combination of several legal systems found in the United States, where both common and code law are reflected in the legal system.

One measure of the importance of the legal system in each country is the number of attorneys per capita. Please see Exhibit 7.1. Judging by that metric, the legal system is called upon to settle commercial disputes much more frequently in the United States than in almost all countries, and particularly China. China's legal system is really only 50 years old; in the 1980s, the country had 3,000 attorneys, and now the number is closer to 150,000. By comparison, the legal system in Japan is much more developed. Even so, as the Japanese economy continues to become more integrated in the global market, the need for attorneys is burgeoning. There are more than 30,000 attorneys there now, and the Japanese government intends to grow that number to 50,000 by 2018.[2]

---

[1] All the provinces of Canada have a common-law system with the exception of Quebec, which is a code-law province. All the states in the United States are common law except Louisiana, which is code law.

[2] Bruce E. Aronson, "The Brave New World of Lawyers in Japan," *Pacific Rim Law & Policy Journal* 21, no. 2 (March 2012), pp. 255–75.

Exhibit 7.1

Lawyers per 100,000 People in Selected Countries

Sources: Randy Peerenboom, "Economic Development and the Development of the Legal Profession in China," presentation at Oxford University, 2006; Council of Bars and Law Societies of Europe, http://www.ccbe.edu, 2010; http://www.oab.org.br, 2010; http://www.abanet.org, 2010; Bruce E. Aronson, "The Brave New World of Lawyers in Japan," *Pacific Rim Law & Policy Journal* 21, no. 2 (March 2012), pp. 255–75.

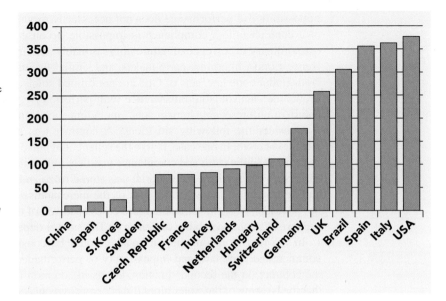

Common vs. Code Law

The basis for common law[3] is tradition, past practices, and legal precedents set by the courts through interpretations of statutes, legal legislation, and past rulings. Common law seeks "interpretation through the past decisions of higher courts which interpret the same statutes or apply established and customary principles of law to a similar set of facts." Code law,[4] in contrast, is based on an all-inclusive system of written rules (codes) of law. Under code law, the legal system is generally divided into three separate codes: commercial, civil, and criminal.

Common law is recognized as not being all-inclusive, whereas code law is considered complete as a result of catchall provisions found in most code-law systems. For example, under the commercial code in a code-law country, the law governing contracts is made inclusive with the statement that "a person performing a contract shall do so in conformity with good faith as determined by custom and good morals." Although code law is considered all-inclusive, it is apparent from the foregoing statement that some broad interpretations are possible in order to include everything under the existing code.

Steps are being taken in common-law countries to codify commercial law even though the primary basis of commercial law is common law, that is, precedents set by court decisions. An example of the new uniformity is the acceptance of the Uniform Commercial Code by most states in the United States. Even though U.S. commercial law has been codified to some extent under the Uniform Commercial Code, the philosophy of interpretation is anchored in common law.

As discussed later in the section on the protection of intellectual property, laws governing intellectual property offer the most striking differences between common-law and code-law systems. Under common law, ownership is established by use; under code law, ownership is determined by registration. In some code-law countries, certain agreements may not be enforceable unless properly notarized or registered; in a common-law country, the same agreement may be binding so long as proof of the agreement can be established. Although every country has elements of both common and code law, the differences in interpretation between common- and code-law systems regarding contracts, sales agreements, and other legal issues are significant enough that an international marketer familiar with only one system must enlist the aid of legal counsel for the most basic legal questions.

Another illustration of how fundamental differences in the two systems can cause difficulty is in the performance of a contract. Under common law in the United States, the

---

[3] Also known as English law.

[4] Also known as the Napoleonic Code. Quoted in Richard Fletcher, Heather Crawford, *International Marketing: An Asia-Pacific Perspective*, Pearson Higher Education AU, 2013

impossibility of performance does not necessarily excuse compliance with the provisions of a contract unless compliance is impossible because of an act of God, such as some extraordinary occurrence of nature not reasonably anticipated by either party of a contract. Hence floods, lightning, earthquakes, and similar events are generally considered acts of God. Under code law, acts of God are not limited solely to acts of nature but are extended to include "unavoidable interference with performance, whether resulting from forces of nature or unforeseeable human acts," including such things as labor strikes and riots.

Consider the following situations: A contract was entered into to deliver a specific quantity of cloth. In one case, before the seller could make delivery, an earthquake caused the destruction of the cloth and compliance was then impossible. In the second case, pipes in the sprinkler system where the material was stored froze and broke, spilling water on the cloth and destroying it. In each case, loss of the merchandise was sustained and delivery could not be made. Were the parties in these cases absolved of their obligations under the contract because of the impossibility of delivery? The answer depends on the system of law invoked.

In the first situation, the earthquake would be considered an act of God under both common and code law, and impossibility of performance would excuse compliance under the contract. In the second situation, courts in common-law countries would probably rule that the bursting of the water pipes did not constitute an act of God if it happened in a climate where freezing could be expected. Therefore, impossibility of delivery would not necessarily excuse compliance with the provisions of the contract. In code-law countries, where the scope of impossibility of performance is extended considerably, the destruction might very well be ruled an act of God, and thus, release from compliance with the contract could be obtained.

Islamic Law

The basis for the *Shari'ah* (Islamic law) is interpretation of the Koran. It encompasses religious duties and obligations, as well as the secular aspect of law regulating human acts. Broadly speaking, Islamic law defines a complete system that prescribes specific patterns of social and economic behavior for all individuals. It includes issues such as property rights, economic decision making, and types of economic freedom. The overriding objective of the Islamic system is social justice.

Among the unique aspects of Islamic law is the prohibition against the payment of interest. The Islamic law of contracts states that any given transaction should be devoid of *riba*, which is defined as unlawful advantage by way of excess of deferment, that is, interest or usury. Prohibiting the receipt and payment of interest is the nucleus of the Islamic system. However, other principles of Islamic doctrine advocate risk sharing, individuals' rights and duties, property rights, and the sanctity of contracts. The Islamic system places emphasis on the ethical, moral, social, and religious dimensions to enhance equality and fairness for the good of society. Another principle of the Islamic legal system is the prohibition against investment in those activities that violate the *Shari'ah*. For example, any investment in a business dealing with alcohol, gambling, and casinos would be prohibited.

Prohibition against the payment of interest affects banking and business practices severely.[5] However, certain acceptable practices adhere to Islamic law and permit the transaction of business. Mortgages for property are difficult because payment of interest is forbidden under Islamic law. Buyers of real property have to use a financier, who buys the property and then sells it to them in return for repayments of the capital. Instead of charging interest, a financier either sells the property at a higher price or sells it at the same price and takes additional payments to cover what would have been interest. Of the other ways to comply with Islamic law in

Banking in Dubai, UAE, requires an understanding of Islamic law and customs. Prohibition against the payment of interest and prohibition against investments in businesses dealing with alcohol and gambling are two of the tenets of Islamic law that affect banking.

[5]Sara Hadman, "Saudi Arabia Issues Its First Sovereign Islamic Bond," *The New York Times*, January 25, 2012.

financial transactions, trade with markup or cost-plus sale (*murabaha*) and leasing (*ijara*) are the most frequently used. In both *murabaha* and *ijara,* a mutually negotiated margin is included in the sale price or leasing payment. These practices meet the requirements of *Shari'ah* by enabling borrowers and lenders to share in the rewards as well as losses in an equitable fashion. They also ensure that the process of wealth accumulation and distribution in the economy is fair and representative of true productivity. Strict fundamentalists often frown on such an arrangement, but it is practiced and is an example of the way the strictness of Islamic law can be reconciled with the laws of non-Islamic legal systems.

Because the laws are based on interpretation of the Koran, the international marketer must have knowledge of the religion's tenets and understand the way the law may be interpreted in each region. Regional courts can interpret Islamic law from the viewpoint of fundamentalists (those that adhere to a literal interpretation of the Koran), or they may use a more liberal translation. A company can find local authorities in one region willing to allow payment of interest on deferred obligations as stipulated in a contract, while in another region, all interest charges may be deleted and replaced with comparable "consulting fees." In yet another, authorities may void a contract and declare any payment of interest illegal. Marketers conducting business in Islamic-law countries must be knowledgeable about this important legal system.

Marxist–Socialist Tenets

As socialist countries become more directly involved in trade with non-Marxist countries, it has been necessary to develop a commercial legal system that permits them to engage in active international commerce. The pattern for development varies among the countries because each has a different background, and each is at a different stage in its development of a market-driven economy. For example, central European countries such as the Czech Republic and Poland had comprehensive codified legal systems before communism took over, and their pre–World War II commercial legal codes have been revised and reinstituted. Consequently, they have moved toward a legal model with greater ease than some others have. Russia and most of the republics of the former Soviet Union and China have had to build from scratch an entire commercial legal system. Under the premise that law, according to Marxist–socialist tenets, is strictly subordinate to prevailing economic conditions, such fundamental propositions as private ownership, contracts, due process, and other legal mechanisms have had to be developed. China and Russia differ, however, in that each has taken a different direction in its political economic growth. Russia is moving toward a democratic system. China is attempting to activate a private sector within a multi-component, or mixed, economy in a socialist legal framework; that is, it tries to "perform its functions according to law and contribute to the development of socialist democracy and political civilization in China."

Both countries have actively passed laws, though the process has been slow and often disjointed. China has implemented hundreds of new laws and regulations governing trade, yet the process is hampered by vaguely written laws, the lack of implementation mechanisms for the new laws, and an ineffective framework for dispute resolution and enforcement. A good example is China's attempt to control what goes on in Chinese cyberspace by applying the States Secrets Law to the Internet. The definition of a state secret is so broad that it can cover any information not cleared for publication with the relevant authorities.

Russia's experience has been similar to China's, in that vaguely worded laws have been passed without mechanisms for implementation. The situation in Russia is often described as chaotic because of the laws' lack of precision. For example, to illegally receive or disseminate commercial secrets has become a crime, but the law provides no exact definition of a commercial secret. Copyright law violations that cause "great damage" are listed but with no clear definition of how much damage constitutes "great." Both China and Russia are hampered by not having the heritage of a legal commercial code to build on, as many of the Eastern-bloc European countries had.

The international marketer must be concerned with the differences among common law, code law, Islamic law, and socialist legal systems when operating between countries; the rights of the principals of a contract or some other legal document under one law may be significantly different from their rights under the other. It should be kept in mind that there could also be differences between the laws of two countries whose laws are based on the same legal system. Thus, the problem of the marketer is one of anticipating the different laws regulating business, regardless of the legal system of the country.

Jurisdiction in International Legal Disputes

LO2

The important factors in the jurisdiction of legal disputes

Determining whose legal system has jurisdiction when a commercial dispute arises is another problem of international marketing. A frequent error is to assume that disputes between citizens of different nations are adjudicated under some supranational system of laws. Unfortunately, no judicial body exists to deal with legal commercial problems arising among citizens of different countries. Confusion probably stems from the existence of international courts such as the World Court at The Hague and the International Court of Justice, the principal judicial organ of the United Nations. These courts are operative in international disputes between sovereign nations of the world rather than between private citizens and/or companies.

Legal disputes can arise in three situations: between governments, between a company and a government, and between two companies. The World Court can adjudicate disputes between governments, whereas the other two situations must be handled in the courts of the country of one of the parties involved or through arbitration. Unless a commercial dispute involves a national issue between nation states, the International Court of Justice or any similar world court does not handle it. Because there is no "international commercial law," the foreign marketer must look to the legal system of each country involved—the laws of the home country, the laws of the countries within which business is conducted, or both.

When international commercial disputes must be settled under the laws of one of the countries concerned, the paramount question in a dispute is: Which law governs? Jurisdiction is generally determined in one of three ways: (1) on the basis of jurisdictional clauses included in contracts, (2) on the basis of where a contract was entered into, or (3) on the basis of where the provisions of the contract were performed.

The most clear-cut decision can be made when the contracts or legal documents supporting a business transaction include a jurisdictional clause. A clause similar to the following establishes jurisdiction in the event of disagreements:

> That the parties hereby agree that the agreement is made in Oregon, USA, and that any question regarding this agreement shall be governed by the law of the state of Oregon, USA.

This clause establishes that the laws of the state of Oregon would be invoked should a dispute arise. If the complaint were brought in the court of another country, it is probable that the same Oregon laws would govern the decision. Cooperation and a definite desire to be judicious in foreign legal problems have led to the practice of foreign courts judging disputes on the basis of the law of another country or state whenever applicable. Thus, if an injured party from Oregon brings suit in the courts of Mexico against a Mexican over a contract that included the preceding clause, it would not be unusual for the Mexican courts to decide on the basis of Oregon law. This tendency assumes, of course, it has been recognized that Oregon law prevailed in this dispute, either as a result of the prior agreement by the parties or on some other basis.

International Dispute Resolution

LO3

The various methods of dispute resolution

When things go wrong in a commercial transaction—the buyer refuses to pay, the product is of inferior quality, the shipment arrives late, or any one of the myriad problems that can arise—what recourse does the international marketer have? Of course, reference to the contract between parties is a place to start. But the importance of contracts and their enforcement varies across countries.[6] The first step in any dispute is to try to resolve the issue informally, ideally through inventive negotiation[7] processes. But if such

---

[6]Kevin Zheng Zhou and Laura Poppo, "Exchange Hazards, Relational Liability, and Contracts in China: The Contingent Role of Legal Enforceability," *Journal of International Business Studies* 41, no. 5 (2010), pp. 861–79; Jagdip Singh, Patrick Lentz, and Edwin J. Nijssen, "First- and Second-Order Effects of Consumers' Institutional Logics on Firm-Consumer Relationships: A Cross-Market Comparative Analysis," *Journal of International Business Studies* 42, no. 2 (2011), pp. 307–33.

[7]See Chapter 19 and John L. Graham, Lynda Lawrence, and William Hernandez Requejo, Inventive Negotiation: *Getting Beyond Yes* (New York: Palgrave Macmillan, 2014).

among acceptable arbitrators to defend their case, and the ICC Court of Arbitration appoints a third member, generally chosen from a list of distinguished lawyers, jurists, and professors.

The history of ICC effectiveness in arbitration has been spectacular. An example of a case that involved arbitration by the ICC concerned a contract between an English business and a Japanese manufacturer. The English business agreed to buy 100,000 plastic dolls for 80 cents each. On the strength of the contract, the English business sold the entire lot at $1.40 per doll. Before the dolls were delivered, the Japanese manufacturer had a strike; the settlement of the strike increased costs, and the English business was informed that the delivery price of the dolls had increased from 80 cents to $1.50 each. The English business maintained that the Japanese firm had committed to make delivery at 80 cents and should deliver at that price. Each side was convinced that it was right.

The Japanese, accustomed to code law, felt that the strike was beyond their control (an act of God) and thus compliance with the original provisions of the contract was excused. The English, accustomed to common law, did not accept the Japanese reasons for not complying because they considered a strike part of the normal course of doing business and not an act of God. The dispute could not be settled except through arbitration or litigation; they chose arbitration. The ICC appointed an arbitrator who heard both sides and ruled that the two parties would share proportionately in the loss. Both parties were satisfied with the arbitration decision, and costly litigation was avoided. Most arbitration is successful, but success depends on the willingness of both parties to accept the arbitrator's rulings.

Contracts and other legal documents should include clauses specifying the use of arbitration to settle disputes. Unless a provision for arbitration of any dispute is incorporated as part of a contract, the likelihood of securing agreement for arbitration after a dispute arises is reduced. A typical arbitration clause is as follows:

> Any controversy or claim arising out of or relating to this contract shall be determined by arbitration in accordance with the International Arbitration Rules of the American Arbitration Association.

Including the number of arbitrators, the place of arbitration (city and/or country), and the language of the arbitration in the clause is also useful.[8]

Although an arbitration clause in a contract can avert problems, sometimes enforcing arbitration agreements can be difficult. Arbitration clauses require agreement on two counts: (1) The parties agree to arbitrate in the case of a dispute according to the rules and procedures of some arbitration tribunal and (2) they agree to abide by the awards resulting from the arbitration. Difficulty arises when the parties to a contract fail to honor the agreements. Companies may refuse to name arbitrators, refuse to arbitrate, or, after arbitration awards are made, refuse to honor the award. In most countries, arbitration clauses are recognized by the courts and are enforceable by law within those countries. More than 120 countries have ratified the Convention on the Recognition and Enforcement of Foreign Arbitral Awards, also known as the New York Convention, which binds them to uphold foreign arbitration awards. Under the New York Convention, the courts of the signatory countries automatically uphold foreign arbitral awards issued in member countries. In addition to the New York Convention, the United States is a signatory of the Inter-American Convention on International Arbitration, to which many Latin American countries are party. The United States is also party to a number of bilateral agreements containing clauses providing for enforcement of arbitral awards. When all else fails, the final step to solve a dispute is litigation.

Litigation

Lawsuits in public courts are avoided for many reasons. Most observers of lawsuits between citizens of different countries believe that almost all victories are spurious because the cost, frustrating delays, and extended aggravation that these cases produce are more oppressive by far than any matter of comparable size. In India, for instance, there is a backlog of more than 3 million cases, and litigating a breach of contract between private parties can

---

[8]Drafting Dispute Resolution Clauses, A Practical Guide, American Arbitration Association

take a decade or more. The best advice is to seek a settlement, if possible, rather than sue. Other deterrents to litigation are the following:

- Fear of creating a poor image and damaging public relations.

- Fear of unfair treatment in a foreign court. (Fear that a lawsuit can result in unfair treatment, perhaps intentionally, is justifiable, because the decision could be made by either a jury or a judge not well versed in trade problems and the intricacies of international business transactions.)

- Difficulty in collecting a judgment that may otherwise have been collected in a mutually agreed settlement through arbitration.

- The relatively high cost and time required when bringing legal action. The Rheem Manufacturing Company, a billion-dollar manufacturer of heating and air conditioning systems, estimates that by using arbitration over litigation, it has reduced the time and cost of commercial-dispute resolution by half.

- Loss of confidentiality. Unlike arbitration and conciliation proceedings, which are confidential, litigation is public.

One authority suggests that the settlement of every dispute should follow four steps: First, try to placate the injured party; if this does not work, conciliate, arbitrate, and, finally, litigate. The final step is typically taken only when all other methods fail. Furthermore, in some cases, problem-solving approaches may be warranted within the context of even litigated disputes.[9] This approach is probably wise whether one is involved in an international dispute or a domestic one.

Protection of Intellectual Property Rights: A Special Problem

LO4

The unique problems of protecting intellectual property rights internationally

Companies spend millions of dollars establishing brand names or trademarks to[10] symbolize quality and design a host of other product features meant to entice customers to buy their brands to the exclusion of all others. Millions more are spent on research to develop products, patented processes,[11] designs, and formulas that provide companies with advantages over their competitors. Such intellectual or industrial properties are among the more valuable assets a company may possess. Brand names such as Apple, Coca-Cola, and Gucci; processes such as xerography; and computer software are invaluable. One financial group estimated that the Marlboro brand had a value of $33 billion, Kellogg's $9 billion, Microsoft $9.8 billion, and Levi's $5 billion; all have experienced infringement of their intellectual property rights. Normally, property rights can be legally protected to prevent other companies from infringing on such assets. Companies must, however, keep a constant vigil against piracy and counterfeiting. Moreover, with increasing frequency, companies are developing new technologies to prevent piracy, but counterfeiters are relentless in their criticism of and technological attacks on even the most sophisticated security measures.

Counterfeiting and Piracy

Counterfeit and pirated goods come from a wide range of industries—apparel, automotive parts, agricultural chemicals, pharmaceuticals, books (yes, even management books such as the one you are reading right now), records, films, computer software, mobile phones, baby formula, hamburgers,[12] auto parts and cars themselves and even stores themselves.[13] Estimates are that more than 10 million fake Swiss timepieces carrying famous brand names such as Cartier and Rolex are sold every year, netting illegal profits of at least

[9]Chang Zhang, David A. Griffith, and S. Tamer Cavusgil, "The Litigated Dissolution of International Distribution Relationships: A Process Framework and Propositions," *Journal of International Marketing* 14, no. 2 (2006), pp. 85–115.

[10]Stephanie Strom, "Trademarks Take on New Importance in Internet Era," *The New York Times,* February 20, 2012; David Barboza, "Apple Defends Right to iPad Name in Shanghai Court," *The New York Times,* February 22, 2012.

[11]Archibald Preuschat, "Apple Loses Dutch Appeal to Block Samsung Tablets," *The Wall Street Journal,* January 24, 2012.

[12]Tiffany Hsu and David Pierson, "Double Trouble in Shanghai," *Los Angeles Times*, February 11, 2012, pp. A1, A6.

[13]Laurie Birkitt and Loretta Chao, "Made in China: Fake Stores," *Los Angeles Times*, August 3, 2011, pp. B1–2.

Exhibit 7.2

Piracy Rates for
Computer Software,
Top and Bottom Ten

Source: From *2013 BSA and IDC
Global Software Piracy Study,*
Business Software Alliance. Reprinted
with permission. *Seventh Annual
BSA/IDC Global Software Piracy
Study* (Washington, DC: Business
Software Alliance), www.bsa.org
/globalstudy. One hundred twenty-six
countries and regions are ranked.

Highest Piracy Rates		Lowest Piracy Rates	
Zimbabwe	91	United States	18
Georgia	90	Japan	19
Moldova	90	Luxembourg	20
Libya	89	New Zealand	20
Venezuela	88	Australia	21
Bangladesh	87	Austria	22
Yemen	87	Denmark	23
Armenia	86	Sweden	23
Belarus	86	Germany	24
Iraq	86	United Kingdom	24

$500 million. Although difficult to pinpoint, lost sales from the unauthorized use of U.S. patents, trademarks, and copyrights amount to more than $300 billion annually. That translates into more than two million lost jobs. Software, music, and movies are especially attractive targets for pirates because they are costly to develop but cheap to reproduce and distribute over the Internet. Pirated music sales are estimated to exceed $5 billion annually and are growing at 6 percent per year. And unauthorized U.S. software that sells for $500 in this country can be purchased for less than $10 in East Asia.

The Business Software Alliance, a trade group, estimates that software companies lost over $21.0 billion in the Asia-Pacific region, $18.1 billion in Europe, and $10.9 billion in North America in 2013. Judging from the press on the topic, one might conclude that China is the biggest piracy problem. However, China has moved fast off the list of 10 worst piracy rates, according to Exhibit 7.2. At this writing, it ranks #38 and piracy has fallen to 74 percent, down from 92 percent just a few years earlier. Moreover, the dollars lost in the United States because of software piracy are the most in the world at $9.7 billion, with China coming in a close second at $8.8 billion. China's progress is due primarily to education programs, enforcement, and Microsoft's historic agreement with Lenovo. We also note that other populous nations have made major progress in reducing software piracy (e.g., Russia down 9 percent, Brazil down 9, Japan and Vietnam both down 4, India down 9 percent) between 2007–2013.[14]

Recent research implies that for companies like Microsoft, some level of piracy actually can serve the company. It can be seen as a kind of product trial that ultimately builds commitment. As updated versions of products become available, purchases may actually follow. Particularly as countries such as China begin to enforce WTO statutes on piracy, customers conditioned on pirated goods may indeed be willing and able to pay for the new versions.

Although counterfeit CDs, toys, and similar products cost companies billions of dollars in lost revenue and have the potential of damaging the product's brand image, the counterfeiting of pharmaceuticals can do serious physical harm. In Colombia, investigators found an illegal operation making more than 20,000 counterfeit tablets a day of the flu drug Dristan, a generic aspirin known as Dolex, and Ponstan 500, a popular painkiller made by Pfizer. The counterfeited pills contained boric acid, cement, floor wax, talcum powder, and yellow paint with high lead levels, all used to replicate the genuine medications' appearance.

Counterfeit drugs range from copies that have the same efficacy as the original to those with few or no active ingredients to those made of harmful substances. A pharmaceutical manufacturers' association estimates that 2 percent of the $327 billion worth of drugs sold each year are counterfeit, or about $6 billion worth. In some African and Latin American nations, as much as 60 percent are counterfeit. The World Health Organization thinks 8 percent of the bulk drugs imported into the United States are counterfeit, unapproved, or substandard. Things are much worse in developing countries—the WTO recently reported that 64 percent of antimalarial drugs were fake. More than 70 percent of drugs consumed in Nigeria are imported from India and China, widely seen as the biggest sources of counterfeit pharmaceuticals.[15]

---

[14]*The Compliance Gap, BSA Global Software Survey* (Washington, DC: Business Software Alliance, 2014), http://www.bsa.org/globalstudy.

[15]"Bad Medicine," *The Economist*, October 13, 2012, pp. 74–75.

Another problem is collusion between the contract manufacturer and illegitimate sellers. In China, exact copies of New Balance shoes were fabricated by contract manufacturers who were New Balance suppliers. They flooded the market with genuine shoes that were sold for as little as $20. Unilever discovered that one of its suppliers in Shanghai made excess cases of soap, which were sold directly to retailers. One of Procter & Gamble's Chinese suppliers sold empty P&G shampoo bottles to another company, which filled them with counterfeit shampoo. Counterfeiting and piracy of intellectual property constitute outright theft, but the possibility of legally losing the rights to intellectual property because of inadequate protection of property rights and/or a country's legal structure is another matter.

Finally, it should be mentioned that some critics argue that MNCs have pushed the current intellectual property regime too far in favor of the firms, particularly with the most recent WTO TRIPS Agreement, to be discussed in more detail subsequently.[16] The critics suggest that the so-called tight rein the firms hold on the production of intellectual property has actually served to limit creativity and the associated benefits to the people that the intellectual property (IP) laws are intended to serve. The conflict is unfolding in interesting ways between the so-called "old and new economies," with traditional MNCs standing against the likes of Google and Wikipedia.[17] Even the French have joined the fray against the American IP legislation.[18] Such arguments pitch antitrust laws against IP laws. The argument goes on.

Inadequate Protection

The failure to protect intellectual property rights adequately in the world marketplace can lead to the legal loss of rights in potentially profitable markets. Because patents, processes, trademarks, and copyrights are valuable in all countries, some companies have found their assets appropriated and profitably exploited in foreign countries without license or reimbursement.[19] Furthermore, they often learn that not only are other firms producing and selling their products or using their trademarks, but also the foreign companies are the rightful owners in the countries where they operate.

There have been many cases in which companies have legally lost the rights to trademarks and have had to buy back these rights or pay royalties for their use. The problems of inadequate protective measures taken by the owners of valuable assets stem from a variety of causes. One of the more frequent errors is assuming that because the company has established rights in the United States, they will be protected around the world or that rightful ownership can be established should the need arise. This assumption was the case with McDonald's in Japan, where enterprising Japanese registered its golden arches trademark. Only after a lengthy and costly legal action with a trip to the Japanese Supreme Court was McDonald's able to regain the exclusive right to use the trademark in Japan. After having to "buy" its trademark for an undisclosed amount, McDonald's maintains a very active program to protect its trademarks.

Similarly, a South Korean company legally used the Coach brand on handbags and leather goods. The company registered the Coach trademark first and has the legal right to use that mark in Korea. The result is that a Coach-branded briefcase that is virtually identical to the U.S. product can be purchased for $135 in South Korea versus $320 in the United States. A U.S. attorney who practices with a South Korean firm noted that he has seen several instances in which a foreign company will come to Korea and naively start negotiating with a Korean company for distribution or licensing agreements, only to have the Korean company register the trademark in its own name. Later, the Korean company will use that

---

[16]Susan Sell, *Power and Ideas, North–South Politics of Intellectual Property and Antitrust* (Albany: State University of New York Press, 1998); Susan Sell, *Intellectual Property Rights: A Critical History* (Boulder, CO: Lynne Rienners Publishers, 2006).

[17]Jonathan Weisman, "Web Protests Piracy Bills, and 4 Senators Change Course," *The New York Times,* January 18, 2012; Ben Sisario, "7 Charged as FBI Closes a Top File-Sharing Site," *The New York Times,* January 20, 2012; Amy Chozick, "A Clash of Media Worlds (and Generations)," *The New York Times,* January 21, 2012.

[18]Eric Pfanner, "Copyright Cheats Face the Music in France," *The New York Times,* February 19, 2012.

[19]John Hagedoorn, Danielle Cloodt, and Hans van Kranenburg, "Intellectual Property Rights and the Governance of International R&D Partnerships," *Journal of International Business Studies* 36, no. 2 (2005), pp. 156–74.

registration as leverage in negotiations or, if the negotiations fall apart, sell the trademark back to the company. Many businesses fail to take proper steps to legally protect their intellectual property. They fail to understand that some countries do not follow the common-law principle that ownership is established by prior use or to realize that registration and legal ownership in one country does not necessarily mean ownership in another.

Prior Use versus Registration

In the United States, a common-law country, ownership of IP rights is established by prior use—whoever can establish first use is typically considered the rightful owner. In many code-law countries, however, ownership is established by registration rather than by prior use—the first to register a trademark or other property right is considered the rightful owner. For example, a trademark in Jordan belongs to whoever registers it first in Jordan. Thus you can find "McDonald's" restaurants, "Microsoft" software, and "Safeway" groceries all legally belonging to Jordanians. After a lengthy court battle that went to the Spanish Supreme Court, Nike lost its right to use the "Nike" brand name for sports apparel in Spain. Cidesport of Spain had been using Nike for sports apparel since 1932 and sued to block Nike (U.S.) sportswear sales. Because Cidesport does not sell shoes under the Nike label, Nike (U.S.) will be able to continue selling its brand of sports shoes in Spain. A company that believes it can always establish ownership in another country by proving it used the trademark or brand name first is wrong and risks the loss of these assets.

Besides the first-to-register issue, companies may encounter other problems with registering. China has improved intellectual property rights protection substantially and generally recognizes "first to invent." However, a Chinese company can capture the patent for a product invented elsewhere; it needs only to reverse-engineer or reproduce the product from published specifications and register it in China before the original inventor. Latvia and Lithuania permit duplicate registration of trademarks and brand names. A cosmetics maker registered Nivea and Niveja cosmetics brands in the former Soviet Union in 1986 and again in Latvia in 1992, but a Latvian firm had registered and had been selling a skin cream called Niveja since 1964. Neither the Soviet nor the Latvian authorities notified either firm. Applicants are responsible for informing themselves about similar trademarks that are already registered. The case has been taken to the Supreme Court of Latvia. It is best to protect IP rights through registration. Several international conventions provide for simultaneous registration in member countries.

International Conventions

Many countries participate in international conventions designed for mutual recognition and protection of intellectual property rights. There are three major international conventions:

1. The Paris Convention for the Protection of Industrial Property, commonly referred to as the Paris Convention, includes the United States and 100 other countries.

2. The Inter-American Convention includes most of the Latin American nations and the United States.

3. The Madrid Arrangement, which established the Bureau for International Registration of Trademarks, includes 26 European countries.

In addition, the World Intellectual Property Organization (WIPO) of the United Nations is responsible for the promotion of the protection of intellectual property and for the administration of the various multilateral treaties through cooperation among its member states.[20] Furthermore, two multicountry patent arrangements have streamlined patent procedures in Europe. The first, the Patent Cooperation Treaty (PCT), facilitates the process for application for patents among its member countries. It provides comprehensive coverage, in that a single application filed in the United States supplies the interested party with an international search report on other patents to help evaluate whether

---

[20]Visit http://www.wipo.org, the home page of the WIPO, for detailed information on the various conventions and the activities of WIPO.

or not to seek protection in each of the countries cooperating under the PCT. The second, the European Patent Convention (EPC), established a regional patent system allowing any nationality to file a single international application for a European patent. Companies have a choice between relying on national systems when they want to protect a trademark or patent in just a few member countries and applying for protection in all 28 member states. Trademark is valid for 10 years and is renewable; however, if the mark is not used within 5 years, protection is forfeited. Once the patent or trademark is approved, it has the same effect as a national patent or trademark in each individual country designated on the application.

The Trade-Related Aspects of Intellectual Property Rights (TRIPs) agreement, a major provision of the World Trade Organization, is the most comprehensive multilateral agreement on intellectual property to date. TRIPs sets standards of protection for a full range of intellectual property rights that are embodied in current international agreements. The three main provisions of the TRIPs agreement required that participating members be in compliance with minimum standards of protection by 2006, set procedures and remedies for the enforcement of IP rights, and make disputes between WTO members with respect to TRIPs obligations subject to the WTO's dispute settlement procedures.[21]

Once a trademark, patent, or other intellectual property right is registered, most countries require that these rights be used and properly policed. The United States is one of the few countries in which an individual can hold a patent without the patented entity being manufactured and sold throughout the duration of the patent period. Other countries feel that in exchange for the monopoly provided by a patent, the holder must share the product with the citizens of the country. Hence, if patents are not used within a specified period, usually from one to 5 years (the average is 3 years), the patent reverts to public domain.

This rule is also true for trademarks; products bearing the registered mark must be sold within the country, or the company may forfeit its right to a particular trademark. McDonald's faced that problem in Venezuela. Even though the McDonald's trademark was properly registered in that code-law country, the company did not use it for more than 2 years. Under Venezuelan law, a trademark must be used within 2 years or it is lost. Thus, a Venezuelan-owned "Mr. McDonalds," with accompanying golden arches, is operating in Venezuela. The U.S. McDonald's Corporation faces a potentially costly legal battle if it decides to challenge the Venezuelan company.

Individual countries expect companies to actively police their intellectual property by bringing violators to court. Policing can be a difficult task, with success depending in large measure on the cooperation of the country within which the infringement or piracy takes place. A lack of cooperation in some countries may stem from cultural differences regarding how intellectual property is viewed. In the United States, the goal of protection of IP is to encourage invention and to protect and reward innovative businesses. In Korea, the attitude is that the thoughts of one person should benefit all. In Japan, the intent is to share technology rather than protect it; an invention should serve a larger, national goal, with the rapid spread of technology among competitors in a manner that promotes cooperation. In light of such attitudes, the lack of enthusiasm toward protecting intellectual property can be better understood. The United States is a strong advocate of protection, and at U.S. insistence, many countries are becoming more cooperative about policing cases of infringement and piracy. After decades of debate, European Union ministers agreed on a common continentwide system for patented inventions. Instead of being forced to submit an application in all EU countries' languages, inventors can submit only one, in English, French, or German. Finally, as the legal system evolves in China, authorities there have now begun enforcing local companies' patents at the expense of foreign firms.

---

[21]For a discussion of TRIPs, visit http://www.wto.org and select Intellectual Property.

People hold signs at a protest by the technology organization New York Tech Meetup against proposed laws to curb Internet piracy outside the offices of US Democratic Senators from New York Chuck Schumer and Kirsten Gillibrand January 18, 2012 on Third Avenue in New York. Schumer and Gillibrand are co-sponsors of the Senate bill PIPA (Protect Intellectual Property Act). SOPA (Stop Online Piracy Act) is the US House version.
 (1) A protest by the technology organization New York Tech Meetup against legislation in the U.S. Congress that would tighten intellectual property laws.
(2) Aside from the United States, the biggest piracy problem is China. Here Jackie Chan helps the Chinese government crack down, forecasting the probable path of IP piracy in China. That is, pirates have turned into policemen historically in the United States, Japan, and Taiwan as the production of intellectual property took off in each country.[22] The same will happen in China during the next decade as artists, researchers, and entrepreneurs there produce new ideas worth protecting.
(3) The HIV/AIDS epidemic is an economic and health catastrophe that many in sub-Saharan Africa and other developing countries[23] believe is exacerbated by drug companies' pricing policies and protection of intellectual property.[24] Here protestors march toward the U.S. embassy in Pretoria, South Africa.

[22]N. Mark Lam and John L. Graham, *China Now, Doing Business in the World's Most Dynamic Market* (New York: McGraw-Hill, 2007).

[23]Amelia Gentleman, "Battle Pits Patent Rights against Low-Cost Generic Drugs," *The New York Times*, January 30, 2007, p. C5; "Clinton, Drug Companies Strike Deal to Lower AIDS Drug Prices," *The Wall Street Journal*, May 8, 2007; Rumman Ahmed, "India Revokes Roche Patent," *The Wall Street Journal*, November 3, 2012, online.

[24]John E. Cook and Roger Bate, "Pharmaceuticals and the Worldwide HIV Epidemic: Can a Stakeholder Model Work?" *Journal of Public Policy & Marketing* 23, no. 2 (2004), pp. 140–52.

Other Managerial Approaches to Protecting Intellectual Property

LO5

How to protect against piracy and counterfeiting

The traditional, but relatively feeble, remedies for American companies operating in countries such as China are several: (1) prevention, that is, engage local representation and diligently register IP with the appropriate agencies;[25] (2) pursue negotiation and alternative dispute resolution; (3) complain to the Chinese authorities; and (4) complain to the U.S. government and World Trade Organization (WTO). Beyond these traditional strategies, research is now being conducted to better understand consumers' motivations with respect to counterfeit brands,[26] and creative thinkers of enterprise have come up with several new ideas that we briefly describe next.[27]

Microsoft.   Bill Gates's negotiation strategy with Chinese software pirates demonstrates his guile, prescience, and patience. He accidentally revealed his strategy in an interview at the University of Washington:

> Although about 3 million computers get sold every year in China, people don't pay for the software. Someday they will, though. And as long as they're going to steal it, we want them to steal ours. They'll get sort of addicted, and then we'll somehow figure out how to collect something in the next decade.

Well, it didn't take a decade for this marketing/product trial approach to work. On April 18, 2006, one day ahead of Chinese President Hu Jintao's arrival in Redmond, Washington, for dinner at Gates's home and on his way to a meeting with President George W. Bush, Gates inked a deal with Lenovo for $1.2 billion of software to be included in the Chinese firm's computers.

Philips.   One of the originators of "open innovation" is Philips Research in the Netherlands. Thirty years ago, it pioneered the concept of partnering[28] to develop and market new ideas. Open innovation for Philips also means that it buys ideas from R&D partners and sells ideas to marketing partners, rather than developing and marketing only its own ideas. One project exemplifies its innovative approach to developing and protecting intellectual property in China. The PHENIX Initiative was a commercial, industrial, and R&D project to develop mobile interactive digital services for the Beijing Olympics. Led by France Telecom, it involved financing and technology contributions from both European and Chinese corporations and governmental organizations.

Although many American firms have established design and R&D centers in China already, U.S. government restrictions on high-tech export and American executives' competitive angst prevent associations such as the PHENIX Initiative for U.S. firms in China. Thus, our arm's-length relationships in China limit both the amount of technology we develop and the degree of protection afforded it compared with European and Asian competitors. Moreover, our pleas for the Chinese government to "protect *our* intellectual property" sound exploitative to both the authorities and the public there.

Warner Bros.   Finally, we suggest an excellent way for IP-rich firms to make money in China currently and in the near future, using the oldest pricing strategy of all: *Charge what the market will bear.* Even with the reluctant help of the Chinese authorities in enforcing the WTO/TRIPs agreement, Chinese consumers will continue the creative copying of foreign intellectual property until they are charged what they perceive as "reasonable" prices. Indeed, we applaud the recent heroic, albeit controversial, marketing strategies of Warner Bros. in China, which nearly halved the prices of its DVDs to $1.88 and distributed the products within days of their release in theaters—earlier than anywhere else in the world.

This pricing approach is quite consistent with one we have long advocated, namely, adjusting prices on the basis of the comparative income levels in developing countries. That is, a fair price (from the Chinese point of view) would take into account the income and purchasing

---

[25]Barbara Demick, "China Gives a Shred about Piracy," *Los Angeles Times*, April 23, 2011, p. A3.

[26]Keith Wilcox, Hyeong Min Kim, and Sankar Sen, "Why Do Consumers Buy Counterfeit Brands?" *Journal of Marketing Research* 46, no. 2 (2009), pp. 247–59.

[27]See Lam and Graham, *China Now*, for more details.

[28]"What's Mine Is Yours," *The Economist*, May 30, 2009, p. 80.

The Bill & Warren Show, By Brent Schlender; Warren Buffett; Bill Gates, *Fortune*, July 20, 1998

power differentials between consumers in the United States and China. For example, at the time, the ratio between U.S. and Chinese GDP per capita at purchase price parity was approximately $40,000 to $6,500. Adjusting the current U.S. price of about $10 for a DVD on Amazon.com, a "reasonable" price to charge in China would be about $1.50. And we particularly appreciate the tactical nuance of adding the $.38 to achieve the very lucky price the Warner Bros. marketers are both charging and getting in China—$1.88!

Warner Bros. is also trying to create a market for high-quality DVD rentals in a partnership with Union Voole Technology in China. Inexpensive video-on-demand systems price the multi-view rentals at less than $1 and deliver via the Internet.

Cyberlaw: Unresolved Issues

LO6

The many issues of evolving cyberlaw

The Internet is by its nature a global enterprise for which no political or national boundaries exist. Although this global reach is its strength, it also creates problems when existing laws do not clearly address the uniqueness of the Internet and its related activities. Existing law is vague or does not completely cover such issues as gambling, the protection of domain names, taxes, jurisdiction in cross-border transactions, contractual issues, piracy (as discussed in the last section), and censorship.[29] The very public dispute between Google and the government of China during 2010 is an important example of the last issue.[30] The European Union, the United States, and many other countries are drafting legislation to address the myriad legal questions not clearly addressed by current law. But until these laws apply worldwide, companies will have to rely on individual-country laws, which may or may not provide protection. When you add together the unprecedented dynamism of the cyber industry to a fledgling legal system as in China, you end up with a rather wild regulatory environment. China is currently trying to monitor and censor text messaging.[31] But perhaps the most interesting battle within the Chinese bureaucracy was over which ministry will regulate the online version of *World of Warcraft*, the most popular such game in the country. The General Administration of Press and Publication and the Ministry of Culture were the two combatants in this interesting game. The Ministry of Culture prevailed and has now set new regulations that can be enforced via 2-year sentences in real-life jail for violations.[32]

Domain Names and Cybersquatters

Unfortunately, the ease with which Web names can be registered and the low cost of registering has led to thousands being registered. **Cybersquatters (CSQs)** buy and register descriptive nouns, geographic names, names of ethnic groups and pharmaceutical substances, and other similar descriptors and hold them until they can be sold at an inflated price. For example, a cybersquatter sold "www.themortgage.com" for $500,000; the record price paid so far is $7.5 million for the domain name "www.business.com." If a cybersquatter has registered a generic domain name that a company wants, the only recourse is to buy it.

Another ploy of CSQs is to register familiar names and known trademarks that divert traffic from intended destinations or to sell competing products. eBay, the world's largest online auction house, was embroiled in a dispute with an entrepreneur in Nova Scotia who registered "www.ebay.ca," thus forcing the U.S. company to use "www.ca.ebay.com" for its newly launched Canadian website until it was successful in regaining the use of "www.ebay.ca"; both addresses now go to the same site.

Cybersquatters register a well-known brand or trademark that misdirects a person to the CSQ's site or to a competing company's site. For example, an adult entertainment website registered "www.candyland.com." Hasbro, the toy company, markets a game for children called "Candy Land." Disturbed by the thought that customers might end up at an adult entertainment site, Hasbro wanted to have the site vacated. It had the option of suing to have it removed or buying the domain name. Hasbro elected to sue, and though the adult website was

---

[29]I. Made Sentana, "BlackBerry to Be Censored in India," *The Wall Street Journal*, January 10, 2011; Ben Fritz and John Horn, "U.S. Filmmakers Chip away at China's Wall," *Los Angeles Times*, August 24, 2011, pp. B1, B4; Farnaz Fassihi, "Iran Mounts New Web Crackdown," *The Wall Street Journal*, January 6, 2012.

[30]"Google and China, Flower for a Funeral," *The Economist*, January 16, 2010, pp. 41–42.

[31]Sharon LaFraniere, "China to Scan Text Messages to Spot 'Unhealthy Content,'" *The New York Times*, January 20, 2010, p. A5.

[32]"China Jails World of Warcraft Cybercrime Group," *Reuters*, December 26, 2013, online.

Potential customers visit a Microsoft booth in Beijing. When Chinese bloggers use Microsoft's service to post messages and type in such terms as "democracy," "capitalism," "liberty," or "human rights," they get a yellow light and a computer warning: "This message includes forbidden language. Please delete the prohibited expression." Microsoft has agreed to this sort of censorship, explaining that it is just following local laws and that the company still provides a most useful service to its Chinese clients. The critics disagree. The argument goes on.

not directly infringing on its trademark, the courts deemed it to be damaging to the reputation of Hasbro and its children's game. The address now takes you directly to a Hasbro site.

Other cybersquatting abuses that can pose a serious threat to business include parody sites, protest sites, and hate sites. A good example is "www.walmartsucks.org," a site highly critical of Walmart. This type of website may be difficult to prevent because the right to free speech is protected. The only defense Walmart might have is to challenge the website's right to use a trade name to direct someone to the site.

It is easy to imagine many situations in which the actions of companies or information posted on a site can lead to a lawsuit when Internet content is unlawful in one country but not in the host country. For example, an American studio that makes a movie with nude scenes could be prosecuted in a country that bans nudity in movies. Not only would the movie studio be liable, but also the Internet service provider could be liable for material posted on its website. Writers and publishers could face libel suits in countries with laws restrictive of free speech, where weak or nonexistent free speech protections are tools to intimidate and censor. Internet publishers or individual website owners fear they can be sued for defamation from any or many jurisdictions, merely because their articles can be downloaded anywhere in the world. Lawsuits involving libel, defamation, and product liability cause companies to voluntarily restrict their website to selected countries rather than leave themselves open to legal action. The Internet is not a libel-free zone.

Most country's courts are inclined to assert jurisdiction over online activity, wherever it originates, so long as harm is experienced locally and the sense is that the party responsible either knew or ought to have known that the harm was a likely consequence of its actions. Most agree, though, that laws that are expressly designed to apply not just in a single country but worldwide are necessary to untangle the legal hassles that are occurring.

Of 100 business leaders polled by the International Chamber of Commerce, more than one-third said legal uncertainty covering Internet operations affected "significant business decisions." The most immediate impact, according to the ICC, is clear: Many online merchants refuse to sell outside their home countries.

Taxes   Another thorny issue in e-commerce concerns the collection of taxes. A typical tax system relies on knowing where a particular economic activity is located. But the Internet enables individual workers to operate in many different countries while sitting at the same desk. When taxes should be collected, where they should be collected, and by whom are all issues under consideration by countries around the world. In the past, a company was deemed to have a taxable presence in a country if it had a permanent establishment there. But whether the existence of a server or a website qualifies as such a presence is not clear. One proposal that has enthusiastic support from tax authorities is for servers to be designated as "virtual permanent establishments" and thus subject to local taxes.

To pinpoint when and where a sale takes place in cyberspace is difficult, and unless elusive taxpayers can be pinpointed, any tax may be difficult to collect. In "brick-and-mortar" sales, the retailer collects, but when the Internet site is in one country and the customer is in another, who collects? One proposal is to have shipping companies such as FedEx or credit card companies collect—obviously, neither party is receiving this suggestion enthusiastically.

The EU Commission has implemented a directive to force foreign companies to levy value-added tax (VAT) on services delivered via the Internet, television, or radio to customers in the European Union. Foreign companies with sales via the Internet of over €100,000 (~$125,000) inside the European Union would have to register in at least one EU country and levy VAT at that country's rate, somewhere between 15 percent and 25 percent. The tax is justified on the basis of leveling the playing field. That is, EU companies have to charge their EU customers VAT, whereas foreign companies supplying the same service to the same customers are duty free. U.S. companies protested, to no avail, calling the new taxes "e-protectionism." [33] Perhaps the most egregious example of strange Internet taxing comes from France. The Ministry of Culture there proposed a tax on online advertising revenues, aimed at American firms such as Google, Microsoft, AOL, Yahoo!, and Facebook, to pay for new subsidies for the French music, movie, and publishing industries.[34] Other countries outside the EU are considering similar internet taxes—not only are multinational companies protesting, so are their own citizens.[35]

Jurisdiction of Disputes and Validity of Contracts

As countries realize that existing laws relating to commerce do not always clearly address the uniqueness of the Internet and its related activities, a body of cyberlaw is gradually being created. Two of the most troubling areas are determining whose laws will prevail in legal disputes between parties located in different countries and establishing the contractual validity of electronic communications. The European Union is having the most difficulty in reconciling the vast differences in the laws among its member states to create a uniform law. For example, a draft regulation debated in Brussels and other European capitals would have required vendors to comply with 28 different, and sometimes bizarre, sets of national rules on consumer protection—ranging from dozens of restrictions on advertising to France's requirement that all contracts must be concluded in French, regardless of whether businesses intend to sell goods for export to France.

The EU Commission has adopted an e-commerce directive that will permit online retailers to trade by the rules of their home country unless the seller had enticed or approached the consumer by way of advertising. Then, any legal action is to take place in the consumer's country of residence. The rationale is that if a company actively seeks customers in a given country, it ought to be willing to abide by that country's consumer protection laws. Whether the directive will be accepted by all 28 member states is still problematic.

The European Commission has begun to review the entire regulatory framework for the technological infrastructure of the information society. The commission is working on various pieces of legislation intended to place electronic commerce on an equal footing with conventional commerce. One of the first steps was to introduce an EU-wide computer network dubbed EEJ net that provides an easy way to resolve small-scale disputes out of court. Problems over deliveries, defective products, or products that do not fit their description can be dealt with by a single one-stop national contact point, or clearinghouse, in each member state. The consumer will be able to find information and support in making a claim to the out-of-court dispute resolution system in the country where the product supplier is based.

Establishing the validity of contractual law for e-commerce is making substantial progress also. India, for example, recently passed a law that recognizes e-mail as a valid form of communication, electronic contracts as legal and enforceable, and digital signatures as binding. Several countries are preparing, or have passed, legislation similar to the United Kingdom's that allows digital signatures to be used in the creation of online contracts that are as legally binding as any paper-based original document.

Commercial Law within Countries

LO7 ▰▰

The legal differences between countries and how those differences can affect international marketing plans

When doing business in more than one country, a marketer must remain alert to the different legal systems. This problem is especially troublesome for the marketer who formulates a common marketing plan to be implemented in several countries. Although differences in languages and customs may be accommodated, legal differences between countries may still present problems for a marketing program.

---

[33]For a report on a resolution on cross-border tax issues proposed by the OECD, see "OECD Launches Project on Improving the Resolution of Cross-Border Tax Disputes," http://www.oecd.org, and select Taxation. The OECD proposes a variety of issues related to the Internet, all of which can be found at this site. Ultimately, the Hungarian government yielded to the public protests and dropped its Internet tax plan; see Rick Lyman, "Hungary Drops Internet Tax Plan after Public Outcry," *The New York Times*, November 1, 2014, p. A6.

[34]"France and the Internet, Helicopters at the Ready," *The Economist*, January 16, 2010, pp. 63–64.

[35]Rick Lyman, "Proposed Internet Tax Draws Hungarians to Streets in Protest," *The New York Times*, October 30, 2012, p. A6.

Marketing Laws

All countries have laws regulating marketing activities in promotion, product development, labeling, pricing, and channels of distribution. We are also beginning to see more restrictions on what we call marketing research in the United States. The latest example is Facebook running media experiments without asking Europeans for their permission—privacy is more closely guarded on the Continent than in the United States.[36] Usually the discrepancies across markets cause problems for trade negotiators, particularly for managers and their firms. For example, the United States does not allow the buying or selling of human organs,[37] and it restricts the use of human stem cells in medical research to develop treatments for a variety of diseases. Other nations have different laws. The ethics of both issues are quite controversial, and adding an international dimension just complicates things even more. In the case of the current international trade in human organs, Europeans can legally travel to foreign countries for transplants. However, the European Union Parliament is considering making it a criminal offense to do so. Meanwhile, the U.S. government is considering relaxing laws regulating stem cell research as scientists in other nations, unfettered by similar restrictions, are making important advances in the field. The latest conundrum in the international market for healthcare services is the assembly of "global babies," including eggs, sperm, and surrogate mothers, all from different legal regimes.[38]

Other examples of prohibitions of product/service offerings are China's ongoing censorship of all media, including Google[39] and Disney movies such as The Croods;[40] the European Union requiring the removal of Google references to *New York Times* content;[41] and Lithuania banning the sale of energy drinks to minors.[42] Other countries restrict distribution in a variety of ways: Cuba has recently closed private venues for movies and video games—they are just beginning to understand free enterprise.[43] A number of countries, including Russia and Argentina, are clamping down on international courier services by placing limits on quantity and frequency of shipments to individuals' addresses.[44] Meanwhile, India has been relaxing limitations on both banking[45] and retailing.[46]

Some countries may have only a few marketing laws with lax enforcement; others may have detailed, complicated rules to follow that are stringently enforced. For example, Sweden banned all television advertising to children in 1991. The United Kingdom,[47] Greece, Norway, Denmark, Austria, and the Netherlands all restrict advertising directed at children. Recently, the European Commission threatened to restrict all advertising of soft drinks and snack foods to children, and PepsiCo volunteered to curb its advertising to kids in response. At the same time, the American food industry is arguing against such actions in the United States. It is interesting to note that the U.S. Federal Trade Commission and the sugared food and toy manufacturers went down a similar path toward restricting advertising to children in the late 1970s. The industry made a few minor concessions at the time but began ignoring previous commitments during the 1980s. All these developments will be interesting to follow as childhood obesity continues to be a major public health issue in all affluent countries.

---

[36]Vindu Goel, "After an Uproar, European Regulators Question Facebook on Psychological Testing," *The New York Times*, July 3, 2014, p. B3.

[37]"Let Livers Go Where They're Needed," *Bloomberg BusinessWeek*, September 11, 2014, online.

[38]Tamara Audi and Arlene Chang, "Assembling the Global Baby," *The Wall Street Journal*, December 11, 2010, pp. C1–2.

[39]Keith Bradshure and Paul Mozur, "Sealed Tight," *The New York Times*, September 2, 2014, pp. B1–2.

[40]Richard Verrier, "China Pulls 'The Croods' from Theaters," *Los Angeles Times*, June 8 2013, p. B3.

[41]Noam Cohen and Mark Scott,"Times Articles Removed from Google Results in Europe," *The New York Times*, October 4, 2014, p. A3.

[42]Sabrina Bachai, "Lithuania Bans the Sale of Energy Drinks to Minors," *Medical Daily*, May 16, 2014.

[43]"Cuba to Close Private Venues for Movies and Video Games," *Associated Press*, November 3, 2013, online.

[44]Andrew E. Kramer, "In Russia, Couriers Halt Parcel Deliveries," *The New York Times*, January 25, 2014, pp. B1–2.

[45]Keith Bradsher and Ellen Barry, "India Gives Foreign Banks New Door into Local Market," *The New York Times*, November 7, 2013, p. B2.

[46]Rajesh Roy, "India Clears Walmart in Probe of 2010 Purchase," *The Wall Street Journal*, October 17, 2013, online.

[47]"Cookie Monster Crumbles," *The Economist*, November 23, 2013, pp. 61–62.

There often are vast differences in enforcement and interpretation among countries with laws that cover the same activities. Laws governing sales promotions in the European Union offer good examples of such diversity. In Austria, premium offers, free gifts, or coupons are considered cash discounts and are prohibited. Premium offers in Finland are allowed with considerable scope as long as the word *free* is not used and consumers are not coerced into buying products. France also regulates premium offers, which are, for all practical purposes, illegal there because selling for less than cost or offering a customer a gift or premium conditional on the purchase of another product is illegal. French law does permit sales twice a year, in January and August, which can legally last four to six weeks. This event is so popular that it is advertised on radio and TV, and special police are even required to control the crowds. One poll indicated that over 40 percent of the French set aside money during the year for sale time, and 56 percent will spend less money on essentials to buy things on sale. The good news here is that many of these restrictions on marketing activities are being softened. Most recently, holiday sales and longer store hours are being allowed in several European countries. China has relaxed some of its restrictions on direct marketing that particularly affected companies such as Mary Kay. However, its laws regulating direct selling are unusually detailed, compared with others around the world. Please see a few articles of the law, excerpted from the 55 total regulations, in Exhibit 7.3. Most agree that China's deep concern about direct selling organizations stems from a long history of grass-roots groups causing civil disorder (recall our description of the Taiping Rebellion in Chapter 3).

The various product comparison laws, a natural and effective means of expression, are another major stumbling block. In Germany, comparisons in advertisements are always subject to the competitor's right to go to the courts and ask for proof of any implied or stated

Exhibit 7.3
Excerpts from Chinese Marketing Laws

Article 5. When undertaking direct selling activities, no direct selling company or its door-to-door salesman may conduct any fraudulent or misleading acts and other drumbeating and sales promotion acts.

Article 23. A direct selling company shall clearly mark the product price on the direct selling product, and the price shall be consistent with the price of the product as showed at the service website. A door-to-door salesman shall sell direct selling products to consumers at the marked price.

Article 24. A direct selling company shall pay remuneration to its door-to-door salesmen at least on a monthly basis. The remunerations paid to any door-to-door salesman by a direct selling company shall be calculated on the basis of the income gained from selling products directly to consumers by the door-to-door salesman himself/herself, and the total remuneration (including commission, bonus, various awards and other economic benefits, and etc.) may not exceed 30% of the income gained from selling products directly to consumers by the door-to-door salesman himself/herself.

Article 29. A direct selling company shall open a special account in the bank designated by the competent commerce department of the State Council together with the administrative department of industry and commerce of the State Council, and put a deposit into it. The deposit shall be RMB 20 million Yuan at the time when a direct selling company is established. After the direct selling company starts operation, the deposit shall be adjusted on a monthly basis, and the amount shall remain at 15% of its sales income from direct selling products of the previous month, but may not exceed RMB 0.1 billion Yuan at the maximum and not less than RMB 20 million Yuan at the minimum. The interest of the deposit shall be owned by the direct selling company.

Article 30. The deposit may be used if:

1. A direct selling company fails to pay remuneration to its door-to-door salesmen without justifiable reasons, or fails to pay the money for returned goods to door-to-door salesmen and consumers;

2. A direct selling company involves itself in such circumstances as suspension of business, merger, dissolution, transfer and bankruptcy and etc., and lacks the ability to pay remuneration to its door-to-door salesmen or to pay the refunds to door-to-door salesmen or consumers; or

3. A direct selling company shall make compensation for any damage to consumers due to the quality of its direct selling products under the law, but it refuses to do so without justifiable reasons or lack the ability to make compensation.

Source: Ministry of Commerce, People's Republic of China Regulations of Direct Selling Administration, August 23, 2005 http://english.mofcom.gov.cn/article/zt_yearboook/lanmua/200804/20080405503301.shtml.

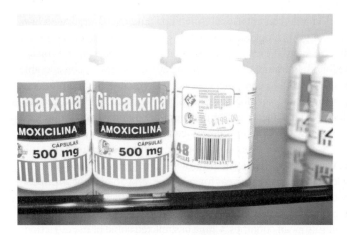

Laws regarding healthcare marketing differ substantially around the world. In Mexico, prescriptions often are not required for powerful drugs. At this farmacia in the Cancun airport, tourists can buy the pictured antibiotic over the counter at bargain prices. Quality is an issue, but availability is not. In the Philippines and other developing countries, you can buy yourself a kidney on the black market—the global price is around $2,000. However, U.S. laws prohibit the buying and selling of human organs.

superiority. In Canada, the rulings are even more stringent: All claims and statements must be examined to ensure that any representation to the public is not false or misleading. Such representation cannot be made verbally in selling or be contained in or on anything that comes to the attention of the public (such as product labels, inserts in products, or any other form of advertising, including what may be expressed in a sales letter). Courts have been directed by Canadian law to take into account, in determining whether a representation is false or misleading, the "general impression" conveyed by the representation as well as its literal meaning. The courts are expected to apply the "credulous person standard," which means that if any reasonable person could possibly misunderstand the representation, the representation is misleading. In essence, puffery, an acceptable practice in the United States, could be interpreted in Canada as false and misleading advertising. Thus, a statement such as "the strongest drive shaft in Canada" would be judged misleading unless the advertiser had absolute evidence that the drive shaft was stronger than any other drive shaft for sale in Canada.

China is experimenting with a variety of laws to control how foreign companies do business, and some of those experiments have gone well, but some badly. Some regulations are being relaxed, such as those controlling foreign advertising companies. Even so, censorship of advertising and program content are constant concerns. Televised ads for "offensive" products such as feminine hygiene pads, hemorrhoid medications, and even athlete's foot ointment are not allowed during the three daily mealtimes. The Chinese authorities banned a LeBron James Nike TV ad because it "violates regulations that mandate all advertisements in China should uphold national dignity and interest and respect the motherland's culture." Apparently LeBron battling a kung fu master isn't appropriate in the land of Confucius. Also, magazines have been ordered to use a direct translation of the often-obscure name that appears on their license or use no English name at all. Thus, *Cosmopolitan* would become "Trends Lady," *Woman's Day* would become "Friends of Health," and *Esquire* would become "Trends Man." The movie *Avatar* also competed for Chinese screens with a government-sponsored film about the life of Confucius; at least temporarily, *Avatar* was allowed to show only on 3D screens, thus allowing Confucius the "appropriate" screen time. A Guns N' Roses album was banned in the country for its objectionable title, *Chinese Democracy*. Such diversity of laws among countries extends to advertising, pricing, sales agreements, and other commercial activities. Indeed, studies suggest that governmental policies affect marketing success in a variety of ways[48] including actually forestalling some firms from taking a marketing orientation in their operations.[49]

There is some hope that the European Union will soon have a common commercial code. One step in that direction is the proposal to harmonize the pan-European regulation of promotions based on the conservative laws that cover promotions in Germany, Austria, and Belgium. However, this proposal is meeting with strong resistance from several groups because of its complex restrictions. Meanwhile, others push for even broader-based harmonization of marketing regulations involving the United States, United Nations, and the WTO.

Although the European Union may sometimes appear a beautiful picture of economic cooperation, there is still the reality of dealing with 28 different countries, cultures, and languages, as well as 28 different legal systems. Even though some of Germany's complicated trade laws were revoked in 2000, groups such as the Center for Combating Unfair Competition, an industry-financed organization, continue to work to maintain the status quo. Before the German law was revoked, the Center's lawyers filed 1,000 lawsuits a year, going after, for example, a grocery store that offered discount coupons or a deli that gave a free cup of coffee to a customer who had already bought 10; its efforts will surely continue.

Although the goal of full integration and a common commercial code has not been totally achieved in the European Union, decisions by the European Court continue to strike down individual-country laws that impede competition across borders. In a recent decision, the European Court ruled that a French cosmetics company could sell its wares by mail in Germany and advertise them at a markdown from their original prices, a direct contradiction of German law. As the Single European Market Act is implemented, many of the legal and trade differences that have existed for decades will vanish. Surprisingly enough, standards set by the European Union for food, software, cars, and other items affect U.S. product standards as well. In many cases, the reconciliation of so many different consumer protection standards that existed in European countries prior to the European Union resulted in rules more rigorous than those for many U.S. products. Consequently, many U.S. products have had to be redesigned to comply with European standards. For example, Carrier air conditioners have been redesigned to comply with European recycling rules; Microsoft has modified contracts with software makers; Internet service providers give consumers a wider choice of technologies; and McDonald's has ceased including soft plastic toys with its Happy Meals and has withdrawn all genetically engineered potatoes from its restaurants worldwide. All this change is because of the need to reconcile U.S. standards with those of the European Union.

Green Marketing Legislation

Multinational corporations also face a growing variety of legislation designed to address environmental issues. Global concern for the environment extends beyond industrial pollution, hazardous waste disposal, and rampant deforestation to include issues that focus directly on consumer products. Green marketing laws focus on environmentally friendly products and product packaging and its effect on solid waste management.

Germany has passed the most stringent green marketing laws that regulate the management and recycling of packaging waste. The new packaging laws were introduced in

---

[48]Stefan Stremersch and Aurelie Lemmens, "Sales Growth of New Pharmaceuticals across the Globe: The Role of Regulatory Regimes," *Marketing Science* 28, no. 4 (2009), pp. 690–708.

[49]Rilian Qu and Christine T. Ennew, "Developing a Market Orientation in a Transitional Economy: The Role of Government Regulation and Ownership Structure," *Journal of Public Policy & Marketing* 24, no. 1 (2005), pp. 82–89.

three phases. The first phase required all transport packaging, such as crates, drums, pallets, and Styrofoam containers, to be accepted back by the manufacturers and distributors for recycling. The second phase required manufacturers, distributors, and retailers to accept all returned secondary packaging, including corrugated boxes, blister packs, packaging designed to prevent theft, packaging for vending machine applications, and packaging for promotional purposes. The third phase requires all retailers, distributors, and manufacturers to accept returned sales packaging, including cans, plastic containers for dairy products, foil wrapping, Styrofoam packages, and folding cartons such as cereal boxes. The requirement for retailers to take back sales packaging has been suspended as long as the voluntary green dot program remains a viable substitute. A green dot on a package identifies manufacturers that have agreed to ensure a regular collection of used packaging materials directly from the consumer's home or from designated local collection points.

Reclaiming recyclables extends beyond packaging to automobiles. Since 2006, manufacturers based in European Union nations must take back any cars they produced that no longer have resale value and pay for proper disposal. Similarly, 85 percent of a scrapped car's material must be recovered for future use.

Many European countries also have devised schemes to identify products that comply with certain criteria that make them more environmentally friendly than similar products. Products that meet these criteria are awarded an "ecolabel" that the manufacturer can display on packaging to signal to customers that it is an environmentally friendly product. The European Union is becoming more aggressive in issuing new directives and in harmonizing ecolabeling and other environmental laws across all member states. Ecolabeling and EU packaging laws are discussed in more detail in the chapter on consumer products (Chapter 13).

Foreign Countries' Antitrust Laws

With the exception of the United States, antitrust laws were either nonexistent or not enforced in most of the world's countries for the better part of the twentieth century. However, the European Union, Japan, China,[50] India,[51] and many other countries have begun to actively enforce their antitrust laws, patterned after those in the United States. Antimonopoly, price discrimination, supply restrictions, and full-line forcing are areas in which the European Court of Justice has dealt severe penalties. For example, before Procter & Gamble was allowed to buy VP-Schickedanz AG, a German hygiene products company, it had to agree to sell off one of the German company's divisions that produced Camelia, a brand of sanitary napkins. Because P&G already marketed a brand of sanitary napkins in Europe, the commission was concerned that allowing P&G to keep Camelia would give the company a controlling 60 percent of the German sanitary products market and 81 percent of Spain's. More recently, the European Union fined Intel $1.45 billion for monopolistic abuses in its marketing in Europe. In addition, the firm must make mandated adjustments in its marketing practices and operations.

The United States also intervenes when non-U.S. companies attempt to acquire American companies. Nestlé's proposed $2.8 billion acquisition of Dreyer's Grand Ice Cream hit a roadblock as U.S. antitrust officials opposed the deal on grounds that it would lead to less competition and higher prices for gourmet ice cream in the United States. At times, companies are subject to antitrust charges in more than one country. Microsoft had a partial victory against antitrust charges brought in the United States, only to face similar anticompetitive charges against Microsoft's Windows operating system in the European Union. The probe is based on possible competitive benefits to European software concerns if legal limits were placed on Microsoft. American companies have faced antitrust violations since the trust-busting days of President Theodore Roosevelt but much less so in other parts of the world. Enforcement of antitrust in Europe was almost nonexistent until the early stages of the European Union established antitrust legislation. And, now China is getting into the game. The Anti-Monopoly Bureau of the Ministry of Commerce considered its first such case and eventually approved the Anheuser-Busch/InBev merger.

---

[50]Andrew Jacobs, Chris Buckley, and Nick Wingfield, "China Starts to Squeeze Tech Firms from U.S.," *The New York Times*, July 29, 2014, pp. B1, 6.

[51]Neha Thirani Bagri, "India Fines 14 Carmakers in Antitrust Case," *The New York Times*, August 27, 2014, p. B6.

U.S. Laws Apply in Host Countries

LO8

The different ways U.S. laws can be applied to U.S. companies operating outside the United States

All governments are concerned with protecting their political and economic interests domestically and internationally; any activity or action, wherever it occurs, that adversely threatens national interests is subject to government control. Leaving the political boundaries of a home country does not exempt a business from home-country laws. Regardless of the nation where business is done, a U.S. citizen is subject to certain laws of the United States. What is illegal for an American business at home can also be illegal by U.S. law in foreign jurisdictions for the firm, its subsidiaries, and licensees of U.S. technology.

Laws that prohibit taking a bribe, trading with the enemy, participating in a commercial venture that negatively affects the U.S. economy, participating in an unauthorized boycott such as the Arab boycott, or any other activity deemed to be against the best interests of the United States apply to U.S. businesses and their subsidiaries and licensees regardless of where they operate. Thus, at any given time a U.S. citizen in a foreign country must look not only at the laws of the host country but also at home law as well.

The question of jurisdiction of U.S. law over acts committed outside the territorial limits of the country has been settled by the courts through application of a long-established principle of international law, the "objective theory of jurisdiction." This concept holds that even if an act is committed outside the territorial jurisdiction of U.S. courts, those courts can nevertheless have jurisdiction if the act produces effects within the home country. The only possible exception may be when the violation is the result of enforced compliance with local law.

Foreign Corrupt Practices Act

Recall from Chapter 5 that the Foreign Corrupt Practices Act (FCPA) makes it illegal for companies to pay bribes to foreign officials, candidates, or political parties. Stiff penalties can be assessed against company officials, directors, employees, or agents found guilty of paying a bribe or of knowingly participating in or authorizing the payment of a bribe. However, also recall that bribery, which can range from lubrication to extortion, is a common business custom in many countries, even though illegal.[52]

The original FCPA lacked clarity, and early interpretations were extremely narrow and confusing. Subsequent amendments in the Omnibus Trade and Competitiveness Act clarified two of the most troubling issues. Corporate officers' liability was changed from having *reason to know* that illegal payments were made to *knowing* of or authorizing illegal payments. In addition, if it is customary in the culture, small (grease or lubrication) payments made to encourage officials to complete routine government actions such as processing papers, stamping visas, and scheduling inspections are not illegal per se.

The debate continues as to whether the FCPA puts U.S. businesses at a disadvantage. Some argue that U.S. businesses are at a disadvantage in international business transactions in those cases in which bribery payments are customary,[53] whereas others contend that it has little effect and, indeed, that it helps companies to "just say no." The truth probably lies somewhere in between. The consensus is that most U.S. firms are operating within the law, and several studies indicate that the FCPA has not been as detrimental to MNCs' interests as originally feared, because exports to developed and developing countries continue to be favorable.

Although U.S. firms seem able to compete and survive without resorting to bribery in the most corrupt societies, it does not mean that violations do not occur or that companies are not penalized for violations.[54] For example, a U.S. environmental engineering firm was found to have made corrupt payments to an Egyptian government official to assist the company in gaining a contract. The company agreed not to violate the FCPA in the future, to pay a civil fine of $400,000, and to reimburse the Department of Justice for the costs of the investigation. Furthermore, the company agreed to establish FCPA compliance procedures and to provide certifications of compliance annually for 5 years. Other firms have paid even larger fines in

---

[52]For discussions of the FCPA, updates, and other information, visit the FCPA home page at http://www.usdoj.gov/criminal/fraud/fcpa.html.

[53]Joe Palazzolo, "Business Slams Bribery Act," *The Wall Street Journal*, November 29, 2011, pp. B1, B8.

[54]Peter Loftus and Jessica Holzer, "J&J Settlement in Bribery Case," *The Wall Street Journal*, April 9, 2011; Ellen Byron, "Avon Bribe Investigation Widens," *The Wall Street Journal*, May 5, 2011, pp. B1–2; Daniel Gilbert and Tom Fowler, "SEC Charges Noble Ex-CEO in Nigerian Bribe Investigation," *The Wall Street Journal*, February 25, 2012.

CROSSING BORDERS 7.2

The Kind of Correspondence an International Marketer Doesn't Want to See

FOR IMMEDIATE RELEASE
FRIDAY, MAY 20, 2005
HTTP://WWW.USDOJ.GOV

CRM
(202) 514-2008
TDD (202) 514-1888

DPC (TIANJIN) LTD. CHARGED WITH VIOLATING THE FOREIGN CORRUPT PRACTICES ACT

WASHINGTON, D.C.—Acting Assistant Attorney General John C. Richter of the Criminal Division today announced the filing of a one-count criminal information charging DPC (Tianjin) Co. Ltd.—the Chinese subsidiary of Los Angeles–based Diagnostic Products Corporation (DPC)—with violating the Foreign Corrupt Practices Act of 1977 (FCPA) in connection with the payment of approximately $1.6 million in bribes in the form of illegal "commissions" to physicians and laboratory personnel employed by government-owned hospitals in the People's Republic of China.

The company, a producer and seller of diagnostic medical equipment, has agreed to plead guilty to the charge, adopt internal compliance measures, and cooperate with ongoing criminal and SEC civil investigations. An independent compliance expert will be chosen to audit the company's compliance program and monitor its implementation of new internal policies and procedures. DPC Tianjin has also agreed to pay a criminal penalty of $2 million.

The bribes were allegedly paid from late 1991 through December 2002 for the purpose and effect of obtaining and retaining business with these hospitals. According to the criminal information and a statement of facts filed in court, DPC Tianjin made cash payments to laboratory personnel and physicians employed in certain hospitals in the People's Republic of China in exchange for agreements that the hospitals would obtain DPC Tianjin's products and services. This practice, authorized by DPC Tianjin's general manager, involved personnel who were employed by hospitals owned by the legal authorities in the People's Republic of China and, thus, "foreign officials" as defined by the FCPA.

In most cases, the bribes were paid in cash and hand-delivered by DPC Tianjin salespeople to the person who controlled purchasing decisions for the particular hospital department. DPC Tianjin recorded the payments on its books and records as "selling expenses." DPC Tianjin's general manager regularly prepared and submitted to Diagnostic Products Corporation its financial statements, which contained its sales expenses. The general manager also caused approval of the budgets for sales expenses of DPC Tianjin, including the amounts DPC Tianjin intended to pay to the officials of the hospitals in the following quarter or year.

The "commissions," typically between 3 percent and 10 percent of sales, totaled approximately $1,623,326 from late 1991 through December 2002, and allowed Depu to earn approximately $2 million in profits from the sales.

DPC Tianjin's parent company, Diagnostic Products Corporation, is the subject of an FCPA enforcement proceeding filed earlier today by the U.S. Securities and Exchange Commission. The SEC ordered the company to cease and desist from violating the FCPA and to disgorge approximately $2.8 million in ill-gotten gains, representing its net profit in the People's Republic of China for the period of its misconduct plus prejudgment interest . . .

recent years, and the Justice Department has agreed not to prosecute firms with "excellent" training programs in place. Firms can also reduce penalties by helping investigations.[55]

U.S. Antitrust Laws that Apply in Foreign Markets

Antitrust enforcement has two purposes in international commerce. The first is to protect American consumers by ensuring that they benefit from products and ideas produced by foreign competitors as well as by domestic competitors. Competition from foreign producers is important when imports are, or could be, a major source of a product or when a single firm dominates a domestic industry. This issue becomes relevant in many joint ventures, particularly if the joint venture creates a situation in which a U.S. firm entering a joint venture with a foreign competitor restricts competition for the U.S. parent in the U.S. market.

The second purpose of antitrust legislation is to protect American export and investment opportunities against any privately imposed restrictions. The concern is that all U.S.-based firms engaged in the export of goods, services, or capital should be allowed to compete on merit and not be shut out by restrictions imposed by bigger or less principled competitors.

The questions of jurisdiction and how U.S. antitrust laws apply are frequently asked but only vaguely answered. The basis for determination ultimately rests with the interpretation

---

[55]Elizabeth Dwoskin and David Voreacos, "The U.S. Goes after Bribery, on a Budget," *Bloomberg Businessweek*, January 23, 2012, pp. 31–32.

of Sections I and II of the Sherman Act. Section I states that "every contract, combination . . . or conspiracy in restraint of trade or commerce among the several states or with foreign nations is hereby declared to be illegal." Section II makes it a violation to "monopolize, or attempt to monopolize, or combine or conspire with any other person or persons, to monopolize any part of the trade or commerce among the several states, or with foreign nations."

The Justice Department recognizes that application of U.S. antitrust laws to overseas activities raises some difficult questions of jurisdiction. It also recognizes that U.S. antitrust-law enforcement should not interfere unnecessarily with the sovereign interest of a foreign nation. At the same time, however, the Antitrust Division is committed to controlling foreign transactions at home or abroad that have a substantial and foreseeable effect on U.S. commerce. When such business practices occur, there is no question in the Antitrust Division of the Department of Justice that U.S. laws apply.

Antiboycott Law

Under the antiboycott law,[56] U.S. companies are forbidden to participate in any unauthorized foreign boycott; furthermore, they are required to report any request to cooperate with a boycott. The antiboycott law was a response to the Arab League boycott of Israeli businesses. The Arab League boycott of Israel has three levels: A primary boycott bans direct trade between Arab states and Israel, a secondary boycott bars Arab governments from doing business with companies that do business with Israel, and a tertiary boycott bans Arab governments from doing business with companies that do business with companies doing business with Israel.[57]

When companies do not comply with the Arab League's boycott directives, their names are placed on a blacklist, and they are excluded from trade with members of the Arab League. Thus U.S. companies are caught in the middle: If they trade with Israel, the Arab League will not do business with them, and if they refuse to do business with Israel in order to trade with an Arab League member, they will be in violation of U.S. law.[58] One hospital supply company that had been trading with Israel was charged with closing a plant in Israel to get itself taken off the Arab League blacklist. After an investigation, the company pled guilty, was fined $6.6 million, and was prohibited from doing business in Syria and Saudi Arabia for 2 years. A less costly fine of $12,000 was paid by a freight forwarder who simply certified that the goods shipped for a third party were not of Israeli origin, were not shipped from Israel, and did not contain any material from Israel.

Extraterritoriality of U.S. Laws

The issue of the extraterritoriality of U.S. laws is especially important to U.S. multinational firms, because the long arm of U.S. legal jurisdiction causes anxiety for heads of state. Foreign governments fear the influence of American government policy on their economies through U.S. multinationals.[59]

Especially troublesome are those instances when U.S. law is in conflict with host countries' economic or political goals. Conflict arises when the host government requires joint ventures to do business within the country and the U.S. Justice Department restricts or forbids such ventures because of their U.S. anticompetitive effects. Host countries see this influence as evidence of U.S. interference. When U.S. MNCs' subsidiaries are prohibited from making a sale in violation of the U.S. Trading with the Enemy Act, host governments react with hostility toward the extraterritorial application of U.S. foreign policy.

---

[56]The antiboycott law applies only to those boycotts not sanctioned by the U.S. government. Sanctioned boycotts, such as the boycotts against trade with Cuba and Iran, are initiated by the United States and must be honored by U.S. firms.

[57]For those non-U.S. companies trading with the Arab League and complying with the boycott, each was required to include a statement on shipping invoices. On an invoice for 10 busses to be shipped from Brazil to Kuwait, the following statement appeared: "We certify that we are the producer and supplier of the shipped goods; we are neither blacklisted by the Arab Boycott of Israel nor are we the head office branch or subsidiary of a boycotted company. No Israeli capital is invested in this firm, no company capital or capital of its owners is invested in any Israeli company; our products are not of Israeli origin and do not contain Israeli raw material or labor."

[58]For a list of current cases against firms violating antiboycott law, visit http://www.bxa.doc.gov and select Antiboycott Compliance, then Antiboycott Case Histories.

[59]Anthony Ferner, Phil Almond, and Trevor Colling, "Institutional Theory and the Cross-National Transfer of Employment Policy: The Case of 'Workforce Diversity' in U.S. Multinationals," *Journal of International Business Studies* 36, no. 3 (2005), pp. 304–21.

This chapter's Global Perspective is a good illustration of the extraterritoriality of U.S. law and how it has an impact on a friendly neighbor as well as a major multinational company.

In an interesting development, MNCs are being held liable for the human-rights abuses of foreign governments. Lawsuits are being brought in U.S. courts against U.S. MNCs, charging them with doing business with oppressive regimes. Unocal Corporation was sued for doing business with Myanmar's (Burma's) military regime, which forced peasants at gunpoint to help build a pipeline for Unocal. Unocal denied the charges. This case was brought under the Alien Claims Act, originally intended to reassure Europe that the fledgling United States would not harbor pirates or assassins. It permits foreigners to sue in U.S. courts for violations of the "the law of nations." Businesses like IBM, Citibank, and Coca-Cola worry that they may be socked with huge jury damages for the misdeeds of oppressive governments. Employment lawyers warn that multinational companies are likely to face more lawsuits from the Third World.

When the intent of any kind of overseas activity is to restrain trade, there is no question about the appropriateness of applying U.S. laws. There is a question, however, when the intent is to conclude a reasonable business transaction. If the U.S. government encourages U.S. firms to become multinational, then the government needs to make provisions for the resolution of differences when conflict arises between U.S. law and host-government laws.

Export Restrictions

LO9

The steps necessary to move goods across country borders

Although the United States requires no formal or special license to engage in exporting as a business, permission or a license to export may be required for certain commodities and certain destinations. Export licensing controls apply to exports of commodities and technical data from the United States; re-exports of U.S.-origin commodities and technical data from a foreign destination to another foreign destination; U.S.- origin parts and components used in foreign countries to manufacture foreign products for exports; and, in some cases, foreign products made from U.S.-origin technical data. Most items requiring special permission or a license for exportation are under the control of the Bureau of Industry and Security (BIS)[60] of the Department of Commerce.

The volume of exports and the number of companies exporting from the United States have grown spectacularly over the last decade. In an effort to alleviate many of the problems and confusions of exporting and to expedite the process, the Department of Commerce has published a revised set of export regulations known as the *Export Administration Regulations (EAR)*. They are intended to speed up the process of granting export licenses by removing a large number of items from specific export license control and concentrating licensing on a specific list of items, most of which pertain to national security, nuclear nonproliferation, terrorism, or chemical and biological weapons. Along with these changes comes a substantial increase in responsibility on the part of the exporter, because the exporter must now ensure that Export Administration Regulations are not violated.

The EAR is intended to serve the national security, foreign policy, and nonproliferation interests of the United States and, in some cases, to carry out its international obligations.[61] It also includes some export controls to protect the United States from the adverse impact of the unrestricted export of commodities in short supply, such as Western cedar. Items that do not require a license for a specific destination can be shipped with the notation "NLR" (no license required) on the Shipper's Export Declaration. Some export restrictions on high-technology products have been recently eased, which we hope marks the beginning of a new trend.

National Security Laws

American firms (as well as firms in other countries),[62] their foreign subsidiaries, or foreign firms that are licensees of U.S. technology cannot sell products to a country in which the sale is considered by the U.S. government to affect national security. Furthermore, responsibility extends to the final destination of the product, regardless of the number of intermediaries that may be involved in the transfer of goods.

In the last century, an extensive export control system was created to slow the spread of sensitive technologies to the former Soviet Union, China, and other communist countries that

---

[60]Formerly known as the Bureau of Export Administration (BXA).

[61]For a primer on Commerce Department export controls, see "Introduction to Commerce Department Export Controls," http://www.bis.doc.gov, and select Export Control basics.

[62]Chester Dawson, "Japan to Ease Ban on Arms Exports," *The Wall Street Journal*, December 27, 2011.

were viewed as major threats to U.S. security. The control of the sale of goods considered to have a strategic and military value was extremely strict. But with the end of the Cold War, export controls were systematically dismantled until 1999, when a congressional committee reported Chinese espionage activities and American aerospace companies transferring sensitive technology irresponsibly. Following the report, legislation was passed again restricting the export of products or technologies that might be used by other countries for defense applications.

The events of September 11, 2001 added another set of restrictions related to weapons of mass destruction (WMD). Unfortunately, many of the products used in WMD are difficult to control because they have dual purposes; that is, they have legitimate uses as well as being important in manufacturing WMD. For example, Iraq, which was allowed to import medical equipment despite a U.N. embargo, purchased, under the pretext of medical benefits, six machines that destroy kidney stones. The manufacturer accepted the claim that Saddam Hussein was concerned about kidney stones in the Iraqi population and began shipping the machines. However, integral components of these machines are high-precision electronic switches that are also used to set off the chain reaction in thermonuclear weapons. When 120 additional switches as "spare parts" were ordered, a red flag went up, and the shipments were stopped.

Countless numbers of dual-purpose technologies are exported from the United States. A sticking point with dual-purpose exports is the intent of the buyer. Silicon Graphics Inc. (SGI) sold computer equipment to a Russian nuclear laboratory that contended it was for nonmilitary use, which would have been legal. However, the Department of Justice ruled that since the sale was made to a government-operated facility involved in both civil and noncivil activities, SGI should have applied for the correct export license. Thus, SGI paid a fine of $1 million plus a $500,000 fine for each of the export violations. National security laws prohibit a U.S. company, its subsidiaries, joint ventures, or licensees from selling controlled products without special permission from the U.S. government. The consequences of violation of the Trading with the Enemy Act can be severe: fines, prison sentences, and, in the case of foreign companies, economic sanctions.

Exports are controlled for the protection and promotion of human rights, as a means of enforcing foreign policy, because of national shortages, to control technology, and for a host of other reasons the U.S. government deems necessary to protect its best interests. In years past, the government restricted trade with South Africa (human rights) and restricted the sale of wheat to the Soviet Union in retaliation for its invasion of Afghanistan (foreign policy). Currently, the government restricts trade with Iran (foreign policy)[63] and the sale of leading-edge electronics (control of technology), and it prohibits the export of pesticides that have not been approved for use in the United States (to avoid the return of residue of unauthorized pesticides in imported food and protect U.S. consumers from the so-called circle of poison). In each of these cases, U.S. law binds U.S. businesses, regardless of where they operate.

Determining Export Requirements	The first step when complying with export licensing regulations is to determine the appropriate license for the product. Products exported from the United States require a general or a validated export license, depending on the product, where it is going, the end use, and the final user. The *general license* permits exportation of certain products that are not subject to EAR control with nothing more than a declaration of the type of product, its value, and its destination. The *validated license,* issued only on formal applications, is a specific document authorizing exportation within specific limitations designated under the EAR.

The responsibility of determining if a license is required rests with the exporter. This is a key point! The steps necessary to determine the type of license required and/or if an item can be shipped are as follows:

- The exporter is responsible for selecting the proper classification number, known as the *Export Control Classification Number (ECCN),* for the item to be exported. The ECCN leads to a description in the *Commerce Control List (CCL),* which indicates the exportability status of the item.

---

[63]Most recently the United States has both punished companies selling to Iran, while lifting restrictions on others. See Rick Gladstone, "U.S. Issues Penalties over Violations of Iran Sanctions," *The New York Times,* February 17, 2014, p. A3; "U.S. Permits Export to Iran of Plane Parts," *Reuters,* April 5, 2014, online.

Chinese air force officers undergo a training session on the latest command center instruments at a training school in Beijing. China successfully test-fired a new type of long-range ground-to-ground missile within its territory as tensions between China and Taiwan intensified after Taiwan's president declared that relations between Taipei and Beijing should be regarded as "special state-to-state relations." Additionally, China and the United States have both shot down their own "errant" satellites with missiles. Much of the electronic technology used in long-range missiles is dual-use; that is, the technology can be used for both nonmilitary and military applications. It is the exporter's responsibility to ensure that the final user of restricted dual-use products complies with export restrictions.

- The exporter must decide from the CCL if the items have end-use restrictions, for example, use in nuclear, chemical, and biological weapons. The exporter must also determine if the product has a dual use, that is, if it can be used in both commercial and restricted applications.

- The exporter is responsible for determining the ultimate end customer and end uses of the product, regardless of the initial buyer. This step includes carefully screening end users and uses of the product to determine if the final destination of the product is to an unapproved user or for an unapproved use. U.S. law requires firms to avoid shipments if the firm has knowledge that customers will use its products for illegal purposes or resell the product to unauthorized end users.

As is true of all the export mechanics that an exporter encounters, the details of exporting must be followed to the letter. Good record keeping, as well as verifying the steps undertaken in establishing the proper ECCN and evaluating the intentions of end users and end uses, is important should a disagreement arise between the exporter and the Bureau of Industry and Security. Penalties can entail denial of export privileges, fines, or both. For example, a 5-year denial of export privileges was imposed on a resident of Pittsfield, Massachusetts, based on his conviction of illegally exporting 150 riot shields to Romania without the required export license. At the time of the shipment, the riot shields were controlled for export worldwide for foreign policy reasons.

ELAIN, STELA, ERIC, and SNAP

Although the procedure for acquiring an export license may seem tedious on first reading, four electronic services facilitate the paperwork and reduce the time necessary to acquire export licenses.

- **ELAIN** (Export License Application and Information Network) enables exporters that have authorization to submit license applications via the Internet for all commodities except supercomputers to all free-world destinations. When approved, licensing decisions are conveyed back to the exporters via the Internet.

- **STELA** (System for Tracking Export License Applications), an automated voice-response system for tracking applications, can be accessed using a touch-tone phone. It provides applicants with the status of their license and classification applications and is available 24 hours a day, seven days a week. STELA can give exporters authority to ship their goods for those licenses approved without conditions.

- **ERIC** (Electronic Request for Item Classification), a supplementary service to ELAIN, allows an exporter to submit commodity classification requests via the Internet to the Bureau of Export administration.

- **SNAP** (Simplified Network Application Process), an alternative to paper license submissions, enables an exporter to submit export and re-export applications, high-performance computer notices, and commodity classification requests via the Internet. Acknowledgments of submissions will be received the same day, and electronic facsimiles of export licenses and other validations can be obtained online. SNAP is one of the changes made by the Department of Commerce to move it from being a paper-based bureaucracy to an all-digital department.

Summary

Businesses face a multitude of problems in their efforts to develop successful marketing programs. Not the least of these problems is the varying legal systems of the world and their effect on business transactions. Just as political climate, cultural differences, local geography, different business customs, and the stage of economic development must be taken into account, so must such legal questions as jurisdictional and legal recourse in disputes, protection of intellectual property rights, extended U.S. law enforcement, and enforcement of antitrust legislation by U.S. and foreign governments. A primary marketing task is to develop a plan that will be enhanced, or at least not adversely affected, by these and other environmental elements. New to the international legal scene is the Internet, which, by its nature, creates a new set of legal entanglements, many of which have yet to be properly addressed. One thing is certain: The freedom that now exists on the World Wide Web will be only a faint memory before long. The myriad questions created by different laws and different legal systems indicate that the prudent path to follow at all stages of foreign marketing operations is one leading to competent counsel, well versed in the intricacies of the international legal environment.

Key Terms

Common law	Marxist–socialist tenets	Litigation	Registration
Code law	Conciliation	Prior use	Cybersquatters (CSQs)
Islamic law	Arbitration		

Questions

1. Define the key terms listed above.
2. How does the international marketer determine which legal system will have jurisdiction when legal disputes arise?
3. Discuss the state of international commercial law.
4. Discuss the limitations of jurisdictional clauses in contracts.
5. What is the "objective theory of jurisdiction"? How does it apply to a firm doing business within a foreign country?
6. Discuss some of the reasons seeking an out-of-court settlement in international commercial legal disputes is probably better than suing.
7. Illustrate the procedure generally followed in international commercial disputes when settled under the auspices of a formal arbitration tribunal.
8. What are intellectual property rights? Why should a company in international marketing take special steps to protect them?
9. In many code-law countries, registration rather than prior use establishes ownership of intellectual property rights. Comment.
10. Discuss the advantages to the international marketer arising from the existence of the various international conventions on trademarks, patents, and copyrights.
11. "The legal environment of the foreign marketer takes on an added dimension of importance since there is no single uniform international commercial law which governs foreign business transactions." Comment.
12. Why is conciliation a better way to resolve a commercial dispute than arbitration?
13. Differentiate between conciliation and arbitration.
14. Assume you are a vice president in charge of a new business-to-business e-commerce division of a well-known major international auto parts manufacturer. A cybersquatter has registered the company name as a domain name. What are your options to secure the domain name for your company? Discuss the steps you should take to ensure worldwide protection of your domain name.
15. Discuss the issues of a website owner being liable for information posted on the site.
16. Discuss the motives of a cybersquatter. What recourse does a company have to defend itself against a cybersquatter?

Chapter 8

Developing a Global Vision through Marketing Research

CHAPTER LEARNING OBJECTIVES

What you should learn from Chapter 8:

LO1 The importance of problem definition in international research

LO2 The problems of availability and use of secondary data

LO3 Sources of secondary data

LO4 Quantitative and qualitative research methods

LO5 Multicultural sampling and its problems in less-developed countries

LO6 Using international marketing research

Global Perspective

JAPAN—TEST MARKET FOR THE WORLD

It was 10:51 p.m. in Tokyo, and suddenly Google was hit with a two-minute spike in searches from Japanese mobile phones. "We were wondering: Was it spam? Was it a system error?" says Ken Tokusei, Google's mobile chief in Japan. A quick call to carrier KDDI revealed that it was neither. Instead, millions of cell phone users had pulled up Google's search box after a broadcaster offered free ringtone downloads of the theme song from *The Man Who Couldn't Marry*, a popular TV show, but had only briefly flashed the web address where the tune was available.

The surge in traffic came as a big surprise to Tokusei and his team. They had assumed that a person's location was the key element of most mobile Internet searches, figuring that users were primarily interested in maps of the part of town they happened to be, timetables for the train home, or the address of the closest yakitori restaurant. The data from KDDI indicated that many Japanese were just as likely to use Google's mobile searches from the couch as from a Ginza street corner.

Japan's cell-phone-toting masses, it seems, have a lot to teach the Internet giant. The country has become a vast lab for Google as it tries to refine mobile search technology. That's because Japan's 110 million cell phone users represent the most diverse—and discriminating—pool of mobile subscribers on the planet. Although Google also does plenty of testing elsewhere, the Japanese are often more critical because they are as likely to tap into the Internet with a high-tech phone as a PC and can do so at speeds rivaling fixed-line broadband. And because Japanese carriers have offered such services for years, plenty of websites are formatted for cell phones.

Tokyo's armies of fashion-obsessed shopaholics have long made the city figure prominently on the map of Western designers. Sure, the suit and tie remain the uniform of the salaryman, but for originality, nothing rivals Tokyo teenyboppers, who cycle in and out of fads faster than a schoolgirl can change out of her uniform and into Goth-Loli gear. (Think Little Bo Peep meets Sid Vicious.) For American and European brands, these young people are a wellspring of ideas that can be recycled for consumers back home (see Crossing Borders 13.3).

But now, instead of just exporting Tokyo cool, some savvy foreign companies are starting to use Japan as a testing ground for new concepts. They're offering products in Japan before they roll them out globally, and more Western retailers are opening new outlets in Tokyo to keep an eye on trends. Ohio-based Abercrombie & Fitch and Sweden's H&M (Hennes & Mauritz) set up shop in Tokyo, and Spain's Zara is expected to double its store count to 50 over the next 3 years. "Twenty-five or 30 years ago, major brands tested their new products in New York," says Mitsuru Sakuraba, who spent 20 years at French fashion house Charles Jourdan. "Now Japan has established a presence as a pilot market."

Some Western companies also have signed on with local partners who can better read the Japanese market. Gola, an English brand of athletic shoes and apparel, has teamed up with EuroPacific (Japan) Ltd., a Tokyo-based retailer of fashion footwear. EuroPacific tweaks Gola's designs for the Japanese market and, a few years ago, came up with the idea of pitching shin-high boxing boots to women. They were a hit with Japanese teens and twenty-somethings, prompting Gola to try offering them in other markets. "They've sold a hell of a lot in Europe," says EuroPacific Director Steve Sneddon.

Sources: Ian Rowley, Hiroko Tashiro, "Testing What's Hot in the Cradle of Cool," *BusinessWeek*, May 7, 2007, p. 46. Used with permission. Kenji Hall, "Japan: Google's Real-Life Lab," *BusinessWeek*, February 25, 2008, pp. 55–57. Used with permission. "Three Windows on Japan," Japan External Trade Organization, 2012, online; World Bank, *World Development Indicators*, 2015.

It's crucial for top executives to get away from their desks and spend time in the marketplace. While detailed marketing research reports are important, decisions at the very top of the largest corporations must still be informed by a sense of the market and customers, obtainable only through direct contact by top executives. Here we see Steven Jobs (left) and Bill Gates (right) going east and west talking with and learning from their customers in the most direct way. Both had heavy international travel schedules, and both found face-to-face meetings with foreign vendors, partners, customers, and regulators to be an inescapable part of trying to understand their international markets. We will all miss Steve Jobs's brilliant marketing imagination and his trademark personal presentations to Apple enthusiasts. Most recently, to mark the twentieth anniversary of Microsoft's entry into Mexico, Gates played and lost a game of Xbox 360 soccer to Mexican national player Rafael Marquez. We wonder: Did he throw the game? We might have also pictured Micha Benoliel, CEO of Open Garden, the developer of FireChat we mentioned in Chapter 1. He was there observing how his firm's new offering was being used in the Hong Kong protests. Facebook's Mark Zuckerberg is learning Chinese and traveling there for similar reasons.[1]

Information is the key component in developing successful marketing strategies, avoiding major marketing blunders, and promoting efficient exchange systems.[2] Information needs range from the general data required to assess market opportunities to specific market information for decisions about product, promotion, distribution, and price. Sometimes the information can be bought from trusted research vendors or supplied by internal marketing research staff. But sometimes even the highest-level executives have to "get their shoes dirty" by putting in the miles, talking to key customers, and directly observing the marketplace in action.[3] Both international and local interpersonal networks are crucial resources for executive decision making.[4] As an enterprise broadens its scope of operations to include international markets, the need for current, accurate information is magnified. Indeed, some researchers maintain that entry into a fast developing, new-to-the-firm foreign market is one of the most daunting and ambiguous strategic decisions an executive can face. A marketer must find the most accurate and reliable data possible within the limits imposed by time, cost, and the present state of the art.

[1]Vindu Goel, Austin Ramzy, and Paul Mozur, "Facebook Lures China, In Mandarin," *The New York Times*, October 24, 2014, pp. B1, 2.

[2]Sudita Basu, John Dickaut, Gary Hecht, Kristy Towry, and Gregory Waymire, "Record Keeping Alters Economic History by Promoting Reciprocity," *PNAS* 106, no. 4 (2009), pp. 1009–14.

[3]Peter Drucker's wisdom improves with age. In his *The Wall Street Journal* article of May 11, 1990 (p. A15), he eloquently the case for direct observation of the marketplace by even the most senior executives. For the most substantive argument in that same vein, see Gerald Zaltman's description of emotional aspects of managerial decision making in "Rethinking Market Research: Putting People Back In," *Journal of Marketing Research* 34 (November 1997), pp. 424–37. Or check Ed Fuller's excellent book on the topic, *You Can't made Lead with Your Feet on the Desk* (New York: Wiley, 2011). Executives also learn about the "big picture" of the international business environment from mass media sources. Unfortunately, the effort to collect news around the world is shrinking fast as newspapers continue to cut reporting staffs, particularly at their international bureaus.

[4]Daniel Z. Levin and Helena Barnard, "Connections to Distant Knowledge: Interpersonal Ties between More- and Less-Developed Countries," *Journal of International Business Studies* 44, no. 7 (2013), pp. 676–98.

Marketing research is traditionally defined as the systematic gathering, recording, and analyzing of data to provide information useful to marketing decision making. Although the research processes and methods are basically the same, whether applied in Columbus, Ohio, or Colombo, Sri Lanka, international marketing research involves two additional complications. First, information must be communicated across cultural boundaries. That is, executives in Chicago must be able to "translate" their research questions into terms that consumers in Guangzhou, China, can understand. Then the Chinese answers must be put into terms (i.e., reports and data summaries) that American managers can comprehend. Fortunately, there are often internal staff and research agencies that are quite experienced in these kinds of cross-cultural communication tasks.

Second, the environments within which the research tools are applied are often different in foreign markets. Rather than acquire new and exotic methods of research, the international marketing researcher must develop the capability for imaginative and deft applications of tried and tested techniques in sometimes totally strange milieus. The mechanical problems of implementing foreign marketing research often vary from country to country. Within a foreign environment, the frequently differing emphases on the kinds of information needed, the often limited variety of appropriate tools and techniques available, and the difficulty of implementing the research process constitute challenges facing most international marketing researchers.

This chapter deals with the operational problems encountered in gathering information in foreign countries for use by international marketers. The emphasis is on those elements of data generation that usually prove especially troublesome in conducting research in an environment other than the United States.

Breadth and Scope of International Marketing Research

The basic difference between domestic and foreign market research is the broader scope needed for foreign research, necessitated by higher levels of uncertainty. Research can be divided into three types on the basis of information needs: (1) general information about the country, area, and/or market; (2) information necessary to forecast future marketing requirements by anticipating social, economic, consumer, and industry trends within specific markets or countries; and (3) specific market information used to make product, promotion, distribution, and price decisions and to develop marketing plans. In domestic operations, most emphasis is placed on the third type, gathering specific market information, because the other data are often available from secondary sources.

A country's political stability, cultural attributes, and geographical characteristics are some of the kinds of information not ordinarily gathered by domestic marketing research departments, but they are required for a sound assessment of a foreign market. This broader scope of international marketing research is reflected in Unisys Corporation's planning steps, which call for collecting and assessing the following types of information:

1. **Economic and demographic.** General data on growth in the economy, inflation, business cycle trends, and the like; profitability analysis for the division's products; specific industry economic studies; analysis of overseas economies; and key economic indicators for the United States and major foreign countries, as well as population trends, such as migration, immigration, and aging.

2. **Cultural, sociological, and political climate.** A general noneconomic review of conditions affecting the division's business. In addition to the more obvious subjects, it covers ecology, safety, and leisure time and their potential impacts on the division's business.

3. **Overview of market conditions.** A detailed analysis of market conditions that the division faces, by market segment, including international.

4. **Summary of the technological environment.** A summary of the state-of-the-art technology as it relates to the division's business, carefully broken down by product segments.

5. Competitive situation. A review of competitors' sales revenues, methods of market segmentation, products, and apparent strategies on an international scope.[5]

Such in-depth information is necessary for sound marketing decisions. For the domestic marketer, most such information has been acquired after years of experience with a single market, but in foreign countries, this information must be gathered for each new market.

There is a basic difference between information ideally needed and that which is collectible and/or used. Many firms engaged in foreign marketing do not make decisions with the benefit of the information listed.[6] Cost, time, and human elements are critical variables. Some firms have neither the appreciation for information nor adequate time or money for the implementation of research. As a firm becomes more committed to foreign marketing and the cost of possible failure increases, greater emphasis is placed on research.

The Research Process

A marketing research study is always a compromise dictated by the limits of time, cost, and the present state of the art. A key to successful research is a systematic and orderly approach to the collection and analysis of data. Whether a research program is conducted in New York or New Delhi, the research process should follow these steps:

1. Define the research problem and establish research objectives.
2. Determine the sources of information to fulfill the research objectives.
3. Consider the costs and benefits of the research effort.
4. Gather the relevant data from secondary or primary sources, or both.
5. Analyze, interpret, and summarize the results.
6. Effectively communicate the results to decision makers.

Although the steps in a research program are similar for all countries, variations and problems in implementation occur because of differences in cultural and economic development. Whereas the problems of research in England or Canada may be similar to those in the United States, research in Germany, South Africa, or Mexico may offer a multitude of difficult distinctions. These distinctions become apparent with the first step in the research process—formulation of the problem. The subsequent text sections illustrate some frequently encountered difficulties facing the international marketing researcher.

Defining the Problem and Establishing Research Objectives

LO1

The importance of problem definition in international research

After examining internal sources of data, the research process should begin with a definition of the research problem and the establishment of specific research objectives.[7] The major difficulty here is converting a series of often ambiguous business problems into tightly drawn and achievable research objectives. In this initial stage, researchers often embark on the research process with only a vague grasp of the total problem. A good example of such a loosely defined problem is that of Russian airline Aeroflot. The company undertook a branding study to inform its marketing decisions regarding improving its long-standing reputation for poor safety standards and unreliable service. This goal is a tough challenge for international marketing researchers.

[5]Apparently companies engage in corporate espionage. See Evan Ramstad, "Chip Executives Arrested in South Korea," *The Wall Street Journal*, February 3, 2010; John J. Fialka, "Hugger-Mugger in the Executive Suite," *The New York Times*, February 2, 2010, p. W10. Apparently governments also get into the industrial competitive intelligence game. See Ken Dilanian, "Russia, China Accused of Cyber Spying," *Los Angeles Times,* August 13, 2011, p. B2; Siobahn Gorman, "China Singled Out for Cyperspying," *The Wall Street Journal,* November 4, 2011.

[6]Bent Petersen, Torben Pedersen, and Marjorie A. Lyles, "Closing the Knowledge Gaps in Foreign Markets," *Journal of International Business Studies* 39, no. 7 (2008), pp. 1097–113.

[7]Scholars in the field also struggle with defining the problem. See Mike W. Peng, "Identifying the Big Question in International Business Research," *Journal of International Business Studies* 35, no. 2 (2004), pp. 99–108; Susan B. Douglas and C. Samuel Craig, "On Improving the Conceptual Foundations of International Marketing Research," *Journal of International Marketing* 14, no. 1 (2006), pp. 1–22.

This first, most crucial step in research is more critical in foreign markets because an unfamiliar environment tends to cloud problem definition. Researchers either fail to anticipate the influence of the local culture on the problem or fail to identify the self-reference criterion (SRC) and therefore treat the problem definition as if it were in the researcher's home environment. In assessing some foreign business failures, it becomes apparent that research was conducted, but the questions asked were more appropriate for the U.S. market than for the foreign one. For example, all of Disney's years of research and experience in keeping people happy standing in long lines could not help Disney anticipate the scope of the problems it would run into with Disneyland Paris. The firm's experience had been that the relatively homogeneous clientele at both the American parks and Tokyo Disneyland were cooperative and orderly when it came to queuing up. Actually, so are most British and Germans. But the rules about queuing in other countries such as Spain and Italy are apparently quite different, creating the potential for a new kind of intra-European "warfare" in the lines. Understanding and managing this multinational customer service problem has required new ways of thinking. Isolating the SRC and asking the right questions are crucial steps in the problem formulation stage.

Other difficulties in foreign research stem from failures to establish problem limits broad enough to include all relevant variables. Information on a far greater range of factors is necessary to offset the unfamiliar cultural background of the foreign market. Consider proposed research about consumption patterns and attitudes toward hot milk-based drinks. In the United Kingdom, hot milk-based drinks are considered to have sleep-inducing, restful, and relaxing properties and are traditionally consumed prior to bedtime. People in Thailand, however, drink the same hot milk-based drinks in the morning on the way to work and see them as invigorating, energy-giving, and stimulating. If one's only experience is the United States, the picture is further clouded, because hot milk-based drinks are frequently associated with cold weather, either in the morning or the evening, and for different reasons each time of day. The market researcher must be certain the problem definition is sufficiently broad to cover the whole range of response possibilities and not be clouded by his or her self-reference criterion.

Indeed, this clouding is a problem that Mattel Inc. ran into headlong. The company conducted a coordinated global research program using focus groups of children in several countries. Based on these findings, the firm cut back on customization and ignored local managers' advice by selling an unmodified Barbie globally. Not only was it dangerous to ignore the advice of local managers; it was also dangerous to ignore parents' opinions involving toys. Kids may like a blonde Barbie, but parents may not. Unfortunately, our predictions about Barbie in a previous edition of this book proved correct: As we mentioned in previous chapters, sales of blonde Barbie dramatically declined in several foreign markets following the marketing research error.

Once the problem is adequately defined and research objectives established, the researcher must determine the availability of the information needed. If the data are available—that is, if they have been collected already by some other agency—the researcher should then consult these **secondary data** sources.

Problems of Availability and Use of Secondary Data

LO2

The problems of availability and use of secondary data

The U.S. government provides comprehensive statistics for the United States; periodic censuses of U.S. population, housing, business, and agriculture are conducted and, in some cases, have been taken for over 100 years. Commercial sources, trade associations, management groups, and state and local governments provide the researcher with additional sources of detailed U.S. market information. Some describe the problem for American marketing researchers is sorting through too much data! Still others argue you can never have enough data.[8]

---

[8]"Open Data: The New Goldmine," *The Economist*, May 18, 2013, p. 73.

CROSSING BORDERS 8.1   Headache? Take Two Aspirin and Lie Down

Such advice goes pretty far in countries such as Germany, where Bayer invented aspirin more than 100 years ago, and the United States. But people in many places around the world don't share such Western views about medicine and the causes of disease. Many Asians, including Chinese, Filipinos, Koreans, Japanese, and Southeast Asians, believe illnesses such as headaches are the result of the imbalance between *yin* and *yang*. *Yin* is the feminine, passive principle that is typified by darkness, cold, or wetness. Alternatively, *yang* is the masculine, active principle associated with light, heat, or dryness. All things result from their combination, and bad things like headaches result from too much of one or the other. Acupuncture and moxibustion (heating crushed wormwood or other herbs on the skin) are common cures. Many Laotians believe pain can be caused by one of the body's 32 souls being lost or by sorcerers' spells. The exact cause is often determined by examining the yolk of a freshly broken egg. In other parts of the world, such as Mexico and Puerto

Rico, illness is believed to be caused by an imbalance of one of the four body humors: "blood—hot and wet; yellow bile—hot and dry; phlegm—cold and wet; and black bile—cold and dry." Even in the high-tech United States, many people believe that pain is often a "reminder from God" to behave properly.

Now Bayer is marketing aspirin as a preventive drug for other ailments, such as intestinal cancer and heart attack. But in many foreign markets for companies such as Bayer, a key question to be addressed in marketing research is how and to what extent aspirin can be marketed as a supplement to the traditional remedies. That is, will little white pills mix well with phlegm and black bile?

Sources: Larry A. Samovar, Richard E. Porter, and Lisa A. Stefani, *Communication between Cultures*, 3rd ed. (Belmont, CA: Wadsworth Publishing, 1998), pp. 224–25; the direct quote is from N. Dresser, *Multicultural Manners: New Rules for Etiquette for a Changing Society* (New York: John Wiley & Sons, 1996), p. 236; see also Andrew Jack, "The Serial Painkiller," *Financial Times*, October 27, 2011.

Availability of Data   While the quantity and quality of marketing-related data available in the United States is unmatched in other countries, things are improving.[9] The data available on and in Japan is a close second, and several European countries do a good job of collecting and reporting data. Indeed, on some dimensions, the quality of data collected in these latter countries can actually exceed that in the United States. However, in many countries, substantial data collection has been initiated only recently.[10] Through the continuing efforts of organizations such as the United Nations and the Organization for Economic Cooperation and Development (OECD), improvements are being made worldwide.

In addition, with the emergence of eastern European countries as potentially viable markets, a number of private and public groups are funding the collection of information to offset a lack of comprehensive market data. Several Japanese consumer goods manufacturers are coordinating market research on a corporate level and have funded dozens of research centers throughout eastern Europe. As market activity continues in eastern Europe and elsewhere, market information will improve in quantity and quality. To build a database on Russian consumers, one Denver, Colorado, firm used a novel approach to conduct a survey: It ran a questionnaire in Moscow's *Komsomolskaya Pravda* newspaper asking for replies to be sent to the company. The 350,000 replies received (3,000 by registered mail) attested to the willingness of Russian consumers to respond to marketing inquiries. The problems of availability, reliability, and comparability of data and of validating secondary data are described in the following sections.

Another problem relating to the availability of data is researchers' language skills. For example, though data are often copious regarding the Japanese market, being able to read Japanese is a requisite for accessing them, either online or in text. This problem may seem rather innocuous, but only those who have tried to maneuver through foreign data can appreciate the value of having a native speaker of the appropriate language on the research team.

[9]"The Government and the Geeks," *The Economist*, February 6, 2010, pp. 65–66.

[10]See GIS analyses based on the 2000 Census in China at http://www.geodemo.com, Demographic Consulting, Inc.

Reliability of Data

Available data may not have the level of reliability necessary for confident decision making for many reasons. Official statistics are sometimes too optimistic, reflecting national pride rather than practical reality, while tax structures and fear of the tax collector often adversely affect data.

Although not unique to them,[11] less developed countries are particularly prone to being both overly optimistic and unreliable in reporting relevant economic data about their countries.[12] China's National Statistics Enforcement Office recently acknowledged that it had uncovered about 60,000 instances of false statistical reports since beginning a crackdown on false data reporting several months earlier.[13] More recently the head of China's National Bureau of Statistics was fired for his involvement in an unfolding corruption scandal.[14] Seeking advantages or hiding failures, local officials, factory managers, rural enterprises, and others file fake numbers on everything from production levels to birthrates. For example, a petrochemical plant reported 1 year's output to be $20 million, 50 percent higher than its actual output of $13.4 million. Finally, if you believe the statistics, until 2000, the Chinese in Hong Kong were the world-champion consumers of fresh oranges—64 pounds per year per person, twice as much as Americans. However, apparently about half of all the oranges imported into Hong Kong, or some $30 million worth, were actually finding their way into the rest of China, where U.S. oranges were illegal.

Willful errors in the reporting of marketing data are not uncommon in the most industrialized countries either. Often print media circulation figures are purposely overestimated even in OECD countries. The European Union (EU) tax policies can affect the accuracy of reported data also. Production statistics are frequently inaccurate because these countries collect taxes on domestic sales. Thus, some companies shave their production statistics a bit to match the sales reported to tax authorities. Conversely, foreign trade statistics may be blown up slightly because each country in the European Union grants some form of export subsidy. Knowledge of such "adjusted reporting" is critical for a marketer who relies on secondary data for forecasting or estimating market demand.

Comparability of Data

LO3

Sources of secondary data

Comparability of available data is the third shortcoming faced by foreign marketers. In the United States, current sources of reliable and valid estimates of socioeconomic factors and business indicators are readily available. In other countries, especially those less developed, data can be many years out of date as well as having been collected on an infrequent and unpredictable schedule. Naturally, the rapid change in socioeconomic features being experienced in many of these countries makes the problem of currency a vital one. Furthermore, even though many countries are now gathering reliable data, there are generally no historical series with which to compare the current information. Comparability of data can even be a problem when the best commercial research firms collect data across countries, and managers are well advised to query their vendors about this problem.

A related problem is the manner in which data are collected and reported. Too frequently, data are reported in different categories or in categories much too broad to be of specific value. The term *supermarket*, for example, has a variety of meanings around the world. In Japan a supermarket is quite different from its American counterpart. Japanese supermarkets usually occupy two- or three-story structures; they sell foodstuffs, daily necessities, and clothing on respective floors. Some even sell furniture, electric home appliances, stationery, and sporting goods; some have a restaurant. General merchandise stores, shopping centers, and department stores are different from stores of the same name in the United States.

---

[11]Yes, even mistakes are made in the United States. Nielsen, the U.S. television research comapny, revealed its own problems recently. See Bill Carter and Emily Steel, "TV Ratings by Neilsen Had Errors for Months," *The New York Times*, October 11, 2014, pp. B1, 7.

[12]"Don't Lie to Me, Argentina," *The Economist*, February 25, 2012, p. 18.

[13]Hung-Gay Fung, Jot Yau, and Gaiyan Zhang, "Reported Trade Figure Discrepancy, Regulatory Arbitrage, and Round-Tripping: Evidence from the China–Hong Kong Trade Data," *Journal of International Business Studies* 42, no. 1 (2011), pp. 152–76.

[14]Neil Gough, "Mixed Signals for China: Conflicting Data Make It Tough to Tell Which Way the Economy is Headed," *The New York Times*, October 21, 2014, pp. B1, 7.

Validating Secondary Data

The shortcomings discussed here should be considered when using any source of information. Many countries have similarly high standards for the collection and preparation of data as those generally found in the United States, but secondary data from any source, including the United States, must be checked and interpreted carefully. As a practical matter, the following questions should be asked to effectively judge the reliability of secondary data sources:

1. Who collected the data? Would there be any reason for purposely misrepresenting the facts?
2. For what purposes were the data collected?
3. How (by what methodology) were the data collected?
4. Are the data internally consistent and logical in light of known data sources or market factors?

Checking the consistency of one set of secondary data with other data of known validity is an effective and often-used way of judging validity. For example, a researcher might check the sale of baby products with the number of women of childbearing age and birthrates, or the number of patient beds in hospitals with the sale of related hospital equipment. Such correlations can also be useful in estimating demand and forecasting sales. As is the case with many data sets, Hofstede's well-worn data sets described in Chapters 4 and 5 have proven valid vis-à-vis a variety of dependent variables, and it is still worthwhile to compare his measures of cultural values to other measures of the same variables.[15]

In general, the availability and accuracy of recorded secondary data increase as the level of economic development increases. There are exceptions; India is at a lower level of economic development than many countries but has accurate and relatively complete government-collected data.

Fortunately, interest in collecting high-quality statistical data rises as countries realize the value of extensive and accurate national statistics for orderly economic growth. This interest in improving the quality of national statistics has resulted in remarkable improvement in the availability of data over the last three decades. However, when no data are available or the secondary data sources are inadequate, it is necessary to begin the collection of primary data.

The appendix to this chapter includes a comprehensive listing of secondary data sources, including websites on a variety of international marketing topics. Indeed, almost all secondary data available on international markets can now be discovered or acquired via the Internet. For example, the most comprehensive statistics regarding international finances, demographics, consumption, exports, and imports are accessible through a single source, the U.S. Department of Commerce at http://www.stat-usa.gov. Many other governmental, institutional, and commercial sources of data can be tapped into on the Internet as well. You can find supplementary information about this text at http://www.mhhe.com/cateora17e.

Gathering Primary Data: Quantitative and Qualitative Research

LO4
Quantitative and qualitative research methods

If, after seeking all reasonable secondary data sources, research questions are still not adequately answered, the market researcher must collect primary data—that is, data collected specifically for the particular research project at hand.[16] The researcher may question the firm's sales representatives,

[15] Linhui Tang and Peter E. Koveos, "A Framework to Update Hofstede's Cultural Values Indices: Economic Dynamics and Institutional Stability," *Journal of International Business Studies* 39, no. 6 (2008), pp. 1045–64; Robbert Maseland and Andre van Hoorn, "Explaining the Negative Correlation between Values and Practices: A Note on the Hofstede-GLOBE Debate," *Journal of International Business Studies* 40, no. 3 (2009), pp. 527–32.

[16] A series of articles in the *Journal of International Business Studies* 42, no. 5 (2011), effectively makes the case for the growing importance of qualitative research methods: See Julian Birkingshaw, Mary Yoko Brannen, and Rosalie Tung, "From a Distance and Generalizable to up Close and Grounded: Reclaiming a Place for Qualitative Methods in International Business Research," pp. 573–81; Yves Doz, "Qualitative Research for International Business," pp. 582–90; Robert A. Burgleman, "Bridging History and Reductionism: A Key Role for Longitudinal Qualitative Research," pp. 591–601; and D. Eleanor Westney and John Van Maanen, "The Casual Ethnography of the Executive Suite," pp. 602–7.

distributors, middlemen, and/or customers to get appropriate market information. Marketing research methods can be grouped into two basic types: quantitative and qualitative research. In both methods, the marketer is interested in gaining knowledge about the market.

In *quantitative research*, usually a large number of respondents are asked to reply either verbally or in writing to structured questions using a specific response format (such as yes/no) or to select a response from a set of choices. Questions are designed to obtain specific responses regarding aspects of the respondents' behavior, intentions, attitudes, motives, and demographic characteristics. Quantitative research provides the marketer with responses that can be presented with precise estimations. The structured responses received in a survey can be summarized in percentages, averages, or other statistics. For example, 76 percent of the respondents prefer product A over product B, and so on. Survey research is generally associated with quantitative research, and the typical instrument used is a questionnaire administered by personal interview, mail, telephone, and, most recently, over the Internet.

Scientific studies, including tightly designed experiments, often are conducted by engineers and chemists in product-testing laboratories around the world. There, product designs and formulas are developed and tested in consumer usage situations. Often those results are integrated with consumer opinions gathered in concurrent survey studies. One of the best examples of this kind of marketing research comes from Tokyo. You may not know it, but the Japanese are the world champions of bathroom and toilet technology. Japan's biggest company in that industry, Toto, has spent millions of dollars developing and testing consumer products. Thousands of people have collected data (using survey techniques) about the best features of a toilet, and at the company's "human engineering laboratory," volunteers sit in a Toto bathtub with electrodes strapped to their skulls to measure brain waves and "the effects of bathing on the human body." Toto is now introducing one of its high-tech (actually low-tech compared with what it offers in Japan) toilets in the U.S. market. It's a $600 seat, lid, and control panel that attaches to the regular American bowl. It features a heated seat and deodorizing fan.

Over the years, Lego has five times aimed its strategic initiatives at girls, with little success. On its sixth try, the company has spent $40 million globally. The new campaign and associated products were designed based primarily on qualitative research methods. The company recruited top product designers and sales strategists from within the firm, had them join forces with outside consultants, and dispatched them in small teams to shadow girls and interview their families over a period of months in Germany, South Korea, the United Kingdom, and the United States. This "Olivia" figure attempts to reflect the girls' reported preferences for thinner shapes and pastel colors, rather than the boxy, primary-colored toys for boys.[19] This time the new product line has been a huge success, boosting Lego's profits by more than $1 billion in the most recent year.[20]

In *qualitative research*, if questions are asked, they are almost always open-ended or in-depth, and unstructured responses, including storytelling,[17] that reflect the person's thoughts and feelings on the subject are sought. Consumers' first impressions about products may be useful. Direct observation of consumers in choice or product usage situations is another important qualitative approach to marketing research.[18] One researcher spent two months observing birthing practices in American and Japanese hospitals to gain insights for the export of healthcare services. Nissan Motors sent a researcher to live with an American family (renting a room in their house for six weeks) to directly observe how Americans use their cars. Most recently the British retailer TESCO

[17]Martine Cardel Gertsen and Anne-Marie Soderberg, "Intercultural Collaboration Stories: On Narrative Inquiry and Analysis as Tools for Research in International Business," *Journal of International Business Studies* 42, no. (2011), pp. 787–804; Julien Cayla and Eric Arnould, "Ethnographic Stories for Market Learning," *Journal of Marketing* 77, no. 4 (July 2013), pp. 1–16.

[18]Christian Madsbjerg and Mikkel B. Rasmussen, "An Anthropologist Walks into a Bar . . ." *Harvard Business Review*, March 2014, pp. 80–88.

[19]Brad Wieners, "Lego Is for Girls," *Bloomberg Businessweek,* December 19, 2011, pp. 68–73.

[20]Rachel Abrams, "Short-Lived Science Line from Lego Girls," *The New York Times*, August 21, 2014, online.

sent teams to live with American families to observe their shopping behaviors in advance of its new entry in the U.S. supermarket battleground with Walmart and others. Anderson Worldwide, Nynex, and Texas Commerce Bank have all employed anthropologists who specialize in observational and in-depth interviews in their marketing research. Qualitative research seeks to interpret what the people in the sample are like—their outlooks, their feelings, the dynamic interplay of their feelings and ideas, their attitudes and opinions, and their resulting actions. The most often used form of qualitative questioning is the focus group interview. However, oftentimes, in-depth interviewing of individuals can be just as effective while consuming far fewer resources.

Qualitative research is used in international marketing research to formulate and define a problem more clearly and to determine relevant questions to be examined in subsequent research. It is also used to stimulate ad message ideas and where interest centers on gaining an understanding of a market rather than quantifying relevant aspects. For example, a small group of key executives at Solar Turbines International, a division of Caterpillar Tractor Company, called on key customers at their offices around the world. They discussed in great depth, with both financial managers and production engineers, potential applications and the demand for a new size of gas-turbine engine the company was considering developing. The data and insights gained during the interviews to a large degree confirmed the validity of the positive demand forecasts produced internally through macroeconomic modeling. The multimillion-dollar project was then implemented. During the discussions, new product features were suggested by the customer personnel that proved most useful in the development efforts.

Qualitative research is also helpful in revealing the impact of sociocultural factors on behavior patterns and in developing research hypotheses that can be tested in subsequent studies designed to quantify the concepts and relevant relationships uncovered in qualitative data collection. Procter & Gamble has been one of the pioneers of this type of research—the company has systematically gathered consumer feedback for some 70 years. It was the first company to conduct in-depth consumer research in China. In the mid-1990s, P&G began working with the Chinese Ministry of Health to develop dental hygiene programs that have now reached millions of consumers there.

Oftentimes the combination of qualitative and quantitative research proves quite useful in consumer markets and business-to-business marketing settings as well. In one study, the number of personal referrals used in buying financial services in Japan was found to be much greater than that in the United States.[21] The various comments made by the executives during interviews in both countries proved invaluable in interpreting the quantitative results, suggesting implications for managers and providing ideas for further research. Likewise, the comments of sales managers in Tokyo during in-depth interviews helped researchers understand why individual financial incentives did not work with Japanese sales representatives.[22]

As we shall see later in this chapter, using either research method in international marketing research is subject to a number of difficulties brought about by the diversity of cultures and languages encountered.

Problems of Gathering Primary Data

The problems of collecting primary data in foreign countries are different only in degree from those encountered in the United States. Assuming the research problem is well defined and the objectives are properly formulated, the success of primary research hinges on the ability of the researcher to get correct and truthful information that addresses the research objectives. Most problems in collecting primary data in international marketing research stem from cultural differences among countries and range from the inability or unwillingness[23] of respondents to communicate their opinions to inadequacies in questionnaire translation.

[21]R. Bruce Money, "Word-of-Mouth Referral Sources for Buyers of International Corporate Financial Services," *Journal of World Business* 35, no. 3 (Fall 2000), pp. 314–29.

[22]R. Bruce Money and John L. Graham, "Sales Person Performance, Pay, and Job Satisfaction: Tests of a Model Using Data Collected in the U.S. and Japan," *Journal of International Business Studies* 30, no. 1 (1999), pp. 149–72.

[23]Fang Wu, Rudolf R. Sinkovics, S. Tamer Cavusgil, and Anthony S. Roath, "Overcoming Export Manufacturers' Dilemma in International Expansion," *Journal of International Business Studies* 38 (2007), pp. 283–302.

CROSSING BORDERS 8.2	**Was Orwell Right in 1949 When He Wrote *1984*?**

Consider the list of what we will loosely call "marketing research" tools circa 2015.

1. Noldus Information Technology Inc. provides facial expression reading technology to measure emotional responses to marketing stimuli (see www.noldus.com and Chapter 16 for more details on this issue.

2. Facial recognition systems and other biometrics were a $7.2 billion business already in 2012.

3. Tax authorities in a number of countries are using Google Inc. Street View service and dedicated iPhone apps to provide evidence in tax fraud cases.

4. Your cell phone contains locational beacons that let electronic readers in retail stores know you are nearby and can deliver a huge variety of marketing communications based on that information. Also, retailers use their security cameras for purposes other than security.

5. High-tech trash cans in London can keep track of who walks by via monitoring their cell phone beacons. Protests forced authorities there to stop the monitoring.

6. Samsung recently reported the theft of two prototype, super-thin televisions from a shipment of 60 sets headed to a Berlin tradeshow. All indications are that a corporate spies stole them.

7. Both the U.S. and European governments are looking to punish corporate spies for cyberattacks and commercial and trade-secret thefts in dozens of American companies.

8. As mentioned earlier, even German Chancellor Angela Merkel's cell phone calls have been listened into by the U.S. National Security Agency.

9. Then there's Target. The father of an unmarried teenager learned about his daughter's pregnancy from the persistent coupons sent for pregnancy-related products based on a prediction of pregnancy, including an approximate due date, by the company's data crawlers.

10. In 2012, Facebook manipulated the emotions of a large sample of users in a psychological experiment.

11. Pro-democracy protestors in Hong Kong fear the police are tracking their online footprints looking for organizers and instigators.

12. Finally, our favorite—an electroencephalogram headset for dogs that measures brain activity combined with appropriate software to determine if Fido likes one dog food better than another.

Privacy and security concerns vary across countries. The European Court of Justice ruled "in a broadly worded directive, that all individuals in the countries within its jurisdiction had the right to prohibit Google from linking to items that were 'inadequate, irrelevant or no longer relevant, or excessive in relation to the purposes for which they were process in the light of the time that has elapsed.'" One of the early consequences of the ruling is that Google has removed aspects of its name-search capability in some European versions of its search engine. The basic issue comes down to an American primary cultural value for freedom of speech versus an equally important value placed on privacy by Europeans. Some interpretations of the European law demand that marketing researchers ask for permission to collect their data and that data banks that include personal information cannot be linked.

Lawyers on both sides of the Atlantic will make fortunes in this fight about the legality of these "marketing research" issues. Our question for you, the future international marketer, is where will you draw the line—when is the use of these hidden privacy intrusive research methods ethical? Using them all on dogs is probably OK!

Sources: Natasha Singer, "Never Forgetting a Face," *The New York Times*, May 18, 2014, pp. B1,2; Marcin Sobczyk, "In Lithuania, the Tax Man Cometh Right after the Google Car Passeth," *The Wall Street Journal*, May 30, 2013, online; Harry McCracken, "Nowhere to Hide: How Retailers Can Find—and Up-Sell—You in the Aisles," *Time*, March 31, 2014, p. 20; Janet Stobart, "London Tosses out Spying Recycle Bins," *Los Angeles Times*, August 15, 2013, p. A3; Jun Yang and Kyunghee Park, "The Curious Case of Samsung's Missing TVs," *Bloomberg BusinessWeek*, December 3–9, 2012, pp. 19–21; Slobhan Gorman and Jared A. Favole, "U.S. Ups Ante for Spying on Firms," *The Wall Street Journal*, February 21, 2013, pp. A1, A16; Danny Hakim, "Europe Moves to Protect Companies' Trade Secrets," *The New York Times*, November 13, 2013, p. B8; Kashmir Hill, "How Target Figured out a Teen Girl was Pregnant before Her Father Did," *Forbes*, February 16, 2012; Michael Cieply, "After an Uproar, European Regulators Question Facebook on Psychological Testing," *The New York Times*, July 3, 2014, p. B3; Michael Forsythe and Alan Wong, "Protesters in Hong Kong on Edge as Police Track their Online Footprints," *The New York Times*, October 28, 2014, online; Nick Leiber, "Innovation: Dog Reader," *Bloomberg BusinessWeek*, October 27–November 2, 2014, p. 45; Jeffrey Toobin, "The Solace of Oblivion: In Europe the Right to Be Forgotten," *New Yorker*, September 29, 2012, online.

Ability to Communicate Opinions

The ability to express attitudes and opinions about a product or concept depends on the respondent's ability to recognize the usefulness and value of such a product or concept. It is difficult for a person to formulate needs, attitudes, and opinions about goods whose use may not be understood, that are not in common use within the community, or that have never been available. For example, someone who has never had the benefits of an office computer will be unable to express accurate feelings or provide any reasonable information about purchase intentions, likes, or dislikes concerning a new computer software package. The more complex the concept, the more difficult it is to design research that will help the respondent communicate meaningful opinions and reactions. Under these circumstances, the creative capabilities of the international marketing researcher are challenged.

No company has had more experience in trying to understand consumers with communication limitations than Gerber. Babies may be their business, but babies often can't talk, much less fill out a questionnaire. Over the years, Gerber has found that talking to and observing both infants and their mothers are important in marketing research. In one study, Gerber found that breast-fed babies adapted to solid food more quickly than bottle-fed babies because breast milk changes flavor depending on what the mother has eaten. For example, infants were found to suck longer and harder if their mother had recently eaten garlic. In another study, weaning practices were studied around the world. Indian babies were offered lentils served on a finger. Some Nigerian children got fermented sorghum, fed by the grandmother through the funnel of her hand. In some parts of tropical Asia, mothers "food-kissed" prechewed vegetables into their babies' mouths. Hispanic mothers in the United States tend to introduce baby food much earlier than non-Hispanic mothers and continue it well beyond the first year. All this research helps the company decide which products are appropriate for which markets. For example, the Vegetable and Rabbit Meat and the Freeze-Dried Sardines and Rice flavors popular in Poland and Japan, respectively, most likely won't make it to American store shelves.

Willingness to Respond

Cultural differences offer the best explanation for the unwillingness or the inability of many to respond to research surveys. The role of the male, the suitability of personal gender-based inquiries, and other gender-related issues can affect willingness to respond. In some countries, the husband not only earns the money but also usually dictates exactly how it is to be spent. Because the husband controls the spending, it is he, not the wife, who should be questioned to determine preferences and demand for many consumer goods. In some countries, women would never consent to be interviewed by a man or a stranger. A French Canadian woman does not like to be questioned and is likely to be reticent in her responses. In some societies, a man would certainly consider it beneath his dignity to discuss shaving habits or brand preference in personal clothing with anyone—most emphatically not a female interviewer.

Anyone asking questions about any topic from which tax assessment could be inferred is immediately suspected of being a tax agent. Citizens of many countries do not feel the same legal and moral obligations to pay their taxes as do U.S. citizens. Tax evasion is thus an accepted practice for many and a source of pride for the more adept. Where such an attitude exists, taxes are often seemingly arbitrarily assessed by the government, which results in much incomplete or misleading information being reported. One of the problems revealed by the government of India in a recent population census was the underreporting of tenants by landlords trying to hide the actual number of people living in houses and flats. The landlords had been subletting accommodations illegally and were concealing their activities from the tax department.

In the United States, publicly held corporations are compelled by the Securities and Exchange Commission (SEC) to disclose certain operating figures on a periodic basis. In many European countries, however, such information is seldom if ever released and then most reluctantly. For example, in Germany attempts to enlist the cooperation of merchants in setting up an in-store study of shelf inventory and sales information ran into strong resistance because of suspicions and a tradition of competitive secrecy. The resistance was overcome by the researcher's willingness to approach the problem step by step. As the retailer gained confidence in the researcher and realized the value of the data gathered, more and more requested information was provided. Besides the reluctance of businesses to respond to surveys, local politicians in underdeveloped countries may interfere with studies in the belief that they could be subversive and must be stopped or hindered. A few moments with local politicians can prevent days of delay. The incentives for completion of

Midnight in New Delhi—both customer service and telephone survey research are being outsourced to lower-wage English-speaking countries. Cost savings of such outsourcing must be balanced with consumer reluctance in cross-cultural communication settings, particularly those involving voluntary responses to marketing research.

questionnaires will also vary across cultures—some that may work in the United States will not in other countries, particularly in those that place a higher value on privacy.

Although such cultural differences may make survey research more difficult to conduct, it is possible. In some communities, locally prominent people could open otherwise closed doors; in other situations, professional people and local students have been used as interviewers because of their knowledge of the market. Less direct measurement techniques and nontraditional data analysis methods may also be more appropriate. In one study, Japanese supermarket buyers rated the nationality of brands (foreign or domestic) as relatively unimportant in making stocking decisions when asked directly; however, when an indirect, paired-comparison questioning technique was used, brand nationality proved to be the most important factor.[24]

Sampling in Field Surveys

LO5

Multicultural sampling and its problems in less-developed countries

The greatest problem in sampling stems from the lack of adequate demographic data and available lists from which to draw meaningful samples. If current, reliable lists are not available, sampling becomes more complex and generally less reliable. In many countries, telephone directories, cross-index street directories, census tract and block data, and detailed social and economic characteristics of the population being studied are not available on a current basis, if at all. The researcher has to estimate characteristics and population parameters, sometimes with little basic data on which to build an accurate estimate.

To add to the confusion, in some South American, Mexican, and Asian cities, street maps are unavailable, and in some Asian metropolitan areas, streets are not identified and houses are not numbered. In contrast, one of the positive aspects of research in Japan and Taiwan is the availability and accuracy of census data on individuals. In these countries, when a household moves, it is required to submit up-to-date information to a centralized government agency before it can use communal services such as water, gas, electricity, and education.

The effectiveness of various methods of communication (mail, telephone, personal interview, and Internet) in surveys is limited. In many countries, telephone ownership is extremely low, making telephone surveys virtually worthless unless the survey is intended to cover only the wealthy.[25] In Sri Lanka, fewer than 19 percent of the residents have landline telephones and less than 7 percent Internet access—that is, only the wealthy.

---

[24]Frank Alpert, Michael Kamins, Tomoaki Sakano, Naoto Onzo, and John L. Graham, "Retail Buyer Beliefs, Attitudes, and Behaviors toward Pioneer and Me-Too Follower Brands: A Comparative Study of Japan and the United States," *International Marketing Review* 18, no. 2 (2001), pp. 160–87.

[25]Paula Vicente and Elizabeth Reis, "Marketing Research with Telephone Surveys: Is It Time to Change?" *Journal of Global Marketing* 23, no. 4 (2010), pp. 321–32.

The adequacy of sampling techniques is also affected by a lack of detailed social and economic information. Without an age breakdown of the total population, for example, the researcher can never be certain of a representative sample requiring an age criterion, because there is no basis of comparison for the age distribution in the sample. A lack of detailed information, however, does not prevent the use of sampling; it simply makes it more difficult. In place of probability techniques, many researchers in such situations rely on convenience samples taken in marketplaces and other public gathering places.

McDonald's got into trouble over sampling issues. The company was involved in a dispute in South Africa over the rights to its valuable brand name in that fast emerging market. Part of the company's claim revolved around the recall of the McDonald's name among South Africans. In the two surveys the company conducted and provided as proof in the proceedings, the majority of those sampled had heard the company name and could recognize the logo. However, the Supreme Court judge hearing the case took a dim view of the evidence because the surveys were conducted in "posh, white" suburbs, whereas 79 percent of the South African population is black. Based in part on these sampling errors, the judge threw out McDonald's case.

Inadequate mailing lists and poor postal service can be problems for the market researcher using mail to conduct research. For example, in Nicaragua, delays of weeks in delivery are not unusual, and expected returns are lowered considerably because a letter can be mailed only at a post office. In addition to the potentially poor mail service within countries, the extended length of time required for delivery and return when a mail survey is conducted from another country further hampers the use of mail surveys. Although airmail reduces this time drastically, it also increases costs considerably.

Language and Comprehension

The most universal survey research problem in foreign countries is the language barrier. Differences in idiom and the difficulty of exact translation create problems in eliciting the specific information desired and in interpreting the respondents' answers.[26] Types of scales appropriate in some cultures, such as reverse-worded items, are problematic in other cultures.[27] Scales have also been found to work differently for native speakers versus bilingual respondents with less intense emotions reported in a second language.[28] Equivalent concepts may not exist in all languages. Family, for example, has different connotations in different countries. In the United States, it generally means only the parents and children. In Italy and many Latin countries, it could mean the parents, children, grandparents, uncles, aunts, cousins, and so forth. The meaning of names for family members can differ too, depending on the context within which they are used. In the Italian culture, the words for aunt and uncle are different for the maternal and paternal sides of the family. The concept of affection is a universal idea, but the manner in which it is manifested in each culture may differ. Kissing, an expression of affection in the West, is alien to many Eastern cultures and even taboo in some.

Literacy poses yet another problem. In some less developed countries with low literacy rates, written questionnaires are completely useless. Within countries, too, the problem of dialects and different languages can make a national questionnaire survey impractical. In India, there are 14 official languages and considerably more unofficial ones. One researcher has used pictures of products as stimuli and pictures of faces as response criteria in a study of eastern German brand preferences to avoid some of the difficulties associated with language differences and literacy in international research. Still others have used other nonverbal kinds of response elicitation techniques, such as pictures and collages.[29]

---

[26]Shi Zhang and Bernd H. Schmitt, "Creating Local Brands in Multilingual International Markets," *Journal of Marketing Research* 38 (August 2001), pp. 313–25; Lera Boroditsky, "Lost in Translation," *The Wall Street Journal*, July 24, 2010.

[27]Nancy Wong, Aric Rindfleisch, and James E. Burroughs, "Do Reverse-Worded Items Confound Measures in Cross-Cultural Research? The Case of the Material Values Scale," *Journal of Consumer Research* 30, no. 1 (June 2003), pp. 72–91.

[28]Bart de Langhe, Stefano Puntoni, Daniel Fernandes, and Stijin M.M. van Osselaer, "The Anchor Contraction Effect in International Marketing Research," *Journal of Marketing Research* 48, no. 2 (April 2011), pp/ 366–80.

[29]Gerald Zaltman, "Rethinking Marketing Research: Putting the People Back In," *Journal of Marketing Research* 34 (November 1997), pp. 424–37.

Marketing researchers in India have to consider the problems of language diversity. Here the primary 13 languages (besides English) are listed on a 20-rupee note.

Furthermore, a researcher cannot assume that a translation into one language will suffice in all areas where that language is spoken. For example, a researcher in Mexico requested a translation of the word *outlet*, as in *retail outlet*, to be used in Venezuela. It was read by Venezuelans to mean an electrical outlet, an outlet of a river into an ocean, and the passageway into a patio. Of course the responses were useless—though interesting. Thus, it will always be necessary for a native speaker of the target country's language to take the "final cut" of any translated material.

In all countries all marketing communications, including research questionnaires, must be written *perfectly*. If not, consumers and customers will not respond with accuracy, or even at all. The obvious solution of having questionnaires prepared or reviewed by a native speaker of the language of the country is frequently overlooked. Even excellent companies such as American Airlines bring errors into their measurement of customer satisfaction by using the same questionnaire in Spanish for their surveys of passengers on routes to Spain and Mexico. A question regarding meal preferences, for example, may cause confusion because to a Spaniard, orange juice is *zumo de naranja*, while a Mexican would order *jugo de naranja*. These apparently subtle differences are no such things to Spanish speakers. Marketers use three different techniques, back translation, parallel translation, and decentering, to help ferret out translation errors ahead of time.

Back Translation.   In back translation, the questionnaire is translated from one language to another, and then a second party translates it back into the original, and the two original language versions are compared. This process often pinpoints misinterpretations and misunderstandings before they reach the public. In one study regarding advertising themes, a soft-drink company wanted to use a very successful Australian advertising theme, "Baby, it's cold inside," in Hong Kong. It had the theme translated from English into Cantonese by one translator and then retranslated by another from Cantonese into English, in which the statement came out as "Small mosquito, on the inside it is very cold." Although "small mosquito" is the colloquial expression for "small child" in Hong Kong, the intended meaning was lost in translation.

Parallel Translation.   Back translations may not always ensure an accurate translation because of commonly used idioms in both languages. Parallel translation is used to overcome this problem. In this process, more than two translators are used for the back translation; the results are compared, differences discussed, and the most appropriate translation selected. Most recently, researchers have suggested augmenting this process by integrating pretesting steps and iteratively adapting the translations.[30]

Decentering.   A third alternative, known as decentering, is a hybrid of back translation. It is a successive process of translation and retranslation of a questionnaire, each time by a different translator. For example, an English version is translated into French and then translated back to

---

[30]Susan P. Douglas and C. Samuel Craig, "Collaborative and Iterative Translation: An Alternative Approach to Back Translation," *Journal of International Marketing* 15, no. 1 (2007), pp. 30–43.

The complexities of the Japanese language confront second graders in Kyoto, where students write some of the 200-plus characters for the sound *shou*. The language commonly uses 15,000 kanji characters, which are borrowed from Chinese. The differences in the structure of the language from English make translation of questionnaires a most daunting task.

English by a different translator. The two English versions are compared, and where there are differences, the original English version is modified and the process is repeated. If there are still differences between the two English versions, the original English version of the second iteration is modified, and the process of translation and back translation is repeated. The process continues to be repeated until an English version can be translated into French and back translated, by a different translator, into the same English. In this process, the wording of the original instrument undergoes a change, and the version that is finally used and its translation have equally comprehensive and equivalent terminologies in both languages.

Regardless of the procedure used, proper translation and the *perfect* use of the local language in a questionnaire are of critical importance to successful research design. Because of cultural and national differences, confusion can just as well be the problem of the researcher as of the respondent. The question itself may not be properly worded in the English version, or English slang or abbreviated words may be translated with a different or ambiguous meaning. Such was the case mentioned earlier with the word *outlet* for *retail outlet*. The problem was not with the translation as much as with the term used in the question to be translated. In writing questions for translation, it is important that precise terms, not colloquialisms or slang, be used in the original to be translated. One classic misunderstanding that occurred in a *Reader's Digest* study of consumer behavior in western Europe resulted in a report that France and Germany consumed more spaghetti than did Italy. This rather curious and erroneous finding resulted from questions that asked about purchases of "packaged and branded spaghetti." Italians buy their spaghetti in bulk; the French and Germans buy branded and packaged spaghetti. Because of this crucial difference, the results underreported spaghetti purchases by Italians. Had the goal of the research been to determine how much branded and packaged spaghetti was purchased, the results would have been correct. However, because the goal was to know about total spaghetti consumption, the data were incorrect. Researchers must always verify that they are asking the right question.

Some of the problems of cross-cultural marketing research can be addressed after data have been collected. For example, we know that consumers in some countries such as Japan tend to respond to rating scales more conservatively than Americans. That is, on a 1 to 7 scale anchored by "extremely satisfied" and "extremely dissatisfied," Japanese tend to answer more toward the middle (more 3s and 5s), whereas Americans' responses tend toward the extremes (more 1s and 7s). Such a response bias can be managed through statistical standardization procedures to maximize comparability.[31] Some translation problems can be detected and mitigated post hoc through other statistical approaches as well.[32]

[31]Hans Baumgartner and Jan-Benedict E. M. Steenkamp, "Response Styles in Marketing Research: A Cross-National Investigation," *Journal of Marketing Research* 38 (May 2001), pp. 143–56; Martijin G. De Jong, Jan-Benedict E. M. Steenkamp, Jean-Paul Fox, and Hans Baumgartner, "Using Item Response Theory to Measure Extreme Response Style in Marketing Research: A Global Investigation," *Journal of Marketing Research* 45, no. 1 (2008), pp. 260–78.

[32]S. Durvasula, R. G. Netemeyer, J. C. Andrews, and S. Lysonski, "Examining the Cross-National Applicability of Multi-Item, Multi-Dimensional Measures Using Generalizability Theory," *Journal of International Business Studies* 37 (2006), pp. 469–83; Martijin G. De Jong, Jan-Benedict E. M. Steenkamp, and Jean-Paul Fox, "Relaxing Measurement Invariance in Cross-National Consumer Research Using a Hierarchical IRT Model," *Journal of Consumer Research* 34 (2007), pp. 260–72; Yi He, Michael A. Merz, and Dana L. Alden, "Diffusion of Measurement Invariance Assessment in Cross-National Empirical Marketing Research: Perspectives from the Literature and a Survey of Researchers," *Journal of International Marketing* 16, no. 2 (2008), pp. 64–83; Martijn G. de Jong, Jan-Benedict E. M. Steenkamp, and Bernard P. Veldkamp, "A Model for the Construction of Country-Specific Yet Internationally Comparable Short-Form Marketing Scales," *Marketing Science* 29, no. 4 (2009), pp. 674–89.

Finally, new work is beginning to criticize the efforts at equivalence in translations via mathematics. In a more "contextualized" approach, not only is the lexical usage negotiated in questionnaire design, but also the context of the research itself. And the results of research also become a matter of cross-cultural negotiation and interpretation.[33]

Multicultural Research: A Special Problem

As companies become global marketers and seek to standardize various parts of the marketing mix across several countries, multicultural studies become more important. A company needs to determine to what extent adaptation of the marketing mix is appropriate.[34] Thus, market characteristics across diverse cultures must be compared for similarities and differences before a company proceeds with standardization on any aspect of marketing strategy. The research difficulties discussed thus far have addressed problems of conducting research within a culture. When engaging in multicultural studies, many of these same problems further complicate the difficulty of cross-cultural comparisons.[35]

Multicultural research involves countries that have different languages, economies, social structures, behavior, and attitude patterns. When designing multicultural studies, it is essential that these differences be taken into account.[36] An important point to keep in mind when designing research to be applied across cultures is to ensure comparability and equivalency of results. Different methods may have varying reliabilities in different countries. Such differences may mean that different research methods should be applied in individual countries.

In some cases, the entire research design may have to be varied between countries to maximize the comparability of the results. For example, in Latin American countries, it may be difficult to attract consumers to participate in either focus groups or in-depth interviews because of different views about commercial research and the value of their time. And Japanese businesspeople as compared to their American counterparts tend not to respond to mail surveys. The latter problem was handled in two recent studies by using alternative methods of questionnaire distribution and collection in Japan. In one study, attitudes of retail buyers regarding pioneer brands were sought. In the U.S. setting, a sample was drawn from a national list of supermarket buyers, and questionnaires were distributed and collected by mail. Alternatively, in Japan, the questionnaires were distributed through contact people at 16 major supermarket chains and then returned by mail directly to the Japanese researchers. The second study sought to compare the job satisfaction of American and Japanese sales representatives. The questionnaires were delivered and collected via the company mail system for the U.S. firm. For the Japanese firm, participants in a sales training program were asked to complete the questionnaires during the program. Although the authors of both studies suggest that the use of different methods of data collection in comparative studies threatens the quality of the results, the approaches taken were the best (only) practical methods of conducting the research.

The adaptations necessary to complete these cross-national studies serve as examples of the need for resourcefulness in international marketing research. However, they also raise serious questions about the reliability of data gathered in cross-national research. Evidence suggests that often insufficient attention is given not only to nonsampling errors and other problems that can exist in improperly conducted multicultural studies but also to the appropriateness of research measures that have not been tested in multicultural contexts.

---

[33]Agnieszka Chidlow, Emmanuella Plakoyiannaki, and Catherine Welch, "Translation in Cross-Language International Business Research: Beyond Equivalence," *Journal of International Business Studies* 45 (2014), pp. 562–82.

[34]Amanda J. Broderick, Gordon E. Greenley, and Rene Dentiste Mueller, "The Behavioral Homogeneity Evaluation Framework: Multi-Level Evaluations of Consumer Involvement in International Segmentation," *Journal of International Business Studies* 38 (2007), pp. 746–63.

[35]Masaski Kotabe, "Contemporary Research Trends in International Marketing," in *Oxford Handbook of International Business*, 2nd edition, ed. Alan Rugman (Oxford: Oxford University Press, 2009), Chapter 17.

[36]James Reardon, Chip Miller, Bram Foubert, Irena Vida, and Liza Rybina, "Antismoking Messages for the International Teenage Segment: The Effectiveness of Message Valence and Intensity across Different Cultures," *Journal of International Marketing* 14, no. 3 (2006), pp. 114–36.

Research on the Internet: A Growing Opportunity

To keep up with the worldwide growth in Internet use is literally impossible. We know that at this writing, there are more than 3 billion users in more than 200 countries. About one tenth of the users are in the United States, but more than half of the hosts are there. The fastest growing market for the Internet is now China, with 600 million users at last count.[37] International Internet use is growing almost twice as fast as American use. Growth in countries such as Costa Rica was dramatically spurred by the local government's decision to reclassify computers as "educational tools," thus eliminating all import tariffs on the hardware. The demographics of users worldwide are as follows: 60 percent male and 40 percent female; average age about 32 years; about 60 percent college educated; median income of about $60,000; usage time about 2.5 hours per week; and main activities of e-mail and finding information. The percentage of Internet users by language is as follows: English, 28 percent; Chinese, 24 percent; Spanish, 8 percent; Japanese, 5 percent; German, 4 percent; Arabic, 3 percent; French, 3 percent; Russian, 3 percent; and all the rest, less than 1 percent each.[38]

For many companies, the Internet provides a new and increasingly important medium for conducting a variety of international marketing research. Indeed, a survey of marketing research professionals suggests that the most important influences on the industry are the Internet and globalization. New product concepts and advertising copy can be tested over the Internet for immediate feedback. Worldwide consumer panels[39] have been created to help test marketing programs across international samples. It has been suggested that there are at least eight different uses for the Internet in international research:

1. **Online surveys and buyer panels.** These can include incentives for participation, and they have better "branching" capabilities (asking different questions based on previous answers) than more expensive mail and phone surveys.

2. **Online focus groups.** Bulletin boards can be used for this purpose.

3. **Web visitor tracking.** Servers automatically track and time visitors' travel through websites.

4. **Advertising measurement.** Servers track links to other sites, and their usefulness can therefore be assessed.

5. **Customer identification systems.** Many companies are installing registration procedures that allow them to track visits and purchases over time, creating a "virtual panel."

6. **E-mail marketing lists.** Customers can be asked to sign up on e-mail lists to receive future direct marketing efforts via the Internet.

7. **Embedded research.** The Internet continues to automate traditional economic roles of customers, such as searching for information about products and services, comparison shopping among alternatives, interacting with service providers, and maintaining the customer–brand relationship. More and more of these Internet processes look and feel like research processes themselves. The methods are often embedded directly into the actual purchase and use situations and therefore are more closely tied to actual economic behavior than traditional research methods. Some firms even provide the option of custom designing products online—the ultimate in applying research for product development purposes.

8. **Observational research (also known as netnography).** Chat rooms, blogs, and personal websites can all be systematically monitored to assess consumers' opinions about products and services. TimeWarner also maintains a laboratory full of iPads, 3D televisions, and Xbox gaming consoles, such that it can use all sorts of high-tech observational devices to measure people's eye movements, heart rates, facial movements, and skin temperatures as they experience visual stimuli such as television programs or video games.[40]

---

[37]World Bank, *World Development Indicators,* 2015.

[38]See http://www.internetworldstats.com.

[39]Information regarding worldwide Internet panels is available at http://www.decisionanalyst.com.

[40]Amy Chozick, "These Lab Specimens Watch 3-D Television," *The New York Times,* January 24, 2012.

Clearly, as the Internet continues to grow, even more types of research will become feasible, and the extent to which new translation software has an impact on marketing communications and research over the Internet will be quite interesting to watch. Some companies now provide translation services for questionnaires, including commonly used phrases such as "rate your satisfaction level."[41] Surveys in multiple languages can be produced quickly, given the translation libraries now available from some application service providers. Finally, as is the case in so many international marketing contexts, privacy is and will continue to be a matter of personal and legal considerations. A vexing challenge facing international marketers will be the cross-cultural concerns about privacy and the enlistment of cooperative consumer and customer groups.

The ability to conduct primary research is one of the exciting aspects about the Internet. However, the potential bias of a sample universe composed solely of Internet respondents presents some severe limitations, and firms vary substantially in their abilities to turn data collected into competitive advantages.[42] Nevertheless, as more of the general population in countries gain access to the Internet, this tool will be all the more powerful and accurate for conducting primary research. Also, the Internet can be used as one of several methods of collecting data, offering more flexibility across countries.

Today the real power of the Internet for international marketing research is the ability to easily access volumes of secondary data. These data have been available in print form for years, but now they are much easier to access and, in many cases, are more current. Instead of leafing through reference books to find two- or 3-year-old data, as is the case with most printed sources, you can often find up-to-date data on the Internet. Such Internet sites as http://www.stat-usa.gov provide almost all data that are published by the U.S. government. If you want to know the quantity of a specific product being shipped to a country, the import duties on a product, and whether an export license is required, it's all there, via your computer. A variety of private firms also provide international marketing information online. See the Appendix of this chapter for more detail.

Estimating Market Demand

The unprecedented events of the crash in world trade during 2009 yielded a scary variety of headlines facing international forecasters—"What Went Wrong with Economics?" "Managing in the Fog," and "Strategic Plans Lose Favor" to name just a few.[43] In assessing current product demand and forecasting future demand, reliable historical data are required.[44] As previously noted, the quality and availability of secondary data frequently are inadequate; nevertheless, estimates of market size must be attempted to plan effectively. Despite limitations, some approaches to demand estimation are usable with minimum information. The success of these approaches relies on the ability of the researcher to find meaningful substitutes or approximations for the needed economic, geographic, and demographic relationships. One interesting example of research creativity is using smuggled goods as an indicator of the demand for a new product. Analysts predicted a poor performance of a new line of Apple iPhones in China judging by the lack of interest in immediately available smuggled phones for prospective buyers there.[45]

When the desired statistics are not available, a close approximation can be made using local production figures plus imports, with adjustments for exports and current inventory levels. These data are more readily available because they are commonly reported by the

---

[41]See, for example, http://www.markettools.com.

[42]Tho D. Nguyen and Nigel J. Barrett, "The Knowledge-Creating Role of the Internet in International Business: Evidence from Vietnam," *Journal of International Marketing* 14, no. 2 (2006), pp. 116–47.

[43]"What Went Wrong with Economics?" *The Economist*, July 18, 2009, pp. 11–12; "Managing in the Fog," *The Economist*, February 28, 2009, pp. 67–68; Joann S. Lublin and Dana Mattioli, "Strategic Plans Lose Favor," *The New York Times*, January 25, 2010, p. B7.

[44]Although more than 25 years old, still the best summary of forecasting methods and their advantages, disadvantages, and appropriate applications is David M. Georgoff and Robert G. Murdick, "Manager's Guide to Forecasting," *Harvard Business Review*, January–February 1986, pp. 110–20.

[45]Pual Mozur and Shanshan Wang, "Glum Sign for Apple in China: Smuggled iPhones Go Begging," *The New York Times*, September 29, 2014, pp. B1, 7.

Everybody wants to see the future—even the ancient Greeks consulted the Oracle of Delphi, who resided in the temple pictured. Modern forecasters may have better tools, but the hazards of the job are still great. Or, as Yogi Berra eloquently put it, "The future ain't what it used to be." *When You Come to a Fork in the Road, Take It!: Inspiration and Wisdom From One of Baseball's Greatest Heroes,* Hyperion Books, 2001

United Nations and other international agencies. Once approximations for sales trends are established, historical series can be used as the basis for projections of growth. In any straight extrapolation however, the estimator assumes that the trends of the immediate past will continue into the future. This assumption can be problematic when the pertinent past has included a major unique event, positive or negative, such as the 2009 crash in world trade.[46] In a rapidly developing economy, extrapolated figures may not reflect rapid growth and must be adjusted accordingly. Given the greater uncertainties and data limitations associated with foreign markets, two methods of forecasting demand are particularly suitable for international marketers: expert opinion and analogy.

Expert Opinion

For many market estimation problems, particularly in foreign countries that are new to the marketer, **expert opinion** is advisable. In this method, experts are polled for their opinions about market size and growth rates. Such experts may be the companies' own sales managers or outside consultants and government officials. The key in using expert opinion to help forecast demand is **triangulation**, that is, comparing estimates produced by different sources. One of the tricky parts is how best to combine the different opinions.

Developing scenarios is useful in the most ambiguous forecasting situations, such as predicting demand for accounting services in emerging markets such as China and Russia or trying to predict the impact of SARS on tourism to Hong Kong. Moreover, statistical analyses of past data are fundamentally weak, because they cannot capture the potential impacts of extreme events[47] such as SARS. Experts with broad perspectives and long experience in markets will be better able to anticipate such major threats to stability and/or growth of market demand.

Analogy

Another technique is to estimate by **analogy**. This method assumes that demand for a product develops in much the same way in all countries, as comparable economic development occurs in each country.[48] First, a relationship must be established between the item to be estimated and a measurable variable[49] in a country that is to serve as the basis for the analogy. Once

---

[46]Don E. Schultz, "Is This the Death of Data," *Marketing News*, September 15, 2009, p. 19.

[47]Pierpaolo Andriani and Bill McKelvey, "Beyond Gaussian Averages: Redirecting International Business and Management Research toward Extreme Events and Power Laws," *Journal of International Business Studies* 38 (2007), pp. 1212–30.

[48]Such an approach was used to predict the depth of the housing market decline in the United States and other markets by making comparisons to the housing boom–bust cycle experienced by Japan in the 1980s and 1990s. See Robert J. Shiller, "Things that Go Boom," *The Wall Street Journal*, February 8, 2007, p. A15.

[49]These variables may include population and other demographics or usage rates or estimates, and so forth. Using combinations of such variables is also referred to as a *chain-ratio* approach to forecasting.

a known relationship is established, the estimator attempts to draw an analogy between the known situation and the country in question. For example, suppose a company wanted to estimate the market growth potential for a beverage in country X, for which it had inadequate sales figures, but the company had excellent beverage data for neighboring country Y. In country Y, per capita consumption is known to increase at a predictable ratio as per capita gross domestic product (GDP) increases. If per capita GDP is known for country X, per capita consumption for the beverage can be estimated using the relationships established in country Y.

Caution must be used with analogy though because the method assumes that factors other than the variable used (in the preceding example, GDP) are similar in both countries, such as the same tastes, taxes, prices, selling methods, availability of products, consumption patterns,[50] and so forth. For example, the 13 million WAP (Wireless Access Protocol) users in Japan led to a serious overestimation of WAP adoptions in Europe—the actual figure of 2 million was less than the 10 million forecasted. Or consider the relevance of the adoption rate of personal computers or cell phones in the United States as they help predict adoption rates in the other four countries listed in Exhibit 8.1. How might Apple Computer use

Exhibit 8.1
Mobile Phone Diffusion Rate (per 100 people)

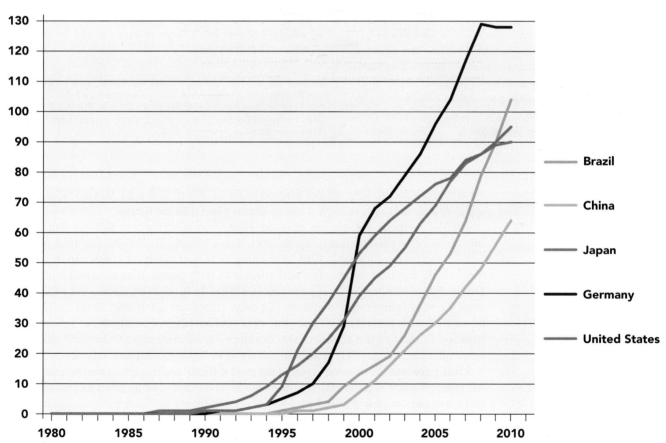

Source: World Bank, *World Development Indicators 2010* (Washington, DC: World Bank, 2012).

[50]Gerard J. Tellis, Stefan Stremerch, and Eden Yin, "The International Takeoff of New Products: The Role of Economics, Culture, and Country Innovativeness," *Marketing Science* 22, no. 2 (2003), pp. 188–208; Sean Dwyer, Hani Mesak, and Maxwell Hsu, "An Exploratory Examination of the Influence of National Culture on Cross-National Product Diffusion," *Journal of International Marketing* 13, no. 2 (2005), pp. 1–27; Roger J. Calantone, David A. Griffith, and Goksel Yalcinkaya, "An Empirical Examination of a Technology Adoption Model for the Context of China," *Journal of International Marketing* 14, no. 4 (2006), pp. 1–27.

CROSSING BORDERS 8.3   Forecasting the Global Healthcare Market

Johns Hopkins Hospital in Baltimore has been expanding its treatment of patients from foreign countries dramatically, burgeoning from 600 to 7,500 in a 6 year period. And there were no hassles with insurance companies and HMOs. In fact, many of these patients paid cash—even for $30,000 surgical procedures! The Mayo Clinic in Rochester, Minnesota, has been serving foreigners for decades. The number there has jumped by about 15 percent in 5 years to more than 1,000 per year. Similar growth is happening in places such as Mount Sinai Hospital in Miami, the University of Texas Cancer Center, and the UCLA Medical Center. The Mayo Clinic has even set up a Muslim prayer room to make patients and their families feel more comfortable. Fast growth, yes (some say exponential), but will it continue? Forecasting this demand so that decisions can be made about staffing and numbers of beds is a daunting project indeed.

Demand in Mexico and Latin America seems to be coming primarily for treatment of infectious and digestive diseases and cancer. Demand from the Middle East stems more from genetic diseases, heart diseases, cancer, and asthma. From Asia, wealthy patients are coming mainly to California for treatment of cancer and coronary diseases. Europeans travel to the United States for mental illness

services, cancer and heart disease, and AIDS treatments. Given that Japan has the world's best success rate for treating stomach cancer, one would forecast that to be a growth sector in the future.

But perhaps the strangest market to forecast is that for prostheses for the global war wounded. Johns Hopkins contracted to replace limbs for soldiers involved in a border clash between Ecuador and Peru at $35,000 per patient. The description in *The Wall Street Journal* article might have been a bit overzealous: "There are wars all over the world, bombs all over the world. Casualty patients are a new and enriching market niche." Forecasting demand for prostheses is in some ways easy—all researchers have to do is track the data on wars worldwide, as listed in Exhibit 6.3 in Chapter 6. Fortunately the demand was falling before 2010. However, the sad reality of the Haitian earthquake meant an estimate of over 40,000 prostheses needed for the survivors of that tragedy.

Sources: "U.S. Hospitals Attracting Patients from Abroad," *USA Today*, July 22, 1997, p. 1A; Ron Hammerle, "Healthcare Becoming a Lot Less Local," *Modern Healthcare*, March 20, 2000, p. 40; Tom Philips, "Haiti Earthquake Creating a Generation of Amputees, Doctors Warn," *Manchester Guardian*, January 21, 2010.

the American data to help predict demand in Japan, South Korea, or Mexico? Despite the apparent drawbacks to analogy, it can be useful when data are limited.

All the methods for market demand estimation described in this section are no substitute for original market research when it is economically feasible and time permits. Indeed, the preferred approach to forecasting is almost always a *combination* of macroeconomic database approaches and interviews with potential and current customers. Triangulation of alternative approaches is always best, and the discussion of discrepancies across sources and methods can raise important questions about current and future forecasting efforts.[51] As adequate data sources become available, as would be the situation in most of the economically developed countries, more technically advanced techniques such as multiple regression analysis or input–output analysis can be used.

Finally, forecasting demand is one of the most difficult and important business activities. All business plans depend entirely on forecasts of a future that no one can see. Even the best companies make big mistakes.

Problems in Analyzing and Interpreting Research Information

Once data have been collected, the final steps in the research process are the analysis and interpretation of findings in light of the stated marketing problem. Both secondary and primary data collected by the market researcher are subject to the many limitations

---

[51]A.N.M. Waheeduzzaman, "Market Potential Estimation in International Markets: A Comparison of Methods," *Journal of Global Marketing* 21, no. 4 (2008), pp. 307–20.

just discussed. In any final analysis, the researcher must take into consideration these factors and, despite their limitations, produce meaningful guides for management decisions.

Accepting information at face value in foreign markets is imprudent. The meanings of words, the consumer's attitude toward a product, the interviewer's attitude, or the interview situation can distort research findings. Just as culture and tradition influence the willingness to give information, so they influence the information given. Newspaper circulation figures, readership and listenership studies, retail outlet figures, and sales volume can all be distorted through local business practices. To cope with such disparities, the foreign market researcher must possess three talents to generate meaningful marketing information.

First, the researcher must possess a high degree of cultural understanding of the market in which research is being conducted. To analyze research findings, the social customs, semantics, current attitudes, and business customs of a society or a subsegment of a society must be clearly understood. At some level, it will be absolutely necessary to have a native of the target country involved in the interpretation of the results of any research conducted in a foreign market.

Second, a creative talent for adapting research methods is necessary. A researcher in foreign markets often is called on to produce results under the most difficult circumstances and short deadlines. Ingenuity and resourcefulness, willingness to use "catch as catch can" methods to get facts, patience (even a sense of humor about the work), and a willingness to be guided by original research findings even when they conflict with popular opinion or prior assumptions are all considered prime assets in foreign marketing research.

Third, a skeptical attitude in handling both primary and secondary data is helpful. For example, it might be necessary to check a newspaper pressrun over a period of time to get accurate circulation figures or to deflate or inflate reported consumer income in some areas by 25 to 50 percent on the basis of observable socioeconomic characteristics. Indeed, where data are suspect, such triangulation through the use of multiple research methods will be crucial.

These essential traits suggest that a foreign marketing researcher should be a foreign national or should be advised by a foreign national who can accurately appraise the data collected in light of the local environment, thus validating secondary as well as primary data. Moreover, regardless of the sophistication of a research technique or analysis, there is no substitute for decision makers themselves getting into the field for personal observation.

Responsibility for Conducting Marketing Research

Depending on the size and degree of involvement in foreign marketing, a company in need of foreign market research can rely on an outside, foreign-based agency or on a domestic company with a branch within the country in question. It can conduct research using its own facilities or employ a combination of its own research force with the assistance of an outside agency.

A trend toward decentralization of the research function is apparent. In terms of efficiency, local analysts appear able to provide information more rapidly and accurately than a staff research department. The obvious advantage to decentralization of the research function is that control rests in hands closer to the market. Field personnel, resident managers, and customers generally have more intimate knowledge of the subtleties of the market and an appreciation of the diversity that characterizes most foreign markets. One disadvantage of decentralized research management is possible ineffective communications with home-office executives. Another is the potential unwarranted dominance of large-market studies in decisions about global standardization. That is to say, larger markets, particularly the United States, justify more sophisticated research procedures and larger sample sizes, and results derived via simpler approaches that are appropriate in smaller countries are often erroneously discounted.

Both Ford and Philips keep track of European technology and consumers and develop products for global markets at their research centers in Aachen, Germany. Some of the best technical universities in Europe are close by in Belgium, the Netherlands, and Germany.

A comprehensive review of the different approaches to multicountry research suggests that the ideal approach is to have local researchers in each country, with close coordination and networking[52] between the client company and the local research companies. Networking among companies, even competing ones, through strategic alliances can also be important in the research and development effort.[53] This cooperation is important at all stages of the research project, from research design to data collection to final analysis. Furthermore, two stages of analysis are necessary. At the individual-country level, all issues involved in each country must be identified, and at the multicountry level, the information must be distilled into a format that addresses the client's objectives. Such recommendations are supported on the grounds that two heads are better than one and that multicultural input is essential to any understanding of multicultural data. With just one interpreter of multicultural data, there is the danger of one's self-reference criterion resulting in data being interpreted in terms of one's own cultural biases. Self-reference bias can affect the research design, questionnaire design, and interpretation of the data.

If a company wants to use a professional marketing research firm, many are available. Most major advertising agencies and many research firms have established branch offices worldwide. Moreover, foreign-based research and consulting firms have seen healthy growth. Of the 25 largest marketing research firms in the world (based on revenues), 15 are based in the United States, including the largest; 3 are in the United Kingdom; 3 are in Japan; 2 are in France; 1 is in Germany; and 1 is in Brazil. The latest count of marketing research firms in China is more than 400 and growing fast. In Japan, where understanding the unique culture is essential, the quality of professional marketing research firms is among the best. A recent study reports that research methods applied by Japanese firms and American firms are generally similar, but with notable differences in the greater emphasis

---

[52]Changsu Kim and Jong-Hun Park, "The Global Research-and-Development Network and Its Effect on Innovation," *Journal of International Marketing* 18, no. 4 (2010), pp. 43–57.

[53]Haisu Zhang, Chengli Shu, Xu Jiang, and Alan J. Malter, "Managing Knowledge for Innovation: The Role of Cooperation, Competition, and Alliance Nationality," *Journal of International Marketing* 18, no. 4 (2010), pp. 74–94; Ruby P. Lee, "Extending the Environment-Strategy-Performance Framework: The Roles of Multinational Corporation Network Strength, Market Responsiveness, and Product Innovation," *Journal of International Marketing,* 18, no. 4 (2010), pp. 58–73.

of the Japanese on forecasting, distribution channels, and sales research. A listing of international marketing research firms is printed annually in April as an advertising supplement in *Marketing News.*

An increasingly important issue related to international marketing research is the growing potential for governmental controls on the activity. In many countries, consumer privacy issues are being given new scrutiny as the Internet expands companies' capabilities to gather data on consumers' behaviors.

Communicating with Decision Makers

LO6

Using international marketing research

Most of the discussion in this chapter has pertained to getting information from or about consumers, customers, and competitors. It should be clearly recognized, however, that getting the information is only half the job. Analyses and interpretation of that information must also be provided to decision makers in a timely manner.[54] High-quality international information systems design will be an increasingly important competitive tool as commerce continues to globalize, and resources must be invested accordingly.[55]

Decision makers, often top executives, should be directly involved not only in problem definition and question formulation but also in the fieldwork of seeing the market and hearing the voice of the customers in the most direct ways when the occasion warrants (as in new foreign markets). Top managers should have a "feel" for their markets that even the best marketing reports cannot provide.

Finally, international marketers face an additional obstacle to obtaining the best information about customers. At the most basic level, marketing research is mostly a matter of interaction with customers. Marketing decision makers have questions about how best to serve customers, and those questions are posed and answered often through the media of questionnaires and research agencies. Even when both managers and customers speak the same language and are from the same culture, communication can become garbled in either direction. That is, customers misunderstand the questions and/or managers misunderstand the answers. Throw in a language/cultural barrier, and the chances of misinformation expand dramatically.

There is no better (or worse) case of such communication problems than the Toyota accelerator problems of 2010. Even great companies can make big mistakes. By not correcting flaws in Toyota product accelerators in the United States soon enough, the world's best automaker did billions of dollars of damage to its annual performance and perhaps its brand equity in the United States. The fundamental communication problem within Toyota was well described at the time:

> There is a cultural element to this penchant for mismanaging crisis. The shame and embarrassment of owning up to product defects in a nation obsessed with craftsmanship and quality raises the bar on disclosure and assuming responsibility. And a high-status company like Toyota has much to lose since its corporate face is at stake. The shame of producing defective cars is supposed to be other firms' problems, not Toyota's, and the ongoing PR disaster reveals just how unprepared the company is for crisis management and how embarrassed it is. In addition, employees' identities are closely tied to their company's image, and loyalty to the firm overrides concerns about consumers.

[54]Anne L. Souchon, Adamantios Diamantopoulos, Hartmut H. Holzmuller, Catherine N. Axxin, James M. Sinkula, Heike Simmet, and Geoffrey R. Durden, "Export Information Use: A Five-Country Investigation of Key Determinants," *Journal of International Marketing* 11, no. 3 (2003), pp. 106–27; Marios Theodosiou and Evangelia Katsikea, "The Export Information System: An Empirical Investigation of Its Antecedents and Performance Outcomes," *Journal of International Marketing* 21, no. 3 (2013), pp. 72–94.

[55]Nicoli Juul Foss and Torben Pedersen, "Organizing Knowledge Processes in the Multinational Corporation: An Introduction," *Journal of International Business Studies* 35, no. 5 (2004), pp. 340–49; Ram Mudambi and Pietro Navarra, "Is Knowledge Power? Knowledge Flows, Subsidiary Power and Rent-Seeking within MNCs," *Journal of International Business Studies* 35, no. 5 (2004), pp. 385–406.

There is also a culture of deference inside corporations that makes it hard for those lower in the hierarchy to question their superiors or inform them about problems. The focus on consensus and group is an asset in building teamwork, but also can make it hard to challenge what has been decided or designed. Such cultural inclinations are not unknown elsewhere around the world, but they are exceptionally powerful within Japanese corporate culture and constitute significant impediments to averting and responding to a crisis.[56]

We would add an additional culture-based explanation: the Japanese penchant for avoiding bad news. Indeed, the Japanese have two words for truth, *tatemae* and *honne*. *Tatemae* is the public, face-saving truth, whereas *honne* is the factual truth, irrespective of the damage it might do to the all-important social relationships within and between Japanese companies.[57] Such internal communication problems have also manifested themselves in other hierarchical, relationship-based cultures such as South Korea and Vietnam.[58] Researchers have identified a number of factors that are associated with better communication within such multinational companies, including frequency of communication instances, face-to-face communication opportunities,[59] employee incentives for sharing information,[60] and cultural similarities.[61] Another study offered "global environmental turbulence"[62] as a

[56]See the excellent article by Jeff Kinston, "A Crisis Made in Japan," *The Wall Street Journal*, February 6–7, 2010, pp. W1–2.

[57]James Day Hodgson, Yoshihiro Sano, and John L. Graham, *Doing Business in the New Japan* (Boulder, CO: Rowman & Littlfield, 2008).

[58]Malcolm Gladwell, *Outliers* (New York: Little Brown, 2008); John U. Farley, Scott Hoenig, Donald R. Lehmann, and Hoang Thuy Nguyen, "Marketing Metrics Use in a Transitional Economy: The Case of Vietnam," *Journal of Global Marketing* 21, no. 3 (2008), pp. 179–90.

[59]Niels Noorderhaven and Anne-Wil Harzing, "Knowledge-Sharing and Social Interaction within MNEs," *Journal of International Business Studies* 40, no. 5 (2009), pp. 719–41.

[60]Gary Oddou, Joyce S. Osland, and Roger N. Blakeney, "Repatriating Knowledge: Variables Influencing the 'Transfer' Process," *Journal of International Business Studies* 40, no. 2 (2009), pp. 181–99.

[61]Martin S. Roth, Satish Jayachandran, Mourad Dakhli, and Deborah A. Colton, "Subsidiary Use of Foreign Marketing Knowledge," *Journal of International Marketing* 17, no. 1 (2009), pp. 1–29.

[62]Ruby P. Lee, Qimei Chen, Daikwan Kim, and Jean L. Johnson, "Knowledge Transfer between MNCs' Headquarters and Their Subsidiaries: Influences on and Implications for New Product Outcomes," *Journal of International Marketing* 16, no. 2 (2008), pp. 1–31.

Exhibit 8.2
Managing the Cultural Barrier in International Marketing Research

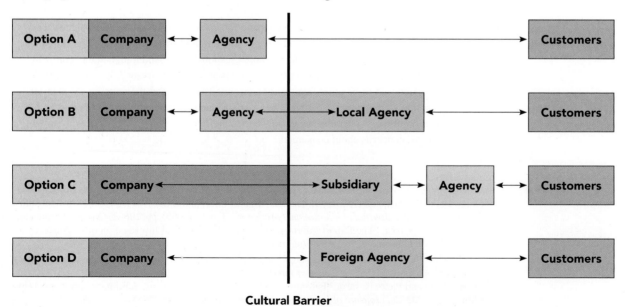

Cultural Barrier

communication-inhibiting factor as well. Certainly Toyota was facing the extreme version of this problem: the precipitous decline in world trade and its own sales contemporaneously with its product quality problems.

Such problems can be exacerbated when research agencies are also involved. The four kinds of company–agency–customer relationships possible are presented in Exhibit 8.2. Options B and C are better suited for managing the cultural barrier across the chain of communication. That is, in both cases, the cultural barrier is bridged *within* a company wherein people that have a common corporate culture and work together on an everyday basis. In B the translation (in the broadest sense of the term—that is, of both questionnaires and reports) is worked out between employees of the international marketing research agency. In C the translation is managed within the company itself. In cases A and D, both cultural and organizational barriers are being crossed simultaneously, thus maximizing the chances for miscommunication. Indeed, these same company–agency–customer considerations are pertinent to other kinds of communications between companies and customers, such as advertising and distribution channel control, and this unique international topic will be addressed again in subsequent chapters.

Summary

The basic objective of the market research function is providing management with information for more accurate decision making. This objective is the same for domestic and international marketing. In foreign marketing research, however, achieving that objective presents some problems not encountered on the domestic front.

Customer attitudes about providing information to a researcher are culturally conditioned. Foreign market information surveys must be carefully designed to elicit the desired data and at the same time not offend the respondent's sense of privacy. Besides the cultural and managerial constraints involved in gathering information for primary data, many foreign markets have inadequate or unreliable bases of secondary information. Such challenges suggest three keys to successful international marketing research: (1) the inclusion of natives of the foreign culture on research teams; (2) the use of multiple methods and triangulation; and (3) the inclusion of decision makers, even top executives, who must on occasion talk directly to or directly observe customers in foreign markets.

Key Terms

Marketing research	Secondary data	Parallel translation	Expert opinion
International marketing research	Primary data	Decentering	Triangulation
Research process	Back translation	Multicultural research	Analogy

Questions

1. Define the key terms listed above.

2. Discuss how the shift from making "market entry" decisions to "continuous operations" decisions creates a need for different types of information and data.

3. Discuss the breadth and scope of international marketing research. Why is international marketing research generally broader in scope than domestic marketing research?

4. The measure of a competent researcher is the ability to utilize the most sophisticated and appropriate techniques and methods available within the limits of time, cost, and the present state of the art. Comment.

5. What is the task of the international marketing researcher? How is it complicated by the foreign environment?

6. Discuss the stages of the research process in relation to the problems encountered. Give examples.

7. Why is the formulation of the research problem difficult in foreign market research?

8. Discuss the problems of gathering secondary data in foreign markets.

9. "In many cultures, personal information is inviolably private and absolutely not to be discussed with strangers." Discuss.

10. What are some problems created by language and the ability to comprehend the questions in collecting primary data? How can a foreign market researcher overcome these difficulties?

11. Discuss how decentering is used to get an accurate translation of a questionnaire.

12. Discuss when qualitative research may be more effective than quantitative research.

13. Sampling presents some major problems in market research. Discuss.

14. Select a country. From secondary sources found on the Internet, compile the following information for at least a 5-year period prior to the present:

principal imports	principal exports
gross national product	chief of state
major cities and population	principal agricultural crop

15. "The foreign market researcher must possess three essential capabilities to generate meaningful marketing information." What are they? Discuss.

Appendix: Sources of Secondary Data

For almost any marketing research project, an analysis of available secondary information is a useful and inexpensive first step. Although there are information gaps, particularly for detailed market information, the situation on data availability and reliability is improving. The principal agencies that collect and publish information useful in international business are presented here, with some notations regarding selected publications.

A. Websites for International Marketing

1. http://www.stat-usa.gov STAT-USA/Internet is clearly the single most important source of data on the Internet. STAT-USA, a part of the U.S. Department of Commerce's Economics and Statistics Administration, produces and distributes at a nominal subscription fee the most extensive government-sponsored business, economic, and trade information databases in the world today, including the National Trade Data Bank, Economic Bulletin Board, and Global Business Procurement Opportunities.

2. http://www.trade.gov/index.asp The website of the Commerce Department's International Trade Administration provides export assistance, including information about trade events, trade statistics, tariffs and taxes, marketing research, and so forth.

3. http://www.usatradeonline.gov Provides import and export information on more than 18,000 commodities, but the user must subscribe.

4. http://www.census.gov/foreign-trade/www/ The U.S. Census Bureau provides a variety of international trade statistics.

5. http://www.cia.gov/library/publications/the-world-factbook/ Find the CIA *World Factbook* here, as well as other pertinent trade information.

6. http://www.customs.ustreas.gov The U.S. Customs Service provides information regarding customs procedures and regulations.

7. http://www.opic.gov The Overseas Private Investment Corporation (OPIC) provides information regarding its services.

8. http://www.exim.gov The Export-Import Bank of the United States (Ex-Im Bank) provides information related to trade financing services provided by the U.S. government.

9. http://www.imf.org The International Monetary Fund (IMF) provides information about the IMF and international banking and finance.

10. http://www.wto.org The World Trade Organization (WTO) provides information regarding its operations.

11. http://www.oecd.org The Organization of Economic Cooperation and Development (OECD) provides information regarding OECD policies and associated data for 29 member countries.

12. http://www.jetro.go.jp The Japan External Trade Organization (JETRO) is the best source for data on the Japanese market.

13. http://www.euromonitor.com Euromonitor is a company providing a variety of data and reports on international trade and marketing.

14. http://publications.worldbank.org *World Development Indicators (WDI) Online* offers the World Bank's comprehensive database on development data, covering more than 600 indicators, 208 economies, and 18 regional income groups.

15. University-based websites. The best such site is Michigan State University's Center for International Business Education and Research (http://globaledge.msu.edu /resourceDesk/).

16. http://www.worldchambers.com The World Network of Chambers of Commerce and Industry provides data and addresses regarding chambers of commerce around the world.

17. http://http://world.wtca.org The World Trade Centers Association provides information about services provided by the World Trade Centers in the United States, including export assistance, trade leads, training programs, and trade missions.

18. http://www.worldtrademag.com *World Trade* magazine provides its annual Resource Guide to products, goods, and services for international trade.

19. http://www.mhhe.com/gilly15e The online learning center that accompanies this text provides supplementary support materials for both instructors and students.

B. U.S. Government Sources

The U.S. government actively promotes the expansion of U.S. business into international trade. In the process of keeping U.S. businesses informed of foreign opportunities, the U.S. government generates a considerable amount of general and specific market data for use by international market analysts. The principal source of information from the U.S. government is the Department of Commerce, which makes its services available to U.S. businesses in a variety of ways. First, information and assistance are available either through personal consultation in Washington, DC, or through any of the US&FCS (U.S. and Foreign Commercial Service) district offices of the International Trade Administration of the Department of Commerce located in key cities in the United States. Second, the Department of Commerce works closely with trade associations, chambers of commerce, and other interested associations in providing information, consultation, and assistance in developing international commerce. Third, the department publishes a wide range of information available to interested persons at nominal cost.

1. National Trade Data Bank (NTDB). The Commerce Department provides a number of the data sources mentioned previously, plus others in its computerized information system in the National Trade Data Bank. The NTDB is a one-step source for export promotion and international trade data collected by 17 U.S. government agencies. Updated each month and released on the Internet, the NTDB enables the reader to access more than 100,000 trade-related documents. The NTDB contains the latest census data on U.S. imports and exports by commodity and country; the complete CIA (Central Intelligence Agency) *World Factbook*; current market research reports compiled by the U.S. and Foreign Commercial Service; the complete *Foreign Traders Index*, which contains over 55,000 names and addresses of individuals and firms abroad that are interested in importing U.S. products; State Department country reports on economic policy and trade practices; the publications *Export Yellow Pages, A Basic Guide to Exporting* and the *National Trade Estimates Report on Foreign Trade Barriers*; the *Export Promotion Calendar*; and many other data series. The NTDB is also available at over 900 federal depository libraries nationwide.

In addition, the Department of Commerce provides a host of other information services. Beyond the material available through the Department of Commerce, consultation and information are available from a variety of other U.S. agencies. For example, the Department of State, Bureau of the Census, and Department of Agriculture can provide valuable assistance in the form of services and information for an American business interested in international operations.

2. http://www.export.gov/tradeleads/index.asp This website connects you to the Export.gov Trade Leads Database, which contains prescreened, time-sensitive leads and Government Tenders gathered through U.S. Commercial Service offices around the world. You can search leads and receive notification when new leads are posted.

3. buyusa.gov Provides details about the services offered by the U.S. Commercial Service.

C. Other Sources

1. Directories

a. Directory of American Firms Operating in Foreign Countries. New York: World Trade Academy Press. Alphabetically lists U.S. firms with foreign subsidiaries and affiliates operating in over 125 countries; also lists the foreign operations grouped by countries.

b. Directory of United States Importers and United States Exporters. New York: Journal of Commerce. Annual. Contain verified business profiles on a total of 60,000 active trading companies. These annual guides also include a product index with the Harmonized Commodity Code numbers, customs information, foreign consulates, embassies, and international banks.

c. Encyclopedia of Global Industries. Detroit: Gale. Alphabetically covers 125 vital international industries, providing in-depth information including statistics, graphs, tables, charts, and market share.

d. Export Yellow Pages. Washington, DC: Venture Publishing–North America; produced in cooperation with the Office of Export Trading Company Affairs and International Trade Administration. Annual. Provides detailed information on over 12,000 export service providers and trading companies, agents, distributors, and companies outside the United States; also includes a product/service index and an alphabetical index.

e. World Directory of Trade and Business Associations. London: Euromonitor, 1995. (Also on CD-ROM.) Contains entries from a broad range of sectors, giving details of publications produced, aims and objectives of the association, and whether they provide assistance in further research.

2. Marketing Guides

a. Exporters Encyclopaedia. Wilton, CT: Dun & Bradstreet. Annual. Comprehensive world marketing guide, in five sections; section two, "Export Markets," gives important market information on 220 countries (import and exchange regulations, shipping services, communications data, postal information, currency, banks, and embassies); other sections contain general export information. Also available are regional guides for Asia-Pacific, Europe, and Latin America and export guides for single countries.

b. U.S. Custom House Guide. Hightstown, NJ: K-III Directory Co. Annual. Provides a comprehensive guide to importing, including seven main sections: import how-to, ports sections, directory of services, tariff schedules (Harmonized Tariff Schedules of the United States), special and administrative provisions, custom regulations, and samples of import documents.

3. General sources of international business and economic data and customized reports. These exemplary websites are generally accessible for corporations with substantial research needs and budgets:

a. Economist Intelligence Unit http://www.eiu.com The Economist Intelligence Unit (EIU) describes itself as providing "a constant flow of analysis and forecasts on more than 200 countries and eight key industries." It helps "executives make informed business decisions through dependable intelligence delivered online, in print, in customized research as well as through conferences and peer interchange." The EIU represents a very high level of analysis. Its products are for sale (an annual subscription runs in the four figures), it facilitates the initial aggregation of information, and it undertakes preliminary analyses. At an intermediate level, within the industries it targets, we have found EIU to be very helpful.

b. Oxford Analytica http://www.oxan.org Oxford Analytica is self-described as "an international, independent consulting firm drawing on a network of over 1,000 senior faculty members at Oxford and other major universities and research institutions around the world." If the CIA Factbook is a Chevy sort of resource and the EIU is a Cadillac, then Oxan is a Lamborghini. Fees run to the five figures, depending on what you order. Among the publicly accessible sources, Oxford Analytica is one of the very best. Its reputation rests "on its ability to harness the expertise of preeminent scholar experts to provide business and government leaders with timely and authoritative analysis of world events. It is a unique bridge between the world of ideas and the world of enterprise." A review of its clients clearly indicates the level of professionalism the firm strives for and apparently attains.

Chapter 9

Economic Development and the Americas

CHAPTER OUTLINE

CHAPTER LEARNING OBJECTIVES

What you should learn from Chapter 9:

LO1 The importance of time zones for trade relationships and marketing operations

LO2 The political and economic changes affecting global marketing

LO3 The connection between the economic level of a country and the marketing task

LO4 The variety of stages of economic development among American nations

LO5 Growth factors and their role in economic development

LO6 Marketing's contribution to the growth and development of a country's economy

LO7 The foundational market metrics of American nations

LO8 The growing importance of trading associations among American nations

Global Perspective

DESYNCHRONOSIS? THE WORLD MAY OPERATE 24/7, BUT PEOPLE DON'T

Some call it circadian dysrhythmia.[1] The medical terms sound much more ominous than just jet lag. But no matter what you call it, it's still a powerful force.

Of course, crossing time zones quickly (usually by jet airliner) is the primary cause of the problem. The more time zones the greater the effects on the person. Also the direction of travel can make a difference. For most people heading west is more difficult – the shorter day makes adjustment tougher. The common symptoms include sleep disturbance, fatigue, sluggishness, headaches, irritability, poorer performance on mental tasks, lack of concentration, and indigestion. All these symptoms make business people less able to conduct international business. Some international executives seem to handle it well though.

Raj Subramaniam, the Senior Vice President of International Marketing at FedEx, has spent almost as much time overseas as he has at the company's Memphis headquarters in the 18 years he has worked there. True, that includes two long-term postings in Hong Kong and Toronto. But even since Subramaniam returned to Tennessee in 2006, he has been logging major miles, visiting FedEx's far-flung offices to oversee global marketing plans and customer service. It's a schedule that suits him, and he takes the opportunity to drop in on old haunts and discover new cities. "The worst thing you can possibly do is stay in the hotel, drink the bottled water, and just look out the window," says the seasoned traveler, who offers a few of his secrets for travelling successfully.

1. Days on the road? I'd say 125 or so, out of which about 100 are outside the U.S.

2. Way to fly? Typically I fly on Cathay Pacific, Emirates, and British Airways. They offer direct flights, and the service is excellent. I'm looking for a reasonable meal and then to read a book and go to sleep. These airlines do a great job of allowing those simple pleasures to happen.

3. Airtime? It's the best time to unplug your electronic leash and read. Right now I'm catching up on a few issues of *Foreign Affairs* magazine.

4. Trip tip? Pack light, and pack running shoes. Travel equals jet lag, so when I get to my destination, I try to hit the gym as quickly as I possibly can.

5. Favorite hotel? The Conrad in Hong Kong. Typically the flight from L.A. lands by 5:30 a.m. I'm at the hotel by 6:30, and I head to the gym. By 7:30, I'm having breakfast on the 59th floor overlooking Victoria Harbor, and by 9:00 I'm in the office. It works beautifully.

Some have a tougher time. Benjamin Southan, correspondent for Businesstraveller.com recounts his story:

In Sydney . . . I'd woken at four in the morning with extreme jet lag and figured I may as well run it off, but I'd packed in a daze—no socks, and no shorts. Well, I could do without socks, I thought, and I had a pair of normal shorts. I could run in those. Big mistake. The loose fit I preferred when lounging around worked less well when running around; my sockless feet rubbed, particularly once I'd warmed up; and it was very warm, even at five in the morning. And because it was going to be a short run, I hadn't bothered to grab a map, or work out where I was going. I kept the harbour to one side, and turned around after 15 minutes or so, taking what I thought was a shortcut as my feet were beginning to hurt. Second big mistake.

An hour later, exhausted, I half-jogged, half-shuffled through the less than salubrious Kings Cross area. No socks, sweat-stained through T-shirt, one hand holding up my shorts, and wondering why no one would meet my eye so I could ask them the way back to the harbour. . . . When I finally found my way back to the hotel, the receptionist alternated between professional concern and personal disgust, with the latter claiming victory. I fell into the lift as the first businessmen were coming down for breakfast, and once in my room pressed the "do not disturb" button and collapsed into bed. I'd allowed myself a day to acclimatize in Sydney before my appointments started, and it was the last trouble I had with jet lag that trip, sleeping for 20 hours and waking only to empty the minibar of chocolate and soft drinks. So much for the weight management.

The latest news? A new app, developed by University of Michigan researchers, tells you when to go to sleep and wake up to best battle desynchronosis—Entrain.

Sources: Benjamin Southan, "Fit to Drop," *Business Traveller* (UK/Europe Edition), October 2009, p. 82. Used with permission. Eugenia Levenson, "Road Warrior," *Fortune*, April 27, 2009, p. 24; Javier Espinoza, "Road Warrior: Beating Jet Lag through Jogging," *The Wall Street Journal*, June 16, 2011; Claire Suddath, "To Cure Jet Lag, Let This App Tell You When It's Bedtime," *Bloomberg BusinessWeek*, April 16, 2014, online.

[1]*Merriam-Webster's Dictionary,* 2013.

Exhibit 9.1
Three Regional Trading Areas Roughly Defined by Time Zones

Source: World Bank, 2015.

Region	Population	GDP
The Americas	.96 billion	$24.8 trillion
Europe, Africa, Middle East	2.25 billion	$27.3 trillion
Asia Pacific	3.92 billion	$22.9 trillion

LO1

The importance of time zones for trade relationships and marketing operations

Time zones make a difference. Jet lag is an important problem. Virtual meetings across time zones are more than just inconvenient; they can disrupt sleep and family life. Indeed, our own studies have demonstrated that among three kinds of distances that international marketers must traverse—miles, time zones, and cultural distances—time zones have the greatest influence on the success of their commercial efforts abroad.[2] Moreover, most countries also maintain good trade relationships with contiguous countries. Thus, we can also see an associated pattern of economic growth and global trade that will extend well into the 21st century. It consists of three multinational market regions that comprise major trading blocs: the Americas, Europe, and Asia. Further, the common time zones give the Europeans advantages in both Africa and the Middle East. Within each trading bloc are fully industrialized countries, as typified by the United States, Germany, and Japan; rapidly industrializing countries such as Brazil, Russia, and China that are close on the heels of the fully industrialized; and other countries that are achieving economic development but at more modest rates. See Exhibit 9.1 for the grossest metrics for each trading bloc.

Many American companies have organized their international operations according to these geographic or temporal, if you like, constraints. For example, Quiksilver manages its global operations from three bases "Avalon Beach" California, for the Americas (and corporate headquarters); St. Jean De Luz, France, for Europe; and Avalon: Beach, New South Wales, Australia, for the Asia/Pacific region. Among its $1.6 billion in global revenues in 2014, approximately 45 percent came from the Americas, 39 percent from Europe, and 16 percent from the Asia/Pacific.

Our presentation of regional market metrics is likewise organized in Chapters 9–11. In this chapter, we first discuss economic development and marketing, then focus on the character of and opportunities for commerce in the Americas. While the United States and Canada are affluent, industrialized countries, most of the countries in the American region better fit the descriptor "developing," and some are doing so very fast indeed. In Chapter 10, we focus on the European Union, as it represents the benchmark for regional commercial and political cooperation, and then we turn to the broader opportunities among its time zone neighbors—the rest of Europe, Africa, and the Middle East. In Chapter 11 we characterize the opportunities in the bustling Asia/Pacific region that includes the majority of people on the planet.

Speaking of flying, Roxy, a Quiksilver brand, sponsors athletes from around the world, including Tora Bright, an Olympic gold medal–winning snowboarder from Australia.

Marketing and Economic Development

LO2

The political and economic changes affecting global marketing

Not many years ago, large parts of the developing world were hostile to foreign investment and imposed severe regulatory barriers to foreign trade. But few nations are content with the economic status quo; now, more than ever, they seek economic growth, improved standards of living, and an

[2]Jennifer D. Chandler and John L. Graham, "Relationship-Oriented Cultures, Corruption, and International Marketing Success," *Journal of Business Ethics* 92(2) (2010), pp. 251–67. See also Kevin K. Boeh and Paul W. Beamish, "Travel Time and the Liability of Distance in Foreign Direct Investment: Location Choice and Entry Mode," *Journal of International Business Studies*, 43 (2012), pp. 525–35.

opportunity for the good life as part of the global consumer world.[3] Latin American and other emerging markets throughout the world will account for 75 percent of the world's total growth in the next two decades and beyond, according to U.S. Department of Commerce estimates. The transition from socialist to market-driven economies, the liberalization of trade and investment policies in developing countries, the transfer of public-sector enterprises to the private sector, and the rapid development of regional market alliances are changing the way countries will trade and prosper in the 21st century.

Argentina,Brazil, Mexico, China, South Korea, Poland, Turkey, India, and Vietnam are some of the countries undergoing impressive changes in their economies and are emerging as vast markets. These and other countries have an ever-expanding and changing demand for goods and services. As countries prosper and their people are exposed to new ideas and behavior patterns via global communications networks, old stereotypes, traditions, and habits are cast aside or tempered, and new patterns of consumer behavior emerge. Luxury cars in China; Avon cosmetics in South Korea; Walmart discount stores in Argentina, Brazil, Mexico, China, and Thailand; McDonald's beefless Big Macs in India; Whirlpool washers and refrigerators in eastern Europe; Sara Lee food products in Indonesia; and Amway products in the Czech Republic exemplify opportunities in emerging markets.

LO3

The connection between the economic level of a country and the marketing task

The economic level of a country is the single most important environmental element to which the foreign marketer must adjust the marketing task. The stage of economic growth within a country affects the attitudes toward foreign business activity,[4] the demand for goods, the distribution systems found within a country, and the entire marketing process.[5] In static economies, consumption patterns become rigid, and marketing is typically nothing more than a supply effort. In a dynamic economy, consumption patterns change rapidly.[6] Marketing constantly faces the challenge of detecting and providing for new levels of consumption, and marketing efforts must be matched with ever-changing market needs and wants. The current level of economic development dictates the kind and degree of market potential that exists, while knowledge of the dynamism of the economy allows the marketer to prepare for economic shifts and emerging markets.[7]

Economic development is generally understood to mean an increase in national production reflected by an increase in the average per capita gross domestic product (GDP) or gross national income (GNI).[8] Besides an increase in average per capita GNI or GDP, most interpretations of the concept also imply a widespread distribution of the increased income. Economic development, as commonly defined today, tends to mean rapid economic growth and increases in consumer demand—improvements achieved "in decades rather than centuries."

---

[3]Stephen Kotkin, "First World, Third World (Maybe Not in That Order)," *The New York Times*, May 6, 2007, p. 7.

[4]Terrance H. Witkowski, "Antiglobal Challenges to Marketing in Developing Countries: Exploring the Ideological Divide," *Journal of Public Policy & Marketing* 24, no. 1 (2005), pp. 7–23.

[5]Ramarao Desiraju, Harikesh Nair, and Pradeep Chintagunta, "Diffusion of New Pharmaceutical Drugs in Developing and Developed Nations," *International Journal of Research in Marketing* 21, no. 4 (2004), pp. 341–57.

[6]Seung Ho Park, Shaomin Li, and David K. Tse, "Market Liberalization and Firm Performance During China's Economic Transition," *Journal of International Business Studies* 37 (2006), pp. 127–47.

[7]Kevin Zheng Zhou, David K. Tse, and Julie Juan Li, "Organizational Changes in Emerging Economies: Drivers and Consequences," *Journal of International Business Studies* 37 (2006), pp. 248–63.

[8]Gross domestic product (GDP) and gross national income (GNI) are two measures of a country's economic activity. GDP is a measure of the market value of all goods and services produced within the boundaries of a nation, regardless of asset ownership. Unlike GNI, GDP excludes receipts from that nation's business operations in foreign countries, as well as the share of reinvested earnings in foreign affiliates of domestic corporations. In most cases and for most applications, the differences between the two are insubstantial. For example, the World Bank reports GDP for China in 2010 as $9.24 trillion and GNI as $9.20 trillion.

Stages of Economic Development

The United Nations classifies a country's stage of economic development on the basis of its level of industrialization. It groups countries into three categories:

MDCs (more-developed countries). Industrialized countries with high per capita incomes, such as Canada, England, France, Germany, Japan, and the United States. Exhibit 9.2 summarizes data regarding the standards of living in the most populous American countries that evince a spectrum of development despite their similar sizes. The reader will notice that those at the lowest levels of development often do not collect or report data suitable for international resources such as Euromonitor International or the World Bank.

LDCs (less-developed countries). Industrially developing countries just entering world trade, many of which are in Asia and Latin America, with relatively low per capita incomes.

LLDCs (least-developed countries). Industrially underdeveloped, agrarian, subsistence societies with rural populations, extremely low per capita income levels, and little world trade involvement. Such LLDCs are found in Central Africa and parts of Asia. Violence and the potential for violence are often associated with LLDCs.

The UN classification has been criticized because it no longer seems relevant in the rapidly industrializing world. In addition, many countries that are classified as LDCs are industrializing at a very rapid rate, whereas others are advancing at more traditional rates of economic development. It is interesting to note in Exhibit 9.2 the differences in income and consumer possessions across the eight most populous American nations.

Countries that are experiencing rapid economic expansion and industrialization and do not exactly fit as LDCs or MDCs are more typically referred to as newly industrialized countries (NICs). These countries have shown rapid industrialization of targeted industries and have per capita incomes that exceed other developing countries. They have moved away from restrictive trade practices and instituted significant free market reforms; as a result, they attract both trade and foreign direct investment. Chile, Brazil, Mexico, South Korea, Singapore, and Taiwan are some of the countries that fit this description. These NICs have become formidable exporters of many products, including steel, automobiles, machine tools, clothing, and electronics, as well as vast markets for imported products.

Brazil provides an example of the growing importance of NICs in world trade, exporting everything from alcohol-based fuels to carbon steel. Brazilian orange juice, poultry,

LO4

The variety of stages of economic development among American nations

Exhibit 9.2
Standards of Living in the Eight Most Populous American Countries

| Country | Population (millions) | GDI/Capita | Medical Resources per 1000 Persons | | Household Ownership % | | |
			Doctors	Hospital Beds	Color TV	Refrigerator	Washing machine
United States	316.4	$54337	2.5	3.0	98.9	99.9	84.6
Brazil	200.4	11017	1.9	2.3	97.6	97.0	54.8
Mexico	117.5	10491	2.2	1.6	94.8	82.7	68.0
Colombia	48.3	7514	1.6	0.8	91.9	78.9	53.9
Argentina	41.5	11334	3.2	2.1	97.1	96.4	95.1
Canada	35.2	51113	2.5	2.7	99.1	99.9	81.9
Peru	30.4	6562	1.7	1.5	70.3	48.7	21.0
Venezuela	30.3	11728	—	0.8	93.5	88.2	70.7

Source: Euromonitor International 2015.

soybeans, and weapons (Brazil is the world's sixth-largest weapons exporter) compete with U.S. products for foreign markets. Embraer, a Brazilian aircraft manufacturer, has sold planes to more than 60 countries and provides a substantial portion of the commuter aircraft used in the United States and elsewhere. Even in automobile production, Brazil is a world player; it ships more than 200,000 cars, trucks, and buses to Third World countries annually. Volkswagen has produced more than 3 million VW Beetles in Brazil and has invested more than $500 million in a project to produce the Golf and Passat automobiles. The firm also recently announced a deal to sell $500 million worth of auto parts to a Chinese partner. General Motors invested $600 million to create what it calls "an industrial complex"—a collection of 17 plants occupied by suppliers such as Delphi, Lear, and Goodyear to deliver preassembled modules to GM's line workers. All in all, auto and auto parts makers are investing more than $2.8 billion aimed at the 200 million people in the Mercosur market, the free trade group formed by Argentina, Brazil, Paraguay, and Uruguay.

Economic Growth Factors

LO5

Growth factors and their role in economic development

Why have some countries grown so rapidly and successfully while others with similar or more plentiful resources languished? Some analysts attribute the faster growth of some to cultural values, others to cheap labor, and still others to an educated and literate population. Certainly all of these factors have contributed to growth, but other important factors are present in all the rapidly growing economies, many of which seem to be absent in those nations that have not enjoyed comparable economic growth.

The factors that existed to some extent during the economic growth of NICs were as follows:

- Political stability in policies affecting their development.

- Economic and legal reforms. Poorly defined and/or weakly enforced contract and property rights are features the poorest countries have in common.

- Entrepreneurship. In all of these nations, free enterprise in the hands of the self-employed was the seed of the new economic growth.

- Planning. A central plan with observable and measurable development goals linked to specific policies was in place.

- Outward orientation. Production for the domestic market and export markets with increases in efficiencies and continual differentiation of exports from competition was the focus.[9]

- Factors of production. If deficient in the factors of production—land (raw materials), labor, capital, management, and technology—an environment existed where these factors could easily come from outside the country and be directed to development objectives.

- Industries targeted for growth. Strategically directed industrial and international trade policies were created to identify those sectors where opportunity existed. Key industries were encouraged to achieve better positions in world markets by directing resources into promising target sectors.

- Incentives to force a high domestic rate of savings and direct capital to update the infrastructure, transportation, housing, education, and training.

---

[9]Cuba still struggles to regain its foothold in international markets after the demise of its robust trade with the Communist Bloc countries in the 1990s. There is some good news though: Tourism dollars are now supporting the redevelopment of "Old Havana," to the tune of more than $1.5 billion in revenues since 1998. A new deepwater container ship port is being developed at Muriel just west of Havana; see Damien Cave, "Former Exit Port for a Wave of Cubans Hopes to Attract Global Shipping," *The New York TImes*, January 28, 2014, p. A4. Also, political detente is making progress; see Michael D. Shear, "Obama Reaches Out to Cuba's Leader, but the Meaning May Elude Grasp," *The New York Times*, December 11, 2013, p. A6.

Brazilian production of coffee (on left) has almost always determined world prices for the brew. Now this commercial dominance is being challenged in two ways. First, Vietnam's burgeoning new production (on right) caused world coffee prices to crash in recent years, from a high of $1.85 per pound in 1997 to about $.50 in 2001. Circa 2015 prices are now back to about $2.00 per pound, after peaking at $3.00 in 2010. And Starbucks is changing the global game in retail coffee distribution—including in its store in the heart of São Paulo, the historical center of coffee production in Brazil and the world.

- Privatization of state-owned enterprises (SOEs) that had placed a drain on national budgets. Privatization released immediate capital to invest in strategic areas and gave relief from a continuing drain on future national resources. Often when industries are privatized, the new investors modernize, thus creating new economic growth.

The final factors that have been present are large, accessible markets with low tariffs. During the early growth of many countries, the first large open market was the United States, later joined by Europe and now, as the fundamental principles of the World Trade Organization (WTO) are put into place, by much of the rest of the world.

Although it is customary to think such growth factors as applying only to industrial growth, the example of Chile shows that economic growth can occur with agricultural development as its economic engine. Chile's economy has expanded at an average rate of 7.2 percent since 1987 and is considered one of the least risky Latin American economies for foreign investment. However, since 1976 when Chile opened up trade, the relative size of its manufacturing sector declined from 27.3 percent of GDP in 1973 to around 11 percent in 2014.[10] Agriculture, in contrast, has not declined. Exports of agricultural

---

[10]World Bank, "World Development Indicators," 2015.

products have been the star performers. Chile went from being a small player in the global fruit market, exporting only apples in the 1960s, to one of the world's largest fruit exporters by 2000. Sophisticated production technology and management methods were applied to the production of table grapes, wine, salmon from fish farms, and a variety of other processed and semiprocessed agricultural products. Salmon farming, begun in the early 1980s, has made salmon a major export item. Salmon exports to the United States are 40,000 tons annually, whereas U.S. annual production of farm-raised salmon is only 31,000 tons. Chile is also a major exporter of the fishmeal that is fed to hatchery-raised salmon.

Chile's production technology has resulted in productivity increases and higher incomes. Its experience indicates that manufacturing is not the only way for countries to grow economically. The process is to continually adapt to changing tastes, constantly improve technology, and find new ways to prosper from natural resources. Contrast Chile today with the traditional agriculturally based economies that are dependent on one crop (e.g., bananas) today and will still be dependent on that same crop 20 years from now. This type of economic narrowness was the case with Chile a few decades ago when it depended heavily on copper. To expand its economy beyond dependency on copper, Chile began with what it did best—exporting apples. As the economy grew, the country invested in better education and infrastructure and improved technology to provide the bases to develop other economic sectors, such as grapes, wine, salmon, and tomato paste.

Regional cooperation and open markets are also crucial for economic growth. As will be discussed in detail in Chapter 10, being a member of a multinational market region is essential if a country is to have preferential access to regional trade groups. As steps in that direction, in 2003 Chile and in 2005 Central American countries (including banana producers) signed free trade agreements with the United States.

Information Technology, the Internet, and Economic Development

In addition to the growth factors previously discussed, a country's investment in information technology (IT) is an important key to economic growth. The cellular phone, the Internet, and other advances in IT open opportunities for emerging economies to catch up with richer ones. New, innovative electronic technologies can be the key to a sustainable future for developed and developing nations alike.

Because the Internet cuts transaction costs and reduces economies of scale from vertical integration, some argue that it reduces the economically optimal size for firms. Lower transaction costs enable small firms in Asia or Latin America to work together to develop a global reach. Smaller firms in emerging economies can now sell into a global market. It is now easier, for instance, for a tailor in Hong Kong to make a suit by hand for an executive in Memphis. One of the big advantages that rich economies have is their closeness to wealthy consumers, and this advantage will erode as transaction costs fall.

The Internet accelerates the process of economic growth by speeding up the diffusion of new technologies to emerging economies. Unlike the decades required for many developing countries to benefit from railways, telephones, or electricity, the Internet is spreading rapidly throughout Latin America and the rest of the world. Information technology can jump-start national economies and allow them to leapfrog from high levels of illiteracy to computer literacy.

Mobile phones and other wireless technologies greatly reduce the need to lay a costly telecom infrastructure to bring telephone service to areas not served. In Caracas, Venezuela, for example, where half of the city's 5 million people live in nonwired slums, cell phones with pay-as-you-go cards have provided service to many residents for the first time. The Internet allows for innovative services at a relatively inexpensive cost. Telecenters in many developing countries provide public telephone, fax, computer, and Internet services where students can read online books and local entrepreneurs can seek potential business partners. Medical specialists from Belgium help train local doctors and surgeons in Senegal via video linkups between classrooms and operating centers and provide them with Internet

Exhibit 9.3
Infrastructure of Most Populous American Countries

Country	Travel by Rail (passenger-km per capita)	Passenger Cars/1000 People	Energy Consumption (tonnes oil equivalent per capita)	Mobile Phones in Use per 1000	Literacy Rate (%)	University Students*
United States	34.5	397	7.2	987	99.9	94
Brazil	—	214	1.4	1353	91.4	—
Mexico	10.1	209	1.6	894	94.6	29
Colombia	1.0	45	0.8	1041	93.8	45
Argentina	166.9	238	2.0	1589	98.0	79
Canada	37.4	432	9.5	734	99.8	—
Peru	2.8	42	0.7	981	94.3	35
Venezuela	—	120	2.7	1018	96.4	78

* Percentage of those eligible within 5 years of high school graduation.

access to medical journals and databases. Traveling there to teach would be prohibitively expensive; via Internet technology, it costs practically nothing.

Objectives of Developing Countries

A thorough assessment of economic development and marketing should begin with a brief review of the basic facts and objectives of economic development.

Industrialization is the fundamental objective of most developing countries. Most countries see in economic growth the achievement of social as well as economic goals. Better education, better and more effective government, the elimination of many social inequities, and improvements in moral and ethical responsibilities are some of the expectations of developing countries. Thus, economic growth is measured not solely in economic goals but also in social achievements. Regarding the last, consider for a moment the tremendous efforts Brazil has undertaken in preparing for the 2016 Olympics.

Because foreign businesses are outsiders, they often are feared as having goals in conflict with those of the host country. Considered exploiters of resources, many multinational firms were expropriated in the 1950s and 1960s. Others faced excessively high tariffs and quotas, and foreign investment was forbidden or discouraged. Today, foreign investors are seen as vital partners in economic development.[11] Experience with state-owned businesses proved to be a disappointment to most governments. Instead of being engines for accelerated economic growth, state-owned enterprises were mismanaged, inefficient drains on state treasuries. Many countries have deregulated industry, opened their doors to foreign investment, lowered trade barriers, and begun privatizing SOEs. The trend toward privatization is currently a major economic phenomenon in industrialized as well as in developing countries.

Infrastructure and Development

One indicator of economic development is the extent of social overhead capital, or infrastructure, within the economy. Infrastructure represents those types of capital goods that serve the activities of many industries. Included in a country's infrastructure are paved roads, railroads, seaports, communication networks, financial networks, and energy supplies and distribution—all necessary to support production and marketing. The quality of an infrastructure directly affects a country's economic growth potential and the ability of an enterprise to engage effectively in business. See Exhibit 9.3 for some comparisons of infrastructure among the eight largest American countries.

---

[11]Heng Liu, Xu Jiang, Jianqi Zhang, and Xinglu Zhou, "Strategic Flexibility and International Venturing by Emerging Market Firms: The Moderating Effects of Institutional and Relational Factors," *Journal of International Marketing* 21, no. 2 (2013), pp. 79–98.

Here in Jamaica, Pepsi partners with a local fast-food company, co-branding and supporting local development efforts.

Infrastructure is a crucial component of the uncontrollable elements facing marketers. Without adequate transportation facilities, for example, distribution costs can increase substantially, and the ability to reach certain segments of the market is impaired. The lack of readily available educational assets hampers not only the ability to communicate to residents (literacy) but also firms' ability to find qualified local marketing managers. To a marketer, the key issue is the impact of a country's infrastructure on a firm's ability to market effectively. Business efficiency is affected by the presence or absence of financial and commercial service infrastructure found within a country—such as advertising agencies, warehousing storage facilities, credit and banking facilities, marketing research agencies, and satisfactory specialized middlemen. Generally speaking, the less developed a country is, the less adequate the infrastructure is for conducting business. Companies do market in less-developed countries, but often they must modify their offerings and augment existing levels of infrastructure.

Countries begin to lose economic development ground when their infrastructure cannot support an expanding population and economy. A country that has the ability to produce commodities for export may be unable to export them because of an inadequate infrastructure. For example, Mexico's economy has been throttled by its archaic transport system. Roads and seaports are inadequate, and the railroad system has seen little modernization since the 1910 Revolution. Please see Exhibit 9.3 for some of the numbers associated with this problem. If it were not for Mexico's highway system (though it, too, is in poor condition), the economy would have come to a halt; Mexico's highways have consistently carried more freight than its railroads. Conditions in other Latin American countries are no better. Shallow harbors and inadequate port equipment in part make a container filled with computers about $1,000 more expensive to ship from Miami to San Antonio, Chile (about 3,900 miles), than the same container shipped from Yokohama, Japan, to Miami (8,900 miles).

Marketing's Contributions

LO6 ▨

Marketing's contribution to the growth and development of a country's economy

How important is marketing to the achievement of a nation's goals? Unfortunately, marketing (or distribution) is not always considered meaningful to those responsible for planning. Economic planners frequently are more production oriented than marketing oriented and tend to ignore or regard distribution as an inferior economic activity. Given such attitudes, economic planners generally are more concerned with the problems of production, investment, and finance than the problems of efficiency of distribution.

Marketing is an economy's arbitrator between productive capacity and consumer demand. The marketing process is the critical element in effectively utilizing production resulting from economic growth; it can create a balance between higher production and higher consumption. An efficient distribution and channel system and all the attendant liaisons match production capacity and resources with consumer needs, wants, and purchasing power.

Marketing luminary, Jagdish Sheth, has offered a most useful guide for making adjustments in emerging markets. He points out five crucial weakness driving the need for different thinking: (1) market heterogeneity—local, fragmented, low-scale, and owner-managed small enterprise; (2) socialpolitical governance—religious, business groups, NGOs, and local communities are more involved; (3) unbranded competition; (4) chronic shortage of resources; and (5) inadequate infrastructure. Among recommendations for changes in marketing theory, strategy, and policy, he lists three adaptations for marketing practice in emerging markets. Rather than adapting global products for local conditions, fusion products may be more appropriate. Holistic medicine would be an example. Rather than diffusion of innovations, the focus of new product development should be on affordability and accessibility. This means cheaper cell phones, not necessarily smarter ones. Or consider Philips' development of cook stoves that we detail in Chapter 13. Finally, national brand advantage will be more important than other sorts of country-of-origin advantages. Sheth's entire article is an important read.[12]

Marketing in a Developing Country

A marketer cannot superimpose a technically elegant marketing strategy on an underdeveloped economy. Marketing efforts must be keyed to each situation, custom tailored for each set of circumstances. A promotional program for a population that is 50 percent illiterate is vastly different from a program for a population that is 95 percent literate. Pricing in a subsistence market poses different problems from pricing in an affluent society. In evaluating the potential in a developing country, the marketer must make an assessment of the existing level of market development and receptiveness within the country, as well as the firm's own capabilities and circumstances.[13]

Level of Market Development

The level of market development roughly parallels the stages of economic development. Exhibit 9.4 illustrates various stages of the marketing process as it evolves in a growing economy. The table is a static model representing an idealized evolutionary process. As discussed previously, economic cooperation and assistance, technological change, and political, social, and cultural factors can and do cause significant deviations in this evolutionary process. However, the table focuses on the logic and interdependence of marketing and economic development. The more developed an economy, the greater the variety of marketing functions demanded, and the more sophisticated and specialized the institutions become to perform marketing functions.

As countries develop, the distribution channel systems develop. In the retail sector, specialty stores, supermarkets, and hypermarkets emerge, and mom-and-pop stores and local brands often give way to larger establishments. In short, the number of retail stores

---

[12]Jagdish M. Sheth, "Impact of Emerging Markets on Marketing: Rethinking Existing Perspectives and Practices," *Journal of Marketing*, 75(4), July 2011, pp. 166–82; for more good ideas in this vein, also see V. Kumar, Amalesh Sharma, Riddhi Shah, and Bharath Rajan, "Establishing Profitable Customer Loyalty for Multinational Companies in the Emerging Economies: A Conceptual Framework," *Journal of International Marketing* 21, no.1 (2013), pp. 57–80.

[13]Donna L. Paul and Rossitza B. Wooster, "Strategic Investments by US Firms in Transition Economies," *Journal of International Business Studies* 39 (March 2008), pp. 249–66.

Exhibit 9.4
Evolution of the Marketing Process

Stage	Substage	Example	Marketing Functions	Marketing Institutions	Channel Control	Primary Orientation	Resources Employed	Comments
Agricultural and raw materials	Self-sufficient	Nomadic or hunting tribes	None	None	Traditional authority	Subsistence	Labor Land	Labor intensive No organized markets
	Surplus commodity product	Agricultural economy, such as coffee, bananas	Exchange	Small-scale merchants, traders, fairs, export-import	Traditional authority	Entrepreneurial Commercial	Labor Mobile phones Land	Labor and land intensive Product specialization Local markets Import oriented
Manufacturing	Small scale	Cottage industry	Exchange Physical distribution	Merchants, wholesalers, export-import	Middlemen	Entrepreneurial Financial	Labor Land Technology Transportation	Labor intensive Product standardization and grading Regional and export markets Import oriented
	Mass production	U.S. economy, 1885–1914	Demand creation Physical distribution	Merchants, wholesalers, traders, and specialized institutions	Producer	Production and finance	Labor Land Technology Transportation Capital	Capital intensive Product differentiation National, regional, and export markets
Marketing	Commercial-transition	U.S. economy, 1915–1929	Demand creation Physical distribution Market information	Large-scale and chain retailers	Producer	Entrepreneurial Commercial	Labor Land Technology Transportation Capital Communication (Internet and mobile phones)	Capital intensive Changes in structure of distribution National, regional, and export markets
	Mass distribution	U.S. economy, 1950 to present	Demand creation Physical distribution Market information Market and product planning, development	Integrated channels of distribution Increase in specialized middlemen	Producer Retailer	Marketing	Labor Land Technology Transportation Capital Communication	Capital and land intensive Rapid product innovation National, regional, and export markets

CROSSING BORDERS 9.1

Marketing in the Third World: Teaching, Pricing, and Community Usage

Much of the marketing challenge in the developing world, which is not accustomed to consumer products, is to get consumers to use the product and to offer it in the right sizes. For example, because many Latin American consumers can't afford a seven-ounce bottle of shampoo, Gillette sells it in half-ounce plastic bottles. And in Brazil, the company sells Right Guard in plastic squeeze bottles instead of metal cans.

But the toughest task for Gillette is convincing Third World men to shave. Portable theaters called mobile propaganda units are sent into villages to show movies and commercials that tout daily shaving. In South African and Indonesian versions, a bewildered bearded man enters a locker room where clean-shaven friends show him how to shave. In the Mexican film, a handsome sheriff is tracking bandits who have kidnapped a woman. He pauses on the trail, snaps a double-edged blade into his razor, and lathers his face to shave. In the end, of course, the smooth-faced sheriff gets the woman. From packaging blades so that they can be sold one at a time to educating the unshaven about the joys of a smooth face, Gillette is pursuing a growth strategy in the developing world.

For another reason, Latin American women appreciate smaller bottles of perfume. Price remains an important consideration, but Mary Kay has found that Latin American women wear a "wardrobe" of fragrances, whereas their European and U.S. counterparts are loyal to a single fragrance.

L'Oreal has struggled in Brazil because the firm eschews door-to-door selling, even though Latin American women are generally used to buying from direct sellers. It will be interesting to see if L'Oreal can succeed there without adapting its fundamental marketing strategies.

What Gillette does for shaving, Colgate-Palmolive does for oral hygiene. Video vans sent into rural India show an infomercial designed to teach the benefits of toothpaste and the proper method of brushing one's teeth. "If they saw the toothpaste tube, they wouldn't know what to do with it," says the company's Indian marketing manager. The people need to be educated about the need for toothpaste and then how to use the product. Toothpaste consumption has doubled in rural Brazil in a six-year period.

Sources: David Wessel, "Gillette Keys Sales to Third World Taste," *The Wall Street Journal*, January 23, 1986, p. 30; "Selling to India," *The Economist*, May 1, 2000; Raja Ramachandran, "Understanding the Market Environment of India," *Business Horizons*, January/February 2000, p. 44; Euromonitor International, 2012; Christina Passariello, "To L'Oreal, Brazil's Women Need Fresh Style of Shopping," *The Wall Street Journal*, January 21, 2011, pp. B1-2.

declines, and the volume of sales per store increases. Additionally, a defined channel structure from manufacturer to wholesaler to retailer develops and replaces the import agent that traditionally assumed all the functions between importing and retailing.

Advertising agencies, facilities for marketing research, repair services,[14] specialized consumer-financing agencies,[15] storage and warehousing facilities, and communications networks (including the Internet and mobile phones) are facilitating agencies created to serve the particular needs of expanded markets and economies. These institutions do not come about automatically, and the necessary marketing structure does not simply appear. Part of the marketer's task when studying an economy is to determine what in the foreign environment will be useful and how much adjustment will be necessary to carry out stated objectives. In some developing countries, it may be up to the marketer to institute the foundations of a modern marketing system. See Crossing Borders 9.1 above.

The limitation of Exhibit 9.4 in evaluating the market system of a particular country is that the system is in a constant state of flux. To expect a neat, precise progression through each successive growth stage, as in the geological sciences, is to oversimplify the dynamic nature of marketing development. So some ventures will not succeed no matter how well planned. A significant factor in the acceleration of market development is that countries or areas of countries have been propelled from the 18th to the 21st century in the span of two decades via borrowed technology.

[14]Ian Alum, "New Service Development Process: Emerging versus Developed Markets," *Journal of Global Marketing* 20, no. 2/3 (2007), pp. 43–56.

[15]Katrijn Gielens and Marnik G. Dekimpe, "The Entry Strategy of Retail Firms into Transition Economies," *Journal of Marketing* 71 (2007), pp. 196–212.

Marketing structures of many developing countries are simultaneously at many stages. It is not unusual to find traditional small retail outlets functioning side by side with advanced, modern markets. This situation is especially true in food retailing, where a large segment of the population buys food from small produce stalls, while the same economy supports modern supermarkets equal to any found in the United States.

Demand in Developing Countries

The data in Exhibit 9.5 represent the diversity of consumption patterns across types of countries. Notice the higher percentages of expenditures for food in developing countries, whereas the costs of housing are more important in affluent countries. Also note the high costs of health goods and medical services associated with the mostly private-sector health-care system of the United States. You may recall from Chapter 4 that the government-based, tax-dollar-supported systems in many other affluent countries deliver equal or better longevity to their citizens, particularly in Japan. Affluence also allows higher proportions to be spent on leisure activities than is the case in developing countries.

Estimating market potential and devising useful segmentation strategies[16] in less-developed countries involves additional challenges. Most of the difficulty arises from the coexistence of three distinct kinds of markets in each country: (1) the traditional rural/agricultural sector, (2) the modern urban/high-income sector,[17] and (3) the often very large transitional sector usually represented by low-income urban slums. The modern sector is centered in the capital city and has jet airports, international hotels, new factories, and an expanding Westernized middle class. The traditional rural sector tends to work in the countryside, as it has for centuries. Directly juxtaposed to the modern sector, the transitional sector contains those moving from the country to the large cities. Production and consumption patterns vary across the three sectors. Latin America currently has a population of about 600 million, about two-thirds of which would be classified as middle class by one definition—that is, within the income per capita band of $5,000 to $20,000 at purchase price parity. The modern sector demands products and services similar to those available in any industrialized country; the remaining 200 million in the transitional and rural sectors, however, demand items indigenous and

---

[16]Tobias Schlager and Peter, "Fitting International Segmentation for Emerging Markets: Conceptual Development and Empirical Illustration," *Journal of International Marketing* 21, no. 2 (2013), pp. 39–61.

[17]Some have referred to this segment as the "new middle class." See Olga Kravets and Ozlem Sandikci, "Competently Ordinary: New Middle Class Consumers in the Emerging Markets," *Journal of Marketing* 78, no. 4 (July 2014), pp. 125–40.

The irony of Parker Brothers' introduction of Monopoly to Ecuador is rather amusing, given President Rafael Correa's announcement of new *anti-monopoly* laws just a year earlier. He was reacting to Carlos Slim's giant Mexican Telmex takeover of Ecuador Telecom.

Exhibit 9.5
Consumption Patterns in Most Populous American Countries

Country	Occupants per Household	Food	Alcohol, Tobacco	Clothing	Housing	Health Goods, Medical Services	Transportation	Communications	Leisure	Education
						Household Expenditures ($/capita)				
United States	2.6	2390	739	1196	6652	7480	3571	864	3209	872
Brazil	3.3	1072	154	289	1283	569	1033	224	300	246
Mexico	3.9	1706	187	221	1454	287	1459	240	339	104
Colombia	3.8	864	143	319	763	139	614	204	248	221
Argentina	3.2	2020	437	343	1781	909	930	532	483	653
Canada	2.6	2609	960	1147	6850	1211	4303	687	2356	431
Peru	4.0	1510	250	180	703	390	365	104	68	122
Venezuela	4.0	1364	250	316	877	463	891	448	493	150

Source: Euromonitor International, 2015.

basic to subsistence.[18] As one authority on developing markets observed, "A rural consumer can live a sound life without many products. Toothpaste, sugar, coffee, washing soap, bathing soap, kerosene are all bare necessities of life to those who live in semiurban and urban areas." One of the greatest challenges of the 21st century is to manage and market to the transitional sector in developing countries. The large-city slums perhaps present the greatest problems for smooth economic development. And perhaps the most frightening trend in 21st century developed countries is the bifurcation of markets into rich and poor, such that they resemble the patterns in emerging markets.[19]

Increasingly marketing research efforts are being focused on the lowest income segments in Latin America. For example, McCann Worldgroup's office in Bogota, Colombia (owned by the global advertising conglomerate Interpublic Group), developed a new division called "Barrio." The launch of the new division is based on a two-year, $2.5 million research project in which McCann sent employees across Latin America to live for a week with families earning between $350 to $700 per month. The agency amassed 700 hours of video recordings and thousands of questionnaires to develop a clearer picture of how consumers behave in the region's poorer districts.

A problem discovered for one of their major clients was a misperception that Nido Rindes Diario, a powdered milk product of Nestle SA, was viewed narrowly as formula appropriate for babies only. A new product positioning was developed, based on the finding that for the poorest families in Latin America, food means survival. One executive explained, "The study found that the meaning of food is energy and strength to work, to carry through the day, to not get sick." To communicate the product's usefulness for the whole family, a radio advertisement was designed using a trumpet and bongo-drum jingle whose verses are a play on the Spanish word *rinde*, which means both long-lasting and productiveness. The jingle suggested that both the consumers of the product and their money would "produce more."

The companies that will benefit in the future from emerging markets in Latin America and elsewhere are the ones that invest when it is difficult and initially unprofitable. In some of the less-developed countries, the marketer will institute the very foundations of a modern market system, thereby gaining a foothold in an economy that will someday be highly profitable. The price paid for entering in the early stages of development may be a lower initial return on investment, but the price paid for waiting until the market becomes profitable may be a blocked market with no opportunity for entry.

Big Emerging Markets (BEMs)   As mentioned previously, the U.S. Department of Commerce estimates that over 75 percent of the expected growth in world trade over the next two decades will come from the more than 130 developing countries; a small core of these countries will account for more than half of that growth.[20] Commerce researchers also predict that imports to the countries identified as big emerging markets (BEMs), with half the world's population and accounting for 25 percent of the industrialized world's GDP today, will soon be 50 percent of that of the industrialized world. With a combined GDP of over $2 trillion, BEMs already account for as large a share of world output as Germany and the United Kingdom combined, and exports to the BEMs exceed exports to Europe and Japan combined.[21]

Big emerging markets share a number of important traits. They

- Are all geographically large.
- Have significant populations.

---

[18]And this doesn't mean "discards" from the United States. See Charles Kenny, "Haiti Doesn't Need Your Old T-Shirt," *Foreign Policy*, November 2001, pp. 30–31.

[19]Nathaniel Popper, "Income Divide Grows in the U.S.," *Los Angeles Times*, December 6, 2011, pp. B1, B8.

[20]Debabrata Talukdar, Sumila Gulyani, and Lawrence F. Salmen, "Customer-Orientation in the Context of Development Projects: Insights from the World Bank," *Journal of Public Policy & Marketing* 24, no. 1 (2005), pp. 100–11.

[21]C. K. Prahalad and Allen Hammond, "Serving the World's Poor, Profitably," *Harvard Business Review* 80, no. 9 (September 2002), pp. 24–32.

- Represent sizable markets for a wide range of products.
- Have strong rates of growth or the potential for significant growth.
- Have undertaken significant programs of economic reform.
- Are of major political importance within their regions.
- Are "regional economic drivers."
- Will engender further expansion in neighboring markets as they grow.

Although these criteria are general and each country does not meet all of them, India, China, Brazil, Mexico, Poland, Turkey, and South Africa are prominent examples of countries the Department of Commerce has identified as BEMs. Other countries such as Egypt, the Philippines,[22] Venezuela, Vietnam, and Colombia may warrant inclusion in the near future. The list is fluid, because some countries will drop off while others will be added as economic conditions change. Inducements for those doing business in BEMs include export–import bank loans and political risk insurance channeled into these areas.

The BEMs differ from other developing countries in that they import more than smaller markets and more than economies of similar size. As they embark on economic development, demand increases for capital goods to build their manufacturing base and develop infrastructure. Increased economic activity means more jobs and more income to spend on products not yet produced locally. Thus, as their economies expand, there is accelerated growth in demand for goods and services, much of which must be imported. Thus, BEM merchandise imports are expected to be nearly $1 trillion higher than they were in 1990; if services are added, the amount jumps beyond the trillion-dollar mark.

Because many of these countries lack modern infrastructure, much of the expected growth will be in industrial sectors such as information technology, environmental technology, transportation, energy technology, healthcare technology, and financial services. What is occurring in the BEMs is analogous to the situation after World War II when tremendous demand was created during the reconstruction of Europe. As Europe rebuilt its infrastructure and industrial base, demand for capital goods exploded; as more money was infused into its economies, consumer demand also increased rapidly. For more than a decade, Europe could not supply its increasing demand for industrial and consumer goods. During that period, the United States was the principal supplier because most of the rest of the world was rebuilding or had underdeveloped economies. Meeting this demand produced one of the largest economic booms the United States had ever experienced. As we shall see later in the chapter, consumer markets and market segments in the BEMs are already booming. Unlike the situation after World War II, however, the competition will be fierce as Japan, China, Europe, the NICs, and the United States vie for these big emerging markets.

The Americas[23]

Within the Americas, the United States, Canada, Central America, and South America have been natural if sometimes contentious trading partners. As in Europe, the Americas are engaged in all sorts of economic cooperative agreements,[24] with NAFTA being the most significant[25] and Mercosur and DR-CAFTA gaining in importance.

North American Free Trade Agreement (NAFTA)

Preceding the creation of the North American Free Trade Agreement (NAFTA), the United States and Canada had the world's largest bilateral trade agreement; each was the other's largest trading partner. Despite this unique commercial relationship, tariff and other trade

---

[22]Bill Johnson, "The CEO of Heinz on Powering Growth in Emerging Markets," *Harvard Business Review*, October 2011, pp. 47–50.

[23]For a comprehensive list of all trade agreements in the Americas, with links to specific documents, visit http://www.sice.oas.org and select Trade Agreements.

[24]Joe Biden, "The Americas Ascendant," *The Wall Street Journal*, June 5, 2013, p. A11.

[25]"Ready to Take Off Again?" *The Economist*, January 4, 2014, pp. 23–24.

Geographic proximity allows Mexicans from Baja, California, to attend Padres baseball games in close-by San Diego. The team maintains this successful store just across the border in Plaza Rio shopping center in Tijuana. And of course, historically, Padre Junipero Serra had visited both places in the late 1700s while establishing the chain of missions in old Spanish California. NAFTA also gave Taco Bell a second shot at making it in Mexico; this store was in Monterrey. The company's 1992, pre-NAFTA incursion failed. Unfortunately the store pictured here also closed in 2010. See why in Crossing Border 9.2 on the next page.

barriers hindered even greater commercial activity. To further support trade activity, the two countries established the United States–Canada Free Trade Area (CFTA), designed to eliminate all trade barriers between the two countries. The CFTA created a single, continental commercial market for all goods and most services. The agreement between the United States and Canada was not a customs union like the European Community; no economic or political union of any kind was involved. It provided only for the elimination of tariffs and other trade barriers.

Shortly after both countries had ratified the CFTA, Mexico announced that it would seek free trade with the United States. Mexico's overtures were answered positively by the United States, and talks on a U.S.–Mexico free trade area began. Mexico and the United States had been strong trading partners for decades, but Mexico had never officially expressed an interest in a free trade agreement until the president of Mexico, Carlos Salinas de Gortari, announced that Mexico would seek such an agreement with the United States and Canada.

Despite the disparity between Mexico's economy and the economies of the other two countries, there were sound reasons for such an alliance. Canada is a sophisticated industrial economy, resource rich, but with a small population and domestic market. Mexico desperately needs investment, technology, exports, and other economic reinforcement to spur its economy. Even though Mexico has an abundance of oil and a rapidly growing population, the number of new workers is increasing faster than its economy can create new jobs. The United States needs resources (especially oil) and, of course, markets. The three need one another to compete more effectively in world markets, and they need mutual assurances that their already dominant trading positions in the others' markets are safe from protection pressures. When NAFTA was ratified and became effective in 1994, a single market of 360 million people with a $6 trillion GNP emerged.

NAFTA required the three countries to remove all tariffs and barriers to trade over 15 years, and by 2008, all tariff barriers had been officially dropped. Some nagging disagreements still persist, such as allowing Mexican trucks and truckers free access to U.S. roads. But for the most part, NAFTA is a comprehensive trade agreement that addresses, and in most cases improves, all aspects of doing business within North America. See Exhibit 9.6 for some of the key provisions of the trade agreement. The elimination of trade and investment barriers among Canada, Mexico, and the United States creates one of the largest and richest markets in the world. Cross-border cooperation seems to ameliorate

CROSSING BORDERS 9.2   Taco Bell Tries Again

It sounds like a fast-food grudge match: Taco Bell took on the homeland of its namesake by reopening for the first time in 15 years in Mexico. Defenders of Mexican culture saw the chain's reentry as a crowning insult to a society already overrun by U.S. chains, from Starbucks and Subway to KFC. "It's like bringing ice to the Arctic," complained pop culture historian Carlos Monsivais.

In Mexico, the company tried to project a more "American" fast-food image by adding French fries—some topped with cheese, sour cream, ground meat, and tomatoes—to the menu of its first store, which opened in late September 2007 in the northern city of Monterrey. Other than the fries and sales of soft-serve ice cream, "our menu comes almost directly from the U.S. menu," said Managing Director Steven Pepper.

Some of the names were changed to protect the sacred: The hard-shelled items sold as "tacos" in the United States were renamed "tacostadas." This made-up word was a play on "tostada," which for Mexicans is a hard, fried disk of cornmeal that is always served flat, with toppings. But while Mexicans eagerly buy many American brands, the taco holds a place of honor in the national cuisine. Mexicans eat them everywhere, any time of day, buying them from basket-toting street vendors in the morning or slathering them in salsa at brightly lit taquerias to wrap up a night on the town.

Taco Bell took pains to say that it was not trying to masquerade as a Mexican tradition. "One look alone is enough to tell that Taco Bell is not a 'taqueria,'" the company said in a half-page newspaper ad. "It is a new fast-food alternative that does not pretend to be Mexican food." It was still a mixed message for Mexicans like Marco Fragoso, a 39-year-old office worker sitting down for

lunch at a traditional taqueria in Mexico City, because the U.S. chain used traditional Mexican names for its burritos, gorditas, and chalupas. "They're not tacos," Fragoso said. "They're folded tostadas. They're very ugly."

Taco Bell failed with an earlier, highly publicized launch in Mexico City in 1992, when it opened a few outlets next to KFC restaurants. Now Taco Bell, KFC, and Pizza Hut are owned by Yum! Brands. But Mexicans were less familiar with foreign chains back then, the economy was on the verge of a crisis, and NAFTA had yet to be signed. The restaurants didn't even last two years. Since then, free trade and growing migration have made U.S. brands ubiquitous in Mexico, influencing everything from how people dress to how they talk.

Graham Allan, president of Yum! Brands, said two years of market research had convinced him that the firm would succeed on the second try. The company built its second store in another Monterrey suburb and planned to open between 8 and 10 more locations in its first year, with plans to eventually reach 300 stores. The first stores were company-owned, and franchise opportunities were to be opened up in later years.

But though marketers like Allen need to be optimistic, it can be tough to stay that way. Taco Bell closed its Monterrey store in 2010. Even the best marketing research cannot guarantee success. This story offers an important lesson in international marketing.

Sources: Michael Arndt, "Tacos without Borders," *BusinessWeek*, September 3, 2007, p. 12; Mark Stevenson, "Another Run for the Border," *Los Angeles Times*, October 15, 2007, p. C4. Used with permission; and Adrian Cerda, "Quiebra Taco Bell en Mexico," *Conteindo*, April 1, 2010.

---

other long-standing areas of conflict such as legal and illegal immigration. NAFTA also has paved the way for Walmart to move into Mexico and the Mexican supermarket giant Gigante to move into the United States. Other cross-border services are also thriving, including entertainment and healthcare.

Furthermore, U.S. and foreign investors with apparel and footwear factories in Asia have been encouraged to relocate their production operations to Mexico.[26] For example, Victoria's Secret lingerie chain opened a new manufacturing plant near Mexico City. The company previously had used contractors in Asia for its lingerie line. Even with wages in Mexico three times the monthly wages in Sri Lanka, the company will still come out ahead because moving goods from Mexico City to the United States is cheaper and faster than moving them from Colombo— the time needed to make a sample can be cut from weeks to days. Mexican goods have no tariffs, whereas Sri Lankan goods carry a 19 percent duty.

---

[26]"Fashion Invasion," *The Economist*, December 8, 2012, p. 67.

Exhibit 9.6
Key Provisions of NAFTA

Market access
Within 10 years of implementation, all tariffs will be eliminated on North American industrial products traded among Canada, Mexico, and the United States. All trade between Canada and the United States not already duty free will be duty free as provided for in CFTA. Mexico will immediately eliminate tariffs on nearly 50 percent of all industrial goods imported from the United States, and remaining tariffs will be phased out entirely within 15 years.

Nontariff barriers
In addition to the elimination of tariffs, Mexico will eliminate nontariff barriers and other trade-distorting restrictions. The U.S. exporters will benefit immediately from the removal of most import licenses that have acted as quotas, essentially limiting the importation of products into the Mexican market. NAFTA also eliminates a host of other Mexican barriers, such as local-content, local-production, and export-performance requirements that have limited U.S. exports.

Rules of origin
NAFTA reduces tariffs only for goods made in North America. Tough rules of origin will determine whether goods qualify for preferential tariff treatment under NAFTA. Rules of origin are designed to prevent free riders from benefiting through minor processing or transshipment of non-NAFTA goods. For example, Japan could not assemble autos in Mexico and avoid U.S. or Canadian tariffs and quotas unless the auto had a specific percentage of Mexican (i.e., North American) content. For goods to be traded duty free, they must contain substantial (62.5 percent) North American content. Because NAFTA rules of origin have been strengthened, clarified, and simplified over those contained in the U.S.–Canada Free Trade Agreement, they supersede the CFTA rules.

Customs administration
Under NAFTA, Canada, Mexico, and the United States have agreed to implement uniform customs procedures and regulations. Uniform procedures ensure that exporters who market their products in more than one NAFTA country will not have to adapt to multiple customs procedures. Most procedures governing rules-of-origin documentation, record keeping, and verification will be the same for all three NAFTA countries. In addition, the three will issue advanced rulings, on request, about whether or not a product qualifies for tariff preference under the NAFTA rules of origin.

Investment
NAFTA will eliminate investment conditions that restrict the trade of goods and services to Mexico. Among the conditions eliminated are the requirements that foreign investors export a given level or percentage of goods or services, use domestic goods or services, transfer technology to competitors, or limit imports to a certain percentage of exports.

Services
NAFTA establishes the first comprehensive set of principles governing services trade. Both U.S. and Canadian financial institutions are permitted to open wholly owned subsidiaries in Mexico, and all restrictions on the services they offer will be lifted. NAFTA opens Mexico's market for international truck, bus, and rail transport and eliminates the requirement to hand off cargo to a Mexican vehicle upon entry into Mexico, saving U.S. industry both time and money. Also, U.S. truck and bus companies will have the right to use their own drivers and equipment for cross-border cargo shipment and passenger service with Mexico.

Intellectual property
NAFTA will provide the highest standards of protection of intellectual property available in any bilateral or international agreement. The agreement covers patents, trademarks, copyrights, trade secrets, semiconductor integrated circuits, and copyrights for North American movies, computer software, and records.

Government procurement
NAFTA guarantees businesses fair and open competition for procurement in North America through transparent and predictable procurement procedures. In Mexico, PEMEX (the national oil company), CFE (the national electric company), and other government-owned enterprises will be open to U.S. and Canadian suppliers.

Standards
NAFTA prohibits the use of standards and technical regulations used as obstacles to trade. However, NAFTA provisions do not require the United States or Canada to lower existing health, environmental, or safety regulations, nor does NAFTA require the importation of products that fail to meet each country's health and safety standards.

Total foreign direct investment in Mexico has averaged more than $20 billion a year since 1995 as companies from all over the world poured money into auto and electronics plants, telecommunications, petrochemicals, and a host of other areas.[27] A large chunk of investment is earmarked for factories that will use Mexico as an export platform for the rest of North America, and increasingly the rest of Latin America.

Job losses have not been as drastic as once feared, in part because companies such as Lucent Technologies established *maquiladora* plants in anticipation of the benefits from NAFTA. The plants have been buying more components from U.S. suppliers, while cutting back on Asian sources. Miles Press, a $2 million maker of directory cards, saw orders from

---

[27]World Bank, *World Development Indicators*, 2015.

CROSSING BORDERS 9.3   In Quebec, They Prefer Pepsi

Up until the 1980s, Coke was king in Quebec. Then the local advertising executives at J. Walter Thompson took a risk. Standard practice for both Coke and Pepsi had been to simply translate U.S. campaigns into French. But being second in the market forced creativity, and based on qualitative research, the ad execs recommended a new selling point: comedy.

It was risky, because while Pepsi had been adopted as a self-effacing term by some Quebecers, it was also a derogatory slur used by non-francophones to describe them. If the marketing plan was seen as offensive, Pepsi could become a pariah.

Claude Meunier, famous for his absurdist humor on *Ding et Dong* television skits, was chosen: to represent Pepsi. The theme of Meunier's ads remained an intractable *joie de vivre* and an undying love of Pepsi. His brief, 30-second spots debuted in 1985 and featured a variety of characters and a humor only Quebecers could appreciate; they became an instant hit.

Pepsi almost matched Coke's sales that same year. By 1986, David had surpassed Goliath and continued to thrive, even though Coke fought back, outspending Pepsi two-to-one on six media campaigns between 1985 and 1993.

"Quebecers had the sentiment that a multinational corporation finally took the trouble to try and understand them, using the same language, with the same accents," says Luc Dupont, a Canadian marketing professor. A nation moored in a sea of English could empathize with a company fighting for purchase in an ocean of Coke. "Subconsciously, Quebecers identify with products that are No. 2," Dupont said. "In addition to the absurd humour and joy of life, they like to say, 'We're different here. We changed things.'"

The Meunier campaign would last 18 years, aided by the fact Meunier became the star of *La Petite Vie*, an early 1990s Quebec sitcom watched by 4 million out of a possible 6 million viewers every Monday night. The Meunier Pepsi campaign won the 1993 CASSIE Best of Show advertising award.

Today, Coke dominates the global market with 51 percent of total sales, compared with Pepsi's 22 percent. But in Quebec, the Pepsi stable of soft drinks owns 61 percent of the market against Coke's 20. It is a dominance unseen anywhere else in North America. "Pepsi's ad campaign allowed us to feed that image of ourselves as different," Dupont said. "Even though in fact, we are not so different." The Pepsi Meunier campaign is taught in textbooks now, Dupont said, as a lesson in how to adapt to your market and change with the times.

We also note that the Quebec province flag is blue and white. while the Canadian flag is red and white. As we will see in Chapter 16, colors often make a difference.

Sources: Konrad Yakabuski, "How Pepsi Won Quebec," *The Globe and Mail*, August 28, 2008, p. B1-2; Rene Bremmer, *The Gazette*, July 11, 2009; Patti Summerfield, "Pepsi Quebec: Deep Roots," *http://strategyonline.ca*, April 1, 2010.

Lucent grow 20 percent in just a few months. Berg Electronics, a $700 million component maker, expects to triple sales to Lucent's Guadalajara plant next year. This ripple effect has generated U.S. service-sector jobs as well. Fisher-Price shifted toy production for the U.S. market from Hong Kong to a plant in Monterrey. Celadon Trucking Services, which moves goods produced for Fisher-Price from Mexico to the United States, added 800 new U.S. drivers to the payroll.

During the protracted economic slump following the dot-com bust in the United States, *maquiladora* plants were closing at an uncomfortable rate. Manufacturing migrated to other low-paying countries such as China, Guatemala, and Vietnam. Most recently, in the depths of the unemployment environment in all three countries, new immigration rules have limited Mexican farm workers from coming north.[28] Even so, the bleak predictions by the critics of NAFTA have not been borne out. The average purchasing power of consumers in all three countries has increased steadily since 1995—see Exhibit 2.7 on page 39 for the evidence.[29]

---

[28]P. J. Huffstutter, "Hiring Foreign Farmworkers Gets Tougher under New Rule," *Los Angeles Times*, February 12, 2010, p. B2.

[29]Andres Martinex, "The Stranger Next Door," *Bloomberg BusinessWeek*, May 12, 2013, pp. 8–9.

NAFTA is a work in progress. Circa 2015, the trade agreement has been a great success;[30] after all, the European Union has been in existence for more than 50 years and has had its ups and downs never mind. NAFTA is a mere babe in arms in comparison. The recent economic downturn has slowed its continuing progress,[31] but generally the economic relationships among the three countries are becoming more intense each day, for the most part quietly and profitably. In short, despite the immediate criticism of NAFTA, in the long run the association has proved most positive as it begins its third decade.

United States–Central American Free Trade Agreement–Dominican Republic Free Trade Agreement (DR-CAFTA)

LO7

The foundational market metrics of American nations

In August 2005, President George Bush signed into law a comprehensive free trade agreement among Costa Rica, the Dominican Republic, El Salvador, Guatemala, Honduras, Nicaragua, and the United States.[32] The agreement includes a wide array of tariff reductions aimed at increasing trade and employment among the seven signatories. Thus, DR-CAFTA represents another important step toward the ultimate goal of a free trade agreement encompassing all the Americas. See Exhibit 9.7 for a listing of American countries involved in trade associations. The statistics included there reflect fundamental measures of their attractiveness to international marketers. Perhaps most useful will be the data reported in the last four columns: the size of the import market, the ease of doing business, and the resources available to consumers, including both money and communication infrastructure. The Ease of Doing Business Index[33] is a ranking based on a combination of 10 different measures, such as ease of "starting a business," "registering property," and "enforcing a contract." For details, see http://www.doingbusiness.org.

Southern Cone Free Trade Area (Mercosur)[34]

LO8

The growing importance of trading associations among American nations

Mercosur (including Argentina, Bolivia, Brazil, Chile, Paraguay, and Uruguay) is the second-largest common-market agreement in the Americas after NAFTA. The Treaty of Asunción, which provided the legal basis for Mercosur, was signed in 1991 and formally inaugurated in 1995. The treaty calls for a common market that would eventually allow for the free movement of goods, capital, labor, and services among the member countries, with a uniform external tariff. Because Mercosur members were concerned about sacrificing sovereign control over taxes and other policy matters, the agreement envisioned no central institutions similar to those of the European Union institutions.

Since its inception, Mercosur has become the most influential and successful free trade area in South America. With the addition of Bolivia and Chile in 1996, Mercosur became a market of 220 million people with a combined GDP of nearly $1 trillion and the third largest free trade area in the world. More recently Colombia and Ecuador have become associate members, with Venezuela to follow shortly; Mexico has observer status as well. Mercosur has demonstrated greater success than many observers expected. The success can be attributed to the willingness of the region's governments to confront some very tough issues caused by dissimilar economic policies related to the automobile and textile trade and to modify antiquated border customs procedures that initially created a bottleneck to smooth border crossings. The lack of surface and transportation infrastructure to facilitate trade and communications is a lingering problem that is being addressed at the highest levels.

Mercosur has pursued agreements aggressively with other countries and trading groups. For example, there are concrete negotiations under way to create a free trade program with

---

[30]Some mistakes have been made. We already mentioned Taco Bell in Mexico, and Target has had problems in Canada. See Ian Austen, "Target Push into Canada Stumbles," *The New York Times*, February 25, 2014, pp. B1, 7.

[31]"Trade with Mexico, Signs of Life," *The Economist*, June 26, 2010, p. 36; "North American Integration, To Each His Own," *The Economist*, February 26, 2011, p. 44.

[32]Beyond NAFTA and DR-CAFTA, the United States has free trade agreements approved for 13 other countries: Australia, Bahrain, Chile, Israel, Jordan, Morocco, Oman, Peru, Singapore, Colombia, South Korea, and Panama.

[33]World Bank, 2015.

[34]See http://www.mercosur.org.uy/.

Exhibit 9.7
American Market Regions Fundamental Market Metrics

(in parentheses) = average annual growth rate, 2006–2011 as a percentage

Association　Country	Population (millions)	GNI* (billions $)	Exports* of Goods (billions $)	Imports* of Goods (billions $)	Ease of Doing Business Index	GNI/ capita* ($)	Internet Users (percentage)
North American Free Trade Agreement (NAFTA)							
United States	316.3 (0.8)	17189.7 (3.0)	1579.6 (4.2)	2268.3 (1.5)	4	54337 (2.2)	84
Mexico	117.5 (1.2)	1232.4 (5.5)	349.7 (6.9)	381.2 (4.3)	51	10491 (4.2)	43
Canada	35.2 (1.1)	1798.8 (3.1)	460.8 (3.5)	461.8 (2.5)	17	51113 (2.0)	86
Dominican Republic–Central American Free Trade Agreement (DR-CAFTA)							
Guatemala	15.5 (2.5)	52.6 (7.4)	10.0 (5.3)	17.5 (3.8)	93	3403 (4.8)	20
Costa Rica	4.7 (1.4)	48.2 (9.5)	11.6 (4.1)	18.0 (3.2)	109	10218 (8.0)	46
El Salvador	6.3 (0.6)	23.3 (2.1)	5.5 (3.7)	10.8 (2.0)	115	3674 (1.4)	23
Nicaragua	6.1 (1.4)	6.8 (11.7)	2.4 (10.3)	5.6 (5.6)	123	1803 (10.2)	16
Honduras	8.1 (2.0)	17.2 (6.6)	7.7 (4.5)	11.1 (1.1)	125	2129 (4.5)	18
Dominican Republic	10.3 (9.8)	58.0 (7.4)	7.6 (5.9)	19.3 (3.9)	112	5623 (8.4)	46
United States	as above						
Caribbean Community and Common Market (CARICOM)							
Antigua	0.1 (1.1)	1.2 (−1.6)	0.1 (−1.76)	0.5 (−7.1)	66	13183 (−2.6)	63
Bahamas	0.4 (1.6)	8.2 (0.1)	1.0 (0.3)	3.3 (0.9)	76	21777 (−1.5)	72
Barbados	0.3 (0.5)	4.1 (−0.9)	0.5 (0.8)	1.8 (−1.3)	84	14440 (−1.4)	75
Belize	0.3 (2.5)	1.6 (5.2)	0.3 (1.6)	0.9 (2.1)	104	4763 (2.6)	32
Dominica	0.1 (0.3)	0.5 (2.6)	0.0 (−1.0)	0.2 (−3.9)	69	6852 (2.3)	59
Grenada	0.1 (0.4)	0.8 (0.6)	0.0 (1.6)	0.4 (−0.5)	102	7614 (0.2)	35
Guyana	0.8 (0.6)	3.0 (9.8)	1.3 (11.7)	1.8 (5.9)	113	3780 (9.2)	33
Haiti	10.3 (1.4)	8.5 (7.9)	0.9 (13.4)	3.4 (8.0)	177	819 (6.5)	11
Jamaica	2.8 (0.5)	14.0 (8.0)	1.6 (−9.1)	6.2 (−4.3)	91	5030 (7.5)	38
St. Kitts	0.1 (1.2)	0.7 (0.6)	0.0 (−2.5)	0.3 (−5.1)	97	13363 (−0.6)	80
St. Lucia	0.2 (1.1)	1.2 (1.8)	0.2 (3.3)	0.6 (−1.9)	59	6544 (0.7)	35
St. Vincent and the Grenadines	0.1 (0.0)	0.7 (1.4)	0.0 (−2.9)	0.4 (−0.7)	75	6601 (1.4)	70
Surinam	0.5 (0.9)	5.1 (11.8)	2.5 (7.8)	2.1 (10.3)	165	9529 (10.8)	37
Trinidad-Tobago	1.3 (0.4)	21.3 (−3.9)	12.8 (−7.3)	8.9 (−1.5)	63	15871 (−4.3)	64
Latin American Integration Association (LAIA, aka ALADI)							
Argentina	41.5 (0.9)	470.0 (20.6)	81.7 (3.1)	73.7 (5.1)	121	11334 (19.5)	60
Bolivia	10.4 (1.6)	28.3 (10.9)	12.3 (11.8)	9.3 (12.9)	158	2722 (9.1)	40
Brazil	200.4 (0.9)	2207.3 (10.0)	242.0 (4.1)	239.6 (6.7)	118	11017 (9.0)	52
Chile	17.6 (0.9)	266.0 (8.6)	76.7 (3.5)	74.6 (5.0)	34	15136 (7.6)	67
Colombia	48.3 (1.4)	363.1 (8.1)	58.8 (9.3)	59.4 (8.4)	42	7514 (6.6)	52
Cuba	11.3 (−0.1)	75.4 (4.7)	6.2 (9.4)	13.8 (−2.1)	—	6691 (4.8)	26
Ecuador	15.1 (1.4)	91.9 (8.8)	24.9 (6.1)	27.3 (7.9)	134	6100 (7.3)	40
Mexico	as above						
Paraguay	6.8 (1.8)	28.8 (10.4)	9.5 (8.0)	12.1 (6.1)	107	4235 (8.5)	37
Peru	30.4 (1.2)	199.3 (8.3)	42.2 (6.3)	42.2 (8.2)	39	6562 (7.1)	39
Uruguay	3.4 (0.3)	53.9 (12.3)	9.1 (8.8)	11.6 (5.1)	85	15831 (12.0)	58
Venezuela	30.3 (1.6)	355.8 (26.7)	89.9 (−1.1)	57.5 (0.5)	180	11728 (24.7)	55

*Current U.S. dollars

Sources: Euromonitor International, 2015; World Bank, 2015.

Mexico, talks with Canada regarding a free trade agreement, and talks between Chile and Mercosur aimed at gradual and reciprocal trade liberalization.

In addition, negotiations have been under way since 1999 for a free trade agreement between the European Union and Mercosur, the first region-to-region free trade accord. A framework agreement was signed in 1995, and the long-term objective is to reach convergence in all areas—cooperation, trade, market access, intellectual property, and political dialogue. The two blocs propose the largest free trade area in the world. The advantages of the accord to Mercosur will mainly come from lifting trade barriers on agricultural and agro-industrial products, which account for the lion's share of Mercosur exports to Europe. However, that point will also be a major stumbling block if the European Union is unwilling to open its highly protected agricultural sector to Brazilian and Argentine imports. Nevertheless, one official of the European Union indicated that the European Union was already in the process of reforming its Common Agricultural Policy. Although negotiations will not be easy, particularly with Europe's current economic problems, Mercosur and the Union should be able to reach an accord. As we shall see in the next section, Mercosur has assumed the leadership in setting the agenda for the creation of a free trade area of the Americas or, more likely, a South American Free Trade Area (SAFTA).

Latin American Progress

A political and economic revolution has been taking place in Latin America over the past three decades. Most of the countries have moved from military dictatorships to democratically elected governments, and sweeping economic and trade liberalization is replacing the economic model most Latin American countries followed for decades. We make this claim despite the recent backsliding of a few countries in the region, such as Venezuela. Privatization of state-owned enterprises and other economic, monetary, and trade policy reforms show a broad shift away from the inward-looking policies of import substitution (that is, manufacturing products at home rather than importing them) and protectionism so prevalent in the past. The trend toward privatization of SOEs in the Americas followed a period in which governments dominated economic life for most of the 20th century. State ownership was once considered the ideal engine for economic growth. Instead of economic growth, however, they ended up with inflated public-sector bureaucracies, complicated and unpredictable regulatory environments, the outright exclusion of foreign and domestic private ownership, and inefficient public companies. Fresh hope for trade and political reforms is now being directed even to communist Cuba.[35]

Today many Latin American countries are at roughly the same stage of liberalization that launched the dynamic growth in Asia during the 1980s and 1990s. In a positive response to these reforms, investors have invested billions of dollars in manufacturing plants, airlines, banks, public works, and telecommunications systems. Because of its size and resource base, the Latin American market has always been considered to have great economic and market possibilities. The population of nearly 600 million is nearly twice that of the United States and 100 million more than the European Community.

The strength of these reforms was tested during the last two decades, a turbulent period both economically and politically for some countries. Argentina, Brazil, and Mexico were affected by the economic meltdown in Asia in 1997 and the continuing financial crisis in Russia. The Russian devaluation and debt default caused a rapid deterioration in Brazil's financial situation; capital began to flee the country, and Brazil devalued its currency. Economic recession in Brazil—coupled with the sharp devaluation of the real—reduced Argentine exports, and Argentina's economic growth slowed. Mexico was able to weather the Russian debt default partly because of debt restructuring and other changes after the major devaluation and recession in the early 1990s. However, competition with Chinese manufacturing has yielded slower growth than predicted at the time of passage of the North American Free Trade Agreement (NAFTA). Other Latin American countries suffered economic downturns that led to devaluations and, in some cases, political instability. Nevertheless, Latin America is still working toward economic reform. Finally, reflected in the

---

[35]Katherine Yung, "When Cuba Opens Up . . . " *Dallas Morning News*, March 11, 2007, pp. D1, D6; "How You'll Advertise in a Newly Capitalist Cuba," *Advertising Age*, June 12, 2011.

data in Exhibit 9.7 is the surprising resilience in the developing countries vis-à-vis the United States and Canada to the lingering economic malaise following the recession of 2008–2009.[36]

Latin American Economic Cooperation

Besides the better-known NAFTA and Mercosur, other Latin American market groups (Exhibit 9.7) have had varying degrees of success. Plagued with tremendous foreign debt, protectionist economic systems, triple-digit inflation, state ownership of basic industries, and overregulation of industry, most Latin American countries were in a perpetual state of economic chaos. In such conditions, trade or integration among member countries stagnated. But as discussed previously, sparked by the success of Mercosur and NAFTA, Latin America has seen a wave of genuine optimism about the economic miracle under way, spurred by political and economic reforms from the tip of Argentina to the Rio Grande. Coupled with these market-oriented reforms is a desire to improve trade among neighboring countries by reviving older agreements or forming new ones. Many of the trade groups are seeking ties to Mercosur, the European Union, or both.

Latin American Integration Association.
The long-term goal of the LAIA, better known by its Spanish acronym, ALADI,[37] is a gradual and progressive establishment of a Latin American common market. One of the more important aspects of LAIA that differs from LAFTA, its predecessor, is the differential treatment of member countries according to their level of economic development. Over the years, negotiations among member countries have lowered duties on selected products and eased trade tensions over quotas, local-content requirements, import licenses, and other trade barriers. An important feature of LAIA is the provision that permits members to establish bilateral trade agreements among member countries. It is under this proviso that trade agreements have been developed among LAIA members.

Caribbean Community and Common Market (CARICOM).[38]
The success of the Caribbean Free Trade Association led to the creation of the Caribbean Community and Common Market. CARICOM member countries continue in their efforts to achieve true regional integration. The group has worked toward a single-market economy and in 2000 established the CSME (CARICOM Single Market and Economy) with the goal of a common currency for all members. The introduction of a common external tariff structure was a major step toward that goal. CARICOM continues to seek stronger ties with other groups in Latin America and has signed a trade agreement with Cuba.

NAFTA to FTAA or SAFTA?

Initially NAFTA was envisioned as the blueprint for a free trade area extending from Alaska to Argentina. The first new country to enter the NAFTA fold was to be Chile, then membership was to extend south until there was a Free Trade Area of the Americas (FTAA) by 2005. The question now is whether there will be an FTAA or whether there will be a tri-country NAFTA in the north and a South American Free Trade Area (SAFTA) led by Brazil and the other member states of Mercosur in the south. The answer to this question rests in part with the issue of fast-track legislation and the policies of President Obama.

Strategic Implications for Marketing
Surfacing in the emerging markets in the Americas and around the world is a vast population whose expanding incomes are propelling them beyond a subsistence level to being viable consumers. As a country develops, incomes change, population concentrations shift, expectations for a better life adjust to higher standards, new infrastructures evolve, and social capital investments are made. Market behavior

---

[36]"Counting Their Blessings," *The Economist*, January 2, 2010, pp. 25–28; Jack Ewing, Vikas Bajaj, and Keith Bradsher, "An Uneven World of Debt," *The New York Times*, February 8, 2010, pp. B1, B3, B6.

[37]http://www.aladi.org, 2015.

[38]http://www.caricom.org, 2015.

People queued for a Chinese-made bus at city center in Havana. China is making major sales and investments in the infrastructures of the developing world, including in Cuba, a member country of LAIA and a fellow "communist" country.

changes, and eventually groups of consumers with common tastes and needs (i.e., market segments) arise.

When incomes rise, new demand is generated at all income levels for everything from soap to automobiles. Furthermore, large households can translate into higher disposable incomes. Young working people in Latin America and Asia usually live at home until they marry. With no rent to pay, they have more discretionary income and can contribute to household purchasing power. Countries with low per capita incomes are potential markets for a large variety of goods; consumers show remarkable resourcefulness in finding ways to buy what really matters to them. In the United States, the first satellite dishes sprang up in the poorest parts of Appalachia. Similarly, in Mexico, homes with color televisions outnumber those with showers.

As incomes rise to middle-class range, demand for more costly goods increases for everything from disposable diapers to automobiles. Incomes for the middle class in emerging markets are less than those in the United States, but spending patterns are different, so the middle class has more to spend than comparable income levels in the United States would indicate. For example, members of the middle class in emerging markets do not own two automobiles and suburban homes, and healthcare and housing in some cases are subsidized, freeing income to spend on refrigerators, TVs, radios, better clothing, and special treats. Exhibit 9.5 illustrates the percentage of household income spent on various classes of goods and services. More household money goes for food in emerging markets than in developed markets, but the next category of high expenditures for emerging and developed countries alike is appliances and other durable goods. Spending by the new rich, however, is a different story. The new rich want to display their wealth; they want to display status symbols such as Rolex watches, Louis Vuitton purses, and Mercedes-Benz automobiles.

One analyst suggests that as a country passes the $5,000 per capita GNP level, people become more brand conscious and forgo many local brands to seek out foreign brands they recognize. At $10,000, they join those with similar incomes who are exposed to the same global information sources. They join the "$10,000 Club" of consumers with homogeneous demands who share a common knowledge of products and brands. They become global consumers. If a company fails to appreciate the strategic implications of the $10,000 Club, it will miss the opportunity to participate in the world's fastest growing global consumer segment. More than 1 billion people in the world now have incomes of $10,000 or better. Companies that look for commonalties among these 1 billion consumers will find growing markets for global brands.

Markets are changing rapidly, and identifiable market segments with similar consumption patterns are found across many countries. Emerging markets will be the growth areas of the 21st century.

Summary

The ever-expanding involvement in world trade of more and more people with varying needs and wants will test old trading patterns and alliances. The global marketer of today and tomorrow must be able to react to market changes rapidly and to anticipate new trends within constantly evolving market segments that may not have existed as recently as last year. Many of today's market facts will likely be tomorrow's historical myths.

Along with dramatic shifts in global politics, the increasing scope and level of technical and economic growth have enabled many nations to advance their standards of living by as much as two centuries in a matter of decades. As nations develop their productive capacity, all segments of their economies will feel the pressure to improve. The impact of these political, social, and economic trends will continue to be felt throughout the world, resulting in significant changes in marketing practices. Furthermore, the impact of information technology will speed up the economic growth in every country. Marketers must focus on devising marketing plans designed to respond fully to each level of economic development.

Brazil and the rest of Latin America continue to undergo rapid political and economic changes that have brought about the opening of most countries in the region to foreign direct investments and international trade. And though emerging markets present special problems, they are promising markets for a broad range of products now and in the future. Emerging markets create new marketing opportunities for MNCs as new market segments evolve. The economic advantages of geography and trade continue to favor market integration and cooperation among American countries on both continents.

Key Terms

Economic development	Newly industrialized countries (NICs)	Infrastructure	Big emerging markets (BEMs)

Questions

1. Define the key terms listed above.
2. Is it possible for an economy to experience economic growth as measured by total GNP without a commensurate rise in the standard of living? Discuss fully.
3. Why do technical assistance programs by more affluent nations typically ignore the distribution problem or relegate it to a minor role in development planning? Explain.
4. Discuss each of the stages of evolution in the marketing process. Illustrate each stage with a particular country.
5. As a country progresses from one economic stage to another, what in general are the marketing effects?
6. Select a country in the agricultural and raw materials stage of economic development and discuss what changes will occur in marketing when it passes to a manufacturing stage.
7. What are the consequences of each stage of marketing development on the potential for industrial goods within a country? For consumer goods?
8. Discuss the significance of economic development to international marketing. Why is the knowledge of economic development of importance in assessing the world marketing environment? Discuss.
9. The Internet accelerates the process of economic growth. Discuss.
10. Discuss the impact of the IT revolution on the poorest countries.
11. Select one country in each of the three stages of economic development. For each country, outline the basic existing marketing institutions and show how their stages of development differ. Explain why.
12. Why should a foreign marketer study economic development? Discuss.
13. The infrastructure is important to the economic growth of an economy. Comment.
14. What are the objectives of economically developing countries? How do these objectives relate to marketing? Comment.
15. Using the list growth factors, evaluate Mexico and Brazil as to their prospects for continued rapid growth. Which factors will be problems for Mexico or Brazil?
16. What is marketing's role in economic development? Discuss marketing's contributions to economic development.
17. Discuss the economic and trade importance of the big emerging markets.

18. One of the ramifications of emerging markets is the creation of a middle class. Discuss.

19. The needs and wants of a market and the ability to satisfy them are the result of the three-way interaction of the economy, culture, and the marketing efforts of businesses. Comment.

20. Discuss the strategic implications of marketing in Mexico.

21. Discuss the consequences to the United States of not being a part of SAFTA.

22. Discuss the strategic marketing implications of NAFTA.

23. Visit the web pages for NAFTA and Mercosur and locate each group's rules of origin. Which group has the most liberal rules of origin? Why is there a difference?

24. NAFTA has been in existence for several years—how has it done? Review Exhibit 9.6, which discusses the initial provisions of the agreement, and, using the Internet, evaluate how well the provisions have been met.

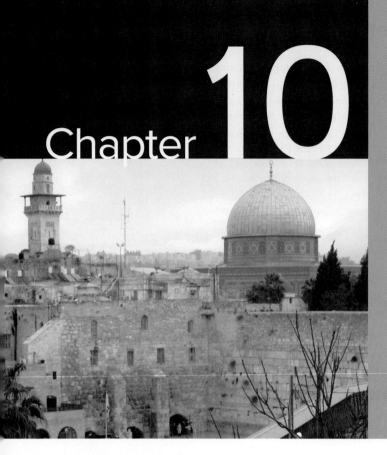

Chapter 10

Europe, Africa, and the Middle East

CHAPTER OUTLINE

CHAPTER LEARNING OBJECTIVES

What you should learn from Chapter 10:

LO1 The reasons for economic union

LO2 Patterns of international cooperation

LO3 The evolution of the European Union

LO4 Evolving patterns of trade as eastern Europe and the former Soviet states embrace free-market systems

LO5 Strategic implications for marketing in the region

LO6 The size and nature of marketing opportunities in the European/African/Middle East regions

Global Perspective

MIGHT FREE TRADE BRING PEACE TO THE MIDDLE EAST?

The nearly complete destruction of the continental European economies by World War II seriously endangered the stability of Europe's social and political institutions. Europe's leaders knew that to rebuild from the ruins, it was essential to form new kinds of international institutions to ensure prosperity, stability, and peace in the region. The first of these institutions was the European Coal and Steel Community, established in 1952 to integrate the coal and steel industries of France, West Germany, Italy, Belgium, the Netherlands, and Luxembourg. Fifty years later, based on the success of this first small experiment in economic interdependence, we now see the European Union with 28 member nations and 6 candidate countries. Until recently the economies have burgeoned, but more important, peace has persisted.

Might such an approach work in the war-torn Middle East? Let's consider the possibilities and potential of a Middle Eastern Union. The crux of the problem is Jerusalem. The holy Old City is a matter of faith to so many. For Christians it is sacred because of its associations with Christ. For Jews it has served as the center for their people—not only in a national way but also, more importantly, in a religious sense. For Muslims only Mecca and Medina are more important spiritual places. And the fighting over the real estate that represents its spiritual events appears perpetual.

Jerusalem can be a primary part of the solution. But we must look beyond the rockets and bombs of the day. We must imagine a safe, prosperous, and peaceful place. Imagine an international shrine. Perhaps the Old City would be administered by Buddhists or Norwegians or the United Nations. Israel would have its grand capital to the west, in the New City, and the Palestinians to the east a bit.

Religious tourism would feed the economies in both countries, as well as the surrounding area. Imagine the possibilities! In 2000, before recent outbreaks of violence, tourism brought in $3.2 billion in revenues for Israel. Compare that with Disneyland in Orange County, California. That park's yearly 10 million visitors spend about $150 each on tickets, food, and souvenirs. Add in the transportation, hotel, and restaurant revenues appreciated in the neighborhood, and that's more than $3 billion a year coming to the Anaheim environs.

The Church of the Holy Sepulcher (built over the tomb of Jesus) would draw Christians. The Wailing Wall is the most holy place for Jews. Muslims would flock to the Dome of the Rock (Mohammed was carried by the angel Gabriel for a visit to Heaven after praying at the Rock). The most enlightened tourists would visit all three. Disney might consult on the queuing problems. Staying open 24/7 would expand capacity by allowing jet-lagged pilgrims access to the more popular places. And outside the Old City are Bethlehem, Hebron, Nazareth, Jericho, the Sea of Galilee, the Dead Sea, and the Red Sea, to name only the more obvious attractions. We're talking $15 billion to $30 billion in annual revenues if things are done right—that's about 10 percent of the current GDP of Israel.

How about Jerusalem as the site for the 2024 or 2028 Olympic games? That's another $5 billion in revenues. And ignoring the dollars for a moment, please consider the sentiments associated with "the 2024 Jerusalem Games" juxtaposed with the disaster of Munich in 1972. And ignoring the dollars for another moment, imagine the spiritual splendor for so many millions visiting the sources of their faith, treading some of the original paths of David, Jesus, and Mohammed.

This little fantasy presumes a peaceful political division of Israel and Palestine along the lines reaffirmed in the Oslo Accords. It presumes a dropping of all commercial boycotts in the region. It presumes that Palestinians won't have to risk being shot while "hopping the fence" to work in Israel. It presumes that companies like Nestlé will be able to integrate the operations of their complementary plants in the area. It presumes that the United States and other countries will send to the region legions of tourists rather than boatloads of weapons. It presumes an open, international, and, most important, a whole Old City of Jerusalem. And it presumes free trade and travel among all nations in the region allowing all to prosper in new ways.

Finally, as Pulitzer Prize–winner Jared Diamond points out, the Middle East, historically referred to as the Fertile Crescent, was the cradle of civilization. It became so long ago because of innovation and trade in the region. One can only imagine what free trade in the area would produce now.

Sources: John L. Graham, "Trade Brings Peace," paper delivered at the Global Ethics and Religion Forum; Clare Hall, Cambridge University conference, *War and Reconciliation: Perspectives of the World Religions,* May 26, 2003, Cambridge, England; Jared Diamond, *Collapse: How Societies Choose to Fail or Succeed* (New York: Viking, 2005); http://www.JerusalemOlympics.org, 2012; John L. Graham, Lynda Lawrence, William Hernandez Requejo, *Inventive Negotiation: Getting Beyond Yes* (New York: Palgrave Macmillan, 2014).

Within a short walk of one another in the Old City of Jerusalem are three of the most important holy sites for Muslims (the Dome of the Rock), Jews (the Wailing Wall), and Christians (the Church of the Holy Sepulchre). Peace in the region would yield a bonanza of religious tourism.[1]

Following the success of the aforementioned European Steel and Coal Community, a global economic revolution began in 1958 when the European Economic Community was ratified and Europe took the step that would ultimately lead to the present-day European Union (EU). Until then, skeptics predicted that the experiment would never work and that the alliance would fall apart quickly. It was not until the single market was established that the United States, Japan, and other countries gave serious thought to creating other alliances. The establishment of common markets, coupled with the trend away from planned economies to the free market system in Latin America, Asia, and eventually the former Soviet Union, created fertile ground that sparked the drive to form trade alliances and free markets the world over. Nation after nation embraced the free market system, implementing reforms in their economic and political systems with the desire to be part of a multinational market region in the evolving global marketplace. Traditions that are centuries old are being altered, issues that cannot be resolved by decree are being negotiated to acceptable solutions, governments and financial systems are restructuring, and companies are being reshaped to meet new competition and trade patterns.

The evolution and growth of multinational market regions—those groups of countries that seek mutual economic benefit from reducing interregional trade and tariff barriers—are the most important global trends today. Organizational form varies widely among market regions, but the universal goals of multinational cooperation are economic benefits for the participants and the associated peace between[2] and within countries.[3] The world is awash in economic cooperative agreements as countries look for economic alliances to expand access

---

[1]Edmund Sanders, "O Little Time of Tourists' Dollars," *Los Angeles Times*, December 20, 2011, pp. A1, A4.

[2]By far the strongest evidence for the "trade causes peace" notion is that provided by Solomon W. Polachek, "Why Democracies Cooperate More and Fight Less: The Relationship between International Trade and Cooperation," *Review of International Economics* 5, no. 3 (1997), pp. 295–309; additional evidence is supplied at http://www.cpbp.org, click on Peace Monitor, then Countries; Jonathan Schell, *The Unconquerable World* (New York: Metropolitan Books, 2003); Thomas Friedman, *The World Is Flat* (New York: Farrar, Straus, and Giroux, 2005); Steven Pinker, *The Better Angels of Our Nature* (New York: Viking, 2011).

[3]Studies of the causes of civil wars supports their belief; see Paul Collier, "The Market for Civil War," *Foreign Policy,* May/June 2003, pp. 38–45; Hernando de Soto, "The Capitalist Cure for Terrorism," *The Wall Street Journal*, October 10, 2014, online.

to free markets. Indeed, part of the efforts of the 193 member countries in the United Nations include mutual economic development; the World Trade Organization, with its 160 members and 24 observers, is wholly dedicated to making trade among nations more efficient.

Regional economic cooperative agreements have been around since the end of World War II. The most successful one is the European Union (EU), the world's largest multinational market region and foremost example of economic cooperation. Multinational market groups form large markets that provide potentially significant opportunities for international business. As it became apparent in the late 1980s that the European Union was to achieve its long-term goal of a single European market, a renewed interest in economic cooperation followed, with the creation of several new alliances. The North American Free Trade Agreement (NAFTA) and the Latin American Integration Association (LAIA) in the Americas and the Association of Southeast Asian Nations (ASEAN) and Asia-Pacific Economic Cooperation (APEC) in the Asian-Pacific Rim are all relatively new or reenergized associations that are gaining strength and importance as multinational market regions.

Along with the growing trend of economic cooperation, concerns about the effect of such cooperation on global competition are emerging. Governments and businesses worry that the European Union, NAFTA, and other cooperative trade groups will become regional trading blocs without trade restrictions internally but with borders protected from outsiders. But as each of these trade groups continues to create new agreements with other countries and groups, the networked global economy and free trade are clearly on the ascendance. The benefits are clear for consumers; however, global companies face richer and more intense competitive environments.

La Raison d'Etre

LO1

The reasons for economic union

Successful economic union requires favorable economic, political, cultural, and geographic factors as a basis for success. Major flaws in any one factor can destroy a union unless the other factors provide sufficient strength to overcome the weaknesses. In general, the advantages of economic union must be clear-cut and significant, and the benefits must greatly outweigh the disadvantages before nations forgo any part of their sovereignty. Many of the associations formed in Africa and Latin America have had little impact because perceived benefits were not sufficient to offset the partial loss of sovereignty.

Economic Factors

Every type of economic union shares the development and enlargement of market opportunities as a basic orientation; usually, markets are enlarged through preferential tariff treatment for participating members, common tariff barriers against outsiders, or both. Enlarged, protected markets stimulate internal economic development by providing assured outlets and preferential treatment for goods produced within the customs union, and consumers benefit from lower internal tariff barriers among the participating countries. In many, but not all cases, external and internal barriers are reduced because of the greater economic security afforded domestic producers by the enlarged market.[4]

Nations with complementary economic bases are least likely to encounter frictions in the development and operation of a common market unit. However, for an economic union to survive, it must have agreements and mechanisms in place to settle economic disputes. In addition, the total benefit of economic integration must outweigh individual differences that are sure to arise as member countries adjust to new trade relationships. The European Union includes countries with diverse economies, distinctive monetary systems, developed agricultural bases, and different natural resources. It is significant that most of the problems encountered by the European Union have arisen over agriculture and monetary policy. In the early days of the European Community (now the European Union), agricultural disputes were common. The British attempted to keep French poultry out of the British market, France banned Italian wine, and the Irish banned eggs and poultry from other member countries. In all cases, the reason given was health and safety, but the stronger motives were the continuation of the age-old policies of market protection. Such skirmishes are not unusual, but they do test the

---

[4]Michele Fratianni and Chan Hoon Oh, "Expanding RTAs, Trade Flows, and the Multinational Enterprise," *Journal of International Business Studies* 40, no. 7 (2009), pp. 1206–27.

strength of the economic union. In the case of the European Union, the European Commission was the agency used to settle disputes and charge the countries that violated EU regulations.

Political Factors

Political amenability among countries is another basic requisite for the development of a supranational market arrangement. Participating countries must have comparable aspirations and general compatibility before surrendering any part of their national sovereignty. State sovereignty is one of the most cherished possessions of any nation and is relinquished only for a promise of significant improvement of the national position through cooperation.

Economic considerations are the basic catalyst for the formation of a customs union group, but political elements are equally important. The uniting of the original European Union countries was partially a response to the outside threat of the Soviet Union's great political and economic power; the countries of western Europe were willing to settle their "family squabbles" to present a unified front to the Russian bear. The communist threat no longer exists, but the importance of political unity to fully achieve all the benefits of economic integration has driven European countries to form the Union (EU).

Geographic and Temporal Proximity

Although geographic and temporal proximity are not absolutely imperative for cooperating members of a customs union, such closeness does facilitate the functioning of a common market. Indeed, research demonstrates that more important than physical distance are differences across time zones.[5] That is, trade tends to travel more easily in north–south directions than it did in ancient times. However, transportation networks (basic to any marketing system) are likely to be interrelated and well developed when countries are close together. Issues of immigration, legal and illegal, also promote closer economic integration between close neighbors. One of the first major strengths of the European Union was its transportation network; the opening of the tunnel between England and France further bound this common market. Countries that are widely separated geographically have major barriers to overcome in attempting economic fusion. However, with increasing efficiencies in communication and transportation, the importance of such factors appears to be waning.

Cultural Factors

As mentioned in the last chapter, the United States has bilateral free trade agreements in progress and approved with several nations in addition to multilateral agreements such as NAFTA and DR-CAFTA (Dominican Republic, Central American Countries, and the U.S.). But generally, cultural similarity eases the shock of economic cooperation with other countries. The more similar the culture, the more likely an agreement is to succeed, because members understand the outlook and viewpoints of their colleagues. Although there is great cultural diversity in the European Union, key members share a long-established Christian heritage and are commonly aware of being European. However, even this aspect of diversity may be unimportant as negotiations proceed with Turkey about EU membership. Language, as a part of culture, has not created as much a barrier for EU countries as was expected. Nearly every educated European can do business in at least two or three languages, so the linguistic diversity of several major languages did not much impede trade.

Patterns of Multinational Cooperation

LO2

Patterns of international cooperation

Of course, at the most general level, the World Trade Organization represents the most important and comprehensive trade agreement in history. However, beyond the WTO, multinational market groups take several other forms, varying significantly in the degree of cooperation, dependence, and interrelationship among participating nations. As mentioned previously, the United States is currently negotiating two huge free trade relationships—the Trans Pacific Partnership with 11 Pacific nations and the Transatlantic Trade and Investment Partnership with the European Union.[6] There

---

[5]Contrast Jared Diamond's *Guns, Germs, and Steel* (New York: W. W. Norton, 1999) and Jennifer Chandler and John L. Graham, "Relationship-Oriented Cultures, Corruption, and International Marketing Success," *Journal of Business Ethics*, 92 (2010), pp. 251–67.

[6]Neil Irwin, "Where Might Obama and the GOP Agree? Here Are Possibilities," *The New York Times*, November 6, 2014, p. B4.

are five fundamental groupings for regional economic integration, ranging from regional cooperation for development, which requires the least amount of integration, to the ultimate integration of political union.

Regional Cooperation Groups. The most basic economic integration and cooperation is the *regional cooperation for development (RCD)*. In the RCD arrangement, governments agree to participate jointly to develop basic industries beneficial to each economy. Each country makes an advance commitment to participate in the financing of a new joint venture and to purchase a specified share of the output of the venture. An example is the project between Colombia and Venezuela to build a hydroelectric generating plant on the Orinoco River. They shared jointly in construction costs, and they share the electricity produced.

Free Trade Area. A free trade area (FTA) requires more cooperation and integration than the RCD. It is an agreement between two or more countries to reduce or eliminate customs duties and nontariff trade barriers among partner countries while members maintain individual tariff schedules for external countries. Essentially, an FTA provides its members with a mass market without barriers to impede the flow of goods and services.[7]

Customs Union. A customs union represents the next stage in economic cooperation. It enjoys the free trade area's reduced or eliminated internal tariffs and adds a common external tariff on products imported from countries outside the union. The customs union is a logical stage of cooperation in the transition from an FTA to a common market. The European Union was a customs union before becoming a common market. Customs unions exist between France and Monaco, Italy and San Marino, and Switzerland and Liechtenstein, to name some examples.

Common Market. A common market agreement eliminates all tariffs and other restrictions on internal trade, adopts a set of common external tariffs, and removes all restrictions on the free flow of capital and labor among member nations. Thus, a common market is a joint marketplace for goods as well as for services (including labor) and for capital. It is a unified economy and lacks only political unity to become a political union. The Treaty of Rome, which established the European Economic Community (EEC) in 1957, called for common external tariffs and the gradual elimination of intramarket tariffs, quotas, and other trade barriers. The treaty also called for the elimination of restrictions on the movement of services, labor, and capital; prohibition of cartels; coordinated monetary and fiscal policies; common agricultural policies; use of common investment funds for regional industrial development; and similar rules for wage and welfare payments. The EEC existed until the Maastricht Treaty created the European Union, an extension of the EEC into a political union.

Political Union. Political union is the most fully integrated form of regional cooperation. It involves complete political and economic integration, either voluntary or enforced. The most notable enforced political union was the Council for Mutual Economic Assistance (COMECON), a centrally controlled group of countries organized by the Soviet Union. With the dissolution of the Soviet Union and the independence of the Eastern European bloc, COMECON was disbanded.

A *commonwealth* of nations is a voluntary organization providing for the loosest possible relationship that can be classified as economic integration. The British Commonwealth includes Britain and countries formerly part of the British Empire. Some of its members still recognize the British monarch as their symbolic head, though Britain has no political authority over any commonwealth country. Its member states had received preferential tariffs when trading with Great Britain, but when Britain joined the European Community, all preferential tariffs were abandoned. A commonwealth can best be described as the weakest of political unions and is mostly based on economic

---

[7]The European Free Trade Area is a good example. See http://www.efta.int/, 2015.

history and a sense of tradition. Heads of state meet every three years to discuss trade and political issues they jointly face, and compliance with any decisions or directives issued is voluntary.

Two new political unions came into existence in the 1990s: the Commonwealth of Independent States (CIS), made up of the republics of the former Soviet Union, and the European Union (EU). The European Union was created when the 12 nations of the European Community ratified the Maastricht Treaty. The members committed themselves to economic and political integration. The treaty allows for the free movement of goods, persons, services, and capital throughout the member states; a common currency; common foreign and security policies, including defense; a common justice system; and cooperation between police and other authorities on crime, terrorism, and immigration issues. Although not all the provisions of the treaty have been universally accepted, each year the EU members become more closely tied economically and politically. Now that the Economic and Monetary Union is in place and most participating members share a common currency, the European Union is headed toward political union as well.

Global Markets and Multinational Market Groups

The globalization of markets, the restructuring of the eastern European bloc into independent market-driven economies, the dissolution of the Soviet Union into independent states, the worldwide trend toward economic cooperation, and enhanced global competition make it important that market potential be viewed in the context of regions of the world rather than country by country.

This section presents basic information and data on markets and market groups in Europe, Africa, and the Middle East. Existing economic cooperation agreements within each of these regions are reviewed. The reader must appreciate that the status of cooperative agreements and alliances among nations has been extremely fluid in some parts of the world. Many are fragile and may cease to exist or may restructure into a totally different form. Several decades will probably be needed for many of the new trading alliances that are now forming to stabilize into semipermanent groups.

Europe

Within Europe, every type of multinational market grouping exists. The European Union, European Economic Area, and the European Free Trade Area are the most established cooperative groups (see Exhibits 10.1 and 10.2). Of escalating economic importance are the fledgling capitalist economies of eastern Europe and the three Baltic states that gained independence from the Soviet Union just prior to its breakup. Key issues center on their economic development and economic alliance with the European Union. Also within the European region is the Commonwealth of Independent States. New and untested, this coalition of 12 former USSR republics may or may not survive in its present form to take its place among the other multinational market groups.

European Integration

LO3

The evolution of the European Union

Despite the ongoing global economic problems affecting it,[8] of all the multinational market groups, none is more secure in its cooperation or more important economically than the European Union (Exhibit 10.3). From its beginning, it has made progress toward achieving the goal of complete economic integration and, ultimately, political union. However, many people, including Europeans, had little hope for the success of the European Economic Community, or the European Common Market as it is often called, because of the problems created by integration and the level of national sovereignty that would have to be conceded to the community. After all, 1,000 years of economic separatism had to be overcome, and the European Common Market is quite heterogeneous. There are language and cultural differences, individual national

---

[8]Gareth Harding, "The Myth of Europe," *Foreign Policy*, January/February 2012, pp. 74–82; Alex Brittain, "Economic Data Signal Two-Speed Europe," *The Wall Street Journal,* February 1, 2012; Floyd Norris, "Europe's Woes Are Reflected in Its Trade Numbers," *The New York Times,* February 17, 2012.

Exhibit 10.1
European Market Regions Fundamental Market Metrics

(in parentheses) = average annual growth rate 2008–2013 as a percentage

Country (year entered union)	Population (millions)	GNI* (billions $)	Exports* of Goods (billions $)	Imports* of Goods (billions $)	Ease of Doing Business Index	GNI/Capita* ($)	Internet Users (percentage)
Association Europeanopean Union (EU)							
Austria (1995)[e]	8.5 (0.4)	412.5 (2.0)	167.1 (–0.7)	173.6 (–0.3)	28	48646 (1.6)	81
Belgium (founder)[e]	11.2 (0.9)	507.4 (1.7)	471.0 (0.0)	447.9 (–0.8)	32	45456 (0.8)	82
Bulgaria (2007)	7.3 (–0.6)	52.0 (3.0)	29.5 (5.6)	34.3 (–1.5)	57	7135 (3.6)	53
Croatia (2013)	4.3 (–0.3)	55.9 (–0.9)	12.7 (–2.0)	21.9 (–6.5)	88	13122 (–0.6)	67
Cyprus (2004)[e]	1.1 (1.2)	21.5 (–0.9)	2.1 (3.6)	6.4 (–10.0)	38	18801 (–2.1)	65
Czech Republic (2004)	10.5 (0.3)	185.3 (–0.2)	162.3 (2.1)	144.3 (0.3)	68	17621 (–0.6)	74
Denmark (1973)	5.6 (0.5)	343.9 (1.6)	110.4 (–1.0)	96.6 (–2.4)	5	61388 (1.2)	95
Estonia (2004)[e]	1.3 (–0.3)	23.7 (3.0)	16.3 (5.5)	18.3 (2.7)	21	18405 (3.3)	80
Finland (1995)[e]	5.4 (0.5)	258.4 (0.9)	74.4 (–5.1)	77.6 (–3.4)	12	47608 (0.4)	92
France (founder)[e]	63.8 (0.5)	2785.1 (1.3)	567.6 (–1.4)	670.5 (–1.3)	35	43647 (0.8)	82
Germany (founder)[e]	80.5 (–0.2)	3736.0 (2.4)	1440.0 (0.6)	1160.6 (0.6)	19	46396 (2.5)	84
Greece (1981)[e]	11.1 (–0.2)	241.5 (–4.2)	36.5 (3.0)	62.1 (–8.3)	89	21830 (–4.0)	60
Hungary (2004)	9.9 (–0.2)	123.2 (2.1)	107.9 (–0.1)	99.1 (–1.8)	52	12429 (2.3)	73
Ireland (1973)[e]	4.6 (0.8)	183.1 (–2.3)	115.5 (–1.9)	66.5 (–4.8)	13	39807 (3.1)	78
Italy (founder)[e]	61.1 (0.5)	2059.1 (–0.1)	517.6 (–1.0)	477.3 (–3.3)	67	33727 (–0.6)	58
Latvia (2004)[e]	2.0 (–1.6)	21.7 (0.5)	13.3 (7.5)	17.8 (1.2)	24	10718 (2.1)	75
Lithuania (2004)	3.0 (–1.5)	44.3 (1.2)	32.6 (6.5)	34.8 (2.2)	25	14900 (2.8)	68
Luxembourg (founder)[e]	0.5 (1.7)	40.7 (0.7)	14.1 (–4.5)	23.9 (–1.5)	56	76704 (–0.9)	94
Malta (2004)[e]	0.4 (0.4)	8.9 (3.2)	5.2 (7.6)	7.5 (5.6)	100	20855 (2.8)	69
Netherlands (founder)[e]	16.8 (0.5)	796.5 (0.6)	575.2 (1.1)	513.1 (0.7)	30	47404 (0.1)	94
Poland (2004)	38.5 (0.1)	495.8 (4.7)	197.8 (3.2)	196.9 (–0.5)	48	12866 (4.6)	63
Portugal (1986)[e]	10.5 (–0.1)	215.4 (–0.4)	62.7 (1.8)	75.6 (–4.4)	29	20537 (–0.3)	62
Romania (2007)	20.0 (–0.7)	183.1 (4.0)	65.8 (5.8)	73.4 (–2.4)	73	9173 (4.7)	50
Slovakia (2004)[e]	5.4 (0.1)	91.7 (2.0)	85.2 (3.1)	79.6 (1.5)	43	16950 (1.9)	78
Slovenia (2004)[e]	2.1 (0.3)	46.6 (–0.7)	28.6 (–0.7)	29.4 (–2.9)	31	22616 (–1.0)	73
Spain (1986)[e]	46.7 (0.4)	1347.5 (–0.8)	311.0 (2.3)	332.3 (–4.4)	46	28852 (–1.3)	72
Sweden (1995)	9.6 (0.8)	574.7 (2.8)	167.7 (–1.8)	159.8 (–1.1)	14	60143 (1.6)	95
United Kingdom (1973)	63.9 (0.8)	2490.7 (1.3)	476.5 (0.4)	645.2 (0.1)	11	38985 (0.6)	90
EU Candidate Countries							
Albania (applied 2009)	3.2 (0.1)	12.7 (4.1)	2.3 (11.5)	4.9 (–1.4)	82	3989 (4.0)	60
Iceland (applied 2009)	0.3 (1.3)	14.2 (8.4)	5.0 (–1.5)	4.8 (–5.1)	13	43121 (7.0)	97
Macedonia (applied 2004)	2.1 (0.2)	10.0 (2.6)	4.3 (1.3)	6.6 (–0.8)	36	4826 (2.4)	61
Montenegro (applied 2008)	0.6 (–0.1)	4.7 (1.4)	0.5 (–4.2)	5.5 (–8.8)	50	7211 (1.5)	57
Serbia (applied 2009)	7.2 (–0.4)	41.3 (6.3)	14.6 (5.9)	20.5 (–3.3)	87	5759 (6.8)	52
Turkey (applied 1987)	75.6 (1.4)	2490.7 (10.4)	151.8 (2.8)	251.7 (4.5)	72	10718 (8.9)	46
European Free Trade Area (EFTA)							
Iceland	as above						
Liechtenstein	0.1	—	—	—	—	—	94
Norway	5.1 (1.3)	519.5 (3.7)	154.3 (–2.1)	89.8 (–0.1)	7	102849 (2.4)	95
Switzerland	8.0 (1.1)	656.7 (2.8)	217.1 (2.5)	191.7 (2.0)	27	81767 (1.7)	87

*Current U.S. $.

[e]Eurozone.

Source: Euromonitor International, 2015; World Bank, 2015.

interests, political differences, and centuries-old restrictions designed to protect local national markets.

Historically, standards have been used to effectively limit market access. Germany protected its beer market from the rest of Europe with a purity law requiring beer sold in Germany to be brewed only from water, hops, malt, and yeast. Italy protected its pasta market by requiring that pasta be made only from durum wheat. Incidentally, the European Court of Justice has struck down both the beer and pasta regulations as trade violations. Such restrictive standards kept competing products, whether from other European countries or elsewhere, out of their respective markets. Skeptics, doubtful that such cultural, legal, and social differences could ever be overcome, held little hope for a unified Europe. Their skepticism has proved wrong. Today, many marvel at how far the European Union has come. Although complete integration has not been fully achieved, a review of the structure of the European Union, its authority over member states, the Single European Act, the European Economic Area, the Maastricht Treaty, and the Amsterdam Treaty will show why the final outcome of full economic and political integration now seems more certain.

Some in Warsaw suggest the picture includes two icons of imperialism. Soviet dictator Joseph Stalin "gave" the people of Poland his 1950s version of great architecture. The Poles have now turned his infamous Palace of Culture and Science into a movie theater (Kinoteka) and office tower. Others see Coca-Cola and its ever-present, powerful advertising as a new kind of control. The argument about globalization goes on.

Exhibit 10.2
The European Economic Area: EU, EFTA, and Associates

Exhibit 10.3
From the European Coal
and Steel Community to
Monetary Union

Source: "Chronology of the EU,"
http://www.europa.eu.int/ (select Abc).
Reprinted with permission from the
European Communities.

Year	Event	Description
1951	Treaty of Paris	European Coal and Steel Community (ECSC) (founding members are Belgium, France, Germany, Italy, Luxembourg, and the Netherlands).
1957	Treaty of Rome	Blueprint, European Economic Community (EEC).
1958	European Economic Community	Ratified by ECSC founding members. Common market is established.
1960	European Free Trade Association	Established by Austria, Denmark, Norway, Portugal, Sweden, Switzerland, and United Kingdom.
1973	Expansion	Denmark, Ireland, and United Kingdom join EEC.
1979	European monetary system	The European Currency Unit (ECU) is created. All members except the UK agree to maintain their exchange rates within specific margins.
1981	Expansion	Greece joins EEC.
1985	1992 Single Market Program	White paper for action introduced to European Parliament.
1986	Expansion	Spain and Portugal join EEC.
1987	**Single European Act**	Ratified, with full implementation by 1992.
1992	Treaty on European Union	Also known as **Maastricht Treaty**. Blueprint for Economic and Monetary Union (EMU).
1993	Europe 1992	Single European Act in force (January 1, 1992).
1993	European Union	Treaty on European Union (Maastricht Treaty) in force, with monetary union by 1999.
1994	European Economic Area	The EEA was formed with EU members and Norway and Iceland.
1995	Expansion	Austria, Finland, and Sweden join EU. Established procedures for expansion to Central and Eastern Europe.
1997	**Amsterdam Treaty**	
1999	Monetary union	Conversion rates are fixed, and euro used by banking and finance industry. Consumer prices are quoted in local currency and in euros.
2002	Banknotes and coins	Circulation of euro banknotes and coins begins January 1, and legal status of national banknotes and coins canceled July 1, 2002.
2004	Expansion	Ten new countries join EU.
2007	Expansion	Bulgaria and Romania join.
2013	Expansion	Croatia joins.

Even though several member states are not fully implementing all the measures, they are making progress. The proportion of directives not yet implemented in all 28 member states has fallen dramatically. Taxation has been one of the areas where implementation lags and reform continues to be necessary. Value-added and registration taxes for automobiles, for example, at one time ranged from 15 percent in Luxembourg to 218 percent in Denmark. Then a midsized Mercedes in Haderslev, Denmark, cost $90,000, nearly triple the amount you would have paid in Flensburg, Germany, just 30 miles south. A Honda Civic cost the British consumer 89 percent more than it cost continental customers. Scotch in Sweden had an $18 tax, nine times the amount levied in Italy. The EU finance ministers have addressed these issues and made some progress, even though tax-raising ability is a sacred power of the nation-state. The full implementation of the legislation is expected to take several years. Although all proposals have not been met, the program for unification has built up a pace that cannot be reversed.

Each month the European Parliament meets for three weeks here in Brussels, Belgium, and then moves for one week to meet in Strasbourg, France. The inconvenience of the fourth week move was a concession to French pride—or perhaps the cheese is better there?

European Union[9]

EU Institutions. The European Union's institutions form a federal pattern with executive, parliamentary, and judicial branches: the European Commission, the Council of Ministers, the European Parliament, and the Court of Justice, respectively. Their decision-making processes have legal status and extensive powers in fields covered by common policies. The European Union uses three legal instruments: (1) regulations binding the member states directly and having the same strength as national laws; (2) directives also binding the member states but allowing them to choose the means of execution; and (3) decisions addressed to a government, an enterprise, or an individual, binding the parties named. Over the years, the Union has gained an increasing amount of authority over its member states.

The European Commission initiates policy and supervises its observance by member states, and it proposes and supervises execution of laws and policies.[10] Commission members act only in the interest of the European Union, and their responsibilities are to ensure that the EU rules and the principles of the common market are respected. For example, in separate actions, the Commission approved the sale of Sun Microsystems to Oracle, but it has pushed Google and others to shorten the time they store consumer data.

The Council of Ministers is the decision-making body of the European Union; it is the Council's responsibility to debate and decide which proposals of the Single European Act to accept as binding on EU members. The Council can enact into law all proposals by majority vote except for changes in tax rates on products and services, which require unanimous vote. The Council, for example, drafted the Maastricht Treaty, which was presented to member states for ratification.

The European Parliament originally had only a consultative role that passed on most Union legislation. It can now amend and adopt legislation, though it does not have the power to initiate legislation. It also has extensive budgetary powers that allow it to be involved in major EU expenditures.

The European Court of Justice (ECJ) is the European Union's Supreme Court. It is responsible for challenging any measures incompatible with the Treaty of Rome and

[9]http://europa.eu.int, 2015.

[10]Jack Ewing and James Kanter, "European Union Gives Hungary Ultimatum," *The New York Times,* January 12, 2012.

It took some selling for the Greeks to adopt the euro instead of the 2,500-year-old drachma. The truck seen here in Athens's Syntagma Square was equipped with video projectors and euro information stands and traveled to 40 Greek towns, informing folks about the new currency. Circa 2012, there has been much talk of returning to the drachma; we shall see.

for passing judgment, at the request of a national court, on the interpretation or validity of points of EU law. The court's decisions are final and cannot be appealed in national courts. For example, Estée Lauder Companies appealed to the ECJ to overrule a German court's decision to prohibit it from selling its Clinique product. The German court had ruled that the name could mislead German consumers by implying medical treatment. The ECJ pointed out that Clinique is sold in other member states without confusing the consumer and ruled in favor of Estée Lauder. This decision marked a landmark case, because many member countries had similar laws that were in essence nontariff trade barriers designed to protect their individual markets. If the German court ruling against Estée Lauder had been upheld, it would have made it difficult for companies to market their products across borders in an identical manner. This case is but one example of the ECJ's power in the European Union and its role in eliminating nontariff trade barriers.

Economic and Monetary Union (EMU).

The EMU, a provision of the Maastricht Treaty, established the parameters of the creation of a common currency for the European Union, the *euro*, and established a timetable for its implementation. In 2002, a central bank was established, conversion rates were fixed, circulation of euro banknotes and coins was completed (see Exhibit 10.4), and the legal tender status of participating members' banknotes and coins was canceled.[11] To participate, members must meet strict limits on several financial and economic criteria, including national deficit, debt, and inflation. The 12 member states employing the euro beginning in January 1, 2001, were Austria, Belgium, Finland, France, Germany, Greece, Ireland, Italy, Luxembourg, the Netherlands, Portugal, and Spain. Denmark voted in 2000 not to join the monetary union, leaving Britain and Sweden still undecided. Denmark's rejection of the euro caused a broader debate about the EU's future. Anti-euro advocates exploited fears of a "European superstate" and local interference from Brussels rather than relying on economic arguments when pushing for rejection. However, in 2007 Slovenia and in 2008 both Malta and Cyprus switched their currencies to the euro.

Exhibit 10.4
The Euro

Source: Euro, http://www.europa.eu.int/euro. Reprinted with permission from the European Communities.

Notes. There are seven euro notes in different colors and sizes, denominated in 500, 200, 100, 50, 20, 10, and 5 euros. The designs symbolize Europe's architectural heritage, with windows and gateways on the front side as symbols of the spirit of openness and cooperation in the European Union. The reverse side features a bridge from a particular age, a metaphor for communication among the people of Europe and the rest of the world.

Coins. There are eight euro coins, denominated in 2 and 1 euros, then 50, 20, 10, 5, 2, and 1 cent. Every coin will carry a common European face—a map of the European Union against a background of transverse lines to which are attached the stars of the European flag. On the obverse, each member state will decorate the coins with their own motifs, for example, the King of Spain or some national hero. Regardless of the motif, every coin can be used and will have the same value in all the member states.

Sign. The graphic symbol for the euro was inspired by the Greek letter epsilon, in reference to the cradle of European civilization and to the first letter of the word *Europe*. It looks like an *E* with two clearly marked, horizontal parallel lines across it. The parallel lines are meant to symbolize the stability of the euro. The official abbreviation is "EUR."

---

[11]Nicholas Kulish, "No Fireworks for Euro as It Reaches the 10-Year Mark," *The New York Times*, December 31, 2011.

Further expansion of the Euro zone is, of course, on hold until the regional economy settles down.

The original 40-year-old operating rules of the EC were proving to be inadequate in dealing with the problems that confront the European Union today. Expansion beyond its present 28 members (see Exhibit 10.1), managing the conversion to the euro and EMU, and speaking with one voice on foreign policy that directly affects the European continent are all issues that require greater agreement among members and thus more responsibility and authority for the institutions of the European Union. The Amsterdam Treaty increases the authority of the institutions of the European Union and is designed to accommodate the changes brought about by the monetary union and the admission of new members.

Expansion of the European Union.   The process of enlargement was for a long time the most important item on the EU's agenda. Ten new countries were added in 2004, some ahead of schedule. Bulgaria and Romania entered as planned in 2007, as did Croatia in 2013. And talks with Turkey, Macedonia, Montenegro, Albania, Iceland, and Serbia are continuing. Negotiations with Turkey have had their ups and downs, but the Muslim majority nation has economically benefited from its new openness.[12] Beyond the current economic doldrums, a broader preoccupation for the European Union is the prospect of illegal immigrants from former Soviet states surging across poorly guarded borders of the newer and/or candidate states and making their way farther west within the EU. The European Union is demanding that borders be sealed, but the new and candidate states are reluctant to jeopardize relations with neighboring communities. Furthermore, the European Union fears a flood of cheap labor even if the borders are closed; it wants a long transition period before freedom of movement of labor, whereas the applicants say their citizens should be allowed to work anywhere in the EU once they are members.

In 2007 the European Union celebrated its golden anniversary. Most would agree that it has been a tremendous success, delivering peace and prosperity to hundreds of millions of people that previously had lived with frequent wars and accompanying economic and social hardships. The 2008–2009 global recession has posed daunting short-term challenges to the integrity of the Union though; and most regions of the 28 nations continue to experience continuing problems. The long-term challenges facing the Union in the next 50 years appear to fall into three categories: (1) improving the Union's economic performance, (2) deciding how to limit the political aspects of union, and (3) deciding about further enlargement. The last problem may well disappear as both multilateral and bilateral agreements continue to multiply around the world and as the WTO continues to gain influence and traction in trade barrier reduction.

Eastern Europe and the Baltic States

LO4

Evolving patterns of trade as eastern Europe and the former Soviet states embrace free-market systems

Eastern Europe and the Baltic states, satellite nations of the former Soviet Union, have moved steadily toward establishing postcommunist market reforms. New business opportunities are emerging almost daily, and the region is described as anywhere from chaotic with big risks to an exciting place with untold opportunities. Both descriptions fit as countries continue to adjust to the political, social, and economic realities of changing from the restrictions of a Marxist–socialist system to some version of free markets and capitalism. However, these countries have neither all made the same progress nor had the same success in economic reform and growth.[13]

---

[12]Stanley Reed, "Turkey Turns Outward," *BusinessWeek,* October 12, 2009, pp. 40–41; "Is Turkey Turning," *The Economist,* June 12, 2010, pp. 55–56.

[13]Clifford J. Schultz II, Timothy J. Burkink, Bruno Grbac, and Natasa Renko, "When Policies and Marketing Systems Explode: An Assessment of Food Marketing in the War-Ravaged Balkans and Implications for Recovery, Sustainable Peace, and Prosperity," *Journal of Public Policy & Marketing* 24, no. 1 (2005), pp. 24–37.

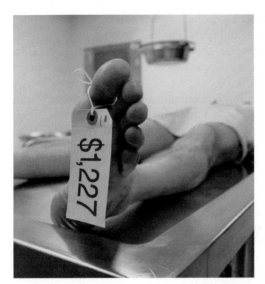

As demand for tobacco declines in more-developed countries, manufacturers direct more marketing efforts in the direction of emerging economies. Indeed, recently Philip Morris published a report estimating the cost savings for the Czech government at $1,227 every time a smoker dies. Apparently, the company did not think through the public relations implications of this grisly bit of research.

Eastern Europe. It is dangerous to generalize beyond a few points about eastern Europe, because each of the countries has its own economic problems and is at a different stage in its evolution from a socialist to a market-driven economy. Most eastern European countries are privatizing state-owned enterprises, establishing free market pricing systems, relaxing import controls, and wrestling with inflation. The very different paths taken toward market economies have resulted in different levels of progress. Countries such as the Czech Republic, which moved quickly to introduce major changes, seem to have fared better than countries such as Hungary, Poland, and Romania, which held off privatizing until the government restructured internally. Moving quickly allows the transformation to be guided mainly by the spontaneity of innovative market forces rather than by government planners or technocrats. Those countries that took the slow road permitted the bureaucrats from communist days to organize effectively to delay and even derail the transition to a market economy.

Yugoslavia has been plagued with internal strife over ethnic divisions, and four of its republics (Croatia, Slovenia, Macedonia, and Bosnia/Herzegovina) seceded from the federation, leaving Serbia and Montenegro in the reduced Federal Republic of Yugoslavia. Soon after seceding, a devastating ethnic war broke out in Croatia and Bosnia/Herzegovina that decimated their economies. A tentative peace maintained by United Nations peacekeepers now exists, but for all practical purposes, the economies of Croatia and Bosnia are worse now than ever before. Most recently, the Kosovo region of Serbia also declared its independence, and political tension remains.

Nevertheless, most countries in the region continue to make progress in building market-oriented institutions and adopting legislation that conforms to that of advanced market economies. The Czech Republic, Hungary, the Slovak Republic, and Poland have become members of the OECD.[14] Joining the OECD means they accept the obligations of the OECD to modernize their economies and to maintain sound macroeconomic policies and market-oriented structural reforms. The four also became members of the European Union in 2004, along with Bulgaria and Romania in 2007. And they are eager to stabilize their developing democracies and their westward tilt in foreign and security policies. Recent complaints about westward migration from the newest members of the EU persist, but history has shown this to be a minor issue in the longer run.[15]

The Baltic States. The Baltic states—Estonia, Latvia, and Lithuania—are a good example of the difference that the right policies can make. All three countries started off with roughly the same legacy of inefficient industry and Soviet-style command economies. Estonia quickly seized the lead by dropping the ruble, privatizing companies and land, letting struggling banks fail, and adopting the freest trading regime of the three countries. Its economic growth has handily outpaced Latvia's and Lithuania's. Since regaining independence in 1991, Estonia's economic reform policy has led to a liberalized, nearly tariff-free, open-market economy.

Although Latvia and Lithuania have made steady progress, government bureaucracy, corruption, and organized crime—common problems found in the countries of the former Soviet Union—continue. These issues represent the most significant hurdles to U.S. trade and investment. The governments and all major political parties support a free market system, yet traces of the Soviet methodology and regulatory traditions at the lower levels of bureaucracy remain visible. All three Baltic countries are WTO members and, as of 2004, EU members.

The Commonwealth of Independent States

Europe (and Asia) has one other trade group that has emerged and persisted since the dissolution of the Soviet Union: the Commonwealth of Independent States (CIS).[16] The series of events after the aborted coup against Mikhail Gorbachev led to the complete dissolution of the USSR. The first Soviet republics to declare independence were the Baltic

---

[14]http://www.oecd.org.

[15]"The Next Wave?" *The Economist*, February 9, 2013, p. 54.

[16]http://www.cisstat.com, 2015.

The hammer and sickle logo of the old USSR has been replaced by signs of free enterprise in Russia. Here in the main shopping district of St. Petersburg, Nike Sport is prominent, along with Coca-Cola red umbrellas.

states, which quickly gained recognition by several Western nations. The remaining 12 republics of the former USSR, collectively known as the Newly Independent States (NIS), regrouped into the Commonwealth of Independent States (see Exhibit 10.5).

The CIS is a loose economic and political alliance with open borders but no central government. The main provisions of the commonwealth agreement are to repeal all Soviet laws and assume the powers of the old regimes; launch radical economic reforms, including freeing most prices; keep the ruble but allow new currencies; establish a European Union–style free trade association; create joint control of nuclear weapons; and fulfill all Soviet foreign treaties and debt obligations.

The 12 members of the CIS share a common history of central planning, and their close cooperation could make the change to a market economy less painful, but differences over economic policy, currency reform, and control of the military may break them apart. How the CIS will be organized and what its ultimate importance will be is anyone's guess.

The three Slavic republics of Russia, Ukraine, and Belarus have interests and history in common, as do the five Central Asian republics. But the ties between these two core groups of the CIS are tenuous and stem mainly from their former Soviet membership. Russia and Ukraine have been involved in a nasty, decade-long dispute over the price and payments

CROSSING BORDERS 10.1   The Big Mac and Moscow Machinations

Many American executives complain about the difficulties of doing business in China. As we report in Chapter 11, their Ease of Doing Business ranking is #99—about in the middle of the 187 nations ranked. Russia comes in worse at #111. (See Exhibit 10.5.) And their ranking will be worse in 2014, particularly if you ask McDonald's about things in Moscow these days.

The *New York Times* reported, "The scene was strait out of the `C.S.I.,' food safety edtion. At a McDonald's in a provincial town northwest of here, health inspectors in lab coats swooped in for a surprise check." Based on their investigation the Russian authorities sued to ban sales of several products including cheeseburgers, fish sandwiches, and some desserts because the calory counts didn't jibe with the menus.

The Russian courts closed nine stores immediately, including the very first and still busiest location in Moscow's Pushkin Square. McDonald's was seemingly at war with Russia for the better part of 2014. Earlier in that year, political tensions began to rise between America and Russia after the conflict over Ukraine and the annexation of Crimea. While dealing with Western sanctions, Russian officials seem to be using McDonald's—a highly visible American presence within the country—as an example.

In August, Russian banned all edible imports—including cheese and vegetables—from the United States, Canada, the European Union, and more in response to Western sanctions. Other American companies are suffering similar harrassment, such as ExxonMobil, Schumberger, Jack Daniels, Visa, and Condé Nast. In the case of Condé Nast, the magazine company is being forced to sell controlling ownership to a Russian partner because foreign media ownership rules have been changed.

The row between Russia and Ukraine started about a decade ago—the issue was a price dispute over natural gas shipped to the Ukraine and the EU via Ukraine pipelines. Leaders of the two countries reached agreements in 2006, 2011, and again in 2014, the last being mediated by the EU. Crimea, with popular beaches, strategic port facilities, fossil fuel resources, and a 77 percent majority of Russian speakers was annexed by Russia in 2014. But, it's hard to imagine Russia being interested in taking more territory from their big CIS (not CSI!) neighbor (note the wide gap in incomes across the two populous countries). And circa 2015, Russia has substantial economic problems of its own, with oil prices dropping below $80 per barrel for the first time in recent memory.

Sources: Khushbu Shah, "Nearly 200 McDonald's in Russian to Undergo Government Inspections," *Eater.com*, October 20, 2014, online; Andrew E. Kramer, "Enduring Russia's Wrath," *The New York Times*, November 7, 2014, pp. B1, 8.

Exhibit 10.5
Commonwealth of Independent States (CIS) Fundamental Market Metrics

(in parentheses) = average annual growth rate 2008–2013 as a percentage

Country	Population (millions)	GNI* (billions $)	Exports* of Goods (billions $)	Imports* of Goods (billions $)	Ease of Doing Business Index	GNI/capita* ($)	Internet Users (percentage)
Armenia[FTAR]	3.0 (0.0)	10.9 (3.8)	1.5 (6.9)	4.4 (–0.2)	40	3670 (3.8)	46
Azerbaijan	9.4 (1.3)	69.4 (8.8)	31.8 (0.8)	11.2 (8.1)	71	7417 (7.4)	59
Belarus[FTAR]	9.4 (–0.2)	69.0 (36.8)	36.5 (2.3)	43.0 (1.8)	64	7307 (37.0)	54
Kazakhstan	16.9 (1.4)	198.9 (17.1)	84.7 (3.5)	48.7 (5.2)	53	11768 (15.5)	54
Kyrgyzstan	5.5 (1.3)	6.9 (12.7)	1.8 (–0.7)	6.1 (8.3)	70	1246 (11.2)	23
Moldova[FTAR]	3.5 (–0.8)	8.8 (9.9)	2.4 (8.6)	5.5 (2.3)	86	2527 (10.9)	49
Russia[FTAR]	143.4 (0.1)	2016.4 (9.9)	523.3 (2.3)	341.3 (3.4)	111	14063 (9.7)	61
Tajikistan	8.2 (2.4)	8.5 (18.1)	1.2 (–3.7)	4.2 (5.2)	141 141 1030	1030 (15.3)	16
Uzbekistan[FTAR]	28.9 (1.4)	58.3 (24.2)	12.4 (3.8)	13.0 (7.0)	156	2016 (22.5)	38
(CIS charter unratified)							
Georgia	4.5 (0.5)	15.8 (6.9)	2.9 (14.2)	7.9 (4.6)	9	3532 (6.4)	43
Turkmenistan	5.2 (1.3)	35.6 (16.7)	18.0 (8.6)	10.0 (12.1)	–	6806 (15.3)	10
Ukraine[FTAR]	45.4 (–0.4)	179.2 (8.8)	64.3 (–0.8)	76.8 (–2.1)	140	3950 (9.2)	42

*Current U.S. $.
[FTAR] = free-trade agreement (CISFTA) ratified
Source: Euromonitor International, 2015; World Bank, 2015.

of gas shipped by the former to the latter.[17] Settlements of this particular point of friction between the close neighbors seems to change with the weather. And we should all hope that the 2014 annexation of Crimea by Russia is the first and last of potential territorial disputes associated with the otherwise astonishingly peaceful disintegration of the Soviet Union.

In 2011, led by Russia and Ukraine, eight of the countries signed a free trade agreement. So far, six of the eight have ratified the agreement, including the two most populous states. Of course, all this economic cooperation is suffering from the short-term political crises.[18]

Many of the new nations in the region have been economically successful since leaving the former USSR. After the USSR collapsed, their economies had all imploded to less than half their peak size during Soviet days. Now, however, they are showing sustained signs of commercial renewal—and multinational icons like Intel have made investments in the area. Although initially Russia experienced serious economic problems, it now has returned to more robust growth in large part due to the successful marketing of its vast energy resources. However, the combination of falling oil and gas prices and its dependency on that industry does not bode well for the immediate future. Also the political disruptions between Ukraine and Russia pose another threat to continued growth in the region.

Africa

In part stimulated by increasing foreign direct investment,[19] particularly from China for infrastructure projects, prospects for enterprise south of the Sahara are on the upswing. Despite global economic problems, growth among African countries has been picking up nicely in the past few years.[20] Ethiopia, Angola, and Malawi each experienced annual

---

[17]Andrew Osborne, "Ukraine Natural-Gas Dispute Intensifies," *The Wall Street Journal*, March 4, 2008, online; Henry Meyer, "Russian Natural-Gas Dispute with Ukraine Threatens New Cutoff to Europe," *Bloomberg,* September 22, 2011; Nina Chestney, "Ukraine-Russia Gas Row—the Sequel—Penciled in Already," *Reuters*, November 5, 2014, online.

[18]"Ukraine Quits CIS, Sets Visa Regime with Russian, Wants Crimea as 'Demilitarized Zone,'" *Reuters*, March 19, 2014, online.

[19]Frank Langfitt, "Will Kenyan Superhighway also Benefit China?" *NPR,* June 21, 2011; "Limited Partnership," *The Economist*, February 1, 2014, page 61.

[20]"The Sun Shines Bright," *The Economist,* December 3, 2011, pp. 82–84.

Cell phone service is widely available even in African countries with per capita incomes among the lowest in the world.

growth rates of greater than 8 percent between 2006 and 2011. Several other countries in the sub-Saharan region have grown faster than 5 percent per annum. The average growth rates in sub-Saharan African countries has been remarkable. As can be seen in Exhibit 10.6, more than half have experienced double-digit increases in GNI, with Eritrea, Ehtiopia, Malawi, Sierra Leone, and Zambia each with average annual grow rates above 20 percent between 2008 and 2013.[21] Yet despite this remarkably good news, Africa's multinational market integration activities can be characterized as a great deal of activity but little progress. All the countries on the continent (save Morocco) have joined a loosely defined African Union,[22] and they are listed in Exhibit 10.6. Including bilateral agreements, an estimated 200 other economic arrangements exist among African countries. Despite the large number and assortment of paper organizations, there has been little actual economic integration because of the political instability[23] that has characterized Africa in recent decades and the unstable economic base on which Africa has had to build. The United Nations Economic Commission for Africa (ECA) has held numerous conferences but has been hampered by governmental inexperience, undeveloped resources, labor problems, and chronic product shortages.

The Economic Community of West African States (ECOWAS), the Southern African Development Community (SADC), and the East African Community (EAC) are the three most active regional cooperative groups. A 15-nation group, ECOWAS has an aggregate gross domestic product of more than $60 billion and is striving to achieve full economic integration. The 20th ECOWAS summit in 1997 approved a plan to accelerate subregional economic integration and development, with emphasis on a full commitment to regional monetary integration and the eventual adoption of a single West African currency. Unfortunately, ECOWAS continues to be plagued with financial problems, conflict within the group, and inactivity on the part of some members. After 30 years, the ECOWAS treaty and its many defined objectives and the way they are to be achieved over a 15-year period in three stages languishes; nothing has been achieved, and free trade remains a deferred dream.

The Southern African Development Community is the most advanced and viable of Africa's regional organizations. Its 15 members encompass a landmass of 7 million square kilometers containing abundant natural resources and a population of more than 250 million. South Africa, the region's dominant economy, has a GDP of more than $200 billion and accounts for 76.8 percent of SADC market share. After years of negotiations, 11 members of SADC approved a free trade agreement aimed at phasing out a minimum of 85 percent of tariffs within eight years and all tariffs circa 2015.

South Africa's economic growth has increased significantly now that apartheid is officially over and the United Nations has lifted the economic embargo that isolated that nation from much of the industrialized world. South Africa has an industrial base that will help propel it into rapid economic growth, with the possibility of doubling its GNP in as few as 10 years. The South African market also has a developed infrastructure—airports, railways, highways, telecommunications—that makes it important as a base for serving nearby African markets too small to be considered individually but viable when coupled with South Africa.

Upbeat economic predictions, a stable sociopolitical environment, and the reinforced vigor of the South African government in addressing the issues of privatization and deregulation while maintaining the long-term goal of making the country more investor friendly bode well for U.S. businesses seeking trading, investment, and joint venture opportunities in South Africa. The country has a fair-sized domestic market of nearly $350 billion with significant growth potential

---

[21]Nicholas Kulsih, "Africans Open Wallets To the Future," *The New York Times*, July 21, 2014, pp. A1, A10.

[22]"Get Still More Serious," *The Economist*, February 6, 2010, p. 14.

[23]Peter Wonacott, "The United States of Africa? Not Yet," *The Wall Street Journal*, July 18, 2014, online.

Exhibit 10.6
African Union Countries and Other Market Groups Fundamental Market Metrics

(in parentheses) = average annual growth rate 2008–2013 as a percentage

Country	Population (millions)	GNI* (billions $)	Exports* of Goods (billions $)	Imports* of Goods (billions $)	Ease of Doing Business Index	GNI/Capita* ($)	Internet Users (percent)
Angola[3]	21.5 (3.2)	110.1 (15.0)	67.1 (–1.4)	28.1 (6.4)	178	5130 (11.4)	19
Benin[2]	10.3 (2.8)	8.0 (6.0)	1.2 (–2.2)	2.2 (–1.2)	175	780 (3.1)	5
Botswana[3]	2.0 (0.9)	15.0 (12.0)	7.6 (9.0)	7.0 (6.1)	65	7418 (11.0)	15
Burkina Faso[2]	16.9 (2.9)	11.9 (8.4)	2.2 (25.5)	3.5 (11.6)	154	705 (5.3)	4
Burundi[4]	10.2 (3.3)	2.7 (17.3)	0.1 (12.9)	0.8 (15.1)	157	268 (13.5)	1
Cameroon	20.9 (2.2)	28.7 (6.6)	4.2 (–0.5)	7.0 (5.3)	162	1370 (4.4)	6
Cape Verde[2]	0.5 (0.6)	1.7 (4.1)	0.1 (16.6)	0.7 (–2.5)	128	3406 (3.5)	38
Central African Republic	4.6 (2.0)	1.5 (–2.8)	0.1 (–1.4)	0.3 (–3.6)	187	335 (–4.6)	4
Chad	11.5 (2.7)	7.4 (7.6)	4.5 (0.8)	3.0 (9.6)	183	641 (4.8)	2
Congo, DR[3]	67.5 (2.8)	19.1 (23.6)	6.3 (7.4)	6.3 (7.9)	183	283 (20.3)	2
Congo, B	4.4 (2.8)	11.2 (10.1)	9.8 (3.4)	5.5 (11.9)	186	2529 (7.1)	7
Cote d'Ivoire[2]	20.3 (2.2)	27.0 (6.7)	13.7 (5.7)	12.9 (10.3)	173	1327 (3.7)	3
Equatorial Guinea	0.8 (2.8)	9.4 (1.3)	14.0 (–2.5)	7.0 (12.4)	164	12464 (–1.5)	16
Eritrea	6.3 (3.3)	3.4 (20.2)	0.3 (96.7)	1.0 (11.4)	185	542 (16.3)	1
Ethiopia	94.1 (2.6)	47.5 (29.3)	3.0 (13.4)	12.0 (7.7)	124	504 (26.0)	2
Gabon	1.7 (2.4)	16.8 (7.3)	9.5 (0.0)	3.9 (8.4)	169	10034 (4.8)	9
Gambia[2]	1.8 (3.2)	0.9 (8.9)	0.1 (45.8)	0.4 (1.7)	148	481 (5.5)	14
Ghana[2]	25.9 (2.3)	43.3 (23.0)	13.7 (21.1)	17.8 (11.6)	62	1670 (20.2)	12
Guinea[2]	11.7 (2.6)	6.3 (15.2)	1.3 (–0.6)	2.2 (9.5)	179	533 (12.2)	2
Guinea Bissau[2]	1.7 (2.4)	1.0 (5.2)	0.2 (10.4)	0.2 (3.8)	181	569 (2.8)	3
Kenya[4]	44.4 (2.7)	44.7 (12.9)	5.9 (3.4)	16.4 (8.1)	122	1009 (9.9)	39
Lesotho[3]	2.1 (1.0)	2.9 (10.5)	0.9 (1.0)	2.3 (2.5)	139	1380 (9.4)	5
Liberia[2]	4.3 (3.2)	1.4 (18.4)	0.5 (17.4)	1.2 (8.3)	149	330 (14.7)	5
Madagascar[3]	22.9 (2.8)	10.5 (7.7)	2.0 (3.1)	3.2 (–3.5)	144	457 (4.7)	2
Malawi[3]	16.4 (3.0)	5.0 (20.4)	1.2 (6.0)	2.7 (4.1)	161	308 (16.9)	5
Mali[2]	15.3 (3.1)	10.0 (5.6)	2.6 (4.4)	3.7 (2.1)	153	655 (2.4)	2
Mauritius[3]	1.2 (0.3)	11.9 (5.8)	2.9 (3.8)	5.4 (3.0)	20	9602 (5.5)	39
Mozambique[3]	25.8 (2.6)	15.5 (16.0)	4.3 (10.1)	8.6 (16.5)	142	602 (13.1)	5
Namibia[3]	2.3 (1.8)	11.9 (10.0)	3.5 (2.3)	7.6 (11.7)	94	5185 (8.1)	14
Niger[2]	17.8 (3.9)	7.6 (9.4)	1.6 (11.9)	1.9 (2.3)	174	429 (5.3)	2
Nigeria[2]	170.9 (2.6)	499.0 (16.2)	91.8 (2.2)	45. (9.9)	138	2920 (13.3)	38
Rwanda[4]	11.8 (2.9)	7.3 (13.1)	0.7 (20.9)	2.5 (16.9)	54	621 (9.9)	9
Sao Tome and Principe	0.2 (2.8)	0.3 (13.7)	0.0 (2.5)	0.1 (4.2)	166	1569 (10.6)	23
Senegal[2]	14.1 (2.9)	15.1 (4.7)	2.4 (4.0)	6.1 (1.2)	176	1068 (1.7)	21
Seychelles[3]	0.1 (0.6)	1.2 (11.9)	0.6 (6.1)	0.9 (–2.5)	77	13240 (11.2)	50
Sierra Leone[2]	6.1 (1.9)	5.0 (21.9)	1.9 (54.4)	1.8 (27.2)	137	821 (19.6)	2
South Africa[3]	52.8 (1.0)	343.3 (8.7)	86.7 (1.4)	101.3 (2.6)	41	6504 (7.7)	49
Swaziland[3]	1.2 (1.6)	3.4 (5.6)	1.9 (2.0)	1.5 (–2.3)	120	2695 (3.9)	25
Tanzania[3,4]	49.2 (3.1)	28.2 (15.8)	5.1 (13.6)	12.3 (11.6)	136	574 (12.3)	4
Togo[2]	6.8 (2.6)	3.5 (6.6)	1.1 (4.3)	2.1 (6.8)	159	512 (3.9)	5
Uganda[4]	37.6 (3.4)	20.6 (17.2)	2.8 (1.0)	4.9 (1.7)	126	548 (13.4)	16
Zambia[3]	14.5 (3.1)	23.8 (23.2)	10.6 (15.4)	10.2 (15.2)	90	1636 (19.4)	15
Zimbabwe[3]	14.1 (2.1)	9.4 (13.6)	3.6 (10.1)	4.3 (7.8)	168	662 (11.4)	19

*Current U.S. $.
[1]Member of Economic Community of West African States (ECOWAS).
[2]Member of Southern African Development Community (SADC).
[3]Member of East African Community.

Source: Euromonitor International, 2015; World Bank, 2015.

and is increasingly becoming free market oriented. It has yet to develop to its full potential, however, because of years of isolation, former inward-looking trade and investment policies, a low savings rate, and a largely unskilled labor force with attendant low productivity.

South Africa has the potential to become the newest big emerging market (BEM), but its development will depend on government action and external investment by other governments and multinational firms. In varying degrees, foreigners are leading the way by making sizable investments.

One of the paradoxes of Africa is that its people are for the most part desperately poor, while its land is extraordinarily rich. East Asia is the opposite: It is a region mostly poor in resources that over the last few decades has enjoyed an enormous economic boom. When several African countries in the 1950s (for example, Congo, the former Zaire) were at the same income level as many East Asian countries (for example, South Korea) and were blessed with far more natural resources, it might have seemed reasonable for the African countries to have prospered more than their Asian counterparts. Although there is no doubt that East Asia enjoyed some significant cultural and historical advantages, its economic boom relied on other factors that have been replicated elsewhere but are absent in Africa. The formula for success in East Asia was an outward-oriented, market-based economic policy coupled with an emphasis on education and healthcare. Most newly industrialized countries have followed this model in one form or another.

The Internet also facilitates education, a fundamental underpinning for economic development. The African Virtual University, which links more than 50 underfunded and ill-equipped African campuses to classrooms and libraries worldwide, grants degrees in computer science, computer engineering, and electrical engineering. South Africa's School Net program links 1,035 schools to the Internet, and the government's Distance Education program brings multimedia teaching to rural schools. Google[24] and other companies are also investing there to build content in Swahili, for example.

Middle East/North Africa (MENA)   The unprecedented and ongoing political turmoil in Middle East/North Africa (MENA) region accelerated dramatically in 2011 and has yielded an associated economic disaster in several countries in the region.[25] The long-term consequences for international trade and marketing are unknown as of yet. There are both positive (greater press freedoms)[26] and negative (new economic sanctions targeting Israel) stories emerging,[27] but the hope is that democracy and freedom in the area will ultimately increase economic opportunities for all.[28] Perhaps the best indication of the possibilities of peace in the region is in the comparative exports of Iraq, Iran, and the UAE in Exhibit 10.7. Both Iraq and Iran have much greater oil reserves, but, in the contexts of their political turmoils, they are exporting less than one-third as much as the UAE.

Even before the current political and economic disruptions, the Middle East had been the least aggressive region in the formation of successfully functioning multinational market groups. The Arab Common Market set goals for free internal trade but has not succeeded. The aim was to integrate the economies of the 22 Arab countries, but before that will be feasible, a long history of border disputes, persisting ideological differences, and internal political turmoil will have to be overcome. The idea is still alive, however, and is a topic of discussion whenever Arab foreign ministers meet. The Arab states on the Persian Gulf, Egypt, and Morocco worked out an agreement on an Arab Free Trade Area, sometimes called the Greater Arab Free Trade Area (GAFTA). This 2005 agreement is still in its early stages of implementation, and its success was uncertain, even before 2011. In Exhibit 10.7, we have organized the Arab-speaking

---

[24]Noam Cohen, "Hungry for Content, Google Tries to Grow Its Own in Africa," *The New York Times,* January 25, 2010, p. B3.

[25]"Arab Spring Economies: Unfinished Business," *The Economist,* February 4, 2012, pp. 49–50.

[26]Sarah A. Topol, "Egypt's Brotherhood TV," *Businessweek.com,* January 19, 2012.

[27]Yitzchok Adlerstein, "Egypt's Petty Palm Embargo," *Los Angeles Times,* October 11, 2011, p. A15.

[28]Jeffrey Goldberg, "The Awakening," *Bloomberg Businessweek,* January 8, 2012, pp. 12–33; Matthew Campbell and Christopher Stephen, "Libya Is Free. Send in the Cinnabons," *Bloomberg Businessweek,* December 17–23, 2012, pp. 17–18.

Old meets new in two big emerging markets. The Grand Bazaar in Istanbul is the oldest and largest covered marketplace in the world, dating back to the 15th century. In modern Istanbul, it competes for customers with the ubiquitous McDonald's. Faint in the background is the Blue Mosque, built in 1616. Of course, the pyramids at Giza near Cairo are much older. But new construction methods and development are competing for the skyline there as well.

Exhibit 10.7
Middle East/North Africa (MENA)

Country	Population (millions)	GNI* (billions $)	Exports* of Goods (billions $)	Imports* of Goods (billions $)	Ease of Doing Business Index	GNI/Capita* ($)	Internet Users (percent)
Arab League Member States							
Algeria	36.0 (1.5)	188.7 (10.9)	74.5 (6.3)	47.2 (17.6)	148	5247 (9.2)	13 (19.7)
Bahrain	1.2 (1.9)	28.6 (2.9)	17.5 (0.2)	13.0 (3.8)	47	23595 (1.0)	90
Comoros	0.7 (2.5)	0.7 (7.50)	0.0 (30.8)	0.3 (9.7)	160	923 (4.9)	7
Djibouti[v]	0.9 (1.9)	1.4 (10.1)	0.1 (11.8)	0.6 (−0.5)	170	1525 (8.1)	10
Egypt	83.7 (2.4)	246.7 (13.2)	28.5 (2.3)	58.3 (3.8)	127	2948 (10.6)	50
Iraq	33.8 (2.8)	204.1 (11.7)	89.5 (28.3)	61.0 (13.1)	155	6043 (8.7)	9
Jordan	6.6 (2.4)	33.4 (8.0)	7.9 (−0.1)	22.1 (5.4)	119	5080 (5.5)	44
Kuwait	4.1 (8.6)	211.9 (7.2)	115.2 (5.6)	29.6 (3.6)	101	51220 (−1.3)	75
Lebanon	4.8 (2.9)	44.8 (8.2)	4.1 (−1.8)	21.2 (4.9)	105	9300 (5.2)	71
Libya[v]	6.4 (1.7)	45.7 (−4.0)	44.0 (−6.7)	27.0 (24. 2)	104	7132 (−5.6)	17
Mauritania	3.9 (2.60)	3.8 (6.2)	2.7 (8.2)	3.3 (10.9)	171	982 (3.5)	6
Morocco	32.9 (1.0)	102.2 (2.9)	21.8 (1.4)	44.9 (1.2)	95	3105 (1.9)	56
Oman	3.6 (7.0)	91.8 (11.7)	56.4 (8.4)	34.3 (8.4)	44	25274 (4.5)	66
Palestine (data included in Israel)							
Qatar	2.0 (6.7)	190.3 (11.9)	136.9 (15.2)	26.9 (−0.7)	45	95984 (4.9)	85
Saudi Arabia	29.3 (2.3)	748.5 (7.2)	375.7 (3.7)	152.0 (8.6)	22	25528 (4.8)	61
Somalia[v]	9.6 (2.3)	—	0.5 (5.2)	1.3 (7.9)	—	—	2
Sudan	38.0 (2.2)	46.7 (15.9)	7.1 (−9.5)	9.9 (1.2)	143 1230	1230 (13.4)	23
Syria[v]	20.8 (2.0)	61.8 (13.6)	3.0 (−27.9)	5.8 (−20.4)	134 2976	2976 (11.4)	26
Tunisia	11.0 (1.1)	46.0 (7.5)	17.1 (−2.5)	24.3 (−0.2)	49 4183	4183 (6.3)	44
United Arab Emirates	8.4 (6.2)	398.4 (4.5)	319.4 (6.0)	237.5 (6.1)	26 47344	47344 (−1.6)	88
Yemen	24.4 (2.4)	35.4 (5.9)	9.5 (4.6)	12.5 (1.9)	129 1451	1451 (3.5)	20
Unaffiliated States							
Iran	76.4 (1.1)	493.4 (23.5)	94.9 (−3.6)	49.9 (−2.9)	152	6458 (22.1)	31
Israel	8.1 (2.0)	284.2 (6.4)	56.9 (2.1)	71.1 (2.0)	33	35268 (4.3)	71
South Sudan	11.3 (4.4)	12.9 (10.3)	—	—	184	1140 (5.7)	—

*Current U.S. $.

[v] = timely reporting of population and GNI disrupted due to ongoing violent conflicts

Source: Euromonitor International, 2015; World Bank, 2015.

You may think Dubai is an odd place—an ostentatious and architecturally spectacular member of the United Arab Emirates that has teetered on the brink of a real estate collapse. So perhaps a change in perspective is in order, say, from outer space. Here's the Dubai coast, seen from the International Space Station. At left are the man-made Palm Jumeirah islands. At right is a development of 300, private, man-made islands shaped like a global map.

countries as defined by the very loose, quasi-political Arab League. In 2011, Sudan divided into two states: Sudan and South Sudan. Palestine recently was recognized by the Arab League, so we have listed it here, but the associated data are not available and thus are subsumed in the data on Israel. The Western Sahara of Morocco is also a matter of political dispute.

Iran, Pakistan, and Turkey, formerly the Regional Cooperation for Development (RCD), have renamed their regional group the Economic Cooperation Organization (ECO). Since reorganizing, Afghanistan and six of the newly independent states were accepted into the ECO. Impressive strides in developing basic industrial production were being made when the RCD was first organized, but the revolution in Iran ended any economic activity. ECO has as its primary goal the development of its infrastructure to pave the way for regional cooperation. Unfortunately, trade volume among ECO members constitutes only 7 percent of their total trade. However, a recent announcement from ECO indicated that there has been an agreement to reduce tariff and nontariff barriers to boost trade.

The other activity in the region, led by Iran, is the creation of the Organization of the Islamic Conference (OIC), a common market composed of Islamic countries. A preferential tariff system among the member states of the OIC and the expansion of commercial services in insurance, transport, and transit shipping are among the issues to be debated at the next conference of Islamic countries. The OIC represents 60 countries and more than 650 million Muslims worldwide. The member countries' vast natural resources, substantial capital, and cheap labor force are seen as the strengths of the OIC.

Of course, the continuing turmoil in Iran and several Arab states and the wars in Syria, Iraq, and Afghanistan remain troubling influences on political and economic relations in the region. Like China, the government of Iran has disrupted Internet communications to head off political demonstrations. Despite the U.S. embargo on Iran and the associated punishment of involved firms and executives, American goods are still being smuggled into the country. The 100 miles by sea from Port Saeed of Dubai to Bandar Abbas in southern Iran seems to be a popular smuggling route. Dubai itself, one of the United Arab Emirates (U.A.E.), has been a prominent center for international investment in the Middle East. However, the Emirate suffered substantially as its aggressive commercial real estate activities collapsed during the 2008–2009 global economic downturn. There are signs of hope that trade can bring peace to the region. For example, a group of Iranian executives is intent on building a modern business school for their country.[29]

[29]Stanley Reed, "Reading Keynes in Tehran," *Bloomberg BusinessWeek*, February 15, 2010, p. 31.

Implications of Market Integration

The degree of differences across regions in economic integration is manifest. The European Union continues to be the global benchmark and therefore serves as the best model for understanding and predicting the processes of change in the other regions described previously. We can expect lessons learned there to be useful for international marketers contemplating entry and operations in the other regions in earlier stages of integration.

Strategic Implications

LO5

Strategic implications for marketing in the region

The complexion of the entire world marketplace has been changed significantly by the coalition of nations into multinational market groups. To international business firms, multinational groups spell opportunity in bold letters through access to greatly enlarged markets with reduced or abolished country-by-country tariff barriers and restrictions. Production, financing, labor, and marketing decisions are affected by the remapping of the world into market groups.

World competition will continue to intensify as businesses become stronger and more experienced in dealing with large market groups. For example, in an integrated Europe, U.S. multinationals had an initial advantage over expanded European firms because U.S. businesses were more experienced in marketing to large, diverse markets and are accustomed to looking at Europe as one market. These U.S. firms did not carry the cumbersome baggage of multiple national organizations dealing in many currencies, with differentiated pricing and administration, with which most EU firms had to contend. The advantage, however, was only temporary as mergers, acquisitions, and joint ventures consolidated operations of European firms in anticipation of the benefits of a single European market. Individual national markets still confront international managers with the same problems of language, customs, and instability, even though they are packaged under the umbrella of a common market. However, as barriers come down and multi-country markets are treated as one common market, a global market will be one notch closer to reality.

Regulation of business activities has been intensified throughout multinational market groups; each group now has management and administrative bodies specifically concerned with business. In the process of structuring markets, rules and regulations common to the group are often more sophisticated than those of the individual countries. Despite the problems and complexities of dealing with the new markets, the overriding message to the astute international marketer continues to be opportunity and profit potential.

Opportunities.   Economic integration creates large mass markets. Many national markets, too small to bother with individually, take on new dimensions and significance when combined with markets from cooperating countries. Large markets are particularly important to businesses accustomed to mass production and mass distribution because of the economies of scale and marketing efficiencies that can be achieved. In highly competitive markets, the benefits derived from enhanced efficiencies are often passed along as lower prices that lead to increased purchasing power.

Most multinational groups have coordinated programs to foster economic growth as part of their cooperative efforts. Such programs work to the advantage of marketers by increasing purchasing power, improving regional infrastructure, and fostering economic development. Despite the problems that are sure to occur because of integration, the economic benefits from free trade can be enormous.

Major savings will result from the billions of dollars now spent in developing different versions of products to meet a hodgepodge of national standards. Philips and other European companies invested a total of $20 billion to develop a common switching system for Europe's several different telephone networks. This figure compares with the $3 billion spent in the United States for a common system and $1.5 billion in Japan for a single system.

Market Barriers.   The initial aim of a multinational market is to protect businesses that operate within its borders. An expressed goal is to give an advantage to the companies within the market in their dealings with other countries of the market group. Analysis of the interregional and international trade patterns of the market groups indicates that such goals have been achieved.

Companies willing to invest in production facilities in multinational markets may benefit from protectionist measures because these companies become a part of the market. Exporters, however, are in a considerably weaker position. This prospect confronts many U.S. exporters who face the possible need to invest in Europe to protect their export markets in the European Union. The major problem for small companies may be adjusting to the EU standards. A company selling in one or two EU member countries and meeting standards there may find itself in a situation of having to change standards or be closed out when an EU-wide standard is adopted.

A manufacturer of the hoses used to hook up deep-fat fryers and other gas appliances to gas outlets faced such a problem when one of its largest customers informed the company that McDonald's was told it could no longer use that manufacturer's hoses in its British restaurants. The same thing happened at Paris Disneyland. Unfortunately, when the common standards were written, only large MNCs and European firms participated, so they had the advantage of setting standards to their benefit. The small company had only two choices: Change or leave. In this particular case, it appears that competitors were working to keep the company out of the market. There were however, enough questions about threaded fittings and compatibility that the company worked with individual countries to gain entrance to their markets—just as it had before a single market existed.

Market Metrics

LO6

The size and nature of marketing opportunities in the European/African/Middle East regions

In this section, we present three tables with fundamental metrics reflecting the size and character of markets in the eight most populous countries in the greater region. Looking across these tables, we see the widest disparity in standards of living, infrastructures, and consumer purchases. As in the Americas, the disparity appears to correlate with latitude, with greater economic development associated with distance from the equator. We also see the lack of data for the least developed countries in Africa and the Middle East. And we have not included in these data direct measures of political instability and other risks—those can be found in other chapters, such as Chapters 5 and 17.

Exhibit 10.8 presents standards of living across the eight countries. The range of GNI per capita is astonishing, with Germany at than $46,396 and the Democratic Republic of Congo at less than $300. Russia, Turkey, and Iran (as best as we can tell) are moving up the development ladder relatively fast.

Exhibit 10.9 compares the infrastructures of the countries. Again we see the wide disparities north to south. Perhaps the most interesting data involve the relative strength of Iran, particularly with regard to the numbers of university students. It is these university students who have been the catalyst for political protests in the country of late. But when it comes to opportunities for development and hiring good marketers of the future, these young people provide some hope.

Exhibit 10.8

Standard of Living in the Eight Most Populous Countries in the Europe/Africa/MENA Region

Country	Population (millions)	GNI per Capita	Medical Resources per 1000 Persons		Household Ownership %		
			Doctors	Hospital Beds	Color TV	Refrigerator	Washing Machine
Nigeria	170.9	2920	0.4	—	47.6	18.3	15.4
Russia	143.4	14063	5.1	9.3	98.2	99.2	84.3
Ethiopia	94.1	505	0.0	0.1	—	—	—
Germany	80.5	46396	4.0	8.3	95.1	99.7	94.5
Egypt	83.7	2948	3.1	1.5	93.8	94.4	95.6
Iran	76.4	6458	0.9	1.2	97.6	87.4	69.1
Turkey	75.6	10718	1.8	2.7	93.8	98.6	96.2
Congo, DR	67.5	283	—	—	—	—	—

Source: Euromonitor International, 2015.

Exhibit 10.9
Infrastructures of the Eight Most Populous Countries of the Europe/Africa/MENA Region

Country	Travel by Rail (passenger-km per capita)	Passenger Cars/1000	Energy Consumption (tones oil equivalent)	Mobile Phones in Use per 1000 People	Literacy Rate %	University Students per 1000 People
Nigeria	4	—	—	745	50	—
Russia	914	288	4.9	1523	100	76
Ethiopia	—	1	—	273	47	—
Germany	1009	545	4.0	1223	100	62
Egypt	488	44	1.0	1192	75	30
Iran	261	153	3.2	854	85	55
Turkey	80	120	1.6	922	96	69
Congo, DR	0	5	—	437	62	8

Source: Euromonitor International, 2015.

Exhibit 10.10 briefly enumerates consumption patterns. For Ethiopia and the Democratic Republic of Congo, we can only guess, and it is quite difficult to imagine conducting systematic primary consumer research in either country. The dollars spent on education in Turkey are promising. Of course, the German statistics jump off the page across the columns. Indeed, perhaps the most shocking datum in this book is the German per capita expenditure on alcohol and tobacco, at some $780/year, more than double the entire annual per capita income in the Democratic Republic of Congo! Of course, we do not blame the Germans, and recall that Canadians spend even more on the psychoactive substances (see Exhibit 9.5 in the previous chapter). Such contrasts in standards of living among human beings are simply incomprehensible.

Marketing Mix Implications

Companies are adjusting their marketing mix strategies to reflect anticipated market changes in the single European market. In the past, companies often charged different prices in different European markets. Nontariff barriers between member states supported price differentials and kept lower-priced products from entering those markets where higher prices were charged. For example, Colgate-Palmolive Company adapted its Colgate toothpaste into a single formula for sale across Europe at one price. Before changing its pricing practices, Colgate sold its toothpaste at different prices in different markets.

Beddedas Shower Gel is priced in the middle of the market in Germany and as a high-priced product in the United Kingdom. As long as products from lower-priced markets could not move to higher-priced markets, such differential price schemes worked.

Exhibit 10.10
Consumption Patterns in the Eight Most Populous Countries in Europe/Africa/MENA Region

Country	People per Household	Household Expenditures ($/capita)								
		Food	Alcohol, Tobacco	Clothing	Housing	Health Goods, Services	Transportation	Communication	Leisure	Education
Nigeria	4.8	1029	25	134	215	37	91	7	25	51
Russia	2.6	2109	628	664	721	278	970	312	343	80
Ethiopia	4.6	—	—	—	—	—	—	—	—	—
Germany	2.0	2950	780	1212	5975	1243	3281	653	2190	247
Egypt	3.8	1052	113	135	527	255	170	73	63	122
Iran	3.4	581	10	132	677	213	217	121	27	74
Turkey	3.7	1783	395	406	1494	245	1295	295	317	100
Congo, DR	6.8	—	—	—	—	—	—	—	—	—

Source: Euromonitor International, 2015.

Now, however, under the EU rules, companies cannot prevent the free movement of goods, and parallel imports from lower-priced markets to higher-priced markets are more likely to occur. Price standardization among country markets will be one of the necessary changes to avoid the problem of parallel imports. With the adoption of the euro, price differentials are much easier to spot, and the consumer can search for the best bargains in brand-name products more easily. Furthermore, the euro is making marketing on the Internet a much simpler task for European firms. On balance, a single currency will make competition in Europe a lot fairer and also a lot tougher.

In addition to initiating uniform pricing policies, companies are reducing the number of brands they produce to focus on advertising and promotion efforts. For example, Nestlé's several brands of yogurt in the European Union were reduced to a single brand. Unilever winnowed its 1,600 brands down to focus on 400 core brands. It plans to develop master brands in certain markets such as the European Union and to market others globally. A major benefit from an integrated Europe is competition at the retail level. Europe lacks an integrated and competitive distribution system that would support small and midsized outlets. The elimination of borders is resulting in increased competition among retailers and the creation of Europewide distribution channels.

Finally, all international marketers should see market integration around the world in a positive light. Trade among close neighbors will always be important—distance does make a difference. But overall, local integration ultimately serves globalization and harmonization of the world trading system, thus reducing the costs of business and delivering greater choice to consumers and greater opportunities to marketers.

Summary

The experiences of the multinational market groups developed since World War II point up both the successes and the hazards such groups encounter. The various attempts at economic cooperation represent varying degrees of success and failure, but almost without regard to their degree of success, the economic market groups have created great excitement among marketers. In the near future, these regional groupings will continue to form trade agreement ties with other nations and regions, thus paving the way for truly globalized markets where consumers dominate.

For companies, the economic benefits possible through cooperation relate to more efficient marketing and production. Marketing efficiency is effected through the development of mass markets, encouragement of competition, improvement of personal income, and various psychological market factors. Production efficiency derives from specialization, mass production for mass markets, and the free movement of the factors of production. Economic integration also tends to foster political harmony among the countries involved; such harmony leads to stability and peace, which are beneficial to the marketer as well as the countries' citizens.

The marketing implications of multinational market groups may be studied from the viewpoint of firms located inside the market or of firms located outside, which wish to sell to the markets. For each viewpoint the problems and opportunities are somewhat different; regardless of the location of the marketer, however, multinational market groups provide great opportunity for the creative marketer who wishes to expand volume. Market groupings make it economically feasible to enter new markets and to employ new marketing strategies that could not be applied to the smaller markets represented by individual countries. At the same time, market groupings intensify competition by protectionism within a market group but may foster greater protectionism between regional markets. Mercosur and ASEAN+3 (to be discussed in the next chapter), for example, suggest the growing importance of economic cooperation and integration. Such developments will continue to confront the international marketer by providing continually growing market opportunities and challenges.

Finally, the European/African/Middle East regions include perhaps the greatest diversity in income levels and cultures possible, providing daunting challenges important opportunities for international marketing managers with responsibilities in the area.

Key Terms

Multinational market regions	Common market	Maastricht Treaty	European Parliament
Free trade area (FTA)	Political union	Single European Act	Amsterdam Treaty
Customs union			

Questions

1. Define the key terms listed above.

2. Elaborate on the problems and benefits that multinational market groups represent for international marketers.

3. Explain the political role of multinational market groups.

4. Identify the factors on which one may judge the potential success or failure of a multinational market group.

5. Explain the marketing implications of the factors contributing to the successful development of a multinational market group.

6. Imagine that the United States was composed of many separate countries with individual trade barriers. What marketing effects might be visualized?

7. Discuss the possible types of arrangements for regional economic integration.

8. Differentiate between a free trade area and a common market. Explain the marketing implications of the differences.

9. It seems obvious that the founders of the European Union intended it to be a truly common market, so much so that economic integration must be supplemented by political integration to accomplish these objectives. Discuss.

10. The European Commission, the Council of Ministers, and the Court of Justice of the European Union have gained power in the last decade. Comment.

11. Select any three countries that might have some logical basis for establishing a multinational market organization and illustrate their compatibility as a regional trade group. Identify the various problems that would be encountered in forming multinational market groups of such countries.

12. U.S. exports to the European Union are expected by some to decline in future years. What marketing actions might a company take to counteract such changes?

13. "Because they are dynamic and because they have great growth possibilities, the multinational markets are likely to be especially rough-and-tumble for the external business." Discuss.

14. Differentiate between a customs union and a political union.

15. Why have African nations had such difficulty in forming effective economic unions?

16. Discuss the implications of the European Union's decision to admit eastern European nations to the group.

Chapter 11

The Asia Pacific Region

CHAPTER LEARNING OBJECTIVES

What you should learn about in Chapter 11:

LO1 The dynamic growth in the region

LO2 The importance and slow growth of Japan

LO3 The importance of the bottom-of-the-pyramid markets

LO4 The diversity across the region

LO5 The interrelationships among countries in the region

LO6 The diversity within China

Global Perspective

FROM THREE-SNAKE WINE AT WALMART TO NEW ZEALAND OYSTERS FROM ALIBABA

Developing markets are experiencing rapid industrialization, growing industrial and consumer markets, and new opportunities for foreign investment. Consider the following illustration: In China, it is just a few shopping days before the Lunar New Year, and the aisles at the local Walmart Supercenter are jammed with bargain hunters pushing carts loaded high with food, kitchen appliances, and clothing. It could be the preholiday shopping rush in any Walmart in Middle America, but the shoppers here are China's nouveau riche. Superstores have proven popular with Chinese consumers, who devote a large part of their spending to food and daily necessities. Walmart has been able to tap into the Chinese sense of social status by offering membership cards that confer not only eligibility for special discounts but social status as well.

Alongside Campbell's soup and Bounty paper towels are racks of dried fish and preserved plums. One shelf is stacked high with multiple brands of *congee*, a popular southern Chinese breakfast dish, and another has *nam yue* peanuts and packets of bamboo shoots. In the liquor section in the back of the store is three-snake rice wine, complete with the dead serpents' bodies coiled together in the potent liquid. About 95 percent of what Walmart sells in China is sourced locally. Gone are the efforts to sell big extension ladders or a year's supply of soy sauce to customers living in tiny apartments.

At present Walmart operates more than 11,000 units in 27 countries, including almost 400 in China. Revenues and profits are growing nicely for its international operations, and overseas expansion is set to continue particularly in China since its entry into the World Trade Organization. As one executive commented, "It boggles the mind to think if everybody washed their hair every day, how much shampoo you would sell [in China]."

The Chinese market can be difficult to tap and may not be profitable for many years for many companies. Most foreign retailers are in a learning mode about the ways and tastes of Asia, which are very different from those on Main Street U.S.A. For example, Pricesmart designed its Beijing store with two huge loading docks to accommodate full-sized diesel trucks in anticipation of the big deliveries needed to keep shelves well packed. What the company found was Chinese distributors arriving with goods in car trunks, on three-wheel pedicabs, or strapped to the backs of bicycles.

That was the good old days. Now contrast that with the latest from Alibaba: On a cold day in April, a group of New Zealand fishermen set out to harvest 50,000 large oysters from the waters of the South Pacific. Once collected, the briny mollusks were transported to processing facilities, packaged four to a container, sealed in chilled polystyrene containers affixed with bright labeling, and put on planes to China. Over the next three days, the oysters traveled thousands of miles to 67 cities across the Chinese mainland. There, they were shipped "still alive" by an army of delivery men to the homes of thousands of shoppers who had ordered them using Tmall, a website operated by Alibaba, the sprawling Internet empire that broke the world's record for IPOs at $25 billion in 2014. That's a lot of clams!

Sources: Keith B. Richburg, "Attention Shenzen Shoppers! U.S. Retail Giants Are Moving into China, and Finding the Learning Curve Formidable," *Washington Post*, February 12, 1997; David Gelles, "Alibaba Is Bringing Luxury, Fast, to China's Middle Class," *The New York Times*, September 10, 2014, online; http://www.walmartstores.com, 2015.

LO1

The dynamic growth
in the region

As the 21st century continues to unfold, so does the dynamism of the Asia Pacific Region.[1] While economic growth rates in North America and Europe have languished, Latin American and MENA have perked up recently. But, the economic miracle begun by Japan in the 1970s and carried on by the Four Asian Tigers in the 1980s has now been embraced by Greater China and the region as a whole. Indeed, marketers in the area are developing strong, new Asian brands,[2] reacting to and creating "a transnational, imagined Asian world" based on the common "globalization, hyper-urban and multicultural experience." As evinced in Chapter 3, the Asia Pacific Region lagged for the last 500 years. But now opportunities abound, brought about by the combination of fast economic growth and half the population of the world.

Dynamic Growth in the Asia Pacific Region

Asia has been the fastest growing area in the world for the past three decades, and the prospects for continued economic growth over the long run are excellent. Beginning in 1996, the leading economies of Asia (Japan, Hong Kong, South Korea, Singapore, and Taiwan) experienced a serious financial crisis, which culminated in the meltdown of the Asian stock markets. A tight monetary policy, an appreciating dollar, and a deceleration of exports all contributed to the downturn. Despite this economic adjustment, the 1993 estimates by the International Monetary Fund (IMF) that Asian economies would have 29 percent of the global output by the year 2000 were on target. Both as sources of new products and technology and as vast consumer markets, the countries of Asia—particularly those along the Pacific Rim—are just beginning to gain their stride.

The Greater China

The term *"The Greater China"* refers to both the People's Republic of China (PRC) and the Republic of China (ROC) or Taiwan.[3] The two separate political units divided in 1949, and each government claimed the other as its territory. The dispute has persisted to this day. Although the ROC was one of the founding members of the United Nations in 1945, the PRC government was officially recognized with a seat on the U.N. Security Council in 1971. Over the years, the relationship between the disputants has been both politically difficult and militarily dangerous. But in the 21st century, direct trade between the formerly hostile neighbors has increased dramatically, easing much of the historical tension in all of East Asia.

The People's Republic of China (PRC).

Aside from the United States, there is no more important single national market than the People's Republic of China (PRC). The economic and social changes occurring in China since it began actively seeking economic ties with the industrialized world have been dramatic. China's dual economic system, embracing socialism along with many tenets of capitalism, produced an economic boom with expanded opportunity for foreign investment and venture capital[4] that has resulted in annual GNP growth averaging nearly 10 percent since 1970. That astonishing growth rate has begun to slow recently, but most analysts see fast growth continuing for China. Indeed, one estimate has China's purchasing power exceeding that of the United States in 2014.[5] All of this growth is dependent on China's ability to deregulate industry, import modern technology, privatize overstaffed and inefficient state-owned enterprises (SOEs), and

[1]Mike W. Peng, Rabi S. Bhagat, and Sea-Jin Chang, "Asia and Global Business," *Journal of International Business Studies* 41, no. 3 (2010), pp. 373–76.

[2]Julien Cayla and Giana M. Eckhardt, "Asian Brands and the Shaping of a Transnational Imagined Community," *Journal of Consumer Research* 35 (2008), pp. 216–30.

[3]Paul Mozur and Jenny W. Hsu, "Taiwan, China Relations Set to Progress," *The Wall Street Journal*, January 15, 2012.

[4]Mark Humphrey-Jenner and Jo-Ann Suchard, "Foreign Venture Capitalists and the Internationalization of Entrepreneurial Companies: Evidence from China," *Journal of International Business Studies* 44, no. 6 (August 2013), pp. 607–21.

[5]Lucy Wescott, "China's Economy Overtakes the U.S. as World's Largest," *Newsweek*, October 8, 2014, online.

continue to attract foreign investment. So far in the 21st century, China's successes have been astonishing; in 2009, China became the world's biggest exporter ahead of Germany, and its aggressive marketing through infrastructure development, particularly in developing countries around the world, impresses as well.[6]

Two major events that occurred in 2000 are having a profound effect on China's economy: admission to the World Trade Organization and the United States's granting normal trade relations (NTR) to China on a permanent basis (PNTR). The PNTR status and China's entry to the WTO cut import barriers previously imposed on American products and services. The United States is obligated to maintain the market access policies that it already applies to China, and has for more than 30 years, and to make its normal trade relation status permanent. After years of procrastination, China has begun to comply with WTO provisions and made a wholehearted and irrevocable commitment to creating a market economy that is tied to the world at large.

An issue that concerns many is whether China will follow WTO rules and lower its formidable barriers to imported goods. Enforcement of the agreement will not just happen. Experience with many past agreements has shown that gaining compliance on some issues is often next to impossible. Some of China's concessions are repeats of unfulfilled agreements extending back to 1979. The United States has learned from its experience with Japan that the toughest work is yet to come. A promise to open markets to U.S. exports can be just the beginning of a long effort at ensuring compliance.

Because of China's size, diversity,[7] and political organization, it can be more conveniently thought of as a group of regions rather than a single country. There is no one-growth strategy for China. Each region is at a different stage economically and has its own link to other regions, as well as links to other parts of the world. Each has its own investment patterns, is taxed differently, and has substantial autonomy in how it is governed. But while each region is separate enough to be considered individually, each is linked at the top to the central government in Beijing. We discuss the diversity within China at the end of this chapter.

China has two important steps to take if the road to economic growth is to be smooth: improving human rights and reforming the legal system. The human rights issue has been a sticking point with the United States because of the lack of religious freedom, the Tiananmen Square massacre in 1989, the jailing of dissidents, and China's treatment of Tibet. The U.S. government's decision to award PNTR reflected, in part, the growing importance of China in the global marketplace and the perception that trade with China was too valuable to be jeopardized over a single issue. However, the issue remains delicate both within the United States and between the United States and China.

Despite some positive changes, the American embassy in China has seen a big jump in complaints from disgruntled U.S. companies fed up with their lack of protection under China's legal system. Outside the major urban areas of Beijing, Shanghai, and Guangzhou, companies are discovering that local protectionism and cronyism make business tough even when they have local partners. Many are finding that Chinese partners with local political clout can rip off their foreign partner and, when complaints are taken to court, influence courts to rule in their favor.

Many of America's best and most experienced companies have stumbled in China due to their misunderstandings of the complex and dynamic market. KFC, and its YUM! Brands corporate parent, with its huge and early presence in the Middle Kingdom this last year felt

---

[6]Gerald Yong Gao, Janet Y. Murray, Masaaki Kotabe, and Jangyong Lu, "A 'Strategy Tripod' Perspective on Export Behaviors: Evidence from Domestic and Foreign Firms Based in an Emerging Economy," *Journal of International Business Studies* 41, no. 3 (2010), pp. 377–96; Yuan Lu, Lianxi Zhou, Garry Bruton, and Weiwen Li, "Capabilities as a Mediator Linking Resources and the International Performance of Entrepreneurial Firms in an Emerging Economy," *Journal of International Business Studies* 41, no. 3 (2010), pp. 451–74.

[7]Diversity across regions also provides other dimensions suitable for market segmentation. See Kineta H. Hung, Flora Fang Gu, and Chi Kin (Bennett) Yim, "A Social Institutional Approach to Identifying Generation Cohorts in China with a Comparison with American Consumers," *Journal of International Business Studies* 38 (2007), pp. 836–53.

China has been pressing bureaucrats to buy locally branded cars. The market share of Chinese brands has plummeted this century from more than 65 percent in 2000 to just 45 percent. European brands garner about 20 percent of the market, Japanese 15 percent, American 11 percent, and Korean 8 percent. Volkswagen (including its Audi luxury sedans, pictured here parked outside the National Peoples Congress) dominates the other foreign carmakers, followed by Hyundai and Toyota. Almost all the foreign companies are deeply involved in joint ventures with Chinese partners.

the sting of a 16 percent drop in same-store sales because of a government investigation of the antibiotics being used by a local chicken supplier.[8] Apple was forced to issue a humiliating apology to consumers for offering "unsatifactory guarantees" that hindered its competitiveness against Samsung. The Korean company has a 20 percent market share in the largest smartphone market in the world, while Apple's languishes at about 8 percent.[9] Even American universities often have a hard time collaborating with their Chinese counterparts—the academic systems are so different in values and standards.[10]

Without doubt, the biggest blunders made by American firms in China have been those by Ford Motor Company executives. In 1912, Dr. Sun Yat-Sen, the first president of China, wrote Henry Ford a personal letter inviting him to "create an industrial empire" in China. One of Ford's assistants sent a terse acknowledgement saying that his boss had "no plans to visit China in the near future."[11] That was strike one. Strike two occurred in 1995. Ford and General Motors were hotly competing for the right to open a major manufacturing plant in China with joint venture partner Shanghai Automotive, the biggest car maker in the country. The mistake: Ford appointed as its first president of Ford of China an American with no China—and little international—experience. GM put together a team of negotiators lead by a most well-connected (*guanxi* in both countries and fluent in Mandarin) naturalized Chinese marketing executive.[12] GM prevailed, and Buicks are everywhere in China. Ford is still trying to catch up. And both are trying to catch up to German, Korean, and Japanese competitors in China.

Actually there are two Chinas—one a maddening, bureaucratic, bottomless money pit, the other an enormous emerging market. There is the old China, where holdovers of the Communist Party's planning apparatus heap demands on multinational corporations, especially in politically important sectors such as autos, chemicals, and telecom equipment. Companies are shaken down by local officials, whipsawed by policy swings, railroaded into bad partnerships, and squeezed for technology. But there is also a new, market-driven China that is fast emerging. Consumer areas, from fast food to shampoo, are now wide open. Even in tightly guarded sectors, the barriers to entry are eroding as provincial authorities, rival ministries, and even the military challenge the power of Beijing's technocrats.

No industry better illustrates the changing rules than information technology. Chinese planners once limited imports of PCs and software to promote homegrown industries, but the Chinese preferred smuggled imports to the local manufacturers. Beijing eventually loosened the restraints, and Microsoft is now the dominant PC operating system. The market's modernization plan calls for imports of equipment and technology of more than $100 billion per year for the foreseeable future. Indeed, China is now the second biggest market for personal computers, following only the United States.

After nearly a decade of frustration in trying to effectively market and service its products in China, IBM took a bold step and entered a venture with the Railways Ministry that allowed IBM to set up IBM service centers dubbed the "Blue Express." The agreement created a national network of service centers in railway stations that has enabled IBM to ship computer parts via the railroad around the country within 24 hours; competitors must book cargo space weeks in advance. In addition, the ministry's staff of more than 300 computer engineers helps out by providing customer services on IBM products.

[8]Julie Jargon, "KFC to Reboot in China," *The Wall Street Journal*, December 5, 2013, p. B3.

[9]"Better Days Ahead," *The Economist*, December 7, 2012, p. 67.

[10]"Campus Collaboration," *The Economist*, January 5, 2013, p. 33.

[11]Keith Bradsher, "After Nearly 90 Years, Ford Wants China to Give It a Second Chance," *The New York Times*, October 21, 2013, p. B7.

[12]N. Mark Lam and John L. Graham, *China Now: Doing Business in the World's Most Dynamic Market* (New York: McGraw-Hill, 2007).

Such innovative thinking by IBM and other marketers often accelerates the development of a more efficient market system. IBM's service centers set an example of effective service before and after sales—important marketing activities. Management training for the thousands of employees of franchises such as Pizza Hut, McDonald's, and KFC has spread expertise throughout the marketing system as the trainees move on to more advanced positions and other companies. Other important markets in China are in the healthcare and environmental areas.

In the long run, the economic strength of China will not be as an exporting machine but as a vast market, particularly if consumers there can overcome the cultural hurdles of thrift and xenophobia. The economic strength of the United States comes from its resources, productivity, and vast internal market that drives its economy. China's future potential might better be compared with America's economy, which is driven by domestic demand, than with Japan's, driven by exports. China is neither an economic paradise nor an economic wasteland, but a relatively poor nation going through a painfully awkward transformation from a socialist market system to a hybrid socialist–free market system, not yet complete and with the rules of the game still being written. Of course, the biggest threat for China is the economic volatility that seems to accompany fast growth[13]—let us hope that the government manages the problem well.

Finally, three other problems face China in the longer run: (1) the well-known environmental decline associated with its fast growth,[14] discussed in Chapter 3; (2) the demographic disaster associated with its one-child policy; and (3) managing the current great transition from rural to urban living. By 2020 the population of the elderly will become manifest as a burden on the economy, eventually dwarfing America's baby boom retirement problem.[15] The one-child policy is also a divisive social issue in China, exacerbated by the recent revelation that a wealthy Chinese couple has produced eight children with the help of surrogates.[16] Eight is a lucky number in China; we assume the couple will stop there.

The third major challenge complicating China's long-run development is what *The Economist* magazine has called a Chinese "apartheid."[17] In trying to manage the surge of rural residents moving to the large cities to work, a two-tiered system of citizenship was created in 1958 with the transition population having fewer privileges than their native urban neighbors. Not only do these 300 million or so transitional citizens face culture-based discrimination, but they also face bureaucratic discrimination in the form of *hakou*, a household registration system. Access to social services such as education and healthcare is limited by law for the rural-to-urban migrants. Moreover, there is no way to earn an "urban citizenship" no matter the length of residence in the cities. Ultimately, when the work ends, the migrant workers must return to their registered homes. The government recognizes the immensity of this problem but has been slow in making reforms.[18]

---

[13]Michael Forsythe and Kevin Hamlin, "The Building Bubble in China," *Bloomberg BusinessWeek,* March 1, 2010, pp. 18–19; Christopher Power, "The Slowdown in China: Who's Exposed," *Bloomberg Businessweek,* July 11, 2011, p. 10; Aaron Back, "China Growth Continues to Slow," *The Wall Street Journal,* December 20, 2011; "Deposit Flight Threatens China's Banks," *Bloomberg Businessweek,* February 27, 2012, pp. 50–51.

[14]David Barboza, "China to Release More Data on Air Pollution in Beijing," *The New York Times,* January 6, 2012; Mark Landler, "U.S. China Reach Agreement on Climate in Step to Global Pact," *The New York Times,* November 12, 2014, pp. A1, 11.

[15]"Illegal Children Will Be Confiscated," *The Economist,* July 23, 2011, p. 12; "One Child Proclivity," *The Economist,* July 19, 2014, p. 40; Tom Orlik, "Aging Chinese Face a Bleak Picture," *The Wall Street Journal,* May 30, 2013, online.

[16]Jonathan Kaiman, "8 Babies and a Rash of Protest," *Los Angeles Times,* January 20, 2012, p. A3.

[17]"Ending Apartheid," *The Economist,* April 19, 2014, special report, p. 7.

[18]Dexter Roberts, "China May Finally Let Its People Go," *Bloomberg Businessweek,* March 19-25, 2012, pp. 21–22. See also the latest research on this important issue: Rongwei Chu and Henry Chiu Hail, "Winding Road toward the Chinese Dream: The U-shaped Relationship between Income and Life Satisfaction among Chinese Migrant Workers," *Social Indicators Research* 118, no. 1 (2014), pp. 235–46.

Hong Kong.   After 155 years of British rule, Hong Kong reverted to China in 1997 when it became a special administrative region (SAR) of the People's Republic of China. The Basic Law of the Hong Kong SAR forms the legal basis for China's "one country, two systems" agreement that guarantees Hong Kong a high degree of autonomy. The social and economic systems, lifestyle, and rights and freedoms enjoyed by the people of Hong Kong prior to the turnover were to remain unchanged for at least 50 years. The Hong Kong government negotiates bilateral agreements (which are then "confirmed" by Beijing) and makes major economic decisions on its own. The central government in Beijing is responsible for foreign affairs and defense of the SAR, as well as, the appointment of the SAR chief executive after his or her election by a 1,200-person committee. This last aspect of control by the PRC central government is the point of contention being protested by pro-democracy advocates.

The Hong Kong dollar continues to be freely convertible, and foreign exchange, gold, and securities markets continue to operate as before. Hong Kong is a free society with legally protected rights. The Hong Kong SAR government continues to pursue a generally noninterventionist approach to economic policy that stresses the predominant role of the private sector. The first test came when the Hong Kong financial markets had a meltdown in 1997 that reverberated around the financial world and directly threatened the mainland's interests. Beijing's officials pretty much kept silent; when they said anything, they expressed confidence in the ability of Hong Kong authorities to solve their own problems.

The decision to let Hong Kong handle the crisis on its own is considered strong evidence that the relationship is working for the best for both sides, considering that China has so much riding on Hong Kong. Among other things, Hong Kong is the largest investor in the mainland, investing more than $100 billion over the last few years for factories and infrastructure. The Hong Kong stock market is the primary source of capital for some of China's largest state-owned enterprises. China Telcom, for example, raised $4 billion in an initial public offering there.

Most business problems that have arisen stem from fundamental concepts such as clear rules and transparent dealings that are not understood the same way on the mainland as they are in Hong Kong. Many thought the territory's laissez-faire ways, exuberant capitalism, and gung-ho spirit would prove unbearable for Beijing's heavy-handed communist leaders. But except for changes in tone and emphasis, even opponents of communist rule concede that Beijing is honoring the "one country, two systems" arrangement.

Two giant pandas, four-year-old male Le Le and two-year-old female Ya Ye, are being loaded onto the Panda Express, a FedEx plane, that is airlifting them from China to the Memphis, Tennessee, zoo for a 10-year visit. Whether it is pandas, time-sensitive deliveries, or cost-saving solutions, FedEx delivers high-value shipments door-to-door to as many as 210 countries. Also, notice the white arrow embedded in the FedEx logo (between the E and the x) that connotes motion. Not only does China use pandas as rewards for trade, it also uses them as enticements. Indeed, it has used "Panda Diplomacy" for some 1,400 years! Two Pandas were offered to Taiwan in 2006, but were rejected—at the time they were called the "Trojan Pandas" by those arguing for refusal. A new government on the island accepted the pair in 2008, and they now reside in the Taipei Zoo.

Taiwan, the Republic of China (ROC).   Mainland–Taiwanese economic relations continue to improve as both have entered the World Trade Organization. As both sides implement WTO provisions, they are ending many restrictions and now implement direct trade—not that they have not been trading. Taiwanese companies have invested more than $50 billion in China, and about 250,000 Taiwanese-run factories are responsible for about 12 percent of China's exports. Estimates of real trade are even higher if activities conducted through Hong Kong front companies are taken into consideration.

It is best to wrap future talks on the One China debate inside a bundle of more concrete issues, such as establishing the "three direct links"—transportation, trade, and communications. The three direct links issue must be faced because each country has joined the WTO, and the rules insist that members communicate about trade disputes and other issues. Trade fits well with both countries' needs. Taiwanese companies face rising costs at home; China offers a nearly limitless pool of cheap labor and engineering talent. Taiwan's tech powerhouses also crave access to China's market.

For Beijing, the Taiwanese companies provide plentiful jobs at a time when bloated SOEs are laying off millions. They also bring the latest technology and management systems, which China needs as a member of the WTO. In any case, Taiwan continues to stand tall in the East Asian economy.

Japan

LO2

The importance and slow growth of Japan

Japan's fast growth in the 1970s and 1980s amazed the world. Then came the early 1990s, and Japan's economy produced a stunning surprise. Almost abruptly, it slowed, sputtered, and stalled. Stagnation set in and it tenaciously persists. Four explanatory themes have emerged, each with a basis in observable fact, namely, Japan's (1) faulty economic policies, (2) inept political apparatus, (3) disadvantages due to global circumstances, and (4) cultural inhibitions.

Each of these four has their proponents, each their own rationale. So let's examine each separately.

Faulty Economic Policies.   A wealth of facts describe Japan's economic pain during the 1990s, but none more so than its stock market collapse. In the early 1990s, its Nikkei index level plummeted from over 35,000 to under 13,000. At this writing, it hovers at about 16,000. Japan's woefully inflated real estate values similarly hit the skids. Its once huge (and to some Americans, alarming) flow of investment into this country simply dried up. The end result found Japan with an economy once accustomed to nearly double-digit annual growth rates struggling, at first just to stay above no-growth levels, and then crashing to "minus growth," that is, a recession, in 1998.

Economic recessions are not, of course, unknown. But the peculiar feature of Japan's 1990's version was its decade-long persistence. Unsurprisingly, most economists sought to convince us that faulty economic policies both triggered the onset and the persistence of Japan's troubles. They explained with commendable brevity: "The bubble burst." But why the bubble, and why did it burst? The most common answer went somewhat as follows: Decades of galloping economic recovery success had bred a prideful national overconfidence. Growing willingness to take exaggerated risks followed. Heavy borrowing soon drove up levels of marginal investment. Eventually, lending agencies began to edge away from confidence toward caution. With the caution flag up, almost suddenly the whole inflated structure collapsed. Caution also filtered down to consumer levels. Spending habits were curtailed. With a fall in product demand, industry was forced to cut back both output and hiring. Unemployment soared to unheard of levels for that nation. The main casualty, however, was the widespread deterioration of national confidence.

No sector was hit harder than Japan's lending institutions, especially its huge, world-class banks. With the crash, the banks looked at loan portfolios splashed with red ink. Lending had to be restricted, a practice that dried up sources of capital needed for financing economic recovery. And so it went, one discouraging development following another, until a verifiable national crisis existed.

Seeing all this, American authorities and economists could not resist the temptation to offer remedies. "Draconian measures are needed," they chanted from across the Pacific. Understandable advice from on high, no doubt, but it reflected ignorance of the Japanese

Exhibit 11.1

Japan's GNI per Capita (current international $, '000)

Source: World Bank, 2015.

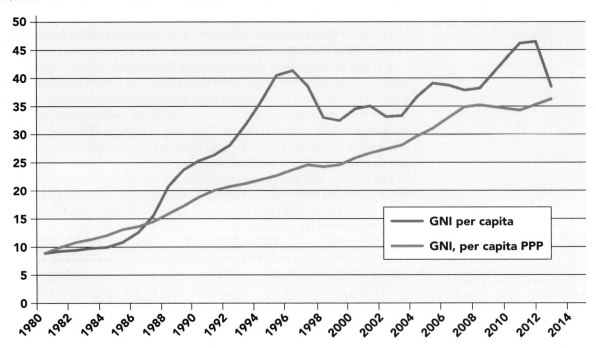

society's cultural prejudice against any action that might call for bold or rapid change. Always remember, Japan values stability above all else. Part of the problem is that most economists focused on overall economic performance and the dramatic slowdown in Japan's growth, tax revenues, and the potential disaster of deflation. And therefore, most economists have missed the real miracle of Japan's economic prowess. Please see Exhibit 11.1.[19]

If we control for purchase price parity (PPP) in the per capita GDP calculations, Japanese growth simply wavered during the 1990s. That is, the PPP calculation takes into account deflation and best reflects the average well-being of the Japanese people. Per capita income fell, but so did prices. You can see that Japan pretty much avoided the Asian financial crisis that resulted in a precipitous economic decline in neighboring South Korea. Indeed, using this metric, the stability of the Japanese economy is miraculous, particularly given the troubles its close neighbors experienced in 1997 and the dimensions of both its stock and property market declines in the early 1990s. It is hard to imagine how the United States's economic performance might respond to simultaneous 60 percent declines in both the NYSE and the housing markets.

The Political Explanation.   Views of economists on Japan's crisis have not been the only ones heard. Political pundits also rose to the challenge. They found two major villains:

Villain #1: The Country's Long Entrenched Liberal Democratic Political Party.

Villain #2: The Hidebound Japanese Bureaucracy.

Back in the 1970s, an authority on just about everything Japanese, one Frank Gibney, had written a seminal book on the nation. He called it *The Fragile Superpower.* His insight into the possible future of Japan's then surging economy was confirmed when the 1990s brought on crisis conditions. "Fragile" proved to be an apt tag.

In a new appraisal, Gibney has written that Japan became the victim of "one-party sickness," an ailment brought on by a 40-year hardening of political arteries. Meanwhile, many observers thought politicians had to share blame with Japan's powerful bureaucracy. Many observers, both inside and outside Japan, had long since come to believe that the bureaucracy actually controlled its elected politicians. Of course, in a consensus-type society,

---

[19]Eamonn Fingleton, "The Myth of Japan's Failure," *The New York Times,* January 6, 2012.

it is not easy, particularly for outsiders, to tell where one institution's power leaves off and another's begins. In any event, to those who championed a political explanation of Japan's woes, these two national institutions were viewed as joint culprits. Meanwhile, other observers, particularly within Japan, were dissatisfied with either the economic or political explanations they were hearing. They felt compelled to look for deeper roots.

Global Circumstances Have Hurt.   The third explanation for Japan's end-of-the-century economic problems has more to do with three circumstances beyond their control. Massive events have affected Japan in the last few years. First, the effects of the economic downturn of 2008–2009 are apparent in Exhibit 11.1. The deep decline in Japanese consumers' purchasing power in 2009 is exceptional over the 30-year period shown. Second, the economic impacts of the 2011 earthquake/tsunami disaster are just beginning to manifest themselves in the data, but the tragedy itself was easy to see. Its economic impact likely will be long lasting. Third, demand for greater oil imports, resulting from the destruction of energy infrastructure and its nuclear power plants, have pushed Japan into an unprecedented trade deficit.[20]

Furthermore, in the longer run, the Japanese population, like the western European population, is shrinking faster than the American. While American babyboomers circa 2005 were at their peak of productivity, both the Japanese and Europeans were about 10 years ahead in adjusting their economic, political, and cultural systems and institutions to population declines and graying hair.[21] And this adjustment is costly—just wait until 2020 in the United States to see how costly.

Japan has had a serious disadvantage in the information age: its complex language. Not only did its three alphabet systems hinder software innovations appropriate for world markets, but also the fundamental indirectness of the Japanese linguistic system hinders electronic information flows in general.[22] So Japan has been late to participate in the information technology explosion that drove the American economy to precarious heights in the late 1990s. We would be the first to argue that Japan is now catching up, particularly as software advances have made the structure of the Japanese language less a hindrance in the digital age. Also, 9/11 caused a slowdown in international travel that pushed Japanese businesspeople to become more adept with e-mail and other electronic communication media.

With American baby boomer households operating at peak consumption levels and oil at historically low real prices, sports utility vehicles (SUVs) became the rage in the United States during 1990–2007. Japanese auto firms, which drove the 1980s boom in Japan, came quite late to the American SUV market. Honda was the last entrant, which in the short run was a huge national economic disadvantage for Japan. But the reluctance to bet so much on big car designs has proven much to the advantage of Japanese car makers. A good argument can be made that they are leading Japan toward a new resurgence, assuming Toyota can regain its former prowess with its hybrid and hydrogen fuel cell technologies.

The Cultural Explanation.   In the mid-1990s, we became aware of what might be called "The Cultural Causation" theory. This theory went something as follows: Immediately after World War II, a shattered Japanese nation arrived at a consensus goal for national recovery. That consensual goal provided the incentive for its spectacular progress, decade after decade. Then during the late 1980s, the Japanese people stepped back and looked around at their manifest achievement. It was easy to conclude they had reached their coveted goal. So the question for them became, "all right, what's next?"

Perhaps more than any other society, the Japanese have an affinity for united effort. They seem inspired by common striving toward a common goal. Lack of one can present a problem.

---

[20]Hiroko Tabuchi, "Rise in Oil Imports Drives a Rare Trade Deficit in Japan," *The New York Times,* January 24, 2012.

[21]The much vaunted Japanese healthcare system is buckling under the weight of the elderly. See "Not All Smiles," *The Economist,* September 10, 2011, pp. 47–48.

[22]Ingo Beyer von Morgenstern, Peter Kenevan, and Ulrich Naiher, "Rebooting Japan's High-Tech Sector," *McKinsey Quarterly,* June 2011.

Others who champion a cultural explanation of Japan's 1990s woes did not limit their reasoning to an absence of a national goal. During most of the 20th century, building a strong enterprise structure provided the key to continuing success. Then with the advent of globalized competition, this inflexible structure became a hindrance. Agility, not structure, became the prime need. As has been pointed out, American corporate enterprise has met this need through wholesale restructuring and a blizzard of mergers, acquisitions, and consolidations. Standard Japanese practices, such as lifetime employment, job promotion based not on merit but on length of service, gender discrimination reciprocal contractor/subcontractor loyalties, and dozens of others have inhibited adaptive corporate measures. To put it simply, the U.S. enterprise scene handled its adjustment to the new economic era better than did the Japanese.

Japan is expected to continue its slow-growth economy during the second decade of the 21st century. Even as large companies have ambitious new growth plans,[23] economic cross-currents continue to roil with unemployment, and Toyota's 2010 quality problems disrupted that crucial company's contributions to the economy. However, economists and governments all over the world are using Japan as a model for policymaking, as Japan was the first to manage a big recession and its fast-graying population by strategically growing its government debt.

India

The wave of change that has been washing away restricted trade, controlled economies, closed markets, and hostility to foreign investment in most developing countries has finally reached India. Since its independence in 1950, the world's largest democracy had set a poor example as a model for economic growth for other developing countries and was among the last of the economically important developing nations to throw off traditional insular policies. As a consequence, India's growth had been constrained and shaped by policies of import substitution and an aversion to free markets. While other Asian countries were wooing foreign capital, India was doing its best to keep it out. Multinationals, seen as vanguards of a new colonialism, were shunned. Aside from textiles, Indian industrial products found few markets abroad other than in the former Soviet Union and eastern Europe.

Now however, times have changed, and India has embarked on the most profound transformation since it won political independence from Britain.[24] A five-point agenda that includes improving the investment climate; developing a comprehensive WTO strategy; reforming agriculture, food processing, and small-scale industry; eliminating red tape; and instituting better corporate governance has been announced. Steps already taken include the following:

Despite world-class scientists, the Indian pharmaceutical industry (with its ownership restrictions, price controls, and weak intellectual property restrictions) does not benefit from innovations and international investments compared with more open emerging economies such as China.

- Privatizing state-owned companies as opposed to merely selling shares in them. The government is now willing to reduce its take below 51 percent and to give management control to so-called strategic investors.

- Recasting the telecom sector's regulatory authority and demolishing the monopolies enjoyed by SOEs.

- Signing a trade agreement with the United States to lift all quantitative restrictions on imports.

- Maintaining momentum in the reform of the petroleum sector.

- Planning the opening of domestic long-distance phone services, housing, real estate, and retail trading sectors to foreign direct investment.

---

[23]Jonathan Soble, "To Rescue Economy, Japan Turns to Supermom," *The New York Times*, January 2, 2015, p. A3.

[24]We highly recommend a special issue on India in the *Journal of MarcroMarketing*. See Alladi Venkatesh, "Special Issue on India: Marcromarketing Perspectives," *Journal of MacroMarketing* 32, no. 3 (2012), pp. 247–51; Gopalkrish R. Iyer, Jagdish M. Sheth, and Arun Sharma, "The Resurgence of India: Triumph of Institutions over Infrastructure?" *Journal of MarcroMarketing* 32, no. 3 (2012), pp. 309–18.

Leaders have quietly distanced themselves from campaign rhetoric that advocated "computer chips and not potato chips" in foreign investment and a *swadeshi* (made-in-India) economy. The new direction promises to adjust the philosophy of self-sufficiency that had been taken to extremes and to open India to world markets. India now has the look and feel of the next China or Latin America.

Foreign investors and Indian reformers still face problems, however. Although India has overthrown the restrictions of earlier governments, reforms meet resistance from bureaucrats, union members, and farmers, as well as from some industrialists who have lived comfortably behind protective tariff walls that excluded competition. Socialism is not dead in the minds of many in India, and religious, ethnic, and other political passions flare easily.

For a number of reasons, India still presents a difficult business environment. Tariffs are well above those of developing world norms, though they have been slashed to a maximum of 65 percent from 400 percent. Inadequate protection of intellectual property rights remains a serious concern. The anti-business attitudes of India's federal and state bureaucracies continue to hinder potential investors and plague their routine operations. Policymakers have dragged their feet on selling money-losing SOEs, making labor laws flexible, and deregulating banking.

In addition, widespread corruption and a deeply ingrained system of bribery make every transaction complicated and expensive. One noted authority on India declared that corrupt practices are not the quaint custom of *baksheesh* but pervasive, systematic, structured, and running from the bottom to the top of the political order. Nevertheless, a survey of U.S. manufacturers shows that 95 percent of respondents with Indian operations plan on expanding, and none say they are leaving. They are hooked on the country's cheap, qualified labor and the potential of a massive market.

With a population now of more than 1.2 billion, India is second in size only to China, and both contain enormous low-cost labor pools. India has a middle class numbering some 250 million, about the population of the United States. Among its middle class are large numbers of college graduates, 40 percent of whom have degrees in science and engineering. India has a diverse industrial base and has become a center for computer software. India is now enjoying an information technology boom. After establishing a reputation among foreign corporations by debugging computer networks in time for Y2K, Indian companies now supply everything from animation work to the browsers used on new-generation wireless phones to e-commerce websites. As discussed previously, India has been an exporter of technical talent to the U.S. Silicon Valley, and now many of these individuals are returning to establish IT companies of their own. Finally, there is a competitive advantage to being on the other side of the world: Wide-awake English speakers are available for 24/7 services for the United States, while their American counterparts sleep.

India not only stands firmly at the center of many success stories in California's Silicon Valley (Indian engineers provide some 30 percent of the workforce there) but is also seeing Internet enthusiasm build to a frenzy on its own shores. Indian entrepreneurs and capital are creating an Indian Silicon Valley, dubbed "Cyberabad," in Bangalore. Exports there are growing 50 percent annually, and each worker adds $27,000 of value per year, an extraordinary figure in a country where per capita GDP is about $1,500. After a little more than a decade of growth, the Indian industry has an estimated 280,000 software engineers in about 1,000 companies. Moreover, large Indian companies are now expanding their own operations abroad, often through major acquisitions in developed countries.[25]

The Four "Asian Tigers"

The most rapidly growing economies in this region during the 1980s and 1990s were the group sometimes referred to as the Four Asian Tigers (or Four Dragons): Hong Kong, South Korea, Singapore, and Taiwan. Often described as the "East Asian miracle," they were the first countries in Asia, after Japan, to move from a status of developing countries to newly

---

[25]Sathyajit R. Gubbi, Preet S. Aulakh, Sougata Ray, M.B. Sarkar, and Raveendra Chittoor, "Do International Acquisitions by Emerging-Economy Firms Create Shareholder Value? The Case of India," *Journal of International Business Studies* 41, no. 3 (2010) pp. 397–418; Sumon Kumar Bhaumik, Nigel Driffield, and Sarmistha Pal, "Does Ownership Structure of Emerging-Market Firms Affect Their Outward FDI? The Case of the Indian Automotive and Pharmaceutical Sectors," *Journal of International Business Studies,* 41, no. 3 (2010), pp. 437–50.

CROSSING BORDERS 11.1   East Comes West and Back Again

Yoga led the way for Indian popular culture coming to the United States. More recently, it has been Bollywood. Think *Slumdog Millionaire*—yes, a British production, but strongly influence by the Indian story, setting, and style. Perhaps the dancing at the end was most representative of the genre. We already mentioned *Monsoon Wedding* in Chapter 4. The Hindi film industry, based in Mumbai, India, is popularly referred to as Bollywood, a term formed by combining the colonial name of Mumbai (Bombay) and Hollywood. Bollywood produces some 1,000 films a year compared with Hollywood, which release about half that in a year. The genre has spread around the world along with the Indian diaspora of some 15 million.

Maybe the singing and dancing from Korea is contagious as well. If you haven't seen "Gangnam Style," you've been living under a rock. And if you've been living under a rock, you can view it on YouTube. Two billion have ahead of you. Other popular Korean cultural exports around the world are competitive electronic sports and kimchi-flavored pot noodles; TV dramas are popular in the Philippines; the French love the films and music. All this yields some $5 billion in export revenues. What is now called k-pop also includes actors and cosmetics. Marketing includes smuggling k-dramas into Hong Kong and organized flash mobs in France demanding k-concerts.

In Vietnam, it's been Korean fast-food offerings from Lotteria. They arrived even before McDonald's, which has finally landed its first store in the country in downtown Ho Chi Minh City. KFC has been there since 1997. Baskin-Robbins and Dunkin' Donuts arrived in 2012. Connections make a difference in Vietnam. The franchisee is one Henry Nguyen, a Harvard and Northwestern grad, whose father-in-law is the country's prime minister.

Sources: Amandeep Takhar, Pauline Maclaran, and Lorna Stevens, "Bollywood Cinema's Global Reach: Consuming the 'Diasphoric Consciousness,'" *Journal of MacroMarketing* 32, no. 3 (2012), pp. 266–79; "Soap, Sparkle, and Pop," *The Economist,* August 9, 2014, pp. 69–70; Mike Ives, "McDonald's Opens in Veitnam, Bringing Big Mac Fans to Fans of Banh Mi," *The New York Times,* February 8, 2014, pp. B1, 5.

industrialized countries. In addition, each has become a major influence in trade and development in the economies of the other countries within their spheres of influence. The rapid economic growth and regional influence of the member countries of the Association of Southeast Nations (ASEAN) over the last decade has prompted the U.S. Trade Representative to pursue free trade agreements—Singapore and South Korea have already signed up. They are vast markets for industrial goods and, as will be discussed later, important emerging consumer markets.

The Four Tigers are rapidly industrializing and extending their trading activity to other parts of Asia. Japan was once the dominant investment leader in the area and was a key player in the economic development of China, Taiwan, Hong Kong, South Korea, and other countries of the region. But as the economies of other Asian countries have strengthened and industrialized, they are becoming more important as economic leaders. For example, South Korea is the center of trade links with north China and the Asian republics of the former Soviet Union. South Korea's sphere of influence and trade extends to Guangdong and Fujian, two of the most productive Chinese Special Economic Zones, and is becoming more important in interregional investment as well.

South Korea exports such high-tech goods as petrochemicals, electronics, machinery, and steel, all of which are in direct competition with Japanese and U.S.-made products. In consumer products, Hyundai, Kia, Samsung, and Lucky-Goldstar (LG) are among the familiar Korean-made brand names in automobiles, microwaves, and televisions sold in the United States. Korea is also making sizable investments outside its borders. A Korean company purchased 58 percent of Zenith, the last remaining TV manufacturer in the United States. At the same time, Korea is dependent on Japan and the United States for much of the capital equipment and components needed to run its factories.

Vietnam   Vietnam's economy and infrastructure were in shambles after 20 years of socialism and war, but this country of more than 91 million is poised for significant growth. A bilateral trade agreement between the United States and Vietnam led to NTR status for Vietnam and lower tariffs on Vietnamese exports to the United States from an average of 40 percent to less than 3 percent. For example, Vietnamese coffee is now in almost every pantry in America, and the new competitiveness has caused prices to sharply decline on the world market.

Vietnam has very few cars; motorbikes deliver almost everything, including moon cakes, in Hanoi.

If Vietnam follows the same pattern of development as other Southeast Asian countries, it could become another Asian Tiger. Many of the ingredients are there: The population is educated and highly motivated, and the government is committed to economic growth. Some factors are a drag on development, however, including poor infrastructure, often onerous government restrictions, minimal industrial base, competition for resources with China,[26] and a lack of capital and technology, which must come primarily from outside the country. Most of the capital and technology are being supplied by three of the Asian Tigers—Taiwan, Hong Kong, and South Korea. American companies such as Intel and Ford [27] are also beginning to make huge investments now that the embargo has been lifted.

Here the great economic divide in Vietnam is displayed: a bright red Ferrari parked near a soccer pitch adjacent to Haiphong Harbor in Vietnam where autos of any sort remain scarce. Notice the admiring motorbiker. At least he's not talking on a cell phone. The prevalence of helmets suggests that most follow the rules—though in the countryside, not so much.

[26]Edward Wong, "Vietnam Enlists Allies to Stave Off China's Reach," *The New York Times*, February 5, 2010, p. A9.

[27]Patrick Barta, "Ford Looks to Southeast Asia for Growth," *The Wall Street Journal*, March 9, 2011.

Bottom-of-the-Pyramid Markets (BOPMs)

LO3

The importance of the bottom-of-the-pyramid markets

C. K. Prahalad and his associates introduced a new concept into the discussion of developing countries and markets—**bottom-of-the-pyramid markets (BOPMs)**[28]—consisting of the 4 billion people across the globe with annual incomes of less than $1,200. These markets are not necessarily defined by national borders but rather by the pockets of poverty across countries. These 4 billion consumers are, of course, concentrated in the LDCs and LLDCs, as defined in the aforementioned U.N. classification scheme, particularly in South Asia and sub-Sahara Africa.

Prahalad's basic point is that these consumers have been relatively ignored by international marketers because of misconceptions about their lack of resources (both money and technology) and the lack of appropriateness of products and services usually developed for more affluent consumers. This dearth of attention is now changing.[29] Three cases demonstrate the commercial viability of such markets and their long-term potential. CEMEX, a Mexican cement company with global operations, pioneered an often profitable program to build better housing for the poor that includes innovative design, financing, and distribution systems. Similarly, Aravind Eye Care System in India began with the problem of blindness among the poor and developed an innovative organization of workflow—from patient identification to postoperative care—that has yielded better vision for consumers and profits for the company. Finally, in her wonderful book about the global economy, Pietra Rivoli[30] tells the story of how small entrepreneurs clothe East Africa with old American t-shirts. All three operations include combinations of products, services, research, and promotions that are appropriate for the lowest-income neighborhoods in the world.

Here we see the start of economic development. As rough as conditions are in this rural school in Lahtora, India, they're even more difficult in Tanzania. But in both places, students are eager to learn. Private schools are becoming more abundant in India as the economy develops. But the tuition remains quite low at some schools, at only $2 per month.[31]

---

[28]C. K. Prahalad, *The Fortune at the Bottom of the Pyramid* (Philadelphia: Wharton School Publishing, 2005).

[29]Madhu Viswanathan, Jose Antonio Rosa, and Julie A. Ruth, "Exchanges in Marketing Systems: The Case of Subsistence Consumer-Merchants in Chennai, India," *Journal of Marketing* 74, no. 3 (2010), pp. 1–17; Nailya Ordabayeva and Pierre Chandon, "Getting Ahead of the Joneses: When Equality Increases Conspicuous Consumption among Bottom-Tier Consumers," *Journal of Consumer Research* 38 (2011).

[30]Pietra Rivoli, *The Travels of a T-Shirt in the Global Economy* (New York: Wiley, 2005).

[31]Vikas Bajaj and Jim Yardley, "Many of India's Poor Turn to Private Schools," *The New York Times*, December 30, 2011.

Exhibit 11.2
Dynamic Transformation of BOPM Clusters

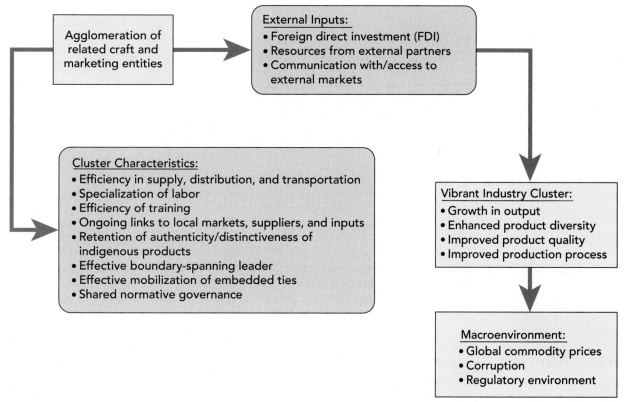

Source: Eric Arnould and Jakki J. Mohr, "Dynamic Transformation for Base-of-the-Pyramid Market Clusters," *Journal of the Academy of Marketing Science* 33, no. 3 (July 2005). Reprinted with kind permission from Springer Science and Business Media.

Note: BOPM = bottom-of-the-pyramid market.

A comprehensive study of the development of the leather-working industry in West Africa presents a new model for creating industries and markets in BOPMs.[32] The authors describe how industry clusters evolve and can be supported by outside investments from commercial and governmental concerns. Exhibit 11.2 represents the ingredients and processes involved in establishing a viable industry cluster in an LLDC. Craftspeople must network and collaborate with one another, vendors, customers, and family to attain efficiencies in production, domestic and international distribution,[33] and other marketing activities. Key to the vibrancy of the industry cluster will be a series of cluster characteristics, external inputs, and macroenvironment factors. The scheme presented might serve as a checklist for stimulating economic development through marketing in BOPMs. Entrepreneurial activities that are networked appear to be perhaps the best way to stimulate economic development, growth, and sustainability[34] from within developing countries. And marketing is key.

Finally, Grameen Bank,[35] a private commercial enterprise in Bangladesh, developed a program to supply phones to 300 villages. There are only eight land phone lines for every

[32]Eric Arnould and Jakki J. Mohr, "Dynamic Transformation for Base-of-the-Pyramid Market Clusters," *Journal of the Academy of Marketing Science* 33, no. 3 (July 2005), pp. 254–74.

[33]Jagdish Bhagwati, *In Defense of Globalization* (Oxford: Oxford University Press, 2004); also see http://www .thebeadchest.com as an interesting example of an international distributor working with African suppliers.

[34]Rajan Varadarajan, "Toward Sustainability: Public Policy, Global Social Innovations for Base-of-the-Pyramid Markets, and Demarketing for a Better World," *Journal of International Marketing* 22, no. 2 (2014), pp. 1–20.

[35]"Rehabilitation and Attack," *The Economist*, April 19, 2014, p. 64.

Exhibit 11.3
Standard of Living in the Eight Most Populous Countries in the Asia Pacific Region

Country	Population (millions)	GNI per Capita*	Medical Resources per 1000 Persons		Household Ownership %		
			Doctors	Hospital Beds	Color TV	Refrigerator	Washing Machine
China	1354	6748	1.6	0.4	97	86	86
India	1246	1426	0.8	15.4	65	23	9
Indonesia	247	3405	0.2	0.5	74	42	31
Pakistan	211	1123	0.8	0.5	71	45	49
Bangladesh	157	934	0.4	0.5	—	—	—
Japan	127	39912	2.3	12.3	97	99	100
Philippines	98	3373	0.0	1.1	74	44	34
Vietnam	91	1794	0.8	3.1	91	52	24

*Current US $.

Source: Euromonitor International, 2015.

1,000 people in Bangladesh, one of the lowest phone-penetration rates in the world. The new network is nationwide, endeavoring to put every villager within two kilometers of a cellular phone. Already cell phone penetration has exploded, growing from 2 per 1,000 to 671 per 1,000 during the last 14 years.[36] The good news is that all these efforts appear to have delivered a decade of growth in these least developed areas of the world.[37]

Market Metrics

LO4

The diversity across the region

Exhibits 11.3–11.5 display the fundamental market metrics for the eight most populous countries of the Asia Pacific region. Notice the great diversity in the way people live across the countries, and once again the north-south disparity is clear as well. The income of the Japanese dominates the first chart, along with the dearth of data for Bangladesh. The general excellence of the Japanese healthcare system that produces the longest lifespans in the world is represented.

Exhibit 11.4 compares the infrastructures of the countries. The Japanese rail system is the best in the world, while in the Philippines, people travel by boat and bus. The Vietnamese have few cars, so most travel by motorbike. It is amazing to see families of five traveling on single motorbikes in the hectic streets of Ho Chi Minh City (Saigon). The emphasis put on university training in the Philippines bodes well for its future growth.

[36]World Bank, "World Development Indicators," 2015.

[37]Charles Kenny, "Best. Decade. Ever." *Foreign Policy,* September 2010, pp. 27–29.

Exhibit 11.4
Infrastructures of the Eight Most Populous Countries of the Asia/Pacific Region

Country	Travel by Rail (passenger-km per capita)	Passenger Cars/1000	Energy Consumption (tonnes oil equivalent)	Mobile Phones in Use per 1000 People	Literacy Rate (%)	University Students per 1000 People
China	806	78	2.1	908	96	27
India	925	19	0.5	711	63	25
Indonesia	81	47	0.7	1229	93	32
Pakistan	124	10	0.3	607	55	10
Bangladesh	63	3	0.2	671	60	13
Japan	3125	312	3.7	1150	100	61
Philippines	—	9	0.3	1045	97	35
Vietnam	54	22	0.6	1324	95	26

Source: Euromonitor International, 2012; World Bank 2015.

Seeing the rough weave of traffic on the streets of old Delhi, India, you likely can understand the need for the elevated expressways. The introduction of Tata Motor's new $2,500 car, the Nano, will only make congestion worse. The country just raised the national speed limit from 80 kph to 100 kph, spurred by a roads revolution, the centerpiece of which is the 3,650-mile golden Quadrilateral highway linking Delhi, Mumbai (Bombay), Chennai (Madras), and Kolkata (Calcutta), the most expensive public works project in the nation's history. However, we wonder: How will the traffic police keep the ubiquitous sacred cows off expressway on-ramps?

Exhibit 11.5 briefly enumerates consumption patterns. Of course, Japan stands out. Also, notice the difference between the Chinese and Indian emphases on education.

Asia Pacific Trade Associations

LO5

The interrelationships among countries in the region

After decades of dependence on the United States and Europe for technology and markets, countries in the Asia Pacific region are preparing for the next economic leap driven by trade, investment, and technology, aided by others in the region. Though few in number, trade agreements among some of the Asian newly industrialized countries are seen as movement toward a regionwide, intra-Asian trade area, with Japan and China at the center of this activity.

In years past, the United States was Japan's single largest trading partner. However, now markets in China and Southeast Asia are increasingly more important in Japanese corporate strategy for trade and direct investment. Once a source of inexpensive labor for products shipped to Japan or to third markets, these countries are now seen as viable markets. Furthermore, Japanese investment across a number of manufacturing industries is geared

Exhibit 11.5
Consumption Patterns in the Eight Most Populous Countries in the Asia/Pacific Region

Country	People per Household	Household Expenditures ($/capita)								
		Food	Alcohol, Tobacco	Clothing	Housing	Health Goods, Services	Transportation	Communication	Leisure	Education
China	3.1	654	89	212	422	166	186	96	81	53
India	4.8	264	25	65	115	31	145	12	11	11
Indonesia	3.9	653	106	62	346	52	200	62	96	68
Pakistan	6.8	364	9	49	168	25	56	18	4	47
Bangladesh	4.3	—	—	—	—	—	—	—	—	—
Japan	2.4	3106	588	771	5839	1071	2766	704	2012	498
Philippines	4.5	871	26	28	253	53	221	65	38	80
Vietnam	3.6	421	33	36	88	65	155	25	16	70

Source: Euromonitor International, 2015.

Exhibit 11.6
Asia Pacific Market Group Fundamental Market Metrics

(in parentheses) = average annual growth rate 2008–2013 as a percentage

Association	Country (year entered union)	Population (millions)	GNI* (billions $)	Exports* of Goods (billions $)	Imports* of Goods (billions $)	Ease of Doing Business Index	GNI/ capita* ($)	Internet Users (percent)
ASEAN Free Trade Area (AFTA)								
	Brunei	0.4 (1.8)	16.0 (6.9)	11.6 (2.4)	3.6 (6.8)	83	39400 (5.0)	90
	Cambodia	15.1 (1.7)	14.7 (8.1)	9.1 (14.1)	13.0 (14.8)	135	974 (6.3)	6
	Indonesia	247.2 (1.0)	841.6 (13.4)	182.6 (5.9)	186.6 (7.6)	116	3405 (12.2)	16
	Laos	6.8 (2.0)	9.9 (12.0)	2.6 (19.1)	2.9 (15.6)	163	1459 (9.8)	13
	Malaysia	29.7 (1.5)	302.1 (5.0)	228.1 (2.7)	205.9 (5.6)	8	10166 (3.4)	67
	Myanmar	48.4 (0.7)	41.1 (26.4)	10.3 (8.4)	11.6 (22.2)	—	848 (10.5)	1
	Philippines	98.4 (1.7)	331.9 (7.2)	56.7 (2.9)	62.4 (1.9)	133	3373 (3.4)	37
	Singapore	5.5 (2.4)	288.8 (7.0)	411.7 (4.0)	373.0 (3.1)	1	52952 (4.5)	73
	Thailand	68.2 (0.6)	363.7 (5.1)	225.4 (5.2)	219.0 (6.8)	18	5332 (4.5)	29
	Vietnam	90.7 (1.1)	162.7 (16.8)	133.3 (16.3)	132.9 (10.5)	98	1794 (15.5)	44
ASEAN +3								
	China	1354.0 (0.5)	9137.2 (12.4)	2210.7 (9.1)	1949.3 (11.5)	99	6748 (11.8)	46
	Japan	127.3 (−0.1)	5082.5 (−0.9)	714.6 (−1.8)	823.3 (1.8)	23	39912 (−0.7)	86
	South Korea	50.2 (0.5)	1316.4 (5.5)	559.6 (5.8)	515.6 (3.4)	6	26212 (4.9)	85
Major Unaffiliated States								
	Afghanistan	30.6 (2.5)	20.9 (16.4)	0.5 (−1.5)	5.4 (12.3)	170	685 (13.6)	6
	Australia	27.6 (1.6)	1639.8 (4.9)	252.2 (6.2)	232.2 (4.0)	11	59478 (3.3)	83
	Bangladesh	156.6 (1.1)	146.3 (14.0)	29.1 (13.6)	36.4 (8.8)	132	934 (12.7)	7
	India	1246.0 (1.5)	1776.9 (14.6)	313.6 (10.0)	465.6 (7.7)	131	1426 (12.9)	15
	New Zealand	4.5 (0.9)	179.5 (4.9)	39.4 (5.2)	39.6 (2.9)	3	40148 (4.0)	83
	Pakistan	210.6 (3.4)	236.5 (18.1)	25.2 (4.2)	44.7 (1.2)	106	1123 (14.2)	11
	Taiwan	23.2 (0.3)	507.6 (5.6)	305.4 (3.6)	269.9 (2.3)	—	21914 (5.3)	—

*Current U.S. $.

Source: Euromonitor International, 2015 and World Bank, 2015.

toward serving local customers and building sophisticated local production and supplier networks.

Present trade agreements include one multinational trade group, the Association of Southeast Asian Nations (ASEAN), which is evolving into the ASEAN Free Trade Area (AFTA); ASEAN+3, a forum for ASEAN ministers plus ministers from China, Japan, and South Korea; and the Asia-Pacific Economic Cooperation (APEC), a forum that meets annually to discuss regional economic development and cooperation.

Association of Southeast Asian Nations (ASEAN) and ASEAN+3

The primary multinational trade group in Asia is ASEAN.[38] Like all multinational market groups, ASEAN has experienced problems and false starts in attempting to unify the combined economies of its member nations. Most of the early economic growth came from trade outside the ASEAN group. Similarities in the kinds of products they had to export, in their natural resources, and other national assets hampered earlier attempts at intra-ASEAN trade. The steps that the countries took to expand and diversify their industrial base to foster intraregional trade when ASEAN was first created have resulted in the fastest growing economies in the region and an increase in trade among members (see Exhibit 11.6).

Four major events account for the vigorous economic growth of the ASEAN countries and their transformation from cheap-labor havens to industrialized nations: (1) the ASEAN governments' commitment to deregulation, liberalization, and privatization of their economies; (2) the decision to shift their economies from commodity based to manufacturing based; (3) the decision to specialize in manufacturing components in which they have a

[38]See http://www.aseansec.org.

For products using high value and time-sensitive component parts such as manufactured in Kuala Lumpur, Malaysia, the air express services, such as provided by this DHL Worldwide Express Boeing 737, are vital.

comparative advantage (which created more diversity in their industrial output and increased opportunities for trade); and (4) Japan's emergence as a major provider of technology and capital necessary to upgrade manufacturing capability and develop new industries.

Although there has never been an attempt to duplicate the supranational government of the European Union, each year the group becomes more interrelated. ASEAN Vision 2020 is the most outward-looking commitment to regional goals ever accepted by the group. Among the targets that will lead to further integration is the commitment to implementing fully and as rapidly as possible the ASEAN Free Trade Area. Toward those ends, the 10 ASEAN nations have signed formal trade agreements with China, Australia, and New Zealand. And in 2011, a political thaw between Myanmar and Western nations helped demonstrate the attractiveness of commercial cooperation.

As in the European Union, businesses are drafting plans for operation within a free trade area. The ability to sell in an entire region without differing tariff and nontariff barriers is one of the important changes that will affect many parts of the marketing mix. Distribution can be centralized at the most cost-effective point rather than having distribution points dictated by tariff restrictions. Some standardization of branding will be necessary because large customers will buy at the regional level rather than bit by bit at the country level. Pricing can be more consistent, which will help reduce the smuggling and parallel importing that occur when different tariff schedules create major price differentials among countries. In essence, marketing can become more regionally and centrally managed.

CROSSING BORDERS 11.2

There's Good Spam and Bad Spam in South Korea

The only country producing more spam that the United States is South Korea. It's estimated that 80 percent of junk e-mail is sent to you via hijacked personal computers. Almost 10 percent comes through South Korean computers—that's second in the world behind the United States and ahead of India.

Particularly pernicious is spam on your smartphone. Thirty-eight million Koreans use the KakaoTalk chat app. As it has surged in popularity, so have spam attacks coming through it. The majority of spam are gambling advertisements, followed by loan, chauffer service, phone contract, and adult adverts. Despite blocking actions by companies and consumers, Korean users still receive sometimes three to four per day. Now users are starting to delete the chat app because of the clatter of spam. This is the bad spam in South Korea.

The good spam is the meat kind, and it's from America. During the Lunar New Year holiday period, common gifts to friends and relatives include imported wines, choice cuts of beef, rare herbal teas, and Spam. Meanwhile, in its home country, Spam is a thrifty staple and a culinary joke retaining its low-rent image. But, in Seoul it is seen as a classy gift sold in the high-end Lotte Department Store.

Indeed, Korea is the biggest international market for the gelatinous pink pork product outside the United States.

The origin of its popularity comes from the 1950s Korean War. At that tragic time of privation in South Korea, the only source of meat was the U.S. military PXs (Post Exchanges). The American servicemen and -women have left, but their spam remains ubiquitous. It is an important part of South Korean culinary culture, but many young people has no idea of its origin, even when they pick "military stew" (*budaejjige*) off a restaurant menu. The stew often served in hole-in-the wall restaurants or at homes includes a dose of kimchi and rice.

"And then there are the gift boxes, which have helped lift Spam's sales in South Korea fourfold in the last decade to nearly 20,000 tons, worth $235 million, last year. The local producer, CJ Cheil Jedang, said it released 1.6 million boxed sets this holiday season alone, boasting of contents that make Koreans 'full of smiles,'" according to one reporter. Meanwhile, the digital spam still deliver the frowns.

Sources: Hyeji Yang, "Koreans Deleting Popular KakoTalk Chat App to Escape Spam," *KoreanBANG*, September 19, 2014; Choe San-Hun, "In South Korea, Spam Is the Stuff Gifts Are Made Of," *The New York Times*, January 26, 2014.

One result of the Asian financial crisis of 1997 to 1998 was the creation of **ASEAN+3** (ASEAN plus China, Japan, and South Korea) to deal with trade and monetary issues facing Asia. Most of East Asia felt that they were both let down and put upon by the West, which they felt created much of the problem by pulling out in the midst of the crisis. The leading financial powers seemingly either declined to take part in the rescue operations, as the United States did in Thailand, or proposed unattainable solutions. The result was the creation of ASEAN+3, consisting of the foreign and finance ministers of each country, which meets annually after the ASEAN meetings. The first meeting was devoted to devising a system whereby the member countries shared foreign exchange reserves to defend their currencies against future attack. Although they were only tentative, the members of ASEAN+3 also discussed creating a common market and even a single currency or, perhaps, a new Asian entity encompassing both Northeast and Southeast Asia. Closer links between Southeast Asia and Northeast Asia are seen as a step toward strengthening Asia's role in the global economy and creating a global three-bloc configuration.

Asia-Pacific Economic Cooperation (APEC)

The other important grouping that encompasses the Asian-Pacific Rim is the Asia-Pacific Economic Cooperation.[39] Formed in 1989, **APEC** provides a formal structure for the major governments of the region, including the United States and Canada, to discuss their mutual interests in open trade and economic collaboration. APEC is a unique forum that has evolved into the primary regional vehicle for promoting trade liberalization and economic cooperation. APEC includes all the major economies around the Pacific Rim, from Russia to Chile to Australia, the most dynamic, fastest growing economies in the world. APEC has as its common goals a commitment to open trade, to increase economic collaboration, to sustain regional growth and development, to strengthen the multilateral trading system, and to reduce barriers to investment and trade without detriment to other economies.

Representatives from APEC member nations meet annually to discuss issues confronting the group, to propose solutions to problems arising from the growing interdependence among their economies, and to continue their quest for ways to lower barriers to trade. Although APEC is still far from being a free trade area, each meeting seems to advance it another step in that direction, notwithstanding the objections of some members.

A Focus on Diversity within China

LO6

The diversity within China

We close this chapter with a section briefly describing the diversity *within* China. Certainly we might include a similar section on India; both have twice the population of the European Union and three times that of the United States. We might also consider the cultural and economic differences in other large countries such as Japan[40] or Vietnam or across the islands of Indonesia. But given our limited room here, and both the fast ascendancy and wide diversity of the Chinese economy, we have chosen to focus on The Greater China.[41] Moreover, recent research has demonstrated region-based strategic choices affect subsidiary performance in China.[42]

Today's China is divided into mutually competitive, complementary economic "warring states" (as some have said), just as it was twenty-two hundred years ago, before being united in the Qin Dynasty. Among these "warring states," four regional economies stand out from the north to the south of the country, along the Pacific Coast:

- The traditional industrial heartland in Northeast China, with the coastal city Dalian as its hub among the three provinces of Liaoning, Jilin, and Heilongjiang.

---

[39]See http://www.apec.org.

[40]Shinobu Kitayama, Keiko Ishii, Toshie Imada, Kosuke Takemura, and Jenny Ramaswamy, "Voluntary Settlement and the Spirit of Independence: Evidence form Japan's 'Northern Frontier,'" *Journal of Personality and Social Psychology* 91, no. 3 (2006), pp. 369–84.

[41]The concept of The Greater China combines the PRC and Taiwan. This combination politically is a matter of ongoing debate, but we adopt it to be comprehensive in our discussion.

[42]Xufei Ma, Tony W. Tong, and Marcus Fitza, "How Much Does Subnational Region Matter to Foreign Subsidiary Performance? *Evidence from Fortune* Global 500 Corporations' Investments in China," *Journal of International Business Studies* 44, no. 1 (2013), pp. 66–87.

Exhibit 11.7
Chinese Administrative
Divisions

Major Economic Regions	Provinces and Other Divisions	Population (millions)	GDP/Capita (U.S. $s)
Northeast China	Liaoning	43.9	14525
	Jilin	27.5	11112
	Heilongjiang	38.3	8832
Beijing–Tianjin IT corridor	Beijing[2]	20.9	21948
	Tianjin[2]	14.4	23453
Yangtze River Delta	Shanghai[2]	24.0	21213
	Jiangsu	79.3	17567
Pearl River Delta	Guangdong	106.2	13784
	Hong Kong[4]	7.2	53203
	Macau[4]	0.6	142564
Others	Henan	94.1	8047
	Shandong	97.1	13262
	Sichuan	81.0	7642
	Hebei	73.1	9116
	Hunan	66.6	8656
	Anhui	60.1	7460
	Hubei	57.9	10034
	Zhejiang	54.9	16120
	Guangxi[1]	47.0	7202
	Yunnan	46.7	5906
	Jiangxi	45.1	7481
	Guizhou	34.9	5397
	Shaanxi	37.6	10052
	Fujian	37.6	13623
	Shanxi	36.2	8197
	Chongquig[2]	29.6	10077
	Gansu	25.8	5721
	Inner Mongolia[1]	24.9	15893
	Taiwan[3]	23.3	39,600
	Xinjiang[1]	22.5	8755
	Hainan	8.9	8316
	Ningxia[1]	6.5	9282
	Qinghai	5.8	8597
	Tibet[1]	3.1	6138

[1]Autonomous Region.
[2]Municipality.
[3]Province of ROC.
[4]Special Administrative Region.
Source: 2013 Statistical Communique of the Provinces on National Economic and Social Development, accessed 2015.

- The Beijing–Tianjin information technology (IT) corridor in north China.
- The Yangtze River Delta, known as the Greater Shanghai area, with its emerging IT manufacturing center of Suzhou.
- The Pearl River Delta, containing Hong Kong, Macau, Guangzhou, and Shenzhen, as the world's manufacturing base for the IT industry.

Today these four regions include about one-quarter of the Mainland's people (i.e., more than 300 million) but account for about half of the GDP of the country. The per capita income of these provinces is greater than $16,000 at PPP, roughly twice the national average. In Exhibit 11.7, we list the economic differences across the regions, provinces, and municipalities. People in the Shanghai municipality make four times the income of those in Guizhou in the inland south of the country. Per capita incomes in the previously separate areas of Hong Kong, Macau, and Taiwan are the highest.

Beyond the economic diversity, the people of China exhibit important ethnic and linguistic differences (see Exhibit 11.8). Han Chinese constitute more than 90 percent of the people, with substantially sized minority groups that include the Zhuang, Manchu, Hui, Miao, Uyghur, Tujia, Yi, Mongol, Tibetan, Buyi, Dong, Yao, Korean, and others. The national language is standard Mandarin, but more than 56 dialects and other languages are

Exhibit 11.8
Map of Greater China

Source: Reprinted courtesy of Oriental Travel—offers tourist information and reservation services for worldwide travelers to the Greater China region. http://www.orientaltravel.com.

spoken across the country. Of course, written Chinese can be read almost universally, but different dialects are almost always mutually indecipherable. This lack of common language causes some interesting problems for television and radio advertisers in the country that print media can usually avoid. For example, the more than 3,000 television stations around the PRC are mandated by the State Administration of Radio, Film, and Television to present programming and advertisements in Mandarin. But such directives are commonly ignored in favor of local languages and dialects that better communicate to consumers both the programming content and the commercial messages. Particularly in Guangdong province, the emphasis on the local Cantonese "language" is pervasive. Television programming in that region is predominantly in Cantonese, but most commercial messages are in Mandarin. Radio programming and commercials both tend to be presented in Cantonese. Moreover, many residents of Guangdong province pay closest attention to the Hong Kong media in Cantonese via satellite. See Crossing Borders 11.3 for some additional interesting details.

Northeast China: Longtime Industrial Heartland

Northeast China was the industrial and technological center of the country in the 1970s and 1980s. Then, large numbers of state-owned enterprises in the petrochemical, steel, and heavy industries dominated production in the old planned economy. While still hugely important, growth in the other three major regions has exceeded that in the Northeast as China moves from communism toward a more free-enterprise orientation.[43]

The three contiguous provinces in Northeast China—Liaoning (43.9 million persons), Jilin (27.5 million), and Heilongjiang (38.3 million)—have long represented a cohesive unit in terms of culture and the political economy. Indeed, the strength of the regional interrelationship is well reflected in how they are described in other parts of the Middle Kingdom: The three are referred to as *dongbei*, meaning Northeast, or *dong sansheng*, meaning Northeastern Three Provinces, instead of identifying each province individually. Finally, perhaps the most important advantage of the region is its juxtaposition with China's most important industrial neighbors. For centuries, goods and ideas have flowed across those borders and continue to do so in the greatest quantities ever. Liaoning has the closest economic ties with Japan, Jilin with South Korea, and Heilongjiang with Russia.

---

[43]"The North-East, Back in the Cold," *The Economist*, January 3, 2015, pp. 31–32.

CROSSING BORDERS 11.3   Comments on Dealing with Dialects in China

The State Administration of Radio, Film, and Television has decided that it needs to put a stop to dialect creep.

In a short news item posted to SARFT's website, a spokesperson reiterated the rules requiring that the dialogue in television dramas be standard Mandarin. SARFT spokesperson Zhu Hong said that the number of television shows making extensive use of dialect is on the rise, and some of the programs showed overlong and excessive uses of dialect not in accordance with the spirit of the country's strong promotion of standard Mandarin and in violation of national rules. Additionally, the practice has an effect on the audience on an aesthetic level.

Zhu Hong also said that province-level radio, film, and television administrative departments and producers needed to strictly follow the rules spelled out in SARFT document #560 (from 2005), the Notice Concerning Further Reiteration the Use of Standard Mandarin in TV Series, and more rigorously review completed shows. The use of standard Mandarin should predominate in shows going into production, under normal circumstances, he noted.

Zhu Hong also stressed that the language in television shows other than local musicals should be predominantly standard Mandarin. In normal circumstances, dialect and non-standard Mandarin should not be used. Major revolutionary and historically themed TV shows, children's series, and shows promoting educational content are to use Mandarin. Leaders portrayed in TV shows are to use Mandarin.

Local dialects can add color to dialogue that is predominantly in Mandarin, but major characters are supposed to have standard speech. This requirement presents difficulties for the accurate, lifelike portrayal of many of China's founding leaders, such as Mao Zedong (from Hunan) and Deng Xiaoping (from Sichuan).

Most recently viewers in Shanghai are upset about losing one of their favorite TV shows. Gao Bowen hosts and preforms *pingtan*, a traditional Shanghai art form that includes telling jokes and stories and singing and playing instruments. His show, "Shanghai Dialect Talk," was forced off the air because its channel began broadcasting on satellite, and the central government forbids dialects being used on that nation-wide medium.

In a more mundane circumstance, a freight carrier active in China and Taiwan once aired a commercial showing one of its competitors trying to tell an old lady that he had a package for her. She did not understand the message in Mandarin, so the hapless delivery guy was forced to stand there repeating the message a few dozen times. The company that made the commercial naturally has their delivery guy walk right up and use the right dialect.

Sources: Joel Martinsen, "Too Much Dialect on the Small Screen," Danwei. org, July 17, 2009; "Chinese Dialects and Accents," tvtroes.org, accessed 2010; Didi Kirsten Tatlow, "Shanghai Laments Loss of TV Show in Local Dialect," *The New York Times*, May 2, 2014, online.

Because of the economic opportunity and proximity, students in this region study Japanese or Russian in foreign language classes instead of English. Korean is also a widely spoken language, with about 2 million minority Koreans residing in this area. The Chinese dialect spoken in this region is similar to Mandarin but with a slight *dongbei* accent.

The Japanese influence in the region goes back to the 1930s, when the Japanese controlled much of northern China through the puppet emperor of Manchukuo (Manchurian State). Fifty years later, the Japanese/Chinese commercial relationship resumed and has blossomed along with China's rise. Japanese investment has flowed into the area since the 1980s, and China is now Japan's most important trading partner, even ahead of the United States.

Dalian at the southern tip of the Liaodong Peninsula is the focus of bi-national relationships. The city has one of the world's largest and most modern port facilities (managed by a Singaporean company), it is only a four-hour flight from Japan, and its high-quality workforce and inexpensive real estate attract Japanese high-tech investments. Companies such as Toshiba, Canon, and Matsushita employ tens of thousands of Chinese workers there, and thousands of Japanese managers and engineers reside there. All this interaction is made easier because some 70,000 Chinese speak fluent Japanese. Finally, Dalian has been able to clean up much of the environmental damage done by decades of industrial abuse and now has become a tree-lined host to high-tech and software companies from around the world.

Both Liaoning and Jilin provinces share borders with North Korea, and both provinces host substantial numbers of Korean minorities. Of the 2 million ethnic Koreans in the country, about 60 percent live in Jilin province. South Korea has taken advantage of this cultural bridge and focused its investments there, particularly since 2002.

China's longest border is with Russia, some 4,600 miles. The most important part of the border commercially is that near Heilongjiang. The long Russian influence in Harbin, the provincial capital—some call it "Little Moscow"—is evident in its architecture, consumption patterns (vodka and ice cream are popular), and its residents' valuable Russian language skills. Although tensions have almost always run high along the border, now the two countries are beginning to cooperate more closely around the trade of energy resources. In particular, Russian oil is flowing fast to feed the white-hot growth of *dongbei*.

Beijing–Tianjin

Central planning has made this region of 35 million not only the political center of the country but the R&D center as well. The Central Business District (CBD), Zhongguancun (known as China's Silicon Valley), and most recently the Olympic Village are among the consequences of the unique political and cultural background of Beijing, the Chinese capital. The 75-mile corridor between Beijing and its coastal cousin Tianjin hosts some 5,000 Chinese high-tech companies, among them Lenovo, and more than 1,000 international IT companies. Perhaps the key to this region is the quality of its higher education. Peking University and Tsinghua University are the most prominent among the 70 universities in the region. The development of the Beijing Central Business District continues with the ambitious goal of rivaling those in Manhattan, Paris, and Japan.

Tianjin is China's third largest industrial city after Shanghai and Beijing, but it is also the fastest growing one. Primary industries include automotive, electronics, metals, and petrochemicals. New emphases are also being put on developing information technology, biotechnology, medicine, and green energies. Motorola's huge investments in the Tianjin Economic and Technology Development Zone have yielded perhaps the biggest mobile phone manufacturing operations in the world.

Shanghai and the Yangtze River Delta

Before World War II, Shanghai was perhaps the most important center for Asia Pacific trade and finance. Now in the 21st century, it has regained its status among several rivals, including Hong Kong, Singapore, Tokyo, and Los Angeles. Shanghai has been undergoing a major industrial renaissance during the past two decades. The traditional share of low value-added manufacturing in textiles and heavy equipment manufacturing industries has declined as many of them move west. Medium value-added industries now account for the vast majority of Shanghai's industrial employment. But new emphases are being put on developing its automobile assembly industry and other high-tech industries, such as computer, telecommunications equipment, and integrated circuit manufacturing.

China's sustained economic growth and accession to the WTO have aided Shanghai's position as a regional trade and financial center. Half the city's GDP derives from financial services industries, such as banking, retailing, finance, trade, insurance, and real estate development. Shanghai's stock exchange appears to have the potential to overtake Hong Kong and Shenzhen. It has a much broader base of industries, complementary economic resources from the Yangtze River Delta and the entire Yangtze River Valley area that extends deep into China's hinterland, and powerful backing from Beijing. Indeed, the Commerce Department reports the fastest growth in U.S. exports among cities away from the coast has been in Ningbo, Chengdu, and Wuhan, all up the Yangtze River Valley from Shanghai.

Pudong, with an area of 200 square miles and a population of more than 2 million, is located on the east bank of the Huangpu River, just across from the urban center of Shanghai. The new airport and Pudong New Area's fast green-field growth effectively represents the modernization of greater Shanghai and China's emergence as an economic power in the new millennium.

Suzhou, an hour's drive west of Shanghai, is emerging as one of China's hottest manufacturing centers. It has replaced the provincial capital Nanjing, two hours away on the Shanghai–Nanjing expressway, to become Jiangsu province's number one economy and foreign trade center. In the last 10 years foreign investors, particularly tens of thousands of Taiwanese firms, have built manufacturing facilities for everything from consumer goods to high-tech products. More than 250,000 managers and engineers from Taiwan now live in the area as well. Suzhou is now ranked in the top ten of the Chinese Cities Comprehensive Competitive Powers Ranking.

A park bench in the resort city of Guilin speaks volumes about the one-child policy in China. One surprise: The beloved child appears to be a girl! Source: Johan de Rooy.

Pearl River Delta

The Greater Pearl River area includes three cities of more than 5 million inhabitants (Hong Kong, Guangzhou, and Shenzhen); five cities with more than 1 million inhabitants (Zhuhai, Huizhou, Foshan, Zhongshan, and Dongguan); and a number of cities that each contain approximately half a million inhabitants, such as Macau.

Shenzhen, a boomtown bordering Hong Kong and a fishing village just 20 years ago, has replaced the provincial capital Guangzhou to lead the local economy. In 1980, Shenzhen was designated as China's first Special Economic Zone. The permanent resident population in Shenzhen in 1980 was only 300,000. Today's population has reached 7 million, reflecting the significance and attractiveness of the city as a manufacturing and transportation base. Proximity to Hong Kong, an international service center, is one of the advantages of Shenzhen. As a manufacturing base for a wide range of industries, Shenzhen can use Hong Kong as a trade platform to expand the global market. In addition, foreign enterprises can supply industrial products to Shenzhen through Hong Kong. As major foreign investors in Shenzhen, Hong Kong companies can form strategic partnerships with multinational companies. With their mainland experience, international exposure, and business acumen, Hong Kong companies and personnel are capable of helping foreign companies reduce their investment and management risks in Shenzhen.

The Other Billion

So far in this section, we have talked about one-fourth of the population of China—the coastal, industrializing, relatively rich folks. But the rural China few Westerners ever see is the part of China that doesn't yet participate in the global economy. The central government pays it some attention, but not much. These one billion people usually receive about 10 percent of the central government budget. That amounts to less than $100 a head for rural roads, water, power supplies, schools, and hospitals.

Development in the region is focused on the large municipalities and cities such as the Chongqing municipality (29.2 million) within Sichuan province (another 81.9 million persons). China's World War II capital, this developing city is 1,500 miles up the Yangtze River from Shanghai. The average income for a Chongqing resident was about $11,000 in 2014, compared with rural neighbors at about 20 percent of that. But the government actually is not spending much in the area. Instead, we find multinational companies funding development. For example, BP has built a $200 million chemical plant in the area, Volvo

A vendor delivers a Christmas tree in Beijing. Since China's reforms and loosening of controls on religion at the end of the 1970s, the number of Christians has risen from 2 million to 50 million. Although restrictions on freedom of religion continue, as economic freedom grows, so do political freedoms, but at a slower pace.

has begun producing its small S40 series there, and Yamaha has a motorcycle plant nearby. Much, much more work needs to be done. But as wages rise along with the recent labor shortages along the east coast, the "market" will pull development westward. "How fast?" is the question of the day. The concept of bottom-of-the-pyramid marketing applies here.

Yum! Brands is looking to expand fast in China. In 2014 it added 700 new KFC, Pizza Hut, and Taco Bell restaurants, to total 4,600 restaurants in more than 1,000 cities. Fast food competitor McDonald's also intends to expand at a similar pace, if from a smaller base. Location decisions are made primarily by consideration of local incomes, particularly in central China. The KFC location decisions in the area are instructive: At last count, of 10 stores in Gansu province, 9 are in the capital city; 28 of 39 restaurants in Hubei are in Wuhan, the capital; and 17 of 25 in Sichuan are located in Chengdu.

Unrest in the countryside also flares up as the economic divide widens, and new communication technologies display the gap. The problems of development for this three-fourths of the population are daunting, and the scale of the potential social frictions are truly frightening. The opportunities for American companies there are very different from those of the bustling east coast.

Although it is difficult to compete with China's low manufacturing costs, imagine marketing in a country with production but little disposable income, no storage, limited transportation that goes to the wrong markets, and no middlemen or facilitating agents to activate the flow of goods from the manufacturer to the consumer. When such conditions exist in developing markets, marketing and economic progress are retarded. To some degree, this problem faces China and many of the republics of the former Soviet Union too. In China, for example, most of the 1.3 billion potential consumers are not accessible because of a poor or nonexistent distribution network. Indeed, the true consumer market in China is probably limited to no more than 25 percent of those who live in the more affluent cities. No distribution and channel system exists to effectively distribute products, so companies must become resourceful to compensate for the poor infrastructure.

Differences in Business Negotiation Styles within The Greater China

In Chapter 19, we discuss in some detail differences in negotiation styles across several national cultures, as well as the dangers of stereotyping. Here we briefly focus on differences in approaches in six regions of the greater China, and we hope it is obvious that people from the various regions listed will not conform exactly to the ethnic characterizations summarized next.[44] Our purpose here is simply to demonstrate the interesting breadth of behavior in Chinese business culture.

Northeastern Negotiators.   Forthrightness is the stereotype of businesspeople in the Northeast, mostly held by their southern neighbors. Negotiators from the three northeastern provinces above the Yangtze are certainly industrious, competent businesspeople. They are generally honest and plainspoken. They are also not known for their risk-taking propensity or creativity.

Beijing Area.   Negotiators from the Beijing area are known for their unusual (within China) bureaucratic sloth and imperialist perspective, both yielding a relative lack of creativity, that is, thinking outside the box. Because they often have defined the box in the first place, they are not used to thinking of ways to escape it. A note of caution about this generalization is particularly necessary though when it comes to the growing cosmopolitanism of managers working in and around the capital city.

Shanghai Area.   Negotiators from the Shanghai area are renowned in China for their shrewdness. They are outgoing, big talkers and big spenders. They try to impress you in ways and to extents you won't see anywhere else in China. For them, anything is

[44]See N. Mark Lam and John L. Graham, *China Now: Doing Business in the World's Most Dynamic Market* (New York: McGraw-Hill, 2007).

CROSSING BORDERS 11.4   Culture Changes, Celebrations Spread from the South

Philip Cheng, a 26-year-old financial analyst, has spent the past four Valentine's Days with his girlfriend, Molly Lam. Last year, they flew to Shanghai together, taking photos of the city's famous skyline and sharing a romantic meal at a cozy Italian restaurant.

However, the young couple's Valentine's Day plans came under a new threat from Cheng's 50-year-old mother. For the first time in decades, Valentine's Day fell on the first day of the Lunar New Year, the biggest holiday on the Chinese calendar. For most Chinese families, Chinese New Year is a major family occasion filled with family visits and big meals. Mrs. Cheng had plans. Her son's choice: girlfriend or mother?

The Chinese New Year shifts each year according to the lunar cycle. Its overlap with Valentine's Day, which hasn't happened since 1953 and won't recur until 2048, forced time-honored Chinese and Western traditions to jockey for space with one another in Hong Kong, where both holidays are celebrated. Earlier in the week, Cheng and his two sisters got a text message from their mother, pleading with them not to miss the family Chinese New Year dinner. Says Cheng's mother, Anna, "Even though we're family, we're all so busy with our own things that we hardly ever see each other. On an occasion like this, I just think it's important for us to be able to share a meal together."

"When the message showed up on my phone, I couldn't believe it," Mr. Cheng recounts with a groan. "I had already been planning to spend the day with my girlfriend." In mainland China, one newspaper pitted the clash of dates as one between "the West's ideal of a paradise for two, and Chinese New Year's ideal of a reunited family."

The calendrical coincidence is frustrated restaurant owners and florists who look to Cupid's big day and the Chinese New Year as the biggest annual moneymakers. "It's a huge blow to the industry," says Elizabeth Tse, chairwoman of the Hong Kong Flower Retailers Association. With Valentine's Day falling on Sunday, husbands and boyfriends won't have to send flowers to their partners' offices, where "having flowers on your desk is seen as a real status symbol," she says. She figures that because of the New Year, many people will visit their relatives and perhaps go to a temple, and then if they go out for a romantic evening, "many will say, 'Forget the flowers, let's just do dinner.'"

In mainland China, celebrating Valentine's Day is a more recent phenomenon, but 5 percent of respondents to a recent poll said they would ditch the lunar holiday to spend it with their lover, and another 5 percent admitted to being torn and confused. Elsa Ma, a 34-year-old telecom marketing manager from the interior mainland city of Wuhan, is traveling to her fiancé's hometown for the long weekend to meet her future in-laws for the first time after an eight-month courtship, and to celebrate Chinese New Year. But she's not giving up Valentine's Day, which "is important to both of us," she says. "Definitely, I will see his parents when I wake up, but the whole day we are going to spend alone."

In Hong Kong, where Valentine's Day has been celebrated for much longer, some restaurants plowed ahead with their usual romantic offerings. At the French restaurant Gaddi's in the Peninsula Hotel, the Valentine's Day *prix fixe* menus were available for $370 a person.

The saying in the Pearl River Delta area is, "They make the rules in Beijing, we interpret the rules here." So change in China has always flowed from the south to the north, since the former has greater exposure to foreign ideas and has for at least the last three centuries. Christmas and Valentine's Day holidays are catching on up north; however, we think it will be some time before $370 per person dinners catch on in Guizhou province, where incomes are about 10 percent of those in Hong Kong.

Sources: N. Mark Lam and John L. Graham, *China Now, Doing Business in the World's Most Dynamic Market* (New York: McGraw-Hill, 2007); Jonathan Cheng, "In Hong Kong, Love's at War with Tradition," *The Wall Street Journal*, February 13, 2010, online.

possible—they are very creative thinkers. But more than anything else, they are successful and really the dominant business group on the Mainland.

The Pearl River Delta.   Chinese in the south have always been the closest to foreign influences, which has yielded their special forms of entrepreneurship and spontaneity. Negotiators are reputed to be relatively honest and forthright. They are less calculating than folks in Shanghai. But they are excellent traders and particularly interested in making short-term gains.

Hong Kong.   The business culture in Hong Kong is distinct from others in China in important ways. Almost all the Chinese you deal with in Hong Kong will be bilingual and speak at least English fluently. Indeed, their English may be better than yours. As Hong Kong executives have learned English, they have also absorbed British culture. However, for most, their first language is Cantonese. Among Chinese speakers around the world, Cantonese is the roughest dialect. It almost always sounds like an argument is going on. But if you get mad, face is lost on both sides of the table, and usually the deal is dead. Finally, humility and indirection are more emphasized in southern than in northern China.

Taiwan.   Both the behavior and the language of the people of Taiwan are considered by other Chinese to be the most conservative. That is, neither Confucius's influence nor the Mandarin spoken has been mitigated by Communist philosophies and rule. Consequently, age, rank, and family play the most powerful roles. Companies tend to be managed directly from the top, and the decision-making style is autocratic. Managers are simultaneously down-to-earth and practical but on occasion daring.

Marketing Opportunities in The Greater China

Everyone knows the Chinese market is huge and growing fast. We also note that across this vast land of opportunity, there are extreme differences in economic well-being, cultures, and political structures. The rich municipalities like Beijing and Shanghai are quite comparable to Paris, New York, or Tokyo in terms of the availability of luxury products. In terms of the stages of economic development, they are large and rich enough to be thought of as "more-developed countries." As in the United States, luxury cars sell better on the coast, and trucks sell better in rural areas of the west. Some of the latter might still be labeled "least-developed countries." However, unlike the United States, in China you cannot sell the same lines of cosmetics or shampoos nationwide.

The U.S. Commerce Department lists the following commercial sectors as particularly inviting for American exporters: automotive components, cleaner coal, construction equipment, education and training services, machine tools, marine industries, healthcare, water and wastewater treatment, rail equipment, renewable energy, and green building. Marketing most of these industrial products in China requires little cultural nuance, except perhaps at the negotiation table. But selling consumer products will require both linguistic and values-based adjustments in integrated marketing communication strategies and tactics.

Finally, the influence of national government policies and regulations of marketing will often be minor compared with that of their local counterparts. The rules themselves may be different from province to province, and certainly their interpretation and enforcement will depend on local values and individual administrators at the provincial and municipal levels. Spending time learning the local differences and building good personal relationships with distribution partners and government officials will be crucial for success. This last piece of advice holds true in every market around the world, but the diversity of the Chinese market will especially challenge the patience and persistence of international marketers for decades to come.

Summary

The Asia Pacific region is the most dynamic of the three regions covered in Chapters 9–11. It includes more than half the people on the planet, and for a variety of reasons, the economies are growing quite fast. In particular, China and India both grew at double-digit rates during the last five years, and *so far* they have fared better than the United States or Europe coming out of the 2008–2009 global recession. Meanwhile economic growth in South Korea, Singapore, Taiwan, and particularly Japan has remained tepid. Now China has become the second most important national market, behind only the United States.

The mix of stages of economic development present a variety of opportunities for international marketers: infrastructure development, new industrial markets, and huge consumer markets. Japan and high-income consumers in many countries also represent important luxury markets. New concepts, such as marketing to the bottom of the pyramid, are also most applicable in south Asia. The countries of the Asia Pacific region are cooperating in two major trade associations, ASEAN+3 and APEC. Finally, we have addressed the diversity in markets, industries, and cultures within China.

Key Terms

"The Greater China"	Bottom-of-the-pyramid	ASEAN	APEC
Purchase price parity (PPP)	markets (BOPMs)	ASEAN+3	
Four Asian Tigers			

Questions

1. Define the key terms listed above.

2. Explain why China's economy languished for the last 500 years but has now burgeoned in the last 20.

3. Why has Japan's economy faltered?

4. What explains the fast growth of the four "Asian Tigers"?

5. Compare the growth success and potentials of India and China. List the advantages and disadvantages of each.

6. Discuss the problems a marketer might encounter when considering the Marxist–socialist countries as markets.

7. What are the market opportunities and challenges in Greater China?

8. What are the political issues swirling around the strong trade relationship between the U.S. and the PRC?

9. Briefly describe three examples of strategies of MNC in China and in India.

10. Should the United States fear China's emergence? Why or why not?

11. Do you expect that China, then India, will follow the growth paths of Japan and South Korea? What factors are similar across the countries, and what is unique about each of these four?

12. Describe the opportunities and threats of entering the market in Bangladesh.

13. Describe the economic interaction of China and its northern neighbors.

14. How are China's marketing strategies abroad similar to and different from those of American firms?

15. What can the United States, Europe, and China learn from the experiences of Japan during the last 20 years?

Chapter 12

Global Marketing Management:

PLANNING AND ORGANIZATION

CHAPTER LEARNING OBJECTIVES

What you should learn from Chapter 12:

LO1 How global marketing management differs from international marketing management

LO2 The need for planning to achieve company goals

LO3 The important factors for each alternative market-entry strategy

LO4 The increasing importance of international strategic alliances

Global Perspective

THE BRITISH SELL ANOTHER TREASURE

The mating dance was unusually long, but then again, the deal was unusually large. Kraft first proposed to purchase the British institution Cadbury for a price of almost $17 billion in early September. Then it had until November 9 to make a formal offer or give up the fight. The courtship unleashed a barrage of bad jokes (e.g., "Cadbury gags on Kraft bid"). It also stirred up atavistic fears across Britain of a faceless American conglomerate wrecking a great British institution and forcing Britons to give up Dairy Milk chocolate and Creme Eggs in favor of Cheez Whiz and Jell-O.

A succession of studies has shown that three-quarters of mergers and acquisitions fail to produce any benefits for shareholders, and more than half actually destroy shareholder value (e.g., Quaker and Snapple, Daimler-Benz and Chrysler, Time Warner and AOL). The danger is particularly pronounced in hostile bids that cross borders and involve much loved brands.

A Kraft–Cadbury deal sounds designed for failure. Todd Stitzer, Cadbury's boss, argues that his firm is an embodiment of a distinctive style of "principled capitalism" that was inspired by its Quaker founders nearly two centuries ago and has been woven into its fabric ever since. Destroy that tradition and "you risk destroying what makes Cadbury a great company."

Chocolate companies as a breed also have a peculiarly intimate relationship with their customers, partly because chocolate is involved in so many childhood, romantic, and festive rituals, and partly because people acquire their chocolate preferences at their mothers' knees. Most Britons would rather eat scorpions than Hershey bars. The giants of the chocolate business have all dominated their respective regions for decades. Britons have been stuffing themselves with Dairy Milk since 1905, Creme Eggs since 1923, and Crunchies since 1929.

A Kraft–Cadbury combination also would create a rotten-toothed behemoth, with $50 billion in annual sales, a significant presence in every market worthy of the name, and a real chance of making up lost ground in China. Kraft has a strong position in mainland Europe and operations in 150 countries. Cadbury is worshipped wherever the British empire once held sway (the company commands 70 percent of the chocolate market in India, for example), and a lot of other places besides (notably, Brazil and Mexico). It also has an unrivaled distribution system among small shops in India and parts of Africa. Skeptics are right to point out that grandiose mergers more often destroy brands than strengthen them, particularly when those brands are such delicate confections as chocolate bars and gooey eggs. But then again, few mergers offer the chance to establish a global empire of taste.

The mating dance was finally consummated in January 2010, for some $19 billion in cash and stock. Among those who do not appreciate this latest marital arrangement was Warren Buffett, whose Berkshire Hathaway group owns 9.4 percent of Kraft. Had he been able, he would have voted against the $19 billion dowry that Kraft paid as too much.

Now, five years later, the British are still cranky about someone stealing their candy. The U.K. government has approved a much tougher set of requirements in their Takeover Code for foreign firms taking over domestic ones. Kraft's closing of Cadbury's sentimental favorite plant in Somerdale, including moving 500 jobs to Poland, stimulated the British ire.

Sources: "Food Fight," *The Economist*, November 7, 2009, p. 63; Graeme Wearden, "Warren Buffett Blasts Kraft's Takeover of Cadbury," http:// guardian.co.uk, January 20, 2010; Ben Morris, "The Cadbury Deal: How It Changed Takeovers," *BBC News*, May 2, 2014, online.

Circa 2015, Netflix had more than 50 million members for its streaming services, one-quarter of which were outside the United States. Another strategy for expanding its business overseas is the creation of its own content. Its first production of this sort is the most successful *House of Cards*. American movie studios are now making about 41 percent of their revenues from international licensing.[3] On the streets of Rome, the series is being advertised as part of a package offered via Sky Atlantic, a new channel on Sky Italia, a Rupert Murdock owned, satellite TV broadcaster. Also being offered are two HBO productions, *Game of Thrones* and *Boardwalk Empire*. The last is a bit ironic—the outdoor advertising is adjacent to the Tiber River, sort of on the boardwalk of the old Roman Empire.

Confronted with slower growth in home markets, increasing global competition for expanding markets, multinational companies are changing their marketing strategies and altering their organizational structures. Netflix is a great example of the first challenge. Currently about 75 percent of its subscribers are in the United States. But top management sees huge opportunities internationally.[1] Their goals are to enhance their competitiveness and to ensure proper positioning to capitalize on opportunities in the global marketplace. Comprehensive decisions must be made regarding key strategic choices, such as standardization versus adaptation, concentration versus dispersion, and integration versus independence. Particularly as national borders become less meaningful, we see the rise of greater international corporate collaboration networks yielding new thinking about traditional concepts of competition and organization.

A recent study of North American and European corporations indicated that nearly 75 percent of the companies are revamping their business processes, that most have formalized strategic planning programs, and that the need to stay cost competitive was considered the most important external issue affecting their marketing strategies. Change is not limited to the giant multinationals but includes midsized and small firms as well.

In fact, the flexibility of a smaller company may enable it to reflect the demands of global markets and redefine its programs more quickly than larger multinationals. Acquiring a global perspective is easy, but the execution requires planning, organization, and a willingness to learn[2] new approaches—from engaging in collaborative relationships to redefining the scope of company operations.

This chapter discusses global marketing management, competition in the global marketplace, strategic planning, and alternative market-entry strategies. It also identifies the elements that contribute to an effective international or global organization.

Global Marketing Management

LO1

How global marketing management differs from international marketing management

In the 1970s, the market segmentation argument was framed as "standardization versus adaptation." In the 1980s, it was "globalization versus localization," and in the 1990s, it was "global integration versus local responsiveness." The fundamental question was whether the global homogenization of consumer tastes allowed global standardization of the marketing mix. The Internet revolution of the 1990s, with its unprecedented global reach, added a new twist to the old debate.

Even today, some companies are calling "global" the way to go. For example, executives at Twix Cookie Bars tried out their first global campaign with a new global advertising agency, Grey Worldwide. With analysis, perhaps a global campaign does make sense

[1]Emily Steel, "Netflix, Growing, Envisions Expansion Abroad," *The New York Times*, July 22, 2014, pp. B1, 2.

[2]Yuping Zeng, Oded Shenkar, Seung-Hyun Lee, and Sangceol Song, "Cultural Differences, MNE Learning Abilities, and the Effect of Experience on Subsidiary Mortality in a Dissimilar Culture: Evidence from Korean MNEs," *Journal of International Business Studies*, 44 (2013), pp. 42–65; Dirk DE Clercq and Lianxi Zhou, "Entrepreneurial Strategic Posture and Performance in Foreign Markets: The Critical Role of International Learning Effort," *Journal of International Marketing* 22, no. 2 (2014), pp. 47–67.

[3]Amol Sharma, "TV Studios Tune into Foreign Markets," *The Wall Street Journal*, November 30, 2014, pp. A1, 14.

The competition among soft drink bottlers in India is fierce. Here Coke and Pepsi combine to ruin the view of the Taj Mahal. Notice how the red of Coke stands out among its competitors in the picture. Of course, now Coca-Cola has purchased Thums Up, a prominent local brand—this is a strategy the company is applying around the world. But the red is a substantial competitive advantage both on store shelves and in outdoor advertising of the sort common in India and other developing countries. We're not sure who borrowed the "monsoon/thunder" slogans from whom.

for Twix. But look at the companies that are going in the other direction. Levi's jeans have faded globally in recent years. While Ford is selling its Fiesta worldwide, it has pared back its stable of brands around the world, giving up control of auto icons like Volvo, Land Rover, and Mazda. And perhaps the most global company of all, Coca-Cola, is peddling two brands in India—Coke and Thums Up. Coke's CEO explained, "Coke has had to come to terms with a conflicting reality. In many parts of the world, consumers have become pickier, more penny-wise, or a little more nationalistic, and they are spending more of their money on local drinks whose flavors are not part of the Coca-Cola lineup." Thums Up is now the biggest selling cola in India with more than a 40 percent market share.

Part of this trend back toward localization is caused by the efficiencies of customization made possible by the Internet and increasingly flexible manufacturing processes. Indeed, a good example of the "mass customization" is Dell Computer Corporation, which maintains no inventory and builds each computer to order. Also crucial has been the apparent rejection of the logic of globalism by trade unionists, environmentalists, and consumers so well demonstrated in Seattle during the World Trade Organization meetings in 1999. Although there is a growing body of empirical research illustrating the risks and difficulties of global standardization, contrary results also appear in the literature.[4] Finally, prominent among firms' standardization strategies is Mattel's unsuccessful

---

[4]Oliver Schilke, Martin Reimann, and Jacquelyn S. Thomas, "When Does International Marketing Standardization Matter to Firm Performance?" *Journal of International Marketing* 17, no. 4 (2009), pp. 24–46.

Constance I. Hays, "Learning to Think Smaller at Coke," The New York Times, February 6, 2000.

Items in the Disney Princess collection are on display at the Licensing International show at New York's Javits Convention Center. Mattel's strategic response to Bratz and Disney's ethnically diverse lines was twofold. First, it sued Bratz owner MGA with an intellectual property rights claim. The lawsuit lasted nine years, and a federal appeals court awarded only legal fees to MGA—no damages. In response, MGA plans more legal action regarding Bratz's loss of brand equity during the years of legal machinations. Second, Mattel bought the rights to produce the Princess dolls. The Disney Princesses have been selling well due to Mattel's marketing efforts.

globalization of blonde Barbie. We correctly predicted in a previous edition of this book that a better approach was that of Disney, with its more culturally diverse line of "Disney Princesses" including Mulan (Chinese) and Jasmine (Arabic). Even though Bratz and Disney Princesses won this battle of the new "toy soldiers," the question is still not completely settled. Mattel continued the war by suing MGA, claiming the company had stolen new product ideas for its Bratz line from Mattel. After nine years of litigation and a variety of judgments going in both directions, in 2013 a federal appeals court ordered Mattel to pay MGA only the legal fees incurred—no damages were awarded. MGA still plans more legal action to recoup its lost brand equity from the years of legal wrangling. Mattel learned its lesson: Rather than fighting Disney, it decided to join forces by purchasing a license to market the Princess line. Profits are up at both companies because of the arrangement.[5]

Indeed, the debate about standardization versus adaptation is itself a wonderful example of the ethnocentrism of American managers and academics alike. That is, from the European or even the Japanese perspective, markets are by definition international, and the special requirements of the huge American market must be considered from the beginning. Only in America can international market requirements be an afterthought.

Moreover, as the information explosion allows marketers to segment markets ever more finely, it is only the manufacturing and/or finance managers in companies who argue for standardization for the sake of economies of scale. From the marketing perspective, customization is always best. The ideal market segment size, if customer satisfaction is the goal, is *one*. According to one expert, "Forward-looking, proactive firms have the ability and willingness . . . to accomplish both tasks [standardization and localization] simultaneously."[6]

We believe things are actually simpler than that. As global markets continue to homogenize and diversify simultaneously, the best companies will avoid the trap of focusing on *country* as the primary segmentation variable. Other segmentation variables are often more

---

[5]Ann Zimmerman, "Maker of Bratz Dolls Wins a Legal Reprieve," *The Wall Street Journal*, December 11, 2009, p. B10; "Mattel Rival to Get $310 Million in Suit," *Associated Press*, August 5, 2011.

[6]Masaaki Kotabe, "Contemporary Research Trends in International Marketing: The 1960s," Chapter 17 in *Oxford Handbook of International Business*, 2nd edition, Alan Rugman (ed.) (Oxford: Oxford University Press, 2008); Richard Kustin, "The World is Flat, Almost: Measuring Marketing Standardization and Profit Performance of Japanese and U.S. Firms," *Journal of Global Marketing* 23, no. 2 (2010), pp. 100–108.

important—for example, region,[7] city,[8] climate, language group, media habits, age,[9] or income, as exemplified in our discussion about the diversity within China in Chapter 11. The makers of Twix apparently think that media habits (i.e., MTV viewership) supersede country, according to their latest segmentation approach. At least one industry CEO concurred regarding media-based segmentation: "With media splintering into smaller and smaller communities of interest, it will become more and more important to reach those audiences wherever [whichever country] they may be. Today, media companies are increasingly delivering their content over a variety of platforms: broadcast—both TV and radio—and cable, online and print, big screen video, and the newest portable digital media including 3-D. And advertisers are using the same variety of platforms to reach their desired audience." Finally, perhaps a few famous Italian brands are the best examples: Salvatore Ferragamo shoes, Gucci leather goods, and Ferrari cars sell to the highest-income segments globally. Indeed, for all three companies, their U.S. sales are greater than their Italian sales.

In the 21st century, standardization versus adaptation is simply not the right question to ask. Rather, the crucial question facing international marketers is what are the most efficient ways to segment markets. Country has been the most obvious segmentation variable, particularly for Americans. But as better communication systems continue to dissolve national borders, other dimensions of global markets are growing in salience.

The Nestlé Way: Evolution Not Revolution

Nestlé certainly hasn't been bothered by the debate on standardization versus adaptation. Nestlé has been international almost from its start in 1866 as a maker of infant formula. By 1920, the company was producing in Brazil, Australia, and the United States and exporting to Hong Kong. Today, it sells more than 2,000 brands and operates in 86 countries. Nestlé is the world's biggest marketer of infant formula, powdered milk, instant coffee, chocolate, soups, and mineral water. It ranks second in ice cream, and in cereals, it ties Ralston Purina and trails only Kellogg Company. Its products are sold in the most upscale supermarkets in Beverly Hills, California, and in huts in Nigeria, where women sell Nestlé bouillon cubes alongside homegrown tomatoes and onions. Although the company has no sales agents in North Korea, its products somehow find their way into stores there, too.

The "Nestlé way" is to dominate its markets. Its overall strategy can be summarized in four points: (1) think and plan long term, (2) decentralize, (3) stick to what you know, and (4) adapt to local tastes. To see how Nestlé operates, take a look at its approach to Poland, one of the largest markets of the former Soviet bloc. Company executives decided at the outset that it would take too long to build plants and create brand awareness. Instead, the company made acquisitions and followed a strategy of "evolution not revolution." It purchased Goplana, Poland's second-best-selling chocolate maker (it bid for the No. 1 company but lost out) and carefully adjusted the end product via small changes every two months over a two-year period until it measured up to Nestlé's standards and was a recognizable Nestlé brand. These efforts, along with all-out marketing, put the company within striking distance of the market leader, Wedel. Nestlé also purchased a milk operation and, as it did in Mexico, India, and elsewhere, sent technicians into the field to help Polish farmers improve the quality and quantity of the milk it buys through better feeds and improved sanitation.

Nestlé's efforts in the Middle East are much longer term. The area currently represents only about 2 percent of the company's worldwide sales, and the markets, individually, are relatively small. Furthermore, regional conflicts preclude most trade among the countries. Nevertheless, Nestlé anticipates that hostility will someday subside, and when that happens, the company will be ready to sell throughout the entire region. Nestlé has set up a network of factories in five countries that can someday supply the entire region with

---

[7]Ricardo Flores, Ruth V. Aguilera, Arash Mahdian, and Pal M. Vaaler, "How Well Do Supranational Regional Grouping Schemes Fit International Business Research Models?" *Journal of International Business Studies* 44 2013), pp. 451–74.

[8]Anthony Goerzen, Christian Geisler Asmussen, and Bo Bernhard Nielsen, "Global Cities and Multinational Enterprise Location Strategy," *Journal of International Business Studies* 44 (2013), pp. 427–50.

[9]Dannie Kjeldgaard and Soren Askegaard, "The Glocalization of Youth Culture: The Global Youth Segment as Structures of Common Difference," *Journal of Consumer Research* 33 (2006), pp. 21–27.

different products. The company makes ice cream in Dubai and soups and cereals in Saudi Arabia. The Egyptian factory makes yogurt and bouillon, while Turkey produces chocolate. And a factory in Syria makes ketchup, a malted-chocolate energy food, instant noodles, and other products. If the obstacles between the countries come down, Nestlé will have a network of plants ready to provide a complete line to market in all the countries. In the meantime, factories produce and sell mostly in the countries in which they are located.

For many companies, such a long-term strategy would not be profitable, but it works for Nestlé because the company relies on local ingredients and markets products that consumers can afford. The tomatoes and wheat used in the Syrian factory, for example, are major local agricultural products. Even if Syrian restrictions on trade remain, there are 14 million people to buy ketchup, noodles, and other products the company produces there. In all five countries, the Nestlé name and the bird-in-a-nest trademark appear on every product.

Nestlé bills itself as "the only company that is truly dedicated to providing a complete range of food products to meet the needs and tastes of people from around the world, each hour of their day, throughout their entire lives."

Benefits of Global Marketing

Few firms have truly global operations balanced across major regional markets. However, when large international market segments can be identified,[10] economies of scale in production and marketing can be important competitive advantages for multinational companies.[11] As a case in point, Black & Decker Manufacturing Company—makers of electrical hand tools, appliances, and other consumer products—realized significant production cost savings when it adopted a pan-European strategy. It was able to reduce not only the number of motor sizes for the European market from 260 to 8 but also 15 different models to 8. Similarly, Ford estimates that by unifying product development, purchasing, and supply activities across several countries, it saves more than $3 billion a year. Finally, while Japanese firms initially dominated the mobile phone business in their home market, international competitors now pose growing challenges via better technologies developed through greater global penetration.

Transfer of experience and know-how across countries through improved coordination and integration of marketing activities is also cited as a benefit of global operations.[12] Global diversity in marketing talent leads to new approaches across markets.[13] Unilever successfully introduced two global brands originally developed by two subsidiaries. Its South African subsidiary developed Impulse body spray, and a European branch developed a detergent that cleaned effectively in European hard water. Aluminum Company of America's (Alcoa) joint venture partner in Japan produced aluminum sheets so perfect that U.S. workers, when shown samples, accused the company of hand-selecting the samples. Line workers were sent to the Japanese plant to learn the techniques, which were then transferred to the U.S. operations. Because of the benefits of such transfers of knowledge, Alcoa has changed its practice of sending managers overseas to "keep an eye on things" to sending line workers and managers to foreign locations to seek out new techniques and processes.

Marketing globally also ensures that marketers have access to the toughest customers. For example, in many product and service categories, the Japanese consumer has been the hardest to please; the demanding customers are the reason that the highest-quality products

[10]Simcha Ronen and Oded Shenkar, "Mapping World Cultures: Cluster Formation, Sources, and Implications," *Journal of International Business Studies* 44 (2013), pp. 867–97; Margaret Fletcher, Simon Harris, and Robert Glenn Richey Jr., "Internationalization Knowledge: What, Why, Where, and When?" *Journal of International Marketing* 21, no. 3 (2013) pp. 47–71.

[11]Natalia Vila and Ines Kuster, "Success and Internationalization: Analysis of the Textile Sector," *Journal of Global Marketing* 21, no. 2 (2008), pp. 109–26; Amar Gande, Christopher Schenzler, and Lemma W. Senbet, "Valuation Effects of Global Diversification," *Journal of International Business Studies* 40, no. 9 (2009), pp. 1515–32.

[12]Nigel Driffield, James H. Love, and Stefan Menghinello, "The Multinational Enterprise as a Source of International Knowledge Flows: Direct Evidence from Italy," *Journal of International Business Studies* 41, no. 2 (2010), pp. 350–59.

[13]Luis Alfonso Dau, "Learning across Geographic Space: Pro-Market Reforms, Multinationalization Strategy, and Profitability," *Journal of International Business Studies* 44 (2013), pp. 235–62.

CROSSING BORDERS 12.1   Swedish Takeout

Fifty years ago in the woods of southern Sweden, a minor revolution took place that has since changed the concept of retailing and created a mass market in a category where none previously existed. The catalyst of the change was and is IKEA, the Swedish furniture retailer and distributor that virtually invented the idea of self-service, takeout furniture. IKEA sells reasonably priced and innovatively designed furniture and home furnishings for a global marketplace.

The name was registered in Agunnaryd, Sweden, in 1943 by Ingvar Kamprad—the IK in the company's name. He entered the furniture market in 1950, and the first catalog was published in 1951. The first store didn't open until 1958 in Almhult. It became so incredibly popular that a year later the store had to add a restaurant for people who were traveling long distances to get there.

IKEA entered the United States in 1985. Although IKEA is global, most of the action takes place in Europe, with more than 70 percent of the firm's $36 billion in sales. Nearly one-fourth of that comes from stores in Germany. This level compares with only about $5 billion in NAFTA countries. The firm has stores in more than 40 countries around the world.

One reason for the relatively slow growth in the United States is that its stores are franchised by Netherlands-based Inter IKEA Systems, which carefully scrutinizes potential franchisees—individuals or companies—for strong financial backing and a proven record in retailing. The IKEA Group, based in Denmark, is a group of private companies owned by a charitable foundation in the Netherlands; it operates more than 350 stores. The Group also develops, purchases, distributes, and sells IKEA products, which are available only in company stores.

Low price is built into the company's lines. Even catalog prices are guaranteed not to increase for one year. The drive to produce affordable products inadvertently put IKEA at the forefront of the environmental movement several decades ago. In addition to lowering costs, minimization of materials and packing addressed natural resource issues. Environmentalism remains an integral operational issue at IKEA. Even the company's catalog is completely recyclable.

On the day that Russia's first IKEA store opened in 2000, the wait to get in was an hour. Highway traffic backed up for miles. More than 40,000 people crammed into the place, picking clean sections of the warehouse. The store still pulls in more than 100,000 customers per week. IKEA has big plans for Russia. Company officials are placing IKEA's simple shelves, kitchens, bathrooms, and bedrooms in millions of Russian apartments that haven't been remodeled since the Soviet days.

One of IKEA's strength is its strategic learning and adjustment in its international expansion. Its approach has been called "flexible replication," wherein a strategic template is fitted to each international context. And now IKEA has opened 16 new stores in China's biggest cities.

Sources: Colin McMahon, "Russians Flock to IKEA as Store Battles Moscow," *Chicago Tribune*, May 17, 2000; "IKEA to March into China's Second-tier Cities [Next]," *SinoCast China Business Daily News*, August 6, 2007, p. 1; "IKEA Struggles to Source Sustainable Timber," *Environmental Data Services*, July 2009, p. 22; Anne VanderMey, "IKEA Takes on China," *Fortune*, December 12, 2011; Anna Jonsson and Nicolai J. Foss, "International Expansion through Flexible Replication: Learning from the Internationalization Experience of IKEA," *Journal of International Business Studies* 42, no. 9 (2011), pp. 1079–102.

and services often emanate from that country. Competing for Japanese customers provides firms with the best testing ground for high-quality products and services.

Diversity of markets served carries with it additional financial benefits. Spreading the portfolio of markets served brings important stability of revenues and operations to many global companies. Companies with global marketing operations suffered less during the Asian market downturn of the late 1990s than did firms specializing in the area. During the global trade crash of 2009, firms with operations in Latin American and China were less affected. Firms that market globally are able to take advantage of changing financial circumstances in other ways as well. For example, as tax and tariff rates ebb and flow around the world, the most global companies are able to leverage the associated complexity to their advantage.

Planning for Global Markets

Planning is a systematized way of relating to the future. It is an attempt to manage the effects of external, uncontrollable factors on the firm's strengths, weaknesses, objectives, and goals to attain a desired end. Furthermore, it is a commitment of resources to a country market to achieve specific goals. In other words, planning is the job of making things happen that might not otherwise occur.

CROSSING BORDERS 12.2   Alligators and the Alligator

Actually, it's a crocodile. Frenchmen Rene Lacoste and Andre Gillier founded the Lacoste firm in 1933 and added the iconic symbol to their shirts, which they exported to the United States for sale as designer goods by retailers such as Brooks Brothers. The brand reached the apex of its popularity in the United States in the 1970s and 1980s, symbolized by its listing in Lisa Birnbach's *Official Preppy Handbook* published in 1980.

Then managers made a great strategic mistake. Rather than raising prices to increase both sales revenues and profits, the firm put the crocodile logo on a wide variety of products: shorts, perfume, sunglasses, tennis shoes, belts, deck shoes, walking shoes, watches, even cars. The products then were distributed to a wider variety of retailers, including such low-end stores as Mervyns. An Izod sales manager for the big Southern California market at the time responded to a question about the success of the company by noting, "We don't know why we're doing so well—we're just scrambling to fill all the orders." But not knowing why the products were selling so well meant that they also couldn't see the coming crash. In the mid-1980s,

the crocodile was ubiquitous, which is not a good position for a designer product. Customers stopped buying, and the decline in sales was dramatic. Only after some 15 years has the company made a reasonable recovery.

Other luxury/designer brands have learned to manage their growth more carefully. Even in the brand craze striking China and high income groups around the world, leather goods maker Louis Vuitton (which often uses alligator to make its products) has chosen to grow relatively slowly. Recently the company expanded its capacity by adding a seventeenth factory in Marsaz, France, that employs 70 people. That is just a drop in the bucket for the $7 billion international marketer.

"Our paradox is how to grow without diluting our image," said CEO Yves Carcelle at the factory opening. It is perhaps the nicest decision an international marketer must make: Raise prices or broaden distribution? Carcelle seems to have learned from his crocodile compatriots.

Source: Christina Passariello, "At Vuitton, Growth in Small Batches," *The Wall Street Journal*, June 27, 2011, pp. B1, B10.

Planning allows for rapid growth of the international function, changing markets, increasing competition, and the turbulent challenges of different national markets. The plan must blend the changing parameters of external country environments with corporate objectives and capabilities to develop a sound, workable marketing program.[14] A strategic plan commits corporate resources to products and markets to increase competitiveness and profits.

Planning relates to the formulation of goals and methods of accomplishing them, so it is both a process and a philosophy. Structurally, planning may be viewed as corporate, strategic, or tactical. International corporate planning is essentially long term, incorporating generalized goals for the enterprise as a whole. Strategic planning is conducted at the highest levels of management and deals with products, capital, research, and the long- and short-term goals of the company. Tactical planning, or market planning, pertains to specific actions and to the allocation of resources used to implement strategic planning goals in specific markets. Tactical plans are made at the local level and address marketing and advertising questions.

A major advantage for a multinational corporation (MNC) involved in planning is the discipline imposed by the process. An international marketer who has gone through the planning process has a framework for analyzing marketing problems and opportunities and a basis for coordinating information from different country markets. The process of planning may be as important as the plan itself, because it forces decision makers to examine all factors that affect the success of a marketing program and involves those who will be responsible for its implementation. Another key to successful planning is evaluating company objectives, including management's commitment and philosophical orientation to international business. Finally, the planning process is a primary medium of organizational learning.

---

[14]Wade M. Danis, Dan S. Chiaburu, and Majorie A. Lyles, "The Impact of Managerial Networking Intensity and Market-Based Strategies on Firm Growth during Institutional Upheaval: A Study of Small and Medium-Sized Enterprises in a Transition Economy," *Journal of International Business Studies* 41, no. 2 (2010), pp. 287–307.

Company Objectives and Resources

Defining objectives clarifies the orientation of the domestic and international divisions, permitting consistent policies. The lack of well-defined objectives has found companies rushing into promising foreign markets only to find activities that conflict with or detract from the companies' primary objectives.

Foreign market opportunities do not always parallel corporate objectives and resources;[15] it may be necessary to change the objectives, alter the scale of international plans, or abandon them. One market may offer immediate profit but have a poor long-run outlook, while another may offer the reverse. Only when corporate objectives are clear can such differences be reconciled effectively.

International Commitment

The planning approach taken by an international firm affects the degree of internationalization to which management is philosophically committed. Such commitment affects the specific international strategies and decisions of the firm.[16] This is particularly important for small, entrepreneurial firms.[17] After company objectives have been identified, management needs to determine whether it is prepared to make the level of commitment required for successful international operations—commitment in terms of dollars to be invested, personnel for managing the international organization, and determination to stay in the market long enough to realize a return on these investments.

A company uncertain of its prospects is likely to enter a market timidly, using inefficient marketing methods, channels, or organizational forms, thus setting the stage for the failure of a venture that might have succeeded with full commitment and support by the parent company.[18] Any long-term marketing plan should be fully supported by senior management and have realistic time goals set for sales growth. Occasionally, casual market entry is successful, but more often than not, market success requires long-term commitment.

Finally, a new series of studies is demonstrating a strong regional preference for multinational companies as they expand their operations. Part of this preference is due to the challenges associated with cultural distance[19] and part with physical distance, particularly that related to the difficulties of doing business across time zones. As we mentioned previously, most countries and companies trade most with their neighbors. Managers' characteristics and preferences also affect this choice.[20] Others report that firms also gain competitive advantages from clustering operations in specific regions.[21] Yet to some degree, researchers question the existence of global strategies, maintaining that only nine American *Fortune* 500 companies deserve the term "global" with respect to their operational coverage of

[15]Jan Kemper, Andreas Engelen, and Malte Brettel, "How Top Management's Social Capital Fosters the Development of Specialized Marketing Capabilities," *Journal of International Marketing* 19, no. 3 (2011), pp. 87–112.

[16]Antonio Navarro, Francisco J. Acedo, Matthew J. Robson, Emilio Ruzo, and Fernando Losada, "Antecedents and Consequences of Firms' Export Commitment: An Empirical Study," *Journal of International Marketing* 18, no. 3 (2010) pp. 41–61.

[17]Lianxi Shou, Aiqi Wu, and Bradley Barnes, "The Effects of Early Internationalization on Performance Outcomes in Young International Ventures: The Mediating Role of Marketing Capabilities," *Journal of International Marketing* 20, no. 4 (2012), pp. 25–45; Panagiotis Ganotakis and James A. Love, "Export Propensity, Export Intensity, and Firm Performance: The Role of the Entrepreneurial Founding Team," *Journal of International Business Studies* 43 (2012), pp. 693–718.

[18]Bradley R. Barnes, Leonidas C. Leonidou, Noel Y.M. Siu, and Constantinos N. Leonidou, "Opportunism as the Inhibiting Trigger for Developing Long-Term–Oriented Western Export–Hong Kong Importer Relationships," *Journal of International Marketing* 18, no. 2 (2010), pp. 35–63.

[19]Magnus Hultman, Constantine S. Katsikeas, and Matthew J. Robson, "Export Promotion Strategy and Performance: The Role of International Experience," *Journal of International Marketing* 19, no. 4 (2011), pp. 17–39.

[20]Elitsa R. Banalieva and Kimberly A. Eddleston, "Home-Region Focus and Performance of Family Firms: The Role of Family vs. Non-Family Leaders," *Journal of International Business Studies* 42, no. 8 (2011), pp. 1060–72.

[21]Joseph Johnson and Gerard J. Tellis, "Drivers of Success for Market Entry into China and India," *Journal of Marketing* 72, no. 3 (2008), pp. 1–13; Jennifer D. Chandler and John L. Graham, "Relationship-Oriented Cultures, Corruption, and International Marketing Success," *Journal of Business Ethics* 92, no. 2 (2010), pp. 251–67.

the planet. We can agree that strategic choices currently favor regional foci, but the trend is toward steadily increasing globalization of trade agreements, trade, and company strategies, as we mentioned in the previous chapter. Competition and the new ease of global communications is forcing managers around the world to make greater commitments to global marketing.

The Planning Process

LO2

The need for planning to achieve company goals

Whether a company is marketing in several countries or is entering a foreign market for the first time, planning is essential to success. The first-time foreign marketer must decide what products to develop, in which markets, and with what level of resource commitment. For the company that is already committed, the key decisions involve allocating effort and resources among countries and product(s), deciding on new market segments to develop or old ones to withdraw from, and determining which products to develop or drop. Guidelines and systematic procedures are necessary for evaluating international opportunities and risks and for developing strategic plans to take advantage of such opportunities. The process illustrated in Exhibit 12.1 offers a systematic guide to planning for the multinational firm operating in several countries.

Phase 1: Preliminary Analysis and Screening—Matching Company and Country Needs.
Whether a company is new to international marketing or heavily involved, an evaluation of potential markets is the first step in the planning process. A critical first step in the international planning process is deciding in which

Exhibit 12.1
International Planning Process

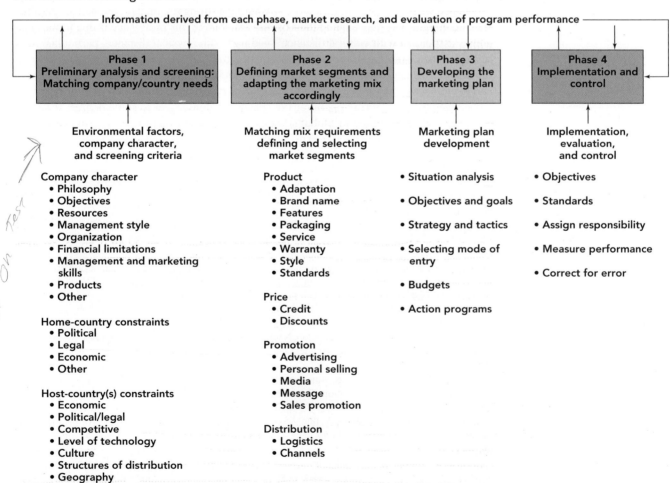

existing country market to make a market investment. A company's strengths and weaknesses (including characteristics of its home country),[22] products, philosophies, modes of operation,[23] and objectives must be matched with a country's constraining factors and market potential.[24] Research has shown three entry criteria to be most useful: analyses of institutional context, cultural context, and transaction costs.[25] In the first part of the planning process, countries are analyzed and screened to eliminate those that do not offer sufficient potential for further consideration. Emerging markets pose a special problem because many have inadequate marketing infrastructures, distribution channels are underdeveloped, and income levels and distribution vary among countries. We also note that in some cases exploitation of unexpected market opportunities can preclude the careful planning advocated herein.[26]

The next step is to establish screening criteria against which prospective countries can be evaluated. These criteria are ascertained by an analysis of company objectives, resources, and other corporate capabilities and limitations. It is important to determine the reasons for entering a foreign market and the returns expected from such an investment. A company's commitment to international business and its objectives for going international are important in establishing evaluation criteria. Minimum market potential, minimum profit, return on investment, acceptable competitive levels, standards of political stability, acceptable legal requirements, and other measures appropriate for the company's products are examples of the evaluation criteria to be established.

Once evaluation criteria are set, a complete analysis of the environment within which a company plans to operate is made. The environment consists of the uncontrollable elements discussed previously and includes both home-country and host-country constraints, marketing objectives, and any other company limitations or strengths that exist at the beginning of each planning period. Although an understanding of uncontrollable environments is important in domestic market planning, the task is more complex in foreign marketing, because each country under consideration presents the foreign marketer with a different set of unfamiliar environmental constraints. This stage in the planning process, more than anything else, distinguishes international from domestic marketing planning.

The results of Phase 1 provide the marketer with the basic information necessary to evaluate the potential of a proposed country market, identify problems that would eliminate the country from further consideration, identify environmental elements that need further

[22]Lutz Kaufmann and Jan-Frederik Roesch, "Constraints on Building and Deploying Marketing Capabilities by Emerging Market Firms in Advanced Markets," *Journal of International Marketing* 20, no. 4 [2012], pp. 1–24; Peter Gabrielsson, Mika Gabrielsson, and Tomi Seppala, "Marketing Strategies for Foreign Expansion of Companies Originating in Small and Open Economies: The Consequences of Strategic Fit and Performance," *Journal of International Marketing* 20, no. 2 (2012), pp. 25–48; Anna Lamin and Grigorios Livanis, "Agglomeration, Catch-Up, and the Liability of Foreignness in Emerging Economies," *Journal of International Business Studies* 44 (2013), pp. 579–606; Gongming Qian, Lee Li, and Alan M. Rugman, "Liability of Country Foreignness and Liability of Regional Foreignness: Their Effects on Geographic Diversification and Firm Performance," *Journal of International Business Studies* 44 (2013), pp. 635–47.

[23]Gabriel R.G. Benito, Bent Petersen, and Lawrence S. Welch, "Towards More Realistic Conceptualizations of Foreign Operation Modes," *Journal of International Business Studies* 40, no. 9 (2009), pp. 1455–70; Paula Hortinha, Carmen Lages, and Luis Filipe Lages, "The Trade-Off between Customer and Technology Orientations: Impact on Innovative Capabilities and Export Performance," *Journal of International Marketing* 19, no. 3 (2011), pp. 36–58.

[24]Namrata Malhotra and C. R. (Bob) Corredoira, "An Organizational Model for Understanding Internationalization Processes," *Journal of International Business Studies* 41, no. 2 (2010), pp. 330–49; Usha C. V. Haley and David M. Boje, "Storytelling the Internationalization of the Multinational Enterprize," *Journal of International Business Studies* (2014), pp. 1115–1132.

[25]Keith D. Brouthers, "Institutional, Cultural, and Transaction Cost Influences on Entry Mode Choice and Performance," *Journal of International Business Studies* 44 (2013), pp. 1–13.

[26]Yanto Chandra, "An Opportunity-Based View of Rapid Internationalization," *Journal of International Marketing* 20, no. 1 (March 2012), pp. 74–102.

analysis, determine which part of the marketing mix can be standardized and which part of and how the marketing mix must be adapted to meet local market needs, and develop and implement a marketing action plan.

Information generated in Phase 1 helps companies avoid the kinds of mistakes that plagued Radio Shack Corporation, a leading merchandiser of consumer electronic equipment in the United States, when it first went international. Radio Shack's early attempts at international marketing in western Europe resulted in a series of costly mistakes that could have been avoided had it properly analyzed the uncontrollable elements of the countries targeted. The company staged its first Christmas promotion in anticipation of December 25 in Holland, unaware that the Dutch celebrate St. Nicholas Day and give gifts on December 6. Furthermore, legal problems in various countries interfered with some plans. German courts promptly stopped a free flashlight promotion in German stores because giveaways violated German sales laws. In Belgium, the company overlooked a law requiring a government tax stamp on all window signs, and poorly selected store sites resulted in many of the new stores closing shortly after opening.

With the analysis in Phase 1 completed, the decision maker faces the more specific task of selecting country target markets and segments, identifying problems and opportunities in these markets, and beginning the process of creating marketing programs.

Phase 2: Defining Target Markets and Adapting the Marketing Mix Accordingly.

A more detailed examination of the components of the marketing mix is the purpose of Phase 2. Once target markets are selected, the marketing mix must be evaluated in light of the data generated in Phase 1. Incorrect decisions at this point lead to products inappropriate for the intended market or costly mistakes in pricing, advertising, and promotion. The primary goal of Phase 2 is to decide on a marketing mix adjusted to the cultural constraints imposed by the uncontrollable elements of the environment that effectively achieves corporate objectives and goals.[27]

The process used by the Nestlé Company is an example of the type of analysis done in Phase 2. Each product manager has a country fact book that includes much of the information suggested in Phase 1. The country fact book analyzes in detail a variety of culturally related questions. In Germany, the product manager for coffee must furnish answers to a number of questions. How does a German rank coffee in the hierarchy of consumer products? Is Germany a high or a low per capita consumption market? (These facts alone can be of enormous consequence. In Sweden the annual per capita consumption of coffee is 8.2 kilograms, in the United States 4.2, and in Japan it's only 3.3.)[28] How is coffee used—in bean form, ground, or powdered? If it is ground, how is it brewed? Which coffee is preferred—Brazilian Santos blended with Colombian coffee, or robusta from the Ivory Coast? Is it roasted? Do the people prefer dark roasted or blonde coffee? (The color of Nestlé's instant coffee must resemble as closely as possible the color of the coffee consumed in the country.)

As a result of the answers to these and other questions, Nestlé produces 200 types of instant coffee, from the dark robust espresso preferred in Latin countries to the lighter blends popular in the United States. Almost $50 million a year is spent in four research laboratories around the world experimenting with new shadings in color, aroma, and flavor. Do the Germans drink coffee after lunch or with their breakfast? Do they take it black or with cream or milk? Do they drink coffee in the evening? Do they sweeten it? (In France, the answers are clear: In the morning, coffee with milk; at noon, black coffee—that is, two totally different coffees.) At what age do people begin drinking coffee? Is it a traditional beverage, as in France; is it a form of rebellion among the young, as in England, where coffee drinking has been taken up in defiance of tea-drinking parents; or is it a gift, as in Japan? There is a coffee boom in tea-drinking Japan, where Nescafé

---

[27]Thomas L. Powers and Jeffrey J. Loyka, "Adaptation of Marketing Mix Elements in International Markets," *Journal of Global Marketing* 23, no. 1 (2010), pp. 65–79.

[28]Coffee Consumption, World Resources Institute, 2012.

As they say, as one door closes, another opens up—indeed, sometimes two! Given all the tea in China, it's particularly amazing that for almost eight years you could buy a mocha frappuccino in the Forbidden City in Beijing. The yellow roof symbolizes Imperial grounds, but we don't think the Emperor had grounds of the coffee sort in mind when he built the place in the 1400s. China joining the WTO some six centuries later opened up the market in new ways to franchisers from around the world. However, unlike the other 1,000-plus Starbucks stores in China, this one stirred strong protests by the local media and was eventually closed in the summer of 2007. Meanwhile, about one month after the Forbidden City store was forbidden in China, the company's first Russian store opened in Moscow. On a cold afternoon in Moscow, Russians and foreign tourists can choose between grabbing a cappuccino at either Starbucks or McDonald's McCafe. The two are just a couple of blocks from each other on Moscow's most famous traditional shopping street, the Arbat. The American companies were smart enough this time around not to try locating in Red Square.

is considered a luxury gift item; instead of chocolates and flowers, Nescafé is toted in fancy containers to dinners and birthday parties. With such depth of information, the product manager can evaluate the marketing mix in terms of the information in the country fact book.

Phase 2 also permits the marketer to determine possibilities for applying marketing tactics across national markets. The search for similar segments across countries can often lead to opportunities for economies of scale in marketing programs. This opportunity was the case for Nestlé when research revealed that young coffee drinkers in England and Japan had identical motivations. As a result, Nestlé now uses principally the same message in both markets.

Frequently, the results of the analysis in Phase 2 indicate that the marketing mix will require such drastic adaptation that a decision not to enter a particular market is made. For example, a product may have to be reduced in physical size to fit the needs of the market, but the additional manufacturing cost of a smaller size may be too high to justify market entry. Also, the price required to be profitable might be too high for a majority of the market to afford. If there is no way to reduce the price, sales potential at the higher price may be too low to justify entry.

The answers to three major questions are generated in Phase 2:

1. Are there identifiable market segments that allow for common marketing mix tactics across countries?

2. Which cultural/environmental adaptations are necessary for successful acceptance of the marketing mix?

3. Will adaptation costs allow profitable market entry?

Based on the results in Phase 2, a second screening of countries may take place, with some countries dropped from further consideration. The next phase in the planning process is the development of a marketing plan.

Phase 3: Developing the Marketing Plan.   At this stage of the planning process, a marketing plan is developed for the target market—whether it is a single country or a global market set. The marketing plan begins with a situation analysis and culminates in the selection of an entry mode and a specific action program for the market. The specific plan establishes what is to be done, by whom, how it is to be done, and when. Included are budgets and sales and profit expectations. Just as in Phase 2, a decision not to enter a specific market may be made if it is determined that company marketing objectives and goals cannot be met.

Phase 4: Implementation and Control.   Although we present the model as a series of sequential phases, the planning process is a dynamic, continuous set of interacting variables with information continuously building among phases. The phases outline a crucial path to be followed for effective, systematic planning.

A "go" decision in Phase 3 triggers implementation of specific plans and anticipation of successful marketing. However, the planning process does not end at this point. All marketing plans require coordination and control during the period of implementation. Many businesses do not control marketing plans as thoroughly as they could, even though continuous monitoring and control could increase their success. An evaluation and control system requires performance-objective action, that is, bringing the plan back on track should standards of performance fall short. Such a system also assumes reasonable metrics of performance are accessible. A global orientation facilitates the difficult but extremely important management tasks of coordinating and controlling the complexities of international marketing.

Utilizing a planning process and system encourages the decision maker to consider all variables that affect the success of a company's plan. Furthermore, it provides the basis for viewing all country markets and their interrelationships as an integrated global unit. By following the guidelines presented in Part Six of this text, "The Country Notebook—A Guide for Developing a Marketing Plan," the international marketer can put the strategic planning process into operation.

With the information developed in the planning process and a country market selected, the decision regarding the entry mode can be made. The choice of mode of entry is one of the more critical decisions for the firm because the choice will define the firm's operations and affect all future decisions in that market.

Alternative Market-Entry Strategies[29]

A company has four different modes of foreign market entry from which to select: exporting, contractual agreements, strategic alliances, and direct foreign investment. The different modes of entry can be further classified on the basis of the equity or nonequity requirements of each mode. The amount of equity required by the company to use different modes affects the risk, return, and control that it will have in each mode. For example, indirect exporting requires no equity investment and thus has a low risk, low rate of return, and little control, whereas direct foreign investment requires the most equity of the four modes and creates the greatest risk while offering the most control and the potential highest return.

Companies most often begin with modest export involvement. As sales revenues grow, the firms often proceed down through the series of steps listed in Exhibit 12.2.[30] Successful smaller firms are often particularly adept at exploiting networks of personal and commercial relationships to mitigate the financial risks of initial entry. Also, experience in larger numbers of foreign markets can increase the number of entry strategies used. In fact, a company in several country markets may employ a variety of entry modes because each country market poses a different set of conditions.[31] For example, JLG Industries in Pennsylvania makes self-propelled aerial work platforms (cherry pickers) and sells them

---

[29]One scholar has pointed out that this is one of the most-often studied topics among international business researchers, and it has perhaps reached its tipping point with respect to new contributions. We would agree. See J. Myles Shaver, "Do We Really Need More Entry Mode Studies," *Journal of International Business Studies* 44 (2013), pp. 23–27.

[30]Gerald Yong Gao and Yigang Pan, "The Pace of MNCs' Sequential Entries: Cumulative Entry Experience and the Dynamic Process," *Journal of International Business Studies* 41, no. 9 (2011), pp. 1572–80.

[31]Susan B. Douglas and C. Samuel Craig, "Convergence and Divergence: Developing a Semiglobal Marketing Strategy," *Journal of International Marketing* 19, no. 1 (2011), pp. 82–100; Ruby P. Lee, "Extending the Environment-Strategy-Performance Framework: The Roles of Multinational Corporation Network Strength, Market Responsiveness, and Product Innovation," *Journal of International Marketing* 18, no. 4 (2010), pp. 58–73; Janet Y Murray, Min Ju, and Gerald Yong Gao, "Foreign Market Entry Timing Revisited: Trade-Off Between Market Share Performance and Firm Survival," *Journal of International Marketing* 20, no. 3 (2012), pp. 50–64; Briger Maekelburger, Christian Schwens, and RuedigerKabst, "Asset Specificity and Foreign Market Entry Mode Choice of Small and Medium-sized Enterprises: The Moderating Influence of Knowledge Safeguards and Institutional Safeguards," *Journal of International Business Studies* 43 (2012), pp. 458–76.

Exhibit 12.2
Alternative Market-Entry Strategies

Look →
For Exam

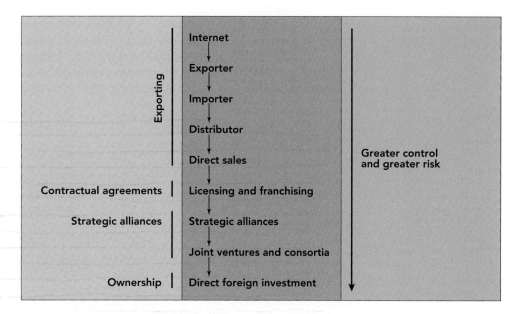

Exporting

- Internet
- Exporter
- Importer
- Distributor
- Direct sales

Contractual agreements | Licensing and franchising

Strategic alliances | Strategic alliances

Joint ventures and consortia

Ownership | Direct foreign investment

Greater control and greater risk

all over the world. The firm actually manufactured in Scotland and Australia beginning in the 1970s, but it was forced to close the plants in the 1990s. However, the company's international sales have burgeoned again. The growth in European business allowed for a simplification of distribution channels through the elimination of middlemen; dealerships have been purchased in Germany, Norway, Sweden, and the United Kingdom. JLG set up dealership joint ventures in Thailand and Brazil, and sales have been brisk despite volatility problems in those countries. The company also has established sales and service businesses from scratch in Scotland, Italy, and South Africa.

Exporting

LO3

The important factors for each alternative market-entry strategy

Exporting accounts for some 10 percent of global economic activity. Exporting can be either direct or indirect. With **direct exporting**, the company sells to a customer in another country. This method is the most common approach employed by companies taking their first international step because the risks of financial loss can be minimized. In contrast, **indirect exporting** usually means that the company sells to a buyer (importer or distributor) in the home country, which in turn exports the product. Customers include large retailers such as Walmart or Sears, wholesale supply houses, trading companies, and others that buy to supply customers abroad.

Early motives for exporting often are to skim the cream from the market or gain business to absorb overhead. Research recommends that a more focused[32] and learning-based approach[33] to a few international markets will work best for new exporters. Careful segmentation of export markets has been shown to be an important influence on venture performance.[34] Early involvement may also be opportunistic and come in the form of an inquiry from a foreign customer or initiatives from an importer in the foreign market. This motive is the case with Pilsner Urquell, the revered Czech beer, which for many years has sold in the United States through Guinness Bass Import Corporation (GBIC). However, the Czech firm severed its relationship with the importer because it wasn't getting the attention of the other imported beers in GBIC's portfolio. The firm established its own sales force of two dozen to handle five key metropolitan areas in the United States. Prices were reduced and a global media plan developed with a British ad agency.

[32]Lance Eliot Brouthers, George Nakos, John Hadarcou, and Keith D. Brouthers, "Key Factors for Successful Export Performance for Small Firms," *Journal of International Marketing* 17, no. 3 (2009), pp. 21–38.

[33]Joseph Johnson, Eden Yin, and Hueiting Tsai, "Persistence and Learning: Success Factors of Taiwanese Firms in International Markets," *Journal of International Marketing* 17, no. 3 (2009), pp. 39–54.

[34]Adamantios Diamantopoulos, Amat Ring, Bodo B. Schlegelmilch, and Eva Doberer, "Drivers of Export Segmentation Effectiveness and Their Impact on Export Performance," *Journal of International Marketing* 22, no. 1 (2014), pp. 39–61.

Exporting is also a common approach for mature international companies with strong marketing and relational capabilities.[35] Some of America's largest companies engage in exporting as their major market-entry method. Indeed, Boeing is the best example, as America's largest exporter. The mechanics of exporting and the different middlemen available to facilitate the exporting process are discussed in detail in Chapter 15.

The Internet.   The Internet is becoming increasingly important as a foreign market entry method. Initially, Internet marketing focused on domestic sales. However, a surprisingly large number of companies started receiving orders from customers in other countries, resulting in the concept of international Internet marketing (IIM). PicturePhone Direct, a mail-order reseller of desktop videoconferencing equipment, posted its catalog on the Internet expecting to concentrate on the northeastern United States. To the company's surprise, PicturePhone's sales staff received orders from Israel, Portugal, and Germany.

Other companies have had similar experiences and are actively designing Internet catalogs targeting specific countries with multilingual websites. Dell Computer Corporation has expanded its strategy of selling computers over the Internet to foreign sites as well. Dell began selling computers via the Internet to Malaysia, Australia, Hong Kong, New Zealand, Singapore, Taiwan, and other Asian countries through a "virtual store" on the Internet. The same selling mode has been launched in Europe.

Amazon.com jumped into the IIM game with both feet. It hired a top Apple Computer executive to manage its fast growing international business. Just 15 months after setting up book and CD e-tailing sites in Germany and the United Kingdom, the new overseas Amazon websites surged to become the most heavily trafficked commercial venues in both markets. Among the companies with the most profitable e-tailing businesses are former catalog companies such as Lands' End and L.L. Bean. Interestingly, Lands' End's success in foreign markets was tainted by unexpected problems in Germany. German law bans "advertising gimmicks"—and that's what regulators there called Lands' End's "unconditional lifetime guarantee." Indeed, the firm took the dispute all the way to the German supreme court and lost. Moreover, the uncertainty swirling around the European Union's approach to taxing Internet sales is continuing cause for great concern. As we will discuss in Chapter 15, most recently the Chinese internet giant, Alibaba, is pushing he envelope on global sales and world trade.

As discussed in Chapter 2, the full impact of the Internet on international marketing is yet to be determined. However, IIM should not be overlooked as an alternative market-entry strategy by the small or large company. Coupled with the international scope of credit card companies such as MasterCard and Visa and international delivery services such as UPS and Federal Express, deliveries to foreign countries can be relatively effortless.

Direct Sales.   Particularly for high-technology and big ticket industrial products, a direct sales force may be required in a foreign country. This requirement may mean establishing an office with local and/or expatriate managers and staff, depending of course on the size of the market and potential sales revenues. International sales management is one of the topics covered in detail in Chapter 17.

Contractual Agreements   *Contractual agreements* are long-term, nonequity associations between a company and another in a foreign market. Contractual agreements generally involve the transfer of technology, processes, trademarks, and/or human skills. In short, they serve as a means of transfer of knowledge rather than equity. Research has shown that when legal systems differ substantially across partners' countries, informal aspects of business relationships will be more important.[36]

Licensing.   A means of establishing a foothold in foreign markets without large capital outlays is licensing. Patent rights, trademark rights, and the rights to use technological

[35]David A. Griffith and Boryana V. Dimitrova, "Business and Cultural Aspects of Psychic Distance and Complementarity of Capabilities in Export Relationships," *Journal of International Marketing* 22, no. 3 (2014), pp. 50–67.

[36]Majid Abdi and Preet S. Aulakh, "Do Country-Level Institutional Frameworks and Interfirm Governance Arrangements Substitute or Complement in International Business Relationships?" *Journal of International Business Studies* 43 (2012), pp. 477–97.

processes are granted in foreign licensing. It is a favorite strategy for small and medium-sized companies, though by no means limited to such companies. Common examples of industries that use licensing arrangements in foreign markets are television programming and pharmaceuticals. Not many confine their foreign operations to licensing alone; it is generally viewed as a supplement to exporting or manufacturing, rather than the only means of entry into foreign markets. The advantages of licensing are most apparent when capital is scarce, import restrictions forbid other means of entry, a country is sensitive to foreign ownership, or patents and trademarks must be protected against cancellation for nonuse. The risks of licensing are choosing the wrong partner, quality and other production problems, payment problems, contract enforcement, and loss of marketing control.[37]

Although licensing may be the least profitable way of entering a market, the risks and headaches are less than those for direct investments. It is a legitimate means of capitalizing on intellectual property in a foreign market, and such agreements can also benefit the economies of target countries. Licensing takes several forms. Licenses may be granted for production processes, for the use of a trade name, or for the distribution of imported products. Licenses may be closely controlled or be autonomous, and they permit expansion without great capital or personnel commitment if licensees have the requisite capabilities. Not all experiences with licensing are successful because of the burden of finding, supervising, and inspiring licensees. The duration of licensing agreements depends to a large degree on technology and market uncertainties—more uncertainty favors shorter contracts. New research is beginning to address the trade-offs surrounding exclusive rights in international licensing. Exclusive rights are more frequently granted in countries with strong intellectual property rights protection and industries with high rates of technological change.[38]

Franchising.   Franchising is a rapidly growing form of licensing in which the franchiser provides a standard package of products, systems, and management services, and the franchisee provides market knowledge, capital, and personal involvement in management. The combination of skills permits flexibility in dealing with local market conditions and yet provides the parent firm with a reasonable degree of control. The key word in the previous sentence is "reasonable"—companies in recent years have chosen to buy back stores from franchisees. Recently Starbucks has taken this step in western provinces of China.[39] The franchiser can follow through on marketing of the products to the point of final sale. It is an important form of vertical market integration. Potentially, the franchise system provides an effective blending of skill centralization and operational decentralization; it has become an increasingly important form of international marketing. In some cases, franchising is having a profound effect on traditional businesses. In England, for example, annual franchised sales of fast foods are estimated at nearly $2 billion, which accounts for 30 percent of all foods eaten outside the home. The key factors that influence success of franchising approaches are monitoring costs (based on physical and cultural distances), the principal's international experience, and the brand equity in the new market.

Prior to 1970, international franchising was not a major activity. A survey by the International Franchising Association revealed that only 14 percent of its member firms had franchises outside of the United States, and the majority of those were in Canada. Now hundreds of thousands of franchises of U.S. firms are located in countries throughout the world. Franchises include soft drinks, motels (including membership "organizations" like Best Western International), retailing, fast foods, car rentals, automotive services, recreational services, and a variety of business services from print shops to sign shops. Canada is the dominant market for U.S. franchisers, with Japan and the United Kingdom second and third in importance. The Asia Pacific Rim has seen rapid growth as companies look to Asia for future expansion.

---

[37]Preet S. Aulakh, Marshall S. Jiang, and Yigang Pan, "International Technology Licensing: Monopoly Rents, Transaction Costs, and Exclusive Rights," *Journal of International Business Studies* 41, no. 4 (2010), pp. 587–605.

[38]For more information in this area see Preet S. Aulakh, Marshall S. Jiang, and Sali Li, "Licensee Technological Potential and Exclusive Rights in International Licensing: A Multilevel Model," *Journal of International Business Studies*, 44, 2013, pages 699–718.

[39]Tang Zhihao, "Starbucks Buys Back Control of Stores," *China Daily*, June 3, 2011, p. 14.

Maybe they can help you find a home with a view of the Black Sea here at the Century 21 office in Istanbul, Turkey. We know they'll be happy to sell you a piece of chicken from the Colonel's place in Eilat, Israel, just across the Red Sea from Aqaba, Jordan.

Despite temporary setbacks during the global economic downturn right after the turn of the millennium, franchising is still expected to be the fastest growing market-entry strategy. Franchises were often among the first types of foreign retail business to open in the emerging market economies of eastern Europe, the former republics of Russia, and China. McDonald's is in Moscow (its first store seated 700 inside and had 27 cash registers), and KFC is in China (the Beijing KFC store has the highest sales volume of any KFC store in the world). The same factors that spurred the growth of franchising in the U.S. domestic economy have led to its growth in foreign markets. Franchising is an attractive form of corporate organization for companies wishing to expand quickly with low capital investment. The franchising system combines the knowledge of the franchiser with the local knowledge and entrepreneurial spirit of the franchisee. Foreign laws and regulations are friendly toward franchising because it tends to foster local ownership, operations, and employment.

Lil'Orbits, a Minneapolis-based company that sells donut-making equipment and ingredients to entrepreneurs, is an example of how a small company can use licensing and franchising to enter foreign markets. Lil'Orbits sells a donut maker that turns out 1.5-inch donuts while the customer waits. The typical buyer in the United States buys equipment and mix directly from the company without royalties or franchise fees. The buyer has a small shop or kiosk and sells donuts by the dozen for takeout or individually along with a beverage.

CROSSING BORDERS 12.3   The Men Who Would Be Pizza Kings

In more senses than one, pizza outlets are mushrooming all over India. The wait for pizza lovers in places like Surat, Kochi, and Bhubaneshwar is finally over. Both American franchisers Domino's and Pizza Hut now have more than 200 stores each in the country. Chennai-based Pizza Corner, having established itself in the south, has now boldly ventured into the north—it has already opened three outlets in Delhi and is planning to increase the number to eight.

While Domino's is trying to dish out a pizza for every ethnic group, Pizza Hut is trying to expose Indians to the pizza's Chinese cousin. It has come up with the "Oriental," which has hot Chinese sauce, spring onions, and sesame seeds as its toppings. It was developed based on the Indian fondness for Chinese food. This is not to say that

Pizza Hut does not pay heed to the spice-soaked Indian version. Apart from the Oriental, it is also dishing out a spicy paneer tikka pizza. Milk shakes are on the menu, too. Most recently an Indian dairy company has been earning market share in both pizzas and ice cream. Things are getting interesting there fast. And, in spite of Kipling's prophesy that the two streams shall never meet, the Indianization of the pizza is truly here.

Sources: Smita Tripathi, "Butter Chicken Pizza in Ludhiana," *Business Standard*, June 17, 2000, p. 2; Rahul Chandawarkar, "Collegians Mix Money with Study Material," *Times of India*, June 22, 2000; Thomas L. Friedman, *The World Is Flat* (New York: Farrar, Straus, and Giroux, 2005); "Dominos Pizza India Plans 500 Stores in Country," *Indian Business Insight*, February 14, 2008, p. 20; Julie Jargon and Arlene Chang, "Yum Brands Bets on India's Young for Growth," *The Wall Street Journal*, December 12, 2009, p. B1; http://www.pizzahut.co.in, 2012.

Successful in the United States, Lil'Orbits ran an advertisement in *Commercial News USA*, a magazine showcasing products and services in foreign countries, that attracted 400 inquiries. Pleased with the response, the company set up an international franchise operation based on royalties and franchise fees. Now a network of international franchised distributors markets the machines and ingredients to potential vendors. The distributors pay Lil'Orbits a franchise fee and buy machines and ingredients directly from Lil'Orbits or from one of the licensed vendors worldwide, from which Lil'Orbits receives a royalty. This entry strategy has enabled the company to enter foreign markets with minimum capital investment outside the home country. The company has more than 20,000 franchised dealers in 85 countries. About 60 percent of the company's business is international.

Although franchising enables a company to expand quickly with minimum capital, there are costs associated with servicing franchisees. For example, to accommodate different tastes around the world, Lil'Orbits had to develop a more pastrylike, less sweet mix than that used in the United States. Other cultural differences have had to be met as well. For example, customers in France and Belgium could not pronounce the trade name Lil'Orbits, so Orbie is used instead. Toppings also had to be adjusted to accommodate different tastes. Cinnamon sugar is the most widely accepted topping, but in China, cinnamon is considered a medicine, so only sugar is used. In the Mediterranean region, the Greeks like honey, and chocolate sauce is popular in Spain. Powdered sugar is more popular than granulated sugar in France, where the donuts are eaten in cornucopia cups instead of on plates.

Strategic International Alliances

LO4

The increasing importance of international strategic alliances

A **strategic international alliance (SIA)** is a business relationship established by two or more companies to cooperate out of mutual need and to share risk in achieving a common objective. Strategic alliances have grown in importance over the last few decades as a competitive strategy in global marketing management. Strategic international alliances are sought as a way to shore up weaknesses and increase competitive strengths—that is, complementarity is key.[40] Firms enter into SIAs for several reasons: opportunities for rapid expansion into new markets, access to new technology,[41] more efficient production and innovation, reduced marketing costs, strategic competitive moves, and access to additional sources of products and capital. Studies have demonstrated that affiliations with prominent financial institutions makes potential partners more attractive,[42] and resource deployment stability enhances alliance performance.[43] Finally, evidence suggests that SIAs often contribute nicely to profits.

Among some of the more prominent SIAs have been Nokia (Finland)/ATT, Alibaba (China)/Microsoft, Tata (India)/Starbucks, and Renault (France)/Nissan (Japan). But perhaps the most visible SIAs are now in the airline industry. American Airlines, Cathay Pacific, British Airways, Japan Airlines, Mexicana, Iberia, Quantas, and eight others are partners in the Oneworld Alliance, which integrates schedules and mileage programs. Competing with Oneworld are the Star Alliance (led by United and Lufthansa) and SkyTeam (led by Air France, Delta, and KLM). These kinds of strategic

In the Star Alliance strategic alliance, Lufthansa and Thai Airlines share several aspects of their operations, including ticketing and reservations, catering, cargo, and airport slots. As the global airline industry continues to consolidate, more strategic partnerships are being formed and disappearing.

[40]Eric Fang and Shaoming Zou, "Antecedents and Consequences of Marketing Dynamic Capabilities in International Joint Ventures," *Journal of International Business Studies* 39, no. 1 (2008), pp. 1–27; Tony W. Tong and Jeffrey J. Reuer, "Competitive Consequences of Interfirm Collaboration: How Joint Ventures Shape Industry Profitability," *Journal of International Business Studies* 41, no. 6 (2010), pp. 1056–73.

[41]http://www.lilorbits.com, 2012.

[42]Jeffrey J. Reurer and Roberto Ragozzino, "Signals and International Alliance Formation: The Roles of Affiliations and International Activities," *Journal of International Business Studies* 45 (2014), pp. 321–37.

[43]Matthew J. Robson, Bodo B. Schlegelmilch, and Brigitte Bojkowszky, "Resource Deployment Stability and Performance in International Research-and-Development Alliances: A Self-Determination Theory Explanation," *Journal of International Marketing* 20, no. 1 (2012), pp. 1–18.

international alliances imply that there is a common objective; that one partner's weakness is offset by the other's strength; that reaching the objective alone would be too costly, take too much time, or be too risky; and that together their respective strengths make possible what otherwise would be unattainable. For example, during the recent turmoil in the global airline industry, Star Alliance began moving in the direction of buying aircraft, a new strategic innovation.

An SIA with multiple objectives involves C-Itoh (Japan), Tyson Foods (United States), and Provemex (Mexico). It is an alliance that processes Japanese-style yakitori (bits of marinated and grilled chicken on a bamboo stick) for export to Japan and other Asian countries. Each company had a goal and made a contribution to the alliance. C-Itoh's goal was to find a lower-cost supply of yakitori; because it is so labor intensive, it was becoming increasingly costly and noncompetitive to produce in Japan. C-Itoh's contribution was access to its distribution system and markets throughout Japan and Asia. Tyson's goal was new markets for its dark chicken meat, a by-product of demand for mostly white meat in the U.S. market. Tyson exported some of its excess dark meat to Asia and knew that C-Itoh wanted to expand its supplier base. But Tyson faced the same high labor costs as C-Itoh. Provemex, the link that made it all work, had as its goal expansion beyond raising and slaughtering chickens into higher value-added products for international markets. Provemex's contribution was to provide highly cost-competitive labor.

Through the alliance, they all benefited. Provemex acquired the know-how to bone the dark meat used in yakitori and was able to vertically integrate its operations and secure a foothold in a lucrative export market. Tyson earned more from the sale of surplus chicken legs than was previously possible and gained an increased share of the Asian market. C-Itoh had a steady supply of competitively priced yakitori for its vast distribution and marketing network. Thus, three companies with individual strengths created a successful alliance in which each contributes and each benefits.

Many companies also are entering SIAs to be in a strategic position to be competitive and to benefit from the expected growth in international markets.[44] As a case in point, when General Mills wanted a share of the rapidly growing breakfast-cereal market in Europe, it joined with Nestlé to create Cereal Partners Worldwide. The European cereal market was projected to be worth hundreds of millions of dollars as health-conscious Europeans changed their breakfast diet from eggs and bacon to dry cereal. General Mills's main U.S. competitor, Kellogg, had been in Europe since 1920 and controlled about half of the market.

For General Mills to enter the market from scratch would have been extremely costly. Although the cereal business uses cheap commodities as its raw materials, it is both capital and marketing intensive; sales volume must be high before profits begin to develop. Only recently has Kellogg earned significant profits in Europe. For General Mills to reach its goal alone would have required a manufacturing base and a massive sales force. Furthermore, Kellogg's stranglehold on supermarkets would have been difficult for an unknown to breach easily. The solution was a joint venture with Nestlé. Nestlé had everything General Mills lacked—a well-known brand name, a network of plants, and a powerful distribution system—except for the one thing that General Mills could provide: strong cereal brands.

The deal was mutually beneficial. General Mills provided the knowledge in cereal technology, including some of its proprietary manufacturing equipment, its stable of proven brands, and its knack for pitching these products to consumers. Nestlé provided its name on the box, access to retailers, and production capacity that could be converted to making General Mills's cereals. In time, Cereal Partners Worldwide intends to extend its marketing effort beyond Europe. In Asia, Africa, and Latin America, Cereal Partners Worldwide will have an important advantage over the competition because Nestlé is a dominant food producer.

---

[44]Tieying Yu, Mohan Subramaniam, and Albert A Cannella Jr., "Competing Globally, Allying Locally: Alliances between Global Rivals and Host-Country Factors," *Journal of International Business Studies* 44 (2013), pp. 117–37.

Exhibit 12.3
Building Strategic Alliances

Primary Relationship Activity	Typical Actions, Interactions, Activities	Key Relationship Skill
Dating	Senior executives leveraging personal networks	Good radar; good relationship self-awareness
	Wondering how to respond to inquiries	
	Wondering how to seek out possibilities	
Imaging	Seeing the reality in possibilities	Creating intimacy
	Creating a shared vision from being together	
	Involving trusted senior managers	
Initiating	Bringing key executives into action	Trust building
	Creating trust through face-to-face time	
Interfacing	Facilitating the creating of personal relationships at many levels	Partnering
	Traveling to partner facilities and engaging in technical conversations	
	Blending social and business time	
Committing	Demonstrating that managers are fully committed to the alliance and each other	Commitment
	Managing the conflict inherent in making hard choices	
	Accepting the reality of the alliance and its relationships	
Fine-tuning	Relying on mature and established relationships	Growing *with* another
	Facilitating interaction and relationships with future successors	

Source: Adapted from Robert E. Spekman, Lynn A. Isabella, with Thomas C. MacAvoy, *Alliance Competence* (New York: Wiley, 2000), p. 81. Reprinted with permission of John Wiley & Sons, Inc.

As international strategic alliances have grown in importance, more emphasis has been placed on a systematic approach to forming them. Most experts in the field agree that the steps outlined in Exhibit 12.3 will lead to successful and high-performance strategic alliances. In particular, we note the wide agreement regarding the importance of building trust in the interpersonal and institutional relationships as a prerequisite of success.[45] Of course, in international business there are no guarantees; the interface between differing ethical, cultural, and legal systems often makes matters more difficult.[46] And a key activity in all the steps outlined in the exhibit is international negotiation, the subject of Chapter 19.[47]

International Joint Ventures.

International joint ventures (IJVs) as a means of foreign market entry have accelerated sharply during the last 30 years. Besides serving as a means of lessening political and economic risks by the amount of the partner's contribution to the venture, IJVs provide a way to enter markets that pose legal and cultural barriers that is less risky than acquisition of an existing company.

[45]Robert E. Spekman, Lynn A. Isabella, with Thomas C. MacAvoy, *Alliance Competence* (New York: Wiley, 2000).

[46]Haisu Zhang, Chegli Shu, Xu Jaing, and Alan J. Malter, "Managing Knowledge for Innovation: The Role of Cooperation, Competition, and Alliance Nationality," *Journal of International Marketing* 18, no. 4 (2010), pp. 74–94; Kai Li, Dale Griffin, Heng Yue, and Longkai Zhao, "National Culture and Capital Structure Decisions: Evidence from Foreign Joint Ventures in China," *Journal of International Business Studies* 42, no. 4 (2011), pp. 477–503; Anupama Phene and Stephen Tallman, "Complexity, Context, and Governance in Biotechnology Alliances," *Journal of International Business Studies* 43, no. 1 (2012), pp. 61–83.

[47]Kam-hon Lee, Gong-ming Qian, Julie H. Yu, and Ying Ho, "Trading Favors for Marketing Advantage: Evidence from Hong Kong, China, and the United States," *Journal of International Marketing* 13 (2005), pp. 1–35; Daniel C. Bello, Constantine S. Katsikeas, and Matthew J. Robson, "Does Accommodating a Self-Serving Partner in an International Marketing Alliance Pay Off?" *Journal of Marketing* 74, no. 6 (2011), pp. 77–93.

A joint venture is different from other types of strategic alliances or collaborative relationships in that a joint venture is a partnership of two or more participating companies that have joined forces to create a separate legal entity. Joint ventures are different from minority holdings by an MNC in a local firm.

Four characteristics define joint ventures: (1) JVs are established, separate, legal entities; (2) they acknowledge intent by the partners to share in the management of the JV; (3) they are partnerships between legally incorporated entities, such as companies, chartered organizations, or governments, and not between individuals; and (4) equity positions are held by each of the partners.

However, IJVs can be hard to manage. The choice of partners and the qualities of the relationships between the executives are important factors leading to success.[48] Several other factors contribute to their success or failure as well: positions of partners in industrial networks,[49] how control is shared, relations with parents, institutional (legal) environments, marketing capabilities, experience, and the extent to which knowledge is shared across partners. Despite this complexity, nearly all companies active in world trade participate in at least one international joint venture somewhere; many companies have dozens of joint ventures. A recent Conference Board study indicated that 40 percent of *Fortune* 500 companies were engaged in one or more IJVs. Particularly in telecommunications and Internet markets, joint ventures are increasingly favored.

Around the Asia Pacific Rim, where U.S. companies face unfamiliar legal and cultural barriers, joint ventures are preferred to buying existing businesses. Local partners can often lead the way through legal mazes and provide the outsider with help in understanding cultural nuances. A JV can be attractive to an international marketer when it enables a company to utilize the specialized skills of a local partner, when it allows the marketer to gain access to a partner's local distribution system, when a company seeks to enter a market where wholly owned activities are prohibited, when it provides access to markets protected by tariffs or quotas, and when the firm lacks the capital or personnel capabilities to expand its international activities.

In China, a country considered to be among the most challenging in Asia, more than 50,000 joint ventures have been established in the 30 years since the government began allowing IJVs there. Among the many reasons IJVs are so popular is that they offer a way of getting around high Chinese tariffs, allowing a company to gain a competitive price advantage over imports. Manufacturing locally with a Chinese partner rather than importing achieves additional savings as a result of low-cost Chinese labor. Many Western brands are manufactured and marketed in China at prices that would not be possible if the products were imported.

A prominent example of a new U.S.–China joint venture is that agreed to by filmmakers James Cameron and and his Cameron Pace Group with two state-owned film production companies in Tianjin. Cameron's hope is that such direct access to the fastest growing film market in the world will help his firm make 3-D productions the global standard. His movie *Avatar* broke all records for Chinese audiences. Cameron expressed frustration with American film producers, who remain reluctant to shoot in the 3-D format.[50]

Consortia.   Consortia are similar to joint ventures and could be classified as such except for two unique characteristics: (1) They typically involve a large number of participants and (2) they frequently operate in a country or market in which none of the participants is currently active. Consortia are developed to pool financial and managerial resources and to

[48]Gokhan Ertug, Ilya R.P. Cuypers, Niels G. Noordenhaven, and Ben M. Mensaou, "Trust between International Joint Venture Partners: Effects of Home Countries," *Journal of International Business Studies* 44 (2013), pp. 263–82.

[49]Sunny Li Sun and Ruby P. Lee, "Enhancing Innovation through International Joint Venture Portfolios: From the Emerging Firm Perspective," *Journal of International Marketing* 21, no. 3 (2013), pp. 1–21; Weilei (Stone) Shi, Sunny Li Sun, Brian C. Pinkham, and Mike W. Ping, "Domestic Alliance Network to Attract Foreign Partners: Evidence from International Joint Ventures in China," *Journal of International Business Studies* 45 (2014), pp. 338–62.

[50]Gabrielle Jaffe, "James Cameron Launches Joint Venture for 3-D Films in China," *Los Angeles Times*, August 9, 2012, p. B3.

lessen risks. Often, huge construction projects are built under a consortium arrangement in which major contractors with different specialties form a separate company specifically to negotiate for and produce one job. One firm usually acts as the lead firm, or the newly formed corporation may exist independently of its originators.

Without a doubt, the most prominent international consortium has been Airbus, Boeing's European competitor in the global commercial aircraft market. Airbus Industrie was originally formed when four major European aerospace firms agreed to work together to build commercial airliners. In 2000, the four agreed to transform the consortium into a global company to achieve operations efficiencies that would allow it to compete better against Boeing. Meanwhile, Boeing joined together with its own consortium to develop the new 787 Dreamliner aircraft.

Sematech, the other candidate for most prominent consortium, was originally an exclusively American operation. Sematech is an R&D consortium formed in Austin, Texas, during the 1980s to regain America's lead in semiconductor development and sales from Japan. Members included firms such as IBM, Intel, Texas Instruments, Motorola, and Hewlett-Packard. However, at the turn of the millennium even Sematech went international. Several of the founding American companies left and were replaced by firms from Taiwan, Korea, Germany, and the Netherlands (still none from Japan). The firm is also broadening its own investment portfolio to include a greater variety of international companies.

All strategic international alliances are susceptible to problems of coordination. For example, some analysts blamed the international breadth of Boeing's 787 Dreamliner consortium for the costly delays in manufacturing the new jet. Further, circumstances and/or partners can change in ways that render agreements untenable, and often such corporate relationships are short lived. Ford and Nissan launched a joint venture minivan in 1992 called the Mercury Villager/Nissan Quest. The car was mildly successful in the U.S. market, but in 2002 the joint venture stopped producing the cars—that's two years earlier than the original contract called for. Now that Nissan is controlled by French automaker Renault, it began producing its own minivan in 2003 for sale in the United States. When General Motors formed a joint venture with Daewoo, its purpose was to achieve a significant position in the Asian car market. Instead, Daewoo used the alliance to enhance its own automobile technology, and by the time the partnership was terminated, GM had created a new global competitor for itself.

Nestlé has been involved in a particularly ugly dissolution dispute with Dabur India. The Swiss firm owned 60 percent and the Indian firm 40 percent of a joint venture biscuit company, Excelcia Foods. Following months of acrimony, Dabur filed a petition with the Indian government accusing Nestlé of indulging in oppression of the minority shareholder and of mismanaging the JV company. In particular, Dabur alleged that Nestlé was purposefully running Excelcia into bankruptcy so that Nestlé could wriggle out of its "non-compete obligations and go after the India-biscuit market using another brand." Nestlé countered that the problem had more to do with the partners' inability to agree on a mutually acceptable business plan. The dispute was eventually settled out of court by Nestlé buying Dabur's 40 percent interest, shortly after which Excelcia was closed in lieu of restructuring.

Direct Foreign Investment

A fourth means of foreign market development and entry is *direct foreign investment*, that is, investment within a foreign country. Companies may invest locally to capitalize on low-cost labor, to avoid high import taxes, to reduce the high costs of transportation to market, to gain access to raw materials and technology, or as a means of gaining market entry.[51] Firms may either invest in or buy local companies[52] or establish new operations facilities. The local firms enjoy important benefits aside from the investments themselves, such as substantial technology transfers and the capability to export to a more diversified customer base. As with the other modes of market entry, several factors have been

[51]Riikka M. Sarala and Eero Vaara, "Cultural Differences, Convergence, and Crossconvergence as Explanations of Knowledge Transfer in International Acquisitions," *Journal of International Business Studies* 41, no. 8 (2010), pp. 1365–90.

[52]Annie Gasparro, "Kellogg Wins Bid for Egyptian Firm," *The Wall Street Journal*, January 2, 2015, p. B3.

found to influence the structure and performance of direct investments: (1) timing[53]—first movers have advantages but are more risky; (2) the growing complexity and contingencies of contracts; (3) transaction cost structures; (4) technology and knowledge transfer;[54] (5) degree of product differentiation; (6) the previous experiences and cultural diversity of acquired firms;[55] and (7) advertising and reputation barriers. This mix of considerations and risks makes for increasingly difficult decisions about such foreign investments. But as off-putting legal restrictions[56] continue to ease with WTO and other international agreements, more and more large firms are choosing to enter markets via direct investment.

The growth of free trade areas that are tariff-free among members but have a common tariff for nonmembers creates an opportunity that can be capitalized on by direct investment. Similar to its Japanese competitors, Korea's Samsung has invested some $500 million to build television tube plants in Tijuana, Mexico, to feed the already huge NAFTA television industry centered there. Kyocera Corporation, a Japanese high-tech company, bought Qualcomm's wireless consumer phone business as a means of fast entry into the American market. Google bought Motorola not only for its technology, but also to enhance its participation in the Chinese market. Nestlé is seeking business in China through its purchase of local candy maker Hsu Fu Chi and, of course, Kraft bought Cadbury. Disney acquired UTV Software Communications Ltd. of India, aiming to open up both broadcast and mobile-gaming businesses in that important market. Microsoft purchased Nokia's mobile phone operations. Finally, Nestlé is building a new milk factory in Thailand to serve the ASEAN Free Trade Area.

A hallmark of global companies today is the establishment of manufacturing operations throughout the world. This trend will increase as barriers to free trade are eliminated and companies can locate manufacturing wherever it is most cost effective. The selection of an entry mode and partners are critical decisions, because the nature of the firm's operations in the country market is affected by and depends on the choices made. The entry mode affects the future decisions because each mode entails an accompanying level of resource commitment, and changing from one entry mode to another without considerable loss of time and money is difficult.

Organizing for Global Competition

An international marketing plan should optimize the resources committed to company objectives. The organizational plan includes the type of organizational arrangements and management process to be used and the scope and location of responsibility. Because organizations need to reflect a wide range of company-specific characteristics—such as size, level of policy decisions, length of chain of command, staff support, source of natural, personnel, and vendor resources, degree of control, cultural differences in decision-making styles,[57] centralization, and type or level of marketing

---

[53]Chris Changwha Chung, Seung-Hyun Lee, Paul W. Beamish, and Takehiko Isobe, "Subsidiary Expansion/Contraction during Times of Economic Crisis," *Journal of International Business Studies* 41, no. 3 (2010), pp. 500–516; Sea-Jin Chang and Nay Hyuk Rhee, "Rapid FDI Expansion and Firm Performance," *Journal of International Business Studies* 42, no. 8 (2011) pp. 995–1015.

[54]Henrik Bresman, Julian Birkinshaw, and Robert Nobel, "Knowledge Transfer in International Acquisitions," *Journal of International Business Studies* 41, no. 1 (2010), pp. 5–20; Julian Birkinshaw, Henrik Bressman, and Robert Nobel, "Knowledge Transfer in International Acquisitions: A Retrospective," *Journal of International Business Studies* 41, no. 1 (2010), pp. 21–26.

[55]Udo Zander and Lena Zander, "Opening the Grey Box: Social Communities, Knowledge, and Culture in Acquisitions," *Journal of International Business Studies* 41, no. 1 (2010), pp. 27–37.

[56]Desislava Dikova, Padma Roa Sahib, and Arjen van Witteloostuijn, "Cross-Border Acquisition Abandonment and Completion: The Effect of Institutional Differences and Organizational Learning in the International Business Service Industry, 1981–2001," *Journal of International Business Studies* 41, no. 2 (2010), pp. 223–45.

[57]Andreas Engelen and Malte Brettel, "A Cross-Cultural Perspective of Marketing Departments' Influence Tactics," *Journal of International Marketing* 19, no. 2 (2011), pp. 73–94; Peter C. Verhoef, Peter S.H. Leeflang, Jochen Reiner, Martin Natter, William Baker, Amir Griinstein, Anders Gustafsson, Pamela Morrison, and John Saunders, "A Cross-National Investigation into the Marketing Department's Influence within the Firm: Toward Initial Empirical Generalizations," *Journal of International Marketing* 19, no. 3 (2011), pp. 59–86.

involvement—trade-offs abound,[58] and devising a standard organizational structure is difficult. Many ambitious multinational plans meet with less than full success because of confused lines of authority, poor communications, and lack of cooperation between headquarters and subsidiary organizations.[59]

A single organizational structure that effectively integrates domestic and international marketing activities has yet to be devised. Companies face the need to maximize the international potential of their products and services without diluting their domestic marketing efforts. Companies are usually structured around one of three alternatives: (1) global product divisions responsible for product sales throughout the world; (2) geographical divisions responsible for all products and functions within a given geographical area; or (3) a matrix organization consisting of either of these arrangements with centralized sales and marketing run by a centralized functional staff, or a combination of area operations and global product management.

Companies that adopt the global product division structure are generally experiencing rapid growth and have broad, diverse product lines. General Electric is a good example, having reorganized its global operations into six product divisions—infrastructure, industrial, commercial financial services, NBC Universal, healthcare, and consumer finance.[60] Geographic structures work best when a close relationship with national and local governments is important.

The matrix form—the most extensive of the three organizational structures—is popular with companies as they reorganize for global competition. A matrix structure permits management to respond to the conflicts that arise among functional activity, product, and geography. It is designed to encourage sharing of experience, resources, expertise, technology, and information among global business units. At its core is better decision making, in which multiple points of view affecting functional activity, product, and geography are examined and shared. A matrix organization can also better accommodate customers who themselves have global operations and global requirements.

A company may be organized by product lines but have geographical subdivisions under the product categories. Both may be supplemented by functional staff support. Exhibit 12.4 shows such a combination. Modifications of this basic arrangement are used by a majority of large companies doing business internationally.

The turbulence of global markets requires flexible organizational structures though. Forty-three large U.S. companies studied indicated that they planned a total of 137 organizational changes for their international operations over a five-year period. Included were such changes as centralizing international decision making, creating global divisions, forming centers of excellence, and establishing international business units. Bausch & Lomb, one of the companies in the study, revamped its international organizational structure by collapsing its international division into a worldwide system of three regions and setting up business management committees to oversee global marketing and manufacturing strategies for four major product lines. Bausch & Lomb's goal was to better coordinate central activities without losing touch at the local level.

To the extent that there is a trend, two factors seem to be sought, regardless of the organizational structure: a single locus for direction and control and the creation of a simple line organization that is based on a more decentralized network of local companies.

Locus of Decision   Considerations of where decisions will be made, by whom, and by which method constitute a major element of organizational strategy. Management policy must be explicit about which decisions are to be made at corporate headquarters, which at international

---

[58]Paula Hortinha, Carmen Lages, and Luis Filipe Lages, "The Trade-Off between Customer and Technology Orientations: Impact on Innovation Capabilities and Export Performance," *Journal of International Marketing* 19, no. 3 (2011), pp. 36–58; Tao (Tony) Gao and Linda Hui Shi, "How Do Multinational Suppliers Formulate Mechanisms of Global Account Coordination? An Integrative Framework and Empirical Study," *Journal of International Marketing* 19, no. 4 (2011), pp. 61–87.

[59]Ingmar Bjorkman, Carl F. Fey, and Hyeon Jeong Park, "Institutional Theory and MNC Subsidiary HRM Practices: Evidence from a Three-Country Study," *Journal of International Business Studies* 38 (2007), pp. 430–46.

[60]Kelly Hewett and William O. Bearden, "Dependence, Trust, and Relational Behavior on the Part of Foreign Subsidiary Marketing Operations: Implications for Managing Global Marketing Operations," *Journal of Marketing* 65, no. 4 (October 2001), pp. 51–66.

Exhibit 12.4
Schematic Marketing Organization Plan Combining Product, Geographic, and Functional Approaches

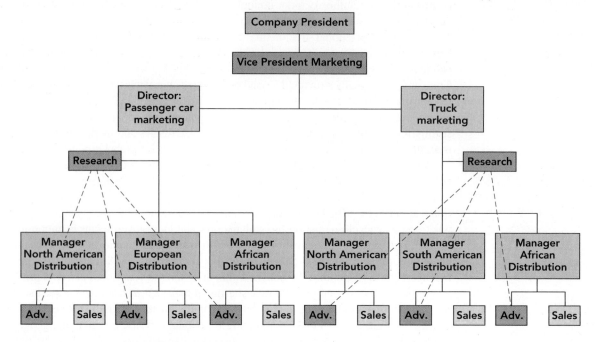

headquarters, which at regional levels, and which at national or even local levels. Most companies also limit the amount of money to be spent at each level. Decision levels for determination of policy, strategy, and tactical decisions must be established. Tactical decisions normally should be made at the lowest possible level, without country-by-country duplication. This guideline requires American headquarters' managers to trust the expertise of their local managers.[61] Of course, the best decisions will be made through interactive consultation, something the geographic distances often preclude.[62]

Centralized versus Decentralized Organizations

An infinite number of organizational patterns for the headquarters' activities of multinational firms exist, but most fit into one of three categories: centralized, regionalized, or decentralized organizations. The fact that all of the systems are used indicates that each has certain advantages and disadvantages. The chief advantages of centralization are the availability of experts at one location, the ability to exercise a high degree of control on both the planning and implementation phases, and the centralization of all records and information.

Some companies effect extreme decentralization by selecting competent local managers and giving them full responsibility for national or regional operations. These executives

[61]Francesco Ciabuschi, Mats Forsgren, and Oscar Martin Martin, "Rationality vs. Ignorance: The Role of MNE Headquarters in Subsidiaries' Innovation Processes," *Journal of International Business Studies* 42, no. 7 (2011), pp. 958–70; Elitsa R. Banalieva and Charles Dhanaraj, "Home-region Orientation in International Expansion Strategies," *Journal of International Business Studie* 44 (2013), pp. 89–116; Christian Homburg and Jana-Kristin Prigge, "Exploring Subsidiary Desire for Autonomy—A Conceptual Framework and Empirical Findings," *Journal of International Marketing* 22(4) (2014), pp. 21–43; Xiaowen Tian and John W. Slocum, "What Determines MNC Subsidiary Performance? Evidence from China," *Journal of World Business* 49 (2014), pp. 421–30.

[62]Esther Tippmann, Pamela Sharkey Scott, and Vincent Mangematin, "Problem Solving in MNCs: How Local and Global Solutins Are (and Are Not) Created," *Journal of International Business Studies* 43 (2012), pp. 746–71; Marc G. Baaij and Arjen H.L. Slangen, "The Role of Headquarters-Subsidiary Geographic Distance in Strategic Decisions by Spatially Disaggregated Headquarters" *Journal of International Business Studies* 44 (2013), pp. 941–52; Sjoerd Beugelskijk and Ram Mudambi, "MNEs as Border-Crossing Multi-Location Enterprises: The Role of Discontinuities in Geographic Space," *Journal of International Business Studies* 44 (2013), pp. 413–26; Shavin Malhotra and Ajai S. Gaur, "Spacial Geography and Control of Foreign Subsidiaries," *Journal of International Business Studies* 45 (2014), pp. 191–210.

are in direct day-to-day contact with the market but lack a broad company view, which can mean partial loss of control for the parent company.

In many cases, whether a company's formal organizational structure is centralized or decentralized, the informal organization reflects some aspect of all organizational systems. This reflection is especially true relative to the locus of decision making. Studies show that even though product decisions may be highly centralized, subsidiaries may have a substantial amount of local influence in pricing, advertising, and distribution decisions. If a product is culturally sensitive, the decisions are more likely to be decentralized.

Summary

Expanding markets around the world have increased competition for all levels of international marketing. To keep abreast of the competition and maintain a viable position for increasingly competitive markets, a global perspective is necessary. Global competition also requires quality products designed to meet ever-changing customer needs and rapidly advancing technology. Cost containment, customer satisfaction, and a greater number of players mean that every opportunity to refine international business practices must be examined in light of company goals. Collaborative relationships, strategic international alliances, strategic planning, and alternative market-entry strategies are important avenues to global marketing that must be implemented in the planning and organization of global marketing management.

Key Terms

Corporate planning	Direct exporting	Franchising	Joint venture
Strategic planning	Indirect exporting	Strategic international	
Tactical planning	Licensing	alliance (SIA)	

Questions

1. Define the key terms listed above.

2. Define strategic planning. How does strategic planning for international marketing differ from that for domestic marketing?

3. Discuss the benefits to an MNC of accepting the global market concept. Explain the three points that define a global approach to international marketing.

4. Discuss the effect of shorter product life cycles on a company's planning process.

5. What is the importance of collaborative relationships to competition?

6. In Phases 1 and 2 of the international planning process, countries may be dropped from further consideration as potential markets. Discuss some of the conditions that may exist in a country that would lead a marketer to exclude a country in each phase.

7. Assume that you are the director of international marketing for a company producing refrigerators. Select one country in Latin America and one in Europe and develop screening criteria to use in evaluating the two countries. Make any additional assumptions that are necessary about your company.

8. "The dichotomy typically drawn between export marketing and overseas marketing is partly fictional; from a marketing standpoint, they are but alternative methods of capitalizing on foreign market opportunities." Discuss.

9. How will entry into a developed foreign market differ from entry into a relatively untapped market?

10. Why do companies change their organizations when they go from being an international to a global company?

11. Formulate a general rule for deciding where international business decisions should be made.

12. Explain the popularity of joint ventures.

13. Compare the organizational implications of joint ventures versus licensing.

14. Visit the websites of General Motors and Ford, both car manufacturers in the United States. Search their sites and compare their international involvement. How would you classify each—as exporter, international, or global?

15. Using the sources in Question 14, list the different entry modes each company uses.

16. Visit the Nestlé Corporation website (http://www.nestle.com/) and the Unilever website (http://www.unilever.com/). Compare their strategies toward international markets. In what ways (other than product categories) do they differ in their international marketing?

Chapter 13

Products and Services for Consumers

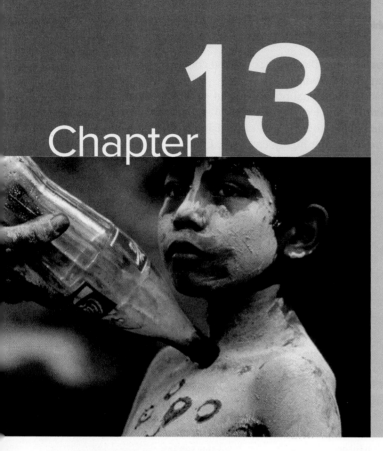

CHAPTER OUTLINE

CHAPTER LEARNING OBJECTIVES

What you should learn from Chapter 13:

LO1 The importance of offering a product suitable for the intended market

LO2 The importance of quality and how quality is defined

LO3 Physical, mandatory, and cultural requirements for product adaptation

LO4 The need to view all attributes of a product to overcome resistance to acceptance

LO5 Country-of-origin effects on product image

Global Perspective

CHINA—DISNEY ROLLS THE DICE AGAIN

With the opening of Disneyland in Anaheim in 1955, the notion of the modern theme park was born. The combination of the rides, various other attractions, and the Disney characters has remained irresistible. Tokyo Disneyland has also proved to be a success, making modest money for Disney through licensing and major money for its Japanese partners. Three-fourths of the visitors at the Tokyo park are repeat visitors, the best kind.

Then came EuroDisney. Dissatisfied with the ownership arrangements at the Tokyo park, the EuroDisney deal was structured very differently. Disney negotiated a much greater ownership stake in the park and adjacent hotel and restaurant facilities. Along with the greater control and potential profits came a higher level of risk.

Even before the park's grand opening ceremony in 1992, protestors decried Disney's "assault" on the French culture. The location was also a mistake—the Mediterranean climate of the alternative Barcelona site seemed much more attractive on chilly winter days in France. Managing both a multicultural workforce and clientele proved daunting. For example, what language was most appropriate for the Pirates of the Caribbean attraction—French or English? Neither attendance nor consumer purchases targets were achieved during the early years: Both were off by about 10 percent. By the summer of 1994, EuroDisney had lost some $900 million. Real consideration was given to closing the park.

A Saudi prince provided a crucial cash injection that allowed for a temporary financial restructuring and a general reorganization, including a new French CEO and a new name, Paris Disneyland. The Paris park returned to profitability, and attendance increased. However, when the temporary holiday on royalties, management fees, and leases expired, the Saudi prince injected another $33 million into the park. Most recently, a new $150 million attraction based on the movie *Ratatouille* has opened, tweaking Disney's offerings for Europeans. Now the Paris park attracts more than 11 million visitors annually.

In 2006 Hong Kong Disneyland opened for business. The Hong Kong government provided the bulk of the investment for the project (almost 80 percent of the $3 billion needed). As in Europe, the clientele is culturally diverse, though primarily Chinese. Performances are done in Cantonese (the local dialect), Mandarin (the national language), and English. The park drew 5.2 million visitors in 2006, but attendance fell sharply to about 4 million in 2007. Disney has had to renegotiate its financial structure and schedule as a consequence. On the positive side of the ledger, the Hong Kong park produced its first profits in 2013 and 2014— $14 million and $31 million, respectively. This has allowed the company to add the first Marvel attraction among all its parks worldwide—Iron Man will be added in 2015.

In 2009 the Chinese government approved a new park in Shanghai to be managed by the Hong Kong groups with a price tag of $4 billion, to be completed also in 2015. The two Chinese parks will offer a somewhat different array of characters and rides toward keeping both north and south Chinese customers pleased with their differentiated "personalities." Disney now has 11 major parks worldwide that attract more than 120 million visitors and deliver about $2 billion in profits annually. Indeed, it continues to be quite interesting to follow Mickey's international adventures; you might say it's been a rollercoaster ride.

Sources: http://www.disney.go.com; Frank Longid, "Disney, China Partner Will Spend $4.4 Billion Building Resort in Shanghai," *Bloomberg News,* April 8, 2011; Brady MacDonald, "Disneyland Paris Pulls Back the Veil on Ratatouille Dark Ride," *Los Angeles Times*, March 7, 2013, online; Brooks Barnes, "Disney to Add Hotel to Its Hong Kong Park," *The New York Times*, February 17, 2014, online.

The opportunities and challenges for international marketers of consumer goods and services today have never been greater or more diverse. New consumers are springing up in emerging markets in eastern Europe, the Commonwealth of Independent States, China and other Asian countries, India, Latin America—in short, globally. Although some of these emerging markets have little purchasing power today, they promise to be huge markets in the future. In the more mature markets of the industrialized world, opportunity and challenge also abound as consumers' tastes become more sophisticated and complex, and as increases in purchasing power provide them with the means of satisfying new demands.

As described in the Global Perspective, Disney is the archetypal American exporter for global consumer markets. The distinction between products and services for such companies means little. Their DVDs are *products*, whereas cinema performances of the same movies are *services*. Consumers at the theme parks (including foreign tourists at domestic sites) pay around $100 to get in the gate, but they also spend about the same amount on hats, T-shirts, and meals while there. And the movies, of course, help sell the park tickets and the associated toys and clothing. Indeed, this lack of distinction between products and services has led to the invention of new terms encompassing both products and services, such as *market offerings*[1] and *business-to-consumer (B2C) marketing*. However, the governmental agencies that keep track of international trade still maintain the questionable product–service distinction, and thus so do we in this chapter and the next.[2] The reader should also note that when it comes to U.S. exports targeting consumers, the totals are about evenly split among the three major categories of durable goods (such as cars and computers), nondurable goods (mainly food, drugs, toys), and services (e.g., tourism and telecommunications).

The trend for larger firms is toward becoming global in orientation and strategy. However, product adaptation is as important a task in a smaller firm's marketing effort as it is for global companies. As competition for world markets intensifies and as market preferences become more global, selling what is produced for the domestic market in the same manner as it is sold at home proves to be increasingly less effective. Some products cannot be sold at all in foreign markets without modification; others may be sold as is, but their acceptance is greatly enhanced when tailored specifically to market needs. In a competitive struggle, quality products and services that meet the needs and wants of consumers at an affordable price should be the goal of any marketing firm.

Quality

LO1

The importance of offering a product suitable for the intended market

Global competition is placing new emphasis on some basic tenets of business. It is shortening product life cycles and focusing on the importance of quality, competitive prices, and innovative products.[3] The power in the marketplace is shifting from a sellers' to a customers' market, and the latter have more choices because more companies are competing for their attention. More competition and more choices put more power in the hands of the customer, and that of course drives the need for quality. Gone are the days when the customer's knowledge was limited to one or at best just a few different products. Today the customer knows what is best, cheapest, and highest quality, largely due to the Internet and the smartphones in their pockets. It is the customer who defines quality in terms of his or her needs and resources. Research has shown that perceived quality can be used as a

---

[1]For example, see Philip Kotler and Kevin Lane Keller, *Marketing Management*, 14th ed. (Upper Saddle River, NJ: Prentice Hall, 2011).

[2]We hope that it is obvious that many of the points we make regarding the development of consumer products are pertinent to consumer services as well, and vice versa. Of course, some distinctions are still substantive. These are focused on in the section entitled "Marketing Consumer Services Globally" later in this chapter.

[3]David A. Griffith and Gaia Rubera, "A Cross-Cultural Investigation of New Product Strategies for Technological and Design Innovations," *Journal of International Marketing* 22, no. 1 (2014), pp. 5–20.

valuable market segmentation variable.[4] For example, new Apple smartphones are the rage in brand-conscious Japan.[5] But Docomo's older-model cell phones also sell well to philanderers (an oddly defined market indeed) because of privacy features.[6] While cell phones that don't roam don't sell in Japan at any price, but in China they do very well indeed. Just ask the folks at UTStarcom, a California firm that has sold low-cost, nonroaming mobile phones in India and Vietnam, as well as China.

American products have always been among the world's best, but competition is challenging us to make even better products. In most global markets, the cost and quality of a product are among the most important criteria by which purchases are made. For consumer and industrial products alike, the reason often given for preferring one brand over another is better quality at a competitive price. Quality, as a competitive tool, is not new to the business world, but many believe that it is the deciding factor in world markets. However, we must be clear about what we mean by quality.

Quality Defined

LO2

The importance of quality and how quality is defined

Quality can be defined on two dimensions: market-perceived quality and performance quality. Both are important concepts, but consumer perceptions of a quality product often have more to do with market-perceived quality than performance quality. The relationship of quality (of course, relative to price) conformance to customer satisfaction is analogous to an airline's delivery of quality. If viewed internally from the firm's perspective (performance quality), an airline has achieved quality conformance with a safe flight and landing. But because the consumer expects performance quality to be a given, quality to the consumer is more than compliance (a safe flight and landing). Rather, cost, timely service, frequency of flights, comfortable seating, and performance of airline personnel from check-in to baggage claim are all part of the customer's experience that is perceived as being of good or poor quality. Considering the number of air miles flown daily, the airline industry is approaching zero defects in quality conformance, yet who will say that customer satisfaction is anywhere near perfection?

We must also note here that industry critics argue strongly that firms frequently and purposefully misrepresent the performance quality of their products in their advertising and public relations campaigns. This criticism has been shown quite valid with respect to the safety and health performance of tobacco products. Auto, pharmaceutical, and food-processing firms are often accused of similar unethical corporate practices. The culpable firms often settle the associated lawsuits out of court. Such corporate malfeasance begs, and often yields, increasing government regulations across countries toward protecting the public's safety and health.[7] These market-perceived quality attributes are embedded in the total product, that is, the physical or core product and all the additional features the consumer expects. Two prominent, negative examples effectively support the notion that customers define quality. Kodak failed to understand that quality to consumers meant the convenience of digital technologies. Nokia clung to the idea that mobile handsets were mainly for calling people.[8]

---

[4]James Argarwal, Naresh K. Malhotra, and Ruth N. Bolton, "A Cross-National and Cross-Cultural Approach to Global Market Segmentation: An Application Using Consumers' Perceived Quality," *Journal of International Marketing* 18, no. 3 (2010), pp. 18–40.

[5]Daisuke Wakabayashi and Mayumi Negishi, "Japan Becomes Surprising Growth Market for Apple," *The Wall Street Journal*, November 11, 2013, pp. B1, 6.

[6]Daisuke Wakabayashi, "Japan's Philanderers Stay Faithful to Their 'Infidelity Phones.'" *The Wall Street Journal*, January 11, 2013, online.

[7]David Glen Mick, Simone Pettigrew, Cornelia Pechmann, and Julie L. Ozanne, *Transformative Consumer Research For Personal and Collective Well-Being* (New York: Routledge, 2012); Robert H. Lustig, *Fat Chance: Beating the Odds Against Sugar, Processed Food, Obesity, and Disease* (New York: Plume, 2012); Nicholas Freudenberg, *Lethal but Legal: Corporations, Consumption, and Protecting Public Health* (New York: Oxford University Press, 2014);

[8]Matthew Lynn, "The Fallen King of Finland," *Bloomberg Businessweek*, September 20, 2010, pp. 7–8; Elizabeth A. Sullivan, "Cowboy Up," *Marketing News*, January 31, 2012, pp. 18–21.

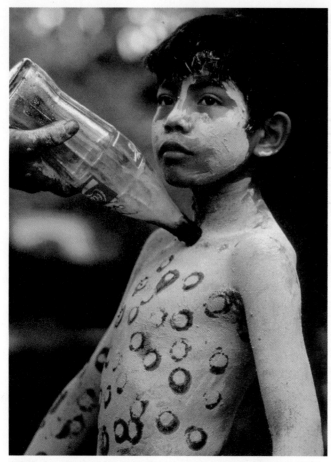

Products are not used in the same ways in all markets. Here, a boy in an eastern Mexican village is prepared for a "Jaguar dance" to bring rain. Clay, ashes, and the globally ubiquitous Coke bottle make for the best cat costumes. Perhaps our favorite example comes from India; in the Punjab region, *lassi* bars, a popular yoghurt drink, are often prepared in top-load washing machines!

In a competitive marketplace in which the market provides choices, most consumers expect performance quality to be a given. Naturally, if the product does not perform up to their standards, it will be rejected. Compare hybrid gas-electric systems for example—Toyota's is designed to save fuel in city driving; General Motors's performs best on the highway during long trips. Which drive system offers higher quality depends on the consumer's needs. Japanese consumers find themselves stuck in traffic more frequently, whereas Americans tend toward road trip types of activities. When there are alternative products, all of which meet performance quality standards, the product chosen is the one that meets market-perceived quality attributes.

Interestingly, China's leading refrigerator maker recognized the importance of these market-perceived quality attributes when it adopted a technology that enabled consumers to choose from 20 different colors and textures for door handles and moldings. For example, a consumer can design an off-white refrigerator with green marble handles and moldings. Why is this important? Because it lets consumers "update their living rooms," where most Chinese refrigerators are parked. The company's motive was simple: It positioned its product for competition with multinational brands by giving the consumer another expression of quality.

Quality is also measured in many industries by objective third parties. In the United States, J.D. Power and Associates has expanded its auto quality ratings, which are based on consumer surveys, to other areas, such as computers. Customer satisfaction indexes developed first in Sweden are now being used to measure customer satisfaction across a wide variety of consumer products and services.[9] Another dimension of quality for imported products is the "fair trade" designation. Fair Trade USA provides a certification that ensures that farmers in emerging economies receive a fair price for the coffee, tea, chocolate, rice, and other products they produce, instead of selling at the lower market price to a middleman.[10] Finally, the U.S. Department of Commerce annually recognizes American firms for the quality of their international offerings— Motorola and the Ritz Carlton Hotel chain have won the prestigious Malcolm Baldrige Quality Award twice. Solar Turbines International, a division of Caterpillar, has also won the Baldridge Award, and it is featured in our next chapter.

Maintaining Quality

Maintaining performance quality is critical, but frequently a product that leaves the factory with performance quality is damaged as it passes through the distribution chain. This damage is a special problem for many global brands for which production is distant from the market and/or control of the product is lost because of the distribution system within the market. When Mars Company's Snickers and other Western confectioneries were introduced to Russia, they were a big hit. Foreign brands such as Mars, Toblerone, Waldbaur, and Cadbury were the top brands—indeed, only one Russian brand placed in the top ten. But within five years, the Russian brands had retaken eight of the top spots, and only one U.S. brand, Mars's Dove bars, was in the top ten.

[9]Claes Fornell, Michael D. Johnson, Eugene W. Anderson, Jaesung Cha, and Barbara Everitt Bryant, "The American Consumer Satisfaction Index: Nature, Purpose, and Findings," *Journal of Marketing* 60, no. 4 (October 1996), pp. 35–46; http://www.cfigroup.com, 2015.

[10]Eve Mitchell, "A Top Importer of Fair Trade," *Los Angeles Times,* January 23, 2012, p. A11.

Red October brand chocolate (on the left) still competes well against foreign rivals Nestlé and Mars on Moscow store shelves. One advertising executive in Moscow reports that Russians are experiencing a renewed nationalism in product preferences. We have no idea what the "for Men" appeal is all about, but it apparently works in Moscow.

What happened? A combination of factors caused the decline of the foreign brands. Russia's Red October Chocolate Factory got its act together; modernized its packaging, product mix, and equipment; and set out to capture the market. Performance quality was also an issue. When the Russian market opened to outside trade, foreign companies eager to get into the market dumped surplus out-of-date and poor-quality products. In other cases, chocolates were smuggled in and sold on street corners and were often mishandled in the process. By the time they made it to consumers, the chocolates were likely to be misshapen or discolored—poor quality compared with Russia's Red October chocolate.

Market-perceived quality was also an issue. Russian chocolate has a different taste because of its formulation—more cocoa and chocolate liqueur are used than in Western brands, which makes it grittier. Thus, the Red October brand appeals more to Russian tastes, even though it is generally priced above Western brands. As evinced by this example, quality is not just desirable, it is essential for success in today's competitive global market, and the decision to standardize or adapt a product is crucial in delivering quality.

Toyota has long been known for its high-quality automobiles. But in 2009, at the height of its dominance of the global automobile industry (GM relinquished the global market-share title that year, during its bankruptcy), it suffered a quality maintenance *tsunami*. Sticky gas pedals appeared to contribute to unintended, sudden acceleration in Toyotas sold in the United States. The quality problem was linked to 34 deaths in the United States since 2000 by interrogators at congressional hearings, which included testimony by Akio Toyoda, the Japanese CEO of Toyota Motor Corporation. This linking of deaths to quality problems will be a matter for the U.S. courts to decide however, and facts in such cases—such as driver error versus mechanical problems—are hard to pin down. Indeed, Ford actually received more complaints about the sudden unintended acceleration problem than Toyota between 2004 and 2009, according to National Highway Traffic Safety Administration figures. But one of the main topics discussed during the congressional hearings was Toyota's consumer complaint handling and internal communications between the U.S. sales subsidiary and decision makers in Japan. The length of time between consumer complaints and the 6 million-car recall was a central issue. In his Japanese-style apology (see Chapter 5) to the American people during the hearings, Toyoda stated, "I myself, as well as Toyota, am not perfect. We never run away from our problems or pretend we don't notice them." But, not "noticing them" was a chief complaint voiced by the firm's critics. As the lawsuits around this issue play out in the years to come, it will be interesting to see the impact of his apology on juries. And of course, the impact of this quality problem and the "late" recall will be determined by the jury of public opinion and the previously loyal customers of the brand.[11] In Exhibit 13.3 later in the chapter, we do note that Toyota's brand equity has recently gained smartly.

Physical or Mandatory Requirements and Adaptation

LO3

Physical, mandatory, and cultural requirements to product adaptation

A product may have to change in a number of ways to meet the physical or mandatory requirements of a new market, ranging from simple package changes to total redesign of the physical core product. In many countries, the term product homologation is used to describe the changes mandated by local product and service standards. A recent study reaffirmed the often-reported finding that mandatory adaptations were more frequently the reason for product adaptation than adapting for cultural reasons.

Some needed changes are obvious with relatively little analysis; a cursory examination of a country will uncover the need to rewire electrical goods for a different voltage

[11]Several articles on the topic including Joseph B. White and Peter Landers, "Toyoda is Wary Star of Kabuki at Capitol," *The Wall Street Journal*, February 25, 2010, pp. A1, A7.

Oliwer Kmiecik, Akio Toyoda's statement to Congress, February 24, 2010

system,[12] simplify a product when the local level of technology is not high, or print multilingual labels where required by law. IKEA issues product safety warnings in 26 languages. Electrolux, for example, offers a cold-wash-only washing machine in Asian countries where electric power is expensive or scarce. Other necessary changes may surface only after careful study of an intended market.

Legal, economic, political, technological, and climatic requirements of the local marketplace often dictate product adaptation. During a period in India when the government strongly opposed foreign investment, PepsiCo. changed its product name to Lehar-Pepsi (in Hindi, *lehar* means "wave") to gain as much local support as possible. The name returned to Pepsi-Cola when the political climate turned favorable. Laws that vary among countries usually set specific package sizes, labeling requirements, and safety and quality standards. The World Health Organization is only beginning to regulate the marketing of high-carcinogen American cigarettes. But videogame content is regulated around the world according to violence levels and sexual content.

The less economically developed a market is, the greater degree of change a product may need for acceptance. One study found that only 1 in 10 products could be marketed in developing countries without modification of some sort. To make a purchase more affordable in low-income countries, the number of units per package may have to be reduced from the typical quantities offered in high-income countries. Razor blades, cigarettes, chewing gum, and other multiple-pack items are often sold singly or two to a pack instead of the more customary 10 or 20. Mary Kay sells its fragrances in Latin America in smaller packages, because women there prefer a wardrobe of fragrances, not just one. Cheetos, a product of PepsiCo.'s Frito-Lay, is packaged in 15-gram boxes in China so it can be priced at 1 yuan, or about 12 cents. At this price, even children with little spending money can afford Cheetos.

Changes may also have to be made to accommodate climatic differences.[13] General Motors of Canada, for example, experienced major problems with several thousand Chevrolet automobiles shipped to a Middle Eastern country; GM quickly discovered they were unfit for the hot, dusty climate. Supplementary air filters and different clutches had to be added to adjust for the problem. Exports of cars made in America have been booming recently, to the extent that Ford is now selling its homologated Mustang for the first time overseas.[14] While this new trend is very good for American-made cars, now China is gearing up to send its autos around the world by requiring its parts makers to meet international standards.[15]

Perhaps our favorite example of product homologation comes from China. Oreos were first introduced there in 1996, but the company didn't adapt them to Chinese tastes until 9 years later. Now they're the top-selling biscuit in the country, after consumer research suggested reducing the sugar content and reducing package sizes and prices. Now Kraft has developed new flavors just for China—the traditional chocolate cookie surrounds a green tea filling or a "fruit duo" filling such as orange/mango or peach/grape.[16] Of course, the integrated marketing communications campaign also helped[17]—we detail that in Chapter 16. Because most products sold abroad by international companies originate in home markets and require some form of modification, companies need a systematic process to identify products that need adaptation.[18]

---

[12]Fortunately, now the USB cable is solving more and more of this problem—see "Edison's Revenge," *The Economist*, October 19, 2013, pp. 65–66.

[13]Philip M. Parker and Nader T. Tavossoli, "Homeostasis and Consumer Behavior across Cultures," *International Journal of Research in Marketing* 17, no. 1 (March 2000), pp. 33–53.

[14]Bil Saporito, "American Idol" *Time*, December 16, 2013, pp. 36–38.

[15]Keith Bradsher, "China Hints at Effort to Export Cars to West," *The New York Times*, October 18, 2013, p. B3.

[16]Sanette Tanaka, "What's Selling Where—Oreo Cookies," *The Wall Street Journal*, August 30, 2012, p. D2.

[17]Julie Jargon, "Kraft Reformulates Oreo, Scores in China," *The Wall Street Journal*, May 1, 2008, pp. B1, B7.

[18]Magnus Hultman, Matthew J. Robson, and Constantine S. Katsikeas, "Export Product Strategy Fit and Performance: An Empirical Investigation," *Journal of International Marketing* 17, no. 4 (2009), pp. 1–23.

Green Marketing and Product Development

A quality issue of growing importance the world over, especially in Europe and the United States, is green marketing. Europe has been at the forefront of the "green movement," with strong public opinion and specific legislation favoring environmentally friendly marketing and products.[19] Green marketing is a term used to identify concern with the environmental consequences of a variety of marketing activities. The European Commission has passed legislation to control all kinds of packaging waste throughout the European Union. Two critical issues that affect product development are the control of the packaging component of solid waste and consumer demand for environmentally friendly products.

In the United States, Japanese car manufacturers took advantage of their gas-guzzling American cousins as consumers became more concerned about the environmental effects of SUVs like General Motors's Hummer. Indeed, even in the United States the Hummer has largely died a timely death. Four-dollar gasoline and the bankruptcy of General Motors in 2009 killed the beast, and not even a Chinese bailout could save the behemoth.[20] Harley Davidson is now producing a plug-in electric motorcycle. It will see how the "electric hog" will sell overseas, where Harley's bad-boy image has worked so well.[21] In China, green opportunities abound. Perhaps one of the largest is related to the explosion of the demand for refrigerators there, which both use electricity and potentially leak air-polluting refrigerants.[22]

The European Commission issued guidelines for ecolabeling that became operational in 1992. Under the directive, a product is evaluated on all significant environmental effects throughout its life cycle, from manufacturing to disposal—a cradle-to-grave approach. A detergent formulated to be biodegradable and nonpolluting would be judged friendlier than a detergent whose formulation would be harmful when discharged into the environment. Aerosol propellants that do not deplete the ozone layer are another example of environmentally friendly products. No country's laws yet require products to carry an ecolabel to be sold, however. The designation that a product is "environmentally friendly" is voluntary, and environmental success depends on the consumer selecting the ecology-friendly product.

Since the introduction of the ecolabel idea, Hoover washing machines early on gained approval for its use. Interestingly enough, the benefits of winning the symbol have resulted in Hoover tripling its market share in Germany and doubling its share of the premium sector of the U.K. washing-machine market. The approval process seems to be deterring many European manufacturers, many of which are using their own, unofficial symbols. The National Consumer Council, a consumer watchdog group, reports that many consumers are so confused and cynical about the myriad symbols that they are giving up altogether on trying to compare the green credentials of similar products.

Laws that mandate systems to control solid waste, while voluntary in one sense, do carry penalties. The EU law requires that packaging material through all levels of distribution, from the manufacturer to the consumer, be recycled or reused. Currently, between 50 percent and 65 percent of the weight of the packaging must be recovered, and between 25 percent and 45 percent of the weight of the totality of packaging materials contained in packaging waste will be recycled.

Each level of the distribution chain is responsible for returning all packaging, packing, and other waste materials up the chain. The biggest problem is with the packaging the customer takes home; by law the retailer must take back all packaging from the customer if no central recycling locations are available. For the manufacturer's product to participate in direct collection and not have to be returned to the retailer for recycling, the manufacturer must

[19]Leonidas C. Leonidou, Constantine S. Katsikeas, Thomas A. Fotiadis, and Paul Christodoulides, "Antecedents and Consequences of an Eco-Friendly Export Marketing Strategy: The Moderating Role of Foreign Public Concern and Competitive Intensity," *Journal of International Marketing* 21, no. 3 (2013), pp. 22–46.

[20]Nick Bunkley, "G.M. Deal for Hummer Falls Apart," *The New York Times*, February 25, 2010, pp. B1, B4.

[21]Bill Saborito, "This Harley Is Electric," *Time*, June 30, 2014, pp. 50–52.

[22]Nicola Twilley, "The Price of Cold," *The New York Times Magazine*, July 27, 2014, pp. 28–32.

CROSSING BORDERS 13.1

In Germany, Video Games Showing Frontal Nudity Are OK, but Blood Is *Verboten*

Video game heroine Lara Croft is an adrenaline junkie unafraid of getting bloody. But in Germany, the buxom starlet of the "Tomb Raider" series doesn't bleed—even if she's being mauled by a tiger.

Although the $25 billion video game industry is global, the games themselves aren't. They reflect the distinct cultures and traditions of different markets, and game publishers carefully tweak their titles and other details to tone down offensive materials. And "offensive" varies from country to country.

Red blood in a game sold in the United States turns green in Australia. A topless character in a European title acquires a bikini top in the United States. Human enemies in an American game morph into robots in Germany. Violent sex scenes in a Japanese game disappear in the American versions.

Of all countries, Germany is one of the trickiest to tackle, publishers say. The country has spent five decades developing one of the world's strictest decency standards for virtually all media, from books and comics to music and games.

If a game features blood splatterings, decapitations, or death cries, it runs the risk of being placed on a government list known as "the index." Being indexed means it can't be sold to anyone under 18, displayed in stores, or advertised on television, in newspapers, or in magazines. Games containing pornography or glorifications of war, Nazism, and racial hatred face the same fate. Most recently the government has announced plans to forbid the sales of such graphic video games to minors.

Finally we note that the Germans are taking another tack against the games—a study there has shown that assigning more homework reduces time spent on games! Meanwhile, in the United States, the Supreme Court has ruled unconstitutional a California law to prevent sale of violent games to minors, on the basis of freedom of speech. Meanwhile, China is going the other way—it has finally opened its market to previously banned video game consoles, which were believed to promote violence. Microsoft's Xbox One is now being offered there.

Sources: A. Phan and S. Sandell, "In Germany, Video Games Showing Frontal Nudity Are OK, but Blood Is *Verboten,*" *Los Angeles Times*, June 9, 2003, p. C1. Used with permission. Melissa Bell, "Supreme Court Rules Violent Video Game Ban Unconstitutional: Was it the Most Violent Game?" *Washington Post*, June 27, 2011; Dina Bass, Edmond Lococo, Tian Chen, and Bruce Einhorn, "Microsoft Looks Abroad For an Xbox One Rescue," *Bloomberg Businessweek*, October 2, 2014, pp. 42, 43.

guarantee financial support for curbside or central collection of all materials. The growing public and political pressure to control solid waste is a strong incentive for compliance.

Although the packaging and solid waste rules are burdensome, there have been successful cases of not only meeting local standards but also being able to transfer this approach to other markets. Procter & Gamble's international operations integrated global environmental concerns as a response to increasing demands in Germany. It introduced Lenor, a fabric softener in a superconcentrated form, and sold it in a plastic refill pouch that reduced packaging by 85 percent. This move increased brand sales by 12 percent and helped set a positive tone with government regulators and activists. The success of Lenor was transferred to the United States, where P&G faced similar environmental pressures. A superconcentrated Downy, the U.S. brand of fabric softener, was repackaged in refill pouches that reduced package sizes by 75 percent, thereby costing consumers less and actually increasing Downy market share. The global marketer should not view green marketing as a European problem; concern for the environment is worldwide (recall our Cambodian monkey with the Coke can in Chapter 3), and similar legislation is sure to surface elsewhere. This discussion is yet another example of the need to adapt products for global marketing.

Products and Culture

To appreciate the complexity of standardized versus adapted products, one needs to understand how cultural influences are interwoven with the perceived value and importance a market places on a product.[23] A product is more than a physical item: It is a bundle of satisfactions (or *utilities*) that the buyer receives. These utilities include

---

[23]Julien Dayla and Giana M. Eckhardt, "Asian Brands and the Shaping of a Transnational Imagined Community," *Journal of Consumer Research* 35 (2008), pp. 216–30.

Cola Turka holds a surprisingly large percentage of shelf space vis-à-vis Coke and Pepsi in this supermarket in Istanbul. The 2-liter bottle is priced at 2.00 lira, just under Coke's 2.05 lira. Cola Turka's TV ads, initially featuring American actor Chevy Chase speaking Turkish, seem to have worked well. Check youtube.com for Cola Turka ads.

its form, taste, color, odor, and texture; how it functions in use; the package; the label; the warranty; the manufacturer's and retailer's servicing; the confidence or prestige enjoyed by the brand; the manufacturer's reputation; the country of origin; and any other symbolic utility received from the possession or use of the goods. In short, the market relates to more than a product's physical form and primary function.[24] The values and customs within a culture confer much of the importance of these other benefits. In other words, a product is the sum of the physical and psychological satisfactions it provides the user.

A product's physical attributes generally are required to create its primary function. The primary function of an automobile, for example, is to move passengers from point A to point B. This ability requires a motor, transmission, and other physical features to achieve its primary purpose. The physical features or primary function of an automobile generally are in demand in all cultures where there is a desire to move from one point to another by ways other than by foot or animal power. Few changes to the physical attributes of a product are required when moving from one culture to another. However, an automobile has a bundle of psychological features that are as important in providing consumer satisfaction as its physical features. Within a specific culture, other automobile features (color, size, design, brand name, price) have little to do with its primary function—the movement from point A to B—but do add value to the satisfaction received.

The meaning and value imputed to the psychological attributes of a product can vary among cultures and are perceived as negative or positive. To maximize the bundle of satisfactions received and to create positive product attributes rather than negative ones, adaptation of the nonphysical features of a product may be necessary. Coca-Cola, frequently touted as a global product, found it had to change Diet Coke to Coke Light when it was introduced in Japan. Japanese women do not like to admit to dieting, because the idea of a diet implies sickness or medicine. So instead of emphasizing weight loss, "figure maintenance" is stressed. Anti-American sentiment is also causing Coke problems with Muslim consumers. At least four new competitors have popped up recently—Mecca Cola, Muslim Up, Arab Cola, and Cola Turka. McDonald's is also responding to such problems with its new McArabia sandwich.

Adaptation may require changes of any one or all of the psychological aspects of a product. A close study of the meaning of a product shows the extent to which the culture determines an individual's perception of what a product is and what satisfaction that product provides.

The adoption of some products by consumers can be affected as much by how the product concept conforms with their norms, values, and behavior patterns as by its physical or mechanical attributes. For example, only recently have Japanese consumers taken an interest in dishwashers—they simply didn't have room in the kitchen. However, very compact designs by Mitsubishi, Toto (a Japanese toilet company), and others are making new inroads into Japanese kitchens. A novelty always comes up against a closely integrated cultural pattern, and this conflict is primarily what determines whether, when, how, and in what form it gets adopted. Some financial services have been difficult to introduce into Muslim countries because the pious have claimed they promoted usury and gambling, both explicitly forbidden in the Koran. The Japanese have historically found all body jewelry repugnant. The Scots have a decided resistance to pork and all its associated products, apparently from days long ago when such taboos were founded on fundamentalist interpretations of the Bible. Filter cigarettes have failed in at least one Asian country because a very low life expectancy hardly places people in the age bracket most prone to fears of lung cancer—even supposing that they shared Western attitudes about death. All these sorts of problems require product offering adaptation by international marketers.

---

[24]C. K. Prahalad, *The Fortune at the Bottom of the Pyramid* (Philadelphia: Wharton School Publishing, 2005).

A Philips Design engineer perfects the technology and efficiency of the stove producing one kind of quality, the engineering sort.

In Africa, as in India, cattle dung is an important source of fuel.

Fuel can be hard to find and hard to transport. Cutting the time and effort spent by as much as 80 percent in rural areas would allow for other productive activities for both women and children, as well as promote personal safety for both groups. In addition to dung and wood, corn cobs and charcoal can be used as fuel.

In Africa and around the world, one of the greatest risks of living in transitional areas (slums) in big cities is the danger of wildfires, often started by careless cooking methods using open fires.

Here you can see the design of the stove. This is the forced air version, using a battery-powered fan to draw air into the top of the flame through the hollow sides of the stove. The forced air model pictured burns at a very high temperature. To contain the heat properly, a ceramic-walled combustion chamber must be used for safety and to ensure a long economic life.

PHILIPS DESIGN
The Product Development Process

In Chapter 5 (page 160) we described Philips's development of a smokeless wood/dung burning stove for India. Herein we portray an effort to apply the technology to develop a new stove to be used in urban slums and rural villages in Africa. The problems are twofold in low-income areas in both regions: (1) traditional cooking methods produce large amounts of unhealthful smoke in homes and (2) traditional open fires are substantial community fire hazards, particularly in densely populated slums. Review the pictures moving clockwise starting with the picture below of the tragic slum fire.

In the Philips Design laboratories in Eindhoven, the Netherlands, two new models of smokeless wood stoves were designed: a forced air model and a natural draft model. Both stoves save large amounts of fuel compared with traditional open fires. They also reduce the amount of smoke produced

Local UNDC personnel help make introductions to rural villagers in Lesotho. Philips makes it a practice to collaborate on almost all R&D projects with organizations around the world: private, public, and NGOs. As one executive put it, "We have smart people at Philips, but we don't have all the smart people."

Here stoves are distributed by the Philips field team to potential users in a rural village. The stoves are free, so everybody is happy.

Before the actual field testing, the stoves were demonstrated to a variety of officials, including the Prime Minister of Lesotho; the Ministers of Trade, Health, Energy, and Natural Resources; the Director General of UNIDO; local NGOs; and local village leaders.

during cooking by injecting air into the top of the combustion chamber. This causes the smoke, which is essentially unburned fuel, to continue burning.

The stoves use 80 percent less fuel and thereby yield four additional advantages: (1) less time is spent looking for and transporting fuel; (2) more time becomes available for other useful activity, such as micro-industry or school; (3) deforestation is reduced dramatically; and (4) CO_2 emissions are cut as significantly as fuel consumption.

Careful design in the laboratory is never good enough though. Field testing is crucial. Philips collaborated with a variety of organizations in the product to perform the field testing: the people and government of Lesotho, the EU delegation to Lesotho, the Industrial Development Corporation (IDC) of South Africa, the United Nations Development Programme (UNDP), and the United Nations Industrial Development Organization (UNIDO).

African Clean Energy (ACE) has now begun producing the Philips-designed cookstove in Lesotho. As of 2013, it had produced 5,000 stoves and will expand capacity to 9,000 per month. Currently, the stoves sell for about $70, and the firm is working to fill orders for 14,000. But prices will come down dramatically with scale.[25]

The entire village received stoves.

A researcher interviews the users about their experiences with the stoves. Almost all of the comments were positive. But some complaints were voiced as well. Representative examples included: "The stoves should be bigger, in order to carry bigger pots," "it is difficult to add fuel when using a big pot," "the pots get black," "one needs to stay with the stove to add fuel," "only one pot can cook at a time," and "the natural draft stove fills up with ash when cooking for a long time."

The field trial report notes the complaints, but the response is overwhelmingly positive. Indeed, the stoves when widely distributed will ultimately sell for around $10. When the field test users were asked at what price they would sell their stoves back to Philips, they responded on average $25–$60.

[25]Jennifer Tweddell, "Partner Spotlight: African Clean Energy (ACE)," *Global Alliance for Clean Cookstoves* (http://www.cleancookstoves.org), April 30, 2013, online.

CROSSING BORDERS 13.2

Seeds of Fashion: Eastern vs. Western Counter-Culture Movements and a Look at the Gothic Lolitas of Harajuku, Japan

Where do new ideas come from? Since its origin, the Gothic Lolita subculture of Harajuku has continued to fascinate people around the world. This group is just one example of the counterculture fashion movements that have emerged from the Harajuku district of Japan, each group identified by a specific look that conveys a visual message. Gothic Lolita fashion infuses Victorian-era clothing with elements of Goth and Japanese *anime* to create a unique form of dress. Adherents take notes from the *Gothic & Lolita Bible* (a quarterly magazine with an estimated circulation of 100,000) and rely on their distinctive appearance to proclaim their subcultural identity. As in other counterculture movements, youths' fantasies of liberation, rebellion, and revolution have become embedded in the cultural mode of a changing nation.

By examining the fashion of the Harajuku, we can gain a more in-depth understanding of group affiliation and construction of self in counterculture movements. Definitive of a counterculture, the Gothic Lolita's in-group behavior and fashion evokes opposition and displays a symbolic rebellion against mainstream Japanese culture. These attitudes are reflected in norm-breaking and attention-grabbing styles.

In the past, youth subcultures generally have emerged from Western society and diffused globally. But the Harajuku subculture began in the East and is moving West, marking a shift in the cultural current. The Harajuku subculture is also an example of the difference between Eastern and Western counterculture movements. Whereas maturity in Western cultures is associated with authority and individuality, in Confucian Japan, maturity is the ability to cooperate with a group, accept compromises, and fulfill obligations to society. Therefore, rebellion in Japanese youth culture means rebellion against adulthood as well. Rather than engaging in sexually provocative or aggressive behaviors to emphasize their maturity and independence, as occurs among Western rebels, Japanese Gothic Lolitas display themselves in a childlike and vulnerable manner to emphasize their immaturity and inability to meet the social responsibilities and obligations of adulthood.

Likely because of this refusal to cooperate with social expectations, mainstream Japan views the subculture as selfish, especially considering its indulgent consumption behaviors. Unlike contemporary Western youth cultures, such as punk and grunge, the Gothic Lolita subculture does not condemn materialism or other aspects of modern consumer culture. Instead, one outfit (as seen in the accompanying photo) can cost as much as

Japanese women in an ad for Angelic Pretty fashions appearing in the *Gothic & Lolita Bible*.

$300–$1,000! Because personal consumption is regarded as both antisocial and immoral in Japanese society, the subculture opposes normative social values by indulging in the conspicuous consumption.

Most participants (aged 13–30 years) are students or have jobs that require them to wear a uniform every day. On Sundays, they feel they have reached the time they can truly be themselves. Their lifestyle is frowned upon, making it very common to see teenagers carrying bags with their "harajuku outfit" on the train and changing at the park so their parents never see their outfits. Others wear the clothing as their normal daily dress, but the vast majority save it for Sundays, when they congregate at Jingu Bridge and Yoyogi Park to show off their fashions, hang out, and meet others like them. Some go just to have their pictures taken by the subculture's magazine photographers, who search for shots of new trends, or by tourists.

Source: Kristen Schiele, "How Subcultures Regain Control through Reclamation: A Case of Commodification in Japan," working paper, Merage School of Business, University of California, Irvine, 2015. Used with permission.

When analyzing a product for a second market, the extent of adaptation required depends on cultural differences in product use and perception between the market the product was originally developed for and the new market. The greater these cultural differences between the two markets, the greater the extent of adaptation that may be necessary.[26] Research has also shown that firms with strong organizational identities can

---

[26]An excellent new book on this topic is John A. Quelch and Katherine E. Jocz's *All Business is Local* (New York: Portfolio/Penguin, 2012).

have more difficulty in adapting products adequately.[27] Another factor favoring adaptation is how a subsidiary is established—acquisition yields greater adaptation than greenfield investment.[28]

When instant cake mixes were introduced in Japan, the consumers' response was less than enthusiastic. Not only do Japanese reserve cakes for special occasions, but they prefer the cakes to be beautifully wrapped and purchased in pastry shops. The acceptance of instant cakes was further complicated by another cultural difference: Many Japanese homes do not have ovens. An interesting sidebar to this example is the company's attempt to correct for that problem by developing a cake mix that could be cooked in a rice cooker, which all Japanese homes have. The problem with that idea was that in a Japanese kitchen, rice and the manner in which it is cooked have strong cultural overtones, and to use the rice cooker to cook something other than rice is a real taboo. Of course, cake mixes were not readily accepted in the United States when they were introduced in 1949. For housewives, it didn't seem like they were baking if all they did was add water. Changing the formula to require adding eggs made the process feel more substantial, and the housewives were won over.

Examples are typically given about cultures other than American, but the need for cultural adaptation is often necessary when a foreign company markets a product in the United States, too. A major Japanese cosmetics company, Shiseido, attempted to break into the U.S. cosmetic market with the same products sold in Japan. After introducing them in more than 800 U.S. stores, the company realized that American taste in cosmetics is very different from Japanese tastes. The problem was that Shiseido's makeup required a time-consuming series of steps, a point that does not bother Japanese women. Success was attained after designing a new line of cosmetics as easy to use as American products.

The problems of adapting a product to sell abroad are similar to those associated with the introduction of a new product at home. Products are not measured solely by their physical specifications. The key characteristics of a new product are related with what it does to and/or for the customer with respect to his or her habits, tastes, and patterns of life. The problems illustrated in the cake mix example have little to do with the physical product or the user's ability to make effective use of it and more with the fact that acceptance and use of the cake mixes would have required upsetting behavior patterns considered correct or ideal.

Finally, there are some interesting surprises in the area of adaptation. An interesting example is Harry Potter. About 20 percent of the sales of his last adventure book in Japan were in English. Japanese consumers were looking for ways to augment English lessons, and the books and associated audiotapes filled that particular need very well. For them Potter is not just entertainment; it's education.

Innovative Products and Adaptation

An important first step in adapting a product to a foreign market is to determine the degree of newness as perceived by the intended market.[29] How people react to newness and how new a product is to a market must be understood. In evaluating the newness of a product, the international marketer must be aware that many products successful in the United States, having reached the maturity or even decline stage in their life cycles, may be perceived as new in another country or culture and thus must be treated as innovations. From a sociological viewpoint, any idea perceived as new by a group of people is an innovation.

[27]Julien Cayla and Lisa Penaloza, "Mapping the Play of Organizational Identity in Foreign Market Adaptation," *Journal of Marketing* 76, no. 6 (November 2012), pp. 38–54.

[28]Arjen H. L. Slangen and Desislava Dikova, "Planned Marketing Adaptation and Multinationals' Choices between Acquisitions and Greenfields," *Journal of International Marketing* 22, no. 2 (2014), pp.68–88.

[29]Junfeng Zhang, C. Anthony Di Benedetto, and Scott Hoenig, "Product Development Strategy, Product Innovation Performance, and the Mediating Role of Knowledge Utilization: Evidence from Subsidiaries in China," *Journal of International Marketing* 17, no. 2 (2009), pp. 42–58.

Whether or not a group accepts an innovation, and the time it takes to do so, depends on the product's characteristics.[30] Products new to a social system are innovations, and knowledge about the diffusion (i.e., the process by which innovation spreads) of innovation is helpful in developing a successful product strategy. Sony's marketing strategies for the U.S. introduction of its PlayStation 2 were well informed by its wild successes achieved six months earlier during the product's introduction in Japan. Marketing strategies can guide and control, to a considerable degree, the rate and extent of new product diffusion because successful new product diffusion is dependent on the ability to communicate relevant product information and new product attributes.

A U.S. cake mix company entered the British market but carefully eliminated most of the newness of the product. Instead of introducing the most popular American cake mixes, the company asked 500 British housewives to bake their favorite cake. Since the majority baked a simple, very popular dry sponge cake, the company brought to the market a similar easy mix. The sponge cake mix represented familiar tastes and habits that could be translated into a convenience item and did not infringe on the emotional aspects of preparing a fancy product for special occasions. Consequently, after a short period of time, the second company's product gained 30 to 35 percent of the British cake mix market. Once the idea of a mix for sponge cake seemed acceptable, the introduction of other flavors became easier.

The goal of a foreign marketer is to gain product acceptance by the largest number of consumers in the market in the shortest span of time. However, as discussed in Chapter 4 and as many of the examples cited have illustrated, new products are not always readily accepted by a culture; indeed, they often meet resistance. Although they may ultimately be accepted, the time needed for a culture to learn new ways, to learn to accept a new product, is of critical importance to the marketer because planning reflects a time frame for investment and profitability. If a marketer invests with the expectation that a venture will break even in three years and seven are needed to gain profitable volume, the effort may have to be prematurely abandoned. The question comes to mind of whether the probable rate of acceptance can be predicted before committing resources and, more critically, if the probable rate of acceptance is too slow, whether it can be accelerated. In both cases, the answer is a qualified yes. Answers to these questions come from examining the work done in diffusion research—research on the process by which innovations spread to the members of a social system.

Diffusion of Innovations

Everett Rogers noted that "crucial elements in the diffusion of new ideas are (1) an innovation, (2) which is communicated through certain channels, (3) over time, (4) among the members of a social system."[31] Rogers continued with the statement that it is the element of time that differentiates diffusion from other types of communications research. The goals of the diffusion researcher and the marketer are to shorten the time lag between introduction of an idea or product and its widespread adoption.

Rogers and others[32] give ample evidence of the fact that product innovations have varying rates of acceptance. Some diffuse from introduction to widespread use in a few years;

---

[30]Changhui Zhou and Jing Li, "Product Innovation in Emerging Market-Based International Joint Ventures: An Organizational Ecology Perspective," *Journal of International Business Studies* 39, no. 7 (2008), pp. 1114–32.

[31]Everett M. Rogers, *Diffusion of Innovations*, 5th ed. (New York: The Free Press, 2003). This book should be read by anyone responsible for product development and brand management, domestic or international.

[32]Marnik G. Dekimpe, Philip M. Parker, and Miklos Sarvary, "Global Diffusion and Technological Innovations: A Couple-Hazard Approach," *Journal of Marketing Research* 38 (February 2000), pp. 47–59; Gerard J. Tellis, Stefan Stremersch, and Eden Yin, "The International Takeoff of New Products: The Role of Economics, Culture, and Country Innovativeness," *Marketing Science* 22, no. 2 (2003), pp. 188–208; Sean Dwyer, Hani Mesak, and Maxwell Hsu, "An Exploratory Examination of the Influence of National Culture on Cross-National Product Diffusion," *Journal of International Marketing* 13, no. 2 (2005), pp. 1–27.

others take decades. Patterns of diffusion also vary substantially, and steady growth is the exception—high-tech products often demonstrate periods of slow growth interspersed with performance jumps[33] or early declines followed by broader takeoffs. As mentioned in Chapter 8, cultural and other national differences affect the takeoff of new products.[34] Also, spillover effects from adopters in neighboring countries can influence diffusion rates. One study shows that the historical spread of stock markets around the world was strongly correlated (r > 0.6) with linguistic distance from English, as we described in Chapters 4 and 5.[35] Analyses of both factors can suggest ideal countries for new product introduction. One study suggests Hong Kong and the United States as candidates for such classification.[36] Another study reports that new product growth is becoming more synchronized across countries.[37]

Patterns of alcoholic beverage consumption converge across Europe only when a 50-year time frame is considered. Microwave ovens, introduced in the United States initially in the 1950s, took nearly 20 years to become widespread; the contraceptive pill was introduced during that same period and gained acceptance in a few years. In the field of education, modern math took only five years to diffuse through U.S. schools, whereas the idea of kindergartens took nearly 50 years to gain total acceptance. Tata Motors' $2,000 minicar introduced in 2008 is having trouble getting off the ground in India. So far, despite tweaking the design, sales have still disappointed. The price has also crept up, but Tata insists it will be patient.[38] A growing body of evidence suggests that an understanding of diffusion theory may suggest ways to accelerate the process of diffusion. Knowledge of this process also may provide the foreign marketer with the ability to assess the time it takes for a product to diffuse—before a financial commitment is necessary. It also focuses the marketer's attention on features of a product that provoke resistance, thereby providing an opportunity to minimize resistance and hasten product acceptance.

At least three extraneous variables affect the rate of diffusion of an object: the degree of perceived newness, the perceived attributes of the innovation, and the method used to communicate the idea.[39] The more innovative a product is perceived to be, the more difficult it is to gain market acceptance. That is, at a fundamental level, innovations are often disruptive.[40] Consider alternative-fuel cars in the United States. Although they are popular with consumers, dealers did not appreciate their low maintenance requirements, which reduced after-sale service revenues. Furthermore, the infrastructure to support hydrogen fuel cell cars has been expensive to build. Thus, some suggest that the technology is inappropriate for the United States, whereas China, without an established infrastructure, could leapfrog the older, gasoline-fueled options. The problem for China, however, is that studies show diffusion of innovations to be slowed by inefficient governmental institutions.[41]

---

[33]Ashish Sood and Gerard J. Tellis, "Technological Evolution and Radical Innovation," *Journal of Marketing* 69 (2005), pp. 152–68.

[34]Deepa Chandrasekaran and Gerard J. Tellis, "Global Takeoff of New Products: Culture, Wealth, or Vanishing Differences," *Marketing Science* 27, no. 5 (2008), pp. 844–60.

[35]Dante M. Pirouz and John L. Graham, "Culture, Globalization, and Stock Price Volatility," working paper, University California, Irvine, 2012.

[36]Yvonne van Everdingen, Dennis Fok, and Stefan Stremersch, "Modeling Global Spillover of New Product Takeoff," *Journal of Marketing Research* 46 (2009), pp. 637–52.

[37]Deepa Chandrasekaran and Gerard J. Tellis, "Getting a Grip on the Saddle: Chasms or Cycles?" *Journal of Marketing* 75, no. 4 (2011), pp. 21–34.

[38]Siddarth Philip, "The World's Cheapest Car Runs Out of Gas," *Bloomberg Businessweek*, April 15–21, 2013, p. 21.

[39]Anita Elberse and Jehoshua Eliashberg, "Demand and Supply Dynamics for Sequentially Released Products in International Markets: The Case of Motion Pictures," *Marketing Science* 22, no. 3 (2003), pp. 329–54.

[40]Jared Diamond, *Collapse* (New York: Viking, 2005).

[41]Roberto Martin N. Galang, "Governmental Efficiency and International Technology Adoption: The Spread of Electronic Ticketing among Airlines," *Journal of International Business Studies* 43 (2012), pp. 631–54.

The Japanese and the Dutch are the world's champions in toilet innovations. Japan's long history of crowding has prompted the culture to focus on cleanliness, frequent bathing, and high-tech bathrooms. Thus, Matsushita's toilet reads your body weight, temperature, and blood pressure. Soon you will also be able to get a readout on glucose and protein levels in your urine! The Dutch are also worried about plumbing—much of their country is below sea level. Sphinx in Maastricht produces a urinal for women and a fly imbedded in the porcelain for their men's urinal. The latter reduces maintenance costs, as the company's research has shown that most men will aim for the fly, which is strategically placed to minimize splash. Both Dutch innovations can be seen in the Schiphol Airport outside of Amsterdam. Other interesting innovations in toilets around the world are: About half of the U.S. states, Hong Kong, and Singapore have passed laws requiring more toilets for women;[42] Sega has designed new mini-games for men's rest rooms that are controlled by players' urine;[43] Intel now puts computer chips in urinals to count uses and schedule maintenance;[44] a low-cost sanitary toilet has been designed especially for slums around the world that includes easy collection of waste for conversion to fertilizer.[45]

In sum, the perception of innovation can often be changed if the marketer understands the perceptual framework of the consumer, as has certainly proved to be the case with the fast global diffusion of Internet use, e-tailing, and health- and beauty-related products and services.

---

[42]"Flushing away Unfairness," *The Economist,* July 10, 2010, p. 60.

[43]Ben Messig, "Sega Brings Gaming to the Bathroom with Urine-Controlled Video Game," *aolnews.com,* January 10, 2011.

[44]Ian King, "Intel Inside," *Bloomberg Businessweek,* October 6-12, pp. 41–42.

[45]Patrick Clark, "Cleaning Up," *Bloomberg Businessweek,* October 17, 2011, p. 20.

Analyzing the five characteristics of an innovation can assist in determining the rate of acceptance or resistance of the market to a product. A product's (1) *relative advantage* (the perceived marginal value of the new product relative to the old), (2) *compatibility* (its compatibility with acceptable behavior, norms, values, and so forth), (3) *complexity* (the degree of complexity associated with product use), (4) *trialability* (the degree of economic and/or social risk associated with product use), and (5) *observability* (the ease with which the product benefits can be communicated) affect the degree of its acceptance or resistance. In general, the rate of diffusion can be postulated as positively related to relative advantage, compatibility, trialability, and observability but negatively related to complexity.

Perhaps one of the most interesting examples of encouraging trial is a new smart phone app developed by Loreal called Makeup Genius. It lets you see yourself in real time wearing Loreal's makeup products that aren't actually applied on your face. "When you smile, pucker up, or wink, the virtual cosmetics actually move along with you."[46] In the first four months of the role out in France and the U.S. the app has been downloaded 1.7 million times. One analyst says that more is spent on research in the cosmetics industry than on the space shuttle. No doubt this is true—Loreal holds more than 35,000 patents and spends 3.7 percent of its revenues on research that includes some 4,000 scientists working in 50 countries. Really. We're not making this up! Another example of ease of triability is the "Beanie-Baby-like" Tsum Tsum stackable stuffed Disney characters sold for $4.95 each. They took off faster than both Makeup Genius and the space shuttle, first in Japan, then the U.S. Because the stack (tsum tsum means stack in Japanese) kids want more than one. And, the first one is really easy to buy.[47]

The evaluator must remember that it is the perception of product characteristics by the potential adopter, not the marketer, that is crucial to the evaluation. A market analyst's self-reference criterion (SRC) may cause a perceptual bias when interpreting the characteristics of a product. Thus, instead of evaluating product characteristics from the foreign user's frame of reference, the marketer might analyze them from his or her frame of reference, leading to a misinterpretation of the product's cultural importance.

Once the analysis has been made, some of the perceived newness or causes for resistance can be minimized through adroit marketing. The more congruent product perceptions are with current cultural values, the less resistance there will be and the more rapid product diffusion or acceptance will be. Finally, we should point out that the newness of the product or brand introduced can be an important competitive advantage; the pioneer brand advantage often delivers long-term competitive advantages in both domestic and foreign markets.[48]

Production of Innovations

Human progress through the millennia has been driven by international trade. Good ideas are borrowed, and even invented, in cross-cultural interactions.[49] Think of the ancient Silk Road or the Silicon Valley of the 21st century.

Working with diverse groups is not always easy, but studies show that diverse groups put more ideas on the table and provide different perspectives on those ideas, thus multiplying creative output—*if* you can overcome the initial problems in communication.[50]

---

[46]Caroline Winter, "Put Your Face One," *Bloomberg BusinessWeek*, September 11, 2014, pp. 67–69).

[47]Brooks Barnes, "Sensing a Tsum Tsum Craze Afoot, Disney Rushes to Supply Fans," *New York Times*, August 11, 2014, p. B6.

[48]Gerald Young Gao, Yigang Pan, David K. Tse, and Chi Kin (Bennett) Yim, "Market Share Performance of Foreign and Domestic Brands in China," *Journal of International Marketing* 14 (2006), pp. 32–51.

[49]Alex Eapen, "Social Structure and Technology Spillovers from Foreign to Domestic Firms," *Journal of International Business Studies* 43 (2012), pp. 244–63.

[50]John L. Graham, Lynda Lawrence, and William Hernández Requejo, *Inventive Negotiation: Getting Beyond Yes* (New York: Palgrave Macmillan, 2014).

A path-breaking study on the long-term impact on work team performance well demonstrates this principal.[51] The details are interesting. Thirty-six teams of four to five mostly undergraduate business majors were formed to work on a variety of cases over a four-month period: 17 teams were culturally homogeneous (all from the same nationality and ethnic background), and 19 were diverse groups ("a white American, a black American, a Hispanic American, and a foreign national from Asia, Latin America, Africa, or the Middle East.")

In weeks 5, 9, 13, and 17, the groups were "required to (1) examine the case from a variety of perspectives, (2) identify the problems that had a bearing on the situation described in the case, (3) generate a list of alternatives that might be employed to deal with the problems they had identified, and (4) to select what they believed was the most effective of the alternatives and provide justification for their recommendation."[52]

On average, both diverse and homogeneous groups increased their idea productivity over the 17-week period (see Exhibit 13.1). Initially, the diverse groups were at a disadvantage, but after working together, they improved faster, and in week 13, they actually overtook their homogeneous counterparts.

As we mentioned in Chapter 8 companies around the world recognize the importance of creative environments and circumstances. For example, Philips' innovation laboratory in Eindhoven, Netherlands has been used to test consumers' reactions to innovations in LED lights in a common sort of living room environment.[53] British inventor/designer conjured the idea for a gravity powered lamp for use in remote villages in developing countries after talking with a charity group about solar energy. His lamp replaces kerosene or battery-powered lamps using a falling weight as in a grandfather clock to produce the energy to power a light bulb for about 30 minutes.[54] Serendipity helped an IBM research chemist develop a new plastic with valuable qualities-she mistakenly neglected to add a called-for ingredient, and like magic, a breakthough.[55] Finally, Lego crowdsourced new product ideas. The most remarkable was a new line targeting girls-their "Research

[51]Warren E. Watson, Kamalesh Kumar, and Larry K Michaelsen, "Cultural Diversity's Impact on Interaction Process and Performance: Comparing Homogeneous and Diverse Task Groups," *Academy of Management Journal* 36, no. 3 (1993), pp. 590–602.

[52]Watson, Kumar, and Michaelson, op cit.

[53]John Gertner, "Lighting the Way," *Fast Company.com*, March 2014, pp. 143–48.

[54]Caroline Winter, "Clean, Cheap Light, Powered by Gravity," *Bloomberg BusinessWeek*, March 18–24, 2013, p. 33.

[55]John Markoff, "Error at IBM Lab Finds New Family of Materials," *The New York Times*, May 16, 2014, p. B6.

Exhibit 13.1
Average Number of Ideas Put on the Table

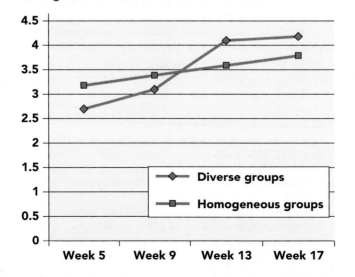

Institute" includes Lego figures such as a paleontologist, an astronomer, and a chemist, all with the respective laboratories. The idea was submitted by an archeologist at the University of Glasgow.[56]

Some consideration must be given to the inventiveness of companies[57] and countries.[58] For example, it is no surprise that more of the new ideas associated with the Internet are being produced in the United States vis-a-vis Japan.[59] The 266 million American users of the Internet far outnumber the 109 million Japanese users.[60] Similarly, America wins the overall R&D expenditure contest. Expenditures are about the same across member countries of the Organization for Economic Cooperation and Development, at about 2 to 3 percent of GDP, so America's large economy supports twice the R&D spending as does Japan, for example. This spending yields about three times the number of U.S. patents granted to American firms versus Japanese firms.

One study suggests that national culture influences innovativeness (individualism enhances creativity[61]), but another argues that corporate culture, not national culture, is key.[62] The Japanese government diagnosed the problem as a lack of business training. Japanese engineers are not versed in marketing and entrepreneurship, and American-style educational programs are being created at a record pace to fill the gap. However, we do note a disturbing trend: The growth of American R&D spending is slower than most other competitive countries. Russia, India, and China are experiencing double-digit growth compared with America's four percent annual growth rate over the last five years.[63] Moreover, in 2009, for the first time in history, more patents were registered by foreign residents in the United States than by U.S. residents.[64]

Many Japanese firms also take advantage of American innovativeness by establishing design centers in the United States—most notable are the plethora of foreign auto design centers in Southern California. At the same time, American automobile firms have established design centers in Europe. Indeed, the Ford Taurus, the car that saved Ford in the 1980s, was a European design.

The stream of research in this area of international marketing is growing.[65] For example, locations with solid intellectual property standards seem to promote innovation.[66] Still burgeoning numbers of other studies show the advantages of globalization-based diversity

[56]Rachel Abrams, "Short-Lived Science Line from Lego for Girls," *The New York Times*, August, 21, 2014, online.

[57]Rohit Deshpandé and John U. Farley, "Organizational Culture, Innovativeness, and Market Orientation in Hong Kong Five Years after Handover: What Has Changed?" *Journal of Global Marketing* 17, no. 4 (2004), pp. 53–75.

[58]Anyone interested in a wonderful book on this topic should read the Pulitzer Prize–winning *Guns, Germs, and Steel: The Fates of Human Societies* by Jared Diamond (New York: Norton, 1999); also see Subin Im, Cheryl Nakata, Heungsooa Park, and Young-Won Ha, "Determinants of Korean and Japanese New Product Performance: An Interrelational and Process View," *Journal of International Marketing* 11, no. 4 (2003), pp. 81–113; David Hillier, Julio Pindado, Valdoceu de Queiroz, and Chabela de la Torre, "The Impact of Country-Level Corporate Governance on Research and Development," Journal of International Business Studies 42, no. 1 (2011), pp. 76–98; Sergey Anokhin and Joakim Wincent, "Start-Up Rates and Innovation: A Cross-Country Examination," *Journal of International Business Studies* 43, no. 1 (2012), pp. 41–60.

[59]Thomas L. Friedman, *The World Is Flat* (New York: Farrar, Straus, and Giroux, 2005).

[60]Euromonitor International, 2015.

[61]Jack A. Goncalo and Barry M. Staw, "Individualism—Collectivism and Group Creativity," *Organizational Behavior and Human Decision Processes* 100 (2006), pp. 96–109.

[62]Gerard J. Tellis, Jaideep C. Prabhu, and Rajesh K. Chandy, "Radical Innovation across Nations: The Preeminence of Corporate Culture," *Journal of Marketing* 73, no. 1 (2009), pp. 3–23.

[63]Euromonitor International, 2015.

[64]Michael Arndt, "Ben Franklin, Where Are You?" *Bloomberg Businessweek*, January 4, 2010, p. 29.

[65]V. Kuma, "Understanding Cultural Differences in Innovation: A Conceptual Framework and Future Research Directions," *Journal of International Marketing* 22, no. 3 (2014), pp. 1–29.

[66]Min Ju, Kevin Zheng Zhou, Gerald Yong Gao, and Jiangyong Lue, "Technological Capability Growth and Performance Outcome: Foreign versus Local Firms in China," *Journal of International Marketing* 21, no. 2 (2013), pp. 1–16.

in promoting innovative thinking.[67] Likewise, international imitation is an important source of innovative ideas.[68] Moreover, while criticisms of Chinese copycats[69] are reminiscent of 1980s-era complaints about the Japanese, innovations in cars, movies, and hotel services are being sparked by American and Chinese R&D collaboration.[70] Finally, note the dramatic growth of U.S.- and Chinese-created patents in the last few years demonstrated in Exhibit 13.2.

Research is also now focusing on the related issue of "conversion-ability" or the success firms have when they take inventions to market. Three main factors seem to favor conversion, at least in the global pharmaceutical industry: patience (nine years seems optimal for taking a newly patented drug to approval), focus on a few important

Exhibit 13.2

U.S. Patents Granted to Invention Teams that Include Both American and Chinese Citizens

Source: http://www.patft.uspto.gov, 2011.

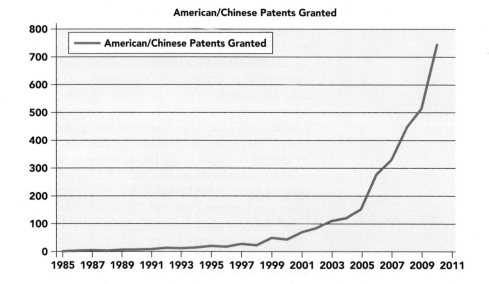

patents favor conversion, at least in the global pharmaceutical industry: patience (nine years seems optimal for taking a newly patented drug to approval), focus on a few important

---

[67]Daniel Lederman, "An International Multilevel Analysis of Product Innovation," *Journal of International Business Studies* 41, no. 4 (2010), pp. 606–19; Maria Jesus Nieto and Alicia Rodriguez, "Offshoring of R&D: Looking Abroad to Improve Innovation Performance," *Journal of International Business Studies* 42, no. 3 (2011), pp. 345–61; Elena Golovko and Giovanni Valentini, "Exploring the Complementarity between Innovation and Export for SME's Growth," *Journal of International Business Studies* 42, no. 3 (2011), pp. 362–80; Arun Kumaraswamy, Ram Mudambi, Harith Saranga, and Arindam Tripathy, "Catch-Up Strategies in the Indian Auto Components Industry: Domestic Firms' Responses to Market Liberalization," *Journal of International Business Studies* 43 (2012), pp. 368–95; Davide Castellani, Alfredo Jimenez, and Antonello Zanfei, "How Remote Are R&D Labs? Distance Factors and International Innovation Activities," *Journal of International Business Studies* 44 (2013), pp. 649–75; Diana A. Filipescu, Shameen Prashantham, Alex Rialp, and Josep Rialp, "Technological Innovation and Exports: Unpacking Their Reciprocal Causality," *Journal of International Marketing* 21, no. 1 (2013), pp. 23–38; Nathan Boso, Vicky M. Story, John W. Cadogan, Milena Micevski, and Selma Kadic-Maglajlic, "Firm Innovativeness and Export Performance: Environmental, Networking, and Structural Contingencies," *Journal of International Marketing* 21, no. 4 (2013), pp. 62–87; Sheryl Winston Smith, "Follow Me to the Innovation Frontier? Leaders, Laggards, and the Differential Effects of Imports and Exports on Technological Innovation," *Journal of International Business Studies* 45 (2014), pp. 248–74; Snehal Awate, Marcus M. Larsen, and Ram Mudambi, "Accessing vs. Sourcing Knowledge: A Comparative Study of R&D Internationalization between Emerging and Advanced Economy Firms," *Journal of International Business Studies*, 2014, online; Lee Li, Gongming Qian, and Zhenming Qian, "Inconsistencies in International Product Strategies and Performance of High-Tech Firms," *Journal of International Marketing* 22, no. 3 (2014), pp. 99–113.

[68]Ruby P. Lee and Kevin Zheng Zhou, "Is Product Imitation Good for Firm Performance? An Examination of Product Imitation Types and Contingency Factors," *Journal of International Marketing* 20, no. 3 (2012), pp. 1–16.

[69]Yu Hua, *China in Ten Words* (New York; Random House, 2011).

[70]"A Back Seat that Augers China's Influence," *Bloomberg Businessweek,* January 23, 2012, pp. 23–24; "Bigger Abroad: Hollywood Goes Global," *The Economist,* February 19, 2011, pp. 69–70; Hugo Martin, "Comforts of Home," *Los Angeles Times,* July 16, 2011, pp. B1–B2; Kevin Wale, "Three Snapshots of Chinese Innovation," *McKinseyQuarterly,* February 2012.

innovations, and experience.[71] Another study demonstrates that strengthening patent protections tends to favor firms in developed countries differentially more than firms in developing countries.[72] If evidence continues to accumulate in this vein, policy makers will have to reconsider the current global application of a "one-size-fits-all" intellectual property system.

Analyzing Product Components for Adaptation

LO4

The need to view all attributes of a product to overcome resistance to acceptance

A product is multidimensional, and the sum of all its features determines the bundle of satisfactions (utilities) received by the consumer. To identify all the possible ways a product may be adapted to a new market, it helps to separate its many dimensions into three distinct components, as illustrated by the Product Component Model in Exhibit 13.3. By using this model, the impact of the cultural, physical, and mandatory factors (discussed previously) that affect a market's acceptance of a product can be focused on the core component, packaging component, and support services component. These components include all a product's tangible and intangible elements and provide the bundle of utilities the market receives from use of the product.

Core Component

The *core component* consists of the physical product—the platform that contains the essential technology—and all its design and functional features. It is on the product platform that product variations can be added or deleted to satisfy local differences. Major

---

[71]Rajesh Chandy, Brigitee Hpostaken, Om Narasimhan, and Jaideep Prabhu, "From Invention to Innovation: Conversion Ability in Product Development," *Journal of Marketing Research* 43 (2006), pp. 494–508.

[72]Brent B. Allred and Walter G. Park, "Patent Rights and Innovative Activity: Evidence from National and Firm-Level Data," *Journal of International Business Studies* 38 (2007), pp. 878–900.

Exhibit 13.3
Product Component Model

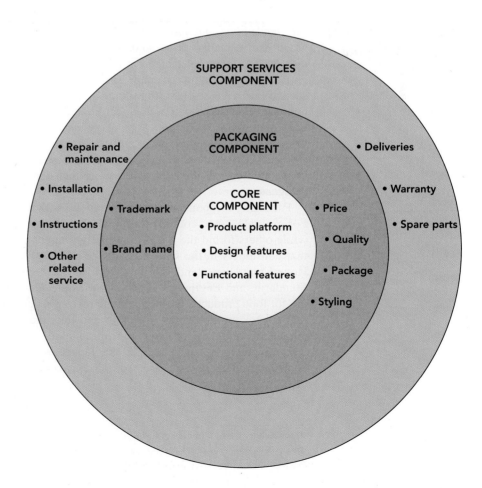

adjustments in the platform aspect of the core component may be costly, because a change in the platform can affect product processes and thus require additional capital investment. However, alterations in design, functional features, flavors, color, and other aspects can be made to adapt the product to cultural variations. In Japan, Nestlé originally sold the same kind of corn flakes it sells in the United States, but Japanese children ate them mostly as snacks instead of for breakfast. To move the product into the larger breakfast market, Nestlé reformulated its cereals to more closely fit Japanese taste. The Japanese traditionally eat fish and rice for breakfast, so Nestlé developed cereals with familiar tastes—seaweed, carrots and zucchini, and coconut and papaya. The result was a 12 percent share of the growing breakfast cereal market.

For the Brazilian market, where fresh orange juice is plentiful, General Foods changed the flavor of its presweetened powdered juice substitute, Tang, from the traditional orange to passion fruit and other flavors. Changing flavor or fragrance is often necessary to bring a product in line with what is expected in a culture. Household cleansers with the traditional pine odor and hints of ammonia or chlorine popular in U.S. markets were not successful when introduced in Japan. Many Japanese sleep on the floor on futons with their heads close to the surface they have cleaned, so a citrus fragrance is more pleasing. Rubbermaid could have avoided missteps in introducing its line of baby furniture in Europe with modest changes in the core component. Its colors were not tailored to European tastes, but worst of all, its child's bed didn't fit European-made mattresses!

Functional features can be added or eliminated depending on the market. In markets where hot water is not commonly available, washing machines have heaters as a functional feature. In other markets, automatic soap and bleach dispensers may be eliminated to cut costs or to minimize repair problems. Additional changes may be necessary to meet safety and electrical standards or other mandatory (homologation) requirements. The physical product and all its functional features should be examined as potential candidates for adaptation.

Packaging Component

The *packaging component* includes style features, packaging, labeling, trademarks, brand name, quality, price, and all other aspects of a product's package. Perhaps the most curious error ever made in packaging was in the 1911 design of the Coca-Cola bottle. It was based on the shape of a cacao seed (the raw source of chocolate), not the seed of Erythoxylon plant (the source of coca and cocaine), the artist apparently having confused coca and cacao in the local library.[73] Apple Computer found out the hard way how important this component can be when it first entered the Japanese market. Some of its personal computers were returned unused after customers found the wrapping on the instruction manual damaged! As with the core component, the importance of each of the elements in the eyes of the consumer depends on the need that the product is designed to serve.

Packaging components frequently require both discretionary and mandatory changes. For example, some countries require labels to be printed in more than one language, while others forbid the use of any foreign language. Meanwhile, one study has found that consumers in the United States respond negatively to bilingual packaging.[74] At Hong Kong Disneyland, the jungle cruise ride commentary is delivered in Cantonese, Mandarin, and English. Several countries are now requiring country-of-origin labeling for food products. Elements in the packaging component may incorporate symbols that convey an unintended meaning and thus must be changed. One company's red-circle trademark was popular in some countries but was rejected in parts of Asia, where it conjured up images of the Japanese flag. Yellow flowers used in another company trademark were rejected in Mexico, where a yellow flower symbolizes death or disrespect.

---

[73]Tim Madge, *White Mischief: A Cultural History of Cocaine* (New York: Thunder's Mouth Press, 2001).

[74]Mahesh Gopinath and Myron Glassman, "The Effect of Multiple Language Product Descriptions on Product Evaluations," *Psychology & Marketing* 25, no. 3 (2008), pp. 233–61.

A well-known baby-food producer that introduced small jars of baby food in Africa, complete with labels featuring a picture of a baby, experienced the classic example of misinterpreted symbols: The company was absolutely horrified to find that consumers thought the jars contained ground-up babies. In China, though not a problem of literacy per se, Brugel, a German children's cereal brand that features cartoon drawings of dogs, cats, birds, monkeys, and other animals on the package, was located in the pet foods section of a supermarket. The label had no Chinese, and store personnel were unfamiliar with the product. It is easy to forget that in low-literacy countries, pictures and symbols are taken literally as instructions and information.

Care must be taken to ensure that corporate trademarks and other parts of the packaging component do not have unacceptable symbolic meanings. Particular attention should be given to translations of brand names and colors used in packaging. When Ford tried to sell its Pinto automobile in Brazil, it quickly found out that the car model's name translated to "tiny male genitals." White, the color symbolizing purity in Western countries, is the color for mourning in others. In China, P&G packaged diapers in a pink wrapper. Consumers shunned the pink package—pink symbolized a girl, and in a country with a one-child-per-family rule where boys are preferred, you do not want anyone to think you have a girl, even if you do.

Reasons a company might have to adapt a product's package are countless. In some countries, laws stipulate specific bottle, can, and package sizes, measurement units, and ingredients and measures thereof.[75] If a country uses the metric system, it will probably require that weights and measurements conform to the metric system. Such descriptive words as "giant" or "jumbo" on a package or label may be illegal. High humidity or the need for long shelf life because of extended distribution systems may dictate extra-heavy packaging for some products. As is frequently mentioned, Japanese attitudes about quality include the packaging of a product. A poorly packaged product conveys an impression of poor quality to the Japanese. It is also important to determine if the packaging has other uses in the market. Lever Brothers sells Lux soap in stylish boxes in Japan because more than half of all soap cakes there are purchased during the two gift-giving seasons. Size of the package is also a factor that may make a difference to success in Japan. One study found that package sizes can actually influence consumption levels.[76] Soft drinks are sold in smaller-size cans than in the United States to accommodate the smaller Japanese hand. In Japan, most food is sold fresh or in clear packaging, while cans are considered dirty. So when Campbell introduced soups to the Japanese market, it decided to go with a cleaner, more expensive pop-top opener.

Labeling laws vary from country to country and do not seem to follow any predictable pattern. In Saudi Arabia, for example, product names must be specific. "Hot Chili" will not do; it must be "Spiced Hot Chili." Prices are required to be printed on the labels in Venezuela, but in Chile putting prices on labels or in any way suggesting retail prices is illegal. Coca-Cola ran into a legal problem in Brazil with its Diet Coke. Brazilian law interprets *diet* to have medicinal qualities. Under the law, producers must give the daily recommended consumption on the labels of all medicines. Coca-Cola had to get special approval to get around this restriction. Until recently in China, Western products could be labeled in a foreign language with only a small temporary Chinese label affixed somewhere on the package. Under the new Chinese labeling law, however, food products must have their name, contents, and other specifics listed clearly in Chinese printed directly on the package—no temporary labels are allowed.

Labeling laws create a special problem for companies selling products in various markets with different labeling laws and small initial demand in each. In China, for example, there is demand for American- and European-style snack foods even though

[75]Stephanie Storm, "After Public Outcry, Cargill Says It Will Label Products Made with a Beef Binder," *The New York Times*, November 6, 2013, p. B3.

[76]Chanthika Pornpitakpan, "How Package Sizes, Fill Amounts, and Unit Costs Influence Product Usage Amounts," *Journal of Global Marketing* 23, no. 4 (2010), pp. 275–87.

that demand is not well developed at this time. The expense of labeling specially to meet Chinese law often makes market entry costs prohibitive. Forward-thinking manufacturers with wide distribution in Asia are adopting packaging standards comparable to those required in the European Union by providing standard information in several different languages on the same package. A template is designed with space on the label reserved for locally required content, which can be inserted depending on the destination of a given production batch.

Support Services Component

The *support services* component includes repair and maintenance, instructions, installation, warranties, deliveries, and the availability of spare parts. Many otherwise successful marketing programs have ultimately failed because little attention was given to this product component.[77] Repair and maintenance are especially difficult problems in developing countries. In the United States, a consumer has the option of obtaining service from the company or from scores of competitive service retailers ready to repair and maintain anything from automobiles to lawn mowers. Equally available are repair parts from company-owned or licensed outlets or the local hardware store. Consumers in a developing country and in many

---

[77]Susanna Khavul, Mark Peterson, Drake Mullens, and Abdul A. Rasheed, "Going Global with Innovations from Emerging Economies: Investment in Customer Support Capabilities Pays Off," *Journal of International Marketing* 18, no. 4 (2010), pp. 22–42.

CROSSING BORDERS 13.3   So, Your Computer Isn't Working?

Most people have two options when the desk beast starts acting up: Call the service center or read the manual. Both are becoming cross-cultural activities. With increasing frequency, service call centers are being staffed by folks in the Philippines, India, the Caribbean, and other developing countries where English is commonly spoken. The savings for the companies can be in the 90 percent range. But for consumers, it was tough enough bridging the technician–layperson gap. Now a cross-cultural layer is being added to the interaction.

At least many manufacturers are getting more adept at adapting user manuals. In some countries, the manuals are treasured for their entertainment value. Mike Adams of the translation and marketing firm Arial Global Reach explains, "Japanese people really enjoy reading documentation, but that's because Japanese documentation is actually fun to look at." Japanese manuals are often jazzed up with creative cartoons. Even program interfaces are animated. Microsoft's much-maligned Clippy the Paperclip was replaced in Japan with an animated dolphin, "And even highly technical Japanese engineers don't feel at all childish when they view or interact with these animations."

Put those cute characters in manuals in other countries and the customer will doubt the seriousness of the firm. Mark Katib, general manager of Middle East Translation Services, says most customers in that part of

the world, as do Americans, prefer uncluttered, nontechnical explanations. He spends most of his time making sure that information is presented in an acceptable manner, not impinging on people's beliefs.

Apparently you cannot give an Italian a command such as "never do this." The consequences for that kind of language are calls from Italians who have broken their machines by doing exactly "this." Instead, Italian manuals must use less demanding language, like "you might consider . . . ."

The Germans will reject manuals with embedded humor. Hungarians like to fix things themselves, so their manuals are more like machine shop guides. Finally, one software maker that developed a WAN (wide-area network) used a flowing stream of text, "WAN WAN WAN WAN" on the package. To a Japanese that's the sound a dog makes, and in Japan no one would buy a product advertising itself by a barking dog.

The main point here is that "technobabble" is hard to translate in any language.

Sources: Michelle Delio, "Read the F***ing Story, then RTFM," *Wired News*, http://www.wired.com, June 4, 2002; Pete Engardio, Aaron Bernstein, and Manjeet Kripalani, "Is Your Job Next?" *BusinessWeek*, February 3, 2003, pp. 50–60; Alli McConnon, "India's Competition in the Caribbean," *BusinessWeek*, December 24, 2007, p. 75; Rudy Hirschheim, "Offshoring and the New World Order," *Communications of the ACM* 12, no. 11 (2009), pp. 132–35.

developed countries may not have even one of the possibilities for repair and maintenance available in the United States, and independent service providers can be used to enhance brand and product quality.[78]

In some countries, the concept of routine maintenance or preventive maintenance is not a part of the culture. As a result, products may have to be adjusted to require less frequent maintenance, and special attention must be given to features that may be taken for granted in the United States.

The literacy rates and educational levels of a country may require a firm to change a product's instructions. A simple term in one country may be incomprehensible in another. In rural Africa, for example, consumers had trouble understanding that Vaseline Intensive Care lotion is absorbed into the skin. *Absorbed* was changed to *soaks into*, and the confusion was eliminated. The Brazilians have successfully overcome the low literacy and technical skills of users of the sophisticated military tanks it sells to Third World countries. The manufacturers include videocassette players and videotapes with detailed repair instructions as part of the standard instruction package. They also minimize spare parts problems by using standardized, off-the-shelf parts available throughout the world. And, of course, other kinds of cultural preferences come into play even in service manuals.

Complementary products must be considered increasingly in the marketing of a variety of high-tech products. Perhaps the best example is Microsoft's Xbox and its competitors. Sales of the Xbox had lagged those of Sony's and Nintendo's game consoles in Japan. Microsoft diagnosed the problem as a lack of games that particularly attract Japanese gamers and therefore developed a series of games to fill that gap. An early offering, a role-playing game called *Lost Odyssey*, was developed by an all-Japanese team.[79]

The Product Component Model can be a useful guide for examining the adaptation requirements of products destined for foreign markets. A product should be carefully evaluated on each of the three components to determine any mandatory and discretionary changes that may be needed.

Marketing Consumer Services Globally

As mentioned at the beginning of the chapter, much of the advice regarding adapting products for international consumer markets also applies to adapting services. Moreover, some services are closely associated with products. Good examples are the support services just described or the customer services associated with the delivery of a Big Mac to a consumer in Moscow. However, services are distinguished by four unique characteristics—intangibility, inseparability, heterogeneity, and perishability—and thus require special consideration.

Products are often classified as tangible, whereas services are *intangible*. Automobiles, computers, and furniture are examples of products that have a physical presence; they are things or objects that can be stored and possessed, and their intrinsic value is embedded within their physical presence. Of course, Lego markets its toys around the world, but its services are also crucial to its competitiveness. There are Legoland Resorts in Denmark, the United Kingdom, the United States, Germany, and Malaysia (the first in Asia). *The Lego Movie* has been a smash hit internationally as well.[80] And one enterprising young woman in Singapore is offering Lego building lessons to kids unfamiliar with the toys.[81]

---

[78]Ikechi Ekeledo and Nadeem M. Firoz, "Independent Service Providers as a Competitive Advantage in Developing Economies," *Journal of Global Marketing* 20 (2007), pp. 39–54.

[79]Yukari Iwatani Kane, "Microsoft Makes Big Push to Woo Japanese with New Xbox Games," *The Wall Street Journal* (online), September 12, 2007.

[80]Gregory Schmidt, "Lego Builds an Empire, Brick by Brick," *The New York Times*, February 15, 2014, pp. B1, 7.

[81]"A Toymaker Taps into a New Market for Selling to Pussycat Mums," *The Economist*, November 16, 2013, p. 72.

Insurance, dry cleaning, hotel accommodations, and airline passenger or freight service, in contrast, are intangible and have intrinsic value resulting from a process, a performance, or an occurrence that exists only while it is being created.

The intangibility of services results in characteristics unique to a service: It is *inseparable* in that its creation cannot be separated from its consumption; it is *heterogeneous* in that it is individually produced and is thus unique; and it is *perishable* in that once created it cannot be stored but must be consumed simultaneously with its creation. Contrast these characteristics with a tangible product that can be produced in one location and consumed elsewhere, that can be standardized, whose quality assurance can be determined and maintained over time, and that can be produced and stored in anticipation of fluctuations in demand.

As is true for many tangible products, a service can be marketed as both an industrial (business-to-business) and a consumer service, depending on the motive of, and use by, the purchaser. For example, travel agents and airlines sell industrial or business services to a business traveler and a consumer service to a tourist. Financial services, hotels, insurance, legal services, and others may each be classified as either a business or a consumer service. As one might expect, the unique characteristics of services result in differences in the marketing of services and the marketing of consumer products.

Services Opportunities in Global Markets

International tourism is by far the largest services export of the United States, ranking behind only capital goods and industrial supplies when all exports are counted. Spending by foreign tourists visiting American destinations such as Orlando or Anaheim is roughly double that spent by foreign airlines on Boeing's commercial jets. Worldwide, tourists spent some $2 trillion last year, and an agency of the United Nations projects that number will grow by four times by 2020. The industry employs some 200 million people all around the world. The five most popular international tourist destinations are, in order, France, the United States, Spain, China, and Italy. Residents of China, the United States, Germany, Russia, and the United Kingdom are the five biggest spenders on international tourism. The growth in recent years of Chinese and Russian travelers has been unusually steep, while the declines in Japanese tourism have been correspondingly deep.[82] And traveler markets within countries are now displaying clear usage segments.[83] Overall, the tourism business declined more than 10 percent during the 2008–2009 recession, and like the economy in general, no quick recovery is expected. The good news is that you may soon be able to actually leave the planet and return on Richard Branson's commercial passenger spaceship—the price for a brief visit to space, a mere $280,000.[84] That's far less than the $20 million required for a longer ride (and a short stay at the International Space Station) on a Russian rocket.

The dramatic growth in tourism, especially before the recession, prompted U.S. firms and institutions to respond by developing new travel services to attract both domestic and foreign customers. For example, the Four Seasons Hotel in Philadelphia created a two-day package that included local concerts and museum visits. In addition to its attractions for kids, Orlando, Florida, has an opera company with performances by world-class singers. The cities of Phoenix, Las Vegas, and San Diego formed a consortium and put together a $500,000 marketing budget specifically appealing to foreign visitors to stop at all three destinations in one trip. Even the smallest hotels are finding a global clientele on the Internet.

---

[82]UN World Tourism Organization, http://mkt.unwto.org/barometer, accessed 2015.

[83]Philemon Oyewole, "Country Segmentation on the International Tourism Market Using Propensity to Travel and to Spend Abroad," *Journal of International Marketing* 23, no. 2 (2010), pp. 152–67.

[84]Mary Kissel, "Space: The Next Business Frontier," *The Wall Street Journal,* December 17, 2011.

Two of the best vistas in the world are Tahiti above the water (Bora Bora is silhouetted in the background) and the coral reefs off Belize under the water. Tourists flock to both from around the world. Services companies follow the tourists, including the Professional Association of Diving Instructors (PADI), which certifies scuba divers and instructors from its headquarters in Costa Mesa, California.

Other top consumer services exports include transportation, financial services, education, telecommunications, entertainment, information, and healthcare, in that order. Consider the following examples of each:

- American airlines are falling all over themselves to capture greater shares of the expanding Latin American travel market through investments in local carriers.

- Insurance sales are burgeoning in Latin America, with joint ventures between local and global firms making the most progress.

- Financial services in China are undergoing a revolution, with new services being offered at a fast pace—new sources of investor information and National Cash Register ATMs popping up everywhere. They are just getting acquainted with ATMs in Poland as well.

- Merrill Lynch is going after the investment-trust business that took off after Japan allowed brokers and banks to enter that business for the first time only in recent years.

- Almost 1 million foreign students (103,000 from India and 98,000 from China) spent more than $20 billion in tuition to attend American universities and colleges in 2013–2014.[85] Executive training is also a viable export for U.S. companies. Now at the K–12 level, private American schools are selling their services abroad as well.[86]

- Currently, phone rates in markets such as Germany, Italy, and Spain are so high that American companies cannot maintain toll-free information hotlines or solicit phone-order catalog sales. Other telecommunications markets are deregulating, creating opportunities for foreign firms. Wireless communications are ubiquitous in Japan and Europe.

- Cable TV sales are exploding in Latin America, and so too are video game sales in South Korea.[87]

- Sporting events are being sold all over the world—Mexican football in Los Angeles, American football in Scotland and Turkey, American baseball in Mexico, and professional soccer in China.

---

[85]Karin Fischer, " International Student Numbers Continue Record-Breaking Growth, Chronicle of Higher Education, November 17, 2014, online.

[86]Caroline Winter, "U.S. Private Schools are Looking East," *Bloomberg Businessweek*, October 6–12, 2014, pp. 25–27.

[87]Paul Mozur, "The Video-Game Nation," *The New York Times*, October 20, 2014, pp. B1, 7.

- Finally, not only are foreigners coming to the United States for healthcare services in growing numbers, but also North American firms are building hospitals abroad as well. Recently two infants, one from Sweden and one from Japan, received heart transplants at Loma Linda Hospital in California—laws in both their countries prohibit such life-saving operations. Beijing Toronto International Hospital opened its doors for some 250 Chinese patients; the services include a 24-hour satellite link for consultations with Toronto. Asian and Mexican competitors are also competing for this global market. The cost of a heart valve replacement with bypass is about $75,000 in the United States, $22,000 in Singapore, and $9,500 in India. Of course, the negative side of this trend is represented by the growing illegal global trade in organs for transplant. New reports are also showing that growth in this area has been less than predicted.[88]

Barriers to Entering Global Markets for Consumer Services

Most other services—automobile rentals, airline services, entertainment, hotels, and tourism, to name a few—are inseparable and require production and consumption to occur almost simultaneously; thus exporting is not a viable entry method for them. The vast majority of services (some 85 percent) enter foreign markets by licensing, franchising, or direct investment. Four kinds of barriers face consumer services marketers in this growing sector of the global marketplace: protectionism, controls on transborder data flows, protection of intellectual property, and cultural requirements for adaptation.

Protectionism.

The European Union is making modest progress toward establishing a single market for services. However, exactly how foreign service providers will be treated as unification proceeds is not clear. Reciprocity and harmonization, key concepts in the Single European Act, possibly will be used to curtail the entrance of some service industries into Europe. The U.S. film and entertainment industry seems to be a particularly difficult sector, although Vivendi's (a French company) purchase of Universal Studios made things a bit more interesting. A directive regarding transfrontier television broadcasting created a quota for European programs, requiring EU member states to ensure that at least 50 percent of entertainment air time is devoted to "European works." The European Union argues that this set-aside for domestic programming is necessary to preserve Europe's cultural identity. The consequences for the U.S. film industry are significant, because more than 40 percent of U.S. film industry profits come from foreign revenues.

Restrictions on Transborder Data Flows.

There is intense concern about how to deal with the relatively new "problem" of transborder data transfers. The European Commission is concerned that data about individuals (e.g., income, spending preferences, debt repayment histories, medical conditions, employment) are being collected, manipulated, and transferred between companies with little regard for the privacy of the affected individuals. A proposed directive by the Commission would require the consent of the individual before data are collected or processed. A wide range of U.S. service companies would be affected by such a directive—insurance underwriters, banks, credit reporting firms, direct marketing companies, and tour operators are a few examples. The directive would have broad effects on data processing and data analysis firms, because it would prevent a firm from electronically transferring information about individual European consumers to the United States for computer processing. Hidden in all the laws and directives are the unstated motives of most countries: a desire to inhibit the activities of multinationals and to protect local industry. As the global data transmission business continues to explode into the new century, regulators will focus increased attention in that direction.

---

[88]"Medecine avec Frontieres," *The Economist*, February 15, 2014, pp. 53–54.

Protection of Intellectual Property.   An important form of competition that is difficult to combat arises from pirated trademarks, processes, copyrights, and patents. You will recall that this topic was covered in detail in Chapter 7, so we just mention it here for completeness.

Cultural Barriers and Adaptation.   Because trade in services frequently involves people-to-people contact, culture plays a much bigger role in services than in merchandise trade.[89] Examples are many: Eastern Europeans are perplexed by Western expectations that unhappy workers put on a "happy face" when dealing with customers.[90] But McDonald's requires Polish employees to smile whenever they interact with customers. Such a requirement strikes many employees as artificial and insincere. The company has learned to encourage managers in Poland to probe employee problems and to assign troubled workers to the kitchen rather than to the food counter. Japanese Internet purchasers often prefer to pay in cash and in person rather than trust the Internet transaction or pay high credit card fees.

As another example, notice if the Japanese student sitting next to you in class ever verbally disagrees with your instructor. Classroom interactions vary substantially around the world. Students in Japan listen to lectures, take notes, and ask questions only after class, if then. In Japan the idea of grading class participation is nonsense. Conversely, because Spaniards are used to large undergraduate classes (hundreds rather than dozens), they tend to talk to their friends even when the instructor is talking. Likewise, healthcare delivery systems and doctor–patient interactions reflect cultural differences. Americans ask questions and get second opinions. Innovative healthcare services are developed on the basis of extensive marketing research. However, in Japan the social hierarchy is reflected heavily in the patients' deference to their doctors. While Japanese patient compliance is excellent and longevity is the best in the world, the healthcare system there is relatively unresponsive to the expressed concerns of consumers.

Japanese also tend to take a few long vacations—7 to 10 days is the norm. Thus, vacation packages designed for them are packed with activities. Phoenix, Las Vegas, and San Diego or Rome, Geneva, Paris, and London in 10 days makes sense to them. The Four Seasons Hotel chain provides special pillows, kimonos, slippers, and teas for Japanese guests. Virgin Atlantic Airways and other long-haul carriers have interactive screens available for each passenger, allowing viewing of Japanese (or American, French, etc.) movies and TV.

Managing a global services workforce is certainly no simple task. Just ask the folks at UPS. Some of the surprises UPS ran into included indignation in France when drivers were told they couldn't have wine with lunch, protests in Britain when drivers' dogs were banned from delivery trucks, dismay in Spain when it was found that the brown

[89]Torsten Ringberg, Gaby Odekerken-Schroder, and Glenn L. Christensen, "A Cultural Models Approach to Service Recovery," *Journal of Marketing* 71 (2007), pp. 184–214; Samart Powpaka, "Empowering Chinese Service Employees: A Reexamination and Extension," *Journal of Global Marketing* 21, no. 4 (2008), pp. 271–93; Haksin Chan and Lisa C. Wan, "Consumer Responses to Service Failures: A Resource Preference Model of Cultural Influences," *Journal of International Marketing* 16, no. 1 (2008), pp. 72–97; Hean Tat Keh and Jin Sun, "The Complexities of Perceived Risk in Cross-Cultural Services Marketing," *Journal of International Marketing* 16, no. 1 (2008), pp. 120–46; Edwin J. Nijssen and Hester van Herk, "Conjoining International Marketing and Relationship Marketing: Exploring Consumers' Cross-Border Relationships," *Journal of International Marketing* 17, no. 1 (2009), pp. 91–115; Sathak Gaurav, Shawn Cole, and Jeremy Tobacman, "Marketing Complex Financial Products in Emerging Markets: Evidence from Rainfall Insurance in India," *Journal of Marketing Research* 48(2011), pp. 150–62; Yadong Luo, Stephanie Lu Wang, Qinqin Zheng, and Vaidyanathan Jayaraman, "Task Attributes and Process Integration in Business Process Offshoring: A Prespective of Service Providers from India and China," *Journal of International Business Studies* 43 (2012), pp. 498–524; Carine Peeters, Catherine Dehon, and Patricia Carcia-Prieto, "The Attention Stimulus of Cultural Differences in Global Services Sourcing," Journal of International Business Studies, 2014, online.

[90]Andrew E. Kramer, "Russian Service, and with Please and Thank You," *The New York Times*, November 2, 2013, pp. A1, 10.

UPS trucks resembled the local hearses, and shock in Germany when brown shirts were required for the first time since 1945 (brown shirts are associated with Nazi rule during World War II).

And while tips of 10 to 20 percent are an important part of services workers' incentives in the United States, this is not the case in Germany, where tips are rounded to the nearest euro. Thus, closer management of service personnel is required in those countries to maintain high levels of customer satisfaction.

Clearly, opportunities for the marketing of consumer services will continue to grow in the 21st century. International marketers will have to be quite creative in responding to the legal and cultural challenges of delivering high-quality services in foreign markets and to foreign customers at domestic locales.

Brands in International Markets

Hand in hand with global products and services are global brands. A *global brand* is defined as the worldwide use of a name, term, sign, symbol (visual and/or auditory), design, or combination thereof intended to identify goods or services of one seller and to differentiate them from those of competitors. Much like the experience with global products, the question of whether or not to establish global brands has no single answer. However, the importance of a brand name, even in the nonprofit sector, is unquestionable.[91] Indeed, Exhibit 13.4 lists the estimated worth (equity) of the 20 top global brands. And as indicated in previous chapters, protecting brand equity is also a big business.

---

[91]John A. Quelch and Nathalie Laidler-Kylander, *The New Global Brands* (Mason, OH: Southwestern, 2006).

Exhibit 13.4
Top Twenty Brands

Rank	Previous	Brand	Country	Sector	Brand Value	Change
1	1	Apple	United States	Electronics	118,863	+21%
2	2	Google	United States	Internet services	107,439	+15%
3	3	Coca-Cola	United States	Beverages	81,563	+3%
4	4	IBM	United States	Business services	72,244	−8%
5	5	Microsoft	United States	Software	61,154	+3%
6	6	GE	United States	Diversified	45,480	−3%
7	8	Samsung	South Korea	Electronics	45,462	+15%
8	10	Toyota	Japan	Automotive	42,492	+20%
9	7	McDonald's	United States	Restaurants	42,254	+1%
10	11	Mercedes-Benz	Germany	Automotive	34,228	+8%
11	12	BMW	Germany	Automotive	34,214	+7%
12	9	Intel	United States	Electronics	34,153	−8%
13	14	Disney	United States	Media	32,223	+14%
14	13	Cisco	United States	Business services	30,396	+6%
15	19	Amazon	United States	Retailing	29,478	+25%
16	18	Oracle	United States	Business services	25,980	+8%
17	15	Hewlett-Packard	United States	Electronics	23,758	−8%
18	16	Gillette	United States	Consumer products	22,845	−9%
19	17	Louis Vuitton	France	Luxury	22,552	−9%
20	20	Honda	Japan	Automotive	21,673	+17%

Source: Interbrand.com, accessed 2014. Reprinted with permission. Also see WPP's ranking which is very different because it is bases on different criteria.

A successful brand is the most valuable resource a company has. The brand name encompasses the years of advertising, goodwill, quality evaluations, product experience, and other beneficial attributes the market associates with the product. Brand image is at the very core of business identity and strategy. Western researchers have personified brands, imbuing them with personalities and images. In a sense, the consumer–brand interaction becomes much like an interpersonal interaction, wherein cultural differences hold heavy sway.[92] This comparison also implies that even global brands must be positioned locally, as a Japanese consumer will see and interact with the Coke brand differently than a French consumer, for example. Research shows that the importance and impact of brands (and the success of their extensions)[93] vary with cultural values around the world.[94] Thus, customers everywhere respond to images,[95] myths, and metaphors that help them define their personal and national identities within a global context of world culture and product benefits.[96]

Global brands play an important role in that process. The value of Sony, Coca-Cola, McDonald's, Toyota, and Marlboro is indisputable. Both Interbrand and WPP rankings estimate the value of Coca-Cola, for decades the world's most valuable brand, at about $81 billion. In fact, one authority speculates that brands are so valuable that companies will soon include a "statement of value" addendum to their balance sheets to include intangibles such as the value of their brands. Please see Exhibit 13.4 for details. One researcher has noted that in the short run, brand equities remain relatively stable, but not so in the long run.[97] The latter is certainly the case when the long run includes the recession of 2008–2009. Google's brand equity increased 25 percent in the period, while GE's declined 10 percent. But the biggest change was the huge decline of Citi, which lost almost half (49 percent) of its brand

[92] Andreas B. Eisingerich and Gaia Rubera, "Drivers of Brand Commitment: A Cross-National Investigation," *Journal of International Marketing* 18, no. 2 (2010), pp. 64–79; Claudiu V. Dimofte, Johny K. Johansson, and Richard P. Bagozzi, "Global Brands in the United States: How Consumer Ethnicity Mediates the Global Brand Effect," *Journal of International Marketing* 18, no. 3 (2010), pp. 81–106.

[93] Sharon Ng, "Cultural Orientation and Brand Dilution: Impact of Motivation Level and Extension Typicality," *Journal of Marketing Research* 47, no. 1 (2010), pp. 186–98; Carlos J. Torelli and Rohini Ahluwalia, "Extending Culturally Symbolic Brands: A Blessing or a Curse?" *Journal of Consumer Research* 38, no. 5 (2012), pp. 933–47.

[94] See the special issue of the *Journal of Global Marketing* 23, no. 3 (2010) on branding, especially Erdener Kaynak and Lianxi Zhou, "Special Issue on Brand Equity, Branding, and Marketing Communications in Emerging Markets," pp. 171–76; Xuehua Wang and Zhilin Yang, "The Effect of Brand Credibility on Consumers' Brand Purchase Intention in Emerging Economies: The Moderating Role of Brand Awareness and Brand Image," pp. 177–88; Wang Zingyuan, Fuan Li, and Yu Wei, "How Do They Really Help? An Empirical Study of the Role of Different Information Sources in Building Brand Trust," pp. 243–52; and Yi-Min Chen, "The Persistence of Brand Value at Country, Industry, and Firm Levels," pp. 253–69. Also see Son K. Lam, Michael Ahearne, and Niels Schillewaert, "A Multinational Examination of the Symbolic-wInstrumental Framework of Consumer-Brand Identification," *Journal of International Business Studies* 43 (2012), pp. 306–31; Carlos J. Torellie, Aysegul Ozsomer, Sergio Wl. Carvalho, Hean Tat Keh, and Natalia Maehle, "Brand Concepts as Representations of Human Values: Do Cultural Congruity and Compatability between Values Matter?" *Journal of Marketing* 76, no. 4 (July 2012), pp. 92–108; Elif Izberk-Bilgin, "Infidel Brands: Unveiling Alternative Meanings of Global Brands at the Nexus of Globlaization, Consumer Culture and Islamism," *Journal of Consumer Research* 39, no. 4 (2012), pp. 663–87.

[95] Xuehua Wang, Zhilin Yang, and Ning Rong Liu, "The Impacts of Brand Personality and Congruity on Purchase Intention: Evidence from the Chinese Mainland's Automobile Market," *Journal of Global Marketing* 22 (2009), pp. 199–215; Francisco Guzman and Audhesh K. Paswan, "Cultural Brands from Emerging Markets: Brand Image across Host and Home Countries," *Journal of International Marketing* 17, no. 3 (2009), pp. 71–86; Ralf van der Lans and 12 coauthors, "Cross-National Logo Evaluation Analysis: An Individual-Level Approach," *Marketing Science* 28, no. 5 (2009), pp. 968–85; Yinlong Zhang and Adwait Khare, "The Impact of Accessible Identities on the Evaluation of Global vs. Local Products," *Journal of Consumer Research* 36 (2009), pp. 525–37.

[96] Douglas B. Holt, "What Becomes an Icon Most?" *Harvard Business Review*, March 2003, pp. 43–49; Yuliya Strizhakova, Robin L. Coulter, and Linda A. Price, "Branded Products as a Passport to Global Citizenship: Perspectives from Developed and Developing Countries," *Journal of International Marketing* 16, no. 4 (2008), pp. 57–85; Lily Dong and Kelly Tian, "The Use of Western Brands in Asserting Chinese National Identity," *Journal of Consumer Research* 36 (2009), pp. 504–22.

[97] A. Coskun Samli and Merici Fevrier, "Achieving and Managing Global Brand Equity: A Critical Analysis," *Journal of Global Marketing* 21, no. 3 (2008), pp. 207–15.

Copying is the highest form of flattery? Not so in the car business. The new QQ model from Chinese company Chery (left) resembles the Matiz or Spark from GM's Daewoo (right)—perhaps a bit too much.

equity in a single year, falling from #19 to #36. Ouch! You can find the most recent rankings for Google and GE in Exhibit 13.4, but Citi dropped even further, to #48. We have included the link to the WPP ranking for your information. Because the two ranking organizations use different criteria (e.g., Interbrand requires companies to have substantial international sales) to estimate brand equity, their rankings are actually very different. For example, WWP ranks Google at #1, with a brand equity of $158 billion. It also ranks China Mobile and International Commercial Bank of China (ICBC) as #15 and #17, respectively.

Global Brands

Naturally, companies with strong brands strive to use those brands globally. In fact, even perceived "globalness" can lead to increases in sales.[98] The Internet and other technologies accelerate the pace of the globalization of brands. Even for products that must be adapted to local market conditions, a global brand can be successfully used with careful consideration.[99] Heinz produces a multitude of products that are sold under the Heinz brand all over the world. Many are also adapted to local tastes. In the United Kingdom, for example, Heinz Baked Beans Pizza (available with cheese or sausage) was a runaway hit, selling more than 2.5 million pizzas in the first six months after its introduction. In the British market, Heinz's brand of baked beans is one of the more popular products. The British consumer eats an average of 16 cans annually, for a sales total of $1.5 billion a year. The company realized that consumers in other countries are unlikely to rush to stores for bean pizzas, but the idea could lead to the creation of products more suited to other cultures and markets.

Ideally a global brand gives a company uniformly positive worldwide brand associations that enhance efficiency and cost savings when introducing other products with the brand name, but not all companies believe a single global approach is the best. Indeed, we know that the same brand does not necessarily hold the same meanings in different countries. In addition to companies such as Apple, Kellogg, Coca-Cola, Caterpillar, and Levi's, which

[98]Jan-Benedict E. M. Steenkamp, Rajeev Batra, and Dana L. Alden, "How Perceived Brand Globalness Creates Brand Value," *Journal of International Business Studies* 34 (2003), pp. 53–65; Claudiu V. Dmofte, Johny K. Johansson, and Ilkka A. Ronkainen, "Cognitive and Affective Reactions of U.S. Consumers to Global Brands," *Journal of International Marketing* 16, no. 4 (2008), pp. 113–35; Vertica Bhardwaj, Archana Kumar, and Youn-Kyun Kim, "Brand Analyses of U.S. Global and Local Brands in India: The Case of Levi's," *Journal of Global Marketing* 23 (2010), pp. 80–94; Bernhard Swoboda, Karin Pennemann, and Markus Taube, "The Effects of Perceived Brand Globalness and Perceived Brand Localness in China: Empirical Evidence on Western, Asian, and Domestic Retailers," *Journal of International Marketing* 20, no. 4 (2012), pp. 72–95; Aysegul Ozsomer, "The Interplay between Global and Local Brands: A Closer Look at Perceived Brand Globalness and Local Iconness," *Journal of International Marketing* 20, no. 2 (2012), pp. 72–95.

[99]Shi Zhang and Bernd H. Schmitt, "Creating Local Brands in Multilingual International Markets," *Journal of Marketing Research* 38 (August 2001), pp. 313–25.

use the same brands worldwide, other multinationals such as Nestlé, Mars, Procter & Gamble, and Gillette have some brands that are promoted worldwide and others that are country specific. Among companies that have faced the question of whether to make all their brands global, not all have followed the same path.[100]

Companies that already have successful country-specific brand names must balance the benefits of a global brand against the risk of losing the benefits of an established brand.[101] And some brand names simply do not translate.[102] The cost of reestablishing the same level of brand preference and market share for the global brand that the local brand has must be offset against the long-term cost savings and benefits of having only one brand name worldwide. In those markets where the global brand is unknown, many companies are buying local brands of products that consumers want and then revamping, repackaging, and finally relaunching them with a new image. Unilever purchased a local brand of washing powder, Biopan, which had a 9 percent share of the market in Hungary; after relaunching, market share rose to about 25 percent.

When Mars, a U.S. company that includes candy and pet food among its product lines, adopted a global strategy, it brought all its products under a global brand, even those with strong local brand names. In Britain, the largest candy market in Europe, M&Ms previously were sold as Treets, and Snickers candy was sold under the name Marathon to avoid association with *knickers*, the British word for women's underpants. To bring the two candy products under the global umbrella, Mars returned the candies to their original names. The pet food division adopted Whiskas and Sheba for cat foods and Pedigree for dog food as the global brand name, replacing KalKan. To support this global division that accounts for more than $4 billion annually, Mars also developed a website for its pet food brands. The site functions as a "global infrastructure" that can be customized locally by any Pedigree Petfoods branch worldwide. For instance, Pedigree offices can localize languages and information on subjects such as veterinarians and cat-owner gatherings.

Finally, researchers are beginning to address the sometimes difficult problem of brand extensions in global markets. Consumers in "Eastern" cultures may be more likely to understand and appreciate brand extensions because of their more holistic thinking than consumers in "Western" cultures, with their more analytical thinking patterns. Obviously more work needs to be done in this area, but important differences across cultures are readily discernible in the acceptance of brand extensions.[103]

National Brands

A different strategy is followed by the Nestlé Company, which has a stable of global and country-specific national brands in its product line. The Nestlé name itself is promoted globally, but its global brand expansion strategy is two-pronged. In some markets, it acquires well-established national brands when it can and builds on their strengths—there are 7,000 local brands in its family of brands. In other markets where there are no strong brands it can acquire, it uses global brand names. The company is described as preferring brands to be local, people to be regional, and technology to be global. It does, however, own some of the world's largest global brands; Nescafé is but one.

---

[100]Prominent among those arguing against global brands are David A. Aaker and Erich Joachimsthaler, "The Lure of Global Branding," *Harvard Business Review*, November–December 1999. For an interesting view of the arguments for and against globalization of brands, see Anand P. Raman, "The Global Face Off," *Harvard Business Review*, June 2003, pp. 35–46.

[101]Stanford A. Westjohn, Nitish Singh, and Peter Magnusson, "Responsiveness to Global and Local Consumer Culture Positioning: A Personality and Collective Identity Perspective," *Journal of International Marketing* 20, no. 21 (2012), pp. 58–73.

[102]Clement S. F. Chow, Esther P. Y. Tang, and Isabel S. F. Fu, "Global Marketers' Dilemma: Whether to Translated the Brand Name into Local Language," *Journal of Global Marketing* 20 (2007), pp. 25–38.

[103]Alokparna Basu Monga and Deborah Roedder John, "Cultural Differences in Brand Extension Evaluation: The Influence of Analytic versus Holistic Thinking," *Journal of Consumer Research* 33 (2007), pp. 529–36; Guoqun Fu, John Saunders, and Riliang Qu, "Brand Extensions in Emerging Markets: Theory Development and Testing in China," *Journal of Global Marketing* 22 (2009), pp. 217–28; Sharon Ng, "Cultural Orientation and Brand Dilution: Impact Level and Extension Typicality," *Journal of Marketing Research* 47, no. 1 (2010), pp. 186–98. ; Carlos J. Torelli and Rohini Ahluwalia, "Extending Culturally Symbolic Brands: A Blessing or a Curse?" *Journal of Consumer Research* 38, no. 5 (February 2012), pp. 933–47.

Unilever is another company that follows a strategy of a mix of national and global brands. In Poland, Unilever introduced its Omo brand detergent (sold in many other countries), but it also purchased a local brand, Pollena 2000. Despite a strong introduction of two competing brands, Omo by Unilever and Ariel by Procter & Gamble, a refurbished Pollena 2000 had the largest market share a year later. Unilever's explanation was that eastern European consumers are leery of new brands; they want brands that are affordable and in keeping with their own tastes and values. Pollena 2000 is successful not just because it is cheaper but because it is consistent with local values.

Multinationals must also consider increases in nationalistic pride that occur in some countries and their impact on brands.[104] In India, for example, Unilever considers it critical that its brands, such as Surf detergent and Lux and Lifebuoy soaps, are viewed as Indian brands. Just as is the case with products, the answer to the question of when to go global with a brand is, "It depends—the market dictates." Use global brands where possible and national brands where necessary. Finally, there is growing evidence that national brands' acceptance varies substantially across regions within countries, suggesting that even finer market segmentation of branding strategies may be efficient.[105]

Country-of-Origin Effect and Global Brands

LO5

Country-of-origin effects on product image

As discussed previously, brands are used as external cues to taste, design, performance, quality, value, prestige, and so forth. In other words, the consumer associates the value of the product with the brand. The brand can convey either a positive or a negative message about the product to the consumer and is affected by past advertising and promotion, product reputation, and product evaluation and experience.[106] In short, many factors affect brand image. One factor that is of great concern to multinational companies that manufacture worldwide is the country-of-origin effect on the market's perception of the product.[107]

Country-of-origin effect (*COE*) can be defined as any influence that the country of manufacture, assembly, or design has on a consumer's positive or negative perception of a product.[108] In 2008, 22 Chinese companies were found to have sold dairy products containing melamine, a toxic chemical that enhances appearance. This has stoked Chinese mainland fears about product quality, particularly of baby formula. During 2013, there was a rush on formula from Hong Kong, perceived to be safer by consumers, to the extent that the government of Hong Kong imposed limits on exports. Company made little difference—only

[104]Tsang-Sing Chan, Geng Cui, and Nan Zhou, "Competition between Foreign and Domestic Brands: A Study of Consumer Purchases in China," *Journal of Global Marketing* 22 (2009), pp. 181–97.

[105]Bart J. Bronnenberg, Sanjay K. Dhar, and Jean-Pierre Dube, "Consumer Package Goods in the United States: National Brands, Local Branding," *Journal of Marketing Research* 44 (2007), pp. 4–13; M. Berk Ataman, Carl F. Mela, and Harald J. van Heerde, "Consumer Package Goods in France: National Brands, Regions Chains and Local Branding," *Journal of Marketing Research* 44 (2007), pp. 14–20.

[106]Jean-Claude Usunier and Ghislaine Cestre, "Product Ethnicity: Revisiting the Match between Products and Countries," *Journal of International Marketing* 15 (2007), pp. 32–72; Ravi Pappu, Pascale G. Quester, and Ray W. Cooksey, "Country Image and Consumer-Based Brand Equity: Relationships and Implications for International Marketing," *Journal of International Business Studies* 38 (2007), pp. 726–45; Nicole Koschate-Fischer, Adamantios Diamantopoulos, and Katharina Oldenkotte, "Are Consumers Willing to Pay More for a Favorable Country Image? A Study of Country-of-Origin Effects on Willingness to Pay," *Journal of International Marketing* 20, no. 1 (2012), pp. 19–41; Mark Florian Herz and Adamantios Diamantopoulos, "Country-Specific Associations Made by Consumers: A Dual-Coding Theory Perspective," *Journal of International Marketing* 21, no. 3 (2013), pp. 95–121; Cathy Yi Chen, Pragya Mathur, and Durairaj Maheswaran, "The Effects of Country-Related Affect on Product Evaluations," *Journal of Consumer Research* 41, no. 4 (December 2014), pp. 1033–46.

[107]Brian R. Chabowski, Saeed Samiee, and G. Tomas M. Hult, "A Bibliometric Analysis of the Global Branding Literature and a Research Agenda," *Journal of International Business Studies* 44 (2013), pp. 622–34.

[108]Charles A. Funk, Jonathan D. Arthurs, Len J. Trevino, and Jeff Joireman, "Consumer Animosity in the Global Value Chain: The Effect of International Production Shifts on Willingness to Purchase Hybrid Products," *Journal of International Business Studies* 41, no. 4 (2010), pp. 639–51; Piyush Sharma, "Country of Origin Effects in Developed and Emerging Markets: Exploring the Contrasting Roles of Materialism and Value Consciousness," *Journal of International Business Studies* 42, no. 2 (2011), pp. 285–306; Olivier Bertrand, "What Goes around Comes around: Effects of Offshore Outsourcing on the Export Performance of Firms," *Journal of International Business Studies* 42, no. 2 (2011), pp. 334–44.

country of manufacture.[109] A company competing in global markets today manufactures products worldwide; when the customer becomes aware of the country of origin, there is the possibility that the place of manufacture will affect product or brand images.[110]

The country, the type of product, and the image of the company and its brands all influence whether the country of origin will engender a positive or negative reaction.[111] A variety of generalizations can be made about country-of-origin effects on products and brands.[112] Consumers tend to have stereotypes about products and countries that have been formed by experience, hearsay, myth, and limited information.[113] Following are some of the more frequently cited generalizations.

Consumers have broad but somewhat vague stereotypes about specific countries and specific product categories that they judge "best": English tea, French perfume, Chinese silk, Italian leather, Japanese electronics, Jamaican rum, and so on. Stereotyping of this nature is typically product specific and may not extend to other categories of products from these countries.

The importance of these types of stereotypes was emphasized recently as a result of a change in U.S. law that requires any cloth "substantially altered" (woven, for instance) in another country to identify that country on its label. Designer labels such as Ferragamo, Gucci, and Versace are affected in that they now must include on the label "Made in China," because the silk comes from China. The lure to pay $195 and up for scarves "Made in Italy" by Ferragamo loses some of its appeal when accompanied with a "Made in China" label. As one buyer commented, "I don't care if the scarves are made in China as long as it doesn't say so on the label." The irony is that 95 percent of all silk comes from China, which has not only the reputation for the finest silk but also a reputation of producing cheap scarves. The "best" scarves are made in France or Italy by one of the haute couture designers.

Ethnocentrism can also have country-of-origin effects; feelings of national pride—the "buy local" effect, for example—can influence attitudes toward foreign products.[114] Honda,

---

[109]John Hannon and Barbara Demick, "Baby Formula Feeds Territorial Discord," *Los Angeles Times*, March 1, 2013, p. A5.

[110]Peter Magnusson, Vijaykumar Krishnan, Stanford A. Westjohn, and Srdan Zdravkovic, "The Spillover Effects of Prototype Brand Transgressions on Country Image and Related Brands," *Journal of International Marketing* 22, no. 1 (2014), pp. 21–38.

[111]Valentyna Melnyk, Kristina Klein, and Franziska Volckner, "The Double-Edged Sword of Foreign Brand Names for Companies from Emerging Countries," *Journal of Marketing* 76, no. 6 (November 2012), pp. 21–37.

[112]Peeter W. J. Verleigh, Jan-Benedict E. M. Steenkamp, and Matthew T. G. Meulenberg, "Country-of-Origin Effects in Consumer Processing of Advertising Claims," *International Journal of Research in Marketing* 22, no. 2 (2005), pp. 127–39.

[113]George Balabanis and Adamantios Diamantopoulos, "Brand Origin Identification by Consumers: A Classification Perspective," *Journal of International Marketing* 16, no. 1 (2008), pp. 39–71; Alfred Rosenbloom and James E. Haefner, "Country-of-Origin Effects and Global Brand Trust: A First Look," *Journal of Global Marketing* 22, no. 4 (2009), pp. 267–79.

[114]Rohit Varman and Russell W. Belk, "Nationalism and Ideology in an Anticonsumption Movement," *Journal of Consumer Research* 36 (2009), pp. 686–700; T.S. Chan, Kenny K. Chan, and Lai-Cheung Leung, "How Consumer Ethnocentrism and Animosity Impair the Economic Recovery of Emerging Markets," *Journal of Global Marketing* 23, no. 3 (2010) pp. 208–25; Jan-Benedict E. M. Steenkamp and Martin G. De Jong, "A Global Investigation into the Constellation of Consumer Attitudes toward Global and Local Products," *Journal of Marketing* 74, no. 6 (2010), pp. 18–40; Alexander Josiassen, "Consumer Disidentification and its Effects on Domestic Product Purchases: An Empirical Investigation in the Netherlands," *Journal of Marketing* 75, no. 2 (2011), pp. 124–40; Eva M. Oberecker and Adamantios Diamantopoulos, "Consumers' Emotional Bonds with Foreign Countries: Does Consumer Affinity Affect Behavioral Intentions?" *Journal of International Marketing* 19, no. 2 (2011), pp. 45–72; George Balabanis and Adamantios Diamantopoulos, "Gains and Losses from the Misperception of Brand Origin: The Role of Brand Strength and Country-of-Origin Image," *Journal of International Marketing* 19, no. 2 (2011), pp. 95–116; Xiaoling Guo, "Living in a Global World: Influence of Consumer Global Orientation on Attitudes toward Global Brands from Developed versus Emerging Countries," *Journal of International Marketing* 21, no. 1 (2013), pp. 1–22; Dana L. Alden, James B. Kelley, Petra Reifler, Julie A. Lee, and Geoffrey N. Soutar, "The Effect of Global Company Animosity on Global Brand Attitudes in Emerging and Developed Markets: Does Perceived Value Matter?" *Journal of International Marketing* 21, no. 2 (2013), pp. 17–38; Cher-Min Fong, Chun-Ling Lee, and Yunzhou Du, "Consumer Animosity, Country of Origin, and Foreign Entry-Mode Choice: A Cross-Country Investigation," *Journal of International Marketing* 22, no. 1 (2014), pp. 62–76; Piyush Sharma, "Consumer Ethnocentrisim: Reconceptualization and Cross-Cultural Validation," *Journal of International Business Studies*, 2014, online.

As they say, "two brands are better than one!" How about four? The four flags you seeing flying on the radar mast of the *Endeavor* at sea among the Galapagos Islands represent Ecuador (bottom), the Bahamas registry of the 85-person cruise ship (right), the National Geographic Society, and Lindblad Expeditions. The latter two are a great example of co-branding. The multifaceted strategic alliance that Lindblad Expeditions has with the National Geographic Society, "enables travelers to participate in the world of natural and cultural history as engaged, active explorers who care about the planet." This is an alliance of two exploration pioneers in an innovative program to reach remote and pristine destinations around the globe. Sustainable and education-based tourism is featured by the alliance.

which manufactures one of its models almost entirely in the United States, recognizes this phenomenon and points out how many component parts are made in America in some of its advertisements. In contrast, others have a stereotype of Japan as producing the "best" automobiles, at least up until 2010. A study completed before the Toyota quality disaster had found that U.S. automobile producers may suffer comparatively tarnished images, regardless of whether they actually produce superior products.

Countries are also stereotyped on the basis of whether they are industrialized, in the process of industrializing, or developing. These stereotypes are less product specific; they are more a perception of the quality of goods and services in general produced within the country.[115] Industrialized countries have the highest quality image, and products from developing countries generally encounter bias.

In Russia, for example, the world is divided into two kinds of products: "ours" and "imported." Russians prefer fresh, homegrown food products but imported clothing and manufactured items. Companies hoping to win loyalty by producing in Russia have been unhappily surprised. Consumers remain cool toward locally produced Polaroid cameras and Philips irons. Yet computers produced across the border in Finland are considered high quality. For Russians, country of origin is more important than brand name as an indicator of quality. South Korean electronics manufacturers have difficulty convincing Russians that their products are as good as Japanese ones. Goods produced in Malaysia, Hong Kong, or Thailand are more suspect still. Eastern Europe is considered adequate for clothing but poor for food or durables. Turkey and China are at the bottom of the heap.

One might generalize that the more technical the product, the less positive is the perception of something manufactured in a less developed or newly industrializing country.[116] There is also the tendency to favor foreign-made products over domestic-made in less-developed countries. Foreign products fare not as well in developing countries because consumers have stereotypes about the quality of foreign-made products, even from industrialized countries. A survey of consumers in the Czech Republic found that 72 percent of Japanese products were considered to be of the highest quality; German goods followed with 51 percent, Swiss goods with 48 percent, Czech goods with 32 percent, and, last, the United States with 29 percent.

One final generalization about COE involves fads that often surround products from particular countries or regions in the world. These fads are most often product specific and generally involve goods that are themselves faddish in nature. European consumers' affection for American products is quite fickle. The affinity for Jeep Cherokees, Budweiser beer, and Bose sound systems of the 1990s has faded to outright animosity toward American brands as a protest of American political policies. This reaction echoes the 1970s and 1980s backlash against anything American, but in the 1990s, American was in. In China, anything Western seems to be the fad. If it is Western, it is in demand, even at prices three and four times higher than those of domestic products. In most cases such fads wane after a few years as some new fad takes over.

---

[115]Jan-Benedict E. M. Steenkamp and Inge Geyskens, "How Country Characteristics Affect the Perceived Value of Web Sites," *Journal of Marketing* 70 (2006), pp. 136–50.

[116]Leila Hamzaoui-Essoussi, "Technological Complexity and Country-of-Origin Effects on Binational Product Evaluation: Investigation in an Emerging Market," *Journal of International Marketing* 23, no. 4 (2010) pp. 306–20.

There are exceptions to the generalizations presented here, but it is important to recognize that country of origin can affect a product or brand's image significantly. Furthermore, not every consumer is sensitive to a product's country of origin.[117] A finding in a recent study suggests that more knowledgeable consumers are more sensitive to a product's COE than are those less knowledgeable. Another study reports that COE varies across consumer groups; Japanese were found to be more sensitive than American consumers.[118] The multinational company needs to take these factors into consideration in its product development and marketing strategy, because a negative country stereotype can be detrimental to a product's success unless overcome with effective marketing.

Once the market gains experience with a product, negative stereotypes can be overcome. Nothing would seem less plausible than selling chopsticks made in Chile to Japan, but it happened. It took years for a Chilean company to overcome doubts about the quality of its product, but persistence, invitations to Japanese to visit the Chilean poplar forests that provided the wood for the chopsticks, and a high-quality product finally overcame doubt; now the company cannot meet the demand for its chopsticks.

Country stereotyping—some call it "nation equity"[119]—can also be overcome with good marketing.[120] The image of Korean electronics and autos improved substantially in the United States once the market gained positive experience with Korean brands. Most recently in the United States, the quality/safety of Chinese-made products has been a source of problems for American-branded toys, foods, and pharmaceuticals. It will be interesting to watch how the new Chinese brands themselves, such as Lenovo computers and Haier appliances, will work to avoid the current negative "nation equity" to which they are suffering association. All of this stresses the importance of building strong global brands like Sony, General Electric, and Levi's. Brands effectively advertised and products properly positioned can help ameliorate a less-than-positive country stereotype.

Private Brands

Private brands owned by retailers are growing as challengers to manufacturers' brands, whether global or country specific. Store brands are particularly important in Europe compared with the United States.[121] In the food retailing sector in Britain and many European countries, private labels owned by national retailers increasingly confront manufacturers' brands. From blackberry jam and vacuum cleaner bags to smoked salmon and sun-dried tomatoes, private-label products dominate grocery stores in Britain and many of the hypermarkets of Europe. Private brands have captured nearly 30 percent of the British and Swiss markets and more than 20 percent of the French and German markets. In some European markets, private-label market share has doubled in just the past five years.

Sainsbury, one of Britain's largest grocery retailers with 420 stores, reserves the best shelf space for its own brands. A typical Sainsbury store has about 16,000 products, of which 8,000 are Sainsbury labels. These labels account for two-thirds of store sales.

---

[117]This appears to be less the case when professional buyers make decisions. See John G. Knight, David K. Holdsworth, and Damien W. Mather, "Country-of-Origin and Choice of Food Imports: An In-Depth Study of European Distribution Chanel Gatekeepers," *Journal of International Business Studies* 38 (2007), pp. 107–25.

[118]Zeynep Gurhan-Canli and Durairaj Maheswaran, "Cultural Variations in Country of Origin Effects," *Journal of Marketing Research* 37 (August 2000), pp. 309–17.

[119]Durairaj Maheswaran, "Nation Equity: Incidental Emotions in Country-of-Origin Effects," *Journal of Consumer Research* 33 (2006), pp. 370–76.

[120]Lys S. Amine, Mike C. H. Chao, and Mark J. Arnold, "Exploring the Practical Effects of Origin, Animosity, and Price-Quality Issues: Two Case Studies of Taiwan and Acer in China," *Journal of International Marketing* 13, no. 2 (2005), pp. 114–50.

[121]Tulin Erdem, Ying Zhao, and An Valenzuela, "Performance of Store Brands: A Cross-Country Analysis of Consumer Store-Brand Preferences, Perceptions, and Risk," *Journal of Marketing Research* 41, no. 1 (2004), pp. 59–72; Jan-Benedict E. M. Steenkamp, Harald J. Van Heere, and Inge Geyskens, "What Makes Consumers Willing to Pay a Price Premium for National Brands over Private Labels?" *Journal of Marketing Research* 47, no. 6 (2010), pp. 1011–24.

The company avidly develops new products, launching 1,400 to 1,500 new private-label items each year, and weeds out hundreds of others no longer popular. It launched its own Novon brand laundry detergent; in the first year, its sales climbed past Procter & Gamble's and Unilever's top brands to make it the top-selling detergent in Sainsbury stores and the second-best seller nationally, with a 30 percent market share. The 15 percent margin on private labels claimed by chains such as Sainsbury helps explain why their operating profit margins are as high as 8 percent, or eight times the profit margins of their U.S. counterparts.

Private labels are formidable competitors, particularly during economic difficulties in the target markets. Buyers prefer to buy less expensive, "more local" private brands during recessions.[122] This strategy also allows retailers to outsource production while still appreciating the advantages of a local brand.[123] Private brands provide the retailer with high margins; they receive preferential shelf space and strong in-store promotions; and perhaps most important for consumer appeal, they are quality products at low prices. Contrast this characterization with manufacturers' brands, which traditionally are premium priced and offer the retailer lower margins than it would get from private labels.

To maintain market share, global brands will have to be priced competitively and provide real consumer value. Global marketers must examine the adequacy of their brand strategies in light of such competition. This effort may make the cost and efficiency benefits of global brands even more appealing.

---

[122]Lien Lamey, Barbara Deleersnyder, Marnik G. Dekimpe, and Jan-Benedict E. M. Steenkamp, "How Business Cycles Contribute to Private-Label Success: Evidence from the United States and Europe," *Journal of Marketing* 76 (2007), pp. 1–15.

[123]Shih-Fen Chen, "A Transaction Cost Rationale for Private Branding and Its Implications for the Choice of Domestic vs. Offshore Outsourcing," *Journal of International Business Studies* 40, no. 1 (2009), pp. 156–75.

Summary

The growing globalization of markets that gives rise to standardization must be balanced with the continuing need to assess all markets for those differences that might require adaptation for successful acceptance. The premise that global communications and other worldwide socializing forces have fostered a homogenization of tastes, needs, and values in a significant sector of the population across all cultures is difficult to deny. However, more than one authority has noted that in spite of the forces of homogenization, consumers also see the world of global symbols, company images, and product choice through the lens of their own local culture and its stage of development and market sophistication. Each product must be viewed in light of how it is perceived by each culture with which it comes in contact. What is acceptable and comfortable within one group may be radically new and resisted within others, depending on the experiences and perceptions of each group. Understanding that an established product in one culture may be considered an innovation in another is critical in planning and developing consumer products for foreign markets. Analyzing a product as an innovation and using the Product Component Model may provide the marketer with important leads for adaptation.

Key Terms

Quality	Green marketing	Diffusion	Global brand
Product homologation	Innovation	Product Component Model	

Questions

1. Define the key terms listed above.

2. Debate the issue of global versus adapted products for the international marketer.

3. Define the country-of-origin effect and give examples.

4. The text discusses stereotypes, ethnocentrism, degree of economic development, and fads as the basis for generalizations about country-of-origin effect on product perception. Explain each and give an example.

5. Discuss product alternatives and the three marketing strategies: domestic market extension, multidomestic markets, and global market strategies.

6. Discuss the different promotional/product strategies available to an international marketer.

7. Assume you are deciding to "go international." Outline the steps you would take to help you decide on a product line.

8. Products can be adapted physically and culturally for foreign markets. Discuss.

9. What are the three major components of a product? Discuss their importance to product adaptation.

10. How can knowledge of the diffusion of innovations help a product manager plan international investments?

11. Old products (that is, old in the U.S. market) may be innovations in a foreign market. Discuss fully.

12. "If the product sells in Dallas, it will sell in Tokyo or Berlin." Comment.

13. How can a country with a per capita GNP of $100 be a potential market for consumer goods? What kinds of goods would probably be in demand? Discuss.

14. Discuss the characteristics of an innovation that can account for differential diffusion rates.

15. Give an example of how a foreign marketer can use knowledge of the characteristics of innovations in product adaptation decisions.

16. Discuss "environmentally friendly" products and product development.

Chapter 14

Products and Services for Businesses

CHAPTER OUTLINE

Global Perspective: Intel, the Boom, and
the Inescapable Bust

Demand in Global Business-to-Business Markets

    The Volatility of Industrial Demand
    Stages of Economic Development
    Technology and Market Demand

Quality and Global Standards

    Quality Is Defined by the Buyer
    ISO 9000 Certification: An International Standard of Quality

Business Services

    After-Sale Services
    Other Business Services

Trade Shows: A Crucial Part of Business-to-Business
Marketing

Relationship Marketing in Business-to-Business Contexts

CHAPTER LEARNING OBJECTIVES

What you should learn from Chapter 14:

LO1 The importance of derived demand in industrial
markets

LO2 How demand is affected by technology levels

LO3 Characteristics of an industrial product

LO4 The importance of ISO 9000 certification

LO5 The growth of business services and nuances of
their marketing

LO6 The importance of trade shows in promoting
industrial goods

LO7 The importance of relationship marketing for
industrial products and services

Global Perspective

INTEL, THE BOOM, AND THE INESCAPABLE BUST

This is what we wrote here in the 1999 edition of this book:

Fortune's cover story, "Intel, Andy Grove's Amazing Profit Machine—and His Plan for Five More Years of Explosive Growth" is capped only by *Time*'s Man of the Year story, "Intel's Andy Grove, His Microchips Have Changed the World—and Its Economy." 1997 was the eighth consecutive year of record revenue ($25.1 billion) and earnings ($6.5 billion) for the company Grove helped found. Yet at the beginning of 1998 the real question was, "Will the world change Intel?" Judging from Intel's own forecasts for a flat first quarter in 1998, Chairman of the Board Grove and his associates were concerned that the financial meltdown in Asian markets would affect Intel's plans for "five more years of explosive growth." Some 30 percent of the firm's record 1997 revenues had come from Asian markets. Indeed, one pundit had earlier predicted, "I see no clear technology threats. The biggest long-term threat to Intel is that the market growth slows." Others warned there's something wrong out there: computer-industry overcapacity.

Actually Intel had an even longer list of threats all posted as a disclaimer to its published forecast: "Other factors that could cause actual results to differ materially are the following: business and economic conditions, and growth in the computing industry in various geographic regions; changes in customer order patterns, including changes in customer and channel inventory levels, and seasonal PC buying patterns; changes in the mixes of microprocessor types and speeds, motherboards, purchased components and other products; competitive factors, such as rival chip architectures and manufacturing technologies, competing software-compatible microprocessors and acceptance of new products in specific market segments; pricing pressures; changes in end users' preferences; risk of inventory obsolescence and variations in inventory valuation; timing of software industry product introductions; continued success in technological advances, including development, implementation and initial production of new strategic products and processes in a cost-effective manner; execution of

manufacturing ramp; excess storage of manufacturing capacity; the ability to successfully integrate any acquired businesses, enter new market segments and manage growth of such businesses; unanticipated costs or other adverse effects associated with processors and other products containing errata; risks associated with foreign operations; litigation involving intellectual property and consumer issues; and other risk factors listed from time to time in the company's SEC reports."

Time's Man of the Year had a lot to worry about—most of all that industrial market booms are always followed by busts. Will the rise truly last five more years?

How is it that the brilliant Mr. Grove didn't see the inescapable bust coming? Hadn't he been in this cyclic business from the beginning? His boom did last, another three and a half years beyond his 1997 prediction, not five. And the bust was an ugly thing. Sales revenues declined by more than 20 percent during 2001, the stock price crashed from a high of $75 a share to below $20, shedding 80 percent of the company's value along the way, and 11,000 layoffs were announced. Ouch! The lesson here is a simple one: In industrial markets, including the global ones, what goes up must come down!

But after taking its lumps in 2009, along with the rest of the world, new Intel CEO Paul Otellini led the firm to record performance in 2011. Global sales revenues jumped from $43.6 billion in 2010 to $54.0 billion a year later. The stock price stands at about $36 circa 2015, and revenues are still well above $50 billion. Remarkable, and volatile, but in the better way this time.

Sources: David Kirkpatrick, "Intel Andy Grove's Amazing Profit Machine—And His Plan for Five More Years of Explosive Growth," *Fortune*, February 17, 1997, pp. 60–75; "Man of the Year," *Time*, January 5, 1998, pp. 46–99; Peter Burrow, Gary McWilliams, Paul C. Judge, and Roger O. Crockett, "There's Something Wrong Out There," *BusinessWeek*, December 29, 1997, pp. 38–49; http://www.intc.com, 2015.

Although everyone likely is familiar with most of the consumer brands described in Chapter 13, sales of such products and services do not constitute the majority of export sales for industrialized countries. Take the United States, for example. As can be seen in Exhibit 14.1, the main product the country sells for international consumption is *technology*. This dominance is reflected in categories such as capital goods and industrial supplies, which together account for some 48 percent of all U.S. exports of goods and services.[1] Technology exports are represented by both the smallest and the largest products—semiconductors and commercial aircraft, the latter prominently including America's export champions, Boeing's 747s. Two of the 10 most valuable companies in the world at this writing—Microsoft and General Electric—are sellers of high-technology industrial products/services.

The issues of standardization versus adaptation discussed in Chapter 13 have less relevance to marketing industrial goods than consumer goods because there are more similarities in marketing products and services to businesses across country markets than there are differences. The inherent nature of industrial goods and the sameness in motives and behavior among businesses as customers create a market where product and marketing mix standardization are commonplace. Photocopy machines are sold in Belarus for the same reasons as in Belgium: to make photocopies. Some minor modification may be necessary to accommodate different electrical power supplies or paper size, but basically, photocopy machines are standardized across markets, as are the vast majority of industrial goods. For industrial products that are basically custom made (specialized steel, customized machine tools, and so on), adaptation takes place for domestic as well as foreign markets.

---

[1]Internet jargon seems to be morphing the manager's lexicon toward B2B and B2C distinctions (i.e., business-to-business and business-to-consumer) and away from the traditional industrial and consumer goods distinctions. International trade statistics, categories, and descriptors have not kept up with these changes. Consequently, we use the adjectives *industrial* and *business-to-business* interchangeably in this book.

Exhibit 14.1

Major Categories of U.S. Exports

Source: U.S. Department of Commerce, http://www.doc.gov, 2015.

Category	Percentage
Services total	**29.5**
Travel (hotels, etc.)	5.6
Passenger fares	1.8
Other transportation (freight and port services)	3.0
Royalties and Licenses	5.9
Private Services*	13.2
• Commercial, professional, and technical services (advertising, accounting, legal, construction, engineering)	
• Healthcare	
• Financial services (banking and insurance)	
• Education and training services (mostly foreign student tuition)	
• Entertainment (movies, books, records)	
• Telecommunications	
[* The Commerce Department no longer breaks out the statistics by the Private Services categories. They are listed here in the order of their historical percentages, first being highest.]	
Merchandise total	**70.5**
Foods, feeds, and beverages (wheat, fruit, meat)	6.2
Industrial supplies (crude oil, plastics, chemicals, metals)	24.3
Capital goods (construction equipment, aircraft, computers, telecommunications)	24.1
Automotive vehicles, engines, and parts	6.4
Consumer goods (pharmaceuticals, tobacco, toys, clothing)	8.6
Other categories	0.9

Note: The United States exports approximately $2.1 trillion worth of services and goods each year. Services exports are the more understated, so these percentages are only reasonable approximations of the importance of each category listed. Each U.S. Commerce Department category comprises many kinds of products or services, including (but certainly not limited to) those listed in parentheses.

Two basic factors account for greater market similarities among industrial goods customers than among consumer goods customers. First is the inherent nature of the product: Industrial products and services are used in the process of creating other goods and services; consumer goods are in their final form and are consumed by individuals and/or households. Second, the motive or intent of the users differ: Industrial consumers are seeking profit, whereas the ultimate consumer is seeking satisfaction. These factors are manifest in specific buying patterns and demand characteristics and in a special emphasis on relationship marketing as a competitive tool. Whether a company is marketing at home or abroad, the differences between business-to-business and consumer markets merit special consideration.

Along with industrial goods, business services are a highly competitive growth market seeking quality and value. Manufactured products generally come to mind when we think of international trade. Yet the most rapidly growing sector of U.S. international trade today consists of business services—accounting, advertising, banking, consulting, construction, hotels, insurance, law, transportation, and travel sold by U.S. firms in global markets. The intangibility of services creates a set of unique problems to which the service provider must respond. A further complication is a lack of uniform laws that regulate market entry. Protectionism, though common for industrial goods, can be much more prevalent for the services provider.

This chapter discusses the special problems in marketing goods and services to businesses internationally, the increased competition and demand for quality in those goods and services, and the implications for the global marketer.

Demand in Global Business-to-Business (B2B) Markets

Gauging demand in industrial markets can involve some huge bets. Shanghai's 30-kilometer, $1.2 billion bullet train line was one example. This product of a Sino–German joint venture was really a prototype for fast things to come in mass transit–dependent China. Indeed, China now has the longest (more than 6000 miles) and fastest (more than 300 mph) high-speed rail service in the world with the help of $58 billion in German subsidies. Alternatively, a big bet that went bad was Iridium LLC; its 72-satellite, $5 billion communications system was unable to sell the associated phones. Iridium badly miscalculated demand for its approach to global telecommunications and was sold in bankruptcy for $25 million. The system remains operational with the U.S. Department of Defense as its primary customer. Most recently, however, Iridium is making a bit of a comeback. It raised $200 million in an IPO in late 2009 to help it build on its successes with machine-to-machine (M2M) commercial subscribers that need coverage in the 90 percent of the planet where mobile phone service does not exist.[2]

Three factors seem to affect the demand in international industrial markets differently than in consumer markets. First, demand in industrial markets is by nature more volatile. Second, stages of industrial and economic development affect demand for industrial products. Third, the level of technology of products and services makes their sale more appropriate for some countries than others.

LO1

The importance of derived demand in industrial markets

The Volatility of Industrial Demand

Consumer products firms have numerous reasons to market internationally—gaining exposure to more customers, keeping up with the competition, extending product life cycles, and growing sales and profits, to name a few. Firms producing products and services for industrial markets have an additional crucial reason for venturing abroad: dampening the natural volatility of industrial markets. Indeed, perhaps the single most important difference between consumer and industrial marketing is the huge, cyclical swings in demand inherent in the latter. It is true that demand for consumer durables such as cars, furniture, or home computers can be quite volatile. In industrial markets, however, three other factors come into play that exacerbate both the ups and downs in demand: Industrial sellers tend to

[2]Arik Hesseldahl, "The Second Coming of Iridium," *BusinessWeek*, October 29, 2009, p. 29; Jan McBride, "Digi Extends Internet of AnyThing to Iridium Satellite Network," *The New York Times*, February 7, 2012.

have small numbers of customers upon which they are more dependent, professional buyers tend to act in concert, and derived demand accelerates changes in markets.[3]

A good example of the first problem is the demise of Apple's sapphire supplier. GT Advanced Technologies was to supply Apple's manufacturing partners with the super-hard sapphire screens for its burgeoning iPhone line. While such a contract might have generated billions of dollars in business for GT, it comes with great risks—huge fluctuations in demand at razor-thin profit margins mean little room for error. A few production problems pushed GT into bankruptcy.[4]

Servers are sold to companies; thus, the demand for them is more volatile than the demand for personal computers being sold to individual consumers. Here Microsoft acknowledges the technology bust of 2000 in its ads for servers in both the United States and Japan. In both countries, the pressure was on CIOs to "do more with less." Executives faced "larger projects" and "shrinking budgets." The American executive is working late; everyone else has gone home. The focus on the Japanese individual executive may look odd to older, more collectivistic Japanese managers. However, Microsoft acknowledged that things were changing in Japan—particularly, information technology decisions were more focused and less consensus-oriented. Younger Japanese will like the independence reflected in the image. Finally, do you think it's a coincidence that both executives are standing near windows?

[3]Ilan Brat, "Crane Migration Hinders Builders," *The Wall Street Journal*, June 18, 2007, pp. B1, B2.
[4]Daisuke Wakabayashi, "Inside Apple's Broken Sapphire Factory," *The Wall Street Journal*, November 20, 2014, pp. B1, 4.

A more recent global campaign for Microsoft B2B offerings mentions nothing about the IT bust of the last decade. The power of the cloud is the important topic now and the pitches are quite similar across media and markets. In the French version we again see the required footnotes about translating English terms into French—see Chapter 4. As you might expect the campaign included placements in airports, trade publications, business periodicals, and sports sections of newspapers.

Purchasing agents at large personal computer manufacturers such as Lenovo, Apple, Acer, Samsung, and Toshiba are responsible for obtaining component parts for their firms as cheaply as possible and in a timely manner. They monitor demand for PCs and prices of components such as microprocessors or disk drives, and changes in either customer markets or supplier prices directly affect their ordering. Declines in PC demand or supplier prices can cause these professionals to slam on the brakes in their buying; in the latter case, they wait for further price cuts. And because the purchasing agents at all the PC companies, here and abroad, are monitoring the same data, they all brake (or accelerate) simultaneously. This is exactly what happened in 2008 in the $14 billion global seaweed market. Certain types of seaweed are used in toothpaste, cosmetics, and chicken patties, and the volatility in industrial demand pushed prices from $0.50/kilogram to $1.80/kilogram and then to $1.00/kilogram, all in three months.[5] Consumers monitor markets as well, but not nearly to the same degree. Purchases of cola, clothing, and cars tend to be steadier.

For managers selling capital equipment and big-ticket industrial services, understanding the concept of derived demand is absolutely fundamental to their success. Derived demand can be defined as demand dependent on another source. Thus, the demand for Boeing 747s is derived from the worldwide consumer demand for air travel services, and the demand for Fluor Corp's global construction and engineering services to design and build oil refineries in China is derived from Chinese consumers' demands for gasoline. Minor changes in consumer

[5]Patrick Barta, "Indonesia Got Soaked When the Seaweed Bubble Burst," *The Wall Street Journal*, October 21, 2008, online.

Exhibit 14.2
Derived Demand Example

Time Period	Consumer Demand for Premolded Fiberglass Shower Stalls			Number of Machines in Use to Produce the Shower Stalls			Demand for the Machines		
Year	Previous Year	Current Year	Net Change	Previous Year	Current Year	Net Change	Replacement	New	Total
1	100,000	100,000	—	500	500	—	50	—	50
2	100,000	110,000	+10,000	500	550	+50	50	50	100
3	110,000	115,000	+5,000	550	575	+25	50	25	75
4	115,000	118,000	+3,000	575	590	+15	50	15	65
5	118,000	100,000	−18,000	590	500	−90	—	−40	−40
6	100,000	100,000	—	500	500	—	10	—	10

Source: Adapted from R. L. Vaile, E. T. Grether, and R. Cox, *Marketing in the American Economy* (New York: Ronald Press, 1952), p. 16.

demand mean major changes in the related industrial demand. In the example in Exhibit 14.2, a 10 percent increase in consumer demand for shower stalls in year 2 translates into a 100 percent increase in demand for the machines to make shower stalls. The 15 percent decline in consumer demand in year 5 results in a complete shutdown of demand for shower-stall–making machines. For Boeing, the September 11 terrorist attacks, the continuing threat of more of the same, and the subsequent armed conflicts in the Middle East combined to dramatically reduce air travel (both vacation and commercial) worldwide, which in turn caused cancellations of orders for aircraft. Moreover, the airlines not only canceled orders, they also mothballed parts of their current fleets. During August 2003, there were 310 jetliners stored in a Mojave Desert facility awaiting demand to pick up again. The commercial aircraft industry has always been and will continue to be one of the most volatile of all. Perhaps the only industry that is more volatile is that for ships: oil tankers and freighters. In 2010, Danish Maersk Line ordered 10 of the biggest container ships ever built. One year later, the port of Singapore was awash in a glut of unused commercial ships.[6]

Industrial firms can take several measures to manage this inherent volatility, such as maintaining broad product lines[7] and broad market coverage, raising prices faster and reducing advertising expenditures during booms,[8] ignoring market share as a strategic goal, eschewing layoffs,[9] and focusing on stability. For most American firms, where corporate cultures emphasize beating competitors, such stabilizing measures are usually given only lip service. Conversely, German and Japanese firms value employees and stability more highly and are generally better at managing volatility in markets.[10]

Some U.S. companies, such as Microsoft and especially General Electric, have been quite good at spreading their portfolio of markets served. Late-1990s declines in Asian markets were somewhat offset by strong American markets, just as late-1980s increases in Japanese demand had offset declines in the United States. Indeed, one of the strange disadvantages of having the previously command economies go private is their integration

[6]"The Danish Armada," *The Economist*, February 26, 2011, p. 73; Keith Bradsher, "Freighter Oversupply Weighs on Shipowners and Banks," *The New York Times*, January 25, 2012.

[7]"Seeking a Stable Formula," *The Economist*, June 26, 2010, p. 67.

[8]Cathy Anterasian and John L. Graham, "When It's Good Management to Sacrifice Market Share," *Journal of Business Research*, 19, 1989, pp. 187–213; Peren Östüran, Ayşegül Özsomer, and Rik Pieters, The Role of Market Orientation in Advertising Spending During Economic Collapse: The Case of Turkey in 2011," *Journal of Marketing Research*, 51(2), 2014, pp. 139–152.

[9]Southwest Airlines management, unlike almost all its competitors, has avoided layoffs during the recent bust in the industry. Refusing to make layoffs has been a founding principle of the organization. "Southwest Airlines December Traffic Rose 4%," *Dow Jones News Service*, January 4, 2008.

[10]Cathy Anterasian, John L. Graham, and R. Bruce Money, "Are American Managers Superstitious about Market Share?" *Sloan Management Review*, Summer 1996, pp. 667–77; John L. Graham, "Culture and Human Resources Management," Chapter 18 in Alan Rugman and Thomas L. Brewer (eds.), *The Oxford Handbook of International Business*, 2nd ed. (Oxford: Oxford University Press, 2008).

into the global market. That is, prior to the breakup of the USSR, Soviets bought industrial products according to a national five-year plan that often had little to do with markets outside of the communist bloc. Their off-cycle ordering tended to dampen demand volatility for companies able to sell there. Now, privately held Russian manufacturers watch and react to world markets just as their counterparts do all over the globe. The increasing globalization of markets will tend to increase the volatility in industrial markets as purchasing agents around the world act with even greater simultaneity. Managing this inherent volatility will necessarily affect all aspects of the marketing mix, including product/service development.

Stages of Economic Development

Perhaps the most significant environmental factor affecting the international market for industrial goods and services is the degree of industrialization. Although generalizing about countries is almost always imprudent, the degree of economic development can be used as a rough measure of a country's industrial market. Rostow's[11] five-stage model of economic development is useful here; demand for industrial products and services can be classified correspondingly. Interestingly, countries in all five stages compete for and actively market themselves as locations for foreign direct investment, which of course helps with their economic development.[12]

> **Stage 1** (*the traditional society*). The most important industrial demand will be associated with natural resources extraction—think parts of Africa and the Middle East.
>
> **Stage 2** (*preconditions for takeoff*). Manufacturing is beginning. Primary needs will be related to agriculture[13] and infrastructure development—for example, telecommunications, construction,[14] and power generation equipment and expertise. Vietnam would fit this category.
>
> **Stage 3** (*takeoff*). Manufacturing of both semidurable and nondurable consumer goods has begun. Goods demanded relate to equipment and supplies to support manufacturing. Russian and Eastern European countries fit this category.
>
> **Stage 4** (*drive to maturity*). These are industrialized economies such as South Korea and the Czech Republic. Their focus is more on low-cost manufacturing of a variety of consumer and some industrial goods. They buy from all categories of industrial products and services.
>
> **Stage 5** (*the age of mass consumption*). These are countries where design activities are going on and manufacturing techniques are being developed, and they are mostly service economies. Japan and Germany are obvious examples of countries that purchase the highest-technology products and services, mostly from other Stage 5 suppliers and consumer products from Stage 3 and 4 countries.

We must also point out the even the most advanced countries around the world still need infrastructure improvements and natural resources. The United States is now providing petroleum refining services and fuel exports for a variety of countries around the world.[15] Conversely, the extent of America's decaying infrastructure will require massive imports from our high-technology neighbors.[16] This topic will come up again in the next chapter.

---

[11]Walt W. Rostow, *The Stages of Economic Growth*, 2nd ed. (London: Cambridge University Press, 1971).

[12]Rick T. Wilson and Daniel W. Baack, "Attracting Foreign Direct Investment: Applying Dunning's Location Advantages Framework to FDI Advertising," *Journal of International Marketing* 20, no. 2 (2012), pp. 96–115.

[13]Bryan Gruley and Shruti Date Singh, "Profit Machine," *Bloomberg Businessweek*, July 5, 2012, pp. 45–49.

[14]"Ready-Mixed Fortunes," *The Economist*, June 22, 2013, pp. 68–69.

[15]Ben Lefebvre, "U.S. Refiner Exports Hit High," *The Wall Street Journal*, October 9, 2013, pp. B1, 2.

[16]"Bridging the Gap," *The Economist*, June 28, 2014, pp. 23–24.

Technology and Market Demand

How demand is affected by technology levels

Another important approach to grouping countries is on the basis of their ability to benefit from and use technology, particularly now that countries are using technology as economic leverage to leap several stages of economic development in a very short time. Perhaps the best indicator of this dimension of development is the quality of the educational system.[17] Despite relatively low levels of per capita GDP, many countries (e.g., China, the Czech Republic, Russia, and Cuba) place great emphasis on education, which affords them the potential to leverage the technology that is transferred.

Not only is technology the key to economic growth, but for many products, it is also the competitive edge in today's global markets. Indeed, being involved in and having access to high-technology markets is a crucial source of innovations for industrial firms.[18] As precision robots and digital control systems take over the factory floor, manufacturing is becoming more science oriented, and access to inexpensive labor and raw materials is becoming less important. The ability to develop the latest information technology and to benefit from its application is a critical factor in the international competitiveness of managers, countries, and companies. Three interrelated trends spur demand for technologically advanced products: (1) expanding economic and industrial growth in Asia, particularly China and India; (2) the disintegration of the Soviet empire; and (3) the privatization of government-owned industries worldwide.

Beginning with Japan, many Asian countries have been in a state of rapid economic growth over the last 30 years. Although this growth has recently slowed, the long-term outlook for these countries remains excellent. Japan has become the most advanced industrialized country in the region, now even developing a commercial airliner industry,[19] while South Korea, Hong Kong, Singapore, and Taiwan (the "Four Tigers") have successfully moved from being cheap labor sources to becoming industrialized nations. China and the Southeast Asian countries of Malaysia, Thailand, Indonesia, and the Philippines are exporters of manufactured products to Japan and the United States. Since overcoming most of their 1990s financial problems, they are continuing to gear up for greater industrialization. In many such emerging markets, local entrepreneurial companies in high-tech industries are competing successfully with more traditional MNCs while balancing both their research and development efforts.[20] Countries at each of the first three levels of industrial development demand technologically advanced products for further industrialization, which will enable them to compete in global markets.

As a market economy develops in the Commonwealth of Independent States (CIS, former republics of the USSR) and other eastern European countries, new privately owned businesses will create a demand for the latest technology to revitalize and expand manufacturing facilities. These countries will demand the latest technology to expand their industrial bases and build modern infrastructures.

Concurrent with the fall of communism, which fueled the rush to privatization in eastern Europe, Latin Americans began to dismantle their state-run industries in hopes

---

[17]For an interesting article on the prospects of technology use in the classroom, see "Catching on at Last," *The Economist*, June 29, 2013, pp. 24–27.

[18]Vishal Bindroo, Babu John Mariadoss, and Rajan Ganesh Pillai, "Customer Clusters as a Source of Innovation-Based Competitive Advantage," *Journal of International Marketing* 20, no. 3 (2012), pp. 17–33.

[19]Chris Cooper and Kiyotaka Matsuda, "Mitsubishi Spreads Its Wings," *Bloomberg Businessweek*, October 27–November 2, 2014, pp. 29–30.

[20]Matthew Hughes, Silvia L. Martin, Robert E. Morgan, and Matthew J. Robson, "Realizing Product-Market Advantage in High-Technology International New Ventures: The Mediating Role of Ambidextrous Innovation," *Journal of International Marketing* 18, no. 4 (2010), pp. 1–22; Cheng Zhang, Peijian Song, and Zhe Qu, "Competitive Action in the Diffusion of Internet Technology Products in Emerging Markets: Implications for Global Marketing Managers," *Journal of International Marketing* 19, no. 4 (2011), pp. 40–60; Elena Vasilchenko and Sussie Morrish, "The Role of Entrepreneurial Networks in the Exploration and Exploitation of Internationalization of Opportunities in Information and Communication Technology Firms," *Journal of International Marketing* 19, no. 4 (2011), pp. 88–105; Nathan Wasburn and B. Tom Hunsaker, "Finding Great Ideas in Emerging Markets," *Harvard Business Review*, September 2011, pp. 115–19.

Construction equipment is crucial in developing countries. Here an American-made compact Kobelco tracked backhoe helps build tourism facilities near Angkor Wat, Cambodia. The American competitor to giant Caterpillar was recently purchased by Fiat.

of reviving their economies. Mexico, Argentina, and Brazil are leading the rest of Latin America in privatizing state-owned businesses. The move to privatization is creating enormous demand for industrial goods as new owners invest heavily in the latest technology. Telmex, a $4 billion joint venture between Southwestern Bell, France Telecom, and Teléfonos de Mexico, invested hundreds of millions of dollars to bring the Mexican telephone system up to the most advanced standards. Telmex is only one of scores of new privatized companies from Poland to Paraguay that are creating a mass market for the most advanced technology.

The fast economic growth in Asia, the creation of market economies in eastern Europe and the republics of the former Soviet Union, and the privatization of state-owned enterprises in Latin America and elsewhere will create expanding demand, particularly for industrial goods and business services, well into the 21st century. The competition to meet this global demand will be stiff; the companies with the competitive edge will be those whose products are technologically advanced, of the highest quality, and accompanied by world-class service.

Quality and Global Standards

As discussed in Chapter 13 the concept of quality encompasses many factors, and the perception of quality rests solely with the customer. The level of technology reflected in the product, compliance with standards that reflect customer needs, support services and follow-through, and the price relative to competitive products are all part of a customer's evaluation and perception of quality. As noted, these requirements are different for consumers versus industrial customers because of differing end uses. The factors themselves also differ among industrial goods customers because their needs are varied. Finally, recent studies have demonstrated that perceptions of industrial product quality also can vary across cultural groups[21] even in the most technologically developed countries.

Business-to-business marketers frequently misinterpret the concept of quality. Good quality as interpreted by a highly industrialized market is not the same as that interpreted by standards of a less industrialized nation. For example, an African government had been buying hand-operated dusters for farmers to distribute pesticides in cotton fields.

---

[21]Nathaniel Popper, "Islamic Banks, Stuffed with Cash, Explore Partnerships in West," *The New York Times*, December 26, 2013, pp. B1, 2.

The duster supplied was a finely machined device requiring regular oiling and good care. But the fact that this duster turned more easily than any other on the market was relatively unimportant to the farmers. Furthermore, the requirement for careful oiling and care simply meant that in a relatively short time of inadequate care, the machines froze up and broke. The result? The local government went back to an older type of French duster that was heavy, turned with difficulty, and gave a poorer distribution of dust but that lasted longer because it required less care and lubrication. In this situation, the French machine possessed more relevant quality features and therefore, in marketing terms, possessed the higher quality.

Likewise, when commercial jet aircraft were first developed, European and American designs differed substantially. For example, American manufacturers built the engines slung below the wings, whereas the British competitor built the engines into the wings. The American design made for easier access and saved on repair and servicing costs, and the British design reduced aerodynamic drag and saved on fuel costs. Both designs were "high quality" for their respective markets. At the time, labor was relatively expensive in the United States, and fuel was relatively expensive in the United Kingdom.

Quality Is Defined by the Buyer

LO3

Characteristics of an industrial product

One important dimension of quality is how well a product or service[22] meets the specific needs of the buyer. When a product falls short of performance expectations, its poor quality is readily apparent. However, it is less apparent but nonetheless true that a product that exceeds performance expectations can also be of poor quality. A product whose design exceeds the wants of the buyer's intended use generally has a higher price or is more complex, reflecting the extra capacity. Quality for many goods is assessed in terms of fulfilling specific expectations—no more and no less. Thus, a product that produces 20,000 units per hour when the buyer needs one that produces only 5,000 units per hour is not a quality product, in that the extra capacity is unnecessary to meet the buyer's use expectations. Indeed, this point is one of the key issues facing personal computer makers. Many business buyers are asking the question, "Do we really need the latest $1,000 PC for everyone?" And more and more often the answer is no, the $500 tablets will do just fine.

This price–quality relationship is an important factor in marketing in developing economies, especially those in the first three stages of economic development described earlier. Standard quality requirements of industrial products sold in the U.S. market that command commensurately higher prices may be completely out of line for the needs of the less developed markets of the world. Labor-saving features are of little importance when time has limited value and labor is plentiful. Also of lesser value is the ability of machinery to hold close tolerances where people are not quality-control conscious, where large production runs do not exist, and where the wages of skillful workers justify selective fits in assembly and repair work. Features that a buyer does not want or cannot effectively use do not enhance a product's quality rating.

This distinction does not mean quality is unimportant or that the latest technology is not sought in developing markets. Rather, it means that those markets require products designed to meet their specific needs, not products designed for different uses and expectations, especially if the additional features result in higher prices. This attitude was reflected in a study of purchasing behavior of Chinese import managers, who ranked product quality first, followed in importance by price. Timely delivery was third and product style/features ranked 11th out of 17 variables studied. Hence, a product whose design reflects the needs and expectations of the buyer—no more, no less—is a quality product.

The design of a product must be viewed from all aspects of use. Extreme variations in climate create problems in designing equipment that is universally operable. Products that

---

[22]Christina Sichtmann, Maren von Selasinsky, and Adamantios Diamantopoulos, "Service Quality and Export Performance of Business-to-Business Service Providers: The Role of Service Employee- and Customer-Oriented Quality Control Initiatives," *Journal of International Marketing* 19, no. 1 (2011), pp. 1–22.

CROSSING BORDERS 14.1

Sewage and Swamps: A Preview of Renewable Energy Technologies

As global climate change continues to manifest itself, the human response is creating a complex goo of opportunities for international marketers. Two are described here. One involves burning sewage gas, the other pine trees from swamps.

If Toyota has its way, its new hydrogen-powered Mirai could revolutionize the automobile industry and save the environment. Instead of an engine, the Mirai uses Toyota Fuel Cell Technology, has two hydrogen tanks, emits only water vapor, and has a range of 300 miles. The car takes just three to five minutes to refuel and was designed to have a premium driving feel, similar to a Lexus. Long known for its focus on sustainability, Toyota hopes that the Mirai will reduce even more CO_2 from the environment; hydrogen generates the least amount of greenhouse gas and can be made from garbage, corn, and solar and wind power. The automaker has partnerships to build 19 fueling stations in California by 2016 and to roll out additional stations along the East Coast later. It is also offering state incentives and carpool lane stickers to encourage local governments and consumers to get on board. General Motors, Honda, Hyundai, Mercedes also have prototypes on the road, and Volkswagen is also in the game.

The momentum behind fuel cells suggests that automakers see their principal challenges—sparse fueling infrastructure and high cost—as potentially more surmountable over the long term than the ones facing battery electric vehicles, including limited range and long charging times. Toyota had already lent more than $7 million to Southern California startup FirstElement Fuel to begin construction of 19 stations across the state, in conjunction with a large state grant. Recently, Honda agreed to a $13.8 million loan that would help FirstElement propose construction of a dozen more stations in California.

Among FirstElement's founding executives are engineers who helped design a unique hydrogen fueling station at the Orange County Sanitation District in Fountain Valley, California, that makes hydrogen out of sewage. The station, which was the first of its kind when it opened in 2011, was a collaboration among the University of California–Irvine, California Air Resources Board, Orange County Sanitation District, Air Products, and FuelCell Energy Inc. Hydrogen for the cars can be derived from a variety of sources, including solar, wind, and even nuclear. All the

companies involved are eyeing opportunities in Asia and Europe as well.

Speaking of Europe, the EU Commission has mandated a 20 percent reduction in greenhouse gas emissions there by 2020. One of the options for meeting that goal is replacing coal (a fossil fuel) with wood (current carbon) as a fuel in electrical power plants. American forests supply the wood scrap that is turned into pellets that can be shipped by sea to Europe and handled there by equipment suited for coal. Critics complain that releasing the CO_2 sequestered in trees adds to the problem. But supporters point out that newly planted forests eat CO_2 faster than the old stands of trees, often from swamps, being converted to pellets. These projects mean both jobs and burgeoning exports for the U.S. companies involved.

Keep your eyes peeled as these and other technology-based industries continue to develop.

Sources: Justin Scheck and Ianthe Jeanne Dugan, "Europe's Green-Fuel Search Turns to America's Forests," *The Wall Street Journal*, May 27, 2013, online; Donya Blaze, "The 2016 Toyota Mirai Could Mean the End of Oil Changes Forever," *NewsOne.com*, November 23, 2014; Sherri Cruz, "Fuel Cell Research Powers Industry," *Orange County Register*, May 5, 2014, online; Kenneth Chang, "A Road Test of Alternative Fuel Visions," *The New York Times*, November 18, 2014, pp. D1, 6; Susan Carter, "In O.C., Toyota Debuts First Commercially Available Hydrogen Fuel-Cell Vehicle," *Orange County Register*, November 20, 2014, online; http://www.nfcrc.uci.edu, accessed 2015. Brian Bremner, Craig Trudell, and Yuki Hagiwara, "Remaking Toyota: The Internal Combustion Engine Is Over. The World's Biggest Auto Company Is Ready," *Bloomberg Businessweek*, January 11, 2015, pp. 44–49.

Trees and wood scrap transformed into easily shipped pellets for power plants.

function effectively in western Europe may require major design changes to operate as well in the hot, dry Sahara region or the humid, tropical rain forests of Latin America. Trucks designed to travel the superhighways of the United States almost surely will experience operational difficulties in the mountainous regions of Latin America on roads that often barely resemble Jeep trails. Manufacturers must consider many variations in making products that will be functional in far-flung markets.

In light of today's competition, a company must consider the nature of its market and the adequacy of the design of its products. Effective competition in global markets means that overengineered and overpriced products must give way to products that meet the specifications of the customer at competitive prices. Success lies in offering products that fit a customer's needs—technologically advanced for some and less sophisticated for others, but all of high quality. To be competitive in today's global markets, the concept of total quality management (TQM) must be a part of all MNCs' management strategy, and TQM starts with talking to customers. Indeed, more and more frequently, industrial customers, including foreign ones, are directly involved in all aspects of the product development process, from generating new ideas to prototype testing.

A lack of universal standards is another problem in international sales of industrial products. The United States has two major areas of concern in this regard for the industrial goods exporter: a lack of common standards for manufacturing highly specialized equipment such as machine tools and computers, and the use of the inch-pound, or English, system of measurement. Conflicting standards are encountered in test methods for materials and equipment, quality control systems, and machine specifications. In the telecommunications industry, the vast differences in standards among countries create enormous problems for the expansion of that industry.

Efforts are being made through international organizations to create international standards. For example, the International Electrotechnical Commission is concerned with standard specifications for electrical equipment for machine tools. The search has also been engaged for ways in which an international roaming umbrella can be established for wireless communications. The U.S. Department of Commerce participates in programs to promote U.S. standards and is active in the development of the Global Harmonization Task Force, an international effort to harmonize standards for several industry sectors. The U.S. Trade Representative participates in negotiations to harmonize standards as well. Recently a key agreement was signed with the European Union to mutually recognize each other's standards in six sectors. The agreements will eliminate the need for double testing (once each on both sides of the Atlantic) and address inspection or certification in telecommunications, medical devices, electromagnetic compatibility, electrical safety, recreation craft, and pharmaceuticals. The agreements cover approximately $50 billion in two-way trade and are expected to equate to a 2 to 3 percent drop in tariffs.

In addition to industry and international organizations setting standards, countries often have standards for products entering their markets. Saudi Arabia has been working on setting standards for everything from light bulbs to lemon juice, and it has asked its trading partners for help. The standards, the first in Arabic, will most likely be adopted by the entire Arab world. Most countries sent representatives to participate in the standard setting. For example, New Zealand sent a representative to help write the standards for the shelf life of lamb. Unfortunately, the United States failed to send a representative until late in the discussions, and thus many of the hundreds of standards written favor Japanese and European products. Also, Saudi Arabia adopted the new European standard for utility equipment. The cost in lost sales to two Saudi cities by just one U.S. company, Westinghouse, was from $15 to $20 million for U.S.-standard distribution transformers. Increasingly, American firms are waking up to the necessity of participating in such standards discussions early on.

In the United States, conversion to the metric system and acceptance of international standards have been slow.[23] Congress and industry have dragged their feet for fear

---

[23]Justin Scheck, "Cooking a Poundcake in a Metric Oven Is No Easy Task," *The Wall Street Journal*, November 23, 2012, online.

conversion would be too costly. But the cost will come from *not* adopting the metric system; the General Electric Company had a shipment of electrical goods turned back from a Saudi port because its connecting cords were six feet long instead of the required standard of two meters.

As foreign customers on the metric system account for more and more American industrial sales, the cost of delaying standardization mounts. Measurement-sensitive products account for one-half to two-thirds of U.S. exports, and if the European Union bars nonmetric imports, as expected, many U.S. products will lose access to that market. About half of U.S. exports are covered by the EU's new standards program.

To spur U.S. industry into action, the Department of Commerce indicated that accepting the metric system will not be mandatory unless you want to sell something to the U.S. government; all U.S. government purchases are to be conducted exclusively in metric. All federal buildings are now being designed with metric specifications, and highway construction funded by Washington uses metric units. Because the U.S. government is the nation's largest customer, this directive may be successful in converting U.S. business to the metric system. The Defense Department now requires metric specifications for all new weapons systems as well.

Despite the edicts from Washington, the National Aeronautics and Space Administration (NASA), which presides over some of the most advanced technology in the world, has resisted metrification. The $100 billion-plus[24] space station contains some metric parts, but most of the major components are made in the United States and are based on inches and pounds. NASA's excuse was that it was too far into the design and production to switch. Unfortunately, the space station is supposed to be an international effort with Russia as one of the partners, and this decision created large problems for systems integration. Worse yet, the cause of the 1999 failure of the $125 million Mars Climate Orbiter was a mix-up between metric and English measurement systems. NASA has agreed to make its next mission to the moon in 2020 metric.[25] Let's see if it keeps its promise. It is hard to believe that the only three countries not officially on the metric system are Liberia, Myanmar, and the United States. It is becoming increasingly evident that the United States must change or be left behind.

ISO 9000 Certification: An International Standard of Quality

LO4

The importance of ISO 9000 certification

With quality becoming the cornerstone of global competition, companies are requiring assurance of standard conformance from suppliers, just as their customers are requiring the same from them. ISO 9000[26] certification has also been found to positively affect the performance and stock prices of firms.

ISO 9000s, a series of five international industrial standards (ISO 9000–9004) originally designed by the International Organization for Standardization in Geneva to meet the need for product quality assurances in purchasing agreements, are becoming a quality assurance certification program that has competitive and legal ramifications when doing business in the European Union and elsewhere. The original ISO 9000 system was promulgated in 1994. In 2000 the system was streamlined, as it was again in 2006. ISO 9000 concerns the registration and certification of a manufacturer's quality system. It is a certification of the existence of a quality control system that a company has in place to ensure it can meet published quality standards. ISO 9000 standards do not apply to specific products. They relate to generic system standards that enable a company, through a mix of internal and external audits, to provide assurance that it has a quality control system. It is a certification

---

[24]The original cost estimate was $16 billion. "International Space Station Marks Its 10th Anniversary," *RIA Novosti*, January 29, 2008.

[25]David B. Williams, "Metric Mission," *Science World*, April 2, 2007, p. 6.

[26]ISO 14001, a parallel environmental management standard, has not experienced the same rate of diffusion as ISO 9000. See Magali Delmas and Ivan Montiel, "The Diffusion of Voluntary International Management Standards: Responsible Care, ISO 9000, and ISO 14001 in the Chemical Industry," *Policy Studies Journal* 36 (2008), pp. 65–82.

The Japanese manufacturer is quite proud of the ISO 9000 quality ratings for its plant in San Jose, Costa Rica.

of the production process only and does not guarantee that a manufacturer produces a "quality" product or service. The series describes three quality system models, defines quality concepts, and gives guidelines for using international standards in quality systems.

To receive ISO 9000 certification, a company requests a certifying body (a third party authorized to provide an ISO 9000 audit) to conduct a registration assessment—that is, an audit of the key business processes of a company. The assessor will ask questions about everything from blueprints to sales calls to filing. "Does the supplier meet promised delivery dates?" and "Is there evidence of customer satisfaction?" are two of the questions asked and the issues explored. The object is to develop a comprehensive plan to ensure that minute details are not overlooked. The assessor helps management create a quality manual, which will be made available to customers wishing to verify the organization's reliability. When accreditation is granted, the company receives certification. A complete assessment for recertification is done every four years, with intermediate evaluations during the four-year period.

Although ISO 9000 is generally voluntary, except for certain regulated products, the EU Product Liability Directive puts pressure on all companies to become certified. The directive holds that a manufacturer, including an exporter, will be liable, regardless of fault or negligence, if a person is harmed by a product that fails because of a faulty component. Thus, customers in the European Union need to be assured that the components of their products are free of defects or deficiencies. A manufacturer with a well-documented quality system will be better able to prove that products are defect free and thus minimize liability claims.

A strong level of interest in ISO 9000 is being driven more by marketplace requirements than by government regulations, and ISO 9000 is now an important competitive marketing tool in Europe and around the world. As the market demands quality and more and more companies adopt some form of TQM, manufacturers are increasingly requiring ISO 9000 registration of their suppliers. Companies manufacturing parts and components in China are quickly discovering that ISO 9000 certification is a virtual necessity, and the Japanese construction industry now requires ISO 9000 as part of the government procurement process. More and more buyers, particularly those in Europe, are refusing to buy from manufacturers that do not have internationally recognized third-party proof of their quality capabilities. ISO 9000 may also be used to serve as a means of differentiating "classes" of suppliers, particularly in high-tech areas where high product reliability is crucial. In other words, if two suppliers are competing for the same contract, the one with ISO 9000 registration may have a competitive edge.

Although more and more countries (now more than 100) and companies continue to adopt ISO 9000 standards, many have complaints about the system and its spread. For example, 39 electronics companies battled against special Japanese software criteria for ISO 9000. Electronics companies also protested against the establishment of a new ISO Health and Safety Standard. Still others are calling for more comprehensive international standards along the lines of America's Malcolm Baldrige Award, which considers seven criteria—leadership, strategic planning, customer and market focus, information and analysis, human resource development, management, and business results. The telecommunications industry recently promulgated an industry-specific TL 9000 certification program, which combines aspects of ISO 9000 and several other international quality standards.

Perhaps the most pertinent kind of quality standard is now being developed by the University of Michigan Business School and the American Society for Quality Control.[27] Using survey methods, their American Customer Satisfaction Index (ACSI) measures

[27]Claes Fornell, Michael D. Johnson, Eugene W. Anderson, Jaesung Cha, and Barbara Everitt Bryant, "The American Consumer Index: Nature, Purpose, and Findings," *Journal of Marketing* 60, no. 4 (October 1996), pp. 35–46; http://www.asq.org, 2008; http://www.cfigroup.com, 2012.

customers' satisfaction and perceptions of quality of a representative sample of America's goods and services. The approach was actually developed in Sweden and is now being used in other European and Asian countries as well. The appeal of the ACSI approach is its focus on results, that is, quality as perceived by product and service users. So far the ACSI approach has been applied only in consumer product and service contexts; however, the fundamental notion that customers are the best judges of quality is certainly applicable to international business-to-business marketing settings as well. Individual industrial marketing firms are seeking even better ways to implement quality improvement programs, including using similar techniques as those employed by ACSI.

Business Services

For many industrial products, the revenues from associated services exceed the revenues from the products. Perhaps the most obvious case is cellular phones, in which the physical product is practically given away to gain the phone services contract. Or consider how inexpensive printers may seem until the costs of operation (i.e., ink cartridges) are included. Indeed, for many capital equipment manufacturers, the margins on after-sale services (i.e., maintenance contracts, overhauls, repairs, and replacement parts) are much higher than the margins on the machinery itself. Furthermore, when companies lease capital equipment to customers, the distinction between products and services almost disappears completely. When a business customer leases a truck, is it purchasing a vehicle or transportation services?

Businesses also buy a variety of services that are not associated with products. Our favorite examples are the at-sea-satellite-launch services now provided by Sea Launch[28], Boeing and SpaceX delivering astronauts to the International Space Station,[29] and the new concept proffered by Microsoft cofounder Paul Allen to launch satellites from high-flying mega-jet aircraft.[30] Other professional services are purchased from advertising and legal agencies,[31] transportation and insurance companies, oil field services, banks and investment brokers, and healthcare providers, to name only a few. Both categories of business services are discussed in this section.

After-Sale Services

Effective competition abroad requires not only proper product design but also effective service, prompt deliveries, and the ability to furnish spare and replacement parts without delay. For example, GE Medical Systems provides a wide range of after-sale services for hospitals that buy MRIs and other equipment—training, information technologies, associated healthcare services, and parts and accessories.[32] In the highly competitive European Union, it is imperative to give the same kind of service a domestic company or EU company can give.

For many technical products, the willingness of the seller to provide installation and training may be the deciding factor for the buyers in accepting one company's product over another's. South Korean and other Asian businesspeople are frank in admitting they prefer to buy from American firms but that Japanese firms often get the business because of outstanding after-sales service. Frequently heard tales of conflicts between U.S. and foreign firms over assistance expected from the seller are indicative of the problems of after-sales service and support. A South Korean executive's experiences with an American engineer and some Japanese engineers typify the situation: The Korean electronics firm purchased semiconductor-chip–making equipment for a plant expansion. The American engineer was slow in completing the installation; he stopped work at 5:00 p.m. and would not work on

[28]W.J. Hennigan, "Sea Launch Looking Up Again with New Rocket Mission," *Los Angeles Times*, September 22, 2011; W. J. Hennigan, "Sea Launch Rocker Carrying Satellite Fails after Liftoff," *Los Angeles Times*, February 2, 2013, p. B2.

[29]Kenneth Chang, "Boeing and SpaceX to Take Americans to Space Station," *The New York Times*, September 17, 2014, p. A19.

[30]Andy Pasztor and Dionne Searcey, "Paul Allen, Supersizing Space Flight," *The Wall Street Journal*, December 14, 2011.

[31]Jennifer Smith, "Asian Law Giant Takes Shape," *The Wall Street Journal*, December 15, 2011.

[32]See http://www.gehealthcare.com, 2012.

weekends. The Japanese, installing other equipment, understood the urgency of getting the factory up and running; without being asked, they worked day and night until the job was finished.

Unfortunately this example is not an isolated case. In another example, Hyundai Motor Company bought two multimillion-dollar presses to stamp body parts for cars. The presses arrived late, even more time was required to set up the machines, and Hyundai had to pay the Americans extra to get the machines to work correctly. Such problems translate into lost business for U.S. firms. Samsung Electronics Company, Korea's largest chipmaker, used U.S. equipment for 75 percent of its first memory-chip plant; when it outfitted its most recent chip plant, it bought 75 percent of the equipment from Japan. Of course, not all American companies have such problems. Indeed, in India Intel recently opened a data center comprising an Internet server farm of hundreds of servers. Already customers in many countries connect and store their servers and have them serviced by Intel at such centers.

Customer training is rapidly becoming a major after-sales service when selling technical products in countries that demand the latest technology but do not always have trained personnel. China demands the most advanced technical equipment but frequently has untrained people responsible for products they do not understand. Heavy emphasis on training programs and self-teaching materials to help overcome the common lack of skills to operate technical equipment is a necessary part of the after-sales service package in much of the developing world. While perhaps McDonald's Hamburger University is the most famous international customer training center, industrial sellers may soon catch up. Cisco Systems, collaborating with the government and a university in Singapore, established the first Cisco Academy Training Centre to serve that region of the world, and Intel established e-Business Solutions Centers in five European countries.

A recent study of international users of heavy construction equipment revealed that, next to the manufacturer's reputation, quick delivery of replacement parts was of major importance in purchasing construction equipment. Furthermore, 70 percent of those questioned indicated they bought parts not made by the original manufacturer of the equipment because of the difficulty of getting original parts. Smaller importers complain of U.S. exporting firms not responding to orders or responding only after extensive delay. It appears that the importance of timely availability of spare parts to sustain a market is forgotten by some American exporters that are used to quick deliveries in the domestic market. When companies are responsive, the rewards are significant. U.S. chemical production equipment manufacturers dominate sales in Mexico because, according to the International Trade Administration, they deliver quickly. The ready availability of parts and services provided by U.S. marketers can give them a competitive edge.

Some international marketers also may be forgoing the opportunity of participating in a lucrative aftermarket. Certain kinds of machine tools use up to five times their original value in replacement parts during an average life span and thus represent an even greater market. One international machine tool company has capitalized on the need for direct service and available parts by changing its distribution system from "normal" to one of stressing rapid service and readily available parts. Instead of selling through independent distributors, as do most machine tool manufacturers in foreign markets, this company established a series of company stores and service centers similar to those found in the United States. The company can render service through its system of local stores, whereas most competitors must dispatch service people from their home-based factories. The service people are kept on tap for rapid service calls in each of its network of local stores, and each store keeps a large stock of standard parts available for immediate delivery. The net result of meeting industrial needs quickly is keeping the company among the top suppliers in foreign sales of machine tools.

International small-package door-to-door express air services, the Internet, and international toll-free telephone service have helped speed up the delivery of parts and have made after-sales technical service almost instantly available. Amdahl, the giant mainframe computer maker, uses air shipments almost exclusively for cutting inventory costs and ensuring premium customer service, which is crucial to competing against larger rivals. With increasing frequency, electronics, auto parts, and machine parts sent by air have become a formidable weapon in cutting costs and boosting competitiveness. Technical advice is only a toll-free call or a computer keyboard away, and parts are air-expressed immediately to the customer. Not only does this approach improve service standards, but it also is often more cost effective than maintaining an office in a country, even though foreign-language speakers must be hired to answer calls.

After-sales services are not only crucial in building strong customer loyalty and the all-important reputation that leads to sales at other companies, but they are also almost always more profitable than the actual sale of the machinery or product.

Other Business Services

LO5

The growth of business services and nuances of their marketing

Trade creates demands for international services.[33] Most business services companies enter international markets to service their local clients abroad.[34] Accounting, banking,[35] advertising, and law firms were among the early companies to establish branches or acquire local affiliations abroad to serve their U.S. multinational clients. Hotels and auto-rental agencies followed the business traveler abroad. Most recently, healthcare services providers have been following firms abroad—Blue Cross is now selling HMO services to American companies operating in Mexico and other countries. Once established, many of these client followers, as one researcher refers to them, expand their client base to include local companies as well. As global markets grow, creating greater demand for business services, service companies become international market seekers.

As mentioned in Chapter 13, the mode of entry for most consumer services firms is licensing, franchising, strategic alliances, or direct. This tendency is so because of the inseparability of the creation and consumption of the services. However, because some business services have intrinsic value that can be embodied in some tangible form (such as a blueprint or architectural design), they can be produced in one country and exported to another. Data processing and data analysis services are good examples. The analysis or processing is completed on a computer located in the United States, and the output (the service) is transmitted via the Internet to a distant customer. Architecture, systems integration,[36] and engineering consulting services are exportable when the consultant travels to the client's site and later returns home to write and submit a report or a design.

Business services firms face most of the same constraints and problems confronting merchandise traders. Protectionism is the most serious threat to the continued expansion of international services trade. The growth of international services has been so rapid during the last decade it has drawn the attention of local companies, governments, and researchers. As a result, direct and indirect trade barriers have been imposed to restrict foreign companies from domestic markets. Every reason, from the protection of infant industries to national security, has been used to justify some of the restrictive practices. A list of more than 2,000 instances of barriers to the free flow of services among nations was recently compiled by the U.S. government. In response to the threat of increasing restriction, the United States has successfully negotiated to open business services markets through both NAFTA and GATT.

---

[33]Perhaps one of the best examples of trade leading demand for services is the critical importance of Japanese trading companies to that country. See Anthony Goerzen and Shige Makino, "Multinational Corporation Internationalization in the Service Sector: A Study of Japanese Trading Companies," *Journal of International Business Studies* 38 (2007), pp. 1149–69.

[34]Lihong Qian and Andrew Delios, "Internationalization and Experience: Japanese Banks' International Expansion, 1980–1998," *Journal of International Business Studies* 39 (2008), pp. 231–48; Jad Mouawad, "Piling on the Luxury," *The New York Times*, May 8, 2014, pp. F1, 4.

[35]Shujing Li, Jiaping Qiu, and Chi Wan, "Corporate Globalization and Bank Lending," *Journal of International Business Studies* 42, no. 8 (2011), pp. 1016–42; Robert Cull, Stephen Haber, and Masami Imai, "Related Lending and Banking Development," *Journal of International Business Studies* 42, no. 3 (2011), pp. 406–26.

[36]Janet Y. Murray, Masaki Kotabe, and Stanford A. Westjohn, "Global Sourcing Strategy and Performance of Knowledge-Intensive Business Services: A Two-Stage Strategic Fit Model," *Journal of International Marketing* 17, no. 4 (2009), pp. 90–105.

Until the GATT and NAFTA agreements, few international rules of fair play governed trade in services. Service companies faced a complex group of national regulations that impeded the movement of people and technology from country to country. At least one study has demonstrated that personnel and intellectual property issues are key drivers of success and failure, particularly in knowledge-based services such as consulting, engineering, education, and information technology. The United States and other industrialized nations want their banks, insurance companies, construction firms, and other business service providers to be allowed to move people, capital, and technology around the globe unimpeded. Restrictions designed to protect local markets range from not being allowed to do business in a country to requirements that all foreign professionals pass certification exams in the local language before being permitted to practice. In Argentina, for example, an accountant must have the equivalent of a high school education in Argentinean geography and history before being permitted to audit the books of a multinational company's branch in Buenos Aires.

Restrictions on cross-border data flows are potentially the most damaging to both the communications industry and other MNCs that rely on data transfers across borders to conduct business.[37] Some countries impose tariffs on the transmission of data, and many others are passing laws forcing companies to open their computer files to inspection by government agencies or are tightly controlling transmission domestically. Most countries have a variety of laws to deal with the processing and electronic transmission of data across borders. In many cases, concern stems from not understanding how best to tax cross-border data flows.

As mentioned earlier, competition in all sectors of the services industry is increasing as host-country markets are being invaded by many foreign firms. The practice of following a client into foreign markets and then expanding into international markets is not restricted to U.S. firms. Service firms from Germany, Britain, Japan, and other countries follow their clients into foreign markets and then expand to include local business as well. Telecommunications, advertising, and construction are U.S. services that face major competition, not only from European and Japanese companies but also from representatives of Brazil, India, and other parts of the world.

Clearly opportunities for the marketing of business services will continue to grow well into the 21st century. International marketers will have to be quite creative in responding to the legal and cultural challenges of delivering high-quality business services in foreign markets and to foreign customers. The success of international business services firms will of course depend on finding high-quality employees (with technical and interpersonal skills and a strong customer orientation)[38] to build and maintain the personal relationships that are so important, particularly when doing business across cultures.[39] We will expand on this last point in Chapters 17 and 19.

Trade Shows: A Crucial Part of Business-to-Business Marketing

LO6

The importance of trade shows in promoting industrial goods

The promotional problems encountered by foreign industrial marketers are little different from the problems faced by domestic marketers. Until recently there has been a paucity of specialized advertising media in many countries.[40] In the last decade, however, specialized industrial media have been developed to provide the industrial marketer with a means of

---

[37]"Brocade," *The Wall Street Journal*, Realtime Narratives, March 10, 2014, online.

[38]Vinh La, Paul Patterson, and Chris Styles, "Client-Perceived Performance and Value in Professional B-2-B Services: An International Perspective," *Journal of International Business Studies* 40, no. 2 (2009), pp. 274–300.

[39]Wenyu Dou, Hairong Li, Nan Zhou, and Chenting Su, "Exploring Relationship Satisfaction between Global Professional Service Firms and Local Clients in Emerging Markets," *Journal of International Business Studies* 41, no. 7 (2010), pp. 1198–217.

[40]Of course, it should be noted that some industrial companies still use nonspecialized media, building brand awareness at all levels. A good example is Intel's sponsorship of the official website of the Tour de France back in 2002.

So you want to buy an Airbus 380? How about kicking the tires of one at the Paris Air Show, the world's biggest aerospace trade show?

communicating with potential customers, especially in western Europe and to some extent in eastern Europe, the Commonwealth of Independent States (CIS), and Asia.

In addition to advertising in print media and reaching industrial customers through catalogs, websites,[41] and direct mail, the trade show or trade fair has become the primary vehicle for doing business in many foreign countries. As part of its international promotion activities, the U.S. Department of Commerce sponsors trade fairs in many cities around the world. Additionally, local governments in most countries sponsor annual trade shows. African countries, for example, host more than 70 industry-specific trade shows.

Trade shows serve as the most important vehicles for selling products, reaching prospective B2B customers, contacting and evaluating potential agents and distributors, and marketing in most countries. Firms that have successfully integrated trade show attendance and follow-up personal selling efforts have been consistently shown to be more profitable.[42] Although important in the United States, trade shows serve a much more important role in other countries. They have been at the center of commerce in Europe for centuries and are where most prospects are found. European trade shows attract high-level decision makers who are attending not just to see the latest products but to buy. Pre-show promotional expenditures are often used in Europe to set formal appointments. The importance of trade shows to Europeans is reflected in the percentage of their media budget spent on participating in trade events and how they spend those dollars. On average, Europeans spend 22 percent of their total annual media budget on trade events, whereas comparable American firms typically spend less than 5 percent. Europeans tend not to spend money on circuslike promotions, gimmicks, and such; rather, they focus on providing an environment for in-depth dealings. More than 2,000 major trade shows are held worldwide every year. The Hanover Industry Fair (Germany), the largest trade fair in the world, has nearly 6,000 exhibitors, who show a wide range of industrial products to 600,000 visitors.[43]

---

[41]For illustrative examples of the burgeoning information available to industrial customers on websites, see http://www.caterpillar.com, http://www.fluor.com, http://www.hewlett-packard.com, and http://www.qualcom.com.

[42]Timothy Smith, Srinath Gopalakrishnan, and Paul M. Smith, "The Complementary Effect of Trade Shows on Personal Selling," *International Journal of Research in Marketing* 21, no. 1 (2004), pp. 61–76.

[43]See http://www.hannovermesse.de/home for details.

The 2016 Mirai (Japanese for "future"), Toyota's first hydrogen fuel-cell vehicle offering, was debuted at the Los Angeles Auto Show in November 2014. In order for the car to become a renewable energy success, it will need an infrastructure of hydrogen fueling stations around the country and around the world. Several automotive companies and entrepreneurial industrial marketers are collaborating in this new marketing venture.

Trade shows provide the facilities for a manufacturer to exhibit and demonstrate products to potential users and to view competitors' products. They are an opportunity to create sales and establish relationships with agents, distributors, franchisees, and suppliers that can lead to more nearly permanent distribution channels in foreign markets. In fact, a trade show may be the only way to reach some prospects. Trade show experts estimate that 80 to 85 percent of the people seen on a trade show floor never have a salesperson call on them. Several websites now specialize in virtual trade shows. They often include multimedia and elaborate product display booths that can be virtually toured. Some of these virtual trade shows last only a few days during an associated actual trade show.[44]

The number and variety of trade shows are such that almost any target market in any given country can be found through this medium.[45] Most remarkable was the Medical Expo in Havana in 2000—the first trade show to be sanctioned by both the U.S. and Cuban governments in more than four decades. More than 8,000 Cuban doctors, nurses, technicians, and hospital administrators attended. This initial event was followed in 2002 with a major food products trade show in Havana. In eastern Europe, fairs and exhibitions offer companies the opportunity to meet new customers, including private traders, young entrepreneurs, and representatives of nonstate organizations. The exhibitions in countries such as Russia and Poland offer a cost-effective way of reaching a large number of customers who might otherwise be difficult to target through individual sales calls. Specialized fairs in individual sectors such as computers, the automotive industry, fashion, and home furnishings regularly take place.

In difficult economic and/or political circumstances, online trade shows become a useful, but obviously less than adequate, substitute. A good example of the kinds of services being developed can be found in Crossing Borders 14.3. During the weakened global economy at the turn of the century, slimmer travel budgets and SARS scares dramatically reduced attendance, and even forced cancellations, of traditionally popular international trade fairs. Political conflicts between the European Union and the United States over Middle East policies resulted in the U.S. Department of Defense discouraging American attendance at the 2003 Paris Air Show. Top American executives at Boeing, Lockheed, and the like dutifully stayed away. Exhibit space declined by 5 percent, and orders announced dropped from $45 billion in 2001 to $32 billion. It is hard to estimate what the costs in terms of international orders are for firms such

[44]See more information see "Virtual Conference and Trade Show Market Forecast 2013–2018," *Market Research Media,* April 7, 2014, online, http://www.marketresearchmedia.com/?p=421.

[45]Keith Bradsher, "Export Fair in China Loses Steam," *The New York Times*, October 16, 2013, pp. B1, 9.

CROSSING BORDERS 14.2

No More Aching Feet, but What about the 15-Ton Russian Tank?

During April 2000, the first stand-alone virtual trade show was staged by ISP Virtual Show. It was aimed at an appropriate audience—Internet service providers (ISPs). The address was ISPVirtualShow.com (the site is down now, but you can still take a look by Googling it). Technology for the show was provided by iTradeFair.com, a website worth the visit.

According to the promoters, "The advantages of a virtual trade show far outweigh those of the physical model. Exhibitors (booths start at $1,995) and attendees (tickets are $99) from all over the world will now be able to exhibit and attend direct from their desktops. There are endless benefits of a virtual show, including massive reductions in costs both in exhibiting and manpower terms, savings on booth space and buildings, accommodations, flights, expenses, the obligatory bar bills and costs of time spent out of the office."

The virtual trade show offers a fresh alternative to the traditional model. Using advanced technology, anyone anywhere in the world can visit the virtual show and access information in his or her own language—making language barriers a thing of the past. Also, if attendees and exhibitors would like to continue a discussion offline, clocks displaying times from all over the world make scheduling easy. Finally, weary executives attending the same trade shows year in, year out will no longer have to suffer aching feet, hot stuffy rooms without air-conditioning, and overpriced, plastic food.

Although this pitch sounds great, we believe that an aspect of real trade shows that the virtual ones miss is the face-to-face contact and the all-important interpersonal relationship building that goes on over drinks or during those "plastic" meals. And there is no virtual way to achieve the same effect as a Russian software developer who displayed a 15-ton Russian tank in his booth at Comtek Trade Show in Moscow, or the Russian jet engine supplier that used scantily clad women dancers to attract crowds to its booth at the Farnborough Air Show. We note that the Air Show organizers banned the dancers, and that created even more of an uproar. Ah, marketing! In any case, we shall see how the new promotional medium of virtual trade shows evolves.

Sources: "ISP Virtual Show: World's First Virtual Trade Show," *M2 Presswire*, October 26, 1999; Jeanette Borzo, "Moscow's Comtek Trade Show Confronts Internet Challenge," *Dow Jones News Service*, April 19, 2000; "ICUEE Is the Demo Expo," *Transmission & Distribution*, August 1, 2005, p. 74; "Russian Firm Banned from Using Scantily Clad Women to Lure Customers to Its Stand At Farnborough Air Show," Daily Mail (UK), July 19, 2008, online; http:// www.iTradeFair.com, 2012.

as Boeing when their top executives cannot mix with potential customers at such a crucial event. We do know that Airbus inked orders for dozens of commercial aircraft from customers in Qatar and the Arab Emirates. Not even the best online trade show imaginable can make up for this apparent step backward in international trade and cooperation.

Relationship Marketing in Business-to-Business Contexts

LO7

The importance of relationship marketing for industrial products and services

The characteristics that yield the uniqueness of industrial products and services lead naturally to **relationship marketing**.[46] The long-term relationships with customers that define relationship marketing fit the characteristics inherent in industrial products and are a viable strategy for business-to-business marketing. The first and foremost characteristic of industrial goods markets is the motive of the buyer: to make a profit. Industrial products fit into a services delivery or manufacturing process, and their contributions will be judged on how well they contribute to that process. For an industrial marketer to fulfill the needs of a customer, the marketer must understand those needs as they exist today and how they will change as the buyer strives to compete in global markets that call for long-term relationships. The key functions of global account managers revolve around the notions of intelligence gathering, coordination with the customer's staff, and reconfiguration (i.e., adapting the practices and process to the changing competitive environment).

---

[46]Linda Hui Shi, J. Chris White, Shaoming Zou, and S. Tamer Cavusgil, "Global Account Management Strategies: Drivers and Outcomes," *Journal of International Business Studies* 41 (2011), pp. 620–38.

The industrial customer's needs in global markets are continuously changing, and suppliers' offerings must also continue to change. The need for the latest technology means that it is not a matter of selling the right product the first time but rather of continuously changing the product to keep it right over time. The objective of relationship marketing is to make the relationship an important attribute of the transaction,[47] thus differentiating oneself from competitors. It shifts the focus away from price to service and long-term benefits. The reward is loyal customers that translate into substantial long-term profits.

Focusing on long-term relationship building will be especially important in most international markets where culture dictates stronger ties between people and companies. Particularly in countries with collectivistic and high-context cultures, such as those in Latin America or Asia, trust will be a crucial aspect of commercial relationships. Constant and close communication with customers will be the single most important source of information about the development of new industrial products and services. Indeed, in a recent survey of Japanese professional buyers, a key choice criterion for suppliers was a trait they called "caring" (those who defer to requests without argument and recognize that in return buyers will care for the long-term interests of sellers). Longer-term and more communication-rich relationships are keys to success in international industrial markets.

As in all areas of international business, the Internet is facilitating relationship building and maintenance in new ways. One study has shown key aspects of managing this aspect of international industrial marketing to include website design, multilingual access, cultural considerations, and effective marketing of the website itself.[48] Cisco Systems is a leader in this area; it not only supplies the hardware that allows B2B commerce to work, but its relationship management practices and process also serve as models for the industry. Cisco's international customers can visit its website to check out product specs and to order. That information is then routed on the Internet through Cisco to its suppliers. A full 65 percent of the orders move directly from the supplier to the customer—Cisco never touches them. Things are built only after they are ordered; thus little, if any, inventory is kept in warehouses. Based on Cisco's success, businesses around the world are beginning to reorganize themselves accordingly.

---

[47]Atul Sharma, Louise Young, and Ian Wilkinson, "The Commitment Mix: Dimensions of Commitment in International Trading Relationships in India," *Journal of International Marketing* 14 (2006), pp. 64–91.

[48]Riyand Eid, Ibrahim Elbeltagi, and Mohammed Zairi, "Making Business-to-Business International Internet Marketing Effective: A Study of Critical Factors Using a Case-Study Approach," *Journal of International Marketing* 14 (2006), pp. 87–109.

Solar Turbines Inc.
A Global Industrial Marketer

With more than 80 percent of its sales outside of the United States, Solar Turbines Inc. is the most global subsidiary of one of America's most global companies. More than half of Caterpillar's 2014 sales of over $50 billion were to customers outside of the United States, making the parent corporation one of the county's leading exporters. Pictured here is work on the road leading to the airport at Serengeti National Park in Tanzania.

Solar Turbines advertises in print and digital media (see examples just below) such as the Oil & Gas Journal in the U.S. and local trade journals in foreign languages. PEMEX is a huge customer in hot and humid Mexico. In the harsh winter conditions of the former Soviet Union and now Russia, oil and gas companies have remained important customers for Solar Turbines for more than 50 years.

Most recently Solar Turbines communicates with its customers, before and after sales, via the pictured iPad App.

Courtesy of Solar Turbines, Inc.

The Project Team

Sales Engineer, who maintains initial Customer contact, prompts analysis of Customer needs, submits a comprehensive proposal to the Customer, monitors execution of the order, and submits the order to the assigned ...

Application Engineer, who is responsible for determining the best product match for Customer requirements and recommending alternative approaches as appropriate. The Application Engineer works closely with ...

Engineering and Control Systems, where gas turbines, gas compressors, and controls are designed and gas turbine packages are customized for the customer based on proven designs.

Solar Turbines sells its products and services through project teams that include both customer personnel and vendors. Solar has followed its American customers around the world, supplying equipment and services for their global ventures. Of course, the firm sells directly to a wide variety of foreign firms as well.

Personal selling is the most important aspect of the promotions mix for industrial companies like Solar. In addition to calling on clients directly, sales engineers attend key trade shows around the world, such as this one in Amsterdam.

Project Manager handles all aspects of the order, maintains liaison with the Customer, controls documentation, arranges quality audits, and is responsible for on-time shipment and scheduling equipment commissioning at the Customer site.

Manufacturing Technicians produce, assemble, and test industrial gas turbines and turbomachinery packages designed to meet specific Customer needs. Manufacturing also arranges shipment of equipment to the Customer site where ...

Customer Services handles installation and start-up of the turbo-machinery, trains personnel, and provides a wide range of vital services to support Customer and operating requirements.

Suppliers are a critical element of all project teams; they provide materials and components that must meet Solar's demanding Quality Standards.

The Venezuelan offshore oil and gas platform pictured here is about a $40 million project for Solar; it includes four sets of turbomachinery. Close coordination among customer, subcontractors, and Solar is required from initial designs through powering up the facility.

Courtesy of Solar Turbines, Inc.

Solar's sales and services efforts don't stop when the machine has been turned on. After-sales services (maintenance contracts, overhaul, and spare parts) often account for one-third of some industrial manufacturers' revenues, and Solar is no exception to that rule. Pictured are company overhaul operations in Indonesia.

Solar's Global Partnerships

Solar sells and distributes its and products and services through a variety of affiliates around the world. Some countries require local content, so the firm often provides the turbines and compressors while local partners develop much of the rest of the package. As a socially responsible manufacturer, Solar also collaborates with customers and affiliates in developing low emissions products.

Seizing the opportunity to turn waste into energy and reduce emissions at the same time, Jinneng Science & Technology Co., Ltd. Has installed eight Solar gas turbine generator sets. The combined heat and power systems operate at high efficiency and use less fuel than separate heat and power systems, translating into a high return on investment. The installation not only makes commercial sense, but also benefits the environment by reducing CO_2 emissions by 536,000 tons per year, the equivalent of eliminating annual emissions from 97,000 automobiles.

Solar Turbines participates in a variety of ways to produce cleaner energy. Here executives and engineers from Qinghua Coking Group visit the San Diego facilities of the American firm to learn more about gas turbine technologies and opportunities.

Since 1992, Solar has offered gas turbine engines with pollution-prevention SoLoNO$_x$™ dry lean-premixed combustion technology. This advanced combustion system provides the most cost effective and environmentally friendly approach to reduce NO$_x$ emissions. More than 2600 gas turbines with SoLoNO$_x$™ technology have been installed worldwide, logging more than 132 million operating hours. Solar's combined experience with dry lean-premixed combustion technology allows the firm to claim superiority in the gas turbine industry.

Toward the continuing development of cleaner and more efficient products Solar Turbines partners with and supports research at engineering schools around the world. Pictured here is the combustion research facility at UC Irvine, just up the coast from Solar Turbines' San Diego headquarters.

Courtesy of Solar Turbines, Inc.

Summary

Industrial (business-to-business) marketing requires close attention to the exact needs of customers. Basic differences across various markets are less than those for consumer goods, but the motives behind purchases differ enough to require a special approach. Global competition has risen to the point that industrial goods marketers must pay close attention to the level of economic and technological development of each market to determine the buyer's assessment of quality. Companies that adapt their products to these needs are the ones that should be most effective in the marketplace.

The demand for products and services in business-to-business markets is by nature more volatile than in most consumer markets.

The demand also varies by level of economic development and the quality of educational systems across countries. Ultimately, product or service quality is defined by customers, but global quality standards such as ISO 9000 are being developed that provide information about companies' attention to matters of quality. After-sale services are a hugely important aspect of industrial sales. The demand for other kinds of business services (e.g., banking, legal services, advertising) is burgeoning around the world. Trade shows are an especially important promotional medium in business-to-business marketing.

Key Terms

Derived demand	ISO 9000s	Relationship marketing
Price–quality relationship	Client followers	

Questions

1. Define the key terms listed above.

2. What are the differences between consumer and industrial goods, and what are the implications for international marketing?

3. Discuss how the various stages of economic development affect the demand for industrial goods.

4. "Industrialization is typically a national issue, and industrial goods are the fodder for industrial growth." Comment.

5. "The adequacy of a product must be considered in relation to the general environment within which it will be operated rather than solely on the basis of technical efficiency." Discuss the implications of this statement.

6. Why hasn't the United States been more helpful in setting universal standards for industrial equipment? Do you feel that the argument is economically sound? Discuss.

7. What roles do service, replacement parts, and standards play in competition in foreign marketing? Illustrate.

8. Discuss the role industrial trade fairs play in international marketing of industrial goods.

9. Describe the reasons an MNC might seek an ISO 9000 certification.

10. What ISO 9000 legal requirements are imposed on products sold in the European Union? Discuss.

11. Discuss the competitive consequences of being ISO 9000 certified.

12. Discuss how the characteristics that define the uniqueness of industrial products lead naturally to relationship marketing. Give some examples.

13. Discuss some of the more pertinent problems in pricing industrial goods.

14. What is the price–quality relationship? How does this relationship affect a U.S. firm's comparative position in world markets?

15. Select several countries, each at a different stage of economic development, and illustrate how the stage affects demand for industrial goods.

16. England has almost completed the process of shifting from the inch–pound system to the metric system. What effect do you think this will have on the traditional U.S. reluctance to make such a change? Discuss the economic implications of such a move.

17. Discuss the importance of international business services to total U.S. export trade. How do most U.S. service companies become international?

18. Discuss the international market environment for business services.

Chapter 15

International Marketing Channels

CHAPTER OUTLINE

CHAPTER LEARNING OBJECTIVES

What you should learn from Chapter 15:

LO1 The variety of distribution channels and how they affect cost and efficiency in marketing

LO2 The Japanese distribution structure and what it means to Japanese customers and to competing importers of goods

LO3 How distribution patterns affect the various aspects of international marketing

LO4 The functions, advantages, and disadvantages of various kinds of middlemen

LO5 The importance of selecting and maintaining middlemen

LO6 The growing importance of e-commerce as a distribution alternative

LO7 The interdependence of physical distribution activities

6 Duane Stanford, "Africa: Coke's Last Frontier," *Bloomberg BusinessWeek*, October 28, 2010.

Global Perspective

CENTRAL PERK IN BEIJING

All 4Ps of marketing—product, price, promotion, and place— are important for retailers, particularly the last. No one has made more profit by creating a "third place" for consumers than Starbucks. As on the TV show *Friends*, friends have a sofa to sit on, talk, and, the retailer hopes, consume. But it doesn't always work out to the retailer's advantage in Beijing:

One first-time Beijing Starbucks visitor reported, "The thing I like most is the comfortable sofa, and I think when I first saw the Starbucks I entered it and sat in the sofa. But, the servant came and told me if you don't consume coffee you can't be here. So I left because at the time I think for students like me, the price of coffee was a little bit high."

Another customer reported not knowing the rules of the game: "I remember when I first went to Starbucks I wanted an ice coffee. . . . But, after finishing the coffee the sugar stayed in the bottom of the cup. I don't know because there are many kinds of sugar. . . . I don't know what kind of sugar is right for me, for my coffee. So I want in the future . . . some service and lessons about what kind of sugar is added to what kind of coffee."

IKEA in Beijing has a larger store and a larger problem of this sort:

With no plans one Saturday, Zhang Xin told his wife, son, and mother to wear something smart and hop into the family sedan. He could have taken them to the Forbidden City or the Great Wall, but he decided on another popular destination—IKEA.

Riding an escalator past a man lying on a display bed with a book opened on his belly, the clan sauntered into the crush of visitors squeezing onto the showroom path, bumping elbows and nicking ankles with their yellow shopping trolleys. Zhang said the family needed a respite from the smog and a reliable lunch. "We just came here for fun," said the 34-year-old office manager. "I suppose we could have gone somewhere else, but it wouldn't have been a complete experience."

Welcome to IKEA Beijing, where the atmosphere is more theme park than store. When the Swedish furniture giant first opened here in 1999, it hoped locals would embrace its European brand of minimalism. A decade later, Beijingers have done just that. Perhaps too much.

Every weekend, thousands of looky-loos pour into the massive showroom to use the displays. Some hop into bed, slide under the covers and sneak a nap; others bring cameras and pose with the decor. Families while away the afternoon in the store for no other reason than to enjoy the air conditioning. Visitors can't seem to resist novelties most Americans take for granted, such as free soda refills and ample seating. They also like the laid-back staffers who don't mind when a child jumps on a couch.

Purchasing anything at *Yi Jia*, as the store is called here, can seem like an afterthought. "It's the only big store in Beijing where a security guard doesn't stop you from taking a picture," said Jing Bo, 30, who was looking for promising backdrops for a photograph of his girlfriend.

The store's success can be traced, in part, to how grounded it is in the capital's zeitgeist. At a time when home ownership is more within reach and incomes are rising, IKEA offers affordable, modern furniture to an emerging middle class clamoring to be *bai ling*, or white collar. It doesn't hurt either that the understated style is a satisfying departure from, say, the faux French imperial designs favored by the older nouveaux riches and gaudy hotels.

"Our values are changing," said Lizzy Hou, a university graduate who moved to Beijing in May from neighboring Hebei province for a teaching job. "We want to be modern. I think IKEA stands for a kind of lifestyle. People don't necessarily want to buy it, but they want to at least experience it."

Yet in the store in Shanghai's Xuhui shopping district, elderly Chinese also have taken to gathering in the cafeteria for free coffee (offered to holders of a family membership card) on weeknights. Just as in Central Perk, they are mostly single, often widowed folks looking to meet prospects!

Though frustrated, IKEA executives hope browsers like Luo will eventually turn into buyers. That's why they don't shoo anyone away for sleeping. It's the promise of China's middle class that has girded their investment here. The privately owned company operates 19 stores in China, though there have been indications that profit remains elusive.

"The brand awareness is great, but the question is, how do we get people to open up their wallets and spend money?" said Linda Xu, a company spokeswoman who rolled her eyes when she came upon a trio of slumbering customers. When Walmart and the French supermarket chain Carrefour entered China in the 1990s, many flocked to the new stores just to look and touch. Now millions of Chinese shop there every day.

Sources: Meera Venkatraman and Teresa Nelson, "From Servicescape to Consumptionscape: A Photo-Elicitation Study of Starbucks in the New China," *Journal of International Business Studies* 39, no. 6 (2008), pp. 1010–26; David Pierson, "Beijing Loves IKEA—But Not for Shopping," *Los Angeles Times*, August 25, 2009, online. For more on this topic, see also Edwin J. Nijssen and Susan P. Douglas, Shafiq Khan, Senior Vice President eCommerce with Luis Babicek, James Nixon, and Robin Chiriboga, Marriott International, 2015. Used with permission. "Consumer World-Mindedness, Social-Mindedness, and Store Image," *Journal of International Marketing* 16, no. 3 (2008), pp. 84–107; Laurie Brukitt, "In China, IKEA Is a Swede Place for Senior Romance, Relaxation," *The Wall Street Journal*, December 1, 2011, pp. A1, A16.

Two visitors to Beijing's IKEA enjoy
a nap on a display sofa.

If marketing goals are to be achieved, a product must be accessible to the target market at an affordable price. Getting the product to the target market can be a costly process if inadequacies within the distribution structure cannot be overcome. Forging an aggressive and reliable channel of distribution may be the most critical and challenging task facing the international marketer. Moreover, some argue that meeting such challenges is a key catalyst to economic development.

Each market contains a distribution network with many channel choices whose structures are unique and, in the short run, fixed. In some markets, the distribution structure is multilayered, complex, inefficient, even strange, and often difficult for new marketers to penetrate; in others, there are few specialized middlemen except in major urban areas; and in yet others, there is a dynamic mixture of traditional and new, evolving distribution systems available on a global scale. Regardless of the predominating distribution structure, competitive advantage will reside with the marketer best able to build the most efficient channels from among the alternatives available. And as global trade continues to burgeon and physical distribution infrastructures lag, the challenges will be even greater in the 21st century.

This chapter discusses the basic points involved in making channel decisions: channel structures; distribution patterns; available alternative middlemen; factors affecting choice of channels; and locating, selecting, motivating, and terminating middlemen.

Channel-of-Distribution Structures

In every country and in every market, urban or rural, rich or poor, all consumer and industrial products eventually go through a distribution process. The distribution process includes the physical handling and distribution of goods, the passage of ownership (title), and—most important from the standpoint of marketing strategy—the buying and selling negotiations between producers and middlemen and between middlemen and customers.

A host of policy and strategic channel selection issues confronts the international marketing manager. These issues are not in themselves very different from those encountered in domestic distribution, but the resolution of the issues differs because of different channel alternatives and market patterns.

Each country market has a distribution structure through which goods pass from producer to user. Within this structure are a variety of middlemen whose customary functions, activities, and services reflect existing competition, market characteristics, tradition, and economic development.

In short, the behavior of channel members is the result of the interactions between the cultural environment and the marketing process. Channel structures range from those with little developed marketing infrastructure, such as those found in many emerging markets, to the highly complex, multilayered system found in Japan.

Import-Oriented Distribution Structure

LO1

The variety of distribution channels and how they affect cost and efficiency in marketing

Traditional channels in developing countries evolved from economies with a strong dependence on imported manufactured goods. In an *import-oriented* or *traditional distribution structure,* an importer controls a fixed supply of goods, and the marketing system develops around the philosophy of selling a limited supply of goods at high prices to a small number of affluent customers. In the resulting seller's market, market penetration and mass distribution are not necessary because demand exceeds supply, and in most cases, the customer seeks the supply from a limited number of middlemen.

This configuration affects the development of intermediaries and their functions. Distribution systems are local rather than national in scope, and the relationship between the importer and any middleman in the marketplace is considerably different from that found in a mass-marketing system. The idea of a channel as a chain of intermediaries performing specific activities and each selling to a smaller unit beneath it until the chain reaches the ultimate consumer is not common in an import-oriented system.

They're in China, but they aren't Peking ducks. The birds are for sale in Guangzhou's Qingping Free Market, the first farmers' market to be opened in China after the Cultural Revolution in 1979. This market was the place where free enterprise found its rebirth. Every kind of food is for sale here—from ducks to dogs, from scorpions to dried lizards on sticks.

Because the importer–wholesaler traditionally performs most marketing functions, independent agencies that provide advertising, marketing research, warehousing and storage, transportation, financing, and other facilitating functions found in a developed, mature marketing infrastructure are nonexistent or underdeveloped. Thus, few independent agencies to support a fully integrated distribution system develop.

Contrast this situation with the distribution philosophy of mass consumption that prevails in the United States and other industrialized nations. In these markets, one supplier does not dominate supply, supply can be increased or decreased within a given range, and profit maximization occurs at or near production capacity. Generally a buyer's market exists, and the producer strives to penetrate the market and push goods out to the consumer, resulting in a highly developed channel structure that includes a variety of intermediaries, many of which are unknown in developing markets.

As China develops economically, its market system and distribution structure are evolving as well.[1] As already discussed, economic development is uneven, and various parts of an economy may be at different stages of development. Channel structures in countries that have historically evolved from an import-oriented base will usually have vestiges of their beginnings reflected in a less than fully integrated system. At the other extreme is the Japanese distribution system with its multiple layers of specialized middlemen.

Japanese Distribution Structure

LO2

The Japanese distribution structure and what it means to Japanese customers and to competing importers of goods

Distribution in Japan has historically been considered a most effective nontariff barrier to the Japanese market.[2] However, the market is becoming more open as many traditional modes of operation are eroding in the face of competition from foreign marketers and as Japanese consumers continue to focus on lower prices. But it still serves as an excellent case study for the pervasive impact culture plays on economic institutions such as national distribution systems. The Japanese distribution structure is different enough from its U.S. or European counterparts that it should be carefully studied by anyone contemplating entry.

[1]Lutz Kaufman and Andreas Jentzsch, "Internationalization Processes: The Case of Automotive Suppliers in China," *Journal of International Marketing* 14 (2006), pp. 52–84.

[2]For a detailed study on this subject, see Frank Alpert, Michael Kamins, Tokoaki Sakano, Naoto Onzo, and John L. Graham, "Retail Buyer Decision Making in Japan: What U.S. Sellers Need to Know," *International Business Review* 6, no. 2 (1997), pp. 91–104; Yoshinobu Sato, "Some Reasons Why Foreign Retailers Have Difficulties in Succeeding in the Japanese Market," *Journal of Global Marketing* 18, no. 1/2 (2004), pp. 21–44.

The Japanese system has four distinguishing features: (1) a structure dominated by many small middlemen dealing with many small retailers, (2) channel control by manufacturers, (3) a business philosophy shaped by a unique culture, and (4) laws that protect the foundation of the system—the small retailer.

The density of middlemen, retailers, and wholesalers in the Japanese market is unparalleled in any Western industrialized country. The traditional Japanese structure serves consumers who make small, frequent purchases at small, conveniently located stores. An equal density of wholesalers supports the high density of small stores with small inventories. It is not unusual for consumer goods to go through three or four intermediaries before reaching the consumer—producer to primary, secondary, regional, and local wholesaler, and finally to retailer to consumer.

While other countries have large numbers of small retail stores, the major difference between small stores (nine or fewer employees) in Japan and the United States is the percentage of total retail sales accounted for by small retailers. In Japan, small stores account for 59.1 percent of retail food sales; in the United States, small stores generate 35.7 percent of food sales. Perhaps the most remarkable data in Exhibit 15.1 are the reductions in spending across types of stores in Japan. Japan is known for its plethora of vending machines, as is well reflected in these data. In all three countries, the steepest growth in spending comes from Internet shopping, with mobile phone usage showing the fastest growth.

As we shall see in a subsequent section, profound changes in retailing are occurring in Japan. Although it is still accurate to describe the Japanese market as having a high density of middlemen, the number of small stores is declining as they are being replaced by larger discount and specialty stores. These small stores serve an important role for Japanese consumers. High population density; the tradition of frequent trips to the store; an emphasis on service, freshness, and quality; and wholesalers who provide financial assistance, frequent deliveries of small lots, and other benefits combine to support the high number of small stores.

Manufacturers depend on wholesalers for a multitude of services to other members of the distribution network. Financing, physical distribution, warehousing, inventory, promotion, and payment collection are provided to other channel members by wholesalers. The system works because wholesalers and all other middlemen downstream are tied to manufacturers by a set of practices and incentives designed to ensure strong marketing support for their products and to exclude rival competitors from the channel. Wholesalers typically act as agent middlemen and extend the manufacturer's control through the channel to the retail level.

Coupled with the close economic ties and dependency created by trade customs and the long structure of Japanese distribution channels is a relationship-oriented business philosophy that emphasizes loyalty, harmony, and friendship. The value system supports long-term dealer–supplier relationships that are difficult to change as long as each party perceives economic advantage. The traditional partner, the insider, generally has the advantage.

A general lack of price competition, the provision of costly services, and other inefficiencies render the cost of Japanese consumer goods among the highest in the world. Indeed, when you just compare paychecks at current exchange rates (i.e., GDP per capita), the Japanese make $38,492 compared to Americans at $53,193. However, if you take into consideration what those paychecks will buy [i.e., GDP per capita at purchase price parity (PPP)], the American advantage grows as goods cost more in Japan and their purchasing

Exhibit 15.1

Sales per Household (in U.S. Dollars) by Type of Retailer (and Average Annual Growth Rate 2009–2014)

Source: Euromonitor International, 2015.

Type of Retailer	Germany	Japan	United States
Grocery retailers	$6,504 (0.5)	$6,313 (–1.4)	$8,157 (1.7)
Nongrocery specialists[a]	6,516 (0.4)	8,546 (–1.9)	9,191 (0.8)
Direct selling	83 (–0.9)	294 (–1.9)	201 (–0.6)
Home, shopping	234 (–11.5)	512 (–5.2)	696 (–5.8)
Internet	1,112 (19.8)	1,300 (10.4)	1,981 (15.9)
Vending	75 (–0.9)	492 (–3.4)	37 (0.6)
Mobile Internet	152 (115.0)	376 (38.0)	347 (44.6)
Internet pure play[b]	704 (22.1)	932 (10.5)	1,034 (19.6)

[a]Includes apparel, shoes, electronics, appliances, health, beauty, home, garden, leisure, personal goods, and mixed categories.

[b]No brick-and-mortar affiliates.

power is equivalent to only 36,315.[3] Such prices create a perfect climate for discounting, which is beginning to be a major factor. The Japanese consumer contributes to the continuation of the traditional nature of the distribution system through frequent buying trips, small purchases, favoring personal service over price, and a proclivity for loyalty to brands perceived to be of high quality. Additionally, Japanese law gives the small retailer enormous advantage over the development of larger stores and competition. All these factors have supported the continued viability of small stores and the established system, though changing attitudes among many Japanese consumers are beginning to weaken the hold traditional retailing has on the market.

Competition from large retail stores had been almost totally controlled by *Daitenho*— the Large-Scale Retail Store Law (and its more recent incarnations). Designed to protect small retailers from large intruders into their markets, the law required that any store larger than 5,382 square feet (500 square meters) must have approval from the prefecture government to be "built, expanded, stay open later in the evening, or change the days of the month they must remain closed." All proposals for new "large" stores were first judged by the Ministry of International Trade and Industry (MITI). Then, if all local retailers *unanimously* agreed to the plan, it was swiftly approved. However, without approval at the prefecture level, the plan was returned for clarification and modification, a process that could take several years (10 years was not unheard of) for approval.

The U.S. government's Structural Impediments Initiative, deregulation, and most recently Walmart are causing changes in Japanese distribution practices. Ultimately, however, only local merchants challenging the traditional ways by giving the consumer quality products at competitive, fair prices can bring about the demise of the traditional distribution system. Specialty discounters are sprouting up everywhere, and entrepreneurs are slashing prices by buying direct and avoiding the distribution system altogether. For example, Kojima, a consumer electronics discounter, practices what it calls "global purchasing" and buys merchandise anywhere in the world as cheaply as possible. Kojima's tie with General Electric enables it to offer a 410-liter GE refrigerator for $640, down from the typical price of $1,925, and to reduce the 550-liter model from $3,462 to $1,585.

Trends: From Traditional to Modern Channel Structures	Today, few countries are sufficiently isolated to be unaffected by global economic and political changes. These currents of change are altering all levels of the economic fabric, including the distribution structure.[4] Traditional channel structures still appear in many places—Nestle touts its distribution "by foot, by bike, and by taxi" in Africa,[5] and Coca-Cola CEO Muhtar Kent promises, "There's nowhere in Africa that we don't go. We go to every town, every village, every township."[6] But such channel structures also are giving way to new forms, new alliances, and new processes—some more slowly than others, but all are changing.[7] For example, Walmart, Tesco, and Carrefour are all having trouble with their biggest stores and are thus downsizing to "compact hypermarkets" of around 3,000–5,000 square meters instead of 10,000 square meters.[8] Or consider the recent successes of eBay in China[9] and the post–earthquake/tsunami surge

---

[3]Constant 2000 international dollars; World Development Indicators, World Bank, 2015.

[4]Katrijn Gielens, Linda M. van de Gucht, Jan-Benedict E. M. Steenkamp, and Marnik G. Dekimpe, "Dancing with the Giant: The Effect of Wal-Mart's Entry into the United Kingdom on the Performance of European Retailers," *Journal of Marketing Research* 45, no. 5 (2008), pp. 519–34; Michael Etgar and Dalia Rachman-Moore, "Geographical Expansion by International Retailers: A Study of Proximate Markets and Global Expansion Strategies," *Journal of Global Marketing* 23 (2010), pp. 5–15.

[5]Devon Maylie, "By Foot, by Bike, by Taxi, Nestle Expands in Africa," *The Wall Street Journal*, December 1, 2011, pp. B1, B16.

[6]Duane D. Stanford, "Coke's Last Round," *Bloomberg BusinessWeek*, November 1, 2011, pp. 55–61.

[7]Suk-Ching Ho, "Evolution versus Tradition in Marketing Systems: The Hong Kong Food Retailing Experience," *Journal of Public Policy & Marketing* 24, no. 1 (2005), pp. 90–99; Bruce Einhorn and Wing-Gar Cheng, "China: Where Retail Dinosaurs Are Thriving," *Bloomberg BusinessWeek*, February 1 & 8, 2010, p. 64.

[8]David Jolly, "Carrefour Rethinks Its 'Bigger Is Better' Strategy," *The New York Times*, January 27, 2012.

[9]Bruce Einhorn, "EBay Finds a Secret Door to China," *Bloomberg BusinessWeek*, April 18, 2011, pp. 39–41.

in Internet shopping in Japan.[10] Pressures for change in a country come from within and without. Multinational marketers are seeking ways to profitably tap market segments that currently are served by costly, traditional distribution systems. In India, the familiar clutter of traditional retailers is fast giving way to the wide aisles of new local and foreign supermarkets. In the United Kingdom Tesco is moving into retail banking in its stores,[11] and Anthropologie is testing the waters there as well.[12] As Carrefour's profits dip in Europe, it is importing new concepts from its hypermarkets in Brazil, such as a reduced number of SKUs.[13] Direct marketing, door-to-door selling, hypermarkets, discount houses, shopping malls, catalog selling, the Internet, and other distribution methods are being introduced in an attempt to provide efficient distribution channels. Importers and retailers also are becoming more involved in new product development;[14] for example, the Mexican appliance and electronics giant Grupo Elektra has formed an alliance with Beijing Automobile Works Group to develop and build low-cost cars for Mexico and export markets.

Some important trends in distribution will eventually lead to greater commonality than disparity among middlemen in different countries. Walmart, for example, is expanding all over the world—from Mexico to Brazil and from Europe to Asia. The only major disappointment for the American juggernaut has been its lack of scale and profits in South Korea; in 2006 the firm sold its five stores there.[15] Avon is expanding into eastern Europe; Amway into China; and L.L. Bean and Lands' End have successfully entered the Japanese market. The effect of all these intrusions into the traditional distribution systems is change that is making discounting, direct marketing, self-service, supermarkets, mass merchandising, and e-commerce concepts common all over the world, elevating the competitive climate to a level not known before.

As U.S. retailers have invaded Europe, staid, nationally based retailers have been merging with former competitors and companies from other countries to form Europewide enterprises. Carrefour, a French global marketer, merged with Promodes, one of its fierce French competitors, to create, in the words of its CEO, "a worldwide retail leader." The U.K. supermarket giant Sainsbury has entered an alliance with Esselunga of Italy (supermarkets), Docks de France (hypermarkets, supermarkets, and discount stores), and Belgium's Delhaize (supermarkets). The alliance provides the four companies the opportunity to pool their experience and buying power to better face growing competition and opportunity afforded by the single European market and the euro.

While European retailers see a unified Europe as an opportunity for pan-European expansion, foreign retailers are attracted by the high margins and prices. Costco, the U.S.-based warehouse retailer, saw the high gross margins that British supermarkets command (7 to 8 percent compared with 2.5 to 3 percent in the United States) as an opportunity. Costco prices were initially 10 to 20 percent cheaper than rival local retailers.

Expansion outside the home country, as well as new types of retailing, is occurring throughout Europe. El Corte Inglés, Spain's largest department store chain, not only is moving into Portugal and other European countries but also was one of the first retailers to offer a virtual supermarket on the Internet (http://www.elcorteingles.es) and to sponsor two 24-hour home shopping channels in Spain. Increasingly smaller retailers are also expanding overseas. Another Spanish retailer, Mango, opened a store in New York City and, along with other European competitors, was taking advantage of low costs of operation in the United States at the time associated with the sinking dollar.

---

[10]Diane Brady, "Japanese Shoppers Loosen Up Online," *Bloomberg BusinessWeek,* April 18, 2011, online.

[11]Kerry Capell, "Eggs, Bread, Milk—and a Mortgage," *Bloomberg BusinessWeek*, March 1, 2010, p. 20.

[12]Michael Arndt, "Urban Outfitters' Grow-Slow Strategy," *Bloomberg BusinessWeek*, March 1, 2010, p. 56.

[13]Christina Passariello, "Carrefour Net Drops Amid Overhaul Effort," *The Wall Street Journal*, February 19, 2010, online.

[14]Goksel Yalcinkaya, Roger J. Calantone, and David A. Griffith, "An Examination of Exploration Capabilities: Implications for Product Innovation and Market Performance," *Journal of International Marketing* 15 (2007), pp. 63–93.

[15]"Wal-Mart Exits Korean Market," *Los Angeles Times*, May 23, 2006, p. C3.

One of Walmart's strengths is its internal Internet-based system, which makes its transactions with suppliers highly efficient and lowers its cost of operations. Indeed, it is buying ailing retailers around the world with the intention of "saving them" with its distribution technologies. This same type of system is available on the Internet for both business-to-business and business-to-consumer transactions. For example, General Motors, Ford Motor Company, and DaimlerChrysler have created a single online site called Covisint (http://www.covisint.com) for purchasing automotive parts from suppliers, which is expected to save the companies millions of dollars. A typical purchase order costs Ford $150, whereas a real-time order via Covisint will cost about $15. Sears Roebuck and Carrefour of France have created GlobalNetXchange (AKA Agentrics, see http://www.gnx.com), a retail exchange that allows retailers and their suppliers to conduct transactions online. Any company with a web browser can access the exchange to buy, sell, trade, or auction goods and services. Described as "one of the most dramatic changes in consumer-products distribution of the decade," the exchange is expected to lower costs for both buyer and supplier. As more such exchanges evolve, one can only speculate about the impact on traditional channel middlemen.

We have already seen the impact on traditional retailing within the last few years caused by e-commerce retailers such as Amazon.com, Dell Computer, eBay, and others—all of which are expanding globally. Most brick-and-mortar retailers are experimenting with or have fully developed websites, some of which are merely extensions of their regular stores, allowing them to extend their reach globally. L.L. Bean, Eddie Bauer, and Lands' End are examples.

One of the most challenging aspects of web sales is delivery of goods. One of the innovative features of the 7dream program at 7-Eleven stores in Japan is the use of convenience stores for pick-up points for web orders. It has worked so well in Japan that Ito-Yokado Corporation, owner of 7-Eleven Japan and 72 percent of the U.S. chain, is exporting the idea to U.S. stores. In the Dallas–Fort Worth area, 250 stores have installed ATM-like machines tied into a delivery and payment system that promises to make 7-Eleven stores a depot for e-commerce. FedEx, UPS, and other package delivery services that have been the backbone of e-commerce delivery in the United States are offering similar services for foreign customers of U.S. e-commerce companies, as well as for foreign-based ones. When goods cross borders, UPS and others offer seamless shipments, including customs and brokerage. Most of these service companies are established in Europe and Japan and are building networks in Latin America and China.

The impact of these and other trends will change traditional distribution and marketing systems. While this latest retailing revolution remains in flux, new retailing and middlemen systems will be invented, and established companies will experiment, seeking ways to maintain their competitive edge. Moreover, it is becoming more dangerous to think of competitors in terms of individual companies—in international business generally, and

Now that Russians can own their homes, they're spending fast in home improvement stores like this one in St. Petersburg. In English it would be called "Super Home."

distribution systems particularly, a networks perspective is increasingly required. That is, firms must be understood in the context of the commercial networks of which they are a part.[16] These changes will resonate throughout the distribution chain before new concepts are established and the systems stabilize. Not since the upheaval that occurred in U.S. distribution after World War II that ultimately led to the Big-Box type of retailer has there been such potential for change in distribution systems. This time, however, such change will not be limited mostly to the United States—it will be worldwide.

Distribution Patterns

LO3

How distribution patterns affect the various aspects of international marketing

Even though patterns of distribution are in a state of change and new patterns are developing, international marketers need a general awareness of the traditional distribution base. The "traditional" system will not change overnight, and vestiges of it will remain for years to come. Nearly every international firm is forced by the structure of the market to use at least some middlemen in the distribution arrangement. It is all too easy to conclude that, because the structural arrangements of foreign and domestic distribution seem alike, foreign channels are the same as or similar to domestic channels of the same name. Only when the varied intricacies of actual distribution patterns are understood can the complexity of the distribution task be appreciated. The following description of differences in retailing should convey a sense of the variety of distribution patterns in general, including wholesalers.

Retail Patterns

Retailing shows even greater diversity in its structure than does wholesaling. In Italy and Morocco, retailing is composed largely of specialty houses that carry narrow lines, whereas in Finland, most retailers carry a more general line of merchandise. Retail size is represented at one end by Japan's giant department store Mitsukoshi, which reportedly enjoys the patronage of more than 100,000 customers every day, and at the other extreme by the market of Ibadan, Nigeria, where some 3,000 one- or two-person stalls serve not many more customers. Some manufacturers sell directly to consumers through company-owned stores such as Cartier and Disney, and some sell through a half-dozen layers of middlemen.

---

[16]Mats Forsgren, Ulf Holm, and Jan Johanson, *Managing the Embedded Multinational: A Business Network View* (Northampton, MA: Edward Elgar, 2005); see also the associated book review by Charles Dhanarah, *Journal of International Business Studies* 38 (2007), pp. 1231–33.

PEMEX (Petróleos Mexicanos), the Mexican national oil company, will not let foreign firms distribute there. However, in Malaysia, a Mobil station sits right across the boulevard from a government-owned PETRONAS (Petroliam Nasional) station.

Exhibit 15.2
Retail Structure in Selected Countries

Source: Euromonitor International, 2015; World Bank, 2015.

Country	All Retailers (000)	People Served per Retailer	Internet Users (percentage)
United States	835	378	84
Canada	152	230	86
Argentina	469	87	60
Germany	282	287	84
Russia	761	180	61
Israel	43	186	71
South Africa	159	333	49
China	6,146	221	46
Japan	849	150	86
Australia	83	377	83

Size Patterns.   The extremes in size in retailing are similar to those that predominate in wholesaling. Exhibit 15.2 dramatically illustrates some of the variations in size and number of retailers per person that exist in some countries. The retail structure and the problems it engenders cause real difficulties for the international marketing firm selling consumer goods. Large dominant retailers can be sold to directly, but there is no adequate way to reach small retailers who, in the aggregate, handle a great volume of sales.[17] In Italy, official figures show there are 931,000 retail stores, or one store for every 63 Italians. Of the 269,000 food stores, fewer than 10,000 can be classified as large. Thus, retailers are a critical factor in adequate distribution in Italy.

Underdeveloped countries present similar problems. Among the large supermarket chains in South Africa, there is considerable concentration. Of the country's 31,000 stores, 1,000 control 60 percent of all grocery sales, leaving the remaining 40 percent of sales to be spread among 30,000 stores. To reach the 40 percent of the market served by those 30,000 stores may be difficult. In black communities in particular, retailing is on a small scale—cigarettes are often sold singly, and the entire fruit inventory may consist of four apples in a bowl.

Retailing around the world has been in a state of active ferment for several years. The rate of change appears to be directly related to the stage and speed of economic development, and even the least developed countries are experiencing dramatic changes. Supermarkets of one variety or another are blossoming in developed and underdeveloped countries alike. Discount houses that sell everything from powdered milk and canned chili to Korean TVs and DVD players are thriving and expanding worldwide.

Direct Selling.   Sometimes called direct marketing,[18] selling directly to the consumer through mail, by telephone, or door-to-door is often the approach of choice in markets with insufficient or underdeveloped distribution systems. The approach, of course, also works well in the most affluent markets. Amway, operating in more than 100 foreign countries, has successfully expanded into Latin America and Asia with its method of direct marketing. Companies that enlist individuals to sell their products are proving to be especially popular in eastern Europe and other countries where many people are looking for ways to become entrepreneurs. In the Czech Republic, for example, Amway Corporation signed up 25,000 Czechs as distributors and sold 40,000 starter kits at $83 each in its first two weeks of business. Avon is another American company that is expanding dramatically overseas.

Direct sales through catalogs have proved to be a successful way to enter foreign markets. In Japan, it has been an important way to break the trade barrier imposed by the Japanese distribution system. For example, a U.S. mail-order company, Shop America,

---

[17]Tomasz Lenartowicz and Sridhar Balasubramanian, "Practices and Performance of Small Retail Stores in Developing Economies," *Journal of International Marketing* 17 (2009), pp. 59–90.

[18]See http://www.dsa.com, the Direct Selling Association's website, for definitions and a plethora of useful information about this industry.

CROSSING BORDERS 15.1   It Depends on What "Not Satisfied" Means

Amway's policy is that dissatisfied customers can get a full refund at any time, no questions asked—even if the returned bottles are empty. This refund policy is a courtesy to customers and a testament that the company stands behind its products, and it is the same all over the world. But such capitalistic concepts are somewhat unfamiliar in China.

The best game in town for months among the rising ranks of Shanghai's entrepreneurs was an $84 investment for a box of soaps and cosmetics that they could sell as Amway distributors. Word of this no-lose proposition quickly spread, with some people repackaging the soap, selling it, and then turning in the containers for a refund. Others dispensed with selling altogether and scoured garbage bins instead, showing up at Amway's Shanghai offices with bags full of bottles to be redeemed.

One salesman got nearly $10,000 for eight sacks full of all kinds of empty Amway containers. And at least one barbershop started using Amway shampoos for free and returning each empty bottle for a full refund. In a few weeks, refunds were totaling more than $100,000 a day. "Perhaps we were too lenient," said Amway's Shanghai chief. Amway changed the policy, only to have hundreds of angry Amway

distributors descend on the company's offices to complain that they were cheated out of their money. Amway had to call a press conference to explain that it wasn't changing its refund policy, simply raising the standard for what is deemed dissatisfaction. If someone returns half a bottle, fine, but for empties, Amway announced it would check records to see if the person had a pattern of return.

But the company did not anticipate the unusual sense of entitlement it had engendered in China. The satisfaction-guaranteed policy did not spell out specifically what dissatisfaction meant, something people in the Western world understood. "We thought that it would be understood here, too." The change in policy left some dissatisfied. One distributor protested, "Don't open a company if you can't afford losses." Despite these initial problems, Amway apparently is learning the market—the company doubled its sales last year in China to $4 billion. And other direct sellers such as Mary Kay cosmetics are also finding similar success in China.

Sources: David Barboza, "Direct Selling Flourishes in China, Providing Jobs and Igniting Criticism," *The New York Times*, December 26, 2009, pp. B1, B5 ; "Amway Bankrolls Harvard CourseA for Chinese Graduates," *Bloomberg Businessweek*, September 24, 2013, online.

teamed up with 7-Eleven Japan to distribute catalogs in its 4,000 stores. Shop America sells items such as compact discs, Canon cameras, and Rolex watches for 30 to 50 percent less than Tokyo stores; a Canon Autoboy camera sells for $260 in Tokyo and $180 in the Shop America catalog.

Many catalog companies are finding they need to open telephone service centers in a country to accommodate customers who have questions or problems. Hanna Andersson (the children's clothing manufacturer), for example, received complaints that it was too difficult to get questions answered and to place orders by telephone, so it opened a service center with 24 telephone operators to assist customers who generate more than $5 million in sales annually. Many catalog companies also have active websites that augment their catalog sales.

Resistance to Change. Efforts to improve the efficiency of the distribution system, new types of middlemen, and other attempts to change traditional ways are typically viewed as threatening and are thus resisted.[19] A classic example is the restructuring of the film distribution business being caused by the fast changing technologies of digitization and piracy. Laws abound that protect the entrenched in their positions. In Italy, a new retail outlet must obtain a license from a municipal board composed of local tradespeople. In a two-year period, some 200

Perhaps the greatest innovation in retailing in the 21st century has been the Apple retail store with its "genius bar," etc. Here you see their store in the shopping center adjacent to the Louvre Museum and its iconic glass pyramid in Paris. The green leaf represents Earth Day—the picture was taken on April 22, 2015. Of course, uber.com and airbnb.com would be candidates for most innovative, but both are harder to picture.

[19]Gardiner Harris, "Walmart Drops Ambitious Expansion Plant for India," *The New York Times*, October 20, 2013, p. B3; Tiffany Hsu, "Checkout for Tesco," *Los Angeles Times*, April 18, 2013, pp. B1, 6; "A Long Way from the Supermarket," *The Economist*, October 18, 2014, pp. 63–64.

applications were made and only 10 new licenses granted. Opposition to retail innovation is everywhere, yet in the face of all the restrictions and hindrances, self-service, discount merchandising, liberal store hours, and large-scale merchandising continue to grow because they offer the consumer convenience and a broad range of quality product brands at advantageous prices. Ultimately the consumer does prevail.

Alternative Middleman Choices

LO4

The functions, advantages, and disadvantages of various kinds of middlemen

A marketer's options range from assuming the entire distribution activity (by establishing its own subsidiaries and marketing directly to the end user) to depending on intermediaries for distribution of the product. Channel selection must be given considerable thought, because once initiated, it is difficult to change, and if it proves inappropriate, future growth and profits may be affected.

The channel process includes all activities, beginning with the manufacturer and ending with the final consumer. This inclusion means the seller must exert influence over two sets of channels: one in the home country and one in the foreign-market country. Exhibit 15.3 shows some of the possible channel-of-distribution alternatives. The arrows show those to whom the producer and each of the middlemen might sell. In the home country, the seller must have an organization (generally the international marketing division of a company) to deal with channel members needed to move goods between countries. In the foreign market, the seller must supervise the channels that supply the product to the end user. Ideally, the company wants to control or be directly involved in the process through the various channel members to the final user. To do less may result in unsatisfactory distribution and the failure of marketing objectives. In practice, however, such involvement throughout the channel process is not always practical or cost effective. Consequently, selection of channel members and effective controls are high priorities in establishing the distribution process.

Once the marketer has clarified company objectives and policies, the next step is the selection of specific intermediaries needed to develop a channel. External middlemen are differentiated according to whether or not they take title to the goods: Agent middlemen work on commission and arrange for sales in the foreign country but do not take title to the merchandise. By using agents, the manufacturer assumes trading risk but maintains the right to establish policy guidelines and prices and to require its agents to provide sales records and customer information. Merchant middlemen actually take title to manufacturers' goods and assume the trading risks, so they tend to be less

Exhibit 15.3
International
Channel-of-Distribution
Alternatives

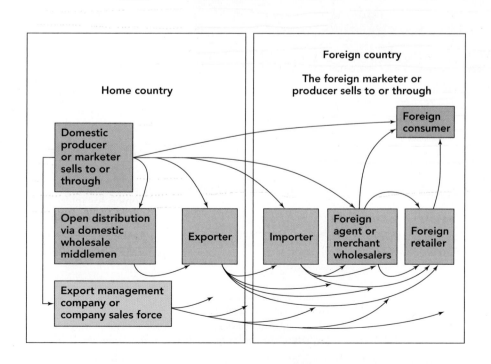

controllable than agent middlemen. Merchant middlemen provide a variety of import and export wholesaling functions involved in purchasing for their own account and selling in other countries. Because merchant middlemen primarily are concerned with sales and profit margins on their merchandise, they are frequently criticized for not representing the best interests of a manufacturer. Unless they have a franchise or a strong and profitable brand, merchant middlemen seek goods from any source and are likely to have low brand loyalty. Ease of contact, minimized credit risk, and elimination of all merchandise handling outside the United States are some of the advantages of using merchant middlemen.

Middlemen are not clear-cut, precise, easily defined entities. A firm that represents one of the pure types identified here is rare. Thus, intimate knowledge of middlemen functions is especially important in international activity because misleading titles can fool a marketer unable to look beyond mere names. What are the functions of a British middleman called a stockist, or one called an exporter or importer? One exporter may, in fact, be an agent middleman, whereas another is a merchant. Many, if not most, international middlemen wear several hats and can be clearly identified only in the context of their relationship with a specific firm.

Only by analyzing middlemen functions in skeletal simplicity can the nature of the channels be determined. Three alternatives are presented: first, middlemen physically located in the manufacturer's home country; next, middlemen located in foreign countries; and finally, government-affiliated middlemen.

Home-Country Middlemen

Home-country middlemen, or *domestic middlemen*, located in the producing firm's country, provide marketing services from a domestic base. By selecting domestic middlemen as intermediaries in the distribution processes, companies relegate foreign-market distribution to others. Domestic middlemen offer many advantages for companies with small international sales volume, those inexperienced with foreign markets, those not wanting to become immediately involved with the complexities of international marketing, and those wanting to sell abroad with minimal financial and management commitment. A major trade-off when using home-country middlemen is limited control over the entire process. Domestic middlemen are most likely to be used when the marketer is uncertain or desires to minimize financial and management investment. A brief discussion of the more frequently used types of domestic middlemen follows.

Remember for a moment the scene in the Pixar movie *Monsters, Inc.*—millions of doors on conveyor belts. That scene is reminiscent of the inside of the Nike's European distribution center in Laakdal, Belgium. The shoes come from a variety of Asian low-cost manufacturers and arrive at the center via Rotterdam and Antwerp and the adjacent canal. Twelve hundred people work at the heavily automated facility where 8 million pairs of shoes are sorted and then shipped to customers all over the continent via truck. Even as sales grow, the company will not need to expand the center, because the trend is for the factories to ship directly to the major European retailers, including the Nike Sport in St. Petersburg pictured in Chapter 10.

Manufacturers' Retail Stores. An important channel of distribution for a large number of manufacturers is the owned, or perhaps franchised, retail store. Disney, Benetton, and many of the classic Italian luxury goods makers take this approach.

Global Retailers. As global retailers like IKEA, Costco, Sears Roebuck, Toys "R" Us,[20] and Walmart expand their global coverage, they are becoming major domestic middlemen for international markets. Their successes seem to result from maintaining their core marketing approaches while localizing the array of products, promotions, and other peripheral aspects of their operations.[21] Walmart, with more

---

[20]Laurie Burkitt and Ann Zimmerman, "Toys 'R' Us Maps an Expansion in China," *The Wall Street Journal*, November 19, 2012, online.

[21]Bernhard Swoboda and Stefan Elsner, "Transferring the Retail Format Successfully into Foreign Countries," *Journal of International Marketing* 21, no. 1 (2013), pp. 81–109.

than 11,000 stores in 15 foreign markets, is an attractive entry point to international markets for U.S. suppliers. Walmart offers an effective way to enter international markets with a minimum of experience. For example, Pacific Connections, a California manufacturer of handbags with $70 million in sales, ventured into overseas markets in Argentina, Brazil, Canada, and Mexico through its ties to Walmart. And as trade restrictions are eased through alliances such as NAFTA, new global retailers are being created—Gigante from Mexico is a good example of this trend.

Export Management Companies. The export management company (EMC) is an important middleman for firms with relatively small international volume or those unwilling to involve their own personnel in the international function. These EMCs range in size from 1 person upward to 100 and handle about 10 percent of the manufactured goods exported. An example of an EMC is a Washington, D.C.–based company that has exclusive agreements with 10 U.S. manufacturers of orthopedic equipment and markets these products on a worldwide basis.

Target, while a strong competitor for Walmart in the United States, has had trouble keeping up abroad. Its biggest international adventure into Canada, circa 2015, has not performed well.[22] If you are driving around Australia, you might see the brand and logo on more than 300 stores down under, such as the one in Mareeba, Victoria. The American company had granted rights to the trademark, but it is otherwise unrelated to the Australian stores.

Typically, the EMC becomes an integral part of the marketing operations of its client companies. Working under the names of the manufacturers, the EMC functions as a low-cost, independent marketing department with direct responsibility to the parent firm. The working relationship is so close that customers are often unaware they are not dealing directly with the export department of the company (see Exhibit 15.4).

The export management company may take full or partial responsibility for promotion of the goods, credit arrangements, physical handling, market research, and information on financial, patent, and licensing matters. An EMC's specialization in a given field often enables it to offer a level of service that could not be attained by the manufacturer

Exhibit 15.4
How Does an EMC Operate?

Most export management companies offer a wide range of services and assistance, including the following:

Researching foreign markets for a client's products. Traveling overseas to determine the best method of distributing the product. Appointing distributors or commission representatives as needed in individual foreign countries, frequently within an already existing overseas network created for similar goods. Exhibiting the client's products at international trade shows, such as U.S. Department of Commerce–sponsored commercial exhibitions at trade fairs and U.S. Export Development Offices around the world.

Handling the routine details in getting the product to the foreign customer—export declarations, shipping and customs documentation, insurance, banking, and instructions for special export packing and marking.

Granting the customary finance terms to the trade abroad and ensuring payment to the manufacturer of the product.

Preparing advertising and sales literature in cooperation with the manufacturer and adapting it to overseas requirements for use in personal contacts with foreign buyers.

Corresponding in the necessary foreign languages.

Making sure that goods being shipped are suitable for local conditions and meet overseas legal and trade norms, including labeling, packaging, purity, and electrical characteristics. Advising on overseas patent and trademark protection requirements.

Source: "The Export Management Company," U.S. Department of Commerce, Washington, DC.

[22]Ian Austen, "Target Push into Canada Stumbles," *The New York Times*, February 24, 2014, online.

without years of groundwork. Traditionally, the EMC works on commission, though an increasing number are buying products on their own account.

Two of the chief advantages of EMCs are minimum investment on the part of the company to get into international markets, and no commitment of company personnel or major expenditure of managerial effort. The result, in effect, is an extension of the market for the firm with negligible financial or personnel commitments.

The major disadvantage is that EMCs seldom can afford to make the kind of market investment needed to establish deep distribution for products because they must have immediate sales payout to survive. Such a situation does not offer the market advantages gained by a company that can afford to use company personnel. Carefully selected EMCs can do an excellent job, but the manufacturer must remember that the EMC is dependent on sales volume for compensation and probably will not push the manufacturer's line if it is spread too thinly, generates too small a volume from a given principal, or cannot operate profitably in the short run. In such cases, the EMC becomes an order taker and not the desired substitute for an international marketing department.

Trading Companies.   Trading companies have a long and honorable history as important intermediaries in the development of trade between nations. Trading companies accumulate, transport, and distribute goods from many countries. In concept, the trading company has changed little in hundreds of years.

The British firm Gray MacKenzie and Company is typical of companies operating in the Middle East. It has some 70 salespeople and handles consumer products ranging from toiletries to outboard motors and Scotch whiskey. The key advantage to this type of trading company is that it covers the entire Middle East.

Large, established trading companies generally are located in developed countries; they sell manufactured goods to developing countries and buy raw materials and unprocessed goods. Japanese trading companies (*sogo shosha*) date back to the early 1700s and operate both as importers and exporters. Some 300 are engaged in foreign and domestic trade through 2,000 branch offices outside Japan and handle more than $1 trillion in trading volume annually. Japanese trading companies account for 61 percent of all Japanese imports and 39 percent of all exports, or about one-fifth of Japan's entire GDP.

For companies seeking entrance into the complicated Japanese distribution system, the Japanese trading company offers one of the easiest routes to success. The omnipresent trading companies virtually control distribution through all levels of channels in Japan. Because trading companies may control many of the distributors and maintain broad distribution channels, they provide the best means for intensive coverage of the market.

U.S. Export Trading Companies.   The Export Trading Company (ETC) Act allows producers of similar products to form export trading companies. A major goal of the ETC Act was to increase U.S. exports by encouraging more efficient export trade services to producers and suppliers to improve the availability of trade finance and to remove antitrust disincentives to export activities. By providing U.S. businesses with an opportunity to obtain antitrust preclearance for specified export activities, the ETC Act created a more favorable environment for the formation of joint export ventures. Through such joint ventures, U.S. firms can take advantage of economies of scale, spread risk, and pool their expertise. In addition, through joint selling arrangements, domestic competitors can avoid interfirm rivalry in foreign markets. Prior to the passage of the ETC Act, competing companies could not engage in joint exporting efforts without possible violation of antitrust provisions. The other important provision of the ETC Act permits bank holding companies to own ETCs.

Immediately after passage of the ETC Act, several major companies (General Electric, Sears Roebuck, Kmart, and others) announced the development of export trading companies. In most cases, these export firms did not require the protection of the ETC Act since they initially operated independently of other enterprises. They provided international sales for U.S. companies to a limited extent, but primarily they operated as trading companies for their own products. To date, many of the trading companies (particularly the bank-owned ones) established after passage of the ETC Act have closed their doors or are languishing.

Complementary Marketers.

Companies with marketing facilities or contacts in different countries with excess distribution capacity or a desire for a broader product line sometimes take on additional lines for international distribution; though the formal name for such activities is complementary marketing, it is commonly called *piggybacking*. General Electric Company has been distributing merchandise from other suppliers for many years. It accepts products that are noncompetitive but complementary and that add to the basic distribution strength of the company itself. The classic example was Gillette distributing batteries in less developed countries, years before Gillette bought Duracell.

Most piggyback arrangements are undertaken when a firm wants to fill out its product line or keep its seasonal distribution channels functioning throughout the year. Companies may work either on an agency or merchant basis, but the greatest volume of piggyback business is handled on an ownership (merchant) purchase-and-resale arrangement. The selection process for new products for piggyback distribution determines whether (1) the product relates to the product line and contributes to it, (2) the product fits the sales and distribution channel presently employed, (3) the margin is adequate to make the undertaking worthwhile, and (4) the product will find market acceptance and profitable volume. If these requirements are met, piggybacking can be a logical way of increasing volume and profit for both the carrier and the piggybacker.

Manufacturer's Export Agent.

The *manufacturer's export agent* (*MEA*) is an individual agent middleman or an agent middleman firm providing a selling service for manufacturers. Unlike the EMC, the MEA does not serve as the producer's export department but has a short-term relationship, covers only one or two markets, and operates on a straight commission basis. Another principal difference is that MEAs do business in their own names rather than in the name of the client. Within a limited scope of operation, the MEAs provide services similar to those of the EMC.

Webb-Pomerene Export Associations.

Webb-Pomerene export associations (*WPEAs*) are another major form of group exporting. The Webb-Pomerene Act of 1918 allowed American business firms to join forces in export activities without being subject to the Sherman Antitrust Act. Thus, WPEAs cannot participate in cartels or other international agreements that would reduce competition in the United States, but they can offer four major benefits: (1) reduction of export costs, (2) demand expansion through promotion, (3) trade barrier reductions, and (4) improvement of trade terms through bilateral bargaining. Additionally, WPEAs set prices, standardize products, and arrange for disposal of surplus products. Although they account for less than 5 percent of U.S. exports, WPEAs include some of America's blue-chip companies in agricultural products, chemicals and raw materials, forest products, pulp and paper, textiles, rubber products, motion pictures, and television.

Foreign Sales Corporation.

A *foreign sales corporation* (*FSC*) is a sales corporation set up in a foreign country or U.S. possession that can obtain a corporate tax exemption on a portion of the earnings generated by the sale or lease of export property. Manufacturers and export groups can form FSCs. An FSC can function as a principal, buying and selling for its own account, or a commissioned agent. It can be related to a manufacturing parent or can be an independent merchant or broker. The WTO in 2003 ruled FSCs to be in violation of international trade rules, thus starting a major trade dispute with the European Union that still simmers and occasionally boils over.

Foreign-Country Middlemen

The variety of agent and merchant middlemen in most countries is similar to that in the United States. International marketers seeking greater control over the distribution process may elect to deal directly with middlemen in the foreign market. They gain the advantage of shorter channels and deal with middlemen in constant contact with the market.

Using foreign-country middlemen moves the manufacturer closer to the market and involves the company more closely with problems of language, physical distribution, communications, and financing. Foreign middlemen may be agents or merchants, they may be associated with the parent company to varying degrees, or they may be hired temporarily for special purposes. Some of the more important foreign-country middlemen are manufacturer's representatives and foreign distributors.

Government-Affiliated Middlemen

Marketers must deal with governments in every country of the world. Products, services, and commodities for the government's own use are always procured through government purchasing offices at federal, regional, and local levels. In the Netherlands, the state's purchasing office deals with more than 10,000 suppliers in 20 countries. About one-third of the products purchased by that agency are produced outside the Netherlands. Finally, regarding the efficiency of the public sector versus the private sector, an important lesson was learned during the 2005 Hurricane Katrina disaster—Walmart planned for and delivered aid better than FEMA (the U.S Federal Emergency Management Agency).

Factors Affecting Choice of Channels

The international marketer needs a clear understanding of market characteristics and must have established operating policies before beginning the selection of channel middlemen. The following points should be addressed prior to the selection process:

1. Identify specific target markets within and across countries.
2. Specify marketing goals in terms of volume, market share, and profit margin requirements.
3. Specify financial and personnel commitments to the development of international distribution.
4. Identify control, length of channels, terms of sale, and channel ownership.

Once these points are established, selecting among alternative middlemen choices to forge the best channel can begin. Marketers must get their goods into the hands of consumers and must choose between handling all distribution or turning part or all of it over to various middlemen. Distribution channels vary depending on target market size, competition, and available distribution intermediaries.

Key elements in distribution decisions include the functions performed by middlemen (and the effectiveness with which each is performed), the cost of their services, their availability, and the extent of control that the manufacturer can exert over middlemen activities.

Although the overall marketing strategy of the firm must embody the company's profit goals in the short and long run, channel strategy itself is considered to have six specific strategic goals. These goals can be characterized as the six Cs of channel strategy: cost, capital, control, coverage, character, and continuity. In forging the overall channel-of-distribution strategy, each of the six Cs must be considered in building an economical, effective distribution organization within the long-range channel policies of the company. It should also be noted that many firms use multiple or hybrid channels of distribution because of the trade-offs associated with any one option. Research has also shown that establishment of a new channel of distribution can add to firm value.[23] Indeed, Dell selling computers at kiosks inside Japan's Jusco supermarkets, Toys "R"

---

[23]Christian Homburg, Josef Vollmayr, and Alexander Hahn, "Firm Value Creation through Major Channel Expansion: Evidence from an Event Study in the United States, Germany, and China," *Journal of Marketing* 78, no. 3 (2014), pp. 38–61.

Us selling toys in food stores, and Starbucks selling packaged ground coffee in Chinese retail outlets[24] are good examples.

Cost   The two kinds of channel costs are (1) the capital or investment cost of developing the channel and (2) the continuing cost of maintaining it. The latter can be in the form of direct expenditure for the maintenance of the company's selling force or in the form of margins, markup, or commissions of various middlemen handling the goods. Marketing costs (a substantial part of which is channel cost) must be considered as the entire difference between the factory price of the goods and the price the customer ultimately pays for the merchandise. The costs of middlemen include transporting and storing the goods, breaking bulk, providing credit, local advertising, sales representation, and negotiations.

Despite the old truism that you can eliminate middlemen but you cannot eliminate their functions or cost, creative, efficient marketing does permit channel cost savings in many circumstances. Some marketers have found, in fact, that they can reduce cost by eliminating inefficient middlemen and thus shortening the channel. Mexico's largest producer of radio and television sets has built annual sales of $36 million on its ability to sell goods at a low price because it eliminated middlemen, established its own wholesalers, and kept margins low. Conversely, many firms accustomed to using their own sales forces in large-volume domestic markets have found they must lengthen channels of distribution to keep costs in line with foreign markets.

Capital Requirements   The financial ramifications of a distribution policy are often overlooked. Critical elements are capital requirement and cash-flow patterns associated with using a particular type of middleman. Maximum investment is usually required when a company establishes its own internal channels, that is, its own sales force. Use of distributors or dealers may lessen the capital investment, but manufacturers often have to provide initial inventories on consignment, loans, floor plans, or other arrangements. Coca-Cola initially invested in China with majority partners that met most of the capital requirements. However, Coca-Cola soon realized that it could not depend on its local majority partners to distribute its product aggressively in the highly competitive, market-share–driven business of carbonated beverages. To assume more control of distribution, it had to assume management control, and that meant greater capital investment from Coca-Cola. One of the highest costs of doing business in China is the capital required to maintain effective distribution.

Control   The more involved a company is with the distribution, the more control it exerts. A company's own sales force affords the most control but often at a cost that is not practical. Both Starbucks and KFC in China have found it worthwhile to keep ownership of stores (rather than selling through franchisees) in several regions.[25] On the opposite end of the control scale were the 22 fake Apple stores in China, discovered and shut down in 2011![26] Each type of channel arrangement provides a different level of control; as channels grow longer, the ability to control price, volume, promotion, and type of outlets diminishes. If a company cannot sell directly to the end user or final retailer, an important selection criterion for middlemen should be the amount of control the marketer can maintain. Of course, there are risks in international distribution relationships as well—opportunism and exploitation are two. Finally, one of the most alarming examples of distribution channels

[24]Annie Gasparro, "Starbucks Shuffles Global Management Team," *The Wall Street Journal*, May 2, 2013, online.

[25]Tang Zhihao, "Starbucks Buys Back Control of Stores," *China Daily,* June 3, 2011, p. 14; David E. Bell, "KFC's Radical Approach to China," *Harvard Business Review,* November 11, 2011.

[26]Nathan Olivarez-Giles, "22 More Fake Apple Stores Found," *Los Angeles Times,* August 13, 2011, p. B2.

out of control regards the current worldwide shortage of fish; retailers and distributors in affluent countries literally feed the demands of their voracious customers and kill the fisheries along the way.[27]

Coverage

Another major goal is full-market coverage to gain the optimum volume of sales obtainable in each market, secure a reasonable market share, and attain satisfactory market penetration. Coverage may be assessed by geographic segments, market segments, or both. Adequate market coverage may require changes in distribution systems from country to country or time to time. Coverage is difficult to extend both in highly developed areas and in sparse markets—the former because of heavy competition and the latter because of inadequate channels.

Recall that the Japanese are the world-champion fish consumers at more than 32 kg per person per year—see Exhibit 4.2. Consequently, just as world prices for cut flowers are set at the Aalsmeer Flower Auction in the Netherlands, world prices for fish are set at the Tsukigi fish market in Tokyo. A big fresh bluefin tuna caught in the Atlantic, iced and shipped by air to Tokyo, can bring as much as $1.76 million at auction (the previous record price was only $396,000 in 2012)[28] and then be shipped by air back to Boston for hungry sushi consumers. Perhaps the market is "too efficient," as the world now faces a shortage of such tuna, and at least for some, Americans are paying too much for fish these days[29].

Many companies do not attempt full-market coverage but seek significant penetration in major population centers. In some countries, two or three cities constitute the majority of the national buying power. For instance, 60 percent of the Japanese population lives in the Tokyo–Nagoya–Osaka market area, which essentially functions as one massive city.

At the other extreme are many developing countries with a paucity of specialized middlemen except in major urban areas. Those that do exist are often small, with traditionally high margins. In China, for example, the often-cited billion-person market is, in reality, confined to fewer than 25 to 30 percent of the population of the most affluent cities. Even as personal income increases in China, distribution inadequacies limit marketers in reaching all those who have adequate incomes. In both extremes, the difficulty of developing an efficient channel from existing middlemen plus the high cost of distribution may nullify efficiencies achieved in other parts of the marketing mix.

To achieve coverage, a company may have to use many different channels—its own sales force in one country, manufacturers' agents in another, and merchant wholesalers in still another.

Character

The channel-of-distribution system selected must fit the character of the company and the markets in which it is doing business. Some obvious product requirements, often the first considered, relate to the perishability or bulk of the product, complexity of sale, sales service required, and value of the product.

Channel captains must be aware that channel patterns change; they cannot assume that once a channel has been developed to fit the character of both company and market, no more need be done. Great Britain, for example, has epitomized distribution through specialty-type middlemen, distributors, wholesalers, and retailers; in fact, all middlemen have traditionally worked within narrow product specialty areas. In recent years, however,

[27]"Japan's Tuna Crisis," *The New York Times*, June 27, 2007, p. A22; Elisabeth Rosenthal, "In Europe, the Catch of the Day is Often Illegal," *The New York Times*, January 15, 2008, pp. A1, A6; Wakatsuki, "Not Working for Scale," op. cit.

[28]Yoko Wakatsuki, "Not Working for Scale: Tuna Sets Record Price," CNNInternational.com, January 5, 2011; Malcolm Foster, "Bluefin Tuna Sells for Incredible Record $1.76 Million at Tokyo Fish Auction," *Huffington Post.com*, January 5, 2013, online.

[29]Paul Greenberg, "Why Are We Importing Our Own Fish?" *The New York Times*, June 22, 2014, p. SR6.

You can buy just about anything at Stockmann's Department Store in Helsinki—men's and women's fashions, hardware (hammers, etc.) and software, bakery goods and garden supplies, fillet of reindeer and furniture, televisions—yes, everything from Audi A3s to zucchini. It even has cold storage services for your mink. But Stockmann's doesn't stock Samsung cell phones. The Korean company hasn't yet penetrated Nokia's home market. Of course, the product line is thin but rich at Cartier's in Paris. And you can find the Samsung at the Grand Bazaar (Kapali Carsi) in Istanbul, billed as the oldest and largest covered marketplace in the world. The 15th-century mall competes for customers with its 20th-century cousin, Akmerkez Etiler, in a high-income neighborhood about 10 miles away. Finally, Louis meets Lenin here on Red Square in Moscow. Russians now go for the luxury brands at the old government department store (still with the unattractive name, Gum), recently transformed into a 800,000-square-foot, indoor, high-end shopping mall. You can see St. Basil's Cathedral in the background, and just 200 meters across the square, Comrade Vladimir Lenin's embalmed body is entombed in a chilly mausoleum. While the old communist isn't too happy about free enterprise disturbing his view, he certainly must be pleased about the 2008 resumption of the annual Red Square May Day military parade after its seventeen-year hiatus. In 2013, the company added injury to insult by building a two-story replica of a Louis Vuitton trunk in the square. The public and government "persuaded" the company to dismantle it as a "violation of historical appearance." The Russians were much faster removing the trunk than the Chinese in forbidding a Starbucks in the Forbidden City.[30]

there has been a trend toward broader lines, conglomerate merchandising, and mass marketing. The firm that neglects the growth of self-service, scrambled merchandising, or discounting may find it has lost large segments of its market because its channels no longer reflect the character of the market.

Continuity Channels of distribution often pose longevity problems. Most agent middlemen firms tend to be small institutions. When one individual retires or moves out of a line of business, the company may find it has lost its distribution in that area. Wholesalers and especially retailers are not noted for their continuity in business either. Most middlemen have little

---

[30]Andrew Roth, "Moscow Says Louis Vuitton Doesn't Go with Red Square," *The New York Times*, November 28, 2013, p. A6.

loyalty to their vendors. They handle brands in good times when the line is making money but quickly reject such products within a season or a year if they fail to produce during that period. Distributors and dealers are probably the most loyal middlemen, but even with them, manufacturers must attempt to build brand loyalty downstream in a channel lest middlemen shift allegiance to other companies or other inducements.

Channel Management

The actual process of building channels for international distribution is seldom easy, and many companies have been stopped in their efforts to develop international markets by their inability to construct a satisfactory system of channels.

Construction of the middleman network includes seeking out potential middlemen, selecting those who fit the company's requirements, and establishing working relationships with them. In international marketing, the channel-building process is hardly routine. The closer the company wants to get to the consumer in its channel contact, the larger the sales force required. If a company is content with finding an exclusive importer or selling agent for a given country, channel building may not be too difficult; however, if it goes down to the level of subwholesaler or retailer, it is taking on a tremendous task and must have an internal staff capable of supporting such an effort.

Locating Middlemen

The search for prospective middlemen should begin with study of the market and determination of criteria for evaluating middlemen servicing that market. The checklist of criteria differs according to the type of middlemen being used and the nature of their relationship with the company. Basically, such lists are built around four subject areas: productivity or volume, financial strength, managerial stability and capability, and the nature and reputation of the business. Emphasis is usually placed on either the actual or potential productivity of the middleman.

The major problems are locating information to aid in the selection and choice of specific middlemen and discovering middlemen available to handle one's merchandise. Firms seeking overseas representation should compile a list of middlemen from such sources as the following: the U.S. Department of Commerce; commercially published directories; foreign consulates; chamber-of-commerce groups located abroad; other manufacturers producing similar but noncompetitive goods; middlemen associations; business publications; management consultants; carriers—particularly airlines; and Internet-based services such as Unibex, a global technology services provider. Unibex provides a platform for small- to medium-sized companies and larger enterprises to collaborate in business-to-business commerce.

Selecting Middlemen

LO5

The importance of selecting and maintaining middlemen

Finding prospective middlemen is less a problem than determining which of them can perform satisfactorily. Low volume or low potential volume hampers most prospects, many are underfinanced, and some simply cannot be trusted. In many cases, when a manufacturer is not well known abroad, the reputation of the middleman becomes the reputation of the manufacturer, so a poor choice at this point can be devastating.

Screening.   The screening and selection process itself should include the following actions: an exploratory letter or e-mail including product information and distributor requirements in the native language sent to each prospective middleman; a follow-up with the best respondents for specific information concerning lines handled, territory covered, size of firm, number of salespeople, and other background information; check of credit and references from other clients and customers of the prospective middleman; and, if possible, a personal check of the most promising firms. Obtaining financial information on prospective middlemen has become easier via such Internet companies as Unibex, which provides access to Dun & Bradstreet and other client information resources.

Experienced exporters suggest that the only way to select a middleman is to go personally to the country and talk to ultimate users of your product to find whom they consider to be the best distributors. Visit each possible middleman once before selecting the one to represent you; look for one with a key person who will take the new product to his or her heart and make it a personal objective to make the sale of that line a success. Furthermore, exporters stress that if you cannot sign one of the two or three customer-recommended distributors, you might be better off having no distributor in that country, because having a worthless one costs you time and money every year and may cut you out when you finally find a good one.

The Agreement.   Once a potential middleman has been found and evaluated, the task of detailing the arrangements with that middleman begins. So far the company has been in a buying position; now it must shift into a selling and negotiating position to convince the middleman to handle the goods and accept a distribution agreement that is workable for the company. Agreements must spell out specific responsibilities of the manufacturer and the middleman, including an annual sales minimum. The sales minimum serves as a basis for evaluation of the distributor; failure to meet sales minimums may give the exporter the right of termination.

Some experienced exporters recommend that initial contracts be signed for one year only. If the first year's performance is satisfactory, they should be reviewed for renewal for a longer period. This time limit permits easier termination, and more important, after a year of working together in the market, a more suitable arrangement generally can be reached.

Motivating Middlemen

The level of distribution and the importance of the individual middleman to the company determine the activities undertaken to keep the middleman motivated. On all levels, the middleman's motivation is clearly correlated with sales volume. Motivational techniques that can be employed to maintain middleman interest and support for the product may be grouped into five categories: financial rewards, psychological rewards, communications, company support, and corporate rapport.

Obviously, financial rewards must be adequate for any middleman to carry and promote a company's products. Margins or commissions must be set to meet the needs of the middleman and may vary according to the volume of sales and the level of services offered. Without a combination of adequate margin and adequate volume, a middleman cannot afford to give much attention to a product.

Being human, middlemen and their salespeople respond to psychological rewards and recognition of their efforts. A trip to the United States or to the parent company's home or regional office is a great honor. Publicity in company media and local newspapers also builds esteem and involvement among foreign middlemen.

In all instances, but particularly when cultural distances are great,[31] the company should maintain a continuing flow of communication in the form of letters, newsletters, and periodicals to all its middlemen. The more personal these are, the better. One study of exporters indicated that the more intense the contact between the manufacturer and the distributor, the better the performance by the distributor. More and better contact naturally leads to less conflict and a smoother working relationship, and relationships are key, particularly in relationship-oriented cultures in emerging markets.[32]

Finally, considerable attention must be paid to the establishment of close rapport between the company and its middlemen. In addition to methods noted, a company should be certain that the conflicts that arise are handled skillfully and diplomatically. Bear in mind that all over the world, business is a personal and vital thing to the people involved.

---

[31]Carl Arthur Solberg, "Product Complexity and Cultural Distance Effects on Managing International Distributor Relationships: A Contingency Approach," *Journal of International Marketing* 16, no. 3 (2008), pp. 57–83; Chenting Su, Zhilin Yang, Guijun Zhuang, Nan Zhou, and Wenyu Dou, "Interpersonal Influence as an Alternative Channel Communication Behavior in Emerging Markets: The Case of China," *Journal of International Business Studies* 40, no. 4 (2009), pp. 668–89.

[32]Gerald A. McDermott and Rafael A. Corredoira, "Network Composition, Collaborative Ties, and Upgrading In Emerging Market Firms: Lessons from the Argentine Autoparts Sector," *Journal of International Business Studies* 41, no. 2 (2010), pp. 308–29.

Controlling Middlemen

The extreme length of channels typically used in international distribution makes control of middlemen especially important.[33] Contracts and good social relations are both useful in managing international channels. Most research has found the latter to be more important.[34] Marketing objectives must be spelled out both internally and to middlemen as explicitly as possible. Standards of performance should include the sales volume objective, inventory turnover ratio, number of accounts per area, growth objective, price stability objective, and quality of publicity. Cultural differences enter into all these areas of management.[35]

Control over the system and control over middlemen are necessary in international business. The first relates to control over the distribution network, which implies overall controls for the entire system to be certain the product is flowing through desired middlemen. Some manufacturers have lost control through "secondary wholesaling" or parallel imports.[36] A company's goods intended for one country are sometimes diverted through distributors to another country, where they compete with existing retail or wholesale organizations.

The second type of control is at the middleman level. When possible, the parent company should know (and to a certain degree control) the activities of middlemen with respect to their volume of sales, market coverage, services offered, prices, advertising, payment of bills, and even profit. Quotas, reports, and personal visits by company representatives can be effective in managing middleman activities at any level of the channel.

Terminating Middlemen

When middlemen do not perform up to standards or when market situations change, requiring a company to restructure its distribution, it may be necessary to terminate relationships. In the United States, this termination is usually a simple action regardless of the type of middlemen; they are simply dismissed. However, in other parts of the world, the middleman often has some legal protection that makes termination difficult. In Colombia, for example, if you terminate an agent, you are required to pay 10 percent of the agent's average annual compensation, multiplied by the number of years the agent served, as a final settlement.

Competent legal advice is vital when entering distribution contracts with middlemen. But as many experienced international marketers know, the best rule is to avoid the need to terminate distributors by screening all prospective middlemen carefully. A poorly chosen distributor may not only fail to live up to expectations but may also adversely affect future business and prospects in the country.

---

[33]Maggie Chuoyan Dong, David K. Tse, and Kineta Hung, "Effective Distributor Governance in Emerging Markets: The Salience of Distributor Role, Relationship Stages, and Market Uncertainty," *Journal of International Marketing* 18, no. 3 (2010), pp. 1–17; Zhilin Yang, Chenting Su, and Kim-Shyan Fam, "Dealing with Institutional Distance in International Marketing Channels," *Journal of Marketing* 76, no. 3 (2012), pp. 41–55.

[34]Kevin Zheng Zhou and Dean Xu, "How Foreign Firms Curtail Local Supplier Opportunism in China: Detailed Contracts, Centralized Control, and Relational Governance," *Journal of International Business Studies* 43 (Zhou 2012), pp. 677–92; Zhilin Yang, Chenting Su, and Kim-Shyan Fam, "Dealing with Institutional Distances in International Marketing Channels: Governance Strategies That Engender Legitimacy and Efficiency," *Journal of Marketing* 76, no. 3 (May 2012), pp. 41–55; Rajdeep Grewal, Alok Kumar, Girish Mallapragada, and Amit Saini, "Marketing Channels in Foreign Markets: Control Mechanisms and the Moderating Role of Multinational Corporation Headquarters-Subsidiary Relationship," *Journal of Marketing Research* 50, no. 3 (Grewal 2013), pp. 378–98; Leonidas C. Leonidou, Saeed Samiee, Bilge Aykol, and Michael A. Talias, "Antecedents and Outcomes of Exporter-Importer Relationship Quality: Synthesis, Meta-Analysis, and Directions for Future Research," *Journal of International Marketing* 22, no. 2 (2014), pp. 21–46; Min Ju, Hongxin Zhao, and Tiedong Wang, "The Boundary Conditions of Export Relational Governance: A 'Strategy Tripod' Perspective," *Journal of International Marketing* 22, no. 2 (2014), pp. 89–106.

[35] Wesley J. Johnston, Shadab Khalil, Megha Jain, and Julian Ming-Sung Cheng, "Determinants of Joint Action in International Channels of Distribution: The Moderating Role of Psychic Distance," *Journal of International Marketing* 20, no. 3 (Johnston 2012), pp. 34–49.

[36]See the discussion of parallel imports in Chapter 18.

The Internet

LO6

The growing importance
of e-commerce as a
distribution alternative

The Internet is an important distribution method for multinational companies and a source of products for businesses and consumers.[37] Indeed, a good argument can be made that the Internet has finally put the consumer in control of marketing and distribution globally. Computer hardware and software companies and book and music retailers were the earliest e-marketers to use this method of distribution and marketing. More recently there has been an expansion of other types of retailing and business-to-business (B2B) services into e-commerce.[38] Technically, e-commerce is a form of direct selling; however, because of its newness and the unique issues associated with this form of distribution, it is important to differentiate it from other types of direct marketing.

E-commerce is used to market B2B services, consumer services, and consumer and industrial products via the World Wide Web. It involves the direct marketing from a manufacturer, retailer, service provider, or some other intermediary to a final user. A good example of a multinational firm with a huge international online presence is Cisco Systems (http://www.cisco.com). Cisco's website appears in 14 languages and has country-specific content for 49 nations. Gateway has global sites in Japan, France, the Netherlands, Germany, Sweden, Australia, the United Kingdom, and the United States, to name a few (http://www.gateway.com). Sun Microsystems and its after-marketing company, SunExpress, have local-language information about more than 3,500 aftermarket products. SunPlaza enables visitors in North America, Europe, and Japan to get information online about products and services and to place orders directly in their native languages.

Besides consumer goods companies such as Lands' End, Levis, and Nike, and the huge general stores of e-tailing—Amazon, Walmart, and China's Alibaba[39]—many smaller and less well-known companies have established a presence on the Internet beyond their traditional markets. An Internet customer from the Netherlands can purchase a pair of brake levers for his mountain bike from California-based Price Point. He pays $130 instead of the $190 that the same items would cost in a local bike store.

For a Spanish shopper in Pamplona, buying sheet music used to mean a 400-kilometer trip to Madrid. Now he crosses the Atlantic to shop—and the journey takes less time than a trip to the corner store. Via the Internet, he can buy directly from specialized stores and high-volume discounters in New York, London, and almost anywhere else.

E-commerce is more developed in the United States than the rest of the world, partly because of the vast number of people who own personal computers and partly because of the much lower cost of access to the Internet than found elsewhere. In addition to language, legal, and cultural differences, the cost of local phone calls (which are charged by the minute in most European countries) initially discouraged extensive use and contributed to slower Internet adoption in Europe. Even the all-powerful Alibaba in China has stumbled in its home market. At least initially the firm's new shopping platform, Tmall Global, designed to deliver foreign goods to Chinese customers, has underwhelmed both consumers and potential investors, perhaps delaying it expected 2015 initial public offering.[40]

Services, the third engine for growth, are ideally suited for international sales via the Internet. All types of services—banking, education, consulting, retailing, hotels,

---

[37]Vinh Nhat Lu and Craig C. Julian, "The Internet, Strategy and Performance: A Study of Australian Export Market Ventures," *Journal of Global Marketing* 21, no. 3 (2008), pp. 231–40.

[38]Carlyle Farrell, "The Role of the Internet in the Delivery of Export Promotion Services: A Web Site Content Analysis," *Journal of Global Marketing* 21, no. 4 (2008), pp. 259–70.

[39]Mark Scott, "Principles Are No Match for Europe's Love of U.S. Web Titans," *The New York Times*, July 7, 2014, pp, B1, 3; "Walmart Plants More Stores and E-Commerce in China," *Reuters*, October 25, 2013, online; Neil Gough and Alexandra Stevenson, "The Rise of Alibaba, and a Tycoon," *The New York Times*, May 8, 2014, pp. B1, 4.

[40]Kathy Chu, "Alibaba Stumbles with Foreign Sales," *The Wall Street Journal*, December 23, 2014, pp. B1, 5.

CROSSING BORDERS 15.2   Gourmet Goes to Paris

Next time you're in in the City of Lights and hankering for a little continental cuisine (the North American kind), stop by Cantine California—if you can find it.

Gourmet stuffed, organic meat tacos are on the menu of this popular food truck. The Parisians call this cool American import "très Brooklyn," which roughly translates into "informality, creativity, and quality." Jordan Feilders, the pictured truck owner is bicultural, having been raised in France with roots in the United States. He blends succulent pork carnitas and chipoltes in adobo and masa harina for his tacos. Many of his ingredients are imported directly from Mexico. He buys the buns for his burgers from a local bakery catering to Muslims. The Tunisian "Ramadan bread" had the right combination of lightness, mildness, chew, and sesame seeds. You can look for the truck near the Apple store at the Louvre—it does stop there. But better, just check Twitter and Facebook to follow its moves.

Where do new markets come from? By examining the strategies of Kogi BBQ—credited by many for launching the gourmet food truck movement in the United States—we can gain a better understanding of the potential for social media as a distribution channel and its ability to create a marketplace. When he co-founded Kogi BBQ, one of the first gourmet food trucks operating in Los Angeles, chef Roy Choi (a bicultural, Korean-born American) faced resistance from consumers, brick-and-mortar restaurants, and local government agencies. Launched during the cold, rainy week leading up to Thanksgiving in 2008, Choi struggled at first to find customers for his Korean barbecue tacos made from a fusion of gourmet Korean and Mexican ingredients.

Although mobile food trucks had operated in California since the 1960s, these "roach coaches" typically parked outside construction sites or bars and served blue-collar customers. While Kogi's food was a significant departure from the tacos, burritos, and quesadillas sold by LA's traditional taco trucks, Kogi initially followed the same distribution strategy, parking outside bars in Hollywood. There, the trucks found few customers and resorted to giving away food. Choi recalled, "the first couple weeks we were out there, people were laughing at us because they just couldn't conceptualize what it was [we were selling]."

Fortunately for Choi and his colleagues, they had hired a marketing consultant, Mike Prasad, who created a Twitter account to promote the truck. Kogi also hosted private, free tastings for local food bloggers, whose subsequent blog entries about Kogi raised awareness in the "foodie" community. Parked outside a bar in the rain, the Kogi truck looked like any other roach coach and drew roach coach customers. However, the unfamiliar flavors and higher prices turned off customers expecting cheap Mexican fast food. But by using social media, Kogi was able to reach a younger, tech-savvy, affluent, foodie customer, where the gourmet

twist on tacos had a greater appeal. Within a few weeks, customers were waiting multiple hours in line to eat, and Kogi was regularly selling out even exotic specials such as Kimchi Quesadilla with Sesame Leaves. Kogi also changed the location strategy. While traditional taco trucks parked in the same locations and waited for the customers to come to them, Kogi began listening to customer requests on Twitter and driving to the neighborhoods with more demand.

Seeing Kogi's long lines, other entrepreneurs found a food truck, started a Twitter account, and joined the market. Within a year, there were almost a hundred gourmet food trucks on the streets of Los Angeles, selling a wide variety of foods. While many of these later entrants attracted large customer followings, none could draw a crowd like Kogi. To gain more customers, Kogi started parking trucks together in "round-ups" of 6, 8, or even 20 trucks selling different foods. Like a mobile, rotating food court, these roundups offered consumers greater variety and convenience and were able to attract far more customers than each truck could alone. To promote the roundups, participating trucks would Tweet not only the location, but also the names of the other trucks in attendance. By mentioning another truck on Twitter, some of the tweeting truck's Twitter followers might then follow the mentioned truck. While promoting their competitors to their own best customers—their Twitter followers—the roundup participants cooperated to increase demand and grow the market.

The gourmet food truck concept has now spread to other cities and countries: first to affluent cities with an existing consumer demand for street food, such as New York, Portland, San Francisco, and Austin, and then to markets where one might not expect customers to eat standing outside a truck, such as Anchorage, Paris, Montreal, London, Madrid, Milan, Sapporo, and, *oui*, Paris. In each market, local entrepreneurs have adapted their product offerings to cater to local tastes, while retaining social media as their primary tool for reaching customers. What was a $400 million industry in 2008 grew by 2014 into an $800 million industry with more than 3,000 trucks. The concept has also spread to other industries, with entrepreneurs launching mobile boutiques, vintage clothing stores, and even art galleries.

Sources: Contributed by Russ Nelson. Julia Moskin, "Food Trucks in Paris? U.S. Cuisine Finds Open Minds, and Mouths," *The New York Times*, June 3, 2012, online; Tamara Best, "Shops on Wheels, but the Goods Aren't Sold from the Trunk," *The New York Times*, November 27, 2014, pp. B1, 2. For more details on this topic see Russel Nelson, *Dynamic Network Models for the Analysis of Cooperation and Competition in New Markets*, doctoral dissertation, the Paul Merage School of Business, August, 2015.

gambling—can be marketed through a website that is globally accessible. As outsourcing of traditional in-house tasks such as inventory management, quality control, and accounting, secretarial, translation, and legal services has become more popular among companies, the Internet providers of these services have grown both in the United States and internationally.

Moreover, online B2B enables companies to enhance their performance[41] in at least three ways. First, it reduces procurement costs by making it easier to find the cheapest supplier, and it cuts the cost of processing the transactions. Estimates suggest that a firm's possible savings from purchasing over the Internet vary from 2 percent in the coal industry to up to 40 percent in electronic components. British Telecom claims that procuring goods and services online will reduce the average cost of processing a transaction by 90 percent and reduce the direct costs of goods and services it purchases by 11 percent. The Ford, GM, and DaimlerChrysler exchange network for buying components from suppliers could reduce the cost of making a car by as much as 14 percent.

Second, it allows better supply-chain management. For example, more than 75 percent of all Cisco orders now occur online, up from 4 percent in 1996. This connection to the supply chain allowed Cisco to reduce order cycle time from six to eight weeks to one to three weeks and to increase customer satisfaction as well.

Third, it makes possible tighter inventory control. With Walmart's direct Internet links between its inventory control system and its suppliers, each sale automatically triggers a replenishment request. Fewer out-of-stock situations, the ability to make rapid inventory adjustments, and reduced ordering and processing costs have made Walmart one of the industry's most efficient companies.

The worldwide potential for firms operating on the Internet is extraordinary, but only if they are positioned properly[42] and well supported by management.[43] The World Wide Web, as a market, is rapidly moving through the stage where the novelty of buying on the Web is giving way to a more sophisticated customer who has more and constantly improving websites from which to choose. In short, web merchants are facing more competition, and web customers have more choice. This situation means that if a company is going to be successful in this new era of marketing, the basics of good marketing cannot be overlooked. For example, Forrester Research has discovered that nearly half the international orders received by U.S. companies go unfilled, even though a typical U.S. company can expect 30 percent of its web traffic to come from foreign countries and 10 percent of its orders to come from abroad.

By its very nature, e-commerce has some unique issues that must be addressed if a domestic e-vendor expects to be a viable player in the international cybermarketplace. International legal issues were discussed in Chapter 7. Particularly, high-flying Google is under censorship attack and other kinds of controls in both China[44] and Italy.[45] Many other issues arise because the host-country intermediary who would ordinarily be involved in international marketing is eliminated. An important advantage of selling direct is that total costs can be lowered so that the final price overseas is considerably less than it would have been through a local-country middleman. However, such activities as translating prospective customer inquiries and orders into English and replying in the customer's language, traditionally done by a local distributor, have to be done by someone. When intermediaries are eliminated, someone, either the seller or the buyer, must

[41]Ruey-Jer (Bryan) Jean, Rudolf R. Sinkovics, and S. Tamer Cavusgil, "Enhancing International Customer-Supplier Relationships through IT Resources: A Study of Taiwanese Electronics Suppliers," *Journal of International Business Studies* 41, no. 7 (2010), pp. 1218–39.

[42]Byeong-Joon Moon and Subash C. Jain, "Determinants of Outcomes of Internet Marketing Activities of Exporting Firms," *Journal of Global Marketing* 20 (2007), pp. 55–72.

[43]Gary Gregory, Munib Karavdic, and Shoaming Zou, "The Effects of E-Commerce on Export Marketing Strategy," *Journal of International Marketing* 15 (2007), pp. 30–57.

[44]Juliet Ye, "Chinese Video Takes Aim at Online Censorship," *The Wall Street Journal*, February 11, 2010, online.

[45]Adam Liptak, "When Free Worlds Collide," *The New York Times*, February 28, 2010, p. Opinion 1.

Global Marketing on the Web at Marriott

The Internet today is the most global of any media. The power of the Internet results from its unique capabilities to:

- Encompass text, audio and video in one platform.
- Operate in a dialogue versus monologue mode.
- Operate simultaneously as mass media *and* personalized media.
- Build global "communities," unconfined by national borders.

However, leveraging these advantages effectively requires dealing with various substantive issues, including:

- Major differences in Internet penetration rates across the globe ranging from 87 percent penetration in North America to 27 percent for the continent of Africa. This difference greatly influences the role of the Web as part of the marketing mix in international markets. Even for advanced EU economies, the variability of adoption is great, ranging from 95 percent in Sweden to 50 percent in Romania. (www.internetworldstats.com).

- Unique issues caused by technology including broadband versus narrow-band, which drive what products and services can be marketed and how. In the narrow-band world, highly graphic and video-based Web sites are not viable. An example is the elaborate photo tours of hotels on www.Marriott.com, which download quickly on broadband connections but take inordinately long on narrow band. Therefore, a site designed for one market can be ineffective in another. Costs to globalize can be enormous if multiple language sites need to be built. For example, translating the 110,000- page Marriott.com Web site is a very costly undertaking, both on a one-time and ongoing basis. Add to that the costs` of translating the back-end systems that feed the site, and the costs rise exponentially. For sites with a lot of constantly changing content and heavy dependence on back-end systems, maintaining foreign language sites can be prohibitively expensive.

- Implications of differing labor costs that affect return on investment (ROI). For example, in the United States, the cost of an online booking for Marriott is less than half that of a phone booking. That differential may not apply in many Third World countries, where labor costs are often very low, making it difficult to justify a Web site investment.

- Different approaches to privacy, access, and infrastructure investment also require changes to strategy by market.

- On privacy. For example, EU laws are much more stringent than U.S. laws; as a result, the e-mail marketing strategy in the European Union is much more cautious than in the United States.

- On access. Some countries regulate access to the Internet. For example, China only allows access to approved sites, whereas the United States does not limit Internet access.

- On infrastructure investment. Some countries have private investment fueling the development of the telecom technology systems required to enable Internet access (e.g., the United States), whereas in other countries, state-owned phone companies have this responsibility. In general, markets that have depended state investment have been laggards in the Internet space.

Apart from all of these issues, one of the most important challenges for companies contemplating a global Internet presence is determining whether they should build "foreign market sites" or "foreign language sites." In an ideal world, with infinite resources, the answer could be to build both. However, that option is rarely possible given resource constraints. This challenge has been a key issue for Marriott International, which has responded in different ways, depending on market situations. In some cases, the company tried one approach before moving to the other. In fact, Marriott's experience in this area is an excellent illustration of the issue.

A good example is the question of using France or French. Should we have a global site in French that caters to ALL French-speaking customers, no matter which country they live in.

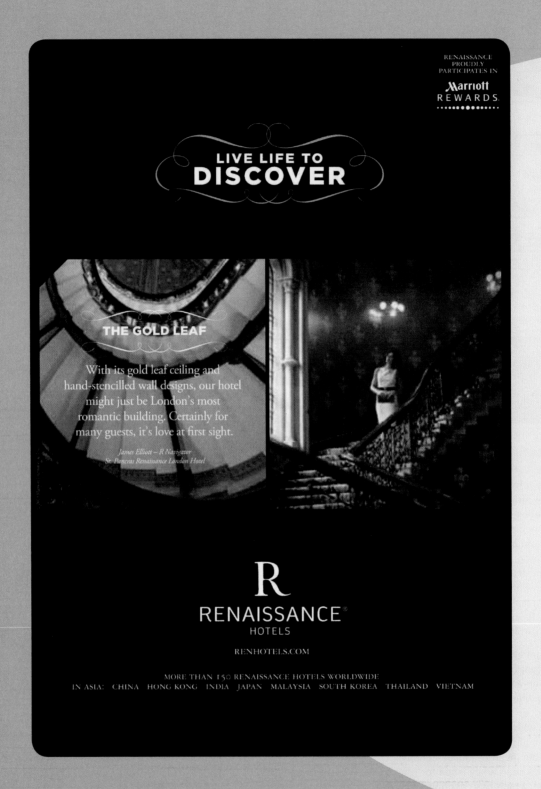

RENAISSANCE
PROUDLY
PARTICIPATES IN

Marriott
REWARDS

LIVE LIFE TO
DISCOVER

THE GOLD LEAF

With its gold leaf ceiling and
hand-stencilled wall designs, our hotel
might just be London's most
romantic building. Certainly for
many guests, it's love at first sight.

James Elliott – R Navigator
St. Pancras Renaissance London Hotel

R
RENAISSANCE®
HOTELS

RENHOTELS.COM

MORE THAN 150 RENAISSANCE HOTELS WORLDWIDE
IN ASIA: CHINA HONG KONG INDIA JAPAN MALAYSIA SOUTH KOREA THAILAND VIETNAM

Or should we have a site in the French language, which addresses the needs of the LOCAL French market? Having a French language site for a global French-speaking market had significant benefits, because there is a sizable French-speaking population in the world, which includes major parts of North and Central Africa and the Caribbean islands. However, in this case, Marriot decided in favor of a local site for France. In summary, the company found that

- The needs of French customers living in France were very different from the needs of customers in French-speaking Africa or Haiti. Customers living in France prefer different destinations than those living in other French-speaking areas, such as the Caribbean.

- Promotional approaches were also different for France than for other French-speaking countries. Using a U.S. example to illustrate, sweepstakes are far more popular and accepted in the United States than in Europe.
- Finally, the French market dwarfed all other French-speaking markets combined. Therefore, if Marriott could only afford to maintain one French site, it was more cost effective to address the largest French market, namely, France.

In 2009 and 2010 Marriott International faced increased pressure from the Province of Quebec authorities in that their French language site did not meet the needs of their local population and thus, was not compliant with their local laws. In the face of fines and other business actions by the Quebec authorities, Marriott International revised their strategy concerning a French language site and decided for a change of strategy in order to be compliant with local Canada laws while at the same time continue to serve the greater France area – France, Belgium, Switzerland, the Levant and the Maghreb. The France site has been turned into a French language portal.

Our approach was similar for the decision about Spanish.

- None of the Spanish-speaking markets was very large for Marriott. Although Spain is the largest economy in the Spanish-speaking world, as of now, the company does not have enough hotels there or enough traffic from Spain to cost effectively build a site uniquely for Spain. That applies to all other Spanish-speaking countries.
- There was greater commonality of destinations among many Spanish-speaking countries—especially the Latin American countries—than among French-speaking countries. For example, the United States is an equally popular destination for almost all Latin American countries.

As in the case of French/France, Marriott initially took the opposite approach to the same question, resulting in eight Spanish sites for various Latin American countries. However, it more quickly found that it was impractical to build, manage, and maintain so many sites and get the returns on investment it desired. Although this scenario may and should change as the individual markets mature and gain critical mass, it appears that it will take some years. Until then, Marriott will maintain one Spanish-language site.

Another crucial game changer for these strategic decisions has been the rise of website personalization. Advances in personalization technologies have enabled single domains for multiple source markets to be relevant to many audiences with the ability to dynamically change images and offers based on a user's data such as IP address and browser language. These technologies are enabling Marriott's language sites to work for many audiences without the need to build additional sites per country.

In summary, the international online marketplace is highly complex and continues to evolve. There is no single approach that fits every situation; even when that appears the case, it may not be for long, as is clear from the experience described. A key focus therefore should be on making good trade-off decisions and maintaining flexibility in strategy.

Source: Shafiq Khan, Senior Vice President eCommerce with Luis Babicek, James Nixon and Robin Chiriboga, Marriott International, 2015. (Photos Courtesy of Marriott.)

assume the functions they performed. Consequently, an e-vendor must be concerned with the following issues.

1. **Culture.** The preceding chapters on culture should not be overlooked when doing business over the Web. The website and the product must be culturally neutral or adapted to fit the uniqueness of a market, because culture does matter.[46] In Japan, the pickiness of Japanese consumers about what they buy and their reluctance to deal with merchants at a distance must be addressed when marketing on the Web. Even a Japanese-language site can offend Japanese sensibilities. As one e-commerce consultant warns: in a product description, you wouldn't say "Don't turn the knob left," because that's too direct. Instead, you would say something like: "It would be much better to turn the knob to the right." To many Europeans, American sites come off as having too many bells and whistles because European sites are more consumer oriented. The different cultural reactions to color can be a potential problem for website designed for global markets. While red may be highly regarded in China or associated with love in the United States, in Spain it is associated with socialism. The point is that when designing a website, culture cannot be forgotten.

2. **Adaptation.** Ideally, a website should be translated into the languages of the target markets. This translation may not be financially feasible for some companies, but at least the most important pages of the site should be translated. Simple translation of important pages is only a stopgap measure however. If companies are making a long-term commitment to sales in another country, web pages should be designed (in all senses of the term—color, use features, etc.) for that market. One researcher suggests that if a website does not have at least multiple languages, a company is losing sales. It is the company's responsibility to bridge the language and cultural gap; the customer will not bother—he or she will simply go to a site that speaks his or her language. As discussed, culture does count, and as competition increases, a country-specific website may make the difference between success and failure.

3. **Local contact.** Companies fully committed to foreign markets are creating virtual offices abroad; they buy server space and create mirror sites, whereby a company has a voice mail or fax contact point in key markets. Foreign customers are more likely to visit sites in their own country and in the local language. In Japan, where consumers seem particularly concerned about the ability to return goods easily, companies may have outlets where merchandise can be returned and picked up. These so-called click-and-mortar models have gained a large following.

4. **Payment.** The consumer should be able to use a credit card number—by e-mail (from a secure page on the website), by fax, or over the phone. Although this accessibility had been an important problem in burgeoning markets like China, customers and banking systems there are now beginning to catch on fast.

5. **Delivery.** For companies operating in the United States, surface postal delivery of small parcels is the most cost effective but takes the longest time. For more rapid but more expensive deliveries, FedEx, UPS, and other private delivery services provide delivery worldwide. For example, Tom Clancy's bestseller *Executive Orders,* shipped express to Paris from Seattle-based Amazon.com, would cost a reader $55.52. The same book delivered in 4 to 10 weeks via surface mail costs $25.52, which is a substantial savings over the cost of the book in

[46]Jan-Benedict E. M. Steenkamp and Inge Geyskens, "How Country Characteristics Affect the Perceived Value of Web Sites," *Journal of Marketing* 70 (2006), pp. 136–50; Abdul R. Ashraf, Narongsak (Tek) Thongpapanl, and Seigyoung Auh, "The Application of the Technology Acceptance Model Under Different Cultural Contexts: The Case of Online Shopping," *Journal of International Marketing* 22, no. 3 (2014), pp. 68–93.

a Paris bookstore, where it sells for $35.38. Delivery is often a crucial problem in other countries. Even Chinese giant Alibaba has difficulties meeting delivery promises there.[47]

6. **Promotion.** Although the Web is a means of promotion, if you are engaging in e-commerce, you also need to advertise your presence and the products or services offered. The old adage "Build a better mouse trap and the world will beat a path to your door" does not work for e-commerce, just as it does not work with other products unless you tell your target market about the availability of the "better mouse trap." How do you attract visitors from other countries to your website? The same way you would at home—except in the local language. Search engine registration, press releases, local newsgroups and forums, mutual links, and banner advertising are the traditional methods. A website should be seen as a retail store, with the only difference between it and a physical store being that the customer arrives over the Internet instead of on foot.

When discussing the Internet and international channels of distribution, the question of how traditional channels will be changed by the Internet must be considered. Already, comparison shopping across the Continent via the Internet is wrenching apart commercial patterns cobbled together over centuries. Before the Internet, Europeans rarely shopped across borders, and car companies, exempt from EU antitrust laws in distribution, offered cars at price differentials of up to 40 percent. The Internet has blown this system apart and allows the European customer to shop easily for the best price.

Not only will the traditional channels change, but so will the Internet, which is still evolving. Much of what is standard practice today may well be obsolete tomorrow as new means of data transmission are achieved, costs of accessing the Web decrease, and new e-commerce models are invented. The Web is rapidly growing—and changing as it grows.

Logistics

LO7

The interdependence of physical distribution activities

When a company is primarily an exporter from a single country to a single market, the typical approach to the physical movement of goods is the selection of a dependable mode of transportation that ensures safe arrival of the goods within a reasonable time for a reasonable carrier cost. As a company becomes global, such a solution to the movement of products could prove costly and highly inefficient for seller and buyer. As some global marketers say, the hardest part is not making the sale but getting the correct quantity of the product to customers in the required time frame at a cost that leaves enough margins for a profit.

At some point in the growth and expansion of an international firm, costs other than transportation are such that an optimal cost solution to the physical movement of goods cannot be achieved without thinking of the physical distribution process as an integrated system. When an international marketer begins producing and selling in more than one country and becomes a global marketer, it is time to consider the concept of *logistics management,* a total systems approach to the management of the distribution process that includes all activities involved in physically moving raw material, in-process inventory, and finished goods inventory from the point of origin to the point of use or consumption.[48]

A *physical distribution system* involves more than the physical movement of goods. It includes the location of plants and warehousing (storage), transportation mode, inventory quantities, and packing. The concept of physical distribution takes into account the interdependence of the costs of each activity; a decision involving one activity affects the cost and efficiency of one or all others. In fact, because of their interdependence, the sum of each of the different activity costs entails an infinite number of "total costs." (*Total cost* of the system is defined as the sum of the costs of all these activities.)

---

[47]Shanshan Wang and Paul Mozur, "Buying Is Easy. Delivery Is Hard." *The New York Times,* November 12, 2014, pp. B1, 10.

[48]An excellent source on this subject is Donald F. Wood et al., *International Logistics,* 2nd ed. (New York: Amacom, 2002).

The idea of interdependence can be illustrated by the classic example of airfreight. One company compared its costs of shipping 44,000 peripheral boards worth $7.7 million from a Singapore plant to the U.S. West Coast using two modes of transportation—ocean freight and the seemingly more expensive airfreight. When considering only rates for transportation and carrying costs for inventory in transit, air transportation costs were approximately $57,000 higher than ocean freight. But when total costs were calculated including warehousing, insurance and inventory expenses, airfreight was actually less costly than ocean freight because of other costs involved in the total physical distribution system.

To offset the slower ocean freight and the possibility of unforeseen delays and to ensure prompt customer delivery schedules, the company had to continuously maintain 30 days of inventory in Singapore and another 30 days' inventory at the company's distribution centers. The costs of financing 60 days of inventory and of additional warehousing at both points—that is, real physical distribution costs—would result in the cost of ocean freight exceeding air by more than $75,000. And ocean freight may even entail additional costs such as a higher damage rate, higher insurance, and higher packing rates.

Substantial savings can result from the systematic examination of logistics costs and the calculation of total physical distribution costs. A large multinational firm with facilities and customers around the world shipped parts from its U.S. Midwest plant to the nearest East Coast port, then by water route around the Cape of Good Hope (Africa), and finally to its plants in Asia, taking 14 weeks. Substantial inventory was maintained in Asia as a safeguard against uncertain water-borne deliveries. The transportation carrier costs were the least expensive available; however, delivery delays and unreliable service caused the firm to make emergency air shipments to keep production lines going. As a result, air shipment costs rose to 70 percent of the total transport bill. An analysis of the problem in the physical distribution system showed that trucking the parts to West Coast ports using higher-cost motor carriers and then shipping them to Asia by sea could lower costs. Transit time was reduced, delivery reliability improved, inventory quantities in Asia decreased, and emergency air shipments eliminated. The new distribution system produced annual savings of $60,000.

Although a cost difference will not always be the case, the examples illustrate the interdependence of the various activities in the physical distribution mix and the total cost. A change of transportation mode can affect a change in packaging and handling, inventory costs, warehousing time and cost, and delivery charges.

The concept behind physical distribution is the achievement of the optimum (lowest) system cost, consistent with customer service objectives of the firm. If the activities in the physical distribution system are viewed separately, without consideration of their interdependence, the final cost of distribution may be higher than the lowest possible cost (optimum cost), and the quality of service may be adversely affected. Additional variables, costs, and risks[49] that are interdependent and must be included in the total physical distribution decision heighten the distribution problems confronting the international marketer. As the international firm broadens the scope of its operations, the additional variables and costs become more crucial in their effect on the efficiency of the distribution system.

One of the major benefits of the European Union's unification is the elimination of transportation barriers among member countries. Instead of approaching Europe on a country-by-country basis, a centralized logistics network can be developed. The trend in Europe is toward pan-European distribution centers. Studies indicate that companies operating in Europe may be able to cut 20 warehousing locations to 3 and maintain the same level of customer service. A German white goods manufacturer was able to reduce its European warehouses from 39 to 10, as well as improve its distribution

---

[49]Thomas Fuller, "Floodwaters Are Gone, but Supply Chain Issues Linger," *The New York Times,* January 20, 2012.

and enhance customer service. By cutting the number of warehouses, it reduced total distribution and warehousing costs, brought down staff numbers, held fewer items of stock, provided greater access to regional markets, made better use of transport networks, and improved service to customers, all with a 21 percent reduction of total logistics costs.

Finally, an abundance of new logistical innovations are being produced around the world. Containers are now being shipped from China to Europe via train, saving 20 days vis-à-vis the 40-day travel time by ship.[50] Also, cargo ships are now reducing transit time by taking an Arctic route. Innovations in container ships include ships too large to fit through the Panama Canal and into most U.S. ports[51] and Rolls Royce's development of a sail-powered bulk carrier.[52] New investments are being made in supersonic passenger jets.[53] Chinese[54] and Brazilian[55] firms are building new port facilities around the world. Meanwhile, the trade infrastructure of the United States continues to falter.[56]

Trade infrastructure is crucial for international competitiveness and cooperation. There is a lot going on in this picture of the Port of Oakland, California. You can see the three apparently full, foreign-owned container ships sitting low in the water—the many empty containers onboard will be heading east to Asian ports and then will return full. The Matson ship moving down the Oakland Estuary is heading to Hawaii with containers and private automobiles onboard. Matson, as a U.S. domestic line founded in 1882, has only one competitor on the Hawaii/mainland route, so it survives with relatively light cargoes—again notice it is high in the water. Finally, if you look very closely in the background, you can see the new east span of the San Francisco Bay Bridge opened in 2014. The old span is also still visible as it is being slowly taken apart piece-by-piece. This crucial commercial link across the bay once carried cargoes by train inland from the Embarcadero at San Francisco. Now it carries only cars in both directions, and the port facilities have moved to Oakland. Sadly, the new bridge is one of the very few major projects undertaken in the country's crumbling infrastructure. We twiddle our thumbs while our international competitors build new ports (Cuba), new airports[57] (South Korea), and new bullet trains (China).

---

[50]Dexter Roberts, Henry Meyer, and Dorthee Tschampa, "When It Doesn't Have To Be There Overnight," *Bloomberg Businessweek*, December 24, 2012, pp. 20–22.

[51]Danny Hakim, "Aboard a Cargo Colossus," *The New York Times*, October 5, 2014, pp. B4, 5.

[52]Robert Wall and Christopher Jasper, "Clipper Ships Return to the High Seas," *Bloomberg Businessweek*, July 7, 2013, pp. 18–19.

[53]Thomas Black, "The Slow Takeoff of Bob Bass's Very Fast Plane," *Bloomberg Businessweek*, November 13, 2014, pp. 23–24.

[54]"The New Masters and Commanders," *The Economist*, June 8, 2013, pp. 63–64.

[55]Damien Cave, "Former Exit Port for a Wave of Cubans Hopes to Attract Global Shipping," *The New York Times*, January 28, 2014, p. A4.

[56]"Bridging the Gap," *The Economist*, June 28, 2014, pp. 23–24.

[57]See http://www.PendletonX.org.

Summary

The international marketer has a broad range of alternatives for developing an economical, efficient, high-volume international distribution system. To the uninitiated, however, the variety may be overwhelming. Careful analysis of the functions performed suggests more similarity than difference between international and domestic distribution systems; in both cases, the three primary alternatives are using agent middlemen, merchant middlemen, or government-affiliated middlemen. In many instances, all three types of middlemen are employed on the international scene, and channel structure may vary from nation to nation or from continent to continent.

The neophyte company in international marketing can gain strength from the knowledge that information and advice are available relative to the structuring of international distribution systems and that many well-developed and capable middleman firms exist for the international distribution of goods. Although international middlemen have become more numerous, more reliable, and more sophisticated within the past decade, traditional channels are being challenged by the Internet, which is rapidly becoming an important alternative channel to many market segments. Such growth and development offer an ever-wider range of possibilities for entering foreign markets.

Key Terms

Distribution process
Distribution structure
Large-Scale Retail Store Law
Agent middlemen
Merchant middlemen
Home-country middlemen
Export management company (EMC)
Trading companies
Export Trading Company (ETC)
Complementary marketing

Questions

1. Define the key terms on this page.
2. Discuss the distinguishing features of the Japanese distribution system.
3. Discuss the ways Japanese manufacturers control the distribution process from manufacturer to retailer.
4. Describe Japan's Large-Scale Retail Store Act and discuss how the Structural Impediments Initiative (SII) is bringing about change in Japanese retailing.
5. "Japanese retailing may be going through a change similar to that which occurred in the United States after World War II." Discuss and give examples.
6. Discuss how the globalization of markets, especially Europe after 1992, affects retail distribution.
7. To what extent, and in what ways, do the functions of domestic middlemen differ from those of their foreign counterparts?
8. Why is the EMC sometimes called an independent export department?
9. Discuss how physical distribution relates to channel policy and how they affect each other.
10. Explain how and why distribution channels are affected as they are when the stage of development of an economy improves.
11. In what circumstances is the use of an EMC logical?
12. In which circumstances are trading companies likely to be used?
13. How is distribution-channel structure affected by increasing emphasis on the government as a customer and by the existence of state trading agencies?
14. Review the key variables that affect the marketer's choice of distribution channels.
15. Account, as best you can, for the differences in channel patterns that might be encountered in a highly developed country and an underdeveloped country.
16. One of the first things companies discover about international patterns of channels of distribution is that in most countries, it is nearly impossible to gain adequate market coverage through a simple channel-of-distribution plan. Discuss.
17. Discuss the various methods of overcoming blocked channels.
18. What strategy might be employed to distribute goods effectively in the dichotomous small/large middleman pattern, which characterizes merchant middlemen in most countries?
19. Discuss the economic implications of assessing termination penalties or restricting the termination of middlemen. Do you foresee such restrictions in the United States?
20. Discuss why Japanese distribution channels can be the epitome of blocked channels.
21. What are the two most important provisions of the Export Trading Company Act?
22. You are the sales manager of a small company with sales in the United States. About 30 percent of your business is mail

order, and the remainder is from your two retail stores. You recently created an e-store on the Web and a few days later received an order from a potential customer from a city near Paris, France. The shipping charges listed on the Web are all for locations in the United States. You don't want to lose this $350 order. You know you can use the postal service, but the customer indicated she wanted the item in about a week. Air express seems logical, but how much will it cost? Consult both the FedEx home page (http://www.fedex.com) and the UPS home page (http://www.ups.com) to get some estimates on shipping costs. Here are some details you will need: value

$350; total weight of the package, 2.5 pounds; package dimensions, 4 inches high by 6 inches wide by 1 inch thick; U.S. zip code, 97035; and French zip code, 91400. (Note: It's not fair to call UPS or FedEx—use the Internet.)

23. Based on the information collected in Question 22, how practical would it be to encourage foreign sales? Your average order ranges from about $250 to $800. All prices are quoted plus shipping and handling. You handle a fairly exclusive line of Southwestern Indian jewelry that sells for about 15 to 20 percent higher in Europe than in the United States. The products are lightweight and high in value.

Chapter 16

Integrated Marketing Communications and International Advertising

CHAPTER LEARNING OBJECTIVES

What you should learn from Chapter 16:

LO1 Local market characteristics that affect the advertising and promotion of products

LO2 The strengths and weaknesses of sales promotions and public relations in global marketing

LO3 When global advertising is most effective; when modified advertising is necessary

LO4 The communication process and advertising misfires

LO5 The effects of a single European market on advertising

LO6 The effect of limited media, excessive media, and government regulations on advertising and promotion budgets

Global Perspective

BARBIE VERSUS MULAN

One of the best examples of integrated marketing communications (IMC) we have found was Mattel's for the new Rapunzel Barbie. The movie character/doll whose ankle-length blonde locks cascade down her pink ball gown, was released on the same day in 2003 in 59 countries, including the United States—the company's biggest product launch ever. In 2003, the first year, Rapunzel Barbie and related merchandise generated $200 million in global sales, nearly half of that outside the United States.

Two developments at the time were changing kids' tastes. One was the rapid worldwide expansion of cable and satellite TV channels, which along with movies and the Internet exposed millions of kids to the same popular icons. For example, Walt Disney Co. then operated 24 Disney-branded cable and satellite channels in 67 countries outside the United States—up from 0 a few years earlier. The other development was the widening international reach of retailing giants such as Walmart Stores Inc., Toys "R" Us Inc., and Carrefour SA, which had opened thousands of stores outside their home markets. Increasingly, the mass retailers entered into exclusive deals with toy and consumer-products companies, allowing them to stage huge, coordinated promotional campaigns.

For example, when Rapunzel Barbie had its debut, Walmart stores in South Korea and China hired local women to dress up like the doll and greet children as they entered. At the same time, the Mattel TV ad campaign was broadcast around the world in 15-, 20-, and 30-second spots—in 35 different languages. Mattel's Barbie website, which has eight language options, featured Rapunzel stories and games. A computer-animated movie, called *Barbie as Rapunzel*, was broadcast on TV and released on video and DVD around the world, and it was even shown in some theaters overseas.

In Madrid, the launch was accompanied by a "premiere" of the movie and special promotions of comb sets and other accessories at Carrefour stores across Spain. After attending the premiere, the kids could and did buy the dolls. For some parents, this meant Christmas shopping later in the year at the often frenetic Toys "R" Us in Madrid for stuffed dragons from the movie or a Barbie laptop computer, a Barbie kitchen set, a Barbie travel van, and a host of other Barbie gadgets and accessories.

Nowadays, few American companies sell toys in the Islamic world. Mattel, the world's largest toy company, has no plans to do so. Perhaps Disney's Jasmine will sell well there, though she's actually inappropriately dressed for many of Islamic faith. Jasmine is just one of the series of "Princess" dolls aimed directly at Barbie's dominance of the doll category. Snow White, Pocahontas, Mulan, and, most recently, Princess Tiana are others in the band. Their diversity may have broader appeal. Disney uses pink in the packaging. Disney is also mindful of the fashion-conscious Barbie critics. Disney Princess is more about tiaras and wands rather than handbags and high heels. Where Barbie is more a role model, and therefore more objectionable to parents, Disney is putting its emphasis on the fantasy. Too bad someone isn't emphasizing education.

Indeed, too bad for Mattel—despite the comprehensiveness of successive integrated marketing communications strategies, sales of Barbie have remained slow. Competitors' more ethnically diverse products better reflect the changing demographics in the U.S. market, as well as, the rest of the world.

Finally, as mentioned in Chapter 12, now Mattel has purchased the rights to sell Disney Princess dolls and is doing well doing so.

Sources: Lisa Bannon and Carlta Vitshum, "One-Toy-Fits-All: How Industry Learned to Love the Global Kid," *The Wall Street Journal*, April 29, 2003, p. A1; Charisse Jones, "Disney Adds African-American Princess Tiana to Royal Family," *USAToday*, February 16, 2009; Paul Ziobro, "Floundering Mattel Tries to Make Things Fun Again," *The Wall Street Journal*, December 23, 2014, pp. A1, 10; Tiffany Hsu, "Other Mattel Dolls Outdo Barbie," *Los Angeles Times*, July 18, 2013, pp. B1, 3; Elizabeth A. Harris and Tanzina Vega, "Race in Toyland: A Nonwhite Doll Crosses Over," *The New York Times*, July 26, 2014, online.

LO1

Local market characteristics that affect the advertising and promotion of products

Integrated marketing communications (IMC) are composed of advertising, sales promotions, trade shows, personal selling, direct selling, and public relations—almost all are included in the Barbie campaign described in the Global Perspective. Indeed, even the original *Wall Street Journal* story was most likely prompted by a company press release. All these mutually reinforcing elements of the promotional mix have as their common objective the successful sale of a product or service. In many markets, the availability of appropriate communication channels to customers can determine entry decisions. For example, most toy manufacturers would agree that toys cannot be marketed profitably in countries without commercial television advertising directed toward children. Thus, product and service development must be informed by research regarding the availability of communication channels. Once a market offering is developed to meet target market needs, intended customers must be informed of the offering's value and availability. Often different messages are appropriate for different communications channels, and vice versa.

For most companies, advertising and personal selling are the major components in the marketing communications mix. In this chapter, the other elements of IMC are briefly discussed first. The goal of most companies, large and small,[1] is to achieve the synergies possible when sales promotions, public relations efforts, and advertising are used in concert. However, the primary focus of this chapter is on international advertising. The topic of the next chapter is global sales management.

Sales Promotions in International Markets

Sales promotions are marketing activities that stimulate consumer purchases and improve retailer or middlemen effectiveness and cooperation. Cents-off, in-store demonstrations, samples, coupons, gifts, product tie-ins, contests, sweepstakes, sponsorship of special events such as concerts, the Olympics, fairs, and point-of-purchase displays are types of sales promotion devices designed to supplement advertising and personal selling in the promotional mix. The Rapunzel Barbie movie premiere is too.

LO2

The strengths and weaknesses of sales promotions and public relations in global marketing

Sales promotions are short-term efforts directed to the consumer or retailer to achieve such specific objectives as consumer product trial or immediate purchase, consumer introduction to the store or brand, gaining retail point-of-purchase displays, encouraging stores to stock the product, and supporting and augmenting advertising and personal sales efforts. For example, Procter & Gamble's introduction of Ariel detergent in Egypt included the "Ariel Road Show," a puppet show (not the Little Mermaid!) that was taken to local markets in villages, where more than half of all Egyptians still live. The show drew huge crowds, entertained people, told about Ariel's better performance without the use of additives, and sold the brand through a distribution van at a nominal discount. Besides creating brand awareness for Ariel, the road show helped overcome the reluctance of the rural retailers to handle the premium-priced Ariel. Perhaps our all-time favorite example in this genre is the Simpsons' international festival, sponsored by Fox in Hollywood. Spain's Simpson trivia champion defeated 11 other global contestants in the "Bart Bowl World Finals." Finally, while all software firms decry piracy in foreign markets as a costly crime, most recognize that in some sense it is actually a form of product trial.

In markets in which the consumer is hard to reach because of media limitations, the percentage of the promotional budget allocated to sales promotions may have to be increased. In some less developed countries, sales promotions constitute the major portion of the promotional effort in rural and less accessible parts of the market. In parts of Latin America, a portion of the advertising sales budget for both Pepsi-Cola and Coca-Cola is spent on carnival trucks, which make frequent trips to outlying villages to promote their products. When a carnival truck makes a stop in a village, it may show a movie or provide some other kind of entertainment; the price of admission is an unopened bottle of the product purchased from

---

[1]Ho Yin Wong and Bill Merrilees, "Determinants of SME International Marketing Communications," *Journal of Global Marketing* 1, no. 4 (2008), pp. 293–306; Chien-Wei Chen, "Integrated Marketing Communications and New Product Performance in International Markets," *Journal of Global Marketing* 24, no. 5 (2011), pp. 397–416.

the local retailer. The unopened bottle is to be exchanged for a cold bottle plus a coupon for another bottle. This promotional effort tends to stimulate sales and encourages local retailers, who are given prior notice of the carnival truck's arrival, to stock the product. Nearly 100 percent coverage of retailers in the village is achieved with this type of promotion. In other situations, village merchants may be given free samples, have the outsides of their stores painted (see pages 2 and 496), or receive clock signs in attempts to promote sales.

An especially effective promotional tool when the product concept is new or has a very small market share is product sampling. Nestlé Baby Foods faced such a problem in France in its attempt to gain share from Gerber, the leader. The company combined sampling with a novel sales promotion program to gain brand recognition and to build goodwill. Because most French people take off for a long vacation in the summertime, piling the whole family into the car and staying at well-maintained campgrounds, Nestlé provided rest-stop structures along the highway where parents could feed and change their babies. Sparkling clean *Le Relais Bébés* were located along main travel routes. Sixty-four hostesses at these rest stops welcomed 120,000 baby visits and dispensed 600,000 samples of baby food during the program. There were free disposable diapers, a changing table, and high chairs for the babies to sit in while dining.

In China, Kraft began a grassroots IMC campaign to educate consumers about the American tradition of pairing milk with cookies. The company created an Oreo apprentice program at 30 Chinese universities that drew 6,000 applicants. Three hundred were trained to become Oreo ambassadors. Some rode around major Chinese cities on bicycles outfitted with wheel covers resembling Oreos, handing out samples to more than 300,000 consumers. Others held Oreo-themed basketball games to reinforce the idea of *dunking* cookies in milk. Television commercials showed kids twisting apart Oreo cookies, licking the cream center, and dipping the halves into glasses of milk. After languishing for many years in China, now Oreo is the best-selling biscuit in the country.

One of our favorite sales promotions is the Microsoft/Burger King collaboration in Japan. To publicize the release of Windows 7, the two companies concocted a seven-patty, 2,120-calorie "Windows 7 Whopper" to sell for ¥777 (you can calculate the US$ price). The first 30 burgers sold each day at each of the company's 15 outlets sold at that price, and then the price doubled the rest of the day. Sales tallied more than 15,000 burgers the first week; YouTube videos showed customers trying to get their mouths around the monster. The publicity was a welcome change for Burger King since reentering the country in 2007. It had been chased out during a price war with 3,200-store-strong McDonald's in 2001. Burger King's return to Japan is part of its larger global strategy, involving expansion into Egypt, Hong Kong, and Poland.[2]

As is true in advertising, the success of a promotion may depend on local adaptation. Furthermore, research has shown that responses to promotions can vary across promotional types and cultures. Major constraints are imposed by local laws, which may not permit premiums or free gifts to be given. Some countries' laws control the amount of discount given at retail, others require permits for all sales promotions, and in at least one country, no competitor is permitted to spend more on a sales promotion than any other company selling the product. Effective sales promotions can enhance the advertising and personal selling efforts and, in some instances, may be effective substitutes when environmental constraints prevent the full utilization of advertising.

International Public Relations

Creating good relationships with the popular press and other media to help companies communicate messages to their publics—customers, the general public, and governmental regulators—is the role of public relations (PR). The job consists of not only encouraging the press to cover positive stories about companies (as in the Barbie story) but also managing unfavorable rumors, stories, and events.[3] Regarding the latter, the distinction between advertising and public relations has become an issue now considered by the

[2]Kenji Hall, "The (Hard to Install) Windows 7 Whopper," *BusinessWeek*, November 16, 2009, p. 28.

[3]Yi Zhao, Ying Zhao, and Kristiaan Helsen, "Consumer Learning in a Turbulent Market Environment: Modeling Consumer Choice Dynamics After a Product-Harm Crisis," *Journal of Marketing Research* 48, no. 2 (2011), pp. 255–67.

United States Supreme Court. Nike was criticized for using "sweatshop" labor in Asia and responded to critics with paid advertising. The Court decided that freedom of speech issues did not pertain to the ads, and the associated civil suit against the firm for false advertising could go forward. Indeed, Nike appears to have exacerbated and extended the problem from a public relations standpoint by taking the case all the way to the Supreme Court.

The importance of public relations in international marketing is perhaps best demonstrated by several recent controversies: (1) the Google China political fight over censorship and hacking;[4] (2) a wave of suicides by employees at Foxconn's factories in China, which makes electronics products for the likes of Apple, Hewlett-Packard, and Dell;[5] (3) the criticism of Ketcham, ironically itself a prominent American public relations firm, that has represented Vladimir Putin and Russia to the tune of tens of millions of dollars since 2006;[6] and (4) the Toyota brake pedal problem mentioned in Chapter 13. The most remarkable scene of all was Akio Toyoda, CEO of Toyota and grandson of the founder, bowing and profusely apologizing at a congressional hearing in Washington, then only days later again bowing in contrition in Beijing. The spectacle was demanded by supporters (there are many in Congress) and critics among the publics and the governments in both countries.[7] Going from the centuries-old "bowing and apologizing" to the 21st-century approach, we note that Toyota is also using social media to address the problem. To both disseminate information and monitor the fluid waters of public opinion, Toyota launched a branded channel of Tweetmeme with the help of Federated Media. Called Toyota Conversations, the channel features news stories, videos, and other information. It also shares tweets from Toyota's Twitter account and its own AdTweets, such as "5 Reasons to Buy a Toyota." Tweetmeme channels can be programmed to pick up only select news sources. So in contrast to the sober tone of stories in the *Los Angeles Times* and elsewhere, the mood is positive and light.[8]

The Toyota PR problem is strikingly reminiscent of the Bridgestone/Firestone Tires safety recall disaster of 2000. The Japanese company then was blamed for more than 100 deaths in the United States because of its defective tires. True to form in such corporate disasters, the Japanese CEO of the American subsidiary "declared his full and personal responsibility" for the deaths at a U.S. Senate hearing. Such an approach is good public relations in Japan. However, in Washington, senators were not interested in apologies. Moreover, the company blamed its customer, Ford Motor Company, for the problems as well, accusing Ford of telling customers to underinflate the tires for a smoother ride. The problem spread to other markets—Saudi Arabia banned imports of vehicles equipped with Firestone tires. Unbelievably, the company's response to the Saudi action has been to denounce it as a violation of WTO agreements. Perhaps the company would have been better off promoting its ISO 9000 rating—remember the picture in Chapter 14 on page 428? By now the Bridgestone problem is certainly forgotten by almost all Americans; in the last edition of our text we wondered in print how long it will take the American public to forgive Toyota. Given its recent climb in the global brand equity rankings on page 404 in Chapter 13, its public relations efforts have paid off handsomely. Of course, Toyota's remedial responses regarding product quality helped as well.

Public relations firms' billings in the international arena have been growing at double-digit rates for some years. Handling such international PR problems as global workplace standards and product safety recalls has become big business for companies serving corporate clients such as Mattel Toys,[9] McDonald's, and, of course, Nike. Fast growth is also being

[4] Amir Efrati and Loretta Chao, "Google Softens Tone on China," *The Wall Street Journal,* January 12, 2012.

[5] David Barboza, "Foxconn Resolves Pay Dispute with Workers," *The New York Times,* January 12, 2012; Charles Duhigg and David Barboza, "In China, Human Costs Are Built into an iPad," *The New York Times*, January 25, 2012. The latter source offers a quite complete discussion of the issue, which seems to have been resolved for the time.

[6] Ravi Somaiya, "PR Firm for Putin's Russia Now Walking a Fine Line," *The New York Times*, September 1, 2014, pp. B1, 4.

[7] David Pierson, "Toyota's President's Whirlwind Apology Tour Lands in China," *Los Angeles Times*, March 2, 2010, pp. B1, B6.

[8] Jessica Guynn, "Toyota Taps Twitter for Positive Spin," *Los Angeles Times,* March 4, 2010, p. B3.

[9] "Mattel Apologizes to China over Recall," *Associated Press,* September 21, 2007.

Piazza Navona in the heart of Rome is one of the favorite places in the Eternal City for both locals and tourists. At its center is a masterpiece of Baroque Roman sculpture, the *Fontana dei Quattro Fiumi* (Fountain of Four Rivers) by Gian Lorenzo Bernini (1651). The four major rivers of the world depicted are the Danube (Europe), Ganges (Asia), Nile (Africa), and Rio de la Plata (the Americas). The Baroque exuberance of the figure representing the Rio de la Plata seems to be protesting the banality of the Samsung advertisement in the background. Samsung has made a common international marketing mistake here, confusing public relations and advertising.[11] Samsung is helping pay for the restoration of the building facing the piazza, and Romans appreciate that. But the advertisement disrupts the aesthetics of the place. Better would have been a smaller, less obtrusive sign simply taking credit for the restoration. It is ironic that the Samsung ad uses the tagline "*messa a fuoco rapida*," which we later learned means "fast focus" in English. The focus on the ad was intentionally made soft, putting the emphasis on the sculpture.

Kelly Slater, 10-time world surfing champion, ended his long-term relationship with corporate sponsor Quiksilver in 2014. As a promised bonus for winning his 10th championship, he took a 3 percent stake in the company rather than the rumored $10 million in cash. In 2015 Kelly's ride with Quiksilver wiped out, so to speak. The firm declared bankruptcy and its stock plummeted by 80%. We don't know if Kelly bailed out in time?

fueled by the expanding international communications industry. New companies need public relations consultation for "building an international profile," as the marketing manager of VDSL Systems explained when hiring MCC, a prominent British firm. Surprising growth is occurring in emerging markets like Russia as well. The industry itself is experiencing a wave of mergers and takeovers, including the blending of the largest international advertising agencies and the most well-established PR firms.

Corporate sponsorships might be classified as an aspect of sales promotions or public relations, though their connections to advertising are also manifest. Proctor & Gamble builds schools in Vietnam and notes the donations with classroom plaques[10]; this is different from the Samsung ad pictured in Italy. Tobacco companies have been particularly creative at using sports event sponsorships to avoid countries' advertising regulations associated with more traditional media. Other prominent examples are Quiksilver's long-term relationship with perennial world champion surfer, Kelly

---

[10]Lauren Coleman-Lochner and Vinicy Chan, "P&G Woos the Hearts, Minds, and Schools of Vietnam," *Bloomberg Businessweek*, July 9–15, 2012, pp. 19–21.

[11]Gaia Pianigiani and Jim Yardley, "Corporate Medicis to the Rescue," *The New York Times*, July 16, 2014, pp. C1, 5.

CROSSING BORDERS 16.1   PR in the PRC

In 1999 an industry was born in China when the Ministry of Labor and Social Security recognized public relations as a profession. These excerpts from the *China Daily* illustrate how institutions evolve in emerging economies:

> More laws are needed to regulate China's fledgling public relations profession, an industry leader said yesterday in Beijing. "To seize the enormous business opportunities promised by China's upcoming entry in the World Trade Organization, we need specific laws to regulate the market, curb malpractice and promote competency of local PR firms," said Li Yue, vice-director of the China International Public Relations Association. Her comments were made during a national symposium on public relations, also known as PR.
>
> Symposium delegates said they were concerned about the disorder in the PR industry and the frequent personnel changes in PR firms. They urged the passage of more laws to put an end to what many consider to be the chaos in the profession. Industry insiders cited a limited talent pool, cut-throat price

wars and low professional standards as the industry's major problems.

> In the 1980s, most Chinese people would think of reception girls, lavish banquets, and the use of connections when public relations were mentioned. Now, public relations firms are seen as helping their clients gain better name recognition of their companies. They also manage corporate images.
>
> Finally, it is interesting to see how corporate and press relations differ across cultures. In China and Taiwan, it is both ethical and legal to offer press organizations compensation for coverage. Arms'-length objectivity of the press is not an issue at the current stage of development of systems there.

Sources: "China: More Regulation of PR Sought," *China Daily*, January 20, 2000, p. 3; "PRW: The Top European PR Consultancies 2000," *PR Week*, June 23, 2000, p. 7; "PR Firms Gaining Experience by Working with Multinational Firms," *Industry Updates*, June 20, 2005; "Ogilvy Public Relations Worldwide/China and JL McGregor Announce Strategic Alliance," *PR Newswire*, June 13, 2007; "Gov't Should Not Buy Media Coverage: Official," *China Post*, December 28, 2010.

Slater; Coca-Cola's sponsorship of European football (soccer) matches; or Kia Motor's sponsorship of the Australian Open tennis tournament. McDonald's executed huge international IMC campaigns surrounding its sponsorship of the 2000 Sydney Olympics. Included were Olympic-themed food promotions, packaging and in-store signs, TV and print ads, and Web chats with superstar athletes such as American basketball player Grant Hill. In addition to the various promotions targeting the 43 million daily customers in their 27,000 restaurants around the world, the firm targeted the athletes themselves. As the official restaurant partner, McDonald's got to operate seven restaurants in Sydney, including the two serving the Olympic Village. During the three weeks of the Games, nearly 1.5 million burgers were served to the athletes, officials, coaches, media staffers, and spectators. McDonald's continued this sort of official corporate support for the Athens (2004), Beijing (2008), and London (2012) games as well. Finally, one of the more innovative sponsorship arrangements was Intel's agreement with the Tour de France to support the official Tour website, http://www.letour.com. Of course, all these aspects of IMC work best when coordinated and reinforced with a consistent advertising campaign, the topic covered in the rest of the chapter.

International Advertising

Global media advertising was still recovering from the slump from the 2008–2009 recession. At $520 billion in 2014, up 5.1 percent from the the previous year, it has almost recovered its 2008 record level. For the top 100 global advertisers, revenues bounced from $118 billion in 2008 to $109 billion in 2009, then to $122 billion in 2010 and $131 billion for 2013. Perhaps the most important overall trend is the astonishing growth of the use of digital media, this year gaining the number two spot in attracting advertising dollars. Print media has fallen behind to number three, and TV, while still number one, is beginning to slip as well. Overall, the shift to digital media is deflationary for the industry. Also, this year mass media advertising in China has surpassed Japan for the first time and is now at number two behind

A Breakthrough in International Advertising Effectiveness

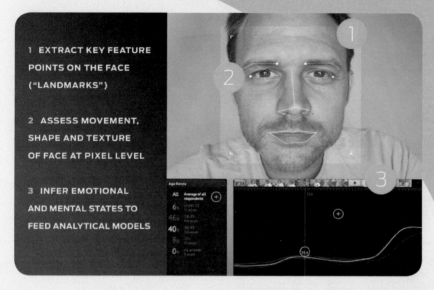

1 EXTRACT KEY FEATURE POINTS ON THE FACE ("LANDMARKS")

2 ASSESS MOVEMENT, SHAPE AND TEXTURE OF FACE AT PIXEL LEVEL

3 INFER EMOTIONAL AND MENTAL STATES TO FEED ANALYTICAL MODELS

Facial-recognition software, much like grocery store laser scanner data in the 1980/1990s, represents a major advance in marketing science.[12] Here we have asked key executives at Affectiva, Inc., an American firm on the forefront of this work, to describe their services. Of particular interest are the cross-cultural differences Rana el Kaliouby and Gabi Zijderveld have observed. Affectiva, a division of advertising giant WWP, counts among its prominent clientele global marketers such as Mars, Kellogg, and Unilever.

Why Emotions Matter in Advertising

Emotions influence every aspect of our lives—from the way we interact with each other to the decisions we make and even to our health. A big portion of our decision-making process is emotional—from what we eat for breakfast to how we decide to buy a house or who to marry!

Emotionally engaged customers are good for business: Emotions are memory markers. In a landmark study, researchers[13] showed that advertisements that elicited the most facial expressions were remembered the most five days after watching; and that strong memory was true for positive as well as negative emotion responses. Our everyday emotions depict how well we remember events, brands, and products. It is these emotions that also influence consumer behavior such as sharing behavior, brand loyalty, and purchase decisions. More than ever before, brands are choosing to build a strong emotional connection with their consumers.

Yet traditional methods of measuring emotional response to brands, products, advertising, and media content, through surveys and focus groups, require viewers to think about and report how they feel—which most people are not able or willing to do. Contemporary neuroscience techniques provide new insight into how the mind works but often require expensive, bulky equipment and lab-type settings that limit and influence the experience and, for that reason, often do not provide true emotion insight.

Affectiva's Affdex automated facial coding and emotion analytics software offers something different. The face is one of the most powerful channels for communicating affect and mood, and by analyzing facial expressions inexpensively and at scale, Affdex introduces a cost-effective neuroscience technique that captures participants' unbiased and unfiltered emotional reactions (e.g., whether a person is engaged, amused, surprised, or confused) in an unobtrusive manner.

Quantification of Facial Behavior
Until recently, the quantification of facial behavior has relied primarily on two approaches: (1) manual coding of muscle movements on the face from photographic images or video segments, typically by an expert observer, and (2) measurement of electrical muscle potentials on the face, known as electromyography (EMG). Neither of these approaches is easily scalable.[14]

[12]Thales Teixeira, Rosalind Picard, and Rana el Kaliouby, "Why, When, and How Much to Entertain Consumers in Advertisements? A Web-Based Facial Tracking Field Study," *Marketing Science*, May 9, 2014, online.

[13]Richard L. Hazzlet and Sasha Yassky Hasslet, "Emotional Response to Television Commercials: Facial EMG vs. Self-Report," *Journal of Advertising Research*, March–April 1999, pp. 7–23.

[14]John L. Graham, "A New System for Measuring Nonverbal Responses to Marketing Appeals," *Marketing in the 80's, 1980 Marketing Educators' Conference Proceedings* 46 (1980), pp. 340–42.

Recent computer vision and machine learning advances have enabled accurate automated facial coding from video material. Among other advantages, automated facial coding allows extensive amounts of data to be analyzed. Typically, these systems comprise several steps: (1) face detection and alignment, (2) shape or texture feature extraction, and (3) facial action or expression classification.

How Affdex Works

Affdex captures facial expressions via a standard computer or device camera as participants view a digital stimulus such as an ad or video. Affdex employs advanced computer vision and machine-learning algorithms within a scalable cloud-based infrastructure to identify the emotions portrayed in a face video.

When a participant opts-in to have his or her camera turned on, Affdex will first identify the face and will then locate the main feature points on the face, such as eyes and mouth. Once the region of interest has been isolated, Affdex analyzes each pixel in the region to describe the color, texture, edges, and gradients of the face, which is then mapped, using machine learning, to a facial expression of emotion (e.g., a smile or smirk). The Affdex algorithms have been tuned to handle a wide variety of conditions—lighting conditions, different ethnicities, and even multiple faces present in a video. Once classification is complete, the emotion data extracted from a video are ready for summarization and aggregation and are presented via the Affdex online dashboard. Expression information is also summarized for addition to a normative database.

Affdex provides two categories of emotion metrics: dimensions of emotion and discrete emotions. Dimensions of emotion are used to characterize the emotional response Discrete emotions are used to describe the specific emotional states.

The dimensions of emotion that Affdex measures include:

- Valence—a measure of the positive (or negative) nature of the participant's experience with the content.

- Attention—a measure of the participant's attention to the screen, using the orientation of the face to assess if he or she is looking directly at the screen or if he or she is distracted (turning away) while viewing content.

- Expressiveness/intensity—a measure of how emotionally engaging content is, computed by accumulating the frequency and intensity of the discrete emotions, including smile, dislike, surprise, and concentration. Unlike valence, expressiveness is independent of the positive or negative aspect of the facial expressions.

The discrete emotion measures includes:

- Enjoyment—the degree to which the participant is displaying a natural, positive smile. The smile classifier looks at the full face rather than just the mouth/lip area, incorporating other facial cues, like the eyes, to accurately indicate a true smile.

- Concentration—the degree to which the participant is frowning (displaying a brow furrow) that is not induced by a dislike response and thus more likely the result of focus, mental effort, or even confusion.

- Surprise—the degree to which the participant is expressing surprise by raising his or her eyebrows.

- Dislike—the degree to which the participant is showing expressions of dislike or even disgust.

- Skepticism/doubt—measured by a smirk, or asymmetric lip movement, this emotion is critical in media testing because it is an indicator that a viewer is not persuaded by a message.

Emotion Norms
To date, Affectiva has amassed the world's largest data repository—Affectiva's emotion insights have been gathered from nearly 11,000 media units (more than 2.6 million face videos) and spans more than 75 countries around the globe.

This has enabled Affectiva to build a global normative database of emotion response to video content that can be filtered and analyzed by geographic region, demographic profile, as well as industries and product categories. With these data, advertisers can perform A/B tests for their content and compare how their ad ranks with respect to other content in their product category or market.

Emotion Analytics in Quantitative and Qualitative Market Research
Affdex can be easily incorporated into existing quantitative and qualitative market research studies to add rich insights into communication and engagement effectiveness.

Today, many market research companies use Affdex facial coding and emotion analytics as part of their methodology for copy testing and other brand effectiveness studies. The Affdex dashboard shows aggregated for all study participants the frame-by-frame emotional reactions to a digital stimulus. When combined with a survey, the Affdex dashboard can also show the survey breaks.

Affdex Discovery is a qualitative solution expressly designed for moderators of focus groups—either in person or online. The Affdex Discovery moderator console shows the emotional responses of each respondent synched with the digital stimulus for moment-by-moment analysis. This enables the moderator to see exactly how each participant reacted at a certain moment in time, providing them with insight to guide discussion and probe deeper.

Typical Advertising Use Cases
Affdex has been used by more than 1,400 brands to assess consumer emotional engagement with their digital content in a variety of different scenarios, including the testing of ad copy, animatics, product testimonials, and concepts. Leveraging the Affdex emotion analytics, advertisers have been able to select the best animatic, optimize scenes and story arcs, create cut-downs, evaluate wear-out effects, determine media spend, and conduct predictive analytics for in-market performance. Media companies are also using Affdex to test movie trailers, characters in TV pilots, and optimal placement of TV promos and ads in pods.

Cross-Cultural Differences
We have amassed 2.7 million face videos from more than 75 countries—more than 7 billion emotion data points. These data have never existed before and are allowing us to gain insight into cross-cultural differences in facial expressions at a scale that was never possible before. When it comes to emotion communication, we all start with the same base of universal, pan-cultural facial expressions. However, while emotion expression is universal, we learn at an early age to alter our expressions based on social circumstance, this is called "Cultural Display Rules." For instance, we may amplify our sadness at funerals and dampen it at weddings. These display rules vary by culture. Our emotion data have confirmed that collectivist cultures, like China and India, are more likely to dampen or mask their emotion, especially negative ones. We don't see evidence of that in individualistic cultures like the United States or Germany. Our studies have shown that people in Western and Latin American countries are a lot more expressive than in Southeast Asia. For example, Spain is almost five times more expressive than Indonesia. Our data have also given us unique insights into the many nuances of a smile, and fleeting expressions of smile, that are difficult to observe with the naked eye but are picked up well by our software. An example of that is the "polite smile" that we see in collectivist cultures.

Exhibit 16.1
Top 20 Global Advertisers

2013	Advertiser	Headquarters	2013 (billions $)	Percent Change from 2012
1	Procter & Gamble	Cincinnati	$11.5	10.0%
2	Unilever	London, Rotterdam	7.9	9.2
3	L'Oreal	Clichy, France	5.9	6.4
4	Toyota	Toyota City, Japan	3.4	1.7
5	General Motors	Detroit	3.3	5.1
6	Volkswagen	Wolfsburg, Germany	3.2	7.9
7	Nestlé	Vevey, Switzerland	3.1	4.1
8	Coca-Cola	Atlanta	2.9	0.1
9	Mars Inc.	McLean, VA	2.9	22.1
10	PepsiCo	Purchase, NY	2.7	9.4
11	Sony Corp.	Tokyo	2.7	−13.2
12	McDonald's Corp.	Oak Brook, IL	2.7	1.8
13	Reckitt Benckiser	Slough, Berkshire, UK	2.5	6.8
14	Ford Motor Co.	Dearborn, MI	2.4	17.7
15	Nissan	Yokohama, Japan	2.2	11.9
16	Samsung	Seoul, South Korea	2.2	6.4
17	Johnson & Johnson	New Brunswick, NJ	2.1	12.7
18	Microsoft	Redmond, WA	2.0	46.8
19	Yum! Brands	Louisville, KY	1.9	15.9
20	Comcast	Philadelphia, PA	1.9	−5.5

Source: *Advertising Age,* 2014. Copyright © 2014 Crain Communication. Reprinted with permission.

only the United States. China ranked number five in 2007 and number ten in 2000. Will we see more evidence of economic problems in Japan in other exhibits to come?[15]

Global mass media advertising is a powerful tool for cultural change,[16] and as such, it receives continuing scrutiny by a wide variety of institutions. One important study has shown that advertising expenditures are generally cyclical, though less so in relationship-oriented countries where managers and regulators favor stability and long-term performance.[17] Most scholars agree that we are just beginning to understand some of the key issues involved in international advertising, but our knowledge will continue to be quite perishable as the revolution continues.

Exhibits 16.1 and 16.2 illustrate the biggest companies and product categories for international advertising. Procter & Gamble was the global champion of spending. The most outstanding datum in the two tables is the uniquely large decline in Sony's spending. This is just one sign of many of Japan's most recent economic woes. Also, we note that global advertising spending is more evenly spread across product/service categories than in previous years. For example, in 2010, ads for personal care items garnered 24 percent of the global total. We also broke out the spending patterns for two emerging markets in Exhibit 16.3a/b. Demonstrated is a key difference in stages of development between China and Russia. Although relatively low in position in Exhibit 16.3b, four Chinese firms appear on the list, but for Russia only one firm is local. We also note the historical dominance of Pepsi in Russia, where Coca-Cola still has not caught up since the days of vodka-for-Pepsi trades with the Soviet Union. Judging by the relative progress of the two countries on this single criterion, China looks like it

---

[15]Indeed, media spending is in decline across categories in Japan except for online advertising. Also, the two biggest Japanese advertisers, Toyota and Sony, rank #18 and #20 in growth of global ad expenditures among the top twenty global companies.

[16]Xin Zhao and Russell W. Belk, "Politicizing Consumer Culture: Advertising's Appropriation of Political Ideology in China's Social Transition," *Journal of Consumer Research* 35, no. 2 (2008), pp. 231–44.

[17]Barbara Deleersnyder, Marnik G. Dekimpe, Jan-Benedict E.M. Steenkamp, and Peter S.H. Leeflang, "The Role of National Culture in Advertising's Sensitivity to Business Cycles: An Investigation across Continents," *Journal of Marketing Research* 46, no. 5 (2009), pp. 623–36.

Exhibit 16.2

Top 100 Advertisers' Global
Spending by Category

Source: *Advertising Age,*
2014. Copyright © 2014 Crain
Communication. Reprinted with
permission.

Category	2013 (billions)	Percent Change from 2012	Percent of Total
Automotive	$16.5	3.6%	11.9%
Retail	16.1	0.2	11.6
Telecommunications, Internet services, ISP	11.2	6.0	8.1
General services	9.0	3.2	6.5
Food, beverages, candy	8.5	−1.2	6.1
Medicine and remedies	8.2	5.8	5.9
Financial services	7.6	−4.7	5.5
Personal care	7.1	2.1	5.1
Restaurants	6.3	5.3	4.6
Insurance	5.3	7.5	3.8

Exhibit 16.3a

Russia's Top Ten
Advertisers ($ millions)

Source: From Special Report
Global Marketing, *Advertising Age,*
2014. Copyright © 2014 Crain
Communication. Reprinted with
permission.

Advertiser	2013	Percent Change from 2012
Procter & Gamble	$89.5	−5.5%
PepsiCo	75.1	−1.3
Mars Inc.	73.3	−5.2
Unilever	69.8	−5.8
L'Oreal	58.1	−6.2
Nestle	49.9	−1.3
Henkel	43.6	−3.7
Novartis	40.6	−3.7
Sistema	38.9	4.9
RB (Reckitt Benckiser)	38.3	−4.2

Exhibit 16.3b

China's Top Ten
Advertisers ($ millions)

Source: From Special Report
Global Marketing, *Advertising Age,*
2014. Copyright © 2014 Crain
Communication. Reprinted with
permission.

Advertiser	2013	Percent Change from 2012
Procter & Gamble	$2460.2	36.1%
L'Oreal	1155.5	7.4
Unilever	1148.0	35.3
Alibaba Group	911.9	162.2
Mars Inc.	739.8	80.7
Yum! Brands	680.7	23.2
Hangzhou Wahaha Group	498.6	24.2
Coca-Cola	490.6	2.0
Guangdong Jiaduobao Drink & Food Co.	442.8	32.9
Tinghsin International Group	418.7	53.2

is further up the ladder of economic development. The Russian list includes only one local
company—Sistema is a holding company selling products and services across several categories including media, finance, petroleum, and retailing. Meanwhile China's list includes four
local companies with e-tailing giant Alibaba's spending exploding. The other three Chinese
companies sell food and/or beverages. Also, the contrast in growth of spending in the two
largest formerly communist countries is stark.

Of all the elements of the marketing mix, decisions involving advertising are those most
often affected by cultural differences among country markets. Consumers respond in terms
of their culture, style, feelings, value systems, attitudes, beliefs, and perceptions. Advertising's function is to interpret or translate the qualities of products and services in terms of
consumer needs, wants, desires, and aspirations. Thus, the emotional appeals, symbols,
persuasive approaches, and other characteristics of an advertisement must coincide with
cultural norms if the ad is to be effective.

Reconciling an international advertising campaign with the cultural uniqueness of markets is the challenge confronting the international or global marketer. The basic framework

and concepts of international advertising are essentially the same wherever employed. Seven steps are involved:

1. Perform marketing research.
2. Specify the goals of the communication.
3. Develop the most effective message(s) for the market segments selected.
4. Select effective media.
5. Compose and secure a budget based on what is required to meet goals.
6. Execute the campaign.
7. Evaluate the campaign relative to the goals specified.

Of these seven steps, developing messages almost always represents the most daunting task for international marketing managers. So, that topic is emphasized here. Nuances of international media are then discussed. Advertising agencies are ordinarily involved in all seven steps and are the subject of a separate section. Finally, the chapter closes with a discussion of broader issues of governmental controls on advertising.

Advertising Strategy and Goals

LO3

When global advertising is most effective; when modified advertising is necessary

The goals of advertising around the world vary substantially. For example, Chinese manufacturers are establishing new brands as their economy expands; Unilever is introducing a new product-line extension, Dove Shampoo, in East Asian markets; and Russia's airline Aeroflot is seeking to upgrade its quality image. All these marketing problems require careful marketing research and thoughtful and creative advertising campaigns in country, regional, and global markets.

Intense competition for world markets and the increasing sophistication of foreign consumers have led to the need for more sophisticated advertising strategies. Increased costs, problems of coordinating advertising programs in multiple countries, and a desire for a broader company or product image have caused multinational companies (MNCs) to seek greater control and efficiency without sacrificing local responsiveness. In the quest for more effective and responsive promotion programs, the policies covering centralized or decentralized authority, use of single or multiple foreign or domestic agencies, appropriation and allocation procedures, copy, media, and research are being examined. More and more multinational companies can be seen to be managing the balance between standardization of advertising themes and customization.[18] And recently, as described in Chapter 13, more companies are favoring the latter.

A case in point is the Gillette Company, which sells 800 products in more than 200 countries. Gillette has a consistent worldwide image as a masculine, sports-oriented company, but its products have no such consistent image. Its razors, blades, toiletries, and cosmetics are known by many names. Trac II blades in the United States are more widely known worldwide as G-II, and Atra blades are called Contour in Europe and Asia. Silkience hair conditioner is known as Soyance in France, Sientel in Italy, and Silkience in Germany. Whether or not global brand names could have been chosen for Gillette's many existing products is speculative. However, Gillette's current corporate philosophy of globalization provides for an umbrella statement, "Gillette, the Best a Man Can Get," in all advertisements for men's toiletries products in the hope of providing some common image.

A similar situation exists for Unilever, which sells a cleaning liquid called Vif in Switzerland, Viss in Germany, Jif in Britain and Greece, and Cif in France. This situation is a result of Unilever marketing separately to each of these countries. At this point, it would be difficult for Gillette or Unilever to standardize their brand names, because each brand is established in its market and therefore has equity. Nortel Networks has used a "local heroes" approach in its international advertising. The company picks local celebrities to pitch standardized messages across national markets for its telecommunications services.

---

[18]Charles R. Taylor, "Who Standardizes Advertising More Frequently, and Why Do They Do So? A Comparison of U.S. and Japanese Subsidiaries' Advertising Practices in the European Union," *Journal of International Marketing* 14 (2006), pp. 98–120; Kineta H. Hung, Stella Yiyan Li, and Russell W. Belk, "Global Understandings: Female Readers' Perceptions of the New Woman in Chinese Advertising," *Journal of International Business Studies* 38 (2007), pp. 1034–51.

These vehicular ads make an effective advertising medium even in a dense London fog. Because most London cabs are black, the Snickers ad catches the eye immediately.

In many cases, standardized products may be marketed globally. But because of differences in cultures, they still require a different advertising appeal in different markets. For instance, Ford's model advertising varies by nation because of language and societal nuances. Ford advertises the affordability of its Escort in the United States, where the car is seen as entry level. But in India, Ford launched the Escort as a premium car. "It's not unusual to see an Escort with a chauffeur there," said a Ford executive.

Finally, many companies are using market segmentation strategies that ignore national boundaries—business buyers or high-income consumers across the globe are often targeted in advertising, for example. Others are proposing newer global market segments defined by "consumer cultures" related to shared sets of consumption-related symbols—convenience, youth, America, internationalism/cosmopolitan orientation,[19] and humanitarianism are examples. Other, more traditional segments are product and region related; those are discussed next.

Product Attribute and Benefit Segmentation

As discussed in the chapters on product and services development (Chapters 13 and 14), a market offering really is a bundle of satisfactions the buyer receives. This package of satisfactions, or utilities, includes the primary function of the product or service, along with many other benefits imputed by the values and customs of the culture. Different cultures often seek the same value or benefits from the primary function of a product—for example, the ability of an automobile to get from point A to point B, a camera to take a picture, or a wristwatch to tell time. But while usually agreeing on the benefit of the primary function of a product, consumers may perceive other features and psychological attributes of the item differently.

Consider the different market-perceived needs for a camera. In the United States, excellent pictures with easy, foolproof operation are expected by most of the market; in Germany and Japan, a camera must take excellent pictures, but the camera must also be state of the art in design. In Africa, where penetration of cameras is less than 20 percent of the households, the concept of picture taking must be sold. In all three markets, excellent pictures are expected (i.e., the primary function of a camera is demanded), but the additional utility or satisfaction derived from a camera differs among cultures. Many products produce expectations beyond the common benefit sought by all.

Dannon's brand of yogurt promotes itself as the brand that understands the relationship between health and food, but it communicates the message differently, depending on the market. In the United States, where Dannon yogurt is seen as a healthy, vibrant food, the brand celebrates its indulgent side. In France, however, Dannon was seen as too pleasure oriented. Therefore, Dannon created the Institute of Health, a real research center dedicated to food and education. The end result is the same message but communicated differently—a careful balance of health and pleasure.

The Blue Diamond Growers Association's advertising of almonds is an excellent example of the fact that some products are best advertised only on a local basis. Blue Diamond had a very

[19]Petra Riefler, Adamantios Diamantopoulos, and Judy A. Siguaw, "Cosmopolitan Consumers as a Target Group for Segmentations," *Journal of International Business Studies* 43 (2013), pp. 285–305.

iPhone 5s

Lumia 635

Hello, Tim.

try "What do I have next?"
see more

cortana when my wife calls
remind me to tell her happy
anniversary

Screens simulated; sequences shortened.

MICROSOFT ADAPTS, LESSONS FROM THE FIELD

Corporate and advertising strategies at Microsoft have been evolving fast in recent years. Satya Nadella has taken over as the company's third CEO. The new organization of the company reflects the dynamism of both cloud and mobile technologies. The acquisition of Nokia's Devices and Services business for over $7 billion in 2014 demonstrated its commitment to mobile devices.

In that same year the topline revenues of the firm were more than $86 billion. The three major sources of that income were Commercial Licensing at $42 billion, Device and Consumer Licensing at almost $19 billion, and Computing and Gaming Hardware at almost $10 billion. The two big expense categories were R&D (44,000 employees) at $11.3 billion and marketing and sales (30,000 employees) at $15.3 billion. The latter included $2.3 billion in advertising expenditures. All very big numbers.

We talked with executives there about some of the challenges they faced in the dynamic global environment of that year. Below we present just one of their very interesting stories.

Mobile Phones and Services, The Challenger Campaign.

The purchase of Nokia put Microsoft marketers in an unfamiliar position. For most of the company's history they have lead the markets in which they've operated. But, with mobile phones Samsung and Apple are dominating competitors. So how should David compare itself to the Goliaths? The decision was made to take a "challenger" position and focus on a competitive appeal based on the superior performance[1] of Microsoft's Cortana personal assistant built into the Windows Phone 8.1. The superiority claim comes partially from the learning and information proactivity that also protects the privacy of users in ways that Apple's Siri cannot.

In this series of ads you can see the company's strategic shift in its advertising. In previous campaigns the advertisements presented how Microsoft products can provide solutions for your life problems. Now, however,

Este não

Este é o Lumia 530 Dual SIM

A ja kupię sobie lepszy smartfon

Moja Lumia 930. Uwielbiam ją.

the advertisements show how Microsoft products can provide better solutions compared to its competitors' products.

In the U.S. a comparative advertising campaign is a relatively straightforward proposition. As you can see in the still photograph from an animated commercial the iPhone and the Lumia were placed side-by-side, and the script included a conversation between a very smart Cortana and a rather simple Siri. The conversation ends with a befuddled Siri saying, "I remember when I was the only phone that talked." Or, in other executions, the commercial ends with Siri commenting on how smart Cortana is, "Now that is a smart phone!" says an enlightened Siri after learning about some of Cortana's unique features.

In many other countries around the world (such as Russia, India, Italy, or Brazil), however, comparative advertising is a touchy subject if allowed at all. This becomes a strategic advertising challenge when considering the desire to have a globally consistent and relevant campaign. Thus we see two adaptations to the original imagery and copy below. First, in Vietnam instead of directly presenting a competitor, the other device is presented as a wrapped gift. It is implied that the gift could be an Apple or a Samsung or another type of gift as it is left to the imagination of the consumer. Although a direct comparison is not made, the viewers can easily fill in the blank and take away the competitive message. A similar effect is achieved in the Poland spot. This time, a pair of hands is shown to represent a consumer waiting to buy a new phone. Without directly portraying a device, the advertisement invites the viewers to elicit a competitor's phone. Once the competitor is established in viewer's mind, the same competitive objective can be achieved.

Finally we note that Cortana is available for specific regions only. In the regions where the service is offered, her voice is adapted to match the everyday language, culture and speech patterns of the country its user lives in. For example, the UK version of Cortana speaks with a British accent and uses British idioms, while the Chinese version, known as Xiao Na, speaks Mandarin Chinese and has an icon featuring a face to go along with the voice.

[1]This claim was well supported by a direct comparison of Cortana, Siri, and Google Now (also a personal assistant feature for Android phones) that appeared in PC Magazine at the time. See Michael Muchmore, "Cortana vs. Google Now vs. Siri: Which Voic Assistant Wins?" *pcmag.com*, May 13, 2014.

successful ad campaign in the United States showing almond growers knee-deep in almonds while pleading with the audience, "A can a week, that's all we ask." The objective of the campaign was to change the perception of almonds as a special-occasion treat to an everyday snack food. The campaign was a success; in addition to helping change the perception of almonds as a snack food, it received millions of dollars' worth of free publicity for Blue Diamond from regional and national news media. The successful U.S. ad was tested in Canada for possible use outside the United States. The Canadian reaction was vastly different; to them, the whole idea was just too silly. And further, Canadians prefer to buy products from Canadian farmers, not American farmers. This response led to the decision to study each market closely and design an advertisement for each country market. The only similarity among commercials airing in markets in New York, Tokyo, Moscow, Toronto, or Stockholm is the Blue Diamond logo.

Regional Segmentation

The emergence of pan-European communications media is enticing many companies to push the balance toward more standardized promotional efforts. As media coverage across Europe expands, it will become more common for markets to be exposed to multiple messages and brands of the same product. To avoid the confusion that results when a market is exposed to multiple brand names and advertising messages, as well as for reasons of efficiency, companies strive for harmony in brand names, advertising, and promotions across Europe.

Along with changes in behavior patterns, legal restrictions are slowly being eliminated, and viable market segments across country markets are emerging. Although Europe will never be a single homogeneous market for every product, that does not mean that companies should shun the idea of developing European-wide promotional programs. A pan-European promotional strategy would mean identifying a market segment across all European countries and designing a promotional concept appealing to market segment similarities.

The Message: Creative Challenges

Global Advertising and the Communications Process

LO4

The communication process and advertising misfires

International communications may fail for a variety of reasons: A message may not get through because of media inadequacy, the message may be received by the intended audience but not be understood because of different cultural interpretations,[20] or the message may reach the intended audience and be understood but have no effect because the marketer did not correctly assess the needs and wants or even the thinking processes[21] of the target market.

In the international communications process, each of the seven identifiable steps ultimately can affect the accuracy of the message. As illustrated in Exhibit 16.4, the process consists of the following:

1. **An information source.** An international marketing executive with a product message to communicate.

2. **Encoding.** The message from the source converted into effective symbolism for transmission to a receiver.

3. **A message channel.** The sales force and/or advertising media that convey the encoded message to the intended receiver.

4. **Decoding.** The interpretation by the receiver of the symbolism transmitted from the information source.

5. **Receiver.** Consumer action by those who receive the message and are the target for the thought transmitted.

6. **Feedback.** Information about the effectiveness of the message that flows from the receiver (the intended target) back to the information source for evaluation of the effectiveness of the process.

[20]Ana Valenzuela, Barbara Mellers, and Judy Strebel, "Pleasurable Surprises: A Cross-Cultural Study of Consumer Responses to Unexpected Incentives," *Journal of Consumer Research* 36 (2010).

[21]Jennifer Aaker, "Accessibility or Diagnosticity? Disentangling the Influence of Culture on Persuasion Processes and Attitudes," *Journal of Consumer Research* 26, no. 4 (March 2000), pp. 340–57.

Exhibit 16.4
The International
Communications Process

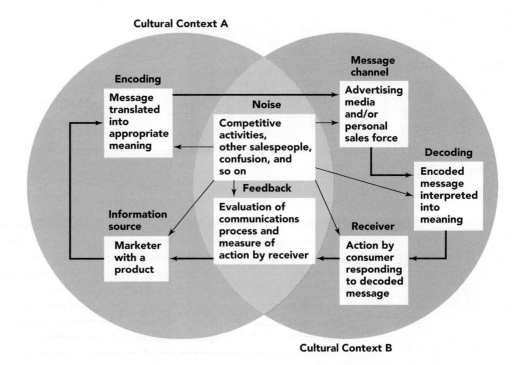

7. **Noise.** Uncontrollable and unpredictable influences such as competitive activities and confusion that detract from the process and affect any or all of the other six steps.

Unfortunately, the process is not as simple as just sending a message via a medium to a receiver and being certain that the intended message sent is the same one perceived by the receiver. In Exhibit 16.4, the communications process steps are encased in Cultural Context A and Cultural Context B to illustrate the influences complicating the process when the message is encoded in one culture and decoded in another. If not properly considered, the different cultural contexts can increase the probability of misunderstandings. Research in the area suggests that effective communication demands the existence of a "psychological overlap" between the sender and the receiver; otherwise, a message falling outside the receiver's perceptual field may transmit an unintended meaning. It is in this area that even the most experienced companies make blunders.

Most promotional misfires or mistakes in international marketing are attributable to one or several of these steps not properly reflecting cultural influences or a general lack of knowledge about the target market. Referring to Exhibit 16.4, the information source is a marketer with a product to sell to a specific target market. The product message to be conveyed should reflect the needs and wants of the target market; however, often the actual market needs and the marketer's perception of them do not coincide. This disconnect is especially true when the marketer relies more on the self-reference criterion (SRC) than on effective research. It can never be assumed that "if it sells well in one country, it will sell in another." For instance, bicycles designed and sold in the United States to consumers fulfilling recreational exercise needs are not sold as effectively for the same reason in a market where the primary use of the bicycle is transportation. Cavity-reducing fluoride toothpaste sells well in the United States, where healthy teeth are perceived as important, but has limited appeal in markets such as Great Britain and the French areas of Canada, where the reason for buying toothpaste is breath control. From the onset of the communications process, if basic needs are incorrectly defined, communications fail because an incorrect or meaningless message is received, even though the remaining steps in the process are executed properly.

The encoding step causes problems even with a "proper" message. At this step, such factors as color,[22] timing, values, beliefs, humor, tastes, and appropriateness of spokespersons[23] can cause the international marketer to symbolize the message incorrectly. For example, the

---

[22]Elizabeth G. Miller, "Shades of Meaning: The Effect of Color and Flavor Names on Consumer Choice," *Journal of Consumer Research* 32 (2005), pp. 86–92.

[23]Drew Martin and Arch G. Woodside, "Dochakuka: Melding Global Inside Local: Foreign-Domestic Advertising Assimilation in Japan," *Journal of Global Marketing* 21 (2007), pp. 19–32.

Red Works! Indeed, it is the most popular color used in national flags, appearing in 31% of them. ["What is the Most Patriotic Color?" *Time*, September 8–15, 2014, p. 42.] Since we first wrote about the color's power some 15 years ago, a lot has been happening.[24] Notice the Coke advantage at work—the red contrasts with the outdoor environment, while the Cristal aqua blends more with the blue sky and trees. Cristal is a popular brand of bottled water actually owned by Coca-Cola and sold in the Yucatan Peninsula in Mexico. The Coke ads are emblazoned on a café in the central plaza of Canas, Costa Rica. Or you can spend it like Beckham—in addition to Vodafone and Nike on his jersey, David Beckham, here in his Manchester United red, also represented Pepsi, Adidas, Castrol, Upper Deck, Marks & Spencer, Police, Meiji, Tokyo Beauty Center, etc., etc., etc. The Spanish soccer power Real Madrid spent $40 million buying Beckham's contract from his British home team, and then the Los Angeles Galaxy moved him there. One disadvantage of the moves south—the white jerseys of the Spanish and American teams don't catch the eye as did the Manchester United red.[25] Most recently Beckham has teamed up with the Red campaign (along with Oprah and Bono) to promote products of firms that donate revenues to the Global Fund to Fight AIDS. Other firms involved in the project include Dell, Microsoft, American Express, Armani, Converse, Hallmark, Apple, and The Gap.[26] We also note that the world's most famous athlete is not Beckham, or even last-day-red-shirt-wearing Tiger Woods. Instead, it's Formula 1 racecar driver Michael Schumacher. The German has made more money than any other sports figure as he dominated the sport most watched on television globally. And the flamboyant red jumpsuit and red Ferraris helped. The other red brands—Marlboro and Vodafone—loved him too. Alas, now Schumacher, like Beckham, shed his original Ferrari red for Mercedes white, and his performance lagged. Maybe it was the color? Finally, we are sad to report that Schumacher suffered severe brain damage in 2014, not in a crash on the race track, but on a ski hill.[27]

[24]Elisabeth A. Sullivan, "Color Me Profitable," *Marketing News*, October 15, 2008, p. 8; Andrew J. Ellion and Daniela Niesta, "Romantic Red: Red Enhances Men's Attraction to Women," *Journal of Personality and Social Psychology* 95, no. 5 (2008), pp. 1150–64; Ravi Mehta and Rui (Juliet) Zhu, "Blue or Red? Exploring the Effect of Color on Cognitive Task Performances," *Science* 323 (2009), pp. 1226–29.

[25]Kristen Korosec, "Manchester United Red," *Marketing News,* September 30, 2010, pp. 14–18.

[26]Ron Nixon, "Little Green for (Red)," *The New York Times,* February 6, 2008, pp. C1, C5.

[27]"Schumacher Moved to Family Estate," *The New York Times*, September 10, 2014, p. B12.

Why would both Coke and McDonald's shed their eye-catching red logos for black and white? You can see the answers at the bottom of page 523 at the end of this chapter. The stadium pictured is in Buenos Aires, is popularly called *La Bombonera,* is officially named *Alberto Armano,* is the home of the club team *Boca Junior,* and was the home team for Argentina's most famous *futbol* player ever, Maradona. The McDonald's (yes, the arches are usually gold, but the brand name is red) sits adjacent to the city square in the old Inca Empire capital at Cuzco, Peru. Finally, even PepsiCo is blushing over Coke's dominance: It's introducing an all-red can in China. If it succeeds there, perhaps Pepsi will just match other countries' flags as well—red, white, and blue works not only in the United States but in Russia and France as well.

marketer wants the product to convey coolness so the color green is used; however, people in the tropics might decode green as dangerous or associate it with disease. Another example of the encoding process misfiring was a perfume presented against a backdrop of rain that, for Europeans, symbolized a clean, cool, refreshing image but to Africans was a symbol of fertility. The ad prompted many viewers to ask if the perfume was effective against infertility.

Problems of literacy, media availability, and types of media create challenges in the communications process at the encoding step. Message channels must be carefully selected if an encoded message is to reach the consumer. Errors such as using the Internet as a medium when only a small percentage of an intended market has access to the Internet, or using print media for a channel of communications when the majority of the intended users cannot read or do not read the language in the medium, are examples of ineffective media channel selection in the communications process.

Decoding problems are generally created by improper encoding, which caused such errors as Pepsi's "Come Alive" slogan being decoded as "Come out of the grave." Chevrolet's brand name for the Nova model (which means new star) was decoded into Spanish as *No Va!,* meaning "it doesn't go." In another misstep, a translation that was supposed to be decoded as "hydraulic ram" was instead decoded as "wet sheep." In a Nigerian ad, a platinum blonde sitting next to the driver of a Renault was intended to enhance the image of the automobile. However, the model was perceived as not respectable and so created a feeling of shame. An ad used for Eveready Energizer batteries with the Energizer bunny was seen by Hungarian consumers as touting a bunny toy, not a battery.

Decoding errors may also occur accidentally, as was the case with Colgate-Palmolive's selection of the brand name Cue for toothpaste. The brand name was not intended to have any symbolism; nevertheless, it was decoded by the French into a pornographic word. In some cases, the intended symbolism has no meaning to the decoder. In an ad transferred from the United States, the irony of tough-guy actor Tom Selleck standing atop a mountain with a steaming mug of Lipton tea was lost on eastern Europeans.

Errors at the receiver end of the process generally result from a combination of factors: an improper message resulting from incorrect knowledge of use patterns, poor encoding producing a meaningless message, poor media selection that does not get the message to the receiver, or inaccurate decoding by the receiver so that the message is garbled or incorrect. Even bad luck comes into play. Recall that French's mustard was boycotted (along with French wines, fries, etc.) by Americans when the Paris government did not go along with the attack on Iraq in 2003—even though the brand name has nothing to do with the country and is an American brand.

City streets in Singapore are alive with advertising. California Fitness Centers in Southeast Asia are owned by America's 24-hour Fitness Centers. Obviously the image of "bodyland" southern California sells well around the world. However, there's an interesting irony in that brand name for Muslim customers. The word *California* first appears in the eleventh-century epic poem *The Song of Roland;* there it literally means the "caliph's domain"—the Caliph of Baghdad ruled the Islamic Empire then. The Spaniards who named California in the early 1500s thought they were in Asia! Moreover, the deeper meaning of the brand name is lost even on the modern Muslims who comprise 15 percent of Singapore's current population!

Finally, the feedback step of the communications process is important as a check on the effectiveness of the other steps. Companies that do not measure their communications efforts are likely to allow errors of source, encoding, media selection, decoding, or receiver to continue longer than necessary. In fact, a proper feedback system (ad testing) allows a company to correct errors before substantial damage occurs.

In addition to the problems inherent in the steps outlined, the effectiveness of the international communications process can be impaired by noise. Noise comprises all other external influences, such as competitive advertising, other sales personnel, and confusion at the receiving end, that can detract from the ultimate effectiveness of the communication. Noise is a disruptive force interfering with the process at any step and is frequently beyond the control of the sender or the receiver. As Exhibit 16.4 illustrates with the overlapping cultural contexts, noise can emanate from activity in either culture or be caused by the influences of the overlapping of the cultural contexts.

The model's significance is that one or all steps in the process, cultural factors, or the marketer's SRC can affect the ultimate success of the communication. For example, the message, encoding, media, and intended receiver can be designed perfectly, but the inability of the receiver to decode may render the final message inoperative. In developing advertising messages, the international marketer can effectively use this model as a guide to help ensure that all potential constraints and problems are considered so that the final communication received and the action taken correspond with the intent of the source.

The growing intensity of international competition, coupled with the complexity of multinational marketing, demands that the international advertiser function at the highest creative level. The creative task is made more daunting by other kinds of barriers to effective communications—legal, linguistic, cultural, media, production, and cost considerations.

Legal Constraints

LO5

The effects of a single European market on advertising

Laws that control comparative advertising vary from country to country in Europe. In Germany, it is illegal to use any comparative terminology; you can be sued by a competitor if you do. Belgium and Luxembourg explicitly ban comparative advertising, whereas it is clearly authorized in the United Kingdom, Ireland, Spain, and Portugal. The directive covering comparative advertising allows implicit comparisons that do not name competitors but bans explicit comparisons between named products. The European Commission issued several directives to harmonize the laws governing advertising. However, member states are given substantial latitude to cover issues under their jurisdiction. Many fear that if the laws are not harmonized, member states may close their borders to advertising that does not respect their national rules.

Comparative advertising is heavily regulated in other parts of the world as well. In Asia, an advertisement showing chimps choosing Pepsi over Coke was banned from most satellite television; the phrase "the leading cola" was accepted only in the Philippines. An Indian court ordered Lever to cease claiming that its New Pepsodent toothpaste was "102% better" than the leading brand. Colgate, the leading brand, was never mentioned in the advertisement, though a model was shown mouthing the word "Colgate" and the image was accompanied by a "ting" sound recognized in all Colgate ads as the ring of confidence. Banning explicit comparisons will rule out an effective advertising approach heavily used by U.S. companies at home and in other countries where it is permitted. Finally, even as comparative advertising restrictions are lifted, international marketers will have to carefully consider consumers' responses to novel advertising campaigns in this genre.[28]

A variety of restrictions on advertising of specific products exist around the world. Advertising of pharmaceuticals is restricted in many countries. For example, critics in Canada complain that laws there have not been revised in 50 years and have been rendered obsolete by the advent of TV and, more recently, the Internet. Toy, tobacco, and liquor advertising is restricted in numerous countries. The French government until recently forbade TV ads for retailers, publishing, cinema, and the press.

Advertising on television is strictly controlled in many countries. China is relaxing some regulations while strengthening others. For example, recently the government began to require concrete proof of ad claims and banned pigs in advertising—the latter in deference to its Muslim minorities. While the Chinese government is doing little to regulate product placement advertisements, the European Union limits product placement in foreign programming but not EU-produced material. In Kuwait, the government-controlled TV network allows only 32 minutes of advertising per day, in the evening. Commercials are controlled to exclude superlative descriptions, indecent words, fearful or shocking shots, indecent clothing or dancing, contests, hatred or revenge shots, ethnic derision, and attacks on competition. Russian law forbids subliminal advertising, but it is still prevalent there because enforcement resources are lacking.

Some country laws against accessibility to broadcast media seem to be softening. Australia ended a ban on cable television spots, and Malaysia is considering changing the rules to allow foreign commercials to air on newly legalized satellite signals. However, with rare exceptions, all commercials on Malaysian television still must be made in Malaysia.

Companies that rely on television infomercials and television shopping are restricted by the limitations placed on the length and number of television commercials permitted when their programs are classified as advertisements. The levels of restrictions in the European Union vary widely, from no advertising on the BBC in the United Kingdom to member states that limit advertising to a maximum of 15 percent of programming daily. The Television without Frontiers directive permits stricter or more detailed rules to the broadcasters under jurisdiction of each member state. In Germany, for example, commercials must be spaced at least 20 minutes apart and total ad time may not exceed 12 minutes per hour. Commercial stations in the United Kingdom are limited to 7 minutes per hour.

Internet services are especially vulnerable as EU member states decide which area of regulation should apply to these services. Barriers to pan-European services will arise if some member states opt to apply television-broadcasting rules to the Internet while other countries apply print-media advertising rules. The good news is that the European Union is addressing the issue of regulation of activities on the Internet. Although most of the attention will be focused on domain names and Internet addresses, the European Commission does recognize that online activities will be severely hampered if subject to fragmented regulation.

Some countries have special taxes that apply to advertising, which might restrict creative freedom in media selection. The tax structure in Austria best illustrates how advertising taxation can distort media choice by changing the cost ratios of various media: Federal

---

[28]Carolyn White Nye, Martin S. Roth, and Terence A. Shimp, "Comparative Advertising in Markets where Brands and Comparative Advertising Are Novel," *Journal of International Business Studies* 39, no. 5 (2008), pp. 851–63.

states, with the exception of Burgenland and Tyrol, tax. ad insertions at 10 percent; states and municipalities tax posters at 10 to 30 percent. Radio advertising carries a 10 percent tax, except in Tyrol, where it is 20 percent. Salzburg, Steiermark, Kärnten, and Vorarlberg impose no tax. There is a uniform tax of 10 percent throughout the country on television ads. Cinema advertising has a 10 percent tax in Vienna, 20 percent in Burgenland, and 30 percent in Steiermark. There is no cinema tax in the other federal states.

Linguistic Limitations

Language is one of the major barriers to effective communication through advertising. The problem involves different languages of different countries, different languages[29] or dialects within one country, and the subtler problems of linguistic nuance, argument style,[30] vernacular, and even accent. Indeed, recently an Irish accent was voted "sexiest" in Britain and Ireland, beating the competition from the Scots, Welsh, Geordies, Brummies, West Country, and "posh English" contenders. For many countries language is a matter of cultural pride and preservation—France is the best example, of course.

Incautious handling of language has created problems in all countries.[31] Some examples suffice. Chrysler Corporation was nearly laughed out of Spain when it translated its U.S. theme that advertised "Dart Is Power." To the Spanish, the phrase implied that buyers sought, but lacked, sexual vigor. The Bacardi Company concocted a fruity bitters with a made-up name, Pavane, suggestive of French chic. Bacardi wanted to sell the drink in Germany, but Pavane is perilously close to *pavian,* which means "baboon." A company marketing tomato paste in the Middle East found that in Arabic the phrase "tomato paste" translates as "tomato glue." In Spanish-speaking countries, you have to be careful of words that have different meanings in the different countries. The word *ball* translates in Spanish as *bola,* which means ball in one country, revolution in another, a lie or fabrication in another, and an obscenity in yet another. Most recently, the product name iPad has raised issues around the world. Even in the United States, women reflexively relate the word "pad" to hygiene products. In Ireland consumers complain that the names iPod and iPad sound exactly the same, and Japanese does not have a sound for the letter "a" in iPad. Adding injury to insult, but in a legal way, other companies in the United States, Switzerland, and Japan already have trademarks for the name.[32]

Tropicana brand orange juice was advertised as *jugo de China* in Puerto Rico, but when transported to Miami's Cuban community, it failed. To the Puerto Rican, *China* translated into *orange,* but to the Cuban-American it was China the country—and the Cuban-Americans were not in the market for "communist" juice. "A whole new range of products" in a German advertisement came out as "a whole new stove of products."

Language raises innumerable barriers that impede effective, idiomatic translation and thereby hamper communication. This barrier is especially apparent in advertising materials and on the Internet. Abstraction, terse writing, and word economy, the most effective tools of the advertiser, pose problems for translators. Communication is impeded by the great diversity of cultural heritage and education that exists within countries and that causes varying interpretations of even single sentences and simple concepts. Some companies have tried to solve the translation problem by hiring foreign translators who live in the United States. This option often is not satisfactory because both the language and the translator change, so the expatriate in the United States is out of touch after a few years. Everyday words have different meanings in different cultures. Even spelling and pronunciation can cause problems: Wrigley had trouble selling its Spearmint gum in Germany until it changed the spelling to Speermint.

---

[29]David Luna and Laura A. Peracchio, "Advertising to Bilingual Consumers: The Impact of Code-Switching on Persuasion," *Journal of Consumer Research* 31, no. 2 (2005), pp. 57–73; David Luna, Dawn Lerman, and Laura A. Peracchio, "Structural Constraints in Code-Switched Advertising," *Journal of Consumer Research* 32 (2005), pp. 416–23.

[30]Lefa Teng and Michel Laroche, "Interactive Effects of Appeals, Arguments, and Competition across North American and Chinese Cultures," *Journal of International Marketing* 14 (2006), pp. 110–28; Sharon Begley, "What's in a Word," *Newsweek,* January 8, 2010, p. 31.

[31]See http://www.engrish.com for a wide range of (mostly) humorous translation problems related to the use of English for Japanese products, signage, and so on.

[32]Brad Stone, "What's in a Name? For Apple, iPad Said More than Intended," *The New York Times,* January 10, 2010, pp. A1, A3.

In addition to translation challenges, low literacy in many countries seriously impedes communications and calls for greater creativity and use of verbal media. Multiple languages within a country or advertising area pose another problem for the advertiser. Even a tiny country such as Switzerland has four separate languages. The melting-pot character of the Israeli population accounts for some 50 languages. A Jerusalem commentator says that even though Hebrew "has become a negotiable instrument of daily speech, this has yet to be converted into advertising idiom." And, we are only just beginning to learn the complex of considerations regarding advertising to bilinguals.[33] Advertising communications must be perfect, and linguistic differences at all levels cause problems. In-country testing with the target consumer group is the only way to avoid such problems.

[33]Aradhna Krihna and Rohini Ahluwalia, "Language Choice in Advertising to Bilinguals: Asymmetric Effects for Multinationals versus Local Firms," *Journal of Consumer Research* 35, no. 4 (2008), pp. 692–705; Jaime Noriega and Edward Blair, "Advertising to Bilinguals: Does the Language of Advertising Influence the Nature of Thoughts?" *Journal of Marketing* 72, no. 5 (2008), pp. 69–83.

The "true ting" in Jamaica is a grapefruit-flavored soft drink. The slogan is, of course, a take-off on "the real thing" advertising of Coca-Cola some decades ago. "Ting" is obviously a Creole version of "thing" for Jamaicans. Perhaps the best billboards ever are the giant bulls posted on hillsides around rural Spain. They were originally meant to advertise Osborne Brandy, but they have evolved into a national symbol. Not even Coca-Cola can make that strong a claim. Finally, GE joined with the Chinese government in promoting a green Beijing Olympics. Ironically, many folks around the world see outdoor advertising itself as a kind of pollution!

绿色创想

CROSSING BORDERS 16.2   How Do You Say "Tapestry" in Swedish?

"Translating from one language to another, unless it is from Greek and Latin, the queens of all languages, is like looking at Flemish tapestries from the wrong side, for although the figures are visible, they are covered by threads that obscure them, and cannot be seen with the smoothness and color of the right side." So said Miguel Cervantes in *Don Quixote*.

In Thailand, is Redalen (a) a town in Norway, (b) a bed sold by Swedish furniture chain IKEA, or (c) something that sounds uncomfortably close to getting to third base?

The answer, it turns out, is all three. IKEA is famous for using tongue-twisting Scandinavian names to help identify its sofas and beds. But as the big-box retailer expands into fast-growing new markets, it is discovering that those hard-to-pronounce names can also have other meanings—and that spells trouble in other languages.

Take Thailand, for example. IKEA launched a new super-store here late last year, its fifth largest. It is packed with shoppers seeking bargains among the flat-pack, assemble-it-yourself furniture or wolfing down Swedish meatballs in the IKEA restaurant.

Reading a standard IKEA catalog aloud, though, can draw strange looks, or worse. Besides the *Redalen* bed, there is the very nice *Jättebra* plant pot, which can sound in part like a crude Thai term for sex, and a host of other problematic words.

To solve that problem, IKEA is saying *adjö* (Swedish for *adieu*) to unintentionally saucy product names and *hej* (hello) to a team of Thai speakers who modify terms so they can't be so easily misinterpreted.

"The Swedish . . . words are important because they bring a unique character to the brand," says one member of the team, Natthita Opaspipat. She spent nearly four years preparing for the launch of IKEA's Bangkok store by carefully scrutinizing terms to see how they sounded in Thai before transliterating them into Thailand's cursive, Sanskrit-influenced alphabet. In some cases, she and other team members change a vowel sound or a consonant to prevent unfortunate misunderstandings.

The ironic part of this Crossing Borders is that, at the top, you read Cervantes in translation!

Source: James Hookway, "Swedish Retailer Hires Local Linguists to Police Racy Translations," *The Wall Street Journal*, June 5, 2012, pp. A1, 16.

Cultural Diversity

The problems associated with communicating to people in diverse cultures present one of the great creative challenges in advertising. One advertising executive puts it bluntly: "International advertising is almost uniformly dreadful mostly because people don't understand language and culture." Communication is more difficult because cultural factors largely determine the way various phenomena are perceived.[34] If the perceptual framework is different, perception of the message itself differs.[35]

Existing perceptions based on tradition and heritages often render advertising campaigns ineffective or worse. For example, marketing researchers in Hong Kong found that cheese is associated with *Yeung-Yen* (foreigners) and thus rejected by some Chinese. Toyota introduced the Prado SUV in China only to learn that the name sounded like the Chinese word for "rule by force." This

---

[34]Nader T. Tavassoli and Yih Hwai Lee, "The Differential Interaction of Auditory and Visual Advertising Elements with Chinese and English," *Journal of Marketing Research* 40, no. 4 (2003), pp. 468–80; Guillaume D. Johnson, Roger M. Elliott, and Sonya A. Grier, "Conceptualizing Multicultural Advertising Effects in the 'New' South Africa," Journal of Global Marketing 23, no. 3 (2010), pp. 171–76; Edwin J. Nijssen and Susan P. Douglas, "Consumer World-Mindedness and Attitudes toward Product Positioning in Advertising: An Examination of Global versus Foreign versus Local Positioning," *Journal of International Marketing* 19, no. 3 (2011), pp. 113–32; Gianfranco Walsh, Edward Shiu, and Louise M. Hassan, "Cross-National Advertising and Behavioral Intentions: A Multilevel Analysis," *Journal of International Marketing* 22, no. 1 (2014), pp. 77–97.

[35]Some of the most important work being done in the area of culture and advertising is represented by Jennifer Aaker and Patti Williams's "Empathy and Pride: The Influence of Emotional Appeals across Cultures," *Journal of Consumer Research* 25 (December 1998), pp. 241–61; Ulrich R. Orth and Denisa Holancova, "Men's and Women's Responses to Sex Role Portrayals in Advertisements," *International Journal of Research in Marketing* 21, no. 1 (2004), pp. 77–88; Aysen Bakir, "Character Portrayal: Examining Gender Roles in Television Commercials Targeted at Children in India and the United States," *Journal of Global Marketing* 26, no. 2 (2013), pp. 57–67.

name reminded some Chinese of the 1937 invasion by Japan—not a nice memory at all. The effectiveness of sex appeals,[36] music,[37] and celebrities[38] varies across cultures as well.

Procter & Gamble's initial advertisement for Pampers brand diapers failed because of cultural differences between the United States and Japan. A U.S. commercial that showed an animated stork delivering Pampers diapers to homes was dubbed into Japanese with the U.S. package replaced by the Japanese package and put on the air. To P&G's dismay, the advertisement failed to build the market. Some belated consumer research revealed that consumers were confused about why this bird was delivering disposable diapers. According to Japanese folklore, giant peaches that float on the river bring babies to deserving parents, not storks.

In addition to concerns with differences among nations, advertisers find that subcultures within a country require attention.[39] People in Hong Kong have 10 different patterns of breakfast eating. The youth of a country almost always constitute a different consuming culture from the older people, and urban dwellers differ significantly from rural dwellers. Besides these differences, there is the problem of changing traditions. In all countries, people of all ages, urban or rural, cling to their heritage to a certain degree but are willing to change some areas of behavior. Indeed, due to the early efforts of Nestlé and the most recent expansion by Starbucks, in tea-drinking Japan, coffee has become the fashionable beverage for younger people and urban dwellers who like to think of themselves as cosmopolitan and sophisticated.

Media Limitations

Media are discussed at length later, so here we note only that limitations on creative strategy imposed by media may diminish the role of advertising in the promotional program and may force marketers to emphasize other elements of the promotional mix. A marketer's creativity is certainly challenged when a television commercial is limited to 10 showings a year with no two exposures closer than 10 days, as is the case in Italy. Creative advertisers in some countries have even developed their own media for overcoming media limitations. In some African countries, advertisers run boats up and down the rivers playing popular music and broadcasting commercials into rural areas as they travel.

Production and Cost Limitations

Creativity is especially important when a budget is small or where there are severe production limitations, such as poor-quality printing and a lack of high-grade paper. For example, the poor quality of high-circulation glossy magazines and other quality publications in eastern Europe has caused Colgate-Palmolive to depart from its customary heavy use of print media for other forms. Newsprint is of such low quality in China that a color ad used by Kodak in the West is not an option. Kodak's solution has been to print a single-sheet color insert as a newspaper supplement.

The necessity for low-cost reproduction in small markets poses another problem in many countries. For example, hand-painted billboards must be used instead of printed sheets because the limited number of billboards does not warrant the production of printed sheets. In Egypt, static-filled television and poor-quality billboards have led companies such as Coca-Cola and Nestlé to place their advertisements on the sails of feluccas, boats that sail along the Nile. Feluccas, with their triangle sails, have been used to transport goods since the time of the pharaohs and serve as an effective alternative to attract attention to company names and logos.

---

[36]Geng Cui and Xiaoyan Yang, "Responses of Chinese Consumers to Sex Appeals in International Advertising: A Test of Congruency Theory," *Journal of Global Marketing* 22, no. 3 (2009), pp. 229–45; Wendy W. N. Wan, Ching-Leung Luk, and Cheris W.C. Chow, "Consumer Responses to Sexual Advertising: The Intersection of Modernization, Evolution, and International Marketing," *Journal of International Business Studies* 45 (2014), pp. 751–82.

[37]Ashok K. Lalwani, May O. Lwin, and Pee Beng Ling, "Does Audiovisual Congruency in Advertisements Increase Persuasion? The Role of Cultural Music and Products," *Journal of Global Marketing* 22 (2009), pp. 139–53.

[38]Somdutta Biswas, Mahmood Hussain, and Kathleen O'Donnell, "Celebrity Endorsements in Advertisements and Consumer Perception: A Cross-Cultural Study," *Journal of Global Marketing* 22 (2008), pp. 121–37.

[39]Victoria Jones, "It's Not Black and White: Advertising and Race in Cultural Context," *Journal of Global Marketing* 23, no. 1 (2010), pp. 45–64.

Media Planning and Analysis

The effect of limited media, excessive media, and government regulations on advertising and promotion budgets

Few doubt that a revolution in communications is under way. Your authors notice it because the changes that occur between the two-year revisions of this textbook are the greatest when it comes to media. Yes, political events and natural disasters can dramatically impact many millions of people overnight, but the network effects of the burgeoning electronic communication media—in the form of PCs, the Internet, and mobile phones—influence not only political events and responses to national disasters but also everyday life for everyone on the planet, from camel markets in Egypt to the international space stations where humans are living off the planet! Perhaps the most eloquent description of the communications revolution comes from Bob Garfield's book, *The Chaos Scenario*:

> … let me just share the 2007 comments of Sir Martin Sorrell, chairman of the WPP Group, the world's largest advertising agency holding company:
>
> "Slowly, the new media will cease to be thought of as new media; they will simply be additional channels of communication. And like all media that were once new but are now just media, they'll earn a well-deserved place in the media repertoire, perhaps through reverse takeovers—*but will almost certainly displace none.*"
>
> The italics are mine. The absurdity was Sir Martin's. Does he not see that the internet is not just some newfangled medium—like TV displacing radio? No, it is a revolutionary advance, along the lines of fire, agriculture, the wheel, the printing press, gunpowder, electricity, radio, manned flight, antibiotics, atomic energy. . . . The digital revolution is already having far-ranging effects on every aspect of our lives, from socialization to communication to information to entertainment to democracy, and these Brave New World effects will only be magnified as the Cowardly Old World collapses before our eyes. Not that this *will* happen.
>
> This *is* happening. Right now.[40]

Strong words from Mr. Garfield, but we agree with his principle point. The changes in media in the 21st century are proceeding at a blinding speed. Next we try to capture them, with due respect to the disrupted world of Sir Sorrell.

Tactical Considerations

Although nearly every sizable nation essentially has the same kinds of media, a number of specific considerations, problems, and differences are encountered from one nation to another. In international advertising, an advertiser must consider the availability, cost, coverage, and appropriateness of the media. And the constant competitive churn among these media makes for a tricky and dynamic landscape for decisions. For example, billboard ads next to highways cannot include paragraphs of text. Moreover, recent research has demonstrated that effectiveness varies across media types,[41] cultures, and products; Chinese consumers in both Taiwan and China view print ads more positively than Americans, for example.[42] Local variations and lack of market data require added attention. Major multinationals are beginning to recognize the importance of planning communications channels as media companies continue to rationalize and evolve. Indeed, media giants such as Disney and Time Warner cover an increasingly broad spectrum of the electronic media, necessitating that MNCs rethink their relationships with media service providers.

Imagine the ingenuity required of advertisers confronted with these situations:

- In Brazil, TV commercials are sandwiched together in a string of 10 to 50 commercials within one station break.

- National coverage in many countries means using as many as 40 to 50 different media.

- Specialized media reach small segments of the market only. In the Netherlands, there are Catholic, Protestant, socialist, neutral, and other specialized broadcasting systems.

[40]Bob Garfield, *The Chaos Scenario* (Nashville, TN: Stielstra Publishing, 2009), p. 11.

[41]Kineta Hung, Stella Yiyan Li, and David K. Tse, "Interpersonal Trust and Platform Credibility in a Chinese Multibrand Online Community," *Journal of Advertising* 40, no. 3 (2011), pp. 99–118.

[42]Carrie La Ferle, Steven M. Edwards, and Wei-Na Lee, "Culture, Attitudes, and Media Patterns in China, Taiwan, and the U.S.: Balancing Standardization and Localization Decisions," *Journal of Global Marketing* 21, no. 3 (2008), pp. 191–206.

- In Germany, TV scheduling for an entire year must be arranged by August 30 of the preceding year, with no guarantee that commercials intended for summer viewing will not be run in the middle of winter.

- In Vietnam, advertising in newspapers and magazines is limited to 10 percent of space and to 5 percent of time, or three minutes an hour, on radio and TV.

Availability.   One of the contrasts of international advertising is that some countries have too few advertising media and others have too many. In some countries, certain advertising media are forbidden by government edict to accept some advertising materials. Such restrictions are most prevalent in radio and television broadcasting. In many countries, there are too few magazines and newspapers to run all the advertising offered to them. Conversely, some nations segment the market with so many newspapers that the advertiser cannot gain effective coverage at a reasonable cost. One head of an Italian advertising agency commented about his country: "One fundamental rule. You cannot buy what you want."

In China the only national TV station, CCTV, has one channel that must be aired by the country's 27 provincial/municipal stations. Recently CCTV auctioned off the most popular break between the early evening news and weather; a secured year-long, daily five-second billboard ad in this break went for $38.5 million. For this price, advertisers are assured of good coverage—more than 96 percent of households have TV sets. One of the other options for advertisers is with the 2,828 TV stations that provide only local coverage.

Cost.   Media prices are susceptible to negotiation in most countries. Agency space discounts are often split with the client to bring down the cost of media. The advertiser may find that the cost of reaching a prospect through advertising depends on the agent's bargaining ability. The per contract cost varies widely from country to country. One study showed that the cost of reaching 1,000 readers in 11 different European countries ranged from $1.58 in Belgium to $5.91 in Italy; in women's service magazines, the page cost per 1,000 circulation ranged from $2.51 in Denmark to $10.87 in Germany. Shortages of advertising time on commercial television in some markets have caused substantial price increases. In Britain, prices escalate on a bidding system. They do not have fixed rate cards; instead, there is a preempt system in which advertisers willing to pay a higher rate can bump already-scheduled spots.

Coverage.   Closely akin to the cost dilemma is the problem of coverage. Two points are particularly important: One relates to the difficulty of reaching certain sectors of the population with advertising and the other to the lack of information about coverage. In many world marketplaces, a wide variety of media must be used to reach the majority of the markets. In some countries, large numbers of separate media have divided markets into uneconomical advertising segments. With some exceptions, a majority of the population of less developed countries cannot be reached readily through the traditional mass medium of advertising. In India, video vans are used to reach India's rural population with 30-minute infomercials extolling the virtues of a product. Consumer goods companies deploy vans year-round except in the monsoon season. Colgate hires 85 vans at a time and sends them to villages that research has shown to be promising.

Because of the lack of adequate coverage by any single medium in eastern European countries, companies must resort to a multimedia approach. In the Czech Republic, for example, TV advertising rates are high, and the lack of available prime-time spots has forced companies to use billboard advertising. In Slovenia the availability of adequate media is such a problem that companies resort to some unusual approaches to get their messages out. For example, in the summer, lasers are used to project images onto clouds above major cities. Vehicle advertising includes cement-mixers, where Kodak ads have appeared. On the positive side, crime is so low that products can be displayed in freestanding glass cabinets on sidewalks; Bosch Siemens (Germany) and Kodak have both used this method.

Lack of Market Data.   Verification of circulation or coverage figures is a difficult task. Even though many countries have organizations similar to the Audit Bureau of Circulation in the United States, accurate circulation and audience data are not assured. For example, the president of the Mexican National Advertisers Association charged that newspaper circulation figures are grossly exaggerated. He suggested that as a rule, agencies should divide these figures in two and take the result with a grain of salt. The situation in China is no better; surveys of habits and market penetration are available only for the cities of Beijing, Shanghai, and Guangzhou. Radio and television audiences are always difficult to measure, but at least in most countries, geographic coverage is known. Research data are becoming more reliable as advertisers and agencies demand better quality data.

Even where advertising coverage can be measured with some accuracy, there are questions about the composition of the market reached. Lack of available market data seems to characterize most international markets; advertisers need information on income, age, and geographic distribution, but such basic data seem chronically elusive except in the largest markets. Even the attractiveness of global television (satellite broadcasts) is diminished somewhat because of the lack of media research available.

An attempt to evaluate specific characteristics of each medium is beyond the scope of this discussion. Furthermore, such information would quickly become outdated because of the rapid changes in the international advertising media field. It may be interesting, however, to examine some of the unique international characteristics of various advertising media. In most instances, the major implications of each variation may be discerned from the data presented.

Newspapers.   The newspaper industry is suffering from lack of competition in some countries and choking because of it in others. Most U.S. cities have just one or two major daily newspapers, but in many countries, there are so many newspapers that an advertiser has trouble achieving even partial market coverage. Uruguay, population 3 million, has 21 daily newspapers with a combined circulation of 553,000. Turkey has 380 newspapers, and an advertiser must consider the political position of each newspaper so that the product's reputation is not harmed through affiliation with unpopular positions. Japan has only five national daily newspapers, but the circulation numbers are unusually large. Connections are necessary to buy advertising space; *Asahi,* Japan's largest newspaper, has been known to turn down more than a million dollars a month in advertising revenue. And even the Japanese giants face a graying population whose younger members are increasingly choosing the electronic media. Circulation rates have been steadily declining there.[43] As can be seen in Exhibit 16.5, the decline in ad revenues going to the print media is dramatic. Over the past five years, the the average loss has been more than 7 percent. The losses are also widespread. This is an ongoing disaster for the industry. Indeed, as we mentioned earlier in the chapter, AdAge.com estimates that spending on online media already exceeds that spent on print.

---

[43]"The Teetering Giants," *The Economist,* February 10, 2010, pp. 72–73.

Exhibit 16.5
Media Spending (US$/household) in Selected Countries (average annual growth rate 2008–2013)

Country	TV	Radio	Print	Cinema	Outdoor	Online
World	90 (1.7)	16 (−2.7)	60 (−7.4)	1 (4.1)	15 (−0.6)	45 (11.4)
China	41 (15.2)	4 (6.5)	21 (6.9)	0.2 (10.4)	11 (8.8)	18 (21.3)
Japan	304 (−1.4)	21 (−4.5)	143 (−7.4)	—	79 (−5.8)	155 (5.4)
Australia	445 (−0.6)	117 (−0.9)	378 (−9.8)	12 (0.0)	57 (0.6)	409 (14.3)
Russia	72 (4.3)	7 (1.3)	14 (−7.6)	3 (13.8)	18 (−3.3)	32 (29.8)
Brazil	154 (9.8)	9 (5.6)	36 (−0.9)	1 (1.9)	6 (8.1)	12 (18.0)
Israel	159 (−2.6)	19 (−6.6)	123 (−10.6)	3 (−1.0)	20 (−9.1)	89 (3.2)
South Africa	104 (10.3)	33 (9.2)	72 (−1.0)	2 (−8.5)	10 (7.7)	6 (17.9)
Canada	254 (−0.3)	117 (−0.2)	181 (−5.7)	—	36 (0.3)	239 (14.4)
USA	532 (1.4)	137 (−3.5)	333 (−10.5)	6 (4.1)	65 (1.3)	277 (12.7)
Germany	130 (−0.6)	24 (−0.1)	281 (−4.5)	2 (−1.3)	25 (−1.5)	131 (9.7)

Source: Euromonitor, 2015.

CROSSING BORDERS 16.3

Advertising Themes that Work in Japan, Including a Polite Duck

Respect for tradition: Mercedes ads stress that it was the first to manufacture passenger cars.

Mutual dependence: Shiseido ads emphasize the partnership (with beauty consultants) involved in achieving beauty.

Harmony with nature: Toyotas are shown in front of Mt. Fuji.

Use of seasons: Commercials are often set in and products are often used in specific seasons only.

Newness and evolution: Products are shown to evolve from the current environment slowly.

Distinctive use of celebrities, including gaijin *(foreigners):* A recent study showed that 63 percent of all Japanese commercials featured hired celebrities.

Aging of society: Seniors are featured often.

Changing families: The changing role of fathers—more time spent at home—is a common theme.

Generation gaps and individualism: Younger characters are shown as more individualistic.

Self-effacing humor: A dented Pepsi can was used in an ad to demonstrate its deference to the more popular Coke.

Polite ducks: The AFLAC duck is going to Japan but with a softer quack. Instead of the American version's abrasive quack, the Japanese actor portrays the duck with a more soothing tone. "The Japanese culture does not like being yelled at," says an AFLAC spokesperson. About 70 percent of the firm's international revenues come from Japan, or some $8 billion. Although this campaign is the first to be shot specifically for Japan, the Japanese have met the duck before. The company, now Japan's largest insurer in terms of individual policies, has also used dubbed voices for American ads, including the loud "quacker." The latest version of the duck ad has been so popular that the jingle associated with it became the most downloaded ringtone in Japan!"

Sources: George Fields, Hotaka Katahira, and Jerry Wind, *Leveraging Japan, Marketing to the New Asia* (San Francisco: Jossey-Bass, 2000); "ALFAC Tames Its Duck for Japanese Market," *Los Angeles Times*, May 13, 2003, p. C7; Lavonne Kuykendall, "Aflac CEO: The Duck Helps Drive Sales in Japan," *Dow Jones Newswire*, February 24, 2010.

In many countries, there is a long time lag before an advertisement can be run in a newspaper. In India and Indonesia, paper shortages delay publication of ads for up to six months. Furthermore, because of equipment limitations, most newspapers cannot be made larger to accommodate the increase in advertising demand.

Separation between editorial and advertising content in newspapers provides another basis for contrast on the international scene. In some countries, it is possible to buy editorial space for advertising and promotional purposes; the news columns are for sale to anyone who has the price. Because there is no indication that the space is paid for, it is impossible to tell exactly how much advertising appears in a given newspaper.

Magazines.   The use of foreign national consumer magazines by international advertisers has been notably low for many reasons. Few magazines have a large circulation or provide dependable circulation figures. Technical magazines are used rather extensively to promote export goods, but as with newspapers, paper shortages cause placement problems. Media planners are often faced with the largest magazines accepting up to twice as many advertisements as they have space to run them in—then the magazines decide what advertisements will be included just before going to press by means of a raffle.

Such local practices may be key factors favoring the growth of so-called international media that attempt to serve many nations. Increasingly, U.S. publications are publishing overseas editions. *Reader's Digest International* has added a new Russian-language edition to its more than 20 other language editions. Other American print media available in international editions range from *Playboy* to *Scientific American* and even include the *National Enquirer*, recently introduced to the United Kingdom. Advertisers have three new magazines through which to reach women in China: Hachette Filipachi Presse, the French publisher, is expanding Chinese-language editions of *Elle*, a fashion magazine; *Woman's Day* is aimed at China's "busy modern" woman; and *L'Evénement*

Sportif is a sports magazine. These media offer alternatives for multinationals as well as for local advertisers. Generally, ad revenues from magazines are about one-third of those from newspapers. As magazines become thinner around the world—showing their lack of advertisements—they share the devastating revenue declines with newspapers.

Radio and Television.

Possibly because of their inherent entertainment value, radio and television have become major communications media in almost all nations. Now high-definition television (HDTV) has taken off worldwide as well. In China, virtually all homes in major cities have a television, and most adults view television and listen to radio daily. Radio has been relegated to a subordinate position in the media race in countries where television facilities are well developed. In many countries, however, radio is a particularly important and vital advertising medium when it is the only one reaching large segments of the population. The audiences for both broadcast media have remained relatively stable, as indicated by the spending statistics in Exhibit 16.5. While television advertising revenues have increased at an average annual rate of about 1.7 percent, radio has declined at almost 3 percent per year during the last five years.

Television and radio advertising availability varies between countries. Some countries do not permit any commercial radio or television, but several of the traditional noncommercial countries have changed their policies in recent years because television production is so expensive. Until recently, France limited commercials to a daily total of 18 minutes but now has extended the time limit to 12 minutes per hour per TV channel. South Korea has two television companies, both government owned, which broadcast only a few hours a day. They do not broadcast from midnight to 6:00 a.m., and they usually cannot broadcast between 10:00 a.m. and 5:30 p.m. on weekdays. Commercials are limited to 8 percent of airtime and shown in clusters at the beginning and end of programs. One advertiser remarked, "We are forced to buy what we don't want to buy just to get on."

Presently, a perfect storm is brewing that may cause commercial television to follow the path of print. First is the surge of growth in spending on digital media, to be discussed in a subsequent section of the chapter. Second, ad skipping devices such as Dish's AdHop

Given the ubiquitous Guinness advertising in Dublin, it's not surprising that Irish livers need assurance. Ireland is behind only the Czech Republic when it comes to per capita consumption of beer. Actually, Royal Liver Assurance is a British pension/insurance company with offices in Dublin (it was established in the 1850s as the Liverpool Liver Burial Society). "Hurling" is a rather brutal form of field hockey popular in Ireland. The Irish government recognizes the causal effects of advertising on consumption—beer ads are not allowed on radio or TV before sports programs and may not be shown more than once per night on any one channel. See http://www.eurocare.org for more information on the consumption of alcohol in Ireland and other European countries.

function are making ads disappear from your TV screen.[44] Third, Netflix streaming and binge watching are also killing the appeal of TV advertising.[45] Of course, all this is happening in the United States, but all such innovations tend to spread around the world. The big question then is how will American politicians spend the billions of dollars they are used to raising for their campaigns?

Satellite and Cable TV.   Of increasing importance in TV advertising is the growth and development of satellite TV broadcasting. Sky Channel, a United Kingdom–based commercial satellite television station, beams its programs and advertising into most of Europe to cable TV subscribers. The technology that permits households to receive broadcasts directly from the satellite via a dish the size of a dinner plate costing about $350 is adding greater coverage and the ability to reach all of Europe with a single message. The expansion of TV coverage will challenge the creativity of advertisers and put greater emphasis on global standardized messages. For a comparison of penetration rates by cable TV, computers, and the Internet in the several countries, see Exhibit 16.5.

Advertisers and governments are both concerned about the impact of satellite TV. Governments are concerned because they fear further loss of control over their airwaves and the spread of "American cultural imperialism." Notice in Exhibit 16.5 that China does not allow the medium. European television programming includes such U.S. shows as *Laguna Beach: the Real Orange County*. *Wheel of Fortune* is the most popular foreign show in the United Kingdom and France, where both the U.S. and French versions are shown. American imports are so popular in France and Germany that officials fear lowbrow U.S. game shows, sitcoms, and soap operas will crush domestic producers. This battle has even reached political levels associated with differences in worldviews represented in the news. The government of France invested in developing, not surprisingly, a French-language "CNN" called *France 24* but has stopped subsidizing an English-language version. *Al-Jazeera*, initially subsidized by Qatar government loans, is currently struggling to break even. Nevertheless, it is the now widely recognized Arabic "CNN" and is commensurately influential in the Middle East.

Parts of Asia and Latin America receive TV broadcasts from satellite television networks. Univision and Televisa are two Latin American satellite television networks broadcasting via a series of affiliate stations in each country to most of the Spanish-speaking world, as well as the United States. *Sabado Gigante,* a popular Spanish-language program broadcast by Univision, is seen by tens of millions of viewers in 16 countries. Star TV, a new pan-Asian satellite television network, has a potential audience of 2.7 billion people living in 38 countries from Egypt through India to Japan, and from Russia to Indonesia. Star TV was the first to broadcast across Asia but was quickly joined by ESPN and CNN. The first Asian 24-hour all-sports channel was followed by MTV Asia and a Mandarin Chinese–language channel that delivers dramas, comedies, movies, and financial news aimed at the millions of overseas Chinese living throughout Asia. Programs are delivered through cable networks but can be received through private satellite dishes.

One of the drawbacks of satellites is also their strength, that is, their ability to span a wide geographical region covering many different country markets. That means a single message is broadcast throughout a wide area. This span may not be desirable for some products; with cultural differences in language, preferences, and so on, a single message may not be as effective. PVI (Princeton Video Imaging) is an innovation that will make regional advertising in diverse cultures easier than it presently is when using cable or satellite television. PVI allows ESPN, which offers this service, to fill visual real estate—blank walls, streets, stadium sidings—with computer-generated visuals that look like they belong in the scene. For instance, if you are watching the "street luge" during ESPN's X-Games, you

---

[44]David Lieberman, "UPDATE: Dish and Disney Finalize Output Deal That Ends Their Ad-Hopper Dispute," *Deadline.com*, March 3, 2014, online.

[45]Emily Steel, "As a Conference, Research Shows Streaming Is Upending TV Business," *The New York Times*, December 9, 2014, p. B3.

will see the racers appear to pass a billboard advertising Adidas shoes that really is not there. That billboard can say one thing in Holland and quite another in Cameroon. And if you are watching in Portland, Oregon, where Adidas might not advertise, you will see the scene as it really appears—without the billboard. These commercials can play in different languages, in different countries, and even under different brand names.

Most satellite technology involves some government regulation. Singapore, Taiwan, and Malaysia prohibit selling satellite dishes, and the Japanese government prevents domestic cable companies from rebroadcasting from foreign satellites. Such restrictions seldom work for long, however. In Taiwan, an estimated 1.5 million dishes are in use, and numerous illicit cable operators are in business. Through one technology or another, Asian households will be open to the same kind of viewing choice Americans have grown accustomed to and the advertising that it brings with it.

Direct Mail.   Direct mail is a viable medium in an increasing number of countries. It is especially important when other media are not available. As is often the case in international marketing, even such a fundamental medium is subject to some odd and novel quirks. For example, in Chile, direct mail is virtually eliminated as an effective medium because the sender pays only part of the mailing fee; the letter carrier must collect additional postage for every item delivered. Obviously, advertisers cannot afford to alienate customers by forcing them to pay for unsolicited advertisements. Despite some limitations with direct mail, many companies have found it a meaningful way to reach their markets. The Reader's Digest Association has used direct mail advertising in Mexico to successfully market its magazines.

In Southeast Asian markets, where print media are scarce, direct mail is considered one of the most effective ways to reach those responsible for making industrial goods purchases, even though accurate mailing lists are a problem in Asia as well as in other parts of the world. In fact, some companies build their own databases for direct mail. Industrial advertisers are heavy mail users and rely on catalogs and sales sheets to generate large volumes of international business. Even in Japan, where media availability is not a problem, direct mail is successfully used by marketers such as Nestlé Japan and Dell Computer. To promote its Buitoni fresh-chilled pasta, Nestlé is using a 12-page color direct mail booklet of recipes, including Japanese-style versions of Italian favorites.

In Russia, the volume of direct mail has gone from just over 150,000 letters per month to more than 500,000 per month in one year. The response rate to direct mailings is as high as 10 to 20 percent in Russia, compared with only 3 to 4 percent or less in the United States. One suggestion as to why it works so well is that Russians are flattered by the attention—needless to say, that will probably change as use of the medium grows.

The Internet.   Although we are still learning about its effectiveness, particularly across cultures,[46] the Internet has emerged as the second or third most important advertising medium globally, depending on the source. However, there is no disagreement about the unprecedented growth rate of companies' spending on online advertising, globally more than 10 percent per year during 2008–2013. Its use in business-to-business communications and promotion via catalogs and product descriptions is rapidly gaining in popularity. Because a large number of businesses have access to the Internet, the Internet can reach a large portion of the business-to-business market.

Although limited in its penetration of households in some countries, the Internet is being used by a growing number of companies as an advertising medium for consumer goods. Many consumer goods companies have e-stores, and others use the Internet as an advertising medium to stimulate sales in retail outlets. Waterford Crystal of Ireland set up its website specifically to drive store traffic. The aim is to promote its products and attract

Very Important

---

[46]Shaojing Sun and Ying Want, "Familiarity, Beliefs, Attitudes, and Consumer Responses toward Online Advertising in China and the United States," *Journal of Global Marketing* 23, no. 2 (2010), pp. 127–38; Jana Moller and Martin Eisend, "A Global Investigation into the Cultural and Individual Antecedents of Banner Advertising Effectiveness," *Journal of International Marketing* 18, no. 2 (2010), pp. 80–98.

Exhibit 16.6
Top Ten Websites in Three Countries (visitors per month)

Rank	Brazil 31.9 million visitors		Portugal 3.8 million visitors		South Korea 28.1 million visitors	
1	Google sites	26.2	Google sites	3.6	NHN Corporation	22.7
2	Microsoft sites	25.2	Microsoft sites	3.4	Daum	20.5
3	UOL	20.6	Portugal Telecom	2.4	SK Group	20.2
4	Yahoo! sites	17.4	Hi5.COM	2.3	gretech	14.7
5	Terra-Telefonica	16.8	Yahoo! sites	1.4	Yahoo! sites	12.2
6	Organizacoes Globo	16.7	UOL	1.3	KT Group	11.8
7	Grupo Brasil Telecom	16.6	Grupo Impresa	1.2	Microsoft sites	11.4
8	Wikimedia sites	10.8	Wikimedia sites	1.1	Google sites	10.4
9	WordPress	10.1	Grupo Brasil Telecom	1.1	eBay	10.0
10	BuscaPe.com Inc.	8	WordPress	1.1	JMnet	10.0

Source: comScore Media Metrix, 2014, online. Reprinted with permission.

people into stores that sell Waterford crystal. Sites list and display almost the entire catalog of the Waterford collection, while stores like Bloomingdale's that stock Waterford support the promotional effort by also advertising on their websites.

For consumer products, the major limitation of the Internet is coverage. In the United States, growing numbers of households have access to a computer. The growing number of Internet households accessible outside the United States generally constitutes a younger, better-educated market segment with higher-than-average incomes. For many companies, this group is an important market niche. Furthermore, this limitation is only temporary as new technology allows access to the Internet via television and as lower prices for personal computers expand the household base. Exhibit 16.6 gives you some idea of the distribution of website visitors in three major markets. Notice the American brand names included in the lists: five for Brazil, six for Portugal, and four for South Korea; also consider the overlap in the Portuguese websites in Brazil and Portugal, as well as the dominance of Google and Microsoft. The great majority of visitors are viewing the local versions of these websites—that is, .br, .pt, and .kr. The most visited in the United States during the same period were Google, Microsoft, Yahoo!, Facebook, AOL, Ask Network, Glam Media, Turner Digital, and Wikipedia, in that order.

As the Internet continues to grow and countries begin to assert control over what is now a medium with few restrictions, increasing limitations will be set. Beyond the control of undesirable information, issues such as pay-per-view, taxes, unfair competition, import duties, and privacy are being addressed all over the world. In Australia, local retailers are calling for changes in laws because of the loss of trade to the Internet; under current law, Internet purchases do not carry regular import duties. The Internet industry is lobbying for a global understanding on regulation to avoid a crazy quilt of confusing and contradictory rules.

Another limitation that needs to be addressed soon is the competition for Internet users. The sheer proliferation of the number of websites makes it increasingly difficult for a customer to stumble across a particular page. Search engines have now become crucial directors of Internet users' attention. Also, serious Internet advertisers or e-marketers will have to be more effective in communicating the existence of their Internet sites via other advertising media. Some companies are coupling their traditional television spots with a website; IBM, Swatch watches, AT&T, and Samsung electronics are among those going for a one-two punch of on-air and online presences. Television spots raise brand awareness of a product regionally and promote the company's website.

Finally, while online advertising is burgeoning in importance globally, it is also morphing more toward social and mobile media. One analyst has declared the death of the banner and website ad in favor of apps such as Facebook, Twitter, and Instagram. And this leads us to the topic of social media.[47]

---

[47]Frahad Manjoo, "Fall of the Banner Ad: The Monster that Swallowed the Web," *The New York Times*, November 6, 2014, pp. 1, B11.

Social Media.   Word-of-mouth (WOM) advertising and peer recommendations have always been key influencers of brand choice, but the power of the Internet has changed the pace and reach of WOM. Social media (such as social networking, blogs, virtual worlds, and video sharing) can be powerful marketing tools, but marketers are just beginning to loosen control and let consumers interact with brands on their own terms. Consumer-generated content is having an impact on brands (both positive and negative), and new media are on the agendas of marketers of all products, not just those targeted at young people. Consumers will create content about brands whether the marketers of those brands like it or not. Thus, it is vital that marketers follow, and participate in, the conversations consumers are having online.

The Internet is not delineated by national boundaries, though we note that word-of-mouth seems to work better in more information-oriented and uncertainty avoidant cultures.[48] In any case, consumers from many different countries and cultures can and do interact online. We are just beginning to understand the potential uses and pitfalls of this medium and the characteristics of its users. One recent study[49] distinguishes social network uses in the United States and those for a sample from abroad (i.e., an aggregate of 11 countries: Brazil, Canada, China, France, Germany, India, Japan, Mexico, Russia, South Korea, and the United Kingdom). For the purposes of the study, the users consisted of consumers who had visited at least one social networking site, such as MySpace, Cyworld, Mixi, and/or Facebook.

By the way, at more than 1 billion users, Facebook dominates social networking around the world. It charges about $1 million a day to run a video ad on Facebook, but at least initially, those "invited" to advertise are screened by the company. The ads will have to judged "meaningful" as rated by users, and if selected, they will play without sound and users will be able to scroll past them without watching them. It will be interesting to see how this works.[50]

More than half the Americans in the sample had watched TV shows or video streams online. In addition, the Americans were significantly more likely to download TV programs, burn or copy a movie or TV show, and download a feature-length film. The Americans also owned significantly more technology than their international counterparts, and both samples owned more technology than those who had never visited a social networking site. More than half of the Americans had used their mobile devices to send or receive SMS (short message service) text and e-mails, browse the Internet for news and information, and receive digital images. Although the international users exhibited similar behaviors, their mobile devices were richer with features. For example, international users are significantly more likely to have MP3s on their mobile devices than those in the United States. Also, see in Exhibit 16.7 that Israelis spend more time on social media sites than any users in any other country. Finally, we note that the median band width speed for the United States, at 16.9 gigabytes, is number 16 among OECD nations. South Korea is first and boasts 75 gigabytes, Netherlands is next with 61.4, and Denmark is at 40, with the United Kingdom at 35.8.[51]

Mobile Phone Applications.   As the number of mobile phones continues to explode around the world, now at more than 7 billion, so do the number of applications available to users. Indeed, it was recently reported that the top 1 percent of mobile phone

---

[48]Desmond Lam, Alvin Lee, and Richard Mizerski, "The Effects of Cultural Values in Word-of-Mouth Communication," *Journal of International Marketing* 17, no. 3 (2009), pp. 55–70; Jan H. Schumann, Florian v. Wangenheim, Anne Stringfellow, Zhilin Yang, Vera Blazevic, Sandra Praxmarer, G. Shainesh, Marcin Komor, Randall M. Shannon, and Fernando R. Jimenez, "Cross-Cultural Differences in the Effect of Received Word-of-Mouth Referral in Relational Service Exchange," *Journal of International Marketing* 18, no. 3 (2010), pp. 62–80; Shu-Chuan Chu and Sejung Marina Choi, "Electronic Word-of-Mouth in Social Networking Sites: A Cross-Cultural Study of the United States and China," *Journal of Global Marketing* 24, no. 3 (2011), pp. 263–81.

[49]"Social Networkers Are Also Heavy Technology Users," *Research Brief from the Center for Media Research*, November 14, 2007, http://www.centerformediaresearch.com.

[50]Reed Albergotti, "Brands Face Tough Screening for Facebook Video Ads," *The Wall Street Journal*, May 5, 2014, online.

[51]"In Broadband, the United States Lags Behind," *The New York Times*, May 28, 2014, p. B2.

Exhibit 16.7

Top 10 Social Media Users:
Average Time Spent on
Social Networking Sites,
October 2011 (hours per
user)

Source: Michael Jung, "Social
Networking Is the Most Popular Online
Activity," http://www.thenewage
.co.za/38836-1021-53-Social
_networking_is_the_most_popular
_online_activity, December 26, 2011,
online.

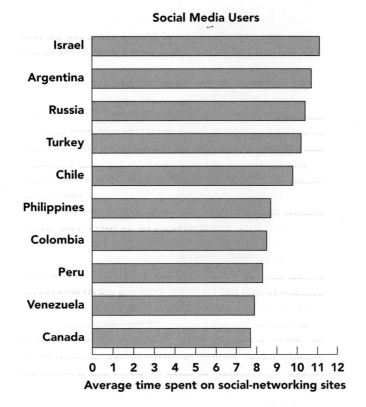

Social Media Users

Average time spent on social-networking sites

users consume half of the world's bandwidth, and the gap is growing![52] As one expert has most eloquently put it, "There is a big shift from holding a phone to your ear to holding it in your hand. It opens the door of information services. It's not the web, but it's a web of services that can be offered on mobile devices. It allows consumers to ask questions and marketers to deliver answers in new ways. Around the world creative people are finding ways to use mobile phones in new ways."[53]

In Uganda, rice farmers who had trouble with aphids texted Farmer's Friend for advice and received a message telling them how to make a pesticide using soap and paraffin. A farmer with blighted tomato plants learned how to control the problem by spraying the plants with a milk-based mixture. Farmer's Friend is one of a range of phone-based services launched in 2009 by MTN, Google, and the Grameen Foundation's "Application Laboratory," or App Lab.

Google Trader is another text-based system that matches buyers and sellers of agricultural produce and commodities. Sellers send a message to say where they are and what they have to offer, which will be available to potential buyers within 30 km for seven days. The user is charged about 10¢ per posting. In its first five weeks of operation, the service received 1 million queries.

Perhaps the best measure of the importance of this creative medium was the incredible response to the Haiti earthquake of 2010. Texting the phrase "Haiti" to the number 90999 automatically donates $10 to the Red Cross. The relief agency received more than $2 million dollars within 24 hours of the earthquake. Twitter also was used as an essential communication medium during the relief efforts and another medium for soliciting and accepting donations.[54] Finally, in Australia mobiles recently represented 52 percent of digital screen time. Other per

---

[52]Kevin J. O'Brien, "Top 1% of Mobile Users Consume Half of World's Bandwidth, and the Gap is Growing," *The New York Times, January* 5, 2012.

[53]Rajeesh Veeraraghavan, Naga Yasodhar, and Kentaro Toyama, "Warana Unwired: Replacing PCs with Mobile Phones in a Rural Sugar Cane Cooperative," *Information Technology & International Development* 5, no. 1 (2009), pp. 81–95.

[54]Jenna Wortham, "$2 Million in Donations for Haiti, via Text Message," *The New York Times*, January 13, 2010, online.

Notice the Chinese Mandarin characters on Steph Curry's jersey. In English they say "Warriors." This jersey was worn by the Golden State team in games during the Chinese New Year in 2015. You can also notice the patch on his right shoulder – it is a goat signifying the Year of the Goat in the Chinese zodiac, or 2015. The red and yellow in the piping connote good luck and wealth/happiness, respectively, in Chinese culture.

THE NBA GOES GLOBAL

The National Basketball Association (NBA) markets its products and services globally with great success. The array of marketing tools employed by the League is impressive – broadcast and print media campaigns for tickets, courtside banner sales, public service announcements, licensing logos internationally, TV around the world, potential teams in Europe, exhibition games in several countries, even video games. Foreign merchandize sales are divided as follows: 40% in China, 33% in Europe/Middle East/Africa, 18% in Asian countries, 6% in Canada, and 3% in Latin America.[1]

But the place the NBA dominates is social media. The numbers for the 2014–15 season are impressive: The NBA's YouTube site had 5.9 million subscribers and 2.5 billion views. The NHL, second best among the major sports leagues, boasted only one-tenth of those numbers. The NBA's Facebook page had 26.8 million "likes" – more than the NFL, MLB, NASCAR, and NHL combined. The bottom line for that banner year was a record 240 million fans, 811 million likes and followers combined across all league, team, and player social platforms, and 31 *billion media impressions*, the last a 130% increase over the previous year.

Internationally, the NBA is the most-followed sports league on social media in China, with more than 100 million followers on Tencent and Sina. NBA has 17 international Facebook destinations; more than 50% of followers are international.

None of this is by chance. The NBA has been a real pioneer in the field (or on this court) working with Silicon Valley firms such as Facebook for almost ten years.[2] Leading these efforts has been Melissa Rosenthal Brenner, Senior Vice President for Digital Media. Her hands-on approach includes following the social media during games using five different platforms: Samsung (an NBA partner), iPhone 6, iPad Air 2, Microsoft Surface, and a laptop. She wants to keep a feel for how her consumers experience the game and the media. The goal of social media is to get consumers to turn on the game.

The players themselves are a most tech-savy and social media conscious group. The NBA Social Media Awards have recognized some of the best

[1] Ira Boudway, "The Global Playbook," *Bloomberg Businessweek*, February 10, 2015, p. 23.
[2] Katherine Rosman, "For the NBA, It's the Most Tweetable Time of the Year," *New York Times*, December 24, 2014, p. E1.

moments which resonated with fans and sparked the most social engagement. In 2013–14, Damian Lillard of the Portland Trail Blazers was designated "Social MVP," and the Houston Rockets garnered the "Team Social MVP," and the "LOL Award" went to Nick Young of the Los Angeles Lakers.

If you click on the globe icon of the NBA.com homepage you will find a NBA Global with a series of foreign home pages listed – focus on NBA Argentina and NBA China. We suggest you go to the actual pages and explore the breadth of marketing information there. Check the most recent numbers with those reported above. That is, please view our limited material in the book as a mere signpost to the very rich virtual territory of NBA Global.

The interactive map on NBA Global shows the home countries of players around the world. For example, five players are from Spain and two from Cameroon, and you can follow any or all via social media. For the first time in history, the NBA now has more than 100 players representing 37 different countries.

Near the top of each page you see the various social media emphasized by the League for the particular market. The Global page includes blogs, Facebook, Twitter, and g$^+$. The Argentina NBA page includes the same four social platforms plus Pinterest and Rss. Most of the rest of the countries are similar to Argentina. But the choices on the NBA China page are limited to only Chinese social media – its own versions of Google, Facebook, and Twitter, they are Tencent Weibo, Tencent Qzone, Tencent WeChat, and Sina Weibo

The NBA's Global Operations.
The NBA has offices in 13 markets worldwide: Beijing, Hong Kong, Johannesburg, London, Madrid, Mexico City, Mumbai, New York/New Jersey, Rio de Janeiro, Shanghai, Seoul, Taipei, and Toronto. In 2008, the NBA launched NBA China with 5 strategic partners that invested $253 million: Disney/ESPN, Bank of China Group Investment, Legend Holdings, China Merchant Group, and Li Ka Shing Foundation.

NBA games and programs are available in 215 countries and territories in 47 languages. NBA TV reaches subscribers in 99 countries and territories. NBA Digital platforms (NBA.com, NBA Mobile, NBA Game Time app) received a record 27 billion page views during the 2013–14 NBA season (regular and

postseason combined). More than 50% of all NBA digital visitors come from fans outside North America. The NBA currently features 18 international web destinations: Africa, Argentina, Australia, Brazil, China, ene-be-a, Germany, Greece, India, Israel, Italy, Japan, Mexico, New Zealand, Philippines, Spain, Taiwan and Turkey. NBA LEAGUE PASS offers fans in more than 200 countries access to a complete season of live NBA games on NBA.com and NBA Mobile. Top five markets for subscriptions have been Australia, Germany, UK, Canada, and France.

More than 30% of NBA product sales are generated outside of the U.S. In 2014, NBA products were shipped to consumers in 130 countries and territories outside the U.S. The NBA has seven dedicated international e-commerce sites: nbastore.com.au (Australia), nbastore.co.nz (New Zealand), LojaNBA.com (Brazil), NBA.tmall.com (China), NBATienda.com (Mexico), NBAStore.eu (Europe, Middle East, and Africa) and NBAStore.in (India), with more international sites slated to launch in 2015. International transactions represent 62% of sales at the NBA Store on Fifth Avenue.

The NBA has relationships with an array of marketing partners to engage fans and activate a wide range of programs and activities. Partners that work with the league around the world include 2K Sports, AB InBev, adidas, BBVA, Cisco, Gatorade, Harman, Nike, SAP and Spalding. Local partnerships with top companies in select regions include America Movil (Mexico), Avea (Turkey), Bell (Canada), Bimbo (Latin America and Spain), and Friesland Campina (Asia, ex-China). In greater China, the NBA has the following marketing and promotional partners: AB InBev (Harbin Beer); Adidas; ANTA; American Airlines; Cathay Financial Group (Taiwan); Castrol, Clear (Unilever); Gatorade; Master Kong; Mengniu Dairy; Nike; SAP; Spalding; Sprite; and ZTE Mobile.

Other Aspects of the NBA's IMC. This season
(2014–15), NBA Global Games included a total of nine NBA teams playing seven regular-season and preseason games in seven cities in six countries. Preseason: Five teams - Brooklyn Nets, Cleveland Cavaliers, Miami Heat, Sacramento Kings, and San Antonio Spurs - playing a series of games in Brazil, China, Germany, and Turkey. Regular

Steph Curry of the Golden State Warriors givens ball handling instructions to Chinese kids in Beijing.

Season: The NBA played games in Mexico City (Houston Rockets vs. Minnesota Timberwolves; Nov. 12) and London (Milwaukee Bucks vs. New York Knicks; Jan. 15). On April 22, 2015, the NBA and the National Basketball Players Association (NBPA) announced that the NBA's first game in Africa will take place Aug. 1 at Ellis Park Arena in Johannesburg, South Africa.

The NBA is committed to growing the game at the grassroots level, and in 2014 the League conducted more than 218 international events in 123 cities and 36 countries outside of the U.S. NBA 3X is the league's international grassroots event platform that combines an exciting 3x3 competition with authentic NBA entertainment and basketball activities. In 2014, NBA 3X and other NBA-branded 3x3 events were staged in 55 cities in 16 countries and featured 27,500 participants and nearly 800,000 attendees.

Jr. NBA is the league's international platform to grow basketball participation at the youth level. Jr. NBA provides top quality basketball instruction for young players and their coaches and promotes the core values of the game, such as sportsmanship, teamwork, a positive attitude, and respect. In 2014, Jr. NBA programs were staged in 70 cities in 13 countries, with participation from more than 215,000 boys and girls and more than 3,700 coaches.

Social Responsibility.

Through NBA Cares, the league and its teams and players have donated more than $242 million to charity, completed more than 3 million hours of hands-on community service, and created more than 915 places where kids and families can live, learn, or play on five continents. Internationally, 179 places built in 26 countries.

Together with FIBA, the NBA hosts 'Basketball without Borders' (BWB) annually: Since 2001, the NBA and FIBA have staged 41 BWB camps in 23 cities in 20 countries on five continents. More than 150 different current and former NBA/WNBA players have joined nearly 140 NBA team personnel from all 30 NBA teams with 33 BWB campers drafted into the NBA. In 2014, BWB included first-time camps in Taipei, Taiwan and Rome, Italy, as well as a return to Johannesburg, South Africa.

month screen times reported were 38 hours for desktop and laptop devices, 29 hours for smartphones (both browsing and apps), and 24 hours for tablets. Finally, application usage dominated total smartphone and tablet usage at 86 percent. Many industry analysts report that companies are having trouble keeping up with this fast-changing consumer behavior.[55]

Other Media.   Restrictions on traditional media or their availability cause advertisers to call on lesser media to solve particular local-country problems. The cinema is an important medium in many countries, as are billboards and other forms of outside advertising. Billboards are especially useful in countries with high illiteracy rates. Hong Kong is clearly the neon capital of the world, with Tokyo's Ginza and New York's Times Square running close seconds. Indeed, perhaps the most interesting "billboard" was the Pizza Hut logo that appeared on the side of a Russian Proton rocket launched to carry parts of the international space station into orbit. Can extraterrestrials read? Do they like pizza?

In Haiti, sound trucks equipped with powerful loudspeakers provide an effective and widespread advertising medium. Private contractors own the equipment and sell advertising space, much as a radio station would. This medium overcomes the problems of illiteracy, lack of radio and television set ownership, and limited print media circulation. In Ukraine, where the postal service is unreliable, businesses have found that the most effective form of direct business-to-business advertising is direct faxing.

In Spain, a new medium includes private cars that are painted with advertisements for products and serve as moving billboards as they travel around. This system, called *Publicoche* (derived from the words *publicidad*, meaning advertising, and *coche*, meaning car), has 75 cars in Madrid. Car owners are paid $230 a month and must submit their profession and "normal" weekly driving patterns. Advertisers pay a basic cost of $29,000 per car per month and can select the type and color of car they are interested in and which owners are most suited to the campaign, based on their driving patterns.

Campaign Execution and Advertising Agencies

The development of advertising campaigns and their execution are managed by advertising agencies. Just as manufacturing firms have become international, so too have U.S., Japanese, and European advertising agencies expanded internationally to provide sophisticated agency assistance worldwide. Local agencies also have expanded as the demand for advertising services by MNCs has developed. Thus, the international marketer has a variety of alternatives available. In most commercially significant countries, an advertiser has the opportunity to employ a local domestic agency, its company-owned agency, or one of the multinational advertising agencies with local branches. There are strengths and weaknesses associated with each. The discussion regarding firm and agency relations in Chapter 8 on pages 255–257 and Exhibit 8.2 are quite pertinent here. Moreover, the agency-company relationships can be complicated and fragile in the international context—Ford and Disneyland Paris recently changed agencies, for example.

A local domestic agency may provide a company with the best cultural interpretation in situations in which local modification is sought,[56] but the level of sophistication can be weak. Moreover, the cross-cultural communication between the foreign client and the local agency can be problematic. However, the local agency may have the best feel for the market, especially if the multinational agency has little experience in the market. Eastern Europe has been a problem for multinational agencies that are not completely attuned to the market. In Hungary, a U.S. baby care company's advertisement of bath soap, showing a woman holding her baby, hardly seemed risqué. But where Westerners saw a young mother, scandalized Hungarians saw

---

[55]"Mobile Dominates Digital Consumer Screen Time," *CMO.com.au*, August 8, 2014, online.

[56]Morris Kalliny and Salma Ghanem, "The Role of the Advertising Agency in the Cultural Message Content of Advertisements: A Comparison of the Middle East and the United States," *Journal of Global Marketing* 22, no. 4 (2009), pp. 313–28.

Two novel media are shown here: (1) Not only do the Russians sell space for space tourists on their rockets; they also sell advertising space! (2) The Japanese beverage company Suntory promotes its products with "Monitor Man" during a football match at National Stadium. "Monitor Man" puts on an LCD display, showing ads for Pepsi and other products, and walks around the stadium. The job requires some muscle, as the equipment weighs about 15 pounds. All this effort is perhaps purposely reminiscent of the Simpson's "Duff Man." Ohhh yaaaa!

an unwed mother. The model was wearing a ring on her left hand; Hungarians wear wedding bands on the right hand. It was obvious to viewers that this woman wearing a ring on her left hand was telling everybody in Hungary she wasn't married. A local agency would not have made such a mistake. Finally, in some emerging markets like Vietnam, local laws require a local advertising partner.

The best compromise is a multinational agency with local branches, because it has the sophistication of a major agency with local representation. Furthermore, a multinational agency with local branches is better able to provide a coordinated worldwide advertising campaign.[57] This ability has become especially important for firms doing business in Europe. With the interest in global or standardized advertising, many agencies have expanded to provide worldwide representation. Many companies with a global orientation employ one, or perhaps two, agencies to represent them worldwide.

Compensation arrangements for advertising agencies throughout the world are based on the U.S. system of 15 percent commissions. However, agency commission patterns throughout the world are not as consistent as they are in the United States; in some countries, agency commissions vary from medium to medium. Companies are moving from the commission system to a reward-by-results system, which details remuneration terms at the outset. If sales rise, the agency should be rewarded accordingly. This method of sharing in the gains or losses of profits generated by the advertising is gaining in popularity and may become the standard. Services provided by advertising agencies also vary greatly, but few foreign agencies offer the full services found in U.S. agencies. (See Exhibit 16.8 for the largest.) The latest news in the industry is that the biggest firms just continue to grow— number two Omincom and number three Publicis have agreed to merge, thus overtaking WPP for top of the board. They will both maintain their corporate offices in New York and Paris, at least temporarily.[58]

---

[57]Among multinational advertising agencies, there appears to be an advantage to early arrival in new markets. See Peter Manusson, Stanford A Westjohn, and David J. Boggs, "Order-of-Entry Effects for Service Firms in Developing Markets: An Examination of Multinational Advertising Agencies," *Journal of International Marketing* 17, no. 2 (2009), pp. 23–41.

[58]"Omnipotent, or Omnishambles?" *The Economist*, August 3, 2013, pp. 53–54.

Exhibit 16.8
World's Top Ten Advertising Agencies

2013	Agency (parent)	Headquarters	Global Revenues ($million 2013)	Percent Change from 2012
1	WPP	Dublin	$17.3	4.8%
2	Omnicom Group	New York	14.6	2.6
3	Publicis Groupe	Paris	9.2	8.7
4	Interpublic Group	New York	7.1	7.0
5	Dentsu	Tokyo	5.8	−9.4
6	Havas	Suresnes, France	2.3	2.1
7	Hakuhodo DY Holdings	Tokyo	1.8	−15.7
8	Alliance Data Systems International	Irvine, TX	1.4	10.6
9	IBM International Experience	Armonk, NY	1.3	74.3
10	MDC Partners	Toronto/New York	1.2	6.1

Source: From Special Report Global Marketing, *Advertising Age*, 2014. Copyright © 2014 Crain Communication. Reprinted with permission.

International Control of Advertising: Broader Issues

In a previous section, specific legal restrictions on advertising were presented. Here broader issues related to the past, present, and future of the international regulation of advertising are considered.

Consumer criticisms of advertising are not a phenomenon of the U.S. market only. Consumer concern with the standards and believability of advertising may have spread around the world more swiftly than have many marketing techniques. A study of a representative sample of European consumers indicated that only half of them believed advertisements gave consumers any useful information. Six of 10 believed that advertising meant higher prices (if a product is heavily advertised, it often sells for more than brands that are seldom or never advertised); nearly eight of 10 believed advertising often made them buy things they did not really need and that ads often were deceptive about product quality. In Hong Kong, Colombia, and Brazil, advertising fared much better than in Europe. The non-Europeans praised advertising as a way to obtain valuable information about products; most Brazilians consider ads entertaining and enjoyable.

European Commission officials are establishing directives to provide controls on advertising as cable and satellite broadcasting expands. Deception in advertising is a thorny issue, because most member countries have different interpretations of what constitutes a misleading advertisement. Demands for regulation of advertising aimed at children is a trend appearing in both industrialized and developing countries.

Decency and the blatant use of sex in advertisements also are receiving public attention. One of the problems in controlling decency and sex in ads is the cultural variations found around the world. An ad perfectly acceptable to a Westerner may be very offensive to someone from the Middle East, or, for that matter, another Westerner. Standards for appropriate behavior as depicted in advertisements vary from culture to culture. Regardless of these variations, concern about decency, sex, and ads that demean women and men is growing. International advertising associations are striving to forestall laws by imposing self-regulation, but it may be too late; some countries are passing laws that will define acceptable standards.

The difficulty that business has with self-regulation and restrictive laws is that sex can be powerful in some types of advertisements. European advertisements for Häagen-Dazs, a premium U.S. ice cream maker, and LapPower, a Swedish laptop computer company, received criticism for being too sexy. Häagen-Dazs's ad showed a couple in various stages of undress, in an embrace, feeding ice cream to each other. Some British editorial writers and radio commentators were outraged. One commented that "the ad was the most blatant and inappropriate use of sex as a sales aid." The ad for LapPower personal computers that the Stockholm Business Council on Ethics condemned featured the co-owner of the company with an "inviting smile and provocative demeanor displayed." (Wearing a low-cut dress, she was bending over a LapPower computer.) The bottom line for both these companies was increased sales. In Britain, ice cream sales soared after the "Dedicated to Pleasure" ads appeared, and in Sweden, the co-owner stated, "Sales are increasing daily." Whether laws are passed or the industry polices itself, advertising and its effect on people's behavior have engendered international concern.

Advertising regulations are not limited to Europe. In Quebec, Canada, not only was advertising to children banned, but also a careful study of the effects demonstrated the substantial effectiveness of the ban in reducing consumption of the fast-food products targeted.[59] The city of Sao Paulo, Brazil, has successfully banned all outdoor advertising in that important commercial center.[60] Indeed, there is an enhanced awareness of the expansion of mass communications and the perceived need to effect greater control in developing countries as well. Malaysia consistently regulates TV advertising to control the effect of the "excesses of Western ways." The government has become so concerned that it will not allow "Western cultural images" to appear in TV commercials. No bare shoulders or exposed armpits are allowed, nor are touching or kissing, sexy clothing, or blue jeans. These are just a few of the prohibitions spelled out in a 41-page advertising code that the Malaysian government has been compiling for more than 10 years.

The assault on advertising and promotion of tobacco products is escalating. In the United States, tobacco firms have agreed to curtail promotion as part of government-supported class-action lawsuits. The European Union Parliament approved larger health warnings on cigarette packs. Most significantly, the World Health Organization (WHO) has launched a global campaign against the tobacco industry.[61] Dr. Gro Harlem Brundtland, director-general of the WHO, explains, "Tobacco is a communicable disease—it's communicated through advertising, marketing and making smoking appear admirable and glamorous." A worldwide ban of tobacco advertising is just one of the stated goals of the new WHO action.

Product placement within TV programming is another area of advertising receiving the attention of regulators. In the United States, complaints have been aired regarding cigarette smoking in movies and on TV. Product placements avoid some of the regulations in markets like China, where ad time is limited. Because these practices are new to China, the growth rate has been initially dramatic. It will be interesting to follow how product placement will be regulated as the practice proliferates.

The advertising industry is sufficiently concerned with the negative attitudes and skepticism of consumers and governments and with the poor practices of some advertisers that the International Advertising Association and other national and international industry groups have developed a variety of self-regulating codes. Sponsors of these codes feel that unless the advertisers themselves come up with an effective framework for control, governments will intervene. This threat of government intervention has spurred interest groups in Europe to develop codes to ensure that the majority of ads conform to standards set for "honesty, truth, and decency." In those countries where the credibility of advertising is questioned and in those where the consumerism movement exists, the creativity of the advertiser is challenged. The most egregious control, however, may be in Myanmar (formerly Burma), where each medium has its own censorship board that passes judgment on any advertising even before it is submitted for approval by the Ministry of Information. There is even a censorship board for calendars. Content restrictions are centered on any references to the government or military, other political matters, religious themes, or images deemed degrading to traditional culture. In many countries, there is a feeling that advertising, and especially TV advertising, is too powerful and persuades consumers to buy what they do not need, an issue that has been debated in the United States for many years.

[59]Tirtha Dhar and Kathy Baylis, "Fast-Food Consumption and the Ban on Advertising Targeting Children: The Quebec Experience," *Journal of Marketing Research* 48, no. 5 (2011), pp. 799–813.

[60]Patrick Burgoyne, "Sao Paulo: The City that Said No to Advertising," *BusinessWeek,* June 18, 2007.

[61]"Russian Government Approves Accession to WHO Tobacco Control Convention," *Interfax*, January 10, 2008.

CROSSING BORDERS 16.4

Is the World Wide Web Actually Building Borders?

We close the chapter with a chilling excerpt from Neil Strauss's article in *The Wall Street Journal*. Food for thought!

If you happen to be reading this article online, you'll notice that right above it, there is a button labeled "like." Please stop reading and click on "like" right now.

Thank you. I feel much better. It's good to be liked.

There's a growing cultural obsession with being blogged, digged, tweeted and liked. Now add Google's +1 to the mix and it's just like being in high school all over again.

Don't forget to comment on, tweet, blog about and StumbleUpon this article. And be sure to "+1" it if you're on the newly launched Google+ social network. In fact, if you don't want to read the rest of this article, at least stay on the page for a few minutes before clicking elsewhere. That way, it will appear to the site analytics as if you've read the whole thing.

Once, there was something called a point of view. And, after much strife and conflict, it eventually became a commonly held idea in some parts of the world that people were entitled to their own points of view.

Unfortunately, this idea is becoming an anachronism. When the Internet first came into public use, it was hailed as a liberation from conformity, a floating world ruled by passion, creativity, innovation and freedom of information. When it was hijacked first by advertising and then by commerce, it seemed like it had been fully co-opted and brought into line with human greed and ambition.

But there was one other element of human nature that the Internet still needed to conquer: the need to belong. The "like" button began on the website

FriendFeed in 2007, appeared on Facebook in 2009, began spreading everywhere from YouTube to Amazon to most major news sites last year, and has now been officially embraced by Google as the agreeable, supportive and more status-conscious "+1." As a result, we can now search not just for information, merchandise and kitten videos on the Internet, but for approval.

You 'like' me! Even rock stars agonize over their Facebook and Twitter stats.

Just as stand-up comedians are trained to be funny by observing which of their lines and expressions are greeted with laughter, so too are our thoughts online molded to conform to popular opinion by these buttons. A status update that is met with no likes (or a clever tweet that isn't retweeted) becomes the equivalent of a joke met with silence. It must be rethought and rewritten. And so we don't show our true selves online, but a mask designed to conform to the opinions of those around us.

Conversely, when we're looking at someone else's content—whether a video or a news story—we are able to see first how many people liked it and, often, whether our friends liked it. And so we are encouraged not to form our own opinion but to look to others for cues on how to feel.

"Like" culture is antithetical to the concept of self-esteem, which a healthy individual should be developing from the inside out rather than from the outside in. Instead, we are shaped by our stats, which include not just "likes" but the number of comments generated in response to what we write and the number of friends or followers we have. I've seen rock stars agonize over the fact that another artist has far more Facebook "likes" and Twitter followers than they do.

Source: Excerpted from Neil Strauss', "The Insidious Evils of 'Like' Culture," *The Wall Street Journal*, July 2, 2011.

Summary

An integrated marketing communications (IMC) program includes coordination among advertising, sales management, public relations, sales promotions, and direct marketing. Global marketers face unique legal, language, media, and production limitations in every market. These must be considered when designing an IMC program. During the late 1990s, many large firms moved toward an advertising strategy of standardization. However, more recently even the most multinational companies have changed emphasis to strategies based on national, subcultural, demographic, or other market segments.

The major problem facing international advertisers is designing the best messages for each market served. The potential for cross-cultural misunderstandings is great in both public relations and the various advertising media. The availability and quality of advertising media also vary substantially around the world.

Marketers may be unable to enter markets profitably for the lack of appropriate advertising media—for example, some products require the availability of TV.

Advances in communication technologies (particularly the Internet) are causing dramatic changes in the structure of the international advertising and communications industries. New problems are being posed for government regulators as well. Despite these challenges, the industry is experiencing dramatic growth as new media are developed and as new markets open to commercial advertising.

Key Terms

Integrated marketing communications (IMC)	Sales promotions	Public relations (PR)	Noise

Questions

1. Define the key terms listed above.
2. "Perhaps advertising is the side of international marketing with the greatest similarities from country to country throughout the world. Paradoxically, despite its many similarities, it may also be credited with the greatest number of unique problems in international marketing." Discuss.
3. Someone once commented that advertising is America's greatest export. Discuss.
4. With satellite TV able to reach many countries, discuss how a company can use satellite TV and deal effectively with different languages, different cultures, and different legal systems.
5. Outline some of the major problems confronting an international advertiser.
6. Defend either side of the proposition that advertising can be standardized for all countries.
7. Review the basic areas of advertising regulation. Are such regulations purely foreign phenomena?
8. How can advertisers overcome the problems of low literacy in their markets?
9. What special media problems confront the international advertiser?
10. After reading the section in this chapter on direct mail, develop guidelines to be used by a company when creating a direct mail program.
11. Will the ability to broadcast advertisements over TV satellites increase or decrease the need for standardization of advertisements? What are the problems associated with satellite broadcasting? Comment.
12. In many of the world's marketplaces, a broad variety of media must be utilized to reach the majority of the market. Explain.
13. Cinema advertising is unimportant in the United States but a major media in such countries as Austria. Why?
14. "Foreign newspapers obviously cannot be considered as homogeneous advertising entities." Explain.
15. Borrow a foreign magazine from the library. Compare the foreign advertising to that in an American magazine.
16. What is sales promotion and how is it used in international marketing?
17. Show how the communications process can help an international marketer avoid problems in international advertising.
18. Take each of the steps in the communications process and give an example of how culture differences can affect the final message received.
19. Discuss the problems created because the communications process is initiated in one cultural context and ends in another.
20. What is the importance of feedback in the communications process? Of noise?

(From page 497) Why would Coke and McDonald's shed the red in their logos?

For the blue-and-yellow-uniformed Maradona and his team *Boca Junior*, Coke's red and white are also the hated colors of their main *futbol* competitor in Buenos Aires, *River Plate*. The negotiations between Coco-Cola and the *Boca Junior* club executives must have been fascinating with millions of dollars on the table, with many thousands of raucous fans acting as a very much involved, and potentially riotous, audience. So, a black-and-white Coke logo was the creative solution. We note that Sinteplast, a large paint company and local sponsor, was able to include its red, white, and blue logo on the stadium—the colors of passion! The red and gold of McDonald's was traded for black in Cuzco because the area is an official UNESCO World Heritage Site, and the money that supports this designation includes rules that preclude "intrusive" advertising.

Chapter 17

Personal Selling and Sales Management

CHAPTER OUTLINE

CHAPTER LEARNING OBJECTIVES

What you should learn from Chapter 17:

LO1 The role of interpersonal selling in international marketing

LO2 The considerations in designing an international sales force

LO3 The steps to recruiting three types of international salespeople

LO4 Selection criteria for international sales and marketing positions

LO5 The special training needs of international personnel

LO6 Motivation techniques for international sales representatives

LO7 How to design compensation systems for an international sales force

LO8 How to prepare Americans for foreign assignments

LO9 The changing profile of the global sales and marketing manager

David J. Cichelli (editor), *2010 Sales Compensation Trends Survey Results* (Scottsdale, AZ: The Alexander Group, Inc., 2010).

Global Perspective

INTERNATIONAL ASSIGNMENTS ARE GLAMOROUS, RIGHT?

"Glamorous" is probably not the adjective the following executives would use:

> The problem as I see it with the company's talk about international managers is that they were just paying lip service to it. When I applied for the posting to Malaysia they gave me all this stuff about the assignment being a really good career move and how I'd gain this valuable international experience and so on. And don't get me wrong, we really enjoyed the posting. We loved the people and the culture and the lifestyle and when it came back to returning home, we weren't really all that keen . . . . The problem was that while I had been away, the company had undergone a wholesale restructuring . . . . This meant that when I got back, my job had been effectively eliminated.

> We have been in the United States for eleven months and I reckon it will be another six to twelve months before my wife and the kids are really settled here. I'm still learning new stuff every day at work and it has taken a long time to get used to American ways of doing things . . . . I mean if the company said, "Oh, we want you to move to South Africa in a year's time," I would really dig my heels in because it was initially very disruptive for my wife when she first came here.

And "glamorous" would not be on the tip of these expatriate spouses' tongues either:

> I found I haven't adapted to Spanish hours. I find it a continual problem because the 2–5 p.m. siesta closure is really awkward. I always find myself where I have to remind myself that from 2–5 I have a blank period that I can't do anything . . . . We started adjusting to the eating schedule. Whether we like it or not, we eat a lot later.

> We've been really fortunate we haven't had to use healthcare services here . . . . The thought of going to, needing to go to a doctor is scary because for me it would have to be someone English speaking or I wouldn't, you know, feel comfortable.

Given these kinds of problems, is that international sales position being offered to you as attractive as it looks? Will it really help your career?

Sources: Nick Forster, "The Myth of the 'International Manager,'" *International Journal of Resource Management* 11, no. 1 (February 2000), pp. 126–42; Mary C. Gilly, Lisa Peñaloza, and Kenneth M. Kambara, "The Role of Consumption in Expatriate Adjustment and Satisfaction," working paper, Paul Merage School of Business, University of California, Irvine, 2015.

David J. Cichelli (editor), *2010 Sales Compensation Trends Survey Results* (Scottsdale, AZ: The Alexander Group, Inc., 2010). Used with permission.

LO1

The role of interpersonal selling in international marketing

The salesperson is a company's most direct tie to the customer; in the eyes of most customers, the salesperson is the company. As presenter of company offerings and gatherer of customer information, the sales representative is the final link in the culmination of a company's marketing and sales efforts.

Growing global competition, coupled with the dynamic and complex nature of international business, increases both the need and the means for closer ties with both customers and suppliers. Particularly in relationship-based cultures such as China, relationship marketing, built on effective communications between the seller and buyer, focuses on building long-term alliances rather than treating each sale as a one-time event.[1] Advances in information technology are allowing for increasingly higher levels of coordination across advertising, marketing research, and personal selling efforts, yielding new roles and functions in customer relationship management (CRM).[2] Similarly, such advances are changing the nature of personal selling and sales management, lead some to forecast substantial reductions in field sales efforts. Others suggest that the new technologies have changed the job, but not the number of highly qualified sales people needed.

In this ever-changing environment of international business, the tasks of designing, building, training, motivating, and compensating an international sales group generate unique problems at every stage of management and development.[3] In this chapter are discussed the alternatives and problems of managing sales and marketing personnel in foreign countries. Indeed, these problems are among the most difficult facing international marketers. In one survey of CEOs and other top executives, the respondents identified "establishing sales and distribution networks" and "cultural differences" as major difficulties in international operations.

Designing the Sales Force

LO2

The considerations in designing an international sales force

The first step in managing a sales force is its design. Based on analyses of current and potential customers, the selling environment, competition, and the firm's resources and capabilities, decisions must be made regarding the numbers,[4] characteristics, and assignments of sales personnel. All these design decisions are made more challenging by the wide variety of pertinent conditions and circumstances in international markets.[5]

[1]Roy Y.J. Chua, Michael W. Norris, and Paul Ingram, "*Guanxi* vs. Networking: Distinctive Configurations of Affect- and Cognition-Based Trust in the Networks of Chinese and American Managers," *Journal of International Business Studies* 40, no. 3 (2009), pp. 490–508; Nikala Lane and Nigel Peircy, "Strategizing the Sales Organization," *Journal of Strategic Marketing* 17, 3-4 (2009), pp. 307–322; Luis Filipe Lages. Garcia Silva, and Chris Styles, "Relationship Capabilities, Quality, and Innovation as Determinants of Export Performance," *Journal of International Marketing* 17, no. 4 (2009), pp. 47–70; Christina Sichtmann, Maren von Selasinsky, and Adamantios Diamantopoulos, "Service Quality and Export Performance of Business-to-Business Service Providers: The Role of Service Employee- and Customer-Oriented Quality Control Initiatives," *Journal of International Marketing* 19, no. 1 (2011), pp. 1–22; Susi Geiger and John Finch, "Buyer-Seller Interactions in Mature Industrial Markets: Blurring the Relational-Transactional Selling Dichotomy," *Journal of Personal Selling & Sales Management* 3, no. 3 (2011), pp. 255–68.

[2]Linda H. Shi, Shaoming Zou, J. Chris White, Regina C. McNally, and S. Tamer Cavusgil, "Global Account Management Capability: Insights from Leading Suppliers," *Journal of International Marketing* 13, no. 2 (2005), pp. 93–113; Linda Hui Shi, J. Chris White, Shaoming Zou, and S. Tamer Cavusgil, "Global Account Management Strategies: Drivers and Outcomes," *Journal of International Business Studies* 41, no. 4 (2010), pp. 620–38.

[3]Despite the importance of this topic, our knowledge of it is just now starting to catch up with practice. See Nikolaos G. Panagopoulos, Nick Lee, Ellen Bolman Pullins, George J. Avlonitis, Pasal Brassier, Paolo Guenzi, Anna Humenberger, Piotr Kwiatec, Terry W. Loe, Elina Oksanen-Ylikoski, Robert M. Peterson, Beth Rogers, and Dan C. Weilbaker, "Internationalizing Sales Research: Current Status, Opportunities, and Challenges," *Journal of Personal Selling & Sales Management* 31, no. 3 (2011), pp. 219–42; Artur Baldauf and Nick Lee, "International Selling and Sales Management: Sales Force Research beyond Geographical Boundaries," *Journal of Personal Selling & Sales Management* 31, no. 3 (2011), pp. 211–19.

[4]Adi Narayan, "Welcome to India, the Land of the Drug Reps," *Bloomberg Businessweek*, September 12, 2011, pp. 26–27.

[5]Tomi Kaamanen, Tatu Simula, and Sami Torstila, "Cross-Border Relocations of Headquarters in Europe," *Journal of International Business Studies* 43, no. 7 (2012), pp. 187–210.

Exhibit 17.1
Cultural Differences in Incentives

Source: David J. Cichelli (ed.), *2012 Sales Compensation Trends Survey* (The Alexander Group, Inc.). Reprinted with permission.

Country	Percentage of incentive pay versus base pay	Percentage of incentives based on team performance
China	36%	25%
Russia	38	21
Japan	36	18
Mexico	37	17
Brazil	36	16
France	38	12
United States	38	11
Germany	38	10
United Kingdom	36	9

Moreover, the globalization of markets and customers, makes the job of international sales manager quite interesting.

As described in previous chapters, distribution strategies will often vary from country to country. Some markets may require a direct sales force, whereas others may not. How customers are approached can differ as well. The hard sell that may work in some countries can be inappropriate in others. Automobiles have been sold door to door in Japan for years, and only recently have stocks been sold over the Internet in Europe. More than 100,000 of Singapore's 6 million inhabitants are involved in home product sales and other forms of direct marketing. The size of accounts certainly makes a difference as well. Selling high-technology products may allow for the greater use of American expatriates, whereas selling consulting services will tend to require more participation by native sales representatives. Selling in information-oriented cultures such as Germany may also allow for greater use of expatriates. However, relationship-oriented countries such as Japan will require the most complete local knowledge possessed only by natives. Writing about Japan, two international marketing experts agree: "Personal selling as a rule has to be localized for even the most global of corporations and industries."[6]

A nice demonstration of the importance and complexity of cultural influences on sales management practices appears in the data presented in Exhibit 17.1. The Alexander Group annually surveys sales managers at more than 100 multinational companies, most with operations around the world, including IBM, Hewlett-Packard, and Samsung. There are no important differences in pay mix practices across countries (i.e., the average percentage of incentive pay ranges between 36 and 38 percent), yet there are important differences in the use of team performance metrics. These differences are strongly ($r = 0.89$) correlated with Hofstede's measures of individualism/collectivism. See pages 167–168.

Once decisions have been made about how many expatriates, local nationals, or third-country nationals a particular market requires, the more intricate aspects of design can be undertaken, such as territory allocation and customer call plans. Many of the most advanced operations research tools developed in the United States can be applied in foreign markets, with appropriate adaptation of inputs, of course.[7] For example, one company has provided tools to help international firms create balanced territories and find optimal locations for sales offices in Canada, Mexico, and Australia.[8] However, the use of such high-tech resource allocation tools requires intricate knowledge of not only

---

[6]Johny K. Johansson and Ikujiro Nonaka, *Relentless: The Japanese Way of Marketing* (New York: Harper Business, 1997), p. 97.

[7]Laia Ferrer, Rafael Pastor, and Alberto Garcia-Villoria, "Designing Salespeople's Routes with Multiple Visits of Customers: A Case Study," *International Journal of Production Economics* 19, no. 1 (2009), pp. 46–54.

[8]See the website for The TerrAlign Group, http://www.terralign.com, for more detailed information.

geographical details but also appropriate call routines. Many things can differ across cultures—the length of sales cycles, the kinds of customer relationships, and the types of interactions with customers. Indeed, more than one study has identified substantial differences in the importance of referrals in the sales of industrial services in Japan vis-à-vis the United States.[9] The implications are that in Japan, sales calls must be made not only on customers but also on the key people, such as bankers, in the all-important referral networks.

Recruiting Marketing and Sales Personnel

LO3

The steps to recruiting three types of international salespeople

The number of marketing management personnel from the home country assigned to foreign countries varies according to the size of the operation, the availability of qualified locals, and other firm characteristics. Increasingly, the number of U.S. home-country nationals (expatriates) assigned to foreign posts is smaller as the pool of trained, experienced locals grows.

The largest personnel requirement abroad for most companies is the sales force, recruited from three sources: expatriates, local nationals, and third-country nationals. A company's staffing pattern may include all three types in any single foreign operation, depending on qualifications, availability, and company needs. Sales and marketing executives can be recruited via the traditional media of advertising (including newspapers, magazines, job fairs, and the Internet), employment agencies or executive search firms,[10] and the all-important personal referrals. The last source will be crucial in many foreign countries, particularly the relationship-oriented ones.

Expatriates

The number of companies relying on expatriate personnel is increasing[11] as the volume of world trade increases and as more companies use locals to fill marketing positions. When products are highly technical, or when selling requires an extensive background of information and applications, an expatriate sales force remains the best choice. The expatriate salesperson may have the advantages of greater technical training, better knowledge of the company and its product line, and proven dependability. Because they are not locals, expatriates sometimes add to the prestige of the product line in the eyes of foreign customers. And perhaps most important, expatriates usually are able to effectively communicate with and influence headquarters' personnel.[12]

The chief disadvantages of an expatriate sales force are the high cost, cultural and legal[13] barriers, and the limited number of high-caliber personnel willing to live abroad for extended periods. Employees are reluctant to go abroad for many reasons: Some find it difficult to uproot families for a two- or three-year assignment, increasing numbers of dual-career couples often require finding suitable jobs for spouses, and many executives believe such assignments impede their subsequent promotions at home. Recall the comments of the executives in the Global Perspective. The loss of visibility at corporate headquarters plus the belief that "out of sight is out of mind" are major reasons for the reluctance to accept a foreign assignment. Companies with well-planned career development programs have the least difficulty. Careful fitting and integration of expatriate employees into foreign offices

[9]R. Bruce Money, Mary C. Gilly, and John L. Graham, "National Culture and Referral Behavior in the Purchase of Industrial Services in the United States and Japan," *Journal of Marketing* 62, no. 4 (October 1998), pp. 76–87.

[10]The largest international executive search firm is Korn/Ferry International (http://www.kornferry.com).

[11]Darin W. White, R. Keith Absher, and Kyle A. Huggings, "The Effects of Hardness and Cultural Distance on Sociocultural Adaptations in an Expatriate Sales Management Population," *Journal of Personal Selling & Sales Management* 31, no. 3 (2011), pp. 325–37.

[12]Nelia S. Brunig, Karan Sonpar, and Xiaoyun Wang, "Host_Country National Networks and Expatriate Effectiveness: A Mixed-Methods Study," *Journal of International Business Studies* 43 (2012), pp. 444–50.

[13]Even if job permits are obtained, other legal problems can also crop up. See James T. Areddy, "China Charges Rio Tinto Employees," *The Wall Street Journal*, February 10, 2010, online.

also can make a big difference.[14] Indeed, the best international companies make it crystal clear that a ticket to top management is an overseas stint. Korn/Ferry International reports in a survey of 75 senior executives from around the world that "international experience" is the attribute identified as second most important for CEOs—experience in marketing and finance positions were first and third, respectively.[15] We should also mention that expatriates working in foreign headquarters offices also face similar dislocation problems as those described previously.[16]

Expatriates commit to foreign assignments for varying lengths of time, from a few weeks or months to a lifetime. Some expatriates have one-time assignments (which may last for years), after which they return to the parent company; others are essentially professional expatriates, working abroad in country after country. Still another expatriate assignment is a career-long assignment to a given country or region; this assignment is likely to lead to assimilation of the expatriate into the foreign culture to such an extent that the person may more closely resemble a local than an expatriate. Because expatriate marketing personnel are likely to cost substantially more than locals, a company must be certain of their effectiveness.

More and more American companies are taking advantage of American employees who are fluent in languages other than English. For example, many U.S. citizens speak Spanish as their first language. The large number of Puerto Ricans working for American multinationals in places like Mexico City is well documented. Recent immigrants and their sons and daughters who learn their parents' languages and about their native cultures will continue to be invaluable assets for firms wishing to enter such markets. Certainly ethnic Chinese- and Vietnamese-Americans are serving as cultural bridges for commerce with those two nations. Indeed, throughout history patterns of commerce have always followed paths of immigration.

Virtual Expatriates

The Internet and other advances in communications technologies,[17] along with the growing reluctance of executives to move abroad, are creating a new breed of expatriate, the virtual one. Also with increasing frequency, virtual international sales teams are being used.[18] The performance of such teams appears mixed, enjoying the advantages of diversity-driven creativity and lower travel costs but suffering the disadvantages of different time zones[19] and cross-cultural communications. According to a PricewaterhouseCoopers survey of 270 organizations, there has been a substantial increase in shorter-term, commute, and virtual assignments in recent years. Virtual expatriates manage operations in other countries but do not move there. They stay in hotels, make long visits, and maintain their families at home. Some spend up to 75 percent of their working time traveling. None leave home without the ubiquitous laptop and cell phone.

---

[14]B. Sebastian Reiche, Maria L. Kraimer, and Anne-Wil Harzing, "Why Do International Assignees Stay? An Organizational Embeddedness Perspective," *Journal of International Business Studies* 42, no. 4 (2011), pp. 521–44.

[15]See "Marketing Is Fastest Route to the Executive Suite," Korn/Ferry International (http://www.kornferry .com).

[16]Boris Groysberg, Nitin Nohria, and Kerry Herman, "The Expat Dilemma," *Harvard Business Review*, November 2011, pp. 150–55; Miriam Moeller and Michael Harvey, "Inpatriate Marketing Managers: Issues Associated with Staffing Global Marketing Positions," *Journal of International Marketing* 19, no. 4 (2011), pp. 1–16.

[17]Peter Burrows, "Virtual Meetings for Real-World Budgets," *Bloomberg Businessweek*, August 9, 2010, pp. 36–37.

[18]Vishag Badrinarayanan, Sreedhar Madhavaram, and Elad Granot, "Global Virtual Sales Teams (GVSTs): A Conceptual Framework of the Influence of Intellectual and Social Capital on Effectiveness," *Journal of Personal Selling & Sales Management*, 31, no. 3 (2011), pp. 311–24.

[19]Amy Dockser Marcus, "To Avoid Jet Lag this Summer, Travel Like a Scientist," *The Wall Street Journal*, May 27, 2013, online; Martin Rooney, "Learning to Laugh through the Pain," *The New York Times*, May 6, 2014, p. B7.

The 2009 travel disruptions caused by the initial stages of H1N1 virus were similar to those from the 2003 SARS outbreak. A worker cleans an American Airlines plane detained at San Jose International Airport in California after a nonstop flight from Tokyo, in which several passengers complained of symptoms similar to SARS, or severe acute respiratory syndrome. Officials found no threat after isolating passengers and crew for two hours. We can expect more such disease-based problems as people on the planet continue to get closer together. International travel can be a lot of work!

Close contact with subordinates and customers is, of course, tougher for virtual expatriates. Moreover, the travel can be a killer[20]—that is, foreign bugs are often more virulent and easier to catch on long international flights (indeed, one doctor calls airplanes "germ tubes"),[21] crime and violence against expatriates and travelers in foreign cities is a real hazard,[22] air pollution,[23] short-hop flights and traffic conditions[24] in less developed countries are dangerous, and living in hotels is lonely. However, virtual expatriates' families do not have to be uprooted, and executives can stay in closer touch with the home office. Finally, from the firm's perspective, a virtual assignment may be the only option and often a good way to avoid the extra expenses of an actual executive move.

Local Nationals The historical preference for expatriate managers and salespeople from the home country is giving way to a preference for local nationals.[25] At the sales level, the picture is clearly biased in favor of the locals because they transcend both cultural and legal barriers. Usually[26] more knowledgeable about a country's business structure and systems[27]

[20]Andreas Schotter and Paul W. Beamish, "The Hassle Factor: An Explanation for Managerial Location Shunning," *Journal of International Business Studies* 44 (2013), pp. 52–54.

[21]Mehul Srivastava and Jason Gale, "In India, Dengue Fever Stalks the Affluent," *Bloomberg Businessweek*, September 20, 2010, pp. 13–14; Joe Sharkey, "For the Traveler, Ebola Is a Small Blip on the Radar," *The New York Times*, October 14, 2014, p. B6; Choe Sang-Hun, "Ebola Prompts North Korea to Bar Tourists," *The New York Times*, October 24, 2014, p. A10.

[22]Nicholas Casey and Jose de Cordoba, "U.S. Warns of Mexico Peril," *The Wall Street Journal*, April 13, 2011; Scott McCartney, "Crisis Abroad: Tips for International Travelers," *The Wall Street Journal*, June 9, 2011; Jennifer Oetzel and Kathleen Getz, "Why and How Might Firms Respond Strategically to Violent Conflict?" *Journal of International Business Studies* 43, no. 2 (2012), pp. 166–86.

[23]Keith Bradsher, "Looking Beyond China, Some Companies Shift Personnel," *The New York Times*, September 10, 2014, pp. B1, 2.

[24]Ola Orekunrin, "The Trauma Epidemic," *The New York Times*, October 18, 2013, p. A23.

[25]Kenneth S. Law, Lynda Jiwen Song, Chi-Sum Wong, and Donghua Chen, "The Antecedents and Consequences of Successful Localization," *Journal of International Business Studies* 40, no. 8 (2009), pp. 1359–73.

[26]Dan V. Caprar, "Foreign Locals: A Cautionary Tale on the Culture of Local Employees," *Journal of International Business Studies* 42, no. 5 (2011), pp. 608–28.

[27]Syeda Nazli Wasti and Syeda Arzu Wasti, "Trust in Buyer-Supplier Relations: The Case of the Turkish Automotive Industry," *Journal of International Business Studies* 39 (2008), pp. 118–31.

Exhibit 17.2
The World's 20 Most
Expensive Cities (in order)

Source: Expatistan.com, 2015.

London	Sydney
Oslo	Hong Kong
Geneva	Brisbane
Zurich	The Hague
New York	Stockholm
Lausanne	Honolulu
Singapore	Amsterdam
Paris	Melbourne
San Francisco	Tokyo
Copenhagen	Washington, DC

The cities are listed in order; London is the most expensive and Washington, DC, is the least expensive of these 20 most expensive.

than an expatriate would be, local salespeople are better able to lead a company through the maze of unfamiliar distribution systems and referral networks. Furthermore, pools of qualified foreign personnel available in some places cost less to maintain than a staff of expatriates.

In Europe and Asia, many locals have earned MBA degrees in the United States; thus, a firm gets the cultural knowledge of the local meshed with an understanding of U.S. business management systems. Although expatriates' salaries may be no more than those of their national counterparts, the total cost of keeping comparable groups of expatriates in a country can be considerably higher (often three times the expense) because of special cost-of-living benefits, moving expenses, taxes, and other costs associated with keeping an expatriate abroad. As can be seen in Exhibit 17.2, only four of the most expensive cities in the world are in the United States.

The main disadvantage of hiring local nationals is the tendency of headquarters personnel to ignore their advice. Even though most foreign nationals are careful to keep relationships at the home office warm, their influence is often reduced by their limited English communication skills and lack of understanding of how home-office politics influence decision making. Another key disadvantage can be their lack of availability; one CEO of a consulting firm that specializes in recruiting managers in China reports that 10 openings exist for every one qualified applicant. Moreover, whereas in the United States hiring experienced salespeople from competitors, suppliers, or vendors is common practice, the same approach in other countries may not work. In places like Japan, employees are much more loyal to their companies and therefore are difficult to lure away even for big money. College recruits can also be hard to hire in Japan because the smartest students are heavily recruited by the largest Japanese firms. Smaller firms and foreign firms are seen in Japan as much more risky employment opportunities. We do note, however, that in recent years Japan's economic growth has been stunted, giving even foreign companies a strong position in recruiting.[28]

One other consideration makes recruiting of local nationals as sales representatives more difficult in many foreign countries. We all know about Americans' aversion to being a salesperson. Personal selling is often derided as a career and represented in a negative light in American media—Arthur Miller's *Death of a Salesman* is of course the best example. Despite the bad press, however, personal selling is the most common job in the United States. Indeed, the United States has been described as "a nation of salesmen."[29] But as negatively as the selling profession is viewed in the United States, in many other countries, it is viewed in even worse ways. Particularly in the more relationship-oriented cultures such as France, Mexico, and Japan, sales representatives tend to be on the bottom rung of the

---

[28]David McNeill, "In Bleak Economy, Japanese Students Grow Frustrated with Endless Job Hunt," *Chronicle of Higher Education*, February 7, 2010, online.

[29]See Earl Shorris's excellent and still pertinent book, *A Nation of Salesmen* (New York: Norton, 1994).

Locals hit the road. Japanese salesmen save on expenses in this "capsule hotel" in Osaka.

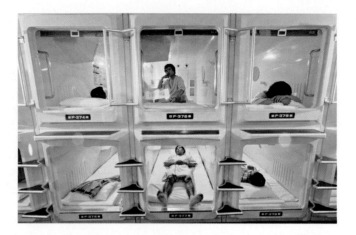

social ladder. Thus, recruiting the brightest people to fill sales positions in foreign operations can be very difficult indeed.

Third-Country Nationals

The internationalization of business has created a pool of third-country nationals (TCNs), expatriates from their own countries working for a foreign company in a third country. The TCNs are a group whose nationality has little to do with where they work or for whom. An example would be a German working in Argentina for a U.S. company. Historically, few expatriates or TCNs spent the majority of their careers abroad, but now a truly "global executive" has begun to emerge. The recently appointed chairman of a division of a major Netherlands company is a Norwegian who gained that post after stints in the United States, where he was the U.S. subsidiary's chairman, and in Brazil, where he held the position of general manager. At one time, Burroughs Corporation's Italian subsidiary was run by a French national, the Swiss subsidiary by a Dane, the German subsidiary by an English person, the French subsidiary by a Swiss, the Venezuelan subsidiary by an Argentinean, and the Danish subsidiary by a Dutch person.

American companies often seek TCNs from other English-speaking countries to avoid the double taxation costs of their American managers. Americans working in Spain, for example, must pay both Spanish and U.S. income taxes, and most American firms' compensation packages for expatriates are adjusted accordingly. So, given the same pay and benefits, it is cheaper for an American firm to post a British executive in Spain than an American.

Overall, the development of TCN executives reflects not only a growing internationalization of business but also an acknowledgment that personal skills and motivations are not the exclusive property of one nation. These TCNs often are sought because they speak several languages and know an industry or foreign country well. More and more companies feel that talent should flow to opportunity, regardless of one's home country.

Host-Country Restrictions

The host government's attitudes toward foreign workers often complicate selecting expatriate U.S. nationals over locals. Concerns about foreign corporate domination, local unemployment, and other issues cause some countries to restrict the number of non-nationals allowed to work within the country. Most countries have specific rules limiting work permits for foreigners to positions that cannot be filled by a national. Furthermore, the law often limits such permits to periods just long enough to train a local for a specific position. Such restrictions mean that MNCs have fewer opportunities for sending home-country personnel to management positions abroad.

In earlier years, personnel gained foreign-country experience by being sent to lower management positions to gain the necessary training before eventually assuming top-level foreign assignments. Most countries, including the United States, control the number of foreigners allowed to work or train within their borders. Since September 11, 2001, U.S. immigration authorities have clamped down even harder on the issuance of all kinds of work visas.

Selecting Sales and Marketing Personnel

LO4

Selection criteria for international sales and marketing positions

To select personnel for international marketing positions effectively, management must define precisely what is expected of its people. A formal job description can aid management in expressing long-range as well as current needs. In addition to descriptions for each marketing position, the criteria should include special requirements indigenous to various countries.

People operating in the home country need only the attributes of effective salespersons, whereas a transnational management position can require skills and attitudes that would challenge a diplomat. International personnel requirements and preferences vary considerably. However, some basic requisites leading to effective performance should be considered because effective executives and salespeople, regardless of what foreign country they are operating in, share certain personal characteristics, skills, and orientations.[30]

Maturity is a prime requisite for expatriate and third-country personnel. Managers and sales personnel working abroad typically must work more independently than their domestic counterparts. The company must have confidence in their ability to make ethical[31] decisions and commitments without constant recourse to the home office, or they cannot be individually effective.

International personnel require a kind of *emotional stability* (some have used the term "hardness," which roughly translates into emotional stability combined with flexibility)[32] not demanded in domestic sales positions.[33] Regardless of location, these people are living in cultures dissimilar to their own; to some extent they are always under scrutiny and always aware that they are official representatives of the company abroad. They need sensitivity to behavioral variations in different countries, but they cannot be so hypersensitive that their behavior is adversely affected.

Managers or salespeople operating in foreign countries need considerable *breadth of knowledge* of many subjects both on and off the job. The ability to speak one or more other languages is always preferable.

The marketer who expects to be effective in the international marketplace needs to have a *positive outlook* on an international assignment. People who do not like what they are doing and where they are doing it stand little chance of success, particularly in a foreign country. Failures usually are the result of overselling the assignment, showing the bright side of the picture, and not warning about the bleak side.

An international salesperson must have a high level of *flexibility*, whether working in a foreign country or at home. Expatriates working in a foreign country must be particularly sensitive to the habits of the market; those working at home for a foreign company must adapt to the requirements and ways of the parent company.

Successful adaptation in international affairs is based on a combination of attitude and effort. A careful study of the customs of the market country should be initiated before the marketer arrives and should be continued as long as facets of the culture are not clear. One useful approach is to listen to the advice of national and foreign businesspeople

[30]Pualo Guenzi, Luigi M. de Luca, and Gabriele Troilo, "Organizational Drivers of Salespeople's Customer Orientation and Selling Orientation," *Journal of Personal Selling & Sales Management* 31, no. 3 (2011), pp. 269–86; Kenneth Le Meunier-FitzHugh and Nigel F. Piercy, "Exploring the Relationship between Market Orientation and Sales and Marketing Collaborations," *Journal of Personal Selling & Sales Management* 31, no. 3 (2011), pp. 287–96.

[31]Kam-hon Lee, Gong-ming Qian, Julie H. Yu, and Ying Ho, "Trading Favors for Marketing Advantage: Evidence from Hong Kong, China, and the United States," *Journal of International Marketing* 13, no. 1 (2005), pp. 1–35; Sergio Roman and Salvador Ruiz, "Relationship Outcomes of Perceived Ethical Sales Behavior: The Customer's Perspective," *Journal of Business Research* 58, no. 4 (2005), pp. 439–52.

[32]White et al., "The Effects of Hardness and Cultural Difference," op. cit.

[33]Willem Verbeke and Richard P. Bagozzi, "Exploring the Role of Self- and Customer-Provoked Embarrassment in Personal Selling," *International Journal of Research in Marketing* 20, no. 3 (2003), pp. 233–58.

Mary Kay Inc.
Direct Selling Goes Global

Mary Kay Ash in 1988 at a Directors' Conference in Mexico City. Over the years, the founder of Mary Kay Inc. has received many awards for her inspirational and entrepreneurial leadership, including being named one of the 25 Most Influential Business Leaders of the Last 25 Years by PBS and the Wharton School of Business in 2004; National Business Hall of Fame election in 1996 by *Fortune*; and one of "America's 25 Most Influential Women" in the 1985 *The World Almanac and Book of Facts*. About her success she explained, "I envisioned a company in which any woman could become just as successful as she wanted to be. The doors would be wide open to opportunity for women who were willing to pay the price and had the courage to dream." Mary Kay established an important corporate ethic in her firm from the beginning: It was first—a company dedicated to making life more beautiful for women. It was founded not on the competitive rule but on the Golden Rule—on praising people to enable their success—and on the principles of placing faith first, family second, and career third. It was a company, as Mary Kay Ash often said, "with heart."

The website in each country is presented in the local native language. Here we see Brazil's. Targeted are two types of Mary Kay partners: (1) cosmetics customers (*quero comprar productos*) and (2) potential Independent Beauty Consultants (*quero ser uma consultora*). Success in the company is predicated on both selling products and developing an active group of Consultants.

Mary Kay Inc. is one of the world's largest direct selling companies, with more than $3.5 billion in annual wholesale sales worldwide. Mary Kay was founded in 1963 by Mary Kay Ash, with the goal of helping women achieve personal growth and financial success. Mary Kay remains committed to enriching women's lives, and today more than 3 million people of all backgrounds are enjoying the advantages of being Mary Kay Independent Beauty Consultants. Mary Kay's high-quality skin care and color cosmetics products are sold in more than 36 countries.

Order of Entry

United States 1963	Sweden 1992	Hong Kong 1999
Australia 1971	Guatemala 1993	Kazakhstan 2000
Canada 1978	Moldova 1993	Philippines 2000
Argentina 1980	Norway 1993	Slovakia 2000
Uruguay 1984	Russia 1993	South Korea 2001
Germany 1986	China 1995	Poland 2006
Malaysia 1988	Portugal 1995	Lithuania 2009
Mexico 1988	Finland 1996	Singapore 2009
New Zealand 1989	Czech Republic 1997	Armenia 2010
Taiwan 1991	Ukraine 1997	Switzerland 2012
United Kingdom 1990	Brazil 1998	Belarus 2013
Spain 1992	El Salvador 1999	Netherlands 2013

The business model is simple: All independent sales force members purchase products from Mary Kay Inc. at a set wholesale price and then sell the products directly to consumers at a retail price. With flexible hours, a clearly defined business plan, and an open-ended opportunity to achieve personal growth and financial success, a Mary Kay business is the ideal choice for many people. Members of the independent sales force are in business for themselves, set their own schedules, build their own customer base, and determine their own level of success.

Starting a Mary Kay independent business costs as little as $100 (plus tax and shipping) for a Mary Kay Starter Kit, which includes educational materials. The organization of the sales force is quite flat, beginning with Independent Beauty Consultants (more than 2 million), then Independent Sales Directors (about 39,000), and Independent National Sales Directors (about 600). More than 300 of the Sales Directors have earned more than $1 million in lifetime commissions. Sales Directors continue to maintain and build their own customer base while building a cadre of Beauty Consultants which they mentor, providing leadership, guidance, and recognition. Sales Directors and National Sales Directors can earn additional income through commissions paid directly by Mary Kay Inc.

While sales management practices are generally consistent worldwide, each market requires some degree of adaptation based on local customs, cultures, and legal frameworks. The company's ability to adapt its programs has been successful in several markets. Examples of the way this adaptation occurs follows:

Armenia. Women in Armenia value spending time with other women. With Mary Kay, they find opportunities for social connection, as well as flexible income and more personal recognition than in many other available jobs. While Armenian consumers may recognize a global brand such as Mary Kay, they are not very familiar with the direct selling model. Even though several direct selling companies already operate in Armenia, traditional retail trade remains more common. Thus a top priority for Mary Kay Armenia is working together with other direct selling companies to establish a favorable reputation for direct selling.

Brazil. Brazil is a great opportunity for direct sellers, but it has a very complicated and high tax system that varies in every state. Importing products is one of the most difficult challenges, as the rules change constantly. That makes planning for inventory levels and obtaining product registrations and operation licenses challenging. However, consistent effort within the company and communication with government officials promise continued success in fast growing Brazil.

Mexico. Through the years Mary Kay Mexico has developed and nourished strong brand awareness among consumers. Customers are very loyal to the company due to the high quality of the products, promotional initiatives, and personal services. Mexicans have a positive view of direct selling—where you can find anything from cosmetics, vitamins, jewelry, shoes, or decorative items being sold in this person-to-person, relationship selling model. Selling these kinds of products to relatives or friends who already intended to purchase them is perceived as a win–win situation.

Poland. Almost half the women in Poland hold jobs—typically with higher qualifications but lower salaries than men. Some stay home, but many women work "two shifts"—a regular job plus caring for family. They have an entrepreneurial spirit and appreciate the family-friendly flexibility of an independent Mary Kay business. But they need their husbands' support. This is an area of potential conflict, as traditional (let's say "old-fashioned") husbands do not accept women leaving the house in the evening for a business meeting or skin care class. However, because of the Mary Kay values of a balanced life (faith first, family second, career third) the business growth of Mary Kay Poland has been consistent.

Spain. Many consumers in Spain are not familiar with direct selling, and as a result, they do not understand the benefits of having an Independent Beauty Consultant offer unique and personal services, along with quality Mary Kay products. One of the company's objectives is to equip the independent sales force with solid business knowledge and professionalism to ensure that Mary Kay stands apart from competitors. The customer service offered to the sales force and that they in turn offer to customers not only helps them understand the benefits of direct selling but also generates trust with consumers.

In the United States, the Mary Kay pink Cadillac is a cultural icon, as well as a powerful incentive for performance, delivering both monetary value and social recognition. Here in Shanghai, China, where General Motors does not manufacture Cadillacs, pink Mercedes serve that purpose. In other countries, other brands of autos are employed including Mitsubishi, Toyota, FAW-Volkswagen, Skoda, and Chevrolet. More than 10,500 women worldwide qualify to drive Mary Kay Career Cars.

At her home, an Independent Mary Kay Beauty Consultant in Canada demonstrates the use of cosmetic kits.

The company's Texas roots are enjoyed during a Sales Directors' weeklong leadership program in Prague, Czech Republic—notice their distinctive black suits, also a mark of social recognition. Of course, around the world, the styles of the suits vary considerably with local fashions.

Training of Independent Beauty Consultants is a key aspect of sales management for the company. Here we see established Consultants in their red jackets attending a career seminar in Seoul, South Korea. The red jackets signify achievement in both sales and recruiting activities.

International sales is hard work.[34] A typical week for this Canadian executive looks like this: Leave Singapore with the flu. Arrive home in Toronto to discover that a frozen pipe has burst. Immediately board a plane for a two-day trip to Chicago. Back to Toronto. On to Detroit, battling jet lag and the flu. Back to Toronto, running through the Detroit airport and throwing his briefcase into a closing door. Take a brief break in flooded house before boarding another plane to China. Reports waking up in a plane and asking his seatmate where they were landing. Seventeen flights in two weeks left him a bit confused.

operating in that country. *Cultural empathy* and cultural intelligence[35] are clearly a part of the basic orientation, because anyone who is antagonistic or confused about the environment is unlikely to be effective.[36] Similar cultural values would be an asset in this area as well.[37] And not only smaller cultural distances but also the direction of the cultural exchange can make a difference. That is, some report that it is easier for an American to work in China than vice versa.[38]

Finally, international sales and marketing personnel must be *energetic* and *enjoy travel*. Many international sales representatives spend about two-thirds of their nights in hotel rooms around the world. Going through the long lines of customs and immigration after a 15-hour flight requires a certain kind of stamina not commonly encountered. Some argue that frequent long flights can damage your health. Even the seductive lights of Paris nights fade after the fifth business trip there.

[34]Fernando Jaramillo, Jay Prakash Mulki, and James S. Boles, "Workplace Stressors, Job Attitude, and Job Behaviors: Is Interpersonal Conflict the Missing Link?" *Journal of Personal Selling & Sales Management* 31, no. 3 (2011), pp. 339–56.

[35]Peter Magnusson, Stanford A. Westjohn, Alexey V. Semenov, Arilova A. Randrianasolo, and Srdan Zdravkovic, "The Role of Cultural Intelligence in Marketing Adaptation and Export Performance," *Journal of International Marketing* 21, no. 4, (201)3, pp. 44–61; Wilhelm Barner-Rasmussen, Mats Ehrnrooth, Alexei Koveshnikov, and Kristiiina Makela, "Cultural and Language Skills Are Resources for Boundary Spanning within the MNC," *Journal of International Business Studies* 45 (2014), pp. 886–905.

[36]Don Y. Lee and Philip L. Dawes, "Gaunxi, Trust, and Long-Term Orientation in Chinese Business Markets," *Journal of International Marketing* 13, no. 2 (2005), pp. 28–56.

[37]Kimmy Wa Chan, Chi Kin (Bennett) Yim, and Simon S.K. Lam, "Is Customer Participation in Value Creation a Double-Edged Sword? Evidence from Professional Financial Services across Cultures," *Journal of Marketing* 74, no. 3 (2010), pp. 48–64; White et al., "The Effects of Hardness and Cultural Difference," op. cit.

[38]"A Tale of Two Expats," *The Economist*, January 1, 2011, pp. 62–64.

Most of these traits can be assessed during interviews and perhaps during role-playing exercises. Paper-and-pencil ability tests, biographical information, and reference checks are of secondary importance. Indeed, as previously mentioned, in many countries, referrals will be the best way to recruit managers and sales representatives, making reference checks during evaluation and selection processes irrelevant.

There is also evidence that some traits that make for successful sales representatives in the United States may not be important in other countries. One study compared sales representatives in the electronics industries in Japan and the United States. For the American representatives, pay and education were both found to be positively related to performance and job satisfaction. In Japan, they were not. That is, the Americans who cared more about money and were more educated tended to perform better and be more satisfied with their sales jobs. Conversely, the Japanese sales representatives tended to be more satisfied with their jobs when their values were consistent with those of their company.[39] The few systematic studies in this genre suggest that selection criteria must be localized, and American management practices must be adapted to foreign markets.

Selection mistakes are costly. When an expatriate assignment does not work out, hundreds of thousands of dollars are wasted in expenses and lost time. Getting the right person to handle the job is also important in the selection of locals to work for foreign companies within their home country. Most developing countries and many European countries have stringent laws protecting workers' rights. These laws are specific as to penalties for the dismissal of employees. Perhaps Venezuela has the most stringent dismissal legislation: With more than three months of service in the same firm, a worker gets severance pay amounting to one month's pay at severance notice plus 15 days' pay for every month of service exceeding eight months plus an additional 15 days' pay for each year employed. Furthermore, after an employee is dismissed, the law requires that person be replaced within 30 days at the same salary. Colombia and Brazil have similar laws that make employee dismissal a high-cost proposition.

Finally, evidence indicates that a manager's culture affects personnel decisions. One study reports "that managers given an identical [personnel selection] problem do not make the same decisions nor do they value the criteria often used in recruitment and promotion decisions equally. For example, they found that Austrian and German managers are more likely to hire compatriots than Italian managers."[40] Thus, we are just scratching the surface of a variety of issues in the area of international sales management research.

Training for International Marketing

LO5

The special training needs of international personnel

The nature of a training program depends largely on both the home culture of the salesperson[41] and the culture of the business system in the foreign market.[42] Also important is whether expatriate or local personnel will be representing the firm. Training for expatriates focuses on the customs and the special foreign sales problems that will be encountered, whereas local personnel require greater emphasis on the

[39]R. Bruce Money and John L. Graham, "Salesperson Performance, Pay, and Job Satisfaction: Tests of a Model Using Data Collected in the U.S. and Japan," *Journal of International Business Studies* 30, no. 1 (1999), pp. 149–72.

[40]Dominique Rouzies, Michael Segalla, and Barton A. Weitz, "Cultural Impact on European Staffing Decisions in Sales Management," *International Journal of Research in Marketing* 20, no. 1 (2003), pp. 425–36.

[41]Richard P. Bagozzi, Willem Verbeke, and Jacinto C. Gavino Jr., "Culture Moderates the Self-Regulation of Shame and Its Effects on Performance: The Case of Salespersons in the Netherlands and the Philippines," *Journal of Applied Psychology* 88, no. 2 (2003), pp. 219–33.

[42]Sergio Roman and Salvador Ruiz, "A Comparative Analysis of Sales Training in Europe: Implications for International Sales Negotiations," *International Marketing Review* 20, no. 3 (2003), pp. 304–26; Guijun Zhuang and Alex Tsang, "A Study on Ethically Problematic Selling Methods in China with a Broader Concept of Gray Marketing," *Journal of Business Ethics* 79, no. 1–2 (2008), pp. 85–101.

company, its products, technical information, and selling methods. In training either type of personnel, the sales training activity is burdened with problems stemming from long-established behavior and attitudes. Local personnel, for instance, cling to habits continually reinforced by local culture. Nowhere is the problem greater than in China or Russia, where the legacy of the communist tradition lingers. The attitude that whether you work hard or not, you get the same rewards, has to be changed if training is going to stick. Expatriates are also captives of their own habits and patterns. Before any training can be effective, open-minded attitudes must be established.

Continual training may be more important in foreign markets than in domestic ones because of the lack of routine contact with the parent company and its marketing personnel. In addition, training of foreign employees must be tailored to the recipients' ways of learning and communicating. For example, the Dilbert cartoon character's theme that worked so well in ethics training courses with a company's American employees did not translate well in many of its foreign offices.

One aspect of training is frequently overlooked: Home-office personnel dealing with international marketing operations need training designed to make them responsive to the needs of the foreign operations. The best companies provide home-office personnel with cross-cultural training and send them abroad periodically to increase their awareness of the problems of the foreign operations.

The Internet now makes some kinds of sales training much more efficient. Users can study text onscreen and participate in interactive assessment tests. Sun Microsystems estimates that its use of the Internet can shorten training cycles by as much as 75 percent. And in some parts of the world where telecommunications facilities are more limited, CD-ROM approaches have proven quite successful. Lockheed Martin has used an interactive CD-ROM-based system to train its employees worldwide on the nuances of the Foreign Corrupt Practices Act and associated corporate policies and ethics.

CROSSING BORDERS 17.1   How Important Are Those Meetings?

In Japan, they're really important. A former American sales manager tells this story:

I worked as general manager of the Japanese subsidiary of an American medical equipment company. Our office was in downtown Tokyo, which made for a two-hour commute for most of our salesmen. Rather than have them come into the office before beginning sales calls every day, I instructed them to go to their appointments directly from home and to come to the office only for a weekly sales meeting. Although this was a common way for a U.S. sales force to operate, it was a disaster in Japan. Sales fell, as did morale. I quickly changed the policy and had everyone come to the office every day. Sales immediately climbed as the salesmen reinforced their group identity.

Now contrast that with how sales representatives are managed at Hewlett-Packard in the United States, as

described by one of its sales executives: "We're really looking at this issue of work/family balance. If someone wants to work at home, they can, and we'll outfit their home offices at our expense, provided they have a good reason to want to work at home. If you want to drive productivity, getting people's work lives and home lives in balance is key."

As a former IBM CEO once put it: "To win, our players have to be on the field. We can't win the game in the locker room. . . . We want our people on the field in front of the customers, not in conference rooms talking to their managers or other staff organizations." At IBM, a new corporate policy limits sales meeting to one per week.

Sources: Clyde V. Prestowitz, *Trading Places—How We Are Giving Away Our Future to Japan and How to Reclaim It* (New York: Basic Books, 1989); Geoffrey Brewer et al., "The Top (25 Best Sales Forces in the U.S.)," *Sales & Marketing Management*, November 1, 1996, p. 38; Erin Strout, "Blue Skies Ahead?" *Sales & Marketing Management*, March 1, 2003, pp. 24–26; http://ibm.com, 2012.

Motivating Sales Personnel

LO6

Motivation techniques
for international sales
representatives

Motivation is especially complicated because the firm is dealing with different cultures, different sources, and different philosophies. Marketing is a business function requiring high motivation regardless of the location of the practitioner. Marketing managers and sales managers typically work hard, travel extensively, and have day-to-day challenges. Selling is hard, competitive work wherever undertaken, and a constant flow of inspiration is needed to keep personnel functioning at an optimal level. National differences must always be considered in motivating the marketing force.[43] In one study, sales representatives in comparable Japanese and American sales organizations were asked to allocate 100 points across an array of potential rewards from work.[44] The results were surprisingly similar. The only real differences between the two groups were in social recognition, which, predictably, the Japanese rated as more important. However, the authors of the study concluded that though individual values for rewards may be similar, the social and competitive contexts still require different motivational systems.

Because the cultural differences reviewed in this and previous chapters affect the motivational patterns of a sales force, a manager must be extremely sensitive to the personal behavior patterns of employees. Individual incentives that work effectively in the United States can fail completely in other cultures.[45] For example, with Japan's emphasis on paternalism and collectivism and its system of lifetime employment and seniority, motivation through individual incentives does not work well because Japanese employees seem to derive the greatest satisfaction from being comfortable members of a group. Thus, an offer of an individual financial reward for outstanding individual effort could be turned down because an employee would prefer not to appear different from peers and possibly attract their resentment. Japanese bonus systems are therefore based on group effort, and individual commission systems are rare. Japanese sales representatives are motivated more by the social pressure of their peers than by the prospect of making more money based on individual effort. Likewise, compensation packages in eastern European countries typically involve a substantially greater emphasis on base pay than in the United States, and performance-based incentives have been found to be less effective. Although some point out that motivational practices are changing even in Japan, such patterns do not change very quickly or without substantial efforts.

Communications are also important in maintaining high levels of motivation; foreign managers need to know that the home office is interested in their operations, and in turn, they want to know what is happening in the parent country. Everyone performs better when well informed. However, differences in languages, culture, and communication styles can make mutual understanding between managers and sales representatives more difficult.

Part of the corporate culture (some say peer pressure) that motivates Japanese sales representatives is the morning calisthenics.

[43]Thomas E. DeCarlo, Raymond C. Rody, and James E. DeCarlo, "A Cross National Example of Supervisory Management Practices in the Sales Force," *Journal of Personal Selling & Sales Management* 19 (1999), pp. 1–14; Ping Ping Fu, Jeff Kennedy, Jasmine Tata, Gary Yukl, Michael Harris Bond, Tai-Kuang Peng, Ekkirala S. Srinivas, John P. Howell, Leonel Prieto, Paul Koopman, Jaap J. Boonstra, Selda Pasa, Marie-Francoise Lacassagne, Hiro Higashide, and Adith Cheosakul, "The Impact of Societal Cultural Values and Individual Social Beliefs on the Perceived Effectiveness of Managerial Influence Strategies: A Meso Approach," *Journal of International Business Studies* 35 (2004), pp. 284–305; David S. Baker and Duleep Delpechitre, "Collectivistic and Individualistic Performance Expectancy in the Utilization of Sales Automation Technology in an International Sales Force," *Journal of Personal Selling & Sales Management* 33, no. 3 (2013), pp. 277–88.

[44]Money and Graham, "Salesperson Performance, Pay, and Job Satisfaction."

[45]Jing Du and Jin Nam Choi, "Pay for Performance in Emerging Markets: Insights from China," *Journal of International Business Studies* 41, no. 4 (2010), pp. 671–89.

Because promotion and the opportunity to improve status are important motivators, a company needs to make clear the opportunities for growth within the firm. In truly global firms, foreign nationals can aspire to the highest positions in the firm. Likewise, one of the greatest fears of expatriate managers, which can be easily allayed, is that they will be forgotten by the home office. Blending company sales objectives and the personal objectives of the salespeople and other employees is a task worthy of the most skilled manager. The U.S. manager must be constantly aware that many of the techniques used to motivate U.S. personnel and their responses to these techniques are based on the seven basic cultural premises discussed in Chapter 5. Therefore, each method used to motivate a foreigner should be examined for cultural compatibility.

Designing Compensation Systems

For Expatriates

LO7

How to design compensation systems for an international sales force

Developing an equitable and functional compensation plan that combines balance, consistent motivation, and flexibility is extremely challenging in international operations. This challenge is especially acute when a company operates in a number of countries, when it has individuals who work in a number of countries, or when the sales force is composed of expatriate and local personnel. Fringe benefits play a major role in many countries. Those working in high-tax countries prefer liberal expense accounts and fringe benefits that are nontaxable (such as company cars) instead of direct income subject to high taxes. Fringe-benefit costs are high in Europe, ranging from 35 to 60 percent of salary.

Pay can be a significant factor in making it difficult for a person to be repatriated. Often those returning home realize they have been making considerably more money with a lower cost of living in the overseas market; returning to the home country means a cut in pay and a cut in standard of living. In many countries expats can afford full-time domestic help due to the low wages abroad that they cannot afford back at home.

Conglomerate operations that include domestic and foreign personnel cause the greatest problems in compensation planning. Expatriates tend to compare their compensation with what they would have received at the home office during the same time, and local personnel and expatriate personnel are likely to compare notes on salary. Although any differences in the compensation level may be easily and logically explained, the group receiving the lower amount almost always feels aggrieved and mistreated.

Short-term assignments for expatriates further complicate the compensation issue, particularly when the short-term assignments extend into a longer time. In general, short-term assignments involve payments of overseas premiums (sometimes called separation allowances if the family does not go along), all excess expenses, and allowances for tax differentials. Longer assignments can include home-leave benefits or travel allowances for the spouse. International compensation programs also provide additional payments for hardship locations and special inducements to reluctant personnel to accept overseas employment and to remain in the position.

For a Global Sales Force

Compensation plans of American companies vary substantially around the globe, reflecting the economic, legal,[46] and cultural differences[47] in the diverse markets served. Asia and Western Europe require the most localization, while practices in the emerging markets are more pliable. For example, one study reports that European managers tend to use larger incentive components in countries with high personal income taxes, as the higher taxes negate the incentive to perform.[48] We note that personal income tax rates are relatively

[46]Marc van Essen, Pursey P.M.A.R. Heugens, Jordan Otten, and J. (Hans) van Oosterhout, "An Institution-Based View of Executive Compensation: A Multilevel Meta-Analytic Test," *Journal of International Business Studies* 43 (2012), pp. 396–423.

[47]Marta M. Elvira and Anabella Davila, *Managing Human Resources in Latin America* (London: Routledge, 2005).

[48]Dominique Rouzies, Anne T. Coughlan, Erin Anderson, and Dawn Iacobucci, "Determinants of Pay Levels and Structures in Sales Organizations," *Journal of Marketing* 73, no. 3 (2009), pp. 92–104.

Exhibit 17.3
Global Similarity to U.S. Compensation Plans

Countries/Regions		Degree of Plan Similarity with the United States					
		Eligibility	Performance Measures	Weighting	Plan Mechanics	Mix/ Leverage	Payout Frequency
Europe	United Kingdom						
	Scandinavia						
	France						
	Germany						
	Spain/Italy						
Southeast Asia	Hong Kong						
	Korea						
	Taiwan						
	Malaysia						
	Indonesia						
	(Singapore)						
	Australia						
Japan							
Canada							
South America							

▭ Similar   ▭ Varies   ▭ Dissimilar

Data represent multiple client projects conducted by the Alexander Group Inc. for primarily high-technology industry sales organizations.

Source: David J. Cichelli (ed.), *2012 Sales Compensation Trends Survey* (The Alexander Group, Inc.). Used with permission.

low in the United States and Japan (less than 30 percent) and relatively high in Western Europe where the study was conducted (above 35 percent). Also, in Europe, work councils (i.e., internal labor union committees) are very much involved in setting rules about compensation companywide, even for salespeople. In Austria and Germany, for example, work councils not only codetermine compensation plans but also must approve them before implementation. Meanwhile in Japan cultural differences play a key role. One study reports, "The teaming environment, all about team rewards, not individual attainment, and a sales cycle highly influenced by relationship building often require a higher reliance on base pay."[49]

As reflected in Exhibit 17.3, some experts feel compensation plans in Japan and southern Europe are most different from the standard U.S. approach. Those same experts believe that generally compensation schemes around the world are becoming more similar to the U.S. system with its emphasis on commissions based on individual performance.[50] However, the data in Exhibit 17.3 still reflect the locations of the larger differences.[51]

Among multinational companies about half describe their sales compensation plans as global in nature and the other half as local. The results of one survey[52] of 85 such companies provide some detail with respect to sales compensation program elements. The

[49]David J. Cichelli (editor), *2010 Sales Compensation Trends Survey Results* (Scottsdale, AZ: The Alexander Group, Inc., 2010).

[50]David J. Cichelli, *Global Sales Compensation Practices Survey* (Scottsdale, AZ: The Alexander Group, Inc., 2006).

[51]Personal interview with David J. Cichelli, Vice President, Alexander Group, March 2012.

[52]Ibid.

Exhibit 17.4
Global versus Local Compensation Practices

More Global	Program Element	Percent of Total				
		Global	Country	World Region	Combination	Not Applicable
↑	Program Design Principles	53.93	21.35	13.48	2.25	8.99
	Program Approval	52.33	19.77	16.28	3.49	8.14
	Formula Mechanics	42.05	27.27	17.05	4.55	9.09
	Pay Competitiveness Philosophy	41.11	31.11	14.44	3.33	10.00
	Performance Measures	37.65	25.88	20.00	5.88	10.59
	Job Grades	36.05	25.58	17.44	3.49	17.44
	Technical Automation Support	32.56	25.58	17.44	5.81	18.60
	Quota Setting Method	24.71	31.75	21.18	11.76	10.59
	Pay Mix	22.99	33.33	25.29	9.20	9.20
	Payout Administration Calculations	26.74	37.21	20.93	6.98	8.14
	Survey Benchmark Companies	21.35	39.33	20.22	6.74	12.36
↓	Quotas—Sales Personnel	12.94	43.53	15.29	15.29	12.94
More Local						

Source: David J. Cichelli (editor), *2010 Sales Compensation Trends Survey Results* (Scottsdale, AZ: The Alexander Group, Inc., 2010). Used with Permission.

participating companies represented a wide variety of industrial sectors, high-tech to entertainment to consumer services, and many are *Fortune* 500 companies, predominantly from the United States, Japan, and Europe. As can be seen in Exhibit 17.4, most companies establish sales compensation practices locally (either at the country or regional levels). The only program elements more often determined at the global level were Program Design Principles (53.9 percent) and Program Approval (52.3 percent).

One company has gone to great lengths to homogenize its worldwide compensation scheme. Beginning in the late 1990s, IBM rolled out what is perhaps the most global approach to compensating a worldwide sales force.[53] The main features of that plan, which applies to 140,000 sales executives in 165 countries, are presented in Exhibit 17.5. The plan was developed in response to "global" complaints from sales representatives that the old plan was confusing and did not provide for work done outside one's territory and that it therefore did not promote cross-border teamwork. IBM sales incentive managers from North America, Latin America, Asia Pacific, and Europe worked together with consultants on the design for some nine months. At first glance it may appear that IBM is making the cardinal error of trying to force a plan developed centrally onto sales offices literally spread around the world and across diverse cultures; however, the compensation plan still allows substantial latitude for local managers. Compensation managers in each country determine the frequency of incentive payouts and the split between base and incentive pay, while following a global scheme of performance measures. Thus, the system allows for a high incentive component in countries like the United States and high base-salary components in countries like Japan.

Perhaps the most valuable.... of global compensation. Among the more important recommendations were:[54]

1. allow the local managers to decide the mix of incentive versus base pay;

2. use consistent training and communication schemes worldwide; and

3. don't assume cultural differences can be managed through the incentive plan.

---

[53]Michele Marchetti, "Gamble: IBM Replaces Its Outdated Compensation Plan with a World Wide Framework. Will It Pay Off?" *Sales & Marketing Management*, July 1996, pp. 65–69. IBM continues to globalize its sales management practices—see Erin Strout, "Blue Skies Ahead? IBM Is Transforming the Way Its Sales Force Does Business," *Sales & Marketing Management*, March 1, 2003, pp. 24–27.

[54]Ibid.

Exhibit 17.5

A Compensation Blueprint:
How IBM Pays 140,000
Sales Executives Worldwide

Source: Adapted from Michele
Marchetti, "Gamble: IBM Replaces Its
Outdated Compensation Plan with a
World Wide Framework. Will It Pay
Off?" *Sales & Marketing Management,*
July 1996, pp. 65–69.

Total Compensation		Plan Components	Payout Frequency	Pay Measurements	Number of Measurements Used to Calculate
Benefits					
Variable Pay →		**Corporate Objectives**	**Annually**	**Bonus payment (based on)** • **Profit** • **Customer satisfaction**	**2**
Incentive Compensation →		**Teamwork**	**Monthly**	**20% of incentive compensation** • **Work team performance** • **Industry performance**	**2**
		Personal Contribution	**Quarterly**	**60% of incentive compensation** • **Growth** • **Solutions** • **Channels/partners** • **Profit contribution**	**1–2**
		Challenges/ Contests	**As earned**	**20% of incentive compensation** • **National** • **Local**	**1–4**
Recognition					
Base Salary					

Evaluating and Controlling Sales Representatives

Evaluation and control of sales representatives in the United States is a relatively simple task.[55] In many sales jobs, emphasis is placed on individual performance, which can easily be measured by sales revenues generated (often compared with past performance, forecasts, or quotas). In short, a good sales representative produces big numbers. However, in many countries the evaluation problem is more complex, particularly in relationship-oriented cultures, where teamwork is favored over individual effort and closer supervision is expected, and may even be appreciated.[56] Performance measures require closer observation and may include the opinions of customers, peers, and supervisors. Of course, managers of sales forces operating in relationship-oriented cultures may see measures of individual performance as relatively unimportant.

One study comparing American and Japanese sales representatives' performance illustrates such differences.[57] Supervisors' ratings of the representatives on identical performance scales were used in both countries. The distribution of performance of the Japanese was statistically normal—a few high performers, a few low, but most in the middle. The American distribution was different—a few high, most in the middle, but almost no low performers. In the United States, poor performers either quit (because they are not making any money), or they are fired. In Japan the poor performers stay with the company and are seldom fired. Thus, sales managers in Japan have a problem their American counterparts do not: how to motivate poor performers. Indeed, sales management textbooks in the United States usually include material on how to deal with "plateaued" salespeople but say little about poor performers because the latter are not a problem.

The primary control tool used by American sales managers is the incentive system. Because of the Internet and smartphones, more and more American sales representatives operate out of offices in their homes and see supervisors infrequently. Organizations have

[55]Rene Y. Darmon and Xavier C. Martin, "A New Conceptual Framework of Sales Force Control Systems," *Journal of Personal Selling & Sales Management* 31, no. 3 (2011), pp. 297–310.

[56]William A. Weeks, Terry W. Loe, Lawrence B. Chonko, Carlos Ruy Martinez, and Kirk Wakefield, "Cognitive Moral Development and the Impact of Perceived Organizational Ethical Climate on the Search for Sales Force Excellence: A Cross-Cultural Study," *Journal of Personal Selling & Sales Management* 26 (2006), pp. 205–17.

[57]Money and Graham, "Salesperson Performance, Pay, and Job Satisfaction."

become quite flat and spans of control increasingly broad in recent years. However, in many other countries spans of control can be quite narrow by American standards—even in Australia and particularly in Japan. In the latter country, supervisors spend much more time with fewer subordinates. Corporate culture and frequent interactions with peers and supervisors are the means of motivation and control of sales representatives in relationship-oriented cultures like Japan.

Preparing U.S. Personnel for Foreign Assignments

LO8

How to prepare Americans for foreign assignments

Estimates of the annual cost of sending and supporting a manager and his or her family in a foreign assignment range from 150 to 400 percent of base salary. The costs in employee morale and money (some estimates are in the $300,000 to $600,000 range) increase substantially if the expatriate requests a return home before completing the normal tour of duty (a normal stay is two to four years). In addition, if repatriation into domestic operations is not successful and the employee leaves the company, an indeterminately high cost in low morale and loss of experienced personnel results. To reduce these problems, international personnel management has increased planning for expatriate personnel to move abroad, remain abroad, and then return to the home country.[58] The planning process must begin prior to the selection of those who go abroad and extend to their specific assignments after returning home. Selection, training, compensation, and career development policies (including repatriation) should reflect the unique problems of managing the expatriate.

Besides the job-related criteria for a specific position,[59] the typical candidate for an international assignment is married, has two school-aged children, is expected to stay overseas three years, and has the potential for promotion into higher management levels. These characteristics of the typical expatriate are the basis of most of the difficulties associated with getting the best qualified personnel to go overseas, keeping them there, and assimilating them on their return.

Overcoming Reluctance to Accept a Foreign Assignment

Despite the strong evidence that international service serves both the employee and the firm well in the long run, many excellent prospects choose to avoid such assignments.[60] Concerns for career and family are the most frequently mentioned reasons for a manager to refuse a foreign assignment. The most important career-related reservation is the fear that a two- or three-year absence will adversely affect opportunities for advancement.[61] This "out of sight, out of mind" fear (as exemplified in the opening Global Perspective) is closely linked to the problems of repatriation. Without evidence of advance planning to protect career development, better qualified and ambitious personnel may decline offers to go abroad. However, if candidates for expatriate assignments are picked thoughtfully, returned to the home office at the right moment, and rewarded for good performance with subsequent promotions at home, companies find recruiting of executives for international assignments eased.

Even though the career development question may be adequately answered with proper planning, concern for family may interfere with many accepting an assignment abroad. Initially, most potential candidates are worried about uprooting a family and settling into a strange environment. Questions about the education of the children (especially those with specific needs), isolation from family and friends, proper healthcare, and, in some countries, the potential for violence reflect the misgivings a family faces when relocating to a

---

[58]Jeffrey P. Shay and Sally A. Baack, "Expatriate Assignment, Adjustment and Effectiveness: An Empirical Examination of the Big Picture," *Journal of International Business Studies* 35, no. 3 (2004), pp. 216–32.

[59]Shung J. Shin, Frederick P. Morgeson, and Michael A. Campion, "What You Do Depends on Where You Are: Understanding How Domestic and Expatriate Work Requirements Depend upon the Cultural Context," *Journal of International Business Studies* 38 (2007), pp. 64–83.

[60]William W. Maddux and Adam D. Galinsky, "Cultural Borders and Mental Barriers: The Relationship between Living abroad and Creativity," *Journal of Personality and Social Psychology* 96, no. 5 (2009), pp. 1047–61.

[61]Mark C. Bolino, "Expatriate Assignments and Intra-Organizational Career Success: Implications for Individuals and Organizations," *Journal of International Business Studies* 38 (2007), pp. 819–35.

foreign country.[62] Special compensation packages have been the typical way to deal with this problem. A hardship allowance, allowances to cover special educational requirements that frequently include private schools, housing allowances, and extended all-expense-paid vacations are part of compensation packages designed to overcome family-related problems with an overseas assignment. Ironically, the solution to one problem creates a later problem when that family returns to the United States and must give up those extra compensation benefits used to induce them to accept the position.

Reducing the Rate of Early Returns

Once the employee and family accept the assignment abroad, the next problem is keeping them there for the assigned time. But the attrition rate of those selected for overseas positions can be very high, though some studies have suggested it is declining overall. One firm with a hospital management contract experienced an annualized failure rate of 20 percent—not high when compared with the construction contractor who started out in Saudi Arabia with 155 Americans and was down to 65 after only two months.

A number of management development approaches generally work for keeping executives motivated,[63] though cultural differences are important considerations.[64] One study found that higher salaries are key in motivating expatriates to remain abroad.[65] Another important study involving more than 6,000 managers in 24 countries determined that individualism yielded both perceptions of higher workloads and stronger influences on job dissatisfaction and turnover intentions.[66]

The most important reasons a growing number of companies are including an evaluation of an employee's family among selection criteria are the high cost of sending an expatriate abroad and increasing evidence that unsuccessful family adjustment[67] is the single most important reason for expatriate dissatisfaction and the resultant request for return home. In fact, a study of personnel directors of more than 300 international firms found that the inability of the manager's spouse to adjust to a different physical or cultural environment was the primary reason for an expatriate's failure to function effectively in a foreign assignment. One researcher estimated that 75 percent of families sent to a foreign post experience adjustment problems with children or have marital discord. One executive suggests that there is so much pressure on the family that if there are any cracks in the marriage and you want to save it, think long and hard about taking a foreign assignment.

Dissatisfaction is caused by the stress and trauma of adjusting to new and often strange cultures. The employee has less trouble adjusting than family members; a company's

---

[62]Alan Paul, "It's China, or the Job," *The Wall Street Journal*, April 9, 2009.

[63]David M. Brock, Oded Shenkar, Amir Shoham, and Ilene C. Siscovick, "Nature Culture and Expatriate Deployment," *Journal of International Business Studies* 39, no. 8 (2008), pp. 1293–309; Shawn M. Carraher, Sherry E. Sullivan, and Madeline M. Crocitto, "Mentoring across Global Boundaries: An Empirical Examination of Home- and Host-Country Mentors on Expatriate Career Outcomes," *Journal of International Business Studies* 39, no. 8 (2008), pp. 1310–26; Christopher Mabey, "Management Development and Firm Performance in Germany, Norway, Spain, and the UK," *Journal of International Business Studies* 39, no. 8 (2008), pp. 1327–42.

[64]Carl P. Maertz Jr., Ahmad Hassan, and Peter Magnusson, "When Learning Is Not Enough: A Process Model of Expatriate Adjustment as Cultural Cognitive Dissonance Reduction," *Organizational Behavior and Human Decision Processes* 108 (2009), pp. 66–78.

[65]Robert Zeithammer and Ryan P. Kellogg, "The Hesitant *Hai Gui*: Return-Migration Preferences of U.S.-Educated Chinese Scientists and Engineers," *Journal of Marketing Research* 50, no. 5 (2013), pp. 644–63.

[66]Liu-Qin Yang, et al., "Individualism-Collectivism as a Moderator of the Work Demands-Strains Relationship: A Cross-Level and Cross-National Examination," *Journal of International Business Studies* 43 (2012), pp. 424–43. Similar findings are also reported in R. Bruce Money and John L. Graham, "Sales Performance, Pay, and Job Satisfaction: Tests of a Model Using Data Collected in the U.S. and Japan," *Journal of International Business Studies* 30, no. 1 (1999), pp. 149–72.

[67]Riki Takeuchi, David P. Lepak, Sophia V. Marinova, and Seokhwa Yun, "Nonlinear Influences of Stressors on General Adjustment: The Case of Japanese Expatriates and Their Spouses," *Journal of International Business Studies* 38 (2007), pp. 928–43.

American expatriates flock to stores like this one in Warsaw. Inside you'll find not only books in English, but also Kraft macaroni and cheese, Bisquick, and other hard-to-find-in-Europe staples of the American diet.

expatriate moves in a familiar environment even abroad and is often isolated from the cultural differences that create problems for the rest of the family. And about half of American expatriate employees receive cross-cultural training before the trip—much more often than their families do. Family members have far greater daily exposure to the new culture but are often not given assistance in adjusting. New consumption patterns must be learned, from grocery shopping to seeking healthcare services.[68] Family members frequently cannot be employed, and in many cultures, female members of the family face severe social restrictions. In Saudi Arabia, for example, the woman's role is strictly dictated. In one situation, a woman's hemline offended a religious official who, in protest, sprayed black paint on her legs. In short, the greater problems of culture shock befall the family. Certainly any recruiting and selection procedure should include an evaluation of the family's ability to adjust.

Families that have the potential and the personality traits that would enable them to adjust to a different environment may still become dissatisfied with living abroad if they are not properly prepared for the new assignment. More and more companies realize the need for cross-cultural training to prepare families for their new homes. One- or two-day briefings to two- or three-week intensive programs that include all members of the family are provided to assist assimilation into new cultures. Language training, films, discussions, and lectures on cultural differences, potential problems, and stress areas in adjusting to a new way of life are provided to minimize the frustration of the initial cultural shock. This cultural training helps a family anticipate problems and eases adjustment. Once the family is abroad, some companies even provide a local ombudsman (someone experienced in the country) to whom members can take their problems and get immediate assistance. Although the cost of preparing a family for an overseas assignment may appear high, it must be weighed against estimates that the measurable cost of prematurely returned families could cover cross-cultural training for 300 to 500 families. Additionally, we also appreciate that single people may also run into completely different values and rituals when it comes to dating and social interactions. Companies that do not prepare employees and their families for culture shock have the highest incidence of premature return to the United States.

Successful Expatriate Repatriation

A Conference Board study reported that many firms have sophisticated plans for executives going overseas but few have comprehensive programs to deal with the return home. Many have noted that too often repatriated workers are a valuable resource neglected or wasted by inexperienced U.S. management.

Low morale and a growing amount of attrition among returning expatriates have many causes. Some complaints and problems are family related, whereas others are career related. The family-related problems generally pertain to financial and lifestyle readjustments. Some expatriates find that in spite of higher compensation programs, their net worths have not increased, and the inflation of intervening years makes it impossible to buy a home comparable to the one they sold on leaving. The hardship compensation programs used to induce the executive to go abroad also create readjustment problems on the return home. Such compensation benefits frequently permitted the family to live at a much higher level abroad than at home (employing yard boys, chauffeurs, domestic help, and so forth). Because most compensation benefits are withdrawn when employees return to the home country, their standard of living decreases, and they must readjust. Unfortunately, little can be done to ameliorate these kinds of problems, short of transferring the managers to other foreign locations. Current thinking suggests that the problem of dissatisfaction with compensation and benefits upon return can be lessened by reducing benefits when overseas. Rather than provide the family abroad with hardship payments, some companies are reducing payments and other benefits on the premise that the assignment abroad is an integral requirement for growth, development, and advancement within the firm.

---

[68]Mary C. Gilly, Lisa Peñaloza, and Kenneth M. Kambara, "The Role of Consumption in Expatriate Adjustment and Satisfaction," working paper, Paul Merage School of Business, University of California, Irvine, 2015.

Family dissatisfaction, which causes stress within the family on returning home, is not as severe a problem as career-related complaints. A returning expatriate's dissatisfaction with the perceived future is usually the reason many resign their positions after returning to the United States. The problem is not unique to U.S. citizens; Japanese companies have similar difficulties with their personnel. The most frequently heard complaint involves the lack of a detailed plan for the expatriate's career when returning home. New home-country assignments are frequently mundane and do not reflect the experience gained or the challenges met during foreign assignment. Some feel their time out of the mainstream of corporate affairs has made them technically obsolete and thus ineffective in competing immediately on return. Finally, there is some loss of status, requiring an ego adjustment when an executive returns home.

Companies with the least amount of returnee attrition differ from those with the highest attrition in one significant way: personal career planning for the expatriate. This planning begins with the decision to send the person abroad. The initial transfer abroad should be made in the context of a long-term company career plan. Under these circumstances, the individual knows not only the importance of the foreign assignment but also when to expect to return and at what level. Near the end of the foreign assignment, the process for repatriation begins. The critical aspect of the return home is to keep the executive completely informed regarding such matters as the proposed return time, new assignment and an indication of whether it is interim or permanent, new responsibilities, and future prospects. In short, returnees should know where they are going and what they will be doing next month and several years ahead.

A report on what MNCs are doing to improve the reentry process suggests five steps:

1. Commit to reassigning expatriates to meaningful positions.
2. Create a mentor program.[69] Mentors are typically senior executives who monitor company activities, keep the expatriate informed on company activities, and act as a liaison between the expatriate and various headquarters departments.
3. Offer a written job guarantee stating what the company is obligated to do for the expatriate on return.
4. Keep the expatriate in touch with headquarters through periodic briefings and headquarters visits.
5. Prepare the expatriate and family for repatriation once a return date is set.[70]

Some believe the importance of preparing the employee and family for culture shock upon return is on a par with preparation for going abroad.

Developing Cultural Awareness

Many businesses focus on the functional skills needed in international marketing, overlooking the importance of cultural intelligence.[71] Just as the idea that "if a product sells well in Dallas, it will sell well in Hong Kong" is risky, so is the idea that

---

[69]John M. Mezias and Terri A. Scandura, "A Needs-Driven Approach to Expatriate Adjustment and Career Development: A Multiple Mentoring Perspective," *Journal of International Business Studies* 36 (2005), pp. 519–38.

[70]Mila B. Lazarova and Jean-Luc Cerdin, "Revisiting Repatriation Concerns: Organizational Support versus Career and Contextual Influences," *Journal of International Business Studies* 38 (2007), pp. 404–29.

[71]This is a topic of much discussion; see P. Christopher Earley and Elaine Mosakowski, "Cultural Intelligence," *Harvard Business Review*, October 2004, pp. 139–46; Orly Levy, Schon Beechler, Sully Taylor, and Nakiye A. Boyacigiller, "What We Talk about When We Talk about 'Global Mindset': Managerial Cognition in Multinational Corporations," *Journal of International Business Studies* 38 (2007), pp. 231–58; William Neburry, Liuba Y. Belkin, and Paradis Ansari, "Perceived Career Opportunities from Globalization: Globalization Capabilities and Attitudes toward Women in Iran and the U.S.," *Journal of International Business Studies* 39 (2008), pp. 814–32; Gary Knight and Daekwan Kim, "International Business Competence and the Contemporary Firm," *Journal of International Business Studies* 40, no. 2 (2009), pp. 255–73; Soon Ang and Linn Van Dyne, *Handbook of Cultural Intelligence* (Armonk, NY: M.E. Sharpe, 2008); John D. Hansen, Tanuja Singh, Dan C. Weilbaker, and Rodrigo Guesalaga, "Cultural Intelligence in Cross-Cultural Selling: Propositions and Directions for Future Research," *Journal of Personal Selling & Sales Management* 31, no. 3 (2011), pp. 243–54.

"a manager who excels in Dallas will excel in Hong Kong." Most expatriate failures are not caused by lack of management or technical skills but rather by lack of an understanding of cultural differences and their effect on management skills. As the world becomes more interdependent and as companies depend more on foreign earnings, there is a growing need for companies to develop cultural awareness among those posted abroad.

Just as we might remark that someone has learned good social skills (i.e., an ability to remain poised and be in control under all social situations), so too good cultural skills can be developed.[72] These skills serve a similar function in varying cultural situations; they provide the individual with the ability to relate to a different culture even when the individual is unfamiliar with the details of that particular culture. Cultural skills can be learned just as social skills can be learned. People with cultural skills can:

- Communicate respect and convey verbally and nonverbally a positive regard and sincere interest in people and their culture.
- Tolerate ambiguity and cope with cultural differences and the frustration that frequently develops when things are different and circumstances change.
- Display empathy by understanding other people's needs and differences from their point of view.
- Remain nonjudgmental about the behavior of others, particularly with reference to their own value standards.
- Recognize and control the SRC, that is, recognize their own culture and values as an influence on their perceptions, evaluations, and judgment in a situation.
- Laugh things off—a good sense of humor helps when frustration levels rise and things do not work as planned.

Finally, we are beginning to see research that is demonstrating the advantages of biculturalism. That is, marketers who have lived for a long period in a second country and are fluent in a second language are much more likely to understand the importance of and be tolerant of cultural differences as they pertain to both management tasks and marketing decision making in international contexts.[73]

The Changing Profile of the Global Manager

LO9

The changing profile of the global sales and marketing manager

Until recently the road to the top was well marked. Surveys of chief executives consistently reported that more than three-quarters had finance, manufacturing, or marketing backgrounds. As the post–World War II period of growing markets and domestic-only competition has faded, however, so too has the narrow one-company, one-industry chief executive. In the new millennium, increasing international competition, the globalization of companies, technology, demographic shifts, and the speed of overall change will govern the choice of company leaders. It will be difficult for a single-discipline individual to reach the top in the future.

The executive recently picked to head Procter & Gamble's U.S. operations is a good example of the effect globalization is having on businesses and the importance of experience, whether in Japan, Europe, or elsewhere. The head of all P&G's U.S. business was

[72]Jon M. Shapiro, Julie L. Ozanne, and Bige Saatcioglu, "An Interpretive Examination of the Development of Cultural Sensitivity in International Business," *Journal of International Business Studies* 39 (2008), pp. 71–87; Dawn R. Deeter-Schmelz and Karen Norman Kennedy, "A Global Perspective on the Current State of Sales Education in the College Curriculum," *Journal of Personal Selling & Sales Management* 31, no. 1 (2011), pp. 55–75.

[73]C. Lakshman, "Biculturalism and Attributional Complexity: Cross-Cultural Leadership Effectiveness," *Journal of International Business Studies* 44 (2013), pp. 922–40; Gundula Lücke, Tatiana Kostova, and Kendall Roth, "Multiculturism from a Cognitive Perspective: Patterns and Implications," *Journal of International Business Studies* 44 (2014), pp. 169–90.

CROSSING BORDERS 17.2 | A Look into the Future: Tomorrow's International Leaders? An Education for the 21st Century

A school supported by the European Union teaches Britons, French, Germans, Dutch, and others to be future Europeans. The European School in a suburb of Brussels has students from 12 nations who come to be educated for life and work, not as products of motherland or fatherland but as Europeans. The European Union runs 10 European Schools in western Europe, enrolling 17,000 students from kindergarten to twelfth grade. Graduates emerge superbly educated, usually trilingual, and very, very European.

The schools are a linguistic and cultural melange. Native speakers of 36 different languages are represented in one school alone. Each year students take fewer and fewer classes in their native tongue. Early on, usually in first grade, they begin a second language, known as the "working language," which must be English, French, or German. A third language is introduced in the seventh year, and a fourth may be started in the ninth.

By the time students reach their eleventh year, they are taking history, geography, economics, advanced math, music, art, and gym in the working language. When the students are in groups talking, they are constantly switching languages to "whatever works."

Besides language, students learn history, politics, literature, and music from the perspective of all the European countries—in short, European cultures. The curriculum is designed to teach the French, German, Briton, and those of other nationalities to be future Europeans.

This same approach is being taken at the MBA level as well. The well-respected European School of Management has campuses in several cities—Berlin, Paris, Oxford, and Madrid. Students spend part of their time at each of the campuses. American MBA programs are beginning to imitate such programs. The University of Chicago School of Business now has campuses in Barcelona and Singapore. The Fuqua School at Duke offers a unique executive MBA program involving travel to several foreign countries and a substantial percentage of teaching delivered interactively over the Internet. This last program attracts students from all over the world who are willing to pay a six-figure tuition.

Sources: Glynn Mapes, "Polyglot Students Are Weaned Early Off Mother Tongue," *The Wall Street Journal*, March 6, 1990, p. A1. Reprinted by permission of *The Wall Street Journal*, © 1990 Dow Jones & Company, Inc. All Rights Reserved Worldwide. See also Kevin Cape, "Tips on Choosing the Right One, International Schools," *International Herald Tribune*, January 25, 2003, p. 7; http://fuqua.duke.edu/mba/executive/global/, 2012.

born in the Netherlands, received an MBA[74] from Rotterdam's Eramus University, then rose through P&G's marketing ranks in Holland, the United States, and Austria. After proving his mettle in Japan, he moved to P&G's Cincinnati, Ohio, headquarters to direct its push into East Asia, and then to his new position. Speculation suggests that if he succeeds in the United States, as he did in Japan, he will be a major contender for the top position at P&G. The CEOs of other major multinational companies, such as Johnson & Johnson and Coca-Cola, similarly share strong international backgrounds.[75]

Fewer companies today limit their search for senior-level executive talent to their home countries. Coca-Cola's former CEO, who began his ascent to the top in his native Cuba, and the former IBM vice chairman, a Swiss national who rose through the ranks in Europe, are two prominent examples of individuals who achieved the top positions of firms outside their home countries. Indeed, 14 *Fortune* 100 companies were found to be headed by immigrant CEOs in one study. Alternatively, American-style diversity[76] is not shared by companies in competitive countries in Asia, for example.[77]

---

[74]Laurie Goering, "Foreign Business Schools Fill a Huge Gap," *Los Angeles Times*, January 14, 2008, p. C4.

[75]Katie Thomas, "J&J's Next Chief is Steeped in Sales Culture," *The New York Times*, February 23, 2012; Alan Rappeport, "Climbing Coke's Corporate Ladder," *Los Angeles Times*, January 1, 2012, p. B2; Leslie Kwoh, "Don't Unpack That Suitcase," *The Wall Street Journal*, May 9, 2012, p. B10.

[76]David Wassel, "U.S. Keeps Foreign PhDs," *The Wall Street Journal*, January 26, 2010, online.

[77]Joel Kotkin, "The Kids Will Be Alright," *The Wall Street Journal*, January 23–24, 2010, p. W9.

Some companies, such as Colgate-Palmolive, believe that it is important to have international assignments early in a person's career, and international training is an integral part of its entry-level development programs. Colgate recruits its future managers from the world's best colleges and business schools. Acceptance is highly competitive, and successful applicants have a BA or MBA with proven leadership skills, fluency in at least one language besides English, and some experience living abroad. A typical recruit might be a U.S. citizen who has spent a year studying in another country or a national of another country who was educated in the United States.

Trainees begin their careers in a two-year, entry-level, total-immersion program that consists of stints in various Colgate departments. A typical rotation includes time in the finance, manufacturing, and marketing departments and an in-depth exposure to the company's marketing system. During that phase, trainees are rotated through the firm's ad agency, marketing research, and product management departments and then work seven months as field salespeople. At least once during the two years, trainees accompany their mentors on business trips to a foreign subsidiary. The company's goal is to develop in their trainees the skills they need to become effective marketing managers, domestically or globally.

On the completion of the program, trainees can expect a foreign posting, either immediately after graduation or soon after an assignment in the United States. The first positions are not in London or Paris, as many might hope, but in developing countries such as Brazil, the Philippines, or maybe Zambia. Because international sales are so important to Colgate (60 percent of its total revenues are generated abroad), a manager might not return to the United States after the first foreign assignment but rather move from one overseas post to another, developing into a career internationalist, which could lead to a CEO position.

Companies whose foreign receipts make up a substantial portion of their earnings and that see themselves as global companies rather than as domestic companies doing business in foreign markets are the most active in making the foreign experience an integrated part of a successful corporate career. Indeed for many companies, a key threshold seems to be that when overseas revenues surpass domestic revenues, then the best people in the company want to work on international accounts. Such a global orientation then begins to permeate the entire organization—from personnel policies to marketing and business strategies. This shift was the case with Gillette, which in the 1990s made a significant recruitment and management-development decision when it decided to develop managers internally. Gillette's international human resources department implemented its international-trainee program, designed to supply a steady stream of managerial talent from within its own ranks. Trainees are recruited from all over the world, and when their training is complete, they return to their home countries to become part of Gillette's global management team.

Foreign-Language Skills

Opinions are mixed on the importance of a second language for a career in international business. There are those whose attitude about another language is summed up in the statement that "the language of international business is English." Indeed, one journalist quipped, "Modern English is the Walmart of languages: convenient, huge, hard to avoid, superficially friendly, and devouring all rivals in its eagerness to expand."[78]

Proponents of language skills argue that learning a language improves not only cultural understanding[79] and business relationships[80] but also the student's

---

[78]Mark Abley, journalist. See also Daisuke Wakabayashi, "English Gets the Last Word in Japan," *The Wall Street Journal*, August 6, 2010, pp. B1–2; Michael Wei and Margaret Conley, "It's a Small World for Students of English," *Bloomberg BusinessWeek*, June 12, 2011.

[79]Lera Boroditsky, "Lost in Translation," *The Wall Street Journal*, July 24, 2010.

[80]Ellen Gamerman, "Just One Word: (That's Chinese for 'Plastics')," *The Wall Street Journal*, March 17–18, 2007, pp. P1, P5.

intelligence![81] Others point out that to be taken seriously in the business community, the expatriate must be at least conversational in the host language. Particularly when it comes to selling in foreign countries, languages are important. Says a Dutch sales training expert, "People expect to buy from sales reps they can relate to, and who understand their language and culture. They're often cold towards Americans trying to sell them products."

Some recruiters want candidates who speak at least one foreign language, even if the language will not be needed in a particular job. Having learned a second language is a strong signal to the recruiter that the candidate is willing to get involved in someone else's culture.

Although most companies offer short, intensive language-training courses for managers being sent abroad, many are making stronger efforts to recruit people who are bilingual or multilingual. According to the director of personnel at Coca-Cola, when his department searches its database for people to fill overseas posts, the first choice is often someone who speaks more than one language. We note that Chinese has now become a popular language in America's schools[82] and English in Chinese schools. Indeed, Disney is opening English language schools in China with Mickey as part of the faculty![83] We applaud the advances in the technology of language training and translation. For example, you can now practice your language skills on you're the smart phone in your pocket.[84] Likewise, there are apps that translate speech, and the technology is headed toward simultaneous translation by computer. Now NTT DoCoMo, the largest mobile-phone operator in Japan, offers service that translates phone calls between Japanese and English, Chinese, or Korean. The firm's computers eavesdrop and translate each person's words in a matter of seconds.[85] And these technologies will improve with time.

But language is much more than getting the translation right. Language guides thinking, decision making, and creativity. We are most pleased to see a special issue of the *Journal of International Business Studies* in 2014 on these broader topics. And we agree with the editors, "Language lies at the heart of international business (IB) activities…"[86] The various researchers begin to provide a glimpse of the importance of this topic: One study reports that asymmetries in language proficiency cause a variety of problems for global teams, including power struggles and out-group affect.[87] A second study demonstrates that language limitations not only complicate cross-cultural adjustments, but also do damage to multinational companies financially.[88] Another study points out the advantages and disadvantages of language-sensitive recruitment efforts.[89] A fourth paper suggests international firms should try to reach an agreement on what they call a *multilingual*

[81]Shirley S. Wang, "Building a More Resilient Brain," *The Wall Street Journal*, October 12, 2010; Gretchen Cuda-Kroen, "Being Bilingual May Boost Your Brain Power," *NPR*, April 4, 2011.

[82]Sam Dillon, "Foreign Languages Fade in Class—Except Chinese," *The New York Times*, January 10, 2010, online.

[83]James T. Areddy and Peter Sanders, "Chinese Learn English the Disney Way," *The Wall Street Journal*, April 20, 2009, pp. B1, B5.

[84]"Linguists Online," *The Economist*, January 5, 2013, p. 52.

[85]"Conquering Babel," *The Economist*, January 5, 2013, pp. 63–64.

[86]Mary Yoko Brannen, Rebecca Piekkari, and Susanne Teitze, "The Multifaceted Role of Language in International Business: Unpacking the Forms, Functions, and Features of a Critical Challenge to MNC Theory and Performance," *Journal of International Business Studies* 45 (2014), pp. 495–507.

[87]Pamela J. Hinds, Tsedal B. Neeley, and Catherine Durnell Camton, "Language as a Lightning Rod: Power Contests, Emotion Regulation and Subgroup Dynamics in Global Teams," *Journal of International Business Studies* 45 (2014), pp. 536–61.

[88]Andrei Kuznetsov and Olga Kusnetsova, "Building Professional Discourse in Emerging Markets: Language, Context, and the Challenge of Sensemaking," *Journal of International Business Studies* 45 (2014), pp. 583–99.

[89]Vesa Peltokorpi and Eero Vaara, "Knowledge Transfer in Multinational Corporations: Productive and Counterproductive Effects of Language-Sensitive Recruitment," *Journal of International Business Studies* 45 (2014), pp. 600–22.

franca—as opposed to a single dominant language or a multilingual approach—which is a combination of languages and procedures of use that make sense for the organization.[90] Other studies in this genre demonstrate how corporate language policies and practices can have negative effects on evaluation processes[91] and strategic human resources management.[92]

We the authors feel strongly that language skills are of great importance; if you want to be a major player in international business in the future, learn to speak other languages, or you might not make it—your competition will be those European students described in Crossing Borders 17.2. A joke that foreigners tell about language skills goes something like this: What do you call a person who speaks three or more languages? Multilingual. What do you call a person who speaks two languages? Bilingual. What do you call a person who speaks only one language? An American! Maybe the rest of the world knows something we don't.

[90]Addy Janssens and Chris Steyaert, "Re-Considering Language within a Cosmopolitan Understanding: Toward a *Multilingual Franca* Approach in International Business Studies," *Journal of International Business Studies* 45 (2014), pp. 623–39.

[91] Martyna Sliwa and Marjana Johansson, "How Non-Native English-Speaking Staff Are Evaluated in Linguistically Deiverse Organizations: A Sociolinguistic Perspective," *Journal of International Business Studies*, online.

[92]Vesa Peltokorpi and Eero Vaara, "Language Policies and Practices in Wholly Owned Foreign Subsidiaries: A Recontextualization Perspective," *Journal of International Business Studies* 43 (2012), pp. 808–33.

Summary

An effective international sales force constitutes one of the international marketer's greatest concerns. The company's sales force represents the major alternative method of organizing a company for foreign distribution and, as such, is on the front line of a marketing organization.

The role of marketers in both domestic and foreign markets is rapidly changing, along with the composition of international managerial and sales forces. Such forces have many unique requirements that are being filled by expatriates, locals, third-country nationals, or a combination of the three. In recent years, the pattern of development

has been to place more emphasis on local personnel operating in their own lands. This emphasis, in turn, has highlighted the importance of adapting U.S. managerial techniques to local needs.

The development of an effective marketing organization calls for careful recruiting, selecting, training, motivating, and compensating of expatriate personnel and their families to ensure the maximization of a company's return on its personnel expenditures. The most practical method of maintaining an efficient international sales and marketing force is careful, concerted planning at all stages of career development.

Key Terms

Expatriate
Local nationals

Third-country nationals
(TCNs)

Separation allowances
Work councils

Repatriation

Questions

1. Define the key terms listed above.
2. Why may it be difficult to adhere to set job criteria in selecting foreign personnel? What compensating actions might be necessary?
3. Why does a global sales force cause special compensation problems? Suggest some alternative solutions.
4. Under which circumstances should expatriate salespeople be utilized?

5. Discuss the problems that might be encountered in having an expatriate sales manager supervising foreign salespeople.

6. "To some extent, the exigencies of the personnel situation will dictate the approach to the overseas sales organization." Discuss.

7. How do legal factors affect international sales management?

8. How does the sales force relate to company organization? To channels of distribution?

9. "It is costly to maintain an international sales force." Comment.

10. Adaptability and maturity are traits needed by all salespeople. Why should they be singled out as especially important for international salespeople?

11. Can a person develop good cultural skills? Discuss.

12. Describe the attributes of a person with good cultural skills.

13. Interview a local company that has a foreign sales operation. Draw an organizational chart for the sales function and explain why that particular structure was used by that company.

14. Evaluate the three major sources of multinational personnel.

15. Which factors complicate the task of motivating the foreign sales force?

16. Why do companies include an evaluation of an employee's family among selection criteria for an expatriate assignment?

17. "Concerns for career and family are the most frequently mentioned reasons for a manager to refuse a foreign assignment." Why?

18. Discuss and give examples of why returning U.S. expatriates are often dissatisfied. How can these problems be overcome?

19. If "the language of international business is English," why is it important to develop a skill in a foreign language? Discuss.

20. The global manager of 2020 will have to meet many new challenges. Draw up a sample résumé for someone who could be considered for a top-level executive position in a global firm.

Chapter 18

Pricing for International Markets

CHAPTER OUTLINE

CHAPTER LEARNING OBJECTIVES

What you should learn from Chapter 18:

LO1 Components of pricing as competitive tools in international marketing

LO2 How to control pricing in parallel import or gray markets

LO3 Price escalation and how to minimize its effect

LO4 Countertrading and its place in international marketing practices

LO5 The mechanics of price quotations

LO6 The mechanics of getting paid

Peter Burrows, "Inside the iPhone Gray Market," *BusinessWeek*, February 12, 2008. Used with permission.

Global Perspective

LESSONS IN THE PRICE OF YOUR OREO, THE WORLD'S FAVORITE COOKIE

The divine drink which builds up resistance and fights fatigue. A cup of this precious drink permits a man to walk for a whole day without food.

Hernando Cortés

The seed pods of the cocoa tree grow on the trunk. Each pod is about the size of a cantaloupe and holds about 40 seeds. The scientific name for the tree is *Theobroma*, which means "food of the gods." Apparently Cortés was right, or he just had a lot of influence. The cocoa seeds are bitter tasting as they contain both theobromine and caffeine.

The Olmecs, Mayans, and Aztecs of pre-Columbian Mesoamerica crushed the dried cocoa beans, mixed them with water and sometimes vanilla and/or chilies, and drank the concoction. This is what Cortés would have been reporting in the preceding epigraph. While he was happy about the gold he was absconding from the Aztecs, the more valuable discovery was the "divine drink" he had held in his hands. The Conquistadors witnessed Moctezuma downing some 50 cups a day of the frothy liquid he called *xocolatl*, a native word for "bitter water." The theobromine and caffeine content would have produced the buzz Cortés experienced and the addiction apparent in the Emperor's court.

The first commercial shipment of chocolate arrived in Seville from Veracruz in 1585. As in the case of sugar, this ushered in enslavements of natives and West Africans to work in growing and harvesting of the cocoa seeds in the Americas.

Like druggist John Pemberton would do some three centuries later to avoid the bitter tastes of coca and cola in his new soda concoction, the Europeans dumped in sugar to make the chocolate drink more palatable. You can get a good idea of why this practice developed by trying a teaspoon of unsweetened baking chocolate from your pantry. Make it a half teaspoon.

In your Mega Stuff Oreo, sugar is the first ingredient by volume and cocoa the fourth. Of course, you recall from Chapter 4, page 101, that sugar is toxic while the cocoa by itself is not. Sugar prices in the United States are about twice those of the world prices (see the accompanying chart) because the U.S. government uses tariffs and price supports to block sugar imports and to stabilize demand for American producers. In the chart, you can observe the superior stability in the U.S. price versus the lower world prices. Also evinced is the impact of the OPEC price cartel on oil prices in the early 1970s (see Exhibit 18.4, page 578 for more details) that stimulated inflation, for both sugar and cocoa prices, and global recession into the 1980s.

With respect to chocolate, the Europeans really pushed other innovations: In 1689, Jamaican Dr. Hans Sloane developed milk chocolate. Solid chocolate, invented in Italy at the end of the 18th century, soon benefited from Swiss, Dutch, German, and British ideas. The Cadbury brothers came out with their first chocolate bar in 1849. Many of the brands popular today are associated with this stream of innovations—Ghirardelli, Nestlé, and Lindt. The mass-production processes developed by Milton Hershey added the characteristic of low price.

The global trade of chocolate has evolved into a mainstream of cocoa leaving Africa for European and American production facilities and consumers. The complex supply chain includes some 5 million farmers around the world, local and foreign cocoa buyers, shipping organizations, grinders, processors, chocolatiers, and distributors. The production and distribution of Cortés's "divine drink" now employs 40 to 50 million people worldwide.

The other side of consumption is the global production of cocoa. About 70 percent comes from the West African nations of Cameroon, Cote d'Ivoire, Ghana, and Nigeria.

Indonesia, Brazil, and Ecuador are also big producers. The top five cocoa bean importing countries are Netherlands, the United States, Germany, Malaysia, and France, in that order.

Villagers in West Africa that produce about 70 percent of the global supply of cocoa "are abandoning the crop because its price is volatile [see the chart], farms are too small to be economical, yields haven't risen for decades, and alternative crops, such as rubber, are more lucrative." Thus, demand is outstripping supply by 50,000 tons per year. As cookie makers bleed off the global cocoa reserve of 1.8 million tons, prices escalate.

New production is limited by climate change—hot, humid conditions are needed. Even so, all of the big companies, such as Nestlé and Mars, are investing tens of millions of dollars in better production methods. Due to shortages, political instability, and now Ebola, cocoa prices have experienced swings of more than 20 percent in 10 of the last 20 years.

The largest five candy companies deliver the most chocolate to consumers worldwide. In order they are Mars ($16.8 billion in global sales of Snickers and M&Ms), Mondelez ($15.5 billion, Cadbury and Oreos), Grupo Bimbo ($14.1 billion, Ricolino and Sarah Lee), Nestlé ($12.8 billion, Crunch bars), and Hershey's ($46.4 billion in global sales, KitKat and Almond Joy).

As attested to in the Hershey's annual report, the cocoa futures contract prices are quite volatile within and across years. While such volatility in prices at the wholesale level gives purchasing agents headaches, it is great news for marketers. It's easy to argue for immediate price increases down the distribution channel (from grocers to consumers) when the cost of your most important ingredient rises

dramatically from 2008 to 2010. Then, when cocoa prices crashed in 2012, if you don't bother to lower your selling prices much or quickly, the practice helps profits. In the United States, the virtual duopoly of Hershey's and Mars makes it easier to maintain price increases vis-à-vis overall inflation rates and the volatility of cocoa prices.

Canada's Competition Bureau recently filed criminal charges against the local affiliates of Nestlé, Cadbury (Mondelez), and Mars, along with a Canadian network of wholesale distributors and three individuals, alleging they conspired to fix the price of chocolate confectionery products in Canada. Hershey's has agreed to plead guilty and has been working with the investigators. In 2013, the four companies settled in the associated law suit by paying $23 million in fines.

The consequences of these market and marketing machinations are the following prices around the world: In China, you can get green tea or blueberry/raspberry cream Oreos for about 10¢ each. In Mexico, your de leche/banana Oreo will cost you about 8¢; the ads suggest twisting the cookies to mix the two flavors. Sounds like a good idea! Advertising can be informative. In Argentina, a tri-chocolate Oreo goes for about 6¢. Here in the United States, out of a one-pound bag, one Oreo is about 7¢ and one Mega Stuff Oreo is 10¢.

Sources: Robert H. Lustig, *Fat Chance: Beating the Odds against Sugar, Processed Food, Obesty, and Disease* (New York: Plume, 2013); Isis Almeida and Olivier Monnier, with Baudelaire Mieu, "Enjoy Those Chocolate Hearts While You Can," *Bloomberg Businessweek*, February 11–17, 2013, pp. 18–19; "What's Selling Where—Oreo Cookies," *The Wall Street Journal*, August 20, 2012, p. D2; Karen Johnson, "Chocolate Price Fixing Is Alleged by Canada," *The Wall Street Journal*, June 7, 2013, p. B6.

Setting and changing prices are key strategic marketing decisions. Prices both set values and communicate in international markets.[1] For example, Hong Kong Disneyland's early attendance was lower than expected, in part driven by what some called an unaffordable opening-day price of $32 a ticket. Setting the right price for a product or service can be the key to success or failure. Even when the international marketer produces the right product, promotes it correctly, and initiates the proper channel of distribution, the effort fails if the product is not properly priced. Although the quality of U.S. products is widely recognized in global markets, foreign buyers, like domestic buyers, balance quality and price in their purchase decisions. An offering's price must reflect the quality and value the consumer perceives in the product. Of all the tasks facing the international marketer, determining what price to charge is one of the most difficult. A plethora of factors must be considered, particularly those related to particular foreign market characteristics, such as economic volatility, development, legal requirements, and so on.[2] It is further complicated when the company sells its product to customers in multiple countries' markets.

LO1

Components of pricing as competitive tools in international marketing

As globalization continues, competition intensifies among multinational and home-based companies. All are seeking a solid competitive position so they can prosper as markets reach full potential. The competition for the diaper market among Kimberly-Clark,

[1]Lorraine Eden and Peter Rodriguez, "How Weak Are the Signals? International Price Indices and Multinational Enterprises," *Journal of International Business Studies* 36, no. 1 (2004), pp. 61–74.
[2]Qun Tan and Carlos M. P. Sousa, "Research on Export Pricing: Still Moving toward Maturity," *Journal of International Marketing* 19, no. 3 (2011), pp. 1–35.

P&G, and the smaller companies illustrates how price becomes increasingly important as a competitive tool and how price competition changes the structure of a market. Whether exporting or managing overseas operations, the manager's responsibility is to set and control the price of goods in multiple markets in which different sets of variables are to be found: different tariffs, costs, attitudes, competition, currency fluctuations, and methods of price quotation.

This chapter focuses on the basic pricing policy questions that arise from the special cost, market, and competitive factors found in foreign markets. A discussion of price escalation and its control and factors associated with price setting and leasing is followed by a discussion of the use of countertrade as a pricing tool and a review of the mechanics of international price quotation. We close the chapter with a brief discussion about the mechanics of getting paid the prices charged—letters of credit and such.

Pricing Policy

Active marketing in several countries compounds the number of pricing problems[3] and variables relating to price policy. For example, one study found wide variations in the volatility of prices across countries. Culture seems to play a role because bigger price swings are seen in more collectivistic countries for an array of products and services—stock prices, housing, milk, and, overall, in the consumer price index[4]. Unless a firm has a clearly thought-out, explicitly defined price policy, expediency rather than design establishes prices. The country in which business is being conducted, the type of product, variations in competitive conditions, and other strategic factors affect pricing activity. Price and terms of sale cannot be based on domestic criteria alone.

Pricing Objectives

In general, price decisions are viewed two ways: pricing as an active instrument of accomplishing marketing objectives, or pricing as a static element in a business decision. If prices are viewed as an active instrument, the company *sets* prices (rather than *following* market prices)[5] to achieve specific objectives,[6] whether targeted returns on profit, targeted sales volumes, or some other specific goals.[7] The company that follows the second approach, pricing as a static element, probably exports only excess inventory, places a low priority on foreign business, and views its export sales as passive contributions to sales volume. When U.S. and Canadian international businesses were asked to rate, on a scale of 1 to 5, several factors important in price setting, total profits received an average rating of 4.70, followed by return on investment (4.41), market share (4.13), and total sales volume (4.06). Liquidity ranked the lowest (2.19).

The more control a company has over the final selling price of a product, the better it is able to achieve its marketing goals. However, controlling end prices is not always possible. The broader the product line and the larger the number of countries involved, the more complex is the process of controlling prices to the end user.

Parallel Imports

LO2

How to control pricing in parallel import or gray markets

In addition to having to meet price competition country by country and product by product, companies have to guard against competition with their own subsidiaries or branches. Because of the different prices possible in different country markets, a product sold in one

[3]Claude Obadia, "Competitive Export Pricing: The Influence of the Information Context," *Journal of International Marketing* 21, no. 2 (2013), pp. 62–78.

[4]Dante Pirouz and John L. Graham, "Culture, Globalization, and Stock Price Volatility," working paper, Merage School of Business, University of California, Irvine, 2015.

[5]Carl Arthur Solberg, Barbara Stottinger, and Attila Yaprak, "A Taxonomy of the Pricing Practices of Exporting Firms: Evidence from Austria, Norway, and the United States," *Journal of International Marketing* 14 (2006), pp. 23–48.

[6]Andrew LaVallee, "Unilever to Test Mobile Coupons," *The Wall Street Journal*, May 29, 2009, p. B8.

[7]Christopher K. Hsee, Jean-Pierre Dube, and Yan Zhang, "The Prominence Effect in Shanghai Apartment Prices," *Journal of Marketing Research* 45, no. 2 (2008), pp. 133–44.

CROSSING BORDERS 18.1   Inside the iPhone Gray Market

You could buy one (indeed, more than one) in Beijing even though they had not yet been shipped there by Apple or AT&T. The gray market for iPhones in China was bustling. Apparently 800,000 to 1 million iPhones, or about one-fourth of the total sold, were "unlocked"—that is, altered to be able to run on networks other than those of Apple's exclusive partners.

This iPhone aftermarket did not take long to develop. By the time the device went on sale on June 29, 2007, software hackers and companies that specialize in unlocking cell phones had already begun searching for ways to make the iPhone work on unsanctioned networks. Within weeks, online forums were buzzing with an answer that emanated from a tiny company based in Prague, Czech Republic.

Pavel Zaboj is a 36-year-old former math student who, together with friends, developed an electronic device called Turbo SIM that was designed to turn cell phones into mobile payment systems. Turns out, Turbo SIM also could be used to trick the iPhone into thinking it was operating on AT&T's network. By mid-August, Zaboj's 10-person firm, Bladox, was flooded with orders, particularly from Canada and Mexico, where Apple addicts did not have to venture far to get an iPhone. Bladox was totally unprepared and could not fill all the orders that rolled in. "We just sat there, open-mouthed," Zaboj says.

Bladox has sold devices used to unlock phones in roughly 100 countries, including French Polynesia and Afghanistan, Brazil, Canada, the Dominican Republic, Indonesia, Israel, Nigeria, Peru, Poland, Russia, and the United Arab Emirates.

The boom was fueled not just by the short supply of a hot product but also by scant evidence of interference from Apple or its partners. Apple-authorized partners—AT&T, O2, Orange, and Deutsche Telekom's T-Mobile—lost hundreds of dollars in monthly fees per subscriber when they avoided a two-year contract in favor of unlocking. But the bulk of the unlocking seems to have been occurring in places where customers had no authorized carrier to choose from anyway.

Apple took in hundreds of dollars per iPhone sale when customers activated service with one of its partners, but most analysts say the unlocking craze also helps spread Apple's brand awareness.

The gray market got another push forward from exchange rates. With the dollar falling, consumers from Europe and elsewhere could get a better deal on an iPhone during a trip to the United States than from buying it at home. Gray marketers saw the same opportunity and began recruiting a range of people to secure iPhones.

Sometimes, it is as simple as asking friends and family members to reach their iPhone limit: five phones at Apple and three at AT&T. One reseller admits he got a friend to print business cards and pose as a small business owner to dupe an Apple Store manager into letting him buy 100 iPhones for his "employees." Chinese retailers also admitted to "getting people like airline stewardesses to bring the iPhones over for us."

Some iPhones on the gray market may have leaked from points closer to the source: the big Chinese factories where they are assembled.

Most recently Apple is selling iPhones through its new partner Unicom (Hong Kong) but is still facing stiff competition from other smart phones. But Apple seemingly could have charged more for the latest version of its iPad, given the rioting over the fashionable product in Beijing.

Sources: Peter Burrows, "Inside the iPhone Gray Market," *BusinessWeek*, February 12, 2008. Used with permission. John Markoff, "Friends and Smugglers Meet Demand for iPhones," *The New York Times*, February 18, 2008, pp. A1, A8; "Lukewarm Reception," *Business China*, January 4, 2010, p. 5; Charles Duhigg and David Barboza, "In China, Human Costs Are Built into an iPad," *The New York Times*, January 25, 2012.

country may be exported to another and undercut the prices charged in that country.[8] For example, to meet economic conditions and local competition, an American pharmaceutical company might sell its drugs in a developing country at a low price and then discover that these discounted drugs are being exported to a third country, where, as parallel imports, they are in direct competition with the same product sold for higher prices by the same firm. This practice is lucrative when wide margins exist between prices for the same products in different countries. A variety of conditions can create a profitable opportunity for a parallel market.

---

[8]We see this in a variety of product areas, including publishing and automobiles. See, respectively, "Seconds to Go," *The Economist,* March 23, 2023, p. 71; Matthew Goldstein, "U.S. Targets Buyers of Chinese-Bound Luxury Cars," *The New York Times*, February 12, 2014, pp, B1, 5.

Restrictions brought about by import quotas and high tariffs also can lead to parallel imports and make illegal imports attractive. India has a three-tier duty structure on computer parts ranging from 50 to 80 percent on imports. As a result, estimates indicate that as much as 35 percent of India's domestic computer hardware sales are accounted for by the gray market.

The possibility of a parallel market occurs whenever price differences are greater than the cost of transportation between two markets. In Europe, because of different taxes and competitive price structures, prices for the same product vary between countries. When this situation occurs, it is not unusual for companies to find themselves competing in one country with their own products imported from another European country at lower prices. Pharmaceutical companies face this problem in Italy, Greece, and Spain because of price caps imposed on prescription drugs in those countries. For example, the ulcer drug Losec sells for only $18 in Spain but goes for $39 in Germany. The heart drug Plavix costs $55 in France and sells for $79 in London. Presumably such price differentials would cease once all restrictions to trade were eliminated in the European Union, and in most cases, this is true. However, the European Union does not prevent countries from controlling drug prices as part of their national health plans.

The drug industry has tried to stop parallel trade in Europe but has been overruled by European authorities. Now the industry is trying a different approach, restricting supplies to meet only local demand according to formulas based on prior demand and anticipated growth. The idea is that a country should receive just enough of a drug for its citizens. Wholesalers that order more with the intention of shipping the drugs to higher-priced markets will not have enough to do so. A number of major pharmaceutical companies have imposed similar restrictions. The companies say these measures are intended to streamline distribution, help prevent medicine shortages, and curtail excess inventory, whereas distributors claim the strategy is aimed at thwarting cross-border drug trading. The fact is, "half of all demand in Britain of several products is being met by imports from low-priced countries" and companies are attempting to curtail parallel imports.

Gray market pharmaceuticals moving from Canada to the United States are estimated to represent about $427 million annually—not a large amount when compared to the $135 billion U.S. drug market, but it can be substantial for specific drugs like Paxil, Zyban, and Viagra. Although importing prescription drugs from a foreign country, including Canada, is against U.S. law, a person can travel to Canada or Mexico to make purchases or buy over the Internet. Technically, buying over the Internet and having the drugs mailed to the United States is illegal. However, the government has taken a relatively lax view toward such purchases, provided the supply does not exceed 90 days.

Naturally, drug companies that have been hit the hardest want to put a stop to the traffic. Glaxo SmithKline, the prescription drug maker, has asked all Canadian pharmacies and wholesalers to "self-certify" that they are not exporting its drugs outside Canada. The company also is warning U.S. customers about imported drugs in a new advertising campaign. Those that fail to comply will have their Glaxo supplies cut off—"Glaxo products are approved by Health Canada for sale in Canada only." Some feel that this move will not solve the problem even if Glaxo is able to stop Canadian sales because Americans will be able to find less expensive drugs in other markets, like Australia and Ireland. The Internet trade will be hard to shut down as long as large price differentials persist among markets. Furthermore, U.S. legislators are passing laws that allow such drug imports.

Exclusive distribution, a practice often used by companies to maintain high retail margins to encourage retailers to provide extra service to customers, to stock large assortments, or to maintain the exclusive-quality image of a product, can create a favorable condition for parallel importing. Perfume and designer brands such as Gucci and Cartier are especially prone to gray markets. To maintain the image of quality and exclusivity, prices for such products traditionally include high profit margins at each level of distribution; characteristically, there are differential prices among markets and limited quantities of product, and distribution is restricted to upscale retailers. Wholesale prices for exclusive brands of fragrances are often 25 percent more in the United States than wholesale prices in other countries. These are ideal conditions for a lucrative gray market for unauthorized dealers in other countries who buy more than they need at wholesale prices lower than U.S. wholesalers pay. They then sell the excess at a profit to unauthorized U.S. retailers but at a price lower than the retailer would have to pay to an authorized U.S. distributor.

The high-priced designer sportswear industry is also vulnerable to such practices. Nike, Adidas, and Calvin Klein were incensed to find their products being sold in one of Britain's leading supermarket chains, Tesco. Nike's Air Max Metallic trainers, which are priced at £120 ($196) in sports shops, could be purchased at Tesco for £50 ($80). Tesco had bought £8 million in Nike sportswear from overstocked wholesalers in the United States (Exhibit 18.1). To prevent parallel markets from developing when such marketing and pricing strategies are used, companies must maintain strong control over distribution and prices.

Companies that are serious about restricting the gray market must establish and monitor controls that effectively police distribution channels. In some countries they may get help from the courts. A Taiwan court ruled that two companies that were buying Coca-Cola in the United States and shipping it to Taiwan were violating the trademark rights of both the Coca-Cola Company and its sole Taiwan licensee. The violators were prohibited from importing, displaying, or selling products bearing the Coca-Cola trademark. In other countries, the courts have not always come down on the side of the trademark owner. The reasoning is that once the trademarked item is sold, the owner's rights to control the trademarked item are lost. In a similar situation in Canada, the courts did not side with the Canadian exporter who was buying 50,000 cases of Coke a week and shipping them to Hong Kong and Japan. The exporter paid $4.25 a case, plus shipping of $1.00 a case, and sold them at $6.00, a nifty profit of 75 cents a case. Coca-Cola sued, but the court ruled that the product was bought and sold legally.

Exhibit 18.1
How Gray Market Goods End Up in U.S. Stores

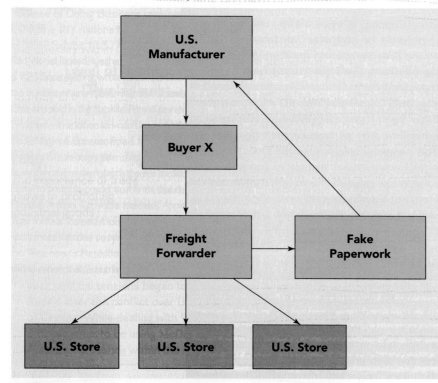

1. A major manufacturer agrees to sell its products, at a price competitive for an overseas market, to "Buyer X" who promises to sell the products overseas.

2. The manufacturer ships the goods to Buyer X.

3. Buyer X has a local freight forwarder at the port take possession of the goods.

4. Instead of shipping the goods to their supposed destination, the freight forwarder (at the behest of Buyer X) sends them to smaller distributors and discount outlets in the United States.

5. The freight forwarder sends a bogus bill of lading to the manufacturer, so the company believes the goods have been sold overseas.

Parallel imports can do long-term damage in the market for trademarked products.[9] Customers who unknowingly buy unauthorized imports have no assurance of the quality of the item they buy, of warranty support, or of authorized service or replacement parts. Purchasers of computers, for example, may not be able to get parts because authorized dealers have no obligation to service these computers. In the case of software, the buyer may be purchasing a counterfeit product and will not be authorized for technical support. Furthermore, when a product fails, the consumer blames the owner of the trademark, and the quality image of the product is sullied.

Approaches to International Pricing

Whether the orientation is toward control over end prices or net prices, company policy relates to the net price received. Cost and market considerations are important; a company cannot sell goods below cost of production and remain in business, and it cannot sell goods at a price unacceptable in the marketplace. Firms unfamiliar with overseas marketing and firms producing industrial goods orient their pricing solely on a cost basis. Firms that employ pricing as part of the strategic mix, however, are aware of such alternatives as market segmentation from country to country or market to market, competitive pricing in the marketplace, price for stability of operations,[10] and other market-oriented pricing factors,[11] including cultural differences in perceptions of pricing.[12]

Full-Cost versus Variable-Cost Pricing

Firms that orient their price thinking around cost must determine whether to use variable cost or full cost in pricing their goods. In variable-cost pricing, the firm is concerned only with the marginal or incremental cost of producing goods to be sold in overseas markets. Such firms regard foreign sales as bonus sales and assume that any return over their variable cost makes a contribution to net profit. These firms may be able to price most competitively in foreign markets, but because they are selling products abroad at lower net prices than they are selling them in the domestic market, they may be subject to charges of dumping. In that case, they open themselves to antidumping tariffs or penalties that take away from their competitive advantage. Nevertheless, variable-cost (or *marginal-cost*) pricing is a practical approach to pricing when a company has high fixed costs and unused production capacity. Any contribution to fixed cost after variable costs are covered is profit to the company.

In contrast, companies following the full-cost pricing philosophy insist that no unit of a similar product is different from any other unit in terms of cost and that each unit must bear its full share of the total fixed and variable cost. This approach is suitable when a company has high variable costs relative to its fixed costs. In such cases, prices are often set on a cost-plus basis, that is, total costs plus a profit margin. Both variable-cost and full-cost policies are followed by international marketers.

Skimming versus Penetration Pricing

Firms must also decide when to follow a skimming or a penetration pricing policy. Traditionally, the decision of which policy to follow depends on the level of competition, the innovativeness of the product, market characteristics, and company characteristics.

---

[9]For an interesting look at how enforcement efforts work, see Kersi D. Anita, Mark E. Bergen, Shantanu Dutta, and Robert J. Fisher, "How Does Enforcement Deter Gray Market Incidence?" *Journal of Marketing* 70 (2006), pp. 92–106.

[10]Apparently executives at General Electric recently forgot that higher prices can help maintain stable operations when backlogs are large. See Kate Linebaugh and Bob Sechler, "GE Profit Slides Amid Margin Squeeze," *The Wall Street Journal*, January 20, 2012.

[11]Pradeep K. Chintagunta and Ramaroa Desiraju, "Strategic Pricing and Detailing Behavior in International Markets," *Marketing Science* 24, no. 1 (2005), pp. 67–80.

[12]Manoj Thomas and Vick Morwitz, "Penny Wise and Pound Foolish: The Left-Digit Effect in Price Cognition," *Journal of Consumer Research* 32, no. 2 (2005), pp. 54–64; Lisa E. Bolton, Hean Tat Keh, and Joseph W. Alba, "How Do Price Fairness Perceptions Differ across Cultures?" *Journal of Marketing Research* 47, no. 3 (2010), pp. 564–76.

CROSSING BORDERS 18.2   Don't Squeeze the Charmin, Mr. Whipple—Or Change the Color

The British pay twice the price as the Germans and the French, and nearly two-and-a-half times as much as Americans, for a standard four-roll pack of toilet paper. Why? Is it price gouging, the impact of the euro, the relative value of the English pound, or just culture?

The answer is rather simple: British consumers insist on a softer, more luxurious texture than their less discriminating continental and American cousins. British toilet paper is four grams heavier per square meter because it contains more fiber than European tissues. Extensive consumer testing has established that British consumers are not willing to be fobbed off with anything less.

Another factor distinguishes the British preference for a special toilet paper roll. Go to any supermarket, and you will be confronted by an extraordinary choice of more than 50 colors, sizes, and brands. Honeysuckle, warm pink, summer peach, pearl white, meadow green, breeze blue, and magnolia are just some of the shades on offer. The reason for this variety apparently is that the British shopper insists that toilet paper match the color scheme of the bathroom. On the continent, consumers settle happily for white, with pink thrown in as a wild alternative.

Procter & Gamble captured 10 percent of the market in less than five months after offering a stronger Charmin, but it may have gone too far. There were complaints that the "wet strength" of Charmin was unsuitable for U.K. toilets. The U.K. sewage system could handle Charmin alone, but the issue was whether the system would get clogged if several rival tissues adopted the stronger tissue. Procter & Gamble agreed to halve the strength of its Charmin toilet tissue. And the P&G product has also been rated worst on a forest-friendly scale by Greenpeace. Complying with this latest criticism will surely raise costs.

Although consumers may be mad about U.K. toilet paper prices, those in India are furious. A recent scandal involving $80 rolls of toilet paper, paid for by corrupt government officials, catalyzed an anticorruption campaign that had led to the imprisonment of cabinet members and CEOs alike.

Sources: "Going Soft," *The Economist*, March 4, 2000; "P&G Unblocks Sewage Row with Toilet Paper Revamp," *Reuters*, May 10, 2000; Timothy Kenny, "Eurasia: Of Toilet Paper, Escalators and Hope," *The Wall Street Journal Europe*, September 16, 2005, p. A9; "Skip it, Eco-Worrier," *The Times (London)*, December 1, 2007, p. 11; Gurcharan Das, "India Says No to $80 Toilet Paper," *The New York Times*, September 3, 2011.

A company uses skimming when the objective is to reach a segment of the market that is relatively price insensitive and thus willing to pay a premium price for the value received. If limited supply exists, a company may follow a skimming approach to maximize revenue and to match demand to supply. When a company is the only seller of a new or innovative product, a skimming price may be used to maximize profits until competition forces a lower price.[13] Skimming often is used in markets with only two income levels: the wealthy and the poor. Costs prohibit setting a price that will be attractive to the lower-income market, so the marketer charges a premium price and directs the product to the high-income, relatively price-insensitive segment. Apparently this was the policy of Johnson & Johnson's pricing of diapers in Brazil before the arrival of P&G. Today such opportunities are fading away as the disparity in income levels is giving way to growing middle-income market segments in many countries. The existence of larger markets attracts competition and, as is often the case, the emergence of multiple product lines, thus leading to price competition.

A penetration pricing policy is used to stimulate market and sales growth by deliberately offering products at low prices. Penetration pricing most often is used to acquire and hold share of market as a competitive maneuver. However, in country markets experiencing rapid and sustained economic growth, and where large shares of the population are moving into middle-income classes, penetration pricing may be used to stimulate market growth even with minimum competition. Penetration pricing may be a more profitable strategy than skimming if it maximizes revenues as a base for fighting the competition that is sure to come.

Regardless of the formal pricing policies and strategies a company uses, the market sets the effective price for a product. Said another way, the price has to be set at

---

[13]Caroline Bingxin Li and Julie Juan Li, "Achieving Superior Financial Performance in China: Differentiation, Cost Leadership, or Both?" *Journal of International Marketing* 16, no. 3 (2008), pp. 1–22.

Chinese wait to enter Beijing's first Walmart outlet. Thousands crowded the Sam's Club store on the far western edge of Beijing as the world's biggest retailer made its first foray into a major Chinese city. Walmart now has nearly 200 stores elsewhere in China; the first opened in 1996. The low-price-for-good-quality strategy of Walmart and other mass retailers such as Costco and Carrefour, the French supermarket chain, have resulted in lower retail prices in China, Japan, and other Asian countries they have entered.

a point at which the consumer will perceive value received, and the price must be within reach of the target market. As a consequence, many products are sold in very small units in some markets to bring the unit price within reach of the target market. Warner-Lambert's launch of its five-unit pack of Bubbaloo bubble gum in Brazil failed—even though bubble gum represents more than 72 percent of the overall gum sector—because it was priced too high for the target market. A relaunch of a single-unit "pillow" pack brought the price within range and enabled the brand to quickly gain a respectable level of sales.

As a country's economy grows and the distribution of wealth becomes more equitable, multiple income levels develop, distinct market segments emerge, and multiple price levels and price/quality perceptions increase in importance. As an example, the market for electronic consumer goods in China changed in just a few years. Instead of a market for imported high-priced and high-quality electronic goods aimed at the new rich versus cheaper, poorer quality, Chinese-made goods for the rest of the market, a multitiered market reflecting the growth of personal income has emerged.

Sony of Japan, a leading foreign seller of high-priced consumer electronic goods, was upstaged in the Chinese market when Aiwa, a competitor, recognized the emergence of a new middle-tier market for good-quality, modestly priced electronic goods. As part of a global strategy focused on slim margins and high turnover, Aiwa of Korea began selling stereo systems at prices closer to Chinese brands than to Sony's. Aiwa's product quality was not far behind that of Sony and was better than top Chinese brands, and the product resembled Sony's high-end systems. Aiwa's recognition of a new market segment and its ability to tap into it resulted in a huge increase in overall demand for Aiwa products.

Pricing decisions that were appropriate when companies directed their marketing efforts toward single market segments will give way to more sophisticated practices. As incomes rise in many foreign markets, the pricing environment a company encounters will be similar to that in the United States. As countries prosper and incomes become more equitably distributed, multiple market segments develop. As these segments emerge, Walmart, Carrefour, and other mass retailers enter the market to offer price-conscious customers good value at affordable prices. This scenario seems to repeat itself in country after country. Within these markets, an effective pricing strategy becomes crucial.

Price Escalation

LO3 ▮▮▮

Price escalation and how
to minimize its effect

People traveling abroad often are surprised to find goods that are relatively inexpensive in their home country priced outrageously high in other countries. Because of the natural tendency to assume that such prices are a result of profiteering, manufacturers often resolve to begin exporting to crack these new, profitable foreign markets only to find that, in most cases, the higher prices reflect the higher costs of exporting. A case in point is a pacemaker for heart patients that sells for $2,100 in the United States. Tariffs and the Japanese distribution system add substantially to the final price in Japan. Beginning with the import tariff, each time the pacemaker changes hands, an additional cost is incurred. The product passes first through the hands of an importer, then to the company with primary responsibility for sales and service, then to a secondary or even a tertiary local distributor, and finally to the hospital. Markups at each level result in the $2,100 pacemaker selling for more than $4,000 in Japan. Inflation results in price escalation, one of the major pricing obstacles facing the MNC marketer. This escalation is true not only for technical products like the pacemaker but also for such products as crude oil, soft drinks, and beer. Estimates indicate that if tariffs and trade barriers on these products were abolished, the consumer would enjoy savings of 6.57 trillion yen.

Costs of Exporting

Excess profits exist in some international markets, but generally the cause of the disproportionate difference in price between the exporting country and the importing country, here termed price escalation, is the added costs incurred as a result of exporting products from one country to another. Specifically, the term relates to situations in which ultimate prices are raised by shipping costs, insurance, financing costs,[14] packing, tariffs, longer channels of distribution, larger middlemen margins, special taxes, administrative costs, and exchange rate fluctuations. The majority of these costs arise as a direct result of moving goods across borders from one country to another and often combine to escalate the final price to a level considerably higher than in the domestic market.

Taxes, Tariffs, and Administrative Costs

A Japanese wholesale store manager of a meat market in Tokyo arranges packs of beef imported from Australia. Earlier in the day, the government had announced plans to raise its tariff on refrigerated beef imports to 50 percent from 38.5 percent, following a spike in imports. The price tag reads: "Premium beef, sirloin steak from Australia @ 258 yen per 100 grams." Tariffs are one of the main causes of price escalation for imported products.

A tariff, or duty, is a special form of taxation. Like other forms of taxes, a tariff may be levied for the purpose of protecting a market or for increasing government revenue. A tariff is a fee charged when goods are brought into a country from another country. The level of tariff is typically expressed as the rate of duty and may be levied as specific, ad valorem, or compound. A specific duty is a flat charge per physical unit imported, such as 15 cents per bushel of rye. Ad valorem duties are levied as a percentage of the value of the goods imported, such as 20 percent of the value of imported watches. Compound duties include both a specific and an ad valorem charge, such as $1 per camera plus 10 percent of its value. Tariffs and other forms of import taxes serve to discriminate against all foreign goods.

Fees for import certificates or for other administrative processing can assume such levels that they are, in fact, import taxes. Many countries have purchase or excise taxes that apply to various categories of goods; value-added or turnover taxes, which apply as the product goes through a channel of distribution; and retail sales taxes. Such taxes increase the end price of goods but in general do not discriminate against foreign goods. Tariffs are the primary discriminatory tax that must be taken into account in reckoning with foreign competition.

In addition to taxes and tariffs, a variety of administrative costs are directly associated with exporting and importing a product. Export and import licenses, other documents, and the physical arrangements for getting the product from port of entry to the

---

[14]Mark Whitehouse, "Number of the Week: Consumers in China and Brazil Discover Credit," *The Wall Street Journal*, October 9, 2010; Alessandra Migliaccio and Sonia Sirletti, "A Country that Needs More Credit Cards," *Bloomberg BusinessWeek*, December 12, 2011, p. 24.

buyer's location mean additional costs. Although such costs are relatively small, they add to the overall cost of exporting. All these taxes, tariffs, and other charges add abut 60 to 70 percent on top of Apple's iPhone price in Brazil. Samsung, facing similar barriers there, has managed to sell its smartphones at lower prices; thus, the market shares for smartphones in Brazil is Samsung at 40+ percent and Apple at just over 13 percent.[15]

Inflation

In countries with rapid inflation or exchange variation, the selling price must be related to the cost of goods sold and the cost of replacing the items. Goods often are sold below their cost of replacement plus overhead, and sometimes are sold below replacement cost. In these instances, the company would be better off not to sell the products at all. When payment is likely to be delayed for several months or is worked out on a long-term contract,

Shoppers look at stacks of discount clothing jutting out on a sidewalk to attract potential buyers at Tokyo's Sugamo shopping district. With the stock market plunging to 16-year lows, talk of deflationary dangers, and a morass of confusion in its political leadership, Japan appeared to be headed toward a serious economic crisis. The central bank played down the possibility of deflation, saying that falling prices show the market is finally opening up to competition.

inflationary factors must be figured into the price. Inflation and lack of control over price were instrumental in an unsuccessful new-product launch in Brazil by the H. J. Heinz Company; after only two years, Heinz withdrew from the market. Misunderstandings with the local partner had resulted in a new fruit-based drink being sold to retailers on consignment; that is, they did not pay until the product was sold. Faced with a rate of inflation of more than 300 percent at the time, just a week's delay in payment eroded profit margins substantially. Soaring inflation in many developing countries has made widespread price controls a constant threat in many countries.

Because inflation and price controls imposed by a country and/or the global marketplace[16] are beyond the control of companies, they use a variety of techniques to inflate the selling price to compensate for inflation pressure and price controls. They may charge for extra services, inflate costs in transfer pricing, or break up products into components and price each component separately.

Inflation causes consumer prices to escalate, and consumers face ever-rising prices that eventually exclude many of them from the market. In contrast, deflation results in ever-decreasing prices, creating a positive result for consumers, but both put pressure to lower costs on everyone in the supply chain.

Deflation

The Japanese economy has been in a deflationary spiral for a number of years. In a country better known for $10 melons and $100 steaks, McDonald's now sells hamburgers for 52 cents, down from $1.09; a flat screen 32-inch color television is down from $4,000 to less than $1,000; and clothing stores compete to sell fleece jackets for $8, down from $25 two years earlier. Consumer prices have dropped to a point that they are similar to those Japanese once found only on overseas shopping trips. The high prices prevalent in Japan before deflation allowed substantial margins for everyone in the distribution chain. As prices continued to drop over several years, those less able to adjust costs to allow some margin with deflated prices fell by the wayside. Entirely new retail categories—100-yen discount shops, clothing chains selling low-cost imported products from China, and warehouse-style department stores—have become more common. Sales at discount stores grew by 78 percent in recent years. Discounting is the way to prosper in Japan, which again helps fuel deflation. While those in the distribution chain adjusted to a different competitive environment or gave up, Japanese consumers were reveling in their newfound spending power. Japanese tourists used to travel to the United States to buy things at much cheaper prices, but as one consumer commented, "Nowadays, I feel prices in Japan are going down and America is no longer cheaper." Although she was

[15]Vincent Bevins and Chris O'Brien, "In Brazil, Apple Has Barriers To Sales," *Los Angeles Times*, July 4, 2013, p. B1, 4.

[16]Charles Forelle, "Greece Defaults, and Tries to Move On," *The Wall Street Journal*, March 10, 2012.

accustomed to returning from trips to the United States carrying suitcases of bargains, she returned from her last two-week vacation with purchases that fit in one fanny pack.

In a deflationary market, it is essential for a company to keep prices low and raise brand value to win the trust of consumers. Whether experiencing deflation or inflation, an exporter has to place emphasis on controlling price escalation.

Exchange Rate Fluctuations

At one time, world trade contracts could be easily written because payment was specified in a relatively stable currency. The American dollar was the standard, and all transactions could be related to the dollar. Now that all major currencies are floating freely relative to one another, no one is quite sure of the future value of any currency. Increasingly, companies are insisting that transactions be written in terms of the vendor company's national currency, and forward hedging is becoming more common. If exchange rates are not carefully considered in long-term contracts, companies find themselves unwittingly giving 15 to 20 percent discounts. Indeed, anyone who wrote a contract with a Russian customer in rubles in 2014 lost a bundle as Russia's currency lost more than 20 percent of its value vis-à-vis the American dollar.[17] The added cost incurred by exchange rate fluctuations on a day-to-day basis must be taken into account, especially where there is a significant time lapse between signing the order and delivery of the goods. Exchange rate differentials mount. Whereas Hewlett-Packard gained nearly half a million dollars' additional profit through exchange rate fluctuations in one year, Nestlé lost a million dollars in six months. Other companies have lost or gained even larger amounts.

During the mid-1990s, Mexico knocked three zeroes off the peso in response to a major devaluation. Venezuela did the same in 2008.[18] In 2005 Turkey knocked six zeroes off its lira toward its potential alignment with the European Union. Both actions affected perceptions of key constituencies. Both bills are worth about 75¢.

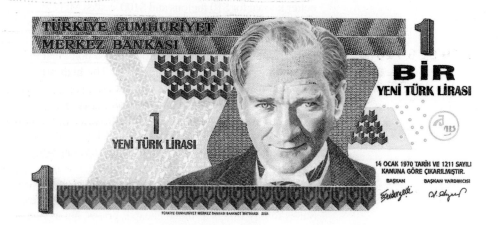

[17]"The Rouble's Rout," *The Economist*, November 15, 2014, p. 77.

[18]Annually *The Economist* publishes its Big Mac index, which predicts currency fluctuations. See "Grease-Proof Paper," *The Economist*, January 25, 2014, p. 63. Also see Ira Iosebashvili, "On Currencies, What's Fair Is Hard To Say," *The Wall Street Journal*, February 22, 2013, p. A12.

Varying Currency Values

In addition to risks from exchange rate variations, other risks result from the changing values of a country's currency relative to other currencies,[19] such as consumers' perceptions of value. Consider the situation in Germany for a purchaser of U.S. manufactured goods from mid-2001 to mid-2003. During this period, the value of the U.S. dollar relative to the euro went from a strong position (U.S.$1 to € 1.8315) in mid-2001 to a weaker position in mid-2003 (U.S.$1 to €0.8499). A strong dollar produces price resistance because a larger quantity of local currency is needed to buy a U.S. dollar. Conversely, when the U.S. dollar is weak, demand for U.S. goods increases because fewer units of local currency are needed to buy a U.S. dollar. The weaker U.S. dollar, compared with most of the world's stronger currencies, that existed in mid-2003 stimulated exports from the United States. Consequently, when the dollar strengthens, U.S. exports will soften.

A woman looks at a poster offering a half-priced bacon and lettuce hamburger, reduced from U.S.$3.20 to $1.60 during a monthly discount at a McDonald's restaurant in downtown Tokyo. McDonald's Japan announced that it would reduce the price of hamburgers by 30 percent for a month to return to customers the profit the company made by the strong yen against U.S. dollars in importing the raw materials from abroad. McDonald's move created goodwill among its customers at a time when it is forced to lower prices to "hike" sales in an economy that is suffering a major downturn. This move is a good example of how differences in the value of currencies can be positive for a company, as in this case, or negative when the value of the dollar is much stronger than the local currency.

When the value of the dollar is weak relative to the buyer's currency (i.e., it takes fewer units of the foreign currency to buy a dollar), companies generally employ cost-plus pricing. To remain price competitive when the dollar is strong (i.e., when it takes more units of the foreign currency to buy a dollar), companies must find ways to offset the higher price caused by currency values. When the rupee in India depreciated significantly against the U.S. dollar, PC manufacturers faced a serious pricing problem. Because the manufacturers were dependent on imported components, their options were to absorb the increased cost or raise the price of PCs.

Currency exchange rate swings are considered by many global companies to be a major pricing problem. Because the benefits of a weaker dollar are generally transitory, firms need to take a proactive stance one way or the other. For a company with long-range plans calling for continued operation in foreign markets that wants to remain price competitive, price strategies need to reflect variations in currency values.

Innumerable cost variables can be identified depending on the market, the product, and the situation. The cost, for example, of reaching a market with relatively small potential may be high. High operating costs of small specialty stores like those in Mexico and Thailand lead to high retail prices. Intense competition in certain world markets raises the cost or lowers the margins available to world business. Only experience in a given marketplace provides the basis for compensating for cost differences in different markets. With experience, a firm that prices on a cost basis operates in a realm of reasonably measurable factors.

Middleman and Transportation Costs

Channel length and marketing patterns vary widely, but in most countries, channels are longer and middleman margins higher than is customary in the United States. The diversity of channels used to reach markets and the lack of standardized middleman markups leave many producers unaware of the ultimate price of a product.

Besides channel diversity, the fully integrated marketer operating abroad faces various unanticipated costs because marketing and distribution channel infrastructures are underdeveloped in many countries. The marketer can also incur added expenses for warehousing and handling of small shipments and may have to bear increased financing costs when dealing with underfinanced middlemen.

[19]Klaus Wertenbrouch, Dilip Soman, and Amitava Chattopadhyay, "On the Perceived Value of Money: The Reference Dependence of Currency Numerosity Effects," *Journal of Consumer Research* 34 (2007), pp. 1–10; Simon Shuster, "Ruble's Collapse Spells Trouble for Vulnerable Putin," *Time*, January 5, 2015, p. 16; Ira Iosebashvili and Ian Talley, "Dollar Hits an 11-Year High," *The Wall Street Journal*, January 3–4, 2015, pp. A1, 2.

Because no convenient source of data on middleman costs is available, the international marketer must rely on experience and marketing research to ascertain middleman costs. The Campbell Soup Company found its middleman and physical distribution costs in the United Kingdom to be 30 percent higher than in the United States. Extra costs were incurred because soup was purchased in small quantities—small English grocers typically purchase 24-can cases of assorted soups (each case being hand-packed for shipment). In the United States, typical purchase units are 48-can cases of one soup purchased by the dozens, hundreds, or carloads. The purchase habits in Europe forced the company into an extra wholesale level in its channel to facilitate handling small orders.

Exporting also incurs increased transportation costs when moving goods from one country to another. If the goods go over water, insurance, packing, and handling are additional costs not generally added to locally produced goods. Such costs add yet another burden because import tariffs in many countries are based on the landed cost, which includes transportation, insurance, and shipping charges. These costs add to the inflation of the final price. The next section details how a price in the home market may more than double in the foreign market.

Sample Effects of Price Escalation

Exhibit 18.2 illustrates some of the effects the factors discussed previously may have on the end price of a consumer item. Because costs and tariffs vary so widely from country to country, a hypothetical but realistic example is used. It assumes that a constant net price is received by the manufacturer, that all domestic transportation costs are absorbed by the various middlemen and reflected in their margins, and that the foreign middlemen have the same margins as the domestic middlemen. In some instances, foreign middleman margins are lower, but it is equally probable that these margins could be greater. In fact, in many instances, middlemen use higher wholesale and retail margins for foreign goods than for similar domestic goods.

Notice that the retail prices in Exhibit 18.2 range widely, illustrating the difficulty of price control by manufacturers in overseas retail markets. No matter how much the manufacturer may wish to market a product in a foreign country for a price equivalent to US$10, there is little opportunity for such control. Even assuming the most optimistic conditions for Foreign Example 1, the producer would need to cut its net by more than one-third to absorb freight and tariff costs if the goods are to be priced the same in both foreign and domestic markets. Price escalation is everywhere: A man's dress shirt that sells for $40 in

Exhibit 18.2
Sample Causes and Effects of Price Escalation

	Domestic Example	Foreign Example 1: Assuming the Same Channels with Wholesaler Importing Directly	Foreign Example 2: Importer and Same Margins and Channels	Foreign Example 3: Same as 2 but with 10 Percent Cumulative Turnover Tax
Manufacturing net	$ 5.00	$ 5.00	$ 5.00	$5.00
Transport, CIF	n.a.	6.10	6.10	6.10
Tariff (20 percent CIF value)	n.a.	1.22	1.22	1.22
Importer pays	n.a.	n.a.	7.32	7.32
Importer margin when sold to	n.a.	n.a.	1.83	1.83
wholesaler (25 percent on cost)				+0.73
Wholesaler pays landed cost	5.00	7.32	9.15	9.88
Wholesaler margin	1.67	2.44	3.05	3.29
(33⅓ percent on cost)				+0.99
Retailer pays	6.67	9.76	12.20	14.16
Retail margin	3.34	4.88	6.10	7.08
(50 percent on cost)				+1.42
Retail price	$10.01	$14.64	$18.30	$22.66

Notes: All figures in U.S. dollars; CIF = cost, insurance, and freight; n.a. = not applicable. The exhibit assumes that all domestic transportation costs are absorbed by the middleman. Transportation, tariffs, and middleman margins vary from country to country, but for the purposes of comparison, only a few of the possible variations are shown.

the United States retails for $80 in Caracas. A $20 U.S. electric can opener is priced in Milan at $70; a $35 U.S.-made automatic toaster is priced at $80 in France.

Unless some of the costs that create price escalation can be reduced, the marketer is faced with a price that may confine sales to a limited segment of wealthy, price-insensitive customers. In many markets, buyers have less purchasing power than in the United States and can be easily priced out of the market. Furthermore, once price escalation is set in motion, it can spiral upward quickly. When the price to middlemen is high and turnover is low, they may insist on higher margins to defray their costs, which, of course, raises the price even higher. Unless price escalation can be reduced, marketers find that the only buyers left are the wealthier ones. If marketers are to compete successfully in the growth of markets around the world, cost containment must be among their highest priorities. If costs can be reduced anywhere along the chain, from manufacturer's cost to retailer markups, price escalation will be reduced. A discussion of some of the approaches to reducing price escalation follows.

Approaches to Reducing Price Escalation

Three methods used to reduce costs and lower price escalation are lowering the cost of goods, lowering tariffs, and lowering distribution costs.

Lowering Cost of Goods

If the manufacturer's price can be lowered, the effect is felt throughout the chain. One of the important reasons for manufacturing in a third country is an attempt to reduce manufacturing costs and thus price escalation. The impact can be profound if you consider that the hourly cost of skilled labor in a Mexican maquiladora is less than $3 an hour including benefits, compared with more than $10 in the United States.

In comparing the costs of manufacturing microwave ovens in the United States and in Korea, the General Electric Company found substantial differences. A typical microwave oven cost GE $218 to manufacture compared with $155 for Samsung, a Korean manufacturer. A breakdown of costs revealed that assembly labor cost GE $8 per oven and Samsung only 63 cents. Perhaps the most disturbing finding for GE was that Korean laborers delivered more for less cost: GE produced four units per person, whereas the Korean company produced nine.

Although Korea remains an important offshore manufacturing location, China has emerged as the global manufacturing powerhouse backed by an inexpensive labor force, rapidly improving production quality, new sources of capital, a more dynamic private sector, and a deliberately undervalued currency. China supplies a growing range of products to the global marketplace. Japan, the land of zero-defect quality control, is increasingly happy with the competence of Chinese workers. Star Manufacturing, a Japanese precision machine tool manufacturing company, moved 30 percent of its production to China because China's cheap labor and cheap resources reduced its production costs by 20 percent. Of course, circa 2012, Chinese labor costs were seeming less competitive than those in other countries such as Vietnam and even Mexico.[20]

Eliminating costly functional features or even lowering overall product quality is another method of minimizing price escalation. For U.S.-manufactured products, the quality and additional features required for the more developed home market may not be necessary in countries that have not attained the same level of development or consumer demand. In the price war between P&G and Kimberly-Clark in Brazil, the quality of the product was decreased to lower the price. Similarly, functional features on washing machines made for the United States, such as automatic bleach and soap dispensers, thermostats to provide four different levels of water temperature, controls to vary water volume, and bells to ring at appropriate times, may be unnecessary for many foreign markets. Eliminating them means lower manufacturing costs and thus a corresponding reduction in price escalation. Lowering manufacturing costs can often have a double benefit: The lower price to the buyer may also mean lower tariffs, because most tariffs are levied on an ad valorem basis.

Lowering Tariffs

When tariffs account for a large part of price escalation, as they often do, companies seek ways to lower the rate. Some products can be reclassified into a different, and lower,

---

[20]Carol Matlack, "The Gulf in Auto Wages," *Bloomberg BusinessWeek*, July 12, 2010, pp. 15, 16; "The End of Cheap Goods," *The Economist*, June 11, 2011, p. 71.

customs classification.[21] An American company selling data communications equipment in Australia faced a 25 percent tariff, which affected the price competitiveness of its products. It persuaded the Australian government to change the classification for the type of products the company sells from "computer equipment" (25 percent tariff) to "telecommunication equipment" (3 percent tariff). Like many products, this company's products could be legally classified under either category. One complaint against customs agents in Russia is the arbitrary way in which they often classify products. Russian customs, for instance, insists on classifying Johnson & Johnson's 2-in-1 Shower Gel as a cosmetic with a 20 percent tariff rather than as a soap substitute, which the company considers it, at a 15 percent tariff.

How a product is classified is often a judgment call. The difference between an item being classified as jewelry or art means paying no tariff for art or a 26 percent tariff for jewelry. For example, a U.S. customs inspector could not decide whether to classify a $2.7 million Fabergé egg as art or jewelry. The difference was $0 tariff versus $700,000. An experienced freight forwarder/customs broker saved the day by persuading the customs agent that the Fabergé egg was a piece of art. Because the classification of products varies among countries, a thorough investigation of tariff schedules and classification criteria can result in a lower tariff.

Besides having a product reclassified into a lower tariff category, it may be possible to modify a product to qualify for a lower tariff rate within a tariff classification. In the footwear industry, the difference between "foxing" and "foxlike" on athletic shoes makes a substantial difference in the tariff levied. To protect the domestic footwear industry from an onslaught of cheap sneakers from the Far East, the tariff schedules state that any canvas or vinyl shoe with a foxing band (a tape band attached at the sole and overlapping the shoe's upper by more than one-quarter inch) be assessed at a higher duty rate. As a result, manufacturers design shoes so that the sole does not overlap the upper by more than one-quarter inch. If the overlap exceeds one-quarter inch, the shoe is classified as having a foxing band; less than one-quarter inch, a foxlike band. A shoe with a foxing band is taxed at 48 percent and one with a foxlike band (one-quarter inch or less overlap) is taxed a mere 6 percent.

There are often differential rates between fully assembled, ready-to-use products and those requiring some assembly, further processing, the addition of locally manufactured component parts, or other processing that adds value to the product and can be performed within the foreign country. For example, a ready-to-operate piece of machinery with a 20 percent tariff may be subject to only a 12 percent tariff when imported unassembled. An even lower tariff may apply when the product is assembled in the country and some local content is added.

Hugh Jackman portraying Wolverine, an X-Men fictional character from Marvel Enterprises. A tariff classification issue arose when the company declared the imported toy characters as nonhuman toys and U.S. Customs said that they were human figure dolls—tariffs on dolls at that time were 12 percent versus 6.8 percent for toys. U.S. Customs alleged that the X-Men figures were human figures and thus should be classified as dolls, not figures featuring animals or creatures, which would mean that they could be classified as toys. Product classifications are critical when tariffs are determined.

Repackaging also may help to lower tariffs. Tequila entering the United States in containers of one gallon or less carries a duty of $2.27 per proof gallon; larger containers are assessed at only $1.25. If the cost of rebottling is less than $1.02 per proof gallon, and it probably would be, considerable savings could result. As will be discussed shortly, one of the more important activities in foreign trade zones is the assembly of imported goods, using local and frequently lower cost labor.

Lowering Distribution Costs

Shorter channels can help keep prices under control. Designing a channel that has fewer middlemen may lower distribution costs by reducing or eliminating middleman markups. Besides eliminating markups, fewer middlemen may mean lower overall taxes. Some countries levy

---

[21]Matthew Dolan, "To Outfox the Chicken Tax, Ford Strips Its Own Vans," *The Wall Street Journal*, September 22, 2009, pp. A1, A14.

a value-added tax on goods as they pass through channels. Goods are taxed each time they change hands. The tax may be cumulative or noncumulative. A cumulative value-added tax is based on total selling price and is assessed every time the goods change hands. Obviously, in countries where value-added tax is cumulative, tax alone provides a special incentive for developing short distribution channels. Where that is achieved, tax is paid only on the difference between the middleman's cost and the selling price. While many manufacturers had to cut prices in wake of Japan's deflation, Louis Vuitton, a maker of branded boutique goods, was able to increase prices instead. A solid brand name and direct distribution have permitted Vuitton's price strategy. Vuitton's leather monogrammed bags have become a Japanese buyer's "daily necessity," and Vuitton distributes directly and sets its own prices.

Using Foreign Trade Zones

Some countries have established foreign or free trade zones (FTZs) or free ports to facilitate international trade. More than 300 of these facilities operate throughout the world, storing or processing imported goods. As free trade policies in Africa, Latin America, eastern Europe, and other developing regions expand, an equally rapid expansion has taken place in the creation and use of foreign trade zones. In a free port or FTZ, payment of import duties is postponed until the product leaves the FTZ area and enters the country. An FTZ is, in essence, a tax-free enclave and not considered part of the country as far as import regulations are concerned. When an item leaves an FTZ and is imported officially into the host country of the FTZ, all duties and regulations are imposed.

Utilizing FTZs can to some extent control price escalation resulting from the layers of taxes, duties, surcharges, freight charges, and so forth. Foreign trade zones permit many of these added charges to be avoided, reduced, or deferred so that the final price is more competitive. One of the more important benefits of the FTZ in controlling prices is the exemption from duties on labor and overhead costs incurred in the FTZ in assessing the value of goods.

By shipping unassembled goods to an FTZ in an importing country, a marketer can lower costs in a variety of ways:

- Tariffs may be lower because duties are typically assessed at a lower rate for unassembled versus assembled goods.
- If labor costs are lower in the importing country, substantial savings may be realized in the final product cost.
- Ocean transportation rates are affected by weight and volume; thus unassembled goods may qualify for lower freight rates.
- If local content, such as packaging or component parts, can be used in the final assembly, tariffs may be further reduced.

All in all, a foreign or free trade zone is an important method for controlling price escalation. Incidentally, all the advantages offered by an FTZ for an exporter are also advantages for an importer. U.S. importers use more than 100 FTZs in the United States to help lower their costs of imported goods. See Exhibit 18.3 for illustrations of how FTZs are used.

Dumping

A logical outgrowth of a market policy in international business is goods priced competitively at widely differing prices in various markets. Marginal (variable) cost pricing, as discussed previously, is a way prices can be reduced to stay within a competitive price range. The market and economic logic of such pricing policies can hardly be disputed, but the practices often are classified as dumping and are subject to severe penalties and fines. Various economists define dumping differently. One approach classifies international shipments as dumped if the products are sold below their cost of production. Another approach characterizes dumping as selling goods in a foreign market below the price of the same goods in the home market.

World Trade Organization (WTO) rules allow for the imposition of a dumping duty when goods are sold at a price lower than the normal export price or less than the cost in the country of origin, increased by a reasonable amount for the cost of sales and profits, when this price is likely to be prejudicial to the economic activity of the importing country. A countervailing duty or *minimum access volume (MAV)*, which restricts the amount a country will import, may be imposed on foreign goods benefiting from subsidies, whether in production, export, or transportation.

Exhibit 18.3
How Are Foreign Trade Zones Used?

There are more than 100 foreign trade zones (FTZs) in the United States, and FTZs exist in many other countries as well. Companies use them to postpone the payment of tariffs on products while they are in the FTZ. Here are some examples of how FTZs in the United States are used.

- A Japanese firm assembles motorcycles, jet skis, and three-wheel all-terrain vehicles for import as well as for export to Canada, Latin America, and Europe.

- A U.S. manufacturer of window shades and miniblinds imports and stores fabric from Holland in an FTZ, thereby postponing a 17 percent tariff until the fabric leaves the FTZ.

- A manufacturer of hair dryers stores its product in an FTZ, which it uses as its main distribution center for products manufactured in Asia.

- A European-based medical supply company manufactures kidney dialysis machines and sterile tubing using raw materials from Germany and U.S. labor. It then exports 30 percent of its products to Scandinavian countries.

- A Canadian company assembles electronic teaching machines using cabinets from Italy; electronics from Taiwan, Korea, and Japan; and labor from the United States, for export to Colombia and Peru.

In all these examples, tariffs are postponed until the products leave the FTZ and enter the United States. Furthermore, in most situations the tariff is at the lower rate for component parts and raw materials versus the higher rate that would be charged if products were imported directly as finished goods. If the finished products are not imported into the United States from the FTZ but are shipped to another country, no U.S. tariffs apply.

Sources: Lewis E. Leibowitz, "An Overview of Foreign Trade Zones," *Europe*, Winter–Spring 1987, p. 12; "Cheap Imports," *International Business*, March 1993, pp. 98–100; "Free-Trade Zones: Global Overview and Future Prospects," http://www.stat-usa.gov, 2015.

For countervailing duties to be invoked, it must be shown that prices are lower in the importing country than in the exporting country and that producers in the importing country are being directly harmed by the dumping. A report by the U.S. Department of Agriculture indicated that levels of dumping by the United States hover around 40 percent for wheat and between 25 and 30 percent for corn, and levels for soybeans have risen steadily over the past four years to nearly 30 percent. These percentages, for example, mean that wheat is selling up to 40 percent below the cost of production. For cotton, the level of dumping for one year rose to a remarkable 57 percent, and for rice, it then stabilized at around 20 percent. The study indicated that these commodities are being dumped onto international markets by the United States in violation of WTO rules. The report found that after many years of accepting agricultural dumping, a few countries have begun to respond by investigating whether some U.S. agricultural exports are dumped. Brazil is considering a case against U.S. cotton before the WTO. Canada briefly imposed both countervailing and antidumping duties on U.S. corn imports; the United States did the same for Chinese apple juice concentrate.

Dumping is rarely an issue when world markets are strong. In the 1980s and 1990s, dumping became a major issue for a large number of industries when excess production capacity relative to home-country demand caused many companies to price their goods on a marginal-cost basis. In a classic case of dumping, prices are maintained in the home-country market and reduced in foreign markets.

Today, tighter government enforcement of dumping legislation is causing international marketers to seek new routes around such legislation. Assembly in the importing country is a way companies attempt to lower prices and avoid dumping charges. However, these *screwdriver plants,* as they are often called, are subject to dumping charges if the price differentials reflect more than the cost savings that result from assembly in the importing country. Another subterfuge is to alter the product so that the technical description will fit a lower duty category. To circumvent a 16.9 percent countervailing duty imposed on Chinese gas-filled, nonrefillable pocket flint lighters, the manufacturer attached a useless valve to the lighters so that they fell under the "nondisposable" category, thus avoiding the duty. Countries see through many such subterfuges and impose taxes. For example, the European Union imposed a $27 to $58 dumping duty per unit on a Japanese firm that assembled and sold office machines in the European Union. The firm was charged with valuing imported parts for assembly below cost.

The U.S. market is currently more sensitive to dumping than in the recent past. In fact, the Uruguay Round of the GATT included a section on antidumping that grew out of U.S.

insistence on stricter controls on dumping of foreign goods in the United States at prices below those charged at home. Changes in U.S. law have enhanced the authority of the Commerce Department to prevent circumvention of antidumping duties and countervailing duties that have been imposed on a country for dumping. The United States and European Union have been the most ardent users of antidumping duties. A question asked by many though: Are dumping charges just a cover for protectionism? Previously, when an order was issued to apply antidumping and countervailing duties on products, companies charged with the violation would get around the order by slightly altering the product or by doing minor assembly in the United States or a third country. This effort created the illusion of a different product not subject to the antidumping order. The new authority of the Department of Commerce closes many such loopholes.

Leasing in International Markets

An important selling technique to alleviate high prices and capital shortages for capital equipment or high-priced durable goods is the leasing system. The concept of equipment leasing has become increasingly important as a means of selling capital equipment in overseas markets. In fact, an estimated $50 billion worth (original cost) of U.S.-made and foreign-made equipment is on lease in western Europe.

The system of leasing used by industrial exporters is similar to the typical lease contracts used in the United States. Terms of the leases usually run one to five years, with payments made monthly or annually; included in the rental fee are servicing, repairs, and spare parts. Just as contracts for domestic and overseas leasing arrangements are similar, so are the basic motivations and the shortcomings. For example:

- Leasing opens the door to a large segment of nominally financed foreign firms that can be sold on a lease option but might be unable to buy for cash.
- Leasing can ease the problems of selling new, experimental equipment, because less risk is involved for the users.
- Leasing helps guarantee better maintenance and service on overseas equipment.
- Equipment leased and in use helps sell other companies in that country.
- Lease revenue tends to be more stable over a period of time than direct sales would be.

The disadvantages or shortcomings take on an international flavor. Besides the inherent disadvantages of leasing, some problems are compounded by international relationships. In a country beset with inflation, lease contracts that include maintenance and supply parts (as most do) can lead to heavy losses toward the end of the contract period. Furthermore, countries where leasing is most attractive are those where spiraling inflation is most likely to occur. The added problems of currency devaluation, expropriation, or other political risks are operative longer than if the sale of the same equipment were made outright. In light of these perils, leasing incurs greater risk than does outright sale; however, there is a definite trend toward increased use of this method of selling internationally, so the benefits must exceed the risk.

Some companies are taking the next step after leasing equipment—charging for the related service rendered. For example, Solar Turbines (the division of Caterpillar we talked about in Chapter 14) will, of course, be happy to sell you a gas-turbine-powered gas compressor for your pipeline. It will be happy to lease you one as well. In fact, Solar Turbines may even sell you the gas compressing services by the cubic meter of gas that combines its equipment and a management contract. This is just like Xerox charging you for copies made rather than selling you the machine.

Countertrade as a Pricing Tool

LO4

Countertrading and its place in international marketing practices

Countertrade is a pricing tool that every international marketer must be ready to employ, and the willingness to accept a countertrade will often give the company a competitive advantage. The challenges of countertrade must be viewed from the same perspective as all other variations in international trade. Marketers must be aware of which markets will likely require countertrades, just as they must be aware of social customs and legal requirements. Assessing this factor along with all other market factors will enhance a marketer's competitive position.

One of the earliest barter arrangements occurred between the Soviet Union and PepsiCo before the ruble was convertible and before most companies were trading with the USSR. PepsiCo wanted to beat Coca-Cola into the Russian market. The only way possible was for PepsiCo to be willing to accept vodka (sold under the brand name Stolichnaya) from Russia and bottled wines (sold under the brand name of Premiat) from Romania to finance Pepsi bottling plants in those countries. From all indications, this arrangement was very profitable for Russia, Romania, and PepsiCo. Pepsi continues to use countertrade to expand its bottling plants. In a recent agreement between PepsiCo and Ukraine, Pepsi agreed to market $1 billion worth of Ukrainian-made commercial ships over an eight-year period. Some of the proceeds from the ship sales will be reinvested in the shipbuilding venture, and some will be used to buy soft-drink equipment and build five Pepsi bottling plants in the Ukraine. PepsiCo dominates the cola market in Russia and all the former Soviet republics in part because of its exclusive countertrade agreement with Russia, which locked Coca-Cola out of the Russian cola market for more than 12 years. After the Soviet Union disintegrated, the Russian economy crashed, and most of the Russian payment system broke down into barter operations. Truckloads of aspirin were swapped by one company, then traded for poultry, which in turn was bartered for lumber, in turn to be exchanged for X-ray equipment from Kazakhstan—all to settle debts. Many of these transactions involved regional electricity companies that were owed money by virtually everyone.

Although cash may be the preferred method of payment, countertrades have been an important part of trade with eastern Europe, the newly independent states, China,[22] and, to a varying degree, some Latin American and African nations. Barter, or countertrades, still constitute between 20 and 40 percent of all transactions in the economies of the former Soviet bloc. Corporate debts to suppliers, payments and services, even taxes—all have a noncash component or are entirely bartered. Many of these countries constantly face a shortage of hard currencies with which to trade and thus resort to countertrades when possible. A recent purchase of 48 F-16 Falcons from Lockheed Martin was pegged at $3.5 billion. The financial package included soft loans and a massive offset program—purchases from Polish manufacturers that more than erased the costs of the deal in foreign exchange. Lockheed has also offered F-16s to Thailand in exchange for frozen chickens.[23] With an economy once short of hard currency, Russia has offered a wide range of products in barter for commodities it needed. For example, Russian expertise in space technology was offered for Malaysian palm oil and rubber, and military equipment was exchanged for crude palm oil or rice from Indonesia.[24] Today, an international company must include in its market-pricing toolkit some understanding of countertrading.

Problems of Countertrading

The crucial problem confronting a seller in a countertrade negotiation is determining the value of and potential demand for the goods offered as payment. Frequently there is inadequate time to conduct a market analysis; in fact, it is not unusual to have sales negotiations almost completed before countertrade is introduced as a requirement in the transaction.

Although such problems are difficult to deal with, they can be minimized with proper preparation. In most cases where losses have occurred in countertrades, the seller has been unprepared to negotiate in anything other than cash. Some preliminary research should be done in anticipation of being confronted with a countertrade proposal. Countries with a history of countertrading are identified easily, and the products most likely to be offered in a countertrade often can be ascertained. For a company trading with developing countries, these facts and some background on handling countertrades should be a part of every pricing toolkit. Once goods are acquired, they can be passed along to institutions that assist companies in selling bartered goods.

Barter houses specialize in trading goods acquired through barter arrangements and are the primary outside source of aid for companies beset by the uncertainty of a countertrade. Although barter houses, most of which are found in Europe, can find a market for bartered

[22]"Trade Financing and Insurance: Countertrade," *Economist Intelligence Unit–Country Finance*, January 22, 2008, p. 101.

[23]John Hudson, "Lockheed Martin Tried to Trade F-16s for Frozen Chickens," http://www.theatlanticwire.com, March 4, 2011.

[24]Zakki P. Hakim, "Ministry Eyes Rice-for-Planes Trade Deal," *Jakarta Post*, September 20, 2005, p. 13.

goods, this effort requires time, which puts a financial strain on a company because capital is tied up longer than in normal transactions.

In the United States, there are companies that assist with bartered goods and their financing. Citibank has created a countertrade department to allow the bank to act as a consultant as well as to provide financing for countertrades. It is estimated that there are now about 500 barter exchange houses in the United States, many of which are accessible on the Internet. Some companies with a high volume of barter have their own in-house trading groups to manage countertrades. The 3M Company (Minnesota Mining and Manufacturing), for example, has a wholly owned division, 3M Global Trading (http://www.3m.com /globaltrading), which offers its services to smaller companies.

The Internet and Countertrading

The Internet may become the most important venue for countertrade activities. Finding markets for bartered merchandise and determining market price are two of the major problems with countertrades. Several barter houses have Internet auction sites, and a number of Internet exchanges are expanding to include global barter.

Some speculate that the Internet may become the vehicle for an immense online electronic barter economy, to complement and expand the offline barter exchanges that take place now. In short, some type of electronic trade dollar would replace national currencies in international trade transactions. This e-dollar would make international business considerably easier for many countries, because it would lessen the need to acquire sufficient U.S. or other hard currency to complete a sale or purchase.

TradeBanc, a market-making service, has introduced a computerized technology that will enable members of trade exchanges to trade directly, online, with members of other trade exchanges anywhere in the world, as long as their barter company is a TradeBanc affiliate (http:// www.tradebanc.com). The medium of exchange could be the Universal Currency proposed by the International Reciprocal Trade Association (IRTA; http://www.irta.com), an association of trade exchanges with members including Russia, Iceland, Germany, Chile, Turkey, Australia, and the United States. The IRTA has proposed to establish and operate a Universal Currency

---

CROSSING BORDERS 18.3   Psychological Pricing in China, the Lucky 8

Retailers in the United States often use prices ending in 99, and this tactic has been shown to be effective in a number of consumer studies. One explanation has to do with consumers' tendency to ignore the digits after the first rather than bothering to round to the closest number. Thus, $2.99 seems more like $2 than $3. Another explanation suggests the prices ending in 99 signal a sale price, and are therefore more attractive to consumers interested in sale prices.

A psychological pricing tactic in Chinese cultures is to include eights in the prices. Eight is attractive to Chinese consumers because it is the luckiest number among all, and the more eights the better. The number eight (八, ba) said in Chinese Mandarin sounds like the word for "prosperity" (发, fa), and it works similarly in Cantonese as well.

Thus, the 88th floor is a lucky and more valuable one in high-rise buildings in the region — in Hong Kong buildings that have far fewer floors can still get premium prices of the penthouse on the 88th floor by simply skipping "unlucky" floors and omitting intermediate floors, particularly the unlucky numbers such as four. And automobile license plates and phone numbers with consecutive

8s can be worth hundreds of thousands of dollars. Finally, the opening ceremonies for the Olympic Games in Beijing began at 8 seconds, 8 minutes after 8pm (local time) on 8/8/08, thus guaranteeing the success of the Games.

Research has also shown a systematic bias in both advertised prices and stock prices for the number eight in Chinese markets. For example, among 499 prices for a variety of products listed in newspapers in Shanghai, Hong Kong, and Taiwan, 39.9 percent ended in 8, and the next most common ending number was 14.7 percent for 5. The unlucky number 4 (related to death) appeared at the end of only 1.4 percent of the prices. A similar study was conducted on Shanghai and Shenzen stock exchange data, and found a strong preference for share prices ending in 8, and an aversion to prices ending in the number 4.

Sources: See C. Simmons and Robert M. Schindler, "Cultural Superstitions and the Price Endings Used in Chinese Advertising," *Journal of International Marketing*, 11(2), 2003, pp. 101–111; N. Mark Lam and John L. Graham, *China Now: Doing Business in the World's Most Dynamic Market* (New York: McGraw-Hill, 2007); Philip Brown and Jason Mitchell, "Culture and Stock Price Clustering: Evidence for the Peoples' Republic of China," *Pacific-Basin Finance Journal*, 16(1/2), 2008, pp. 95–120; Jason Chow, "Will Lafite's Red '8' Be Lucky in China?" *The Wall Street Journal*, November 1, 2010.

Clearinghouse, which would enable trade exchange members to easily trade with one another using this special currency. When the system is in full swing, all goods and services from all the participating affiliates would be housed in a single database. The transactions would be cleared by the local exchanges, and settlement would be made using IRTA's Universal Currency, which could be used to purchase anything from airline tickets to potatoes.

Price Quotations

LO5

The mechanics of price quotations

In quoting the price of goods for international sale, a contract may include specific elements affecting the price, such as credit, sales terms, and transportation. Parties to the transaction must be certain that the quotation settled on appropriately locates responsibility for the goods during transportation and spells out who pays transportation charges and from what point. Price quotations must also specify the currency to be used, credit terms, and the type of documentation required. Finally, the price quotation and contract should define quantity and quality. A quantity definition might be necessary because different countries use different units of measurement. In specifying a ton, for example, the contract should identify it as a metric or an English ton and as a long or short ton. Quality specifications can also be misunderstood if not completely spelled out. Furthermore, there should be complete agreement on quality standards to be used in evaluating the product. For example, "customary merchantable quality" may be clearly understood among U.S. customers but have a completely different interpretation in another country. The international trader must review all terms of the contract; failure to do so may have the effect of modifying prices even though such a change was not intended.

Administered Pricing

Administered pricing is an attempt to establish prices for an entire market. Such prices may be arranged through the cooperation of competitors; through national, state, or local governments; or by international agreement. The legality of administered pricing arrangements of various kinds differs from country to country and from time to time. A country may condone price fixing for foreign markets but condemn it for the domestic market, for instance.

In general, the end goal of all administered pricing activities is to reduce the impact of price competition or eliminate it. Price fixing by business is not viewed as an acceptable practice (at least in the domestic market),[25] but when governments enter the field of price administration, they presume to do it for the general welfare to lessen the effects of "destructive" competition. The Chinese government not only sets price caps for products and services,[26] but it also fines foreign firms for just talking about planned price hikes.[27]

The point at which competition becomes destructive depends largely on the country in question. To the Japanese, excessive competition is any competition in the home market that disturbs the existing balance of trade or gives rise to market disruptions. Few countries apply more rigorous standards in judging competition as excessive than Japan, but no country favors or permits totally free competition. Economists, the traditional champions of pure competition, acknowledge that perfect competition is unlikely and agree that some form of workable competition must be developed.

The pervasiveness of price-fixing attempts[28] in business is reflected by the diversity of the language of administered prices; pricing arrangements are known as agreements, arrangements, combines, conspiracies, cartels, communities of profit, profit pools, licensing, trade associations, price leadership, customary pricing, or informal interfirm agreements.[29] The arrangements themselves vary from the completely informal, with no

---

[25]Jerry Hirsch and Ken Bensinger, "Car-Parts Firms Admit Price Fixing," *Los Angeles Times,* January 31, 2012, pp. B1, B6.

[26]Laurie Brukitt, "China May Cap Prices of Movie Tickets," *The Wall Street Journal,* January 9, 2012.

[27]Paul Sonne and Laurie Burkitt, "China Fines Unilever for Price Comments," *The Wall Street Journal,* May 7, 2011.

[28]Recent cases of illegal price fixing and monopoly pricing include Bridgestone tires in the United States and Mercedes in China. See, respectively, Jaclyn Trop, "Bridgestone Admits Guilt in U.S. Fixing Case," *The New York Times,* February 14, 2014, pp. B4; Chris Buckley, "China Says Mercedes Violated Pricing Law," *The New York Times,* August 19, 2014, p. B3.

[29]Dana Nunn and Miklos Sarvary, "Pricing Practices and Firms' Market Power in International Cellular Markets: An Empirical Study," *International Journal of Research in Marketing* 21, no. 4 (2004), pp. 377–95.

spoken or acknowledged agreement, to highly formalized and structured arrangements. Any type of price-fixing arrangement can be adapted to international business, but of all the forms mentioned, cartels are the most directly associated with international marketing.

Cartels   A cartel exists when various companies producing similar products or services work together to control markets for the types of goods and services they produce.[30] The cartel association may use formal agreements to set prices, establish levels of production and sales for the participating companies, allocate market territories, and even redistribute profits. In some instances, the cartel organization itself takes over the entire selling function, sells the goods of all the producers, and distributes the profits.

The economic role of cartels is highly debatable, but their proponents argue that they eliminate cutthroat competition and rationalize business, permitting greater technical progress and lower prices to consumers. However, most experts doubt that the consumer benefits very often from cartels.

The Organization of Petroleum Exporting Countries (OPEC) is probably the best known international cartel. Its power in controlling the price of oil has resulted from the percentage of oil production it controls.[31] In the early 1970s, when OPEC members provided the industrial world with 67 percent of its oil, OPEC was able to quadruple the price of oil. See Exhibit 18.4. You can also see the extreme volatility of oil prices over the years. Also, notice the inflation in the late 1970s and 1980s and the deflation of the most recent years, both evinced in the comparison of the nominal and real prices of oil. The sudden rise in price from $3 a barrel to

Oil prices quadrupled in the mid-1970s because of OPEC's control of supplies. The $100+ per barrel oil you see in this picture was caused by burgeoning demand in China and around the world in 2008. Pertamina is the Indonesian national oil company. Indonesia terminated its membership in OPEC in 2009. Circa 2015, prices had dropped to below $50 per barrel because of slackening demand worldwide and new production in the United States.

---

[30]Paul Sonne and Laurence Norman, "P&G, Unilever Fined for Detergent Cartel," *The Wall Street Journal,* April 13, 2011; Steffen Brenner, "Self-Disclosure in International Cartels," *Journal of International Business Studies* 42, no. 2 (2011), pp. 221–34.

[31]For an extensive discussion of OPEC and the associated history of Middle East oil production, see Andrew Scott Cooper, *The Oil Kings* (New York: Simon & Schuster, 2011).

Exhibit 18.4
The Volatility of Oil Prices
(Average spot, US$/barrel)

Source; World Bank, 2015.

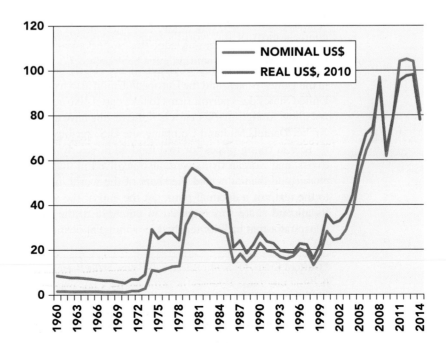

This signage near Guilin, China, at first glance suggests to foreigners the gasoline price posting typical in most countries. But, no: This listing refers to available octanes. In China, the government controls pricing at its state-owned gas stations, so there is no reason to look for bargains or to smile at the prices! Circa 2012, gas prices were fixed at about $6/gallon, compared with $10 in Turkey, $8 in the United Kingdom, $1 in Egypt, and $.06 in oil-rich, car-poor Venezuela.

$11 or more a barrel was a primary factor in throwing the world into a major recession. In 2000, OPEC members lowered production, and the oil price rose from $10 to more than $30, creating a dramatic increase in U.S. gasoline prices. Non-OPEC oil-exporting countries benefit from the price increases, while net importers of foreign oil face economic repercussions.

One important aspect of cartels is their inability to maintain control for indefinite periods. Greed by cartel members and other problems generally weaken the control of the cartel. OPEC members tend to maintain a solid front until one decides to increase supply, and then others rapidly follow suit. In the short run, however, OPEC can affect global prices. Indeed, at this writing, the price for crude oil has tanked to less than $50 per barrel.[32] Such a drop helps consumers, at least in the short run. Producers are punished. For oil- and gas-dependent Russia, this caused a 20 percent decline in the ruble vis-à-vis the U.S. dollar in 2014. Such dramatically cheaper oil also makes renewable energy programs let practical.[33] Finally, with both Europe and Japan fighting a deflation, falling oil prices may exacerbate the problem. And the prospect of Iraq and Iran bumping their stabled production, and the volatility you see in Exhibit 18.4, will continue.

A lesser-known cartel, but one that has a direct impact on international trade, is the cartel that exists among the world's shipping companies. Every two weeks about 20 shipping-line managers gather for their usual meeting to set rates on tens of billions of dollars of cargo. They do not refer to themselves as a cartel but rather operate under such innocuous names as "The Trans-Atlantic Conference Agreement" (http://www.tacaconf.com). Regardless of the name, they set the rates on about 70 percent of the cargo shipped between the United States and northern Europe. Shipping between the United States and Latin American ports and between the United States and Asian ports also is affected by shipping cartels. Not all shipping lines are members of cartels, but a large number are; thus they have a definite impact on shipping. Although legal, shipping cartels are coming under scrutiny by the U.S. Congress, and new regulations may soon be passed.

Another cartel is the diamond cartel controlled by De Beers. For more than a century, De Beers has smoothly manipulated the diamond market by keeping a tight control over world supply.[34] The company mines about half the world's diamonds and takes in another 25 percent through contracts with other mining companies. In an attempt to control the other 25 percent, De Beers runs an "outside buying office" where it spends millions buying up diamonds to protect prices. The company controls most of the world's trade in rough gems and uses its market power to keep prices high.

The legality of cartels at present is not clearly defined. Domestic cartelization is illegal in the United States, and the European Union also has provisions for controlling cartels. The United States does permit firms to take cartel-like actions in foreign markets, though it does not allow foreign-market cartels if the results have an adverse impact on the U.S. economy. Archer Daniels Midland Company, the U.S. agribusiness giant, was fined $205 million for its role in fixing prices for two food additives, lysine and citric acid. German, Japanese, Swiss, and Korean firms were also involved in that cartel. The group agreed on prices to charge and then allocated the share of the world market each company would get—down to the tenth of a decimal point. At the end of the year, any company that sold more than its allotted share was required to purchase in the following year the excess from a co-conspirator that had not reached its volume allocation target.

---

[32]Clifford Kraus, "U.S. Oil Prices Fall Below $80 a Barrel," *The New York Times*, November 4, 2014, p. B3.

[33]Bill Saporito, "Green Squeeze, Cheap Gas Slows Hybrids and EVs—For Now," *Time*, November 10, 2014, p. 20.

[34]Eric Onstad, "De Beers May Spurn Low-Margin Russian Supply," *Reuters News*, July 20, 2007.

The De Beers company is one of the world's largest cartels, and for all practical purposes, it controls most of the world's diamonds and thus is able to maintain artificially high prices for diamonds. One of the ways in which it maintains control is illustrated by a recent agreement with Russia's diamond monopoly, in which De Beers will buy at least $550 million in rough gem diamonds from Russia, or about half of the country's annual output. By controlling supply from Russia, the second largest producer of diamonds, the South African cartel can keep prices high.

Although EU member countries have had a long history of tolerating price fixing, the European Union is beginning to crack down on cartels in the shipping, automobile, and cement industries, among others. The unified market and single currency have prompted this move. As countries open to free trade, powerful cartels that artificially raise prices and limit consumer choice are coming under closer scrutiny. However, the EU trustbusters are fighting tradition—since the trade guilds of the Middle Ages, cozy cooperation has been the norm. In each European country, companies banded together to control prices within the country and to keep competition out.

Government-Influenced Pricing

Companies doing business in foreign countries encounter a number of different types of government price setting. To control prices, governments may establish margins, set prices and floors or ceilings, restrict price changes, compete in the market, grant subsidies, and act as a purchasing monopsony or selling monopoly.[35] The government may also influence prices by permitting, or even encouraging, businesses to collude in setting manipulative prices. As an aside, of course, some companies need no help in price fixing—which often is illegal.[36]

The Japanese government traditionally has encouraged a variety of government-influenced price-setting schemes, However, in a spirit of deregulation that is gradually moving through Japan, Japan's Ministry of Health and Welfare will soon abolish regulation of business hours and price setting for such businesses as barbershops, beauty parlors, and laundries. Under the current practice, 17 sanitation-related businesses can establish such price-setting schemes, which are exempt from the Japanese Anti-Trust Law.

Governments of producing and consuming countries seem to play an ever-increasing role in the establishment of international prices for certain basic commodities. There is, for example, an international coffee agreement, an international cocoa agreement, and an international sugar agreement. And the world price of wheat has long been at least partially determined by negotiations between national governments.

---

[35]"Apple, EU Reach iTunes Pricing Deal," *The Wall Street Journal*, January 9, 2008, online.

[36]John R. Wilke, "Two U.K. Airlines Settle Price-Fixing Claims," *The Wall Street Journal*, February 15, 2008, p. A4.

Despite the pressures of business, government, and international price agreements, most marketers still have wide latitude in their pricing decisions for most products and markets.

Getting Paid: Foreign Commercial Payments

The sale of goods in other countries is further complicated by additional risks encountered when dealing with foreign customers. Risks from inadequate credit reports on customers, problems of currency exchange controls, distance, and different legal systems, as well as the cost and difficulty of collecting delinquent accounts, require a different emphasis on payment systems. In U.S. domestic trade, the typical payment procedure for established customers is an *open account*—that is, the goods are delivered, and the customer is billed on an end-of-the-month basis. However, the most frequently used term of payment in foreign commercial transactions for both export and import sales is a letter of credit, followed closely in importance by commercial dollar drafts or bills of exchange drawn by the seller on the buyer. Internationally, open accounts are reserved for well-established customers, and cash in advance is required of only the poorest credit risks or when the character of the merchandise is such that not fulfilling the terms of the contract may result in a heavy loss. Because of the time required for shipment of goods from one country to another, advance payment of cash is an unusually costly burden for a potential customer and places the seller at a definite competitive disadvantage.

LO6

The mechanics of getting paid

Terms of sales are typically arranged between the buyer and seller at the time of the sale. The type of merchandise, amount of money involved, business custom, credit rating of the buyer, country of the buyer, and whether the buyer is a new or old customer must be considered in establishing the terms of sale. The five basic payment arrangements—letters of credit, bills of exchange, cash in advance, open accounts, and forfaiting—are discussed in this section.

Letters of Credit

Export letters of credit opened in favor of the seller by the buyer handle most American exports. Letters of credit shift the buyer's credit risk to the bank issuing the letter of credit. When a letter of credit is employed, the seller ordinarily can draw a draft against the bank issuing the credit and receive dollars by presenting proper shipping documents. Except for cash in advance, letters of credit afford the greatest degree of protection for the seller.

The procedure for a letter of credit begins with completion of the contract. (See Exhibit 18.5 for the steps in a letter-of-credit transaction.) A *letter of credit* means that once the seller has accepted the credit, the buyer cannot alter it in any way without permission of the seller. Added protection is gained if the buyer is required to confirm the letter of credit through a U.S. bank. This irrevocable, confirmed letter of credit means that a U.S. bank accepts responsibility to pay regardless of the financial situation of the buyer or foreign bank. From the seller's viewpoint, this step eliminates the foreign political risk and replaces the commercial risk of the buyer's bank with that of the confirming bank. The confirming bank ensures payment against a confirmed letter of credit. As soon as the documents are presented to the bank, the seller receives payment.

"That's as worthless as a three-dollar bill"—so the old saying goes. Cuba actually has two currencies, the Cuban peso and the Cuban convertible peso (CUC). The latter is what you see here, and you can exchange it for euros or Canadian dollars, but not U.S. dollars. The convertible Cuban peso's current value is about U.S.$1.08. The Cuban peso can be used only for domestic transactions and is worth about one-sixth of its convertible brother.

Exhibit 18.5
A Letter-of-Credit Transaction

Here is what typically happens when payment is made by an irrevocable letter of credit confirmed by a U.S. bank. Follow the steps in the illustration below.

1. Exporter and customer agree on terms of sale.
2. Buyer requests its foreign bank to open a letter of credit.
3. The buyer's bank prepares a letter of credit (LC), including all instructions, and sends the letter of credit to a U.S. bank.
4. The U.S. bank prepares a letter of confirmation and letter of credit and sends to seller.
5. Seller reviews LC. If acceptable, arranges with freight forwarder to deliver goods to designated port of entry.
6. The goods are loaded and shipped.

7. At the same time, the forwarder completes the necessary documents and sends documents to the seller.
8. Seller presents documents, indicating full compliance, to the U.S. bank.
9. The U.S. bank reviews the documents. If they are in order, issues seller a check for amount of sale.
10. The documents are airmailed to the buyer's bank for review.
11. If documents are in compliance, the bank sends documents to buyer.
12. To claim goods, buyer presents documents to customs broker.
13. Goods are released to buyer.

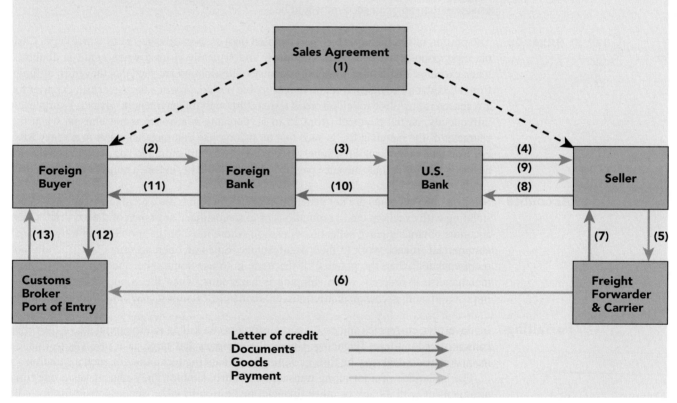

Source: Based on "A Basic Guide to Exporting," U.S. Department of Commerce, International Trade Administration, Washington, DC.

The international department of a major U.S. bank cautions that a letter of credit is not a guarantee of payment to the seller. Rather, payment is tendered only if the seller complies exactly with the terms of the letter of credit. Because all letters of credit must be exact in their terms and considerations, it is important for the exporter to check the terms of the letter carefully to be certain that all necessary documents have been acquired and properly completed; otherwise, leverage can flow to the buyer, which now has possession of the goods.

The process of getting a letter of credit can take days, if not weeks. Fortunately, this process is being shortened considerably as financial institutions provide letters of credit on the Internet. As one example, AVG Letter of Credit Management LLC uses eTrade Finance Platform (ETFP), an e-commerce trade transaction system that enables exporters, importers, freight forwarders, carriers, and trade banks to initiate and complete trade transactions over the Internet. The company advertises that the efficiencies afforded by the Internet make it possible to lower the cost of an export letter of credit from $500-plus to $25.[37]

Bills of Exchange

Another important form of international commercial payment is bills of exchange drawn by sellers on foreign buyers. In letters of credit, the credit of one or more banks is involved, but with bills of exchange (also known as *dollar drafts*), the seller assumes all risk until the actual dollars are received. The typical procedure is for the seller to draw a draft on the buyer and present it with the necessary documents to the seller's bank for collection. The documents required are principally the same as for letters of credit. On receipt of the draft, the U.S. bank forwards it with the necessary documents to a correspondent bank in the buyer's country; the buyer is then presented with the draft for acceptance and immediate or later payment. With acceptance of the draft, the buyer receives the properly endorsed bill of lading that is used to acquire the goods from the carrier.

Dollar drafts have advantages for the seller because an accepted draft frequently can be discounted at a bank for immediate payment. Banks, however, usually discount drafts only with recourse; that is, if the buyer does not honor the draft, the bank returns it to the seller for payment. An accepted draft is firmer evidence in the case of default and subsequent litigation than an open account would be.

Cash in Advance

The portion of international business handled on a cash-in-advance basis is not large. Cash places unpopular burdens on the customer and typically is used when credit is doubtful, when exchange restrictions within the country of destination are such that the return of funds from abroad may be delayed for an unreasonable period, or when the American exporter for any reason is unwilling to sell on credit terms. Although full payment in advance is employed infrequently, partial payment (from 25 to 50 percent) in advance is not unusual when the character of the merchandise is such that an incomplete contract can result in a heavy loss. For example, complicated machinery or equipment manufactured to specification or special design would necessitate advance payment, which would be, in fact, a nonrefundable deposit.

Open Accounts

Sales on open accounts are not generally made in foreign trade except to customers of long standing with excellent credit reputations or to a subsidiary or branch of the exporter. Open accounts obviously leave sellers in a position where most of the problems of international commercial finance work to their disadvantage. Sales on open accounts are generally not recommended when the practice of the trade is to use some other method, when special merchandise is ordered, when shipping is hazardous, when the country of the importer imposes difficult exchange restrictions, or when political unrest requires additional caution.

Forfaiting

Inconvertible currencies and cash-short customers can kill an international sale if the seller cannot offer long-term financing. Unless the company has large cash reserves to finance its customers, a deal may be lost. Forfaiting is a financing technique for such a situation.

The basic idea of a forfaiting transaction is fairly simple: The seller makes a one-time arrangement with a bank or other financial institution to take over responsibility for collecting the account receivable. The exporter offers a long financing term to its buyer but intends to sell its account receivable, at a discount, for immediate cash. The forfaiter buys the debt, typically a promissory note or bill of exchange, on a nonrecourse basis. Once the exporter sells the paper, the forfaiter assumes the risk of collecting the importer's payments. The forfaiting institution also assumes any political risk present in the importer's country.[38]

Forfaiting is similar to factoring, but it is not the same. In *factoring*, a company has an ongoing relationship with a bank that routinely buys its short-term accounts receivable at a discount—in other words, the bank acts as a collections department for its client. In forfaiting, however, the seller makes a one-time arrangement with a bank to buy a specific account receivable.

All these ways of payment and the associated fees and, of course, the prices to be paid are most often negotiated between buyers and sellers. This leads us to the topic of the next chapter, international negotiations.

---

[37]"QuestaWeb Offers Totally Automated Letter of Credit Feature," *Business Wire*, March 3, 2008.

[38]For more information about forfaiting, visit http://www.afia-forfaiting.org.

Summary

Pricing is one of the most complicated decision areas encountered by international marketers. Rather than deal with one set of market conditions, one group of competitors, one set of cost factors, and one set of government regulations, international marketers must take all these factors into account, not only for each country in which they are operating but also often for each market within a country. Market prices at the consumer level are much more difficult to control in international than in domestic marketing, but the international marketer must still approach the pricing task on a basis of established objectives and policy, leaving enough flexibility for tactical price movements. Controlling costs that lead to price escalation when exporting products from one country to another is one of the most challenging pricing tasks facing the exporter. Some of the flexibility in pricing is reduced by the growth of the Internet, which has a tendency to equalize price differentials between country markets.

The continuing growth of Third World markets coupled with their lack of investment capital has increased the importance of countertrades for most marketers, making countertrading an important tool to include in pricing policy. The Internet is evolving to include countertrades, which will help eliminate some of the problems associated with this practice.

Pricing in the international marketplace requires a combination of intimate knowledge of market costs and regulations, an awareness of possible countertrade deals, infinite patience for detail, and a shrewd sense of market strategy. Finally, letters of credit and other issues related to getting paid are discussed.

Key Terms

Parallel market	Skimming	Countervailing duty	Cartel
Gray market	Penetration pricing policy	Countertrade	Letters of credit
Exclusive distribution	Price escalation	Barter	Bills of exchange
Variable-cost pricing	Dumping	Administered pricing	Forfaiting
Full-cost pricing			

Questions

1. Define the key terms listed above.

2. Discuss the causes of and solutions for parallel imports and their effect on price.

3. Why is it so difficult to control consumer prices when selling overseas?

4. Explain the concept of price escalation and why it can mislead an international marketer.

5. What are the causes of price escalation? Do they differ for exports and goods produced and sold in a foreign country?

6. Why is it seldom feasible for a company to absorb the high cost of international transportation and reduce the net price received?

7. Price escalation is a major pricing problem for the international marketer. How can this problem be counteracted? Discuss.

8. Volatile currency values have an impact on export strategies. Discuss.

9. "Regardless of the strategic factors involved and the company's orientation to market pricing, every price must be set with cost considerations in mind." Discuss.

10. "Price fixing by business is not generally viewed as an acceptable practice (at least in the domestic market), but when governments enter the field of price administration, they presume to do it for the general welfare to lessen the effects of 'destructive' competition." Discuss.

11. Do value-added taxes discriminate against imported goods?

12. Explain specific tariffs, ad valorem tariffs, and compound tariffs.

13. Suggest an approach a marketer may follow in adjusting prices to accommodate exchange rate fluctuations.

14. Explain the effects of indirect competition and how they may be overcome.

15. Why has dumping become such an issue in recent years?

16. Cartels seem to rise again, after they have been destroyed. Why are they so appealing to business?

17. Discuss the different pricing problems that result from inflation versus deflation in a country.

18. Discuss the various ways in which governments set prices. Why do they engage in such activities?

19. Why are costs so difficult to assess in marketing internationally?

20. Discuss the major problems facing a company that is countertrading.

21. If a country you are trading with has a shortage of hard currency, how should you prepare to negotiate price?

22. Of the four types of countertrades discussed in the text, which is the most beneficial to the seller? Explain.

23. Discuss how FTZs can be used to help reduce price escalation.

24. One free trade zone is in Turkey. Visit http://www.esbas.com.tr and discuss how it might be used to help solve the price escalation problem of a product being exported from the United States to Turkey.

25. Visit Global Trading (a division of 3M) at http://www.mmm.com/globaltrading/edge.html and select "The Competitive Edge" and "Who We Are." Then write a short report on how Global Trading could assist a small company that anticipates having merchandise from a countertrade.

Chapter 19

Inventive Negotiations with International Customers, Partners, and Regulators

CHAPTER OUTLINE

CHAPTER LEARNING OBJECTIVES

What you should learn from Chapter 19:

LO1 The problems associated with cultural stereotypes

LO2 How culture influences behaviors at the negotiation table

LO3 Common kinds of problems that crop up during international business negotiations

LO4 The similarities and differences in communication behaviors in several countries

LO5 How differences in values and thinking processes affect international negotiations

LO6 Important factors in selecting a negotiation team

LO7 How to prepare for international negotiations

LO8 Managing all aspects of the negotiation process

LO9 The importance of follow-up communications and procedures

LO10 The basics of inventive international negotiations

William Hernandez Requejo and John L. Graham, *Global Negotiation: The New Rules* (New York: Palgrave Macmillan, 2009). Reproduced with permission of Palgrave Macmillan.

PART FIVE

Global Perspective

A JAPANESE *AISATSU*

It is not so much that speaking only English is a disadvantage in international business. Instead, it's more that being bilingual is a huge advantage. Observations from sitting in on an *aisatsu* (a meeting or formal greeting for high-level executives typical in Japan) involving the president of a large Japanese industrial distributor and the marketing vice president of an American machinery manufacturer are instructive. The two companies were trying to reach an agreement on a long-term partnership in Japan.

Business cards were exchanged and formal introductions made. Even though the president spoke and understood English, one of his three subordinates acted as an interpreter for the Japanese president. The president asked everyone to be seated. The interpreter sat on a stool between the two senior executives. The general attitude between the parties was friendly but polite. Tea and a Japanese orange drink were served.

The Japanese president controlled the interaction completely, asking questions of all Americans through the interpreter. Attention of all the participants was given to each speaker in turn. After this initial round of questions for all the Americans, the Japanese president focused on developing a conversation with the American vice president.

During this interaction, an interesting pattern of nonverbal behaviors developed. The Japanese president would ask a question in Japanese. The interpreter then translated the question for the American vice president. While the interpreter spoke, the American's attention (gaze direction) was given to the interpreter. However, the Japanese president's gaze direction was at the American. Thus, the Japanese president could carefully and unobtrusively observe the American's facial expressions and nonverbal responses. Conversely, when the American spoke, the Japanese president had twice the response time. Because the latter understood English, he could formulate his responses during the translation process.

What is this extra response time worth in a strategic conversation? What is it worth to be able to carefully observe the nonverbal responses of your top-level counterpart in a high-stakes business negotiation?

Sources: James Day Hodgson, Yoshihiro Sano, and John L. Graham, *Doing Business with the New Japan* (Boulder, CO: Rowman & Littlefield, 2008); John L. Graham, Lynda Lawrence, and William Hernandez Requejo, Inventive Negotiation: *Getting Beyond Yes* (New York: Palgrave Macmillan, 2014). Also see http://www.InventiveNegotiation.com.

I (John Graham) had been in China a couple of weeks. I was tired. The fog had delayed my flight from Xian to Shanghai by four hours. I was standing in a long line at the counter to check in *again*. I started chatting with the older chap in line ahead of me. Juhani Kari introduced himself as a Finnish sales manager at ABB. He asked me what I did for a living. I responded, "I teach international business." He replied, "There is no such thing as international business. There's only interpersonal business." A wise man, indeed!

Face-to-face negotiations are an omnipresent activity in international commerce.[1] Once global marketing strategies have been formulated, once marketing research has been conducted to support those strategies, and once product/service, pricing, promotion, and place decisions have been made, then the focus of managers turns to implementation of the plans. In international business, such plans are almost always implemented through face-to-face negotiations with business partners and customers from foreign countries. The sales of goods and services, the management of distribution channels, contracting for marketing research and advertising services, licensing and franchise agreements, and strategic alliances all require managers from different cultures to sit and talk with one another to exchange ideas and express needs and preferences.[2]

Executives must also negotiate with representatives of foreign governments who might approve a variety of their marketing actions or be the actual ultimate customer for goods and services. In many countries, governmental officials may also be joint venture partners and, in some cases, vendors.[3] For example, negotiations for the television broadcast rights for the 2012 Summer Olympics in London included NBC, the International Olympic Committee, and United Kingdom governmental officials. Some of these negotiations can become quite complex, involving several governments, companies, and cultures.[4] Good examples are the European and North American talks regarding taxing the Internet, the continuing interactions regarding global environmental issues, or the ongoing WTO negotiations begun in Doha, Qatar, in 2001. All these activities demand a new kind of "business diplomacy."

One authority on international joint ventures suggests that a crucial aspect of all international commercial relationships is the negotiation of the original agreement. The seeds of success or failure often are sown at the negotiation table, vis-à-vis (face-to-face), where

---

[1]Several excellent books have been published on the topic of international business negotiations. Among them are Lothar Katz, *Negotiating International Business* (Charleston, SC: Booksurge, 2006); Camille Schuster and Michael Copeland, *Global Business, Planning for Sales and Negotiations* (Fort Worth, TX: Dryden, 1996); Robert T. Moran and William G. Stripp, *Dynamics of Successful International Business Negotiations* (Houston: Gulf, 1991); Pervez Ghauri and Jean-Claude Usunier (eds.), *International Business Negotiations* (Oxford: Pergamon, 1996); Donald W. Hendon, Rebecca Angeles Henden, and Paul Herbig, *Cross-Cultural Business Negotiations* (Westport, CT: Quorum, 1996); Sheida Hodge, *Global Smarts* (New York: Wiley, 2000); and Jeanne M. Brett, *Negotiating Globally* (San Francisco: Jossey-Bass, 2014). In addition, Roy J. Lewicki, David M. Saunders, and John W. Minton's *Negotiation: Readings, Exercises, and Cases*, 3rd ed. (New York: Irwin/McGraw-Hill, 1999) is an important book on the broader topic of business negotiations. The material from this chapter draws extensively on William Hernandez Requejo and John L. Graham, *Global Negotiation: The New Rules* (New York: Palgrave Macmillan, 2008); James Day Hodgson, Yoshihiro Sano, and John L. Graham, *Doing Business with the New Japan* (Boulder, CO: Rowman & Littlefield, 2008); and N. Mark Lam and John L. Graham, *China Now: Doing Business in the World's Most Dynamic Market* (New York: McGraw-Hill, 2007). See also http://www.GlobalNegotiationResources.com, 2010; John L. Graham, Lynda Lawrence, and William Hernandez Requejo, Inventive Negotiation: *Getting Beyond Yes* (New York: Palgrave Macmillan, 2014); and http://www.InventiveNegotiation.com.

[2]David G. Sirmon and Peter J. Lane, "A Model of Cultural Differences and International Alliance Performance," *Journal of International Business Studies* 35, no. 4 (2004), pp. 306–19; we also note that consumers worldwide are negotiating more as the economic doldrums persist: "Let's Make a Deal," *The Economist*, February 7, 2009, p. 57.

[3]Keith Bradsher, "As Deadline Nears, GM's Sale of Hummer Faces Several Big Obstacles," *The New York Times*, February 24, 2010, p. B5.

[4]R. Bruce Money provides an interesting theoretical perspective on the topic in "International Multilateral Negotiations and Social Networks," *Journal of International Business Studies* 29, no. 4 (1998), pp. 695–710. Lively anecdotes are included in Jiang Feng, "Courting the Olympics: Beijing's Other Face," *Asian Wall Street Journal*, February 26, 2001, p. 6; Ashling O'Connor, "After 54 Years, the Olympic Clock Is Ticking," *Times of London*, February 10, 2003, p. 35; Manjeet Kripalani, "Tata: Master of the Gentle Approach," *BusinessWeek*, February 25, 2008, pp. 64–66.

not only are financial and legal details agreed to but also, perhaps more important, the ambiance of cooperation and trust is established.[5] Indeed, the legal details and the structure of international business ventures are almost always modified over time, usually through negotiations. But the atmosphere of cooperation initially established face-to-face at the negotiation table persists—or the venture fails.

Business negotiations between business partners from the same country can be difficult. The added complication of cross-cultural communication can turn an already daunting task into an impossible one.[6] However, if cultural differences are taken into account, oftentimes wonderful business agreements can be made that lead to long-term, profitable relationships across borders. The purpose of this final chapter is to help prepare managers for the challenges and opportunities of international business negotiations. To do this, we will discuss the dangers of stereotypes, the impact of culture on negotiation behavior, and the implications of cultural differences for managers and negotiators.

The Dangers of Stereotypes

LO1

The problems associated with cultural stereotypes

The images of John Wayne, the cowboy, and the samurai, the fierce warrior, often are used as cultural stereotypes in discussions of international business negotiations.[7] Such representations almost always convey a grain of truth—an American cowboy kind of competitiveness versus a samurai kind of organizational (company) loyalty. One Dutch expert on international business negotiations argues, "The best negotiators are the Japanese because they will spend days trying to get to know their opponents. The worst are Americans because they think everything works in foreign countries as it does in the USA."[8] There are, of course, many Americans who are excellent international negotiators and some Japanese who are ineffective. The point is that negotiations are not conducted between national stereotypes; negotiations are conducted between people, and cultural factors often make huge differences.

Recall our discussions about the cultural diversity *within* countries from Chapters 4 and 11 and consider their relevance to negotiation. For example, we might expect substantial differences in negotiation styles between English-speaking and French-speaking Canadians. The genteel style of talk prevalent in the American Deep South is quite different from the faster speech patterns and pushiness more common in places like New York City. Experts tell us that negotiation styles differ across genders in America as well. Still others tell us that the urbane negotiation behaviors of Japanese bankers are very different from the relative aggressiveness of those in the retail industry in that country. Finally, age and experience can also make important differences. The older Chinese executive with no experience dealing with foreigners is likely to behave quite differently from her young assistant with undergraduate and MBA degrees from American universities.

The focus of this chapter is culture's influence on international negotiation behavior. However, it should be clearly understood that individual personalities and backgrounds and a variety of situational factors also heavily influence behavior at the negotiation table— and it is the manager's responsibility to consider these factors.[9] Remember: Companies and countries do not negotiate—people do. Consider the culture of your customers and business partners, but treat them as individuals.

[5]Constantine Katsikeas, Dionysis Skarmeas, and Daniel C. Bello, "Developing Successful Trust-Based International Exchange Relationships," *Journal of International Business Studies* 40, no. 1 (2009), pp. 132–55.

[6]James K. Sebenius, "The Hidden Challenge of Cross-Border Negotiations," *Harvard Business Review*, March–April, 2002, pp. 76–82.

[7]Nurit Zaidman discusses how stereotypes are formed in "Stereotypes of International Managers: Content and Impact on Business Interactions," *Group & Organizational Management*, March 1, 2000, pp. 45–54.

[8]Samfrits Le Poole comments on the American stereotype in "John Wayne Goes to Brussels," in Roy J. Lewicki, Joseph A. Litterer, David M. Saunders, and John W. Minton (eds.), *Negotiation: Readings, Exercises, and Cases*, 2nd ed. (Burr Ridge, IL: Irwin, 1993). The quote is from the Spanish newspaper *Expansion*, November 29, 1991, p. 41.

[9]Stephen E. Weiss provides the most complete recent review of the international negotiations literature— "International Business Negotiations Research," in B. J. Punnett and O. Shenkar (eds.), *Handbook for International Management Research* (Ann Arbor: University of Michigan Press, 2004), pp. 415–74.

The Europeans stereotype themselves. This postcard was purchased at the European Parliament gift store in Brussels. Of course, not all Dutch are cheap; there are sober Irish, and so on. Now that the European Union has expanded to 28 countries, a larger card will be required. But we're fairly certain they'll have a humorous perspective on all the new entrants.

The Pervasive Impact of Culture on Negotiation Behavior

LO2

How culture influences behaviors at the negotiation table

The primary purpose of this section is to demonstrate the extent of cultural differences in negotiation styles and how these differences can cause problems in international business negotiations. The material in this section is based on a systematic study of the topic over the last three decades in which the negotiation styles of more than 1,000 businesspeople in 17 countries (20 cultures) were considered.[10] The countries studied were Japan, Korea, Taiwan, China (Tianjin, Guangzhou, and Hong Kong), the Philippines, the Czech Republic, Russia, Israel, Norway, Germany, France, the United Kingdom, Spain, Brazil, Mexico, Canada (English-speaking and French-speaking), and the United States. The countries were chosen because they constitute America's most important present and future trading partners.

---

[10]The following institutions and people provided crucial support for the research on which this material is based: U.S. Department of Education; Toyota Motor Sales USA Inc.; Solar Turbines Inc. (a division of Caterpillar Tractors Co.); the Faculty Research and Innovation Fund and the International Business Educational Research (IBEAR) Program at the University of Southern California; Ford Motor Company; Marketing Science Institute; Madrid Business School; and Professors Nancy J. Adler (McGill University), Nigel Campbell (Manchester Business School), A. Gabriel Esteban (University of Houston, Victoria), Leonid I. Evenko (Russian Academy of the National Economy), Richard H. Holton (University of California, Berkeley), Alain Jolibert (Université des Sciences Sociales de Grenoble), Dong Ki Kim (Korea University), C. Y. Lin (National Sun-Yat Sen University), Hans-Gunther Meissner (Dortmund University), Alena Ockova (Czech Management Center), Sara Tang (Mass Transit Railway Corporation, Hong Kong), Kam-hon Lee (Chinese University of Hong Kong), and Theodore Schwarz (Monterrey Institute of Technology, Monterrey, CA).

Looking broadly across the several cultures, two important lessons stand out. The first is that regional generalizations very often are not correct. For example, Japanese and Korean negotiation styles are quite similar in some ways, but in other ways, they could not be more different. The second lesson learned from this study is that Japan is an exceptional place: On almost every dimension of negotiation style considered, the Japanese are on or near the end of the scale. Sometimes Americans are on the other end. But actually, most of the time Americans are somewhere in the middle. The reader will see this evinced in the data presented in this section. The Japanese approach, however, is most distinct, even *sui generis*.

LO3

Common kinds of problems that crop up during international business negotiations

Cultural differences cause four kinds of problems in international business negotiations, at the levels of:[11]

1. Language
2. Nonverbal behaviors
3. Values
4. Thinking and decision-making processes

The order is important; the problems lower on the list are more serious because they are more subtle. For example, two negotiators would notice immediately if one were speaking Japanese and the other German. The solution to the problem may be as simple as hiring an interpreter or talking in a common third language, or it may be as difficult as learning a language. Regardless of the solution, the problem is obvious. Cultural differences in nonverbal behaviors, in contrast, are almost always hidden below our awareness. That is to say, in a face-to-face negotiation, participants nonverbally—and more subtly—give off and take in a great deal of information.[12] Some experts argue that this information is more important than verbal information. Almost all this signaling goes on below our levels of consciousness.[13] When the nonverbal signals from foreign partners are different, negotiators are most likely to misinterpret them without even being conscious of the mistake. For example, when a French client consistently interrupts, Americans tend to feel uncomfortable without noticing exactly why. In this manner, interpersonal friction often colors business relationships, goes undetected, and, consequently, goes uncorrected. Differences in values and thinking and decision-making processes are hidden even deeper and therefore are even harder to cure. We discuss these differences here, starting with language and nonverbal behaviors.

Differences in Language and Nonverbal Behaviors

LO4

The similarities and differences in communication behaviors in several countries

Americans are clearly near the bottom of the languages skills list, though Australians assert that Australians are even worse. It should be added, however, that American undergrads recently have begun to see the light and are flocking to language classes and study-abroad programs. Unfortunately, foreign language teaching resources in the United States are inadequate to satisfy the increasing demand. In contrast, the Czechs are now throwing away a hard-earned competitive advantage: Young Czechs will not take Russian anymore. It is easy to understand why, but the result will be a generation of Czechs who cannot leverage their geographic advantage because they will not be able to speak to their neighbors to the east.

The language advantages of the Japanese executive in the description of the *aisatsu* that opened the chapter were quite clear. However, the most common complaint heard from American managers regards foreign clients and partners breaking into side conversations in their native languages. At best, this is seen as impolite, and quite often American negotiators are likely to attribute something sinister to the content of the foreign talk—"They're plotting or telling secrets."

---

[11]For additional details, see William Hernandez Requejo and John L. Graham, *Global Negotiation: The New Rules* (New York: Palgrave Macmillan, 2008); http://www.GlobalNegotiationResources.com, 2010.

[12]Mark Bauerlein, "Why Gen-Y Johnny Can't Read Nonverbal Cues," *The Wall Street Journal*, August 28, 2009, online.

[13]Jan Ulijn, Anne Francoise Rutowski, Rajesh Kumar, and Yunxia Zhu, "Patterns of Feelings in Face-to-Face Negotiation: A Sino-Dutch Pilot Study," *Cross Cultural Management* 12, no. 3 (2005), pp. 103–18.

Japanese negotiators exchange business cards at the front end of a meeting. Even more important than the nonverbal demonstration of respect in the "little ritual" is the all-important information about the relative status of the negotiators, clearly communicated by job title and company. Japanese executives literally do not know how to talk to one another until the status relationship is determined, because proper use of the language depends on knowledge of the relative status of the negotiators.

This perception is a frequent American mistake. The usual purpose of such side conversations is to straighten out a translation problem. For instance, one Korean may lean over to another and ask, "What'd he say?" Or the side conversation can regard a disagreement among the foreign team members. Both circumstances should be seen as positive signs by Americans—that is, getting translations straight enhances the efficiency of the interactions, and concessions often follow internal disagreements. But because most Americans speak only one language, neither circumstance is appreciated. By the way, people from other countries are advised to give Americans a brief explanation of the content of their first few side conversations to assuage the sinister attributions.

Data from simulated negotiations are also informative. In our study, the verbal behaviors of negotiators in 15 of the 21 cultures (six negotiators in each of the 15 groups) were videotaped. The numbers in the body of Exhibit 19.1 represent the percentages of statements that were classified into each category listed. That is, 7 percent of the statements made by Japanese negotiators were classified as promises, 4 percent as threats, 7 percent as recommendations, and so on. The verbal bargaining behaviors used by the negotiators during the simulations proved to be surprisingly similar across cultures. Negotiations in all 15 cultures studied were composed primarily of information-exchange tactics—questions and self-disclosures. Note that the Japanese appear on the low end of the continuum of self-disclosures. Their 34 percent (along with Spaniards and English-speaking Canadians) was the second lowest across all 15 groups, suggesting that they are the most reticent about giving information, except for the Israelis. Overall, however, the verbal tactics used were surprisingly similar across the diverse cultures.

Exhibit 19.2 provides analyses of some linguistic aspects and nonverbal behaviors for the 15 videotaped groups. Although these efforts merely scratch the surface of these kinds of behavioral analyses, they still provide indications of substantial cultural differences.[14] Note that, once again, the Japanese are at or next to the end of the continuum on almost every dimension of the behaviors listed. Their facial gazing and touching are the least among the 15 groups. Only the northern Chinese used the word *no* less frequently, and only the English-speaking Canadians and Russians used more silent periods than did the Japanese.

A broader examination of the data in Exhibits 19.1 and 19.2 reveals a more meaningful conclusion: The variation across cultures is greater when comparing linguistic aspects of language and nonverbal behaviors than when the verbal content of negotiations is considered. For example, notice the great differences between Japanese and Brazilians in Exhibit 19.1 vis-à-vis Exhibit 19.2.

Following are further descriptions of the distinctive aspects of each of the 15 cultural groups videotaped. Certainly, conclusions about the individual cultures cannot be drawn from an analysis of only six businesspeople in each culture, but the suggested cultural differences are worthwhile to consider briefly.

Japan.   Consistent with most descriptions of Japanese negotiation behavior, the results of this analysis suggest their style of interaction is among the least aggressive (or most polite). Threats, commands, and warnings appear to be deemphasized in favor of more positive promises, recommendations, and commitments. Particularly indicative of their polite conversational style was their infrequent use of *no* and *you* and facial gazing, as well as more frequent silent periods.

Korea.   Perhaps one of the more interesting aspects of the analysis is the contrast of the Asian styles of negotiations. Non-Asians often generalize about Asians; the findings demonstrate, however, that this generalization is a mistake. Korean negotiators used

---

[14]Thomas W. Leigh and John O. Summers, "An Initial Evaluation of Industrial Buyers' Impressions of Salespersons' Nonverbal Cues," *Journal of Personal Selling & Sales Management*, Winter 2002, pp. 41–53.

Exhibit 19.1
Verbal Negotiation Tactics (The "What" of Communications)

Bargaining Behaviors and Definitions	JPN	KOR	TWN	CHN**	RUSS	ISRL	GRM	UK	FRN	SPN	BRZ	MEX	FCAN	ECAN	USA
Promise. A statement in which the source indicates its intention to provide the target with a reinforcing consequence, which the source anticipates the target will evaluate as pleasant, positive, or rewarding.	7†	4	9	6	5	12	7	11	5	11	3	7	8	6	8
Threat. Same as promise, except that the reinforcing consequences are thought to be noxious, unpleasant, or punishing.	4	2	2	1	3	4	3	3	5	2	2	1	3	0	4
Recommendation. A statement in which the source predicts that a pleasant environmental consequence will occur to the target. Its occurrence is not under the source's control.	7	1	5	2	4	8	5	6	3	4	5	8	5	4	4
Warning. Same as recommendation, except that the consequences are thought to be unpleasant.	2	0	3	1	0	1	1	1	3	1	1	2	3	0	1
Reward. A statement by the source that is thought to create pleasant consequences for the target.	1	3	2	1	3	2	4	5	3	3	2	1	1	3	2
Punishment. Same as reward, except that the consequences are thought to be unpleasant.	1	5	1	0	1	3	2	0	3	2	3	0	2	1	3
Normative appeals. A statement in which the source indicates that the target's past, present, or future behavior will conform with social norms or is in violation of social norms.	4	3	1	1	1	5	1	1	0	1	1	1	3	1	2
Commitment. A statement by the source to the effect that its future bids will not go below or above a certain level.	15	13	9	10	1	10	9	13	10	9	8	9	8	14	13
Self-disclosure. A statement in which the source reveals information about itself.	34	36	42	36	40	30	47	39	42	34	39	38	42	34	36
Question. A statement in which the source asks the target to reveal information about itself.	20	21	14	34	27	20	11	15	18	17	22	27	19	26	20
Command. A statement in which the source suggests that the target perform a certain behavior.	8	13	11	7	7	9	12	9	9	17	14	7	5	10	6

*For each group, n = 6.

**Northern China (Tianjin and environs).

†Read "7 percent of the statements made by Japanese negotiators were promises."

Source: From William Hernandez Requejo and John L. Graham, *Global Negotiation: The New Rules* (New York: Palgrave Macmillan, 2009). Reproduced with permission of Palgrave Macmillan.

Exhibit 19.2

Linguistic Aspects of Language and Nonverbal Behaviors ("How" Things Are Said)

Bargaining Behaviors (per 30 minutes)	Cultures*														
	JPN	KOR	TWN	CHN**	RUSS	ISRL	GRM	UK	FRN	SPN	BRZ	MEX	FCAN	ECAN	USA
Structural Aspects															
"No's." The number of times the word *no* was used by each negotiator.	1.9	7.4	5.9	1.5	2.3	8.5	6.7	5.4	11.3	23.2	41.9	4.5	7.0	10.1	4.5
"You's." The number of times the word *you* was used by each negotiator.	31.5	35.2	36.6	26.8	23.6	64.4	39.7	54.8	70.2	73.3	90.4	56.3	72.4	64.4	55.1
Nonverbal Behaviors															
Silent periods. The number of conservational gaps of 10 seconds or longer.	2.5	0	0	2.3	3.7	1.9	0	2.5	1.0	0	0	1.1	0.2	2.9	1.7
Conversational overlaps. Number of interruptions.	6.2	22.0	12.3	17.1	13.3	30.1	20.8	5.3	20.7	28.0	14.3	10.6	24.0	17.0	5.1
Facial gazing. Number of minutes negotiators spent looking at opponent's face.	3.9	9.9	19.7	11.1	8.7	15.3	10.2	9.0	16.0	13.7	15.6	14.7	18.8	10.4	10.0
Touching. Incidents of bargainers touching one another (not including handshaking).	0	0	0	0	0	0	0	0	0.1	0	4.7	0	0	0	0

*For each group, n = 6.

**Northern China (Tianjin and environs).

Source: From William Hernandez Requejo and John L. Graham, *Global Negotiation: The New Rules* (New York: Palgrave Macmillan, 2009). Reproduced with permission of Palgrave Macmillan.

CROSSING BORDERS 19.1   Poker Faces and Botox Injections

We often hear from American executives the complaint that their Japanese counterparts are "hard to read" at the negotiation table; that is, they use "poker faces." However, when we videotape and count negotiators' facial movements (smiles and frowns), we see no differences between Japanese and Americans. It appears that because of differences in the timing and meaning of facial expressions across the two cultures, the Americans are unable to interpret the Japanese facial expressions, so they mistakenly report seeing nothing.

Now it seems that American executives are seeking their own poker-face advantage through the new wonder of science, Botox. Shots of the new drug are being used to freeze and sculpt their faces into "semipermanent serenity." Says one American executive, "When you look strong and

tough and not afraid, people respect you more . . . showing less expression really makes a statement."

Paul Ekman, a University of California psychologist who studies facial expressions, describes this trend as "very scary." Facial expressions have evolved to serve a purpose, to aid in the formation of basic human bonds through subconscious facial movements. Take those away, and how can we tell friend or foe, mate or murderer?

Rather than preparing for your international negotiations using Botox, we instead recommend a good book, a nice round of golf, or perhaps a good, old-fashioned facial!

Sources: Suein L. Hwang, "Some Type A Staffers Dress for Success with a Shot of Botox," *The Wall Street Journal*, June 31, 2002, p. B1; James D. Hodgson, Yoshihiro Sano, and John L. Graham, *Doing Business with the New Japan* (Boulder, CO: Rowman & Littlefield, 2008).

---

considerably more punishments and commands than did the Japanese. Koreans used the word *no* and interrupted more than three times as frequently as the Japanese. Moreover, no silent periods occurred between Korean negotiators.

China (Northern).   The behaviors of the negotiators from northern China (i.e., in and around Tianjin) were most remarkable in the emphasis on asking questions (34 percent).[15] Indeed, 70 percent of the statements made by the Chinese negotiators were classified as information-exchange tactics. Other aspects of their behavior were quite similar to the Japanese, particularly the uses of *no* and *you* and silent periods.[16]

Taiwan.   The behavior of the businesspeople in Taiwan was quite different from that in China and Japan but similar to that in Korea. The Chinese in Taiwan were exceptional in the length of time of facial gazing—on average, almost 20 of 30 minutes. They asked fewer questions and provided more information (self-disclosures) than did any of the other Asian groups.

Russia.   The Russians' style was quite different from that of any other European group, and, indeed, was quite similar in many respects to the style of the Japanese. They used *no* and *you* infrequently and used the most silent periods of any group. Only the Japanese did less facial gazing, and only the Chinese asked a greater percentage of questions.

---

[15]The Chinese emphasis on questions is consistent with other empirical findings: Dean Tjosvold, Chun Hui, and Haifa Sun, "Can Chinese Discuss Conflicts Openly? Field and Experimental Studies of Face Dynamics," *Group Decision and Negotiation* 13 (2004), pp. 351–73.

[16]There is a burgeoning literature on negotiations with Chinese. See Catherine H. Tinsley and Jeanne M. Brett, "Managing Workplace Conflict in the U.S. and Hong Kong," *Organizational Behavior and Human Decision Process* 85 (2001), pp. 360–381; Pervez Ghauri and Tony Fang, "Negotiating with the Chinese: A Socio-Cultural Analysis," *Journal of World Business* September 22, 2001, pp. 303–12; Vivian C. Sheer and Ling Chen, "Successful Sino-Western Business Negotiation: Participants' Accounts of National and Professional Cultures," *Journal of Business Communication*, January 1, 2003, pp. 50–64; Rajesh Kumar and Verner Worm, "Social Capital and the Dynamics of Business Negotiations between the Northern Europeans and the Chinese," *International Marketing Review* 20, no. 3 (2003), pp. 262–86; John L. Graham and N. Mark Lam, "The Chinese Negotiation," *Harvard Business Review*, October 2003, pp. 82–91; Anna Stark, Kim-Shyan Fam, David S. Waller, and Zhilong Tian, "Chinese Negotiation Practice, Perspective from New Zealand Exporters," *Cross Cultural Management* 12, no. 3 (2005), pp. 85–102.

Israel.   The behaviors of the Israeli negotiators were distinctive in three respects. They used the lowest percentage of self-disclosures, apparently holding their cards relatively closely. Yet they also used, by far, the highest percentages of promises and recommendations. They were also at the end of the scale for the percentage of normative appeals at 5 percent, with the most frequent references being to competitors' offers. Perhaps most important, the Israeli negotiators interrupted one another much more frequently than negotiators from any other group. This important nonverbal behavior is most likely to blame for the "pushy" stereotype often used by Americans to describe their Israeli negotiation partners.

Germany.   The behaviors of the Germans are difficult to characterize because they fell toward the center of almost all the continua. However, the Germans were exceptional in the high percentage of self-disclosures (47 percent) and the low percentage of questions (11 percent).

United Kingdom.   The behaviors of the British negotiators were remarkably similar to those of the Americans in all respects.

Spain.   *Diga* is perhaps a good metaphor for the Spanish approach to negotiations evinced in our data. When you make a phone call in Madrid, the usual greeting on the other end is not *hola* ("hello") but instead *diga* ("speak"). It is not surprising then that the Spaniards in the videotaped negotiations likewise used the highest percentage of commands (17 percent) of any of the groups and gave comparatively little information (self-disclosures, only 34 percent). Moreover, except for the Israelis, they interrupted one another more frequently than any other group, and they used the terms *no* and *you* very frequently.

France.   The style of the French negotiators was perhaps the most aggressive of all the groups. In particular, they used the highest percentage of threats and warnings (together, 8 percent). They also used interruptions, facial gazing, and *no* and *you* very frequently compared with the other groups, and one of the French negotiators touched his partner on the arm during the simulation.

Brazil.   The Brazilian businesspeople, like the French and Spanish, were quite aggressive. They used the second-highest percentage of commands of all the groups. On average, the Brazilians said the word *no* 42 times, *you* 90 times, and touched one another on the arm about 5 times during 30 minutes of negotiation. Facial gazing was also high.

Mexico.   The patterns of Mexican behavior in our negotiations are good reminders of the dangers of regional or language-group generalizations.[17] Both verbal and nonverbal behaviors were quite different from those of their Latin American (Brazilian) or continental (Spanish) cousins. Indeed, Mexicans answer the telephone with the much less demanding *bueno* (short for "good day"). In many respects, the Mexican behavior was very similar to that of the negotiators from the United States.

French-Speaking Canada.   The French-speaking Canadians behaved quite similarly to their continental cousins. Like the negotiators from France, they too used high percentages of threats and warnings and even more interruptions and eye contact. Such an aggressive interaction style would not mix well with some of the more low-key styles of some of the Asian groups or with English speakers, including English-speaking Canadians.

English-Speaking Canada.   The Canadians who speak English as their first language used the lowest percentage of aggressive persuasive tactics (threats, warnings, and punishments totaled only 1 percent) of all 15 groups. Perhaps, as communications researchers suggest, such stylistic differences are the seeds of interethnic discord as witnessed in Canada over the years. With respect to international negotiations, the English-speaking Canadians used noticeably more interruptions and *no*'s than negotiators from either of Canada's major trading partners, the United States and Japan.

---

[17]T. Lenartowicz and J. P. Johnson, "A Cross-National Assessment of the Values of Latin American Managers: Contrasting Hues or Shades of Gray?" *Journal of International Business Studies* 34, no. 3 (May 2003), pp. 266–81.

United States.   Like the Germans and the British, the Americans fell in the middle of most continua. They did interrupt one another less frequently than all the others, but that was their sole distinction.

These differences across the cultures are quite complex, and this material by itself should not be used to predict the behaviors of foreign counterparts. Instead, great care should be taken with respect to the aforementioned dangers of stereotypes. The key here is to be aware of these kinds of differences so that the Japanese silence, the Brazilian "no, no, no . . . ," or the French threat is not misinterpreted.

Differences in Values

LO5

How differences in values and thinking processes affect international negotiations

Four values—objectivity, competitiveness, equality, and punctuality—that are held strongly and deeply by most Americans seem to frequently cause misunderstandings and bad feelings in international business negotiations.

Objectivity.   "Americans make decisions based upon the bottom line and on cold, hard facts." "Americans don't play favorites." "Economics and performance count, not people." "Business is business." Such statements well reflect American notions of the importance of objectivity.

The single most important book on the topic of negotiation, *Getting to Yes*,[18] is highly recommended for both American and foreign readers. The latter will learn not only about negotiations but also, perhaps more important, about how Americans think about negotiations. The authors are emphatic about "separating the people from the problem," and they state, "Every negotiator has two kinds of interests: in the substance and in the relationship." This advice is probably worthwhile in the United States or perhaps in Germany, but in most places in the world, such advice is nonsense. In most places in the world, particularly in collectivistic, high-context cultures, personalities and substance are not separate issues and cannot be made so.

For example, consider how important nepotism is in Chinese or Hispanic cultures. Experts tell us that businesses don't grow beyond the bounds and bonds of tight family control in the burgeoning "Chinese Commonwealth." Things work the same way in Spain, Mexico, and the Philippines by nature. And, just as naturally, negotiators from such countries not only will take things personally but also will be personally affected by negotiation outcomes. *Guanxi*, the Chinese word for personal connections, is key for negotiators working in China. Long-term reciprocity is the basis of commercial interactions there, and Western concepts like objectivity almost always take a back seat.[19] What happens to them at the negotiation table will affect the business relationship, regardless of the economics involved.

Competitiveness and Equality.[20]   Simulated negotiations can be viewed as a kind of experimental economics wherein the values of each participating cultural group are roughly reflected in the economic outcomes. The simple simulation used in our research represented the essence of commercial negotiations—it had both competitive and cooperative aspects. At least 40 businesspeople from each culture played the same buyer–seller game, negotiating over the prices of three products. Depending on the agreement reached, the "negotiation pie" could be made larger through cooperation (as high as $10,400 in joint profits) before it was divided between the buyer and seller. The results are summarized in Exhibit 19.3.

The Japanese were the champions at making the pie big. Their joint profits in the simulation were the highest (at $9,590) among the 20 cultural groups involved. The American pie was more average sized (at $9,030), but at least it was divided relatively equitably (51.8 percent of the profits went to the buyers). Conversely, the Japanese (and others) split their pies in

---

[18]Roger Fisher, William Ury, and Bruce Patton, *Getting to Yes: Negotiating Agreement without Giving In,* 3rd ed. (New York: Penguin, 2011).

[19]Flora F. Gu, Kineta Hung, and David K. Tse, "When Does Guanxi Matter? Issues of Capitalization and Its Dark Sides," *Journal of Marketing* 72, no. 4 (2008), pp. 12–28.

[20]Of course, the opposite of equality is hierarchy, and the latter is more prevalent in China. For example, see Ray Friedman, Shu-Chen Chi, and Leigh Anne Liu, "An Expectancy Model of Chinese-American Differences in Conflict Avoiding," *Journal of International Business Studies* 37 (2006), pp. 76–91.

Exhibit 19.3
Cultural Differences in
Competitiveness and
Equality

Source: William Hernandez Requejo and
John L. Graham, *Global Negotiation:
The New Rules* (New York: Palgrave
Macmillan, 2009). Reproduced with
permission of Palgrave Macmillan.

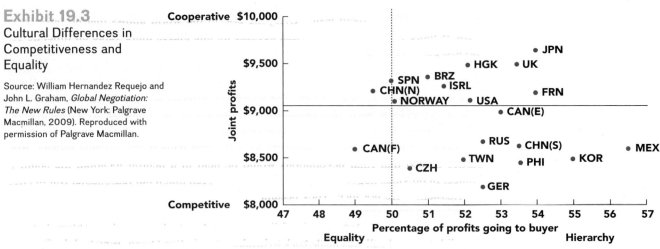

Note: Based on at least 40 businesspeople in each cultural group.

strange (perhaps even unfair)[21] ways, with buyers making higher percentages of the profits (53.8 percent). The implications of these simulated business negotiations are completely consistent with the comments of other authors and the adage that in Japan the buyer is "king." By nature, Americans have little understanding of the Japanese practice of giving complete deference to the needs and wishes of buyers. That is not the way things work in America. American sellers tend to treat American buyers more as equals, and the egalitarian values of American society support this behavior. Moreover, most Americans will, by nature, treat Japanese buyers more frequently as equals. Likewise, American buyers will generally not "take care of" American sellers or Japanese sellers. The American emphasis on competition and individualism represented in these findings is quite consistent with the work of Geert Hofstede[22] detailed in Chapter 4, which indicated that Americans scored the highest among all the cultural groups on the individualism (versus collectivism) scale. Moreover, values for individualism/collectivism have been shown to directly influence negotiation behaviors in several other countries.[23]

Finally, not only do Japanese buyers achieve better results than American buyers, but compared with American sellers ($4,350), Japanese sellers also get more of the commercial pie ($4,430). Interestingly, when shown these results, Americans in executive seminars still often prefer the American seller's role. In other words, even though the American sellers make lower profits than the Japanese, many American managers apparently prefer lower profits if those profits are yielded from a more equal split of the joint profits. A new study has likewise demonstrated that Americans and Japanese have different views about fairness.[24]

Finally, the Japanese emphasis on hierarchical relationships seems to hamper internal communications; subordinates don't pass along bad news, for example. This reticence seems to have been a major problem during the Toyota product quality issues mentioned in previous chapters. These differences in approaches also have influenced interactions externally with U.S. government regulators. One analysis described Toyota's problem as follows: "Its secretive corporate culture in Japan clashed with the U.S. requirements that automakers disclose safety threats."[25]

[21]Concepts of fairness clearly vary across cultures; see Nancy R. Buchan, Rachael T. S. Croson, and Eric J. Johnson, "When Do Fair Beliefs Influence Bargaining Behavior: Experimental Bargaining in Japan and the United States," *Journal of Consumer Research* 31, no. 2 (2004), pp. 181–90.

[22]Geert Hofstede, *Culture's Consequences*, 2nd ed. (Thousand Oaks, CA: Sage, 2001).

[23]John L. Graham, "Culture's Influence on Business Negotiations: An Application of Hofstede's and Rokeach's Ideas," in Farok J. Contractor and Peter Lorange (eds.), *Cooperative Strategies and Alliances* (Amsterdam: Pergamon, 2002), pp. 461–92. Also see Roy J. Lewicki, David M. Saunders, and John W. Minton, *Essentials of Negotiation*, 2nd ed. (New York: McGraw-Hill, 2001).

[24]Nancy R. Buchan, Rachel T. A. Croson, and Eric J. Johnson, "When Do Fair Beliefs Influence Bargaining Behavior? Experimental Bargaining in Japan and the United States," *Journal of Consumer Research* 31 (2004), pp. 181–90.

[25]Kate Linebaugh, Dionne Searcey, and Norihiko Shirouzu, "Secretive Culture Led Toyota Astray," *The Wall Street Journal*, February 8, 2010, online.

Time. "Just make them wait." Everyone else in the world knows that no negotiation tactic is more useful with Americans, because no one places more value on time, no one has less patience when things slow down, and no one looks at their wristwatches more than Americans do. The material from Chapter 5 on P-time versus M-time is quite pertinent here. Edward T. Hall[26] in his seminal writing is best at explaining how the passage of time is viewed differently across cultures and how these differences most often hurt Americans.

Even Americans try to manipulate time to their advantage, however. As a case in point, Solar Turbines Incorporated (a division of Caterpillar) once sold $34 million worth of industrial gas turbines and compressors for a Russian natural gas pipeline project. Both parties agreed that final negotiations would be held in a neutral location, the south of France. In previous negotiations, the Russians had been tough but reasonable. But in Nice, the Russians were not nice. They became tougher and, in fact, completely unreasonable, according to the Solar executives involved.

The Americans needed a couple of discouraging days to diagnose the problem, but once they did, a crucial call was made back to headquarters in San Diego. Why had the Russians turned so cold? They were enjoying the warm weather in Nice and weren't interested in making a quick deal and heading back to Moscow! The call to California was the key event in this negotiation. Solar's headquarters people in San Diego were sophisticated enough to allow their negotiators to take their time. From that point on, the routine of the negotiations changed to brief, 45-minute meetings in the mornings, with afternoons at the golf course, beach, or hotel, making calls and doing paperwork. Finally, during the fourth week, the Russians began to make concessions and to ask for longer meetings. Why? They could not go back to Moscow after four weeks on the Mediterranean without a signed contract. This strategic reversal of the time pressure yielded a wonderful contract for Solar.

Differences in Thinking and Decision-Making Processes

When faced with a complex negotiation task, most Westerners (notice the generalization here) divide the large task up into a series of smaller tasks. Issues such as prices, delivery, warranty, and service contracts may be settled one issue at a time, with the final agreement being the sum or the sequence of smaller agreements. In Asia, however, a different approach is more often taken wherein all the issues are discussed at once, in no apparent order, and concessions are made on all issues at the end of the discussion. The Western sequential approach and the Eastern holistic approach do not mix well.[27]

That is, American managers often report great difficulties in measuring progress in Japan. After all, in America, you are half done when half the issues are settled. But in Japan, nothing seems to get settled. Then, surprise, you are done. Often Americans make unnecessary concessions right before agreements are announced by the Japanese. For example, one American department store buyer traveling to Japan to buy six different consumer products for his chain lamented that negotiations for his first purchase took an entire week. In the United States, such a purchase would be consummated in an afternoon. So, by his calculations, he expected to have to spend six weeks in Japan to complete his purchases. He considered raising his purchase prices to try to move things along faster. But before he was able to make such a concession, the Japanese quickly agreed on the other five products in just three days. This particular businessperson was, by his own admission, lucky in his first encounter with Japanese bargainers.

This American businessperson's near-blunder reflects more than just a difference in decision-making style. To Americans, a business negotiation is a problem-solving activity,

[26]Edward T. Hall, "The Silent Language in Overseas Business," *Harvard Business Review*, May–June 1960, pp. 87–96.

[27]East–West differences in thinking are studied in detail in Joel Brockner, Ya-Ru Chen, Elizabeth A. Mannix, Kwok Leung, and Daniel P. Skarlicki, "Culture and Procedural Fairness: When the Effects of What You Do Depend on How You Do It," *Administrative Science Quarterly*, March 1, 2000, pp. 138–57. Most important is Richard E. Nisbett, *The Geography of Thought: How Asians and Westerners Think Differently . . . and Why* (New York: The Free Press, 2003). Also, for a discussion of related communication problems in international work teams, see Jeanne Brett, Kristin Behfar, and Mary C. Kern, "Managing Multicultural Teams," *Harvard Business Review*, November 2006, pp. 84–91.

the best deal for both parties being the solution. To a Japanese businessperson, a business negotiation is a time to develop a business relationship with the goal of long-term mutual benefit. The economic issues are the context, not the content, of the talks. Thus, settling any one issue really is not that important. Such details will take care of themselves once a viable, harmonious business relationship is established. And, as happened in the case of our retail goods buyer, once the relationship was established—signaled by the first agreement—the other "details" were settled quickly.

American bargainers should anticipate such a holistic approach and be prepared to discuss all issues simultaneously and in an apparently haphazard order. Progress in the talks should not be measured by how many issues have been settled. Rather, Americans must try to gauge the quality of the business relationship. Important signals of progress can be the following:

- Higher-level foreigners being included in the discussions.
- Questions beginning to focus on specific areas of the deal.
- A softening of attitudes and positions on some of the issues—"Let us take some time to study this issue."
- At the negotiation table, increased talk among themselves in their own language, which may often mean they're trying to decide something.
- Increased bargaining and use of the lower-level, informal, and other channels of communication.

Implications for Managers and Negotiators

Considering all the potential problems in cross-cultural negotiations, particularly when you mix managers from relationship-oriented cultures with those from information-oriented ones, it is a wonder that any international business gets done at all. Obviously, the economic imperatives of global trade make much of it happen despite the potential pitfalls. But an appreciation of cultural differences can lead to even better international commercial transactions—it is not just business deals but highly profitable business relationships that are the real goal of international business negotiations.[28]

Four steps lead to more efficient and effective international business negotiations. They are as follows: (1) selection of the appropriate negotiation team;[29] (2) management of preliminaries, including training, preparations, and manipulation of negotiation settings; (3) management of the process of negotiations, that is, what happens at the negotiation table; and (4) appropriate follow-up procedures and practices. Each is discussed in this section.

Negotiation Teams

LO6

Important factors in selecting a negotiation team

One reason for global business successes is the large numbers of skillful international negotiators. These are the managers who have lived in foreign countries and speak foreign languages. In many cases, they are immigrants to the United States or those who have been immersed in foreign cultures in other capacities (Peace Corps volunteers and Mormon missionaries are common examples). More business schools are beginning to reemphasize language training and visits abroad. Indeed, it is interesting to note that the original Harvard Business School catalog of 1908–1909 listed courses in German, French, and Spanish correspondence within its curriculum.

The selection criteria for international marketing and sales personnel previously detailed in Chapter 17 are applicable in selecting negotiators as well. Traits such as maturity, emotional stability, breadth of knowledge, optimism, flexibility, empathy, and stamina are all important, not only for marketing executives involved in international negotiations but also for the technical experts who often accompany and support them. In studies conducted at Ford Motor Company and AT&T, three additional traits were found to be important predictors of negotiator success with international clients and partners: willingness to use team assistance, listening skills, and influence at headquarters.

[28]Noriko Yagi and Jill Kleinberg, "Boundary Work: An Interpretive Ethnographic Perspective on Negotiating and Leveraging Cross-Cultural Identity," *Journal of International Business Studies* 42, no. 5 (2011), pp. 629–53.

[29]C. Leonidou, Constantine S. Katsikeas, and John Hadjimarcou, "Building Successful Export Business Relationships," *Journal of International Marketing*, January 1, 2002, pp. 96–101.

Willingness to use team assistance is particularly important for American negotiators. Because of a cultural heritage of independence and individualism, Americans often make the mistake of going it alone against greater numbers of foreigners. One American sitting across the negotiation table from three or four Chinese negotiators is unfortunately an all too common sight. The number of brains in the room does make a difference. Moreover, business negotiations are social processes, and the social reality is that a larger number of nodding heads can exercise greater influence than even the best arguments. It is also much easier to gather detailed information when teams are negotiating rather than individuals. For example, the Japanese are quite good at bringing along junior executives for the dual purposes of careful note taking and training via observation. Compensation schemes that overly emphasize individual performance can also get in the way of team negotiating—a negotiation team requires a split commission, which many Americans naturally eschew. Finally, negotiators may have to request the accompaniment of senior executives to better match up with client's and partner's negotiation teams. Particularly in relationship-oriented cultures, rank speaks quite loudly in both persuasion and the demonstration of interest in the business relationship.

The single most important activity of negotiations is listening.[30] The negotiator's primary job is collecting information with the goal of enhancing creativity. This goal may mean assigning one team member the sole responsibility of taking careful notes and not worrying about speaking during the meetings. It may also mean that knowing the language[31] of clients and partners will be crucial for the most complete understanding of their needs and preferences. The importance of listening skills in international business negotiations cannot be overstated.

Women can get the job done. Here U.S. Secretary of State Hillary Clinton meets with German Chancellor Angela Merkel.

Bringing along a senior executive is important because influence at headquarters is crucial to success. Indeed, many experienced international negotiators argue that half the negotiation is with headquarters. The representatives' lament goes something like this: "The better I understand my customer, the tougher time I have with headquarters." Of course, this misery associated with boundary-spanning roles is precisely why international negotiators and sales executives make so much money.

Finally, it is also important to reiterate a point made in Chapter 5: Gender should not be used as a selection criterion for international negotiation teams, despite the great differences in the roles of women across cultures. Even in countries where women do not participate in management, American female negotiators are treated as foreigners first. For obvious reasons it may not be appropriate for female managers to participate in some forms of business entertainment—common baths in locker rooms at Japanese golf course clubhouses, for example. However, it is still important for female executives to establish personal rapport at restaurants and other informal settings. Indeed, one expert on cross-gender communication suggests that women may actually have some advantages in international negotiations:

In general, women are more comfortable talking one-on-one. The situation of speaking up in a meeting is a lot closer to boys' experience of using language to establish their position in a large group than it is to girls' experience of using language to maintain intimacy. That's something that can be exploited. Don't wait for the meeting; try to make your point in advance, one-to-one. This is what the Japanese do, and in many ways American women's style is a lot closer to the Japanese style than to American men's.[32]

[30]Donald J. Lund, Lisa K. Scheer, and Irina V. Kozlenkova, "Culture's Impact on the Importance of Fairness in Interorganizational Relationships," *Journal of International Marketing* 21, no. 3 (2013), pp. 21–43.

[31]Helene Tenzer, Markus Pudelko, and Anne-Wil Harzing, "The Impact of Language Barriers on Trust Formation in Multinational Teams," *Journal of International Business Studies* 43 (2012), pp. 591–613; Christian Troster and Daan van Knippenberg, "Leader Openness, Nationality Dissimilarity, and Voice in Multinational Management Teams," *Journal of International Business Studies* 43 (2012) pp. 591–613; Stefan Volk, Tine Kohler, and Markus Pudelko, "Brain Drain: The Cognitive Neuroscience of Foreign Language Processing in Multinational Corporations," *Journal of International Busniess Studies* 45 (2014), pp. 862–85.

[32]Deborah Tannen, *You Just Don't Understand: Men and Women in Conversation* (New York: William Morrow, 1990).

Negotiation Preliminaries

Many companies in the United States provide employees with negotiations training.[33] For example, through his training programs, Chester Karrass[34] has taught more people (some 400,000) to negotiate than any other purveyor of the service[35]—notice his ads in almost all in-flight magazines of domestic U.S. air carriers. However, very few companies provide training for negotiations with managers from other countries. Even more surprising is the lack of cultural content in the training of the government's diplomats. Instead, in most schools of diplomacy the curricula cover language skills, social and diplomatic skills, and knowledge specific to the diplomatic profession, including diplomatic history and international relations, law, economics, politics, international organizations, and foreign policies. Cultural differences in negotiation and communication styles are seldom considered.

Things are different at Ford Motor Company. Ford does more business with Japanese companies than any other firm. Ford owns a part of Mazda, it built a successful mini-van with Nissan, and it buys and sells component parts and completed cars from and to Japanese companies. But perhaps the best measure of Ford's Japanese business is the 8,000 or so U.S.-to-Japan round-trip airline tickets the company buys annually. Ford has made a large investment in training its managers with Japanese responsibilities. More than 2,000 of its executives have attended a three-day program on Japanese history and culture and the company's Japanese business strategies. Furthermore, more than 1,000 Ford managers who work face-to-face with Japanese have attended a three-day program entitled "Managing Negotiations: Japan" (MNJ). The MNJ program includes negotiation simulations with videotape feedback, lectures with cultural differences demonstrated via videotapes of Japanese–American interactions, and rehearsals of upcoming negotiations. The company also conducts similar programs on Korea and the People's Republic of China.

In addition to MNJ, the broader Japan training efforts at Ford must be credited for Ford's successes in Japan. Certainly, MNJ alumni can be seen exercising influence across and up the ranks regarding Japanese relationships. But the organizational awareness of the cultural dimensions of the Japanese business system was quickly raised as well by its broader, three-day program on Japanese business strategies. Remember the story about the Russians in Nice? Two critical events took place. First, the Solar Turbines negotiators diagnosed the problem. Second, and equally important, their California superiors appreciated the problem and approved the investments in time and money to outwait the Russians. So it is that the Ford programs have targeted not only the negotiators working directly with the Japanese but also their managers, who spend most of their time in the company's Detroit headquarters. Negotiators need information specific to the cultures in which they work. Just as critical, their managers back in the United States need a basic awareness of and appreciation for the importance of culture in international business so that they will be more amenable to the "odd-sounding" recommendations coming from their people in Moscow, Rio, or Tokyo.

Any experienced business negotiator will tell you that there is never enough time to get ready. Given the time constraints of international negotiations, preparations must be accomplished efficiently—the homework must be done before the bargaining begins.[36] We recommend the following checklist to ensure proper preparation and planning for international negotiations:

1. Assessment of the situation and the people
2. Facts to confirm during the negotiation

[33]The Harvard Program on Negotiations provides a range of negotiations courses (http://www.pon.harvard.edu). Also, negotiations courses are the most popular in MBA programs around the country; see Leigh Thompson and Geoffrey J. Leonardelli, "Why Negotiation Is the Most Popular Business Course," *Ivey Business Journal* (Online), July/August 2004, p. 1.

[34]See Karrass's website for information regarding his programs: http://www.karrass.com. A key portal with information on negotiations in 50 different countries and links to several associated websites is http://www.GlobalNegotiationResources.com.

[35]Lee Edison provides an interesting description of what he calls "The Negotiation Industry," in an article he wrote for *Across the Board* 37, no. 4 (April 2000), pp. 14–20. Other commentators on training for international business negotiators include Yeang Soo Ching, "Putting a Human Face on Globalization," *New Straits Times*, January 16, 2000, p. 10; A. J. Vogl, "Negotiation: The Advanced Course," *Across the Board*, April 1, 2000, p. 21; and R. V. Veera, "MIT Preparing Students for New Millennium," *New Straits Times*, July 21, 2002, p. 5.

[36]Steven E. Weiss, "Negotiating the Renault–Nissan Alliance: Insights from Renault's Experience," in *Negotiation and Persuasion*, Michael Benoliel, ed. (Singapore: World Scientific Publishing, 2011).

En los negocios no se consigue lo que se merece, se consigue lo que se negocia.

Ahora, más que nunca, la gente de éxito acude a Karrass.

La revista **Forbes** lo dijo en pocas palabras: "Claro, hay docenas de tipos –demasiados– que corren de acá para allá dando cursos, pero la lista de clientes de Karrass es de otra casta: Mobil, General Motors, Ford, IBM, General Electric, Arco, Shell, ITT, Phillips Petroleum, –9 de las 15 empresas más grandes de los Estados Unidos –y 140 más." Añadió **Forbes:**

Kaiser Aluminum & Chemical, que gastó en el transcurso de varios años, cerca de $15,000 dólares en cursos de Karrass, pidió que sus empleados identificaran ahorros específicos logrados al negociar mejor. El total sumó millones de dólares. Un ejecutivo de ventas de Boeing dijo lo mismo acerca de una sola negociación en el Medio Oriente. En General Electric, reconocida por sus programas internos de capacitación, el 90 por ciento de los empleados se

Dr. Chester L. Karrass

Continúa en la siguiente página

Through his books and training courses, Chester Karrass has taught more people to negotiate than anyone else in the world. His firm offers seminars in dozens of countries and advertises in in-flight magazines, here in Spanish.

3. Agenda

4. Best alternative to a negotiated agreement (BATNA)[37]

5. Concession strategies

6. Team assignments

Preparation and planning skill is at the top of almost everyone's list of negotiator traits, yet it seems many Americans are still planning strategies during over-ocean flights when they should be trying to rest. Quick wits are important in business negotiations, and arduous travel schedules and jet lag dull even the sharpest minds. Obviously, information about the other side's goals and preferences should be sought ahead of time. Also important are clear directions from headquarters and detailed information about market conditions.

No matter how thorough the preliminary research, negotiators should always make a list of key facts to reconfirm at the negotiation table. Information gathered about foreign customers (and their networks)[38] and markets almost always includes errors, and things can change during those long airline flights. Next, anticipate that managers from other cultures may put less emphasis on a detailed agenda, but having one to propose still makes sense and helps organize the meetings.

The most important idea in *Getting to Yes* is the notion of the **best alternative to a negotiated agreement (BATNA)**.[39] This notion is how power in negotiations is best measured. Even the smallest companies can possess great power in negotiations if they have many good alternatives and their large-company counterparts do not. It is also important to plan out and write down concession strategies. Concessions can often snowball, and writing them down ahead of time helps negotiators keep them under control.

Finally, specific team assignments should be made clear—who handles technical details, who takes notes, who plays the tough guy, who does most of the talking for the group, and so forth. Also, in relationship-oriented cultures, the selection of intermediaries and the seniority of negotiators will be crucial considerations.

At least seven aspects of the negotiation setting should be manipulated ahead of time if possible:

1. Location

2. Physical arrangements

3. Number of parties

4. Number of participants

5. Audiences (news media, competitors, fellow vendors, etc.)

6. Communications channels

7. Time limits

Location speaks loudly about power relations. Traveling to a negotiating counterpart's home turf is a big disadvantage, and not just because of the costs of travel in money and fatigue. A neutral location may be preferred—indeed, many trans-Pacific business negotiations are conducted in Hawaii. The weather and golf are nice, and the jet lag is about equal.

---

[37]The most instructive story we have ever seen regarding how to build one's BATNA is found in Daniel Michael, "In Clandestine World of Airplane Contracts, An Inside Look at a Deal," *The Wall Street Journal*, March 10, 2003, p. A1. It is a must-read for anyone interested in the topic of international business negotiations.

[38]James Nebus and Carlos Rufin, "Extending the Bargaining Power Model: Explaining Bargaining Outcomes among Nations, MNEs, and NGOs," *Journal of International Business Studies* 41, no. 6 (2010), pp. 996–1015.

[39]Fisher, Ury, and Patton, *Getting to Yes*.

Different negotiation settings have different advantages and disadvantages. Of course, teleconferencing saves money, but meetings tend to be rushed. Golf course negotiations are perhaps the most leisurely, but thoughtful responses are more likely as golfers can consider reactions to statements made at the tee as they chase down their errant shots. E-mail also allows for thoughtful reactions in a similar way. Here an executive "negotiates" a putt at China's first golf course, the Chuan Shan Hot Spring Golf Club.

Location is also an important consideration because it may determine legal jurisdiction if disputes arise. If you must travel to your negotiating counterpart's city, then a useful tactic is to invite clients or partners to work in a meeting room at your hotel. You can certainly get more done if they are away from the distractions of their offices.

Physical arrangements can affect cooperativeness in subtle ways. In high-context cultures, the physical arrangements of rooms can be quite a source of embarrassment and irritation if handled improperly. To the detriment of their foreign business relationships, Americans tend to be casual about such arrangements. Furthermore, views about who should attend negotiations vary across cultures. Americans tend to want to get everyone together to "hammer out an agreement" even if opinions and positions are divergent. Japanese prefer to talk to everyone separately, then, once everyone agrees, to schedule inclusive meetings. Russians tend toward a cumulative approach, meeting with one party and reaching an agreement, then both parties calling on a third party, and so on. In addition, the importance of not being outnumbered in international business negotiations has already been mentioned.

Audiences can have crucial influences on negotiation processes. Purchasing executives at PetroBras, the Brazilian national oil company, are well known for putting competitive bidders in rooms adjacent to one another to increase competitive pressures on both vendors. Likewise, news leaks to the press played a crucial role in pushing along the negotiations between General Motors and Toyota regarding a joint venture production agreement.

As electronic media become more available, efficient, and sometimes necessary (e.g., the war in Iraq or the SARS outbreak mentioned in Chapter 17), more business can be conducted without face-to-face communication. However, Americans should recognize that their counterparts in many other countries do not necessarily share their attraction to the Internet[40] and teleconferencing.[41] Indeed, recent research has shown that when using e-mail, trust is harder to build.[42] Additionally, businesspeople in Hong Kong tend to negotiate more competitively when using e-mail than in face-to-face settings.[43] A conversation

[40]Jan M. Uljn, Andreas Lincke, and Yunus Karakaya, "Non-Face-to-Face International Business Negotiation: How Is National Culture Reflected in This Medium," *IEEE Transactions on Professional Communication* 44, no. 2 (June 2001), pp. 126–37.

[41]Tim Ambler and Chris Styles, *The Silk Road to International Marketing* (London: Financial Times and Prentice Hall, 2000).

[42]Charles E. Naquin and Gaylen D. Paulson, "Online Bargaining and Interpersonal Trust," *Journal of Applied Psychology* 88, no. 1 (2003), pp. 113–20.

[43]Guang Yang, "The Impact of Computer-Mediated Communication on the Processes and Outcomes of Buyer–Seller Negotiations," unpublished doctoral dissertation, Merage School of Business, University of California, Irvine, 2003.

CROSSING BORDERS 19.2 — The Digital Impact on International Negotiations

All in all, e-commerce is good for global marketing. It allows domestic firms to internationalize more quickly and at less cost. It allows international firms to communicate internally and externally with greater efficiency. Fax replaced telex, which, in turn, replaced the telegram. But e-mail is only partly replacing mail, fax, and phone. It is better seen as a different, more informal medium than fax and more convenient than phone. For networking purposes, e-mail is easily copied and relayed, though excess should be avoided. Many of us have learned to screen out e-mails addressed to multiple recipients.

Above all, e-mail can nurture, but not create, the long-term relationships so crucial to international marketing. The decision by Boeing to enter into an automated relationship with Dell was made not by two machines but by

personal contact between executives on both sides. The success of the Procter & Gamble–Walmart relationship rests with the personal relationships and interactions between P&G's key account team and Walmart's buyers. Although non-Thais can learn a great deal about Thailand from the Internet, they can never really understand Thai customers, the way they do business, and their feelings toward products unless they interact directly. Understanding culture requires personal experiential learning, the wellspring of social information.

Sources: Reprinted with permission from Tim Ambler and Chris Styles, *The Silk Road to International Marketing* (London: Financial Times and Prentice Hall, 2000); Guang Yang, *The Impact of Computer Mediated Communication on the Process and Outcomes of Buyer–Seller Negotiations*, unpublished doctoral dissertation, Merage School of Business, University of California, Irvine, 2003.

over a long dinner may actually be the most efficient way to communicate with clients and partners in places like Mexico, Malaysia, and China.

Finally, it is important to manipulate time limits. Recall the example about the Russians and Americans in Nice. The patience of the home office may be indispensable, and major differences in time orientation should be planned for when business negotiations are conducted in most other countries.

At the Negotiation Table

LO8

Managing all aspects of the negotiation process

The most difficult aspect of international business negotiations is the actual conduct of the face-to-face meeting. Assuming that the best representatives have been chosen, and assuming those representatives are well prepared and that situational factors have been manipulated in one's favor, things can still go sour at the negotiation table. Obviously, if these other preliminaries have not been managed properly, things will go wrong during the meetings. Even with great care and attention to preliminary details, managing the dynamics of the negotiation process is almost always the greatest challenge facing Americans seeking to do business in other countries.

Going into a business negotiation, most people have expectations about the "proper" or normal process of such a meeting, the *ritual*, so to speak.[44] Based on these expectations, progress is measured and appropriate bargaining strategies are selected. That is, things may be done differently in the latter stages of a negotiation than they were in the earlier. Higher-risk strategies may be employed to conclude talks—as in the final two minutes of a close soccer match. But all such decisions about strategy are made relative to perceptions of progress through an expected course of events.

Differences in the expectations held by parties from different cultures are one of the major difficulties in any international business negotiation. Before these differences are discussed, however, it is important to point out similarities. Everywhere around the world we have found that business negotiations proceed through four stages:

1. Nontask sounding
2. Task-related exchange of information
3. Persuasion
4. Concessions and agreement

[44]Sometimes these expectations are referred to as "the spirit of the deal" or the "social contract." See Ron S. Fortgang, David A. Lax, and James K. Sebenius, "Negotiating the Spirit of the Deal," *Harvard Business Review*, January–February 2003, pp. 66–74.

Exhibit 19.4
Summary of Japanese, American, and Chinese Business Negotiation Styles

Category	Japanese	Americans	Chinese
Language	Most Japanese executives understand English, though interpreters are often used.	Americans have less time to formulate answers and observe Japanese nonverbal responses because of a lack of knowledge of Japanese.	Often Chinese negotiators will understand at least some English, but will prefer an interpreter.
Nonverbal behaviors	The Japanese interpersonal communication style includes less eye contact, fewer negative facial expressions, and more periods of silence.	American businesspeople tend to "fill" silent periods with arguments or concessions.	Similar in quantities to Americans in most respects, yet difficult to read.
Values	Indirectness and face saving are important. Vertical buyer–seller relationships, with sellers depending on goodwill of buyers *(amae)*, is typical.	Speaking one's mind is important; buyer–seller relationships are horizontal.	Relationship-oriented, *guanxi*, and face are key, looking for a "way" to compromise, truth is secondary.
Four Stages of Business Negotiations			
1. Nontask sounding	Considerable time and expense devoted to such efforts is the practice in Japan.	Very short periods are typical.	Long, expensive, formal, intermediaries are key.
2. Task-related exchange of information	The most important step: High first offers with long explanations and in-depth clarifications.	Information is given briefly and directly. "Fair" first offers are more typical.	Indirectness, explanations first, intermediaries.
3. Persuasion	Persuasion is accomplished primarily behind the scenes. Vertical status relations dictate bargaining outcomes.	The most important step: Minds are changed at the negotiation table, and aggressive persuasive tactics are often used.	Questions, competing offers, delays.
4. Concessions and agreement	Concessions are made only toward the end of negotiations—a holistic approach to decision making. Progress is difficult to measure for Americans.	Concessions and commitments are made throughout—a sequential approach to decision making.	Holistic approach, revisiting closed issues, goal is long-term relationship. Progress is difficult to measure for Americans.

Sources: N. Mark Lam and John L. Graham, *China Now, Doing Business in the World's Most Dynamic Market* (New York: McGraw-Hill, 2007); James Day Hodgson, Yoshihiro Sano, and John L. Graham, *Doing Business with the New Japan* (Boulder, CO: Rowman & Littlefield, 2008).

The first stage, nontask sounding, includes all those activities that might be described as establishing rapport or getting to know one another,[45] but it does not include information related to the "business" of the meeting. The information exchanged in the second stage of business negotiations regards the parties' needs and preferences. The third stage, persuasion, involves the parties' attempts to modify one another's needs and preferences through the use of various persuasive tactics. The final stage of business negotiations involves the consummation of an agreement, which is often the summation of a series of concessions or smaller agreements.

Despite the consistency of this process across diverse cultures, the content and duration of the four stages differ substantially. For example, Exhibit 19.4 details procedural differences in Japan, the United States, and China as well as differences in language, nonverbal behavior, and values.

Nontask Sounding.   Americans always discuss topics other than business at the negotiation table (e.g., the weather, family, sports, politics, business conditions in general) but not for long. Usually the discussion is moved to the specific business at hand after 5 to 10 minutes. Such preliminary talk, known as nontask sounding, is much more than just friendly or polite; it helps negotiators learn how the other side feels that particular day.

[45] Bradely R. Barnes, Leonidas C. Leonidou, Noel Y. M. Siu, and Constantinos N. Leonidou, "Interpersonal Factors As Drivers of Quality and Performance in Western-Hong Kong Inter-Organizational Relationships," *Journal of International Marketing*, 2014, in press; Martin R. Haas and Jonathon N. Cummings, "Barriers to Knowledge Seeking within MNC Teams: Which Differences Matter Most?" *Journal of International Business Studies*, 2014, online.

During nontask sounding, one can determine if a client's attention is focused on business or distracted by other matters, personal or professional.

Learning about a client's background and interests also provides important cues about appropriate communication styles. To the extent that people's backgrounds are similar, communication can be more efficient. Engineers can use technical jargon when talking to other engineers. Sports enthusiasts can use sports analogies. Those with children can compare the cash drain of "putting a kid through college," and so on.

During these initial stages of conversation, judgments, too, are made about the "kind" of person(s) with whom one is dealing: Can this person be trusted?[46] Will he be reliable? How much power does she have in her organization? All such judgments are made before business discussions ever begin.

These preliminary nontask discussions have a definite purpose. Although most people are often unaware of it, such time almost always is used to size up one's clients. Depending on the results of this process, proposals and arguments are formed using different jargon and analogies. Or if clients are distracted by other personal matters or if the other people seem untrustworthy, the decision may be to discuss no business at all. This assessment sounds like a lot to accomplish in 5 to 10 minutes, but that's how long it usually takes in the information-oriented United States. Such is not the case in relationship-oriented countries like China or Brazil; the goals of the nontask sounding are identical, but the time spent is much, much longer. Instead of five minutes, it might take five meetings. Indeed, this is why the Japanese government maintains generous tax deductions for business entertainment.[47]

In the United States, firms resort to the legal system and their lawyers when they've made a bad deal because of a mistake in sizing up a customer or vendor. In most other countries, the legal system cannot be depended upon for such purposes. Instead, executives in places like Korea and Egypt spend substantial time and effort in nontask sounding so that problems do not develop later. Americans need to reconsider, from the foreigner's perspective, the importance of this first stage of negotiations if they hope to succeed in Seoul or Cairo.

Task-Related Exchange of Information.   Only when nontask sounding is complete and a trusting personal relationship[48] is established should business be introduced. American executives are advised to let foreign counterparts decide when such substantive negotiations should begin, that is, to let them bring up business.

A task-related information exchange implies a two-way communication process. However, observations suggest that when Americans meet executives from some cultures across the negotiation table, the information flow is unidirectional. Japanese, Chinese, and Russian negotiators all appear to ask "thousands" of questions and give little feedback. The barrage of questions severely tests American negotiators' patience, and the lack of feedback causes them great anxiety. Both can add up to much longer stays in these countries, which means higher travel expenses.

---

[46]Trust is a key negotiation concept that is receiving growing attention in diverse areas. See Alaka N. Rao, Jone L. Pearce, and Katherine Xin, "Governments, Reciprocal Exchange, and Trust among Business Associates," *Journal of International Business Studies* 36, no. 1 (2005), pp. 104–18; on the chemical basis of trust, see Michael Kosfeld, Markus Heinrichs, Paul J. Zak, Urs Fischbacher, and Ernst Fehr, "Oxytocin Increases Trust in Humans," *Nature* 435 (June 2005), pp. 673–76; Lai Si Tsui-Auch and Guido Mollering, "Wary Managers: Unfavorable Environments, Perceived Vulnerability, and the Development of Trust in Foreign Enterprises in China," *Journal of International Business Studies* 41, no. 6 (2010), pp. 1016–35; Jeffrey H. Dyer and Wujin Chu, "The Determinants of Trust in Supplier-Automaker Relationships in the U.S., Japan, and Korea," *Journal of International Business Studies* 42, no. 1 (2011), pp. 10–27, 28–34; John Paul McDuffie, "Inter-Organizational Trust and the Dynamics of Distrust," *Journal of International Business Studies* 42, no. 1 (2011), pp. 35–47; Akbar Zaheer and Darcy Fudge Kamal, "Creating Trust in Piranha-Infested Waters: The Confluence of Supplier and Host Country Contexts," *Journal of International Business Studies* 42, no. 1 (2011), pp. 48–55; Crystal X. Jiang, Roy Y.J. Chua, Masaaki Kotabe, and Janet Y. Murray, "Effects of Cultural Ethnicity, Firm Size, and Firm Age on Senior Executive Trust in Their Overseas Business Partners: Evidence from China," *Journal of International Business Studies* 42, no. 9 (2011), pp. 1150–73.

[47]"Kanpai!" *The Economist*, December 14, 2013, p. 80.

[48]Andreas Engelen, Fritz Lackhoff, and Susanne Schmidt, "How Can Chief Marketing Officers Strengthen Their Influence? A Social Capital Perspective Across Six Country Groups," *Journal of International Marketing* 21, no. 4 (2013), pp. 88–109.

CROSSING BORDERS 19.3   Fishing for Business in Brazil

How important is nontask sounding? Consider this description about an American banker's meeting in Brazil, as recounted by an observer:

Introductions were made. The talk began with the usual "How do you like Rio?" questions—Have you been to Ipanema, Copacabana, Corcovado, etc.? There was also talk about the flight down from New York. After about five minutes of this chatting, the senior American quite conspicuously glanced at his watch, and then asked his client what he knew about the bank's new services.

"A little," responded the Brazilian. The senior American whipped a brochure out of his briefcase, opened it on the desk in front of the client, and began his sales pitch.

After about three minutes of "fewer forms, electronic transfers, and reducing accounts receivables," the Brazilian jumped back in, "Yes, that should make us more competitive . . . and competition is important here in Brazil. In fact, have you been following the World Cup *fútbol* (soccer) matches recently? Great games." And so the reel began to whir, paying out that monofilament line, right there in that hot high-rise office.

After a few minutes' dissertation on the local *fútbol* teams, Pélé, and why *fútbol* isn't popular in the United States, the American started to try to crank the Brazilian back in. The first signal was the long look at his watch, then the interruption, "Perhaps we can get back to the new services we have to offer."

The Brazilian did get reeled back into the subject of the sale for a couple of minutes, but then the reel started to sing again. This time he went from efficient banking transactions to the nuances of the Brazilian financial system to the Brazilian economy. Pretty soon we were all talking about the world economy and making predictions about the U.S. presidential elections.

Another look at his Rolex, and the American started this little "sport fishing" ritual all over again. From my perspective (I wasn't investing time and money toward the success of this activity), this all seemed pretty funny. Every time the American VP looked at his watch during the next 45 minutes, I had to bite my cheeks to keep from laughing out loud. He never did get to page two of his brochure. The Brazilian just wasn't interested in talking business with someone he didn't know pretty well.

Source: William Hernandez Requejo and John L. Graham, *Global Negotiation: The New Rules* (New York: Palgrave Macmillan, 2009). Reproduced with permission of Palgrave Macmillan.

Certainly an excellent negotiation tactic is to "drain" information from one's negotiation counterparts. But the oft-reported behaviors of Chinese, Japanese, and Russians may not necessarily represent a sophisticated negotiation ploy. Indeed, reference to Exhibit 19.2 provides some hints that differences in conversational styles—silent periods occurred more frequently in negotiations in all three cultures—may be part of the explanation. Indeed, in careful studies of conversational patterns of Americans negotiating with Japanese, the Americans seem to fill the silent periods and do most of the talking. These results suggest that American negotiators must take special care to keep their mouths shut and let foreign counterparts give them information.

Exchanging information across language barriers can be quite difficult as well. Most of us understand about 80 to 90 percent of what our same-culture spouses or roommates say—that means 10 to 20 percent is misunderstood or misheard. That latter percentage goes up dramatically when someone is speaking a second language, no matter the fluency levels or length of acquaintance. And when the second language capability is limited, entire conversations may be totally misunderstood. Using multiple communication channels during presentations—writing, exhibits, speaking, repetition—works to minimize the inevitable errors.

In many cultures, negative feedback is very difficult to obtain. In high-context cultures such as Mexico and Japan, speakers are reluctant to voice objections lest they damage the all-important personal relationships. Some languages themselves are by nature indirect and indefinite. English is relatively clear, but translations from languages like Japanese can leave much to be understood. In more collectivistic cultures like China, negotiators may be reluctant to speak for the decision-making group they represent, or they may not even know how the group feels about a particular proposal. All such problems suggest the importance of having natives of customer countries on your negotiation team and of spending extra time in business and informal entertainment settings trying to understand better the information provided by foreign clients and partners. Conversely, low-context German executives often complain that American presentations include too much "fluff"—they are interested in copious information only, not the hyperbole and hedges so common in American speech. Negative feedback from Germans can seem brutally frank to higher-context Americans.

A final point of potential conflict in information exchange has to do with first offers. Price padding varies across cultures, and Americans' first offers tend to come in relatively close to what they really want. "A million dollars is the goal, let's start at $1.2 million" seems about right to most Americans. Implicit in such a first offer is the hope that things will get done quickly. Americans do not expect to move far from first offers. Negotiators in many other countries do not share the goal of finishing quickly, however. In places like China, Brazil, or Spain, the expectation is for a relatively longer period of haggling, and first offers are more aggressive to reflect these expectations. "If the goal is 1 million, we better start at 2," makes sense there. Americans react to such aggressive first offers in one of two ways: They either laugh or get angry. And when foreign counterparts' second offers reflect deep discounts, Americans' ire increases.

A good example of this problem regards an American CEO shopping for a European plant site. When he selected a $20 million plot in Ireland, the Spanish real estate developer he had visited earlier called wondering why the American had not asked for a lower price for the Madrid site before choosing Dublin. He told the Spaniard that his first offer "wasn't even in the ballpark." He wasn't laughing when the Spaniard then offered to beat the Irish price. In fact, the American executive was quite angry. A potentially good deal was forgone because of different expectations about first offers. Yes, numbers were exchanged, but information was not. Aggressive first offers made by foreigners should be met with questions, not anger.

Persuasion.   In Japan, a clear separation does not exist between task-related information exchange and persuasion. The two stages tend to blend together as each side defines and refines its needs and preferences. Much time is spent in the task-related exchange of information, leaving little to "argue" about during the persuasion stage. Conversely, Americans tend to lay their cards on the table and hurry through the information exchange to persuasion. After all, the persuasion is the heart of the matter. Why hold a meeting unless someone's mind is to be changed? A key aspect of sales training in the United States is "handling objections." So the goal in information exchange among Americans is to quickly get those objections out in the open so they can be handled.

This handling can mean providing clients with more information. It can also mean getting mean. As suggested by Exhibit 19.2, Americans make threats and issue warnings in negotiations. They do not use such tactics often, but negotiators in many other cultures use such tactics even less frequently and in different circumstances. For example, notice how infrequently the Mexicans and English-speaking Canadians used threats and warnings in the simulated negotiations. Others have found Filipino and Chinese negotiators to use a less aggressive approach than Americans.[49] Indeed, in Thailand or China, the use of such aggressive negotiation tactics can result in the loss of face and the destruction of important personal relationships. Such tough tactics may be used in Japan but by

You want him on your side! Banana salespeople such as this fellow in Agra, India, are known worldwide for their negotiation skills—they're hawking a perishable product that shows the wear. In Japan they even have a negotiation strategy named for them: Outrageously high first offers are derogated as *"banana no tataki uri,"* the banana sale approach.

---

[49]X. Michael Song, Jinhong Xie, and Barbara Dyer, "Antecedents and Consequences of Marketing Managers' Conflict Handling Procedures," *Journal of Marketing* 64 (January 2000), pp. 50–66; Alma Mintu-Wimsatt and Julie B. Gassenheimer, "The Moderating Effects of Cultural Context in Buyer–Seller Negotiation," *Journal of Personal Selling & Sales Management* 20, no. 1 (Winter 2000), pp. 1–9.

buyers only and usually only in informal circumstances—not at the formal negotiation table. Americans also get angry during negotiations and express emotions that may be completely inappropriate in foreign countries. Such emotional outbursts may be seen as infantile or even barbaric behavior in places like Hong Kong and Bangkok.

The most powerful persuasive tactic is actually asking more questions. Foreign counterparts can be politely asked to explain why they must have delivery in two months or why they must have a 10 percent discount. Chester Karrass, in his still useful book *The Negotiation Game*,[50] suggests that it is "smart to be a little dumb" in business negotiations. Repeat questions; for example, "I didn't completely understand what you meant—can you please explain that again?" If clients or potential business partners have good answers, then perhaps a compromise on the issue is best. Often, however, under close and repeated scrutiny, their answers are not very good. When their weak position is exposed, they are obliged to concede. Questions can elicit key information, the most powerful yet passive persuasive device. Indeed, the use of questions is a favored Japanese tactic, one they use with great effect on Americans.

Third parties and informal channels of communication are the indispensable media of persuasion in many countries, particularly the more relationship-oriented ones. Meetings in restaurants or meetings with references and mutual friends who originally provided introductions may be used to handle difficult problems with partners in other countries. The value of such informal settings and trusted intermediaries is greatest when problems are emotion laden. They provide a means for simultaneously delivering difficult messages and saving face. Although American managers may eschew such "behind the scenes" approaches, they are standard practice in many countries.

Concessions and Agreement.   Comments made previously about the importance of writing down concession-making strategies and understanding differences in decision-making styles—sequential versus holistic—are pertinent here. Americans often make concessions early, expecting foreign counterparts to reciprocate. However, in many cultures no concessions are made until the end of the negotiations. Americans often get frustrated and express anger when foreign clients and partners are simply following a different approach to concession making, one that can also work quite well when both sides understand what is going on.

After Negotiations

LO9

The importance of follow-up communications and procedures

Tung Chee Hwa, at the time Chief Executive of the Hong Kong Special Administrative Region, consummated the deal with the Mouse for Asia's new Walt Disney World, which opened in 2005.

Contracts between American firms are often longer than 100 pages and include carefully worded clauses regarding every aspect of the agreement. American lawyers go to great lengths to protect their companies against all circumstances, contingencies, and actions of the other party. The best contracts are written so tightly that the other party would not think of going to court to challenge any provision. The American adversarial system requires such contracts.

In most other countries, particularly the relationship-oriented ones, legal systems are not depended upon to settle disputes.[51] Indeed, the term *disputes* does not reflect how a business relationship should work. Each side should be concerned about mutual benefits of the relationship and therefore should consider the interests of the other. Consequently, in places like Japan written contracts are very short—two to three pages—are purposely loosely written, and primarily contain comments on principles of the relationship. From the Japanese point of view, the American emphasis on tight contracts is tantamount to planning the divorce before the wedding.

In other relationship-oriented countries, such as China, contracts are more a description of what business partners view their respective responsibilities to be. For complicated business

---

[50]Chester Karrass, *The Negotiation Game* (New York: Crowell, 1970).

[51]Kevin Zheng Zhou and Laura Poppo, "Exchange Hazards, Relational Reliability, and Contracts in China," *Journal of International Business Studies* 41, no. 5 (2010), pp. 861–81; Jagdip Singh, Patrick Lentz, and Edwin J. Nijssen, "First- and Second-Order Effects of Consumer Institutional Logics on Firm–Consumer Relationships: A Cross-Market Comparative Analysis," *Journal of International Business Studies* 42, no. 2 (2011), pp. 307–33.

relationships, they may be quite long and detailed. However, their purpose is different from the American understanding. When circumstances change, then responsibilities must also be adjusted, despite the provisions of the signed contract. The notion of enforcing a contract in China makes little sense.

Informality being a way of life in the United States, even the largest contracts between companies are often sent through the mail for signature. In America, ceremony is considered a waste of time and money. But when a major agreement is reached with foreign companies, their executives may expect a formal signing ceremony involving CEOs of the respective companies. American companies are wise to accommodate such expectations.

Finally, follow-up communications are an important part of business negotiations with partners and clients from most foreign countries. Particularly in high-context cultures, where personal relationships are crucial, high-level executives must stay in touch with their counterparts. Letters, pictures, and mutual visits remain important long after contracts are signed. Indeed, warm relationships at the top often prove to be the best medicine for any problems that may arise in the future.

Inventive International Negotiations

LO10

The basics of inventive international negotiations

Getting to "yes" sometimes isn't good enough. Perhaps the most famous negotiation parable involves an argument over an orange. The most obvious approach was to simply cut it in half, each person getting a fair share. But when the negotiators began talking to each other, exchanging information about their interests, a better solution to the problem became obvious: The person who wanted the orange for juice for breakfast took that part, and the person wanting the rind for making marmalade took that part. Both sides ended up with more. Neither agreement is particularly creative, but the parable of the orange becomes a story about invention when both parties decide to cooperate to plant more orange trees.

Perhaps the two most instructive examples of inventive negotiating involve pairs of American and Japanese companies, even competitors. One of the best international agreements ever struck was the joint venture between General Motors and Toyota for a plant in Fremont, California. Those negotiations, completed in 1984, resulted in a 25-year relationship between two tough global competitors that yielded award-winning innovations in both manufacturing processes and automobile technology. A crucial feature of the talks was the use of a facilitator (in Japanese, *shokai-sha* or *chukai-sha*), from day one and throughout the meetings. This approach is standard operating procedure among the Japanese, but the concept is foreign to U.S. executives, except when deal making has devolved into dispute resolution. Even longer lasting and more fruitful is the relationship negotiated between Boeing and Mitsubishi. Mitsubishi Japanese Zeroes fought air battles with Boeing B-17s during World War II. But in 1953, Boeing established a subsidiary in Japan. In 1960, Emperor Akihito met with William Allen, Boeing's CEO, and by 1969, they signed their first contract. Their continued collaborative efforts have produced many inventive business arrangements: Boeing buys composite plastic wings for its new 787 Dreamliner from Japanese designers and suppliers, then sells the completed 787s back to Japanese airlines, all with a nice subsidy from the Japanese government. Obviously, inventive thinking even after agreements were reached has been a standard feature of Mitsubishi's and Boeing's long-term relationship.

At business schools these days, we are beginning to learn a lot about creative processes. Courses are being offered and dissertations being proffered with "innovation" as the key buzz word, both at academic conferences and in corporate boardrooms. The more we hear about innovation and creative processes, the more we are beginning to appreciate that the Japanese approach to international business negotiations, by nature, uses many of the techniques commonly emphasized in any discussion of inventive processes. Indeed, there appears to be a deeply fundamental explanation for why the Japanese have been able to build such a successful society, despite their lack of natural resources and relative isolation. Japanese society has its own obstacles to invention—hierarchy and collectivism are two. But, they have developed a negotiation style that in many ways obviates such disadvantages. The procedures we advocate herein coincide nicely with an approach to international negotiations that comes naturally to the Japanese.

Exhibit 19.5
How Inventive Negotiation Works

1. Inventive negotiation is older than history, and more advanced than the future – and it's based on the most basic human talent: imagination.

2. It begins with a glimmer of hope, the vision that things can be better—even worldchanging.

3. You have to find just the right partners and sell them on your vision.

4. Then you build relationships—with those on the other side.

5. You create the system that makes these relationships happen.

6. You add exactly the right people in specific situations, including facilitators.

7. You consider culture and encourage diversity.

8. You meet in the right places and the right spaces, at just the right pace.

9. You leverage emotion and overcome power and corruption.

10. You encourage changing roles.

11. You use tools of innovation.

12. And you use the tools of improvisation.

13. You keep improving the relationships in new ways.

14. And even when you think you've created the best outcome possible, you keep using these strategies to create an even better, longer-lasting, and more sustainable outcome.

Source: John L. Graham, Lynda Lawrence, William Hernandez Requejo, *Inventive Negotiation: Getting Beyond Yes* (New York: Palgrave Macmillan, 2014). See also www.InventiveNegotiation.com.

We also must give credit to the luminaries in field who have long advocated invention in negotiations. Howard Raiffa and his colleagues recommend:

> . . . the teams should think and plan together informally and do some joint brainstorming, which can be thought of as "dialoguing" or "prenegotiating." The two sides make no tradeoffs, commitments, or arguments about how to divide the pie at this early stage.[52]

Roger Fisher and William Ury title their Chapter 4 in *Getting to Yes*[53] "Invent[ing] Options for Mutual Gain." David Lax and James Sebenius, in their book, *3D-Negotiations*,[54] go past getting to yes and talk about "creative agreements" and "great agreements." Our goal here is to push these ideas to the forefront in thinking about business negotiations. The field generally is still stuck in the past, talking about "making deals" and "solving problems." Even the use of terms like "win–win" expose the vestiges of the old competitive thinking. Our point is that a business negotiation is not something that can be won or lost, and the competitive metaphor limits invention. The problem-solving metaphor does as well. Accept only creative outcomes!

The ideas listed in Exhibit 19.5 can be used in all stages of international business negotiations: planning, execution, and follow-up. Application of principles of invention will be practically and overtly appropriate in at least three points in your negotiations. We noted Howard Raiffa's suggestion that they be used in pre-negotiation meetings; we also advocate their use when impasses are reached. For example, in the negotiations regarding the multi-billion dollar Rio Urubamba natural gas project in Peru, the involved firms and environmentalist groups reached what at the time seemed to be an irreconcilable difference: Roads and a huge pipeline through the pristine forest would be an ecological disaster. The creative solution? Think of the remote gas field as an offshore platform, run the pipeline underground, build no roads, and fly in personnel and equipment as needed.

After negotiators have "gotten to yes," a scheduled review of the agreement may actually get your business relationship past "yes" to truly inventive outcomes. Perhaps you schedule such a review six months after implementation of the agreement has begun. But the point is that time must be set aside for an *inventive* discussion of how to improve on the

---

[52]Howard Raiffa with John Richardson and David Metcalfe, *Negotiation Analysis* (Cambridge, MA: Belknap, 2002), p. 196.

[53]Fisher, Ury, and Patton, *Getting to Yes*.

[54]David J. Lax and James K. Sebenius, *3D Negotiations* (Boston: Harvard Business School Press, 2006).

business relationship. The emphasis of such a session should always be putting new ideas on the table—answers to the question, "What haven't we thought of?"[55]

Conclusions

Despite the litany of potential pitfalls facing international negotiators, things are getting better. The stereotypes of American managers as "innocents abroad" or cowboys are becoming less accurate. Likewise, we hope it is obvious that the stereotypes of the reticent Japanese or the pushy Brazilian evinced in the chapter may no longer hold so true. Experience levels are going up worldwide, and individual personalities are important. So you can find talkative Japanese, quiet Brazilians, and effective American negotiators. But culture still does, and always will, count. We hope that it is fast becoming the natural behavior of American managers to take culture into account.

English author Rudyard Kipling said some one hundred years ago: "Oh, East is East, and West is West, and never the twain shall meet." Since then most have imbued his words with an undeserved pessimism. Some even wrongly say he was wrong.[56] The problem is that not many have bothered to read his entire poem, *The Ballad of East and West:*

> Oh, East is East, and West is West, and never the twain shall meet,
> Till Earth and Sky stand presently at God's great Judgment Seat;
> But there is neither East nor West, border, nor breed, nor birth,
> When two strong men stand face to face, though they come from the ends of the earth!

The poem can stand some editing for these more modern times. It should include the other directions—North is North and South is South. And the last line properly should read, "When two strong *people* stand face to face." But Kipling's positive sentiment remains. Differences between countries and cultures, no matter how difficult, can be worked out when people talk to each other in face-to-face settings. Kipling rightly places the responsibility for international cooperation not on companies or governments but instead directly on the shoulders of individual managers, present and future, like you. Work hard!

---

[55]More information regarding inventive negotiations can be found at http://www.InventiveNegotiation.com.
[56]Michael Elliot, "Killing off Kipling," *Newsweek*, December 29, 1977, pp. 52–55.

Summary

Because styles of business negotiations vary substantially around the world, it is important to take cultural differences into account when meeting clients, customers, and business partners across the international negotiation table. In addition to cultural factors, negotiators' personalities and backgrounds also influence their behavior. Great care should be taken to get to know the individuals who represent client and customer companies. Cultural stereotypes can be quite misleading.

Four kinds of problems frequently arise during international business negotiations—problems at the levels of language, nonverbal behaviors, values, and thinking and decision-making processes. Foreign-language skills are an essential tool of the international negotiator. Nonverbal behaviors vary dramatically across cultures, and because their influence is often below our level of awareness, problems at this level can be serious. Whereas most Americans value objectivity, competitiveness, equality, and punctuality, many foreign executives may not. As for thinking and decision making, Western business executives tend to address complex negotiations by breaking deals down into smaller issues and settling them

sequentially; in many Eastern cultures, a more holistic approach is used in discussions.

Much care must be taken in selecting negotiation teams to represent companies in meetings with foreigners. Listening skills, influence at headquarters, and a willingness to use team assistance are important negotiator traits. Americans should be careful to try to match foreign negotiation teams in both numbers and seniority. The importance of cross-cultural training and investments in careful preparations cannot be overstated. Situational factors such as the location for meetings and the time allowed must also be carefully considered and managed.

All around the world, business negotiations involve four steps: nontask sounding, task-related information exchange, persuasion, and concessions and agreement. The time spent on each step can vary considerably from country to country. Americans spend little time on nontask sounding or getting to know foreign counterparts. Particularly in relationship-oriented cultures, it is important to let the customers bring up business when they feel comfortable with the personal relationship. Task-related information goes quickly in the United States as well. In other countries, such as Japan, the most time is spent on the second stage, and careful understandings of partners are the focus. Persuasion is the most important part of negotiations from the American perspective. Aggressive persuasive tactics (threats and warnings) are used frequently. Such persuasive tactics, though they may work well in some cultures, will cause serious problems in others. Because Americans tend to be deal oriented, more care will have to be taken in follow-up communications with foreign clients and partners who put more emphasis on long-term business relationships. Finally, a new emphasis is being put in inventive negotiation processes in international commerce.

Key Terms

Stereotypes	Nontask sounding	Task-related	Inventive in
Best alternative to a negotiated		information exchange	negotiations
agreement (BATNA)			

Questions

1. Define the key terms listed above.

2. Why can cultural stereotypes be dangerous? Give some examples.

3. List three ways that culture influences negotiation behavior.

4. Describe the kinds of problems that usually come up during international business negotiations.

5. Why are foreign-language skills important for international negotiators?

6. Describe three cultural differences in nonverbal behaviors and explain how they might cause problems in international business negotiations.

7. Why is time an important consideration in international business negotiations?

8. What can be different about how a Japanese manager might address a complex negotiation compared with an American negotiator?

9. What are the most important considerations in selecting a negotiation team? Give examples.

10. What kinds of training are most useful for international business negotiators?

11. Name three aspects of negotiation situations that might be manipulated before talks begin. Suggest how this manipulation might be done.

12. Explain why Americans spend so little time on nontask sounding and Brazilians so much.

13. Why is it difficult to get negative feedback from counterparts in many foreign countries? Give examples.

14. Why won't getting mad work in Mexico or Japan?

15. Why are questions the most useful persuasive tactic?

16. What is the parable of the orange, and how does it relate to international negotiations?

PART SIX

Country Notebook
THE COUNTRY NOTEBOOK—A GUIDE FOR DEVELOPING A MARKETING PLAN

THE COUNTRY NOTEBOOK OUTLINE

Cultural Analysis

Economic Analysis

Market Audit and Competititve Marlet Analysis

Preliminary Marketing Plan

The first stage in the planning process is a preliminary country analysis. The marketer needs basic information to evaluate a country market's potential, identify problems that would eliminate a country from further consideration, identify aspects of the country's environment that need further study, evaluate the components of the marketing mix for possible adaptation, and develop a strategic marketing plan. One further use of the information collected in the preliminary analysis is as a basis for a country notebook.

Many companies, large and small, have a country notebook for each country in which they do business. The country notebook contains information a marketer should be aware of when making decisions involving a specific country market. As new information is collected, the country notebook is continually updated by the country or product manager. Whenever a marketing decision is made involving a country, the country notebook is the first database consulted. New-product introductions, changes in advertising programs, and other marketing program decisions begin with the country notebook. It also serves as a quick introduction for new personnel assuming responsibility for a country market.

This section presents four separate guidelines for collection and analysis of market data and preparation of a country notebook: (1) guideline for cultural analysis, (2) guideline for economic analysis, (3) guideline for market audit and competitive analysis, and (4) guideline for preliminary marketing plan. These guidelines suggest the kinds of information a marketer can gather to enhance planning.

The points in each of the guidelines are general. They are designed to provide direction to areas to explore for relevant data.

In each guideline, specific points must be adapted to reflect a company's products and/or services. The decision as to the appropriateness of specific data and the depth of coverage depends on company objectives, product characteristics, and the country market. Some points in the guidelines are unimportant for some countries or some products and should be ignored. Preceding chapters of this book provide specific content suggestions for the topics in each guideline.

I. CULTURAL ANALYSIS

The data suggested in the cultural analysis include information that helps the marketer make market planning decisions. However, its application extends beyond product and market analysis to being an important source of information for someone interested in understanding business customs and other important cultural features of the country.

The information in this analysis must be more than a collection of facts. Whoever is responsible for the preparation of this material should attempt to interpret the meaning of cultural information. That is, how does the information help in understanding the effect on the market? For example, the fact that almost all the populations of Italy and Mexico are Catholic is an interesting statistic but not nearly as useful as understanding the effect of Catholicism on values, beliefs, and other aspects of market behavior. Furthermore, even though both countries are predominantly Catholic, the influence of their individual and unique interpretation and practice of Catholicism can result in important differences in market behavior.

Guideline

I. Introduction
   Include short profiles of the company, the product to be exported, and the country with which you wish to trade.
II. Brief discussion of the country's relevant history
III. Geographical setting
   A. Location
   B. Climate
   C. Topography
IV. Social institutions
   A. Family
      1. The nuclear family
      2. The extended family
      3. Dynamics of the family
         a. Parental roles
         b. Marriage and courtship
      4. Female/male roles (changing or static?)
   B. Education
      1. The role of education in society
         a. Primary education (quality, levels of development, etc.)
         b. Secondary education (quality, levels of development, etc.)
         c. Higher education (quality, levels of development, etc.)
      2. Literacy rates
   C. Political system
      1. Political structure
      2. Political parties
      3. Stability of government
      4. Special taxes
      5. Role of local government

   D. Legal system
      1. Organization of the judiciary system
      2. Code, common, socialist, or Islamic-law country?
      3. Participation in patents, trademarks, and other conventions
   E. Social organizations
      1. Group behavior
      2. Social classes
      3. Clubs, other organizations
      4. Race, ethnicity, and subcultures
   F. Business customs and practices
 V. Religion and aesthetics
   A. Religion and other belief systems
      1. Orthodox doctrines and structures
      2. Relationship with the people
      3. Which religions are prominent?
      4. Membership of each religion
      5. Any powerful or influential cults?
   B. Aesthetics
      1. Visual arts (fine arts, plastics, graphics, public art, colors, etc.)
      2. Music
      3. Drama, ballet, and other performing arts
      4. Folklore and relevant symbols
VI. Living conditions
   A. Diet and nutrition
      1. Meat and vegetable consumption rates
      2. Typical meals
      3. Malnutrition rates
      4. Foods available
   B. Housing
      1. Types of housing available
      2. Do most people own or rent?
      3. Do most people live in one-family dwellings or with other families?
   C. Clothing
      1. National dress
      2. Types of clothing worn at work
   D. Recreation, sports, and other leisure activities
      1. Types available and in demand
      2. Percentage of income spent on such activities
   E. Social security
   F. Healthcare
VII. Language
   A. Official language(s)
   B. Spoken versus written language(s)
   C. Dialects
VIII. A Briefing on Negotiation Style (ours and theirs)
 IX. Executive summary
     After completing all of the other sections, prepare a *two-page* (maximum length)
     summary of the major points and place it at the front of the report. The purpose of
     an executive summary is to give the reader a brief glance at the critical points of
     your report. Those aspects of the culture a reader should know to do business in the
     country but would not be expected to know or would find different based on his or
     her SRC should be included in this summary.
  X. Sources of information
 XI. Appendixes

II. ECONOMIC ANALYSIS

The reader may find the data collected for the economic analysis guideline are more straightforward than for the cultural analysis guideline. There are two broad categories of information in this guideline: general economic data that serve as a basis for an evaluation of the economic soundness of a country, and information on channels of distribution and media availability. As mentioned previously, the guideline focuses only on broad categories of data and must be adapted to particular company and product needs.

Guideline

I. Introduction

II. Population
   A. Total
      1. Growth rates
      2. Number of live births
      3. Birthrates
   B. Distribution of population
      1. Age
      2. Sex
      3. Geographic areas (urban, suburban, and rural density and concentration)
      4. Migration rates and patterns
      5. Ethnic groups

III. Economic statistics and activity
   A. Gross national product (GNP or GDP)
      1. Total
      2. Rate of growth (real GNP or GDP)
   B. Personal income per capita
   C. Average family income
   D. Distribution of wealth
      1. Income classes
      2. Proportion of the population in each class
      3. Is the distribution distorted?
   E. Minerals and resources
   F. Surface transportation
      1. Modes
      2. Availability
      3. Usage rates
      4. Ports
   G. Communication systems
      1. Types
      2. Availability
      3. Usage rates
   H. Working conditions
      1. Employer–employee relations
      2. Employee participation
      3. Salaries and benefits
   I. Principal industries
      1. What proportion of the GNP does each industry contribute?
      2. Ratio of private to publicly owned industries
   J. Foreign investment
      1. Opportunities?
      2. Which industries?
   K. International trade statistics
      1. Major exports
         a. Dollar value
         b. Trends
      2. Major imports
         a. Dollar value
         b. Trends

        3. Balance-of-payments situation
          a. Surplus or deficit?
          b. Recent trends
        4. Exchange rates
          a. Single or multiple exchange rates?
          b. Current rate of exchange
          c. Trends
    L. Trade restrictions
        1. Embargoes
        2. Quotas
        3. Import taxes
        4. Tariffs
        5. Licensing
        6. Customs duties
   M. Extent of economic activity not included in cash income activities
        1. Countertrades
          a. Products generally offered for countertrading
          b. Types of countertrades requested (barter, counterpurchase, etc.)
        2. Foreign aid received
   N. Labor force
        1. Size
        2. Unemployment rates
   O. Inflation rates
IV. Developments in science and technology
   A. Current technology available (computers, machinery, tools, etc.)
   B. Percentage of GNP invested in research and development
   C. Technological skills of the labor force and general population
V. Channels of distribution (macro analysis)
This section reports data on all channel middlemen available within the market.
Later, you will select a specific channel as part of your distribution strategy.
   A. Retailers
        1. Number of retailers
        2. Typical size of retail outlets
        3. Customary markup for various classes of goods
        4. Methods of operation (cash/credit)
        5. Scale of operation (large/small)
        6. Role of chain stores, department stores, and specialty shops
   B. Wholesale middlemen
        1. Number and size
        2. Customary markup for various classes of goods
        3. Method of operation (cash/credit)
   C. Import/export agents
   D. Warehousing
   E. Penetration of urban and rural markets
VI. Media
This section reports data on all media available within the country or market.
Later, you will select specific media as part of the promotional mix and strategy.
   A. Availability of media
   B. Costs
        1. Television
        2. Radio
        3. Print
        4. Internet
        5. Other media (cinema, outdoor, etc.)
        6. Social media and
        7. Accordingly.

      C. Agency assistance
      D. Coverage of various media
      E. Percentage of population reached by each medium
   VII. Executive summary
      After completing the research for this report, prepare a two-page (maximum) summary of the major economic points and place it at the front
  VIII. Sources of information
    IX. Appendixes

III. MARKET AUDIT AND COMPETITIVE MARKET ANALYSIS

Of the guidelines presented, this is the most product or brand specific. Information in the other guidelines is general in nature, focusing on product categories, whereas data in this guideline are brand specific and are used to determine competitive market conditions and market potential.

    Two different components of the planning process are reflected in this guideline. Information in Parts I and II, Cultural Analysis and Economic Analysis, serve as the basis for an evaluation of the product or brand in a specific country market. Information in this guideline provides an estimate of market potential and an evaluation of the strengths and weaknesses of competitive marketing efforts. The data generated in this step are used to determine the extent of adaptation of the company's marketing mix necessary for successful market entry and to develop the final step, the action plan.

    The detailed information needed to complete this guideline is not necessarily available without conducting a thorough marketing research investigation. Thus another purpose of this part of the country notebook is to identify the correct questions to ask in a formal market study.

Guideline

    I. Introduction
   II. The product
      A. Evaluate the product as an innovation as it is perceived by the intended market
        1. Relative advantage
        2. Compatibility
        3. Complexity
        4. Trialability
        5. Observability
      B. Major problems and resistances to product acceptance based on the preceding evaluation
  III. The market
      A. Describe the market(s) in which the product is to be sold
        1. Geographical region(s)
        2. Forms of transportation and communication available in that (those) region(s)
        3. Consumer buying habits
          a. Product-use patterns
          b. Product feature preferences
          c. Shopping habits
        4. Distribution of the product
          a. Typical retail outlets
          b. Product sales by other middlemen
        5. Advertising and promotion
          a. Advertising media usually used to reach your target market(s)
          b. Sales promotions customarily used (sampling, coupons, etc.)
        6. Pricing strategy
          a. Customary markups
          b. Types of discounts available
      B. Compare and contrast your product and the competition's product(s)
        1. Competitors' product(s)
          a. Brand name
          b. Features
          c. Package
        2. Competitors' prices

        3. Competitors' promotion and advertising methods
        4. Competitors' distribution channels
    C. Market size
        1. Estimated industry sales for the planning year
        2. Estimated sales for your company for the planning year
    D. Government participation in the marketplace
        1. Agencies that can help you
        2. Regulations you must follow
IV. Executive summary
    Based on your analysis of the market, briefly summarize (two-page maximum) the major problems and opportunities requiring attention in your marketing mix, and place the summary at the front of the report.
V. Sources of information
VI. Appendixes

IV. PRELIMINARY MARKETING PLAN

Information gathered in Guidelines I through III serves as the basis for developing a marketing plan for your product or brand in a target market. How the problems and opportunities that surfaced in the preceding steps are overcome or exploited to produce maximum sales and profits are presented here. The action plan reflects, in your judgment, the most effective means of marketing your product in a country market. Budgets, expected profits and losses, and additional resources necessary to implement the proposed plan are also presented.

Guideline

I. The marketing plan
    A. Marketing objectives
        1. Target market(s) (specific description of the market)
        2. Sales forecast years 1–5
        3. Profit forecast years 1–5
        4. Market penetration and coverage
    B. SWOT Analysis
        1. Strengths
        2. Weaknesses
        3. Opportunities
        4. Threats
    C. Product adaptation or modification—Using the product component model as your guide, indicate how your product can be adapted for the market.
        1. Core component
        2. Packaging component
        3. Support services component
    D. Promotion mix
        1. Advertising
            a. Objectives
            b. Media mix
            c. Message
            d. Costs
        2. Sales promotions
            a. Objectives
            b. Coupons
            c. Premiums
            d. Costs
        3. Personal selling
        4. Other promotional methods
    E. Distribution: From origin to destination
        1. Port selection
            a. Origin port
            b. Destination port

2. Mode selection: Advantages/disadvantages of each mode
   a. Railroads
   b. Air carriers
   c. Ocean carriers
   d. Motor carriers
3. Packing
   a. Marking and labeling regulations
   b. Containerization
   c. Costs
4. Documentation required
   a. Bill of lading
   b. Dock receipt
   c. Air bill
   d. Commercial invoice
   e. Pro forma invoice
   f. Shipper's export declaration
   g. Statement of origin
   h. Special documentation
5. Insurance claims
6. Freight forwarder. If your company does not have a transportation or traffic management department, then consider using a freight forwarder. There are distinct advantages and disadvantages to hiring one.

F. Channels of distribution (micro analysis). This section presents details about the specific types of distribution in your marketing plan.
   1. Retailers
      a. Type and number of retail stores
      b. Retail markups for products in each type of retail store
      c. Methods of operation for each type (cash/credit)
      d. Scale of operation for each type (small/large)
   2. Wholesale middlemen
      a. Type and number of wholesale middlemen
      b. Markup for class of products by each type
      c. Methods of operation for each type (cash/credit)
      d. Scale of operation (small/large)
   3. Import/export agents
   4. Warehousing
      a. Type
      b. Location

G. Price determination
   1. Cost of the shipment of goods
   2. Transportation costs
   3. Handling expenses
      a. Pier charges
      b. Wharfage fees
      c. Loading and unloading charges
   4. Insurance costs
   5. Customs duties
   6. Import taxes and value-added tax
   7. Wholesale and retail markups and discounts
   8. Company's gross margins
   9. Retail price

H. Terms of sale
   1. EX works, FOB, FAS, C&F, CIF
   2. Advantages/disadvantages of each

I. Methods of payment
  1. Cash in advance
  2. Open accounts
  3. Consignment sales
  4. Sight, time, or date drafts
  5. Letters of credit
II. Pro forma financial statements and budgets
  A. Marketing budget
    1. Selling expense
    2. Advertising/promotion expense
    3. Distribution expense
    4. Product cost
    5. Other costs
  B. Pro forma annual profit and loss statement (first year through fifth year)
III. Resource requirements
  A. Finances
  B. Personnel
  C. Production capacity
IV. Executive summary
  After completing the research for this report, prepare a two-page (maximum) summary of the major points of your successful marketing plan, and place it at the front of the report.
V. Sources of information and links to data bases.
VI. Appendixes
  The intricacies of international operations and the complexity of the environment within which the international marketer must operate create an extraordinary demand for information. When operating in foreign markets, the need for thorough information as a substitute for uninformed opinion is equally important as it is in domestic marketing. Sources of information needed to develop the country notebook and answer other marketing questions are discussed in Chapter 8 and its appendix.

Summary

Market-oriented firms build strategic market plans around company objectives, markets, and the competitive environment. Planning for marketing can be complicated even for one country, but when a company is doing business internationally, the problems are multiplied. Company objectives may vary from market to market and from time to time; the structure of international markets also changes periodically and from country to country; and the competitive, governmental, and economic parameters affecting market planning are in a constant state of flux. These variations require international marketing executives to be especially flexible and creative in their approach to strategic marketing planning.

GLOSSARY

a

administered pricing The attempt to establish prices for an entire market through the cooperation of competitors, through national, state, or local governments, or by international agreement. Its legality differs from country to country and from time to time.

aesthetics Philosophically, the creation and appreciation of beauty; collectively, the arts, including folklore, music, drama, and dance.

AFTA ASEAN (Association of Southeast Asian Nations) Free Trade Area; a multinational trade group that evolved from ASEAN. *See* **APEC; ASEAN+3**

agent middlemen In an international transaction, intermediaries who represent the principal (home manufacturer/marketer) rather than themselves; agent middlemen work on commission and arrange for sales in the foreign country but do not take title to the merchandise. *See* **home-country middlemen; merchant-middlemen**

Amsterdam Treaty *See* **Treaty of Amsterdam**

analogy A method of market estimation that assumes that demand for a product develops in much the same way in all countries as comparable economic development occurs in each country.

APEC The Asian-Pacific Economic Cooperation; a forum that meets annually to discuss regional economic development. *See* **AFTA; ASEAN+3**

arbitration A procedure, used as an alternative to **litigation**, in which parties in a dispute may select a disinterested third party or parties as referee to determine the merits of the case and make a judgment that both parties agree to honor.

ASEAN (Association of Southeast Asian Nations) A multinational regional trade group including Brunei, Cambodia, Indonesia, Laos, Malaysia, Myanmar, Philippines, Singapore, Thailand, and Vietnam.

ASEAN+3 A forum for ministers of the Association of Southeast Asian Nations plus ministers from China, Japan, and South Korea. *See* **AFTA; APEC**

b

back translation The process in which a document, such as a questionnaire, or phrase is translated from one language to another and then translated by a second party into the original language. Back translations can be used to verify that the first translation, as of a marketing slogan, has the intended meaning for the targeted audience. *See* **decentering; parallel translation**

balance of payments The system of accounts that records a nation's international financial transactions.

balance of trade The difference in value over a period of time between a country's imports and exports.

barter The direct exchange of goods between two parties in a transaction. *See* **compensation deals; counterpurchase; countertrade**

BATNA Acronym for "best alternative to a negotiated agreement," a notion discussed in *Getting to Yes*, by Fisher, Ury, and Patton.

big emerging markets (BEMs) Used to describe the core group of populous nations that will account for much of the growth in world trade among developing and newly industrialized countries.

bills of exchange A form of international commercial payment drawn by sellers on foreign buyers; in transactions based on bills of exchange, the seller assumes all risk until the actual dollars are received, making them riskier for the seller than **letters of credit.**

bottom-of-the-pyramid markets (BOPM) These consist of the 4 billion people around the world with annual incomes of $1,200 or less per capita. They are not necessarily defined by national borders, but are rather pockets of poverty particularly concentrated in south Asia and sub-Sahara Africa.

bribery The use of funds, usually illegally, to influence decisions made by public employees and government officials. Such payments often range into the millions of dollars in international commerce.

c

capital account The portion of a **balance of payments** statement that shows a record of direct investment, portfolio investment, and short-term capital movements to and from countries.

cartel An arrangement in which various companies producing similar products or services work together to control markets for the goods and services they produce. The Organization of Petroleum Exporting Countries (OPEC) is the best known international cartel.

client followers Companies, often providers of services, that follow companies that first moved into a foreign market; for example, an American insurance company setting up in Mexico to serve a U.S. auto company that had previously opened a factory there.

code law A legal system based on an all-inclusive system of written rules, or codes, of law; generally divided into three separate codes: commercial, civil, and criminal. In the United States, Louisiana is the one state to use code law. *See* **common law**

Commerce Control List (CCL) A directory, organized by a series of **Export Control Classification Numbers,** that indicates U.S. rules for the exportability of items. Exporters must use the list to determine if there are end-use restrictions on certain items, such as uses in nuclear, chemical, and biological weapons, and determine if a product has a dual use—that is, both in commercial and restricted applications. *See* **Export Administration Regulations**

Commerce Country Chart (CCC) A directory of information that a U.S. exporter needs to consult, along with the **Commerce Control List,** to determine if the exporter needs a license to export or reexport a product to a particular destination. *See* **Export Control Classification Number**

common law The body of law based on tradition, past practices, and legal precedents set by courts through interpretations of statutes, legal legislation, and past rulings. Common law, which is used in all states in the United States except Louisiana, uses past decisions to interpret statutes and apply them to present situations. Also known as English law. *See* **code law**

common market An agreement that eliminates all tariffs and other restrictions on internal trade, adopts a set of common external tariffs, and removes all restrictions on the free flow of capital and labor among member nations.

compensation deals Transactions that involve payment in both goods and cash. *See* **barter; counterpurchase; countertrade**

complementary marketing The process by which companies with excess marketing capacity in different countries or with a desire for a broader product line take on additional lines for international distribution; commonly called *piggybacking*.

conciliation A nonbinding agreement between parties to resolve disputes by asking a third party to mediate differences. Also known as *mediation*. *See* **arbitration; litigation**

confiscation The seizing of a company's assets without payment. Prominent examples involving U.S. companies occurred in Cuba and Iran. *See* **domestication; expropriation**

Confusion philosophy The 2,500-year-old teachings of Chinese philosopher, Confucius, still strongly influence cultures in East Asia today. Primary among his teachings were a deep respect for elders, rulers, and husbands.

controllable elements The aspects of trade over which a company has control and influence; they include marketing decisions covering product, price, promotion, distribution, research, and advertising. *See* **uncontrollable elements**

corporate planning The formulation of long-term, generalized goals for an enterprise as a whole. *See* **strategic planning; tactical planning**

counterpurchase A type of **countertrade** in which a seller receives payment in cash but agrees in a contract to buy goods from the buyer for the total monetary amount involved in the first transaction or for a set percentage of that amount; also known as *offset trade*. *See* **barter; compensation deals**

countertrade A type of transaction in which goods are imported and sold by a company from a country in exchange for the right or ability to manufacture and/or sell goods in that country. Countertrade can substitute for cash entirely or partially and is used extensively in trade between U.S. firms and the former Soviet bloc, along with other emerging markets. *See* **barter; compensation deals; counterpurchase**

countervailing duty A fee that may, under **World Trade Organization** rules, be imposed on foreign goods benefiting from subsidies, whether in production, export, or transportation; may be applied in conjunction with *minimum access volume,* which restricts the amount of goods a country will import.

cultural borrowing The phenomenon by which societies learn from other cultures' ways and borrow ideas to solve problems or improve conditions.

cultural congruence A marketing strategy in which products are marketed in a way similar to the marketing of products already in the market in a manner as congruent as possible with existing cultural norms.

cultural elective *See* **elective**

cultural exclusive *See* **exclusive**

cultural imperative *See* **imperative**

cultural sensitivity An awareness of the nuances of culture so that a culture can be viewed objectively, evaluated, and appreciated; an important part of foreign marketing.

cultural values The system of beliefs and customs held by a population in a given *culture*. A book by Geert Hofstede describes a study of 66 nations and divides the cultural values of those nations into four primary dimensions: the Individualized/Collectivism Index, the Power Distance Index, the Uncertainty Avoidance Index, and the Masculinity/Femininity Index (which is not considered as useful as the other three).

culture The human-made part of human environment—the sum total of knowledge, beliefs, arts, morals, laws, customs, and any other capabilities and habits acquired by humans as members of society.

current account The portion of a **balance of payments** statement that shows a record of all merchandise exports, imports, and services, plus unilateral transfers of funds.

customs-privileged facilities Areas, as in international transactions, where goods can be imported for storage and/or processing with tariffs and quota limits postponed until the products leave the designated areas. *See* **foreign-trade zones**

customs union A stage in economic cooperation that benefits from a *free trade area*'s reduced or eliminated internal tariffs and adds a common external tariff on products imported from countries outside the union. *See* **common market; political union**

cybersquatters Persons or businesses that buy, usually for a nominal fee, and register as website names descriptive nouns, celebrity names, variations on company trademarks, geographic and ethnic group names, and pharmaceutical and other descriptors and then hold them until they can be sold at an inflated price. Sometimes called *CSQ*.

d

dealers The middlemen selling industrial goods or durable goods directly to customers; their actions are the last steps in the **distribution channel.**

decentering A method of translation, a variation on **back translation,** that is a successive process of translation and retranslation of a document, such as a questionnaire, each time by a different translator. The two original-language versions are then compared, and if there are differences, the process is repeated until the second original-language version is the same as the first. *See* **parallel translation**

derived demand Demand that is dependent on another source; it can be fundamental to the success of efforts to sell capital equipment and big-ticket industrial services. For example, the demand for commercial airliners is derived from the demand for air travel.

diffusion (of innovations) The adoption or spread of products across markets by increasing numbers of consumers.

direct exporting The type of exporting in which a company sells to a customer in another country. *See* **indirect exporting**

distribution channels The various routes through which marketers must negotiate their goods to deliver them to the consumer. Distribution channel structures range from those with little developed marketing infrastructure, as found in many emerging markets, to those with highly complex, multilayered systems, as found in Japan. Consideration for channel structure involves "the six Cs": cost, capital, control, coverage, character, and continuity.

distribution process   The physical handling of goods, the passage of ownership (title), and—especially important from a marketing viewpoint—the buying and selling negotiations between the producers and middlemen and between middlemen and customers. *See* **distribution structure**

distribution structure   The system, present in every country's market, through which goods pass from producer to user; within the structure are a variety of middlemen. *See* **distribution process**

domestication   A process by which a host country gradually transfers foreign investments to national control and ownership through a series of government decrees mandating local ownership and greater national involvement in company management. *See* **confiscation; expropriation**

domestic environment uncontrollables   Factors in a company's home country over which the company has little or no control or influence. They include political and legal forces, the economic climate, level of technology, competitive forces, and economic forces. *See* **uncontrollable elements**

dumping   An export practice, generally prohibited by laws and subject to penalties and fines, defined by some as the selling of products in foreign markets below the cost of production and by others as the selling of products at below the prices of the same goods in the home market.

e

economic development   Generally, an increase in national production that results in an increase in average per capita gross domestic product.

economic dualism   The coexistence of modern and traditional sectors within an economy, especially as found in less-developed countries.

ELAIN   Export License Application and Information Network; an electronic service that enables authorized exporters to submit license applications via the Internet for all commodities except supercomputers and to all free-world destinations. *See* **ERIC; SNAP; STELA**

elective   A business custom (as in a foreign country) to which adaptation is helpful but not necessary. *See* **exclusive; imperative**

EMU   The Economic and Monetary Union; formed by the **Maastricht Treaty,** which also formed the European Union.

ERIC   Electronic Request for Item Classification; a supplementary service to **ELAIN** that allows an exporter to submit commodity classification requests via the Internet to the Bureau of Export administration. *See* **SNAP; STELA**

European Parliament   The legislative body of the European Union, similar in concept to the U.S. House of Representatives. That is, more populous countries have more representatives.

exclusive   A business custom (as in a foreign country) in which an outsider must not participate. *See* **elective; imperative**

exclusive distribution   A practice in which a company restricts which retailers can carry its product; often used by companies to maintain high retail margins, to maintain the exclusive-quality image of a product, and to encourage retailers to provide extra service to customers.

expatriate   A person living away from his or her own country. In international sales, expatriates from the selling company's home country may be the best choice for the sales force when products are highly technical or when selling requires an extensive knowledge of the company and its product line. *See* **local nationals**

expert opinion   A method of market estimation in which experts are polled for their opinions about market size and growth rates; used particularly in foreign countries that are new to the marketer.

Export Administration Regulations (EAR)   A set of rules issued by the U.S. Department of Commerce, designed to alleviate many of the problems and confusions of exporting; they are intended to speed up the process of granting export licenses by concentrating license control on a list of specific items, most of which involve national security. Exporters must ensure that their trade activities do not violate the provisions of EAR. *See* **Commerce Control List; Export Control Classification Number**

Export Control Classification Number (ECCN)   Under the provisions of the U.S. **Export Administration Regulations (EAR),** a classification number that a U.S. exporter must select for an item to be exported; the number corresponds to a description in the **Commerce Control List,** which indicates the exportability of the item.

export documents   The various items of documentation for an international transaction, as required by the exporting government, by established procedures of foreign trade, and, in some cases, by the importing government.

export management company (EMC)   An important middleman for firms with relatively small international volume or those unwilling to involve their own personnel in the international function. These EMCs range in size from 1 person upward to 100 and handle about 10 percent of the manufactured goods exported. Typically, the EMC becomes an integral part of the marketing operations of its client companies. Working under the names of the manufacturers, the EMC functions as a low-cost, independent marketing department with direct responsibility to the parent firm. The working relationship is so close that customers are often unaware they are not dealing directly with the export department of the company.

export regulations   Restrictions placed by countries on the selling of goods abroad; among reasons they may be imposed are to conserve scarce goods for home consumption and to control the flow of strategic goods actual or potential enemies. *See* **import regulations**

Export Trading Company (ETC) Act   An act allowing producers of similar products in the United States to form an export trading company; the act created a more favorable environment for the formation of joint export ventures, in part by removing antitrust disincentives to trade activities.

expropriation   The seizure of an investment by a government in which some reimbursement is made to the investment owner; often the seized investment becomes nationalized. *See* **confiscation; domestication**

f

factual knowledge   A type of knowledge or understanding of a foreign culture that encompasses different meanings of color, different tastes, and other traits of culture that a marketer can observe and study, anticipate, and absorb. *See* **interpretive knowledge**

FCPA Foreign Corrupt Practices Act. The act prohibits U.S. businesses and their representatives from openly paying bribes to officials or foreign governments, or using middlemen as conduits for a bribe when the U.S. official knows that the middleman's payment will be used for a bribe.

foreign environment uncontrollables Factors in the foreign market over which a business operating in its home country has little or no control or influence. They include political and legal forces, economic climate, geography and infrastructure, level of technology, structure of distribution, and level of technology. *See* **domestic environment uncontrollables**

foreign-trade zones (FTZs) Regions or ports that act as holding areas for goods before quotas or customs duties are applied. In the United States, more than 150 FTZs allow companies to land imported goods for storage or various processing such as cleaning or packaging before the goods are officially brought into the United States or reexported to another country. *See* **customs-privileged facilities**

forfaiting A financing technique that may be used in an international transaction in which the seller makes a one-time arrangement with a bank or other financial institution to take over responsibility for collecting the account receivable.

Four Asian Tigers Refers to Hong Kong, Taiwan, Singapore, and South Korea as they fast achieved affluence in the 1980s and 90s.

franchising A form of **licensing** in which a company (the franchiser) provides a standard package of branded products, systems, and management services to the franchisee, which in foreign markets has market knowledge. Franchising permits flexibility in dealing with local market conditions while providing the parent firm with a degree of control.

free trade area (FTA) A type of regional cooperation that involves an agreement between two or more countries to reduce or eliminate customs duties and nontariff trade barriers among partner countries while members maintain individual tariff schedules for external countries. An FTA requires more cooperation than the arrangement known as the regional cooperation for development.

full-cost pricing A method of pricing based on the view that no unit of a similar product is different from any other unit of a similar product and that each unit must bear its full share of the total fixed and variable cost, whether sold in the home market or abroad. *See* **skimming; variable-cost pricing**

g

GATT General Agreement on Tariffs and Trade; a trade agreement signed by the United States and 22 other countries shortly after World War II. The original agreement provided a process to reduce **tariffs** and created an agency to patrol world trade; the treaty and subsequent meetings have produced agreements significantly reducing tariffs.

global awareness A frame of reference, important to the success of a businessperson, that embodies tolerance of cultural differences and knowledge of cultures, history, world market potential, and global economic, social, and political trends.

global brand The worldwide use of a name, term, sign, symbol (visual or auditory), design, or a combination thereof to identify goods or services of a seller and to differentiate them from those of competitors.

global marketing The performance of business activities designed to plan, price, promote, and direct the flow of a company's goods and services to consumers or users in more than one nation for a profit. The most profound difference between global and domestic marketing involves the orientation of the company toward markets and planning activities around the world.

global marketing concept A perspective encompassing an entire set of country markets, whether the home market and one other country or the home market and 100 other countries, and viewing them as a unit, identifying groups of prospective buyers with similar needs as a global market segment, and developing a market plan that strives for standardization wherever it is effective in cost and cultural terms.

global orientation A means of operating by which a company acts as if all the company's markets in a company's scope of operations (including the domestic market) were approachable as a single global market, with the company standardizing the marketing mix where culturally feasible and cost effective.

gray market (parallel market) When products intended to be sold in one market, exclusively at a particular low price (often a government controlled low price), are sold in a second market (usually illegally) where market prices are higher. Take for example, pharmaceuticals available in Canada at a regulated low price that are then shipped to customers in the United States by Canadian exporters, at prices lower than those set by the companies in the U.S., which reflect the higher costs of FDA approval in the U.S.

green marketing Consideration and concern for the environmental consequences of product formulation, marketing, manufacturing, and packaging.

greenhouse-gas emissions These are gases resulting primarily from the use of fossil fuels that tend to trap heat in the earth's atmosphere and are causal factors in global climate change. The main problem compounds are carbon dioxide, methane, nitrous oxide, and fluorinated gases.

h

home-country middlemen In international transactions, the intermediaries, located in the producer's home country, who provide marketing services from a domestic base; also known as *domestic middlemen*. Home-country middlemen offer advantages for companies with small international sales volume or for those inexperienced in international trade. *See* **agent middlemen; merchant middlemen**

homologation A term used to describe changes in a product that are mandated by local standards for product and service **quality.**

i

imperative A business custom (as in a foreign country) that must be recognized and accommodated. *See* **elective; exclusive**

import jobbers In international transactions, business entities that purchase goods directly from the manufacturer and sell to wholesalers and retailers and to industrial customers.

import regulations Restrictions placed by countries on the sale of goods from outside markets; among the reasons they are imposed are to protect health, conserve foreign exchange, serve as economic reprisals, protect home industry, and provide revenue from tariffs. Exporters to markets under such regulations may have to go through various steps to comply with them. *See* **export regulations**

indirect exporting   The type of exporting in which a company sells to a buyer (an importer or distributor) in the home country; the buyer in turn exports the product.

infrastructure   The collective assortment of capital goods that serve the activities of many industries and support production and marketing.

innovation   An idea perceived as new by a group of people; when applied to a product, an innovation may be something completely new or something that is perceived as new in a given country or culture. *See* **product diffusion**

integrated marketing communications (IMCs)   The collective arrangement of efforts and methods to sell a product or service, including advertising, sales promotions, trade shows, personal selling, direct selling, and public relations.

international marketing   The performance of business activities designed to plan, price, promote, and direct the flow of a company's goods and services to consumers or users in more than one nation for a profit.

international marketing research   The form of **marketing research** involving two additional considerations: (1) the need to communicate information across national boundaries, and (2) the challenge of applying established marketing techniques in the different environments of foreign markets, some of which may be strange or vexing milieus for the marketer.

International Monetary Fund (IMF)   A global institution that, along with the World Bank Group, was created to assist nations in becoming and remaining economically viable.

interpretive knowledge   An ability to understand and to appreciate fully the nuances of different cultural traits and patterns. *See* **factual knowledge**

invention in negotiations   The use of creative processes such as joint brainstorming in informal side-bar negotiations. This assumes a collaborative approach to negotiations rather than a competitive one, and assumes long-term, mutually beneficial commercial and personal relationships are the goal of the negotiation.

Islamic law   The *Shari'ah;* the legal system based on an interpretation of the Koran. Islamic law encompasses religious duties and obligations as well as the secular aspect of law regulating human acts. Among its provisions is a prohibition of the payment of interest.

ISO 9000s   A series of international industrial standards (ISO 9000–9004) originally designed by the International Organization for Standardization to meet the need for product quality assurances in purchasing agreements.

j

joint venture   A partnership of two or more participating companies that join forces to create a separate legal entity. *See* **strategic international alliance**

justice or fairness   One of three principles of ethics (the others are **utilitarian ethics** and **rights of the parties**); it tests an action by asking if the action respects the canons of justice or fairness to all parties involved.

l

Large-Scale Retail Store Law   In Japan competition from large retail stores has been almost totally controlled by *Daitenho*—the Large-Scale Retail Store Law (and its more recent incarnations). Designed to protect small retailers from large intruders into their markets, the law required that any store larger than 5,382 square feet (500 square meters) must have approval from the prefecture government to be "built, expanded, stay open later in the evening, or change the days of the month they must remain closed." All proposals for new "large" stores were first judged by the Ministry of International Trade and Industry (MITI). Then, if all local retailers *unanimously* agreed to the plan, it was swiftly approved. However, without approval at the prefecture level, the plan was returned for clarification and modification, a process that could take several years (10 years was not unheard of) for approval.

Large-Scale Retail Store Location Act   A regulatory act in Japan, implemented under pressure from the United States in 2000; it replaced the protective Large-Scale Retail Store Law and relaxed restrictions on the opening of large retailers near small shops and abolished the mandate on the number of days a store must be closed.

letters of credit   Financing devices that, when opened by a buyer of goods, allow the seller to draw a draft against the bank issuing the credit and receive dollars by presenting proper shipping document. Except for cash in advance, letters of credit afford the seller the greatest degree of protection. *See* **bills of exchange**

licensing   A contractual means by which a company grants patent rights, trademark rights, and the rights to use technology to another company, often in a foreign market; a favored strategy of small and medium-sized companies seeking a foothold in foreign markets without making large capital outlays. *See* **franchising**

linguistic distance   The measure of difference between languages; an important factor in determining the amount of trade between nations.

litigation   The process in which a dispute between parties is contested in a formal judicial setting; commonly instigated by a lawsuit asserting one party's version of the facts.

local nationals   Persons living in their home country; historically the persons preferred by **expatriate** managers to form the sales force. Local nationals are more knowledgeable about a country's business structure than an expatriate would be, and they are generally less expensive to field and maintain.

logistics management   A total systems approach to management of the distribution process that includes all activities involved in physically moving raw material, in-process inventory, and finished goods inventory from the point of origin to the point of use or consumption.

lubrication   The use of funds to expedite actions of public employees and government officials. The payments made to minor officials may or may not be illegal and are usually of inconsequential amounts.

m

Maastricht Treaty   Treaty signed by 12 nations of the European Community creating the European Union.

Manifest Destiny The notion that Americans were a chosen people ordained by God to create a model society; it was accepted as the basis for U.S. policy during much of the 19th and 20th centuries as the nation expanded its territory.

maquiladoras Also known as *in-bond companies* or *twin plants*, a type of customs-privileged facility that originated in Mexico in the 1970s and provided U.S. companies with a favorable means to use low-cost Mexican labor. They operated through an agreement with the Mexican government allowing U.S. companies to import parts and materials into Mexico without import taxes, provided the finished products are reexported to the United States or another country. *See* **customs-privileged facilities**

marketing research The systematic gathering, recording, and analyzing of data to provide information useful in marketing decision making. *See* **international marketing research**

Marxist-socialist tenets The set of views in which law is subordinate to prevailing economic conditions. Marxist-socialist tenets influenced the legal systems of Russia and other republics of the former Soviet Union, as well as China, forcing these nations to revamp their commercial legal code as they become involved in trade with non-Marxist countries.

merchant middlemen In international transactions, the intermediaries, located in the foreign market, who take title to the home-country manufacturer's goods and sell on their own account. Manufacturers using merchant middlemen have less control over the **distribution process** than those using **agent middlemen.** *See* **home-country middlemen**

Mercosur An evolving South American union, also called the Southern Cone Free Trade Area, formed in 1991 with the goal of creating a **common market** and **customs union** among the participating countries. The original signers were Argentina, Brazil, Paraguay, and Uruguay; Bolivia and Chile later signed agreements with Mercosur.

merge-in-transit A distribution method in which goods shipped from several supply locations are consolidated into one final customer delivery point while they are in transit and then shipped as a unit to the customer.

monochromatic time (M-time) Describing a view of time, typical of most North Americans, Swiss, Germans, and Scandinavians, as something that is linear and can be saved, wasted, spent, and lost. M-time cultures tend to concentrate on one thing at a time and value promptness. *See* **P-time**

Monroe Doctrine A cornerstone of U.S. foreign policy as enunciated by President James Monroe, it proclaimed three basic dicta: no further European colonization in the New World, abstention of the United States from European political affairs, and nonintervention of European governments in the governments of the Western Hemisphere. *See* **Roosevelt Corollary**

multicultural research Inquiry, analysis, and study of more than two countries and cultures that takes into account differences in language, economic structure, social structure, behavior, and attitude patterns. Different methods of research may have varying reliability in different countries.

multinational market regions The groups of countries that seek mutual economic benefit from reducing interregional tariffs and barriers to trade.

n

NAFTA North American Free Trade Agreement. NAFTA is a comprehensive trade agreement that addresses, and in many cases improves, all aspects of doing business within North America. By eliminating trade and investment barriers among Canada, the United States, and Mexico, it created one of the largest and richest markets in the world.

nationalism An intense feeling of national pride and unity; an awakening of a nation's people to pride in their country. Nationalism can take on an antiforeign business bias.

newly industrialized countries (NICs) Countries that are experiencing rapid economic expansion and industrialization.

noise The term for an impairment to the communications process comprising external influences, such as competitive advertising, other sales personnel, and confusion at the "receiving end." Noise can disrupt any step of the communications process and is frequently beyond the control of the sender or the receiver.

nongovernmental organizations (NGOs) Large advocacy organizations, usually not-for-profit, often multinational, and run by citizens rather than companies or governments. Prominent examples are Green Peace, Amnesty International, and the Red Cross.

nontariff barriers Restrictions, other than **tariffs,** placed by countries on imported products; they may include quality standards, sanitary and health standards, **quotas,** embargoes, boycotts, and antidumping penalties.

nontask sounding The part of the negotiation process in which conversation covers topics other than the business at hand; nontask sounding is commonly a preliminary phase and precedes **task-related information exchange.**

o

open account In U.S. domestic trade, the typical payment procedure for established customers, in which the goods are delivered and the customer is billed on an end-of-the-month basis.

Opium Wars Two wars fought between China and Britain over the British run opium trade in China during the middle 1800s. The British navy attacked Chinese ports in retribution for a Chinese ban on the drug, and the Treaty of Nanjing signed in 1842 allowed greater European access to Chinese ports generally, a resumption of the opium trade, and ceding of Hong Kong to British control.

orderly market agreements (OMAs) Agreements, similar to **quotas,** between an importing country and an exporting country for a restriction on the volume of exports. Also known as **voluntary export restraints.**

p

parallel imports International transactions in which importers buy products from distributors in one country and sell them in a second country to distributors that are not part of the manufacturer's regular distribution system.

parallel market (gray market) When products intended to be sold in one market, exclusively at a particular low price (often a government controlled low price), are sold in a second market (usually illegally) where market prices are higher. Take for example, pharmaceuticals available in Canada at a regulated low price that are then shipped to customers in the United States by Canadian exporters, at prices lower than those set by the companies in the U.S., which reflect the higher costs of FDA approval in the U.S.

parallel translation   A method of translation in which two translators are used to make a **back translation;** the results are compared, differences are discussed, and the most appropriate translation is used. The method addresses the use of common idioms in the languages being translated. *See* **decentering**

penetration pricing policy   A low price policy directed at gaining market share from competitors.

physical distribution system   The overall network for the physical movement of goods, including plants and warehousing, transportation mode, inventory quantities, and packaging.

planned change   A marketing strategy in which a company deliberately sets out to change those aspects of a foreign culture resistant to predetermined marketing goals. *See* **unplanned change**

political and social activists (PSAs)   PSAs are individuals who participate in efforts to change the practices and behaviors of corporations and governments, with tactics that can range from peaceful protest to terrorism.

political union   A fully integrated form of regional co-operation that involves complete political and economic integration, either voluntary or enforced; the most notable example was the now disbanded Council for Mutual Economic Assistance (COMECON), a centrally controlled group of countries organized by the Soviet Union.

polychromatic time (P-time)   A view of time, as held in "high context" cultures, in which the completion of a human transaction is more important than holding to schedules. P-time is characterized by the simultaneous occurrence of many things. *See* **M-time**

predatory pricing   A practice by which a foreign producer intentionally sells its products in another country for less than the cost of production to undermine the competition and take control of the market.

price escalation   The pricing disparity in which goods are priced higher in a foreign market than in the home market; caused by the added costs involved in exporting products from one country to another.

price–quality relationship   The balance between a product's price and how well the product performs. Often the price–quality of a product is ideal if it meets basic expectations and no more, allowing it to be priced competitively.

primary data   Data collected, as in market research, specifically for a particular research project. *See* **secondary data**

principle of justice or fairness   *See* **justice or fairness**

principle of rights of the parties   *See* **rights of the parties**

principle of utilitarian ethics   *See* **utilitarian ethics**

prior use   The principle, as observed in the United States and other common-law nations, that ownership of intellectual property rights usually goes to whoever can establish first use.

Product Component Model   A tool for characterizing how a product may be adapted to a new market by separating the product's

many dimensions into three components: support services, packaging, and core component.

product diffusion   The process by which product **innovations** spread; successful product diffusion will depend on the ability to communicate relevant product information and new product attributes.

product homologation   A term used to describe changes in a product that are mandated by local standards for product and service **quality.**

protectionism   The use by nations of legal barriers, exchange barriers, and psychological barriers to restrain entry of goods from other countries.

public relations (PR)   The effort made by companies to create positive relationships with the popular press and general media and to communicate messages to their publics, including customers, the general public, and government regulators.

purchase price parity (PPP)   GDP at PPP corrects GDP for differentials across countries in the costs of consumer purchases. The PPP correction allows for direct comparisons of the overall well-being of consumers across countries.

q

quality   The essential character of something, such as a good or service; defined in two dimensions: market-perceived quality and performance quality. Consumer perception of a product's quality often has more to do with market-perceived quality than performance quality.

quotas   Specific unit or dollar limits applied to a particular type of good by the country into which the good is imported. *See* **tariff**

r

relationship marketing   The aspect of marketing products that depends on long-term associations with customers; an important factor in business-to-business contexts and especially important in most international markets, where culture dictates strong ties between people and companies.

repatriation   The process of bringing a local national back to his/her home country after an assignment abroad.

research process   The process of obtaining information; it should begin with a definition of the research problem and establishment of objectives, and proceed with an orderly approach to the collection and analysis of data.

reserves account   The portion of a **balance-of-trade** statement that shows a record of exports and imports of gold, increases or decreases in foreign exchange, and increases or decreases in liabilities to foreign banks.

rights of the parties   One of three principles of ethics (the others are **utilitarian ethics** and **justice or fairness**); it tests an action by asking if the action respects the rights of the individuals involved.

Roosevelt Corollary   An extension of U.S. policy applied to the Monroe Doctrine by President Theodore Roosevelt, stating that the United States would not only prohibit non-American intervention in Latin American affairs but would also police Latin America and guarantee that all Latin American nations would meet their international obligations. *See* **Monroe Doctrine**

rural/urban migration As countries develop industrially, huge numbers of agricultural workers move to cities causing major difficulties in urban infrastructure capacity and big city slums around the world.

S

sales promotion Marketing activities that stimulate consumer purchases and improve retailer or middlemen effectiveness and cooperation.

secondary data Data collected by an independent agency or individual other than the firm conducting research; often useful in market research. *See* **primary data**

self-reference criterion (SRC) An unconscious reference to one's own cultural values, experience, and knowledge as a basis for a decision.

separation allowances Payment of overseas premiums to employees who take on short-term foreign assignments and travel without their families; allowances generally compensate for all excess expenses and any tax differential.

silent language Term used by Edward T. Hall for the non-spoken and symbolic meanings of time, space, things, friendships, and agreements, and how they vary across cultures; from Hall's seminal article "The Silent Language of Business."

Single European Act An agreement, ratified in 1987, designed to remove all barriers to trade and to make the European Community a single internal market.

skimming A method of pricing, generally used for foreign markets, in which a company seeks to reach a segment of the market that is relatively price insensitive and thus willing to pay a premium price for the value received; may be used to sell a new or innovative product to maximize profits until a competitor forces a lower price. *See* **full-cost pricing; variable-cost pricing**

SNAP Simplified Network Application Process; an electronic service offered by the U.S. Department of Commerce as an alternative to paper license submissions that enables an exporter to submit export and reexport applications, high-performance computer notices, and commodity classification requests via the Internet. *See* **ELAIN; ERIC; STELA**

social institutions The methods and systems, including family, religion, school, the media, government, and corporations, that affect the ways in which people relate to one another, teach acceptable behavior to succeeding generations, and govern themselves.

sovereignty The powers exercised by a state in relation to other countries, as well as the supreme powers of a state as exercised over its own inhabitants.

special drawing rights (SDRs) A means of monetary measurement that represents an average base of value derived from the value of a group of major currencies. Known as "paper gold," it is used by the **IMF** to report most monetary statistics in a unit more reliable than a single currency, such as dollars.

stage of economic development A classification describing the (stage of) maturity and sophistication of a nation's economy as it evolves over time. The best known model, by Walt Rostow, describes five stages, starting with the traditional society and finally reaching the age of high mass consumption.

STELA System for Tracking Export License Applications; an automated voice response system for exporters that enables license applicants to track the status of their license and classification applications with U.S. authorities. *See* **ELAIN; ERIC; SNAP**

strategic international alliance (SIA) A business relationship established by two or more companies to cooperate out of mutual need and to share risk in achieving a common objective.

strategic planning A type of planning conducted at the highest levels of management, dealing with products, capital, and research and the long- and short-term goals of a company. *See* **corporate planning; tactical planning**

subornation The giving of large sums of money—frequently not fully accounted for—designed to entice an official to commit an illegal act on behalf of the one offering the money.

sustainable development An approach toward economic growth that has been described (by Joke Waller-Hunter) as a cooperative effort among businesses, environmentalists, and others to seek growth with "wise resource management, equitable distribution of benefits, and reduction of negative efforts on people and the environment from the process of economic growth."

t

tactical planning A type of planning that pertains to specific actions and to the allocation of resources used to implement strategic planning goals in specific markets; also known as *market planning*; generally conducted at the local level. *See* **corporate planning; strategic planning**

Taiping Rebellion The most costly civil war in human history in China during 1851–1864. Some estimates have the death toll at between 20–40 million.

tariff A fee or tax that countries impose on imported goods, often to protect a country's markets from intrusion from foreign countries. *See* **nontariff barriers; quotas**

task-related information exchange The point in the negotiation process at which nontask communication, or **nontask sounding,** is completed and substantial negotiations begin including information about needs and preferences.

third-country nationals (TCNs) Expatriates from one country working for a foreign company in a third country. *See* **expatriate; local nationals**

terms of sale The set of rules and costs applying to a transaction, covering such categories as price, freight, and insurance. In international trade, terms of sale often sound similar to those in domestic commerce but generally have different meanings. Also known as *trade terms.*

The Greater China Refers to both the People's Republic of China (PRC or Mainland China) and the Republic of China (Taiwan).

trading companies Business entities that accumulate, transport, and distribute goods from many countries.

transfer pricing The pricing of goods transferred from a company's operations or sales units in one country to its units elsewhere; also known as *intracompany pricing.* In transfer pricing, prices may be adjusted to enhance the ultimate profit of the company as a whole.

Treaty of Amsterdam   Treaty, concluded in 1997, that addressed issues left undone by the **Maastricht Treaty** and identified priority measures necessary to bring a single market in Europe fully into effect and to lay a solid foundation for both a single currency and an enlargement of the European Union into central and eastern Europe. *See* **Single European Act**

triangulation   A term borrowed from naval charting meaning using at least three differing measures of the same concept to verify the accuracy of any one method. For example, regarding forecast of demand, separate opinions of experts, sales representatives, and quantitative economic analyses might be compared.

24-Hour Rule   A U.S. requirement, part of the Cargo and Container Security Initiative, mandating that sea carriers and NVOCCs (Non-Vessel Operating Common Carriers) provide U.S. Customs with detailed descriptions (manifests) of the contents of containers bound for the United States 24 hours before a container is loaded on board a vessel.

U

uncontrollable elements   Factors in the business environment over which the international marketer has no control or influence; may include competition, legal restraints, government controls, weather, consumer preferences and behavior, and political events. *See* **controllable elements**

United States–Canada Free Trade Agreement   An agreement, known as CFTA, between the United States and Canada designed to eliminate all trade barriers between the two nations.

unplanned change   A marketing strategy in which a company introduces a product into a market without a plan to influence the way the market's culture responds to or resists the company's marketing message. *See* **planned change**

utilitarian ethics   One of three principles of ethics (the others are **rights of the parties** and **justice or fairness**); it tests an action by asking if it optimizes the "common good" or benefits of all constituencies.

V

variable-cost pricing   A method of pricing goods in foreign markets in which a company is concerned only with the marginal or incremental costs of producing goods for sale in those markets. Firms using variable-cost pricing take the view that foreign sales are bonus sales. *See* **full-cost pricing; skimming**

voluntary export restraints (VERS)   Agreements, similar to **quotas,** between an importing country and an exporting country for a restriction on the volume of exports. Also known as **orderly market agreements (OMAs).**

W

work councils   In Europe, work councils (that is, internal labor union committees) are very much involved in setting rules about compensation and other human resources policies companywide, even for sales people. In Austria and Germany, for example, work councils not only codetermine compensation plans, but also must approve them before implementation.

World Trade Organization (WTO)   World Trade Organization. The organization formed in 1994 that encompasses the **GATT** structure and extends it to new areas that had not been adequately covered previously. The WTO adjudicates trade disputes. All member countries have equal representation.

PHOTO CREDITS

Front Matter

Page 6: © Bobby Yip/Reuters/Corbis; p. 11: © Hero Images/Getty Images; p. 27: © John Graham; p. 28: © Dave G. Houser/Corbis; p. 30: © Jim Watson/AFP/Getty Images; p. 31: © John Graham; p. 33: © Photodisc Green/Getty Images; p. 34: © John Graham.

Chapter1

Opener: © John Graham; p. 4 (left): © Bobby Yip/Reuters/Corbis; p. 4 (right): © Feng Li/Getty Images; p. 5: © Lee Jin-man/AP Images; p. 6 (left): © Str/AP Images; p. 6 (right): © Milos Bicanski/Getty Images; p. 8, p. 12, p. 15 (left): © John Graham; p. 15 (right): © Neil Thomas/Africa Media Online; p. 23 (both): © Oleksiy Maksymenko Photography/Alamy.

Chapter2

Opener, p. 31 (left): © Cliff Jette/The Gazette/AP Images; p. 31 (right): © Allstarphotos/Newscom; p. 42: © John Graham; p. 44 (left): © Sharon Hoogstraten; p. 44 (right): © Conn. Attorney General/AP Images; p. 46: © John Graham; p. 47: © Tom McHugh/Science Source; p. 51: "Globalization" by Gifford Myers. Photo by John Graham.; p. 52 (top): © Mike Nelson/AFP/Getty Images; p. 52 (bottom): © Jane Mingay/AP Images.

Chapter3

Opener: © narvikk/Getty Images; p. 60: © Dave G. Houser/Corbis; p. 67: © Roundabout Water Solutions; p. 68, p. 70 (both), p. 72: © John Graham; p. 73 (left): © narvikk/Getty Images; p. 73 (right), p. 75 (both): © John Graham; p. 82: © Education Images/UIG/Getty Images; p. 83: © John Graham.

Chapter4

Opener, p. 101, p. 102 (Floriad), p. 102 (Aalsmeer Auction), p. 102 (Pope), p. 102 (Amsterdam market), p. 102 (black tulip): © John Graham; p. 102 (Dutch harbor): © Iberfoto/Superstock; p. 103 (Inside Aalsmeer), p. 103 (bidders), p. 103 (loading trucks): © John Graham; p. 103 (Night Watch): © Rijksmuseum, Amsterdam/SuperStock; p. 103 (sunflowers): © Tsugufumi Matsumoto/AP Images; p. 103 (Potato Eaters): © SuperStock; p. 110: © Cary Wolinsky/Trillium Studios; p. 117 (top): © Mahmoud Mahmoud/AFP/Getty Images; p. 117 (bottom): © John Graham; p. 119 (both): Courtesy of IBM; p. 122: © Maxim Marmur/AP Images; p. 126: © Joe McNally/Getty Images.

Chapter5

Opener, p. 132: © John Graham; p. 134: © POOL/Reuters/Corbis; p. 137 (left): © Michael Nicholson/Corbis; p. 137 (right): © Pictorial Press Ltd/Alamy; p. 142 (left): © Ed Kashi/Corbis; p. 142 (right): © Andy Rain/Bloomberg News/Getty Images; p. 149 (left): © Kyodo News/Newscom; p. 149 (right): © Hasan Jamali/AP Images; p. 153: © John Graham; p. 154: © Phillippe Lopez/AFP/Getty Images; p. 162 (top): © Stringer Shanghai/Reuters/Corbis; p. 162 (bottom): © John Graham.

Chapter6

Opener, p. 172: © Eric Feferberg/AFP/Getty Images; p. 175: © Olivier Laban-Mattei/AFP/Getty Images; p. 177: © Behrouz Mehri/AFP/Getty Images; p. 182 (both): © John Graham; p. 184 (top): © Claude Paris/AP Images; p. 184 (middle): © AP Images; p. 184 (bottom): © Georges Gobet/AFP/Getty Images; p. 185 (top): © Klaus-Dietmar Gabbert/epa/Corbis; p. 185 (middle): © Reuters/Corbis; p. 185 (bottom): Courtesy of Sea Shepherd Conservation Society; p. 186: © EPA/Newscom; p. 187, p. 194: © John Graham.

Chapter7

Opener, p. 202: © Derek Berwin/The Image Bank/Getty Images; p. 213 (top left): © Stan Honda/AFP/Getty Images; p. 213 (top right): © Mike Clark/AFP/Getty Images; p. 213 (bottom): © Christian Schwetz/AP Images; p. 216: © Ng Han Guan/AP Images; p. 220 (top left), p. 220 (top right): © John Graham; p. 220 (bottom): © Pat Roque/AP Images; p. 228: © Roger Ressmeyer/Corbis.

Chapter8

Opener, p. 232 (left): © Jim Watson/AFP/Getty Images; p. 232 (right): © Greg Baker/AP Images; p. 239: © Studio 101/Alamy; p. 243: © Brian Lee/Corbis; p. 245, p. 245 (close-up): © John Graham; p. 246: © Cary Wolinsky/Trillium Studios; p. 250, p. 254 (both): © John Graham.

Chapter9

Opener: © Benjamin Lowy/Getty Images; p. 264: © Julian Finney/Getty Images; p. 268 (top left): © Benjamin Lowy/Getty Images; p. 268 (top right): © imageBROKER/Alamy; p. 268 (bottom), p. 271, p. 275, p. 279 (left): © John Graham; p. 279 (right): © Monica Rueda/AP Images; p. 287: © John Graham.

Chapter10

Opener, p. 292 (both), p. 298, p. 300: © John Graham; p. 301: © AFP Photo/Louisa Gouliamaki/Newscom; p. 303: © Shuji Kobayashi/The Image Bank/Getty Images; p. 304, p. 306, p. 309 (left): © John Graham; p. 309 (right): © Amr Nabil/AP Images; p. 310: © NASA/AP Images.

Chapter11

Opener: © Ng Han Guan/AP Images; p. 320: © Stephen Shaver/UPI/Newscom; p. 322: © Ng Han Guan/AP Images; p. 326: © Sherwin Crasto/AP Images; p. 329 (top): © Hoang Dinh Nam/AFP/Getty Images; p. 329 (bottom): © John Graham; p. 330 (left): © Ruth Fremson /The New York Times/Redux; p. 330 (right): © John Graham; p. 333 (left): © Jeremy Woodhouse/Getty Images; p. 333 (right): © Amit Bhargava/Bloomberg News/Getty Images; p. 335: © JIMIN LAI/AFP/Getty Images; p. 341: © John Graham; p. 342: © Goh Chai Hin/AFP/Getty Images.

Chapter12

Opener, p. 348, p. 349 (all): © John Graham; p. 350: © Richard Drew/AP Images; p. 359 (all), p. 364 (both), p. 365: © John Graham.

Chapter13

Opener, p. 378: © Kenneth Garrett/Alamy; p. 379, p. 383: © John Graham; p. 384 (engineer), p. 384 (stove): Courtesy of African Clean Energy (Pty) Ltd.; p. 384 (dung): © ephotocorp/Alamy; p. 384 (carrying wood): Courtesy of African Clean Energy (Pty) Ltd.; p. 384 (slum fire): © Gideon Mendel/Corbis; p. 384 (UNDC personnel), p. 385 (demonstrating stove), p. 385 (distributing stoves): Courtesy of African Clean Energy (Pty) Ltd.; p. 385 (selling stoves): Courtesy of Global Alliance for Clean Cookstoves; p. 385 (village receives stoves), p. 385 (carrying stoves), p. 385 (interviewing stove users): Courtesy of African Clean Energy (Pty) Ltd.; p. 386: © Sam Granado/Dallas Morning News/Newscom; p. 390 (top): © Michael Edrington/The Image Works; p. 390 (bottom left), p. 390 (bottom right), p. 401 (both): © John Graham; p. 406 (both): © Behring/SIPA/Newscom; p. 410: © John Graham.

Chapter14

Opener: © Adam Berry/Bloomberg via Getty Images; p. 418 (both), p. 419 (both): Courtesy of Microsoft; p. 423: © John Graham; p. 425: © Tatyana Alekseeva-Sabeva/iStock/Getty; p. 428: © John Graham; p. 433: © Eric Feferberg/AFP/Getty Images; p. 434: © David Becker/Getty Images; p. 437 (top): © John Graham; p. 437 (all), p. 438 (all): Courtesy of Solar Turbines Inc.; p. 440 (bottom): © John Graham.

Chapter15

Opener: © John Graham; p. 444: © ChinaFotoPress/ChinaFotoPress via Getty Images; p. 445, p. 449 (both), p. 450 (both): © John Graham; p. 452: © Kristy Sparow/Getty Images; p. 454, p. 455, p. 460, p. 461 (all): © John Graham; p. 466: © Marta Nascimento/REA/Redux; p. 468 (both), p. 469 (both), p. 470, p. 471: Courtesy of Marriott; p. 475: © John Graham.

Chapter16

Opener: © Nick Wass/AP Images; p. 483 (top): © John Graham; p. 483 (bottom): © Cameron Spencer/Getty Images; p. 485, p. 486, p. 487: Affectiva; p. 491 (both): © John Graham; p. 492 (both), p. 493: Courtesy of Microsoft; p. 496 (top left), p. 496 (top right): © John Graham; p. 496 (bottom left): © Tom Purslow/Manchester United via Getty Images; p. 496 (bottom right: © Mark Baker/AP Images; p. 497 (both), p. 498, p. 501 (top): © John Graham; p. 501 (bottom left): © Denis Doyle/AP Images; p. 501 (bottom right): Courtesy of GE; p. 509 (all): © John Graham; p. 514: © Nick Wass/AP Images; p. 515 (both), p. 516: Courtesy of NBA Global; p. 517: © Bai Xuefei/Xinhua Press/Corbis; p. 519 (left): © Yuri Kochetkov European Press Agency/Newscom; p. 519 (right): © Tatsuyuki Tayama/Fujifotos/The Image Works.

Chapter17

Opener, p. 530: © David Paul Morris/Getty Images; p. 532: © Roger Ressmeyer/Corbis; p. 534 (both), p. 535 (all): Courtesy of Mary Kay Inc.; p. 536 (both): © David McIntyre/Stock Photo; p. 539: © Tom Wagner/Corbis; p. 546: © John Graham.

Chapter18

Opener: © AF archive/Alamy; p. 563: © Greg Baker/AP Images; p. 564, p. 565: © Katsumi Kasahara/AP Images; p. 566 (both): © John Graham; p. 567: © AP Images; p. 570: © AF archive/Alamy; p. 577: © Dadang Tri/Reuters /Corbis; p. 578: © John Graham; p. 579: © Susan Van Etten/PhotoEdit, Inc; p. 580: © John Graham.

Chapter19

Opener, p. 590: © Photodisc Green/Getty Images; p. 599: © Ralph Orlowski/Getty; p. 601: Used by permission of KARRASS, LTD. Beverly Hills, CA.; p. 602 (left): © Jon Feingersh/Blend Images/Getty Images; p. 602 (right): © Macduff Everton/Corbis; p. 607: © John Graham; p. 608: © Anat Givon/AP Images.

Country Notebook: © John Graham.

NAME INDEX

Page numbers with n indicate notes.

SUBJECT INDEX

Page numbers with n indicate notes.